About the author

Respected wine critic and vigneron James Halliday has a career that spans over forty years, but he is most widely known for his witty and informative writing about wine. As one of the founders of Brokenwood in the Lower Hunter Valley region of New South Wales, and thereafter founder of Coldstream Hills in the Yarra Valley, Victoria, James is an unmatched authority on every aspect of the wine industry, from the planting and pruning of vines through to the creation and marketing of the finished product. His winemaking has led him to sojourns in Bordeaux and Burgundy, and he is constantly in demand as a wine judge in Australia and overseas.

James Halliday has contributed to more than 55 books on wine since he began writing in 1979. His books have been translated into Japanese, French, German, Danish, Icelandic and Polish, and have been published in the UK, the US, as well as Australia. He is also the author of *James Halliday's Wine Atlas of Australia*.

Wine zones and regions of Australia

NEW SOUTH WALES			
WINE ZONE		WINE REGION	
Big Rivers	(A)	Murray Darling	1
		Perricoota	2
		Riverina	3
		Swan Hill	4
Central Ranges	(B)	Cowra	5
		Mudgee	6
		Orange	7
Hunter Valley	(C)	Lower Hunter	8
		Upper Hunter	9
Northern Rivers	(D)	Hastings River	10
Northern Slopes	(E)	New England	11
South Coast	(F)	Shoalhaven Coast	12
		Southern Highlands	13
Southern New South Wales	(G)	Canberra District	14
		Gundagai	15
		Hilltops	16
		Tumbarumba	17
Western Plains	(H)		

SOUTH AUSTRALIA			
WINE ZONE		WINE REGION	
Adelaide Super Zone includes Mount Lofty Ranges, Fleurieu and Barossa wine regions			
Barossa		Barossa Valley	18
		Eden Valley	19
Fleurieu	(J)	Currency Creek	20
		Kangaroo Island	21
		Langhorne Creek	22
		McLaren Vale	23
		Southern Fleurieu	24
Mount Lofty Ranges		Adelaide Hills	25
		Adelaide Plains	26
		Clare Valley	27
Far North	(K)	Southern Flinders Ranges	28
Limestone Coast	(L)	Coonawarra	29
		Mount Benson	30
		Mount Gambier*	31
		Padthaway	32
		Robe	33
		Wrattonbully	34
Lower Murray	(M)	Riverland	35
The Peninsulas	(N)	Southern Eyre Peninsula*	36

VICTORIA			
WINE ZONE		WINE REGION	
Central Victoria	(P)	Bendigo	37
		Goulburn Valley	38
		Heathcote	39
		Strathbogie Ranges	40
Gippsland	(Q)	Upper Goulburn	41
		Alpine Valleys	42
North East Victoria	(R)	Beechworth	43
		Glenrowan	44
		King Valley	45
		Rutherglen	46
North West Victoria	(S)	Murray Darling	47
		Swan Hill	48
Port Phillip	(T)	Geelong	49
		Macedon Ranges	50
		Mornington Peninsula	51
		Sunbury	52
		Yarra Valley	53
Western Victoria	(U)	Ballarat*	54
		Grampians	55
		Henty	56
		Pyrenees	57

* Regions that have taken, or are likely to take, steps to secure registration.

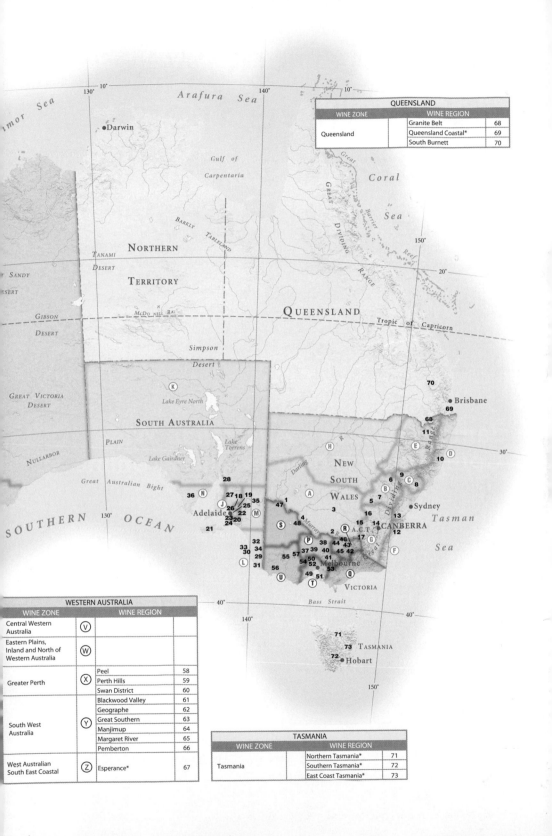

THE BESTSELLING
AND DEFINITIVE
GUIDE TO
AUSTRALIAN
WINES

James Halliday
Australian
Wine Companion

2009 Edition

Hardie Grant Books

Published in 2008 by
Hardie Grant Books
85 High Street
Prahran, Victoria 3181, Australia
www.hardiegrant.com.au

The *Australian Wine Companion* is a joint venture between
James Halliday and Explore Australia Publishing Pty Ltd.

The map in this publication incorporates data copyright
© Commonwealth of Australia (Geoscience Australia) 2004.
Geoscience Australia has not evaluated the data as altered and incorporated
within this publication and therefore gives no warranty regarding accuracy,
completeness, currency or suitability for any particular purpose.

Australian wine zones and wine regions data copyright
© Australian Wine and Brandy Corporation, April 2005

ISBN 978 1 74066 647 3

Typeset by Megan Ellis
Cover photograph courtesy Getty Images
Printed and bound in Australia by McPherson's Printing Group

10 9 8 7 6 5 4 3 2 1

Contents

Introduction

I commenced my introduction to the 2008 edition of the *Wine Companion* with the following paragraph:

'From a feast to a famine, from a world of unlimited opportunity to one clouded with uncertainty, changes have swept across the face of the Australian wine industry with unprecedented speed and power. The 2007 and 2008 calendar years may well prove to be turning points taking grapegrowers, winemakers and wine marketers down paths previously undreamed of.'

The wisdom of hindsight gives me no cause to change my views. For many reasons, the short- to medium-term future of the industry continues to be clouded with uncertainties at all levels.

Barely a day goes by without doomsday predictions of the consequences of climate change, based on the assumptions that it is real, it is permanent and it is likely to be catastrophic. Every now and then, scientists of various persuasions have the temerity to challenge these assumptions.

In February and March 2008, there were numerous reports in newscasts and newspapers suggesting that the earth had in fact cooled slightly between the years 1998 and 2008. On 9 April, *The Australian* gave front-page (and more) coverage to a speech by respected academic Professor Don Aitkin entitled 'A cool look at global warming'.

Having robustly challenged the idea that human activity is to blame for global warming (anthropogenic global warming, or AGW) and that CO_2 emissions are responsible for warming at an alarming and unprecedented rate, he argued that Australia faces two environmental issues of great significance. The first is how to manage water supplies and the second is to find acceptable alternatives to oil-based energy.

It is the first of these issues that casts a long shadow over the wine industry, as we have known it since Federation. Well over two-thirds of the country's production has traditionally come from the Big Rivers Zone of New South Wales, the North West Zone of Victoria, the Lower Murray Zone (Riverland) and the Langhorne Creek region of South Australia. The Murray Darling system, which provided water for these regions (and significantly for the Barossa Valley and McLaren Vale regions), is in dire straits, with little or no chance of recovery in the short term. If and when moderate flows return, the pecking order of the past will be radically changed.

Urban populations and the environment will have priority, and the price per megalitre of whatever is left for horticulture will be much higher. There will thus be a two-way squeeze on these areas: lower yields and higher costs, which on a crude measure might result in a 200% increase in grape prices if viticulture is to remain economically viable. If that, or anything like it, were to remain the case, it is hard to imagine there will be many customers for those grapes.

It is altogether too simplistic to say that in the short term this would in fact benefit the industry, forcing a move from quantity to quality. Australia's dominant share of the UK and the US markets would disappear, and the range of wine on offer to the rapidly emerging Asian markets would be limited.

Despite these uncertainties, the number of new winery entries continues to defy the odds. In the 2005 edition of the *Wine Companion*, there were a mind-boggling 377 new entrants; in 2006, 172; in 2007, 230; in 2008, 218; and this year, 169, bringing the total to over 1100 in just five years, or more than the total number of all Australian wineries in the 2000 edition.

The *Wine Companion* cannot go beyond its present 768 pages, though happily a further 822 wineries appear on www.winecompanion.com.au. The combination of these two sources covers 2483 wineries, more than any other publication.

The continued growth of the wine industry – most obviously noted in the 169 wineries making their first appearance in the 2009 *Wine Companion*, but also in the ever-growing number of wines being tasted – has meant I have had no choice but to enrol the help of another taster. Up until this point of time I, and I alone, have compiled all the tasting notes.

The choice of someone to assist is very important, as it is a continuing, not a one-off, role. Thus, securing the help of Ben Edwards, head of the Australian Sommeliers Association, a top-flight wine show judge with a world view of wine quality, has been a major step. We know each other well and mutually respect each other's palate. That said, Ben is not a clone, and his involvement will bring a breath of fresh air to the *Companion*. I place on record my gratitude for his willingness to add another dimension to an already busy life.

Australian vintage 2008: a snapshot

The uncertainties facing the industry over the next few years are eerily similar to the weather patterns that prevailed over the 2008 growing season. If you focused on South Australia and Victoria you would find that a combination of drought and an all-time, all-state record heatwave for Adelaide of 15 consecutive days, from 3 to 17 March inclusive, with temperatures over 35°C, led to a freakishly early start to vintage and to a vicious compression in the ripening patterns, flooding wineries with grapes of every variety. One winemaker described it as a bathtub and gumboot year as makers struggled to find enough fermentation capacity.

In these states there was no pattern to the normal order of ripening of red varieties nor to the supposed differences between cooler and warmer sites in the regions. The one saving grace was that a significant part of the crop was picked by the end of February, before the heatwave took hold, and included most white varieties. In late March/early April a few loads of red grapes from McLaren Vale and the Barossa Valley ranged between 20 and 31° baumé. If yeasts could be found to ferment 31° baumé grapes to dryness, the alcohol would be close to 30% by volume: 75% of brandy spirit strength without distillation! In fact, those loads went straight to the marc heap.

The Limestone Coast went in part against the trend. The moderating influence of the Southern Ocean kept extreme heat to four days, and after a frenzied start to the vintage, some of the major wineries deliberately slowed the pace, more than satisfied with the quality of shiraz and cabernet sauvignon.

In Western Australia good rainfall and moderate temperatures until a hot January (in some parts) led to a perfect ripening season in Great Southern, Pemberton, Geographe and Margaret River, bird damage and an April season break (hence rainfall) the only problems. In the north (Peel, Perth Hills and the Swan Valley), the coldest December then the warmest January on record finally led to frantic picking and space issues in the wineries similar to the east.

The dual impact of drought, and heat after the cool February had passed, created challenges throughout all Victorian regions. Curiously, while most finished harvest at record early dates in March, some continued well into April.

Much of New South Wales had one of the coolest and wettest growing seasons of the past 100 years, the Hunter Valley, Mudgee, Southern Highlands and Hastings River all suffering. Semillon was picked in a small rainfree window from 14 to 18 January, but no more than 30 % of the reds were picked. In contradistinction, Canberra, Cowra and the Riverina all had near-perfect growing seasons and hence very good wines.

They were joined by Tasmania, where warmer-than-usual growing season temperatures led to a relatively early start and early (and rapid) harvest of excellent grapes, the yields well above average in the north. In the south, severe drought resulted in smaller berries and yields only slightly below normal, but in most parts the quality is very promising. In Queensland, the Granite Belt was similarly blessed with the first good rainfall in years and mild temperatures leading up to harvest.

Finally, most of the white grapes from the majority of regions were picked before the heat, and chardonnay from southern Victoria and Tasmania in particular looks full of promise.

The size of the harvest was uncertain. Up until the end of 2007, official estimates were for 1.22 million tonnes. Early in 2008, that estimate was (surprisingly) lifted to 1.6 million tonnes. This was in part derived from increased yield forecasts for regions outside the Murray Darling/Riverina/Langhorne Creek regions and to a slightly more optimistic assessment for the latter regions, optimism that seems to have been well founded.

Twenty-four hours before the *Companion* went to press, a media release from the Winemakers' Federation of Australia dropped a bombshell. The opening paragraphs stated the harvest 'has come in above expectations in both size and quality, reaching a total of 1.83 million tonnes. This figure is significantly larger than estimations made at the start of the growing season, and is in fact almost double some early predictions'.

The figure explains why Foster's had to write down the value of its bulk wine stocks, with all the major companies floating in a sea of excess chardonnay. If nothing else, it shows just how unpredictable harvests are in times of heat, drought, and rain alike. In the twinkling of an eye, the industry has gone from surplus to shortage and back to surplus again.

Any prediction of the size of the 2009 harvest will be exquisitely difficult, depending as it will on the amount of water available from the Murray Darling to each of the stakeholders. The outlook is still grim, but so it was in the months leading up to 2008.

How to use the *Wine Companion*

The *Australian Wine Companion* is arranged with wineries in alphabetical order; the index lists the wineries by region, which adds a search facility. The entries should be self-explanatory, but here I will briefly take you through the information provided for each entry, using Brookland Valley as an example.

Wineries

Brookland Valley ★★★★★

Caves Road, Wilyabrup, WA 6280
T (08) 9755 6042 **F** (08) 9755 6214 **www**. brooklandvalley.com.au **Open** 7 days 10–5
Winemaker Ross Pamment **Est**. 1984 **Cases** 130 000
Brookland Valley has an idyllic setting, plus its much enlarged Flutes Café (one of the best winery restaurants in the Margaret River region) and its Gallery of Wine Arts, which houses an eclectic collection of wine, food-related art and wine accessories. After acquiring a 50% share of Brookland Valley in 1997, Hardys moved to full ownership in 2004. The quality and consistency of the wines are, quite literally, awesome. Exports to the UK, the US and other major markets.

Winery name   Brookland Valley

Although it might seem that stating the winery name is straightforward, this is not necessarily so. To avoid confusion, wherever possible, I use the name that appears most prominently on the wine label and do not refer to any associated trading name.

Winery rating

The effort to come up with a fair winery rating continues. I looked at the ratings for this and the previous two years; if the wines tasted this year justified a higher rating than last year, the higher rating has been given. If, on the other hand, the wines are of lesser quality, I took into account the track record over the past two years (or longer where the winery is well known) and made a judgement call on whether it should retain its ranking, or be given a lesser one. If lesser, I have usually dropped the rating by only half a star where the prior record has been consistent. Where no wines were submitted by a well-rated winery which had a track record of providing samples, I used my discretion to roll over last year's rating. Unless there are extenuating circumstances (including frost, bushfire, etc.), it is most unlikely I will carry over ratings in the future. In other words, no tastings, no ratings.

The other comment is that, as in prior years (and in the future), the larger wineries tend to have a wide range of products, in a perfect world priced in line with their quality. Thus, for both small wineries, which may only make a handful of different wines, and large, the rating is heavily biased by the performance of the best wines of that producer. To do otherwise would be to deny a five-star rating to any of the 20 or more largest wineries and many others. To find the full list of ratings you need to refer to www.winecompanion.com.au.

The precise meanings attached to the winery star rating are as follows; the percentage at the end of each rating is that of the total number of wineries in the *Wine Companion*. Bear in mind there are another 822 wineries which either have low or no ratings.

★★★★★ Outstanding winery regularly producing wines of exemplary quality and typicity. Will have at least two wines rated at 94 points or above, and have had a five-star rating for the previous two years. 8%

★★★★★ Outstanding winery capable of producing wines of very high quality, and did so this year. Also will usually have at least two wines rated at 94 points or above. 12.5%

★★★★☆ Excellent winery able to produce wines of high to very high quality, knocking on the door of a five-star rating. Will have one wine rated at 94 points or above, and two (or more) at 90 or above; others at 87 to 89. 20.5%

★★★★ Very good producer of wines with class and character. Will have two (or more) wines rated at 90 points or above (or possibly one at 94 or above). 23%

★★★☆ A solid, usually reliable maker of good, sometimes very good wines. Will have one wine at 90 points or above; others at 87 to 89. 13.5%

★★★ A typically good winery, but often has a few lesser wines. Will have some wines at 87 to 89 points. 17%

★★☆ Has the potential to, and normally aspires to, improve. No wines rated above 86 points. 1%

NR A winery, often new, the wines of which I have not tasted in the past 12 months. Will only appear once under this rating. 4.5%

Contact details Caves Road, Wilyabrup, WA 6280 **T** (08) 9755 6042

The details are usually those of the winery and cellar door, but in a few instances may simply be of the winery; this occurs when the wine is made under contract and is sold only through retail.

Region Margaret River

The mapping of Australia into zones, regions and subregions with legally defined boundaries is now largely complete for regions. The registration of subregions is stalled, and there is no fixed date by which all applications for registration of regions or subregions must be completed. A full list of zones, regions and subregions appears on pages 38 to 41. Occasionally you will see 'Warehouse' as the region. This means the wine is made from purchased grapes, in someone else's winery. In other words, it does not have a vineyard or winery in the ordinary way.

www.brooklandvalley.com.au

An increasingly important reference point, often containing material not found (for space reasons) in this book.

Open 7 days 10–5

Although a winery might be listed as not open or open only on weekends, some may in fact be prepared to open by appointment. Many will, some won't; a telephone call will establish whether it is possible or not. Virtually every winery that is shown as being open only for weekends is in fact open on public holidays as well. Once again, a telephone call will confirm this.

Winemaker Ross Pamment

In the large companies the winemaker is simply the head of a team; there may be many executive winemakers actually responsible for specific wines.

Est. 1984

A more or less self-explanatory item, but keep in mind that some makers consider the year in which they purchased the land to be the year of establishment, others the year in which they first planted grapes, others the year they first made wine, others the year they first offered wine for sale, and so on. There may also be minor complications where there has been a change of ownership or break in production.

Cases 130 000

This figure (representing the number of cases produced each year) is merely an indication of the size of the operation. Some winery entries do not feature a production figure: this is either because the winery (principally, but not exclusively, the large companies) regards this information as confidential or because the information was not available at the time of going to press. NFP = not for publication.

Summary Brookland Valley has an idyllic setting, plus its much enlarged Flutes Café (one of the best winery restaurants in the Margaret River region) and its Gallery of Wine Arts, which houses an eclectic collection of wine, food-related art and wine accessories. After acquiring a 50% share of Brookland Valley in 1997, Hardys moved to full ownership in 2004. The quality and consistency of the wines are, quite literally, awesome. Exports to the UK, the US and other major markets.

My summary of the winery. Little needs be said, except that I have tried to vary the subjects I discuss in this part of the winery entry.

New wineries

 The vine leaf symbol indicates the 169 wineries that are new entries in this year's *Wine Companion*.

Tasting notes

Ratings

94–100	♟♟♟♟♟	**Outstanding.** Wines of the highest quality, usually with a distinguished pedigree.
90–93	♟♟♟♟♟	**Highly recommended.** Wines of great quality, style and character, worthy of a place in any cellar.
87–89	♟♟♟♟	**Recommended.** Wines of above-average quality, fault-free, and with clear varietal expression.

In order to compress the amount of material in this year's *Wine Companion*, but also to preserve a like-on-like comparison with prior years, the 2.5- to 3.5-glass-rated wines will appear on www.winecompanion.com.au (2196 in all).

♟♟♟♟♟ **Verse 1 Margaret River Shiraz 2006** An exceptionally good wine; medium-bodied, with blackberry, plum, spice and pepper supported by fine tannins and skilled use of oak. Screwcap. 13° alc. **Rating 95 To 2021 $20**

The tasting note opens with the vintage of the wine tasted. This note will have been made within the 12 months prior to publication. Even that is a long time, and during the life of this book the wine will almost certainly change. Remember also that tasting is a highly subjective and imperfect art. NV = non vintage. The price of the wine is listed where information is available. Notes for wines 94 points or over, for wines offering particularly good value, and for unusual wines, are printed in red.

To 2021

I have simply provided a (conservative) 'best by' date. Modern winemaking is such that, even if a wine has 10 or 20 years' future during which it will gain much greater complexity, it can be enjoyed at any time over the intervening months and years.

Screwcap

This is the closure used for this particular wine. The closures in use for the wines tasted are (in descending order): screwcap 68% (last year 65%), one-piece natural cork 17% (last year 22%) and Diam 5% (last year 6%). The remaining 10% (in approximate order of importance) are ProCork, Twin Top, Crown Seal, Zork, Vino-Lok and Synthetic. I believe the percentage of screwcap closures will continue to rise.

13° alc

I have endeavoured to always include this piece of information, which is in one sense self-explanatory. What is less obvious is the increasing concern of many Australian winemakers about the rise in levels of alcohol; much research and practical experiment (picking earlier, higher fermentation temperatures in open fermenters, etc.) are occurring. Reverse osmosis and yeast selection are two of the research fields of particular promise.

Winery of the year

Brookland Valley

Once the database assembled over the past 12 months yielded its secrets, close on a dozen wineries emerged as serious contenders for the Winery of the Year title. That most of these were not selected was not due to any shortcomings, but simply that two of the group had a particularly spectacular array of wines released over the past 12 months.

By chance (or perhaps not) they are both part of the Constellation Wines group, previously known as Hardys. They are Brookland Valley in Margaret River and Bay of Fires in Tasmania. Until I put pen to paper and began to articulate how I came to choose one over the other, I had made up my mind it was to be Bay of Fires.

I jumped ship at the last moment because Brookland Valley has eight wines rated 94 points or above; they cover Rose, Semillon, Semillon Sauvignon Blanc, Chardonnay (three different wines), Shiraz and Cabernet Sauvignon. That range of itself puts Brookland Valley into a unique position, as no other winery has such a five-glass coverage across so many varietal wines.

There was another reason, although it was barely necessary: four of the eight have a RRP (recommended retail price) of $20 or less. These are from the Verse 1 range, and are Rose, Chardonnay, Semillon, Sauvignon Blanc and Shiraz.

If all this were not enough, the wines were showered with trophies and gold medals during the wine show year, which technically ended with the Sydney Wine Show in February 2008.

Quite obviously, this refutes the commonly held view that the big winery groups do not make great wine. When it comes to quality wine (as opposed to beverage wine), the winemaking teams – in this instance headed by Ross Pamment – fight tigerishly to protect their bailiwick, their independence and their quality standards. At this level, their attitude is on all fours with that of boutique owner-winemakers.

Best of the best of Australian wine

I make my usual disclaimer: while there were two periods of intense tasting activity in the 12 months during which the tasting notes for this edition were made, and while some wines were tasted more than once, an over-arching comparative tasting of all the best wines is simply not possible, however desirable it might be.

So the points for the individual wines scoring 94 or above stand uncorrected by the wisdom of hindsight. Nonetheless, the link between variety and region (or, if you prefer, between variety and terroir) is in most instances strikingly evident. It is for this reason that I have shown the region for each of the best wines. While the short-term focus of the export industry was (until 2007) the paramount necessity of reducing stock either in bulk or under the generic bottling of BOB (buyer own brand), medium and longer term prosperity will depend on a sense of place, of regional identity.

Brand Australia has been the foundation upon which the success of the past 20 years has been built, but all recognise it is time to move on. While some naysayers may regard this as marketing rhetoric, the truth is that Australia is blessed with an unmatched range of terroir (including climate in that deceptively simple term), enabling it to make wines ranging from the uniquely complex fortified wines of Rutherglen (fashioned from frontignac and muscadelle, known locally as muscat and tokay), to the 100 Year Old Para Liqueur of Seppelt in the Barossa Valley, all the way through to the exceptional sparkling wines of Tasmania, grown in a climate every bit as cool as that of Champagne.

This is one of the principal reasons for the wines with the same points to be arranged by region, even though the main text is alpha-ordered. I should also point out that the cut-off for listing the wines of each variety differs considerably, depending on the strength of the class concerned.

Best of the best by variety

Riesling

The 2007 vintage was generally regarded as a difficult one for the variety, but prior vintages and many exceptions (that is, the '07s) led to a long list (too long to reproduce) of rieslings scoring 94 points (in addition to those wines listed below). A considerable number of these wines came from Western Australia and Tasmania. For the record, 51 wines scored 94 points (not listed here due to space constraints). Eden Valley supplanted Clare Valley for the wines scoring 95 points or above, and once the 94-point wines were taken into account, there was a freakish three-way tie between the Eden Valley, Great Southern and Tasmania, each with 13 wines.

RATING	WINE	REGION
96	2006 Paulett Antonina	Clare Valley
96	2003 Wilson Vineyard Polish Hill River Museum	Clare Valley
96	2007 Leo Buring Leonay DWK17	Eden Valley
96	2002 Peter Lehmann Reserve	Eden Valley
96	2007 Pewsey Vale Prima	Eden Valley
96	2002 Pewsey Vale The Contours	Eden Valley
96	2007 Forest Hill Vineyard Block 1	Great Southern
96	2007 Howard Park	Great Southern
96	2007 Seppelt Drumborg	Henty
96	2006 Abbey Creek Vineyard	Porongurup
96	2006 Bay of Fires	Tasmania
96	2003 Craigow	Tasmania
95	2007 Shaw & Smith	Adelaide Hills
95	2007 Twofold	Clare Valley
95	2007 Henschke Julius	Eden Valley
95	2006 Orlando St Helga	Eden Valley
95	2003 Wroxton Single Vineyard	Eden Valley
95	2007 Frankland Estate Isolation Ridge Vineyard	Frankland River
95	2007 West Cape Howe	Great Southern
95	2006 Frogmore Creek FGR	Tasmania
95	2006 Waterton Vineyards	Tasmania

Chardonnay

Members of the ABC (Anything But Chardonnay) club should be made to taste a cross-section of these wines, or the 35 at 95 points, and the 112 at 94 points. The four leading regions (for all chardonnays 94 points or above; the 94-point wines not listed here due to space constraints) are Margaret River (33), Yarra Valley (29), Mornington Peninsula (26) and Adelaide Hills (13).

RATING	WINE	REGION
97	2006 Shaw & Smith M3 Vineyard	Adelaide Hills
97	2006 Bindi Wine Growers Quartz	Macedon Ranges
97	2005 Leeuwin Estate Art Series	Margaret River
96	2006 Ashton Hills	Adelaide Hills
96	2006 Yalumba FDW[7c]	Adelaide Hills
96	2005 Heggies Vineyard Reserve	Eden Valley
96	2006 Clyde Park Vineyard Reserve	Geelong
96	2006 Ashbrook Estate	Margaret River
96	2005 Brookland Valley	Margaret River
96	2005 Chapman Grove Atticus	Margaret River
96	2005 Cullen	Margaret River
96	2005 Lenton Brae	Margaret River
96	2006 Vasse Felix Heytesbury	Margaret River
96	2007 Victory Point	Margaret River
96	2005 Stonier KBS Vineyard	Mornington Peninsula
96	2006 Tuck's Ridge Buckle Vineyard	Mornington Peninsula
96	2006 Forest Hill Vineyard Block 8	Mount Barker
96	2006 Freycinet	Tasmania
96	2006 Oakridge 864	Yarra Valley
96	2006 Toolangi Vineyards Estate	Yarra Valley
96	2005 Yering Station Reserve	Yarra Valley

Semillon

Imitation, they say, is the sincerest form of flattery, and the winemakers at Peter Lehmann have taken this to the highest level with the aid of the very cool 2002 vintage. It will be interesting to see whether future vintages of this wine have the same success, but I suspect it won't be an annual affair. For the record, 28 semillons scored 94 points (not listed here due to space constraints); in all, the Hunter Valley produced 33 wines scoring 94 points or above.

RATING	WINE	REGION
96	2002 Peter Lehmann Reserve Margaret	Barossa Valley
96	2004 Alkoomi Wandoo	Frankland River
96	2007 Tamburlaine Members Reserve	Hunter Valley
96	2006 Tower Estate	Hunter Valley
96	2002 Tyrrell's Museum Release Vat 1	Hunter Valley
96	2001 Tyrrell's Single Vineyard HVD	Hunter Valley
95	2006 Henschke Louis	Eden Valley
95	2002 Audrey Wilkinson Vineyard	Hunter Valley
95	2002 Brokenwood ILR Reserve	Hunter Valley
95	2007 Capercaillie The Creel	Hunter Valley
95	2007 McLeish Estate	Hunter Valley
95	2003 McWilliam's Mount Pleasant Elizabeth	Hunter Valley

95	2002 McWilliam's Mount Pleasant Lovedale	Hunter Valley
95	2002 Meerea Park Alexander Munro	Hunter Valley
95	2005 Poole's Rock	Hunter Valley
95	1999 Tower Estate Museum Release	Hunter Valley
95	2001 Tower Estate Museum Release	Hunter Valley
95	2003 Tyrrell's Single Vineyard Stevens	Hunter Valley
95	2000 Tyrrell's Vat 1	Hunter Valley
95	2007 Ashbrook Estate	Margaret River
95	2006 Brookland Valley	Margaret River
95	2007 Redgate OFS	Margaret River

Sauvignon blanc

Just as 2007 was a difficult year for riesling in South Australia, so it was for sauvignon blanc, which is the explanation for the unusually low representation from the Adelaide Hills – a region that normally dominates this field to a greater extent. For the variety to show its best, the one constant is the need for a cool region. An additional 24 sauvignon blancs were rated at 94 points (not listed here due to space constraints), with Adelaide Hills (9) and Yarra Valley (5) leading the way for those rated 94 points or above.

RATING	WINE	REGION
96	2005 Geoff Weaver Ferus Lenswood	Adelaide Hills
96	2007 De Bortoli Reserve Release	Yarra Valley
95	2007 O'Leary Walker	Adelaide Hills
95	2007 SC Pannell	Adelaide Hills
95	2007 Shaw & Smith	Adelaide Hills
95	2006 Bannockburn Vineyards	Geelong
95	2007 Howard Park	Great Southern
95	2007 Wise Pemberton	Margaret River
95	2007 Chalkers Crossing	Tumbarumba
95	2007 PHI Lusatia Park Vineyard	Yarra Valley

Sauvignon semillon blends

This is the fastest growing wine segment in the market (supported by varietal sauvignon blanc), and at the top end is the nigh-on exclusive preserve of the Margaret River wines. The maritime climate replicates that of Bordeaux, the Old World home of the blend (the percentage of muscadelle is rapidly decreasing in Bordeaux).

RATING	WINE	REGION
96	2005 Cape Mentelle Wallcliffe	Margaret River
96	2006 Cape Mentelle Wallcliffe	Margaret River
95	2005 Suckfizzle	Margaret River
95	2007 Voyager Estate	Margaret River
95	2007 Wise	Margaret River
94	2007 Steinborner Family Vineyards Caroliene	Barossa Valley/ Adelaide Hills
94	2007 Grosset	Clare Valley

94	2007 Henschke Eleanor's Cottage	Eden Valley
94	2007 Yalumba	Eden Valley
94	2007 Feet First	Frankland River
94	2007 Tatler Over the Ditch	Hunter Valley/ Marlborough
94	2007 Amberley Estate	Margaret River
94	2007 Brookland Valley Verse 1	Margaret River
94	2007 Cape Mentelle	Margaret River
94	2007 Chalice Bridge Estate	Margaret River
94	2007 Cullen Mangan Vineyard	Margaret River
94	2007 Cullen	Margaret River
94	2007 Deep Woods Estate	Margaret River
94	2007 Driftwood Estate	Margaret River
94	2007 Hay Shed Hill Block 1	Margaret River
94	2007 Lenton Brae	Margaret River
94	2007 Pierro LTC	Margaret River
94	2007 Sandalford Estate Reserve	Margaret River
94	2007 Stella Bella	Margaret River
94	2007 Thompson Estate	Margaret River
94	2007 Vasse Felix	Margaret River
94	2007 Witchcliffe Estate	Margaret River
94	2007 Goundrey	Mount Barker

Other white wines

Aligote, arneis, aucerot, biancone, chasselas, chenin blanc, clairette, cortese, fiano, flora, garganega, gewurztraminer, gouais, kerner, marsanne, muller thurgau, ondenc, petit manseng, petit meslier, picolit, pinot gris, roussanne, schonburger, siegerrebe, silvaner, taminga, verduzzo, vermentino and viognier are all commercially grown and made into white wines or blends: those that follow are by far the most important varieties in this 'other' category.

RATING	WINE	REGION
96	2005 Yalumba The Virgilius Viognier	Eden Valley
96	2006 Yalumba The Virgilius Viognier	Eden Valley
96	2006 Yeringberg Marsanne Roussanne	Yarra Valley
95	2006 Petaluma Viognier	Adelaide Hills
95	1999 Tahbilk 1927 Vines Marsanne	Nagambie Lakes
94	2007 Haan Viognier Prestige	Barossa Valley
94	2005 Turkey Flat Butchers Block Marsanne Viognier	Barossa Valley
94	2007 Henschke Joseph Hill Gewurztraminer	Eden Valley
94	2007 Seppelt Coborra Drumborg Vineyard Pinot Gris	Henty
94	2006 Happs Viognier	Margaret River
94	2006 McHenry Hohnen Vintners 3 Amigos Marsanne Chardonnay Roussanne	Margaret River
94	2005 Coriole The Optimist Reserve Chenin Blanc	McLaren Vale
94	2007 Primo Estate Joseph Pinot Grigio d'Elena	McLaren Vale
94	2006 Allies Saone Viognier	Mornington Peninsula
94	2007 Paringa Estate Pinot Gris	Mornington Peninsula

94	2006 Vincognita Nangkita Vineyard Madeleine's Viognier	Southern Fleurieu
94	2007 Green Vineyards Cardinia Ranges Pinot Gris	Yarra Valley
94	2006 De Bortoli Estate Grown Viognier	Yarra Valley
94	2006 Yering Station MVR Marsanne Viognier Roussanne	Yarra Valley

Sparkling

The best sparkling wines are now solely sourced either from Tasmania or from the coolest sites in the coolest regions in the southern parts of the mainland. Altitude plays a major role. Thus, for example, it is the Upper Yarra Valley (while not an officially recognised subregion) that supplies the Yarra Valley makers of these wines.

RATING	WINE	REGION
96	2000 Bindi Wine Growers Extended Lees Aged	Macedon Ranges
96	2003 Clover Hill	Tasmania
96	1999 Freycinet Radenti Pinot Noir	Tasmania
96	1999 Yarrabank Late Disgorged	Yarra Valley
95	2001 Clover Hill Blanc de Blanc	Tasmania
95	2004 Josef Chromy Sparkling	Tasmania
95	2004 Domaine Chandon Brut Rose Vintage	Yarra Valley
95	2004 Domaine Chandon Vintage Brut	Yarra Valley
95	2003 Yarrabank Cuvee	Yarra Valley
94	NV Silver Wings Winemaking #2 Brut Rose	Macedon Ranges
94	NV Silver Wings Winemaking Brut	Macedon Ranges
94	2002 Houghton Pinot Noir	Pemberton
94	2000 Hardys Sir James Pinot Noir	Tumbarumba
94	2002 Bay of Fires Arras	Tasmania
94	NV Bay of Fires Tigress Pinot	Tasmania
94	NV Bay of Fires Tigress Sparkling Rose	Tasmania
94	2003 Clover Hill Blanc de Blanc	Tasmania
94	NV Jansz Tasmania Premium Rose	Tasmania
94	2004 Jansz Tasmania Premium Vintage Rose	Tasmania
94	2000 Kreglinger Vintage Brut	Tasmania
94	2004 Domaine Chandon Tasmanian Cuvee	Tasmania
94	2004 Domaine Chandon Z*D Vintage Brut	Yarra Valley
94	NV Dominique Portet Brut Rose LD	Yarra Valley
94	2004 Oakridge Limited Release Blanc de Blanc	Yarra Valley

I would like to make mention of two wines that will be eagerly sought by the small percentage of wine drinkers who understand the peculiarities of the style and who, better still, are prepared to cellar them for a year or more. The Seppelt Show Reserve is missing only because it is not made every year.

RATING	WINE	REGION
94	NV Rockford Black Shiraz	Barossa Valley
94	NV Turkey Flat Sparkling Shiraz	Barossa Valley

Sweet

Once dominated by barrel-fermented semillons, this group is now an eclectic range of aromatic varieties, reliant on either botrytis or freeze concentration, an esoteric Rhône Valley–inspired late harvest viognier marsanne, and a bedrock of botrytis semillons.

RATING	WINE	REGION
95	2007 Waterton Vineyards Dessert Riesling	Tasmania
95	2004 Craigow Botrytis Riesling	Tasmania
95	2007 Frogmore Creek Iced Gewurztraminer	Tasmania
95	2007 Pooley Coal River Late Harvest Riesling	Tasmania
94	2005 Munari Late Harvest Viognier Marsanne	Heathcote
94	2006 Crawford River Nektar	Henty
94	2003 Brown Brothers Cellar Door Release Late Harvested Botrytis Semillon	King Valley
94	2006 Keith Tulloch Wine Botrytis Semillon	Hunter Valley
94	2007 Scarborough Wine Co Late Harvest Semillon	Hunter Valley
94	2006 Tamar Ridge Botrytis Riesling	Tasmania
94	2006 De Bortoli Noble One	Riverina
94	2006 Nugan Estate Cookoothama Darlington Point Botrytis Semillon	Riverina

Rose

The number of roses on the market continues to grow, seemingly unabated and unstoppable. There are no rules: they can be bone-dry, slightly sweet or very sweet. They can be and are made from almost any red variety, red blends or red and white blends. They may be a convenient way of concentrating the red wine left after the rose is run off (bleeding, or saignee) from the fermenter shortly after the grapes are crushed or made from the ground up using grapes and techniques specifically chosen for the purpose. The vast majority of wines fall in the former camp; those listed mainly come from the latter.

RATING	WINE	REGION
94	2007 Charles Melton Rose Of Virginia	Barossa Valley
94	2007 Turkey Flat	Barossa Valley
94	2007 Willow Bridge Estate	Geographe
94	2006 Vinea Marson	Heathcote
94	2007 Brookland Valley Verse 1	Margaret River
94	2007 SC Pannell Grenache Rose	McLaren Vale
94	2007 Angove's Nine Vines Grenache Shiraz Rose	Riverland
94	2007 De Bortoli Pinot Noir Rose	Yarra Valley

Pinot noir

What I term the dress circle around Melbourne (Geelong, Gippsland, Macedon Ranges, Mornington Peninsula and Yarra Valley) and Tasmania have an iron grip on the production of the best pinot noirs, and there is no likelihood of that grip loosening any time soon. If climate change is the cause of recent vintage peculiarities, Ballarat and Henty will join the club, albeit with relatively few producers. For the record, 75 pinot noirs scored 94 points (not listed here due to space constraints). For those scoring 94 points or above, three regions dominated: Mornington Peninsula (31), Tasmania (27) and Yarra Valley (26).

RATING	WINE	REGION
96	2006 Tomboy Hill The Tomboy	Ballarat
96	2006 by Farr Sangreal	Geelong
96	2006 Bindi Wine Growers Block 5	Macedon Ranges
96	2006 Hurley Vineyard Harcourt	Mornington Peninsula
96	2006 Tuck's Ridge Buckle Vineyard	Mornington Peninsula
96	2006 Stoney Rise	Tasmania
95	2006 Tomboy Hill Smythes Creek	Ballarat
95	2006 Bass Phillip 21	Gippsland
95	2006 Bindi Wine Growers Original Vineyard	Macedon Ranges
95	2006 Hurley Vineyard Estate	Mornington Peninsula
95	2006 Kooyong Single Vineyard Selection Ferrous	Mornington Peninsula
95	2006 Moorooduc The Moorooduc	Mornington Peninsula
95	2006 Paringa Estate	Mornington Peninsula
95	2006 Paringa Estate Reserve Special Barrel Selection	Mornington Peninsula
95	2005 Port Phillip Estate Morillon Tete De Cuvee	Mornington Peninsula
95	2005 Scorpo	Mornington Peninsula
95	2006 The Cups Estate Raimondo Reserve	Mornington Peninsula
95	2006 Yabby Lake Vineyard	Mornington Peninsula
95	2006 Bay of Fires Tigress	Tasmania
95	2006 Bream Creek	Tasmania
95	2005 Bream Creek Reserve	Tasmania
95	2006 `ese Vineyards	Tasmania
95	2006 Home Hill	Tasmania
95	2005 Stefano Lubiana Estate	Tasmania
95	2005 Stefano Lubiana Sasso	Tasmania
95	2005 Tamar Ridge Kayena Vineyard	Tasmania
95	2006 Diamond Valley Vineyards Reserve	Yarra Valley
95	2006 Giant Steps Tarraford Vineyard	Yarra Valley
95	2006 Hillcrest Vineyard Reserve	Yarra Valley
95	2005 Labyrinth Viggers Vineyard	Yarra Valley
95	2006 Mayer Close Planted	Yarra Valley
95	2006 Yering Station Reserve	Yarra Valley
95	2006 Yering Station	Yarra Valley

Shiraz

Shiraz is grown across the length and breadth of Australia's wine regions, and any analysis of those regions (other than the dominant Barossa Valley) has little relevance unless one is looking at style and/or domestic and market preferences. Even if one is looking for vines more than 100 years old, they will be found in the Hunter Valley, Goulburn Valley/Nagambie Lakes, Coonawarra, McLaren Vale, Clare Valley, Eden

Valley, Langhorne Creek and, of course, the major repository of the Barossa Valley. It is the most quintessential Australian variety, making its two icons, Penfolds Grange and Henschke Hill of Grace. For the record, 39 shirazs scored 96 points, 101 scored 95 points and 242 scored 94 points (the latter not listed here due to space constraints). The major contributors brought no surprise: the Barossa (96) and McLaren Vale (59), but third place to the Hunter Valley (33) was not something I would have predicted.

RATING	WINE	REGION
97	2004 Yabby Lake Vineyard Roc	Mornington Peninsula
96	2005 Ngeringa Syrah	Adelaide Hills
96	2005 Gibson Barossavale Australian Old Vine Collection	Barossa Valley
96	2006 Glaetzer Amon-Ra Unfiltered	Barossa Valley
96	2002 Grant Burge Meshach	Barossa Valley
96	2006 Groom	Barossa Valley
96	2005 John Duval Eligo	Barossa Valley
96	2006 John Duval Entity	Barossa Valley
96	2005 Peter Lehmann The 1885	Barossa Valley
96	2005 Rolf Binder Veritas Hanisch	Barossa Valley
96	2006 Schubert Estate Goose-yard Block	Barossa Valley
96	2006 St Hallett Blackwell	Barossa Valley
96	2005 Torbreck Vintners The Factor	Barossa Valley
96	2004 Torbreck Vintners The RunRig	Barossa Valley
96	2004 Trevor Jones Reserve Wild Witch	Barossa Valley
96	2006 Turkey Flat	Barossa Valley
96	2006 Clonakilla Syrah	Canberra District
96	2006 Leasingham Single Vineyard Release Provis	Clare Valley
96	2004 O'Leary Walker Claire Reserve	Clare Valley
96	2004 Henschke Hill Of Grace	Eden Valley
96	2005 Maverick Trial Hill	Eden Valley
96	2005 Clayfield	Grampians
96	2006 Grampians Estate Black Sunday Friends Reserve	Grampians
96	2006 The Story Westgate Vineyard	Grampians
96	2005 Pyramids Road	Granite Belt
96	2005 Forest Hill Vineyard Block 9	Great Southern
96	2006 Bindi Wine Growers Pyrette	Heathcote
96	2006 Vinea Marson Syrah	Heathcote
96	2006 Henty Estate	Henty
96	2005 Brokenwood Graveyard Vineyard	Hunter Valley
96	2006 Tyrrell's Winemaker's Selection Vat 9	Hunter Valley
96	2004 Saltram Metala Original Plantings	Langhorne Creek
96	2005 Woodlands Colin	Margaret River
96	2004 Gemtree Vineyards Obsidian	McLaren Vale
96	2004 Hardys Chateau Reynella Cellar 1	McLaren Vale
96	2006 Mitolo Savitar	McLaren Vale
96	2005 Paxton Elizabeth Jean 100 Year	McLaren Vale
96	2005 Primo Estate Shale Stone	McLaren Vale
96	2005 SC Pannell	McLaren Vale
96	2005 Wirra Wirra RSW	McLaren Vale

96	2006 Paringa Estate Reserve Special Barrel Selection	Mornington Peninsula
96	2005 Plantagenet Great Southern	Mount Barker
96	2002 Tahbilk Eric Stevens Purbrick	Nagambie Lakes
96	2006 Mt Billy Antiquity	Southern Fleurieu
96	2006 De Bortoli Reserve Release Syrah	Yarra Valley

Shiraz viognier

In best Australian Tall Poppy Syndrome fashion, it has already become fashionable in some quarters to challenge the remarkable synergy obtained by co-fermenting around 5% of viognier with shiraz. The enhancement of colour, aroma and flavour is remarkable, as is the softening and smoothing of texture. Yes, it is not a panacea for lesser quality grapes and, yes, it is and should remain a subtext to the thrust of shiraz's flavour. Nonetheless, the wines in this group offer hedonistic pleasure second to none. Overall, the blend works best in temperate to cool regions; the Barossa Valley and McLaren Vale are well behind the wines of those cooler climates.

RATING	WINE	REGION
97	2007 Clonakilla	Canberra District
96	2005 Wolf Blass Gold Label	Adelaide Hills
96	2005 Torbreck Vintners The Descendant	Barossa Valley
96	2006 Clonakilla	Canberra District
95	2006 Spinifex	Barossa Valley
95	2006 Turner's Crossing Vineyard	Bendigo
95	2006 Boireann	Granite Belt
95	2005 Goundrey	Mount Barker
95	2005 Yarra Yering Dry Red No. 2	Yarra Valley
95	2006 Yering Station	Yarra Valley
94	2006 Mr Riggs Wine Company	Adelaide
94	2004 Mount Torrens Vineyards Solstice	Adelaide Hills
94	2006 Saltram Pepperjack	Barossa Valley
94	2006 Pondalowie Vineyards	Bendigo
94	2006 Clyde Park Vineyard Megan's Block	Geelong
94	2005 Willow Bridge Estate Family Reserve	Geographe
94	2006 Wovenfield Reserve	Geographe
94	2004 Barwang Vineyard	Hilltops
94	2006 d'Arenberg The Laughing Magpie	McLaren Vale
94	2005 Hardys Starvedog Lane	McLaren Vale
94	2005 Millbrook Estate	Perth Hills
94	2005 Western Range Julimar	Perth Hills
94	2006 Centennial Vineyards Reserve	Southern Highlands
94	2006 De Bortoli Estate Grown	Yarra Valley
94	2006 De Bortoli Gulf Station	Yarra Valley
94	2005 Diamond Valley Vineyards	Yarra Valley
94	2006 Diamond Valley Vineyards	Yarra Valley
94	2005 YarraLoch Stephanie's Dream SV	Yarra Valley

Cabernet sauvignon

The affinity of cabernet sauvignon with a maritime climate is put beyond doubt by its home in Bordeaux's Medoc region. So it comes as no surprise to find that most (but not all) of Australia's top-quality cabernets come from regions with climates similar to Bordeaux (conspicuously Coonawarra) and/or are within 50 km of the sea with no intervening mountain range (Margaret River, McLaren Vale and Langhorne Creek). A further 62 cabernets scored 94 points (not listed here due to space constraints). All up, Margaret River's first place with 17 wines was to be expected, but McLaren Vale (14) edging out Coonawarra (13) into third place was, in racing parlance, a boil over.

RATING	WINE	REGION
96	2005 Leasingham Single Vineyard Release Schobers	Clare Valley
96	2006 Balnaves of Coonawarra The Tally Reserve	Coonawarra
96	2005 Wynns Coonawarra Estate John Riddoch	Coonawarra
96	2005 Ferngrove Majestic	Frankland River
96	2005 Forest Hill Vineyard Block 5	Great Southern
96	2005 Chalkers Crossing	Hilltops
96	2004 Bremerton Reserve Cabernet	Langhorne Creek
96	2002 Brookland Valley Reserve	Margaret River
96	2002 Houghton Gladstones	Margaret River
96	2004 Howard Park Leston	Margaret River
96	2005 Sandalford Prendiville Reserve	Margaret River
96	2004 Hardys Reynell Basket Pressed	McLaren Vale
96	2002 Tahbilk Eric Stevens Purbrick	Nagambie Lakes
96	2005 Polleters	Pyrenees
95	2006 Bird in Hand Mount Lofty Ranges	Adelaide Hills
95	2004 Grant Burge Cameron Vale	Barossa Valley
95	2005 Grant Burge Shadrach	Barossa Valley
95	2005 Majella Coonawarra	Coonawarra
95	2005 Parker Coonawarra Estate Terra Rossa	Coonawarra
95	2005 Wynns Coonawarra Estate Messenger Vineyard	Coonawarra
95	2004 Zema Estate Family Selection	Coonawarra
95	2005 Henschke Cyril Henschke	Eden Valley
95	2005 Wild Duck Creek Estate Reserve	Heathcote
95	1997 Crawford River	Henty
95	2003 Cape Mentelle	Margaret River
95	2005 Clairault Estate	Margaret River
95	2004 Moss Wood	Margaret River
95	2005 Suckfizzle	Margaret River
95	2004 Thompson Estate	Margaret River
95	2005 Woodside Valley Estate Baudin	Margaret River
95	2004 Clarendon Hills Hickinbotham Vineyard	McLaren Vale
95	2005 d'Arenberg The Coppermine Road	McLaren Vale
95	2005 Hardys Chateau Reynella Basket Press	McLaren Vale
95	2006 Pertaringa Rifle & Hunt	McLaren Vale
95	2006 Wirra Wirra The Angelus	McLaren Vale
95	2006 Stonehaven Fatherwoods	Padthaway

| 95 | 2005 Bream Creek | Tasmania |
| 95 | 2005 Olsen Wines Victoria Personal Reserve | Yarra Valley |

Cabernet and family

This group revolves around the grapes of Bordeaux and primarily blends thereof, but with some single varieties, most notably merlot, the majority comes from moderately cool regions. Also included are the classic Australian cabernet and shiraz (or vice versa) blends.

RATING	WINE	REGION
96	2005 Wendouree Cabernet Malbec	Clare Valley
96	2004 Brand's Laira Coonawarra The Patron	Coonawarra
96	2005 Cullen Diana Madeline	Margaret River
96	2004 Pierro Reserve Cabernet Sauvignon Merlot	Margaret River
96	2006 Paramoor The Fraser Shiraz Cabernet Sauvignon Merlot	Macedon Ranges
96	2004 Houghton Jack Mann	Swan Valley
95	2005 Wicks Estate Eminence Shiraz Cabernet	Adelaide Hills
95	2001 Yalumba The Reserve	Barossa Valley
95	2005 Haan Merlot Prestige	Barossa Valley
95	2005 Grosset Gaia	Clare Valley
95	2005 Lindemans Pyrus	Coonawarra
95	2006 Majella The Musician Cabernet Shiraz	Coonawarra
95	2005 Majella Merlot	Coonawarra
95	2004 Murdock The Editorial	Coonawarra
95	2005 Moombaki Reserve	Denmark
95	2005 Henschke Lenswood Abbott's Prayer	Eden Valley
95	2002 Irvine James Irvine Grand Merlot	Eden Valley
95	2005 Wild Duck Creek Estate The Blend	Heathcote
95	2004 Lake Breeze Arthur's Reserve Cabernet Sauvignon Petit Verdot Malbec	Langhorne Creek
95	2005 Pierro Cabernet Sauvignon Merlot LTCf	Margaret River
95	2005 Stella Bella Cabernet Sauvignon Merlot	Margaret River
95	2006 Woodlands Reserve de la Cave Cabernet Franc	Margaret River
95	2004 Pirramimma ACJ	McLaren Vale
95	2004 Primo Estate Joseph Cabernet Sauvignon Merlot	McLaren Vale
95	2005 Picardy Merlot Cabernet Sauvignon Cabernet Franc	Pemberton
95	2005 Warrenmang Luigi Tribute	Pyrenees
95	2005 Penfolds Bin 389 Cabernet Shiraz	South Australia
95	2005 Mount Mary Quintet	Yarra Valley
95	2005 Yarra Yering Dry Red No. 1	Yarra Valley

Shiraz and family

A class utterly dominated by Rhône Valley blends of some or all of shiraz, grenache and mourvedre.

RATING	WINE	REGION
96	2005 Tim Smith Mataro Grenache Shiraz	Barossa Valley
95	2006 John Duval Plexus Shiraz Grenache Mourvedre	Barossa Valley
95	2005 Laughing Jack Limited Three Old Vine Grenache	Barossa Valley
95	2006 Spinifex Indigene	Barossa Valley
95	2005 The Islander Estate Vineyards Old Rowley Bush Vine Grenache	Kangaroo Island
95	2006 SC Pannell Grenache	McLaren Vale
95	2005 SC Pannell Shiraz Grenache	McLaren Vale

Fortified wines

A relatively small but immensely impressive group of wines, as quintessentially Australian as a Driza-Bone.

RATING	WINE	REGION
100	100 Year Old Para Liqueur 1907	Barossa Valley
97	NV Seppeltsfield Rare Tawny DP90	Barossa Valley
97	NV All Saints Estate Rare Muscat	Rutherglen
97	NV All Saints Rare Tokay	Rutherglen
97	NV Campbells Isabella Rare Tokay	Rutherglen
97	NV Morris Old Premium Liqueur Muscat	Rutherglen
97	NV Morris Old Premium Rare Muscat	Rutherglen
97	NV Morris Old Premium Rare Tokay	Rutherglen
97	NV Seppelt Rare Tokay DP59	Rutherglen
96	NV Penfolds Great Grandfather Rare Old Liqueur Tawny	Barossa Valley
96	NV Seppeltsfield Amontillado DP116	Barossa Valley
96	NV Campbells Merchant Prince Rare Muscat	Rutherglen
96	NV Morris Old Premium Tawny Port	Rutherglen
96	NV Seppeltsfield Rare Muscat GR113	Rutherglen
96	NV Stanton & Killeen Rare Muscat	Rutherglen
95	NV Seppeltsfield Oloroso DP38	Barossa Valley
95	NV Seppeltsfield Oloroso Sherry DP118	Barossa Valley
95	NV Baileys of Glenrowan Winemaker's Selection Old Muscat	Glenrowan
95	NV Baileys of Glenrowan Winemaker's Selection Old Liqueur Tokay	Glenrowan
95	NV All Saints Grand Tokay	Rutherglen
95	NV Buller Rare Liqueur Muscat	Rutherglen
95	NV Morris Cellar Reserve Grand Tokay	Rutherglen
95	NV John Kosovich Limited Release Liqueur Muscat	Swan Valley

Best wineries of the regions

The nomination of the best wineries of the regions has evolved in two ways: five red stars for wineries with a particularly distinguished track record over the past three years, and five black stars for those who have been consistently at or near the top for this period. While I have deliberately refused to bind myself to this yardstick, the red-starred wineries have in almost all instances achieved five-star ratings for each of the past three years, and most of those with black stars have had maximum ratings in two of the past three years, including (importantly) this year.

ADELAIDE HILLS
Ashton Hills ★★★★★
Bird in Hand ★★★★★
Deviation Road ★★★★★
Geoff Weaver ★★★★★
Hahndorf Hill Winery ★★★★★
K1 by Geoff Hardy ★★★★★
Longview Vineyard ★★★★★
Mount Torrens Vineyards ★★★★★
New Era Vineyards ★★★★★
Ngeringa ★★★★★
Paracombe Wines ★★★★★
Petaluma ★★★★★
Pike & Joyce ★★★★★
Romney Park Wines ★★★★★
Setanta Wines ★★★★★
Shaw & Smith ★★★★★
Tilbrook ★★★★★
Wicks Estate Wines ★★★★★

BALLARAT
Tomboy Hill ★★★★★

BAROSSA VALLEY
Charles Cimicky ★★★★★
Charles Melton ★★★★★
Deisen ★★★★★
Dutschke Wines ★★★★★
First Drop Wines ★★★★★
Gibson Barossavale ★★★★★
Glaetzer Wines ★★★★★

Grant Burge ★★★★★
Haan Wines ★★★★★
Hentley Farm Wines ★★★★★
Heritage Wines ★★★★★
John Duval Wines ★★★★★
Kaesler Wines ★★★★★
Kalleske ★★★★★
Langmeil Winery ★★★★★
Laughing Jack ★★★★★
Leo Buring ★★★★★
Massena Vineyards ★★★★★
Maverick Wines ★★★★★
Murray Street Vineyard ★★★★★
Orlando ★★★★★
Penfolds ★★★★★
Peter Lehmann ★★★★★
Rockford ★★★★★
Rohrlach Family Wines ★★★★★
Rolf Binder Veritas Winery ★★★★★
Russell Wines ★★★★★
Saltram ★★★★★
Schubert Estate ★★★★★
Seppeltsfield ★★★★★
Sheep's Back ★★★★★
Spinifex ★★★★★
St Hallett ★★★★★
Teusner ★★★★★
Thorn-Clarke Wines ★★★★★
Torbreck Vintners ★★★★★
Trevor Jones/Kellermeister ★★★★★
Turkey Flat ★★★★★

Westlake Vineyards ★★★★★
Wolf Blass ★★★★★
Yalumba ★★★★★
Yelland & Papps ★★★★★

BAROSSA VALLEY/ADELAIDE HILLS
Fox Gordon ★★★★★

BEECHWORTH
battely wines ★★★★★
Giaconda ★★★★★
Smiths Vineyard ★★★★★

BENDIGO
BlackJack Vineyards ★★★★★
Bress ★★★★★
Pondalowie Vineyards ★★★★★
Turner's Crossing Vineyard ★★★★★

CANBERRA DISTRICT
Clonakilla ★★★★★

CENTRAL VICTORIA ZONE
Silver Wings Winemaking ★★★★★

CLARE VALLEY
Annie's Lane ★★★★★
Grosset ★★★★★
Jim Barry Wines ★★★★★
Kilikanoon ★★★★★
Leasingham ★★★★★
Mitchell ★★★★★
Mount Horrocks ★★★★★
Neagles Rock Vineyards ★★★★★
O'Leary Walker Wines ★★★★★
Olssen ★★★★★
Paulett ★★★★★
Pikes ★★★★★
Taylors ★★★★★
Wendouree ★★★★★
Wilson Vineyard ★★★★★

CLARE VALLEY/HEATHCOTE
Twofold ★★★★★

COONAWARRA
Balnaves of Coonawarra ★★★★★
Leconfield ★★★★★
Lindemans ★★★★★
Majella ★★★★★
Murdock ★★★★★
Parker Coonawarra Estate ★★★★★
Punters Corner ★★★★★
Wynns Coonawarra Estate ★★★★★
Yalumba The Menzies ★★★★★
Zema Estate ★★★★★

EDEN VALLEY
Henschke ★★★★★
Pewsey Vale ★★★★★
Poonawatta Estate ★★★★★
Torzi Matthews Vintners ★★★★★

GEELONG
Bannockburn Vineyards ★★★★★
by Farr ★★★★★
Clyde Park Vineyard ★★★★★
Curlewis Winery ★★★★★
Farr Rising ★★★★★
Grassy Point Wines ★★★★★
Scotchmans Hill ★★★★★
Shadowfax ★★★★★

GEOGRAPHE
Capel Vale ★★★★★
Willow Bridge Estate ★★★★★

GIPPSLAND
Bass Phillip ★★★★★
Phillip Island Vineyard ★★★★★

GLENROWAN
Baileys of Glenrowan ★★★★★

GOULBURN VALLEY
Tahbilk ★★★★★

GRAMPIANS
Best's Wines ★★★★★
Clayfield Wines ★★★★★
Grampians Estate ★★★★★
Mount Langi Ghiran Vineyards
    ★★★★★
Seppelt ★★★★★
The Story Wines ★★★★★
Westgate Vineyard ★★★★★

GRANITE BELT
Boireann ★★★★★

GREAT SOUTHERN
Alkoomi ★★★★★
Castle Rock Estate ★★★★★
Duke's Vineyard ★★★★★
Ferngrove ★★★★★
Forest Hill Vineyard ★★★★★
Frankland Estate ★★★★★
Gilberts ★★★★★
Goundrey ★★★★★
Harewood Estate ★★★★★
Howard Park ★★★★★
West Cape Howe Wines ★★★★★

HEATHCOTE
Domaines Tatiarra ★★★★★
Greenstone Vineyard ★★★★★
Heathcote Estate ★★★★★
Heathcote II ★★★★★
Heathcote Winery ★★★★★
Jasper Hill ★★★★★
La Pleiade ★★★★★
Mount Camel Ridge Estate ★★★★★
Munari Wines ★★★★★
Occam's Razor ★★★★★
Shelmerdine Vineyards ★★★★★
Syrahmi ★★★★★
Vinea Marson ★★★★★
Wild Duck Creek Estate ★★★★★

HENTY
Crawford River Wines ★★★★★
Henty Estate ★★★★★

HILLTOPS
Barwang Vineyard ★★★★★
Chalkers Crossing ★★★★★

HUNTER VALLEY
Audrey Wilkinson Vineyard ★★★★★
Brokenwood ★★★★★
Capercaillie ★★★★★
Chateau Pâto ★★★★★
Chatto Wines ★★★★★
De Iuliis ★★★★★
Keith Tulloch Wine ★★★★★
Lake's Folly ★★★★★
McWilliam's Mount Pleasant
    ★★★★★
Margan Family ★★★★★
Meerea Park ★★★★★
Mistletoe Wines ★★★★★
Oakvale ★★★★★
Piggs Peake ★★★★★
Scarborough Wine Co ★★★★★
Stonehurst Cedar Creek ★★★★★
Tamburlaine ★★★★★
Tatler Wines ★★★★★
Thomas Wines ★★★★★
Tower Estate ★★★★★
Tulloch ★★★★★
Tyrrell's ★★★★★

KANGAROO ISLAND
The Islander Estate Vineyards ★★★★★

KING VALLEY
Brown Brothers ★★★★★

LANGHORNE CREEK
Bremerton Wines ★★★★★
John's Blend ★★★★★

MACEDON RANGES
Bindi Wine Growers ★★★★★
Curly Flat ★★★★★
Domaine Epis ★★★★★
Granite Hills ★★★★★
Hanging Rock Winery ★★★★★

MCLAREN VALE

Arakoon ★★★★
Chalk Hill ★★★★★
Chapel Hill ★★★★★
Clarendon Hills ★★★★★
Coriole ★★★★★
d'Arenberg ★★★★★
Five Geese ★★★★★
Gemtree Vineyards ★★★★★
Geoff Merrill Wines ★★★★★
Hardys ★★★★★
Kay Bros Amery ★★★★★
Linda Domas Wines ★★★★★
Maxwell Wines ★★★★★
Mitolo Wines ★★★★★
Mr Riggs Wine Company ★★★★★
Olivers Taranga Vineyards ★★★★★
Paxton ★★★★★
Penny's Hill ★★★★★
Pirramimma ★★★★★
Possums Vineyard ★★★★★
Primo Estate ★★★★★
Richard Hamilton ★★★★★
Samuel's Gorge ★★★★★
SC Pannell ★★★★★
Serafino Wines ★★★★★
Shingleback ★★★★★
The Old Faithful Estate ★★★★★
Wirra Wirra ★★★★★

MARGARET RIVER

Amberley Estate ★★★★★
Ashbrook Estate ★★★★★
Brookland Valley ★★★★★
Cape Mentelle ★★★★★
Chalice Bridge Estate ★★★★★
Chapman Grove Wines ★★★★★
Clairault ★★★★★
Cullen Wines ★★★★★
Devil's Lair ★★★★★
Driftwood Estate ★★★★★
Evans & Tate ★★★★★
Gralyn Estate ★★★★★
Hay Shed Hill Wines ★★★★★
Howard Park ★★★★★
Leeuwin Estate ★★★★★

Lenton Brae Wines ★★★★★
McHenry Hohnen Vintners ★★★★★
Moss Wood ★★★★★
Pierro ★★★★★
Redgate ★★★★★
Rockfield Estate ★★★★★
Sandalford ★★★★★
Stella Bella Wines ★★★★★
Thompson Estate ★★★★★
Vasse Felix ★★★★★
Voyager Estate ★★★★★
Wise Wine ★★★★★
Woodlands ★★★★★
Woodside Valley Estate ★★★★★

MORNINGTON PENINSULA

Allies Wines ★★★★★
Darling Park ★★★★★
Eldridge Estate of Red Hill ★★★★★
Hurley Vineyard ★★★★★
Kooyong ★★★★★
Main Ridge Estate ★★★★★
Merricks Creek Wines ★★★★★
Montalto Vineyards ★★★★★
Moorooduc Estate ★★★★★
Paringa Estate ★★★★★
Port Phillip Estate ★★★★★
Prancing Horse Estate ★★★★★
Red Hill Estate ★★★★★
Scorpo Wines ★★★★★
Stonier Wines ★★★★★
Ten Minutes by Tractor ★★★★★
The Cups Estate ★★★★★
Tuck's Ridge ★★★★★
Willow Creek Vineyard ★★★★★
Yabby Lake Vineyard ★★★★★

MURRAY DARLING

Trentham Estate ★★★★★

NEW ENGLAND

Blickling Estate ★★★★★

ORANGE

Printhie Wines ★★★★★

PADTHAWAY
Henry's Drive Vignerons ★★★★★
Stonehaven ★★★★★

PEMBERTON
Bellarmine Wines ★★★★★
Fonty's Pool Vineyards ★★★★★
Picardy ★★★★★
Smithbrook ★★★★★

PERTH HILLS
Millbrook Winery ★★★★★
Western Ranges Winery ★★★★★

PORT PHILLIP ZONE
Three Wise Men ★★★★★

PYRENEES
Amherst Winery ★★★★★
Dalwhinnie ★★★★★
Polleters ★★★★★
Summerfield ★★★★★
Taltarni ★★★★★
Warrenmang Vineyard & Resort
   ★★★★★

RIVERINA
De Bortoli ★★★★★
McWilliam's ★★★★★

RUTHERGLEN
All Saints Estate ★★★★★
Buller ★★★★★
Campbells ★★★★★
Morris ★★★★★
Stanton & Killeen Wines ★★★★★
Warrabilla ★★★★★

SOUTH WEST AUSTRALIAN ZONE
Larry Cherubino Wines ★★★★★

SOUTHERN FLEURIEU
Mt Billy ★★★★★
Salomon Estate ★★★★★

STRATHBOGIE RANGES
Maygars Hill Winery ★★★★★

SUNBURY
Craiglee ★★★★★

SWAN VALLEY
Faber Vineyard ★★★★★
Houghton ★★★★★

TASMANIA
`ese Vineyards ★★★★★
Bay of Fires ★★★★★
Bream Creek ★★★★★
Clover Hill/Lalla Gully ★★★★★
Craigow ★★★★★
Dalrymple ★★★★★
Domaine A ★★★★★
Freycinet ★★★★★
Frogmore Creek ★★★★★
Jansz Tasmania ★★★★★
Pirie Estate ★★★★★
Pooley Wines ★★★★★
Puddleduck Vineyard ★★★★★
Stefano Lubiana ★★★★★
Stoney Rise ★★★★★
Tamar Ridge ★★★★★
Waterton Vineyards ★★★★★
Winstead ★★★★★

UPPER GOULBURN
Delatite ★★★★★

YARRA VALLEY
Carlei Estate & Carlei Green
   Vineyards ★★★★★
De Bortoli ★★★★★
Diamond Valley Vineyards ★★★★★
Domaine Chandon ★★★★★
Dominique Portet ★★★★★
Gembrook Hill ★★★★★
Giant Steps/Innocent
   Bystander ★★★★★
Hillcrest Vineyard ★★★★★

Killara Estate ★★★★★
Labyrinth ★★★★★
Mayer ★★★★★
Mount Mary ★★★★★
Oakridge ★★★★★
PHI ★★★★★
Punch ★★★★★
Seville Estate ★★★★★
Stuart Wines ★★★★★
Tarrawarra Estate ★★★★★
Toolangi Vineyards ★★★★★
Wantirna Estate ★★★★★
Warramate ★★★★★

Wedgetail Estate ★★★★★
Yarra Yarra ★★★★★
Yarra Yering ★★★★★
Yarrabank ★★★★★
YarraLoch ★★★★★
Yering Station ★★★★★
Yeringberg ★★★★★

SOUTHEAST AUSTRALIA/VARIOUS
Hewitson ★★★★★
Journeys End Vineyards ★★★★★
Tapanappa ★★★★★
Two Hands Wines ★★★★★

Ten of the best new wineries

As ever, ten of the best, not the best ten, although this year the outcome was nearly the same thing. The Barossa Valley provided half of the wineries, perhaps a reflection of the storehouse it has of great shiraz.

ALLIES WINES Mornington Peninsula / PAGE 56
Barney Flanders and David Chapman call Allies a collaboration. Both are originally from a restaurant background, Barney on the floor and David in the kitchen. One thing led to another as they followed separate paths into the wine industry, and then joined forces on the Mornington Peninsula, producing quite beautiful wines, albeit in limited quantities.

CHAPMAN GROVE WINES Margaret River / PAGE 155
Bruce Dukes is the contract winemaker for Chapman Grove, which has 30 ha of high-quality vineyards. Top label wines under the Atticus label are singularly impressive, led by (what else?) chardonnay; the 2005 and '06 vintages are both stunning.

FIRST DROP WINES Barossa Valley / PAGE 233
If nothing else, this shows what a virtual winery can achieve. The business is owned by Matt Gant and John Retsas. Matt was led away from his geography degree from the University of London by lecturer Tim Unwin, who took his students on a field trip to Burgundy and Champagne, leading Matt to Australia, where he won the Wine Society's Young Winemaker of the Year Award in 2004, and the Young Gun Wine Award in '07. John learned his trade at St Hallett, Chain of Ponds, and is now general manager of Schild Estate.

LARRY CHERUBINO WINES South West Australia Zone / PAGE 365
It should have come as no surprise to anyone that when Larry Cherubino set up his own business in 2005 he hit the ground running. His distinguished winemaking career started at Hardys Tintara, then Houghton for a number of years, and thereafter as a Flying Winemaker in high demand in Australia, NZ, South Africa, the US and Italy. This, too, is a virtual winery operation.

MAVERICK WINES Barossa Valley / PAGE 406
A perfectly timed exercise by four very astute wine professionals who acquired four vineyards in the Eden Valley and Barossa Valley during the 2004–06 years of surplus. Their 30 ha are the foundation for a singularly impressive portfolio.

ROHRLACH FAMILY WINES Barossa Valley / **PAGE 546**

Brothers Kevin, Graham and Wayne Rohrlach, with wives Lyn, Lynette and Kaylene, are third-generation growers of 95 ha of prime vineyard land. Until 2000, the grapes were sold to two leading Barossa wineries, but in that year some of the grapes were held back for vinification under the Rohrlach label. In 2003, the family received the ultimate accolade when the Barons of the Barossa gave them the title 'Vignerons of the Year'. It is not hard to see why.

RUSSELL WINES Barossa Valley / **PAGE 554**

John Russell (and wife Rosalind) came to the Barossa in 1990 to create the Barossa Music Festival (with great success). The wine bug bit, and in 1994 they planted the first 14 ha of vines, now increased to 32 ha on three vineyards. Shawn Kalleske makes the wines, optimising the quality of grapes he receives for the label.

THE OLD FAITHFUL ESTATE McLaren Vale / **PAGE 638**

This is a fifty-fifty joint venture between American specialist wine importer John Larchet (with one half), and a quartet of Nick Haselgrove, Warren Randall, Warren Ward and Andrew Fletcher, all of whom know McLaren Vale like the back of their hand (with the other half). Focused on the US market, the venture is able to pay top dollar for top-quality grapes, and the wines are skillfully made by the equally experienced Nick Haselgrove.

THE STORY WINES Grampians / **PAGE 640**

This is a story indeed, taking the varied backgrounds of people who have made their way into the wine industry one step further, for founder, owner and winemaker Rory Lane had as his qualification a degree in ancient Greek literature. Not wanting to put this to the test of real world wealth creation, he enrolled in a post-graduate wine technology and marketing course at Monash University, and the rest is history.

YELLAND & PAPPS Barossa Valley / **PAGE 730**

This is the venture of Michael and Susan Papps (née Yelland), set up after their marriage, in 2005. Michael had lived in the Barossa Valley for 20 years working at local wineries, bottling facilities and wine technology businesses, while Susan worked in New York for a year, studying at the Windows of the World Wine School. Once again, a virtual winery, the production limited by the scarcity of the high-quality grapes they have managed to secure. The prices are a breath of fresh air.

Ten dark horses

This is a highly subjective selection of ten wineries who have excelled over the past 12 months. Thus, they are not new wineries, nor ten of the best (both covered elsewhere), but do have that little bit extra.

ANGOVE'S Riverland / PAGE 62
Has always offered great value with its estate-grown wines, but has significantly expanded the range with offerings from the Clare Valley, McLaren Vale, Coonawarra and Padthaway, all priced under $20, some under $10 (not cheap and nasty). A gold medal Grenache Rose ($15) rounds off the portfolio to perfection.

BAY OF SHOALS Kangaroo Island / PAGE 89
Jacques Lurton's The Islander Estate is the top producer on the island, but John Willoughby's 10-ha vineyard (planned in '94) is producing consistently good chardonnay, sauvignon blanc and cabernet sauvignon. The cellar door is open seven days, great for tourists to this heaven-sent destination.

CASSEGRAIN Hastings River / PAGE 146
John Cassegrain has shrugged off the troubled and now terminated merger with Simon Gilbert Wines, producing a wide range of wines from grapes grown in New England and Hastings River, covering trendy varieties such as tempranillo and durif as well as long-term successes with semillon and chardonnay. This is another quality outpost for tourists on the north coast of New South Wales.

DOMAINE EPIS Macedon Ranges / PAGE 209
Qualifies in every way as a 'dark horse' – forgetting to send wine samples for the two prior editions of this book seems to have been a good way for the winery to keep under the radar. Long-term Essendon guru and former player Alex Epis has the equally legendary Stuart Anderson (Balgownie Estate founder, long since retired to the Macedon Ranges) as his consultant winemaker, and the meticulous care of Epis's two vineyards does the rest. The mail list is the best way to unearth these lovely wines.

GEMTREE VINEYARDS McLaren Vale / PAGE 253
Picking the best grapes from 130 ha of estate vineyards (and selling the remaining two-thirds) gives the Buttery family a huge advantage, and when only 1% goes to make its flagship Obsidian Shiraz (the '04 was the Hyatt Advertiser Wine of the Year in 2007), the quality comes as no surprise. Then there are wines full of left-field interest such as Albarino, Tempranillo and Petit Verdot and a White Lees Shiraz, using the lees from white wines to add texture.

GIANT STEPS/INNOCENT BYSTANDER Yarra Valley / PAGE 256

Consummate marketer/owner/winemaker Phil Sexton may be none-too-pleased to find his winery in the 'dark horse' category, but the fact is the wines from 2006 (predominantly 2006, but also '05) are of consistently high quality, those under the second Innocent Bystander label offering compelling value for money. The capacious winery restaurant in the main street of Healesville is another drawcard.

HENRY'S DRIVE VIGNERONS Padthaway / PAGE 293

A 1992 decision by the Longbottom family to plant a few vines on their large grazing property (owned since the 1940s) has been an acorn to oak story, but I'll wager that few wine professionals would know they now have 300 ha of vines and produce a jaw-dropping 170 000 cases of excellent wine (led by shiraz at four price points from $18 to $55), much of which is exported to the UK, the US and other major markets.

PAXTON McLaren Vale / PAGE 483

I should, I suppose, declare an interest here. David Paxton designed the original Coldstream Hills vineyards and also two Upper Yarra vineyards associated with Coldstream Hills. He is a hugely experienced viticulturist and it is very interesting that his family's five McLaren Vale vineyards were certified biodynamic by 2006. Son Michael makes the wines to very high standards; definitely a label to watch.

SCORPO WINES Mornington Peninsula / PAGE 569

Notwithstanding my disclaimer in the introduction, Scorpo was a contender for Winery of the Year, with seven wines rated at 94 points or above. Contract winemaker Sandro Mosele handled the 2006 vintage with impeccable skill, producing top results with chardonnay, pinot noir and shiraz. It makes the decision of veteran landscape architect Paul Scorpo to buy a derelict apple and cherry orchard in 1997 and plant 6 ha of vines look like a very astute move.

TAMBURLAINE Lower Hunter Valley / PAGE 623

History shows that winery-generated wine clubs built as an add-on to mail/website lists seldom succeed, the benefits to members usually illusory. Tamburlaine is the exception to the rule, going from strength to strength as it has progressively doubled its production of Members Reserve wines from its Hunter Valley and Orange vineyards. Nine of its current wines rate 90 points or above, spanning all the core varieties other than pinot noir, all made with a sure touch by the winemaking team headed by Mark Davidson.

Special value wines

As always, these are lists of ten of the best value wines, not the ten best wines in each price category. There are literally dozens of wines with similar points and prices, and the choice is necessarily an arbitrary one. I have, however, attempted to give as much varietal and style choice as the limited numbers allow.

TEN OF THE BEST VALUE Whites $10 and under

87	2007 De Bortoli Sacred Hill Traminer Riesling	$6.95
87	2007 De Bortoli Sacred Hill Colombard Chardonnay	$6.95
89	2007 McWilliam's Inheritance Semillon Sauvignon Blanc	$6.99
87	2007 Beelgara Estate Range Semillon Sauvignon Blanc	$7.95
88	2007 Westend Estate Outback Semillon Sauvignon Blanc	$7.95
89	2007 Yalumba Oxford Landing Sauvignon Blanc	$7.95
88	2006 Jindalee Estate Circle Collection Chardonnay	$8.95
89	2007 Arrowfield Estate Bowman's Crossing Semillon Sauvignon Blanc	$9
89	2006 SplitRock Vineyard Estate Reserve Hunter Valley Semillon	$10
90	2007 Zilzie Selection 23 Sauvignon Blanc	$10

TEN OF THE BEST VALUE Reds $10 and under

88	2007 (Geoff Merrill) Mount Hurtle Grenache Rose	$8
89	2005 Andrew Peace Blue Sand Cabernet Merlot	$8.95
88	2006 Jindalee Estate Circle Collection Shiraz	$8.95
89	2006 Warburn Estate Premium Reserve Cabernet Merlot	$9
88	2005 Byrne & Smith Woolpunda Red Block Shiraz	$9
89	2006 Angove's Long Row Cabernet Sauvignon	$9.99
90	2005 Llangibby Estate Adelaide Hills Tempranillo Shiraz Cabernet Sauvignon	$10
90	2006 Sinclair Jeremy Cabernet Shiraz	$10
89	2006 Jacob's Creek Shiraz	$10
89	2004 Koonowla The Ringmaster Shiraz	$10

It is in these two groups that the effect of the wine surplus is most evident, forcing down the price (or upping the quality) of wines that would normally be far more expensive.

TEN OF THE BEST VALUE Whites $10–$15

93	2007 Tyrrell's Lost Block Semillon	$13
94	2007 Charles Sturt University Orange Chardonnay	$13.20
94	2006 Chateau Francois Pokolbin Mallee Semillon	$14
94	2006 Wynns Coonawarra Estate Riesling	$14
93	2007 Picardy Pannell Family Trial Batch Pemberton Sauvignon Blanc	$14
93	2007 Tahbilk Marsanne	$14.90
94	2007 Jim Barry Watervale Riesling	$14.95
93	2007 Yalumba Mawson's Wrattonbully Sauvignon Blanc	$14.95
94	2007 Bellarmine Pemberton Chardonnay	$15
94	2006 Ducketts Mill Riesling	$15

TEN OF THE BEST VALUE Reds $10–$15

90	2007 McPherson Cabernet Sauvignon	$10.95
91	2006 Warburn Estate Stephendale Shiraz	$11
90	2006 Yalumba Y Series Shiraz Viognier	$11.95
91	2006 Trentham Estate Pinot Noir	$12.50
94	2005 Lindemans Reserve Padthaway Shiraz	$13.95
93	2005 Dalfarras Shiraz Viognier	$14.95
93	2005 Quarisa Treasures Coonawarra Cabernet Merlot	$14.95
95	2006 Possums Vineyard Willunga Shiraz	$15
95	2006 Zilzie Shiraz	$15
94	2007 Angove's Nine Vines Grenache Shiraz Rose	$15

Australia's geographical indications

The process of formally mapping Australia's wine regions is all but complete, although will never come to a complete halt – for one thing, climate change is lurking in the wings. The division into states, zones, regions and subregions follows; those regions or subregions marked with an asterisk are not yet registered, and may never be, but are in common usage. In two instances I have gone beyond the likely finalisation: it makes no sense to me that the Hunter Valley should be a zone, the region Hunter, and then subregions which are all in the Lower Hunter Valley. I have elected to stick with the traditional division between the Upper Hunter Valley on the one hand, and the Lower on the other.

I am also in front of the game with Tasmania, dividing it into Northern, Southern and East Coast, and, to a lesser degree, have anticipated that the Queensland Coastal region will seek recognition under this or some similar name.

In early 2008, New England Australia in New South Wales became the most recent region to be formally registered. It is cumbersome name, but designed to head off objections from other parts of the world (for example, in the US) with the 'New England' name. For the purposes of this book, I have dropped the word 'Australia' from the regional name, simply to avoid confusion.

State/Zone	Region	Subregion
NEW SOUTH WALES		
Big Rivers	Murray Darling Perricoota Riverina Swan Hill	
Central Ranges	Cowra Mudgee Orange	Orange Foothills★
Hunter Valley	Hunter Lower Hunter Valley★ Upper Hunter Valley★	Broke Fordwich Mount View★ Pokolbin★ Rothbury★
Northern Rivers	Hastings River	

State/Zone	Region	Subregion
Northern Slopes	New England	
South Coast	Shoalhaven Coast	
	Southern Highlands	
Southern New South Wales	Canberra District	
	Gundagai	
	Hilltops	
	Tumbarumba	
Western Plains		

SOUTH AUSTRALIA

Adelaide (Super Zone, includes Mount Lofty Ranges, Fleurieu and Barossa)		
Barossa	Barossa Valley	
	Eden Valley	High Eden
Far North	Southern Flinders Ranges	
Fleurieu	Currency Creek	
	Kangaroo Island	
	Langhorne Creek	
	McLaren Vale	
	Southern Fleurieu	
Limestone Coast	Coonawarra	
	Mount Benson	
	Mount Gambier★	
	Padthaway	
	Robe	
	Wrattonbully	
Lower Murray	Riverland	
Mount Lofty Ranges	Adelaide Hills	Lenswood
		Piccadilly Valley
	Adelaide Plains	Polish Hill River★
	Clare Valley	Watervale★
The Peninsulas	Southern Eyre Peninsula★	

State/Zone	Region	Subregion
VICTORIA		
Central Victoria	Bendigo	
	Goulburn Valley	Nagambie Lakes
	Heathcote	
	Strathbogie Ranges	
	Upper Goulburn	
Gippsland		
North East Victoria	Alpine Valleys	
	Beechworth	
	Glenrowan	
	King Valley	
	Rutherglen	
North West Victoria	Murray Darling	
	Swan Hill	
Port Phillip	Geelong	
	Macedon Ranges	
	Mornington Peninsula	
	Sunbury	
	Yarra Valley	
Western Victoria	Ballarat★	
	Grampians	Great Western
	Henty	
	Pyrenees	
WESTERN AUSTRALIA		
Central Western Australia		
Eastern Plains, Inland and North of Western Australia		
Greater Perth	Peel	
	Perth Hills	
	Swan District	Swan Valley

State/Zone	Region	Subregion
South West Australia	Blackwood Valley	
	Geographe	
	Great Southern	Albany
		Denmark
		Frankland River
		Mount Barker
		Porongurup
	Manjimup	
	Margaret River	
	Pemberton	
West Australian South East Coastal	Esperance★	

QUEENSLAND

Queensland	Granite Belt	
	Queensland Coastal★	
	South Burnett	

TASMANIA

Tasmania	Northern Tasmania★	
	Southern Tasmania★	
	East Coast Tasmania★	

AUSTRALIAN CAPITAL TERRITORY

NORTHERN TERRITORY

Australian vintage charts

Each number represents a mark out of ten for the quality of vintages in each region.

red wine   white wine

NSW

	2004	2005	2006	2007
Lower Hunter Valley				
red	8	7	6	8
white	8	9	7	10
Upper Hunter Valley				
red	6	7	6	7
white	8	9	7	8
Mudgee				
red	8	7	8	5
white	7	9	7	7
Cowra				
red	6	7	6	7
white	5	8	6	6
Orange				
red	9	8	9	6
white	7	9	8	7
Riverina				
red	7	6	6	7
white	8	6	7	7
Canberra District				
red	8	9	8	8
white	8	9	9	8
Southern Highlands				
red		8	8	3
white		9	8	5
Perricoota				
red	7	9	7	7
white	8	6	8	9
Gundagai				
red	7	9	8	6
white	7	8	7	7
Hilltops				
red	9	9	10	6
white	6	8	9	6

	2004	2005	2006	2007
Tumbarumba				
red	5	7	7	7
white	6	9	9	9
Hastings River				
red	7	9	6	8
white	8	9	7	7
Shoalhaven				
red	7	9	7	4
white	7	8	8	4

VIC

	2004	2005	2006	2007
Yarra Valley				
red	10	9	9	7
white	8	9	9	8
Mornington Peninsula				
red	10	9	9	9
white	10	7	8	8
Geelong				
red	8	8	8	7
white	8	7	8	7
Macedon Ranges				
red	8	7	9	8
white	9	8	8	8
Sunbury				
red	8	7	8	8
white	7	8	7	7
Grampians				
red	10	10	8	8
white	6	9	8	7
Pyrenees				
red	10	10	9	8
white	9	9	8	7
Henty				
red	9	9	8	4
white	9	8	9	8

	2004	2005	2006	2007
Bendigo				
red	9	8	8	6
white	9	7	8	7
Heathcote				
red	10	8	9	7
white	9	9	7	6
Goulburn Valley				
red	9	8	9	8
white	7	8	8	7
Upper Goulburn				
red	7	9	8	**
white	7	9	8	4
Strathbogie Ranges				
red	8	9	7	**
white	8	8	8	7
Glenrowan & Rutherglen				
red	9	7	7	**
white	6	7	7	**
King Valley				
red	8	7	8	**
white	9	9	7	**
Alpine Valleys				
red	9	8	8	**
white	9	10	7	**
Beechworth				
red	10	8	8	**
white	8	8	7	**
Gippsland				
red	10	9	9	9
white	9	9	8	8
Murray Darling				
red	7	8	8	8
white	7	8	9	8

	2004	2005	2006	2007

SA

Barossa Valley

9	7	10	7
7	8	7	6

Eden Valley

8	8	7	8
9	9	8	7

Clare Valley

9	9	8	7
8	9	7	6

Adelaide Hills

8	7	7	8
7	8	9	6

Adelaide Plains

8	8	7	8
7	9	8	7

Coonawarra

7	8	7	7
6	7	6	7

Padthaway

7	8	8	8
7	7	7	7

Mount Benson & Robe

7	8	7	7
8	9	7	7

Wrattonbully

4	8	9	6
7	8	7	6

McLaren Vale

9	8	8	7
7	8	7	6

Southern Fleurieu

7	8	8	8
8	8	8	8

Langhorne Creek

8	9	8	8
7	8	9	8

Kangaroo Island

8	8	8	7
7	8	7	8

Riverland

8	8	9	8
8	9	8	9

WA

Margaret River

9	9	7	8
8	9	9	8

Great Southern

7	9	6	8
8	9	8	9

Manjimup

9	7	6	8
5	9	8	9

Pemberton

8	9	6	9
8	9	8	9

Geographe

9	7	6	8
9	8	8	9

Swan District

9	9	7	8
7	8	8	7

Peel

8	10	9	9
7	10	9	9

Perth Hills

9	10	8	8
7	9	7	7

QLD

Granite Belt

7	9	8	8
9	9	7	7

South Burnett

6	9	7	8
6	10	8	8

TAS

Northern Tasmania

6	10	8	7
8	9	7	8

Southern Tasmania

7	10	9	7
8	9	8	8

★★ Frost and bushfire smoke taint precludes ratings; virtually no wine made in these regions.

Plantings and production

The table on page 45 tells the tale of the roller-coaster ride the industry has had over the past five vintages, with no immediate end in sight. The imponderable is the future of the Big Rivers Zone of New South Wales, the Lower Murray Zone and the Langhorne Creek region of South Australia. In the last of the three high-yielding vintages in 2006, these regions provided two-thirds of the total Australian grape crush. While the Riverina region (part of the Big Rivers Zone) would appear to have secured water for at least several years to come, supply to the other regions is at a desperately low level, and with no short-term prospects of improving. If the water does return, it may be too late, and the cost of securing it too high.

The sharp decline in the percentage of red grapes crushed in 2007 is not due to any change of preference or market demand, but simply the much lower yield per hectare in that vintage for red grapes. Since chardonnay, which dwarfs all other white varieties, is in over-supply, and the demand for red wine in both export and domestic markets continues, it is probable there will be a reversion to the pattern of earlier years.

The mini table below throws up some unexpected outcomes. The trendy white varieties (sauvignon blanc is given honorary status, even though it has been around for a long time) are on the ascendancy, while only the newest arrivals of tempranillo and zinfandel have traction in the red wine field. Sangiovese and nebbiolo are extremely difficult varieties to grow and make well, but their decline is nonetheless surprising. Petit verdot is in the opposite camp: easy to grow, and easy to make, retaining colour and flavour even in warm, irrigated regions. Its decline verges on the inexplicable.

| | 2004 | | 2007 | |
	Hectares (total)	Hectares (bearing)	Hectares (total)	Hectares (bearing)
PINOT GRIS	329	207	2,469	1,362
VIOGNIER	683	462	1,369	1,059
SAUVIGNON BLANC	3,425	3,033	5,545	4,545
SANGIOVESE	511	486	479	450
NEBBIOLO	121	105	90	84
PETIT VERDOT	1,623	1,526	1,387	1,335
TEMPRANILLO	257	194	354	317
ZINFANDEL	95	88	136	118

	2003	2004	2005	2007
CHARDONNAY				
hectares	24,138	28,008	30,507	32,151
tonnes	233,747	311,273	378,287	366,936
RIESLING				
hectares	3,987	4,255	4,326	4,432
tonnes	28,994	36,404	41,237	31,002
SAUVIGNON BLANC				
hectares	2,953	3,425	4,152	5,545
tonnes	21,028	39,774	38,355	36,515
SEMILLON				
hectares	6,283	6,278	6,282	6,752
tonnes	77,096	99,237	96,727	75,170
OTHER WHITE				
hectares	24,700	23,925	23,365	24,303
tonnes	196,209	266,794	253,837	192,026
TOTAL WHITE				
hectares	62,051	65,891	68,632	73,183
tonnes	557,074	753,482	808,443	701,649
CABERNET SAUVIGNON				
hectares	28,171	29,313	28,621	27,909
tonnes	225,723	319,955	284,062	183,052
GRENACHE				
hectares	2,322	2,292	2,097	2,011
tonnes	19,866	24,987	25,418	15,602
MOURVEDRE				
hectares	1,092	1,040	963	794
tonnes	11,822	13,992	10,149	6,596
MERLOT				
hectares	10,352	10,804	10,816	10,790
tonnes	92,865	123,944	132,586	90,461
PINOT NOIR				
hectares	4,270	4,424	4,231	4,393
tonnes	27,949	41,690	36,887	26,251
SHIRAZ				
hectares	37,106	39,182	40,508	43,417
tonnes	309,000	436,691	415,421	283,741
OTHER RED				
hectares	12,268	11,235	10,797	11,309
tonnes	85,297	101,816	105,460	63,339
TOTAL RED				
hectares	95,491	98,290	98,033	100,623
tonnes	772,522	1,063,075	1,009,983	669,042
TOTAL GRAPES				
hectares	157,492	164,181	166,665	173,776
tonnes	1,329,596	1,816,556	1,818,426	1,370,690
PERCENTAGE (TONNES)				
White	41.90%	41.48%	44.46%	51.18%
Red	58.10%	58.52%	55.54%	48.82%

Wine and food or food and wine?

It all depends on your starting point: there are conventional matches for overseas classics such as caviar (champagne), fresh foie gras (sauternes, riesling or rose), and new season Italian white truffles (any medium-bodied red). Here the food flavour is all important, the wine merely incidental.

At the other extreme come 50-year-old classic red wines: Grange, or Grand Cru Burgundy, or First Growth Bordeaux, or a Maurice O'Shea Mount Pleasant Shiraz. Here the food is, or should be, merely a low-key foil, but at the same time must be of high quality.

In the Australian context I believe not enough attention is paid to the time of year, which – particularly in the southern states – is or should be a major determinant in the choice of both food and wine. And so I shall present my suggestions in this way, always bearing in mind how many ways there are to skin a cat.

Spring

SPARKLING
Oysters, cold crustacea, tapas, any cold hors d'oeuvres

YOUNG RIESLING
Cold salads, sashimi

GEWURZTRAMINER
Asian

YOUNG SEMILLON
Antipasto, vegetable terrine

PINOT GRIS, COLOMBARD
Crab cakes, whitebait

VERDELHO, CHENIN BLANC
Cold smoked chicken, gravlax

MATURE CHARDONNAY
Grilled chicken, chicken pasta, turkey, pheasant

ROSE
Caesar salad, trout mousse

YOUNG PINOT NOIR
Seared kangaroo fillet, grilled quail

MERLOT
Pastrami, warm smoked chicken

YOUNG MEDIUM-BODIED CABERNET SAUVIGNON
Rack of baby lamb

LIGHT- TO MEDIUM-BODIED COOL CLIMATE SHIRAZ
Rare eye fillet of beef

YOUNG BOTRYTISED WINES
Fresh fruits, cake

Summer

CHILLED FINO
Cold consommé

2–3-YEAR-OLD SEMILLON
Gazpacho

2–3-YEAR-OLD RIESLING
Seared tuna

**YOUNG BARREL-FERMENTED
SEMILLON SAUVIGNON BLANC**
Seafood or vegetable tempura

YOUNG OFF-DRY RIESLING
Prosciutto & melon/pear

COOL-CLIMATE CHARDONNAY
Abalone, lobster, Chinese-style prawns

**10-YEAR-OLD SEMILLON OR
RIESLING**
Braised pork neck

MATURE CHARDONNAY
Smoked eel, smoked roe

OFF-DRY ROSE
Chilled fresh fruit

YOUNG LIGHT-BODIED PINOT NOIR
Grilled salmon

AGED PINOT NOIR (5+ YEARS)
Coq au vin, wild duck

YOUNG GRENACHE/SANGIOVESE
Osso bucco

MATURE CHARDONNAY (5+ YEARS)
Braised rabbit

**HUNTER VALLEY SHIRAZ
(5–10 YEARS)**
Beef spare ribs

MERLOT
Saltimbocca, roast pheasant

**MEDIUM-BODIED CABERNET
SAUVIGNON (5 YEARS)**
Barbecued butterfly leg of lamb

ALL WINES
Parmagiana

Autumn

AMONTILLADO
Warm consommé

**BARREL-FERMENTED MATURE
WHITES**
Smoked roe, bouillabaisse

COMPLEX MATURE CHARDONNAY
Sweetbreads, brains

FULLY AGED RIESLING
Chargrilled eggplant, stuffed capsicum

AGED MARSANNE
Seafood risotto, Lebanese

SOUTHERN VICTORIAN PINOT NOIR
Peking duck

AGED PINOT NOIR
Grilled calf's liver, roast kid, lamb or
pig's kidneys

**MATURE MARGARET RIVER
CABERNET MERLOT**
Lamb fillet, roast leg of lamb with garlic
and herbs

COOL CLIMATE MERLOT
Lamb loin chops

**MATURE GRENACHE/RHONE
BLENDS**
Moroccan lamb

**RICH, FULL-BODIED HEATHCOTE
SHIRAZ**
Beef casserole

YOUNG MUSCAT
Plum pudding

Winter

DRY OLOROSO SHERRY
Full-flavoured hors d'oeuvres

SPARKLING BURGUNDY
Borscht

VIOGNIER
Pea and ham soup

AGED SEMILLON (10+ YEARS)
Vichysoisse (hot)

SAUVIGNON BLANC
Coquilles St Jacques, pan-fried scallops

MATURE CHARDONNAY
Quiche Lorraine

CHARDONNAY (10+ YEARS)
Cassoulet

MATURE SEMILLON SAUVIGNON BLANC
Seafood pasta

YOUNG TASMANIAN PINOT NOIR
Squab, duck breast

MATURE PINOT NOIR
Mushroom ragout, ravioli

MATURE MERLOT
Pot au feu

10-YEAR-OLD HEATHCOTE SHIRAZ
Char-grilled rump steak

15–20-YEAR-OLD FULL-BODIED BAROSSA SHIRAZ
Venison, kangaroo fillet

COONAWARRA CABERNET SAUVIGNON
Braised lamb shanks/shoulder

MUSCAT (OLD)
Chocolate-based desserts

TOKAY (OLD)
Creme brûlée

VINTAGE PORT
Dried fruits, salty cheese

Acknowledgements

It is, I suppose, inevitable that the production of a book such as this should involve many people in a long chain of events, some seemingly trivial, others of fundamental importance.

The starting point is the making of the thousands of bottles of wine that I (and Ben Edwards) taste each year, and the end point is the appearance of the book on retailers' shelves across Australia in August 2008.

My foremost thanks must go to the winemakers for sending the wines to me at their cost and, in particular, those who treat submission dates as serious deadlines rather than an approximate wish list on my part. Those who ignored the deadlines are increasingly likely to fall on their own sword as the competition for space in the book intensifies.

Next are those responsible for getting the wines to me, whether by the excellent parcel delivery service of Australia Post, by courier or by hand delivery. I am reliant on the goodwill and tolerance of many people involved in what may seem a warped version of trivial pursuits as the wines are received; placed in bins; in due course fork-lifted up one storey and removed from those bins; unpacked; listed; entered into the database, with precise names cross-checked, alcohol, price and closure type recorded; tasting sheets printed for the day's tasting of 150 to 170 wines, initially arranged by producer, but then re-sorted by variety; moved on to a long tasting bench; opened; poured at the same pace as I taste; the Riedel glasses returned to washing racks; washed, rinsed and dried (my task each day); the tasting notes dictated; the database now returning the notes to a winery-by-winery sequence; proofed by me (and at least three others at subsequent stages before going to print).

In the meantime, my office team has been busy chasing up new, missing or inconsistent details regarding the wineries, and many of the wines, with special emphasis on new wineries.

Then there is the ever-patient but deadline conscious team at Hardie Grant, working on the cover design (surely brilliant), page design, paper type and two-colour printing, which give rise to the galley pages for proofreading again and again.

To my team of the newly conscripted Ben Edwards, Paula Grey, Beth Anthony, Marcus Hutson; Bev and Chris Bailey (Coldstream Post Office); Pam Holmes (and others at Coldstream Hills); John Cook (programmer); and the Hardie Grant team of Jasmin Chua (senior editor), Megan Ellis (typesetter) and Sandy Cull (cover designer), my heartfelt thanks. This is as much their book as it is mine.

Australian wineries
and wines

A note on alphabetical order
Wineries beginning with 'The' are listed under 'T'; for example,
'The Blok Estate'. Winery names that include a numeral are treated
as if the numeral is spelt out; for example, '5 Blind Mice'
is listed under 'F'.

Abbey Creek Vineyard

2388 Porongurup Road, Porongurup, WA 6324 **Region** Porongurup
T (08) 9853 1044 **F** (08) 9454 5501 **Open** By appt
Winemaker Castle Rock Estate (Robert Diletti) **Est.** 1990 **Cases** 800
This is the family business of Mike and Mary Dilworth, the name coming from a winter creek running alongside the vineyard, and a view of The Abbey in the Stirling Range. The 1.6-ha vineyard is equally split between riesling, pinot noir and cabernet sauvignon planted in 1990 and '93. The rieslings have had significant show success.

ΨΨΨΨΨ **Porongurup Riesling 2006** Extremely fine and crisp; a very long and pure lime/mineral palate, with an extended finish. Long future. Multi-trophy winner, WA Wine Show '07. Screwcap. 12° alc. **Rating** 96 **To** 2016 $19

ΨΨΨΨΨ **Porongurup Riesling 2003** Vibrant colour and personality, showing minimal development; strong lemon flavour and fine acidity, gives way to a very fine and fresh finish. **Rating** 91 **To** 2012 $20
Porongurup Sauvignon Blanc 2007 Good concentration, and pure varietal gooseberry aromas; the palate is generous, fine, long and shows just a little mineral complexity on the finish. Screwcap. 13.8° alc. **Rating** 91 **To** 2009 $19

ΨΨΨΨ **Porongurup Pinot Noir 2006** Light cherry fruit, with a little spice, and pronounced acidity on the finish. Screwcap. 13.9° alc. **Rating** 88 **To** 2009 $30

Abbey Rock

1 Onkaparinga Valley Road, Balhannah, SA 5242 **Region** Adelaide Hills
T (08) 8398 0192 **F** (08) 8398 0188 **www**.abbeyrock.com.au **Open** 7 days 11–4.30
Winemaker Les Sampson **Est.** 2001 **Cases** 30 000
An expanding business with wines sourced from a number of regions spread across SA. The premium wines are made from pinot noir and chardonnay near Hahndorf in the Adelaide Hills, and from chardonnay, semillon, shiraz and grenache in the Clare Valley. In all, plantings have grown to 148 ha, and production has increased from 18 000 cases. Exports to the UK, the US and other major markets.

ΨΨΨΨ **Sweet Briar Clare Valley Cabernet Franc Rose 2007** Good flavour and vibrant red fruits on the pleasantly dry finish. Screwcap. 11° alc. **Rating** 88 **To** 2010 $22
Christine Adelaide Hills Pinot Noir Chardonnay 2006 Quite clean with red berry fruits, a fine mousse and good texture; well-handled sweetness makes for an approachable, appealing style. Cork. 13.5° alc. **Rating** 87 **To** 2011 $32

Abercorn

Cassilis Road, Mudgee, NSW 2850 **Region** Mudgee
T 1800 000 959 **F** (02) 6373 3108 **www**.abercornwine.com.au **Open** Thurs–Mon 10.30–4.30
Winemaker Tim Stevens **Est.** 1996 **Cases** 3000
Tim Stevens is a busy man these days. In 1996 he acquired the then-25-year-old Abercorn Vineyard, and in late 2005 purchased the very well-known adjacent vineyard and winery, Huntington Estate. Over the years he has developed his skills as a winemaker, enabling him to keep the style of the Abercorn and Huntington wines quite distinct. He describes that of Abercorn as the 'modern, smooth, regional style', with the A Reserve and The Growers Revenge leading the way.

Acacia Ridge ★★★

169 Gulf Road, Yarra Glen, Vic 3775 **Region** Yarra Valley
T (03) 9730 1492 **F** (03) 9730 2292 **www**.acaciaridgeyarravalley.com **Open** Wed–Sun 11–5
Winemaker Gary Mills, Geoff Wright (Contract) **Est.** 1996 **Cases** 500

Tricia and Gavan Oakley began the establishment of 4 ha each of pinot noir, shiraz and cabernet sauvignon in 1996. Most of the grapes are sold to three other Yarra Valley winemakers, and when the Oakleys decided to have part of the production vinified for the Acacia Ridge label, they and some other small vignerons set up a marketing and grape-sharing co-operative known as Yarra Valley Micromasters. It is through this structure that the Oakleys obtain their Chardonnay, which complements the Cabernet Merlot and Shiraz made from their own plantings.

ȚȚȚȚ   **Yarra Valley Shiraz 2006** A medium-bodied spicy palate with good flavour; quite plummy, but as yet a little one-dimensional; good potential. Screwcap. 13.5° alc. **Rating** 88 **To** 2012 $25

Acreage Vineyard & Winery   ★★★

681 Gardner and Holman Road, Drouin South, Vic 3818 **Region** Gippsland
T (03) 5627 6383 **F** (03) 5627 6135 **Open** 7 days 10–5
Winemaker Terry Blundell **Est.** 1997 **Cases** 450
Terry and Jan Blundell commenced the planting of their vineyard in 1997 with chardonnay and pinot noir. In 2003 shiraz, merlot and cabernet sauvignon were added, taking the total plantings to 2.5 ha. The cellar door, with views to the Baw Baw Ranges, is only 65 mins from the Melbourne CBD.

ȚȚȚȚ   **Unwooded Chardonnay 2007** Has more grip and texture than most of its ilk, with citrussy/minerally notes on the finish. Screwcap. 13° alc. **Rating** 87 **To** 2010 $15

Across the Lake

79 Mt Shadforth Road, Denmark, WA 6333 **Region** Central Western Australia Zone
T (08) 9848 1838 **www.**acrossthelakewines.com.au **Open** By appt
Winemaker The Vintage Wineworx (Dr Diane Miller) **Est.** 1999 **Cases** 400
The Taylor family has been farming (wheat and sheep) for over 40 years at Lake Grace; a small diversification into grapegrowing started as a hobby, but has developed into a little more than that with 2 ha of shiraz. They were motivated to support their friend Bill (WJ) Walker, who had started growing shiraz three years previously, and has since produced a gold medal–winning wine. Having learnt the hard way which soils are suitable, the Taylors intend to increase their plantings.

ȚȚȚȚȚ   **Shiraz 2005** Good red-purple; a soft, generous medium-bodied palate with a mix of blackberry and black cherry fruit supported by fine, ripe tannins. Gold medal, WA Wine Show '07. Screwcap. 13.3° alc. **Rating** 94 **To** 2015 $25

ȚȚȚȚȚ   **Shiraz 2006** Elegant light- to medium-bodied wine, with bell-clear cool-grown varietal fruit in a cherry spectrum; touches of spice and balanced tannins. Crowd pleaser. **Rating** 90 **To** 2014 $15

Ada River   ★★★★

2330 Main Road, Neerim South, Vic 3831 **Region** Gippsland
T (03) 5628 1661 **F** (03) 5628 1661 **Open** W'ends & public hols 10–6
Winemaker Peter Kelliher **Est.** 1983 **Cases** 1500
The Kelliher family first planted vines on their dairy farm at Neerim South in 1983, extending the vineyard in '89 and increasing plantings further by establishing the nearby Manilla Vineyard in '94. Until 2000, Ada River leased a Yarra Valley vineyard; it has relinquished that lease and in its place established a vineyard at Heathcote in conjunction with a local grower.

ȚȚȚȚȚ   **Reserve Heathcote Shiraz 2006** More concentration and more noticeable alcohol than the varietal; thickly textured, and quite long, with little hint of portiness on the finish. Screwcap. **Rating** 90 **To** 2016 $45

🍷🍷🍷🍷 **Heathcote Cabernet Sauvignon 2006** Blueberry and cassis with a little mineral in the background; good flavour with chewy texture, and fine fruit on the finish. Screwcap. **Rating** 89 **To** 2014 $25
Heathcote Shiraz 2006 Ripe and juicy, with blue and blackberry fruit; good flavour but lacks a little complexity. Screwcap. **Rating** 88 **To** 2014 $25
Heathcote Merlot 2006 Quite plummy, with a little spice and mint; medium-bodied with good persistence. Screwcap. **Rating** 87 **To** 2012 $25

Adinfern Estate

Bussell Highway, Cowaramup, WA 6284 **Region** Margaret River
T (08) 9755 5272 **F** (08) 9755 5206 **www**.adinfern.com **Open** 7 days 11–5.30
Winemaker Merv Smith, Matt Thomas, Transview Pty Ltd (Kevin McKay, Michael Langridge) **Est.** 1996 **Cases** 3500
Merv and Jan Smith have farmed their property as a fine wool and lamb producer for over 30 years, but in 1996 diversified with the development of a 25-ha vineyard planted to sauvignon blanc, semillon, chardonnay, pinot noir, merlot, shiraz, cabernet sauvignon and malbec. One hundred tonnes of grapes are sold to other makers, 25 retained for Adinfern Estate. Exports to Belgium, Singapore and Hong Kong.

🍷🍷🍷🍷 **Margaret River Shiraz 2006** Spice and oak lead the bouquet, the medium-bodied palate with plush plum and blackberry fruit; good length. **Rating** 88 **To** 2015 $19
Margaret River Shiraz 2005 Bright light- to medium-bodied mix of mint, leaf, spice and cherry fruit aromas and flavours; fresh, early-drinking style. Diam. 13.1° alc. **Rating** 88 **To** 2010 $19
Margaret River Cabernet Sauvignon 2005 Light-bodied, as most of the Adinfern wines are, and has minty/leafy overtones, but does have length and fine texture; drink now. Screwcap. 13.4° alc. **Rating** 87 **To** 2011 $19

Affleck

154 Millynn Road, Bungendore, NSW 2621 **Region** Canberra District
T (02) 6236 9276 **F** (02) 6236 9090 **www**.affleck.com.au **Open** Fri–Wed 9–5
Winemaker Ian Hendry **Est.** 1976 **Cases** 500
The cellar door and mail-order price list says that the wines are 'grown, produced and bottled on the estate by Ian and Susie Hendry with much dedicated help from family and friends'. The original 2.5-ha vineyard has been expanded to 7 ha.

🍷🍷🍷🍷 **Canberra District Chardonnay 2006** Bright green-straw; gentle white and yellow peach on the mid-palate; very early picking does shorten the finish a little, but will sustain the wine in the future. Screwcap. 12° alc. **Rating** 88 **To** 2014 $24
Canberra District Rose 2007 Light fresh cherry and strawberry fruit, with just a flick of sweetness; serve well chilled. Screwcap. 12.5° alc. **Rating** 87 **To** 2009 $20

Ainsworth & Snelson

22 Gourlay Street, St Kilda East, Vic 3183 **Region** Warehouse
T (03) 9530 3333 **F** (03) 9530 3446 **www**.ainsworthandsnelson.com **Open** Not
Winemaker Brett Snelson **Est.** 2002 **Cases** 5000
Brett Snelson and Gregg Ainsworth take a handcrafted regional approach to the production of their wines. They use traditional techniques which allow the emphasis to remain on terroir, sourcing grapes from the Clare Valley, Yarra Valley, Barossa and Coonawarra. Brett Snelson keeps his winemaking skills sharp with an annual vintage in Rousillon. Exports to the UK, France, Denmark, Norway, Hong Kong and Singapore.

🍷🍷🍷🍷 **Clare Valley Riesling 2007** Generously flavoured fruit, predominant lime and a touch of tropical passionfruit/pineapple; no minerality; quick developing. Screwcap. **Rating** 88 **To** 2012 $24

Albert River Wines

869 Mundoolun Connection Road, Tamborine, Qld 4270 **Region** Queensland Coastal
T (07) 5543 6622 **F** (07) 5543 6627 **www**.albertriverwines.com.au **Open** Wed–Sun 10–4
Winemaker Contract **Est.** 1998 **Cases** 3000
Albert River is one of the high-profile wineries in the Gold Coast hinterland. David and
Janette Bladin, with a combined 30 years' experience in tourism and hospitality, have acquired
and relocated two of Qld's most historic buildings, Tamborine House and Auchenflower House.
The winery itself is housed in a newly constructed annex to Auchenflower House; the Bladins
have established 4 ha of vineyards on the property, and have another 50 ha under contract. All
of its distribution is through cellar door, mail order and local restaurants. Exports to Japan.

 ## Alderley Creek Wines

2653 Bucketts Way, Stroud, NSW 2138 **Region** Northern Rivers
T (02) 4994 5556 **F** (02) 9555 8534 **www**.alderleycreekwines.com.au **Open** Fri 12–5,
w'ends 10–5
Winemaker David Fatches (Contract) **Est.** 1999 **Cases** 600
In 2006 John and Dianne Stephens purchased this property and 1.2 ha of previously planted
chambourcin and verdelho as a retirement project. The vineyard is between Booral and Stroud
on the way to the Barrington Tops. Alderley House was built in 1833 as part of a horse stud,
breeding the horses ridden by the Australian Light Horse regiments in the Second Boer War
and World War I. After various uses over the decades, it has now been returned to its original
state, surrounded by English-style gardens.

Alexandra Bridge Wines

PO Box 255, South Perth, WA 6951 **Region** Margaret River
T (08) 9368 0099 **F** (08) 9368 0133 **www**.alexandrabridgewines.com.au **Open** Not
Winemaker Brian Fletcher **Est.** 1999 **Cases** 9000
Alexandra Bridge is the operating arm of Australian Wine Holdings. The 800-tonne winery,
commissioned in 2000, was the first built in the Karridale area at the southern end of the
Margaret River. The Brockman Vineyard, planted in three stages commencing in 1995, is
estate-owned and has a total of 30.5 ha of semillon, sauvignon blanc, chardonnay, shiraz and
cabernet sauvignon. The grapes coming from the Brockman Vineyard are supplemented by
long-term supply agreements with other Margaret River growers. Exports to Europe and
Southeast Asia.

Alkoomi

Wingebellup Road, Frankland River, WA 6396 **Region** Frankland River
T (08) 9855 2229 **F** (08) 9855 2284 **www**.alkoomiwines.com.au **Open** 7 days 10–5
Winemaker Michael Staniford, Merv Lange, Ryan Charuschenko **Est.** 1971 **Cases** 90000
For those who see the wineries of WA as suffering from the tyranny of distance, this most
remote of all wineries shows there is no tyranny after all. It is a story of unqualified success due
to sheer hard work, and no doubt to Merv and Judy Lange's aversion to borrowing a single
dollar from the bank. The substantial production is entirely drawn from the ever-expanding
estate vineyards – now over 100 ha. Wine quality across the range is impeccable, always with
precisely defined varietal character. Exports to all major markets.

 TTTTT **Wandoo Frankland River Semillon 2004** Pale, brilliant colour; the first
hints of toast on the bouquet, with long, fine lemon and grass flavours, the oak
seamlessly woven through the fruit. Screwcap. 12.3° alc. **Rating** 96 **To** 2014 $28
Black Label Frankland River Riesling 2007 Fresh and vibrant lime-accented
aromas and flavours around a core of citrussy acidity; very good length and line;
flawless. Screwcap. 13.5° alc. **Rating** 94 **To** 2017 $19.95
Black Label Frankland River Sauvignon Blanc 2007 A spotlessly clean
bouquet with no hint of sweetness or reduction; attractive gooseberry and
passionfruit mix on a long, quite intense palate. **Rating** 94 **To** 2009 $19.95

Blackbutt 2004 Medium–bodied; gently complex cedar and cigar box overtones to blackcurrant and mulberry fruit; fine, lingering tannins. Cork. 14° alc. **Rating** 94 **To** 2015 $47

♥♥♥♥♀ **Black Label Frankland River Chardonnay 2006** Bright green–yellow; fine, intense grapefruit, nectarine and melon fruit on a long palate, sustained by fine acidity and appropriate oak. Screwcap. 13° alc. **Rating** 92 **To** 2013 $19.95
White Label Frankland River Semillon Sauvignon Blanc 2007 A generous wine with lots of citrus and dried straw; vibrant, fresh and crisp on the finish. Screwcap. 13° alc. **Rating** 91 **To** 2009 $13.50

♥♥♥♥ **Black Label Frankland River Shiraz Viognier 2006** Light colour, good hue; light– to medium–bodied, clean, fresh and lively, but lacks the expected depth and texture; what's going on at Alkoomi? Screwcap. 13.5° alc. **Rating** 89 **To** 2012 $20
Black Label Frankland River Cabernet Sauvignon 2005 Cedary/savoury/earthy overtones to light– to medium–bodied red and blackcurrant fruit; less weight and conviction than expected. Screwcap. 14.5° alc. **Rating** 88 **To** 2010 $19.95

All Saints Estate

All Saints Road, Wahgunyah, Vic 3687 **Region** Rutherglen
T (02) 6035 2222 **F** (02) 6035 2200 **www.**allsaintswine.com.au **Open** Mon–Sat 9–5.30, Sun 10–5.30
Winemaker Dan Crane **Est.** 1864 **Cases** 40 000
The winery rating reflects the fortified wines, but the table wines are more than adequate. The Terrace restaurant makes this a most enjoyable stop for any visitor to the northeast. The faux castle, modelled on a Scottish castle beloved of the founder, is classified by the Historic Buildings Council. All Saints and St Leonards were wholly owned by Peter Brown, tragically killed in a road accident in late 2005. Ownership has passed to Peter's three children, Eliza, Angela and Nicholas, and it is the intention to keep the business in the family. Exports to the US.

♥♥♥♥♥ **Rare Rutherglen Tokay NV** Dark olive mahogany; a sumptuous palate based on 50-year-old solera; another level of complexity altogether, again with a rich tapestry of rancio followed by a drying finish. Vino-Lok. 18° alc. **Rating** 97 **To** 2009 $110
Rare Rutherglen Muscat NV Mid-brown; deliciously fresh and lively with a surge of fruit at once very complex yet vibrant; Christmas pudding with spice; long cleansing finish. Vino-Lok. 18° alc. **Rating** 97 **To** 2009 $110
Grand Rutherglen Tokay NV The next step in a clear flavour progression, much darker and headed towards olive-brown; great concentration tea leaf, some burnt toffee and cake; material up to 25 years old. Vino-Lok. 18° alc. **Rating** 95 **To** 2009 $62
Family Cellar Durif 2006 Retains the lightness of the Estate version, but adds more complexity, and a lightly silky texture which is most unlike durif; obviously this is a grape the family has a true understanding of. Screwcap. 14.8° alc. **Rating** 94 **To** 2016 $50
Grand Rutherglen Muscat NV Brown hues now dominant; extremely rich, luscious and viscous burnt toffee and spice; mouthfilling; long finish. Vino-Lok. 18° alc. **Rating** 94 **To** 2009 $62

♥♥♥♥♀ **Classic Rutherglen Tokay NV** Bright golden brown; is indeed classic tokay, with tea leaf, Christmas cake and toffee flavours, then a long, dry finish. Vino-Lok. 18° alc. **Rating** 93 **To** 2009 $31
Classic Rutherglen Muscat NV Pale reddish-brown; clear-cut raisined muscat with notes of glacé fruit and treacle; very good balance and length. Vino-Lok. 18° alc. **Rating** 93 **To** 2009 $31
Family Cellar Marsanne 2006 Honeysuckle and dried straw define this wine; nice freshness and vibrancy on the finish too, with a little amaro twist to the aftertaste. Screwcap. 13.5° alc. **Rating** 90 **To** 2014 $28

Estate Rutherglen Durif 2006 An essay into durif with poise; loaded with succulent dark fruits and elements of spice, the fruit envelopes the palate, but does not weigh it down. Screwcap. 14.8° alc. **Rating** 90 **To** 2014 $24

ΨΨΨΨ **Limited Release Chardonnay Viognier 2006** The viognier plays a starring role, with ample levels of peach and apricot fruit, and good weight and texture across the palate. Screwcap. 14.2° alc. **Rating** 89 **To** 2009 $20

Family Cellar Shiraz 2006 Full-bodied, with chewy, leathery fruit and plenty of oak; quite bright on the palate, but the alcohol dominates a little. Screwcap. 14.5° alc. **Rating** 89 **To** 2014 $50

Pierre Limited Release Cabernet Sauvignon Merlot Cabernet Franc Malbec 2006 A medium-bodied, soft, fleshy and fruitful wine; nicely balanced and easily consumed. Screwcap. 14.2° alc. **Rating** 89 **To** 2009 $28

Chardonnay Viognier 2006 While the blend doesn't have much intellectual justification, it works well enough here to produce a gently fruity medium-bodied palate free of oak. Screwcap. 13.5° alc. **Rating** 88 **To** 2011 $20

Shiraz 2006 Bright and juicy, with red and black fruits framed by tar and leather. Screwcap. 14.4° alc. **Rating** 88 **To** 2012 $24

Barrel Reserve Shiraz 2004 An honest medium-bodied shiraz with appropriate flavour and structure, but lacking the spark to excite. Cork. 14° alc. **Rating** 87 **To** 2011 $24

Allandale

132 Lovedale Road, Lovedale, NSW 2321 **Region** Lower Hunter Valley
T (02) 4990 4526 **F** (02) 4990 1714 **www**.allandalewinery.com.au **Open** Mon–Sat 9–5, Sun 10–5
Winemaker Bill Sneddon, Rod Russell **Est.** 1978 **Cases** 20 000
Owners Wally and Judith Atallah have overseen the growth of Allandale from a small cellar door operation to a substantial business. Allandale has developed a reputation for its Chardonnay, but offers a broad range of wines of consistently good quality, including red wines variously sourced from the Hilltops, Orange and Mudgee. Exports to the UK, the US and other major markets.

ΨΨΨΨ **Hunter Valley Semillon 2007** Tight and focused lemon sherbet fruit, with hints of dried straw; good texture, but a little lean. Screwcap. 11° alc. **Rating** 89 **To** 2015 $19

Hunter Valley Chardonnay 2006 Developed green-gold; extremely rich and complex; partial barrel fermentation adds substantially to the impact of ripe stone fruit flavours. Screwcap. 13.5° alc. **Rating** 89 **To** 2009 $19

Allies Wines

15 Hume Road, Somers, Vic 3927 (postal) **Region** Mornington Peninsula
T 0439 370 530 **F** (03) 5983 1523 **www**.allies.com.au **Open** Not
Winemaker Barney Flanders, David Chapman **Est.** 2003 **Cases** 1000
Barney Flanders and David Chapman call Allies a collaboration; both come from a restaurant background dating back many years, Barney on the floor and David in the kitchen. In 1997 they turned their sights to wine; Barney graduated from CSU with a wine science degree in '99, and has since worked in the Mornington Peninsula, Yarra Valley, Trentino, Sonoma and Côte Rôtie. David left the restaurant scene in 2004 and is studying wine science at CSU. They own no vineyards, and have made wine since '03 from various vineyard sources in various regions, but in '06 took on the management of the 20-ha Merricks Grove Vineyard in Merricks North, which will henceforth supply the core of the material for their Pinot Noir and Chardonnay releases. At the top end of those releases come the limited-production Garagiste-branded wines.

ΨΨΨΨΨ **Stone Axe Vineyard Heathcote Shiraz 2006** Vivid crimson-purple; very fragrant, with an elegant medium-bodied palate; pure blackberry and spice fruit running through to a bright finish. A great exercise in restraint from vineyard to winery to bottle. Screwcap. 13.2° alc. **Rating** 95 **To** 2026 $24

Garagiste Chardonnay 2006 A classy wine, pure and elegant; the citrus and nectarine palate has immaculate balance, and great length courtesy of French clones 76 and 95 and the Yabby Lake origin. Screwcap. 13° alc. **Rating** 94 **To** 2013 $36

Saone Mornington Peninsula Viognier 2006 Strong varietal expression throughout, with apricot blossom aromas and predominant, though not aggressive, palate impact, the 11% chardonnay a seamless component; unusually, will match a wide range of food. Screwcap. 13.5° alc. **Rating** 94 **To** 2011 $24

Garagiste Pinot Noir 2006 Great clarity for an unfined, unfiltered wine; seductive dark cherry and plum aromas and flavours; immaculate structure and texture, and all the length one could wish for. MV6, indigenous yeasts, 11 months French oak (35% new). Screwcap. 13° alc. **Rating** 94 **To** 2013 $35

ΨΨΨΨ **Mornington Peninsula Pinot Noir 2006** More savoury, spicier and lighter-bodied than the Garagiste, notwithstanding higher alcohol; has good length, with tangy/forest-floor characters. Screwcap. 13.4° alc. **Rating** 90 **To** 2011 $27.95

Alta Wines

PO Box 63, Mt Torrens, SA 5244 **Region** Adelaide Hills
T 0434 077 059 **F** (08) 8389 5193 **Open** Not
Winemaker Sarah Fletcher **Est.** NA **Cases** 8000

Sarah Fletcher comes to Alta with an impressive winemaking background: a degree from Roseworthy, and thereafter seven years working for Orlando Wyndham. She came face to face with grapes from all over Australia, and developed a particular regard for those coming from the Adelaide Hills. She became financially involved with Alta in 2005. The range is being extended with varieties suited to the cool climate of the Adelaide Hills. Exports to the UK, Canada and Hong Kong.

ΨΨΨΨ **Adelaide Hills Pinot Noir 2006** Plenty of structure and presence; black cherry and plum plus some savoury, but fine, tannins. A wine with time in front of it. Screwcap. 14° alc. **Rating** 90 **To** 2012 $28

ΨΨΨΨ **Adelaide Hills Sauvignon Blanc 2007** A clean bouquet, but both it and the palate are somewhat muted; a sustained dry finish is the strong point. Screwcap. 12.5° alc. **Rating** 89 **To** 2009

Adelaide Hills Pinot Grigio 2007 Early-picked pear and green apple aromas and flavours, then pronounced acidity on the back-palate and finish gives the wine bite. Screwcap. 13° alc. **Rating** 87 **To** 2009

Amadio Wines

Lot 26–27 South Para Road, Kersbrook, SA 5231 **Region** Adelaide Hills
T (08) 8337 5144 **F** (08) 8336 2462 **www**.amadiowines.com.au **Open** Not
Winemaker Danniel Amadio **Est.** 2004 **Cases** 50 000

Danniel Amadio says he has followed in the footsteps of his Italian grandfather, selling wine from his cellar (cantina) direct to the consumer, cutting out wholesale and distribution. He also draws upon the business of his parents, built not in Italy, but in Australia. Amadio Wines has over 250 ha of vineyards, primarily in the Adelaide Hills, and also small parcels of contract-grown grapes from Clare Valley, McLaren Vale and Langhorne Creek, covering just about every variety imaginable, and – naturally – with a very strong representation of Italian varieties. No samples received; the rating is that of last year. Exports to the US, Canada, China, Sweden and Malaysia.

Amarok Estate ★★★

Lot 547 Caves Road, Wilyabrup, WA 6284 (postal) **Region** Margaret River
T (08) 9756 6888 **F** (08) 9756 6555 **Open** Not
Winemaker Kevin McKay (Contract) **Est.** 1999 **Cases** NA

John and Libby Staley, with their youngest daughter, Megan, her husband, Shane, and youngest grandson, Lewis, have all had hands-on involvement in the establishment of 20 ha of vineyards – clearing bushland, rock picking, stick picking and planting, etc. The soils are gravelly loam over a clay granite base; the vineyard has a western aspect and is 5 km from the Indian Ocean.

Ambar Hill   ★★★

364 Mt Stirling Road, Glen Aplin, Qld 4381 **Region** Granite Belt
T 0409 631 292 **F** (07) 3899 9410 **www**.ambarhill.com.au **Open** Not
Winemaker Jim Barnes **Est.** 2001 **Cases** 1000
Graham and Judy Dalton have planted 4 ha of shiraz, cabernet, merlot, verdelho, chardonnay and semillon, with the first wine produced in 2003. Both have varied backgrounds stretching back to Canberra in the Whitlam era. Graham is an economist-turned-restaurateur, previously a prison reform consultant and running the Qld Farmer's Federation. The wines, incidentally, are sold wholesale through Fino Food + Wine of Bulimba, Qld.

ΨΨΨΨ   **Chardonnay Verdelho 2006** Has more freshness and activity in the mouth than the 2007 (also well made); a nice citrussy tang to the array of gentle stone fruit flavours; has length. Screwcap. 13.5° alc. **Rating** 88 **To** 2010 $16.50
Shiraz 2006 The amount of choc-mint and vanilla oak may appeal to cellar door customers, but is really over the top for the good varietal fruit which is underneath. Screwcap. 14.4° alc. **Rating** 87 **To** 2012 $16.50
Shiraz 2005 Was tasted after a series of the greatest Australian shirazs from the 2006 vintage, and given the benefit of the doubt; pleasant shiraz fruit with a large serve of mocha and vanilla oak. Screwcap. 13° alc. **Rating** 87 **To** 2012 $16.50

Amberley Estate   ★★★★★

Thornton Road, Yallingup, WA 6282 **Region** Margaret River
T (08) 9750 1113 **F** (08) 9750 1155 **www**.amberleyestate.com.au **Open** 7 days 10–4.30
Winemaker Paul Dunnewyk **Est.** 1986 **Cases** 120 000
Based its initial growth on its ultra-commercial, fairly sweet Chenin Blanc, which continues to provide the volume for the brand. However, the quality of all the other wines has risen markedly over recent years as the 31 ha of estate plantings have become fully mature. Purchased by Canadian company Vincor in early 2004. Exports to the UK and the US.

ΨΨΨΨΨ   **Margaret River Semillon Sauvignon Blanc 2007** Intense and crisp; a lovely clean and clear profile of tropical and gooseberry fruit; lively and long. **Rating** 94 **To** 2010 $21.50

ΨΨΨΨ℉   **First Selection Margaret River Cabernet Sauvignon 2004** Dense blackcurrant and blackberry fruit, with oak very evident from the bouquet through to the finish and aftertaste; a silky, fleshy palate, with ripe tannins. **Rating** 94 **To** 2014 $36
First Selection Margaret River Shiraz 2004 Tangy spicy elements give the wine life and interest, as do fine, silky but persistent tannins; will continue to slowly grow in bottle. Screwcap. 14° alc. **Rating** 91 **To** 2020 $38

ΨΨΨΨ   **Margaret River Shiraz 2006** Spicy, leafy aromas, the palate showing more fruit sweetness; positive oak. **Rating** 89 **To** 2014 $21.50
Margaret River Chardonnay 2006 Workmanlike wine, with balanced fruit and oak, but lacks the definition expected in Margaret River. Screwcap. 13° alc. **Rating** 87 **To** 2010 $22.50
First Selection Margaret River Cabernet Sauvignon 2002 Uninspiring colour, and the palate, too, lacks focus and impact; the structure is adequate, the oak more than so. At sixes and sevens. Cork. 13.5° alc. **Rating** 87 **To** 2012 $38

Amherst Winery

Talbot-Avoca Road, Amherst, Vic 3371 **Region** Pyrenees
T (03) 5463 2105 **F** (03) 5463 2502 **www**.amherstwinery.com **Open** W'ends &
public hols 10–5
Winemaker Graham Jukes (Red), Paul Lesock (White) **Est.** 1989 **Cases** 2000
Norman and Elizabeth Jones have planted 4 ha of vines on a property with an extraordinarily
rich history, a shorthand reflection of which is seen in the name Dunn's Paddock Shiraz.
Samuel Knowles was a convict who arrived in Van Diemen's Land in 1838. He endured
continuous punishment before fleeing to SA in 1846 and changing his name to Dunn. When,
at the end of 1851, he married 18-year-old Mary Therese Taaffe in Adelaide, they walked from
Adelaide to Amherst pushing a wheelbarrow carrying their belongings, arriving just before
gold was discovered. The lease title of the property shows that Amherst Winery is sited on
land once owned by Samuel Dunn. Exports to China.

ΨΨΨΨΨ **Dunn's Paddock Pyrenees Shiraz 2006** Vibrant red berry fruits with a touch
of spice; medium-bodied, with good flavour and bright, fine and supple on the
finish. Screwcap. 14.1° alc. **Rating** 94 **To** 2015 $25

Amicus

Rifle Range Road, McLaren Vale, SA 5171 **Region** McLaren Vale
T (08) 8373 6811 **F** (08) 8299 9500 **www**.amicuswines.com.au **Open** Not
Winemaker Walter Clappis, Kimberly Clappis **Est.** 2002 **Cases** 2000
Amicus is a venture bred in the purple. Its owners are 30-year industry veteran (and former
Ingoldby owner) Walter William Wilfred Clappis (he has always provided his name in full), wife
Kerry, plus Amanda and Tony Vanstone and Robert and Diana Hill, known in an altogether
different environment. The grapes come in part from the Clappis' McLaren Vale vineyard (run
on biodynamic principles) and from grapes purchased from growers in Langhorne Creek. No
samples received; the rating is that of last year.

Amietta Vineyard

NR

30 Steddy Road, Lethbridge, Vic 3332 **Region** Geelong
T (03) 5281 7407 **F** (03) 5281 7427 **www**.amietta.com.au **Open** By appt
Winemaker Nicholas Clark, Janet Cockbill **Est.** 1995 **Cases** 450
Janet Cockbill and Nicholas Clark are multi-talented. Both are archaeologists, but Janet manages
to combine part-time archaeology, part-time radiography at Geelong Hospital and part-time
organic viticulture. Nicholas Clark studied viticulture at CSU, and both he and Janet worked
vintage in France at Michel Chapoutier's biodynamic Domaine de Beates in Provence in 2001.
Plantings include lagrein and carmenere. Amietta is producing cameo wines of some beauty.

Anderson

Lot 12 Chiltern Road, Rutherglen, Vic 3685 **Region** Rutherglen
T (02) 6032 8111 **F** (02) 6032 7151 **www**.andersonwinery.com.au **Open** 7 days 10–5
Winemaker Howard Anderson, Christobelle Anderson **Est.** 1992 **Cases** 2000
Having notched up a winemaking career spanning over 30 years, including a stint at Seppelt
(Great Western), Howard Anderson and family started their own winery, initially with a
particular focus on sparkling wine but now extending across all table wine styles. There are
4 ha of estate shiraz and 1 ha each of durif and petit verdot, with yields controlled at a very
low 2.5 tonnes per ha.

ΨΨΨΨΨ **Rutherglen Durif 2004** Restrained alcohol and low pH take this wine into a
different realm than most of Northeast Victoria durifs; well-balanced red fruits
(rather than black) and ripe tannins. Screwcap. 13.9° alc. **Rating** 94 **To** 2012 $21

ΨΨΨΨΨ **Melanie Sweet Shiraz 2005** Has all the ingredients to grow and become very
complex with age; good spirit; blackcurrant, Christmas pudding and licorice
flavours (vintage port style). Cork. 18.5° alc. **Rating** 90 **To** 2020 $25

�Y�YY **Winemaker's Selection Chardonnay 2004** Elegant, light-bodied chardonnay developing slowly; ripe peach and melon with appropriately subtle oak presumably from cool, high-altitude vineyards. Screwcap. 12.8° alc. **Rating** 89 **To** 2010 $25
Cellar Block Shiraz 2002 Abundant, layered blackberry, earth and dark chocolate fruit with a touch of alcohol-derived sweetness; multiple show awards; love it or leave it style. Cork. 15.5° alc. **Rating** 89 **To** 2015 $35
Pinot Noir Chardonnay 1999 Deep yellow-straw; a complex, full-bodied wine with toasty/bready aromas and flavours, in no way reliant on residual sweetness. Upper King Valley. Cork. 12.4° alc. **Rating** 89 **To** 2009 $23
Methode Champenoise Chenin Blanc 2002 It is difficult to make sows' ears into silk purses, but Howard Anderson succeeds; the wine has spent 5 years on yeast lees, and is hand-disgorged in batches of 300 bottles; recommended drinking within 12 months of purchase. Cork. 12° alc. **Rating** 88 **To** 2009 $23

Andrew Harris Vineyards ★★★☆

Sydney Road, Mudgee, NSW 2850 **Region** Mudgee
T (02) 6373 1477 **F** (02) 6373 1296 **www**.andrewharris.com.au **Open** 7 days 9–5
Winemaker Lisa Bray **Est.** 1991 **Cases** 65 000
Andrew and Deb Harris got away to a flying start after purchasing a 300-ha sheep station and planting it with 106 ha of vines. The early red wine releases had considerable show success, and these days the Personal Selection range is of good quality. Exports to the UK, the US, Denmark, Switzerland, Dubai, Malaysia, Thailand, China, Japan and NZ.

YYYY **Highfields Mudgee Semillon 2006** Tight and restrained, with a little lemon sherbet on the finish; could show a little more concentration. Screwcap. 11° alc. **Rating** 87 **To** 2014 $14.95

Andrew Peace Wines ★★★☆

Murray Valley Highway, Piangil, Vic 3597 **Region** Swan Hill
T (03) 5030 5291 **F** (03) 5030 5605 **www**.apwines.com **Open** Mon–Fri 8–5, Sat 12–4, Sun by appt
Winemaker Andrew Peace, Nina Viergutz **Est.** 1995 **Cases** 400 000
The Peace family has been a major Swan Hill grapegrower since 1980, with 100 ha of vineyards, moving into winemaking with the opening of a $3 million winery in '96. The modestly priced wines are aimed at supermarket-type outlets in Australia and exports to all major markets.

YYYY **Blue Sand Cabernet Merlot 2005** Nicely balanced varietal fruit flavours and tannins; redcurrant and blueberry; smooth, supple finish; keenly priced. Screwcap. 13° alc. **Rating** 89 **To** 2012 $8.95
Blue Sand Semillon Sauvignon Blanc 2007 Some development, but good hue; ripe flavours in a tropical pineapple spectrum balanced by acidity on the finish. Screwcap. 12.5° alc. **Rating** 87 **To** 2009 $10.95
Eighth Horse Chardonnay 2007 Lighter-bodied and fresher than the Blue Sand; yellow peach with a hint of sweetness acceptable at this price. Screwcap. 13° alc. **Rating** 87 **To** 2009 $9.95
Eighth Horse Shiraz 2007 Pleasant shiraz fruit on the light- to medium-bodied palate, with subliminal oak and a whisper of sweetness; drink immediately. Screwcap. 13.5° alc. **Rating** 87 **To** 2009 $9.95
Blue Sand Shiraz 2006 Light- to medium-bodied; still fresh, with a mix of red and black fruits; simple, but honest. Screwcap. 13° alc. **Rating** 87 **To** 2009 $10.95

Andrew Seppelt Wines ★★★★

PO Box 278, Greenock, SA 5360 **Region** Barossa Valley
T (08) 8562 8373 **F** (08) 8562 8414 **www**.andrewseppelt.com **Open** Not
Winemaker Andrew Seppelt **Est.** 2001 **Cases** 275

This is a small 'side project' of Andrew Seppelt and Bill Jahnke, which began in 2001. The idea was to push the winemaking envelope way beyond the norm, indeed in some ways standing it on its head. The shiraz was kept in a 1.5-tonne open fermenter with aggressive cap-wetting/plunging early in the fermentation, backing off towards the end, but with the temperature kept at around 20°C until dryness, whereafter it was lifted to 28°C and held for seven days, followed by three weeks maceration on skins. Says Andrew Seppelt, 'The wine smelled horrid – volatile and flat – but that's how I remember the wines at this stage when I was working in Provence'. Malolactic fermentation was spontaneous, and cleaned out the volatile acidity, the wine eventually being bottled unfined and unfiltered. The Shiraz Cabernet is made in a more traditional fashion. The wines will be sold exclusively through a private mailing list on the website at $180 each.

🍷🍷🍷🍷🍷 **Shiraz Cabernet Sauvignon 2005** Deeply coloured and massively proportioned; more silky than the Shiraz, and a bit of varietal integrity, but the alcohol is very potent. Cork. 15.1° alc. **Rating** 92 **To** 2020 $180

🍷🍷🍷🍷 **Shiraz 2005** Amazing concentration, but very alcoholic; porty fruit, cold tea and quite sweet on the palate. Massively proportioned but little charm or grace. Cork. 15.5° alc. **Rating** 89 **To** 2025 $180

Angas Plains Estate

Lot 52 Angas Plains Road, Langhorne Creek, SA 5255 **Region** Langhorne Creek
T (08) 8537 3159 **F** (08) 8537 3353 **www**.angasplainswines.com.au **Open** W'ends & public hols 11–5
Winemaker Peter Douglas (Contract) **Est.** 2000 **Cases** 3000
Angas Plains Estate is a 10 min–drive south of the historic town of Strathalbyn, on the banks of the Angas River. Owners Phillip and Judy Cross employ organic measures to tend their 25 ha of shiraz, cabernet sauvignon and chardonnay. Exports to the US, China and Malaysia.

🍷🍷🍷🍷🍷 **PJ's Langhorne Creek Cabernet Sauvignon 2006** Plush and remarkably rich fruit given the restrained alcohol; redcurrant, cassis and raspberry flavours supported by soft, ripe tannins; good length. Diam. 14° alc. **Rating** 92 **To** 2016 $25
PJ's Langhorne Creek Shiraz 2006 Abundant plum and blackberry fruit to the medium-bodied palate; good texture and balance, supported by fine tannins. Diam. 14° alc. **Rating** 90 **To** 2014 $19

Angelicus

Lot 10 Angels Road, Manjimup, WA 6258 **Region** Pemberton
T (08) 9772 3003 **F** (08) 9772 3153 **www**.angelicus.com.au **Open** W'ends & public hols 10.30–4
Winemaker John Ward **Est.** 1997 **Cases** 500
Dr John and Sue Ward moved from Sydney to Middlesex in the Pemberton Region with the sole aim of establishing a premium–quality vineyard, having taken two years to select the right site. It's a busy life; John continues to work as a medical practitioner and Sue manages the vineyard, following on many years in the hospitality industry as a caterer and restaurateur. They have planted pinot noir, sauvignon blanc, merlot, cabernet sauvignon, chardonnay and tempranillo.

🍷🍷🍷🍷🍷 **Pemberton Pinot Noir 2005** Light- to medium-bodied; a savoury, spicy style, with lots of stem and forest floor, yet not abrasive. Has considerable length, one up for Pemberton pinot. Screwcap. 14.5° alc. **Rating** 93 **To** 2012 $22
Pemberton Sauvignon Blanc 2006 A complex bouquet and palate; barrel fermentation in French oak has certainly added to both flavour and texture, though partially at the expense of varietal character, only the finish breaking free; nonetheless, will have broad appeal. Screwcap. 12.2° alc. **Rating** 92 **To** 2010 $18

Angove's

★★★★☆

Bookmark Avenue, Renmark, SA 5341 **Region** Riverland
T (08) 8580 3100 **F** (08) 8580 3155 **www.**angoves.com.au **Open** Mon–Fri 9–5
Winemaker Warrick Billings, Shane Clohesy, Tony Ingle **Est.** 1886 **Cases** 1.5 million
Exemplifies the economies of scale achievable in the Riverland without compromising
potential quality. Very good technology provides wines which are never poor and sometimes
exceed their theoretical station in life; the white varietals are best. The 480-ha vineyard
is currently being redeveloped with changes in the varietal mix. Angove's expansion into
Padthaway, the Clare Valley, McLaren Vale and Coonawarra (these latter three via contract-
grown fruit) has resulted in premium wines to back up its Riverland wines. Exports to all
major markets.

ΤΤΤΤΤ **Nine Vines Grenache Shiraz Rose 2007** An aromatic red cherry and
raspberry bouquet flows into a vibrant, fresh and long palate with a dry finish.
Multiple gold medals; no surprise. Screwcap. 12.5° alc. **Rating** 94 **To** 2009 $15

ΤΤΤΤΤ **Nine Vines Shiraz Viognier 2006** The viognier has a very marked impact
on the bouquet, and also to the black cherry and plum fruit in great abundance
on the palate; good tannin and oak support. Screwcap. 14.5° alc. **Rating** 93
To 2012 $15

Vineyard Select Clare Valley Riesling 2006 Fragrant apple, spice and lime
aromas lead into a balanced, long palate; gold medal at the local derby, Clare Valley
Show '06. Screwcap. 13° alc. **Rating** 93 **To** 2016 $14.95

Red Belly Black Chardonnay 2006 An attractive wine, with good finesse and
focus to the melon and nectarine fruit; good oak integration. Screwcap. 14° alc.
Rating 92 **To** 2012 $14.99

Vineyard Select Clare Valley Riesling 2007 Quite ripe with fresh lime
and hints of floral and some riper, more exotic fruits; fresh acidity on the finish.
Screwcap. 13° alc. **Rating** 90 **To** 2014 $14.95

ΤΤΤΤ **Long Row Cabernet Sauvignon 2006** Good colour; a clean bouquet with no
reduction, then attractive juicy red and black fruits with a savoury twist of tannins
and oak on the finish. Great value. Screwcap. 14° alc. **Rating** 89 **To** 2009 $9.99

Vineyard Select McLaren Vale Shiraz 2005 An attractive medium-bodied
wine, with a mix of red and black fruits, dark chocolate, fine tannins and balanced
oak; overall quite juicy. Cork. 14.5° alc. **Rating** 89 **To** 2011 $18

Vineyard Select Coonawarra Cabernet Sauvignon 2005 A clear expression
of cabernet fruit on the medium-bodied blackcurrant and cassis palate; soft tannins
and muted oak; easy finish. Cork. 14.5° alc. **Rating** 88 **To** 2011 $18

Nine Vines Tempranillo Shiraz 2006 Fragrant red fruits wound around
a minerally core; good balance and length. Screwcap. 13.5° alc. **Rating** 88
To 2011 $13.95

Long Row Shiraz 2005 Light- to medium-bodied; smooth, balanced black and
red fruits; does not aim for complexity, just balance and drinkability at the price.
Screwcap. 14.5° alc. **Rating** 87 **To** 2009 $9.95

Angullong Wines

★★★

Four Mile Creek Road, Orange, NSW 2800 (postal) **Region** Orange
T (02) 6366 4300 **F** (02) 6466 4399 **www.**angullong.com.au **Open** Not
Winemaker Jon Reynolds **Est.** 1998 **Cases** 5000
The Crossing family (Bill and Hatty, and third generation James and Ben) have owned a
2000-ha sheep and cattle station for over half a century. Located 40 km south of Orange on
the lower slopes of the Orange region, overlooking the Belubula Valley, 217 ha of vines have
been planted since 1998. In all, there are 13 varieties, with shiraz, cabernet sauvignon and
merlot leading the way. Most of the production is sold to Hunter Valley wineries. Exports
to Denmark.

ΤΤΤΤ **Fossil Hill Orange Barbera 2007** Spicy and bright red fruits; good length
and weight, and certainly some drinking interest; acidity keeps the wine fresh and
vibrant. Screwcap. 14° alc. **Rating** 88 **To** 2012 $20

Fossil Hill Orange Shiraz Viognier 2006 A pleasing aromatic style, with a little apricot flesh and juicy red fruits. Screwcap. 15° alc. **Rating** 87 **To** 2014 $20

Angus the Bull   ★★★

PO Box 3016, South Yarra, Vic 3141 **Region** Southeast Australia
T (03) 9820 4077 **F** (03) 9820 4677 **www**.angusthebull.com **Open** Not
Winemaker Hamish MacGowan **Est.** 2002 **Cases** 20 000
Hamish MacGowan, who describes himself as 'a young Australian wine industry professional', has taken the virtual winery idea to its ultimate conclusion, with a single wine (Cabernet Sauvignon) designed to be drunk with premium red meat, or, more particularly, a perfectly cooked steak.

 Cabernet Sauvignon 2005 A light- to medium-bodied, pleasant, albeit modest, wine with no rough edges; no thrills either. Fully priced. Screwcap. 14.5° alc. **Rating** 87 **To** 2009 $20
Cabernet Sauvignon 2006 Attractive, welcoming light- to medium-bodied cassis, raspberry and blackberry fruit; minimal tannins, and some light oak influence. Screwcap. 14.5° alc. **Rating** 87 **To** 2011 $20

Angus Wines   ★★★★☆

Captain Sturt Road, Hindmarsh Island, SA 5214 **Region** Southern Fleurieu
T (08) 8555 2320 **F** (08) 8555 2323 **www**.anguswines.com.au **Open** W'ends & public hols 11–5
Winemaker Boar's Rock (Mike Farmilo), Angas Buchanan **Est.** 1995 **Cases** 3000
Susan and Alistair Angus are pioneer viticulturists on Hindmarsh Island, having established 3.75 ha of shiraz and 1.25 ha of semillon. Part is bottled under the Angus Wines label; some is sold in bulk to other wineries. Every aspect of packaging and marketing the wine has a sophisticated touch. No samples received; the rating is that of last year. Exports to the UK, the US and other major markets.

Annapurna Estate   ★★★

Simmonds Creek Road, Mt Beauty, Vic 3698 **Region** Alpine Valleys
T (03) 5754 1356 **F** (03) 5754 4517 **www**.annapurnaestate.com.au **Open** Wed–Sun, public & school hols 10–5
Winemaker Ezio Minutello **Est.** 1989 **Cases** 25 000
Ezio and Wendy Minutello began the establishment of the 21-ha vineyard at 550 m on Mt Beauty in 1989, planted to pinot noir, chardonnay, pinot gris and merlot. Finally, in 1999, the first wines were released. Annapurna, the second-highest mountain after Mt Everest, is Nepalese for 'goddess of bountiful harvest and fertility'. Ironically, it did not save the 2007 vintage, entirely lost to smoke taint.

Annie's Lane   ★★★★★

Quelltaler Road, Watervale, SA 5452 **Region** Clare Valley
T (08) 8843 0003 **F** (08) 8843 0096 **www**.annieslane.com.au **Open** Mon–Fri 8.30–5, w'ends 11–4
Winemaker Alan MacKenzie **Est.** 1851 **Cases** 230 000
The Clare Valley portfolio of Foster's, the name coming from Annie Weyman, a turn-of-the-century local identity. A series of outstanding wines have been produced since 1996, Copper Trail being the flagship release. Exports to the UK, the US and Europe.

 Copper Trail Clare Valley Shiraz 2005 Great colour and depth; a rich, supple, round medium- to full-bodied palate; fleshy and blackberry and plum fruit; ripe tannins. **Rating** 94 **To** 2020 $36.95

 Copper Trail Clare Valley Riesling 2006 Beginning to show some development; citrus/lime and a touch of toast before balanced acidity on the finish. Screwcap. 12° alc. **Rating** 92 **To** 2013 $53.95

Clare Valley Rose 2007 Vivid crimson-purple; attractive red cherry and strawberry fruit; dry, and finishes with cleansing acidity. Screwcap. 14° alc. **Rating** 91 **To** 2009 $19.95

Clare Valley Riesling 2007 Clean, lifted and full of lime juice; good concentration and racy acidity on the finish. Screwcap. 12° alc. **Rating** 90 **To** 2015 $19.95

Clare Valley Shiraz 2006 Medium- to full-bodied; good fruit, oak and tannin management in a round, mouthfilling style driven by ripe, but not jammy, blackberry fruit; will be long lived. Screwcap. 14.5° alc. **Rating** 90 **To** 2020 $19.95

Clare Valley Cabernet Merlot 2006 Attractive blackcurrant and cassis fruit with total extract and tannins kept at bay to preserve the clean and enjoyable lines of the wine. Screwcap. 14° alc. **Rating** 90 **To** 2016 $19.95

ȚȚȚȚ   Semillon Sauvignon Blanc 2007 Rich, very ripe, mouthfilling fruit at the tropical end of the spectrum; certainly has depth. Clare Semillon/Adelaide Hills Sauvignon Blanc. Screwcap. 12° alc. **Rating** 89 **To** 2013 $19.95

Anodyne Wines

165 Camp Road, Greta, NSW 2334 **Region** Lower Hunter Valley
T (02) 4938 6272 **F** (02) 4938 6004 **www**.camproadestate.com.au **Open** Not
Winemaker David Hook **Est.** 1998 **Cases** 1500

Duncan and Libby Thomson, cardiac surgeon and cardiac scrub nurse respectively, say Heartland Vineyard is the result of a seachange that got a little out of hand. 'After looking one weekend at some property in the Hunter Valley to escape the Sydney rat-race, we stumbled upon the beautiful 90 acres that has become our vineyard.' They have built a rammed-earth house on the property, and the vineyard is now a little over 5 ha, with shiraz, semillon, merlot, barbera, verdelho and viognier. Stress returned to the seachange when a trademark dispute caused them to drop the Heartland Vineyard name and substitute Anodyne Wines (anodyne is a Greek-derived word which means to relieve stress and to soothe — appropriate in the circumstances).

ȚȚȚȚ   Semillon 2007 Generous wine, the higher alcohol adding body and mouthfeel, but diminishing finesse; ready now or in a year or two, no longer. Screwcap. 12.4° alc. **Rating** 87 **To** 2010 $10

Verdelho 2007 Has good life and freshness, with an appealing citrus and tropical mix; clean finish. Screwcap. 13.1° alc. **Rating** 87 **To** 2011 $12

Anvers Wines

Lot 11 Main Road, McLaren Vale, SA 5171 **Region** Adelaide Hills
T (08) 8323 9603 **F** (08) 8323 9502 **www**.anvers.com.au **Open** 7 days 10–5
Winemaker Kym Milne **Est.** 1998 **Cases** 7000

Myriam and Wayne Keoghan established Anvers Wines with the emphasis on quality rather than quantity. The first Cabernet Sauvignon was made in 1998, and volume has increased markedly since then. The quality of the wines is exemplary, no doubt underwriting the increase in production and expansion of markets both across Australia and in most major export markets.

ȚȚȚȚȚ   The Warrior Shiraz 2005 Good colour; has the flavour and structure complexity expected from the three-regional blend (Adelaide Hills/McLaren Vale/Langhorne Creek); overall extract well controlled, and the length is good, with a quite juicy finish. Cork. 14.5° alc. **Rating** 93 **To** 2015 $45

ȚȚȚȚ   McLaren Vale Shiraz 2005 Smoky aromas, the flavours in a sweet prune and blackberry spectrum; curiously, only medium-bodied. Cork. 14.9° alc. **Rating** 89 **To** 2013 $28

Apsley Gorge Vineyard

The Gulch, Bicheno, Tas 7215 **Region** East Coast Tasmania
T (03) 6375 1221 **F** (03) 6375 1589 **Open** By appt
Winemaker Brian Franklin **Est.** 1988 **Cases** NA
While nominally situated at Bicheno on the east coast, Apsley Gorge is in fact some distance inland, taking its name from a mountain pass. Clearly, it shares with the other east coast wineries the capacity to produce Chardonnay and Pinot Noir of excellent quality. Brian Franklin travels to Burgundy each year for the vintage, putting into practice at Apsley Gorge what he learns in Burgundy.

Pinot Noir 2006 A complex wine, with disguised power; a mix of dark plum, spice, briar and forest floor; good length. Screwcap. **Rating** 92 **To** 2014 $21

Chardonnay 2006 Surprising development in both colour and flavour on the palate; somewhat broad, though undeniably flavoursome. Screwcap. **Rating** 88 **To** 2010 $44

Arakoon

229 Main Road, McLaren Vale, SA 5171 **Region** McLaren Vale
T (08) 8323 7339 **F** (02) 6566 6288 **www**.arakoonwines.com.au **Open** By appt
Winemaker Raymond Jones **Est.** 1999 **Cases** 3000
Ray and Patrik Jones' first venture into wine came to nothing: a 1990 proposal for a film about the Australian wine industry with myself as anchorman. Five years too early, say the Joneses. In 1999 they took the plunge into making their own wine, and exporting it along with the wines of others. As the quality of the wines has increased, so has the originally zany labelling been replaced with simple, but elegant, labels. Exports to Sweden, Denmark, Germany, Singapore and Malaysia.

Doyen Willunga McLaren Vale Shiraz 2006 Similar colour but almost a role reversal with Clarendon; fruit more defined and slightly longer perhaps; 100% French oak (part new). Screwcap. 14.5° alc. **Rating** 95 **To** 2022 $45
Clarendon Shiraz 2006 Deep colour; medium- to full-bodied; very rich, round and deep; blackberry, dark chocolate and mocha; ripe tannins; a mix of French and American oak. Screwcap. 14.5° alc. **Rating** 94 **To** 2020 $32

Sellicks Beach McLaren Vale Shiraz 2006 Has the supple, round texture and mouthfeel of the other Arakoon wines; slightly lighter in body, slightly less complex, but still satisfying. Screwcap. 14.5° alc. **Rating** 93 **To** 2016 $20

Full Bodied Red McLaren Vale Grenache Shiraz Mataro 2005 A little more serious than its label might suggest, but that's Arakoon; some Turkish delight may be an autosuggestion alongside spicy fruit and soft tannins. Screwcap. 14.5° alc. **Rating** 89 **To** 2010 $18
The Lighthouse McLaren Vale Cabernet Sauvignon 2006 Very developed colour, as is the wine; soft chocolatey early-drinking style. Screwcap. 14.5° alc. **Rating** 87 **To** 2011 $20

Aramis Vineyards

PO Box 208, Marleston, SA 5033 **Region** McLaren Vale
T (08) 8238 0000 **F** (08) 8234 0485 **www**.aramisvineyards.com **Open** Not
Winemaker Scott Rawlinson **Est.** 1998 **Cases** 4000
The estate vineyards have been planted to just two varieties: shiraz (18 ha) and cabernet sauvignon (8 ha). Viticulturist David Mills is a third-generation McLaren Vale resident and has been involved in the establishment of the vineyards from the beginning. Winemaker Scott Rawlinson was with Mildara Blass for eight years before joining the Aramis team under the direction of owner Lee Flourentzou. Exports to the UK, the US, Canada, Singapore and Hong Kong.

Arimia Margaret River

Quininup Road, Wilyabrup, WA 6280 (postal) **Region** Margaret River
T (08) 9287 2411 **F** (08) 9287 2422 **www**.arimia.com.au **Open** By appt
Winemaker Mark Warren **Est.** 1998 **Cases** 6000
Anne Spencer and Malcolm Washbourne purchased their 55-ha property overlooking the
Indian Ocean, and its northern boundaries marked by the Cape Naturaliste National Park, in
1997. Quininup Creek meanders through the property, providing the water source for its blue-
green dam. The name is a combination of daughters Mia and Ariann. They have planted a 6-ha
Joseph's Coat array of varieties, the Short Story wines coming from the traditional range of
white varietals (semillon, sauvignon blanc, verdelho, chardonnay), the Full Story wines featuring
cabernet sauvignon, merlot, petit verdot, shiraz, grenache, mourvedre and zinfandel.

ΨΨΨΨΨ **Mud Larks Sauvignon Blanc 2007** Spotlessly clean and vibrant gooseberry
and asparagus; the structure and length both good, ditto value. Screwcap. 12.7° alc.
Rating 90 **To** 2009 $15.95
Waverider White 2007 Abundant fruit in a tropical spectrum on both bouquet
and palate, despite the semillon dominance; has good length, and even better value.
Semillon/Sauvignon Blanc. Screwcap. 13.5° alc. **Rating** 90 **To** 2010 $13.95

ΨΨΨΨ **Shiraz Grenache Mourvedre 2004** Much deeper colour than the '05; complex
dark fruits, licorice, leather and spice, the tannins still needing to soften; very
different from the '05. Screwcap. 13.8° alc. **Rating** 89 **To** 2012 $25.95
Rockpool Red 2005 Hold your breath: a blend of Shiraz/Cabernet Sauvignon/
Merlot/Grenache/Mourvedre/Petit Verdot/Zinfandel, none particularly ripe, but
gets points for effort. Screwcap. 13.5° alc. **Rating** 87 **To** 2009 $13.95
Pickled Fairies Verdelho 2007 Typical varietal fruit salad aromas and flavours,
enlivened by a touch of squeezed lemon on the finish. Screwcap. 13.5° alc.
Rating 87 **To** 2010 $15.95
Smiling Dogs Shiraz Viognier 2005 Good hue; a light- to medium-bodied
savoury, spicy palate, without the usual fruit lift and sweetness from viognier; does
have fair length. Screwcap. 14° alc. **Rating** 87 **To** 2010 $19.95
Shiraz Grenache Mourvedre 2005 Light- to medium-bodied wine;
fresh, juicy red berry fruits matched by spicy/savoury tannins; 100% estate,
co-fermented. Screwcap. 13.8° alc. **Rating** 87 **To** 2010 $25
Valmai Zinfandel 2005 Very light-bodied, but does have some attractive confit
red fruit flavours, and is not threatened by tannins. Screwcap. 14.8° alc. **Rating** 87
To 2009 $25.95

Arlewood Estate

PO Box 139, Cowaramup, WA 6284 **Region** Margaret River
T (08) 9755 6267 **F** (08) 9755 6267 **www**.arlewood.com.au **Open** By appt
Winemaker Ian Bell, Mark Messenger **Est.** 1988 **Cases** 7000
A series of events in 2007 have led to major changes in the Arlewood Estate structure. The
Gosatti family sold the Harmans Road vineyard to Vasse Felix, but retained ownership of the
brand and all stock. It will continue to have access to the cabernet sauvignon and merlot up
to and including the 2009 vintage, and will acquire white grapes from more southerly parts
of the region. Exports to the UK, the US, Singapore, Malaysia and Hong Kong.

ΨΨΨΨΨ **Sussex Loc. 3991 Margaret River Semillon Sauvignon Blanc 2006** Rich,
ripe and supple; medium- to full-bodied, with abundant tropical honeyed fruit
flavours, crisp acidity cleaning and lengthening the finish; 197 dozen made; Semillon
(62%)/Sauvignon Blanc (38%). Screwcap. 13° alc. **Rating** 93 **To** 2010 $38
Margaret River Chardonnay 2006 Classic Margaret River style, with great
depth and texture, yet not heavy; ripe nectarine fruit coalesces with the French
oak on the complex palate. Screwcap. 13.5° alc. **Rating** 93 **To** 2014 $38
Single Vineyard Margaret River Shiraz 2005 Bright colour; medium-bodied,
with a complex array of black fruits, licorice and spice; French oak integrated and
balance, the tannins supple. Screwcap. 14.5° alc. **Rating** 91 **To** 2018 $22

ㅜㅜㅜㅜ **Margaret River Sauvignon Blanc Semillon 2007** Complex, with a strong
suggestion of some barrel ferment; good texture; grass and herb flavours with
a twist of ripe citrus on the finish; Sauvignon Blanc (60%)/Semillon (40%).
Screwcap. 14° alc. **Rating** 89 **To** 2010 $22

Margaret River Cabernet Sauvignon 2005 Light colour; very savoury/
foresty/minty, but has length and controlled tannins; simply needed riper fruit
and richness. Screwcap. 14.5° alc. **Rating** 87 **To** 2011 $38

Armstrong Vineyards ★★★★

4 East Parkway, Colonel Light Gardens, SA 5041 (postal) **Region** Grampians
T (08) 8277 6073 **F** (08) 8277 6035 **Open** Not
Winemaker Tony Royal **Est.** 1989 **Cases** 1000
Armstrong Vineyards is the brain- or love-child of Tony Royal, former Seppelt (Great Western)
winemaker, former CEO of Seguin Moreau Australia, and now CEO and joint owner of
Portavin Integrated Wine Services. Armstrong Vineyards has 6.7 ha of shiraz, the first 2 ha
planted in 1989, the remainder in 1995–96. Low yields (4.5–5.5 tonnes per ha) mean the wine
will always be produced in limited quantities. Exports to the UK, Hong Kong and China.

ㅜㅜㅜㅜ **Syrah Viognier 2005** Some development, with gamey flavours of roasted meats
and spice framing the soft and quite forward fruit; good flavour, but finishes short.
Rating 88 **To** 2014

Arranmore Vineyard ★★★

Rangeview Road, Carey Gully, SA 5144 **Region** Adelaide Hills
T (08) 8390 3034 **F** (08) 8390 0005 **www**.arranmore.com.au **Open** By appt
Winemaker John Venus **Est.** 1998 **Cases** 1000
One of the tiny operations which dot the landscape of the beautiful Adelaide Hills. At
an altitude of around 550 m, the 2-ha vineyard is planted to clonally selected pinot noir,
chardonnay and sauvignon blanc. Exports to the UK.

ㅜㅜㅜㅜ **The Tiers Adelaide Hills Pinot Rose 2007** Abounds with strawberry pinot
fruit in a generously framed palate; great lunch wine, straddling rose and (dry red)
pinot; not sweet. Screwcap. 13.1° alc. **Rating** 88 **To** 2009 $20

Adelaide Hills Black Pinot 2005 Strongly foresty, with a green stemmy
character which some will find off-putting; nonetheless, does have length.
Screwcap. 14.2° alc. **Rating** 87 **To** 2012 $39

Arrivo ★★★★

22 Kanmantoo Road, Aldgate, SA 5154 (postal) **Region** Adelaide Hills
T (08) 8370 8072 **F** (08) 8303 6621 **Open** Not
Winemaker Peter Godden, Sally McGill **Est.** 1998 **Cases** 120
While the establishment date of Arrivo is 1998, when Peter Godden and partner Sally
McGill established a nursery block of 35 vines of nebbiolo, the inspiration goes back to
'90, while Peter was still at Roseworthy College, heading off the following year to become
assistant winemaker to Joe Grilli at Primo Estate. In '95 and '96 Peter spent much time in
Barolo, Italy, working the '96 vintage at leading producer Vietti. In the meantime, Sally had
become a leading Italian wine exporter and importer/distributor with Red+White. By 2001
they had propagated sufficient vines from the original 35 to plant 1 ha of vineyard, using
a unique trellis and training system derived from Barolo, but with an Australian twist. Not
only is the trellis complicated and unique, but so are the amazingly complicated fermentation
techniques being used by Peter Godden, best known these days for his work with the AWRI.
Exports to the UK.

ㅜㅜㅜㅜ **Rosato di Nebbiolo 2007** Cherry, strawberry and spicy fruit aromas and
flavours; slightly unexpected sweetness on the finish. Screwcap. 13° alc. **Rating** 88
To 2009 $26

Arrowfield Estate ★★★★

Golden Highway, Jerrys Plains, NSW 2330 **Region** Upper Hunter Valley
T (02) 6576 4041 **F** (02) 6576 4144 **www**.arrowfieldestate.com.au **Open** 7 days 10–5
Winemaker Barry Kooij, Adrianna Mansueto **Est.** 1968 **Cases** 80 000
Arrowfield continues in the ownership of the Inagaki family, which has been involved in
the Japanese liquor industry for over a century. It has 47 ha of low-yielding, old vines in the
Upper Hunter Valley, and also buys grapes from other parts of Australia, making varietal wines
appropriate to those regions. In 2007 it merged with Mornington Peninsula winery Red Hill
Estate, the merged group trading as InWine Group Australia, with Brenton Martin installed as
CEO. Exports to all major markets.

ΨΨΨΨΨ **Shiraz Viognier 2006** Vibrant red fruits and lifted aromas redolent of violets; the
    medium-bodied palate is focused, fine and fresh and has lovely lingering acidity.
    Screwcap. 14.5° alc. **Rating** 93 **To** 2018 $17
    Cabernet Merlot 2005 An attractive cabernet blend, showing plenty of cassis
    and cedar; fleshy on the mid-palate with good flavour. Screwcap. 14.5° alc.
    Rating 92 **To** 2016 $17
    Sophie's Bridge Shiraz 2006 Red fruits dominate, with a little spice on the
    medium-bodied palate; fresh finish; overall appeal, top value. Screwcap. 14° alc.
    Rating 90 **To** 2015 $12

ΨΨΨΨ **Bowman's Crossing Semillon Sauvignon Blanc 2007** Has unexpected
    flavour and length in a ripe citrus spectrum, with judicious balance of acidity
    and subliminal sweetness; great value. Screwcap. 12° alc. **Rating** 89 **To** 2009 $9
    Show Reserve Hunter Valley Shiraz 2006 Distinctly regional with savoury/
    earthy undertones to the medium-bodied black fruits; slightly hard acidity; needs
    patience. Screwcap. 14.5° alc. **Rating** 89 **To** 2015 $25
    Reserve Hunter Valley Semillon 2004 A generous Hunter semillon, with
    good flavour depth and weight on the finish; quite forward and ready now.
    Screwcap. 11.5° alc. **Rating** 88 **To** 2010 $25

Arundel ★★★★☆

Arundel Farm Estate, PO Box 136, Keilor, Vic 3036 **Region** Sunbury
T (03) 9335 3422 **F** (03) 9335 4912 **www**.arundel.com.au **Open** Not
Winemaker Bianca Hayes, Mark Hayes **Est.** 1995 **Cases** 1000
Arundel was built around an acre of cabernet and shiraz planted in the 1970s, but abandoned.
When the Conwell family purchased the property in the early '90s, the vineyard was
resurrected, and the first vintage made by Rick Kinzbrunner in '95. Thereafter the cabernet
was grafted over to shiraz, the block slowly increased to 1.6 ha, and an additional 4 ha of
shiraz and 1.6 ha of viognier and marsanne planted. No samples received; the rating is that
of last year.

Ashbrook Estate

379 Harmans Road, Wilyabrup via Cowaramup, WA 6284 **Region** Margaret River
T (08) 9755 6262 **F** (08) 9755 6290 **Open** 7 days 10–5
Winemaker Tony Devitt, Brian Devitt **Est.** 1975 **Cases** 14 000
A fastidious maker of consistently excellent estate-grown table wines which shuns publicity
and the wine show system alike and is less well known than it deserves to be, selling much of
its wine through the cellar door and by an understandably very loyal mailing list clientele. All
of the white wines are of the highest quality, year in, year out. Exports to the UK, Canada,
Denmark, Germany, Indonesia, Japan, Singapore and Hong Kong.

ΨΨΨΨΨ **Margaret River Chardonnay 2006** An extremely complex wine; some
    deliberate funky characters of white Burgundy; grapefruit and nectarine fruit with
    well-balanced and integrated oak. Screwcap. **Rating** 96 **To** 2014 $29
    Margaret River Semillon 2007 An intense, herbaceous bouquet; exceptional
    finesse for a wine of 14° alcohol; very good overall character and presence; great
    length. Screwcap. 14° alc. **Rating** 95 **To** 2014 $20

🍷🍷🍷🍷🍷 **Margaret River Verdelho 2007** A tropical fruit bouquet; the palate has good length and abundant character, offering passionfruit with a squeeze of citrus; a model for other verdelhos to follow. Screwcap. 14° alc. **Rating** 93 **To** 2010 $19.99
Margaret River Sauvignon Blanc 2007 A gentle mix of grass, herbs, gooseberry and tropical fruits with balanced acidity; plenty of texture. Screwcap. 14° alc. **Rating** 93 **To** 2009 $22
Margaret River Shiraz 2004 In the typically elegant, light- to medium-bodied style of the estate; plum, blackberry, black cherry and spice flavours with a subtle infusion of French oak. Screwcap. 14.5° alc. **Rating** 93 **To** 2017 $27
Margaret River Cabernet Merlot Cabernet Franc 2003 Also includes a touch of petit verdot; is developing nicely, with a harmonious blend of sweet berry and more savoury/earthy characters, the palate fine, long and balanced. Screwcap. 13.5° alc. **Rating** 93 **To** 2014 $27
Margaret River Riesling 2007 Good depth of flavour in a tropical spectrum plus a touch of citrus; has length; good within the maritime limitations for riesling. Screwcap. 13.5° alc. **Rating** 90 **To** 2014 $20

Ashley Wines

392 Redesdale Road, Metcalfe, Vic 3448 **Region** Heathcote
T (03) 5423 2002 **F** (03) 5423 2002 **www**.ashleywines.com.au **Open** By appt
Winemaker Granite Hills (Llew Knight) **Est.** 1997 **Cases** 450
Steve Ashley planted his vineyard with the help of friends and family in 1997, with 3 ha of shiraz and 0.75 ha each of merlot and cabernet sauvignon. It is situated at the very southern (and coolest) end of the Heathcote region, with picking usually in late April. The quality of the grapes, and the skill of Llew Knight as contract winemaker, has been reflected in the track record of the wines in wine shows, where there has been a 100% success rate with the entries. No samples received; the rating is that of last year.

Ashton Hills

Tregarthen Road, Ashton, SA 5137 **Region** Adelaide Hills
T (08) 8390 1243 **F** (08) 8390 1243 **Open** W'ends & most public hols 11–5.30
Winemaker Stephen George **Est.** 1982 **Cases** 1500
Stephen George wears three winemaker hats: one for Ashton Hills, drawing upon a 3.5-ha estate vineyard high in the Adelaide Hills; one for Galah Wines; and one for Wendouree. It would be hard to imagine three wineries with more diverse styles, from the elegance and finesse of Ashton Hills to the awesome power of Wendouree. The Riesling, Chardonnay and Pinot Noir have moved into the highest echelon.

🍷🍷🍷🍷🍷 **Adelaide Hills Chardonnay 2006** Aromatic nectarine fruit on the bouquet; a superbly precise palate reflecting new and used barrel ferment French oak, lees stirring and partial mlf; flawless wine. Screwcap. 13.5° alc. **Rating** 96 **To** 2013 $32.50

🍷🍷🍷🍷🍷 **Reserve Merlot 2003** Light- to medium-bodied, but has long and harmonious flavour and structure; black olive, spice and earth accents to the core of largely red fruit; delicate tannins; ready now. Screwcap. 13.5° alc. **Rating** 93 **To** 2011 $45
Adelaide Hills Riesling 2007 Lemon, thyme and mineral aromas; crisp, intense and long, with a bone-dry finish. Screwcap. 13° alc. **Rating** 92 **To** 2017 $25
Three Pinot Gris Gewurztraminer Riesling 2007 Gewurztraminer does most of the talking, injecting a strong spicy lychee component to a delicious wine. Screwcap. 13.5° alc. **Rating** 91 **To** 2011 $23.75
Reserve Adelaide Hills Pinot Noir 2006 Slightly unconvincing, hazy colour; spicy, savoury, minty, forest-floor characters to the core of plum and black cherry fruit; has length, and needs time. Screwcap. **Rating** 91 **To** 2015 $61

Audrey Wilkinson Vineyard ★★★★★

Oakdale, De Beyers Road, Pokolbin, NSW 2320 **Region** Lower Hunter Valley
T (02) 4998 7411 **F** (02) 4998 7824 **www**.audreywilkinson.com.au **Open** Mon–Fri 9–5,
w'ends & public hols 9.30–5
Winemaker Jeff Byrne **Est.** 1999 **Cases** 15 000
One of the most historic properties in the Hunter Valley, set in a particularly beautiful location,
and with a very attractive cellar door. In 2004 it was acquired by Brian Agnew and family,
and is no longer part of the Pepper Tree/James Fairfax wine group. The wines are made
from 33 ha of estate-grown grapes, the lion's share to shiraz, the remainder (in descending
order) to chardonnay, verdelho, malbec, semillon, tempranillo, merlot, cabernet sauvignon,
gewurztraminer, muscat and zinfandel; the vines were planted between the 1970s and '90s.

ŸŸŸŸŸ **Semillon 2002** Typical top-quality Hunter Semillon, developing with grace as it
builds palate richness; winner of two trophies at the Hunter Valley Wine Show '07.
Cork. 10° alc. **Rating** 95 **To** 2012 $27.50
Museum Reserve Shiraz 2006 Bright deep crimson; lovely concentration, with
ripe red and dark fruits on the bouquet; a pure core of red fruits draws out the
even finish. Screwcap. 13.5° alc. **Rating** 95 **To** 2020 $40

ŸŸŸŸŸ **Oakdale Shiraz 2006** Lively bright-red fruits; a pure expression of shiraz with
spice; medium-bodied, long and fine. Screwcap. 14° alc. **Rating** 92 **To** 2018 $16
Hunter Valley Chardonnay 2007 Pale lemon; good varietal aromas of fresh
melons and hints of citrus; oak handling adds to the richness. Screwcap. 13.5° alc.
Rating 90 **To** 2016 $18.95
Hunter Valley Verdelho 2007 Attractive varietal bouquet with good
concentration and lively texture. Screwcap. 13.9° alc. **Rating** 90 **To** 2011 $18.95

ŸŸŸŸ **Pioneer Series Shiraz 2006** Deeper than the Oakdale, but not as complex;
good flavour and concentration, but finishes a little short. Screwcap. 14° alc.
Rating 89 **To** 2015 $20
Pioneer Series Cabernet Malbec 2006 A lifted style, with focused red fruits
on the bouquet; a little one-dimensional on the palate, but the flavour is sound
and the length satisfactory. Screwcap. 12.5° alc. **Rating** 88 **To** 2012 $20
Hunter Valley Rose 2007 Clean and bright with good fruit and well-handled
level of sweetness. Screwcap. 12.5° alc. **Rating** 87 **To** 2009 $18.95

🍇 Aussie Vineyards ★★★

32 Hartley Road, North Tamborine, Qld 4272 **Region** Granite Belt
T (07) 5545 2000 **F** (07) 5545 2038 **www**.aussievineyards.com.au **Open** 7 days 10–4
Winemaker Jon Heslop **Est.** 2005 **Cases** 110 000
This is the venture of entrepreneur Craig Gore, who has managed to ship more than 100 000
cases to the US in the 2007 calendar year, and is now turning his attention to the local market.
Here the aim is (to use the words of Business Development Manager Zach Wilson) 'to
become Qld's most recognised wine brand … by bringing consumer-driven products to the
domestic market and backing it with heavy promotion and marketing programs'. Specifically,
this is achieved through NASCAR and Champ Car marketing programs. Some of this has a
ring of deja vu about it, but time will tell. In Australia there are two ranges, a regional range
extending from the Granite Belt to the Limestone Coast, Coonawarra and Barossa, and a
three-varietal estate range grown on the estate vineyards at Ballandean, with merlot, cabernet
sauvignon and shiraz the chosen varietals. Winemaker Jon Heslop has a broad and impressive
winemaking background.

ŸŸŸŸ **Au Limestone Coast Chardonnay 2006** Light-bodied, but has the regional
marker of a touch of grapefruit; long, tight, persistent palate, with an airbrush of
oak. Screwcap. 13.8° alc. **Rating** 88 **To** 2012 $16.50
Au Granite Belt Merlot 2005 Undoubted varietal character; ripe fruit
salad with tropical and dried fruit components; slightly phenolic finish. Clever
packaging. Screwcap. 13.8° alc. **Rating** 88 **To** 2009 $22

Au Granite Belt Shiraz 2005 Light-bodied; spicy/savoury notes run through the bouquet and palate, with plum and black cherry fruit providing the framework and balance. Screwcap. 13.8° alc. **Rating** 87 **To** 2013 $22

Austin's Wines

870 Steiglitz Road, Sutherlands Creek, Vic 3331 **Region** Geelong
T (03) 5281 1799 **F** (03) 5281 1673 **www**.austinswines.com.au **Open** By appt
Winemaker Scott Ireland, Richard Austin **Est.** 1982 **Cases** 20 000
Pamela and Richard Austin have quietly built their business from a tiny base, and it has flourished. The vineyard has been progressively extended to 60 ha, and production has soared from 700 cases in 1998. Scott Ireland is now full-time resident winemaker in the capacious onsite winery, and the quality of the wines is admirable. Exports to the UK, the US and other major markets.

Geelong Pinot Noir 2006 Bright, clear colour; fresh and lively red cherry and plum; a silky palate with good length and intensity; will develop. Screwcap. 14° alc. **Rating** 94 **To** 2013 $29.50

Reserve Pinot Noir 2003 Has held hue well; clear-cut cherry and plum fruit, but the finish is still somewhat short. (First tasted Oct '04.) **Rating** 91 **To** 2012 $45

Six Foot Six Geelong Shiraz 2005 Very ripe black fruits and sweet oak combine for an early developing style. Screwcap. 15° alc. **Rating** 88 **To** 2011 $17.90
Geelong Chardonnay 2006 Developed colour; somewhat broad yellow peach and melon fruit, partially offset by acidity on the finish. Screwcap. 14.5° alc. **Rating** 87 **To** 2010
Six Foot Six Geelong Pinot Noir 2006 Fresh but light; small red fruits, then a savoury finish. Screwcap. 14° alc. **Rating** 87 **To** 2010 $17.90

Australian Domaine Wines

PO Box 13, Walkerville, SA 5081 **Region** Various SA
T (08) 8340 3807 **F** (08) 8346 3766 **www**.ausdomwines.com.au **Open** By appt
Winemaker Pikes (Neil Pike), Andrew Braithwaite **Est.** 1998 **Cases** 5000
Australian Domaine Wines is the reincarnation of Barletta Bros, who started their own brand business for leading Adelaide retailer Walkerville Cellars, which they then owned. The wines are made at Pikes using tanks and barrels owned by the Barlettas. Grapes are sourced from the Clare Valley, McLaren Vale and the Barossa Valley. No samples received; the rating is that of last year. Exports to the UK, the US and other major markets.

Australian Old Vine Wine

Farm 271, Rossetto Road, Beelbangera, NSW 2680 **Region** Riverina
T (02) 6963 5239 **F** (02) 6963 5239 **www**.australianoldvine.com.au **Open** 7 days 10–4
Winemaker Piromit Wines (Dom Piromalli) **Est.** 2002 **Cases** 2000
Elio and Marie Alban have registered the name Australian Old Vine Wine Pty Ltd for their business, designed to draw attention to their 7 ha of 50-year-old shiraz and 3 ha of 40-year-old cabernet sauvignon. Wines coming from the younger chardonnay, semillon and chambourcin plantings are released under the Australian Sovereign label. Ultimately, the plan is to buy grapes from old vines in the Barossa Valley and McLaren Vale for an Old Vine blend. Exports to Canada, Russia and Poland.

Alban Estate Limited Release Chambourcin 2005 Brilliant hue; typical fleshy, juicy fruits, a dash of mint and chocolate, and no structure whatsoever, even at 15.5°. So be it. Screwcap. 15.5° alc. **Rating** 87 **To** 2009 $15
Alban Estate Semillon Botrytis 2005 Retains some freshness; typical cumquat, peach and vanilla flavours; good acidity. Screwcap. 11° alc. **Rating** 87 **To** 2011 $20

Avenue Wines

124 Seventh Avenue, Joslin, SA 5070 (postal) **Region** South Australia
T (08) 8228 4188 **F** (08) 8228 4199 **www**.avenuewines.com.au **Open** Not
Winemaker George Ochota **Est.** 2004 **Cases** 2000
The Ochota family established a vineyard in the Clare Valley in the 1960s, which eventually
led to George Ochota becoming an amateur winemaker in the mid-'90s; after winning
numerous medals he decided it was time to take the plunge into commercial winemaking,
buying grapes from the Clare Valley (including the former family vineyard), Langhorne Creek,
McLaren Vale and Barossa.

ΨΨΨΨΨ **Barossa Valley Shiraz 2004** Much more elegant than the '05; silky, spicy
texture and flavour; black fruits, fine tannins and integrated oak, with a long finish.
Screwcap. 14.5° alc. **Rating** 94 **To** 2024 $18

ΨΨΨΨΨ **Clare Valley Riesling 2006** Developed green-yellow; has considerable lime
fruit flavours, the finish lifted and extended by grainy/lemony acidity. Watervale.
Screwcap. 11° alc. **Rating** 92 **To** 2013 $15

McLaren Vale Shiraz 2004 While the bouquet is not convincing, the palate is
far more settled, with fine black fruits and dark chocolate; good finish. Screwcap.
14.5° alc. **Rating** 91 **To** 2024 $18

Barossa Valley Shiraz 2005 Medium-bodied; blackberry and plum fruit, the
oak not oppressive; alcohol heat comes through on the finish and aftertaste; 2 years
in French and American oak, the alcohol as high as the bottle is heavy. Screwcap.
16° alc. **Rating** 90 **To** 2025 $18

Clare Valley Shiraz 2004 Deep colour; potent blackberry, prune, plum and
licorice flavours; overall, more in the style of the '05, particularly with the oak
impact. Screwcap. 15° alc. **Rating** 90 **To** 2020 $20

ΨΨΨΨ **Clare Valley Shiraz 2005** Thicker than the Barossa Shiraz, and medium- to full-
bodied; here the alcohol is obvious from the word go, with mid-palate sweetness,
then a drop-kick finish. Screwcap. 15° alc. **Rating** 89 **To** 2025 $18

Langhorne Creek Shiraz 2005 Dusty Christmas cake characters to an intense
and powerful palate, the high alcohol evident throughout. Screwcap. 15.5° alc.
Rating 89 **To** 2015 $18

Clare Valley Riesling 2007 Generous, full-flavoured tropical citrus mix; early
developing style, typical of the vintage. Polish Hill River. Screwcap. 11.5° alc.
Rating 88 **To** 2012 $15

Langhorne Creek Shiraz 2004 Challenging aspects to the bouquet, possibly
slightly reduced; the palate line wanders until a quite direct and powerful finish.
Screwcap. 15° alc. **Rating** 88 **To** 2014 $18

Clare Valley Cabernet Merlot 2004 Ultra-ripe blackcurrant fruit, and ripe
tannins to match; typical Avenue style. Screwcap. 15° alc. **Rating** 88 **To** 2014 $18

Clare Valley Rose 2007 Brisk and bright; small red fruits, then a bracing, dry
finish. Grenache/Merlot/Shiraz. Screwcap. 11.5° alc. **Rating** 87 **To** 2009 $15

McLaren Vale Shiraz 2005 The sweetest of the four wines, that sweetness
driven by alcohol rather than residual sugar, and resulting in some sweet and sour
notes. Screwcap. 15° alc. **Rating** 87 **To** 2015 $18

B'darra Estate

1415 Stumpy Gully Road, Moorooduc, Vic 3933 **Region** Mornington Peninsula
T (03) 5978 8447 **F** (03) 5978 8977 **www**.bdarraestate.com.au **Open** W'ends 11–5
Winemaker Gavin Perry **Est.** 1998 **Cases** 2000
Gavin and Linda Perry fell in love with Bedarra Island (off the north Qld coast) when they
stayed there, hence the name of their property, which they acquired in 1998. They planted
5 ha of vines in 1999, and are progressively developing the 21-ha holding. In 2007 some
of the vines were grafted over to pinot gris, with the first vintage expected in '09. Exports
to China.

ΨΨΨΨ Sauvignon Blanc 2007 A quiet bouquet, but has lots of tension and thrust on the crisp and long palate; that said, does not have much varietal character. Screwcap. 13.5° alc. **Rating** 88 **To** 2009 $16
Chardonnay 2005 Bright yellow-green; rich peachy wine, ripe and ready to roll. Screwcap. **Rating** 87 **To** 2010 $16
Pinot Noir 2005 Deep colour; ripe spicy plummy fruit, but the choice and amount of oak is oppressive; a pity. Diam. **Rating** 87 **To** 2011 $18

B3 Wines

PO Box 648, Kent Town, SA 5071 **Region** Barossa Valley
T (08) 8363 2211 **F** (08) 8363 2231 **www**.b3wines.com.au **Open** Not
Winemaker Peter Basedow, Michael Basedow, Richard Basedow, Craig Stansborough
Est. 2001 **Cases** NA
Peter, Michael and Richard Basedow are the three Brothers Basedow (as they call themselves), fifth-generation Barossans, with distinguished forefathers. Grandfather Oscar Basedow established the Basedow winery (no longer in family ownership) in 1896, while Martin Basedow established the Roseworthy Agricultural College. Their father, John Oscar Basedow, died in the 1970s, having won the 1970 Jimmy Watson Trophy for his '69 Cabernet Sauvignon, a high point for the family. This is a virtual winery enterprise, grapes being purchased mainly from the Barossa Valley, Coonawarra, Adelaide Hills and Eden Valley. Exports to the US, Canada and Asia.

ΨΨΨΨΨ John Oscar Barossa Shiraz 2005 Essency blackberry fruit aromas, which follow through on the palate; good concentration; the balance of fruit and tannin provides for a long and supple finish. Cork. 14.5° alc. **Rating** 93 **To** 2018 $40
Eden Valley Riesling 2007 Clean, fine and focused fruit, with a strong core of minerals running right through to the vibrant citrus finish. Screwcap. 12.5° alc. **Rating** 91 **To** 2015 $18
Barossa Semillon 2006 Bright straw colour; good fruit, with generous levels of ripeness and flavour; looks good as a young wine. Screwcap. 12.5° alc. **Rating** 90 **To** 2012 $12.90
Barossa Grenache Shiraz Mourvedre 2005 The typical sweet fruit opening of this blend, but builds authority on the finish, with more savoury notes from the shiraz and mourvedre. Screwcap. 14.5° alc. **Rating** 90 **To** 2014 $18

ΨΨΨΨ Adelaide Hills Sauvignon Blanc 2007 Clean and pristine fruit aromas, with nuances of tropical fruits; good flavour on the finish. Screwcap. 13° alc. **Rating** 89 **To** 2011 $18
Barossa Shiraz 2005 A generous style with ample sweet fruit and soft tannins; will have special appeal to some. Cork. 15° alc. **Rating** 89 **To** 2012 $18
Pauline Barossa Cabernet Shiraz 2005 Chocolate-tinged aromas together with ample levels of sweet fruit, and a fine, supple texture across the palate. Cork. 15° alc. **Rating** 89 **To** 2014 $25
Barossa Chardonnay 2007 Ripe stone fruit and nectarine on the bouquet, with just a little hint of nuttiness on the finish; early drinking. Screwcap. 13.5° alc. **Rating** 87 **To** 2010 $12.90
Barossa Cabernet Merlot 2005 Pleasant, if slightly obvious, sweet fruit flavours; minimal tannins and oak contribution. Cork. 14.5° alc. **Rating** 87 **To** 2010 $12.90
Barossa Cabernet Sauvignon 2005 Well-articulated cabernet fruit, again with a hint of sweetness for broad market appeal. Cork. 14.5° alc. **Rating** 87 **To** 2010 $18

Bacchus Hill

100 O'Connell Road, Bacchus Marsh, Vic 3340 **Region** Sunbury
T (03) 5367 8176 **F** (03) 5367 8176 **www**.bacchushill.com.au **Open** W'ends 10–5, Mon–Fri by appt
Winemaker Bruno Tassone **Est.** 2000 **Cases** 3200

Lawyer Bruno Tassone migrated from Italy when he was eight, and watched his father carry on the Italian tradition of making wine for home consumption. Tassone followed the same path before purchasing a 35-ha property with wife Jennifer. Here they have planted 18 ha of riesling, semillon, sauvignon blanc, chardonnay, pinot noir, merlot, shiraz, cabernet sauvignon, chenin blanc and nebbiolo. A move to screwcaps would be of great advantage for the older wines. Exports to Canada.

Back Pocket ★★★★

90 Savina Lane, Severnlea, Qld 4352 (postal) **Region** Granite Belt
T 0418 196 035 **F** (07) 4683 5184 **www**.backpocket.com.au **Open** Not
Winemaker Peter Scudamore-Smith (Contract) **Est.** 1997 **Cases** 600
Mal Baisden and Lel Doon purchased the 20-ha Back Pocket property in 1997; it had long been used for fruit growing, with a small patch of shiraz planted in the early '80s. It was expanded to the present total of 1.2 ha with additional plantings of tempranillo and graciano in '02 and '06. The cleverly named Old Savina Shiraz recognises the efforts of the Savina family who planted the shiraz; Arabia, a budget-priced shiraz; Castanets, 100% tempranillo; and Pickpocket, a rose produced from the juice run-off to concentrate the shiraz.

ΨΨΨΨΩ **Old Savina Shiraz 2005** Well made; medium-bodied, with black cherry fruit supported by integrated French oak; a fractionally broken line. Screwcap. 12.5° alc. **Rating** 90 **To** 2015 $26
Castanets 2007 Maraschino cherry aromas leap from the glass, replicated on the palate along with black cherry; despite the modest alcohol, is fully ripe; lovely wine for Spanish or Italian food. Screwcap. 12.5° alc. **Rating** 90 **To** 2009 $19

ΨΨΨΨ **Pickpocket 2007** Light but bright and fresh small red fruit flavours; nice dry finish. Screwcap. 13° alc. **Rating** 87 **To** 2009 $19
Arabia 2005 Light-bodied, with savoury/spicy overtones to red cherry fruits, and a flick of French oak. Very sophisticated packaging. Screwcap. 13° alc. **Rating** 87 **To** 2011 $16
Old Savina Shiraz 2003 Light- to medium-bodied; soft red and black cherry/plum fruit; minimal tannin and oak impact. Screwcap. 12.5° alc. **Rating** 87 **To** 2009

BackVintage Wines ★★★

2/177 Sailors Bay Road, Northbridge, NSW 2063 (postal) **Region** Warehouse
T (02) 9967 9880 **F** (02) 9967 9882 **www**.backvintage.com.au **Open** Not
Winemaker Rob Moody (Contract) **Est.** 2003 **Cases** 10 000
BackVintage Wines is a virtual winery with a difference; not only does it not own vineyards, nor a winery, it sells only through its website, or by fax or phone. While Robin Moody is shown as winemaker, his role is limited to sourcing wines (with the assistance of Nick Bulleid in the selection process, blending and bottling where the wine has not already been packaged as a cleanskin). As the tasting notes indicate, the experience of Robin Moody (former long-term Southcorp winemaker) and Nick Bulleid shows, and they have done their job well.

ΨΨΨΨ **Eden Valley Riesling 2006** A minerally wine, with washed pebbles and savoury lime juice flavours on the finish; ready to enjoy now. Screwcap. 12.6° alc. **Rating** 89 **To** 2011 $10.95
McLaren Vale Shiraz 2005 Has red fruits and a touches of spice; fleshy and forward; ready now. Screwcap. 14° alc. **Rating** 87 **To** 2011 $10.95
Barossa Shiraz 2005 Quite earthy, with tar and dark fruits, and chewy, somewhat drying, tannins on the finish. Screwcap. 14.5° alc. **Rating** 87 **To** 2013 $12.95

Baddaginnie Run ★★★★

PO Box 579, North Melbourne, Vic 3051 **Region** Strathbogie Ranges
T (03) 9348 9310 **F** (03) 9348 9370 **www**.baddaginnierun.net.au **Open** Not
Winemaker Toby Barlow **Est.** 1996 **Cases** 1500

Winsome McCaughey and Professor Snow Barlow (Professor of Horticulture and Viticulture at the University of Melbourne) spend part of their week in the Strathbogie Ranges, and part in Melbourne. The business name, Seven Sisters Vineyard, reflects the seven generations of the McCaughey family associated with the land since 1870; Baddaginnie is the nearby township. The 27-ha vineyard is one element in a restored valley landscape, 100000 indigenous trees having been replanted. The wines are made by son Toby Barlow, former Mitchelton winemaker. Exports to Canada.

ŶŶŶŶŶ **Strathbogie Ranges Shiraz 2005** Good red-purple; an attractive medium-bodied palate with blackberry and plum flavours; good line and length. **Rating** 92 To 2014 $21
Strathbogie Ranges Shiraz 2006 Pure expression of shiraz from a moderately cool environment; good colour; medium-bodied, with a long, black fruit-driven finish. Screwcap. 14.5° alc. **Rating** 90 To 2016 $24

ŶŶŶŶ **Strathbogie Ranges Verdelho 2007** Has plenty of varietal fruit in a mainline fruit salad spectrum, toughening up very slightly on the finish. Screwcap. 14.2° alc. **Rating** 87 To 2009 $18
Strathbogie Ranges Viognier 2007 Reflects the dilemma with this variety of how to obtain varietal distinction without oily phenolics, in the end having neither; does have length, however. Screwcap. 14° alc. **Rating** 87 To 2009 $20

Badger's Brook

874 Maroondah Highway, Coldstream, Vic 3770 **Region** Yarra Valley
T (03) 5962 4130 **F** (03) 5962 4130 **www**.badgersbrook.com.au **Open** Wed–Sun 11–5
Winemaker Contract **Est.** 1993 **Cases** 2000
Situated next door to the well-known Rochford, it has 10 ha of vineyard, planted mainly to chardonnay, sauvignon blanc, pinot noir, shiraz and cabernet sauvignon, with a few rows each of viognier, roussanne, marsanne and tempranillo. All of the wines are Yarra Valley–sourced, including the second Storm Ridge label. Now houses the smart brasserie restaurant Bella Vedere Cucina with well-known chef Gary Cooper in charge. Exports to Asia.

ŶŶŶŶŶ **Yarra Valley Shiraz Viognier 2004** Bright colour; fresh and lively, light- to medium-bodied, with good flavours in the red cherry/raspberry spectrum, and that particular apricot acidity on the finish. Screwcap. 14° alc. **Rating** 90 To 2014 $22

Bago Vineyards ★★★

Milligans Road, off Bago Road, Wauchope, NSW 2446 **Region** Hastings River
T (02) 6585 7099 **F** (02) 6585 7099 **www**.bagovineyards.com.au **Open** 7 days 11–5
Winemaker Jim Mobbs, John Cassegrain (Consultant) **Est.** 1985 **Cases** NA
Jim and Kay Mobbs began planting the Broken Bago Vineyards in 1985 with 1 ha of chardonnay; total plantings now 12.5 ha. Regional specialist John Cassegrain is consultant winemaker.

ŶŶŶŶ **Albarino 2007** Shows considerable promise; lemon sherbet fruit; crisp, minerally finish. Screwcap. **Rating** 89 To 2009 $20

Baileys of Glenrowan

Cnr Taminick Gap Road/Upper Taminick Road, Glenrowan, Vic 3675 **Region** Glenrowan
T (03) 5766 2392 **F** (03) 5766 2596 **www**.baileysofglenrowan.com.au **Open** 7 days 10–5
Winemaker Paul Dahlenburg **Est.** 1870 **Cases** 15 000
Just when it seemed that Baileys would remain one of the forgotten outposts of the Foster's group, the reverse has occurred. Since 1998 Paul Dahlenburg has been in charge of Baileys, and has overseen an expansion in the vineyard to 143 ha and the construction of a 2000-tonne winery. The cellar door has a heritage museum, winery-viewing deck, contemporary art gallery and landscaped grounds, preserving much of the heritage value. Baileys has also picked up the pace with its Muscat and Tokay, reintroducing the Winemaker's Selection at the top of the tree, while continuing the larger-volume Founder series. No red or fortified wine will be released from the 2007 vintage due to frost and bushfires. Exports to the UK and NZ.

ΨΨΨΨΨ **Winemaker's Selection Old Tokay NV** Obvious age showing from its mahogany/olive-green colour; classic tea-leaf, butterscotch and malt flavours; great harmony with the spirit; a long finish, at once sweet yet dry and spicy. Cork. 16.5° alc. **Rating** 95 **To** 2009 $55

Winemaker's Selection Old Muscat NV Gloriously rich, luscious and powerful; retains the essence of raisin muscat, but complexed by rancio and oriental spices; again, perfect harmony with the fortifying spirit. Cork. 17° alc. **Rating** 95 **To** 2009 $55

Founder Liqueur Muscat NV Intense, lively, grapey varietal character of raisins and plum pudding; acidity gives more lift and intensifies the flavour, yet does not bite; the volatile component of the acidity appears low. Cork. 17° alc. **Rating** 94 **To** 2009 $22

ΨΨΨΨΨ **1920's Block Shiraz 2006** Has an abundance of dark fruits and oak, hints of mocha and fresh acidity on the quite tannic finish; very long indeed, and needs time. Screwcap. 15° alc. **Rating** 93 **To** 2025 $30

Founder Liqueur Tokay NV Moderate age; classic tea-leaf, butterscotch and malt aromas and flavours; a lingering sweetness through the palate, then a final farewell is (commendably) almost dry. Cork. 17° alc. **Rating** 93 **To** 2009 $22

1904 Block Shiraz 2005 Strongly savoury, with spice, earth and leather nuances to the blackberry fruit, augmented by French oak; fine, lingering tannins to close. Screwcap. 14.5° alc. **Rating** 92 **To** 2020 $45

Founder Tawny Port NV Tawny as it is made in North East Victoria, more luscious and raisined than classic South Australian Tawnys. Clean, modern packaging a feature for the fortified range. **Rating** 92 **To** 2009 $23.95

Shiraz 2006 Ample dark fruits, with hints of dried leather and even a little spice; firm on the palate, but with thrust and vibrancy. Screwcap. 14° alc. **Rating** 91 **To** 2018 $20

Balgownie Estate   ★★★★☆

Hermitage Road, Maiden Gully, Vic 3551 **Region** Bendigo
T (03) 5449 6222 **F** (03) 5449 6506 www.balgownieestate.com.au **Open** 7 days 11–5
Winemaker Tobias Ansted **Est.** 1969 **Cases** 10 000
Balgownie Estate continues to grow in the wake of its acquisition by the Forrester family. A $3 million upgrade of the winery coincided with a doubling of the size of the vineyard to 35 ha, and in 2004 Balgownie Estate opened a cellar door in the Yarra Valley (see separate entry). Exports to the UK, the US and other major markets.

ΨΨΨΨΨ **Bendigo Cabernet Sauvignon 2005** Less about the variety and more about the region, showing a strong savoury personality, supported by plenty of dark fruits; dense, but with a lightness on the finish that belies the concentration. Screwcap. 14° alc. **Rating** 93 **To** 2020 $31

Balgownie Estate (Yarra Valley)   ★★★★

Cnr Melba Highway/Gulf Road, Yarra Glen, Vic 3775 **Region** Yarra Valley
T (03) 9730 0700 **F** (03) 9730 2647 www.balgownieestate.com.au **Open** 7 days 10–5
Winemaker Tobias Ansted **Est.** 2004 **Cases** 2500
Balgownie Estate opened a very attractive rammed-earth cellar door in 2004, offering the full range of Balgownie wines (the Chardonnay and Pinot Noir are sourced from the Yarra Valley). The cellar door caters for large-group wine events.

ΨΨΨΨΨ **Chardonnay 2006** A heady blend of roasted nuts and classy French oak on the bouquet, with a fine, focused and intense palate that is long, fresh and harmonious. Screwcap. 13.5° alc. **Rating** 94 **To** 2012 $19.50

ΨΨΨΨ **Pinot Noir 2006** Spice, forest floor, stem and dark fruits in a light-bodied frame; not forced, and well-balanced. Screwcap. 13.5° alc. **Rating** 89 **To** 2012 $19.50

 ## Ballanclea

Ballanclea Road, Ceres, Vic 3221 (postal) **Region** Geelong
T (03) 5272 1438 **Open** Not
Winemaker Waurn Ponds Estate (Duncan MacGillivray) **Est.** 1990 **Cases** 200
Sally Lucock runs a beautiful and historic sheep and crop farm in the Barrabool Hills. When
she acquired the property she found a small vineyard planted in the mid-1980s with no less
than 14 varieties, providing the same sort of challenge that a far larger vineyard might pose.
Paul van Prooyen is the vineyard consultant/manager and the wines are now made at the
Deakin University, Waurn Ponds Estate.

ΥΥΥΥ **Chardonnay Semillon Riesling Sauvignon Blanc 2006** Geelong's answer to
Margaret River's classic dry white; has length. Cork. **Rating** 87 **To** 2009 $20

Ballandean Estate

Sundown Road, Ballandean, Qld 4382 **Region** Granite Belt
T (07) 4684 1226 **F** (07) 4684 1288 **www.**ballandeanestate.com **Open** 7 days 9–5
Winemaker Dylan Rhymer, Angelo Puglisi **Est.** 1970 **Cases** 12 000
The senior winery of the Granite Belt, owned by the ever-cheerful and charming Angelo
Puglisi, but who is an appalling correspondent. The white wines are of diverse but interesting
styles, the red wines smooth and usually well made. The estate speciality, Sylvaner Late Harvest,
is a particularly interesting wine of great character and flavour if given 10 years' bottle age, but
is only produced sporadically.

Ballast Stone Estate Wines

Myrtle Grove Road, Currency Creek, SA 5214 **Region** Currency Creek
T (08) 8555 4215 **F** (08) 8555 4216 **Open** 7 days 10.30–5
Winemaker John Loxton, Marty O'Flaherty **Est.** 2001 **Cases** 80 000
The Shaw family have been vintners for over 35 years, commencing plantings in McLaren Vale
in the early 1970s. Extensive vineyard holdings are now held in McLaren Vale and Currency
Creek, with a modern winery in Currency Creek. The family produces approximately 80 000
cases under the Ballast Stone Estate label as well as supplying others. Exports to the UK, the
US and other major markets.

ΥΥΥΥΥ **Emetior McLaren Vale Currency Creek Shiraz 2002** Very good colour and
hue; very concentrated, with luscious black fruits wrapped in dark chocolate and a
frame of oak; still exceptionally youthful and will live beyond the lifetime of many
of us. Screwcap. 14.5° alc. **Rating** 93 **To** 2032 $40

ΥΥΥΥ **McLaren Vale Currency Creek Shiraz 2005** An attractive array of savoury,
spicy dark berry fruits; light- to medium-bodied; thins fractionally on the finish.
Screwcap. 14° alc. **Rating** 89 **To** 2013 $20
Currency Creek Chardonnay 2007 Gets over the line largely on price, but
also thanks to restrained winemaking giving good balance. Screwcap. 13.5° alc.
Rating 87 **To** 2009 $15
Currency Creek McLaren Vale Cabernet Sauvignon 2005 Aromas of mint,
herb and dark chocolate flow through into a light- to medium-bodied palate, with
a distinctly savoury finish. Screwcap. 14° alc. **Rating** 87 **To** 2012 $20

Balnaves of Coonawarra

Main Road, Coonawarra, SA 5263 **Region** Coonawarra
T (08) 8737 2946 **F** (08) 8737 2945 **www.**balnaves.com.au **Open** Mon–Fri 9–5,
w'ends 12–5
Winemaker Pete Bissell **Est.** 1975 **Cases** 10 000
Grapegrower, viticultural consultant and vigneron Doug Balnaves has 52 ha of high-quality
estate vineyards. The wines are invariably excellent, often outstanding, notable for their supple

mouthfeel, varietal integrity, balance and length; the tannins are always fine and ripe, the oak subtle and perfectly integrated. Coonawarra at its best. Exports to the UK, the US and other major markets.

ＹＹＹＹＹ **The Tally Reserve Cabernet Sauvignon 2006** Beautifully crafted and delineated cassis fruit, framed by gently toasty oak and some floral notes; the palate is rich, deep, fine and very long; the brightness of fruit at the core is the essence of this wine. ProCork. **Rating** 96 **To** 2030 $90
Shiraz 2006 A wine of beauty and balance; black fruit framed by well-handled toasty oak, very fine tannins and a long, supple and fine finish. Screwcap. 15° alc. **Rating** 95 **To** 2020 $28
Cabernet Sauvignon 2006 Has great poise; essency cassis, with hints of earth and a mineral complexity at its core; full-bodied, with fine-grained tannins; will reward patient cellaring. ProCork. **Rating** 94 **To** 2025 $35

ＹＹＹＹＹ **The Blend 2006** Vibrant colour; has great concentration, and ample levels of fruit and complexity; bright, fine and focused, and very good value for money. Screwcap. 14.5° alc. **Rating** 93 **To** 2015 $19
Cabernet Merlot 2006 Quite minty, and very tannic; time is needed for the tannins to soften and become more approachable, but the concentration and fruit quality is definitely there. ProCork. **Rating** 92 **To** 2018 $24

ＹＹＹＹ **Chardonnay 2006** Plenty of nectarine and peach flavour, but lacking the usual Balnaves finesse. Screwcap. **Rating** 87 **To** 2012 $28

Balthazar of the Barossa ★★★★☆

PO Box 675, Nuriootpa, SA 5355 **Region** Barossa Valley
T (08) 8562 2949 **F** (08) 8562 2949 **www.**balthazarbarossa.com **Open** At the Small Winemakers Centre, Chateau Tanunda
Winemaker Anita Bowen **Est.** 1999 **Cases** 870
Anita Bowen announced her occupation as 'a 40-something sex therapist with a 17-year involvement in the wine industry'; she is also the wife of a high-ranked executive with Foster's. Anita undertook her first vintage at Mudgee, then McLaren Vale, and ultimately the Barossa; she worked at St Hallet while studying at Roseworthy College. A versatile lady, indeed. As to her wine, she says, 'Anyway, prepare a feast, pour yourself a glass (no chalices, please) of Balthazar and share it with your concubines. Who knows? It may help to lubricate thoughts, firm up ideas and get the creative juices flowing!' Exports to the US, Canada and Singapore.

ＹＹＹＹＹ **Shiraz 2005** Full of life and movement; juicy plum, blackberry and licorice fruit; good oak and tannins; long finish. ProCork. 14.5° alc. **Rating** 95 **To** 2020 $45

ＹＹＹＹＹ **Ishtar Adelaide Hills Sauvignon Blanc 2007** Aromatic passionfruit and gooseberry aromas, joined by sweet lime juice on the palate; a seductive wine with broad appeal. Screwcap. 12.5° alc. **Rating** 90 **To** 2009 $19
Shiraz 2004 Good texture and structure; blackberry, licorice and plum; fine-grained tannins and controlled oak. ProCork. 14.5° alc. **Rating** 90 **To** 2020 $45

ＹＹＹＹ **Ishtar Viognier 2007** Has plenty of impact, with tangy fruit and a zesty, lingering finish; a minor problem with a lack of clear varietal character, but could develop nicely. Screwcap. 14.5° alc. **Rating** 89 **To** 2011 $19
Ishtar Grenache Shiraz Mourvedre 2005 Light- to medium-bodied; gently sweet red berry fruits, with some spicy elements; minimal tannin structure. Screwcap. 15° alc. **Rating** 88 **To** 2012 $19

Banderra Estate NR

Sandhills Road, Forbes, NSW 2871 **Region** Central Ranges Zone
T (02) 6852 1437 **F** (02) 6852 1437 **Open** Mon–Sat 9–5, Sun 12–5
Winemaker John Saleh, Andrew McEwin, Jill Lindsay (Contract) **Est.** 1920 **Cases** 300

Formerly Sand Hills Vineyard, Banderra Estate dates back to the 1920s, and the ownership of Jacques Jenet. The Salet family became owners a number of years ago, and have re-established estate plantings of chardonnay, colombard, semillon, shiraz, merlot and cabernet sauvignon, with a little pinot noir and mataro, a total of 3.6 ha. As well as the historic cellar door, the wines will also be available at an outlet at the McFeeters Car Museum in Forbes.

Banks Road

600 Banks Road, Marcus Hill, Vic 3222 **Region** Geelong
T (03) 9822 6587 **F** (03) 9822 5077 **www.**banksroadwine.com.au **Open** W'ends 10–4
Winemaker Darren Burke, William Derham **Est.** 2001 **Cases** 2000
Banks Road, owned and operated by William Derham, has two vineyards: the first, 2.5 ha, is on the Bellarine Peninsula at Marcus Hill, planted to pinot noir and chardonnay; the second is at Harcourt in the Bendigo region, planted to 3 ha of shiraz and cabernet sauvignon, the vines ranging from 8 to 12 years of age.

ΨΨΨΨΩ **CDR Geelong Pinot Gris 2007** Marked pear and apple aromas, then a palate with abundant flavour and length, devoid of phenolics. **Rating** 90 **To** 2010
Geelong Pinot Noir 2006 Aromatic plum and dark cherry aromas lead into a palate with abundant flavour; still building complexity; good potential. Screwcap. 14° alc. **Rating** 90 **To** 2012 $25

ΨΨΨΨ **Bendigo Merlot 2004** Somewhat unexpected; the varietal expression is as good as the colour; attractive sweet cassis fruit with touches of leaf, olive and mint, the tannins fine. Screwcap. 13.4° alc. **Rating** 89 **To** 2012
Geelong Pinot Gris 2006 Clean, fresh and crisp; no hint of reduction; has above-average flavour in a typical pear, apple and musk spectrum; good finish. Screwcap. 13.6° alc. **Rating** 88 **To** 2009 $25
Geelong Shiraz 2005 A light- to medium-bodied mix of red and black fruits, with a lively finish, but lacks tannin support. Screwcap. 14° alc. **Rating** 88 **To** 2011 $30
Bendigo Cabernet Merlot 2004 Some spicy earthy leathery overtones, but there is a solid foundation of blackcurrant fruit and appropriate tannins. Screwcap. 13.8° alc. **Rating** 88 **To** 2012
Bendigo Shiraz 2004 Relatively early picked and quite developed notwithstanding its screwcap; strong spice and leaf components but also flashes of red fruits; ready now. Screwcap. 13.7° alc. **Rating** 87 **To** 2010

🍃 Banksia Grove

215 Heathcote-Redesdale Road, Heathcote, Vic 3523 **Region** Heathcote
T (03) 9948 0311 **F** (03) 9948 0322 **www.**banksiagrovewine.com.au **Open** By appt
Winemaker Ian Leamon, John Ellis (Contract) **Est.** 2002 **Cases** 1500
When Kim and Bernadette Chambers purchased the Banksia Grove vineyard in early 2002, they inherited some of the oldest vines in Heathcote, planted in the late 1970s. The prior owners had sold the grapes each year, and made no wine. The Chambers have worked hard to restore the somewhat dilapidated vineyard they inherited, and have extended the plantings by 2 ha, so that there are now 5 ha of shiraz, and 0.6 ha each of cabernet sauvignon and chardonnay. They have deliberately delayed the release of the wines, with both '02 Shiraz and '03 Shiraz available in early '08 (along with other wines in the portfolio).

ΨΨΨΨΨ **Heathcote Shiraz 2003** Intense but elegant wine, which is maturing beautifully; fine tannins support the core of blackberry fruit, with cedary notes from the French oak; the texture is impeccable. High-quality cork. 14.5° alc. **Rating** 94 **To** 2015 $34

ΨΨΨΨΩ **Heathcote Cabernet Sauvignon 2005** The dense blackcurrant fruit comes from 30-year-old vines, the richness supported by round tannins and cedary French oak. Cork. 14.5° alc. **Rating** 92 **To** 2020 $32

ɣɣɣɣ   **Heathcote Chardonnay 2006** Supple and rich, but with a touch of fruit sweetness on the mid-palate, and is developing quickly. Cork. 13.5° alc. **Rating** 88 **To** 2011 $27

Bannockburn Vineyards   ★★★★★

Midland Highway, Bannockburn, Vic 3331 (postal) **Region** Geelong
T (03) 5281 1363 **F** (03) 5281 1349 www.bannockburnvineyards.com **Open** By appt
Winemaker Michael Glover **Est.** 1974 **Cases** 10 000
With the qualified exception of the Cabernet Merlot, which can be a little leafy and gamey, Bannockburn produces outstanding wines across the range, all with individuality, style, great complexity and depth of flavour. The low-yielding estate vineyards play their role. Winemaker Michael Glover is determined to enhance the reputation of Bannockburn. Exports to Canada, Dubai, Korea, China, Singapore and Hong Kong.

ɣɣɣɣɣ   **Geelong Sauvignon Blanc 2006** Brilliant green-yellow; a very complex wine, reflecting wild yeast, no added acid, one-third each stainless steel, old barriques and new puncheons all working to perfection. Has tremendous energy and texture; a special wine. Cork. 14° alc. **Rating** 95 **To** 2011 $23
Geelong Pinot Noir 2005 A fragrant, highly spiced bouquet; has intense flavours, again quite spicy on the very long palate; 25% whole bunch component works very well. A selection of half of the best barrels; from the 30-year-old Olive Hill Vineyard. Cork. 13.5° alc. **Rating** 94 **To** 2015 $55

ɣɣɣɣ   **Geelong Shiraz 2004** Undoubtedly complex, but the Joseph's Coat of aromas and flavours, coupled with the high alcohol, leave question marks over the wine. Cork. 15° alc. **Rating** 88 **To** 2013 $47

Banrock Station   ★★★

Holmes Road (off Sturt Highway), Kingston-on-Murray, SA 5331 **Region** Riverland
T (08) 8583 0299 **F** (08) 8583 0288 www.banrockstation.com **Open** 7 days 10–5
Winemaker Paul Kassebaum **Est.** 1994 **Cases** NFP
The eco-friendly $1 million visitor centre at Banrock Station is a major tourist destination. Owned by Constellation, the Banrock Station property covers over 1700 ha, with 240 ha of vineyard and the remainder being a major wildlife and wetland preservation area. Recycling of all waste water and use of solar energy build on the preservation image. Each bottle of Banrock Station wine sold generates funds for wildlife preservation, with $2 million already contributed. The wines have consistently offered excellent value. Exports to all major markets.

ɣɣɣɣ   **Chardonnay 2007** Unapologetically old-fashioned on 'ain't broke, don't fix' philosophy; has depth and a fair slab of phenolics. 'Help us help the earth' neck tag pulls purse strings. Twin top. 13° alc. **Rating** 87 **To** 2009 $9

Barambah   ★★★★

GPO Box 799, Brisbane, QLD 4001 **Region** South Burnett
T 1300 781 815 **F** 1300 138 949 www.barambah.com.au **Open** Not
Winemaker Peter Scudamore-Smith MW (Contract) **Est.** 1995 **Cases** 1000
Barambah has been purchased by Brisbane couple Jane and Steve Wilson. They live in a historic 19th-century West End home, but have owned a 1600-ha cattle property, Barambah Station, for the past six years. This made them near-neighbours of Barambah, and they had ample opportunity to watch the development of the 7-ha estate vineyard and the quality of its wines. When the opportunity came to purchase the winery and vineyard, they obtained consultancy advice from Peter Scudamore-Smith MW. His response was so positive they did not hesitate to buy the property.

ɣɣɣɣɣ   **First Grid Shiraz 2006** Unequivocally full-bodied, redolent with blackberry, prune, leather and licorice fruit, plus some American oak in the mix; will handsomely repay cellaring. Screwcap. 14° alc. **Rating** 90 **To** 2016 $29

ꕥꕥꕥꕥ **First Grid Chardonnay 2007** No shortage of ripe fruit flavour, plus some oak influence; despite whole bunch pressing, seems a little tough and phenolic. Screwcap. 13° alc. **Rating** 87 **To** 2010 $24
First Grid Cabernet Sauvignon 2006 Medium-bodied; a mix of clearly varietal berry fruit and savoury tannins; a bit disjointed, but could improve in bottle. Screwcap. 14° alc. **Rating** 87 **To** 2012 $32

Barfold Estate ★★★★
57 School Road, Barfold, Vic 3444 **Region** Heathcote
T (03) 5423 4225 **F** (03) 5423 4225 **Open** 7 days 10–5
Winemaker Craig Aitken **Est.** 1998 **Cases** 900
Craig and Sandra Aitken acquired their farm property at Barfold in the southwestern corner of the Heathcote wine region, a cooler portion of the region producing spicy characters in shiraz, and currently being mooted by local winemakers as a future Redesdale subregion that will encompass Barfod, Redesdale, Metcale and Mia Mia. So far they have planted 3.8 ha of shiraz and 0.4 ha of cabernet sauvignon; a small planting of viognier is planned.

ꕥꕥꕥꕥꕥ **Heathcote Shiraz 2006** Dense purple-crimson; lush blackberry, licorice, plum and a hint of spice; appropriate tannins, but curiously a little loose on the finish. Screwcap. 14.5° alc. **Rating** 91 **To** 2020 $25

ꕥꕥꕥꕥ **Heathcote Viognier 2007** Achieves enough peachy apricot-accented varietal fruit to satisfy, while avoiding tough phenolics on the finish. Screwcap. 13.5° alc. **Rating** 87 **To** 2010 $20

Barley Stacks ★★★
1 Lizard Park Drive, Kilkerran, SA 5573 **Region** The Peninsulas Zone
T (08) 8834 1258 **F** (08) 8834 1287 **www**.barleystackswines.com **Open** 7 days 10–4.30
Winemaker John Zilm **Est.** 1997 **Cases** 3000
Rod and Toni Gregory have 11 ha of organically managed vineyard near Maitland, on the western side of the Yorke Peninsula, planted to chardonnay, viognier, shiraz and cabernet sauvignon. All the wines are made onsite, which also has facilities to cater for concerts or festivals, and tours by arrangement. Exports to Canada.

ꕥꕥꕥꕥ **Ketrice The Peninsulas Cabernet Sauvignon 2006** Leafy cabernet, with essency cassis at the core; good acid and nice focus on the finish. Screwcap. 14.5° alc. **Rating** 88 **To** 2014

Barmah Park Wines NR
945 Moorooduc Road, Moorooduc, Vic 3933 **Region** Mornington Peninsula
T (03) 5978 8049 **F** (03) 5978 8088 **www**.barmahparkwines.com.au **Open** 7 days 10–5
Winemaker Ewan Campbell (Contract) **Est.** 2000 **Cases** 2000
Tony Williams planted 1 ha of pinot gris and 2 ha of pinot noir (using two clones, MV6 and G5V15), having the first vintage made in 2003. In '05 a substantial restaurant was opened, offering breakfast in the vines until 11.30 am, and lunch from noon to 5 pm.

Barnadown Run ★★★★
390 Cornella Road, Toolleen, Vic 3551 **Region** Heathcote
T (03) 5433 6376 **F** (03) 5433 6386 **www**.barnadownrun.com.au **Open** 7 days 10–5
Winemaker Andrew Millis **Est.** 1995 **Cases** 1400
Named after the original pastoral lease of which the vineyard forms part, established on the rich terra rossa soil for which Heathcote vineyards are famous. Owner Andrew Millis carries out both the viticulture and winemaking at the 5-ha vineyard, which is planted to cabernet sauvignon, merlot, shiraz and viognier. Exports to the UK, the US, Hong Kong and Singapore.

🍷🍷🍷🍷♀ **Heathcote Shiraz 2004** Pencilly oak frames vibrant fruits on the bouquet, the palate is rich and ripe with a hint of mint; supple and full flavoured; has length. Cork. 15° alc. **Rating** 91 **To** 2018 $27

🍷🍷🍷🍷 **Heathcote Merlot 2004** Great colour, and plenty of ripe red berry fruits, plus a little plum on the mid-palate; quite firm on the finish. Cork. 14° alc. **Rating** 89 **To** 2012 $27
Henry Bennett's Voluptuary 2004 Sweet fruited and ample, but lacks a little complexity; clean and juicy finish. Cork. 14.5° alc. **Rating** 87 **To** 2014 $38
Heathcote Cabernet Sauvignon 2004 Loads of sweet fruit again, as with the other wines; ripe with just a little shrivel, but fairly good fruit delineation. Cork. 14.5° alc. **Rating** 87 **To** 2016 $27

Barokes Wines   ★★★

100 Market Street, South Melbourne, Vic 3205 (postal) **Region** Warehouse
T (03) 9698 1349 **F** (03) 9690 8114 **www**.wineinacan.com **Open** Not
Winemaker Steve Barics **Est.** 2003 **Cases** 150 000
Barokes Wines packages its wines in aluminium cans. The filling process is patented, and the wine has been in commercial production since 2003. The wines show normal maturation and none of the cans used since start-up shows signs of corrosion. Wines are supplied in bulk by large wineries in southeastern Australia, with Peter Scudamore-Smith acting as blending consultant. The wines are perfectly adequate for the market they serve, with remarkably even quality. Exports to all major markets with increasing success, with production rising from 60 000 to 150 000 cases (24 cans per case).

Barossa Ridge Wine Estate

Light Pass Road, Tanunda, SA 5352 **Region** Barossa Valley
T (08) 8563 2811 **F** (08) 8563 2811 **Open** By appt
Winemaker Marco Litterini **Est.** 1987 **Cases** 1800
A grapegrower turned winemaker with a small list of interesting red varietals, shunning the more common Rhône varietals and looking to Bordeaux. Increasing retail distribution in Australia; exports to Switzerland, Germany, Malaysia and Thailand.

🍷🍷🍷🍷🍷 **Litterini Barossa Valley Shiraz Cabernet 2006** A rich, succulent, velvety palate, ranging through black cherry, red and blackcurrant, and perfectly balanced and integrated oak; soft tannins. Screwcap. 14.5° alc. **Rating** 94 **To** 2016 $29.95

Barossa Valley Estate

Seppeltsfield Road, Marananga, SA 5355 **Region** Barossa Valley
T (08) 8562 3599 **F** (08) 8562 4255 **www**.bve.com.au **Open** 7 days 10–4.30
Winemaker Stuart Bourne **Est.** 1985 **Cases** NFP
Barossa Valley Estate is owned by Constellation, marking the end of a period during which it was one of the last significant co-operative-owned wineries in Australia. Across the board, the wines are full flavoured and honest. E&E Black Pepper Shiraz is an upmarket label with a strong reputation and following; the Ebenezer range likewise. Exports to all major markets.

🍷🍷🍷🍷🍷 **Ebenezer Barossa Valley Shiraz 2004** Medium-bodied, but intense and long, with lovely definition to the black cherry and plum fruit, showing no hint of thickness or sweetness; fine tannins sustain the long finish. Cork. 14.5° alc. **Rating** 95 **To** 2015 $37.50

🍷🍷🍷🍷♀ **E Bass Shiraz 2005** Firm and fresh in a 'new' Barossa Valley style; medium-bodied, with controlled alcohol; a tangy mix of red and black fruits; good finish. Screwcap. 14.5° alc. **Rating** 90 **To** 2015 $22.50
E&E Sparkling Shiraz 2003 Similar philosophy in winemaking practices as used for Leasingham Classic Clare Sparkling Shiraz; quite oaky, and quite sweet; points a compromise. Cork. 14.5° alc. **Rating** 90 **To** 2009 $54.99

ΨΨΨΨ   E Minor Shiraz 2005 Developed colour; slightly savoury minty notes on a light-
to medium-bodied palate; soft tannins. Screwcap. 14° alc. **Rating** 87 **To** 2011
$16.50

Barratt   ★★★★☆
Uley Vineyard, Cornish Road, Summertown, SA 5141 **Region** Adelaide Hills
T (08) 8390 1788 **F** (08) 8390 1788 **www.**barrattwines.com.au **Open** Fri–Sun &
most public hols 11.30–5
Winemaker Lindsay Barratt **Est.** 1993 **Cases** 1800
Lindsay and Carolyn Barratt own two vineyards at Summertown: Uley Vineyard and
Bonython Vineyard (total 8.4 ha). Part of the production is sold to other makers, the Barratt
wines being made at the winery facility at the Adelaide Hills Business and Tourism Centre in
Lobethal. Limited quantities are exported to the UK, Canada and Asia.

ΨΨΨΨΨ   Piccadilly Valley Adelaide Hills Chardonnay 2006 Creamy stone fruits and
fine levels of toasty oak; quite peachy on the palate, with richness and finesse on
the finish. Screwcap. 14° alc. **Rating** 93 **To** 2012 $29
Piccadilly Sunrise Adelaide Hills Rose 2007 Very dry and very precise, with
wild strawberries, minerals and a hint of briar in the background; fresh and clean
too. Screwcap. 13.5° alc. **Rating** 90 **To** 2009 $21
The Reserve Piccadilly Valley Adelaide Hills Pinot Noir 2006 Slightly riper
and darker fruit aromas than The Bonython; good weight, and silky on the palate.
Screwcap. 14° alc. **Rating** 90 **To** 2009 $45

ΨΨΨΨ   The Bonython Piccadilly Valley Adelaide Hills Pinot Noir 2006 Quite
lifted and showing savoury notes on the bouquet; light-bodied, the palate has
more varietal character and charm. Screwcap. 14° alc. **Rating** 88 **To** 2009 $24

Barretts Wines   ★★★★☆
Portland-Nelson Highway, Portland, Vic 3305 **Region** Henty
T (03) 5526 5251 **Open** 7 days 11–5
Winemaker Rod Barrett **Est.** 1983 **Cases** 1000
Has a low profile, selling its wines locally, but deserves a far wider audience. The initial releases
were made at Best's, but since 1992 all wines have been made (with increasing skill) on the
property by Rod Barrett, emulating John Thomson at Crawford River Wines. The 5.5-ha
vineyard is planted to riesling, pinot noir and cabernet sauvignon. No samples received; the
rating is that of last year.

Barrgowan Vineyard   ★★★★
30 Pax Parade, Curlewis, Vic 3222 **Region** Geelong
T (03) 5250 3861 **F** (03) 5250 3840 **Open** By appt
Winemaker Dick Simonsen **Est.** 1998 **Cases** 150
Dick and Dib (Elizabeth) Simonsen began the planting of their 0.5 ha of shiraz (with five
clones) in 1994, intending to simply make wine for their own consumption. As all five
clones are in full production, the Simonsens expect a maximum production of 200 cases,
and have accordingly released small quantities of Shiraz, which sells out quickly. The vines
are hand-pruned, the grapes hand-picked, the must basket-pressed, and all wine movements
are by gravity.

ΨΨΨΨΨ   Simonsen Shiraz 2005 Lissom mouthfeel and texture; fine, very long and silky
fruit supported by fine, savoury tannins. Screwcap. **Rating** 91 **To** 2012 $25
Simonsen Shiraz 2006 Medium-bodied; supple, round and smooth, with good
structure and length; just a little over-oaked. Screwcap. **Rating** 90 **To** 2013 $25

Barringwood Park

60 Gillams Road, Lower Barrington, Tas 7306 **Region** Northern Tasmania
T (03) 6492 3140 **F** (03) 6492 3360 **www.**barringwoodpark.com.au **Open** Jan & Feb
7 days, March–Dec Wed–Sun & public hols 10–5
Winemaker Tom Ravich (Contract) **Est.** 1993 **Cases** 1500

Judy and Ian Robinson operate a sawmill at Lower Barrington, 15 mins south of Devonport on the main tourist trail to Cradle Mountain, and when they planted 500 vines in 1993 the aim was to do a bit of home winemaking. In a thoroughly familiar story, the urge to expand the vineyard and make wine on a commercial scale came almost immediately, and they embarked on a six-year plan, planting 1 ha a year in the first four years and building the cellar and tasting rooms during the following two years.

▼▼▼▼▼ **Mill Block Pinot Noir 2006** While light- to medium-bodied, has intense plum, black cherry and spice aromas and flavours; supple and smooth in the mouth, superfine tannins providing the structure; trophy Best Pinot Noir Australian Boutique Wine Awards '07. Screwcap. 13.5° alc. **Rating** 94 **To** 2013 $30

▼▼▼▼ **Meunier Rose 2007** Strawberry blossom aromas; a sweet fruit entry to the mouth, but dries off along the palate; unusual, but quite appealing. **Rating** 89 **To** 2009 $20

IJ Vintage Pinot Noir Chardonnay Pinot Meunier 2004 Intense citrus and stone fruit flavours; a very long palate, with low dosage; bottle-fermented and two and a half years on lees; will improve further with cork age. 12.5° alc. **Rating** 89 **To** 2012 $32

Northbank Chardonnay 2006 Proclaims its Tasmanian origin with a stainless steel shaft of acidity around which the grapefruit and honeydew melon fruit is built; clean finish. Screwcap. 12.6° alc. **Rating** 88 **To** 2013 $24

Pinot Gris 2007 An obvious tinge of bronze; a rich, broad, mouthfilling style, sweet nashi pear and lychee aromas and flavours, bordering on Alsace; the alcohol does heat the finish. Screwcap. 14° alc. **Rating** 88 **To** 2009 $25

Schonburger 2007 Distinctive rose petal pastille aromas and flavours, with some sweetness on the finish, A point or two for being there. Screwcap. 13° alc. **Rating** 87 **To** 2009 $23

Pinot Meunier 2004 Colour still good; the wine continues to hang in there far longer than might have been expected; some earthy leathery flavours, but no rough tannin extract. **Rating** 87 **To** 2009 $18

Barristers Block

6 The Parkway, Leabrook, SA 5068 (postal) **Region** Adelaide Hills
T 0427 076 237 **F** (08) 8364 2930 **www.**barristersblock.com.au **Open** Not
Winemaker Richard Langford, Simon Greenleaf (Contract) **Est.** 2004 **Cases** 2000

Owner Jan Siemelink-Allen has had 20 years in the industry, and five years in SA's Supreme Court in a successful battle to reclaim ownership of 10 ha of cabernet sauvignon and shiraz in Wrattonbully after a joint venture collapsed; it is not hard to imagine the origin of the name. In 2006 she and her family purchased an 8-ha vineyard planted to sauvignon blanc and pinot noir near Woodside in the Adelaide Hills, adjoining Shaw & Smith's vineyard. Jan, as well as having senior management positions, is a member of the SA Premier's Wine Industry Advisory Council; no rose-tinted spectacles here.

▼▼▼▼ **Wrattonbully Cabernet Sauvignon 2005** A powerful wine; savoury/spicy aspects to blackcurrant and mulberry fruit; has good tannin structure, with just a flash of heat on the finish. Zork. 15° alc. **Rating** 89 **To** 2015 $25

Adelaide Hills Sauvignon Blanc 2007 A clean bouquet, and a firm palate with good acidity; in common with many '07s, lacks varietal fruit flair. Screwcap. 12.4° alc. **Rating** 88 **To** 2010 $21

Barossa Shiraz 2006 Developed but deep colour; very ripe pruney/jammy fruit, with some slightly gamey overtones. Zork. 15.5° alc. **Rating** 87 **To** 2013 $25

Barossa Valley Sparkling GSM 2005 The varietal base is very evident, driving the sweet fruit flavours; modest cellaring will reward. Cork. 14.5° alc. **Rating** 87 **To** 2011 $18

Bartagunyah Estate

7 Survey Road, Melrose, SA 5483 **Region** Southern Flinders Ranges
T (08) 8666 2136 **F** (08) 8666 2136 **www**.smartaqua.com.au/bartagunyah **Open** By appt
Winemaker Charles Melton, O'Leary Walker **Est.** 2000 **Cases** NA
Rob and Christine Smart have established 3 ha of shiraz, 2 ha of cabernet sauvignon and 1 ha of viognier on a property adjoining the southern ridge of the beautiful and rugged Mt Remarkable. The Smarts offer four-wheel drive and mountain-bike tours to take in both the scenery and the abundant wildlife of the Flinders Ranges.

ΨΨΨΨ **Shiraz Cabernet Sauvignon 2005** On the upper limit of alcohol for the fruit weight; sweet blackberry and blackcurrant flavours; gentle extraction has helped considerably. Screwcap. 15.5° alc. **Rating** 89 **To** 2015 $20

Barton Estate ★★★☆

2307 Barton Highway, Murrumbateman, NSW 2582 **Region** Canberra District
T (02) 6230 9553 **F** (02) 6230 9565 **www**.bartonestate.com.au **Open** Not
Winemaker Brindabella Hills, Kyeema Estate **Est.** 1997 **Cases** 900
Bob Furbank and wife Julie Chitty are both CSIRO plant biologists: he is a biochemist (physiologist) and she a specialist in plant tissue culture. In 1997 they acquired the 120-ha property forming part of historic Jeir Station, and have since planted 8 ha to 15 varieties, the most substantial plantings to cabernet sauvignon, shiraz, merlot, riesling and chardonnay, the Joseph's Coat completed with micro quantities of other varieties.

ΨΨΨΨΨ **Riesling 2004** Has developed slowly but very well; still fresh and quite delicate, but with lovely lime juice fruit and a long, clean finish. Screwcap. 12° alc. **Rating** 94 **To** 2014 $18

ΨΨΨΨ **Synergy Cabernets Merlot 2004** Relatively light-bodied, but does have surprising line, length and balance; for those looking for subtlety, not blood and thunder. Screwcap. 13.5° alc. **Rating** 89 **To** 2012 $18
Shiraz 2004 Light- to medium-bodied; spicy earthy wine; while not released in early '08 when tasted, is now fully developed, the tannins soft and fine. Screwcap. 13.5° alc. **Rating** 87 **To** 2010 $18
Synergy Cabernets Merlot 2003 Developed colour, verging on brown; the very stained and compromised cork tells why screwcap is the better choice; this wine may well have had more depth than the '04, but has lost it. 13.5° alc. **Rating** 87 **To** 2009 $18

Barwang Vineyard

Barwang Road, Young, NSW 2594 (postal) **Region** Hilltops
T (02) 6382 3594 **F** (02) 6382 2594 **www**.mcwilliams.com.au **Open** Not
Winemaker Jim Brayne, Russell Cody **Est.** 1969 **Cases** NFP
Peter Robertson pioneered viticulture in the Young region when he planted his first vines in 1969 as part of a diversification program for his 400-ha grazing property. When McWilliam's acquired Barwang in 1989, the vineyard amounted to 13 ha; today the plantings exceed 100 ha. Wine quality has been exemplary from the word go: always elegant, restrained and deliberately understated, repaying extended cellaring.

ΨΨΨΨΨ **Shiraz Viognier 2004** Has a really lovely, silky mouthfeel, delicate yet long; mistakenly credited with 83 points in the 2008 Wine Companion, not 93. Screwcap. 13° alc. **Rating** 94 **To** 2012 $23
Cabernet Sauvignon 2005 In typical Barwang style, elegantly poised with precise but supple cassis/blackcurrant fruit, fine tannins and restrained French oak. **Rating** 94 **To** 2020 $22.95

ΨΨΨΨΨ **Shiraz Viognier 2006** Plenty of ripe blackberry fruit, the viognier contribution evident but not over the top; good length and balance. **Rating** 90 **To** 2014 $22.95

Barwick Wines

Yelverton North Road, Dunsborough, WA 6281 **Region** Margaret River
T (08) 9755 7100 **F** (08) 9755 7133 **www**.barwickwines.com **Open** 7 days 11–4
Winemaker Nigel Ludlow **Est.** 1997 **Cases** 120 000
The production gives some guide to the size of the three estate vineyards. The first is the 83-ha Dwalganup Vineyard in the Blackwood Valley region; the second, the 38-ha St John's Brook Vineyard in Margaret River; and the third, the 73-ha Treenbrook Vineyard in Pemberton. Taken together, the three vineyard holdings place Barwick in the top 10 wine producers in WA. The wines are released under four labels: at the bottom, the Crush Label; next, the White Label estate range; next, the Black Label single vineyard wines from any one of the three regions; and at the top, the Platinum Label, which, confusingly, is in fact called The Collectables, from small parcels of estate-grown grapes. Exports to the UK, the US and other major markets.

ΨΨΨΨΨ **Margaret River Semillon 2007** A lively wine, with grass through to citrus aromas and flavours; the zesty palate has good length, and the faintest touch of sweetness. Screwcap. 12.5° alc. **Rating** 90 **To** 2013 $17.95
Sauvignon Blanc Semillon 2007 Gentle tropical passionfruit courtesy of the sauvignon blanc is supported by grassy/minerally notes from the semillon; good balance. Screwcap. 12.5° alc. **Rating** 90 **To** 2012 $14.95
Margaret River Chardonnay 2007 Complex barrel ferment aromas and flavours on a bed of quite sweet melon and nectarine fruit; good mouthfeel and length. **Rating** 90 **To** 2011 $18

ΨΨΨΨ **Margaret River Shiraz 2006** Plenty of activity, with quite potent barrel ferment inputs; blackberry fruit and firm tannins. **Rating** 88 **To** 2015 $18

Barwite Vineyards

PO Box 542, Mansfield, Vic 3724 **Region** Upper Goulburn
T 0408 525 135 **F** (03) 5776 9800 **www**.barwitevineyards.com.au **Open** Not
Winemaker Delatite (Jane Donat) **Est.** 1997 **Cases** 1000
David Ritchie and a group of fellow grape and wine enthusiasts established their substantial vineyard in 1997 on a slope facing the mouth of the Broken River and thereon to Mt Stirling. Pinot noir (28 ha) and chardonnay (9 ha) were planted for Orlando, to be used in sparkling wine. Given the reputation of the region for the production of aromatic white wines, 4.5 ha of riesling were also planted, the intention being to sell the grapes. However, since 2003 some of the best parcels have been kept aside for the Barwite label.

ΨΨΨΨ **Upper Goulburn Riesling 2006** Quite distinctive aromas and flavours, halfway between citrus and stone fruit; a slightly congested finish. Screwcap. 12.5° alc. **Rating** 87 **To** 2009 $17

Basket Range Wines

PO Box 65, Basket Range, SA 5138 **Region** Adelaide Hills
T 0427 021 915 **F** (08) 8390 1515 **www**.basketrangewine.com.au **Open** By appt
Winemaker Phillip Broderick **Est.** 1980 **Cases** 400
A tiny operation known to very few, run by civil and Aboriginal rights lawyer Phillip Broderick, a most engaging man with a disarmingly laid-back manner. He has recently established a new vineyard with 1.3 ha each of cabernet sauvignon, merlot and pinot noir, plus a splash (0.3 ha) of petit verdot which will see production increase as it comes into bearing. Great to see Phillip is continuing to quietly make and release his wines after a quarter of a century in the saddle.

ŶŶŶŶ **Adelaide Hills Cabernet Sauvignon Merlot Petit Verdot 2005** Bright hue; a light- to medium-bodied, fresh, relatively early-picked style, with a mix of cassis, redcurrant, mint and leaf; has length. Screwcap. 13.5° alc. **Rating** 89 **To** 2014 $23

Bass Fine Wines ★★★★☆

Upper McEwans Road, Rosevears, Tas 7270 **Region** Northern Tasmania
T (03) 6331 0136 **F** (03) 6331 0136 **Open** Not
Winemaker Guy Wagner **Est.** 1999 **Cases** 3000
Owner/winemaker Guy Wagner had been carrying on the business as a classic negociant (in Burgundian terms), originally buying wine from various vineyards in bottle and/or in barrel, but from 2000 also purchasing grapes, the wines made at other existing wineries. Prior to the '06 vintage, he completed the construction of a new winery, at which he now makes his own wines, and offers contract winemaking services for others.

ŶŶŶŶŶ **Bass Strait Riesling 2007** Pristine riesling fruit on the bouquet, with great line and generosity on the finish; very long and with good texture. Screwcap.
Rating 93 **To** 2020
Riverview Riesling 2007 Pale straw colour; prominent aromas of fresh lemons and minerals; focused and fine with great acidity and a chalky, dry finish. Screwcap.
Rating 90 **To** 2015
Bass Strait Riesling 2006 Good flavour, with quite exotic citrus fruits, and typical generosity on the finish; good line and texture. **Rating** 90 **To** 2016

ŶŶŶŶ **Riverview Chardonnay 2007** Plenty of cashew and riper stone fruits on the bouquet; a full-flavoured palate, though less complex than the bouquet. **Rating** 89 **To** 2012
Strait Chardonnay 2007 Abundant oak impact on the bouquet, but the fruit intensity and freshness come through on the palate to provide balance; finishes a fraction short. Screwcap. **Rating** 89 **To** 2011
Strait Pinot Noir 2007 Excellent colour; a very pure and linear pinot, with clear black cherry fruit and crisp acidity; needs to build flesh, and light and shade. Screwcap. **Rating** 89 **To** 2012

Bass Phillip ★★★★★

Tosch's Road, Leongatha South, Vic 3953 **Region** Gippsland
T (03) 5664 3341 **F** (03) 5664 3209 **Open** By appt
Winemaker Phillip Jones **Est.** 1979 **Cases** 1500
Phillip Jones has retired from the Melbourne rat-race to handcraft tiny quantities of superlative Pinot Noir which, at its best, has no equal in Australia. Painstaking site selection, ultra-close vine spacing and the very, very cool climate of South Gippsland are the keys to the magic of Bass Phillip and its eerily Burgundian Pinots. Tastings are sporadic (there was a mega-tasting in 2006) and the rating is very much that of the best, not the lesser, wines.

ŶŶŶŶŶ **21 Pinot Noir 2006** Bass Phillip on song; strong purple-red; powerful, intense and focused dark plum and a dusting of spice; will develop superbly over 5–10 years; 21st-anniversary release made from all four estate vineyards (for the first time) Diam. 12.8° alc. **Rating** 95 **To** 2016 $80

battely wines ★★★★★

1375 Beechworth-Wangaratta Road, Beechworth, Vic 3747 **Region** Beechworth
T (03) 5727 0505 **F** (03) 5727 0506 **www.**battelywines.com.au **Open** By appt
Winemaker Russell Bourne **Est.** 1998 **Cases** 500
Dr Russell Bourne is an anaesthetist and former GP at Mt Beauty, who has always loved the food, wine and skiing of North East Victoria. He completed his oenology degree at CSU in 2002 following his '98 acquisition of the former Brown Brothers Everton Hills vineyard. He has since planted 1.6 ha of shiraz and viognier, with further Rhône Valley varietal plantings planned, including counoise. Since 2001 all wines have come from the estate vineyards, which have increased to 2.3 ha. Exports to the UK and the US.

ΨΨΨΨ **Durif 2005** Typical deep colour; achieves the depth of flavour common with this variety, but keeps an uncommon degree of elegance to the almost silky black fruits; heavily stained cork the only issue. 14.5° alc. **Rating** 94 **To** 2015 $35

Battle of Bosworth ★★★★☆

Edgehill Vineyards, Gaffney Road, Willunga, SA 5172 **Region** McLaren Vale
T (08) 8556 2441 **F** (08) 8556 4881 **www.**battleofbosworth.com.au **Open** By appt
Winemaker Joch Bosworth **Est.** 1996 **Cases** 5000
The 75-ha Edgehill Vineyard, established many years ago by Peter and Anthea Bosworth, was taken over by son Joch Bosworth in 1996. He set about converting 10 ha of shiraz, cabernet sauvignon and chardonnay to fully certified A-grade organic viticulture. The regime prohibits the use of herbicides and pesticides; the weeds are controlled by soursob, the pretty yellow flower considered a weed by many, which carpets the vineyards in winter, but dies off in early spring as surface moisture dries, forming a natural weed mat. Organic viticulture is never easy, and when Joch moved to make the first wines from the vines, the Battle of Bosworth name was a neat take. Exports to the UK, the US and other major markets.

ΨΨΨΨΨ **McLaren Vale Shiraz 2006** Lovely concentration and focus; dark chocolate fruits, fruitcake spice and warm but vibrant fruit right across the palate; long and quite luscious. Screwcap. 14.5° alc. **Rating** 93 **To** 2015 $25
McLaren Vale Shiraz Viognier 2006 Highly aromatic, displaying good viognier influence; quite obvious oak, and chewy dark fruits on the palate; good flavour, but pulls up just a little short. Screwcap. 14.5° alc. **Rating** 92 **To** 2016 $24
McLaren Vale Chardonnay Viognier 2007 Has considerable life and vivacity given the vintage; citrus-tinged melon, white peach and an autosuggestion of apricot. Certified organic. Screwcap. 13.5° alc. **Rating** 90 **To** 2011 $18
McLaren Vale Cabernet Sauvignon 2006 Richly fruited but with finesse to the structure; fine tannins and fresh acidity support the generous black fruits on offer. Screwcap. 14.5° alc. **Rating** 90 **To** 2014 $25

ΨΨΨΨ **The War of the Rose 2007** Small red fruit aromas and flavours in a maraschino cherry spectrum, but with no sweetness on the bright, fresh finish. Screwcap. 13.5° alc. **Rating** 89 **To** 2009 $18

Bay of Fires

40 Baxters Road, Pipers River, Tas 7252 **Region** Northern Tasmania
T (03) 6382 7666 **F** (03) 6382 7027 **www.**bayoffireswines.com.au **Open** 7 days 10–5
Winemaker Fran Austin **Est.** 2001 **Cases** NFP
In 1994 Hardys purchased its first grapes from Tasmania, with the aim of further developing and refining its sparkling wines, a process which quickly gave birth to Arras. The next stage was the inclusion of various parcels of chardonnay from Tasmania in the '98 Eileen Hardy, then the development in 2001 of the Bay of Fires brand, offering wines sourced from various parts of Tasmania. The winery was originally that of Rochecombe, then Ninth Island, and now, of course, Bay of Fires. Its potential has now been fully realised in the most impressive imaginable fashion. Exports to all major markets.

ΨΨΨΨΨ **Riesling 2006** A very good wine 12 months ago, then with considerable potential for development, now fully realised, with a vibrant mix of lime, apple and mineral, finishing with crisp acidity. Top gold, Tas Wine Show '08. Screwcap. 12.4° alc. **Rating** 96 **To** 2016 $21.50
Tigress Pinot Noir 2006 Very good colour and clarity; silky, supple, slinky cherry and plum; positive oak, good finish, and a lingering finish. Gold, Sydney Wine Show '08. Screwcap. 13.5° alc. **Rating** 95 **To** 2013 $27.50
Riesling 2007 A clean but restrained bouquet, then leaps into life on the palate, with delicate but beautifully focused lime and passionfruit flavours, tied by a bow of perfect acidity. Screwcap. 12° alc. **Rating** 94 **To** 2015 $30

Pinot Noir 2006 Brilliant clear colour; slightly more texture and complexity than the Tigress, with obvious barrel ferment and sous bois notes; needs time. Screwcap. 13.5° alc. **Rating** 94 **To** 2014 $37

Tigress Pinot Chardonnay NV Highly aromatic strong stone fruit and mandarin abundant flavour, richer than Arras, but less fine. Cork. 12.5° alc. **Rating** 94 **To** 2010 $28.50

Arras 2002 Complex toasty grilled nuts on the bouquet, with lively citrus aromas; good texture and clean fruit, with a lingering, toasty finish. **Rating** 94 **To** 2013 $60

Tigress Sparkling Rose NV Salmon-pink; round, mouthfilling and supple; hints of spicy red fruits and a creamy mouthfeel; long finish. Cork. 13° alc. **Rating** 94 **To** 2009 $28.50

♥♥♥♥♡ **Non Vintage Pinot Noir Chardonnay NV** Highly aromatic, with strong stone fruit and mandarin, and abundant overall flavour; perhaps a little short on finesse. 12.5° alc. **Rating** 91 **To** 2010 $38

Chardonnay 2007 Obvious barrel ferment inputs on the bouquet, but the fine, intense fruit of the palate more than handles the oak; has an authoritative lingering finish. Screwcap. 13° alc. **Rating** 90 **To** 2014 $38

Pinot Gris 2007 Fresh and lively, with a fragrant mix of pear and citrus on a long and lingering finish. Screwcap. 13.5° alc. **Rating** 90 **To** 2010 $31

♥♥♥♥ **Tigress Chardonnay 2007** Elegant nectarine and tangerine flavours; complexed by some barrel ferment/charry oak characters; good length and balance. Screwcap. 13° alc. **Rating** 89 **To** 2011 $28.50

Bay of Shoals

Cordes Road, Kingscote, Kangaroo Island, SA 5223 **Region** Kangaroo Island
T (08) 8553 0289 **F** (08) 8553 2081 **www.**bayofshoalswines.com.au **Open** 7 days 11–5
Winemaker Ruth Pledge, Paul Bailey (Consultant) **Est.** 1994 **Cases** 2500
John Willoughby's vineyard overlooks the Bay of Shoals, which is the northern boundary of Kingscote, Kangaroo Island's main town. Planting of the vineyard began in 1994, and has now reached 10 ha (riesling, chardonnay, sauvignon blanc, cabernet sauvignon and shiraz). In addition, 460 olive trees have been planted to produce table olives.

♥♥♥♥♡ **Kangaroo Island Riesling 2005** Fragrant, floral apple and lime blossom; still very fresh; lime juice flavours supported by a streak of mineral; deserved gold, Aus Small Winemakers Show '07. Screwcap. 12.5° alc. **Rating** 93 **To** 2014 $18

Kangaroo Island Riesling 2006 Very much in the style of the '07, the juicy fruit just a little stronger and sweeter; supple and smooth, has good length and aftertaste. Screwcap. 13.5° alc. **Rating** 92 **To** 2013 $18

Kangaroo Island Riesling 2007 Very impressive for its maritime climate; abundant tropical lime juice flavours, yet retains balance, line and focus, finishing with good acidity. Screwcap. 12.5° alc. **Rating** 91 **To** 2012 $18

Kangaroo Island Shiraz 2006 A clean, elegant and lively shiraz, with black cherry, blackberry and spicy notes on a smooth, long palate; well-handled oak. Screwcap. 14° alc. **Rating** 91 **To** 2016 $20

Kangaroo Island Shiraz 2005 Yet another attractive medium-bodied wine, with a gently complex fusion of spicy black fruits, spice, warm oak and ripe but fine tannins. Screwcap. 14.5° alc. **Rating** 90 **To** 2015 $20

♥♥♥♥ **Kangaroo Island Chardonnay 2007** Elegantly framed light-bodied chardonnay, with melon fruit and some spicy creamy nuances; the palate is a little short. Screwcap. 12.5° alc. **Rating** 88 **To** 2012 $18

Kangaroo Island Vintage Fortified 2007 This is a competent attempt, with strong black fruits, spice and dark chocolate; best of all, not too sweet, although a slightly softer spirit might have been better. Screwcap. 18.5° alc. **Rating** 88 **To** 2016 $20

Kangaroo Island Sauvignon Blanc 2007 The varietal fruit is suppressed on both bouquet and palate but the wine is fault-free and does have overall presence and balanced acidity. Screwcap. 13° alc. **Rating** 87 **To** 2009 $18

Kangaroo Island Sauvignon Blanc 2006 In similar style to the '07, with plenty of fruit without phenolic characters; simply non-specific varietal flavours. Screwcap. 13.5° alc. **Rating** 87 **To** 2009 $18

Kangaroo Island Cabernet Sauvignon 2006 Firm, earthy fruit is true to the variety, but makes for the only Bay of Shoals wine not to beguile the palate; maybe all it needs is a few years in bottle. Screwcap. 13.5° alc. **Rating** 87 **To** 2015 $20

Kangaroo Island Cabernet Sauvignon 2005 Savoury, earthy, leafy, minty aromas and flavours on a medium–bodied palate; the suspicion is that the site is too cold for cabernet sauvignon. Screwcap. 13.5° alc. **Rating** 87 **To** 2011 $20

Beckett's Flat

49 Beckett Road, Metricup, WA 6280 **Region** Margaret River
T (08) 9755 7402 **F** (08) 9755 7344 **www.**beckettsflat.com.au **Open** 7 days 11–5 (winter), 11–6 (summer)
Winemaker Belizar Ilic **Est.** 1992 **Cases** 8000
Belizar (Bill) and Noni Ilic opened Beckett's Flat in 1997. Situated just off the Bussell Highway, midway between Busselton and the Margaret River, it draws upon 14 ha of estate vineyards, first planted in 1992. The wines, which are made onsite, include a range of kosher wines under the Five Stones label. Exports to the US, Canada and Singapore.

    ♀♀♀♀♀ **Single Vineyard Estate Margaret River Sauvignon Blanc 2007** Good varietal definition; fresh-cut grass and a mere hint of tropical fruits; precise and fine, with terrific length of flavour. Screwcap. 13° alc. **Rating** 92 **To** 2009 $17.50
Single Vineyard Estate Margaret River Verdelho 2007 Super-clean and lively, with spice and honeysuckle framed by ample ripe fruits; very long and very clean on the finish. Screwcap. 14° alc. **Rating** 90 **To** 2009 $17.50

Beckingham Wines ★★★

6–7/477 Warrigal Road, Moorabbin, Vic 3189 **Region** Mornington Peninsula
T 0400 292 264 **www.**beckinghamwines.com.au **Open** W'ends 10–5
Winemaker Peter Beckingham **Est.** 1998 **Cases** 3500
Peter Beckingham is a chemical engineer who has turned a hobby into a part-time business, moving operations from the driveway of his house to a warehouse in Moorabbin. The situation of the winery may not be romantic, but it is eminently practical, and more than a few winemakers in California have adopted the same solution. His friends grow the grapes, and he makes the wine, both for himself and as a contract maker for others.

    ♀♀♀♀ **Edgehill Mornington Peninsula Chardonnay 2006** An aromatic and fresh bouquet; enters the palate with good nectarine and grapefruit flavours, but falters slightly on the finish. Screwcap. 14.5° alc. **Rating** 88 **To** 2011 $15

Beelgara Estate

Farm 576 Rossetto Road, Beelbangera, NSW 2680 **Region** Riverina
T (02) 6966 0200 **F** (02) 6966 0298 **www.**beelgara.com.au **Open** Mon–Sat 10–5, Sun 11–3
Winemaker Rod Hooper, Danny Toaldo, Sean Hampel **Est.** 1930 **Cases** 600 000
Beelgara Estate was formed in 2001 after the purchase of the 60-year-old Rossetto family winery by a group of growers, distributors and investors. There is far greater emphasis on bottled table wine (albeit at low prices), spreading its wings to premium regions, but still maintaining excellent value for money.

    ♀♀♀♀ **Estate Range Semillon Sauvignon Blanc 2007** Lively, fresh lemongrass and gooseberry, impressive for the vintage. A very large estate, covering the whole of southeast Australia. Screwcap. 13° alc. **Rating** 87 **To** 2009 $7.95

Rascals Prayer Sauvignon Blanc 2007 Well made; a gentle touch of tropical gooseberry fruit, the acid adjustment spot-on; impressive outcome at the price. Screwcap. 12° alc. **Rating** 87 **To** 2009 $12.95

Belalie Bend   ★★★★

Mannanarie Road, Jamestown, SA 5491 **Region** Southern Flinders Ranges
T (08) 8664 1323 **F** (08) 8664 1923 **www**.belaliebend.com.au **Open** By appt
Winemaker Emma Bowley **Est.** 2001 **Cases** 350
Emma Bowley obtained her wine science degree from CSU, and after a varied career working for large Australian wine companies, and thereafter in the US and Italy, decided to turn her attention to smaller wineries where she could have a hands-on winemaking role. Emma works as a contract winemaker in the Clare Valley, while she and husband Guy have established a vineyard in Jamestown. One ha each of shiraz, cabernet sauvignon and riesling were planted in 2001, followed by 1.5 ha each of mourvedre and shiraz the following year.

ꝐꝐꝐꝐꝐ **Jamestown Southern Flinders Ranges Shiraz 2005** Deep, dense colour; full-bodied rich and strongly structured wine with layers of blackberry and licorice supported by ripe tannins; theoretically should be very long lived. Zork. 14.5° alc. **Rating** 92 **To** 2020 $35

ꝐꝐꝐꝐ **Jamestown Southern Flinders Ranges Cabernet Sauvignon 2005** Dense, deep colour; full-bodied, almost impenetrable palate, with black fruits and enveloping, though ripe, tannins. Zork. 14.5° alc. **Rating** 89 **To** 2014 $35

Belgravia Vineyards   ★★★★

84 Byng Street, Orange, NSW 2800 **Region** Orange
T (02) 6361 4441 **F** (02) 6365 0646 **www**.belgravia.com.au **Open** Sun–Thurs 10–8, Fri–Sat 10–late
Winemaker David Lowe, Jane Wilson (Contract) **Est.** 2003 **Cases** 6000
Belgravia is an 1800-ha mixed farming property (sheep, cattle and vines) 20 km north of Orange. There are now 190 ha of vineyard with 10 ha devoted to the Belgravia brand. In 2006 Belgravia opened its cellar door at the heritage-listed former Union Bank building in Orange, which also operates as a wine bar and restaurant. Exports to the UK and Denmark.

ꝐꝐꝐꝐꝐ **Reserve Orange Cabernet Sauvignon 2006** An elegant, unforced medium-bodied palate, with super-fresh cassis and blackcurrant fruit, a fine web of French oak, and almost delicate tannins. Screwcap. 14.5° alc. **Rating** 92 **To** 2016 $26

ꝐꝐꝐꝐ **Orange Viognier 2006** Positive varietal fruit expression of apricot and peach in a rounded palate, and no phenolic toughness on the finish. Screwcap. 15° alc. **Rating** 89 **To** 2011 $18
Union Bank Orange Rose 2007 Fresh floral aromas of strawberry and cherry are reflected in the crisp, dry palate; nice rose; good value. Screwcap. 13° alc. **Rating** 89 **To** 2009 $14
Reserve Orange Shiraz 2005 Exceptionally bright colour; spicy, savoury, earthy cool-grown style; needs a touch more sweet fruit on the mid-palate. Screwcap. 14.3° alc. **Rating** 89 **To** 2013 $26
Reserve Orange Merlot 2006 Concentrated, powerful and somewhat extractive, but there is an undertow of varietal fruit; may reward those with patience. Screwcap. 14° alc. **Rating** 89 **To** 2016 $26
Orange Riesling 2007 A solid wine, with quite fleshy tropical fruit; short finish. Screwcap. 12.2° alc. **Rating** 87 **To** 2011 $18

Bella Ridge Estate   ★★★★

78 Campersic Road, Herne Hill, WA 6056 **Region** Swan District
T (08) 9250 4962 **F** (08) 9246 0244 **www**.bellaridge.com.au **Open** By appt
Winemaker Alon Arbel **Est.** 2003 **Cases** 3000

Alon Arbel came to WA from Israel in search of strong, easterly sea breezes to power his passion for windsurfing. Here he met wife-to-be, Jodi, and, after working overseas and travelling, they returned to Perth. A year out from completing a degree in engineering, Alon switched to Curtin University's oenology and viticulture course, which he duly completed. Entirely fortuitously, Jodi's parents, Frank and Lois, discovered a 10-ha property (8 ha under vine) on the foothills of the Darling Scarp, with plantings dating back to 1966. The 2003 purchase of the property was a couple of months before the commencement of the '04 vintage, by which time they had managed to erect a 30-tonne winery, crushing 20 tonnes of fruit for their own label and 10 tonnes for contract clients. Since then they have grafted the plantings to an ultra-eclectic mix, which includes the Japanese variety kyoho. Exports to Singapore.

ΨΨΨΨΩ **Shiraz 2005** Dark fruit and smoky oak aromas are followed by quite a viscous, yet lively, palate. Screwcap. 15° alc. **Rating** 90 **To** 2014 $30

ΨΨΨΨ **Chardonnay Viognier 2005** The influence of the viognier is very evident on both bouquet and palate, oak also part of the mix; a slightly congested finish, and demands food. Screwcap. 13.5° alc. **Rating** 88 **To** 2009 $23
Reserve Red 2005 Has concentration and good depth of fruit; a little simple, perhaps, but good texture and weight. Screwcap. **Rating** 88 **To** 2012 $50
Semillon 2007 A pungent, fresh and zesty wine; falls away a little on the finish, but will likely build more flavour with age. Screwcap. 13° alc. **Rating** 87 **To** 2012 $20

Bellarine Estate   ★★★★☆

2270 Portarlington Road, Bellarine, Vic 3222 **Region** Geelong
T (03) 5259 3310 **F** (03) 5259 3393 **www**.bellarineestate.com.au **Open** 7 days 11–4
Winemaker Anthony Brain **Est.** 1995 **Cases** 7000
Important changes were made at Bellarine Estate prior to the 2007 vintage, with an onsite winery commissioned, and Anthony Brain (with extensive cool-climate winemaking experience), installed as winemaker. The 12-ha vineyard is planted to chardonnay, pinot noir, shiraz, merlot, viognier and sauvignon blanc. The winery was opened in time for the 2007 vintage and offers small-run bottling services for others. Julian's Restaurant is open for lunch seven days and dinner Fri/Sat evenings. Exports to the US.

ΨΨΨΨΨ **Phil's Fetish Geelong Pinot Noir 2006** Very good wine; a complex bouquet and palate abounding with dark plum flavours; silky mouthfeel in a medium-bodied context; good length. Screwcap. 13.8° alc. **Rating** 94 **To** 2010 $32

ΨΨΨΨ **Nine Lives Geelong Sauvignon Blanc 2007** Spicy aromas reflect partial French oak barrel fermentation; relatively delicate palate with sweet gooseberry fruit and a balanced, dry finish. Screwcap. 12.7° alc. **Rating** 89 **To** 2010 $25
James' Paddock Geelong Chardonnay 2006 Bright colour; oak asserts itself from start to finish even though the underlying fruit is quite bold. Screwcap. 13.8° alc. **Rating** 89 **To** 2011 $28

Bellarmine Wines   ★★★★★

PO Box 1450, Manjimup, WA 6258 **Region** Pemberton
T (08) 9776 0667 **F** (08) 9776 0657 **www**.bellarmine.com.au **Open** Not
Winemaker Robert Paul (Consulant) **Est.** 2000 **Cases** 5000
This substantial operation is owned by German residents Dr Willi and Gudrun Schumacher. Long-term wine lovers, the Schumachers decided to establish a vineyard and winery of their own, using Australia partly because of its stable political climate. The venture was managed by Mike and Tam Bewsher, both of whom have extensive knowledge of the wine industry but sadly left in April 2008. There are 20 ha of chardonnay, riesling, sauvignon blanc, pinot noir, shiraz, merlot and petit verdot. Exports to Germany.

ΨΨΨΨΨ **Pemberton Riesling 2007** Lively, fresh lime sherbet flavours, the residual sugar perfectly balanced in Kabinett Mosel style; very good length and a zesty finish. Screwcap. 11° alc. **Rating** 94 **To** 2014 $18

Pemberton Sauvignon Blanc 2007 Has lovely citrus, grass and mineral aromas and flavours giving bite and character; intensity without heaviness. **Rating** 94 To 2012 $15

Pemberton Chardonnay 2007 Has the elegance which is the mark of all Bellarmine wines, with beautifully focused nectarine fruit supported by a gossamer web of French oak. Screwcap. 14° alc. **Rating** 94 **To** 2012 $15

♟♟♟♟♟ **Pemberton Riesling Auslese 2007** An attractive wine, though with not quite the intensity and vibrancy of the best vintages; lime juice, spice and balancing acidity. Screwcap. 7.5° alc. **Rating** 92 **To** 2012 $15

Pemberton Riesling Dry 2007 Gentle floral lime blossom aromas; a delicate palate, with good length and balance. Will blossom with further time in bottle. Screwcap. 12° alc. **Rating** 91 **To** 2015 $18

Bellbrae Estate

520 Great Ocean Road, Bellbrae, Vic 3228 **Region** Geelong
T (03) 5264 8480 **F** (03) 5222 6182 **www**.bellbraeestate.com.au **Open** W'ends & public hols 11–5 (winter), 7 days (Jan)
Winemaker Matthew di Sciascio, Peter Flewellyn **Est.** 1999 **Cases** 1800
Bellbrae Estate (and the Longboard Wines brand) is the venture of friends Richard Macdougall and Matthew di Sciascio. Sharing a common love of wine, surf and coastal life, they decided to establish a vineyard and produce their own wine. In 1998 Richard purchased a small sheep grazing property with 8 ha of fertile, sheltered north-facing slopes on the Great Ocean Road near Bellbrae, and with Matthew's help as business associate, Bellbrae Estate was born. Since 2003 all the wines have been Geelong-sourced; at the Geelong Wine Show '07, Bellbrae won the trophy for Most Successful Exhibitor.

♟♟♟♟♟ **Southside Sauvignon Blanc 2007** Stacked full of flavour, with very lively lemony acidity giving the wine great length; trophy, Geelong Wine Show '07. **Rating** 94 **To** 2010 $22

♟♟♟♟♟ **Gundrys Geelong Shiraz 2006** Redolent of blackberry, plum, prune, licorice and spice – all things nice; soft tannins and appropriate oak. Screwcap. 14.5° alc. **Rating** 93 **To** 2020 $33

Longboard Geelong Yarra Valley Shiraz Cabernet 2006 Firm blackberry and blackcurrant fruits are neatly balanced; medium- to full-bodied, with a storehouse of flavour for many years. Screwcap. 14° alc. **Rating** 92 **To** 2020 $19

Longboard Pinot Noir 2006 Deep and bright hue; plenty of plummy fruit on the entry, but falters ever so slightly on the finish. **Rating** 90 **To** 2012 $22

Addiscott Pinot Noir 2006 Excellent texture and structure to blood plum and black cherry fruit; fine tannins, good length; possibly verges on dry red. **Rating** 90 **To** 2013 $33

Bellvale Wines

95 Forresters Lane, Berrys Creek, Vic 3953 **Region** Gippsland
T (03) 5668 8230 **F** (03) 5668 8230 **www**.bellvalewine.com.au **Open** By appt
Winemaker John Ellis **Est.** 1998 **Cases** 2000
John Ellis is the third under this name to be actively involved in the wine industry. His background as a former 747 pilot, and the knowledge he gained of Burgundy over many visits, sets him apart from the others. He has established 17 ha of pinot noir and chardonnay on the red soils of a north-facing slope. He chose a density of 7150 vines per ha, following as far as possible the precepts of Burgundy, but limited by tractor size, which precludes narrower row spacing and even higher plant density. Exports to the UK, the US and other major markets.

♟♟♟♟♟ **The Quercus Vineyard Gippsland Pinot Noir 2006** A truly spicy wine, with whole bunch stemmy character lifting the varietal red fruits; very fresh and lively with razor-like acidity holding the palate together for a very long time. Cork. 12.5° alc. **Rating** 94 **To** 2014 $35

ΨΨΨΨΩ **The Athena Vineyard Gippsland Chardonnay 2006** Obvious barrel ferment
characters on the bouquet; a textured and complex palate with ripe nectarine fruit;
belies its low alcohol. Screwcap. 12.5° alc. **Rating** 93 **To** 2014 $30

Belvoir Park Estate   ★★★★☆

39 Belvoir Park Road, Big Hill, Vic 3453 **Region** Bendigo
T (03) 5435 3075 **www**.belvoirparkwines.com.au **Open** W'ends & public hols 11–5
Winemaker Ian Hall, Achilles Kalanis **Est.** 1997 **Cases** 1000
Ian and Julie Hall have established 2 ha of shiraz and 0.5 ha of cabernet sauvignon on deep,
granite-based soils. As is common with small winery vineyards, the vines are hand-pruned
and all the grapes hand-picked, followed by small batch processing in the winery via open
fermenters and a basket press. The quality of the wines has improved in leaps and bounds.

ΨΨΨΨΩ **Bendigo Riesling 2007** Made with restraint; tight minerally structure, long
and lingering, fine lime juice flavours; surprise packet, especially from this region.
Screwcap. 12° alc. **Rating** 91 **To** 2015 $18
Reserve Shiraz 2006 Medium-bodied; quite fresh black fruits and a touch of
spice; has length, well-balanced tannins and oak. Diam. 13.5° alc. **Rating** 91
To 2015 $30

Ben Potts Wines   ★★★★

Step Road, Langhorne Creek, SA 5255 (postal) **Region** Langhorne Creek
T (08) 8537 3029 **F** (08) 8537 3284 **www**.benpottswines.com.au **Open** Not
Winemaker Ben Potts **Est.** 2002 **Cases** 800
Potts is the sixth generation to be involved in grapegrowing and winemaking in Langhorne
Creek, the first being Frank Potts, founder of Bleasdale Vineyards. Ben completed the
oenology degree at CSU, and ventured into winemaking on a commercial scale in 2002 (aged
25). Fiddle's Block Shiraz is named after great-grandfather Fiddle; Lenny's Block Cabernet
Sauvignon Malbec after grandfather Len; and Bill's Block Malbec after father Bill. No samples
received; the rating is that of last year. Exports to Europe, China, Hong Kong and Singapore.

Ben's Run   ★★★

PO Box 127, Broke, NSW 2330 **Region** Lower Hunter Valley
T (02) 6579 1310 **F** (02) 6579 1370 **www**.bensrun.com.au **Open** Not
Winemaker Pooles Rock (Patrick Auld) **Est.** 1997 **Cases** 1000
Ben's Run, say the owners, 'is named for our kelpie dog for graciously allowing part of his
retirement run to be converted into a showpiece shiraz-only vineyard'. Norman Marran was
the pioneer of the Australian cotton industry, with a distinguished career as a former director
of both the Australian Wheat Board and the Grains Research Corporation, and is currently
chairman of a leading food research company. Exports to the US, Canada, Hong Kong and
Malaysia.

ΨΨΨΨ **Single Vineyard Shiraz 2005** Light-bodied; savoury earthy regional overtones
to predominantly red fruit flavours; fine tannins, the oak (24 months) not over the
top. Diam. 13.1° alc. **Rating** 87 **To** 2013 $18

Bendbrook Wines   ★★★☆

Section 19, Pound Road, Macclesfield, SA 5153 **Region** Adelaide Hills
T (08) 8388 9773 **F** (08) 8388 9373 **www**.bendbrookwines.com.au **Open** By appt
Winemaker Contract **Est.** 1998 **Cases** 2000
John and Margaret Struik have established their 6-ha vineyard on either side of a significant
bend in the Angas River, which runs through the property, with cabernet sauvignon on one
side and shiraz on the other. The name comes from the bend in question, which is indirectly
responsible for the flood which occurs every 4–5 years. The Struiks have restored what was
known as the Postmaster's Residence, which is now their home.

ŶŶŶŶ   Goat Track Shiraz 2005 Basic blackberry fruit runs through a medium-bodied
palate, with some touches of leather, earth and spice to add length and interest.
Screwcap. 14.5° alc. **Rating** 88 **To** 2012 $33
Cracklin' Rosey 2006 The full character of this rose really only manifests
itself on the finish and aftertaste, the viognier making a contribution. Cabernet
Sauvignon/Shiraz/Viognier. Screwcap. 14° alc. **Rating** 87 **To** 2009 $17
Goat Track Shiraz 2006 Slightly hazy colour; light-bodied; spicy/savoury
overtones to red cherry fruit; not entirely ripe. Screwcap. 13.5° alc. **Rating** 87
To 2010 $33

Bended Knee Vineyard   ★★★★

PO Box 334, Buninyong, Vic 3357 **Region** Ballarat
T (03) 5341 8437 **F** (03) 5341 8437 **www**.bendedknee.com.au **Open** Not
Winemaker Peter Roche **Est.** 1999 **Cases** 300
Peter and Pauline Roche began the development of their property in 1999. They have 0.5 ha
each of chardonnay and pinot noir at moderately high density, and 0.2 ha of ultra-close-
planted pinot noir at the equivalent of 9000 vines per ha. Here four clones have been used:
114, 115, G5V15 and 777. The Roches say, 'We are committed to sustainable viticulture and
aim to leave the planet in better shape than we found it.' Ducks, guinea fowl and chooks are
vineyard custodians, and all vine canopy management is done by hand, including pruning and
picking. Although production is tiny, Bended Knee can be found at some of Melbourne's best
restaurants. The sold out sign has meant no wines available for tasting in this edition.

Bent Creek Vineyards   ★★★☆

Lot 10 Blewitt Springs Road, McLaren Flat, SA 5171 **Region** McLaren Vale
T (08) 8383 0414 **F** (08) 8344 7703 **www**.bentcreekvineyards.com.au **Open** Sundays &
public hols 11–5
Winemaker Peter Polson, Tim Geddes **Est.** 2001 **Cases** 5000
Peter Polson is now the sole owner of Bent Creek, which has acquired a second vineyard
of 5 ha at McLaren Vale. As a parallel development, Tim Geddes is now assisting Peter in the
winemaking.

ŶŶŶŶ   McLaren Vale Cabernet Merlot 2006 A big wine with good varietal intensity,
and a sweet mid-palate. Screwcap. 15.2° alc. **Rating** 89 **To** 2015 $20
McLaren Vale Chardonnay 2006 A rich style, with plenty of oak, warm fruit
and cashew aromas; quite nutty on the palate; plenty of flavour. Screwcap. 13.5° alc.
Rating 88 **To** 2012 $20

Benwarin Wines   ★★★★

PO Box 1014, Surry Hills, NSW 2010 (postal) **Region** Lower Hunter Valley
T (02) 8354 1375 **F** (02) 8354 1376 **www**.benwarin.com.au **Open** Not
Winemaker Monarch Winemaking Services **Est.** 1999 **Cases** 7000
Allan Bagley and wife Janneke have planted a substantial 18.57-ha vineyard with shiraz,
verdelho, sangiovese, chambourcin, semillon and chardonnay. Until 2004 most of the grapes
were sold to others, but since then all of the production has gone to the Benwarin label. The
yield is restricted to 2 tonnes per acre, and the wines have been consistent medal winners.
Exports to Canada.

ŶŶŶŶŶ   Hunter Valley Semillon 2007 Clearly defined lemon, herb and lanolin varietal
fruit on both bouquet and palate; generous, but not excessively so. Screwcap. 12° alc.
Rating 90 **To** 2014 $15

ŶŶŶŶ   Hunter Valley Verdelho 2007 Classic Hunter verdelho, with ripe fruit salad,
plus a touch of banana offset by juicy acidity on the finish. Screwcap. 13.5° alc.
Rating 89 **To** 2011 $15

Berrigan Wines

38 Dumfries Road, Floreat, WA 6014 (postal) **Region** Swan District
T (08) 9383 7526 **F** (08) 9383 7516 **www.**berriganwines.com.au **Open** Not
Winemaker Ryan Sudano, Daniel Berrigan **Est.** 1998 **Cases** 500
Berrigan Wines is situated on Creighton Farm, one of the oldest farms in the Swan District,
dating back to 1849. The Berrigan family, headed by Thomas John Berrigan, has planted
verdelho, merlot, shiraz and cabernet sauvignon, and the wines are sold through the website.

♀♀♀♀♀ Creighton Farm Shiraz 2006 Spicy plum and blackberry fruit in abundance;
rich and long, but a little warm on the finish. **Rating** 90 **To** 2013 $15

Berrys Bridge

633 Carapooee Road, Carapooee, Vic 3478 **Region** Pyrenees
T (03) 5496 3220 **F** (03) 8610 1621 **www.**berrysbridge.com.au **Open** W'ends 10.30–4.30,
or by appt
Winemaker Jane Holt **Est.** 1990 **Cases** 1200
While the date of establishment is 1990, Roger Milner purchased the property in 1975. In
the mid-1980s, with Jane Holt, he began the construction of the stone house-cum-winery.
Planting of the existing 7-ha vineyard commenced in 1990, around the time that Jane began
viticulture and oenology studies at CSU. Exports to the US and Switzerland.

♀♀♀♀♀ Pyrenees Shiraz 2005 Massive full-bodied wine, with tannins making a
statement from the first sip, and casting a savoury web over the palate flavours;
hands right off for another 5 years. ProCork. 15° alc. **Rating** 90 **To** 2020 $40

♀♀♀♀ Cabernet Sauvignon Merlot 2005 In vineyard style, of massive proportions
with Stygian black fruits and inevitably powerful tannins. To be fair, not to be
released until Nov '08 and will be long lived, likely to improve with the years.
ProCork. 15° alc. **Rating** 89 **To** 2020 $30

Best's Wines ★★★★★

111 Best's Road, Great Western, Vic 3377 **Region** Great Western
T (03) 5356 2250 **F** (03) 5356 2430 **www.**bestswines.com **Open** Mon–Sat 10–5, Sun
11–4
Winemaker Viv Thomson, Adam Wadewitz **Est.** 1867 **Cases** 22 000
Best's winery and vineyards are among Australia's best-kept secrets. Indeed the vineyards,
with vines dating back to 1867, have secrets which may never be revealed: for example,
certain vines planted in the Nursery Block have defied identification and are thought to
exist nowhere else in the world. The cellars, too, go back to the same era, constructed by
butcher-turned-winemaker Henry Best and his family. Since 1920, the Thomson family has
owned the property, with father Viv and sons Ben, Bart and Marcus representing the fourth
and fifth generations, consistently producing elegant, supple wines which deserve far greater
recognition than they receive. The Bin 0 Shiraz is a classic, the Thomson Family Shiraz
magnificent. Exports to the UK and other major markets.

♀♀♀♀♀ Thomson Family Great Western Shiraz 2005 The depth to this wine speaks
volumes about the quality of fruit; powerful and full of dark fruits, there is an
elegance and poise that draws this wine out to a very long and satisfying finish.
Cork. **Rating** 95 **To** 2020 $120
Bin No. 1 Great Western Shiraz 2005 Super-elegant light- to medium-
bodied wine; black fruits are supported by a fine web of silky tannins and perfectly
judged oak. Screwcap. 14.5° alc. **Rating** 94 **To** 2021 $27

♀♀♀♀♀ Concongella Vineyard Great Western Chardonnay 2005 Tight, restrained
and very youthful citrus bouquet; elements of roasted nuts, and fine, vibrant acidity
on the quite ample and long finish. Screwcap. 13.5° alc. **Rating** 93 **To** 2014 $30
Bin No. 0 Great Western Shiraz 2005 Slightly briny aromas, with rich, ripe
dark fruits beneath; silky texture and fine acid, with just a little toast coming

through on the finish; truly medium–bodied with lively, fine tannin structure. Screwcap. 14.5° alc. **Rating** 93 **To** 2014 $50

Bin No. 1 Great Western Shiraz 2006 Highly aromatic with very good fruit intensity; good texture and weight and abundance of fleshy fruit across the palate; fine and firm on the finish. Screwcap. 14° alc. **Rating** 93 **To** 2018 $30

Concongella Vineyard Great Western Pinot Noir 2006 Firm and savoury, with dark plums and a touch of mint; good flavour and depth; quite bright on the finish. Screwcap. **Rating** 91 **To** 2012 $38

Thirteen Acre Great Western Cabernet Sauvignon 2005 Classic cabernet, with cassis, cedar and a mere hint of mint; very firm and dry on the palate, needs time to fully show its best. Screwcap. 14.5° alc. **Rating** 91 **To** 2016 $30

Chardonnay 2006 Very well crafted; smooth melon, peach and nectarine fruit glides across the tongue, with oak a minor player. Screwcap. 14° alc. **Rating** 90 **To** 2011 $17

♈♈♈♈ **Riesling 2006** Classic slatey, citrus Bouquet; fine acid balance and very good concentration and length; clean and fine on the finish. Screwcap. 12.5° alc. **Rating** 89 **To** 2014 $18

Chardonnay 2007 Aromas of melon, nectarine and a whisp of toast; good flavour, with bright acidity on the finish. Screwcap. 14° alc. **Rating** 89 **To** 2012 $18

Shiraz 2005 Elegant, bright red and black fruits on the light- to medium-bodied palate; Best's third-tier wine, and a pretty good one at that; early drinking. Screwcap. 14.5° alc. **Rating** 89 **To** 2010 $17

Cabernet Merlot 2005 Hints of cassis and redcurrant, with a little mint showing through in the background; clean, fine and focused. Screwcap. 14° alc. **Rating** 88 **To** 2011 $18

Salvation Hills Great Western Merlot 2005 Quite defined red fruits, with a little tomato leaf in the background; quite juicy and certainly ripe, with good acidity and depth. Screwcap. 14.5° alc. **Rating** 87 **To** 2010 $28

Bethany Wines ★★★★☆

Bethany Road, Bethany via Tanunda, SA 5352 **Region** Barossa Valley
T (08) 8563 2086 **F** (08) 8563 0046 **www.**bethany.com.au **Open** Mon–Sat 10–5, Sun 1–5
Winemaker Geoff Schrapel, Robert Schrapel **Est.** 1977 **Cases** 25 000

The Schrapel family has been growing grapes in the Barossa Valley for over 140 years, but the winery has only been in operation since 1977. Nestled high on a hillside on the site of an old quarry, Geoff and Rob Schrapel produce a range of consistently well-made and attractively packaged wines. They have 36 ha of vineyards in the Barossa Valley, 8 ha in the Eden Valley and (recently and interestingly) 2 ha each of chardonnay and cabernet sauvignon on Kangaroo Island. Exports to the UK, the US and other major markets.

♈♈♈♈♈ **Grio Shiraz 2005** Lively and attractive red and dark fruits; excellent concentration and thrust, the tannins fine and in balance, as is the alcohol. Cork. 14.5° alc. **Rating** 95 **To** 2025 $85

♈♈♈♈♉ **Barossa Cabernet Merlot 2005** An attractive wine, with lifted, aromatic cassis fruits; very fine tannins and a long satisfying finish. Cork. 14.5° alc. **Rating** 93 **To** 2016 $29.90

Barossa Shiraz Cabernet 2005 A somewhat developed bouquet, the palate soft and fleshy, and ready to go; hints of cassis frame the supple blackberry fruit. Screwcap. 14° alc. **Rating** 90 **To** 2012 $21

♈♈♈♈ **Barossa Semillon 2006** Glowing yellow–green, very developed; rich and complex, but clogs up on the finish; lees and partial oak more suited to chardonnay, though no shortage of flavour. Screwcap. 11.5° alc. **Rating** 87 **To** 2009 $18

Bettenay's

Cnr Harmans South Road/Miamup Road, Wilyabrup, WA 6284 **Region** Margaret River
T (08) 9755 5539 **F** (08) 9755 5539 **www**.bettenaysmargaretriver.com.au **Open** 7 days 11–5
Winemaker Greg Bettenay, Peter Stanlake (Consultant) **Est.** 1989 **Cases** NA
Greg Bettenay began planting the 11.75 ha of vineyards in 1989 (cabernet sauvignon, chardonnay, shiraz, sauvignon blanc, semillon and merlot). The development now extends to two farm vineyard cottages and a luxury treetop spa apartment known as The Lakeside Loft.

ŢŢŢŢŢ **Margaret River Chardonnay 2006** Has the texture and depth expected of
    Margaret River; stone fruit, with creamy cashew elements, the oak evident but not
    dominant. Screwcap. 14° alc. **Rating** 90 **To** 2012 $32

Bidgeebong Wines

352 Byrnes Road, Wagga Wagga, NSW 2650 **Region** Gundagai
T (02) 6931 9955 **F** (02) 6931 9966 **www**.bidgeebong.com **Open** Mon–Fri 9–4
Winemaker Andrew Birks, Keiran Spencer **Est.** 2000 **Cases** 12 000
Encompasses what the founders refer to as the Bidgeebong triangle – between Young, Wagga Wagga, Tumbarumba and Gundagai – which provides grapes for the Bidgeebong brand. A winery was completed in 2002, and will eventually be capable of handling 2000 tonnes of grapes for Bidgeebong's own needs, and those of other local growers and larger producers who purchase grapes from the region. Exports to the UK, Canada, India, Singapore and China.

ŢŢŢŢ **The Icon Series Chardonnay 2006** Given its Rolls Royce background, it is a
    little disappointing; does have appealing nectarine and citrus fruit, and the French
    oak is appropriate, but doesn't have enough thrust. Screwcap. 13.5° alc. **Rating** 89
    To 2012 $31
    The Icon Series Shiraz 2005 Interesting wine, the savoury Tumbarumba
    component punching above its weight, and the oak still to fully integrate. Gundagai
    (80%)/Tumbarumba (20%). Screwcap. 14.8° alc. **Rating** 89 **To** 2015 $35
    Tumbarumba Merlot 2006 Cool-grown savoury earthy olive overtones to the
    red fruits somewhere in the glass; just another face of Janus aka merlot. Screwcap.
    14° alc. **Rating** 87 **To** 2011 $22
    Gundagai Shiraz 2005 Warm-grown shiraz in traditional mode, with a veneer
    of oak and ripe tannins; laconic Australian style. Screwcap. **Rating** 87 **To** 2014 $22

big shed wines

1289 Malmsbury Road, Glenlyon, Vic 3461 **Region** Macedon Ranges
T (03) 5348 7825 **F** (03) 5348 7825 **www**.bigshedwines.com.au **Open** 7 days,
winter 10–6, summer 10–7
Winemaker Ken Jones **Est.** 1999 **Cases** 1200
Founder and winemaker Ken Jones was formerly a geneticist and molecular biologist at Edinburgh University, and the chemistry of winemaking comes easily. The estate-based wine comes from 2 ha of pinot noir; the other wines are made from purchased grapes grown in various parts of Central Victoria.

ŢŢŢŢŢ **Reserve Shiraz 2005** A big volume of sweet, spicy red and black fruits on the
    medium- to full-bodied palate; ripe tannins add good thrust to the long finish.
    Screwcap. 14.7° alc. **Rating** 93 **To** 2020 $23

ŢŢŢŢ **Semillon 2006** Quite developed toasty/lemony aromas and flavours; a big wine,
    but short finish. Misapplied screwcap. Best Wine Kyneton Wine Show '07. 13.7° alc.
    Rating 89 **To** 2009 $25
    Sparkling Shiraz 2005 Has some complexity; black, spicy fruits with sweetness
    held within bounds, and has some length. Cork. 14.5° alc. **Rating** 87 **To** 2013 $27

Bimbadeen Estate   **NR**

Cnr Bimbadeen Road/Mount View Road, Mount View, NSW 2325 **Region** Lower
Hunter Valley
T (02) 4990 1577 **F** (02) 4991 3689 **www**.bimbadeen.com.au **Open** By appt
Winemaker Mark Davidson **Est.** 2000 **Cases** NA
Bimbadeen Estate has 1.2 ha of semillon, shiraz and verdelho, but is primarily driven by its
six self-contained villas perched high on the side of the Brokenback Range, with panoramic
views out across the Hunter Valley, and which deserve the hyperbole often encountered in
describing ventures of this kind.

Bimbadgen Estate   ★★★★☆

790 McDonalds Road, Pokolbin, NSW 2320 **Region** Lower Hunter Valley
T (02) 4998 7585 **F** (02) 4998 7732 **www**.bimbadgen.com.au **Open** 7 days 10–5
Winemaker Simon Thistlewood, Jane Hoppe **Est.** 1968 **Cases** 50 000
Established as McPherson Wines, then successively Tamalee, Sobels, Parker Wines and now
Bimbadgen, this substantial winery has had what might be politely termed a turbulent history.
It has over 50 ha of estate plantings, mostly with relatively old vines, supplemented by a
separate estate vineyard at Yenda (19 ha) for the lower-priced Ridge series, and purchased
grapes from various premium regions. Exports to all major markets.

ΨΨΨΨΨ **Signature Hunter Valley Semillon 2006** Vibrant colour; a classy semillon, very
powerful and concentrated, but not phenolic; has the structure for a long life (and
higher points still). Screwcap. 11° alc. **Rating** 93 **To** 2021 $40
Signature Hunter Valley Semillon 2007 Fine, tight, lemon fruit bouquet, with
fresh acid hints of dried straw and reasonable length; doesn't excite for the price.
Screwcap. 10.5° alc. **Rating** 91 **To** 2015 $40
Estate Hunter Valley Chardonnay 2007 A rich, ripe and brassy wine, with
yellow peaches and figs on offer; full-flavoured, with plenty of sweet fruit and a
little buttery toast on the finish. Screwcap. 14° alc. **Rating** 90 **To** 2010 $27.95
Art Series Shiraz Viognier 2006 Medium-bodied with fragrant red fruits;
not obviously influenced by the viognier, but quite silky texture is an indicator.
Screwcap. 15° alc. **Rating** 90 **To** 2014 $50
Estate Myall Road Botrytis Semillon 2006 A strong citrus element cuts
through the centre of lively, sweet and luscious fruits; fine, even and fresh on the
finish. Screwcap. 10.5° alc. **Rating** 90 **To** 2014 $26.95

ΨΨΨΨ **Estate Hunter Valley Semillon 2006** A classic Hunter bouquet, but a little
developed for age; dried straw mingled with lemon fruits and quite fine acid; ready
to go now. Screwcap. 11° alc. **Rating** 88 **To** 2010 $19.95
Hunter Valley Verdelho 2007 Well made, and with plenty of varietal fruit salad
flavours; a twist of minerally/lemony acidity rounds it off. Screwcap. 12.5° alc.
Rating 88 **To** 2009 $19.95
Signature Hunter Valley Shiraz 2006 A medium-bodied palate; black cherry,
plum and licorice; still to come out of its vinous nappies, needing 3–4 years
to start to show its true colours. Ambitious price. Screwcap. 14° alc. **Rating** 88
To 2021 $50
Estate Hunter Valley Orange Shiraz 2006 Dark-fruited, briney and slightly
leathery shiraz; very tannic, but lots of fruit to accompany the structure; very dry
on the finish. Screwcap. 14° alc. **Rating** 88 **To** 2014 $23.95
Estate Orange Merlot 2006 Quite leafy on the bouquet, with oak coming
through after; a bit lean and hard on the palate, but a good attempt at making
merlot properly. Screwcap. 15° alc. **Rating** 87 **To** 2011 $23.95
Estate Orange Sangiovese 2005 A light-bodied wine with red fruits and
a little briary note; the high acid and plentiful tannins are true to the variety.
Screwcap. 14.5° alc. **Rating** 87 **To** 2009 $26.95

Bindi Wine Growers ★★★★★

343 Melton Road, Gisborne, Vic 3437 (postal) **Region** Macedon Ranges
T (03) 5428 2564 **F** (03) 5428 2564 **Open** Not
Winemaker Michael Dhillon, Stuart Anderson (Consultant) **Est.** 1988 **Cases** 2000
One of the icons of Macedon. The Chardonnay is top-shelf, the Pinot Noir as remarkable (albeit in a very different idiom) as Bass Phillip, Giaconda or any of the other tiny-production, icon wines. The addition of Heathcote-sourced Shiraz under the Pyrette label confirms Bindi as one of the greatest small producers in Australia. Notwithstanding the tiny production, the wines are exported (in small quantities, of course) to the UK, the US and other major markets.

ᵠᵠᵠᵠᵠ **Quartz Chardonnay 2006** While shares similar complexity to that of Composition, this has far more intensity and precision throughout, with tremendous thrust to the finish and aftertaste; great wine. Diam. 13.5° alc. **Rating** 97 **To** 2017 $70

Block 5 Pinot Noir 2006 The deepest and most profound of the three Bindi Pinots, almost brooding in its intensity, yet the mouthfeel is supple and silky; will thrive for many years to come. Diam. 13.5° alc. **Rating** 96 **To** 2020 $95

Pyrette Heathcote Shiraz 2006 Totally seductive and delicious; smooth, velvety blackberry and plum fruit gains velocity across the palate, the line as precise as it is pure, the oak and tannins perfectly balanced in support. Cork. 14° alc. **Rating** 96 **To** 2021 $40

Extended Lees Aged Sparkling 2000 From low-yielding vines (unusual for sparkling wine), barrel-aged for 6 years on lees, disgorged Jan '08; light, bright gold, the palate has a richness and concentration rarely encountered outside of Champagne, before a low-dosage, high-acid finish rounds off a superb blanc de blancs. 12° alc. **Rating** 96 **To** 2014 $45

Composition Chardonnay 2006 Complex structure and flavour, nectarine and melon playing hide and seek with oak and creamy cashew, the fruit emerging on the minerally finish to strike the final note. Diam. 13.5° alc. **Rating** 95 **To** 2015 $45

Original Vineyard Pinot Noir 2006 Has much greater upfront, delicious, cherry and plum fruit than Composition, albeit with some spicy characters; has vibrant poise, line and length. Diam. 13.5° alc. **Rating** 95 **To** 2016 $70

ᵠᵠᵠᵠᵠ **Composition Pinot Noir 2006** Marginally the lightest colour of the three Bindi Pinots; very fine and distinctly spicy/savoury flavours, dark plum emerging on the long, expanding finish. Diam. 13.5° alc. **Rating** 93 **To** 2013 $50

Bird in Hand ★★★★★

Bird in Hand Road, Woodside, SA 5244 **Region** Adelaide Hills
T (08) 8389 9488 **F** (08) 8389 9511 **www.**birdinhand.com.au **Open** 7 days 11–5
Winemaker Andrew Nugent, Kym Milne, Sam Scott **Est.** 1997 **Cases** 40 000
This very successful wine and olive oil property took its name from a 19th-century gold mine. It is the venture of the Nugent family, headed by Dr Michael Nugent. Son Andrew Nugent is a Roseworthy graduate, and his wife, Susie, manages the olive oil side of the business. The family also has properties on the Fleurieu Peninsula and in the Clare Valley, the latter providing both riesling and shiraz (and olives from 100-year-old wild olive trees). In 2007 a state-of-the-art winery and a straw and mud barrel cellar were completed. Exports to the UK, the US and other major markets.

ᵠᵠᵠᵠᵠ **Mount Lofty Ranges Cabernet Sauvignon 2006** Has intensely focused and precise varietal expression; blackcurrant at the core, supported by positive savoury tannins and correct oak. Screwcap. 14.5° alc. **Rating** 95 **To** 2026 $30

Mount Lofty Ranges Shiraz 2006 Medium-bodied; rich blackberry, licorice and spice fruit; ripe tannins provide good structure; well-integrated French oak. Screwcap. 14.5° alc. **Rating** 94 **To** 2016 $30

Mount Lofty Ranges Merlot 2006 Has more mouthfeel and weight than most merlots without losing varietal expression; a foundation of cassis/redcurrant with glints of black olive and spice. Screwcap. 14.5° alc. **Rating** 94 **To** 2016 $30

ŢŢŢŢŢ **Nest Egg Adelaide Hills Cabernet Sauvignon 2005** A complex wine, with distinct savoury/black olive overtones to the blackcurrant fruit; just a hint of bitterness in an otherwise excellent wine. Cork. 14.5° alc. **Rating** 93 **To** 2015 $60
Honeysuckle Clare Valley Riesling 2007 Full and round, with soft passionfruit/sweet lime flavours, with some autosuggestion of honeysuckle. Intriguing and different. Screwcap. 13.5° alc. **Rating** 92 **To** 2013 $25
Adelaide Hills Chardonnay 2007 Classic, cool region chardonnay with nectarine, grapefruit and melon; the vintage may have nipped away a little of the drive on the finish. Screwcap. 13.5° alc. **Rating** 92 **To** 2013 $25
Joy 2004 Salmon-pink; has the complexity the Sparkling Pinot Noir doesn't have (although the varietal background is the same) with spicy, biscuity edges to the red fruit flavours; serious wine. Cork. 13° alc. **Rating** 92 **To** 2012 $60
Two in the Bush Adelaide Hills Semillon Sauvignon Blanc 2007 A well-balanced, flavoursome palate, with a seamlessly married mix of herb, grass and tropical flavours; good length. 12° alc. **Rating** 91 **To** 2010 $20
Adelaide Hills Sauvignon Blanc 2007 A gooseberry, asparagus and tropical mix in a light frame; finishes with lemony, minerally acidity; clean, dry and crisp. Screwcap. 12.5° alc. **Rating** 90 **To** 2010 $25

ŢŢŢŢ **Two in the Bush Adelaide Hills Chardonnay 2007** A direct, fruit-driven style, with ripe peachy fruit and some offsetting lemony acidity. Screwcap. 13.5° alc. **Rating** 89 **To** 2011 $20
Adelaide Hills Sparkling Pinot Noir 2007 Pale-pink blush; delicate, but near-perfect balance; offers strawberries with a twist of lemon, then a clear finish; a simple but delicious aperitif style. Diam. 12° alc. **Rating** 89 **To** 2009 $25
Adelaide Hills Pinot Noir Rose 2007 Pale, bright pink; fresh, crisp and lively strawberry flavours; light-bodied, but has good balance and line. Screwcap. 12.5° alc. **Rating** 88 **To** 2009 $20
Two in the Bush Adelaide Hills Mount Lofty Ranges Shiraz 2006 The colour lacks the vibrancy of the Bird in Hand Shiraz, as does the fruit flavour, although the length is there on a savoury, slightly green, finish, Screwcap. 14° alc. **Rating** 87 **To** 2010 $20

Birdwood Estate   NR

Mannum Road, Birdwood, SA 5234 (postal) **Region** Adelaide Hills
T (08) 8263 0986 **F** (08) 8263 0986 **Open** Not
Winemaker Oli Cucchiarelli **Est.** 1990 **Cases** 700
Birdwood Estate draws upon 7 ha of estate vineyards progressively established since 1990. The quality of the white wines has generally been good. The tiny production is principally sold through retail in Adelaide.

Biscay Wines

Lot 567 Barossa Valley Highway, Tanunda, SA 5352 **Region** Barossa Valley
T (08) 8563 0297 **F** (08) 8563 0187 **Open** By appt
Winemaker John Hongell, Trevor Hongell **Est.** 1998 **Cases** 1000
While John and Carolyn Hongell are the owners, this is very much a family business. Son Trevor is vineyard manager and budding winemaker; daughter-in-law Daniela is in charge of sales and marketing; and the Hongells' three other children, Geoff, Ian and Jenny, provide their support for the vineyard. In his various previous lives, John Hongell was a brewer, then production director for Dalgety Wines, and then manager of Saltram. Long experience in the industry taught him that sales were far better pulled by demand than pushed by supply, and, despite significant sales in the US and Canada, production has been deliberately restricted during the establishment phase.

ŸŸŸŸŸ **John Hongell Old Vine Barossa Valley Grenache Shiraz 2006** Two-thirds
60-year-old grenache which drives the tangy, fruit bouquet; has more savoury grip
to the palate than is common in the Barossa Valley, giving the wine distinction.
Screwcap. 15° alc. **Rating** 91 **To** 2014 $19
John Hongell Barossa Valley Shiraz 2005 Distinctly savoury, spicy, bitter
chocolate edges to the blackberry fruit all giving good texture and balance; good
drier style. Screwcap. 14.5° alc. **Rating** 90 **To** 2015 $20

ŸŸŸŸ **John Hongell Barossa Valley Shiraz Viognier 2005** Moderately fragrant;
it's not clear whether viognier co-fermented or simply blended, but the wine is
supple and smooth. Screwcap. 15° alc. **Rating** 89 **To** 2015 $35

Bishops Vineyard ★★★☆

86 Acton Road, Acton Park, Tas 7170 (postal) **Region** Southern Tasmania
T (03) 6248 7342 **F** (03) 6248 7342 **www.**bishopsvineyard.com.au **Open** Not
Winemaker Julian Alcorso (Contract) **Est.** 1999 **Cases** 350
Phillip and Maree Bishop planted the first vines on their property in 1999, keeping things
under control with 0.5 ha of each of chardonnay and pinot noir. The property overlooks
Frederick Henry Bay and Ralph's Bay, a 15-min drive from Hobart. Skilled contract wine-
making has paid rewards, and a cellar door is planned to open in 2008.

ŸŸŸŸ **Chardonnay 2007** Very much in the vineyard style; white and yellow peach fruit
in a soft, rounded profile; rapidly developing. **Rating** 89 **To** 2010 $25
Pinot Noir 2006 Clear and bright colour with some development showing;
highly fragrant cherry and plum on entry, then a distinct savoury twist on the
finish; broken line. **Rating** 89 **To** 2011 $26

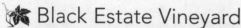 # Black Estate Vineyard ★★★

Patons Road, Axe Creek, Vic 3551 **Region** Bendigo
T (03) 5442 8048 **F** (03) 5442 8048 **www.**blackestate.com.au **Open** By appt
Winemaker Greg Dedman (Contract) **Est.** 1999 **Cases** 250
Robert and Leanne Black purchased their 8-ha property in 1997; it was part of a larger block
which in the latter part of the 19th century was home to the then-renowned 14-ha Hercynia
Vineyard. They completed planting of their 1-ha shiraz vineyard in the spring of 1999, and
the 2004 Black Estate Shiraz was their third commercial vintage.

ŸŸŸŸ **Shiraz 2005** Very ripe fruit characters run throughout the wine; prunes and dried
fruits, with rustic tannins and warmth from the alcohol. Better picked earlier.
Screwcap. 15° alc. **Rating** 88 **To** 2013 $20

Blackbilly Wines ★★★★

Kangarilla Road, McLaren Vale, SA 5171 **Region** McLaren Vale
T 0419 383 907 **F** (08) 8323 9747 **www.**blackbilly.com **Open** By appt
Winemaker Nick Haselgrove, Warren Randall **Est.** 2003 **Cases** 7500
Blackbilly has emerged from the numerous changes in the various Haselgrove wine interests.
These days the people behind Blackbilly are Nick Haselgrove, Warren Randall, Warren Ward
and Andrew Fletcher. Blackbilly is able to access the 400 ha of vines owned by Tinlins, along
with smaller suppliers in McLaren Vale. Exports to all major markets.

ŸŸŸŸŸ **McLaren Vale Shiraz 2006** Dense colour; full-bodied and rich, but supple;
blackberry fruit with the regional subtext of dark chocolate; ripe, soft tannins.
Screwcap. 14.5° alc. **Rating** 93 **To** 2021 $21.95
McLaren Vale Grenache Shiraz Mourvedre 2006 A fractionally reduced
bouquet; has textural and structural interest; spicy earthy verging on peppery notes
to the core of red and black fruits. Screwcap. 14.5° alc. **Rating** 90 **To** 2013 $21.95

🍷🍷🍷🍷 **Adelaide Hills Sauvignon Blanc 2007** Clean, fresh mineral and grass aromas; lively flavours, introducing citrus and asparagus; good for the vintage. Screwcap. 12° alc. **Rating** 89 **To** 2009 $17.95
Adelaide Hills Chardonnay 2007 A somewhat oaky but complex bouquet, then a strongly worked palate, with some nutty mlf characters, and again oaky. Screwcap. 13° alc. **Rating** 87 **To** 2009 $17.95
Adelaide Hills Pinot Gris 2007 Lemony acidity adds to the length, though not so much to varietal character; however, the wine is clean and dry, with enough depth for food. Screwcap. 13.5° alc. **Rating** 87 **To** 2009 $21.95
McLaren Vale Sparkling Shiraz NV A clear varietal shiraz base and perfectly judged dosage (sweetness) for wide appeal. **Rating** 87 **To** 2011 $29.95

Blackboy Ridge Estate   ★★★☆
PO Box 554, Donnybrook, WA 6239 **Region** Geographe
T (08) 9731 2233 **F** (08) 9731 2233 **www.**blackboyridge.com.au **Open** By appt
Winemaker David Crawford (Contract) **Est.** 1978 **Cases** 1000
The 22-ha property on which Blackboy Ridge Estate is established was partly cleared and planted to 2.5 ha of semillon, chenin blanc, shiraz and cabernet sauvignon in 1978. When current owners Adrian Jones and Jackie Barton purchased the property in 2000 the vines were already some of the oldest in the region. The vineyard and the owners' house is on gentle north-facing slopes, with extensive views over the Donnybrook area. A cellar door is planned for late 2008.

🍷🍷🍷🍷 **Geographe Rose 2007** Interesting rose; while low alcohol, has more texture than many without compromising the red fruits from the cabernet and shiraz grapes. Screwcap. 12.5° alc. **Rating** 87 **To** 2009 $14

Blackets/TK Wines   ★★★★☆
PO Box 5405, Sydney, NSW 2001 **Region** Adelaide Hills
T (02) 9232 5714 **F** (02) 9231 6660 **www.**blackets.com.au **Open** Not
Winemaker Tim Knappstein (Contract) **Est.** 2007 **Cases** 3800
Sydney barrister Paul Blacket and wife Christine purchased the Lenswood Vineyard from Tim and Annie Knappstein in 2004. Planting of the 25.5 ha of chardonnay, sauvignon blanc, semillon, gewurztraminer and pinot noir had begun in 1981 and continued through to 2005, and has been under the care of the same vineyard manager for the past 20 years. The Blackets also acquire pinot noir and shiraz from a neighbouring high-altitude Adelaide Hills vineyard, with an Eden Valley Riesling in the planning pipeline, plus shiraz and cabernet partly owned by them with members of the Kilikanoon group and others. TK Wines is also owned by Paul Blacket; production is now focused solely on the Lenswood vineyards.

🍷🍷🍷🍷🍷 **Blackets Adelaide Hills Gewurztraminer 2007** Pronounced spice, lychee and rose petal aromas; a fairly full-bodied, rich and powerful palate has overtones of Alsace; a striking wine. Screwcap. 13.5° alc. **Rating** 92 **To** 2012 $20
Blackets Isabella Adelaide Hills Chardonnay 2007 Classy nectarine and grapefruit aroma and flavour, with a framework of integrated French oak; 25-year-old vines. Screwcap. 14° alc. **Rating** 92 **To** 2013 $26
Blackets Adelaide Hills Sauvignon Blanc 2007 Curiously, has less pronounced varietal character than the Gewurztraminer; gooseberry and grass, plus a touch of passionfruit on a nicely balanced palate. Screwcap. 13.5° alc. **Rating** 90 **To** 2010 $20
TK Wines Adelaide Hills Sauvignon Blanc 2007 While squarely in the herbal spectrum, with grass, snow pea and asparagus, has good mouthfeel and length. Screwcap. 12.5° alc. **Rating** 90 **To** 2009 $19.95

BlackJack Vineyards ★★★★★

Cnr Blackjack Road/Calder Highway, Harcourt, Vic 3453 **Region** Bendigo
T (03) 5474 2355 **F** (03) 5474 2355 **www.**blackjackwines.com.au **Open** W'ends &
public hols 11–5
Winemaker Ian McKenzie, Ken Pollock **Est.** 1987 **Cases** 2500
Established by the McKenzie and Pollock families on the site of an old apple and pear
orchard in the Harcourt Valley and is best known for some very good Shirazs. Ian McKenzie,
incidentally, is not to be confused with Ian McKenzie formerly of Seppelt (Great Western). A
welcome return to top form. Exports to NZ.

ŶŶŶŶŶ   **Block 6 Bendigo Shiraz 2005** Slightly more plush and lush than the Bendigo
Shiraz, also veering more to blackberry/black fruits; fine tannins and good oak.
Screwcap. 14.5° alc. **Rating** 95 **To** 2022 $35
Bendigo Shiraz 2005 Very good structure, texture and balance, back to best
BlackJack form; black and red fruit components plus a dash of spice, and silky
tannins. Screwcap. 14.5° alc. **Rating** 94 **To** 2018 $35
Major's Line Bendigo Shiraz 2005 Intense aromas and flavours of blackberry,
plum, licorice and spice running through the medium-bodied palate; oak and
tannins give precise support. Screwcap. 14.5° alc. **Rating** 94 **To** 2020 $25

ŶŶŶŶ   **Chortle's Edge Bendigo Shiraz 2005** Light- to medium-bodied in a pleasing
fruit-forward style; a firm finish suggests a couple of years in the cellar will be
worthwhile. Screwcap. 14.5° alc. **Rating** 89 **To** 2012 $18
Bendigo Cabernet Merlot 2005 A fine mix of cassis and olive with a slightly
sweet and sour underlay, but does have length and structure. Screwcap. 14.5° alc.
Rating 88 **To** 2015 $25

Blackwood Crest Wines ★★★★☆

RMB 404A, Boyup Brook, WA 6244 **Region** Blackwood Valley
T (08) 9767 3029 **F** (08) 9767 3029 **Open** By appt 10–5
Winemaker Max Fairbrass **Est.** 1976 **Cases** 3000
Blackwood Crest has been holding a low profile while developing its 8-ha vineyards and a
100-tonne winery. It has been a 30-year project, and progresses as time allows, fitting that Max
Fairbrass's grandparents took up the property as virgin bush in 1908.

ŶŶŶŶ   **Late Harvest Botrytis Riesling 2007** Low level of botrytis, but has some
nuances to lift the wine; citrus and a hint of sweetness. Screwcap. 12.5° alc.
Rating 87 **To** 2010 $19

Blamires Butterfly Crossing ★★★

410 Harcourt Road, Sutton Grange, Vic 3448 **Region** Bendigo
T (03) 5474 2567 **www.**butterflycrossing.com.au **Open** W'ends & public hols 11–5,
or by appt
Winemaker Bill Blamires **Est.** 2001 **Cases** 1000
Bill and Sandra Blamires acquired their property after a two-year search of the southern
Bendigo area for what they considered to be an ideal location. They have firmly planted their
faith in shiraz (6 ha) with merlot, cabernet sauvignon, chardonnay and viognier contributing
another 0.5 ha. The vineyard is bisected by Axe Creek, and the butterflies that frequent the
creek (in the absence of drought) are the source of the name for the property.

ŶŶŶŶ   **Shiraz 2006** Lively light- to medium-bodied palate, with an array of spicy black
fruits balanced tannins and good length. Screwcap. 14.3° alc. **Rating** 89 **To** 2015
$16.50
Cabernet Shiraz 2006 A substantial wine, even if a little rustic, with strong black
fruits and a note of briar plus tannins for the longer haul. Screwcap. 14.3° alc.
Rating 88 **To** 2014 $16.50

Blanche Barkly Wines ★★★★

14 Kingower-Brenanah Road, Kingower, Vic 3517 **Region** Bendigo
T (03) 5438 8223 **www.**bendigowine.org.au **Open** W'ends & public hols 10–5 or by appt
Winemaker David Reimers, Arleen Reimers **Est.** 1972 **Cases** 500
The Reimers are happy with their relatively low profile; yields from the 30+-year-old, dry-grown vines are low, and the quality of the wines is reward in itself. Limited availability makes the mailing list the best way of securing the wines.

♥♥♥♥♡ **Johann Bendigo Cabernet Sauvignon 2004** Good concentration of dark fruit; quite pure and focused, with good line through to the ample finish. Cork. 13.2° alc. **Rating** 91 **To** 2016

Bleasdale Vineyards ★★★★☆

Wellington Road, Langhorne Creek, SA 5255 **Region** Langhorne Creek
T (08) 8537 3001 **F** (08) 8537 3224 **www.**bleasdale.com.au **Open** Mon–Sun 10–5
Winemaker Michael Potts, Paul Hotker **Est.** 1850 **Cases** 100 000
One of the most historic wineries in Australia, drawing upon 63.5 ha of vineyards that are flooded every winter by diversion of the Bremer River, which provides moisture throughout the dry, cool growing season. The wines offer excellent value for money, all showing that particular softness which is the hallmark of the Langhorne Creek region. Exports to all major markets.

♥♥♥♥♥ **Bremerview Langhorne Creek Shiraz 2005** An interesting wine; distinct spice, and an elegant fruit-tannin interplay, all more cool climate than warm characters; caresses the mouth; very good finish. Diam. 14.5° alc. **Rating** 94 **To** 2018 $16.50

♥♥♥♥♡ **Frank Potts 2005** A clean, clear-cut array of red and black fruits; balanced tannins and oak run through a long finish. Cork. 14.5° alc. **Rating** 91 **To** 2015 $28
Langhorne Creek Malbec 2004 Typical strong colour, retaining hue; sweet, juicy, dark berry varietal fruit has good length; excellent example of a 100% Malbec. Cork. 14.5° alc. **Rating** 91 **To** 2014 $13.50
Mulberry Tree Cabernet Sauvignon 2004 Great colour; strong varietal expression of blackcurrant, mint and cassis; firm but ripe tannins. Great value. Cork. 14.5° alc. **Rating** 90 **To** 2014 $16.50

♥♥♥♥ **Langhorne Creek Shiraz Cabernet Sauvignon 2005** Light- to medium-bodied; clean and fresh red and black cherry fruit, fine tannins and good length; great value. Screwcap. 14.5° alc. **Rating** 89 **To** 2015 $13.50
Langhorne Creek Malbec 2005 Brightly coloured and highly perfumed; just a little spice, with black olive and redcurrant on the palate. Screwcap. 14.5° alc. **Rating** 89 **To** 2012 $13.50
Langhorne Creek Shiraz Cabernet Sauvignon 2004 Light- to medium-bodied; a savoury, spicy mix of flavours give the wine an edge; a balanced and precise finish. Screwcap. 14° alc. **Rating** 88 **To** 2014 $13.50
The Wise One Wood Matured Tawny NV Youthful red; abundant raisin fruit and soft acid; good balance. Cork. 18° alc. **Rating** 88 **To** 2009 $15
Langhorne Creek Verdelho 2007 Quite firm, with citrus and mineral more to the fore than is fruit salad; does have length. Screwcap. 13° alc. **Rating** 87 **To** 2012 $13.50
Mulberry Tree Cabernet Sauvignon 2005 A soft, light- to medium-bodied palate; black fruits plus touches of mocha and coffee; minimal tannins. Screwcap. 14° alc. **Rating** 87 **To** 2012 $16.50

Blickling Estate   ★★★★★

Green Valley Road, Bendemeer, NSW 2355 **Region** New England
T (02) 6769 6786 **F** (02) 6769 6740 **www.**blickling.com.au **Open** 7 days 9–5
Winemaker First Creek Wines **Est.** 1999 **Cases** 7000
Rolf Blickling has established his 10-ha vineyard, planted to riesling, chardonnay, sauvignon blanc, pinot noir, cabernet sauvignon and shiraz, at an elevation of 950 m. Frosts in spring and April underline how cool the climate is, necessitating careful site selection. The cellar door also operates a lavender and eucalyptus oil distillery. This is the leader of the pack in New England, perhaps in part due to skilled contract winemaking in the Hunter Valley.

ΨΨΨΨΨ **Riesling 2006** Attractive wine; abundant mix of citrus and tropical fruit on both bouquet and palate; early developing style. Screwcap. 13.3° alc. **Rating** 94 **To** 2013 $20.50
Wooded Chardonnay 2006 Full green-straw colour, striking; intense nectarine and citrus; fruit foremost, oak in the background; good line and length. **Rating** 94 **To** 2011 $20

ΨΨΨΨ **Cabernet Sauvignon 2006** Has overcome the challenges of the vintage well; shows cassis, mint, berry and leaf, just a whisker away from full ripeness; well made. Screwcap. 13.5° alc. **Rating** 89 **To** 2014 $26
Shiraz 2005 Bright colour; light- to medium-bodied; attractive juicy red fruits, long, almost citrussy, finish; not 100% ripe. Screwcap. 12.5° alc. **Rating** 88 **To** 2012 $23.50
Unwooded Chardonnay 2006 Bright green-yellow; fresh, tangy, citrussy; a little lean. **Rating** 87 **To** 2009 $18
Reserve Cabernet Sauvignon 2005 Some minty aspects; has elegance; not over-extracted. Screwcap. 14° alc. **Rating** 87 **To** 2010 $40

Blind Man's Bluff Vineyards   ★★★

Lot 15 Bluff Road, Kenilworth, Qld 4574 **Region** Queensland Coastal
T (07) 5472 3168 **F** (07) 5472 3168 **www.**blindmansbluff.com.au **Open** Wed–Sun 10–5
Winemaker Peter Scudamore-Smith (Contract) **Est.** 2001 **Cases** 600
Blind Man's Bluff Vineyards is situated 45 mins from Qld's Sunshine Coast. Noel Evans' dream of establishing a vineyard, when joined by his partner Tricia Toussaint and family members, turned into reality in 2001, when the property was planted to chardonnay, shiraz and verdelho. Various cellar door activities have made the winery a state finalist for tourism.

ΨΨΨΨ **Granite Belt Cabernet Sauvignon 2006** Clear blackcurrant varietal fruit on both bouquet and palate; not so much structure or complexity, but respectable nonetheless. Screwcap. 13.5° alc. **Rating** 89 **To** 2012 $25
Liaisons Chardonnay 2007 Crisp, fresh melon and citrus aromas and flavours all pointing to early picking, and working well; dry finish. Screwcap. 11.5° alc. **Rating** 88 **To** 2009 $28
Sophist Red 2007 A rose in sheep's clothing; interesting alcohol, with sweet notes on the palate and finish (a touch of residual sugar); conceivably reverse osmosis-reduced alcohol; Shiraz. Screwcap. 10° alc. **Rating** 87 **To** 2009 $18

Bloodwood

4 Griffin Road, Orange, NSW 2800 **Region** Orange
T (02) 6362 5631 **F** (02) 6361 1173 **www.**bloodwood.com.au **Open** By appt
Winemaker Stephen Doyle **Est.** 1983 **Cases** 4000
Rhonda and Stephen Doyle are two of the pioneers of the burgeoning Orange district. The wines are sold mainly through the cellar door and by an energetically and informatively run mailing list. Has an impressive track record across the full gamut of varietal (and other) wine styles. Exports to the UK.

ΨΨΨΨΨ **Schubert 2005** Intense, beautifully structured wine, which gradually builds flavour through the length of the palate, with seamless stone fruit and oak; Chardonnay. Screwcap. 14° alc. **Rating** 94 **To** 2015 $25

ΨΨΨΨ♀ **Riesling 2007** A clean bouquet, then a major impact of sweet citrus and tropical fruit in the palate; a touch of residual sugar balanced by acidity. Screwcap. 12.5° alc. **Rating** 90 **To** 2013 $20
Pinot Noir 2006 At the bigger end of the spectrum, but retains varietal character with satsuma plum and spice fruit; good texture and finish. Screwcap. **Rating** 90 **To** 2012 $35

ΨΨΨΨ **Big Men in Tights 2007** Bright fuschia; always more serious than the label suggests ('Caution: may contain traces of nuts'); spicy red fruits, and a balanced, but dry, finish. Screwcap. 13° alc. **Rating** 89 **To** 2009 $15
Chardonnay 2006 Strong barrel ferment inputs on both bouquet and palate frame the stone fruit and melon, but are slightly over the top; may settle down with time. Screwcap. 14° alc. **Rating** 89 **To** 2013 $24
Maurice 2004 Elegant light-bodied wine with strong cedary overtones to the spicy fruits and the palate; fine tannins aid the length. Screwcap. 13.5° alc. **Rating** 89 **To** 2012 $30
Shiraz 2004 Lively, fresh and crisp wine which is developing without haste but which needs no cellaring; savoury spicy flavours do the talking. Screwcap. 14° alc. **Rating** 88 **To** 2011 $24
Cabernet Sauvignon 2004 Light- to medium-bodied; cedary, spicy, leafy, earthy nuances to the cassis blackcurrant fruit; not entirely flavour ripe. Screwcap. 14° alc. **Rating** 88 **To** 2013 $24

Blue Metal Vineyard ★★★★

Lot 18 Compton Park Road, Berrima, NSW 2577 **Region** Southern Highlands
T (02) 4877 1877 **F** (02) 4877 1866 **www**.bluemetalvineyard.com **Open** Thurs–Mon 10–5 or by appt
Winemaker Alison Eisermann **Est.** 1999 **Cases** 1300
The 11-ha Blue Metal Vineyard is situated on part of a cattle station at an elevation of 790 m; the name comes from the rich red soil that overlies the cap of basalt rock. A wide range of grape varieties are planted, including sauvignon blanc, pinot gris, merlot, cabernet sauvignon, sangiovese and petit verdot. The wines have been very competently made. Exports to the UK.

ΨΨΨΨ♀ **Ignis Reserve Cabernet Sauvignon 2006** Has greater concentration than the Signature, still medium-bodied, but with quite velvety cassis and blackcurrant fruit on the mid-palate; good length. Screwcap. 13.5° alc. **Rating** 90 **To** 2016 $45

ΨΨΨΨ **Signature Pinot Gris 2007** A subliminal touch of residual sugar on the back-palate and finish helps the stature and varietal flavour of the wine; will satisfy pinot gris devotees. Screwcap. 13° alc. **Rating** 88 **To** 2009 $25
Ignis Reserve Merlot 2006 Has unexpectedly ripe fruit flavours which are not particularly varietal, curious given the cool region and modest alcohol; not easy to unravel the threads here. Screwcap. 13.5° alc. **Rating** 88 **To** 2014 $45
Signature Cabernet Sauvignon 2006 Surprisingly ripe fruit flavours ranging from cassis into plum and mulberry, then a twist of corrected acidity on the finish. Screwcap. 13.5° alc. **Rating** 88 **To** 2012 $25

Blue Poles Vineyard

PO Box 34, Mount Lawley, WA 6929 **Region** Margaret River
T 0408 096 411 **F** (08) 9370 5354 **www**.bluepolesvineyard.com.au **Open** Not
Winemaker Vasse River Wines (Sharna Kowalczuk) **Est.** 2001 **Cases** 400
Geologists Mark Gifford and Tim Markwell formed a joint venture to locate and develop Blue Poles Vineyard. Their search was unhurried, and contact with the University of Bordeaux

(supplemented by extensive reading of technical literature) showed that a portion of the property included a block that mimicked some of the best vineyards in St Emilion and Pomerol, leading to the planting of merlot and cabernet franc in 2001. Further soil mapping and topography also identified blocks best suited to shiraz and Rhône Valley white varietals, which were planted in '03. The vineyard maintenance has proceeded with minimal irrigation, and no fertilisers.

🍷🍷🍷🍷 **Margaret River Viognier 2007** Very lively and tangy, entirely fruit-driven, with plenty of flavour, but would the real viognier please stand up. Screwcap. 14° alc. **Rating** 87 **To** 2011 $20

Blue Pyrenees Estate ★★★★

Vinoca Road, Avoca, Vic 3467 **Region** Pyrenees
T (03) 5465 1111 **F** (03) 5465 3529 **www**.bluepyrenees.com.au **Open** Mon–Fri 10–4.30, w'ends & public hols 10–5
Winemaker Andrew Koerner, Chris Smales **Est.** 1963 **Cases** 50 000

Forty years after Remy Cointreau established Blue Pyrenees Estate (then known as Chateau Remy), it sold the business to a small group of Sydney businessmen led by John Ellis (no relation to John Ellis of Hanging Rock). Former Rosemount senior winemaker Andrew Koerner heads the winery team. The core of the business is the 180-ha estate vineyard, much of it fully mature. Exports to all major markets.

🍷🍷🍷🍷½ **Midnight Cuvee 2001** Presumably a long period on yeast lees, but fine citrus/nectarine/lemon flavours drive the long, lingering palate; impressive. Cork. 11.5° alc. **Rating** 92 **To** 2011 $32

🍷🍷🍷🍷 **Reserve Shiraz Viognier 2004** Medium-bodied; more savoury and earthy than most shiraz viognier blends, with a strong spicy background. Cork. **Rating** 89 **To** 2012 $34

Vintage Brut 2004 Fresh citrus rind flavours with brisk acidity and good length; aperitif style; Chardonnay/Pinot Noir/Pinot Meunier. Cork. 12° alc. **Rating** 89 **To** 2012 $24

Methode Traditionelle Brut Rose 2001 Small red fruits centred around strawberry; low dosage and brisk acidity; chilled aperitif style. Whole bunch-pressed estate-grown pinot noir. Cork. 11.5° alc. **Rating** 88 **To** 2009 $24

Blue Wren ★★★

433 Cassilis Road, Mudgee, NSW 2850 **Region** Mudgee
T (02) 6372 6202 **F** (02) 6372 6206 **www**.bluewrenwines.com.au **Open** 7 days 10.30–4.30
Winemaker Frank Newman **Est.** 1998 **Cases** 4000

Roy Hofmeier and Vikki Williams purchased Blue Wren from the Anderson family in 2005. They have now combined the Bombira Vineyard with the former Augustine vineyards purchased in 2007, with a total of 10.3 ha of shiraz, 9.2 ha of cabernet sauvignon, 2.4 ha of gewurztraminer, 2.2 ha of chardonnay, and lesser amounts of pinot noir, verdelho and gewurztraminer. Production has risen accordingly.

Blue Yabby Estate ★★★

PO Box 45, Gol Gol, NSW 2738 **Region** Murray Darling
T (03) 5024 8502 **F** (03) 5024 8551 **www**.sunraysianurseries.com.au **Open** Not
Winemaker Glen Olsen (Contract) **Est.** 2004 **Cases** 250

Corey and Belinda Jessup have spent a lifetime in the wine industry. In 2004, after 14 years with the company, they entered into a management buy-out with the owners of Sunraysia Nurseries, Peter and Lois Smith. Sunraysia is one of the largest growers of vines, citrus trees, avocados, olives, pistachio and pomegranate trees in Australia. It seemed no more than sensible to vertically integrate the business by establishing 36 ha of the main varieties; most of the grapes are contracted to a large, local winery, with just enough retained to take winemaking beyond the hobby stage, with a local contract winemaker presiding. The Blue Yabby name has a great story which space prevents me from telling.

ΨΨΨΨ **Adversity Shiraz 2006** Good colour; plenty of plum and blackberry fruit, with spicy tannins on the finish; copes well with 18 months in American oak. Screwcap. 14.8° alc. **Rating** 89 **To** 2012 $20

Bluestone Acres Vineyard

PO Box 206, Wandin North, Vic 3139 **Region** Yarra Valley
T (03) 5964 4909 **F** (03) 5964 3936 **www**.bluestoneacres.com.au **Open** Not
Winemaker Paul Evans **Est.** 2000 **Cases** 700
Graeme and Isabel Ross have 1.2 ha of merlot, 1.15 ha of shiraz and 1 ha of sauvignon blanc on a north-facing slope. The soil is predominantly grey loam in the merlot and shiraz blocks, with a vein of volcanic red clay loam running through part of the shiraz and most of the sauvignon blanc block; a vein of basalt adds spice to the salt of the sauvignon blanc. Integrated pest management is used in the vineyard (no insecticides) and sprays are held to a minimum.

Boat O'Craigo ★★★☆

458 Maroondah Highway, Healesville, Vic 3777 **Region** Yarra Valley
T (03) 5962 6899 **F** (03) 5962 5140 **www**.boatocraigo.com.au **Open** Thurs–Mon 10.30–5.30
Winemaker Al Fencaros, The YarraHill (Contract) **Est.** 1998 **Cases** 3500
Steve Graham purchased the property which is now known as Boat O'Craigo (a tiny place in a Scottish valley where his ancestors lived) in 2003. It has two quite separate vineyards: a 12-ha hillside planting on one of the highest sites in the Yarra Valley, and 7.5 ha at Kangaroo Ground on the opposite side of the valley. Exports to China and Hong Kong.

ΨΨΨΨ **Rob Roy Yarra Valley Pinot Noir 2006** Light- to medium-bodied; savoury/ foresty characters throughout; has length, but needs more fleshy fruit on the mid-palate. Screwcap. 13.3° alc. **Rating** 88 **To** 2010 $24
Black Spur Yarra Valley Sauvignon Blanc 2007 Overall, in a grassy/herbal spectrum, with good balance and length, albeit without setting the pulse racing. Screwcap. 12.5° alc. **Rating** 87 **To** 2009 $18
Black Spur Yarra Valley Chardonnay 2006 Light-bodied; clean, fresh melon and nectarine fruit; 30% barrel ferment component barely visible; fair length. Screwcap. 13° alc. **Rating** 87 **To** 2010 $20

Bochara Wines

1099 Glenelg Highway, Hamilton, Vic 3300 **Region** Henty
T (03) 5571 9309 **F** (03) 5571 9309 **www**.bocharawine.com.au **Open** Fri–Sun 11–5, or by appt
Winemaker Martin Slocombe **Est.** 1998 **Cases** 1000
This is the small business of experienced winemaker Martin Slocombe and former Yalumba viticulturist Kylie McIntyre. They have established 1 ha each of pinot noir and sauvignon blanc, 1.6 ha of shiraz and cabernet sauvignon, and 0.5 ha of pinot meunier, supplemented by grapes purchased from local growers. The modestly priced but well-made wines are principally sold through the cellar door sales cottage on the property, which has been transformed from a decrepit weatherboard shanty with one cold tap to a fully functional two-room tasting area, and through a number of local restaurants and bottle shops. The label design, incidentally, comes from a 1901 poster advertising the subdivision of the original Bochara property into smaller farms.

ΨΨΨΨΨ **Pinot Noir 2006** Vivid crimson, almost magenta; intense plum and cherry varietal fruit, which shows no sign of overripeness; lovely savoury twist on the finish; cellar special. Screwcap. 14.8° alc. **Rating** 94 **To** 2015 $28

ΨΨΨΨΨ **Arcadia Brut Cuvee Blanc de Noir 2004** Spicy, lively bone-dry style, with attractive texture; overall, complex and satisfying in an elegant mode. Cork. 12° alc. **Rating** 90 **To** 2014 $29

♥♥♥♥   Melville Forest Cabernet Sauvignon 2004 Strong earth and cedar overtones to the medium-bodied black fruits; overall, correct but slightly austere. Screwcap. 14.5° alc. **Rating** 89 **To** 2012 $28

Boggy Creek Vineyards   ★★★☆

1657 Boggy Creek Road, Myrrhee, Vic 3732 **Region** King Valley
T (03) 5729 7587 **F** (03) 5729 7600 **www.**boggycreek.com.au **Open** 7 days 10–5
Winemaker Graeme Ray **Est.** 1978 **Cases** 10 000
Graeme and Maggie Ray started their vineyard in 1978, planting small quantities of riesling and chardonnay. Since then the vineyard has grown to over 40 ha with the addition of cabernet sauvignon, shiraz, barbera, pinot gris and other experimental lots. It is situated on northeast-facing slopes at an altitude of 350 m, with warm summer days and cool nights. Exports to the US, Canada, China, Hong Kong and Singapore.

♥♥♥♥   King Valley Shiraz 2005 Light- to medium-bodied, with a pleasing range of spice, licorice and black fruits; fine tannins to close. Screwcap. **Rating** 89 **To** 2013 $22
King Valley Pinot Gris 2005 Fragrant pear aromas and flavours, showing no signs of collapsing; pure varietal rendition. Screwcap. 13.5° alc. **Rating** 88 **To** 2010 $26

Bogong Estate   NR

Cnr Mountain Creek Road/Damms Road, Mt Beauty, Vic 3699 **Region** Alpine Valleys
T 0419 567 588 **F** (03) 5754 1320 **www.**pinotnoir.com.au **Open** 7 days 11–5
Winemaker Bill Tynan, Kate Tynan **Est.** 1997 **Cases** 4500
Bill Tynan and family began the establishment of their 10-ha pinot noir vineyard a decade ago and have been relentless pursuers of different techniques, wine styles and labels. The zany nature of some of this should not hide the fact that the Tynans are totally committed to their production of pinot noir in a number of guises. They have four clones (D5V12, MV6, 114 and 115) grown in separate blocks with differing soil and site climate characteristics. Wild/ indigenous yeasts are used in 1-tonne open fermenters, then basket-pressed. Wine styles (in the glass) tend to challenge conventional taste wisdom.

Boireann   ★★★★★

26 Donnellys Castle Road, The Summit, Qld 4377 **Region** Granite Belt
T (07) 4683 2194 **www.**boireannwinery.com.au **Open** 7 days 10–4.30
Winemaker Peter Stark **Est.** 1998 **Cases** 900
Peter and Therese Stark have a 10-ha property set amongst the great granite boulders and trees which are so much a part of the Granite Belt. They have established 1.5 ha of vines planted to no fewer than 11 varieties, including the four Bordeaux varieties which go to make a Bordeaux-blend; shiraz and viognier; grenache and mourvedre providing a Rhône blend, and there will also be a straight merlot. Tannat (French) and barbera and nebbiolo (Italian) make up the viticultural League of Nations. Peter Stark is a winemaker of exceptional talent, producing cameo amounts of red wines which are quite beautifully made and of a quality equal to Australia's best. The loss of the 2007 crop to frost was a devastating blow, but Boireann will surely bounce back to its best in '08, albeit with only 75% of a normal crop.

♥♥♥♥♥   Granite Belt Shiraz Viognier 2006 Vivid crimson-purple; as ever, superb winemaking and attention to detail; layers of vibrant fruit with viognier lift, and tannins built for a long life. Will flourish for decades; 650 bottles. Diam. 13.8° alc. **Rating** 95 **To** 2026 $50
Granite Belt Mourvedre Shiraz Grenache 2006 A voluminous, lifted bouquet; an intense palate, almost pungent, with a Joseph's Coat of dark fruit and spice flavours; superfine tannins; Mourvedre (40%)/Shiraz (30%)/Grenache (20%)/ Tannat (10%); 1000 bottles. Diam. 13.8° alc. **Rating** 94 **To** 2020 $27

The Lurnea Granite Belt Merlot Cabernet Franc Petit Verdot 2006
Strong purple-crimson; a powerful wine, with considerable personality and velocity; a pulsing array of blackcurrant and cassis fruit, the tannins fine but persistent; 900 bottles. Diam. 13.5° alc. **Rating** 94 **To** 2015 $27

ҮҮҮҮҮ **Granite Belt Cabernet Sauvignon 2006** Very pure and clear expression of varietal fruit on the mid-palate in a cassis spectrum, then authoritative tannins on the finish; 900 bottles. Diam. 13.8° alc. **Rating** 93 **To** 2016 $22
Granite Belt Merlot 2006 A substantial wine with plenty of plum and blackcurrant fruit, likewise tannins; very well made, though doesn't have distinctive varietal character; 760 bottles. Diam. 13.3° alc. **Rating** 91 **To** 2015 $24
Granite Belt Shiraz Cabernet Sauvignon 2007 Spicy, rich and bright; plenty of tannin and fruit, with good flavour; needs time. Cork. 13..5° alc. **Rating** 90 **To** 2016 $20
Granite Belt Grenache Mourvedre 2006 Light, bright hue; distinctly savoury, the mourvedre making a major statement, though there is a skein of bright red juicy fruit running throughout. Diam. 13.5° alc. **Rating** 90 **To** 2013 $15

ҮҮҮҮ **Granite Belt Rose 2007** Very good colour; vibrant fruit flavours of red berry, with pronounced acidity and length. Frost destroyed the whole crop, leaving just 150 litres (200 bottles) of this wine as the sole return for the year. Cabernet Sauvignon/Petit Verdot/Mourvedre. Diam. 13° alc. **Rating** 89 **To** 2009 $20
Granite Belt Barbera 2006 Deep colour; plum, blackberry and multi-spice aromas; very youthful and flavoursome, but lacks the usual finesse and polish of Boireann. Diam. 14° alc. **Rating** 88 **To** 2012 $24

Borambola Wines   ★★★

Sturt Highway, Wagga Wagga, NSW 2650 **Region** Gundagai
T (02) 6928 4210 **F** (02) 6928 4210 **www**.borambola.com **Open** 7 days 11–4 by appt
Winemaker Chris Derrez **Est.** 1995 **Cases** 1000
Borambola Homestead was built in the 1880s, and in the latter part of that century was the centre of a pastoral empire of 1.4 million ha, ownership of which passed to the McMullen family in 1992. It is situated in rolling foothills 25 km east of Wagga Wagga in the Gundagai region. Nine and a half ha of vines surround the homestead (shiraz, cabernet sauvignon and chardonnay).

ҮҮҮҮ **Bunya Bunya Chardonnay 2006** Bright green–straw; fragrant stone fruit aromas track directly through to the well-flavoured palate; drink-me-quick style. Screwcap. 14° alc. **Rating** 88 **To** 2009 $18
Hiraji's Spell Shiraz 2006 Medium- to full-bodied; solid blackberry and plum fruit; rich, soft tannins. Screwcap. 14° alc. **Rating** 88 **To** 2012 $20

Borrodell on the Mount   ★★★★

Lake Canobolas Road, Orange, NSW 2800 **Region** Orange
T (02) 6365 3425 **F** (02) 6365 3588 **www**.borrodell.com.au **Open** 7 days 10–5
Winemaker Chris Derrez, Lucy Maddox, Peter Logan **Est.** 1995 **Cases** 2000
Barry Gartrell and Gaye Stuart-Nairne have planted 5.25 ha of pinot noir, sauvignon blanc, pinot meunier, traminer and chardonnay adjacent to a cherry, plum and heritage apple orchard and truffiere. It is a 10-min drive from Orange, and adjacent to Lake Canobolas, at an altitude of 1000 m. The wines have been consistent medal winners at regional and small winemaker shows.

ҮҮҮҮҮ **Orange Rose 2007** As roses go, pretty delicious; a mix of strawberry, raspberry and a squeeze of lemon; bright, clean finish; great summer drink. Screwcap. **Rating** 90 **To** 2009 $15

ҮҮҮҮ **Orange Sauvignon Blanc 2007** A tight, minerally structure; exclusively in the grass/herb/snow pea/asparagus spectrum, but is not bitter, and has length. Screwcap. 12.2° alc. **Rating** 89 **To** 2010 $22

Winemakers Daughter 1 Orange Gewurztraminer 2007 Good balance and length; surprising it doesn't have far more residual sugar given the alcohol; marginally better than Daughter 2; unusual arrangement – same grapes, different winemakers; this made by Chris Derrez. Screwcap. 7.3° alc. **Rating** 88 **To** 2010 $20
Winemakers Daughter 2 Orange Gewurztraminer 2007 Slightly softer and broader than Daughter 1; some question regarding residual sugar; neither wine shows much varietal fruit, though no fault; winemaker Peter Logan. Screwcap. 7.3° alc. **Rating** 87 **To** 2010 $20

Botobolar ★★★

89 Botobolar Road, Mudgee, NSW 2850 **Region** Mudgee
T (02) 6373 3840 **F** (02) 6373 3789 **www**.botobolar.com **Open** Mon–Sat 10–5, Sun 10–3
Winemaker Kevin Karstrom **Est.** 1971 **Cases** 3000
One of the first (possibly the first) fully organic vineyards in Australia, with present owner Kevin Karstrom continuing the practices established by founder Gil Wahlquist. Preservative-free reds and low-preservative dry whites extend the organic practice of the vineyard to the winery. Dry Red is consistently the best wine to appear under the Botobolar label, with gold-medal success at the Mudgee Wine Show. Its preservative-free red wines are in the top echelon of this class. Exports to Denmark.

 Preservative Free Dry Red 2007 Bright colour; fresh fruit plus some tannin structure to help protect the wine; admirable; Shiraz/Cabernet Sauvignon. Screwcap. 13.5° alc. **Rating** 89 **To** 2009 $17

Bowen Estate ★★★

Riddoch Highway, Coonawarra, SA 5263 **Region** Coonawarra
T (08) 8737 2229 **F** (08) 8737 2173 **Open** 7 days 10–5
Winemaker Doug Bowen, Emma Bowen **Est.** 1972 **Cases** 12 000
Bluff-faced regional veteran Doug Bowen, now with daughter Emma at his side in the winery, presides over one of Coonawarra's landmarks. For reasons I do not begin to understand, the wines no longer have the edge they once possessed. Exports to the UK, the US, China, Indonesia, Singapore and NZ.

 Coonawarra Chardonnay 2006 Somewhat lean and citrussy on the bouquet and palate; quite grippy on the finish, with an acid cut for freshness. Screwcap. 14° alc. **Rating** 89 **To** 2015 $20.20
Coonawarra Shiraz 2005 Savoury and spicy; gentle red and black fruits, not dominated by oak. Screwcap. 14.5° alc. **Rating** 87 **To** 2012 $29.90

Bowman's Run NR

1305 Beechworth-Wodonga Road, Wooragee, Vic 3747 **Region** Beechworth
T (03) 5728 7318 **Open** Most w'ends & by appt
Winemaker Fran Robertson, Andrew Doyle **Est.** 1989 **Cases** 200
Struan and Fran Robertson have 1 ha of cabernet sauvignon, 0.5 ha of riesling and small plots of shiraz and traminer dating back to 1989. The tiny winery came on-stream in 2000, part of a larger general agricultural holding.

Boynton's Feathertop ★★★★☆

Great Alpine Road, Porepunkah, Vic 3741 **Region** Alpine Valleys
T (03) 5756 2356 **F** (03) 5756 2610 **www**.boynton.com.au **Open** 7 days 10–5
Winemaker Kel Boynton **Est.** 1987 **Cases** 20 000
Kel Boynton has a beautiful 16-ha vineyard, framed by Mt Feathertop rising into the skies above it. Overall, the red wines have always outshone the whites. The initial very strong American oak input has been softened in more recent vintages to give a better fruit/oak balance. The wines are released under the Boynton Reserve and Feathertop labels. The 2007 vintage, blitzed by drought and smoke taint, was a near-impossible challenge.

ΨΨΨΨ   Feathertop Alpine Valleys Merlot 2005 Attractive red berry fruit on the bouquet and entry to the mouth, then savoury tannins on the finish; a wine in two parts, though it is varietal. Screwcap. 13.5° alc. **Rating** 88 **To** 2011 $20
Alpine Valleys Pinot Gris 2007 Pear, apple and citrussy acidity; surprisingly, not smoke-tainted. Screwcap. 13.5° alc. **Rating** 87 **To** 2009 $20

 # Brammar Estate

583 Steels Creek Road, Yarra Glen, Vic 3775 **Region** Yarra Valley
T (03) 5965 2407 **www**.brammarestatewinery.com.au **Open** Sat & public hols 10–5, Sun 11–5
Winemaker Dr Ian Brammar **Est.** 1998 **Cases** 250
Dr Ian Brammar, and wife Phillippa, have a tiny patchwork quilt vineyard planted to sauvignon blanc, semillon, pinot gris, gewurztraminer, chardonnay, verdelho, viognier, pinot noir, shiraz, merlot, cabernet franc and cabernet sauvignon. Given the tiny amounts planted, the blends of pinot gris and gewurztraminer; chardonnay and verdelho; sauvignon blanc and semillon; and merlot, cabernet sauvignon and cabernet franc may not seem so quixotic. They say their aim is to specialise in small batches of red and white wines which are made entirely from estate-grown grapes, hand-picked, and fermented, matured, and bottled on the estate.

Brand's Laira Coonawarra

Riddoch Highway, Coonawarra, SA 5263 **Region** Coonawarra
T (08) 8736 3260 **F** (08) 8736 3208 **www**.mcwilliams.com.au **Open** Mon–Fri 8–5, w'ends 10–4
Winemaker Jim Brayne, Peter Weinberg **Est.** 1966 **Cases** NFP
Part of a substantial investment in Coonawarra by McWilliam's, which first acquired a 50% interest from the Brand family, moved to 100%, and followed this with the purchase of 100 ha of additional vineyard land. Significantly increased production of the smooth wines for which Brand's is known has followed. The estate plantings include the 100-year-old Stentiford block.

ΨΨΨΨΨ   The Patron 2004 Superb colour; exceptionally bright, flavoursome and juicy cassis and blackcurrant fruit, the oak perfectly integrated, the tannins soft; a long and perfectly balanced finish; Cabernet Sauvignon Trophy, National Wine Show '07. **Rating** 96 **To** 2024 $60

ΨΨΨΨΨ   Cabernet Sauvignon 2005 Classic Coonawarra cabernet style, made in a fractionally old-fashioned, unadorned fashion; fragrant berry fruit with notes of tobacco and earth running through to a long finish. Screwcap. 15° alc. **Rating** 92 **To** 2015 $22.95
Chardonnay 2006 Clean, fresh, light- to medium-bodied; has good length and brightness; driven by fruit rather than oak. **Rating** 90 **To** 2010 $19.95
Merlot 2005 Bright colour; a mix of snow pea, spice and redcurrant fruit; appropriate medium-bodied structure; fine tannins on a smooth finish. Screwcap. 15° alc. **Rating** 90 **To** 2013 $22.99
The Patron 2005 Medium-bodied; ripe cassis and blackcurrant fruit, the tannins persistent and a little earthy; does have length and line. **Rating** 90 **To** 2015 $60

ΨΨΨΨ   Shiraz 2005 A typically elegant wine, with length and intensity, even if slightly on the lean side. **Rating** 88 **To** 2015 $22.95

Brandy Creek Wines

570 Buln Buln Road, Drouin East, Vic 3818 **Region** Gippsland
T (03) 5625 4498 **www**.brandycreekwines.com.au **Open** Wed–Sun & public hols 10–5, Fri–Sat nights
Winemaker Peter Beckingham (Contract) **Est.** 2005 **Cases** 1200
Marie McDonald and Rick Stockdale purchased the property on which they have since established their vineyard, cellar door and café restaurant in 1997. One ha each of pinot gris and tempranillo were progressively planted over the '99, 2001 and '02 vintages, with other

varieties purchased from local growers in the region. The café (and surrounding vineyard) is situated on a northeast-facing slope with spectacular views out to the Baw Baw Ranges.

ΥΥΥΥΩ **Longford Vineyard Shiraz 2006** More savoury than the Bairnsdale Vineyard, notwithstanding higher alcohol, although there are also some riper notes and vanilla on the medium-bodied palate. Screwcap. 14.9° alc. **Rating** 90 **To** 2016 $24

ΥΥΥΥ **Bairnsdale Vineyard Shiraz 2006** Good hue; solid, robust medium- to full-bodied black fruits with a touch of licorice; balanced tannins and oak. Screwcap. 14.4° alc. **Rating** 89 **To** 2015 $24
Pinot Noir 2006 Not great, but certainly not bad, with clear varietal fruit expression in a spicy savoury spectrum, and a touch of mint. Screwcap. 13.5° alc. **Rating** 88 **To** 2011 $22
Pinot Gris 2006 Pleasant pear and sweet citrus fruit; has length, and a dry finish. Screwcap. 13.8° alc. **Rating** 87 **To** 2009 $25

Brangayne of Orange ★★★★☆

837 Pinnacle Road, Orange, NSW 2800 **Region** Orange
T (02) 6365 3229 **F** (02) 6365 3170 **www.**brangayne.com **Open** Mon–Fri 11–1, 2–4, Sat 10–5 or by appt
Winemaker Simon Gilbert **Est.** 1994 **Cases** 2500
Orchardists Don and Pamela Hoskins decided to diversify into grapegrowing in 1994 and have progressively established 25.7 ha of high-quality vineyards. Right from the outset, Brangayne has produced high-quality wines across all mainstream varieties, remarkably ranging from Pinot Noir to Cabernet Sauvignon. Exports to the UK, Canada and Spain.

ΥΥΥΥΩ **Cabernet Sauvignon 2005** A complex layered bouquet of cassis and floral notes; dark, dense and quite tannic, with plenty of fruit to soak up the structure. Screwcap. 14.5° alc. **Rating** 92 **To** 2018 $35
Tristan Cabernet Sauvignon Shiraz Merlot 2004 Concentrated and fleshy, with a vibrant core of red fruit coursing through the mid-palate; generous on the finish. Cork. 14.5° alc. **Rating** 91 **To** 2015 $29
Chardonnay 2007 A vibrant wine, with stone fruits and nectarine aromas and flavours; good line and persistence across the palate. Screwcap. 13° alc. **Rating** 90 **To** 2009 $19.50

ΥΥΥΥ **Pinot Noir 2006** Ripe dark cherry fruits, with toasty oak and some briary notes on the bouquet; quite rich, and very toasty on the finish. Screwcap. 14.3° alc. **Rating** 89 **To** 2010 $27

Brave Goose Vineyard ★★★★☆

PO Box 633, Seymour, Vic 3660 **Region** Goulburn Valley
T (03) 5799 1229 **F** (03) 5799 0636 **www.**bravegoosevineyard.com.au **Open** By appt
Winemaker John Stocker, Don Lewis **Est.** 1988 **Cases** 400
Dr John Stocker and wife Joanne must be among the most highly qualified boutique vineyard and winery operators in Australia. John Stocker is the former chief executive of CSIRO and chairman of the Grape and Wine Research & Development Corporation for seven years, and daughter Nina has completed the Roseworthy postgraduate oenology course. Moreover, they established their first vineyard (while living in Switzerland) on the French/Swiss border in the village of Flueh. On returning to Australia in 1987 they found a property on the inside of the Great Dividing Range with north-facing slopes and shallow, weathered ironstone soils. Here they have established 2.5 ha each of shiraz and cabernet sauvignon, and 0.5 ha each of merlot and gamay, selling the majority of grapes from the 20-year-old vines, but making small quantities of Cabernet Merlot, Merlot and Gamay. The brave goose in question was the sole survivor of a flock put into the vineyard to repel cockatoos and foxes.

ΥΥΥΥΩ **Shiraz 2006** Good colour depth; abundant ripe blackberry fruit; fine tannins give a slightly milky texture, unusual but not unpleasant; will improve. Screwcap. 13.8° alc. **Rating** 90 **To** 2016 $25

Merlot 2006 This is a very useful example of that elusive and frustrating variety, with a correct balance of redcurrant, snow pea and olive flavours, the tannins largely unseen. Cork. 13.5° alc. **Rating** 90 **To** 2013 $25

Braydon Estate ★★★★

40 Londons Road, Lovedale, NSW 2325 (postal) **Region** Lower Hunter Valley
T (02) 4990 9122 **F** (02) 4990 9133 **Open** Not
Winemaker Pothana (David Hook) **Est.** 1998 **Cases** NA
This will be the last time Braydon Estate will be found in the Wine Companion. The vines have been removed and no more wine is to be made, but all of the existing stock will be sold through the Small Winemakers Centre, Pokolbin or by mail order.

ŶŶŶŶŶ **Home Paddock Hunter Valley Semillon 2006** Firm, tightly structured and slowly building weight; notes of herb, grass and lanolin; good length. Screwcap. 11° alc. **Rating** 90 **To** 2016 $14

ŶŶŶŶ **Home Paddock Hunter Valley Shiraz 2006** Dense crimson-purple; ultra-rich black fruit flavours, but with regionality evident; soft and fleshy, slightly loose texture and structure. Screwcap. 13.7° alc. **Rating** 89 **To** 2014 $18
Home Paddock Hunter Valley Shiraz 2005 Medium- to full-bodied; a mix of ripe plum and blackberry fruits; well-balanced tannins and oak; should age well. Screwcap. 13° alc. **Rating** 89 **To** 2015 $18

Braydun Hill Vineyard ★★★★☆

38–40 Hepenstal Road, Hackham, SA 5163 **Region** McLaren Vale
T (08) 8382 3023 **F** (08) 8326 0033 www.braydunhill.com.au **Open** By appt
Winemaker Rebecca Kennedy **Est.** 2001 **Cases** 1600
It is hard to imagine there would be such an interesting (and inspiring) story behind a 4-ha vineyard planted between 1998 and '99 by the husband and wife team of Tony Dunn and Carol Bradley, wishing to get out of growing angora goats and into grapegrowing. The extension of the business into winemaking was totally unplanned, forced on them by the liquidation of Normans in late 2001. With humour, courage and perseverance, they have met obstacles and setbacks which would have caused many to give up, and have produced wines since 2001 which leave no doubt this is a distinguished site capable of producing wines of high quality. Exports to Japan, Taiwan and Singapore.

ŶŶŶŶŶ **Single Vineyard McLaren Vale Shiraz 2006** Dense colour; unequivocally full-bodied, with a stentorian blast of black fruits, dark chocolate, persistent tannins and oak; is in balance, but needs patience. Cork. 15° alc. **Rating** 93 **To** 2020 $28

Bream Creek ★★★★★

Marion Bay Road, Bream Creek, Tas 7175 **Region** Southern Tasmania
T (03) 6231 4646 **F** (03) 6231 4646 **Open** At Potters Croft, Dunally, tel (03) 6253 5469
Winemaker Winemaking Tasmania (Julian Alcorso) **Est.** 1975 **Cases** 3500
Until 1990 the Bream Creek fruit was sold to Moorilla Estate, but since then the winery has been independently owned and managed under the control of Fred Peacock, legendary for the care he bestows on the vines under his direction. Peacock's skills have seen both an increase in production and also a vast lift in wine quality across the range, headed by the Pinot Noir. The 1996 acquisition of a second vineyard in the Tamar Valley has significantly strengthened the business base of the venture.

ŶŶŶŶŶ **Pinot Noir 2006** Deeply coloured; an extremely complex wine with gamey overtones (not brett) and spice to the dark plum fruit; great flavour profile and length. Screwcap. **Rating** 95 **To** 2014 $26
Reserve Pinot Noir 2005 Bright and lively with red berries and five spice on the bouquet; vibrant palate, with good acid, and a clean-fruited finish; velvety, long and supple. Top gold, Tas Wine Show '08. Diam. **Rating** 95 **To** 2012 $34

Cabernet Sauvignon 2005 Great colour; vibrant and complex with redcurrant and cassis framed by cedar and plentiful fine-grained tannins; long and fine. Diam. **Rating** 95 **To** 2014 $24

ŢŢŢŢ **Chardonnay 2006** A complex wine, with nutty aromas and a touch of smoke; tightens up with acidity on the finish. Scewcap. **Rating** 87 **To** 2012 $22

🍇 Bremer River Vineyards ★★★

c/- Post Office, Langhorne Creek, SA 5255 (postal) **Region** Langhorne Creek
T 0408 844 487 **F** (08) 8370 0362 **Open** Not
Winemaker Bleasdale (Michael Potts) **Est.** 1990 **Cases** 300
Brian and Pat Silcock began the establishment of their Langhorne Creek vineyard in 1970, ultimately planting 10 ha each of shiraz and cabernet sauvignon, plus 2 ha of merlot. In 2002 they decided to have a small part of the grape production vinified, selling direct into selected SA restaurants and bottle shops, as well as through a mail list.

ŢŢŢŢ **Langhorne Creek Shiraz 2004** Medium-bodied; supple, smooth plum and blackberry fruit; falls away slightly on the finish, but commendable value. Cork. 14.5° alc. **Rating** 88 **To** 2011 $15

Bremerton Wines

Strathalbyn Road, Langhorne Creek, SA 5255 **Region** Langhorne Creek
T (08) 8537 3093 **F** (08) 8537 3109 www.bremerton.com.au **Open** 7 days 10–5
Winemaker Rebecca Willson **Est.** 1988 **Cases** 35 000
The Willsons have been grapegrowers in the Langhorne Creek region for some considerable time but their dual business as grapegrowers and winemakers has expanded significantly. Their vineyards have more than doubled to over 100 ha (predominantly cabernet sauvignon, shiraz and merlot), as has their production of wine under the Bremerton label. In 2004 sisters Rebecca and Lucy (marketing) took control of the business, marking the event with (guess what) revamped label designs. Can fairly claim to be the best producer in Langhorne Creek. Exports to all major markets.

ŢŢŢŢŢ **Reserve Cabernet 2004** Focused and pure, showing cassis, cedar and alluring florals on the bouquet; the palate is fine and supple, incredibly long and offers brilliant vibrancy and thrust on the finish. Cork. 14.5° alc. **Rating** 96 **To** 2025 $40
Old Adam Shiraz 2005 Deep crimson hue; a very complex bouquet full of dense dark fruits, nice toasty oak and a touch of spice; medium- to full-bodied; the palate is lively, fresh, deep and complex; very long finish. Cork. 15° alc. **Rating** 95 **To** 2025 $40
B.O.V. 2005 Complex, supple and concentrated; bright-fruited with a strong personality and long, superfine tannins on the finish; built for the long haul; Shiraz/Cabernet Sauvignon. Cork. 15.5° alc. **Rating** 94 **To** 2020 $75

ŢŢŢŢŢ **Selkirk Langhorne Creek Shiraz 2006** Generous, round and supple mouthfeel to black cherry and blackberry fruit; both tannins and oak have been sensitively employed in a strongly regional wine. Screwcap. 14.5° alc. **Rating** 92 **To** 2016 $22
Langhorne Creek Racy Rose 2007 Bright and vibrant colour; a focused and fresh spray of red fruit aromas and flavours; good length, dry finish. Screwcap. **Rating** 91 **To** 2009 $16
Langhorne Creek Verdelho 2007 A clean and floral bouquet; offers a mix of tropical fruit with a touch of pear; lively, fresh acidity and a clear-cut finish. Screwcap. 13° alc. **Rating** 90 **To** 2009 $18
Tamblyn Cabernet Sauvignon Shiraz Malbec Merlot 2006 An attractive array of aromatic, juicy red fruits; has good thrust and length, notwithstanding low tannin levels; ready now. Screwcap. 14.5° alc. **Rating** 90 **To** 2012 $18

ŢŢŢŢ **Special Release Malbec 2006** Typical juicy jammy fruit flavours and minimal structure; I'm not convinced about its use outside of cabernet blends. Screwcap. 15° alc. **Rating** 89 **To** 2014 $24

Langhorne Creek Sauvignon Blanc 2007 Nicely made, but overall lacks varietal fruit impact for higher points; summer seafood style. Screwcap. 11.5° alc. **Rating** 87 **To** 2009 $18.50

Bress ★★★★★

3894 Calder Highway, Harcourt, Vic 3453 **Region** Bendigo
T (03) 5474 2262 **F** (03) 5474 2553 **www**.bress.com.au **Open** W'ends & public hols 11–5 or by appt
Winemaker Adam Marks **Est.** 2001 **Cases** 5000

Adam Marks has made wine in all parts of the world since 1991, and made the brave decision (during his honeymoon in 2000) to start his own business. He has selected Margaret River semillon and sauvignon blanc as the best source of white Bordeaux-style wine in Australia; Yarra Valley as the best pinot noir region; and shiraz from Heathcote for precisely the same reason. In early 2005 the Marks family acquired the former Mt Alexander Vineyard and cellar door, expanding the business overnight. Exports to the Maldives and Indonesia.

🍷🍷🍷🍷🍷 **Macedon Yarra Pinot Noir 2007** Fragrant aromas of those usually elusive violets and red fruits; a pure and uncluttered palate, delicate but quite intense and long; low alcohol no hindrance. Screwcap. 12.5° alc. **Rating** 94 **To** 2015 $18

Heathcote Shiraz 2006 Some colour development; medium-bodied; supple blackberry, plum and licorice fruit with fine, savoury tannins giving very good structure. Screwcap. 13.5° alc. **Rating** 94 **To** 2019 $38

🍷🍷🍷🍷½ **Heathcote & Bendigo Shiraz 2006** A little more colour development than expected; strongly savoury spicy earthy aromas and flavours underlying ripe plummy fruit. Screwcap. 13.5° alc. **Rating** 92 **To** 2016 $18

Briagolong Estate ★★★☆

Valencia–Briagolong Road, Briagolong, Vic 3860 **Region** Gippsland
T (03) 5147 2322 **F** (03) 5147 2341 **www**.briagolongestate.com.au **Open** By appt
Winemaker Gordon McIntosh **Est.** 1979 **Cases** 400

This is very much a weekend hobby for medical practitioner Gordon McIntosh, who invests his chardonnay and pinot noir with Burgundian complexity. He has made several decisions since 2003. First, having had his best vintage in the 1990s ('98) destroyed by TCA cork taint, he has moved to screwcaps. Next, he has introduced the Foothills of Gippsland range at a lower price point (but still estate-grown). Third, he has increased the price of the Estate Chardonnay and Pinot Noir, limited to exceptional barrels, which will not be released every year. Like many others in southern Vic, the 2007 vintage was ruined by smoke taint, and no wine will be released from this vintage; in the meantime, stocks of mature wines will be sold.

🍷🍷🍷🍷½ **Gippsland Pinot Noir 2005** Developing nicely; spicy, foresty, earthy overtones to light, plum-accented fruit; good length and balance; controlled extract and tannins. Screwcap. 13.5° alc. **Rating** 90 **To** 2012 $31

🍷🍷🍷🍷 **Gippsland Chardonnay 2005** Nutty, creamy, toasty bottle-developed flavours offset by balanced acidity in a citrus spectrum. Screwcap. 12.5° alc. **Rating** 89 **To** 2011 $31

Brian Barry Wines ★★★★

PO Box 128, Stepney, SA 5069 **Region** Clare Valley
T (08) 8363 6211 **F** (08) 8362 0498 **Open** Not
Winemaker Brian Barry, Judson Barry **Est.** 1977 **Cases** 6000

Brian Barry is an industry veteran with a wealth of winemaking and show-judging experience. His is nonetheless in reality a vineyard-only operation (16 ha of riesling, 4 ha of cabernet sauvignon, 2 ha of shiraz, 1.2 ha of merlot and 0.4 ha of cabernet franc), with a substantial part of the output sold as grapes to other wineries. The wines are made under contract at various wineries under Brian's supervision. As one would expect, the quality is reliably good. Exports to the UK and the US.

ŢŢŢŢŢ Dux Riesling 2007 Scented lemon and lime blossom aromas; an intense, mineral tinged citrus palate with a touch of CO_2. Zork. **Rating** 92 **To** 2010 $85

ŢŢŢŢ Juds Hill Clare Valley Riesling 2006 Soft lime, apple and spice flavours; good balance, but falls away slightly on the finish; I wonder why these old vines aren't producing more excitement. Screwcap. 11.5° alc. **Rating** 89 **To** 2015 $20
Juds Hill Vineyard Clare Valley Shiraz 2004 Strong pencilly oak aromas; very ripe fruit with mocha and fruitcake coming through on the finish, but the oak is overdone. Screwcap. 14.5° alc. **Rating** 88 **To** 2016 $28

Briar Ridge ★★★★☆

Mount View Road, Mount View, NSW 2325 **Region** Lower Hunter Valley
T (02) 4990 3670 **F** (02) 4990 7802 **www**.briarridge.com.au **Open** 7 days 10–5
Winemaker Karl Stockhausen, Mark Woods **Est.** 1972 **Cases** 18 000
Semillon and shiraz have been the most consistent performers, underlying the suitability of these varieties to the Hunter Valley. The Semillon, in particular, invariably shows intense fruit and cellars well. Briar Ridge has been a model of stability, and has the comfort of over 48 ha of estate vineyards, from which it is able to select the best grapes. It also has not hesitated to venture into other regions, notably Orange. Exports to the US and Canada.

ŢŢŢŢŢ **Signature Release Karl Stockhausen Hunter Valley Shiraz 2006** Pure and aromatic blackberry, cherry and plum; medium-bodied, and a silky texture and mouthfeel; classic Hunter, with very fine tannins. Screwcap. 13.5° alc. **Rating** 94 **To** 2026 $29

ŢŢŢŢŢ **Signature Release Chairman's Selection Orange Chardonnay 2006** Has the fruit freshness and drive from the cool region; nectarine and grapefruit aromas and flavours preserved by barrel fermentation and maturation in 1-year-old oak; good balance. Screwcap. 14° alc. **Rating** 92 **To** 2013 $26
Stockhausen Semillon 2007 An extremely elegant, indeed delicate, wine, running counter to the normal, richer character of the vintage; could develop into something special. Screwcap. 12° alc. **Rating** 90 **To** 2017 $26

ŢŢŢŢ **Old Vines Shiraz 2005** Has started to develop some of the leathery earthy notes which will come with bottle age; how old is old is the question the back label doesn't answer. Screwcap. 14.8° alc. **Rating** 87 **To** 2014 $23
Cold Soaked Cabernet Sauvignon 2006 No claim of origin, though by inference from the Hunter Valley; whether or not, pleasant medium-bodied palate with varietal blackcurrant and cassis, the pre-fermentation 'cold soak' having done its job. Screwcap. 14.5° alc. **Rating** 87 **To** 2016 $23
Red Trio Cabernet Merlot Shiraz 2006 Touted as an early-drinking style, and is, but has the generosity of simple cassis-accented fruit to stay around for a year or two. Screwcap. 13.8° alc. **Rating** 87 **To** 2011 $18

Briarose Estate ★★★★☆

Bussell Highway, Augusta, WA 6290 **Region** Margaret River
T (08) 9758 4160 **F** (08) 9758 4161 **www**.briarose.com.au **Open** 7 days 10–4.30
Winemaker The Vintage Wineworx (Dr Diane Miller), Bill Crappsley (Consultant)
Est. 1998 **Cases** 10 000
Brian and Rosemary Webster began the development of the estate plantings in 1998, which now comprise sauvignon blanc (2.33 ha), semillon (1.33 ha), cabernet sauvignon (6.6 ha), merlot (2.2 ha) and cabernet franc (1.1 ha). The winery is situated at the southern end of the Margaret River region, where the climate is distinctly cooler than that of northern Margaret River.

ŢŢŢŢŢ **Margaret River Sauvignon Blanc Semillon 2007** A complex wine; slightly sweaty notes on the bouquet were obviously acceptable to the Perth Wine Show judges, who gave it a gold medal; powerful palate structure, with a mix of kiwi fruit, herb and grass, and a long finish Screwcap. 12.5° alc. **Rating** 92 **To** 2011 $27

Margaret River Sauvignon Blanc 2007 Relatively light-bodied, with delicate but clear varietal fruit in a gooseberry and citrus spectrum. Screwcap. 12.5° alc. **Rating** 90 **To** 2009 $25

Margaret River Cabernet Merlot 2005 Very good colour and hue; a medium-bodied mix of black and redcurrant fruit, with firm, ripe tannins on a long finish. Screwcap. 13.5° alc. **Rating** 90 **To** 2017 $25

Reserve Margaret River Cabernet Sauvignon 2005 Savoury earthy cedary notes, with just a touch of cassis; quite firm and dry tannins; austere style; trophy Best Cabernet, Perth Wine Show '07. Screwcap. 14° alc. **Rating** 90 **To** 2017 $32

Blackwood Cove 2005 Restrained, austere, Bordeaux-style blend, with a tight mix of predominantly blackcurrant fruit, and with some notes of earth and tobacco; from the coolest corner of the Margaret River. Cork. 14° alc. **Rating** 90 **To** 2020 $36

Brick Kiln

PO Box 56, Glen Osmond, SA 5064 **Region** McLaren Vale
T (08) 8357 2561 **F** (08) 8357 3126 **www**.brickiln.com.au **Open** Not
Winemaker McLaren Vintners **Est.** 2001 **Cases** 1500
This is the venture of Malcolm and Alison Mackinnon, Garry and Nancy Watson, and Ian and Pene Davey. They purchased the 8-ha Nine Gums Vineyard, which had been planted to shiraz in 1995–96, in 2001. The majority of the grapes are sold, with a lesser portion contract-made for the partners under the Brick Kiln label, which takes its name from the Brick Kiln Bridge adjacent to the vineyard. Exports to the UK, the US, Canada, Singapore and Hong Kong.

ΨΨΨΨΨ **Six Partners Reserve McLaren Vale Shiraz 2006** The brighter of the two shirazs from this producer; similar fruit, but better focus and precision on the finish. Screwcap. 14.8° alc. **Rating** 90 **To** 2015 $21.50

ΨΨΨΨ **McLaren Vale Shiraz 2006** Very deep, with a little grape shrivel evident; deep and dark, and quite warm-fruited; finishes a little short. Screwcap. 14.7° alc. **Rating** 88 **To** 2014 $21.50

Brindabella Hills

156 Woodgrove Close, via Hall, ACT 2618 **Region** Canberra District
T (02) 6230 2583 **F** (02) 6230 2023 **www**.brindabellahills.com.au **Open** W'ends, public hols 10–5
Winemaker Dr Roger Harris, Brian Sinclair **Est.** 1986 **Cases** 1150
Distinguished research scientist Dr Roger Harris presides over Brindabella Hills, which increasingly relies on estate-produced grapes, with small plantings of cabernet sauvignon, cabernet franc, merlot, shiraz, chardonnay, sauvignon blanc, semillon and riesling, and a subsequent planting of sangiovese and brunello. Wine quality has been consistently impressive.

ΨΨΨΨΨ **Canberra District Shiraz 2006** Lifted red berry and red apple aromas, with very fine acidity and lovely texture; very elegant, with real suppleness and finesse. Screwcap. 13.4° alc. **Rating** 92 **To** 2014 $25

Canberra District Riesling 2007 Fine and steely; lime juice core and a lovely precise finish; very long and should age gracefully. Screwcap. 12.5° alc. **Rating** 91 **To** 2018 $20

Brini Estate Wines

RSD 600 Blewitt Springs Road, McLaren Vale, SA 5171 (postal) **Region** McLaren Vale
T (08) 8383 0080 **F** (08) 8383 0104 **www**.briniwines.com.au **Open** Not
Winemaker Brian Light (Contract) **Est.** 2000 **Cases** 4500
The Brini family has been growing grapes in the Blewitt Springs area of McLaren Vale since 1953. In 2000 John and Marcello Brini established Brini Estate Wines to vinify a portion of the grape production; up to that time it had been sold to companies such as Penfolds, Rosemount Estate and d'Arenberg. The flagship Sebastian Shiraz is produced from dry-grown

vines planted in 1947, the Shiraz Grenache from dry-grown vines planted in 1964. Skilled winemaking, coupled with impeccable fruit sources, has resulted in a new star in the McLaren Vale firmament. Exports to the UK and Hong Kong.

ΨΨΨΨΨ **Sebastian McLaren Vale Shiraz 2005** Focused and elegant, with a lively array of aromas and fruit flavours; spice, earth, blackberry, plum, vanilla and dark chocolate are all to be found on the long palate. Screwcap. 14.5° alc. **Rating** 94 **To** 2015 $28

ΨΨΨΨΨ **Blewitt Springs Shiraz 2005** A fresh, medium-bodied palate with lively plum, blackberry, licorice and dark chocolate flavours leading the way; 18 months in oak hasn't overly intruded. Screwcap. 14.5° alc. **Rating** 92 **To** 2013 $18

Brocks View Estate

PO Box 396, Yankalilla, SA 5203 **Region** Southern Fleurieu
T (08) 8558 2233 **Open** Not
Winemaker Phillip Christiansen (Contract) **Est.** 1998 **Cases** NA
Peter and Julie Brocksopp have planted a single ha of shiraz at Carrickalinga, with coastal views out over Yankalilla Bay, giving rise to the slogan 'from vines with a view'. The close-density planting on gravel loam over red clay soils is managed organically, with minimal irrigation, the vines hand-pruned and hand-picked.

ΨΨΨΨΨ **Southern Fleurieu Shiraz 2005** Medium- to full-bodied, with an attractive array of black fruits and dark chocolate, ripe tannins and oak seamlessly integrated; excellent balance, even better value. Cork. 14.5° alc. **Rating** 93 **To** 2013 $18

Broke Estate/Ryan Family Wines

Wollombi Road, Broke, NSW 2330 **Region** Lower Hunter Valley
T (02) 6579 1065 **F** (02) 6574 5199 **www**.ryanwines.com.au **Open** W'ends & public hols 11–5
Winemaker Matthew Ryan **Est.** 1988 **Cases** 2000
This is the flagship operation of the Ryan family, with 25 ha of largely mature vineyards, the lion's share to chardonnay, but also including meaningful plantings of semillon, sauvignon blanc, shiraz, merlot, barbera, tempranillo, cabernet sauvignon and cabernet franc. No samples received; the rating is that of last year.

Broke's Promise Wines ★★★★

725 Milbrodale Road, Broke, NSW 2330 **Region** Lower Hunter Valley
T (02) 6579 1165 **F** (02) 9972 1619 **www**.brokespromise.com.au **Open** W'ends 10–5
Winemaker Margan Family **Est.** 1996 **Cases** 700
Joe and Carol Re purchased Broke's Promise in 2005 from Jane Marquard and Dennis Karp, and have continued the winemaking arrangements with Andrew Margan. The 3.5-ha vineyard (chardonnay, barbera, shiraz, semillon and verdelho) is complemented by an olive grove and an art gallery.

ΨΨΨΨΨ **Hunter Valley Shiraz 2006** Good colour; highly flavoured, almost tangy, medium-bodied palate with spicy, lifted fruits of the kind a touch of viognier can give; good line and length. 14.5° alc. **Rating** 93 **To** 2015 $20

ΨΨΨΨ **Hunter Valley Chardonnay 2007** Pleasant stone fruits on bouquet and palate; even structure, good balance. Screwcap. 13° alc. **Rating** 87 **To** 2010 $18

Broken Gate Wines

57 Rokeby Street, Collingwood, Vic 3066 (postal) **Region** Southeast Australia
T (03) 9417 5757 **F** (03) 8415 1991 **www**.brokengate.com.au **Open** Not
Winemaker Contract **Est.** 2001 **Cases** 6000

Broken Gate is a partnership between Brendan Chapman and Josef Orbach. Chapman has an extensive liquor retailing background, and is presently bulk wine buyer for Swords Wines, responsible for the purchase of 160 000 litres of wine across Australia. Josef Orbach lived and worked in the Clare Valley from 1994 to '98 at Leasingham Wines, while also leading the restoration of the Clarevale Winery Co-op building. Exports to China and Singapore.

🍷🍷🍷🍷 **Side Gate Geelong Yarra Valley Chardonnay 2006** Totally fruit-driven; some grapefruit and melon; touch of grip on the finish adds length; handy 375 ml bottle. Screwcap. 13.6° alc. **Rating** 87 **To** 2011 $9

Brokenwood   ★★★★★

401-427 McDonalds Road, Pokolbin, NSW 2321 **Region** Lower Hunter Valley
T (02) 4998 7559 **F** (02) 4998 7893 **www**.brokenwood.com.au **Open** 7 days 9.30–5
Winemaker Iain Riggs, PJ Charteris **Est.** 1970 **Cases** 100 000
Deservedly fashionable winery producing consistently excellent wines. Has kept Graveyard Shiraz as its ultimate flagship wine, while extending its reach through many of the best eastern regions for its broad selection of varietal wine styles. Its big-selling Hunter Semillon remains alongside Graveyard, and there is then a range of wines coming from regions including Orange, Central Ranges, Beechworth, McLaren Vale, Cowra and elsewhere. The two-storey Albert Room (named in honour of the late Tony Albert, one of the founders) tasting facility was opened in 2006. Exports to all major markets.

🍷🍷🍷🍷🍷 **Graveyard Vineyard Hunter Valley Shiraz 2005** A classic style, with savoury, earthy (though fine) tannins evident now, but will progressively soften allowing the emphasis to shift to the black cherry/blackberry fruit. Perfect balance for the long haul. Screwcap. 14° alc. **Rating** 96 **To** 2025 $100
ILR Reserve Semillon 2002 A superbly fine, crisp and delicate wine, still to fully show its wares; if the cork holds, will be very long lived, gaining more character over the years ahead. **Rating** 95 **To** 2015 $45
Hunter Valley Shiraz 2005 A younger brother to Graveyard, but certainly comes from the same bed. Easier to enjoy now and over the next 10 years. From young vines on the Graveyard Block. Screwcap. 14° alc. **Rating** 94 **To** 2015 $35
Hunter Valley Shiraz 2006 Vivid crimson; excellent balance and mouthfeel to perfectly ripened fruit; from young vines in Graveyard Block and declassified portions of Graveyard Old Vines. Screwcap. 14° alc. **Rating** 94 **To** 2020 $40

🍷🍷🍷🍷🍷 **Forest Edge Vineyard Orange Chardonnay 2006** Lively, intense and long flavours ranging from ripe apple through to the tropical end of the spectrum; sophisticated use of barrel ferment oak. Screwcap. 14° alc. **Rating** 91 **To** 2011 $30
Hunter Valley Semillon 2007 Water-white; an ultra-crisp and fresh web of mineral, grass and spice, rather like a toned-down Chablis. Screwcap. 11.5° alc. **Rating** 90 **To** 2013 $20

🍷🍷🍷🍷 **Cricket Pitch Sauvignon Blanc Semillon 2007** Cleverly made to precise specifications; gently tropical fruit on the mid-palate with just an airbrush of oak, tightened up on the finish by the semillon; an anywhere, anytime wine. Screwcap. 13° alc. **Rating** 89 **To** 2010 $17
McLaren Vale Sangiovese 2006 Light but bright hue; a fresh evocation of varietal briary/sour cherry fruit, with suitably fine-grained tannins. Screwcap. 14° alc. **Rating** 89 **To** 2014 $30
Indigo Vineyard Beechworth Pinot Noir 2005 Some slightly stewed fruit characters on the bouquet; showing more dry red than pinot varietal character on the palate, but time may help. Screwcap. 14° alc. **Rating** 88 **To** 2012 $30
Umpire's Vineyard Cowra Semillon Chardonnay Sauvignon Blanc 2006 Simple dehydration gives a wine akin to crystallised fruit in liquid form, finished off with a dash of lemon; for the punters. Screwcap. 10° alc. **Rating** 88 **To** 2009 $22
Cricket Pitch Sauvignon Blanc Semillon 2006 Development evident notwithstanding the screwcap; some honeyed notes give the impression of a touch of sweetness; better younger. Screwcap. 13.5° alc. **Rating** 87 **To** 2009 $17

Indigo Vineyard Beechworth Chardonnay 2006 A complex bouquet and palate, but the alcohol hits hard, a pity given the high-quality ingredients. Screwcap. 14° alc. **Rating** 87 **To** 2011 $30

Brook Eden Vineyard   ★★★★

Adams Road, Lebrina, Tas 7254 **Region** Northern Tasmania
T (03) 6395 6244 **F** (03) 6395 6211 **www**.brookeden.com.au **Open** Thurs–Tues 10–5 Aug–June
Winemaker Contract **Est.** 1988 **Cases** 1100
Peter McIntosh and Sue Stuart purchased Brook Eden from Sheila Bezemer in 2004. At 41° south and at an altitude of 160 m it is one of the coolest sites in Tasmania, and (in the words of the new owners) 'represents viticulture on the edge'. While the plantings remain small (1 ha pinot noir, 0.75 ha chardonnay and 0.25 ha riesling and pinot gris), yield has been significantly reduced, resulting in earlier picking and better quality grapes. Exports to Malaysia and Singapore.

♥♥♥♥♀ **Pinot Noir 2006** Well made, neatly balanced black cherry, plum, spice and briar notes; remarkable flavour given the alcohol. Screwcap. 12° alc. **Rating** 92 **To** 2012 $34

♥♥♥♥ **Chardonnay 2006** Has much riper stone fruit flavours than many, moving into ripe peach territory; silver medal, National Cool Climate Wine Show '07. Screwcap. 13° alc. **Rating** 88 **To** 2012 $25
Friends Pinot Rose 2007 Pale salmon; aromatic and spicy, with a long, bone-dry finish; genuine food style. Screwcap. 13.5° alc. **Rating** 88 **To** 2009 $23
Riesling 2007 Delicate and fresh, but not much intensity to the citrus and passionfruit flavours; may develop. Screwcap. 13° alc. **Rating** 87 **To** 2013 $23

Brookhampton Estate   NR

South Western Highway, Donnybrook, WA 6239 **Region** Geographe
T (08) 9731 0400 **F** (08) 9731 0500 **www**.brookhamptonestate.com.au **Open** 7 days 11–4 (closed public hols)
Winemaker James Kellie (Contract) **Est.** 1998 **Cases** NA
Brookhampton Estate, situated 3 km south of Donnybrook, wasted no time in establishing 115 ha of vines, with three fashionable red varietals to the fore – shiraz (28 ha), merlot (17 ha) and cabernet sauvignon (14.5 ha), with lesser amounts of tempranillo, grenache and barbera; white varieties planted are sauvignon blanc, semillon, chardonnay and viognier.

Brookland Valley   ★★★★★

Caves Road, Wilyabrup, WA 6280 **Region** Margaret River
T (08) 9755 6042 **F** (08) 9755 6214 **www**.brooklandvalley.com.au **Open** 7 days 10–5
Winemaker Ross Pamment **Est.** 1984 **Cases** 130 000
Brookland Valley has an idyllic setting, plus its much enlarged Flutes Café (one of the best winery restaurants in the Margaret River region) and its Gallery of Wine Arts, which houses an eclectic collection of wine, food-related art and wine accessories. After acquiring a 50% share of Brookland Valley in 1997, Hardys moved to full ownership in 2004. The quality, and consistency, of the wines is, quite literally, awesome. Exports to the UK, the US and other major markets.

♥♥♥♥♥ **Chardonnay 2005** A vibrant and pure wine, with outstanding finesse, elegance and length to the citrus and nectarine fruit; oak present in a carefully judged support role; trophy, National Wine Show '07. **Rating** 96 **To** 2013 $36
Reserve Margaret River Cabernet Sauvignon 2002 Good colour; fragrant blackcurrant, cassis, herb and black olive permeate both the bouquet and palate, which is long, intense and supple; lovely now, better still in another 5 years. Cork. 14° alc. **Rating** 96 **To** 2017 $62

Semillon 2006 Immaculate winemaking; a long, intense and perfectly balanced palate; herb and lemon fruit with just a touch of oak; lingering finish. **Rating** 95 **To** 2015 $36

Verse 1 Margaret River Shiraz 2006 An exceptionally good wine; medium-bodied, with blackberry, plum, spice and pepper supported by fine tannins and skilled use of oak. **Rating** 95 **To** 2021 $20

Verse 1 Semillon Sauvignon Blanc 2007 Highly aromatic; good intensity, structure and line to the mix of lemon and tropical fruit; minerally notes on the finish. **Rating** 94 **To** 2010 $20

Chardonnay 2006 Fragrant stone fruit and barrel ferment inputs on the bouquet; abundant melon and white peach on the smooth and supple palate; good length. **Rating** 94 **To** 2013 $36

Verse 1 Margaret River Chardonnay 2006 Extremely complex barrel ferment/wild yeast aromas, then a high-flavoured, fruit-driven palate with oak receding into the background. **Rating** 94 **To** 2011 $20

Verse 1 Margaret River Rose 2007 Lovely mouthfeel to the intense, silky red fruit flavours, the long palate finishing bone-dry; serious rose. Screwcap. 12.5° alc. **Rating** 94 **To** 2009 $18.99

Margaret River Sauvignon Blanc 2007 A spotlessly clean bouquet leads into a bright, fresh minerally palate; full fruit expression still to appear – and may never do so. Screwcap. 13.5° alc. **Rating** 89 **To** 2010 $30

Brookwood Estate

Treeton Road, Cowaramup, WA 6284 **Region** Margaret River
T (08) 9755 5604 **F** (08) 9755 5870 **www.**brookwood.com.au **Open** 7 days 11–5
Winemaker Bronnley Cahill **Est.** 1996 **Cases** 2600
Trevor and Lyn Mann began the development of their 50-ha property in 1996, and now have 1.3 ha each of semillon, sauvignon blanc and chenin blanc, 1.2 ha shiraz and 1 ha of cabernet sauvignon. A winery was constructed in 1999 to accommodate the first vintage. Winemaking is now in the hands of Bronnley Cahill (Trevor and Lyn's daughter), with the experienced eye of Lyn in the background. Exports to Germany and Hong Kong.

Margaret River Semillon Sauvignon Blanc 2007 Fresh, lively and very well focused; semillon provides good structure, sauvignon blanc the fragrant fruit in a tropical spectrum; immaculate balance. Screwcap. 13.5° alc. **Rating** 93 **To** 2011 $19.95

Margaret River Shiraz 2006 Rich, soft blackberry fruit in abundance, supported by gently sweet oak. **Rating** 89 **To** 2013 $29.95

Margaret River Sauvignon Blanc 2007 A clean, herbaceous bouquet; well made and balanced, but doesn't have much vigour to the gentle tropical fruits. Screwcap. 13° alc. **Rating** 87 **To** 2009 $19.95

Margaret River Cabernet Sauvignon 2006 Bright but light colour; fresh raspberry, cassis and redcurrant fruit; minimal structure. Screwcap. 13.5° alc. **Rating** 87 **To** 2011 $35

Broomstick Estate

4 Frances Street, Mount Lawley, WA 6050 (postal) **Region** Margaret River
T (08) 9271 9594 **F** (08) 9271 9741 **www.**broomstick.com.au **Open** Not
Winemaker Mark Warren (Happs) **Est.** 1997 **Cases** 1000
Robert Holloway and family purchased the property on which the vineyard is now established in 1993 as an operating dairy farm. In 1997, 5.5 ha of shiraz was planted. Over the following years 3.8 ha of merlot and then (in 2004) 5.3 ha of chardonnay and 2 ha of sauvignon blanc were added. The Holloways see themselves as grapegrowers first and foremost, but make a small amount of wine under the Broomstick Estate label.

Margaret River Shiraz 2006 Light- to medium-bodied; supple without over-much texture, but nice flavour. **Rating** 87 **To** 2012 $19.50

Brothers in Arms ★★★★

PO Box 840, Langhorne Creek, SA 5255 **Region** Langhorne Creek
T (08) 83537 3182 **F** (08) 8537 3383 **www.**brothersinarms.com.au **Open** Not
Winemaker Justin Lane **Est.** 1998 **Cases** 30 000
The Adams family has been growing grapes at Langhorne Creek since 1891, when the first
vines at the famed Metala vineyards were planted. Guy Adams is the fifth generation to own
and work the vineyard, and over the past 20 years has both improved the viticulture and
expanded the plantings to the present 40 ha (shiraz and cabernet sauvignon). It was not until
1998 that they decided to hold back a small proportion of the production for vinification
under the Brothers in Arms label. Exports to the UK, the US and other major markets.

ŶŶŶŶŶ **Cabernet Sauvignon 2005** As much McLaren Vale character as Langhorne
Creek, thanks to dark chocolate woven through the blackberry fruit; ripe tannins
and sweet oak help an easy access style. Screwcap. **Rating** 90 **To** 2015 $50

ŶŶŶŶ **Formby & Adams Cutting Edge Cabernet Shiraz 2006** Attractively sweet,
juicy red and black fruits, with nuances of spice and licorice plus ripe tannins;
good line and length. Screwcap. 14.5° alc. **Rating** 89 **To** 2013 $19
No. 6 Shiraz Cabernet 2005 A thick, almost viscous palate, with dried fruit
and dark chocolate flavours; soft, ripe tannins. Screwcap. **Rating** 88 **To** 2014 $22

Brown Brothers ★★★★★

Milawa-Bobinawarrah Road, Milawa, Vic 3678 **Region** King Valley
T (03) 5720 5500 **F** (03) 5720 5511 **www.**brownbrothers.com.au **Open** 7 days 9–5
Winemaker Wendy Cameron, Joel Tilbrook, Catherine Looney, Geoff Alexander
Est. 1885 **Cases** 1.1 million
Draws upon a considerable number of vineyards spread throughout a range of site climates,
ranging from very warm to very cool. A relatively recent expansion into Heathcote has added
significantly to its armoury. It is known for the diversity of varieties with which it works,
and the wines represent good value for money. Deservedly one of the most successful family
wineries – its cellar door receives the greatest number of visitors in Australia. Exports to all
major markets.

ŶŶŶŶŶ **Patricia Shiraz 2004** Still, dense, deep purple-red; full-bodied wine, replete with
blackberry, plum and prune fruits supported by substantial but ripe tannins and oak;
with a screwcap would be immortal. Cork. 14.5° alc. **Rating** 94 **To** 2019 $44.95
Cellar Door Release Late Harvested Botrytis Semillon 2003 Interesting
wine; traditional Brown Brothers approach resulted in alcohol 13° to 14°; here
much lower alcohol and bright acidity to go with luscious fruit; has flourished in
bottle. Cork. 8.5° alc. **Rating** 94 **To** 2009 $21

ŶŶŶŶŶ **Shiraz Mondeuse & Cabernet 2005** Full-bodied, rich and dense, with intense
black fruits and equally robust tannins; the components are in balance, and the
wine needs, and will repay, extended cellaring, cork permitting. 13.5° alc.
Rating 93 **To** 2020 $39.95
Patricia Merlot 2004 Plenty of substance and structure without going too far;
merlot varietal character is evident though not razor-sharp; trophy (Best Merlot),
Hobart Wine Show '06. Cork. 14.5° alc. **Rating** 93 **To** 2015 $45
Victoria Shiraz 2005 Has rather more oak evident than is usual for Brown
Brothers, allied with good texture and complexity; juicy blackberry/blueberry
fruit rounds off an appealing wine. **Rating** 92 **To** 2014 $17.90
Patricia Cabernet Sauvignon 2003 Medium- to full-bodied; good texture,
structure and weight, with pleasant earthy overtones to the cabernet fruit; falters
fractionally on the finish. Cork. 14.5° alc. **Rating** 92 **To** 2020 $45
Patricia Pinot Noir Chardonnay Brut 2001 Vibrant and lively, showing
its cool-climate origins in the minerally/citrussy flavours, and in the brisk, but
balanced, acidity. Cork. 12.5° alc. **Rating** 91 **To** 2010 $39

ΨΨΨΨ Cellar Door Release Vermentino 2006 Particularly well made; an interesting variety for a warm climate; one-third barrel ferment has subtly added to the structure; an appealing mix of stone fruit and citrus with acidity woven through on the finish. Screwcap. 13.5° alc. **Rating** 89 **To** 2009 $15.90
Cellar Door Release Heathcote Durif 2005 Deeply coloured; rich, mouthcoating black fruits and dark chocolate; powerful but ripe tannins; good texture. Cork. 15° alc. **Rating** 89 **To** 2015 $19.90
Pinot Noir Chardonnay Pinot Meunier NV Bright colour; a quite serious sparkling, with good intensity and length, before a lingering, dry finish. Cork. 12.5° alc. **Rating** 89 **To** 2009 $18.90
Cellar Door Release Banksdale Viognier 2006 Given complexity by wild yeast fermentation and oak maturation, but the alcohol dulls the edge of the varietal character. Screwcap. 15° alc. **Rating** 87 **To** 2010 $16.90
Heathcote Sangiovese 2006 Crystal-clear light-bodied red fruits ready to roll without any delay. Screwcap. 14.5° alc. **Rating** 87 **To** 2009 $18.90
Victoria Tempranillo 2005 Some slightly reduced sour cherry aromas, with a lemony tang to the palate often present in Australian tempranillo. Screwcap. 14° alc. **Rating** 87 **To** 2009 $15.90
Zibibbo Rosa NV An exceptionally clever cellar door style; bright, fresh cherry and raspberry flavours, the sweetness balanced by acidity. Zibibbo is an Italian synonym for muscat of alexandria. Cork. 8° alc. **Rating** 87 **To** 2009 $15
Special Late Harvested Orange Muscat & Flora 2007 Orange blossom aromas; moderately sweet grapey flavours and gentle acidity; aims to please, and does. Screwcap. 9.5° alc. **Rating** 87 **To** 2010 $14

Brown Hill Estate

Cnr Rosa Brook Road/Barrett Road, Rosa Brook, WA 6285 **Region** Margaret River
T (08) 9757 4003 **F** (08) 9757 4004 **www.**brownhillestate.com.au **Open** 7 days 10–5
Winemaker Nathan Bailey **Est.** 1995 **Cases** 3000
The Bailey family's stated aim is to produce top-quality wines at affordable prices, via uncompromising viticultural practices emphasising low yields per ha, in conjunction with the family being involved in all stages of production with minimum outside help. They have 7 ha each of shiraz and cabernet sauvignon, 4 ha of semillon and 2 ha each of sauvignon blanc and merlot, and by the standards of the Margaret River, the prices are indeed affordable.

ΨΨΨΨΨ Lakeview Margaret River Sauvignon Blanc Semillon 2007 Semillon adds to the length and focus, with an attractive lemony cast to the gooseberry fruit; good length and finish. Screwcap. 13.5° alc. **Rating** 92 **To** 2012 $16
Croesus Reserve Margaret River Merlot 2006 Light- to medium-bodied; an elegant wine, with good varietal expression, unforced and supple. Screwcap. 14.8° alc. **Rating** 90 **To** 2013 $25

ΨΨΨΨ Fimiston Reserve Margaret River Shiraz 2006 More developed colour than Chaffers; more complex but less focused; medium-bodied, with fruit supported by vanilla oak. Screwcap. 14.8° alc. **Rating** 89 **To** 2014 $25
Ivanhoe Reserve Margaret River Cabernet Sauvignon 2006 Medium-bodied, with pleasant cassis, blackcurrant and spice flavours; good tannins and fair length. Screwcap. 14.8° alc. **Rating** 89 **To** 2012 $25
Chaffers Margaret River Shiraz 2006 Good hue; medium-bodied black cherry and plum fruit with some touches of spice; balanced tannins and oak. Screwcap. 14.5° alc. **Rating** 88 **To** 2014 $18
Charlotte Margaret River Sauvignon Blanc 2007 Gentle tropical fruit balanced by citrussy/minerally acidity. Screwcap. 13.5° alc. **Rating** 87 **To** 2009 $16

Brown Magpie Wines

125 Larcombes Road, Modewarre, Vic 3240 **Region** Geelong
T (03) 5261 3875 **F** (03) 5261 3875 **www**.brownmagpiewines.com **Open** 7 days 12–3
Winemaker Loretta Breheny, Shane Breheny, Karen Coulston (Consultant)
Est. 2000 **Cases** 5000
Shane and Loretta Breheny own a 20-ha property predominantly situated on a gentle, north-facing slope, with cypress trees on the western and southern borders providing protection against the wind. Over 2001 and '02, 9 ha of vines were planted, with pinot noir (5 ha) taking the lion's share, followed by pinot gris (2 ha), shiraz (1.5 ha) and 0.25 ha each of chardonnay and sauvignon blanc. Viticulture is Loretta Breheny's love; winemaking (and wine) is Shane's.

ΨΨΨΨΨ **Geelong Shiraz 2006** Light- to medium-bodied; has a delicious array of spicy red and black fruits on a fresh and very long palate; trophy, Geelong Wine Show '07. **Rating** 94 **To** 2015 $29

ΨΨΨΨΨ **Modewarre Mud Shiraz 2006** Bright, youthful colour; dominated by red fruits and spice, with layers of bright fruits across the palate; juicy, fresh and vibrant, with fine, silky, medium-bodied texture. Screwcap. 14° alc. **Rating** 93 **To** 2018 $33
Modewarre Mud Shiraz 2005 A rich wine, with layers of black fruits, licorice and spice; good extract, tannins and oak. **Rating** 92 **To** 2016 $33
Pinot Noir 2006 Dense colour; a very rich and plush wine; remarkably, not obviously extractive, though it is very ripe. **Rating** 90 **To** 2012 $24

ΨΨΨΨ **Geelong Pinot Gris 2007** A very complex bouquet, with the suggestion of some oak somewhere in the mix; the palate follows suit, with a hint of sweetness, but lots of complexity. **Rating** 89 **To** 2009 $20
Blanc de Noir 2006 Pale bronze; an unexpectedly full palate, with nutty/creamy notes offset by powerful acidity. **Rating** 89 **To** 2010 $24

Browns of Padthaway

Keith Road, Padthaway, SA 5271 **Region** Padthaway
T (08) 8765 6040 **F** (08) 8765 6003 **www**.browns-of-padthaway.com **Open** By appt
Winemaker Contract **Est.** 1993 **Cases** 35 000
The Brown family has for many years been the largest independent grapegrower in Padthaway, a district in which most of the vineyards were established and owned by Wynns, Seppelt, Lindemans and Hardys, respectively. Since 1998, after a slow start, Browns has produced excellent wines and wine production has increased accordingly. Exports to the UK, the US, Germany, Malaysia, Thailand, Japan and NZ.

ΨΨΨΨΨ **Myra Family Reserve Cabernet Sauvignon 2004** Attractive and generous blackcurrant and mulberry fruit, with plum tannins and good oak; surprise packet, ready now but will hold. Cork. 14.5° alc. **Rating** 92 **To** 2015 $24

ΨΨΨΨ **Edward Family Reserve Malbec 2003** Good colour; very strong varietal character of plum jam and prunes; soft tannins; good overall balance; ageing remarkably well. Cork. 14.5° alc. **Rating** 88 **To** 2013 $24
Unwooded Chardonnay 2006 Nectarine, melon and peach; fruit-driven, and, though not especially complex, is well balanced. **Rating** 87 **To** 2010 $16
Verdelho 2007 Has plenty of flavour in the typical verdelho fruit salad spectrum, but needs a touch more vibrancy. **Rating** 87 **To** 2009 $16

Bruny Island Wines

★★★

4391 Main Road, Lunawanna, Bruny Island, Tas 7150 (postal) **Region** Southern Tasmania
T (03) 6293 1088 **F** (03) 6293 1088 **Open** W'ends & hols or by appt (closed June–Aug)
Winemaker Bernice Woolley **Est.** 1998 **Cases** 200
Richard and Bernice Woolley have established the only vineyard on Bruny Island, the southernmost commercial planting in Australia. They have a total of 2 ha of chardonnay and pinot noir, not all in production. Bernice has a degree in marketing from Curtin University,

and she and Richard have operated budget-style holiday accommodation on the property since 1999.

🍷🍷🍷🍷 **Unwooded Chardonnay 2006** Has melon, white peach and nectarine flavours and enough lemony acidity to give length. Screwcap. 13.3° alc. **Rating** 87 **To** 2011 $25
Reserve Pinot Noir 2006 Colour more advanced than the varietal; light- to medium-bodied, and less grippy than the varietal, though still a tweak of green on the finish. Screwcap. 13.6° alc. **Rating** 87 **To** 2011 $35

🌿 Buckley's Run Vineyard ★★☆

50 Stony Creek Road, Red Hill, Vic 3937 (postal) **Region** Mornington Peninsula
T (03) 5989 3112 **F** (03) 5989 3085 **Open** At The Local Collection, Wed–Sun 11–5, Mornington Flinders Road
Winemaker Precision Wine (Phillip Kittle, Andrew Thomson) **Est.** 2000 **Cases** NFP
In 1998 Gabrielle Johnston purchased the 17-ha property; 3 ha of pinot gris had been established, and the property also has 165 olive trees and is an established Arabian horse stud. Most of the grapes have been sold over the years, but with small amounts made under the Buckley's Run label by a passing parade of winemakers. In 2006 Gabrielle Johnston joined with five other small vineyards without their own cellar door to form a group called The Local Collection (TLC as a double entendre) at Noels Gallery with over 20 wines available for tasting and matching with the food at the restaurant.

Buller (Rutherglen)

Three Chain Road, Rutherglen, Vic 3685 **Region** Rutherglen
T (02) 6032 9660 **F** (02) 6032 8005 **www**.buller.com.au **Open** Mon–Sat 9–5, Sun 10–5
Winemaker Andrew Buller **Est.** 1921 **Cases** 4000
The Buller family is very well known and highly regarded in North East Victoria, and the business benefits from vines that are now 80 years old. The rating is for the superb releases of Museum fortified wines. Limited releases of Calliope Shiraz and Shiraz Mondeuse can also be good. Exports to the UK and the US.

🍷🍷🍷🍷🍷 **Rare Rutherglen Liqueur Muscat NV** Deep brown with a touch of olive on the rim; full and deep, almost into chocolate, with intense raisined fruit; richly textured, with great structure to the raisined/plum pudding fruit flavours, and obvious rancio age. Clean finish and aftertaste. Diam. 18° alc. **Rating** 95 **To** 2009 $100
Rare Rutherglen Liqueur Tokay NV Medium deep golden-brown; a mix of sweet tea leaf and Christmas cake is a highly aromatic entry point for the bouquet; the palate has a sweet core of muscadelle fruit, and rancio, tea leaf, nutty and cake elements surrounding the core. Diam. 18° alc. **Rating** 94 **To** 2009 $100

🍷🍷🍷🍷🍷 **Fine Old Classic Rutherglen Muscat NV** Some age evident in the colour; very sweet raisin fruit needs more rancio cut, but is good value. **Rating** 92 **To** 2009 $22

🍷🍷🍷🍷 **Fine Old Classic Rutherglen Tokay NV** A mix of tea leaf and dried muscadelle aromas, the palate following down the same track, with distilled muscadelle fruit stemming directly (in flavour terms) from the fruit base; good balance and richness. Cork. 18° alc. **Rating** 89 **To** 2009 $20
Black Dog Creek Riesling 2006 Well made; a firm mineral structure to the apple and pear fruit; dry finish; from 'selected Vic regions'. Screwcap. 12.5° alc. **Rating** 87 **To** 2010 $14

Buller (Swan Hill)

Murray Valley Highway, Beverford, Vic 3590 **Region** Swan Hill
T (03) 5037 6305 **F** (03) 5037 6803 **www**.buller.com.au **Open** Mon–Sat 9–5
Winemaker Richard Buller (Jnr) **Est.** 1951 **Cases** 120 000

This is a parallel operation to the Calliope winery at Rutherglen, similarly owned and operated by third-generation Richard and Andrew Buller. It offers traditional wines which in the final analysis reflect both their Riverland origin and a fairly low-key approach to style in the winery. The estate vineyard of 27.5 ha is planted to a wide variety of grapes, and additional grapes are purchased from growers in the region. Exports to the UK, the US and Canada.

ΨΨΨΨΩ **Gold Botrytis Semillon 2006** Rich and sweet, of course; botrytis evident but not overwhelming; balanced acidity a major plus. Screwcap. 10.5° alc. **Rating** 90 **To** 2010 $20

ΨΨΨΨ **Beverford Durif 2004** Once again shows the power of durif able to express itself even when grown in a warm, high-crop environment; blackberry jam fruit, then a savoury finish. Screwcap. 13.5° alc. **Rating** 88 **To** 2011 $12
Beverford Moscato 2007 New breed; very sweet and grapey tropical fruit; could reduce the alcohol even further with 50% soda water. Being less than 7° alcohol, technically not wine. Screwcap. 5.5° alc. **Rating** 87 **To** 2009 $12
Beverford Moscato Rosso 2007 An interesting low-alcohol style with a mix of strawberries, sugar and lemon juice; within its terms of reference, well made. Screwcap. 7° alc. **Rating** 87 **To** 2009 $12
Beverford Cabernet Sauvignon 2005 Has more weight and structure than many at this price point and origin; strong blackcurrant fruit and supporting tannins. Screwcap. 14.5° alc. **Rating** 87 **To** 2010 $11

Buller View Wines   ★★★

PO Box 457, Reservoir, Vic 3073 **Region** Upper Goulburn
T (03) 9355 7070 **F** (03) 9355 7353 www.bullerviewwines.com.au **Open** Not
Winemaker Karen Coulson (Contract) **Est.** 1996 **Cases** 1500
Pasquale 'Charlie' Orrico migrated from his native Calabria in 1956, establishing a successful commercial building enterprise in Melbourne. Childhood memories of winemaking on his grandfather's vineyard remained with Charlie, and in 1982 he and his wife, Maria, purchased land near Mansfield with the intention of establishing a vineyard. This eventuated in 1996, with the planting of 2 ha of merlot and 1 ha of cabernet sauvignon. From 2002 the estate-grown fruit has been processed onsite. It has to be said that Charlie Orrico has gone where angels fear to tread by choosing to plant merlot and cabernet sauvignon, rather than earlier ripening varieties.

ΨΨΨΨ **Cabernet Sauvignon Merlot 2006** Strong varietal cabernet, with bright cassis fruit on the bouquet and fine acid on the finish; an elegant style. Cork. 14° alc. **Rating** 88 **To** 2012 $18

🍇 Bullock Creek Vineyard   ★★★★

111 Belvoir Park Road, Ravenswood North, Vic 3453 **Region** Bendigo
T (03) 5435 3207 **F** (03) 5435 3207 **Open** W'ends 11–6, or by appt
Winemaker Langanook (Matt Hunter), Bob Beischer **Est.** 1978 **Cases** 200
Bob and Margit Beischer purchased the 2-ha vineyard (and surrounding land) in 1998, initially selling the grapes to Bendigo TAFE, where Bob was undertaking viticultural and winemaking studies, thus seeing their grapes vinified. The long-term plan was to build their own winery, and this was completed for the 2006 vintage. Prolonged drought has kept the yields very low. The estate-grown wines are released under the Bullock Creek Vineyard label; the Bullock Creek Wines label is for those made incorporating some locally grown grapes.

ΨΨΨΨΩ **Shiraz 2006** Saturated colour; plum, blackberry and a touch of licorice; controlled oak, likewise extract; long finish. Screwcap. 14.5° alc. **Rating** 93 **To** 2026 $25

ΨΨΨΨ **Marong Shiraz 2006** More developed than the varietal Shiraz, the high alcohol showing through clearly; black fruits and vanillin oak; a big difference in the two wines, this far from bad. Screwcap. 15° alc. **Rating** 89 **To** 2015 $20

Bendigo Cabernet Sauvignon 2006 Picked far too late, with consequent alcohol heat; reverse osmosis would have solved the problem; a great pity, with very good fruit underneath. Screwcap. 15.8° alc. **Rating** 88 **To** 2016 $30

Bulong Estate

70 Summerhill Road, Yarra Junction, Vic 3797 (postal) **Region** Yarra Valley
T (03) 5967 1358 **F** (03) 5967 1350 **www**.bulongestate.com **Open** 7 days 11–5
Winemaker Matt Carter **Est.** 1994 **Cases** 2000
Judy and Howard Carter purchased their beautifully situated 45-ha property in 1994, looking down into the valley below and across to the nearby ranges with Mt Donna Buang at their peak. Most of the grapes from the immaculately tended vineyard are sold, with limited quantities made onsite for the Bulong Estate label. The wines in the current release portfolio show confident winemaking across the range.

Pinot Noir 2006 Bright colour; fresh and lively red fruits dance in the mouth, the finish long and fine; great early-drinking pinot. Screwcap. 13.5° alc. **Rating** 93 **To** 2011 $21
Chardonnay 2006 Altogether elegant very slow-developing wine; supple nectarine fruit has absorbed barrel ferment (50% new American oak); from three of the excellent Dijon clones. Screwcap. 12.5° alc. **Rating** 91 **To** 2013 $21
Cabernet Franc 2005 Retains bright colour, and has very good varietal expression; fragrant red fruits linked to touches of cedar and spice; good structure; above average. Cork. 14° alc. **Rating** 90 **To** 2013 $21

Pinot Gris 2007 Crisp citrussy acidity gives the wine life and vitality, leaving pear flavours on the mid-palate intact. Screwcap. 13.5° alc. **Rating** 88 **To** 2009 $18

Bundaleer Wines

PO Box 41, Hove, SA 5048 **Region** Southern Flinders Ranges
T (08) 8296 1231 **F** (08) 8296 2484 **www**.bundaleerwines.com.au **Open** At North Star Hotel, Nott Street, Melrose Wed–Sun 11–5
Winemaker Angela Meaney **Est.** 1998 **Cases** 2000
Bundaleer is a joint venture between third-generation farmer Des Meaney and manufacturing industry executive Graham Spurling (whose family originally came from the Southern Flinders Ranges). Planting of the 8-ha vineyard (shiraz and cabernet sauvignon) began in 1998, the first vintage in 2001. It is situated in a region known as the Bundaleer Gardens, on the edge of the Bundaleer Forest, 200 km north of Adelaide. This should not be confused with the Bundaleer Shiraz brand made by Bindi. Exports to the UK, Hong Kong and Japan.

Eden Valley Riesling 2007 Better focus than the Clare, with more lemon fruits, and a longer line on the finish; a more generous and textural wine. Screwcap. 13° alc. **Rating** 90 **To** 2016 $17

Clare Valley Riesling 2007 Very pale colour; lifted aromas of lime juice and a hint of talc; slightly coarse flavours, but has good acidity and length on the finish. Screwcap. 12.5° alc. **Rating** 88 **To** 2015 $17

Bundaleera Vineyard ★★★☆

449 Glenwood Road, Relbia, Tas 7258 (postal) **Region** Northern Tasmania
T (03) 6343 1231 **F** (03) 6343 1250 **Open** W'ends 10–5
Winemaker Pirie Consulting (Andrew Pirie) **Est.** 1996 **Cases** 1000
David (a consultant metallurgist in the mining industry) and Jan Jenkinson have established 2.5 ha of vines on a sunny, sheltered north to northeast slope in the North Esk Valley. The 12-ha property on which their house and vineyard are established gives them some protection from the urban sprawl of Launceston; Jan is the full-time viticulturist and gardener for the immaculately tended property.

ŸŸŸŸŸ **Pinot Noir 2006** Deep colour; abounding with black and red fruits on the palate and the long finish; needs time, and will flourish in the years ahead. Screwcap. 14.2° alc. **Rating** 92 **To** 2014 $27.50

ŸŸŸŸ **Riesling 2007** Quite tightly wound fruit, with the abundance of the '07 acidity; will only go onward and upward from here. Screwcap. 12.9° alc. **Rating** 88 **To** 2017 $18

Bungawarra

Bents Road, Ballandean, Qld 4382 **Region** Granite Belt
T (07) 4684 1128 **F** (07) 4684 1128 **www**.bungawarrawines.com.au **Open** 7 days 10–4.30
Winemaker Jeff Harden **Est.** 1975 **Cases** 1500
Now owned by Jeff Harden, Bungawarra draws upon 4 ha of mature vineyards which over the years have shown themselves capable of producing red wines of considerable character, as the wines from 2006 amply demonstrate.

ŸŸŸŸŸ **Shiraz 2006** Strong colour; inky blackberry, dark chocolate and licorice; particularly milky vanilla oak; ripe tannins. **Rating** 93 **To** 2015 $24

ŸŸŸŸ **Cabernet Sauvignon 2006** Light- to medium-bodied; cassis, berry; sweetened by oak. **Rating** 87 **To** 2011 $24

Bunnamagoo Estate   ★★★★

Bunnamagoo, Rockley, NSW 2795 (postal) **Region** Central Ranges Zone
T 1300 304 707 **F** (02) 6377 5231 **www**.bunnamagoowines.com.au **Open** Not
Winemaker Robert Black **Est.** 1995 **Cases** 14 000
Bunnamagoo Estate (on one of the first land grants in the region) is situated near the historic town of Rockley. Here a 6-ha vineyard planted to chardonnay, merlot and cabernet sauvignon has been established by Paspaley Pearls, a famous name in the pearl industry. Increasing production has led to the decision to build a winery and cellar door in Henry Lawson Drive, Mudgee, opening in 2009, with Robert Black now full-time winemaker.

ŸŸŸŸŸ **Shiraz 2006** Dense colour; medium-bodied, and while the fruit flavours are unambiguously ripe, they are not jammy, nor is the finish hot; balanced oak and tannins; good length. Screwcap. 15° alc. **Rating** 92 **To** 2012 $23.95
Cabernet Sauvignon Merlot 2006 Supple and smooth; good and fresh cassis and blackcurrant plus well-handled French oak; good length and finish. ProCork. 14.5° alc. **Rating** 91 **To** 2016 $21.95
Pinot Noir Chardonnay 2005 Elegant and fresh mix of strawberry and citrus fruit, 24 months on lees having added some textural complexity and a touch of toast; finely balanced and long. Cork. 13° alc. **Rating** 90 **To** 2011 $24.95

ŸŸŸŸ **Cabernet Sauvignon 2005** Cool-grown elements of spice and leaf partially offset by cedar and vanilla oak; fine, silky tannins help the finish. Cork. 14.2° alc. **Rating** 89 **To** 2015 $23.95
Semillon 2007 Oak part of the make-up of the wine on both bouquet and palate; seems a little flat in fruit terms, especially acidity; earlier picking may be better. Screwcap. 13.5° alc. **Rating** 87 **To** 2011 $21.95

Burge Family Winemakers

Barossa Way, Lyndoch, SA 5351 **Region** Barossa Valley
T (08) 8524 4644 **F** (08) 8524 4444 **www**.burgefamily.com.au **Open** Fri, Sat, Mon 10–5
Winemaker Rick Burge **Est.** 1928 **Cases** 3800
Rick Burge and Burge Family Winemakers (not to be confused with Grant Burge, although the families are related) has established itself as an icon producer of exceptionally rich, lush and concentrated Barossa red wines. Rick Burge's sense of humour was evident with the Nice Red (a Merlot/Cabernet made for those who come to the cellar door and ask, 'Do you have

a nice red?'). After the frost and drought 2007 vintage production fell by 70%, and hence the decision to delay the release of the '06 reds, 2008 marked 80 years of continuous winemaking by three generations of the family. Exports to the US and other major markets.

ΨΨΨΨΨ **Olive Hill Barossa Valley Shiraz Mourvedre Grenache 2005** One of the best examples going around of this blend, although shiraz (71%) is by far the dominant partner; offers a complex spray of spicy black fruits with wafts of dark chocolate and mocha. Cork. 14.5° alc. **Rating** 94 **To** 2020 $32

ΨΨΨΨΨ **Draycott Barossa Valley Shiraz 2005** A very attractive medium-bodied wine with plum, blackberry and black cherry fruit; good length, restrained alcohol and fine tannins. Cork. 14.5° alc. **Rating** 93 **To** 2015 $36
Draycott Barossa Valley Shiraz 2006 Carries its alcohol with aplomb; medium- to full-bodied traditional Barossa Valley style, its blackberry and mocha flavours have exemplary mouthfeel and structure; cork permitting, will be long lived. Cork. 15° alc. **Rating** 92 **To** 2021 $36
Olive Hill Barossa Valley Shiraz Mourvedre Grenache 2006 Always one of the better SGM blends from the Barossa Valley, manfully carrying its alcohol, partly because the shiraz is 68%, and the wine is 100% French oak-matured; all up, an abundance of ripe black fruits. Cork. 15.5° alc. **Rating** 92 **To** 2015 $32
Wilsford Founders Reserve Three Generations Blend Old Tawny Port NV Most attractive briary, nutty, Christmas cake and spice flavours; life and freshness from clean rancio finish. Cork. 19° alc. **Rating** 92 **To** 2009 $36
Garnacha Dry Grown Barossa Valley Grenache 2005 Lots of juicy varietal fruit, but has positive tannin structure to give distinction; well above the norm for the Barossa. Cork. 15° alc. **Rating** 90 **To** 2012 $25
The Homestead Barossa Valley Cabernet Sauvignon 2005 Solid blackcurrant fruit, with touches of earth and chocolate to a medium- to full-bodied palate; good tannins. Cork. 14° alc. **Rating** 90 **To** 2018 $25

ΨΨΨΨ **D & OH Barossa Valley Shiraz Grenache 2005** Medium-bodied; the juicy berry grenache contribution is evident, but shiraz rules the roost in flavour and structure, though still an easy-drinking style. Screwcap. 14° alc. **Rating** 89 **To** 2010 $22
Olive Hill Barossa Valley Semillon 2007 Ripe and rich in the mouth, but doesn't have the thrust or vitality of new generation Barossa semillons – white burgundy style of yore. Screwcap. 12.5° alc. **Rating** 87 **To** 2009 $22

Burgi Hill Vineyard ★★★
290 Victoria Road, Wandin North, Vic 3139 **Region** Yarra Valley
T (03) 5964 3568 **F** (03) 5964 3568 **www**.burgihill.com.au **Open** By appt
Winemaker Christopher Sargeant, Dominique Portet **Est.** 1974 **Cases** 300
The 4.5-ha vineyard now operated by Christopher Sargeant and family was established over 30 years ago and is planted to chardonnay, sauvignon blanc, pinot noir, merlot and cabernet sauvignon. For many years the grapes were sold, but now some are vinified for Burgi Hill.

ΨΨΨΨ **Yarra Valley Merlot 2005** Earth, spice and olive aromas and flavours around red fruits are varietal; good length and texture. Cork. **Rating** 87 **To** 2011 $23

Burke & Wills Winery ★★★★
3155 Burke & Wills Track, Mia Mia, Vic 3444 **Region** Heathcote
T (03) 5425 5400 **F** (03) 5425 5401 **www**.wineandmusic.net **Open** By appt
Winemaker Andrew Pattison **Est.** 2003 **Cases** 1500
After 18 years at Lancefield Winery in the Macedon Ranges, Andrew Pattison moved his operation a few miles north in 2004 to set up Burke & Wills Winery at the southern edge of Heathcote, continuing to produce wines from both regions. While establishing 1 ha of shiraz, 0.5 ha gewurztraminer and smaller plantings of merlot, malbec and petit verdot at Burke &

Willa, he still retains an 18-year-old vineyard at Malmsbury at the northern end of the Macedon Ranges, with 1 ha of cabernet and 0.5 ha each of pinot noir and chardonnay. Additional grapes come from contract growers in Heathcote and Bendigo. Exports to the UK.

� **Heathcote Shiraz 2006** Strong articulation of variety and region; medium-bodied, with good length to the black fruits plus touches of licorice and spice; French oak would have been even better. Screwcap. 14° alc. **Rating** 92 **To** 2018 $25

♟♟♟♟ **Dig Tree Macedon Ranges Cabernet Sauvignon 2006** Bright crimson; bright, fresh cassis flavours; a touch of mint and fine tannins; perhaps the day will come for cabernet in this region. Screwcap. 14° alc. **Rating** 88 **To** 2012 $18
Dig Tree Macedon Ranges Pinot Noir 2005 Light colour; earthy/savoury elements, but also some ripe, slightly stewy, fruit; shortens somewhat. Screwcap. 13.5° alc. **Rating** 87 **To** 2011 $18

Burton Premium Wines ★★★★

PO Box 242, Killara, NSW 2071 **Region** McLaren Vale
T (02) 9416 6631 **F** (02) 9416 6681 **www.**burtonpremiumwines.com **Open** Not
Winemaker Boar's Rock (Mike Farmilo), Pat Tocaciu (Contract) **Est.** 1998 **Cases** 3000
Burton Premium Wines has neither vineyards nor winery, purchasing its grapes from McLaren Vale and Coonawarra, and having its wines made in various locations by contract winemakers. It brings together the marketing and financial skills of managing director Nigel Burton, and the extensive wine experience (as a senior wine show judge) of Dr Ray Healy, who is director in charge of winemaking. Exports to Thailand, Vietnam, Korea and Singapore.

♟♟♟♟♟ **McLaren Vale Shiraz 2004** A medium-bodied palate, neatly bringing together black fruits, dark chocolate and mocha, supported by good tannin and oak extract; understated length. Cork. 14.5° alc. **Rating** 90 **To** 2012 $32.45

♟♟♟♟ **Coonawarra Cabernet Sauvignon 2004** Minty, leafy, savoury overtones to a long but not especially generous palate; firm tannins. Twin top. 13.5° alc. **Rating** 88 **To** 2014 $32.45

Butlers Lane of Glenlyon ★★★

70 Butlers Lane, Glenlyon, Vic 3461 **Region** Macedon Ranges
T (03) 5348 7525 **F** (03) 5348 7529 **www.**butlerslane.com.au **Open** W'ends & public hols 11–5, or by appt
Winemaker Neil Prestegar **Est.** 1998 **Cases** 600
After holidaying in the area for 20 years, Neil and Telle Prestegar decided the time had come to take up permanent residence after Neil retired from his engineering company in 1998. Not wishing to do things by halves, they created a trout-filled dam, extensive gardens and a picturesque vineyard, with 2.5 ha of sauvignon blanc, 1.5 ha of pinot noir and 1 ha of merlot. They purchase grapes from local growers to make their Shiraz and Cabernet Sauvignon (in addition to the estate-based varietals).

♟♟♟♟ **Shiraz 2005** Slightly unconvincing colour; medium-bodied; oak obvious in a mix of black fruits, spice and mocha; spicy/savoury tannins. Cork. 14° alc. **Rating** 87 **To** 2014 $20
Yandoit Preservative Free Shiraz 2006 Developed colour, and generally shows why SO_2 is used by all but a handful of makers, here (as is usual) catering for those unable to tolerate SO_2; cannot be pointed by normal standards. Screwcap. 13.5° alc. **Rating** 87 **To** 2008 $20

by Farr

PO Box 72, Bannockburn, Vic 3331 **Region** Geelong
T (03) 5281 1979 **F** (03) 5281 1433 **www.**byfarr.com.au **Open** Not
Winemaker Gary Farr, Nick Farr **Est.** 1999 **Cases** 3000

In 1994 Gary Farr and family planted 12 ha of clonally selected viognier, chardonnay, pinot noir and shiraz at a density of 7000 vines per ha on a north-facing hill directly opposite the Bannockburn Winery. The quality of the wines is exemplary, their character subtly different from those of Bannockburn itself due, in Farr's view, to the interaction of the terroir of the hill and the clonal selection. Exports to the UK, the US, India, Malaysia, Hong Kong and Singapore.

ŸŸŸŸŸ **Sangreal 2006** Slightly brighter hue than the varietal; a steel fist in a velvet glove, with quite beautiful plum and spice fruit, and a super-long and fine palate, opening further on the finish; Pinot Noir. Cork. 13.5° alc. **Rating** 96 **To** 2015 $60
Geelong Chardonnay 2006 Typical complexity, with obvious barrel ferment inputs, yet has a certain delicacy and excellent focus to the supple nectarine and citrus-tinged fruit; long, fine finish. Cork. 13.5° alc. **Rating** 95 **To** 2012 $55
Geelong Shiraz 2006 Captures all that is best in cool-grown shiraz; a multiplicity of flavours without the least hint of heaviness or dead fruit; a smooth, silky texture, with blood plums and spice, tannins perfect. Cork. 14.5° alc. **Rating** 95 **To** 2015 $50
Geelong Pinot Noir 2006 Classic structure and texture in Farr style; very fine tannins supporting the plum and cherry fruit, oak playing the correct support role. Cork. 14° alc. **Rating** 94 **To** 2012 $55

ŸŸŸŸŸ **Farrago 2006** Complex nut, pear and stone fruit aromas and flavours; good oak, and has considerable length. Chardonnay/Viognier. Cork. 13.5° alc. **Rating** 92 **To** 2013 $50

Byrne & Smith Wines ★★★

PO Box 640, Unley, SA 5061 **Region** South Australia
T (08) 8272 1911 **F** (08) 8272 1944 **www.**byrneandsmith.com.au **Open** Not
Winemaker Duane Coates (Contract) **Est.** 1999 **Cases** 30 000
Byrne & Smith is a substantial business with two vineyards totalling 53 ha at Stanley Flat in the northern Clare Valley, and a third vineyard of 106 ha near Waikerie in the Riverland. The majority of the grapes are sold, and the wines being marketed also use purchased grapes from regions as far away as the Margaret River. Exports to the UK, the US, Canada, Germany and Denmark.

ŸŸŸŸ **Woolpunda Red Block Shiraz 2005** At the price, there can be no complaints about the wine; medium-bodied, with blackberry and plum fruit, plus notes of mocha on a balanced palate. Screwcap. 14° alc. **Rating** 88 **To** 2012 $9
Thomson Estate Back Block Cabernet Tempranillo 2005 Fresh and lively, with the green/lemony acidity which tempranillo seems to have in Australia; no structure to speak of. Screwcap. 13.5° alc. **Rating** 87 **To** 2009 $11

Cahills Wines NR

448–484 Booie Road, Kingaroy, Qld 4610 **Region** South Burnett
T (07) 4163 1563 **Open** 7 days 10–4
Winemaker Crane Winery (Bernie Cooper) **Est.** 1998 **Cases** 100
When Cindy and John Cahill purchased a former 66-ha dairy farm in 1996, they did so with the intention of planting a vineyard. John Cahill worked for Lindemans for 13 years in Sydney, Brisbane and Cairns, and developed marketing skills from this experience. Nonetheless, they have hastened slowly, planting 1.2 ha of shiraz (in 1998) and chardonnay (in 2000), slowly extending the plantings since. An olive grove has also been established. They make the Shiraz onsite; the Unwooded Chardonnay is processed at Crane Winery.

Caledonia Australis ★★★★☆

PO Box 626, North Melbourne, Vic 3051 **Region** Gippsland
T (03) 9329 5372 **F** (03) 9328 3111 **www.**caledoniaaustralis.com **Open** Not
Winemaker Martin Williams **Est.** 1995 **Cases** 6000

The reclusive Caledonia Australis is a Pinot Noir and Chardonnay specialist, with 33 ha in two separate vineyard locations. The vineyards are in the Leongatha area, on red, free-draining, high-ironstone soils, on a limestone or marl base, and the slopes are east- to northeast-facing. Small-batch winemaking has resulted in consistently high-quality wines. Exports to the US, Singapore, Hong Kong and Japan.

ŸŸŸŸŸ **Gippsland Chardonnay 2005** Quite toasty on the bouquet, with grapefruit and grilled nuts; the palate is rich and lively, and very fresh, with lovely texture, and a little grip on the finish; very long. Screwcap. 13.5° alc. **Rating** 94 **To** 2015 $28

ŸŸŸŸŸ **Mount Macleod Gippsland Chardonnay 2005** More savoury than the standard wine, with strong marzipan, and grapefruit aromas; quite fleshy and fine on the finish, but with a little less concentration. Screwcap. 13.8° alc. **Rating** 90 **To** 2014 $19.95

ŸŸŸŸ **Gippsland Pinot Noir 2005** Bottle development obvious but not excessive; earthy, briary, forest-floor tones dominate; needs more fruit flesh. Screwcap. 13.5° alc. **Rating** 89 **To** 2011 $28

Cambewarra Estate

520 Illaroo Road, Cambewarra, NSW 2540 **Region** Shoalhaven Coast
T (02) 4446 0170 **F** (02) 4446 0170 **www**.cambewarraestate.com.au **Open** Thurs–Sun 10–5 & public & school hols
Winemaker Tamburlaine **Est.** 1991 **Cases** 3000
Louise Cole owns and runs Cambewarra Estate, near the Shoalhaven River on the central southern coast of NSW, the wines made at Tamburlaine in the Hunter Valley. Cambewarra continues to produce attractive wines which have had significant success in wine shows, comprehensively emerging on top in the local (Kiama) wine show, with Keith Tulloch as chairman of judges.

ŸŸŸŸ **Amanda Verdelho 2006** Above-average depth to the tropical fruit salad flavour; a hint of residual sugar well-justified. Screwcap. 13° alc. **Rating** 87 **To** 2009 $19

Campania Hills

447 Native Corners Road, Campania, Tas 7026 **Region** Southern Tasmania
T (03) 6260 4387 **Open** By appt
Winemaker Winemaking Tasmania (Julian Alcorso) **Est.** 1994 **Cases** 500
This is the former Colmaur, purchased by Jeanette and Lindsay Kingston in 2005. They had just sold a business they had built up over 22 years and thought they were returning to country life and relaxation when they purchased the property, with 1.5 ha of vines equally split between pinot noir and chardonnay (plus 700 olive trees). Says Lindsay Kingston, somewhat wryly, 'We welcome visitors. The last lot stayed three hours.'

Campbells

Murray Valley Highway, Rutherglen, Vic 3685 **Region** Rutherglen
T (02) 6032 9458 **F** (02) 6032 9870 **www**.campbellswines.com.au **Open** Mon–Sat 9–5, Sun 10–5
Winemaker Colin Campbell **Est.** 1870 **Cases** 40 000
A wide range of table and fortified wines of ascending quality and price, which are always honest. As so often happens in this part of the world, the fortified wines are the best, with the extremely elegant Isabella Rare Tokay and Merchant Prince Rare Muscat at the top of the tree; the winery rating is for the fortified wines. A feature of the Vintage Room at the cellar door is an extensive range of back vintage releases of small parcels of wine not available through any other outlet, other than to Cellar Club members. Exports to the UK, the US and other major markets.

ŸŸŸŸŸ **Isabella Rare Rutherglen Tokay NV** Very deep olive-brown; broodingly complex, deep and concentrated aromas, then layer upon layer of flavour in the mouth; of almost syrupy consistency; incredibly intense and complex, with the varietal tea-leaf/muscadelle fruit continuity. Cork. 18° alc. **Rating** 97 **To** 2009 $94

Merchant Prince Rare Rutherglen Muscat NV Dark brown, with olive-green on the rim; particularly fragrant, with essency, raisiny fruit; has an almost silky viscosity to the intense flavours which flood every corner of the mouth, but yet retains elegance. Cork. 18° alc. **Rating** 96 **To** 2008 $94

Grand Rutherglen Tokay NV Olive mahogany; much, much more complex than the Classic, with all the key varietal characteristics enhanced by rancio; the palate is very long, and has no stale characters whatsoever. Cork. 17.5° alc. **Rating** 94 **To** 2009 $65

Grand Rutherglen Muscat NV Full olive-brown; highly aromatic; a rich and complex palate is silky smooth, supple and long, the strong raisin fruit balanced by the clean, fresh, lingering acid (and spirit) cut on the finish. Cork. 17.5° alc. **Rating** 94 **To** 2009 $65

ŸŸŸŸŸ **Classic Rutherglen Tokay NV** Medium brown; has clear-cut varietal character on both the bouquet and palate, with tea leaf, toffee and cake flavours; a delicious balance between youth and full maturity; doesn't cloy. Cork. 17.5° alc. **Rating** 93 **To** 2009 $34.60

Classic Rutherglen Muscat NV Spicy/raisiny complexity starting to build; a large increase in intensity and length over the Rutherglen Muscat. Cork. 17.5° alc. **Rating** 92 **To** 2009 $34.60

Rutherglen Tokay NV Bright, light golden-brown; classic mix of tea-leaf and butterscotch aromas lead into an elegant wine which dances in the mouth; has balance and length. Cork. 17.5° alc. **Rating** 92 **To** 2009 $16.90

Bobbie Burns Rutherglen Shiraz 2006 Vibrant purple hue; deftly handled with lively red fruits and an undercurrent of leather and spice; medium-bodied, with chewy tannins on the finish. Cork. 14.5° alc. **Rating** 91 **To** 2014 $18.90

Rutherglen Muscat NV Bright, clear tawny-gold; a highly aromatic bouquet, spicy and grapey, is mirrored precisely on the palate, which has nigh-on perfect balance. Cork. 17.5° alc. **Rating** 91 **To** 2009 $16.90

ŸŸŸŸ **Rutherglen Trebbiano 2007** A humble variety prone to over-crop, but Campbells has been growing it for decades (and used to call it Chablis); a more than passable alternative to pinot gris. Screwcap. 13.5° alc. **Rating** 87 **To** 2010 $16.50

Camyr Allyn Wines   ★★★☆

Camyr Allyn North, Allyn River Road, East Gresford, NSW 2311 **Region** Upper Hunter Valley
T (02) 4938 9577 **F** (02) 4938 9576 **www.**camyrallynwines.com.au **Open** Wed–Mon 10–5
Winemaker James Evers **Est.** 1999 **Cases** 2500
John and Judy Evers purchased the Camyr Allyn North property in 1997, and immediately set about planting 4.4 ha of verdelho, merlot and shiraz. The wines are made at the Northern Hunter winery at East Gresford by James Evers, who worked for Mildara Blass in Coonawarra for some time. The promotion and packaging of the wines is innovative and stylish.

ŸŸŸŸŸ **Hunter Valley Shiraz 2006** Has clear varietal and regional expression; slightly savoury edges to the core of plum and blackberry fruit are appealing, as is the oak and tannin balance. Screwcap. 13.8° alc. **Rating** 91 **To** 2021 $20

ŸŸŸŸ **Hunter Valley Sparkling Shiraz 2005** Quite elegant; well-balanced light-bodied example; with or without food; good length and nice dry finish. Cork. 12.5° alc. **Rating** 88 **To** 2010 $26

Hunter Valley Rose 2007 An attractive collage of red fruit flavours which manage to deal with the unusually high alcohol; dry finish. Screwcap. 14.5° alc. **Rating** 87 **To** 2009 $18

Hunter Valley Merlot 2006 Lots of green and black olive, herb and earth flavours; difficult to do much more with this variety in the Hunter Valley; alcohol mercifully restrained. Screwcap. 13.8° alc. **Rating** 87 **To** 2010 $20

Cannibal Creek Vineyard

260 Tynong North Road, Tynong North, Vic 3813 **Region** Gippsland
T (03) 5942 8380 **F** (03) 5942 8202 **www**.cannibalcreek.com.au **Open** 7 days 11–5
Winemaker Patrick Hardiker **Est.** 1997 **Cases** 2500
The Hardiker family moved to Tynong North in 1988, initially only grazing beef cattle, but aware of the viticultural potential of the sandy clay loam and bleached subsurface soils weathered from the granite foothills of the Black Snake Ranges. Plantings began in 1997, using organically based cultivation methods. The family decided to make their own wine, and a heritage-style shed built from locally milled timber was converted into a winery and cellar door. Exports to the UK and China.

ΨΨΨΨΨ **Pinot Noir 2005** Good mouthfeel, line and length; gently spicy plum and black cherry fruit; impeccable balance and texture; surprise packet ageing impressively. Diam. 14° alc. **Rating** 92 **To** 2012 $28
Sauvignon Blanc 2007 Nice varietal gooseberry aromas, with a hint of tropical fruits in the background; nice weight and texture. Cork. 13° alc. **Rating** 90 **To** 2009 $24

ΨΨΨΨ **Hardiker Pinot Noir 2006** Quite pale in colour, but clearly varietal, and surprisingly firm on the finish. Cork. 13° alc. **Rating** 87 **To** 2009 $16

Canobolas-Smith

Boree Lane, off Cargo Road, Lidster via Orange, NSW 2800 **Region** Orange
T (02) 6365 6113 **F** (02) 6365 6113 **www**.canobolassmithwines.com.au
Open W'ends & public hols 11–5
Winemaker Murray Smith **Est.** 1986 **Cases** 2000
Canobolas-Smith has established itself as one of the leading Orange region wineries, and its three labels are particularly distinctive. Over the years it has produced some quite outstanding Chardonnays. Much of the wine is sold from the cellar door, which is well worth a visit. Exports to the US and Asia.

ΨΨΨΨΨ **Chardonnay 2005** In typical Canobolas-Smith style, elegant and precise; a slightly hard edge of acidity just takes the wine out of top tier. Screwcap. 14° alc. **Rating** 91 **To** 2015 $40

ΨΨΨΨ **Reserve Shiraz 2005** Both aromas and flavours seem far riper than the alcohol would suggest, with essence/confiture overtones; unusual, but certainly no shortage of flavour. Screwcap. 13.9° alc. **Rating** 89 **To** 2015 $35

Canonbah Bridge

Merryanbone Station, Warren, NSW 2824 (postal) **Region** Western Plains Zone
T (02) 6833 9966 **F** (02) 6833 9980 **www**.canonbahbridge.com **Open** Not
Winemaker Shane McLaughlin, Hunter Wine Services (John Hordern) **Est.** 1999
Cases 25 000
The 32-ha vineyard has been established by Shane McLaughlin on the very large Merryanbone Station, a Merino sheep stud which has been in the family for four generations. The wines are at three price points: at the bottom is Bottle Tree, from southeastern Australia; then Ram's Leap, specific regional blends; and at the top, Canonbah Bridge, either estate or estate/regional blends. Exports to the UK, the US and other major markets.

ΨΨΨΨ **Western Plains McLaren Vale Shiraz Grenache Mourvedre 2004** No shortage of flavour or extract to this unashamedly robust wine, ripe fruits countered by drying tannins. Cork. 14° alc. **Rating** 87 **To** 2012 $19.95

Cape Banks ★★★★

PO Box 1096, Mount Gambier, SA 5290 **Region** Limestone Coast Zone
T (08) 8725 2439 **F** (08) 8725 2490 **Open** Not
Winemaker O'Leary Walker Wines **Est.** 2000 **Cases** 2500
Stephen Hambour and John Sandery began the establishment of the Cape Banks vineyard in 2000, with a planting of 10.7 ha of pinot noir. Six ha of chardonnay and 3 ha of sauvignon blanc were added in '02, with 3 more ha of the latter planted in '03 and '06. Riesling (3.3 ha) and pinot gris (1 ha), both planted '03, complete what is a substantial vineyard, on the face of it perfectly suited to the very cool Mount Gambier climate. Most of the grapes are sold, with a plan to ultimately make 500 cases of each of the varieties grown, with a Sparkling Chardonnay and a Pinot Noir the first two releases.

ΥΥΥΥΥ **Kongorong Pinot Noir 2006** Fresh and fragrant; light- to medium-bodied strawberry and cherry flavours on the unforced palate; wholly commendable; lovely now. Screwcap. 14° alc. **Rating** 91 **To** 2010 $24.50

Cape Barren Wines ★★★★☆

Lot 20, Little Road, Willunga, SA 5172 **Region** McLaren Vale
T (08) 8556 4374 **F** (08) 8556 4364 **www**.capebarrenwines.com.au **Open** By appt
Winemaker Brian Light (Contract) **Est.** 1999 **Cases** 5000
Lifelong friends and vignerons Peter Matthews and Brian Ledgard joined forces in 1999 to create Cape Barren Wines. In all they have 62 ha of vineyards throughout the McLaren Vale region, the jewel in the crown being 4 ha of 70-year-old shiraz at Blewitt Springs, which provides the grapes for the Old Vine Shiraz. The McLaren Vale Grenache Shiraz Mourvedre and McLaren Vale Shiraz come from their other vineyards; most of the grapes are sold. Exports to the UK, the US and other major markets.

ΥΥΥΥΥ **Old Vine McLaren Vale Shiraz 2005** Super-powerful McLaren Vale shiraz, with dense and ripe (but not jammy) black fruits on the rich palate; very good tannin and oak management; Gold medal, National Wine Show '07. Cork. **Rating** 94 **To** 2020 $31.25

ΥΥΥΥΥ **Native Goose McLaren Vale Shiraz 2006** Medium-bodied; an attractive melange of blackberry, plum, spice and dark chocolate; fine, savoury tannins; good length; value. Diam. 14.5° alc. **Rating** 92 **To** 2016 $20
Native Goose McLaren Vale GSM 2006 Medium-bodied, with a seamless marriage of the components in a whirl of red cherry, black cherry and raspberry flavours. Screwcap. 14.5° alc. **Rating** 90 **To** 2012 $23

ΥΥΥΥ **Silly Goose Crisp Dry White 2007** A lively, fresh palate with vibrant grassy flavours dominant, a touch of tropical fruit in the background; Sauvignon Blanc/Semillon/Viognier. Screwcap. 13° alc. **Rating** 88 **To** 2010 $19

Cape Bernier Vineyard ★★★

GPO Box 1743, Hobart, Tas 7001 **Region** Southern Tasmania
T (03) 6253 5443 **F** (03) 6253 6087 **www**.capebernier.com.au **Open** Not
Winemaker Winemaking Tasmania (Julian Alcorso) **Est.** 1999 **Cases** 750
Alastair Christie and family have established 2 ha of Dijon clone pinot noir, another 1.5 ha of chardonnay and 0.5 ha of pinot gris on a north-facing slope overlooking historic Marion Bay. The property is not far from the Bream Creek vineyard, and is one of several developments in the region changing the land use from dairy and beef cattle to wine production and tourism.

Cape Grace ★★★★☆

Fifty One Road, Cowaramup, WA 6284 **Region** Margaret River
T (08) 9755 5669 **F** (08) 9755 5668 **www**.capegracewines.com.au **Open** 7 days 10–5
Winemaker Robert Karri-Davies, Mark Messenger (Consultant) **Est.** 1996 **Cases** 2000

Cape Grace Wines can trace its history back to 1875, when timber baron MC Davies settled at Karridale, building the Leeuwin lighthouse and founding the township of Margaret River; 120 years later, Robert and Karen Karri-Davies planted just under 6 ha of vineyard to chardonnay, shiraz and cabernet sauvignon, with smaller amounts of merlot, semillon and chenin blanc. Robert is a self-taught viticulturist; Karen has over 15 years of international sales and marketing experience in the hospitality industry. Winemaking is carried out on the property; consultant Mark Messenger is a veteran of the Margaret River region. Exports to Singapore and Hong Kong.

ΨΨΨΨΨ **Margaret River Chardonnay 2006** Lovely wine, reflecting the great synergy between the variety and the region; fluid nectarine, white peach and grapefruit with a fine sheen of barrel ferment French oak; very good length and balance. Screwcap. 13° alc. **Rating** 95 **To** 2016 $35

ΨΨΨΨ **Margaret River Cabernet Shiraz 2006** Just bordering on medium-bodied, with fresh, predominantly red, fruits, a dusting of spice and a sprinkle of tannins; has length rather than depth. Screwcap. 13.2° alc. **Rating** 89 **To** 2016 $24

Cape Horn Vineyard   ★★★★

Stewarts Bridge Road, Echuca, Vic 3564 **Region** Goulburn Valley
T (03) 5480 6013 **F** (03) 5480 6013 **www**.capehornvineyard.com.au **Open** 7 days 11–5
Winemaker Ian Harrison, John Ellis (Contract) **Est.** 1993 **Cases** 2000
The unusual name comes from a bend in the Murray River which was considered by riverboat owners of the 19th century to resemble Cape Horn, which is depicted on the wine label. The property was acquired by Echuca GP Dr Sue Harrison and her schoolteacher husband Ian in 1993. Ian Harrison has progressively planted their 11-ha vineyard to chardonnay, shiraz, cabernet sauvignon, zinfandel, marsanne and durif.

ΨΨΨΨΨ **Goulburn Valley Marsanne 2007** An attractive wine; honeysuckle and lychee flavours; good acidity and length; an impressive surprise packet. Screwcap. 13° alc. **Rating** 90 **To** 2013 $18
Goulburn Valley Durif 2004 Good varietal character; plenty of black fruits, but not porty, dead fruit or sweet characters; soft tannins, long finish. Diam. 13.8° alc. **Rating** 90 **To** 2011 $21

Cape Jaffa Wines   ★★★★

Limestone Coast Road, Cape Jaffa, SA 5276 **Region** Mount Benson
T (08) 8768 5053 **F** (08) 8768 5040 **www**.capejaffawines.com.au **Open** 7 days 10–5
Winemaker Derek Hooper **Est.** 1993 **Cases** 30 000
Cape Jaffa was the first of the Mount Benson wineries and all of the production now comes from the substantial estate plantings of 16.4 ha, which include the four major Bordeaux red varieties, plus shiraz, chardonnay, sauvignon blanc and semillon. The winery (built of local rock) has been designed to allow eventual expansion to 1000 tonnes, or 70 000 cases. Exports to the UK, Canada, Thailand, Cambodia, Philippines, Hong Kong and Singapore.

ΨΨΨΨΨ **Siberia 2002** A concentrated wine, which has retained vigour and focus thanks to the cool, low-yielding vintage; very attractive spicy, almost tangy, nuances to the black fruits; long finish; Shiraz. Cork. 13° alc. **Rating** 94 **To** 2012 $34.95

ΨΨΨΨ **Mount Benson Shiraz 2004** A lively medium-bodied palate, which has retained good freshness to its mix of red and black fruits; fine tannins. Screwcap. 13.5° alc. **Rating** 89 **To** 2012 $20
Unwooded Chardonnay 2007 Lively and citrussy, though with some slightly green/herbal notes. Screwcap. 13.5° alc. **Rating** 87 **To** 2010 $19
Brocks Reef Shiraz 2005 The entry to the mouth is pleasing, with supple, velvety fruit, but there is a distracting note of sweetness. Screwcap. **Rating** 87 **To** 2012 $17
Brocks Reef Cabernet Merlot 2005 Extremely ripe fruit and ripe tannins; less ripe might have been better. Screwcap. 14.5° alc. **Rating** 87 **To** 2012 $17

Cape Lavender

4 Carter Road, Metricup, WA 6280 **Region** Margaret River
T (08) 9755 7552 **F** (08) 9755 7556 **www.**capelavender.com.au **Open** 7 days 10–5
Winemaker Peter Stanlake, Eion Lindsay **Est.** 1999 **Cases** 3500
With 11.5 ha of vines, a much-awarded winery restaurant, and lavender fields which help make unique wines, this is a business with something extra. There are a number of lavender wines, moving from sparkling through table to port, which have been infused with lavandula angustifolia. There is also a conventional estate range of Semillon, Sauvignon Blanc, Chardonnay, Merlot, Shiraz and Cabernet Sauvignon, made without lavender.

ΨΨΨΨΨ **Estate Margaret River Chardonnay 2005** Developing slowly; fragrant and lively citrus fruit stemming from low alcohol; good length and finish; apparently unwooded. Screwcap. 12° alc. **Rating** 90 **To** 2011 $27

ΨΨΨΨ **Estate Margaret River Shiraz 2005** Ripe red and dark fruit, with a mere suggestion of spice; medium-bodied with good flavour on the finish. Screwcap. 15° alc. **Rating** 87 **To** 2012 $27

Cape Lodge Wines

Caves Road, Yallingup, WA 6282 (postal) **Region** Margaret River
T (08) 9755 6311 **F** (08) 9755 6322 **www.**capelodge.com.au **Open** Not
Winemaker Jan Macintosh **Est.** 1998 **Cases** 1000
Cape Lodge has evolved from a protea farm in the early 1980s, through a small luxury B&B operation in '93, and a multimillion-dollar investment propelled it to the top 100 hotels of the world in the *Condé Nast Traveler* magazine gold list of '05, the fourth-best restaurant in the world for food by the same publication, and the best 5-star resort in Australia and Asia Pacific by a conference of its peers. Since 2001 it has been owned by Malaysians Seng and So Ong, who were responsible for the major expansion to 22 rooms, a restaurant and a 14 000-bottle wine cellar. In 1998, 1.5 ha each of sauvignon blanc and shiraz were planted, the wine sold exclusively through the Cape Lodge resort.

ΨΨΨΨ **Margaret River Shiraz 2004** Light- to medium-bodied; spicy earthy black fruits with fine tannins and restrained oak; early-drinking style; ready now. Screwcap. 14° alc. **Rating** 88 **To** 2011 $44
Margaret River Sauvignon Blanc 2007 Strongly herbaceous, minerally style; crisp, fresh summer drinking; ambitious price. Screwcap. 13.9° alc. **Rating** 87 **To** 2009 $36

Cape Mentelle

Wallcliffe Road, Margaret River, WA 6285 **Region** Margaret River
T (08) 9757 0888 **F** (08) 9757 3233 **www.**capementelle.com.au **Open** 7 days 10–4.30
Winemaker Robert Mann, Simon Burnell, Tim Lovett **Est.** 1970 **Cases** 90 000
Part of the LVMH (Louis Vuitton Möet Hennessy) group. Since the advent of Dr Tony Jordan as Australasian CEO, there has been a concerted and successful campaign to rid the winery of the brettanomyces infection which particularly affected the Cabernet Sauvignon. The Chardonnay and Semillon Sauvignon Blanc are among Australia's best, the potent Shiraz usually superb, and the berry/spicy Zinfandel makes one wonder why this grape is not as widespread in Australia as it is in California. Exports to all major markets.

ΨΨΨΨΨ **Wallcliffe Sauvignon Blanc Semillon 2005** Wild yeast, new French oak fermentation and mlf provide greater depth and richness than other Margaret River blends; beautifully poised and balanced. Screwcap. 13° alc. **Rating** 96 **To** 2013 $40
Wallcliffe Sauvignon Blanc Semillon 2006 A beautifully crafted and balanced wine; literally takes off on the mid-palate through to the finish, with fantastic drive; great citrus and mineral flavour. Screwcap. **Rating** 96 **To** 2015

Margaret River Chardonnay 2006 Super-fragrant citrus-tinged melon and stone fruit; a long, clear and vibrant palate, with barrel ferment nuances adding texture and complexity; balanced finish; trophy, WA Wine Show '07. Screwcap. 13.5° alc. **Rating** 95 **To** 2010 $43

Margaret River Cabernet Sauvignon 2003 Finally, back to where the wine should have been for years; bright, clear and fresh, with no hint of brett, just delicious cassis and blackcurrant fruit in an elegant, medium-bodied frame. Cork. 14.5° alc. **Rating** 95 **To** 2023 $79

Margaret River Sauvignon Blanc Semillon 2007 Sophisticated winemaking; a harmonious and seamless fusion of the two varieties and partial barrel ferment; has length and intensity. Screwcap. 13° alc. **Rating** 94 **To** 2012 $25

Margaret River Shiraz 2005 Powerful and intense, with a firm, clearly delineated structure founded on firm tannins and integrated oak; blackberry, spice and pepper attest to this relatively cool part of Margaret River. Screwcap. 15° alc. **Rating** 94 **To** 2025 $36

Margaret River Zinfandel 2005 A complex wine in both flavour and structure terms, yet not heavy or extractive, and carrying its alcohol with ridiculous ease, as it does in California. Screwcap. 15.5° alc. **Rating** 94 **To** 2018 $53

ŸŸŸŸ **Marmaduke 2005** An interesting wine, reflecting the Shiraz 66%/Grenache 21%/Mourvedre 4% blend, all unusual for Margaret River; spicy, sweet berry fruits with just a hint of savoury notes from the grenache and mourvedre. Screwcap. 14.5° alc. **Rating** 89 **To** 2010 $17

Trinders Margaret River Cabernet Merlot 2005 Medium-bodied; blackcurrant fruit and savoury tannins outweigh the sweeter, red fruit/cassis components of the merlot; worth cellaring. Screwcap. 14° alc. **Rating** 89 **To** 2015 $30

Margaret River Marsanne Roussanne 2006 Basically in a slightly chalky, dry mode reminiscent of the Rhône; needs more time to soften and evolve. Screwcap. 14° alc. **Rating** 88 **To** 2013 $28

Georgiana 2007 Really doesn't have much to say, although no fault; pleasant tropical fruit, good acidity; Chenin Blanc/Chardonnay/Sauvignon Blanc/Semillon. Screwcap. 13° alc. **Rating** 87 **To** 2009 $17

Cape Naturaliste Vineyard   ★★★★

Lot 77, Caves Road, Yallingup, WA 6282 **Region** Margaret River
T (08) 9755 2538 **F** (08) 9755 2538 **www.**capenaturalistevineyard.com.au
Open Wed–Mon 10.30–5
Winemaker Ian Bell, Barney Mitchell, Craig Brent-White **Est.** 1997 **Cases** 4000
Cape Naturaliste Vineyard has a long and varied history, going back 150 years when it was a coach inn for travellers journeying between Perth and Margaret River. Later it became a dairy farm, and in 1970 was purchased by a mining company intending to extract the mineral sands. The government stepped in and declared it a national park, whereafter (in 1980) Craig Brent-White purchased the property. In '97 the 9-ha vineyard was planted to cabernet sauvignon, shiraz, merlot, semillon and sauvignon blanc. The vineyard is run on an organic/biodynamic basis. The quality of the wines would suggest the effort is well worthwhile. Exports to Singapore and Hong Kong.

ŸŸŸŸŸ **Torpedo Rocks Margaret River Shiraz 2005** Fresh, bright, light- to medium-bodied cool-climate shiraz, with liqueur cherry, plum and spice flavours on a long palate. Screwcap. **Rating** 93 **To** 2015 $35

Torpedo Rocks Margaret River Semillon 2006 The fruit has the tensile strength to absorb barrel ferment and 10 months with lees stirring in French oak; touches of lime and lemon on the finish. Screwcap. 12° alc. **Rating** 90 **To** 2015 $29

ŸŸŸŸ **Margaret River Sauvignon Blanc 2007** Aromas of gooseberry and nettle flow through into a soft palate; lacks arrive on finish. Screwcap. 12.6° alc. **Rating** 87 **To** 2009 $23

Capel Vale

Lot 5 Stirling Estate, Mallokup Road, Capel, WA 6271 **Region** Geographe
T (08) 9727 1986 **F** (08) 6364 4882 **www.**capelvale.com **Open** 7 days 10–4
Winemaker Justin Hearn, Ryan Carter **Est.** 1974 **Cases** NFP
Dr Peter Pratten's Capel Vale has expanded its viticultural empire to the point where it is entirely an estate-run business, with 165 ha of vineyards spread through Mount Barker, Pemberton, Margaret River and Geographe, planted to 13 varieties. Its wines cross every price point and style from fighting varietal to ultra-premium; always known for its Riesling, powerful red wines are now very much part of the portfolio. Exports to all major markets.

♥♥♥♥♥ **Shiraz 2005** Plenty of depth of flavour to the assemblage of spicy black fruits; careful manipulation of and balance between acid, fruit and oak. Gold medal, National Wine Show '06; mis-entered (typographical error) in 2007 *Wine Companion*. Screwcap. 15.3° alc. **Rating** 94 **To** 2011 $23
Debut Cabernet Merlot 2005 Long, fine and intense black and red fruits plus nuances of spice and mint; very high-quality tannin structure. **Rating** 94 **To** 2017 $17.95

♥♥♥♥♡ **Cellar Exclusive Geographe Viognier 2007** A powerful wine, with strong apricot and honey fruit; has above-average length and structure. **Rating** 93 **To** 2012 $26.95
Cellar Exclusive Margaret River Cabernet Merlot Petit Verdot Malbec 2005 Strong varietal expression of cabernet, with blackcurrant and a suggestion of red fruits; the palate is soft and supple, but with real backbone at the core; fine and complex on the finish. Screwcap. 14.5° alc. **Rating** 93 **To** 2015 $26.95
Debut Sauvignon Blanc Semillon 2007 Good length, focus and line to the mix of sweet lime and gooseberry fruit; minerally acidity tightens and lengthens the finish. Screwcap. 12.5° alc. **Rating** 91 **To** 2010 $16.95
Pemberton Semillon Sauvignon Blanc 2007 Aromas and flavours of grass, herb, asparagus and gooseberry; a long, clear-cut palate; Semillon 66%. Screwcap. 12.5° alc. **Rating** 90 **To** 2011 $21.99

♥♥♥♥ **Whispering Hill Mount Barker Riesling 2007** Ripe citrus fruits, with elements of candied lemon zest; quite rich and full, but falls away a little at the end. Screwcap. 12° alc. **Rating** 89 **To** 2012 $24.95
Debut Shiraz 2005 Light but bright colour; attractive lifted red fruit flavours offset by balanced, powdery tannins; 4% viognier lifts the flavour. Screwcap. 14° alc. **Rating** 89 **To** 2010 $16.99
Debut Merlot 2005 Light- to medium-bodied, but has appealing fruit flavours which are right in the small berry and snow pea frame for cool-grown merlot; lack of structure irrelevant for an early-drinking style. Screwcap. 14° alc. **Rating** 88 To 2009 $16.99
Whispering Hill Mount Barker Shiraz 2005 A little confectionery bouquet, with Turkish delight and red fruits; quite spicy, but slightly loose on the finish; good flavour. Screwcap. 14° alc. **Rating** 87 **To** 2012 $49.95

Capercaillie ★★★★★

4 Londons Road, Lovedale, NSW 2325 **Region** Lower Hunter Valley
T (02) 4990 2904 **F** (02) 4991 1886 **www.**capercailliewine.com.au **Open** Mon–Sat 9–5, Sun 10–5
Winemaker Daniel Binet **Est.** 1995 **Cases** 6000
A highly successful winery established by the late Alasdair Sutherland, winemaking now under the direction of the talented Daniel Binet. The Capercaillie wines are particularly well made, with generous flavour. Following the example of Brokenwood, its fruit sources are spread across southeastern Australia, although the portfolio includes high-quality wines which are 100% Hunter Valley. Exports to the UK, Japan, Singapore and Dubai.

ＹＹＹＹＹ The Creel Hunter Valley Semillon 2007 A flowery and scented bouquet leads into a long palate, full of the high-toned flavours of the vintage. Delicious wine; gold at Hunter Valley Wine Show '07. Screwcap. 11° alc. **Rating** 95 **To** 2016 $19
The Ghillie Hunter Valley Shiraz 2003 Lives up to all expectations when first tasted three years ago; elegant and focused; spotlessly clean and pure; lovely ripe plum and blackberry fruit; medium-bodied, with perfect control of tannins and extract; minimum 20 years. Screwcap. 14° alc. **Rating** 94 **To** 2023 $60
Ceilidh Shiraz 2006 A fragrant array of red fruit aromas, then an elegance in the mouth which gives no hint of the alcohol; the oak also restrained. Masterly winemaking. Hunter Valley 50%/McLaren Vale 35%/Barossa 15%. Screwcap. 15° alc. **Rating** 94 **To** 2016 $30
The Ghillie Hunter Valley Shiraz 2006 Has similar elegance to the Ceilidh, and a not dissimilar fruit-driven flavour profile, showing its extra class through length on the palate. Screwcap. 14° alc. **Rating** 94 **To** 2016 $50

ＹＹＹＹＹ The Clan 2006 A blend of Cabernet Sauvignon (Hilltops)/Petit Verdot (McLaren Vale)/Merlot (Mudgee); while still coming together, the components are well-balanced and the outcome will assuredly be a harmonious medium-bodied wine. Points as of today, not the future. Screwcap. 15° alc. **Rating** 91 **To** 2015 $30
Hunter Valley Semillon 2007 At the grassy/minerally end of the spectrum, but certainly has length, with attractive lemony acidity. Screwcap. 11° alc. **Rating** 90 **To** 2015 $30
Dessert Style Gewurztraminer 2006 Bright green-yellow; some apricot, spice and lychee; good length and balance; drink now. Screwcap. 10° alc. **Rating** 90 **To** 2009 $18

Carbunup Crest Vineyard   ★★★★☆

PO Box 235, Busselton, WA 6280 **Region** Margaret River
T (08) 9755 7775 **F** (08) 9754 2618 **www**.carbunupcrest.com.au **Open** Not
Winemaker Flying Fish Cove (Elizabeth Reed) **Est.** 1998 **Cases** 4500
Carbunup Crest is owned by the Meares family, with Kris Meares managing the business. Initially it operated as a grapevine rootling nursery, but it has gradually converted to grapegrowing and winemaking. There are 12 ha of vines made up of cabernet sauvignon, merlot, shiraz, semillon, sauvignon blanc and chardonnay (1 ha). The dry-grown vines produced grapes with excellent flavour, excellence reflected in the wines.

ＹＹＹＹＹ Shiraz 2006 A clean, fresh, bright style right from the opening whistle; supple black cherry and plum on a medium-bodied palate, with soft, ripe tannins to close. Screwcap. 13.2° alc. **Rating** 92 **To** 2011 $19.85
Shiraz 2005 A well-balanced, fruit-driven, medium-bodied palate; spicy, peppery black cherry and plum fruit; silky tannins. Screwcap. 13.8° alc. **Rating** 91 **To** 2013 $19.85
Semillon Sauvignon Blanc 2007 A lively bouquet, and a fresh, vibrant palate driven equally by grassy/lemony semillon and gooseberry/passionfruit sauvignon blanc. Screwcap. 12.5° alc. **Rating** 90 **To** 2010 $17.50
Chardonnay 2006 A well-balanced but flavourful palate driven by nectarine and citrus fruit; restrained oak completes the picture. Screwcap. 13.6° alc. **Rating** 90 **To** 2011 $19.60
Cabernet Merlot 2006 Attractive cassis, blackcurrant, plum and spice fruit supported by soft tannins on a light- to medium-bodied palate; minimal oak, but has finesse. Screwcap. 13° alc. **Rating** 90 **To** 2011 $18.75

ＹＹＹＹ Cabernet Merlot 2005 Attractive medium-bodied palate with savoury/olive components among the base of black and redcurrant fruit; ripe, fine tannins and good length. Screwcap. 13.8° alc. **Rating** 89 **To** 2012 $18.75

Cardinham Estate ★★★

Main North Road, Stanley Flat, SA 5453 **Region** Clare Valley
T (08) 8842 1944 **F** (08) 8842 1955 **Open** 7 days 10–5
Winemaker Scott Smith, Brett Stevens **Est.** 1981 **Cases** 5000
The Smith family has progressively increased the vineyard to its present level of 60 ha, the largest plantings being of cabernet sauvignon, shiraz and riesling. It entered into a grape supply contract with Wolf Blass, which led to an association with then Quelltaler winemaker Stephen John. The joint venture then formed has now terminated, and Cardinham is locating its 500-tonne winery on its Emerald Vineyard and using only estate-grown grapes. This has seen production rise, especially with the staples of Riesling, Cabernet Merlot and Stradbroke Shiraz. Exports to the US and Hong Kong.

🍷🍷🍷🍷 **Clare Valley Riesling 2007** Quite austere lime juice and talc personality; good flavour, but a little tart on the finish. Screwcap. 12.6° alc. **Rating** 87 **To** 2015 **$18**

Carlaminda Estate NR

59 Richards Road, Ferguson, WA 6236 **Region** Geographe
T (08) 9728 3002 **F** (08) 9728 3092 **www**.carlaminda.com **Open** Wed–Sun 11–4
Winemaker Quirinus Olsthoorn **Est.** 2003 **Cases** 800
Quirinus Olsthoorn is primarily a cattle breeder, but has established 6 ha of semillon, shiraz, viognier and tempranillo on his property, the first plantings dating back to 1994. Until 2003 the grapes were sold, but since then part of the production has been retained for the Carlaminda Estate label. Quirinus' French wife Anita runs a small, 'maybe the smallest in Australia', French bistro, which is said to be very successful. Exports to the Netherlands.

Carlei Estate & Carlei Green Vineyards ★★★★★

1 Albert Road, Upper Beaconsfield, Vic 3808 **Region** Yarra Valley
T (03) 5944 4599 **F** (03) 5944 4599 **www**.carlei.com.au **Open** W'ends by appt
Winemaker Sergio Carlei **Est.** 1994 **Cases** 10 000
Carlei Estate has come a long way in a short time, with Sergio Carlei graduating from home winemaking in a suburban garage to his own (commercial) winery in Upper Beaconsfield, which falls just within the boundaries of the Yarra Valley. Along the way Carlei acquired a Bachelor of Wine Science from CSU, and has established a 2.25-ha vineyard with organic and biodynamic accreditation adjacent to the Upper Beaconsfield winery. His contract winemaking services are now a major part of the business, and are a showcase for his extremely impressive winemaking talents. Exports to the US, Canada, China, Singapore and Malaysia.

🍷🍷🍷🍷🍷 **Estate Yarra Valley Chardonnay 2006** Tight and sharply focused, with good thrust to the palate, citrus and nectarine to the fore, oak in the background. Screwcap. **Rating** 94 **To** 2015 **$45**

Green Vineyards Cardinia Ranges Pinot Gris 2007 Pink colour tinge perfectly acceptable for the variety; pear, spice, musk and rose petal aromas; lively palate and crisp acidity; has attitude. Screwcap. 13.5° alc. **Rating** 94 **To** 2009 **$26**

Green Vineyards Yarra Valley Pinot Noir 2004 Rich, ripe damson plum fruit on a full, round and fleshy palate; very good balance, structure and length; somehow retains elegance. Diam. 13.5° alc. **Rating** 94 **To** 2011 **$29**

Green Vineyards Yarra Valley Pinot Noir 2005 Bright, clear colour; the excellent length and persistence is the first impression on tasting, then the array of fine black cherry and plum fruit; lovely tannins to a high-quality pinot. Screwcap. **Rating** 94 **To** 2015 **$30**

Estate Heathcote Nord Shiraz 2005 Excellent hue; from the northern end of the Mt Camel Cambrian soil; a silky, supple, spicy medium-bodied palate, unforced, elegant and long. Diam. **Rating** 94 **To** 2018 **$55**

🍷🍷🍷🍷½ **Estate Heathcote Sud Shiraz 2005** From decomposed pink granitic Heathcote soil; more advanced colour than the Nord, firmer and with more depth to the black fruits, but not the same length. Diam. **Rating** 93 **To** 2015 **$55**

Green Vineyards Yarra Valley Chardonnay 2005 Attractive peach and ripe melon fruit; well-integrated French oak; just off the pace on the finish. Diam. 13.5° alc. **Rating** 92 **To** 2013 $29

Green Vineyards Heathcote Shiraz 2005 Good hue; generous ripe fruits, with a mix of blackberry, plum and an overlay of mocha; soft, ripe tannins. Diam. **Rating** 91 **To** 2013 $26

Green Vineyards Central Victorian Cabernet Sauvignon 2004 Medium-bodied; cedary, earthy overtones to blackcurrant and blackberry fruit; the tannins are a trifle edgy, needing to soften. Cork. 14.5° alc. **Rating** 91 **To** 2016 $29

ȲȲȲȲ **Estate Yarra Valley Pinot Noir 2004** Strongly savoury/spicy/stalky characters throughout, the fruit seemingly on the wane. Diam. **Rating** 89 **To** 2009 $49

Green Vineyards Yarra Valley Chardonnay 2006 Some deliberately funky characters to a nicely built and flavoured wine, which is, however, somewhat short. Diam. **Rating** 88 **To** 2011 $29

Green Vineyards Central Victorian Cabernet Sauvignon 2005 Medium-bodied; moderately sweet blackcurrant/cassis offset by light but savoury tannins. Diam. **Rating** 88 **To** 2014 $29

 # Carrickalinga Creek Vineyard

Lot 10 Willson Drive, Normanville, SA 5204 **Region** Southern Fleurieu
T 0403 009 149 **www**.ccvineyard.com.au **Open** Fri–Sat & public hols 11–5.30
Winemaker Tim Geddes (Contract) **Est.** 2001 **Cases** 600
Tim Anstey and Helen Lacey acquired their north-sloping property 2 km from the St Vincent Gulf in the wake of Tim's retirement from university teaching. The choice of region was driven by Dr John Gladstones' enthusiasm for the mild, maritime climate of the lower Fleurieu Peninsula for red grapes in particular. In 2001 they planted 1 ha each of shiraz and cabernet sauvignon, followed later by 1 ha of chardonnay and 0.3 ha of viognier. The purpose-built cellar door, opened in late '07, is on a hillside with spectacular views of both the coast and surrounding hills. Tim Geddes calls the shots with the winemaking; Tim Anstey is 'cellar hand'.

ȲȲȲȲȲ **Shiraz 2005** Developing convincingly, with spicy black fruits and a touch of dark chocolate stolen from McLaren Vale; 18 months in oak has not been overdone. Value. Screwcap. 14.5° alc. **Rating** 90 **To** 2015 $17

ȲȲȲȲ **Cabernet Sauvignon 2005** Rich, medium- to full-bodied wine, again with some dark chocolate notes of McLaren Vale; quite juicy fruit, but jumps around on the palate; patience required. Screwcap. 14.5° alc. **Rating** 88 **To** 2014 $17

Chardonnay 2007 A slightly fuzzy bouquet, but has pleasing citrus and stone fruit flavours; good length, and well priced. Screwcap. 13.5° alc. **Rating** 87 **To** 2009 $15

Casa Freschi

PO Box 45, Summertown, SA 5141 **Region** Langhorne Creek
T 0409 364 569 **F** (08) 8390 3232 **www**.casafreschi.com.au **Open** Not
Winemaker David Freschi **Est.** 1998 **Cases** 1000
David Freschi graduated with a degree in Oenology from Roseworthy College in 1991 and spent most of the decade working overseas in California, Italy and NZ. In 1998 he and his wife decided to trade in the corporate world for a small family-owned winemaking business, with a core of 2.5 ha of vines established by his parents in '72; an additional 2 ha of nebbiolo have now been planted adjacent to the original vineyard. Says David, 'The names of the wines were chosen to best express the personality of the wines grown in our vineyard, as well as to express our heritage.' The 3-ha vineyard was established in 2004–05. No samples received; the rating is that of last year. Exports to the US and Canada.

Cascabel

Rogers Road, Willunga, SA 5172 (postal) **Region** McLaren Vale
T (08) 8557 4434 **F** (08) 8557 4435 **Open** Not
Winemaker Susana Fernandez, Duncan Ferguson **Est.** 1997 **Cases** 2500
Cascabel's proprietors, Duncan Ferguson and Susana Fernandez, planted a 5-ha mosaic of southern Rhône and Spanish varieties. The choice of grapes reflects the winemaking experience of the proprietors in Australia, the Rhône Valley, Bordeaux, Italy, Germany and NZ – and also Susana Fernandez's birthplace, Spain. Production has moved steadily towards the style of the Rhône Valley, Rioja and other parts of Spain. Exports to the UK, the US, Switzerland, Japan and Spain.

Fleurieu Shiraz 2005 A potent mix of blackberry, dark chocolate, spice and black pepper followed by very firm tannins which will take years to soften; the components are in balance. Screwcap. 15° alc. **Rating** 92 **To** 2025 $33
McLaren Vale Tempranillo Graciano 2005 Spicy, tangy, earthy aromas and flavours, with notable tannin input from the graciano (aka grenache); has good length. Screwcap. 14.5° alc. **Rating** 92 **To** 2013 $39

Tipico 2005 Good hue; a typical savoury/spicy/Christmas cake array of flavours on the light- to medium-bodied palate, with fair length. Grenache/Monastrell/Shiraz. Screwcap. 14.5° alc. **Rating** 89 **To** 2013 $25
McLaren Vale Monastrell 2005 Extremely ripe fruit, with strong, mouthcoating sweetness, not from residual sugar as much as alcohol and fruit; may lose some with time in bottle. Screwcap. 15° alc. **Rating** 88 **To** 2020 $40
Eden Valley Riesling 2007 Some odd aromas, hard to pin down, but a far more conventional palate, finishing with firm acidity. A likely victim of the hot, dry vintage. Screwcap. 12° alc. **Rating** 87 **To** 2010 $23

Casella Wines

Wakely Road, Yenda, NSW 2681 **Region** Riverina
T (02) 6961 3000 **F** (02) 6961 3099 **www.**casellawines.com.au **Open** Not
Winemaker Alan Kennett, Phillip Casella **Est.** 1969 **Cases** 12 million
A modern-day fairytale success story, transformed overnight from a substantial, successful but non-charismatic business making 650 000 cases in 2000. Its opportunity came when the US distribution of Lindemans Bin 65 Chardonnay was taken away from WJ Deutsch & Sons, leaving a massive gap in its portfolio, which was filled by yellow tail. It built its US presence at a faster rate than any other brand in history. Exports to all major markets, and is now rapidly penetrating the UK market. It has been aided in all markets by making small batches (500 dozen or so) of Reserve and Limited Release wines, and by spreading its net for these across three states.

yellow tail The Reserve Shiraz 2006 Very fragrant; blackcurrant, spice and plum on a voluptuous, rich palate, flooded with fruit. Gold medal, National Wine Show '07. 14° alc. **Rating** 94 **To** 2016 $17
yellow tail Limited Release Wrattonbully Cabernet Sauvignon 2004 Lush, mouthfilling cassis and blackcurrant fruit is supported by ripe tannins and quality French oak. Cork. 14° alc. **Rating** 94 **To** 2012 $45

yellow tail Limited Release McLaren Vale Shiraz 2004 Medium-bodied, reflecting its relatively low alcohol; fruit-driven and well balanced; no hint of sweetness. Cork. 14° alc. **Rating** 90 **To** 2014 $45

Yendah Mornington Peninsula Pinot Grigio 2007 Some brassy colour hues acceptable for the variety; pear and musk aromas; the palate has good length and similar true-to-variety flavours. Screwcap. 12° alc. **Rating** 89 **To** 2009 $16
yellow tail Limited Release Shiraz 2005 Seductive crowd pleaser, with lots of soft red and black fruits, oak and distinct sweetness on the finish. **Rating** 89 **To** 2012

Yendah McLaren Vale Shiraz Viognier 2006 The viognier has a marked influence on the bouquet and palate; abundant plum, black cherry and blackberry fruit, with savoury tannins on the finish. Screwcap. 14° alc. **Rating** 89 **To** 2011 $16

yellow tail Limited Release Wrattonbully Cabernet Sauvignon 2005 Pleasant black fruits; soft oak and tannins; some sweetness evident. **Rating** 89 **To** 2011

yellow tail The Reserve Riesling 2006 Workmanlike; plenty of flavour, sweetness offset by citrus and mineral acidity; fair length. Screwcap. 12.5° alc. **Rating** 88 **To** 2009 $16

Yendah Viognier 2007 Lots of flavour, possibly from some skin contact and oak, but needs more fruit definition. Screwcap. 14° alc. **Rating** 88 **To** 2010 $17

yellow tail The Reserve Shiraz 2005 A quite complex amalgam of red fruits, licorice and plum with slightly leathery notes somewhere in the mix; finishes with some sweetness. Synthetic cork means no future. 14° alc. **Rating** 88 **To** 2009 $16

yellow tail Merlot 2006 Light, bright red; fresh red fruit flavours, cassis-accented, with residual sugar well-hidden. Screwcap. 13.5° alc. **Rating** 87 **To** 2009 $9.99

Casley Mount Hutton Winery ★★★

'Mount Hutton', Texas Road, Stanthorpe, Qld 4380 **Region** Granite Belt
T (07) 4683 6316 **F** (07) 4683 6345 **Open** Fri–Sun 10–5
Winemaker Grant Casley **Est.** 1999 **Cases** NA
Grant and Sonya Casley have established 9 ha of sauvignon blanc, chenin blanc, semillon, chardonnay, cabernet sauvignon, merlot and shiraz, making the wine onsite. Wine sales are by mail order and through the cellar door, which offers all the usual facilities, and meals by prior arrangement.

ŸŸŸŸ **Verdelho 2007** Fragrant full fruit bouquet; full-bodied; fruit salad with a twist of lemon; possible skin contact; finishes a little short. Diam. 12.6° alc. **Rating** 88 **To** 2009 $28

Reserve Cabernet Sauvignon 2005 Dense inky colour; powerful but over-extracted, and a hollow mid-palate; blended with shiraz might have been great. Diam. 14.5° alc. **Rating** 87 **To** 2012 $28

Cassegrain

764 Fernbank Creek Road, Port Macquarie, NSW 2444 **Region** Hastings River
T (02) 6582 8377 **F** (02) 6582 8378 **www.**cassegrainwines.com.au **Open** 7 days 9–5
Winemaker John Cassegrain **Est.** 1980 **Cases** 60 000
The short-lived merger of Cassegrain and Simon Gilbert Wines (now Prince Hill Wines) has largely been unwound, although the Cassegrain winery production remains at a high level, with a wide range of Premium, Reserve and Limited Release labels. The winery has recently been upgraded, with the building of a temperature-controlled bottle maturation facility. Exports to the UK and other major markets.

ŸŸŸŸŸ **Reserve Semillon 2002** Already on plateau of development; some toast offsets firms acidity. Cork. 10.5° alc. **Rating** 94 **To** 2010 $26.95

ŸŸŸŸŸ **Edition Noir Northern Slopes Tempranillo 2007** Fine, vibrant and focused with a mineral, slightly savoury, edge; fresh and focused with persistent dark fruit on the finish. Screwcap. 13.5° alc. **Rating** 91 **To** 2014 $22.95

Riesling 2006 Quite aromatic, good lime/citrus/mineral; fresh acidity on finish. Screwcap. 12° alc. **Rating** 90 **To** 2011 $19.95

Semillon 2006 Vibrant, lemony fruit, but acidity very high. Screwcap. 10° alc. **Rating** 90 **To** 2013 $16.95

Fromenteau Chardonnay 2006 Good ripe melon aromas, with fresh citrus fruits on the palate; nice weight and good texture; even finish. Screwcap. 13.5° alc. **Rating** 90 **To** 2014 $26.95

Durif 2006 Good example; quite luscious fruit backed up by tannins; slight prune. Screwcap. 14° alc. **Rating** 90 **To** 2011 $26.95

ŶŶŶŶ   **Rose 2007** Firm, crisp, dry; ideal for summer lunches; some red fruits, slight
reduction. Screwcap. 13° alc. **Rating** 89 **To** 2009 $16.95
Reserve Falerne Merlot Cabernet Sauvignon Durif Tempranillo 2005 A
big wine with lots of savoury flavours; pithy cherries, black olives and some tarry
notes; a somewhat tannic and dry finish. Cork. 13.5° alc. **Rating** 89 **To** 2015 $32
Edition Noir New England Durif 2006 Dark, juicy, and full of black fruit;
quite chewy, but not heavy, with well-handled oak on the palate. Screwcap. 14° alc.
Rating 89 **To** 2015 $26.95
Reserve Shiraz 2004 Light- to medium-bodied; pleasant mouthfeel; some
spicy, savoury overtones to black fruits; fine tannins. Cork. 13.5° alc. **Rating** 88
To 2009 $32
Merlot and Cabernet 2006 Clean, fresh and vibrant, with red fruits framed
by good oak; one-dimensional but fleshy and appealing. Screwcap. 13.5° alc.
Rating 88 **To** 2009 $18.95
Gewurztraminer 2007 Light rose petal spice aromas; crisp and fresh; a touch of
sulphide. Screwcap. 13° alc. **Rating** 87 **To** 2009 $17.95
Chardonnay 2007 Quite subdued bouquet, but rich peach flesh on the palate,
and a little spice from the oak; a clean, minerally finish. Screwcap. 13.5° alc.
Rating 87 **To** 2009 $18.95
Verdelho 2007 Good varietal character, with generous tropical fruits and a little
spice; well-handled oak adds to the finished article. Screwcap. 13.5° alc. **Rating** 87
To 2009 $16.95
Edition Noir Hunter Valley Viognier 2007 Quite varietal, with a spice and
apricot bouquet; rich and ample, but a little short on the finish; good flavour
though. Screwcap. 14° alc. **Rating** 87 **To** 2010 $19.95

Castagna   ★★★★

88 Ressom Lane, Beechworth, Vic 3747 **Region** Beechworth
T (03) 5728 2888 **F** (03) 5728 2898 **www**.castagna.com.au **Open** By appt
Winemaker Julian Castagna **Est.** 1997 **Cases** 2000
The elegantly labelled wines of Castagna come from 4 ha of biodynamically managed estate
shiraz and viognier being established (the latter making up 15% of the total). Winemaker Julian
Castagna is intent on making wines which reflect the terroir as closely as possible, and declines
to use cultured yeast or filtration.

ŶŶŶŶ   **Genesis Syrah 2005** Complex luscious, ripe, sweet fruit; some slightly gamey
notes. 14° alc. **Rating** 89 **To** 2014 $75

Castle Rock Estate   ★★★★★

Porongurup Road, Porongurup, WA 6324 **Region** Porongurup
T (08) 9853 1035 **F** (08) 9853 1010 **www**.castlerockestate.com.au **Open** Mon–Fri 10–4,
w'ends & public hols 10–5
Winemaker Robert Diletti **Est.** 1983 **Cases** 3000
An exceptionally beautifully sited vineyard, winery and cellar door on a 55-ha property
with sweeping vistas from the Porongurups, operated by the Diletti family. The standard of
viticulture is very high, and the site itself ideally situated (quite apart from its beauty). The
two-level winery, set on the natural slope, maximises gravity flow, in particular for crushed
must feeding into the press. The Rieslings have always been elegant and have handsomely
repaid time in bottle; the Pinot Noir is the most consistent performer in the region. Exports
to Japan and Singapore.

ŶŶŶŶŶ   **Riesling 2007** Pale straw; dry slate mineral bouquet with pure lemon fruit on
the palate; high levels of acid provide a long, fine finish. Dyed-in-the-wool stayer.
Screwcap. 13° alc. **Rating** 94 **To** 2018 $20
Pinot Noir 2006 Bright colour; pure varietal fruit, with spice and savoury
nuances; fine tannins and good acidity; long and supple on the finish. Screwcap.
Rating 94 **To** 2013 $30

Shiraz 2005 A really vibrant wine with juicy fruits, roasted meats and plenty of cool peppery spice. Full-bodied with ample fine-grained tannins, and a long, savoury finish. Screwcap. 15° alc. **Rating** 94 **To** 2018 $26

𝔜𝔜𝔜𝔜𝔜 **Cabernet Merlot 2005** Cool-grown cabernet, with a little cedar and black olive supporting essency cassis fruit; plentiful fine-grained tannins on the firm finish. Screwcap. **Rating** 91 **To** 2015 $21
Sauvignon Blanc 2007 Very pale colour; strong pungent varietal aromas with fresh-cut grass and plenty of zippy acid on the finish. Screwcap. 13.5° alc. **Rating** 90 **To** 2011 $18

Catherine Vale Vineyard   ★★★☆

656 Milbrodale Road, Bulga, NSW 2330 **Region** Lower Hunter Valley
T (02) 6579 1334 **F** (02) 6579 1299 **www**.catherinevale.com.au **Open** W'ends & public hols 10–5, or by appt
Winemaker Hunter Wine Services (John Hordern) **Est.** 1994 **Cases** 2000
Former schoolteachers Bill and Wendy Lawson have established Catherine Vale as a not-so-idle retirement venture. Part of the production from the 5.8-ha vineyard is sold to contract winemaker John Hordern; the remainder is vinified for Catherine Vale.

𝔜𝔜𝔜𝔜𝔜 **The Grays Semillon 2006** Carries higher than normal alcohol (for the Hunter) with ease, retaining fruit brightness and thrust to the minerally finish. Screwcap. 12° alc. **Rating** 90 **To** 2015 $14

𝔜𝔜𝔜𝔜 **Buzz's Verdelho 2006** Lighter style; has a touch of elegance, but needs more conviction and depth. Screwcap. 13.5° alc. **Rating** 87 **To** 2009 $14
Winifred Barbera 2006 Has enough fruit ripeness even though only light-bodied, and with pronounced varietal acidity backing up the plum and smoky coffee aromas and flavours. Screwcap. 13.5° alc. **Rating** 87 **To** 2012 $18

Celestial Bay   ★★★★☆

33 Welwyn Avenue, Manning, WA 6152 (postal) **Region** Margaret River
T (08) 9450 4191 **F** (08) 9313 1544 **www**.celestialbay.com.au **Open** Not
Winemaker Bernard Abbott **Est.** 1999 **Cases** 8000
Michael and Kim O'Brien had a background of farming in the Chittering Valley when they purchased their 104-ha property. It is very much a family enterprise, with son Aaron studying viticulture and oenology at Curtin University, and daughter Daneka involved in marketing and sales. Under the direction of vineyard manager Sam Juniper, 52 ha of vines have been rapidly planted. The plantings are totally logical: semillon and sauvignon blanc; chardonnay; shiraz; and cabernet sauvignon, merlot, malbec and petit verdot. Winemaker Bernard Abbott celebrated his 23rd Margaret River vintage in 2008. Exports to the UK, the US, Malaysia, Taiwan, China, Singapore and Hong Kong.

𝔜𝔜𝔜𝔜𝔜 **Margaret River Shiraz 2005** A supple medium-bodied palate, with spicy notes and fine-grained tannins adding to the complexity of the flavour and structure; good length; will be long-lived. Screwcap. 14.5° alc. **Rating** 91 **To** 2017 $22
Margaret River Cabernet Sauvignon 2005 Good focus and intensity to a medium-bodied palate with blackcurrant and cassis; fine tannins, and just a hint of mint. Screwcap. 14° alc. **Rating** 90 **To** 2015 $22

𝔜𝔜𝔜𝔜 **Margaret River Cabernet Merlot 2005** Cassis, redcurrant and blackcurrant fruit offset by touches of grass, herb and olive on a fractionally green finish. Screwcap. 13.7° alc. **Rating** 88 **To** 2013 $19.95
Goose Chase Ruby Red 2006 Light- to medium-bodied; a lively, spicy, savoury red fruit mix; dances in the mouth; ready now. Screwcap. 14° alc. **Rating** 88 **To** 2010 $14.95
Margaret River Chardonnay 2007 Full-bodied, ripe peachy fruit, the alcohol catching up fast on the palate; demands food. Screwcap. 14.5° alc. **Rating** 87 **To** 2009 $19.95

Margaret River Petit Verdot 2006 Vibrant blueberry fruits, and a hint of spice; quite fleshy, with plenty of oak, but not overly complex. Screwcap. **Rating** 87 To 2012 $25

Cellarmasters

Cnr Barossa Valley Way/Siegersdorf Road, Tanunda, SA 5352 **Region** Barossa Valley
T (08) 8561 2200 **F** (08) 8561 2299 **www**.cellarmasters.com.au **Open** Not
Winemaker Nick Badrice, John Schwartzkopff, Sally Blackwell, Neil Doddridge, Mark Starick **Est.** 1982 **Cases** 800 000
Dorrien Estate is the physical base of the vast Cellarmasters network which, wearing its retailer's hat, is by far the largest direct-sale outlet in Australia. It buys substantial quantities of wine from other makers either in bulk or as cleanskin (unlabelled bottles), or with recognisable but subtly different labels of the producers concerned. It also makes wine on its own account at Dorrien Estate, many of which are quite excellent, and of trophy quality. (Chateau Dorrien is an entirely unrelated business.) Purchased by private equity firm Archer Capital in 2007.

Black Wattle Padthaway Coonawarra Shiraz 2005 A super-elegant but quite complex medium-bodied palate; there is an almost silky texture to the fine, savoury tannins. Screwcap. 14.5° alc. **Rating** 94 **To** 2017 $23.95

Black Wattle Robe Cabernet Sauvignon 2006 Strong cassis and blackcurrant fruit, solid oak and ripe tannins; just a little heavy-footed. Screwcap. 14.5° alc. **Rating** 92 **To** 2016 $35.95

Centennial Vineyards

'Woodside', Centennial Road, Bowral, NSW 2576 **Region** Southern Highlands
T (02) 4861 8700 **F** (02) 4681 8777 **www**.centennial.net.au **Open** 7 days 10–5
Winemaker Tony Cosgriff **Est.** 2002 **Cases** 10 000
Centennial Vineyards is a substantial development jointly owned by wine professional John Large and investor Mark Dowling, covering 133 ha of beautiful grazing land, with 29.5 ha planted to sauvignon blanc, riesling, verdelho, chardonnay, albarino, pinot gris, pinot noir, pinot meunier, cabernet sauvignon and tempranillo. Production from the estate vineyards is supplemented by purchases of grapes from other regions, including Orange. The consistency of the quality of the wines is wholly commendable, and reflects the skilled touch of Tony Cosgriff in a region which often throws up climatic challenges. Exports to the US, Denmark, Singapore, China and Korea.

Reserve Shiraz Viognier 2006 Very lively and very intense, yet with a silky texture; lovely black fruits with splashes of red and that viognier lift; unquestionably works best in cool regions. Cork. 14.8° alc. **Rating** 94 **To** 2016 $30

Reserve Pinot Gris 2007 Has much more personality than most, driven by pear and green apple flavours, and – best of all – not by sweetness; thoroughly commendable. Screwcap. 13.5° alc. **Rating** 93 **To** 2010 $24
Woodside Chardonnay 2006 As ever, an elegant style, with melon and stone fruit supported by a touch of French oak; sweet citrussy acidity to close. Screwcap. 13.7° alc. **Rating** 91 **To** 2013 $22
Reserve Orange Merlot 2005 Light- to medium-bodied; fragrant and fruity, with gossamer tannins and delicate oak; will never be better than now. ProCork. 13.5° alc. **Rating** 90 **To** 2009 $28
Woodside Single Vineyard Tempranillo 2006 A fresh, lively, light- to medium-bodied palate with raspberry and cherry fruit plus a twist of dried lemon zest; well made. Screwcap. 13.8° alc. **Rating** 90 **To** 2012 $22.95
Pinot Noir Chardonnay NV Fine mousse; extremely crisp, low dosage, aperitif style, with citrus fruits dominant; extended lees contact showing in the fine mousse rather than flavour; time on cork will help. cork. 11.5° alc. **Rating** 90 To 2012 $28

Cordon Cut Chardonnay 2006 Late cordon cut and desiccation of bunches on the vine has worked well, intensifying both fruit and acidity, but without botrytis; 1 barrel made. Screwcap. 11° alc. **Rating** 90 **To** 2012 $26

ŶŶŶŶ **Woodside Unwooded Chardonnay 2006** Well made (within the context of the style); gentle stone fruit and a touch of mineral on the finish. Screwcap. 13° alc. **Rating** 87 **To** 2010 $19

Sparkling Tempranillo Rose 2006 Red fruits from strawberry to raspberry; a crisp, clean finish which is not sweet. Cork. 12.5° alc. **Rating** 87 **To** 2009 $26.95

Ceravolo Wines   ★★★★

Suite 16, 172 Glynburn Road, Tranmere, SA 5073 (postal) **Region** Adelaide Plains
T (08) 8336 4522 **F** (08) 8365 0538 **www**.ceravolo.com.au **Open** Not
Winemaker Colin Glaetzer, Ben Glaetzer (Contract) **Est.** 1985 **Cases** 20 000
Joe Ceravolo, dental surgeon-turned-vigneron, and wife Heather have been producing single-vineyard wines from their family-owned estate since 1999, centred around Shiraz, but with Chardonnay and Merlot in support. Conspicuous success at the London International Wine Challenge led both to exports and the registration of the Adelaide Plains region under the GI legislation. Further significant wine show success has added to the reputation of the brand. Wines are released under the Ceravolo, St Andrews Estate and Red Earth labels. Exports to the UK, the US and other major markets.

ŶŶŶŶŶ **Adelaide Plains Petit Verdot 2006** Great colour; strongly floral aromas with blueberry and hints of cassis; juicy and mouthfilling, the palate has a flamboyant personality with plenty of flavour. Cork. 15° alc. **Rating** 93 **To** 2014 $25

Adelaide Plains Sangiovese Rose 2007 Some red fruits, and a nice dry, clean and savoury palate; perfect for antipasto on a hot day. Screwcap. 13° alc. **Rating** 90 **To** 2010 $17

Adelaide Plains Shiraz 2005 Bright and juicy shiraz with good flavour, if a little one-dimensional, but very vibrant and lively on the finish. Cork. 14.5° alc. **Rating** 90 **To** 2014 $22

Adelaide Plains Cabernet Sauvignon 2006 Bright varietal fruit with nuances of red and dark berries, plus a hint of cedar on the tightly focused and supple finish. Cork. 14° alc. **Rating** 90 **To** 2016 $20

ŶŶŶŶ **Adelaide Hills Pinot Grigio 2007** Bright fruit on the bouquet, and good varietal concentration on the palate; clean, fresh and crisp, and ready to go. Screwcap. 13° alc. **Rating** 89 **To** 2009 $17.95

Red Earth Adelaide Plains Cabernet Sauvignon 2006 Ripe and concentrated, with a chewy mouthful of tannin on the finish. Cork. 14° alc. **Rating** 87 **To** 2014 $17

Adelaide Plains Sangiovese 2006 Good flavour, with varietal nuances of sour cherry, and controlled tannins. Screwcap. 14° alc. **Rating** 87 **To** 2012 $17.95

Ceres Bridge Estate   ★★★

84 Merrawarp Road, Stonehaven, Vic 3221 **Region** Geelong
T (03) 5271 1200 **F** (03) 5271 1200 **Open** W'ends 12–5
Winemaker Challon Murdock **Est.** 1996 **Cases** 500
Challon and Patricia Murdock began the long, slow and at times very frustrating process of establishing their vineyard in 1996. They planted 1.8 ha of chardonnay in that year, but 50% of the vines died over the next two years in the face of drought and inadequate water supply. Instead of deciding it was all too difficult, they persevered by planting 1.2 ha of pinot noir in 2000, with replanting in '01, and then in '05 signified the intention to become serious by planting between 0.5 ha and 1 ha each of shiraz, nebbiolo, sauvignon blanc, viognier, tempranillo and pinot grigio.

ŶŶŶŶ **Geelong Pinot Noir 2006** Massive extraction of colour and flavour, dragging the wine towards dry red character; may fine itself down a little with a few years in bottle, and a cheap punt. Screwcap. 14.4° alc. **Rating** 87 **To** 2012 $16.95

Chain of Ponds

Adelaide Road, Gumeracha, SA 5233 **Region** Adelaide Hills
T (08) 8389 1415 **F** (08) 8389 1877 **Open** Mon–Fri 9.30–4.30, w'ends &
public hols 10.30–4.30
Winemaker Greg Clack **Est.** 1993 **Cases** 30 000
The Chain of Ponds brand has been separated from the over 200 ha of vineyards which were
among the largest in the Adelaide Hills. It now has contract growers throughout the Adelaide
Hills for the Chain of Ponds label, two single vineyard reds from Kangaroo Island, and the
Norello blends with a SA appellation. Exports to the UK, the US, Canada, Singapore and NZ.

ŸŸŸŸŸ **The Corkscrew Road Adelaide Hills Chardonnay 2004** Developing
impressively, this cork is doing its job well; has layers of nectarine and citrus fruit,
with seamless oak; long finish. Cork. 13.5° alc. **Rating** 94 **To** 2012 $30

ŸŸŸŸŸ **The Red Semi Adelaide Hills Semillon + Sauvignon Blanc 2006** Comes
alive on a long and intense palate, with a seamless varietal flow of grass, citrus and
snow pea; bright finish. Screwcap. 12.5° alc. **Rating** 93 **To** 2012 $18
Williams Vineyard Kangaroo Island Shiraz 2003 A medium-bodied wine
with restrained but spicy/savoury flavours and fine tannins, the French oak now
fully absorbed. Cork. 14° alc. **Rating** 90 **To** 2013 $25

ŸŸŸŸ **Novello Rosso 2007** Fresh, vibrant and with a hint of spice; has good overall
flavour. Screwcap. 12.5° alc. **Rating** 89 **To** 2009 $16
The Ledge Adelaide Hills McLaren Vale Shiraz 2003 Light- to medium-
bodied; the cool Adelaide Hills component (54%) is very dominant; spicy flavours,
with some minty notes; fine tannins. Cork. 15° alc. **Rating** 89 **To** 2011 $28.50
The Amadeus Adelaide Hills Cabernet Sauvignon 2003 The bouquet
has some errant notes; the palate, however, is firm and focused, with earthy
blackcurrant fruit; a wine in two parts. Cork. 14.5° alc. **Rating** 89 **To** 2018 $28.50
**Florance Vineyard Kangaroo Island Cabernet Sauvignon Cabernet
Franc Merlot 2003** Solid, medium- to full-bodied, briary earthy blackberry
fruits and ripe tannins; some sweeter red fruit notes on the finish catch you
unprepared, but are a pleasant surprise. Cork. 14° alc. **Rating** 89 **To** 2013 $25
Adelaide Hills Pinot Grigio 2006 That typically neutral taste profile; has length,
isn't sweet, but is basically blotting paper for food. Screwcap. 14° alc. **Rating** 87
To 2009 $18
The Amadeus Adelaide Hills Cabernet Sauvignon 2004 At the ripe end
of the flavour spectrum, notwithstanding moderate alcohol; some sweet and sour
components. Cork. 14° alc. **Rating** 87 **To** 2012 $30

Chalice Bridge Estate

★★★★★

796 Rosa Glen Road, Margaret River, WA 6285 **Region** Margaret River
T (08) 9433 5200 **F** (08) 9433 5211 **www.chalicebridge.com.au Open** By appt
Winemaker Bob Cartwright (Consultant) **Est.** 1998 **Cases** 40 000
Planting of the vineyard began in 1998; there are now over 28 ha each of cabernet sauvignon
and shiraz, 27 ha of chardonnay, 12.5 ha of semillon, 18 ha of sauvignon blanc and 7 ha of
merlot, making up the total plantings of 122 ha; it is the second-largest single vineyard in
Margaret River. The 2006 appointment of former Leeuwin Estate senior winemaker Bob
Cartwright was major news, adding thrust to a growing business. Sensible pricing also helps.
Exports to the UK, the US and other major markets.

ŸŸŸŸŸ **Margaret River Semillon Sauvignon Blanc 2007** Fine and intense, with
lovely fruit flavour and balance; grassy/minerally semillon provides the structure,
sauvignon blanc the sweet lemon juice and passionfruit; great length, and great
value. Screwcap. 12.5° alc. **Rating** 94 **To** 2010 $16.95
Margaret River Shiraz 2004 First tasted in Oct '05; two years later, still right
up there, fresh and bright, with black fruit flavours, the tannins showing no sign of
softening yet. Screwcap. 14° alc. **Rating** 94 **To** 2015 $22.95

♥♥♥♥♀ **Margaret River Sauvignon Blanc 2007** Spotlessly clean; a fresh and delicate array of grass, gooseberry and passionfruit aromas and flavours; crisp minerally acidity adds to class. Screwcap. 12.5° alc. **Rating** 93 **To** 2009 $16.95
Margaret River Chardonnay 2006 Generous but not flabby peach, nectarine and melon supported by subtle oak; good length and balance. Screwcap. 13.5° alc. **Rating** 90 **To** 2011 $22.95
Margaret River Merlot 2005 Far greater structure than many merlots; has varietal olive and blackcurrant fruit, the tannins needing a little taming, and best left alone for a couple of years. Screwcap. 14.5° alc. **Rating** 90 **To** 2018 $22.95

♥♥♥♥ **Margaret River Classic White 2007** A crisp wine with a mix of predominantly grassy/mineral aromas and flavours, but also touches of nectarine and melon; no oak obvious. Screwcap. 13.5° alc. **Rating** 89 **To** 2010 $16.95
Margaret River Shiraz 2005 Fresh and relatively light-bodied, a pretty wine which belies its alcohol; red fruits and minimal tannins. Screwcap. 14.5° alc. **Rating** 89 **To** 2013 $22.99
Calamus Red 2005 Light- to medium-bodied; a neatly balanced and composed blend of varieties, the oak and tannins likewise. Shiraz/Merlot/Cabernet Sauvignon. Screwcap. 13.5° alc. **Rating** 89 **To** 2018 $16.95
Margaret River Cabernet Sauvignon 2005 Medium-bodied; fine tannins run through the length of the palate with blackcurrant fruit in attendance; needs a touch more fruit weight. Screwcap. 14.5° alc. **Rating** 89 **To** 2013 $22.95

Chalk Hill   ★★★★★

PO Box 205, McLaren Vale, SA 5171 **Region** McLaren Vale
T (08) 8556 2121 **F** (08) 8556 2221 **www**.chalkhill.com.au **Open** Not
Winemaker Emmanuelle Bekkers **Est.** 1973 **Cases** 7000
The growth of Chalk Hill has accelerated after passing from parents John and Diana Harvey to grapegrowing sons Jock and Tom. Both Jock and Tom are heavily involved in wine industry affairs in varying capacities (Tom was a participant in the second intake of the Wine Industry Future Leaders Program) and the business has strong links with Greening Australia. (Chalk Hill donates 25c for each bottle sold, the highest per-bottle donation in the Australian wine industry.) Further acquisitions mean the vineyards now span each subregion of McLaren Vale, and have been planted to both the exotic (albarino, barbera and sangiovese) and the mainstream (shiraz, cabernet sauvignon, grenache, chardonnay and cabernet franc). Exports to all major markets; exports to the US and Canada under the Wits End label.

♥♥♥♥♥ **Reserve McLaren Vale Shiraz 2004** Has plenty of mocha to frame the ample blackberry fruits of the bouquet; there is so much fruit on the palate it is almost sweet, but the finish is fine, dry and even a little chalky; an impressive wine with a lot of flavour. Cork. 15.5° alc. **Rating** 94 **To** 2025
McLaren Vale Barbera 2006 An unusually rich and complex wine, showing none of the limitations the variety often has; layers of black fruits and exotic spices; balanced finish. Screwcap. 15° alc. **Rating** 94 **To** 2021 $24.95

♥♥♥♥♀ **McLaren Vale Shiraz 2004** Deep colour; dark fruits with a slight green edge which adds to the aromatics; a hint of sulphide, but good fruit flavour on the finish; good development potential. Screwcap. 14.5° alc. **Rating** 91 **To** 2018 $20

♥♥♥♥ **Sidetrack 2005** Light- to medium-bodied; a supple, smooth array of spicy berry fruits, ready now. Shiraz (60%)/Cabernet Sauvignon (30%)/Grenache (10%). Screwcap. 14.5° alc. **Rating** 89 **To** 2010 $14.95
McLaren Vale Sangiovese 2006 Makes a strong varietal statement; red and sour cherry flavours, the tannins still to fully resolve. Screwcap. 15° alc. **Rating** 89 **To** 2013 $24.95
Moscato 2007 A clever wine made in a Petillant (slightly effervescent) style; very sweet grapey/juicy flavours, and needed slightly more acidity or less sweetness. Screwcap. 8° alc. **Rating** 87 **To** 2009 $14.95

Chalkers Crossing ★★★★★

285 Grenfell Road, Young, NSW 2594 **Region** Hilltops
T (02) 6382 6900 **F** (02) 6382 5068 **www**.chalkerscrossing.com.au **Open** 7 days 10–4
Winemaker Celine Rousseau **Est.** 2000 **Cases** 7000
Owned and operated by Ted and Wendy Ambler, Chalkers Crossing's 10-ha Rockleigh
Vineyard was planted in 1997–98. It also purchases grapes from Tumbarumba and Gundagai.
Winemaker Celine Rousseau was born in France's Loire Valley, trained in Bordeaux and has
worked in Bordeaux, Champagne, Languedoc, Margaret River and the Perth Hills. This Flying
Winemaker (now an Australian citizen) has exceptional skills and dedication. Exports to the
UK, Canada, Ireland, Sweden, Denmark, China, Singapore and Japan.

♀♀♀♀♀ **Hilltops Cabernet Sauvignon 2005** Strong colour; powerful, intense varietal
blackcurrant and dark chocolate fruit on both bouquet and palate; perfect tannin
and oak structure and balance. Cork. 14.5° alc. **Rating** 96 **To** 2020 $28
Tumbarumba Sauvignon Blanc 2007 A complex bouquet and palate,
reflecting partial barrel ferment and lees contact; smoky, spicy overtones to sweet
gooseberry and tropical fruit; clean, dry finish. Screwcap. 13° alc. **Rating** 95
To 2010 $18
Hilltops Semillon 2006 Masterly winemaking; barrel ferment French oak plus
lees for 10 months, yet the oak influence is very subtle, adding as much to texture
as flavour; will age well. Screwcap. 13.5° alc. **Rating** 94 **To** 2016 $18
Hilltops Shiraz 2006 Tar, anise and blackberry fruits; the medium-bodied palate
is vibrant, focused, long and even, with real depth to the fruit. Screwcap. 15.5° alc.
Rating 94 **To** 2015 $27

♀♀♀♀♀ **Hilltops Cabernet Sauvignon 2006** Blueberry and violet aromas; rich, yet
strict mouthfeel, with many flavours coruscating to the finale; very tannic, but
should show well with time. Screwcap. 14.5° alc. **Rating** 93 **To** 2018 $27
Hilltops Riesling 2007 A very dry, slightly austere wine, with tight focused lime
juice and a strong mineral core. Screwcap. 12.5° alc. **Rating** 90 **To** 2014 $18
Tumbarumba Chardonnay 2006 Quite a complex bouquet with mealy fruit,
complemented by a generous palate; has length. **Rating** 90 **To** 2011 $22

Chalmers/Murray Darling Collection ★★★☆

PO Box 84, Euston, NSW 2737 **Region** Murray Darling
T 0400 261 932 **F** (03) 5026 3228 **www**.murraydarlingcollection.com.au **Open** Not
Winemaker Sandro Mosele (Contract) **Est.** 1989 **Cases** 4000
In March 2008, founders Bruce and Jenny Chalmers sold (to Macquarie Diversified
Agriculture Fund) what was the largest vine nursery propagation business in Australia, plus
650 ha of planted vines, an additional 600 ha available for planting, plus 1500 ha of protected
forest along a 14-km Murray River frontage. The Chalmers have, however, kept the brands and
the winemaking side of the business, with a five-year grape-supply contract from Macquarie.

♀♀♀♀ **Fiano 2007** Has subdued aromas, but a lively, fresh and crisp palate, with notes of
lemon juice, green pear and faint nutty characters. Screwcap. 12.5° alc. **Rating** 87
To 2009 $22

Chambers Rosewood ★★★☆

Barkly Street, Rutherglen, Vic 3685 **Region** Rutherglen
T (02) 6032 8641 **www**.chambersrosewood.com.au **Open** Mon–Sat 9–5, Sun 10–5
Winemaker Bill Chambers, Stephen Chambers **Est.** 1858 **Cases** 20 000
I happen to know that Bill Chambers declines to provide samples of his Rare Muscat and
Tokay to Robert Parker, so do not feel the least miffed that I should likewise be deprived,
but, consistently with my (further amended) winery rating system, I only rate the wines I
taste, not those I remember or have precious, part-consumed bottles of. Hence the demotion
from 5 stars to 3.5 stars. The irony is that the table wines are better than they have ever been
previously. Exports to all major markets.

Chapel Hill ★★★★★

Chapel Hill Road, McLaren Vale, SA 5171 **Region** McLaren Vale
T (08) 8323 8429 **F** (08) 8323 9245 **www**.chapelhillwine.com.au **Open** 7 days 12–5
Winemaker Michael Fragos, Bryn Richards **Est.** 1979 **Cases** 50 000
A leading medium-sized winery in the region; in 2000 Chapel Hill was sold to the Swiss
Thomas Schmidheiny group, which owns the respected Cuvaison winery in California as well
as vineyards in Switzerland and Argentina. Wine quality is as good, if not better, than ever.
Winemaker Michael Fragos was named (international) Winemaker of the Year at London's
International Wine & Spirit Competition '08. The substantial production comes from 43 ha
(shiraz, cabernet sauvignon, chardonnay, verdelho, albarino, sangiovese and merlot) together
with purchased grapes. Exports to the UK, the US and other major markets.

𝟵𝟵𝟵𝟵𝟵 **McLaren Vale Shiraz 2005** Typical McLaren Vale abundance of supple
black fruits and dark chocolate, but without excessive alcohol; ripe tannins and
controlled oak; very well made. Screwcap. 14.5° alc. **Rating** 94 **To** 2019 $25
McLaren Vale Cabernet Sauvignon 2005 Lush and plush, with a dark
chocolate imprint of McLaren Vale making its mark on ripe blackcurrant fruit;
tannins and oak well handled. Screwcap. 14.5° alc. **Rating** 94 **To** 2019 $25

𝟵𝟵𝟵𝟵𝟵 **Bush Vine McLaren Vale Grenache 2006** Very dark plum fruits with a little
tar and a hint of chocolate in the background; lovely texture and weight, showing
grenache plushness to the finish. Screwcap. 15° alc. **Rating** 93 **To** 2012 $30
McLaren Vale Shiraz 2006 A deep and dark warm-fruited wine with chocolate
fruits, fruitcake elements of spice and a long, slightly savoury finish. Screwcap.
14.5° alc. **Rating** 91 **To** 2015 $25
Il Vescovo McLaren Vale Sangiovese 2005 Strong varietal character, with
a mix of black, red and sour cherries; persistent, fine tannins and good length;
the upwards march of sangiovese continues. Screwcap. 14.2° alc. **Rating** 91
To 2015 $20
Il Vescovo Adelaide Hills Tempranillo 2006 A pristine array of red berry
fruits; light- to medium-bodied, but has persistent length thanks to fine tannins;
oak barely visible. Screwcap. 13.5° alc. **Rating** 91 **To** 2016 $20
Il Vescovo McLaren Vale Sangiovese 2006 Vibrant sour cherry fruits with
hints of briar and spice; quite tannic, with pronounced acid, displaying Tuscany's
most important variety well. Screwcap. 14.2° alc. **Rating** 90 **To** 2011 $20

𝟵𝟵𝟵𝟵 **Il Vescovo Adelaide Hills Pinot Grigio 2007** Adelaide Hills has an
appropriate climate for this variety, the wine having an extra degree of flavour and
mouthfeel to the citrus-tinged pear and lychee fruit. Screwcap. 13° alc. **Rating** 89
To 2009 $19.95
Il Vescovo McLaren Vale Sangiovese 2007 Fresh and very crisp; spiced red
and black cherry fruit, then lingering, pushy acidity. Screwcap. 14.2° alc. **Rating** 89
To 2009 $19.95
Il Vescovo McLaren Vale Sangiovese Rose 2007 A savoury, fairly dry style,
with a generous helping of red fruits on the finish. Screwcap. 13.5° alc. **Rating** 88
To 2009 $14

Chaperon Wines ★★★☆

'Grange Hill', Gallaghers Lane, Eastville, Vic 3463 **Region** Bendigo
T (03) 5435 7427 **www**.chaperon.com.au **Open** W'ends & public hols 10–5, or by appt
Winemaker Russell Clarke **Est.** 1994 **Cases** 400
In 1856 English immigrant Edward Bond purchased land in the Maldon area, followed by an
adjoining property in 1871. Here he established the 'Grange Hill' winery and vineyard, which
flourished in the 1880s, leading to the establishment of a second winery and second vineyard.
It disappeared in the 20th century, but in 1994 Russell Clarke and Angelina Chaperon bought
the property and began replanting the vineyard and restoring the old winery buildings. They
have chosen to bypass irrigation and practise organic viticulture in growing 1.2 ha of bush
vine grenache and mourvedre, and 1.8 ha of trellised shiraz.

♟♟♟ Shiraz 2005 Deep, dense blackish purple; a ripe and rich mid-palate; lacks drive and thrust, but has good overall flavour. Screwcap. 16.1° alc. **Rating** 89 To 2012 $25

❧ Chapman Grove Wines ★★★★★

PO Box 1460, Margaret River, WA 6285 **Region** Margaret River
T (08) 9757 7444 **F** (08) 9757 7477 **www**.chapmangrove.com.au **Open** Not
Winemaker Bruce Dukes (Contract) **Est.** 2006 **Cases** 7000
The contract-made wines come from the extensive estate vineyards of 30 ha planted to chardonnay, semillon, sauvignon blanc, shiraz, cabernet sauvignon and merlot. The standard Chapman Grove range offers six varietal wines (including a Shiraz Rose) and two ultra premium wines Chardonnay and Shiraz under the Atticus label.

♟♟♟♟♟ Atticus Margaret River Chardonnay 2005 Very similar in style to the '06, and every bit as good, if not better; silky fruit in a fine web of quality oak and minerally acidity. Screwcap. 14.2° alc. **Rating** 96 **To** 2015 $50
Atticus Margaret River Chardonnay 2006 Intense, tight and precise, with high-quality melon and citrus/grapefruit flavours driving through the long palate and finish, oak a mere garnish. Screwcap. 13.5° alc. **Rating** 95 **To** 2016 $50
Atticus Margaret River Cabernet Sauvignon 2005 Only medium-bodied, but has a long, intense and refined palate, blackcurrant fruit, tannins and oak all precisely where they should be. Screwcap. 13.5° alc. **Rating** 94 **To** 2015 $50

♟♟♟♟♟ Atticus Margaret River Shiraz 2004 A medium-bodied wine with abundant flavour and texture in a strongly spicy spectrum; has good balance and texture, but not in the class of the chardonnays. Screwcap. 14° alc. **Rating** 91 **To** 2013 $50
Margaret River Semillon Sauvignon Blanc 2006 Well balanced, much of the structure and flavour from the semillon component; grassy, citrussy, minerally notes, with a clean, fresh finish. Screwcap. 12.5° alc. **Rating** 90 **To** 2010 $18
Margaret River Chardonnay 2005 Inevitably diminished in the shadow of Atticus, but a well-flavoured wine, with long nectarine and melon fruit, the oak influence minimal. Screwcap. 13.9° alc. **Rating** 90 **To** 2012 $23

♟♟♟♟ Margaret River Merlot 2005 Light-bodied, but the fresh redcurrant/cassis fruit sits well, and the wine has not been forced. Screwcap. 13.5° alc. **Rating** 88 To 2012 $18
Margaret River Cabernet Sauvignon 2005 Pleasant wine, with some similarities to Atticus flavour, but none of its refinement or texture. Screwcap. 13.5° alc. **Rating** 88 **To** 2011 $23

❧ Chapple's Cairn Curran Estate NR

329 Seers Road, Welshmans Reef, Vic 3462 **Region** Bendigo
T (03) 5475 1039 **F** (03) 5475 1049 **www**.chapplewine.com **Open** 7 days 11–5
Winemaker Arthur Chapple, Mark Chapple, James Chapple **Est.** 2000 **Cases** 800
This is the venture of father Arthur, son Mark and grandson James Chapple. Together they have planted a little under 3 ha of shiraz and 0.4 ha of chardonnay on a site overlooking the Cairn Curran Reservoir, midway between the historical goldmining towns of Maldon and Newstead. The basket-pressed Shiraz is made in three distinctly different styles labelled Bold Red, Winemakers Classic and Reserve, all French oak–matured. Slightly unexpectedly, all three wines have the same price ($25).

Charles Cimicky ★★★★★

Gomersal Road, Lyndoch, SA 5351 **Region** Barossa Valley
T (08) 8524 4025 **F** (08) 8524 4772 **Open** Tues–Sat 10.30–4.30
Winemaker Charles Cimicky **Est.** 1972 **Cases** 15 000

These wines are of very good quality, thanks to the sophisticated use of new oak in tandem with high-quality grapes. Happily, Charles Cimicky submitted wines for this edition, underlining in no uncertain fashion the quality of his wines. Exports to the UK, the US, Switzerland, Canada, Malaysia and Hong Kong.

ΤΤΤΤΤ **Reserve Barossa Valley Shiraz 2005** Saturated purple-red; a full-bodied palate, as rich and mouthfilling as the colour suggests; very much in the house style; a big frame, still to completely fill out. Cork. 14.5° alc. **Rating** 94 **To** 2020 $65

Trumps Barossa Valley Shiraz 2006 Dense purple-red; potent blackberry, prune and licorice fruit, with persistent but fine tannins; oak is a net contributor. Three trophies Barossa Valley Wine Show '07. Cork. 14.5° alc. **Rating** 94 **To** 2016 $20

The Autograph Barossa Valley Shiraz 2005 Slightly more developed hue than the Reserve; more spicy, and more light and shade in the flavoursome texture; a particularly long finish, oak in restraint. Cork. 14.5° alc. **Rating** 94 **To** 2017 $40

Charles Melton ★★★★★

Krondorf Road, Tanunda, SA 5352 **Region** Barossa Valley
T (08) 8563 3606 **F** (08) 8563 3422 **www**.charlesmeltonwines.com.au **Open** 7 days 11–5
Winemaker Charlie Melton, Nicola Ormond **Est.** 1984 **Cases** 18 000
Charlie Melton, one of the Barossa Valley's great characters, with wife Virginia by his side, makes some of the most eagerly sought à la mode wines in Australia. Inevitably, the Melton empire grew in response to the insatiable demand, with a doubling of estate vineyards to 13 ha (and the exclusive management and offtake of a further 10 ha) and the erection of an additional barrel store. The expanded volume has had no adverse effect on the wonderfully rich, sweet and well-made wines. Exports to all major markets.

ΤΤΤΤΤ **Grains of Paradise Shiraz 2005** A full-bodied yet elegant wine, full of dark brooding fruits and nuances of tar and earth; a rich and quite luscious palate, which relies on the depth of the fruit for its balance. Screwcap. 14.5° alc. **Rating** 95 **To** 2025 $55

Rose Of Virginia 2007 Vivid purple-red; vibrant red fruits with a twist of lemon; fresh and lively, breezing over the effects of drought. Always one of the best roses in Australia. Screwcap. 12° alc. **Rating** 94 **To** 2009 $20

Voices of Angels Shiraz 2005 Deeper colour than the Grains of Paradise, but more aromatic, with an array of red and dark fruits and plenty of spicy fruitcake; the palate is full-bodied and quite tannic, yet lively and fresh, pointing to a good long life ahead. Screwcap. 14.5° alc. **Rating** 94 **To** 2020 $55

ΤΤΤΤΩ **Nine Popes 2005** Plush raspberry fruits and the autosuggestion of Provencale garrigue on the bouquet; loaded with sweet fruit and framed by well-handled oak, structure for a long life ahead. Screwcap. 14.5° alc. **Rating** 92 **To** 2016 $55

Barossa Valley Cabernet Sauvignon 2005 Bright red and black fruits on the bouquet; good concentration, and abundant cassis fruit on the palate. Screwcap. 14.5° alc. **Rating** 91 **To** 2016 $42

Charles Sturt University Winery ★★★★☆

McKeown Drive (off Coolamon Road), Wagga Wagga, NSW 2650 **Region** Big Rivers Zone
T (02) 6933 2435 **F** (02) 6933 4072 **www**.csu.edu.au/winery/ **Open** Mon–Fri 11–5, w'ends 11–4
Winemaker Andrew Drumm **Est.** 1977 **Cases** 15 000
A totally new $2.5 million commercial winery was opened in 2002, complementing the $1 million experimental winery opened in '01. The commercial winery was funded through the sale of wines produced under the CSU brand, which always offer exceptional value. Following the University's acquisition of the former University of Sydney campus in Orange, it now has 7.7 ha of estate plantings at Wagga Wagga and 17 ha of mature vineyards at Orange, the latter planted to chardonnay, sauvignon blanc, shiraz, cabernet sauvignon and merlot. Interestingly, this teaching facility is using screwcaps for all its wines, white and red, recalling

its pioneering use in 1977. Moreover, since 2005 its sparkling wines have been released under crown seal.

🍷🍷🍷🍷🍷 **Orange Chardonnay 2007** Clever winemaking both in the picking decision and in the judicious use of a touch of French oak; has lovely nectarine grapefruit and melon flavours; simply unbeatable value. Screwcap. 13.5° alc. **Rating** 94 **To** 2012 $13.20

🍷🍷🍷🍷🍷 **Limited Release The College Muscat NV** Lovely clean grapey muscat, with just enough aged complexity to provide a luscious, textural mouthful of Rutherglen heaven. Screwcap. 18° alc. **Rating** 92 **To** 2020 $15.40
Limited Release Sparkling Shiraz NV A good example of sparkling red; varietal with a little savoury edge to the blackberry coulis on the palate; well-handled sugar in this wine leads to a harmonious finish. Crown seal. 14° alc. **Rating** 90 **To** 2009 $19.80

🍷🍷🍷🍷 **Limited Release Orange Chardonnay 2007** Clean and well defined, if a little soft; nectarines and hints of orange peel on the finish. Screwcap. 13° alc. **Rating** 88 **To** 2009 $18.15
Big Rivers Hilltops Orange Cabernet Sauvignon Merlot Cabernet Franc 2005 Bright and clean, with nice fragrance and lift to the palate; great price for a ready-to-go red. Screwcap. 13.9° alc. **Rating** 87 **To** 2009 $13.20
Limited Release Pinot Noir Chardonnay 2004 Very dry, and quite deeply coloured; pushing the edge of the aldehydic style, but quite good flavour. Crown Seal. 12° alc. **Rating** 87 **To** 2009 $19.80

Chartley Estate ★★★

38 Blackwood Hills Road, Rowella, Tas 7270 **Region** Northern Tasmania
T (03) 6394 7198 **F** (03) 6394 7598 **www**.chartleyestatevineyard.com.au **Open** Not
Winemaker Winemaking Tasmania (Julian Alcorso) **Est.** 2000 **Cases** 1250

The Kossman family began the establishment of 2 ha each of pinot gris, sauvignon blanc and pinot noir, and 1 ha of riesling, in 2000. Although the vines are still relatively young, some attractive wines from each variety have been made. Exports to Taiwan.

🍷🍷🍷🍷 **Sauvignon Blanc 2007** A restrained bouquet and palate, with some minerally edges; overall, good weight and length. **Rating** 87 **To** 2009 $20
Black Crow Pinot Noir 2006 Bright fruits on both bouquet and palate, in straightforward, early-drinking style. **Rating** 87 **To** 2011 $25

Chateau Dorrien ★★★

Cnr Seppeltsfield Road/Barossa Valley Way, Dorrien, SA 5352 **Region** Barossa Valley
T (08) 8562 2850 **F** (08) 8562 1416 **www**.chateaudorrien.com.au **Open** 7 days 10–5
Winemaker Fernando Martin, Ramon Martin **Est.** 1985 **Cases** 3500

The Martin family, headed by Fernando and Jeanette, purchased the old Dorrien winery from the Seppelt family in 1984; in '90 the family purchased Twin Valley Estate, and moved the winemaking operations of Chateau Dorrien to the Twin Valley site. All the Chateau Dorrien group wines are sold at Chateau Dorrien; Twin Valley is simply a production facility. In 2006 the Martin family purchased a 32-ha property at Myponga, with over 15 ha of mature vineyards which will now provide the grapes for San Fernando Estate, as the vineyard has been renamed.

🍷🍷🍷🍷 **Barossa Valley Shiraz 2005** A generous helping of vanilla oak is the principal driver of a light- to medium-bodied wine, which is ageing pleasantly. Diam. 14.6° alc. **Rating** 87 **To** 2013 $20

Chateau Francois

Broke Road, Pokolbin, NSW 2321 **Region** Lower Hunter Valley
T (02) 4998 7548 **F** (02) 4998 7805 **Open** W'ends 9–5, or by appt
Winemaker Don Francois **Est.** 1969 **Cases** 200

I have known former NSW Director of Fisheries Dr Don Francois for almost as long as I have been involved with wine, which is a very long time indeed. I remember his early fermentations of sundry substances other than grapes (none of which, I hasten to add, were the least bit illegal) in the copper bowl of an antiquated washing machine in his laundry. He established Chateau Francois one year before Brokenwood, and our winemaking and fishing paths have crossed many times since. Some years ago Don suffered a mild stroke, and no longer speaks or writes with any fluency, but this has not stopped him from producing a range of absolutely beautiful semillons which flourish marvellously with age. I should add that he is even prouder of the distinguished career of his daughter, Rachel Francois, at the NSW bar. The semillon vines are now approaching 40 years, producing exceptional wine year after year, sold for the proverbial song. Five-star value.

YYYYY **Pokolbin Mallee Semillon 2006** Delicious and classic semillon, as yet saying little on the bouquet, but with long, intense and precise fruit on the palate; great now or later style; great bargain. Screwcap. 11° alc. **Rating** 94 **To** 2020 $14

YYYYY **Pokolbin Shiraz 1999** Shows that regional flavour does not require high alcohol, especially from vines nearing 40 years old; has particularly good length and mouthfeel; ready now and a great bargain. Cork. 12° alc. **Rating** 91 **To** 2013 $14

YYYY **Pokolbin Mallee Semillon 2001** Appropriate pale gold-straw colour; some ripe, slightly caramelised fruit and toast; fresh acidity to close and provide length. Cork. 11° alc. **Rating** 89 **To** 2012 $14

Chateau Leamon

5528 Calder Highway, Bendigo, Vic 3550 **Region** Bendigo
T (03) 5447 7995 **F** (03) 5447 0855 **www**.chateauleamon.com.au **Open** Wed–Mon 10–5
Winemaker Ian Leamon **Est.** 1973 **Cases** 2500

One of the longest-established wineries in the region, with estate and locally grown shiraz and cabernet family grapes providing the excellent red wines. No samples received; the rating is that of last year. Exports to the UK, Canada and Singapore.

Chateau Pâto

67 Thompsons Road, Pokolbin, NSW 2321 **Region** Lower Hunter Valley
T (02) 4998 7634 **F** (02) 4998 7860 **Open** By appt
Winemaker Nicholas Paterson **Est.** 1980 **Cases** 500

Nicholas Paterson took over responsibility for this tiny winery following the death of father David Paterson during the 1993 vintage. The winery has 2.5 ha of shiraz (the first plantings), with 0.5 ha each of chardonnay, marsanne, roussanne and viognier and 0.25 ha of mourvedre; most of the grapes are sold, with a tiny quantity of shiraz being made into a marvellous wine. David Paterson's legacy is being handsomely guarded.

YYYYY **Hunter Wine Country DJP Shiraz 2006** A true Hunter shiraz, with spicy leather nuances framed by red berry fruits; deeply complex, with a rush of black fruits on the palate, and a dry, savoury finish. Screwcap. 14.7° alc. **Rating** 94 **To** 2025 $42

Chateau Tanunda

9 Basedow Road, Tanunda, SA 5352 **Region** Barossa Valley
T (08) 8563 3888 **F** (08) 8563 1422 **www**.chateautanunda.com **Open** 7 days 10–5
Winemaker Tim Smith **Est.** 1890 **Cases** 10 000

This is one of the most imposing winery buildings in the Barossa Valley, built from stone quarried at nearby Bethany in the late 1880s. It started life as a winery, then became a specialist brandy distillery until the death of the Australian brandy industry, whereafter it was simply used as storage cellars. It is now completely restored, and converted to a major convention facility catering for groups of up to 400. The winemaking philosophy has been taken back to its roots, with small-batch processing. The large complex also houses a cellar door where the Chateau Tanunda wines are sold; Chateau Bistro and the Barossa Small Winemakers Centre offer wines made by small independent winemakers in the region. It is a sister winery to Cowra Estate, as both are owned by the Geber family. Exports to the UK, Germany Switzerland, Sweden, Denmark, Belgium and China.

ΨΨΨΨΨ **Terroirs of the Barossa Ebenezer District Shiraz 2005** Medium-bodied; quite firm and savoury, with black fruits, spice and earth; most restrained and elegant; an interesting trio with same alcohol and winemaking; 80-year-old vines. Cork. 14.5° alc. **Rating** 93 **To** 2018 $48

The Everest Old Bushvine Grenache 2005 Has good focus and length in a medium-bodied frame; while varietal sweet confiture flavours are there, the slinky, long finish is impressive, as is the price. Cork. 15.5° alc. **Rating** 93 **To** 2015 $160

Terroirs of the Barossa Greenock Shiraz 2005 Medium-bodied; richer, riper and rounder, with a mix of licorice, blackberry and dark chocolate; more texture. Cork. 14.5° alc. **Rating** 92 **To** 2015 $48

The Chateau 100 Year Old Vines Shiraz 2005 Abundant flavour, the sweetness of the fruit suggesting a higher alcohol than 14.5°; nice oak, but needs more authoritative tannins to provide full balance. Cork. 14.5° alc. **Rating** 91 **To** 2025 $55

The Chateau The Everest Shiraz 2005 Medium- to full-bodied, with good balance of fully ripe black fruits, oak and tannins; comes from the best barrels of 50 parcels of wine; the length of labour and the weight of the bottle presumably reflected in the challenging price. Cork. 15° alc. **Rating** 90 **To** 2015 $160

Terroirs of the Barossa Lyndoch Shiraz 2005 Deeper but more developed colour; with black fruits and some prune; doesn't have quite the same persistence; nonetheless, part of a family. Cork. 14.5° alc. **Rating** 90 **To** 2015 $48

The Chateau Barossa Valley Cabernet Sauvignon 2005 Dense, rich and ripe, with blackcurrant fruit verging on confit, but not falling over that line; has good balance and length. Cork. 14.5° alc. **Rating** 90 **To** 2013 $28

ΨΨΨΨ **The Chateau Barossa Valley Riesling 2007** Flowery, ripe fruit aromas; a mix of tropical and citrus on the palate; good early-drinking style. Screwcap. 13.5° alc. **Rating** 89 **To** 2011 $22

Barossa Tower Shiraz 2006 Rich and ripe plum, blackberry and licorice; good length and ripe tannins; minimal oak. Screwcap. 14.5° alc. **Rating** 89 **To** 2015 $18

Barossa Tower Semillon Chardonnay Sauvignon Blanc 2006 The Barossa goes to WA for inspiration (classic dry white) and succeeds, with a fresh and zesty wine, with good length; value. Screwcap. 12° alc. **Rating** 88 **To** 2009 $15

Barossa Tower Grenache Shiraz Mourvedre 2006 Has an attractive savoury, almost lemony, tang which counters any suggestion of cosmetic/confit fruit; fine tannins, good balance. Screwcap. 14.5° alc. **Rating** 88 **To** 2012 $18

The Three Graces Barossa Valley Cabernet Sauvignon Cabernet Franc Merlot 2006 Carries on with the attractive fruit of the '06 Cabernet, albeit lightened with these extra varieties, not native to the Barossa Valley, as it were. Screwcap. 14° alc. **Rating** 88 **To** 2012 $28

The Chateau Shiraz 2005 Similar, but less sweet/opulent fruit than the 100 Year Old Shiraz, allows tannins to provide better balance, albeit with a fairly soft landing. Cork. 14.5° alc. **Rating** 87 **To** 2015 $28

Grand Barossa Shiraz 2005 Medium-bodied, well-balanced blackberry and plum fruit, plus some vanilla oak, but lacks structure and texture. Cork. 14.5° alc. **Rating** 87 **To** 2011 $25

Barossa Tower Merlot 2006 Depth and richness the wine does not have; light- to medium-bodied spice, olive and some red fruits it does, despite the limitations of the region. Screwcap. 14° alc. **Rating** 87 **To** 2011 $18

Barossa Tower Cabernet Sauvignon 2006 Plenty of blackcurrant fruit with ripe tannins and warm vanilla oak; easy-going style. Screwcap. 14.5° alc. **Rating** 87 To 2012 $18

Barossa Tower Zinfandel 2006 Light-bodied; a fragrant red berry, citrus and spice mix which is authentic varietal character; minimal tannins; drink now. Screwcap. 14.5° alc. **Rating** 87 **To** 2009 $18

Chatsfield

O'Neil Road, Mount Barker, WA 6324 **Region** Mount Barker
T (08) 9851 1704 **F** (08) 9851 2660 **www**.chatsfield.com.au **Open** By appt
Winemaker The Vintage Wineworx (Dr Diane Miller) **Est.** 1976 **Cases** 2000
Irish-born medical practitioner Ken Lynch can be proud of his achievements at Chatsfield, as can most of the various contract winemakers who have taken the high-quality estate-grown material and made some impressive wines, notably the Riesling and spicy, licorice Shiraz. No samples received; the rating is that of last year. Exports to the UK.

Chatto Wines

McDonalds Road, Pokolbin, NSW 2325 **Region** Lower Hunter Valley
T (02) 4998 7293 **F** (02) 4998 7294 **www**.chattowines.com.au **Open** 7 days 9–5
Winemaker Jim Chatto **Est.** 2000 **Cases** 7000
Jim Chatto spent several years in Tasmania as the first winemaker at Rosevears Estate. He has since moved to the Hunter Valley but has used his Tasmanian contacts to buy small parcels of riesling and pinot noir. Possessed of a particularly good palate, he has made wines of excellent quality under the Chatto label. He was a star Len Evans Tutorial scholar and is an up-and-coming wine show judge, and was recently appointed chief winemaker for Pepper Tree Estate. Exports to the US and Canada.

ŢŢŢŢŢ **Tasmania Pinot Noir 2006** Vibrant and tangy, with cherry blossom and fraises du bois aromas and flavours; natural acidity provides a long, lingering finish and aftertaste. Screwcap. 13.5° alc. **Rating** 94 **To** 2015 $40

Hunter Valley Shiraz 2006 Vibrant and lively; plum and blackberry fruit with balanced oak; great mouthfeel and thrust through to the finish. Will become a classic. **Rating** 94 **To** 2026

🍇 Chellodene Wines   **NR**

Cnr Farley Road/Setterburg Road, Kingston-on-Murray, SA 5331 **Region** Riverland
T (08) 8583 0176 **F** (08) 8583 0176 **Open** By appt
Winemaker Josephine Lamattina, Jon Foster **Est.** 2000 **Cases** 2500
Just as oaks from acorns grow, so has Chellodene. Josephine Lamattina and Jon Foster decided to crush 1 tonne of grapes in 2000, strictly for their own enjoyment. However, sharing the wines with friends led to requests for winemaking for both friends and neighbours, with the news spreading so that some of Chellodene's clients come from far away. In 2007 they crushed 36 tonnes of nine varieties, making everything from rose to fortified wines.

Chestnut Hill Vineyard

1280 Pakenham Road, Mount Burnett, Vic 3781 **Region** Gippsland
T (03) 5942 7314 **F** (03) 5942 7314 **www**.chestnuthillvineyard.com.au **Open** W'ends & public hols 10.30–5.30, or by appt
Winemaker Charlie Javor **Est.** 1995 **Cases** 1200
Charlie and Ivka Javor started Chestnut Hill with small plantings of chardonnay, sauvignon blanc and pinot noir in 1985 and have slowly increased the vineyards to a little over 3 ha. Less than an hour's drive from Melbourne, the picturesque vineyard is situated among the rolling hills in the Dandenongs near Mt Burnett. The label explains, 'Liberty is a gift we had never experienced in our homeland,' Croatia, from which they emigrated in the late 1960s.

ŸŸŸŸ♀ **Mount Burnett Chardonnay 2006** A subdued bouquet; the palate has fresh fig, melon and a little buttered toast; richly textured, almost chewy, and finishes with plenty of flavour. Diam. **Rating** 90 **To** 2012

ŸŸŸŸ **Mount Burnett Sauvignon Blanc 2007** Bright, with a savoury, mineral complexity; quite textural and very dry, but with nice definition on the finish. Diam. **Rating** 89 **To** 2009

Cheviot Bridge/Long Flat

9th Floor, 564 St Kilda Road, Melbourne, Vic 3004 (postal) **Region** Upper Goulburn
T (03) 8656 7000 **F** (03) 9510 3277 **www.**cheviotbridge.com.au **Open** Not
Winemaker Hugh Cuthbertson **Est.** 1998 **Cases** NFP
Cheviot Bridge/Long Flat brings together a highly experienced team of wine industry professionals and investors, who provided the $10 million-plus required to purchase the Long Flat range of wines from Tyrrell's; the purchase took place in the second half of 2003. The bulk of the business activity is that of virtual winery, acquiring bulk and/or bottled wine from various third-party suppliers. The current releases are very meritorious, both in terms of quality and price. The brands include Cheviot Bridge Yea Valley, Cheviot Bridge CB, Kissing Bridge, Thirsty Lizard, Long Flat, The Long Flat Wine Co and Terrace Vale (see separate entry). Exports to all major markets.

ŸŸŸŸŸ **Cheviot Bridge Yea Valley Shiraz 2006** Lively, fresh and intense red and black fruits on an elegant, medium-bodied palate, with superfine tannins running through the finish. Screwcap. **Rating** 94 **To** 2016 $28

ŸŸŸŸ♀ **Cheviot Bridge Pyrenees Shiraz 2006** Strong purple-red; full-bodied, but not extractive; good regional/varietal expression to the array of black fruits, and flickers of licorice and spice; good length and tannin structure. Terrific value. Screwcap. 14.5° alc. **Rating** 93 **To** 2016 $16
Long Flat Destinations Clare Valley Riesling 2006 Faint tropical overtones to an apple and lime core; good structure; flavour in a lighter mode. Screwcap. 13° alc. **Rating** 90 **To** 2012 $15.95
Cheviot Bridge Yea Valley Chardonnay 2006 Slow-developing medium-bodied style, with seamless fusion of melon fruit with French oak; good length and balance. Screwcap. **Rating** 90 **To** 2012 $28

ŸŸŸŸ **Long Flat Destinations Yarra Valley Pinot Noir 2006** Light- to medium-bodied cherry, plum and spice fruit with a savoury finish; good structure and balance. Continues to impress. Screwcap. 13.5° alc. **Rating** 89 **To** 2012 $15.95
Cheviot Bridge Yea Valley Shiraz 2005 Deceptively light in colour; likewise enters the mouth with fairly light red fruits, but the texture picks up on the back-palate and finish. Screwcap. 14° alc. **Rating** 89 **To** 2011 $19.99
Long Flat Destinations Barossa Valley Shiraz 2006 Bright, clear colour; a light- to medium-bodied palate with a lively mix of black cherry, plum and blackberry fruit; balanced finish. Screwcap. 14.5° alc. **Rating** 89 **To** 2014 $15.95
Long Flat Destinations Coonawarra Cabernet Sauvignon 2004 Has more weight and structure than expected, and, similarly, varietal character expressed by blackcurrant fruit and fine, ripe tannins. Screwcap. 14° alc. **Rating** 89 **To** 2013 $15.95
Long Flat Destinations Coonawarra Cabernet Sauvignon 2005 Medium- to full-bodied, and over-delivers on price; savoury blackcurrant and mulberry fruit, with plenty of tannin support. Screwcap. 14.5° alc. **Rating** 89 **To** 2013 $15.99
Long Flat Destinations Yarra Valley Chardonnay 2006 Well enough made, but is lacking in concentration; what is there is good, and is regional in character, but it stops there. Screwcap. 13° alc. **Rating** 88 **To** 2010 $15.99
Cheviot Bridge Adelaide Hills Chardonnay 2005 Lively, tangy, citrussy, with some sauvignon blanc-like flavours; still fresh and quite long; minimal oak. Screwcap. 14° alc. **Rating** 88 **To** 2011 $16

Cheviot Bridge Yea Valley Cabernet Sauvignon 2006 Strong blackcurrant fruit and even stronger oak add up to abundant flavour, if not finesse. **Rating** 88 **To** 2013 $19.95

Long Flat Destinations Adelaide Hills Sauvignon Blanc 2006 A relatively closed bouquet, but opens up to tropical passionfruit and gooseberry flavours on the palate. Screwcap. 13° alc. **Rating** 87 **To** 2009 $15.95

Long Flat White Semillon Sauvignon Blanc 2007 Pretty good effort for '07, anchored in semillon and filled with a touch of sweetness. Value at this price. Zork. **Rating** 87 **To** 2009 $9

Chidlow's Well Estate

6245 Old Northam Road, Chidlow, WA 6556 **Region** Perth Hills
T (08) 9572 3681 **F** (08) 9572 3750 **www.chidlowswell.com.au Open** By appt
Winemaker Rob Marshall, Julie Smith **Est.** 1995 **Cases** 850
Chidlow is around 60 km east of Perth and was originally known as Chidlow's Well. The 3-ha vineyard is now owned and managed by Peter Costa and Sandy Gray, who continue to grow the chardonnay, chenin blanc, verdelho and shiraz planted on the vineyard by the former owners.

ΨΨΨΨ   **Perth Hills Verdelho 2007** Vibrant and juicy, with orange peel and good flavour and weight. Screwcap. 13.2° alc. **Rating** 87 **To** 2010 $17

Chislehurst Estate

6121 Putty Road, Howes Valley, NSW 2330 (postal) **Region** Hunter Valley Zone
T (02) 6579 4566 **F** (02) 6579 4566 **Open** Not
Winemaker Hunter Wine Services (John Hordern) **Est.** 1989 **Cases** 700
John and Beatrice (Bea) Feaks established the Chislehurst vineyard in 1989. The 4 ha of plantings are on the historic Putty Road, 50 km to the west of Cessnock, but isolated by the Yengo National Park and the Brokenback Range. Its elevation is 100 m higher than the Hunter proper, which also differentiates the wine styles from those of the Hunter.

ΨΨΨΨ   **Chardonnay 2003** Still bright yellow-green; honeyed/toasty notes surround the core of yellow peach fruit; good balance and longevity. Screwcap. 13.5° alc. **Rating** 87 **To** 2009 $10

Verdelho 2003 A mix of toasty development and fresh lively acidity on the finish; a touch of reduction. Screwcap. 13.5° alc. **Rating** 87 **To** 2009 $10

Chrismont

251 Upper King River Road, Cheshunt, Vic 3678 **Region** King Valley
T (03) 5729 8220 **F** (03) 5729 8253 **www.chrismont.com.au Open** 7 days 11–5
Winemaker Warren Proft **Est.** 1980 **Cases** 10 000
Arnold (Arnie) and Jo Pizzini have established 85 ha of vineyards in the Whitfield area of the upper King Valley. They have planted riesling, sauvignon blanc, chardonnay, pinot gris, cabernet sauvignon, merlot, shiraz, barbera, marzemino and arneis. The La Zona range ties in the Italian heritage of the Pizzinis and is part of the intense interest in all things Italian. Exports to the US and Sweden.

ΨΨΨΨΨ   **King Valley Riesling 2006** A hint of reduction on the bouquet; good flavour, with lemon and a mineral core that carries through on the finish. Screwcap. 12.5° alc. **Rating** 90 **To** 2014 $16

King Valley Merlot 2005 Fresh and vibrant, with Italian-like savoury, drying tannins; good depth and structure, and shows the heritage of its makers; made for food. Screwcap. 14° alc. **Rating** 90 **To** 2012 $22

ΨΨΨΨ   **Limited Release King Valley Petit Manseng 2006** Made from a variety found in southwest France, this wine is all about texture; subdued on the bouquet, the palate offers an array of flavours, from fresh fig, lemon and hazelnut; very interesting. Screwcap. 14° alc. **Rating** 89 **To** 2009 $22

King Valley Chardonnay 2004 Very toasty bouquet and palate, but with lively citrus fruits at the core; quite youthful for its age, but should be enjoyed soon. Screwcap. 13.5° alc. **Rating** 89 **To** 2009 $20

La Zona Sangiovese Cabernet 2004 A Super-Tuscan blend, with a savoury streak at its core; very tannic on the finish; the question is whether that savoury fruit will remain over time. Cork. 14° alc. **Rating** 89 **To** 2012 $55

La Zona King Valley Sangiovese 2005 A savoury wine with red cherries and a hint of mint; quite tannic, as you would expect from sangiovese. Screwcap. 14° alc. **Rating** 88 **To** 2009 $22

La Zona King Valley Barbera 2004 A high-toned, incisive mix of plum, black cherry and spice intermingling with notes of mint and citrus. Screwcap. 14° alc. **Rating** 88 **To** 2012 $22

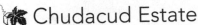

Chudacud Estate   NR

Lot 22 Ward Road, Boyup Brook, WA 6244 **Region** Blackwood Valley
T (08) 9764 4053 **F** (08) 9764 4053 **Open** Wed–Sun & public hols 10–5
Winemaker Ian Duncan, Jennifer Duncan **Est.** 2001 **Cases** NFP
Jennifer Duncan explains the background to Chudacud in fine style. 'This was my husband's dream and my nightmare!!!! Anyone with the slightest notion that wandering through the vineyard hand-in-hand is romantic – think again. It's damn hard work, but I must admit when the cork comes out of the bottle it makes it all worthwhile.' To that I can only add 'Amen'. Their 1 ha of shiraz planted in 2001 (after they moved from the city in '00) makes them the smallest winery in the Blackwood Valley. However, given the absence of food in the Blackwood wine country, the Duncans are building a commercial kitchen which will consist of six barbecues where patrons can choose from rump steak, lamb, fish or chicken and cook their own, accompanied by gourmet salad. It's an old idea, but one which works very well.

Churchview Estate   ★★★★☆

Cnr Bussell Highway/Gale Road, Metricup, WA 6280 **Region** Margaret River
T (08) 9755 7200 **F** (08) 9755 7300 **www**.churchview.com.au **Open** Mon–Sat 9.30–5.30
Winemaker Paul Green **Est.** 1998 **Cases** 17 000
The Fokkema family, headed by Spike Fokkema, immigrated from the Netherlands in the 1950s. Their business success in the following decades led to the acquisition of the 100-ha Churchview Estate property in '97, and to the progressive establishment of 70 ha of vineyards. Exports to the UK and other major markets.

 The Bartondale Reserve Margaret River Chardonnay 2006 Bright green-straw; well-handled barrel ferment inputs into a wine with intense, perfectly ripened fruit. Screwcap. 14.5° alc. **Rating** 92 **To** 2014 $25.50

The Bartondale Reserve Margaret River Cabernet Sauvignon 2005 Retains crimson hue; an elegant, medium- to full-bodied palate, with bright blackcurrant fruit, and firm tannins. Screwcap. 14.5° alc. **Rating** 91 **To** 2015 $32.75

The Bartondale Reserve Margaret River Marsanne 2007 Well made, protecting both the distinctively chalky texture of the variety and the honeysuckle fruit, with a short period in French oak; will develop even further with time. Screwcap. 13.5° alc. **Rating** 90 **To** 2015 $25.50

The Bartondale Reserve Margaret River Shiraz 2005 Much fuller, deeper and (seemingly) riper than the varietal, although the alcohol denies this; blackberry, plum and lingering tannins define the palate; will be long lived. Screwcap. 14.5° alc. **Rating** 90 **To** 2017 $32.75

Margaret River Cabernet Merlot 2005 Good hue; medium-bodied fresh cassis-accented fruits with balanced tannins. Gold medal, Qld Wine Awards '06. Screwcap. 14.5° alc. **Rating** 90 **To** 2013 $19.95

Margaret River Noble Riesling 2007 Curious how well this style does in the Margaret River; very attractive lime juice, with perfectly balanced acidity. Screwcap. 10.5° alc. **Rating** 90 **To** 2012 $22.50

ŶŶŶŶ   **Margaret River Sauvignon Blanc Semillon 2007** A clean and positive bouquet foretelling the ripe sauvignon fruit extending beyond the normal range, but slightly grippy on the finish. Screwcap. 12° alc. **Rating** 87 **To** 2009 $16.95
Margaret River Unwooded Chardonnay 2007 A relatively unexpressive bouquet, but has a volume of melon/stone fruit chardonnay (plus some phenolics) on the palate; food style. Screwcap. 13.5° alc. **Rating** 87 **To** 2010 $16.95
Margaret River Rose 2007 Pale pink; fresh cherry but very light, which – paradoxically – is a plus, for it has been left dry rather than pushed by sugar. Screwcap. 12.5° alc. **Rating** 87 **To** 2009 $14.95
Margaret River Shiraz 2005 Light- to medium-bodied, with bright juicy red fruits in an essentially simple flavour spectrum and texture; ready now. Screwcap. 14.5° alc. **Rating** 87 **To** 2009 $19.95

Cicada Wines

PO Box 808, Riverwood, NSW 2210 **Region** Warehouse
T (02) 9594 4980 **F** (02) 9594 5290 **www**.cicadawines.com **Open** Not
Winemaker Contract **Est.** 2005 **Cases** NFP
Cicada Wines is an ultimate virtual winery, created by a group of wine lovers and professionals who scour Australia for quality wines which have already been bottled but are, when purchased, cleanskin. They have succeeded in finding some good wines.

ŶŶŶŶŶ   **Black Prince Barossa Valley Shiraz 2005** Essency blackberry fruit aroma and flavour; leather and savoury flavours follow through on the long and quite tannic finish, balancing the ripe fruit. Screwcap. 13.8° alc. **Rating** 92 **To** 2016 $18.95

Cirko V   ★★★

148 Markwood-Tarrawingee Road, Markwood, Vic 3678 **Region** King Valley
T (03) 5727 0535 **F** (03) 5727 0487 **www**.cirko-v.com.au **Open** At Tinkers Hill
Winemaker Rick Kinzbrunner (Contract) **Est.** 2003 **Cases** 400
The derivation of the name Cirko V is, to put it mildly, eclectic. Cirko is Esperanto for circus, and V is an abbreviation of vie, French for life. Inspired partly by Cirque du Soleil and Circus Oz, Kristy Taylor and Peter Lumsden decided to undertake a major seachange, giving up their jobs, selling the various properties they had acquired and moving to the King Valley, buying an existing vineyard planted to 4 ha of shiraz, 2 ha of merlot and 1 ha of viognier. They intend to sell most of the wine through the Tinkers Hill cellar door, and a wine club.

ŶŶŶŶ   **Viognier 2006** Has plenty of overall flavour, but is somewhat tough; best appreciated with turkey or free-range chicken. Screwcap. 14.5° alc. **Rating** 87 **To** 2010 $29

Clair de Lune Vineyard

8805 South Gippsland Highway, Kardella South, Vic 3951 **Region** Gippsland
T (03) 5655 1032 **www**.clairdelune.com.au **Open** 7 days 11.30–5.30
Winemaker Brian Gaffy **Est.** 1997 **Cases** 500
Brian Gaffy married a successful 20-year career in civil engineering with a long-term involvement in the Bundaburra Wine & Food Club in Melbourne. His interest in wine grew, leading to studies at the Dookie Agricultural College, with particular input from Martin Williams MW and Denise Miller. He has now planted a total of 4 ha on the rolling hills of the Strzelecki Range to sauvignon blanc, chardonnay, pinot noir and a mixed block of shiraz/merlot/cabernet.

ŶŶŶŶŶ   **Gippsland Shiraz 2007** Spice, roasted meats and pepper on the bouquet; red fruits come through on the palate, with some toughness that needs time to settle down; no doubt about the intensity of fruit. Diam. **Rating** 92 **To** 2013 $28

ŶŶŶŶ   **Sauvignon Blanc 2007** Light-bodied, but has length and an unexpected citrussy bite to the finish, moving through light asparagus and gooseberry notes on the way. Screwcap. 11.9° alc. **Rating** 89 **To** 2009 $25

South Gippsland Wooded Chardonnay 2006 A soft and fleshy wine, with ripe stone fruits and a hint of buttery complexity; fresh, but lacks a little focus. Screwcap. 11.9° alc. **Rating** 87 **To** 2009 $30

Pinot Rose 2007 Fresh, light-bodied strawberry fruit, with cleansing acidity and a dry finish. Screwcap. 12° alc. **Rating** 87 **To** 2009 $25

Clairault ★★★★★

Caves Road, Wilyabrup, WA 6280 **Region** Margaret River
T (08) 9755 6225 **F** (08) 9755 6229 www.clairaultwines.com.au **Open** 7 days 10–5
Winemaker Will Shields **Est.** 1976 **Cases** 30 000
Bill and Ena Martin, with sons Conor, Brian and Shane, acquired Clairault several years ago and have expanded the vineyards on the 120-ha property. The 12 ha of vines established by the former owners (they are up to 30 years old) are being supplemented by another 70 ha of vines, with a ratio of 70% red varieties to 30% white. Deeply concerned about the environment and consumer health, Clairault has joined with ERA (Environmentally Responsible Agriculture) to implement the elimination of chemical use and the introduction of biological farming. Exports to the UK, the US, Canada, Singapore and Hong Kong.

🍷🍷🍷🍷🍷 **Estate Margaret River Cabernet Sauvignon 2005** Classic cabernet aroma and flavour, blackcurrant and cassis offset by flecks of black olive and earth; fine cedary oak and tannins on a long finish. Screwcap. 15° alc. **Rating** 95 **To** 2025 $44

Estate Margaret River Chardonnay 2006 A complex bouquet, with strong barrel ferment inputs; an intense and equally complex palate with nectarine and cashew; good minerality. Screwcap. 14° alc. **Rating** 94 **To** 2015 $32

🍷🍷🍷🍷🍷 **Margaret River Cabernet Sauvignon 2005** Has a sweeter and slightly softer fruit profile than the Estate, but the medium-bodied palate has very good balance, line and length. Screwcap. 15° alc. **Rating** 93 **To** 2015 $24

Margaret River Semillon Sauvignon Blanc 2007 Classic Margaret River style; good focus, intensity and length; marries tropical fruit with a lemon juice dressing. Screwcap. 13° alc. **Rating** 91 **To** 2012 $22

Margaret River Shiraz 2005 Has well above-average weight and depth for Margaret River shiraz, with ripe berry fruits offset by fine but ripe tannins; good oak use. Screwcap. **Rating** 91 **To** 2017 $24

Margaret River Sauvignon Blanc 2007 Has more tropical, passionfruit and gooseberry aromas and flavours than many others from the vintage. Screwcap. 12.5° alc. **Rating** 90 **To** 2010 $22

Margaret River Shiraz 2004 Light- to medium-bodied; retains good freshness to its bright, red cherry, plum and spice fruit which belie the alcohol; fine tannins. Screwcap. 15° alc. **Rating** 90 **To** 2014 $22

Margaret River Cabernet Merlot 2005 Nicely well pitched and weighted, with supple, silky yet distinctly tangy flavours on the long, light- to medium-bodied palate; should please all comers. Screwcap. 14.5° alc. **Rating** 90 **To** 2015 $24

🍷🍷🍷🍷 **Estate Margaret River Riesling 2007** A firm, minerally palate; overall, subdued varietal fruit. a dual function of vineyard and region. Screwcap. 12.5° alc. **Rating** 89 **To** 2012 $22

Margaret River Chardonnay 2007 Tangy, lively, light- to medium-bodied wine with delicate nectarine and grapefruit flavours, backed by appropriately subtle oak. Screwcap. 13° alc. **Rating** 89 **To** 2012 $24

Clancy Fuller ★★★★☆

PO Box 34, Tanunda, SA 5352 **Region** Barossa Valley
T (08) 8563 0080 **F** (08) 8563 0080 **Open** Not
Winemaker Chris Ringland **Est.** 1996 **Cases** 550
This is the venture of industry veterans who should know better: Paul Clancy, long responsible for the Wine Industry Directory which sits in every winery office in Australia; and Peter Fuller, who has built up by far the largest public relations business for all sectors of the wine

industry. They own 2 ha of dry-grown 120-year old shiraz at Bethany, and 2 ha of shiraz and grenade at Jacob's Creek. No samples received; the rating is that of last year.

Clarendon Hills

Brookmans Road, Blewitt Springs, SA 5171 **Region** McLaren Vale
T (08) 8364 1484 **F** (08) 8364 1484 **Open** By appt
Winemaker Roman Bratasiuk **Est.** 1989 **Cases** NA
Age and experience, it would seem, have mellowed Roman Bratasiuk — and the style of his wines. Once formidable and often rustic, they are now far more sculpted and smooth, at times bordering on downright elegance. The quality and consistency of the 2004 wines is, quite simply, outstanding. These are great ambassadors for Australia in the US market. Exports to the UK, the US and other major markets.

ΨΨΨΨΨ **Astralis Syrah 2004** A wine of precision and distinction, with immaculate fruit, oak and tannin balance, a light year away from the original Astralis style. Whether the price is justified is a decision for the purchaser, but the closure is a real concern for long life (stained cork). Cork. 14.5° alc. **Rating** 95 **To** 2015 $450
Hickinbotham Vineyard Cabernet Sauvignon 2004 Unusually perfumed cassis fruit on the bouquet; a svelte palate, long and harmonious, with excellent fruit and oak balance and integration; ripe tannins. Cork. 14.5° alc. **Rating** 95 **To** 2014 $120
Brookman Vineyard Shiraz 2004 Richer, riper, but also more developed than Astralis; mocha and chocolate notes, and does have good length with fine tannins and good acidity. Similar stained cork. Cork. 14.5° alc. **Rating** 94 **To** 2015 $120
Hickinbotham Vineyard Shiraz 2004 Has a somewhat cooler-grown fruit profile than Brookman, with spicy notes and lively acidity; has length and poise. Cork. 14.5° alc. **Rating** 94 **To** 2014 $120
Romas Vineyard Old Vine Grenache 2004 Deep and clear colour; a powerful varietal statement, with blackberry, raspberry and cherry fruit, sustained tannins and perfect balance. Poor-quality cork. 14.5° alc. **Rating** 94 **To** 2011 $120

ΨΨΨΨΨ **Sandown Cabernet Sauvignon 2004** Much riper fruit aromas than Hickinbotham, and the palate is likewise riper; while not porty, lacks the finesse of the Hickinbotham. Cork. 14.5° alc. **Rating** 92 **To** 2013 $90

Clayfield Wines

25 Wilde Lane, Moyston, Vic 3377 **Region** Grampians
T (03) 5354 2689 **F** (03) 5354 2679 **www.**clayfieldwines.com **Open** Mon–Sat 10–5, Sun 11–4
Winemaker Simon Clayfield **Est.** 1997 **Cases** 1000
Former long-serving Best's winemaker Simon Clayfield and wife Kaye are now doing their own thing. They planted 2 ha of shiraz and merlot between 1997 and '99. Additional grapes are purchased from local growers and, when the quality is appropriate, incorporated in the Grampians Shiraz. Production is modest, but the quality is high; production from the 2007 vintage was, nonetheless, severely cut by frost. Exports to the US, Canada and Maldives.

ΨΨΨΨΨ **Grampians Shiraz 2005** Classic example of Grampians shiraz, the fruit flavours and texture reflecting the continental climate with warm days giving generosity, cool to cold nights the spice and acidity, here beautifully balanced. Screwcap. 15° alc. **Rating** 96 **To** 2025 $45

ΨΨΨΨΨ **Massif Grampians Shiraz 2005** Impressive wine in its own right at half the price of the Grampians Shiraz; simply doesn't have the same velvety intensity, but has abundant cool-grown flavour. Screwcap. 15.2° alc. **Rating** 92 **To** 2015 $24

Claymore Wines ★★★★

Leasingham Road, Leasingham, SA 5452 **Region** Clare Valley
T (08) 8843 0200 **F** (08) 8843 0200 **www.**claymorewines.com.au **Open** Wed–Mon 11–4
Winemaker David Mavor, Ben Jeanneret **Est.** 1998 **Cases** 10 000
Claymore Wines is the venture of two medical professionals imagining that it would lead the
way to early retirement (which, of course, it did not). The starting date depends on which
event you take: the first 4-ha vineyard at Leasingham purchased in 1991 (with 70-year-old
grenache, riesling and shiraz); '96, when a 16-ha block at Penwortham was purchased and
planted to shiraz, merlot and grenache; '97, when the first wines were made; or '98, when
the first releases came onto the market, the labels inspired by U2, Pink Floyd and Lou Reed.
Exports to the US, Denmark, Malaysia, Taiwan, Singapore and Hong Kong.

ΨΨΨΨΨ **Joshua Tree Clare Valley Riesling 2007** Herb, slate and lime aromas and
flavours on a quite long palate, with citrus and mineral acidity. Screwcap. 12° alc.
Rating 91 **To** 2014 $18
Walk on the Wild Side Clare Valley Shiraz Viognier 2006 Bright hue;
attractive, lifted, vigorous fruit; fresh finish and aftertaste. Screwcap. 15° alc.
Rating 90 **To** 2014 $20

ΨΨΨΨ **Nirvana Reserve Clare Valley Shiraz 2004** Some sweet and sour characters;
ripe fruit on entry, then a tangy, almost citrussy, finish; has length. Cork. 14° alc.
Rating 89 **To** 2014 $35
Dark Side of the Moon Clare Valley Shiraz 2005 Full-bodied; a very ripe
style with prune, jammy blackberry fruit, the alcohol adding to the fruit sweetness,
then finishing with sharp acidity. Screwcap. 15° alc. **Rating** 87 **To** 2012 $25

Clearview Estate Mudgee NR

Cnr Sydney Road/Rocky Water Hole Road, Mudgee, NSW 2850 **Region** Mudgee
T (02) 6372 4546 **F** (02) 6372 7577 **Open** Mon–Fri 10–3 (Mar–Dec), w'ends 10–4,
or by appt
Winemaker Robert Stein Vineyard **Est.** 1995 **Cases** 1500
Paul and Michelle Baguley acquired the 11-ha vineyard from the founding Hickey family in
2006. Paul brings 10 years' experience as a viticulturist, and Paul and Michelle have introduced
additional wine styles.

Cleggett Wines ★★★

'Shalistin', Strathalbyn Road, Langhorne Creek, SA 5255 **Region** Langhorne Creek
T (08) 8537 3133 **F** (08) 8537 3102 **www.**cleggettwines.com.au **Open** 7 days 10–6
(summer), Thurs–Tues 10–6 (winter)
Winemaker Stephen Clark, Chris Day, Duane Coates (Consultant) **Est.** 2000 **Cases** 1500
The Cleggett family first planted grape vines at Langhorne Creek in 1911. In 1977 a sport
(a natural mutation) of cabernet sauvignon produced bronze-coloured grapes; cuttings were
taken and increasing quantities of the vine were gradually established, and called malian. Ten
years later one of the malian vines itself mutated to yield golden-white bunches, and this
in turn was propagated with the name shalistin. There are now 4 ha of shalistin and 2 ha of
malian in bearing. Shalistin is made as a full-bodied but unoaked white wine; malian produces
both an early- and a late-harvest rose-style wine. Exports to the UK.

ΨΨΨΨ **Legend Series Langhorne Creek Cabernet Sauvignon 2006** Light- to
medium-bodied; pleasant, gently sweet mint, cassis and blackcurrant fruit; supple
finish. Diam. 14.5° alc. **Rating** 88 **To** 2013 $20
Illawarra Block Langhorne Creek Shiraz 2006 Fragrant red and black fruit
aromas; distinct sweetness on the palate is aimed at the popular market sector.
Screwcap. 14° alc. **Rating** 87 **To** 2009 $20

Clemens Hill

686 Richmond Road, Cambridge, TAS 7170 **Region** Southern Tasmania
T (03) 6248 5985 **F** (03) 6248 5985 **Open** By appt
Winemaker Winemaking Tasmania **Est.** 1994 **Cases** 900
The Shepherd family acquired Clemens Hill in 2001 after selling their Rosabrook winery
in the Margaret River. They also have a shareholding in Winemaking Tasmania, the contract
winemaking facility run by Julian Alcorso, who makes the Clemens Hill wines. The estate
vineyards have now been increased to 3.8 ha (pinot noir and sauvignon blanc). Following
the death of Joan Shepherd in 2006, John took John Schuts, an assistant winemaker at Julian
Alcorso's Winemaking Tasmania, into partnership.

ŸŸŸŸŸ **Reserve Pinot Noir 2005** Flavours of plum and dark berry, with exemplary
texture and structure; a long and lingering finish. **Rating** 94 **To** 2015 $52

ŸŸŸŸ **Sauvignon Blanc 2007** Clean and quite fresh, but muted varietal character;
some tropical notes, but lacks thrust. **Rating** 88 **To** 2009 $25.75

Clonakilla

★★★★★

Crisps Lane, Murrumbateman, NSW 2582 **Region** Canberra District
T (02) 6227 5877 **F** (02) 6227 5871 **www**.clonakilla.com.au **Open** 7 days 10–5
Winemaker Tim Kirk **Est.** 1971 **Cases** 9000
The indefatigable Tim Kirk, with an inexhaustible thirst for knowledge, is the winemaker
and manager of this family winery founded by Tim's father, scientist Dr John Kirk. It is not
at all surprising that the quality of the wines is excellent, especially the Shiraz Viognier, which
has paved the way for numerous others to follow, but remains the best example in Australia.
Exports to all major markets.

ŸŸŸŸŸ **Canberra District Shiraz Viognier 2007** Vivid colour; it is hard to imagine
how more flavour could be generated at this alcohol, even if it is only 1 tonne
to the acre; a perfumed bouquet and an Arabian night of dark berry flavours;
the tannins show masterly winemaking at work; only 150 dozen made. Screwcap.
14° alc. **Rating** 97 $90
Syrah 2006 Estate-grown, and normally part of the Shiraz Viognier; whole berry
fermentation with indigenous yeasts, and then 20 months in French oak, has
produced a wine of rare finesse and length, the aftertaste weaving magic normally
reserved for great pinot noir. Screwcap. 14° alc. **Rating** 96 **To** 2026 $80
Canberra District Shiraz Viognier 2006 Exceptionally powerful, rich and
concentrated; a full-bodied, lush, velvety texture and mouthfeel; black fruits and
spice seem to subdue the viognier lift, but this is an exception tasted just prior to
bottling. Screwcap. 14° alc. **Rating** 96 **To** 2026 $80
Hilltops Shiraz 2007 Deep, impenetrable purple; immediately fills the sense
with its array of black fruits and spices all held within a delicate web of fine,
ripe tannins and oak. Amazing achievement to tame droughted, low-yield fruit.
Screwcap. 14.5° alc. **Rating** 95 **To** 2022 $30

ŸŸŸŸŸ **Canberra District Riesling 2007** Colour showing early development; a solid
wine with plenty of ripe citrus flavour and structure; rather less finesse. Screwcap.
12.5° alc. **Rating** 90 **To** 2011 $26

Cloudbreak Wines

5A/1 Adelaide Lobethal Road, Lobethal, SA 5241 **Region** Adelaide Hills
T 0431 245 668 **www**.cloudbreakwines.com.au **Open** W'ends & public hols 11–4
Winemaker Simon Greenleaf, William Finlayson **Est.** 2001 **Cases** 300
Owners Will Finlayson and Simon Greenleaf met 16 years ago while both working at
Petaluma. A long-term plan to make their own wine came after Simon had done vintages in
France, Chile and Spain, and Will in Oregon. In 1998 Simon's parents bought a 7-ha property,
at which time it was completely overgrown with blackberries. Will says, 'We had limited funds

so we did it all ourselves, from clearing the land to growing the cuttings and eventually putting the posts in – it took months of work.' Two varieties were planted first: pinot noir, using Burgundy clones 114 and 115; and pinot gris, followed by sauvignon blanc and chardonnay.

ㅇㅇㅇㅇㅇ **Adelaide Hills Chardonnay 2007** A fraction advanced yellow-green; firm, cool-grown style, with intensity and length to the nectarine and grapefruit flavours; well made. Screwcap. **Rating** 90 **To** 2012 $32

Adelaide Hills Pinot Noir 2007 Strong colour; flush with fully ripe plum and black cherry without straying into dry red territory; a little one-dimensional now, but will develop with time. Screwcap. **Rating** 90 **To** 2013 $34

ㅇㅇㅇㅇ **Adelaide Hills Pinot Gris 2007** Above-average flavour, though not strictly varietal, more to stone fruit and apple; good length. Screwcap. 13.5° alc. **Rating** 87 **To** 2009 $28

🍇 Cloudscape   ★★★

60 Pollards Lane, Drummond, Vic 3461 **Region** Macedon Ranges
T (03) 5423 9225 **F** (03) 5423 9225 **www**.cloudscapewines.com.au **Open** W'ends & public hols 12–5, or by appt
Winemaker Andre Deutsch **Est.** 2001 **Cases** 300
Andre Deutsch and Jan Ward began the development of their vineyard in 2001 with the planting of 2 ha of pinot noir. The non-irrigated vines have been grown using organic and biodynamic principles, which they believe will best express the terroir of the vineyard, which is on the north-facing slope of the plug of an extinct volcano, with red sandy loam soil. While waiting for the vines to mature, they have purchased grapes grown elsewhere, commencing with a 2004 Cabernet Sauvignon Merlot and Cabernet Franc. In a bold move, the wines are not filtered and free of added preservatives and fining agents.

ㅇㅇㅇㅇ **No Added Preservatives Cabernet Sauvignon Merlot Franc 2004** Has clung on to life better than anticipated, not unlike the Virgin Hills wines during their preservative-free period; however, this style demands a screwcap if not consumed within 18 months or so of vintage. Cork. 13.2° alc. **Rating** 87 **To** 2006 $20

Clovely Estate   ★★★☆

Steinhardts Road, Moffatdale via Murgon, Qld 4605 **Region** South Burnett
T (07) 3876 3100 **F** (07) 3876 3500 **www**.clovely.com.au **Open** 7 days 10–5
Winemaker Luke Fitzpatrick **Est.** 1998 **Cases** 30 000
Clovely Estate has the largest vineyards in Qld, having established 174 ha of immaculately maintained vines at two locations just to the east of Murgon in the Burnett Valley. There are 127 ha of red grapes (including 74 ha of shiraz) and 47 ha of white grapes. The attractively packaged wines are sold in four tiers: Clovely Estate at the top (not produced every year); Left Field, strongly fruity and designed to age; Fifth Row, for early drinking; and Queensland, primarily designed for the export market (the UK and other major markets). The estate also has a second cellar door at 210 Mulgrave Road, Red Hill.

ㅇㅇㅇㅇㅇ **Double Pruned South Burnett Shiraz 2005** Medium-bodied; a nice mix of blackberry, plum and more savoury/spicy elements; balanced oak and tannins; no question above-average for South Burnett. Double pruning pioneered 25 years ago by Dr Brian Freeman in the Riverina; significantly delays ripening and sharply reduces yield; 110 dozen made. Cork. 14.9° alc. **Rating** 90 **To** 2015 $60

ㅇㅇㅇㅇ **Reserve South Burnett Shiraz 2006** Essency blackberry pastille fruit; good flavour and with a hint of leather and earth; long and full on the finish, if a little one-dimensional. Screwcap. 14.2° alc. **Rating** 89 **To** 2014 $28

Clover Hill/Lalla Gully   ★★★★★

60 Clover Hill Road, Lebrina, Tas 7254 **Region** Northern Tasmania
T (03) 6395 6114 **F** (03) 6395 6257 **www**.taltarni.com.au **Open** By appt
Winemaker Loïc Le Calvez **Est.** 1986 **Cases** 10 000
Clover Hill was established by Taltarni in 1986 with the sole purpose of making a premium
sparkling wine. It has 21.7 ha of vineyards: 13.1 ha of chardonnay, 7.3 ha of pinot noir and
1.24 ha of pinot meunier. The sparkling wine quality is excellent, combining finesse with
power and length. The 17.5-ha Lalla Gully property is situated in a sheltered amphitheatre,
with a site climate 1°–2°C warmer than Clover Hill, the fruit ripening a week or so earlier.
Exports to the UK, the US and other major markets.

ŶŶŶŶŶ **Clover Hill 2003** Glints of gold introduce a palate with a rippling of stone fruit,
ripe apple, red berry and spice flavours augmented by a touch of brioche, followed
by a long, well-balanced finish. Cork. 13° alc. **Rating** 96 **To** 2009 $41.99
Clover Hill Blanc de Blanc 2001 A pure fruit line of stone fruit, apple and
citrus drives the wine from start to finish; lemony minerally acidity the closing
notes on the finish; 6 cuvees and 4 years yeast lees. Cork. 13° alc. **Rating** 95
To 2009 $51.99
Clover Hill Blanc de Blanc 2003 Tighter and more linear, with a mineral
thread wrapped around the pure lemon core; very fine, fragrant, long and complex;
should age gracefully over time. Cork. **Rating** 94 **To** 2016 $49.95

ŶŶŶŶŶ **Clover Hill 2004** A rich, creamy mouthfeel, with toast and citrus on the palate;
very fine and persistent bead and quite long on the finish. Cork. **Rating** 91
To 2014 $43.95
Lalla Gully Pinot Gris 2007 Bright green-straw; light-bodied, with lively citrus
and grass aromas and flavours; not varietal, but has life and drive. Screwcap. 13° alc.
Rating 90 **To** 2009 $23.95

ŶŶŶŶ **Lalla Gully Riesling 2007** Has a foundation of lime and mineral flavours,
with good length, but a bit hollow on the mid- to back-palate. Screwcap. 12° alc.
Rating 89 **To** 2013 $21.95
Lalla Gully Riesling 2006 Starting to show some development, but has good
flavour, with lemon and slate on the finish. **Rating** 88 **To** 2012 $21.95
Lalla Gully Sauvignon Blanc 2007 Firmly on the minerally side of the divide,
with restrained fruit, but does have length and a fresh finish. Screwcap. 12.5° alc.
Rating 87 **To** 2011 $23.95

Clown Fish   ★★★★

PO Box 342, Cowaramup, WA 6284 **Region** Margaret River
T (08) 9755 5195 **F** (08) 9755 9441 **www**.cowaramupwines.com.au **Open** Not
Winemaker Naturaliste Vintners (Bruce Dukes) **Est.** 1996 **Cases** 2500
Russell and Marilyn Reynolds run a 17-ha biodynamic vineyard with the aid of sons
Cameron (viticulturist) and Anthony (assistant winemaker). Plantings began in 1996, and
have been expanded to cover 4.2 ha of merlot, 4 ha of cabernet sauvignon, 2.3 ha each of
chardonnay and sauvignon blanc, and 2.1 ha each of shiraz and semillon. Notwithstanding low
yields and the discipline which biodynamic grapegrowing entails, wine prices are modest.

ŶŶŶŶŶ **Margaret River Sauvignon Blanc Semillon 2007** Very well made; tightly
focused citrus, grass and mineral flavours; long, dry, balanced finish. **Rating** 92
To 2010 $17.95

ŶŶŶŶ **Margaret River Shiraz 2006** Juicy red and black fruits, with notes of spice
and leaf on the light-bodied palate; good length. Screwcap. 13.5° alc. **Rating** 87
To 2012 $18.95

Clyde Park Vineyard

2490 Midland Highway, Bannockburn, Vic 3331 **Region** Geelong
T (03) 5281 7274 **F** (03) 5281 7309 **www**.clydepark.com.au **Open** W'ends & public
hols 11–5
Winemaker Simon Black, Terry Jongebloed **Est.** 1979 **Cases** 6000
Clyde Park Vineyard was established by Gary Farr, but was sold by him many years ago, and
has passed through several changes of ownership. It is now owned by Terry Jongebloed and
Sue Jongebloed-Dixon. It has significant mature plantings of pinot noir (3.4 ha), chardonnay
(3.1 ha), sauvignon blanc (1.5 ha), shiraz (1.2 ha) and pinot gris (0.9 ha), and the quality of its
wines is exemplary. Exports to the UK.

ŶŶŶŶŶ **Reserve Chardonnay 2006** Matches and marries finesse and complexity, never
easy; finely focused citrus and melon fruit with a delicate supporting web of
French oak; long finish. Screwcap. 13° alc. **Rating** 96 **To** 2014 $44
Reserve Pinot Noir 2006 An interesting contrast to the varietal; finer and more
vibrant on the fore- and mid-palate, the mouthfeel more silky, the tannins finer
still; great length; made from the oldest vines. Screwcap. 13.5° alc. **Rating** 94
To 2014 $49
Megan's Block Shiraz Viognier 2006 Typical lifted aromatics, with a mix of
mint and apricot; typical supple, smooth palate, finishing with fresh acidity. Gold
medal, Geelong Wine Show '07. **Rating** 94 **To** 2012 $32

ŶŶŶŶŶ **Pinot Noir 2006** A powerful Pinot, the strong structure built around fine but
persistent tannins; plum, spice and black cherry fruit; a lingering, peacock's-tail
finish. Screwcap. 13.5° alc. **Rating** 93 **To** 2013 $32
Chardonnay 2006 Vibrant mid-gold; pure varietal chardonnay with stone fruits
and a complex savoury twist; fine and focused on the finish with good length.
Rating 92 **To** 2012 $30
Pinot Gris 2007 Good level of ripeness showing some exotic fruit characters;
lovely texture on the palate, with good weight and some grip on the fresh, long
finish. Screwcap. 13.5° alc. **Rating** 91 **To** 2009 $30
Shiraz 2006 Bright, firm, spicy cool-grown style; not overly generous, but does
have length and balance. **Rating** 90 **To** 2013 $32

Coal Valley Vineyard ★★★★☆

257 Richmond Road, Cambridge, Tas 7170 **Region** Southern Tasmania
T (03) 6248 5367 **F** (03) 6248 4175 **www**.coalvalley.com.au **Open** Thurs–Sun 9–4
(closed Jul)
Winemaker Andrew Hood (Contract) **Est.** 1991 **Cases** 600
Since acquiring Coal Valley Vineyard in 1999, Gill Christian and Tod Goebel have increased
the original 1-ha hobby vineyard to 5 ha of riesling, chardonnay, pinot noir, tempranillo,
cabernet sauvignon and merlot. The cellar door now has a 100-seat restaurant/conference
facility, while Tod now makes the Cabernet Sauvignon onsite, and dreams of making all the
wines. More remarkable was their concurrent lives, one in India, the other in Tasmania (flying
over six times a year) and digging 4000 holes for the new vine plantings. Exports to Canada.

ŶŶŶŶŶ **Riesling 2007** Very fine, crisp and delicate; a beautiful expression of a lower
alcohol but dry style, with excellent length and finesse; the acidity may upset some
tasters. Screwcap. 11.6° alc. **Rating** 94 **To** 2015 $24

ŶŶŶŶŶ **Chardonnay 2006** Intense and aromatic; grapefruit and melon flavours with the
steely core of Tasmanian acidity; barrel ferment oak well integrated, and very good
line and length. Screwcap. 13.8° alc. **Rating** 93 **To** 2016 $25
Pinot Noir 2006 Good colour; plum and black cherry on a firm palate, with a
structure of fine but persistent tannins. Screwcap. 13.5° alc. **Rating** 91 **To** 2012 $32

ŶŶŶŶ **Cabernet Merlot 2006** Dense crimson-purple; fragrant blackcurrant, cassis
and mint aromas lead into a powerful mid-palate, the tannins just a little green;
impressive Tasmania. Screwcap. 14° alc. **Rating** 89 **To** 2016 $30

Vintage Sparkling 2004 Intense stone fruit and citrus on a long and even palate; very good balance, but just a little simple. Cork. 11.8° alc. Rating 89 To 2012 $30

Coates Wines

PO Box 859, McLaren Vale, SA 5171 **Region** McLaren Vale
T 0417 882 557 **F** (08) 8363 9925 **www**.coates-wines.com **Open** Not
Winemaker Duane Coates **Est.** 2003 **Cases** 1500
Duane Coates has a Bachelor of Science, a Master of Business Administration and a Master of Oenology from Adelaide University; for good measure he completed the theory component of the Masters of Wine degree in 2005. Having made wine in various parts of the world, and in SA for a number of important brands, he is more than qualified to make and market the Coates wines. Nonetheless, his original intention was to simply make a single barrel of wine employing various philosophies and practices outside the mainstream, and with no intention of moving to commercial production. The key is organically grown grapes and the refusal to use additives and fining agents. A deliberately low level of new oak (20%) is part of the picture. Exports to the US, Canada, Germany and Sweden.

♀♀♀♀ **Consonance Shiraz Cabernet Sauvignon 2006** Quite rich and ripe, with a tight core of fruit surrounded by toast; a little heat on the finish. McLaren Vale/Langhorne Creek. Cork. **Rating** 89 **To** 2012 $20

Cobaw Ridge

31 Perc Boyers Lane, East Pastoria via Kyneton, Vic 3444 **Region** Macedon Ranges
T (03) 5423 5227 **F** (03) 5423 5227 **www**.cobawridge.com.au **Open** Thurs–Mon 12–5
Winemaker Alan Cooper **Est.** 1985 **Cases** 1500
Nelly and Alan Cooper established Cobaw Ridge's 6-ha vineyard at an altitude of 610 m in the hills above Kyneton. The plantings of cabernet sauvignon have been removed and partially replaced by lagrein, a variety which sent me scuttling to Jancis Robinson's seminal book on grape varieties: it is a northeast Italian variety typically used to make delicate rose, but at Cobaw Ridge it is made into an impressive full-bodied dry red. This success has prompted Alan Cooper to remove 0.5 ha of chardonnay and plant vermentino in its place. The Coopers' son Joshua is taking a circuitous route via Europe and elsewhere in Australia to commencing a Wine Science at Adelaide University and will become the sixth generation of the family on the land. Exports to the UK.

♀♀♀♀♀ **Shiraz Viognier 2006** An essay of pepper in shiraz; very spicy with cool red fruits on the palate; fine tannins and ample acidity providing a fresh, savoury finish. Cork. **Rating** 92 **To** 2016 $42
Chardonnay 2006 Bright green-yellow; tight lemon and mineral palate, with nice weight and texture. **Rating** 90 **To** 2010 $32

♀♀♀♀ **Lagrein 2006** Great colour, and full of blueberry fruits and toasty oak; good flavour, albeit a little short on the finish. Cork. **Rating** 87 **To** 2011 $48

Cody's

New England Highway, Ballandean, Qld 4382 **Region** Granite Belt
T (07) 4684 1309 **F** (07) 5572 6500 **www**.codys.com.au **Open** 7 days 10–5
Winemaker Sirromet (Adam Chapman) **Est.** 1995 **Cases** NA
John Cody has established 2.5 ha of cabernet sauvignon, merlot and shiraz at his Ballandean vineyard. The wines are contract-made by Adam Chapman at Sirromet, and are sold by mail order and through the cellar door, which offers the usual facilities.

♀♀♀♀ **Tempranillo 2006** Light-bodied; fresh, lively red fruits; needs more structure, but no fault. **Rating** 87 **To** 2009 $12

Cofield Wines

Distillery Road, Wahgunyah, Vic 3687 **Region** Rutherglen
T (02) 6033 3798 **F** (02) 6033 0798 **www**.cofieldwines.com.au **Open** Mon–Sat 9–5,
Sun 10–5
Winemaker Damien Cofield, David Whyte **Est.** 1990 **Cases** 13 000
Sons Damien (winery) and Andrew (vineyard) have now taken over responsibility for the
business from parents Max and Karen. Collectively, they have developed an impressively broad-
based product range with a strong cellar door sales base. The Pickled Sisters Café is open for
lunch Wed–Mon (tel 02 6033 2377). A 20-ha property at Rutherglen was purchased in 2007,
which has 5.3 ha already planted to shiraz, and planting of durif and sangiovese followed.

ȲȲȲȲȲ **T XIV Pinot Noir Chardonnay NV** Fine, tight, reserved green apple and nashi
pear aromas and flavours; crisp, long, dry finish; cellar to 2012 is good advice.
Tumbarumba. 12° alc. **Rating** 90 **To** 2012 $24.85
T XV11 Sparkling Shiraz NV Good-quality base wine and well-judged dosage,
produce a sparkling shiraz which is neither oaky nor sweet, and will certainly
repay extended cellaring on cork. Cork. 15.1° alc. **Rating** 90 **To** 2020 $28

ȲȲȲȲ **Max's Blend Rutherglen Shiraz Durif 2006** A big wine with lots of dark
fruited flavour; sweet, ample and quite tannic on the finish. Cork. 15.2° alc.
Rating 87 **To** 2012 $19.50

Coldstream Hills   **NR**

31 Maddens Lane, Coldstream, Vic 3770 **Region** Yarra Valley
T (03) 5964 9410 **F** (03) 5964 9389 **www**.coldstreamhills.com.au **Open** 7 days 10–5
Winemaker Andrew Fleming, Greg Jarratt, James Halliday (Consultant) **Est.** 1985 **Cases** NA
Founded by the author, who continues to be involved as a consultant, but acquired by
Southcorp in mid-1996, thus it is now a small part of Foster's. Expansion plans already then
underway have been maintained, with well in excess of 100 ha of owned or managed estate
vineyards as the base. Chardonnay and Pinot Noir continue to be the principal focus; Merlot
came on-stream in 1997, Sauvignon Blanc around the same time, Reserve Shiraz and Viognier
later still. Vintage conditions permitting, Chardonnay, Pinot Noir and Cabernet Sauvignon are
made in both varietal and Reserve form, the latter in restricted quantities. In the 2006 and
'07 calendar years, the wines won 11 trophies, 17 gold, 17 silver and 52 bronze medals. Tasting
notes are written by Andrew Fleming. Exports to the UK, the US and Singapore.

Amphitheatre Pinot Noir 2006 The palate is a seamless union of dark cherries,
fine spice and gaminess with fine, persistent tannins, a silky texture and underlying
toasty oak; first release, made entirely from the north-facing A Block, and
represents a small selection of the finest barrels; unfiltered. Screwcap. 14°alc.
Rating NR **To** 2018 $120
2006 Coldstream Hills Reserve Chardonnay Displays regional cool-climate
characters of citrus and stone fruit, underpinned by barrel ferment characters of
grilled nuts and toasty oak; minerally notes are evident and provide additional
complexity. Screwcap. **Rating** NR **To** 2018 $46.90
2007 Coldstream Hills Pinot Noir Fragrant cherry and blueberry fruit
characters, with underlying gaminess and spice; medium-bodied; toasty oak is
evident but does not dominate; fine silky tannins and good length. Screwcap.
Rating NR **To** 2011 $28.90
2007 Coldstream Hills Sauvignon Blanc Fragrant lantana and gooseberry,
with underlying passionfruit and lychee aromas, plus mineral and stalky notes;
a fine and elegant style. Screwcap. **Rating** NR **To** 2009 $25.90
2007 Coldstream Hills Chardonnay Vibrant citrus and nectarine fruit aromas,
with underlying toasty oak and minerality; the palate has attractive citrus and
stone fruit, with barrel ferment cashew adding further complexity. Screwcap.
Rating NR **To** 2011 $26.90

2007 Coldstream Hills Limited Release Viognier Intense lime zest, pear and frangipani aromas; lime and apricot flavours with underlying floral notes; fresh acidity, good balance and length. Screwcap. **Rating** NR To 2010, $28.90

2006 Coldstream Hills Reserve Pinot Noir Varietal cherry and plum characters with underlying gamey notes and spice; savoury characters from stalk inclusion are evident, with attractive toasty French oak; the palate is round with silky texture and length. Screwcap. **Rating** NR To 2016 $75

2006 Coldstream Hills Merlot Ripe, concentrated, complex dark plum and cherry fruit, with black olive varietal character; toasty cedary oak adds complexity without dominating. Screwcap. **Rating** NR To 2015 $26.90

2006 Coldstream Hills Cabernet Sauvignon Medium-bodied; blackcurrant and bramble fruit characters dominate, with toasty oak and dark chocolate providing additional complexity. Screwcap. **Rating** NR To 2015 $28.90

2005 Coldstream Hills Reserve Cabernet Sauvignon Classic cool-climate blackcurrant and dark cherry aromas and flavours along with dark chocolate notes on the palate; medium-bodied, with harmonious toasty, cedary oak and fine, yet persistent, tannins. Screwcap. **Rating** NR To 2018 $51.90

2001 Coldstream Hills Pinot Noir Chardonnay Attractive toasty, bready notes with underlying lemon and yeast autolysis characters; youthful lemony chardonnay flavours on the palate, with textural support from the pinot; crisp and balanced finish, with fine acidity and length. Cork. **Rating** NR To 2010

Coliban Valley Wines ★★★★

Metcalfe-Redesdale Road, Metcalfe, Vic 3448 **Region** Heathcote
T 0417 312 098 **F** (03) 9813 3895 **www**.heathcotewinegrowers.com.au **Open** W'ends 10–5
Winemaker Helen Miles **Est.** 1997 **Cases** 500
Helen Miles (with a degree in science) and partner Greg Miles have planted 2.8 ha of shiraz, 1.2 ha of cabernet and 0.4 ha of merlot near Metcalfe, in the cooler southwest corner of Heathcote. The granitic soils and warm climate allow organic principles to be used successfully. The shiraz is dry-grown, while the cabernet sauvignon and merlot receive minimal irrigation.

ΨΨΨΨΨ **Heathcote Cabernet Merlot 2005** Crimson-purple; appropriate picking response for the region gives a medium-bodied wine with sweet cassis fruit and supple mouthfeel. Diam. 13° alc. **Rating** 90 To 2013 $20

ΨΨΨΨ **Heathcote Shiraz 2006** A dense wine with lots of oak and mocha aromas and flavours; very toasty on the finish, but impressive for its depth. Cork. 15° alc. **Rating** 89 To 2014

 ## Collector Wines ★★★★☆

12 Bourke Street, Collector, NSW 2581 (postal) **Region** Canberra District
T (02) 6116 8722 **F** (02) 6286 9482 **www**.collectorwines.com.au **Open** Not
Winemaker Alex McKay **Est.** 2007 **Cases** 750
Owner and winemaker Alex McKay makes two Canberra District Shirazs, the Marked Tree Red from parcels of shiraz from vineyards in and around Murrumbateman, and the Reserve from a single patch of mature shiraz grown on an elevated granite saddle near Murrumbateman. Collector Wines 2005 Marked Tree Red was awarded NSW Wine of the Year for 2007.

ΨΨΨΨ **Reserve Shiraz 2006** Deeper colour than the Marked Tree, and highly aromatic with red fruits, roast meats, spice and great texture; rich and generous on the palate, and wonderfully long; a lovely wine. Screwcap. 13.5° alc. **Rating** 95 To 2020 $46.95

ΨΨΨΨΨ **Marked Tree Red Shiraz 2006** Vibrant purple hue; highly aromatic, with spicy/savoury red and dark fruits; medium-bodied with plenty of grip on the finish, and should age gracefully. Screwcap. 13.5° alc. **Rating** 91 To 2018 $26.95

Colville Estate ★★★

PO Box 504, McLaren Vale, SA 5171 **Region** McLaren Vale
T 0414 826 168 **F** (08) 8556 3742 **Open** Not
Winemaker Tim Geddes (Contract) **Est.** 2001 **Cases** 1300
Peter Easterbrook has a 25-year career as a professional grapegrower in McLaren Vale, and over an extended period has (with wife Jennie) planted 20 ha of shiraz, 4 ha of cabernet sauvignon and 2 ha each of grenache and merlot. The estate is run using non-chemical regimes, relying on composting and natural fertilisers. Most of the grapes are sold, a small amount retained and made for export to Canada and Asia.

ϙϙϙϙ **McLaren Vale Shiraz 2004** Swathed in all-encompassing American oak, albeit with some dark fruits underneath that oak; dusty cork. Cork. 14.5° alc. **Rating** 87 To 2011 $18

Conte Estate Wines ★★★★

Lot 51 Sand Road, McLaren Flat, SA 5171 **Region** McLaren Vale
T 0414 942 072 **F** (08) 8383 0125 **www.conteestatewines.com.au Open** By appt
Winemaker Danial Conte, Steve Conte **Est.** 2003 **Cases** 10 000
Steve and Maria Conte, assisted by son Danial, have a large vineyard, predominantly established since 1960 but with 2.5 ha of shiraz planted 100 years earlier in the 1860s. In all there are 18 ha of shiraz, 12 ha of grenache, 7 ha each of cabernet sauvignon and sauvignon blanc, 6 ha of chardonnay and 1.66 ha of gewurztraminer. While continuing to sell a large proportion of the production, winemaking has become a larger part of the business.

ϙϙϙϙϙ **The Gondola McLaren Vale Grenache Shiraz 2006** Has more weight and structure than the Fifth Wave Grenache; a medium-bodied array of black and red cherry, spice and licorice. Cork. 14.5° alc. **Rating** 90 To 2012 $18

ϙϙϙϙ **Rock Hill McLaren Vale Shiraz 2006** Has better line and texture than the Reserve Over the Hill; blackberry, plum and spice, with a dusting of chocolate; stained cork. 14.5° alc. **Rating** 89 To 2013 $18
The Numb Hand Pruner McLaren Vale Grenache 2006 Light colour sets the tone for a pleasing café summer-style red, best served slightly chilled on a hot day; raspberry- and cherry-accented fruit. Cork. 14.5° alc. **Rating** 89 To 2009 $18
Pink Hit McLaren Vale Gewurztraminer 2007 The bouquet is not particularly varietal, but the fresh, zesty palate does have grapefruit and varietal lychee/stone fruit flavours; good for vintage. Screwcap. 13.5° alc. **Rating** 88 To 2010 $15
Primrose Lane McLaren Vale Chardonnay 2007 A soft entry and fore-palate, but melon and grapefruit flavours, plus a touch of oak, run through quite a long finish. Screwcap. 13.5° alc. **Rating** 88 To 2009 $15
Reserve Over the Hill McLaren Vale Shiraz 2006 Medium-bodied; a mix of spicy black fruits, regional chocolate and some sweet and sour notes; stained cork. 14.5° alc. **Rating** 88 To 2010 $25
Reserve Hunt Road McLaren Vale Cabernet Sauvignon 2006 Weak colour; light- to medium-bodied blackcurrant/cassis fruit in clear varietal mode, though lacking structure for higher points. Cork. 14.5° alc. **Rating** 87 To 2014 $25

Coobara Wines ★★★★☆

PO Box 231, Birdwood, SA 5234 **Region** Adelaide Hills
T (08) 8568 5375 **F** (08) 8568 5375 **www.coobarawines.com.au Open** By appt
Winemaker David Cook, Mark Jamieson **Est.** 1992 **Cases** 2500
David Cook has worked in the wine industry for over 18 years, principally with Orlando, but also with Jim Irvine, John Glaetzer and the late Neil Ashmead. As well as working full time for Orlando, he undertook oenology and viticulture courses, and – with support from his parents – planted 4 ha of cabernet sauvignon and merlot on the family property at Birdwood. In 1993 they purchased the adjoining property, planting 2 ha of riesling, and thereafter lifting

the plantings of merlot and cabernet sauvignon to 4 ha each, plus 2.8 ha of shiraz and 0.5 ha of riesling. In 2003 David decided to commence wine production, a fortuitous decision given that the following year their long-term grape purchase contracts were not renewed. Coobara is an Aboriginal word meaning 'place of birds'.

TTTTT **Adelaide Hills Riesling 2007** A fragrant and floral orange and lime blossom bouquet tightens up impressively on the minerally palate and lingering finish. Screwcap. 10.5° alc. **Rating** 94 **To** 2017 $18

TTTTT **Adelaide Hills Cabernet Merlot 2006** A fresh and clean bouquet, then a light- to medium-bodied palate with delicious red fruits and just enough savoury tannins to hold structure; ready. Screwcap. 14° alc. **Rating** 91 **To** 2014 $18
Adelaide Hills Shiraz 2006 Firm, but not aggressive or extractive flavours and texture; cool-grown red and black fruits plus a dash of spicy tannins. Screwcap. 14° alc. **Rating** 90 **To** 2015 $18

TTTT **Adelaide Hills Merlot 2006** An abundance of spicy black fruits interwoven with threads of black olive; more flavour than finesse. Screwcap. 14° alc. **Rating** 89 **To** 2014 $18

Cooks Lot   ★★★★

Cassilis Road, Mudgee, NSW 2850 **Region** Mudgee
T (02) 9550 3228 **F** (02) 9550 4390 **Open** By appt
Winemaker Duncan Cook, Ian McRae **Est.** 2002 **Cases** 2500
Duncan Cook has established his cellar door and café (open Tues–Sat 10–5) at the Parklands Resort. As well as leasing the cellar door and restaurant, he is planting a little over 1 ha of vines, again on a lend-lease basis. In the meantime he is producing wines from Mudgee and Orange. Winemaking is split between Miramar Winery and Lowe Family, although Duncan is halfway through his oenology degree at CSU, and will gradually take over the winemaking. The cellar door and café have artworks by Amber Subaki, an illustrator who specialises in nudes and portraits, and who designed the Cooks Lot label.

TTTTT **Mudgee Chardonnay 2005** Fresh, clean, well-defined varietal fruit in a stone fruit/citrus spectrum doesn't show heat from alcohol; subtle oak; developing slowly. Screwcap. 14.6° alc. **Rating** 90 **To** 2012 $17.95
Pinot Gris 2007 A very aromatic pear and musk bouquet; plenty of similar fruit flavours on the palate without any oiliness or reliance on residual sugar; well above average. Screwcap. 13.1° alc. **Rating** 90 **To** 2010 $19.95

TTTT **Mudgee Riesling 2006** Unusual, strongly herbal/pyrazine aromas; a touch of spritz on the palate enlivens the wine a little, though basically old-fashioned. Screwcap. 12.2° alc. **Rating** 87 **To** 2009 $17.95
Mudgee Cabernet Merlot 2006 Light- to medium-bodied wine, opening quietly, but surprising with its tenacious savoury finish. Screwcap. 13.7° alc. **Rating** 87 **To** 2013 $17.95

Coolangatta Estate   ★★★★

1335 Bolong Road, Shoalhaven Heads, NSW 2535 **Region** Shoalhaven Coast
T (02) 4448 7131 **F** (02) 4448 7997 **www.**coolangattaestate.com.au **Open** 7 days 10–5
Winemaker Tyrrell's **Est.** 1988 **Cases** 5000
Coolangatta Estate is part of a 150-ha resort with accommodation, restaurants, golf course etc; some of the oldest buildings were convict-built in 1822. It might be thought that the wines are tailored purely for the tourist market, but in fact the standard of viticulture is exceptionally high (immaculate Scott Henry trellising), and the contract winemaking is wholly professional. It has a habit of bobbing up with gold medals at Sydney and Canberra wine shows. Its 2001 Semillon has been a prolific gold-medal winner up to '08, and the '05 looks as if it will follow in its elder brother's footsteps.

ŢŢŢŢŢ **Aged Release Estate Grown Semillon 2001** Showing plenty of toasty development and with a brightness of pure lemon fruits at the core; very long and focused, with real harmony of flavour on the finish. Multiple golds. Cork. 10.4° alc. **Rating** 94 **To** 2011 $29

ŢŢŢŢ **Alexander Berry Chardonnay 2007** Bright pale-yellow; good flavour with citrus and a little nutmeg; toasty finish. Screwcap. 13.8° alc. **Rating** 87 **To** 2009 $22

Coombe Farm Vineyard ★★★★

11 St Huberts Road, Coldstream, Vic 3770 **Region** Yarra Valley
T (03) 9739 1131 **F** (03) 9739 1154 **www.coombefarm.com.au Open** 7 days 10–5
Winemaker Wine Network, Chris Bolden **Est.** 1999 **Cases** 3000
Coombe Farm Vineyard is owned by Pamela, Lady Vestey (Dame Nellie Melba's grand-daughter), Lord Samuel Vestey and the Right Honourable Mark Vestey. The vineyard is planted to chardonnay (20 ha), pinot noir (19 ha), merlot and cabernet sauvignon (7 ha each) and viognier and pinot gris (3 ha each). The vast majority of the fruit is sold to eager winemakers in the region; a small amount is made for Coombe Farm. Exports to the UK.

ŢŢŢŢŢ **Yarra Valley Chardonnay 2006** Elegant and restrained; seamless oak and other winemaking inputs to the nectarine and melon fruit; typical Yarra length and acidity; 600 cases made. Screwcap. 13° alc. **Rating** 93 **To** 2016 $24.95
Yarra Valley Pinot Noir 2006 Very foresty/savoury/spicy/earthy style, with no compromise: take it or leave it; clones MV6, 114 and 115; 400 cases made. Screwcap. 13.5° alc. **Rating** 90 **To** 2012 $24.95

ŢŢŢŢ **Yarra Valley Pinot Gris 2006** Has a bit more flavour and interest than most, with apple, musk and spice; good balance and length; dry finish; 100 cases made. Screwcap. 13° alc. **Rating** 89 **To** 2009 $20.95
Yarra Valley Viognier 2006 Early days, perhaps, but there's not a lot of distinct varietal fruit; on the other hand, the phenolics are controlled; 100 cases made. Screwcap. 13° alc. **Rating** 88 **To** 2010 $20.95

Coombend Estate **NR**

Coombend via Swansea, Tas 7190 **Region** East Coast Tasmania
T (03) 6257 8881 **F** (03) 6257 8884 **Open** 7 days 10–5
Winemaker Tamar Ridge (Andrew Pirie) **Est.** 1985 **Cases** 3000
In 2005 Tamar Ridge acquired Coombend Estate, including all the assets and the business name. Tamar Ridge has immediately commenced the establishment of a large vineyard which will dwarf the existing 1.75 ha of cabernet sauvignon, 2.25 ha of sauvignon blanc, 0.5 ha of pinot noir and 0.3 ha of riesling. Exports to Sweden.

Cooper Burns ★★★★☆

1 Golden Way, Nuriootpa, SA 5353 (postal) **Region** Barossa Valley
T (08) 8683 9181 **F** (08) 8683 9181 **www.cooperburns.com.au Open** Not
Winemaker Mark Cooper, Russell Burns **Est.** 2004 **Cases** 500
Cooper Burns is the winemaking partnership of Mark Cooper and Russell Burns. It is a virtual winery focusing on small-batch, handmade wine from the Barossa Valley (grapes are sourced from Kalimna, Koonunga Hill and Moppa at the northern end of the valley). In 2006 production was increased to add a Shiraz Viognier and Grenache to the existing single-vineyard Shiraz.

ŢŢŢŢŢ **Barossa Valley Shiraz 2006** Concentrated mulberry and fruitcake aromas; pushing the ripeness limits, the palate is thickly textured, and delivers plenty of fruit on the finish. Screwcap. 14.5° alc. **Rating** 91 **To** 2016 $35
Barossa Valley Shiraz Viognier 2006 Good concentration, and quite lifted; dark and dense on the palate, with ample chewy tannins. Screwcap. 14.5° alc. **Rating** 90 **To** 2016 $30

Cope-Williams ★★★★

221 Ochiltrees Road, Romsey, Vic 3434 **Region** Macedon Ranges
T (03) 5429 5595 **F** (03) 5429 6009 **www**.copewilliams.com.au **Open** By appt
Winemaker David Cowburn **Est.** 1977 **Cases** 4000

One of Macedon's pioneers, specialising in sparkling wines that are full flavoured but also producing excellent Chardonnay and Pinot Noir table wines in warmer vintages. A traditional 'English Green'–type cricket ground and Real Tennis complex are available for hire and are booked out most days from spring through until autumn. The facilities have in fact been leased to an independent operator, which Gordon Cope-Williams says will allow him to concentrate on the estate vineyards (3 ha of chardonnay, 2.5 ha of pinot noir, 0.5 ha of cabernet sauvignon and merlot) and the sparkling wines made from the chardonnay and pinot noir. Exports to Switzerland and NZ.

ŸŸŸŸŸ **R.O.M.S.E.Y. Macedon Ranges Brut NV** Complex and intense, bordering on Champagne; good balance and length; twist of citrus to nutty bready notes; Pinot Noir/Chardonnay. Cork. 12° alc. **Rating** 90 **To** 2010
Macedon Ranges Rose NV Fresh pink; vibrant cherry/strawberry fruit; crisp and long palate; bright finish. Cork. 12° alc. **Rating** 90 **To** 2010

ŸŸŸŸ **Macedon Ranges Riche NV** Bright, pale green–gold; extra dosage well equilibrated; supple, sweetened citrus flavours; Pinot Noir 60%/Chardonnay 40%. Cork. 12° alc. **Rating** 89 **To** 2010
Coniston NV Red–salmon; soft, spicy red fruits; touch of sweetness; easy access; Sparkling Pinot Noir/Cabernet Sauvignon/Merlot. Cork. 12° alc. **Rating** 87 **To** 2009

Coriole ★★★★★

Chaffeys Road, McLaren Vale, SA 5171 **Region** McLaren Vale
T (08) 8323 8305 **F** (08) 8323 9136 **www**.coriole.com **Open** Mon–Fri 10–5, w'ends & public hols 11–5
Winemaker Simon White **Est.** 1967 **Cases** 35 000

Justifiably best known for its Shiraz, which – in both the rare Lloyd Reserve and standard forms – is extremely impressive; it was also one of the first wineries to catch on to the Italian fashion with Sangiovese, but its white varietal wines lose nothing by comparison. Also produces high-quality olive oil. Exports to the UK, the US and other major markets.

ŸŸŸŸŸ **The Optimist Reserve McLaren Vale Chenin Blanc 2005** Utterly unexpected; the best youngish Chenin Blanc I've tasted from Australia, with bright lemon and melon fruit, excellent texture, structure, and above all, length. Cork. 13° alc. **Rating** 94 **To** 2012 $30
The Dancing Fig McLaren Vale Shiraz Mourvedre 2006 Very attractive wine, the mourvedre greatly enhancing the structure, but also the flavour spectrum, with warm spice, blackberry, plum and chocolate plus fine tannins; great value. Screwcap. 14.5° alc. **Rating** 94 **To** 2016 $22
Mary Kathleen Reserve McLaren Vale Cabernet Merlot 2001 Re-release 2008. Complex and rich, with almost velvety structure unrecognisable from that first tasted in Oct '03; now a confident wine in the prime of its life, with a touch of regional chocolate an added extra. Cork. 13.5° alc. **Rating** 94 **To** 2013 $46

ŸŸŸŸŸ **McLaren Vale Sangiovese 2006** The cherry fruit of the bouquet flows into the fore-palate, before savoury, powdery but insistent tannins run through the finish; dead-set Italian-food style. Screwcap. 14° alc. **Rating** 92 **To** 2011 $19.95
Fiano 2007 Floral aromas of fruit spice, herb and citrus; elegant and supple mouthfeel with good balance, oak nowhere to be seen; a historic southern Italian variety. Screwcap. 13° alc. **Rating** 91 **To** 2010 $22.95

Brunello Clone McLaren Vale Sangiovese 2005 Slight brick colour; not to be undertaken lightly, a deadly serious wine which seeks to instil fear and respect, not love; Italian restaurant essential. Cork. 14° alc. **Rating** 90 **To** 2015 $35

McLaren Vale Chenin Blanc 2007 Coriole achieves more with this bland variety than others; 30-year-old vines also help; pear, citrus and passionfruit flavours; good length and a crisp finish. Screwcap. 13° alc. **Rating** 90 **To** 2009 $13.95

Nebbiolo Rose 2007 Spicy cherry and rose petal flavours; cerebral, dry style; very good with food. Langhorne Creek. Screwcap. 13° alc. **Rating** 90 **To** 2009 $19.95

Redstone Shiraz 2005 Medium-bodied; good texture and structure to the predominantly black fruits and dark chocolate palate; the tannins are positive, but not threatening. Screwcap. 14.5° alc. **Rating** 90 **To** 2012 $17.95

Mary Kathleen Reserve McLaren Vale Cabernet Merlot 2005 Powerful full-bodied wine, with potent blackcurrant fruit and formidable tannins; unapproachable and, for 5 years at least, points nominal. Cork. 13.9° alc. **Rating** 90 **To** 2025 $42

ŸŸŸŸ **The Old Barn Adelaide Hills Chardonnay 2007** Old Barn is the stone cellar door at which the 250 cases of this wine are sold; light-bodied and crisp nectarine and citrus; subtle oak. Screwcap. 13° alc. **Rating** 89 **To** 2011 $20

The Dancing Fig McLaren Vale Shiraz Mourvedre 2004 Strong dark chocolate wafts up on the first whiff, proclaiming the region; strong tannin structure gives varietal impact on the finish; needs more mid-palate fruit for higher points. Screwcap. 14° alc. **Rating** 89 **To** 2013 $19.95

Redstone Cabernet Merlot 2005 Honest, solidly structured and built wine, with a mix of predominantly black fruits and some regional chocolate. Screwcap. 14.5° alc. **Rating** 89 **To** 2012 $14.95

Redstone Cabernet Sauvignon 2006 Medium- to full-bodied; positive varietal character from start to finish, the blackcurrant supported by positive tannins; needs a year or two in peace. Screwcap. 14.5° alc. **Rating** 89 **To** 2015 $18.50

Counterpoint Vineyard   NR

107 McAdams Lane, Moonambel, Vic 3478 **Region** Pyrenees
T (03) 5467 2245 **F** (03) 5467 2245 **www.**counterpointvineyard.com.au **Open** W'ends & public hols Sept–Apr
Winemaker Campbell McAdam **Est.** 1976 **Cases** 400
Noreen and Campbell McAdam established the vineyard in 1976 an operated it at weekends until 2002, when they built a winery and moved to the property full time. They make a single estate wine from 2 ha of shiraz and cabernet sauvignon, generally a blend, but in some years a straight Shiraz. In addition, they have a 'playground' of other red and white varieties from which tiny batches of wines are released from time to time.

Cowra Estate   NR

Boorowa Road, Cowra, NSW 2794 **Region** Cowra
T (02) 9907 7735 **F** (02) 9907 7734 **Open** At The Quarry Restaurant Tues–Sun 10–4
Winemaker Tim Smith **Est.** 1973 **Cases** 5000
Cowra Estate was purchased from the family of founder Tony Gray by South African–born food and beverage entrepreneur John Geber in 1995. A vigourous promotional campaign has gained a higher domestic profile for the once export-oriented brand. John Geber is actively involved in the promotional effort and rightly proud of the wines. The Quarry Wine Cellars and Restaurant offer visitors a full range of Cowra Estate's wines, plus wines from other producers in the region. The Geber family, incidentally, also owns Chateau Tanunda in the Barossa Valley. Exports to Switzerland and Denmark.

Cowrock Vineyards ★★★

28 Dequetteville Terrace, Kent Town DC, SA 5067 (postal) **Region** Margaret River
T (08) 8331 3000 **F** (08) 8331 3377 **Open** Not
Winemaker Jodie Opie **Est.** 2006 **Cases** NFP
Global Wine Ventures Ltd is the phoenix arisen from the ashes of Xanadu Wines Ltd. The wines will be predominantly sourced from the 44-ha Cowrock Vineyard, situated 20 km south of the Margaret River township. Distribution in Australia is through Red+White, and it is anticipated exports will follow in the US, the UK and select parts of Asia.

ΨΨΨΨΨ **Margaret River Sauvignon Blanc Semillon 2006** Fresh and vibrant, with zesty, citrussy fruit running through the length of the palate and finish; leaves the mouth fresh. Screwcap. 12.5° alc. **Rating** 90 **To** 2010 $15

Craiglee ★★★★★

Sunbury Road, Sunbury, Vic 3429 **Region** Sunbury
T (03) 9744 4489 **F** (03) 9744 4489 **www**.craiglee.com.au **Open** Sun & public hols 10–5, or by appt
Winemaker Patrick Carmody **Est.** 1976 **Cases** 2500
A winery with a proud 19th-century record which recommenced winemaking in 1976 after a prolonged hiatus. Produces one of the finest cool-climate Shirazs in Australia, redolent of cherry, licorice and spice in the better (warmer) vintages, lighter-bodied in the cooler ones. Mature vines and improved viticulture have made the wines more consistent (and even better) over the past 10 years or so. Exports to the UK, the US, Hong Kong and Italy.

ΨΨΨΨΨ **Shiraz 2005** Good colour; classic blackberry and plum fruit, crushed black pepper and licorice; immaculate balance and French oak inputs. Diam. 14.5° alc. **Rating** 95 **To** 2020 $45

ΨΨΨΨΨ **Chardonnay 2006** Quite a toasty bouquet with fig, melon and minerals; thickly textured, with roasted nuts and a zesty, slightly lemony finish. Diam. 14.5° alc. **Rating** 90 **To** 2012 $27
Pinot Noir 2006 Bright savoury cherry aromas with a little toasty spice; light-bodied with good persistence of flavour on the finish. Diam. 14.5° alc. **Rating** 90 **To** 2014 $30

Craigow ★★★★★

528 Richmond Road, Cambridge, Tas 7170 **Region** Southern Tasmania
T (03) 6248 5379 **www**.craigow.com.au **Open** 7 days Christmas to Easter (except public hols), or by appt
Winemaker Winemaking Tasmania (Julian Alcorso) **Est.** 1989 **Cases** 1500
Craigow has substantial vineyards, with 5 ha of pinot noir and another 5 ha (in total) of riesling, chardonnay and gewurztraminer. Barry and Cathy Edwards have moved from being grapegrowers with only one wine made for sale to a portfolio of six wines, while continuing to sell most of their grapes. Craigow has an impressive museum release program; the best are outstanding, while others show the impact of sporadic bottle oxidation.

ΨΨΨΨΨ **Riesling 2003** Glowing yellow-green; flowery lime blossom aromas and a remarkably intense lime- and apple-flavoured palate, still wonderfully youthful, sustained by natural acidity. Gold medal and Chairman's Trophy (mine), Tas Wine Show '07. **Rating** 96 **To** 2014 $19
Botrytis Riesling 2004 Very powerful, intense and long; massive botrytis impact; long, lingering acidity; glorious overall flavour and finish; remarkable wine in every respect. Screwcap. 10.3° alc. **Rating** 95 **To** 2010 $55
Sauvignon Blanc 2007 A spotlessly clean bouquet; a very tight and precise palate neatly balanced between herbal/mineral and tropical fruit; has excellent thrust through to the finish. Gold medal, Sydney Wine Show '08. Screwcap. 12.7° alc. **Rating** 94 **To** 2011 $24

ΨΨΨΨΨ **Pinot Noir 2005** Savoury, spicy forest floor underneath cherry and plum fruit; good length, and has continued to flourish over the past year. Cork. 13.6° alc. **Rating** 93 **To** 2012 $28
Riesling 2006 Washed river stones and lemon zest aromas and flavours, with extreme intensity and length, underwritten by acidity, guaranteed to flourish in bottle. Screwcap. **Rating** 90 **To** 2016 $28

ΨΨΨΨ **Gewurztraminer 2005** Developing at a snail's pace; the fruit/acid balance is perfect, the length good; it is just that the varietal character has gone walkabout. Perhaps best not to worry about that. Screwcap. 13.6° alc. **Rating** 88 **To** 2013 $23
Pinot Noir 2006 Extremely deep colour and stacked with all the flavour the colour suggests; completely locked up, and will take time for the pinot varietal character to express itself. Pending release. Diam. 12.7° alc. **Rating** 87 **To** 2014

Crane Winery ★★★

Haydens Road, Kingaroy, Qld 4610 **Region** South Burnett
T (07) 4162 7647 **F** (07) 4162 8381 **www.**cranewines.com.au **Open** 7 days 10–4
Winemaker John Crane, Bernie Cooper **Est.** 1996 **Cases** 2000
Founded by John and Sue Crane, the winery has 8 ha of estate plantings but also purchases grapes from 20 other growers in the region. Sue Crane's great-grandfather established a vineyard planted to shiraz 100 years ago (in 1898) and which remained in production until 1970. The vineyard was sold to Bernard and Judy Cooper on condition that John Crane made the 2005–07 vintages. Both Bernie and Judy Cooper have strong chemistry and microbiology backgrounds, which are of great assistance in taking over the winemaking responsibility.

ΨΨΨΨ **Bin 2 Shiraz 2005** Light- to medium-bodied; clean cherry and plum fruit with fine, gently savoury tannins; not forced. Twin top. 13.5° alc. **Rating** 87 **To** 2011 $16
Liqueur Verdelho NV A Crane speciality, with biscuity/cake/cumquat jam notes before spirit arrives on the finish to thin the flavour out. Cork. 16.5° alc. **Rating** 87 **To** 2009 $18

Craneford ★★★★☆

Moorundie Street, Truro, SA 5356 **Region** Barossa Valley
T (08) 8564 0003 **F** (08) 8564 0008 **www.**cranefordwines.com **Open** Mon–Fri 10–5
Winemaker Carol Riebke, John Glaetzer (Consultant) **Est.** 1978 **Cases** 35 000
Since Craneford was founded in 1978 it has undergone a number of changes of both location and ownership. The biggest change came in 2004 when the winery, by then housed in the old country fire station building in Truro, was expanded and upgraded. In 2006 John Glaetzer joined the team as consultant winemaker, with Carol Riebke the day-to-day winemaker. Grapes are sourced from a number of small growers, with the emphasis on quality. Exports to all major markets.

ΨΨΨΨ **Adelaide Hills Viognier 2007** Well-judged ripeness, allowing development of some pear, peach and apricot varietal expression without the penalty of a thick phenolic finish. Screwcap. 13.5° alc. **Rating** 88 **To** 2011 $25
Allyson Parsons Barossa Valley Semillon Sauvignon Blanc 2007 Generously built and flavoured, with ripe tropical fruit; waste no time. Screwcap. 13° alc. **Rating** 87 **To** 2009 $15.50

Crawford River Wines ★★★★★

741 Hotspur Upper Road, Condah, Vic 3303 **Region** Henty
T (03) 5578 2267 **F** (03) 5578 2240 **www.**crawfordriverwines.com **Open** By appt
Winemaker John Thomson, Belinda Thomson **Est.** 1975 **Cases** 5000
Time flies, and it seems incredible that Crawford River has celebrated its 30th birthday. Once a tiny outpost in a little-known wine region, Crawford River has now established itself as one of the foremost producers of Riesling (and other excellent wines) thanks to the unremitting attention to detail and skill of its founder and winemaker, John Thomson. His exceptionally

talented and (dare I say) attractive daughter Belinda has returned full time after completing her winemaking degree and working along the way in Marlborough (NZ), Bordeaux, Ribera del Duero (Spain), Bolgheri and Tuscany, and the Nahe (Germany), with Crawford River filling in the gaps. Severe frosts in the spring of 2006 led to secondary bud shoot, and thanks to skilled viticulture, the small '07 crop ripened well, with only cabernet sauvignon lacking structure, hence the first Crawford River rose. Exports to the UK, Ireland, Canada, Japan and Southeast Asia.

ㅜㅜㅜㅜㅜ **Cabernet Sauvignon 1997** The colour (of course) shows 10-year development; cedary, earthy, briary aromas likewise, but the palate is in full flight, still with some cassis berry fruit, balanced by fine tannins and good acidity on the finish. Cork. 13° alc. **Rating** 95 **To** 2011
Riesling 2007 Lovely fruit purity and concentration; light and racy, but with real depth and weight; very long, pure and with an intriguing core of minerality. Screwcap. 13° alc. **Rating** 94 **To** 2015 $33.50
Nektar 2006 As always, a super racy style, with great acidity, pure and precise fruit, and a long and harmonious finish; give it a few years. Screwcap. 12.5° alc. **Rating** 94 **To** 2018 $33.50

ㅜㅜㅜㅜㅜ **Sauvignon Blanc Semillon 2007** Lots of ripe fruit aromas, with a hint of fresh-cut grass; nice weight and texture, and the small amount of sweetness balances out the racy acidity. Screwcap. 12.5° alc. **Rating** 90 **To** 2009 $25

ㅜㅜㅜㅜ **Rose 2007** Pale salmon-pink; a dry, gently spicy/savoury, European/Tavel style. Screwcap. 13.5° alc. **Rating** 87 **To** 2009

Creed of Barossa   ★★★☆

Lyndoch Hill Retreat, cnr Barossa Valley Way, Hermann Thumm Drive, Lyndoch, SA 5351
Region Barossa Valley
T (08) 8524 4046 **F** (08) 8524 4046 **www**.creedwines.com **Open** 7 days 10–5
Winemaker Daniel Eggleton **Est.** 2005 **Cases** 10 000
This is the venture of luxuriantly bearded Mark Creed and business partner (and winemaker) Daniel Eggleton. Their first wine (an intriguing blend of shiraz, cabernet franc and viognier) was made in 2004, with a number of different Shirazs, Merlot, Cabernet Franc and a little Grenache in the pipeline. The partners also own a consulting wing, called C & E Dry Grown Projects Pty Ltd, to make wines for others, and to collaboratively market and distribute those wines. Prior to the 2007 vintage the partners built a small winery, and in mid-2008 moved the cellar door to the Lyndoch Hill Retreat complex, which includes a restaurant, accommodation, conference facilities and garden. Exports to the UK, the US, Canada, Phillipines, Malaysia, China and NZ.

ㅜㅜㅜㅜ **The Pretty Miss Shiraz Cabernet Franc Viognier 2006** I'm not persuaded that the use of viognier in every red blend under the sun is a good idea (although this is a left-field blend from go to whoa) but the flavours are quite appealing. Screwcap. 15.5° alc. **Rating** 89 **To** 2012 $24
The Marque Merlot Cabernet Franc 2006 Strongly influenced by French oak and, perhaps, the high alcohol, both giving a soft sweetness which is left field – but then so is the match of region and varieties in the first place. Screwcap. 15.5° alc. **Rating** 87 **To** 2012 $30

Crittenden Estate   ★★★★

25 Harrisons Road, Dromana, Vic 3936 **Region** Mornington Peninsula
T (03) 5981 8322 **F** (03) 5981 8366 **www**.crittendenwines.com.au **Open** 7 days 11–4
Winemaker Garry Crittenden, Rollo Crittenden **Est.** 2003 **Cases** 5000
The wheel of fortune has turned full circle, with son Rollo Crittenden returning to the (new) family wine business established by father Garry in 2003. In so doing, both father and son have severed ties with Dromana Estate, the old family business. For good measure, winemaking will be moved to a new winery at Patterson Lakes, but off the Mornington Peninsula Highway. Exports to the UK.

$\mathbb{Y}\mathbb{Y}\mathbb{Y}\mathbb{Y}\mathbb{Y}$ **Mornington Peninsula Chardonnay 2005** Complex flavour and structure; integrated French oak accompanies nectarine and white peach fruit, with some creamy/nutty mlf notes; good length. Screwcap. 14° alc. **Rating** 93 **To** 2012 $27

$\mathbb{Y}\mathbb{Y}\mathbb{Y}\mathbb{Y}$ **Mornington Peninsula Pinot Noir 2006** Fresh, light-bodied Pinot with slightly spicy/savoury edges to the cherry and strawberry fruit; clean finish. Screwcap. 13.5° alc. **Rating** 89 **To** 2011 $30

Pinocchio Heathcote Sangiovese 2006 One of the early movers outside SA with the variety; has hallmark spicy, sour cherry fruit encased in savoury tannins. Screwcap. 13.5° alc. **Rating** 89 **To** 2012 $23

Geppetto Sauvignon Blanc Semillon 2007 Well put together; has plenty of gooseberry and lemongrass fruit, finishing relatively dry. Screwcap. 12.5° alc. **Rating** 88 **To** 2009 $17

Mornington Peninsula Pinot Grigio 2007 Has quite clear pear and musk flavours, and finishes relatively dry. Screwcap. 13° alc. **Rating** 88 **To** 2009 $28

Cut Cane Mornington Peninsula Cabernet 2005 A skein of confit fruit runs alongside notes of chocolate, earth and briar; what was the baumé before canes were cut? Interesting wine. Screwcap. 13.5° alc. **Rating** 88 **To** 2013 $30

Mornington Peninsula Sauvignon Blanc 2007 Plenty of flavour in a tropical spectrum, with soft passionfruit and pineapple elements; finishes slightly short. Screwcap. 13° alc. **Rating** 87 **To** 2009 $20

Pinocchio Moscato 2007 A sunburst of fresh grape flavours; drink as is, or add soda water to lighten the flavour and the alcohol even further, but serve ice-cold either way. Screwcap. 7.5° alc. **Rating** 87 **To** 2010 $23

Mornington Peninsula Pinot Noir 2005 Close to an expressive rosé, light in colour and body, with just a twist of tannin on the finish. Screwcap. 13.5° alc. **Rating** 87 **To** 2009 $27

Cullen Wines   ★★★★★

Caves Road, Cowaramup, WA 6284 **Region** Margaret River
T (08) 9755 5277 **F** (08) 9755 5550 **www**.cullenwines.com.au **Open** 7 days 10–4
Winemaker Vanya Cullen, Trevor Kent **Est.** 1971 **Cases** 20 000
One of the pioneers of Margaret River, which has always produced long-lived wines of highly individual style from the substantial and mature estate vineyards. The vineyard has now progressed beyond organic to biodynamic certification, and, subsequent to that, has become the first vineyard and winery in Australia to be certified carbon neutral. This requires the calculation of all of the carbon used and carbon dioxide emitted in the winery, and the carbon is then offset by the planting of new trees. Winemaking is now in the hands of Vanya Cullen, daughter of the founders; she is possessed of an extraordinarily good palate. It is impossible to single out any particular wine from the top echelon; all are superb. Exports to all major markets.

$\mathbb{Y}\mathbb{Y}\mathbb{Y}\mathbb{Y}\mathbb{Y}$ **Margaret River Chardonnay 2005** Immediately proclaims its origins, thanks to the depth and complexity of the fruit, oak simply completing the picture; great mouthfeel, with exquisite purity and line. Screwcap. 14° alc. **Rating** 96 **To** 2018 $60

Diana Madeline 2005 As ever, has fine but persistent tannins running from the fore-palate through to the finish; the deep and intense fruit will sustain the wine until those tannins loosen their grip. All five Bordeaux varieties present led by Cabernet Sauvignon (75%). Screwcap. 14° alc. **Rating** 96 **To** 2018 $90

Margaret River Sauvignon Blanc Semillon 2007 Highly sophisticated winemaking produces a complex, textured and intense palate with a particularly long finish, the fruit and oak seamlessly married; Sauvignon Blanc (80%)/French oak (50%). Screwcap. 13° alc. **Rating** 94 **To** 2013 $35

Mangan Vineyard Margaret River Sauvignon Blanc Semillon 2007 Extremely tight focus and excellent intensity; semillon drives the palate with lemon and mineral running through a long finish; Semillon (63%)/oak (37%). Screwcap. 13.5° alc. **Rating** 94 **To** 2015 $35

🍷🍷🍷🍷♀ **Mangan Margaret River Merlot Petit Verdot Malbec 2006** Elegant but concentrated multi-flavoured palate, from cassis to mint and briar, a savoury finish with balanced tannins. Screwcap. 14° alc. **Rating** 93 **To** 2021 $45

Cumulus Wines

PO Box 41, Cudal, NSW 2864 **Region** Orange
T (02) 6390 7900 **F** (02) 6364 2388 **www**.cumuluswines.com.au **Open** Not
Winemaker Debbie Lauritz, Andrew Bilankij, Phillip Shaw (Consultant) **Est.** 2004
Cases 200 000

Cumulus Wines has had a turbulent history in the short time it has been in business. Hopefully, the acquisition of a 51% share by the huge Berardo Group of Portugal (with numerous world-size wine investments in Portugal, Canada and Madeira) will see long-term stability. This is an asset-rich business, with over 500 ha of vineyards planted to all the mainstream varieties, the lion's share going to shiraz, cabernet sauvignon, chardonnay and merlot. The wines are released under three brands: Rolling, from the Central Ranges region; Climbing, solely from Orange fruit; and a third, yet to be named, super-premium from the best of the estate vineyard blocks. Exports to the UK and the US.

🍷🍷🍷🍷🍷 **Climbing Shiraz 2006** Plum, black cherry, spice and pepper attesting to a cool climate; silky, supple texture with fine-grained tannins and quality oak. Screwcap. 13.8° alc. **Rating** 95 **To** 2021 $20

🍷🍷🍷🍷♀ **Climbing Orange Pinot Gris 2007** Distinct pear and musk aromas and flavours; has above-average intensity and length on the palate, again with varietal character to the fore. Screwcap. 13.5° alc. **Rating** 90 **To** 2009 $19.95
Rolling Shiraz 2006 Good colour; soft, fleshy fruit with a juicy mid-palate, and soft tannins to close; good oak. Screwcap. 14° alc. **Rating** 90 **To** 2012 $17

🍷🍷🍷🍷 **Climbing Orange Merlot 2006** A fragrant wine, with unambiguous if severe varietal character expressed through a mix of red fruits/cassis, a dash of black olive and persistent tannins. Screwcap. 13.5° alc. **Rating** 88 **To** 2012 $21.95
Climbing Orange Cabernet Sauvignon 2006 Good varietal expression, albeit slightly austere, the tannins fractionally dry; the plus comes from the clear-cut blackcurrant fruit. Screwcap. 13.5° alc. **Rating** 88 **To** 2012 $21.95

Curlewis Winery
★★★★★

55 Navarre Road, Curlewis, Vic 3222 **Region** Geelong
T (03) 5250 4567 **F** (03) 5250 4567 **www**.curlewiswinery.com.au **Open** By appt
Winemaker Rainer Breit **Est.** 1998 **Cases** 2500

Rainer Breit and partner Wendy Oliver purchased their property in 1996 with 1.6 ha of what were then 11-year-old pinot noir vines. Rainer Breit, a self-taught winemaker, uses the full bag of pinot noir winemaking tricks: cold-soaking, hot-fermentation, post-ferment maceration, part inoculated and partly wild yeast use, prolonged lees contact, and bottling the wine neither fined nor filtered. While Rainer and Wendy are self-confessed 'pinotphiles', they have planted a little chardonnay and buy a little locally grown shiraz and chardonnay. Exports to Canada, Sweden, Malaysia, Singapore and Hong Kong.

🍷🍷🍷🍷🍷 **Geelong Pinot Noir 2006** Very good colour; has plenty of attitude to its firmly structured plum and cherry fruit; long finish; built to age. Diam. 13.5° alc. **Rating** 94 **To** 2013 $42

🍷🍷🍷🍷♀ **Geelong Chardonnay 2006** Again very developed colour, though the hue is good; much fruit weight in a melon/nectarine/grapefruit spectrum; oak in the back seat. Diam. 14° alc. **Rating** 92 **To** 2012 $38
Bel Sel Geelong Pinot Noir 2006 Very funky savoury, earthy, briary style; firm finish; likely to polarise opinions. Diam. 13° alc. **Rating** 90 **To** 2012 $25

🍷🍷🍷🍷 **Bel Sel Geelong Chardonnay 2006** Very developed colour; nutty toasty over-tones to stone fruit; acidity tightens the finish. Diam. 14° alc. **Rating** 89 **To** 2011 $25

Curly Flat

263 Collivers Road, Lancefield, Vic 3435 **Region** Macedon Ranges
T (03) 5429 1956 **F** (03) 5429 2256 **www**.curlyflat.com **Open** W'ends 1–5 or by appt
Winemaker Phillip Moraghan, Phillip Dean **Est.** 1991 **Cases** 6000
Phillip and Jeni Moraghan began developing Curly Flat in 1992, drawing in part on Phillip's working experience in Switzerland in the late 1980s, and with a passing nod to Michael Leunig. With ceaseless help and guidance from the late Laurie Williams (and others), the Moraghans painstakingly established 8.5 ha of pinot noir, 3.4 ha of chardonnay and 0.6 ha of pinot gris, and a multi-level, gravity-flow winery. Exports to the UK, Japan and Hong Kong.

ΨΨΨΨΨ **Macedon Ranges Chardonnay 2006** A lovely wine with real focus; restrained aromas of lemon, nectarine and a lick of toasty oak; the palate is clearly defined, very long and extremely powerful on the finish. Screwcap. 13.5° alc. **Rating** 95 To 2012 $38
Macedon Ranges Pinot Noir 2005 Dark brooding black cherry, dark plum and loads of spice; very concentrated on the palate, and the fruit holds on and opens up over an extraordinarily long time. Screwcap. 13.8° alc. **Rating** 94 To 2012 $46

Currency Creek Estate

Winery Road, Currency Creek, SA 5214 **Region** Currency Creek
T (08) 8555 4069 **F** (08) 8555 4100 **www**.currencycreekwines.com.au **Open** 7 days 10–5
Winemaker John Loxton **Est.** 1969 **Cases** 10 000
For over 35 years this family-owned vineyard and relatively low-profile winery has produced some outstanding wood-matured whites and pleasant, soft reds selling at attractive prices. In all, there are 60 ha of vines, shiraz taking the lion's share with 40 ha, then cabernet sauvignon (10 ha), sauvignon blanc and chardonnay (4 ha each), and riesling and semillon (1 ha each). It will be apparent from this that the essential part of the grape production is sold. Exports to the UK, the US and Canada.

ΨΨΨΨΨ **The Black Swamp Cabernet Sauvignon 2005** Mid-garnet; showing some development, there is a silky edge to the texture, neatly complementing the savoury cassis fruit. Screwcap. 14° alc. **Rating** 91 To 2014 $20
Ostrich Hill Shiraz 2005 A generous example of cool-climate shiraz; plums and blackberries and just a little spice on show, with fine-grained tannins on the finish. Screwcap. 14° alc. **Rating** 90 To 2015 $20

ΨΨΨΨ **Personal Stock Tawny NV** Lots of rancio and good flavour; just a fraction broad on the finish. Vino–Lok 19.5° alc. **Rating** 89 To 2020 $25.95
Sedgeland Sauvignon Blanc 2007 Good varietal sauvignon; clean, with the right amount of herbaceousness. Screwcap. 13.5° alc. **Rating** 88 To 2011 $15

Cuttaway Hill Estate

PO Box 2034, Bowral, NSW 2576 **Region** Southern Highlands
T (02) 4871 1004 **F** (02) 4871 1005 **www**.cuttawayhillwines.com.au **Open** Not
Winemaker Mark Bourne, Monarch Winemaking Services **Est.** 1998 **Cases** 15 000
Owned by the O'Neil family, Cuttaway Hill Estate is one of the largest vineyard properties in the Southern Highlands, with a total of 38 ha on three vineyard sites. The original Cuttaway Hill vineyard at Mittagong has 17 ha of chardonnay, merlot, cabernet sauvignon and shiraz. The Allambie vineyard of 6.9 ha, on the light sandy loam soils of Ninety Acre Hill, is planted to sauvignon blanc, pinot gris and pinot noir. The third and newest vineyard is 14.2 ha at Maytree, west of Moss Vale, in a relatively drier and warmer meso-climate. Here cabernet sauvignon, merlot and pinot noir (and a small amount of chardonnay) have been planted. The standard of both viticulture and contract winemaking is evident in the quality of the wines, not to mention the growth in production and sales. Exports to the UK, the US, Canada and Ireland.

ŶŶŶŶ♀ **Southern Highlands Chardonnay 2006** A faint whiff of dried lemon peel on the bouquet does not repeat itself on the light-bodied palate, where melon and nectarine fruit lead the way. Screwcap. 13.5° alc. **Rating** 90 **To** 2010 $17.99

ŶŶŶŶ **Southern Highlands Sauvignon Blanc 2007** Offers a mix of herb, citrus and mineral on the brisk, fresh palate and finish. Screwcap. 12.5° alc. **Rating** 88 **To** 2009 $18

Southern Highlands Semillon Sauvignon Blanc 2007 A well-assembled blend with a mix of gooseberry, passionfruit and citrus, slowing slightly on the finish. Screwcap. 10.5° alc. **Rating** 88 **To** 2010 $18

Southern Highlands Pinot Gris 2007 Varietal pear flavours, with restrained alcohol and a crisp, dry finish are what the variety needs. Screwcap. 13° alc. **Rating** 88 **To** 2009 $22

Southern Highlands Pinot Noir 2006 Light-bodied, savoury/spicy aromas and flavours, but with clear varietal character; does shorten on the finish. Screwcap. 14° alc. **Rating** 88 **To** 2010 $21.99

Laurence Sparkling Chardonnay Pinot Noir 2005 Fine, with fresh-cut fruit flavours of apple, citrus and a dash of strawberry; good finish; will improve further on cork. 12° alc. **Rating** 88 **To** 2012 $30

Cypress Post   ★★★

PO Box 1124, Oxley, Qld 4075 **Region** Granite Belt
T (07) 3375 4083 **F** (07) 3375 4083 **www.**cypresspost.com.au **Open** Not
Winemaker Peter Scudamore-Smith MW (Contract) **Est.** 2000 **Cases** 300
The Olsen family – headed by Drs Michael (a consultant botanist) and Catherine Olsen – has a strong botanical and conservation background continuing over two generations. The property has been registered under the Land for Wildlife program, and will continue to be run on these principles, blending science and caring for the future.

ŶŶŶŶ **10 Clones Granite Belt Syrah 2005** The claim to 10 clones is interesting, and unique to Cypress Post; that said, this is a lively, spicy wine with a brisk line and finish. Screwcap. 13.5° alc. **Rating** 87 **To** 2012 $25

D'Angelo Estate   ★★★☆

41 Bayview Road, Officer, Vic 3809 **Region** Yarra Valley
T 0417 055 651 **F** (03) 5943 1032 **www.**dangelowines.com.au **Open** By appt
Winemaker Benny D'Angelo **Est.** 1994 **Cases** 2000
The business dates back to 1994 when Benny D'Angelo's father planted a small block of pinot noir for home winemaking. One thing led to another, with Benny taking over winemaking and doing well in amateur wine shows. This led to the planting of more pinot and some cabernet sauvignon, increasing the vineyard to 2.8 ha. Expansion continued with the 2001 acquisition of a 4-ha site at Officer, which has been planted to six clones of pinot noir, and small parcels of cabernet sauvignon and shiraz. Grapes are also purchased from a wide range of vineyards stretching from Gippsland to Langhorne Creek.

ŶŶŶŶ **Gin Gin Bin Officer Pinot Grigio 2006** A savoury wine, with hazelnut, dried straw and the merest hint of lemon; quite fleshy, with good flavour on the finish. Screwcap. 14° alc. **Rating** 88 **To** 2009 $20

Fugiastro Officer Pinot Noir 2005 Brick hues; this wine is fully developed, and exhibits true gamey/stemmy character; complex, with real personality. Screwcap. 13.4° alc. **Rating** 88 **To** 2009 $25

Gin Gin Bin Officer Blanc de Noir NV Quite creamy mouthfeel, with a strong citrus current and some nutty complexity on the finish. Cork. 11.5° alc. **Rating** 88 **To** 2009 $20

d'Arenberg

Osborn Road, McLaren Vale, SA 5171 **Region** McLaren Vale
T (08) 8329 4888 **F** (08) 8323 9862 **www.**darenberg.com.au **Open** 7 days 10–5
Winemaker Chester Osborn, Jack Walton **Est.** 1912 **Cases** 250 000
Nothing, they say, succeeds like success. Few operations in Australia fit this dictum better than d'Arenberg, which has kept its near-100-year-old heritage while moving into the 21st century with flair and elan. As at last count (without question now outdated) it has 252 ha of vineyard on five properties planted to 19 varieties, and has 120 growers in McLaren Vale. There is no question that its past, present and future revolve around its considerable portfolio of richly robed red wines, shiraz, cabernet sauvignon and grenache being the cornerstones, but with 24 varietal labels spanning the gulf between roussanne and mourvedre. The quality of the wines is unimpeachable, the prices logical and fair. It has a profile in the both the UK and the US which far larger companies would love to have.

ㅇㅇㅇㅇㅇ **The Dead Arm Shiraz 2006** The Dead Arm rarely fails to deliver an uncompromising essay on McLaren fruit; deeply concentrated with levels of dark chocolate, blackberry, nuances of florals and a freshness that belies its weight and power. Good value. Screwcap. **Rating** 95 **To** 2030 $60
The Coppermine Road Cabernet Sauvignon 2005 More savoury restraint than many McLaren Vale cabernets; medium-bodied, with black fruits and savoury tannins; 22 months in French oak. Screwcap. 14.5° alc. **Rating** 95 **To** 2029 $60
The Laughing Magpie Shiraz Viognier 2006 Rich, velvety, luscious fruit flavours saying more about McLaren Vale than viognier; chocolate rather than apricot; however, no niggles about the wine. Screwcap. 14.5° alc. **Rating** 94 **To** 2020 $30
The Derelict Vineyard McLaren Vale Grenache 2004 A powerful wine, which could only come from McLaren Vale and relatively old vines. It has tannin structure seldom seen in the Barossa, and no cosmetic overtones to the black fruits, chocolate and spices. Cork. 14.5° alc. **Rating** 94 **To** 2024 $30
The Derelict Vineyard McLaren Vale Grenache 2006 Shows McLaren Vale grenache to perfection; has excellent structure underpinning the delicious red fruit flavours. Screwcap. **Rating** 94 **To** 2012 $30
The Ironstone Pressings Grenache Shiraz Mourvedre 2006 A very serious example of this Southern Rhône blend; dark and minerally, with briary notes and a hint of spice; chewy, long, and with really vibrant fruit on the finish, this would reward a charry steak well. Screwcap. **Rating** 94 **To** 2016 $65
The Coppermine Road Cabernet Sauvignon 2006 Full-bodied, rich, gutsy wine overflowing with blackcurrant fruit, cassis and tannins; good oak sustains the long finish. Screwcap. **Rating** 94 **To** 2026 $60
Galvo Garage Cabernet Sauvignon Merlot Petit Verdot Cabernet Franc 2005 Excellent colour; full-bodied, powerful wine, the merlot and some cabernet from Adelaide Hills has considerable presence and focus, and will develop very well in bottle, with fine tannins helping. Screwcap. 14.5° alc. **Rating** 94 **To** 2020 $30

ㅇㅇㅇㅇㅇ **Galvo Garage Cabernet Sauvignon Merlot Petit Verdot Cabernet Franc 2006** A full-bodied array of predominantly black fruits with integrated tannins and oak; has all the ingredients. Screwcap. **Rating** 93 **To** 2021 $30
The Noble Viognier Semillon Marsanne Riesling 2005 Extremely rich and luscious; a creamy, honeyed viscosity, the volatile acidity well controlled. Screwcap. 8° alc. **Rating** 92 **To** 2009 $35
The Noble McLaren Vale Riesling 2007 Lavish levels of botrytis, with the inherent structure of riesling, leaves a very sweet wine that is clean, vibrant and with good levels of acidity. Screwcap. **Rating** 92 **To** 2014 $25
d'Arry's Original Shiraz Grenache 2005 Very much in the mainstream of the style, welding together ripe juicy fruit flavours, warm spices and a dash of regional chocolate; good length and balance. Screwcap. 14.5° alc. **Rating** 91 **To** 2018 $18

The Cadenzia Grenache Shiraz Mourvedre 2006 Medium-bodied and full of life; juicy red fruits, slight savoury nuances and fresh acidity on the finish, a very good expression of the blend. Screwcap. **Rating** 91 **To** 2014 $25

Sticks & Stones Tempranillo Grenache Shiraz 2006 A medium-bodied array of multi-spice, multi-fruit flavours expected from this iconoclastic blend, made its own by d'Arenberg some years ago. Screwcap. **Rating** 91 **To** 2014 $30

The Noble Chardonnay Semillon 2006 Intensely fragrant and aromatic, with an acceptable level of volatile acidity; the low alcohol is interesting, normally found with botrytis rieslings. Screwcap. 8° alc. **Rating** 90 **To** 2009 $20

The Dry Dam Riesling 2007 Fresh, crisp and focused; early picking and retention of a touch of sugar balanced by zesty acidity lifts the wine above normal for McLaren Vale. Screwcap. 11.5° alc. **Rating** 90 **To** 2013 $15

The Lucky Lizard Adelaide Hills Chardonnay 2007 Tangy grapefruit dominant, plus some stone fruit; subtle oak; has good length and thrust. Screwcap. **Rating** 90 **To** 2012 $25

The Footbolt Shiraz 2005 Attractive medium-bodied regional wine, with black fruits, dark chocolate and spice intermingling; soft tannins and balanced oak. Screwcap. 14.5° alc. **Rating** 90 **To** 2013 $19.95

The Ironstone Pressings Grenache Shiraz Mourvedre 2005 Overall savoury/spicy characters to the bouquet and medium-bodied palate; one might have expected more weight and density, but maybe it is hiding its light at the moment. Screwcap. 15° alc. **Rating** 90 **To** 2015 $60

The Twentyeight Road Mourvedre 2006 Slightly charry, earthy notes, with elements of tar and black fruits; good acid and chewy tannins are the drivers on the palate. Screwcap. **Rating** 90 **To** 2016 $35

Vintage Fortified Shiraz 2005 Impenetrable colour; neutral spirit, with blackberry, dark chocolate and anise flavours; not too sweet; dodgy cork a real challenge for future development. **Rating** 90 **To** 2025 $19.95

Vintage McLaren Vale Fortified Shiraz Chambourcin 2005 Why this blend? Impenetrable colour; made in dry Portuguese style, and is better than the label would suggest, with sultry black fruits and dark chocolate. Cork. 17.5° alc. **Rating** 90 **To** 2015 $19.95

ŸŸŸŸ **The Broken Fishplate Sauvignon Blanc 2007** Water-white; crisp, fresh, unembroidered wine; mineral, herb and a touch of tropical fruit. Screwcap. 13° alc. **Rating** 89 **To** 2009 $19

The Last Ditch McLaren Vale Adelaide Hills Viognier 2007 A peppery viognier, with apricot fruit coming in second; quite rich, and nicely even on the finish. Screwcap. 13.5° alc. **Rating** 89 **To** 2009 $19.95

The Dead Arm Shiraz 2005 Some reduced characters blur the profile of the usually opulent fruit, introducing some bitter notes; not likely to recover. Screwcap. 14.5° alc. **Rating** 89 **To** 2012 $60

The Stump Jump Grenache Shiraz Mourvedre 2006 Light, bright red-purple; fresh, spicy berry fruit; a delicious, lively, drink-now café style. Screwcap. 14.5° alc. **Rating** 89 **To** 2009 $11.95

The Noble McLaren Vale Riesling 2006 Has considerable intensity, though little of the finesse a wine from the Mosel-Saar-Ruwer would have with similar alcohol and residual sugar. Cork. 9.5° alc. **Rating** 89 **To** 2009 $25

The Olive Grove McLaren Vale Adelaide Hills Chardonnay 2007 Plenty of ripe stone fruit and melon; oak a minor support role; easy-access style. Screwcap. **Rating** 88 **To** 2010 $16.95

The High Trellis McLaren Vale Cabernet Sauvignon 2006 Light- to medium-bodied, with blackcurrant fruit skirted by touches of olive, leaf and mint; easy drinking. Screwcap. 14° alc. **Rating** 88 **To** 2011 $19.95

The Peppermint Paddock Sparkling Chambourcin NV The best use for chambourcin? Juicy and vibrant with good flavour, depth, and thrust on the finish. Cork. 14° alc. **Rating** 88 **To** 2009 $28

The Hermit Crab McLaren Vale Adelaide Hills Viognier Marsanne 2007
Pleasant weight and mouthfeel, a gentle cocktail of flavours, with fair acidity; will grow character with time in bottle. Screwcap. 13.5° alc. **Rating** 87 **To** 2011 $16.95
The Stump Jump Riesling Sauvignon Blanc Roussanne Marsanne 2007
Clean and crisp with the riesling playing the major role; hints of citrus and cleansing acidity on the finish. Screwcap. **Rating** 87 **To** 2009 $11.95
d'Arry's Original Shiraz Grenache 2000 Mooching along contentedly, and has gained more on the swings than lost on the roundabouts since last tasted in Jan '02; appealing gentle spicy/cedary flavours. **Rating** 87 **To** 2007 $19.95

Dal Zotto Estate

Main Road, Whitfield, Vic 3733 **Region** King Valley
T (03) 5729 8321 **F** (03) 5729 8490 **www.**dalzotto.com.au **Open** 7 days 10–5
Winemaker Otto Dal Zotto, Michael Dal Zotto **Est.** 1987 **Cases** 13 000
The Dal Zotto family is a King Valley institution; ex tobacco growers, then contract grapegrowers and now primarily focused on their Dal Zotto Estate range. Led by Otto and Elena Dal Zotto, and with sons Michael and Christian handling winemaking and sales/marketing respectively, the family is delivering increasing amounts of wine from its 48-ha vineyard. The cellar door has now relocated to a more accessible position in the centre of Whitfield and is also home to Rinaldo's Restaurant. Exports to the UK, Canada, Hong Kong and China.

King Valley Barbera 2005 Good colour, with slightly spicy and distinct mineral complexity; high levels of acid, but with fairly tame tannins; the palate is very long, fine and quite poised on the finish. Screwcap. 13.5° alc. **Rating** 93 **To** 2012 $22
King Valley Sangiovese Cabernet 2005 Bright cherry fruit, with some briary notes, high levels of cleansing acid, and an appealing savoury tannin structure. Screwcap. 13.5° alc. **Rating** 91 **To** 2012 $17
King Valley Riesling 2006 Quite a ripe wine, with limes and riper citrus fruit; fresh, vibrant and with a slightly chalky minerality to the finish. Screwcap. 12.5° alc. **Rating** 90 **To** 2014 $15

King Valley Prosecco 2006 Delicate and lively; this is not about complexity, but about balance and freshness; a more than acceptable alternative style; overpriced, though, for what it is. Crown Seal. 12.5° alc. **Rating** 89 **To** 2009 $36
King Valley Sangiovese 2006 Light-bodied, with a little savoury twist to the finish; certainly varietal, but lacking a little stuffing and complexity. Screwcap. 13.5° alc. **Rating** 88 **To** 2011 $22
Brillando 2006 Vibrant light-red fruit aromas; juicy, simple, fun and dry enough to be enjoyed with appropriate food. Crown Seal. 13° alc. **Rating** 88 **To** 2009 $25

Dalfarras

PO Box 123, Nagambie, Vic 3608 **Region** Nagambie Lakes
T (03) 5794 2637 **F** (03) 5794 2360 **Open** At Tahbilk
Winemaker Alister Purbrick, Alan George **Est.** 1991 **Cases** 15 000
The personal project of Alister Purbrick and artist wife Rosa (née Dalfarra), whose paintings adorn the labels of the wines, a redesign in 2004 brilliantly successful. Alister, of course, is best known as winemaker at Tahbilk, the family winery and home, but this range of wines is intended to (in Alister's words) 'allow me to expand my winemaking horizons and mould wines in styles different from Tahbilk'. It now draws upon 23 ha of its own plantings in the Goulburn Valley.

Shiraz Viognier 2005 Elegantly framed; gentle blackberry fruit, the viognier influence perfectly judged; does look as if it will mature fairly quickly. **Rating** 93 **To** 2012 $14.95

Dalrymple ★★★★★

1337 Pipers Brook Road, Pipers Brook, Tas 7254 **Region** Northern Tasmania
T (03) 6382 7222 **F** (03) 6382 7222 **www**.dalrymplevineyards.com.au **Open** 7 days 10–5
Winemaker Dr Bertel Sundstrup **Est.** 1987 **Cases** 6000
A partnership between Jill Mitchell and her sister and brother-in-law, Anne and Bertel
Sundstrup, inspired by father Bill Mitchell's establishment of the Tamarway Vineyard in the
late 1960s. In 1991 Tamarway reverted to the Sundstrup and Mitchell families and it, too, will
be producing wine in the future, probably under its own label but sold from the Dalrymple
cellar door. As production has grown (significantly), so has wine quality across the board. The
winery was purchased by Yalumba in late 2007.

 Chardonnay 2006 An intense wine built around special Tasmanian acidity; tight
grapefruit and nectarine, with the oak swallowed up by that fruit; long finish, long
life. Screwcap. 13.1° alc. **Rating** 94 **To** 2012 $18
Reserve Pinot Noir 2006 An elegant, aromatic bouquet, then a light- to
medium-bodied palate with fine plum and black cherry fruit; lingering finish.
Screwcap. 14.4° alc. **Rating** 94 **To** 2013 $40

Pinot Noir 2006 Curiously, a fraction deeper in colour than the Reserve; more
grip and power; darker fruit flavours. Screwcap. 14.5° alc. **Rating** 92 **To** 2014 $30

Dalwhinnie ★★★★★

448 Taltarni Road, Moonambel, Vic 3478 **Region** Pyrenees
T (03) 5467 2388 **F** (03) 5467 2237 **www**.dalwhinnie.com.au **Open** 7 days 10–5
Winemaker David Jones, Gary Baldwin (Consultant) **Est.** 1976 **Cases** 4500
David and Jenny Jones are making wines with tremendous depth of fruit flavour, reflecting
the relatively low-yielding but very well-maintained vineyards. It is hard to say whether the
Chardonnay, the Cabernet Sauvignon or the Shiraz is the more distinguished. A further 8 ha
of shiraz (with a little viognier) were planted in the spring of 1999 on a newly acquired block
on Taltarni Road. A 50-tonne contemporary high-tech winery now allows the wines to be
made onsite, with three single vineyard Shirazs in the pipeline under the Eagles Series, South
West Rocks and Goddess labels. On the other side of the ledger, the Pinot Noir has been
discontinued. Exports to the UK and other major markets.

 Moonambel Shiraz 2006 Complex and layered with red fruits, ironstone, earth
and hints of tar and mint; the texture of the wine is attractively silky, with a long
and supple finish. Cork. 13.5° alc. **Rating** 95 **To** 2018 $55
Moonambel Cabernet 2006 A layered, complex wine, fully integrated and
showing generous levels of fruit, savoury oak and ample, quite slippery, fine-
grained tannins. Cork. 13.5° alc. **Rating** 94 **To** 2018 $48

Moonambel Chardonnay 2005 Rich and full in the mouth, surprisingly so
at the modest alcohol; peach and nectarine fruit plus solid oak. Diam. 13.5° alc.
Rating 92 **To** 2012 $38

Darling Park ★★★★★

232 Red Hill Road, Red Hill, Vic 3937 **Region** Mornington Peninsula
T (03) 5989 2324 **F** (03) 5931 0326 **www**.darlingparkwinery.com **Open** Fri–Mon 11–5
(7 days Jan)
Winemaker Judy Gifford **Est.** 1986 **Cases** 2000
Josh and Karen Liberman and David Coe have energetically expanded the range of Darling
Park's wines while maintaining a high-quality standard. The Art of Wine club offers back
vintages, as well as previews of upcoming releases. Wine labels feature artworks from the
owners' collections, with artists including Sidney Nolan, Arthur Boyd, John Perceval and
Charles Blackman.

ΨΨΨΨΨ **Reserve Chardonnay 2005** Fine, intense and tight, with a lovely framework of nectarine, melon and citrus fruit, the barrel ferment influence restrained; has very good mouthfeel and length. Screwcap. 13.5° alc. **Rating** 94 **To** 2013 $30
Shiraz 2006 Bright and lively, with a seductive and slightly aromatic array of spices to go with the core of red berry fruits; fine tannins and subtle oak; the touch of viognier works well. Screwcap. 14.5° alc. **Rating** 94 **To** 2016 $29

ΨΨΨΨ **Pinot Noir 2006** Clear varietal expression, with a mix of small red and black fruits, and a savoury carpet underneath. Screwcap. 14.3° alc. **Rating** 89 **To** 2011 $29
Cane Cut Pinot Gris 2006 Candied fruit and orange rind aromas; a fine level of richness, without any heaviness; good persistence on the finish. Screwcap. 12.5° alc. **Rating** 89 **To** 2012 $27
Pinot Gris 2007 Pleasant pear and citrus aromas and flavours; right in the mainstream, and certainly won't frighten the horses. Screwcap. 13.5° alc. **Rating** 87 **To** 2009 $25
Pinot Gris Viognier 2007 A blend of convenience more than logic, but does have modest success, thanks to the unexpected ally of lemony acidity. Screwcap. 13.5° alc. **Rating** 87 **To** 2010 $24

Darlington Vineyard ★★★

Holkam Court, Orford, Tas 7190 **Region** Southern Tasmania
T (03) 6257 1630 **F** (03) 6257 1630 **Open** Thurs–Mon 10–5
Winemaker Hood Wines (Andrew Hood) **Est.** 1993 **Cases** 600
Peter and Margaret Hyland planted a little under 2 ha of vineyard in 1993. The first wines were made from the 1999 vintage, forcing retired builder Peter Hyland to complete their home so that the small building in which they had been living could be converted into a cellar door. The vineyard looks out over the settlement of Darlington on Maria Island, the site of Diego Bernacci's attempt to establish a vineyard and lure investors by attaching artificial bunches of grapes to his vines.

ΨΨΨΨ **Riesling 2006** Soft, ripe, tropical fruit ranging through pineapple to lime, supported by gentle acidity. **Rating** 89 **To** 2010 $17
Pinot Noir 2006 Despite its alcohol, a relatively light-bodied, savoury style with a somewhat herbal finish; does have redeeming length. **Rating** 87 **To** 2010 $22

David Franz ★★★★☆

PO Box 677, Tanunda, SA 5352 **Region** Barossa Valley
T (08) 8563 0705 **F** (08) 8563 0708 **www**.david-franz.com **Open** Not
Winemaker David Franz Lehmann **Est.** 1998 **Cases** 1500
How do you distill down 10 well-typed pages of background into a meagre few lines when it involves a cast of characters which are the very essence of all that is great about the Barossa Valley? It's about a guy who first tried his hand at graphic design at university, switching to an architecture interior design course for two years (equally unfulfilling), then working around Australia, before spending three successful years gaining a diploma in hospitality business management. Next he headed overseas with his new wife Nicki, working a traumatic vintage in South Africa, then escaping to England to work anywhere, as backpackers do, with side trips to Europe. Their third and final trip to France was cut short by the discovery that Nicki was pregnant, forcing a return to Australia. So who is David Franz? Well, he is one of Margaret and Peter Lehmann's sons, who has finally acknowledged that wine is in his blood. With help from his parents along the way, including some financial help, he established David Franz. And I personally know what it is like making wine with stainless-steel dairy minivats, plastic tubs, a hand-operated basket press and a one-inch mono pump. End of page one.

ΨΨΨΨΨ **Benjamin's Promise Shiraz 2002** Deeply focused blackberry fruit runs through a very long, medium- to full-bodied palate; balanced tannins and oak. Cork. 14.2° alc. **Rating** 94 **To** 2022 $32

ŸŸŸŸŸ **Benjamin's Promise Shiraz 1998** A big, soft, plum and blackberry, plushy palate, with the consistent streak of fruit sweetness in all of these Franz reds. Cork. 15° alc. **Rating** 90 **To** 2013 $40

ŸŸŸŸ **Stonewell Hill Semillon 2005** A generous mix of lemon and fruit salad flavours; ingenious winemaking techniques and mouthfilling flavour; 50 dozen made. Screwcap. 11.3° alc. **Rating** 89 **To** 2009 $23
Bethany Road Cabernet Sauvignon 2004 Has riper fruit flavours than the alcohol would suggest, with that house style of sweetness running through the palate; a challenging price. Cork. 14.1° alc. **Rating** 89 **To** 2014 $44
Old Redemption Tawny NV Has considerable biscuity complexity; the fiery spirit on the finish can catch the unwary by surprise, but there is no shortage of character or flavour. Diam. 19.9° alc. **Rating** 89 **To** 2009 $42
Georgie's Walk Cabernet Sauvignon 2002 There is a line of confit sweetness across the length of the palate which is at odds with cabernet; on the other hand, there is good extract. Cork. 14.6° alc. **Rating** 88 **To** 2012 $32
Eden Valley Riesling 2005 A big, generous and broad style; seems much riper than 11.5° alc., the flavours moving into a stone fruit/pineapple/apricot range; some phenolics and sweetness. Screwcap. 11.5° alc. **Rating** 87 **To** 2009 $23
Benjamin's Promise Shiraz 2003 Shows the problems of the vintage, with some confit fruit characters along with slightly sweet and sour notes. Cork. 14.3° alc. **Rating** 87 **To** 2012 $32

David Hook Wines   ★★★★☆

Cnr Broke Road/Ekerts Road, Pokolbin, NSW 2320 **Region** Lower Hunter Valley
T (02) 4998 7121 **www**.davidhookwines.com.au **Open** 7 days 10–5
Winemaker David Hook **Est.** 1984 **Cases** 5000
David Hook has over 20 years' experience, as a winemaker for Tyrrell's and Lake's Folly, also doing the full Flying Winemaker bit, with jobs in Bordeaux, the Rhône Valley, Spain, the US and Georgia. He and his family began establishing the vineyard in 1984. In 2004 they moved the winery home to its present address. The estate-owned Pothana Vineyard has been in production for 25 years, and the wines made from it are given the 'Old Vines' banner. This vineyard is planted on the Belford Dome, an ancient geological formation which provides red clay soils over limestone on the slopes, and sandy loams along the creek flats, the former for red wines, the latter for white. Exports to the US and Japan.

ŸŸŸŸŸ **Pothana Vineyard Old Vines Belford Semillon 2004** Has fulfilled all the promise it showed three years ago; still youthful, but with an appealing array of lemon, herb and mineral flavours; almost silky finish. Screwcap. 10.5° alc. **Rating** 94 **To** 2014 $22

ŸŸŸŸŸ **Pothana Vineyard Belford Shiraz 2006** A lively, dark-fruited shiraz; there is real depth and a chewy element, and the finish is fresh, vibrant and truly focused. Screwcap. 14.5° alc. **Rating** 93 **To** 2015 $30
Pothana Vineyard Belford Chardonnay 2007 Nectarine and a hint of peach bouquet; medium-bodied palate with good intensity and follow-through on the creamy yet fresh finish. Screwcap. 13.5° alc. **Rating** 90 **To** 2009 $25
The Gorge Hunter Valley Shiraz 2006 Stacked with plum and black cherry; the primary fruit is still dominating the regional character, but the Hunter will have its turn in due course. Screwcap. 13.5° alc. **Rating** 90 **To** 2016 $18

ŸŸŸŸ **The Gorge Barbera 2005** Bramble, blackberry and spice aromas and flavours; medium-bodied, with controlled tannins on a good finish; Orange/Hunter Valley. Screwcap. 13.5° alc. **Rating** 89 **To** 2013 $18
The Gorge Central Ranges Sauvignon Blanc 2007 Herbaceous/asparagus fruit which is balanced by a touch of sweetness. Screwcap. 11.5° alc. **Rating** 87 **To** 2009 $18

Dawson & Wills

PO Box 4154, Dandenong South, Vic 3164 **Region** Strathbogie Ranges
T (03) 5790 4259 **F** (03) 9768 5887 **Open** Not
Winemaker Scott McCarthy (Contract) **Est.** 1998 **Cases** 750
This is a weekend and weekday night busman's holiday for Rob Wills and Frank Dawson.
Rob is a professional viticulturist with a day job of running a vineyard in the Goulburn Valley,
while Frank Dawson is an engineer manufacturing equipment for the farming, mining and
construction industries. As neighbours, they first formed a partnership agisting sheep and
cattle, and this in turn led to the establishment of their vineyard, which has 3.6 ha of sauvignon
blanc, 2.5 ha of pinot noir, 1 ha each of cabernet sauvignon and tempranillo, and a few vines
of merlot.

ɣɣɣɣ **Tempranillo 2006** The strange conundrum that appears again and again with
Australian tempranillo: quite bright red fruits followed by a distinctly lemony
finish. Young vines perhaps. Screwcap. **Rating** 87 **To** 2010 $19

De Beaurepaire Wines

182 Cudgegong Road, Rylstone, NSW 2849 **Region** Mudgee
T 0427 791 473 **F** (02) 6379 1474 **www.**debeaurepairewines.com **Open** W'ends &
public hols 11–4, or by appt
Winemaker David Lowe, Jane Wilson (Contract) **Est.** 1998 **Cases** 2000
This is the substantial retirement business of former clinical psychologist Janet de Beaurepaire
and investment banker Richard de Beaurepaire. Beaurepaire Ridge Vineyard is situated on
the 200-ha Woodlawn property, one of the oldest properties west of the Blue Mountains, at
an altitude of 570–600 m. While part of the Mudgee GI, the Rylstone climate is significantly
cooler than other parts of the region. It is planted to 55 ha of shiraz, merlot, cabernet
sauvignon, petit verdot, semillon, chardonnay, viognier and verdelho. The property is bounded
on two sides by the Cudgegong River, which provides irrigation for the vineyard.

ɣɣɣɣ **Captain Starlight Series Semillon Sauvignon Blanc 2006** A clean and fresh
mix of citrus, passionfruit and herb; lemony acidity gives thrust to the finish; good
length. Diam. 12.9° alc. **Rating** 89 **To** 2010 $18

De Bortoli

De Bortoli Road, Bilbul, NSW 2680 **Region** Riverina
T (02) 6966 0100 **F** (02) 6966 0199 **www.**debortoli.com.au **Open** Mon–Sat 9–5, Sun 9–4
Winemaker Darren De Bortoli **Est.** 1928 **Cases** 3 million
Famous among the cognoscenti for its superb Noble One, which in fact accounts for only a
minute part of its total production, this winery turns around low-priced varietal and generic
wines which are invariably competently made and equally invariably provide value for money.
These come in part from 250 ha of estate vineyards, but mostly from contract-grown grapes.
The rating is in part a reflection of the exceptional value for money offered across the range.
Exports to all major markets.

ɣɣɣɣɣ **Noble One 2006** Very intense botrytis characters, with marmalade, peaches and
cream and just a little hint of spice; very long and very sweet. Screwcap. 10.5° alc.
Rating 94 **To** 2012 $32.90
Black Noble NV A unique wine, fortified and long barrel-aged Noble One as
its base; super-intense, yet elegant, and shows no hint of volatile acidity; flavours of
exotic spices and mandarin. Cork. 17.5° alc. **Rating** 94 **To** 2009 $37

ɣɣɣɣɣ **Old Boys 21 Years Old Tawny NV** High-quality tawny, with potent rancio;
intense and long, with spiced biscuit and cake flavours; balanced acidity. Cork.
19° alc. **Rating** 92 **To** 2009 $45
Deen De Bortoli Vat 8 Shiraz 2006 Abundant plum and blackberry fruit on
both bouquet and palate; slightly chippy/charry oak doesn't spoil the party; quite
complex and well priced. Surprise gold-medal winner, Sydney Wine Show '08.
Screwcap. 14° alc. **Rating** 90 **To** 2010 $11.99

Deen De Bortoli Vat 1 Durif 2006 Typical purple-crimson; stacked full of ripe plum and prune fruit, backed by appropriate tannins and acidity; perfect ripeness and alcohol. Screwcap. 13.5° alc. **Rating** 90 **To** 2010 $11.95

Sero King Valley Merlot Sangiovese 2006 An unexpectedly and particularly powerful wine; plenty of red fruits before very strong tannins take over; demands both patience and food. Screwcap. 14° alc. **Rating** 90 **To** 2014 $14.99

ŢŢŢŢ **Deen De Bortoli Vat 5 Botrytis Semillon 2006** Quite a strong raisin bouquet; hints of marmalade come through on the finish; very good value. Screwcap. 11° alc. **Rating** 89 **To** 2011 $12.95

Show Liqueur Muscat NV Mahogany, with an olive-green rim; strong raisiny varietal fruit; overall abundant flavour. Cork. 18° alc. **Rating** 89 **To** 2009 $24

8 Year Old Tawny Port NV Good rancio and balance; spicy, biscuity aromas and flavours; not too sweet. Cork. 18.5° alc. **Rating** 88 **To** 2009 $24

Montage Chardonnay Semillon 2007 Bright and lively, the grassy/citrussy semillon component contributing substantially to both flavour and length; value plus. Screwcap. 13° alc. **Rating** 87 **To** 2009 $9.50

Wild Vine Shiraz 2006 Simple, bright, fresh red fruits, and a slightly sweet, clean finish; serve slightly chilled in summer and don't think about it. Screwcap. 13.5° alc. **Rating** 87 **To** 2009 $8.99

Sacred Hill Shiraz Cabernet 2007 About as much as you can expect at this price; bright, fresh red fruits; zero tannin and oak influence; perhaps just a tiny touch of residual sugar. Screwcap. 13.5° alc. **Rating** 87 **To** 2009 $6.95

Deen Vat 2 Sauvignon Blanc 2007 Well constructed; not intense, but has crowd-pleasing tropical fruit balanced by appropriate acidity. Screwcap. 12° alc. **Rating** 87 **To** 2009 $11.99

Deen De Bortoli Vat 7 Chardonnay 2007 Pleasant melon and peach fruit with subliminal oak; good balance, and even better value. Screwcap. 13.5° alc. **Rating** 87 **To** 2009 $11.95

Sacred Hill Traminer Riesling 2007 Heady pineapple and spice aromas and flavours; rich and unambiguously sweet; serve ice-cold with Chinese takeaway. Screwcap. 12.5° alc. **Rating** 87 **To** 2009 $6.95

Sacred Hill Colombard Chardonnay 2007 Clean, bright and ripe fruit, soft and round in the mouth; ideal commercial style. Screwcap. **Rating** 87 **To** 2009 $6.95

Sero King Valley Shiraz Tempranillo 2006 Medium-bodied; bright plum, black cherry, spice and dried lemon rind; direct style, good length. Screwcap. 14° alc. **Rating** 87 **To** 2010 $14.95

Deen De Bortoli Vat 9 Cabernet Sauvignon 2006 Has more depth and weight than many at or near this price point; blackcurrant and fine tannins are varietal. Screwcap. 14° alc. **Rating** 87 **To** 2010 $11.95

De Bortoli (Hunter Valley)   ★★★★

532 Wine Country Drive, Pokolbin, NSW 2320 **Region** Lower Hunter Valley
T (02) 4993 8800 **F** (02) 4993 8899 **www.**debortoli.com.au **Open** 7 days 10–5
Winemaker Steve Webber **Est.** 2002 **Cases** 35 000
De Bortoli extended its wine empire in 2002 with the purchase of the former Wilderness Estate, giving it an immediate and substantial presence in the Hunter Valley courtesy of the 26 ha of established vineyards; this was expanded significantly by the subsequent purchase of an adjoining 40-ha property. Exports to all major markets.

ŢŢŢŢŞ **Murphy Vineyard Semillon 2006** Pale green-straw; the colour belies its age; very smooth and supple, the finish long, but quite soft; a left-field style. Screwcap. **Rating** 90 **To** 2012 $34

Hunter Valley Shiraz 2006 Attractive and lively fruit ranging through plum, blackberry and spice; a silky palate, with good length, oak merely a prop; will develop. Screwcap. 13.5° alc. **Rating** 90 **To** 2016 $20.50

De Bortoli (Victoria)

Pinnacle Lane, Dixons Creek, Vic 3775 **Region** Yarra Valley
T (03) 5965 2271 **F** (03) 5965 2464 **www.**debortoli.com.au **Open** 7 days 10–5
Winemaker Steve Webber **Est.** 1987 **Cases** 350 000
The quality arm of the bustling De Bortoli group, run by Leanne De Bortoli and husband
Steve Webber, ex-Lindemans winemaker. The top label (De Bortoli), the second (Gulf Station)
and the third label (Windy Peak) offer wines of consistently good quality and excellent value –
the complex Chardonnay and the Pinot Noirs are usually of outstanding quality. The volume
of production, by many times the largest in the Yarra Valley, simply underlines the quality/value
for money ratio of the wines. This arm of the business has 247 ha of vineyards in the Yarra
Valley, and 170 ha in the King Valley. These viticultural resources to one side, Steve Webber
was *Gourmet Traveller* Winemaker of the Year in 2007, recognition he thoroughly deserved.
Exports to all major markets.

Reserve Release Yarra Valley Sauvignon 2007 Very fragrant gooseberry plus
hints of apple and citrus on the bouquet; a long palate with great movement and
delineation, the focus on pristine fruit, not barrel ferment oak. Screwcap. 12.5° alc.
Rating 96 **To** 2011 $40
Reserve Release Yarra Valley Syrah 2006 As ever, immaculately crafted with
perfect line, length and flow; likewise red and black fruits and quality French oak;
a hint of viognier; perfect tannins. Screwcap. 14° alc. **Rating** 96 **To** 2026 $59
Estate Yarra Valley Chardonnay 2006 Complex aromas; the palate has tight
focus and extreme length; distinct affinities with Chablis. Screwcap. 13° alc.
Rating 95 **To** 2016 $30
Reserve Release Yarra Valley Syrah 2005 Super-elegant, restrained but very
complex wine, all the components seamlessly welded together; spicy, savoury notes
to the medium-bodied black fruits sustain the long finish, aided by fine tannins.
Screwcap. 14° alc. **Rating** 95 **To** 2025 $49
Estate Grown Yarra Valley Sauvignon 2007 Walks down a different path than
all other sauvignon blancs except PHI and Geoff Weaver; structural and textural
qualities are foremost, but there is clear herb and gooseberry fruit, the use of oak
creating texture, not flavour. Screwcap. 12° alc. **Rating** 94 **To** 2011 $32
Reserve Release Yarra Valley Chardonnay 2005 An understated wine of
great finesse, an exercise in texture and structure creating a wholly individual style;
tight melon fruit, a touch of apple, and the oak deliberately held to provide texture
rather than flavour; cerebral. Screwcap. 13° alc. **Rating** 94 **To** 2015 $49
Estate Grown Yarra Valley Viognier 2006 An imperious wine with great
impact, thrust and length, yet only mildly reflecting its varietal make-up. It has
exceptional length and a lingering aftertaste, wholly free from oily phenolics.
Screwcap. 13.5° alc. **Rating** 94 **To** 2012 $24.95
Yarra Valley Pinot Noir Rose 2007 Pale salmon-pink; a serious rose with far
more texture and structure than usual; definitely a food style for a wide variety of
dishes. Screwcap. 13.5° alc. **Rating** 94 **To** 2009 $23
Estate Grown Yarra Valley Pinot Noir 2006 A pure and intense evocation
of pinot; plum and black cherry fruit; complex texture thanks to fine tannins and
controlled oak; long finish. Screwcap. 13° alc. **Rating** 94 **To** 2013 $38
Reserve Release Yarra Valley Pinot Noir 2006 A fragrant burst of red
fruits, spice and some French oak on the bouquet; a lively, complex palate, with
an interplay of bright fruit, supple tannins and oak; long finish – all at a modest
alcohol. Screwcap. 13° alc. **Rating** 94 **To** 2013 $59
Gulf Station Yarra Valley Shiraz Viognier 2006 Highly scented and spicy;
vibrant and medium-bodied, with clarion-clear line and length to its effusive red
fruits, fine tannins and subtle oak. Screwcap. 14° alc. **Rating** 94 **To** 2020 $20.99
Estate Grown Yarra Valley Shiraz Viognier 2006 Typical bright hue; a highly
fragrant bouquet leaps out of the glass; finely structured, with extreme length to
the spicy fruits and subtle oak. Screwcap. 14° alc. **Rating** 94 **To** 2016 $35

Estate Grown Yarra Valley Cabernet Sauvignon 2006 Bright crimson-purple; an elegant, medium-bodied wine, with carefully crafted cabernet fruit supported by high-quality oak and ripe tannins; very good line and flow. Screwcap. 14° alc. **Rating** 94 **To** 2021 $36

ɷɷɷɷɷ **Gulf Station Yarra Valley Cabernet Sauvignon 2006** Medium-bodied; tightly focused, classic blackcurrant and cassis supported by fine but persistent tannins and French oak; very good wine. Screwcap. 14° alc. **Rating** 93 **To** 2020 $20.95

Windy Peak Yarra Valley Pinot Noir 2007 Very good colour; ripe red and black cherry aromas, with undoubted varietal character on a palate with well above-average texture and structure; oak unseen; outstanding value. Screwcap. 13° alc. **Rating** 92 **To** 2009 $15.99

Gulf Station Yarra Valley Pinot Noir 2007 While it appears to be driven simply by dark plum and cherry fruit, structural and flavour complexity come through strongly on the spicy, long, finish. Screwcap. 13.5° alc. **Rating** 92 **To** 2012 $20.95

Gulf Station Riesling 2007 Interesting style; aimed to increase mouthfeel and structure with a trade-off in fruit flavour; with three months in stainless steel and in oak with lees stirring. Screwcap. 11° alc. **Rating** 91 **To** 2012 $20.99

Gulf Station Yarra Valley Sauvignon Blanc 2007 A subdued bouquet; but the palate delivers a zesty mix of herb and asparagus, with textural impact from partial barrel ferment in old oak. Screwcap. 11.5° alc. **Rating** 91 **To** 2010 $20.95

Windy Peak Shiraz Viognier 2006 A delicious and fragrant light-bodied wine, bursting with juicy red fruits, simply demanding to be opened on any pretence and in any company. Screwcap. 14° alc. **Rating** 90 **To** 2009 $15.95

Gulf Station Chardonnay 2006 Texture and mouthfeel are the key components; gentle melon and nectarine fruit, plus citrussy acidity to close; minimal oak. Screwcap. 13° alc. **Rating** 90 **To** 2011 $20.99

Estate Grown Yarra Valley Viognier 2007 Clear varietal apricot flesh and nuances of clove and cinnamon; good texture and weight, and ready to go now. Screwcap. 13° alc. **Rating** 90 **To** 2010 $22

ɷɷɷɷ **Windy Peak Sauvignon Blanc Semillon 2007** Typical spotless and finely crafted wine, even at this price level and volume; gooseberry and citrus flavours; sourced from no less than eight regions across Vic and NSW thanks to the '07 vintage. Screwcap. 12.5° alc. **Rating** 87 **To** 2009 $14

Windy Peak Viognier 2007 Apricot blossom aromas; a soft, fleshy palate with some continuing apricot varietal expression; soft finish. Screwcap. 13° alc. **Rating** 87 **To** 2009 $14

De Iuliis   ★★★★★

21 Broke Road, Pokolbin, NSW 2320 **Region** Lower Hunter Valley
T (02) 4993 8000 **F** (02) 4998 7168 **www**.dewine.com.au **Open** 7 days 10–5
Winemaker Michael De Iuliis **Est.** 1990 **Cases** 10 000
Three generations of the De Iuliis family have been involved in the establishment of their 45-ha vineyard. The family acquired the property in 1986 and planted the first vines in 1990, selling the grapes from the first few vintages to Tyrrell's but retaining increasing amounts for release under the De Iuliis label. Winemaker Michael De Iuliis has completed postgraduate studies in oenology at the Roseworthy campus of Adelaide University and was a Len Evans Tutorial scholar. He has been responsible for lifting the quality of the wines into the highest echelon.

ɷɷɷɷɷ **Limited Release Hunter Valley Shiraz 2006** Deeper colour and a more complex array of aromas than the Show Reserve; positive oak frames dark fruits, leather and spice; an emphatic, complex and lingering full-bodied finish. Screwcap. 14.3° alc. **Rating** 95 **To** 2020 $40

Show Reserve Hunter Valley Shiraz 2006 Concentrated and ample sweet fruits; full-bodied and quite oaky, but a vibrant and lively finish, with an aromatic element that is appealing. Screwcap. 14° alc. **Rating** 94 **To** 2025 $28

TTTTT Hunter Valley Semillon 2007 A classic semillon bouquet and entry to the mouth; a mix of grass, herb, lemon and mineral; long finish. Screwcap. 10.5° alc. Rating 92 To 2017 $16

Limited Release Hunter Valley Chardonnay 2006 Has slightly unexpected finesse to the texture and structure, perhaps due to whole-bunch pressing; melon and stone fruit with very good French oak balance and integration. Screwcap. 13.5° alc. Rating 92 To 2011 $20

Show Reserve Hunter Valley Chardonnay 2006 More elegant and understated than the Limited Release; an interesting difference in style, here touches of citrus as well as melon and stone fruit. Screwcap. 13.5° alc. Rating 92 To 2012 $18

Charlie Hunter Valley Shiraz 2006 Deep magenta; plenty of warm, ripe fruit aromas, and a little spice framing the red fruits; good generosity and texture, helped by fine-grained tannins. Screwcap. 14° alc. Rating 92 To 2018 $25

de Mestre Wines

'Inverway', Warrangunyah Road, Ilford, NSW 2850 **Region** Mudgee
T (02) 9221 5711 **F** (02) 9233 6181 **www**.demestrewines.com.au **Open** By appt
Winemaker Paul de Mestre **Est.** 1999 **Cases** NA
de Mestre Wines, with Paul de Mestre at the head, has established 16 ha of low-yielding viognier, shiraz and cabernet sauvignon on a gently sloping, north-facing hill 750 m above sea level. The soil, of volcanic origin, is 460 million years old, and also (intriguingly) includes marine deposits. The wines are made and bottled onsite, with full participation of the three de Mestre children.

TTTT Sofala Road Shiraz 2005 Black cherry, licorice and warm spices are supported by oak and tannins on the medium-bodied palate; a faint touch of bitterness on the aftertaste. Diam. 15° alc. Rating 89 To 2015 $26

Dead Horse Hill

Myola East Road, Toolleen, Vic 3551 **Region** Heathcote
T (03) 5433 6214 **F** (03) 5433 6164 **Open** By appt
Winemaker Jencie McRobert **Est.** 1994 **Cases** 500
Jencie McRobert (and husband Russell) 'did a deal with Dad' for approximately 65 ha of her parents' large sheep and wheat farm at Toolleen, 20 km north of Heathcote. It took a number of years for the 4-ha dry-grown shiraz vines to achieve reasonable yields, but they are now yielding between 3.7 and 5 tonnes per ha of high-quality fruit. Jencie's introduction to wine came partly through the family dining table and partly from meeting Steve Webber, then working for Lindemans at Karadoc, when she was working in soil conservation and salinity management in the Mallee. She subsequently completed a course at CSU, and makes the wine at De Bortoli in the Yarra Valley with the odd bit of assistance from Webber.

TTTTT Heathcote Shiraz 2007 Crimson-purple; archetypal Heathcote flavour and structure; black fruits with fine spices and whispers of bitter chocolate; tannins and extract controlled; best years in front of it. Screwcap. 14° alc. Rating 93 To 2020 $28

Deakin Estate

Kulkyne Way, via Red Cliffs, Vic 3496 **Region** Murray Darling
T (03) 5029 1666 **F** (03) 5024 3316 **www**.deakinestate.com.au **Open** Not
Winemaker Phil Spillman **Est.** 1980 **Cases** 500 000
Part of the Katnook Estate, Riddoch and Deakin Estate triumvirate, which constitutes the Wingara Wine Group, now 60% owned by Freixenet of Spain. The Sunnycliff label is still used for export purposes but no longer appears on the domestic market. Deakin Estate draws on over 300 ha of its own vineyards, making it largely self-sufficient, and produces competitively priced wines of consistent quality and impressive value. Exports to the UK, the US, Canada, NZ and Asia.

ŶŶŶŶ   **Chardonnay 2006** An honest, well-priced wine with yellow peach fruit and a
touch of oak; screwcap a boon. Screwcap. 14° alc. **Rating** 87 **To** 2009 $10
Crackerjack River Bend Shiraz Viognier 2005 Easy, soft, early-drinking style
with flavours of red cherry, a dusting of spice and citrussy acidity. Screwcap. 14.5°
alc. **Rating** 87 **To** 2009 $15
Brut NV Good mousse with a quite fine bead; clean, fresh chardonnay stone fruit
and citrus to the fore; well balanced; a surprise; Chardonnay/Pinot Noir. Cork.
12.5° alc. **Rating** 87 **To** 2009 $10

Deep Woods Estate   ★★★★

Commonage Road, Yallingup, WA 6282 **Region** Margaret River
T (08) 9756 6066 **F** (08) 9756 6366 **www**.deepwoods.com.au **Open** Tues–Sun 11–5,
7 days during hols
Winemaker Travis Clydesdale **Est.** 1987 **Cases** 20 000
The Gould family acquired Deep Woods Estate in 1992, when the first plantings were four
years old. In 2005, the business was purchased by Perth businessman Peter Fogarty and family,
who also own Lake's Folly in the Hunter Valley, and Millbrook in the Perth Hills. The 32-ha
property has 16-ha plantings of cabernet sauvignon, shiraz, merlot, cabernet franc, chardonnay,
sauvignon blanc, semillon and verdelho. Vineyard and cellar door upgrades are underway.
Exports to Switzerland, Belgium, Denmark and Ireland.

ŶŶŶŶŶ   **Margaret River Semillon Sauvignon Blanc 2007** Classic Margaret River
style, with the length of flavour immediately obvious; grass, lemon, herb and
passionfruit on a stylish wine. Screwcap. 12.5° alc. **Rating** 94 **To** 2011 $18.95

ŶŶŶŶ   **Ivory Margaret River Semillon Sauvignon Blanc 2007** Relatively light-
bodied, some tropical fruit notes alongside more citrussy/herbal flavours on the
back-palate. Screwcap. 13° alc. **Rating** 87 **To** 2010 $13.95
Margaret River Verdelho 2007 Light- to medium-bodied; fruit salad
flavours enlivened by a jab of citrus on the finish. Screwcap. 13° alc. **Rating** 87
To 2010 $16.95

Deetswood Wines   ★★★☆

Washpool Creek Road, Tenterfield, NSW 2372 **Region** New England
T (02) 6736 1322 **F** (02) 6736 1322 **www**.deetswoodwines.com.au **Open** Fri–Mon
10–5, or by appt
Winemaker Contract **Est.** 1996 **Cases** 1500
Deanne Eaton and Tim Condrick established their micro-vineyard in 1996, planting 2 ha of
semillon, chardonnay, pinot noir, shiraz, merlot and cabernet sauvignon. At the end of the 19th
century German immigrant Joe Nicoll planted vines and made wines for family use, and there
is still one vine surviving on the site today from the original plantings. The wines are normally
consistent both in quality and style, offering further proof that this is a very interesting area.

ŶŶŶŶ   **Semillon 2007** Taut, crisp, mineral-accented; clean; needs time. **Rating** 89
To 2013 $16

Deisen   ★★★★★

PO Box 61, Tanunda, SA 5352 **Region** Barossa Valley
T (08) 8563 2298 **F** (08) 8563 2298 **www**.deisen.com.au **Open** Not
Winemaker Sabine Deisen **Est.** 2001 **Cases** 1000
Deisen (owned by Sabine Deisen and Les Fensom) once again proves the old adage that
nothing succeeds like success. In the first year, 3.5 tonnes of grapes produced five barrels
of shiraz and two of grenache. Since that time, production has grown slowly but steadily
with bits and pieces of traditional winemaking equipment (small crushers, open tanks and
hand-plunging, all housed in a small tin shed, now extended to a slightly larger tin shed).
The number of wines made and the tiny quantities of some (20 dozen is not uncommon) is
staggering. The style of all the wines is remarkably similar: sweet and luscious fruit; soft, ripe
tannins; and a warmth from the alcohol (toned down in recent releases). Exports to the US.

♟♟♟♟♟ Topnotch Barossa Shiraz 2006 An abundant, voluptuous cascade of blackberry, plum and licorice fruit with perfectly balanced tannins and oak, the alcohol no issue whatsoever. Cork. 14.8° alc. **Rating** 94 **To** 2020 $50

♟♟♟♟♀ Barossa Shiraz 2004 Super-ripe, confit plum fruit aromas and flavours; a deliberate winemaking decision pushing the envelope to the limits, but will have great appeal to some. Cork. 15.5° alc. **Rating** 92 **To** 2020 $56
Barossa Cabernet Sauvignon 2006 A soft, medium- to full-bodied palate with appealing blackcurrant, cassis and mocha; fruit sweetness and gentle tannins are the marks of the label. Cork. 14.3° alc. **Rating** 92 **To** 2016 $43
Barossa Shiraz Cabernet Sauvignon 05/06 Full of ripe blackberry, blackcurrant, plum and prune fruit, oak a bystander; slightly callow and needs time; free-spirited winemaking. Cork. 14.5° alc. **Rating** 91 **To** 2016 $48
Winter Sun 04/05 As always, densely packed with fruit, but with a pleasing dry overall mouthfeel; does shorten fractionally on the finish; Shiraz/Mataro. Cork. 14.7° alc. **Rating** 91 **To** 2015 $49
Barossa GSM 2005 No question that this is a very good example of synergy of Grenache/Shiraz/Merlot, with good structure and powerful fruit flavour; some ripe tannin support. Screwcap. 14.2° alc. **Rating** 90 **To** 2014 $18
Barossa Mataro 2006 Medium- to full-bodied, 10% shiraz contributing to both flavour and structure; blackberry, chocolate and tobacco ripple through the palate, oak a servant to the cause. Cork. 14.6° alc. **Rating** 90 **To** 2015 $37

♟♟♟♟ Early Harvest Barossa Shiraz 2004 Some herbal aromas; extremely interesting wine; shows sweetness rather than early picking; certainly not green on the palate; may have a touch of residual sugar. Cork. 11.5° alc. **Rating** 89 **To** 2017 $29
Tim's Block Barossa Shiraz 2005 Rich and very ripe fruit, with some pruney/ jammy nuances; fine tannins provide a partial offset. Screwcap. 14.6° alc. **Rating** 89 **To** 2015 $20
A Little Barossa Grenache 2005 Very typical Barossa sweet meat/confiture grenache flavours, bolstered on the finish by 10% shiraz; great with Mediterranean food. Cork. 14.5° alc. **Rating** 89 **To** 2013 $26
Barossa Late Grenache 2005 No-holds-barred Barossa Valley style, but seems to have some degree of sweetness beyond that conferred by alcohol; I have to admit not my personal style. Cork. 15° alc. **Rating** 89 **To** 2014 $37
Barossa Riesling 2004 Glowing yellow-green; stacked full of flavour; very difficult to make such small quantities; the touch of residual sugar will help the wine age; 150 bottles. Screwcap. 11.9° alc. **Rating** 88 **To** 2012 $30

del Rios of Mt Anakie   ★★★★☆
2320 Ballan Road, Anakie, Vic 3221 **Region** Geelong
T (03) 9497 4644 **F** (03) 9499 9266 **www.**delrios.com.au **Open** W'ends 10–5
Winemaker Gus del Rio **Est.** 1996 **Cases** 5000
From a Spanish heritage, Gus del Rio established the 14-ha vineyard in 1996 on the slopes of Mt Anakie, northwest of Geelong (chardonnay, pinot noir, cabernet sauvignon, sauvignon blanc, shiraz, merlot and marsanne). The vines are hand-pruned, the fruit hand-picked and the wines are made onsite in the fully equipped winery, which includes a bottling and labelling line able to process over 150 tonnes.

♟♟♟♟♟ Cabernet Sauvignon 2002 Long and intense; achieving ripeness in this super-cool vintage is no mean feat; attractive cedar, chocolate and blackcurrant fruit merge with fine tannins. Screwcap. 14° alc. **Rating** 94 **To** 2013 $30

♟♟♟♟♀ Sauvignon Blanc 2007 Light- to medium-bodied; lemon, asparagus and gooseberry flavours, the finish just a fraction blurred. **Rating** 90 **To** 2009 $18

♟♟♟♟ Rose 2007 Fresh, bright pink; floral red fruits on the bouquet lead into a somewhat severe, bone-dry style made for drinking with summer seafood. **Rating** 87 **To** 2009 $16

Delamere

Bridport Road, Pipers Brook, Tas 7254 **Region** Northern Tasmania
T (03) 6382 7190 **F** (03) 6382 7250 **Open** 7 days 10–5
Winemaker Richard Richardson **Est.** 1983 **Cases** 2000
Richie Richardson produces elegant, rather light-bodied wines that have a strong following.
The Chardonnay has been most successful, a textured, complex, malolactic-influenced wine
with a great, creamy feel in the mouth.

♟♟♟♟♟ **Reserve Pinot Noir 2006** Bright, light red; fresh and lively, in a red fruit
spectrum; just a touch of forest and green acidity. **Rating** 90 **To** 2012 $35

Delatite

Stoneys Road, Mansfield, Vic 3722 **Region** Upper Goulburn
T (03) 5775 2922 **F** (03) 5775 2911 **www**.delatitewinery.com.au **Open** 7 days 10–5
Winemaker Jane Donat **Est.** 1982 **Cases** 20 000
With its sweeping views across to the snow-clad Alps, this is uncompromising cool-climate
viticulture, and the wines naturally reflect that. Light but intense Riesling and spicy Traminer
flower with a year or two in bottle, and in the warmer vintages the red wines achieve flavour
and mouthfeel. In spring 2002 David Ritchie (the viticulturist in the family) embarked on a
program to adopt biodynamics, commencing with the sauvignon blanc and gewurztraminer.
He says, 'It will take time for us to convert the vineyard and change our mindset and practices,
but I am fully convinced it will lead to healthier soil and vines.' The rating from the last edition
has been retained; almost all the '07 crop was lost to frost. Exports to Japan and Malaysia.

♟♟♟♟ **Polly Sparkling Gewurztraminer 2006** Bright green-straw; gewurztraminer
is more obvious on the scented lychee bouquet than the palate, which is more
lemony than spicy; nonetheless, a fresh sparkler. Crown. 12° alc. **Rating** 88
To 2009 $29

Derwent Estate

329 Lyell Highway, Granton, Tas 7070 **Region** Southern Tasmania
T (03) 6263 5802 **F** (03) 6263 5802 **www**.derwentestate.com.au **Open** Mon–Fri 10–4
summer, Sun 11–3 Dec–Jan, closed winter
Winemaker Winemaking Tasmania (Julian Alcorso) **Est.** 1993 **Cases** 1200
The Hanigan family established Derwent Estate as part of a diversification program for their
400-ha mixed farming property: 10 ha of vineyard have been planted, since 1993, to riesling,
pinot noir, chardonnay, cabernet sauvignon and pinot gris.

♟♟♟♟♟ **Pinot Noir 2006** Vivid red-purple; delicious plum, black cherry, very pure and
fine; balance finish, no green acid. Screwcap. **Rating** 94 **To** 2013 $28

♟♟♟♟♟ **Reserve Pinot Noir 2006** Abundant colour, and all of the depth of fruit which
the colour promises; a long finish with good balance, but deserves time. **Rating** 90
To 2013 $35
Cabernet Merlot 2006 Good colour; ripe and focused with a touch of cassis and
some violet; a little simple, but very well made. Screwcap. **Rating** 90 **To** 2014 $28

Deviation Road ★★★★★

Lobethal-Mount Torrens Road, Charleston, SA 5244 **Region** Adelaide Hills
T (08) 8389 4455 **F** (08) 8389 4407 **www**.deviationroad.com **Open** 7 days 11–5
Winemaker Kate Laurie, Hamish Laurie **Est.** 1999 **Cases** 1000
Deviation Road was created in 1998 by Hamish Laurie, great-great-grandson of Mary Laurie,
SA's first female winemaker. He initially joined with father Dr Chris Laurie in 1992 to help
build the Hillstowe Wines business; the brand was sold to Banksia Wines in 2001, but the
Laurie family retained the vineyard, which now supplies Deviation Road with its grapes.
Wife Kate Laurie joined the business in 2001, having studied winemaking and viticulture
in Champagne, then spending four years at her family's Stone Bridge winery in Manjimup.

All the wines except the Sangiovese (WA) and Riesling (other Adelaide Hills growers) come from the 16-ha family vineyards, but only account for a small portion of the annual grape production of those vineyards.

☗☗☗☗☗ **Reserve Adelaide Hills Shiraz 2005** Excellent texture and structure to the full-bodied palate, which is replete with blackberry, licorice, spice and pepper, the tannins fine, the oak well integrated. Screwcap. 15° alc. **Rating** 95 **To** 2020 $34
Reserve Adelaide Hills Chardonnay 2006 Minimal bottle development 18 months from vintage; lively, bright and crisp aromas, then tangy, lively grapefruit and nectarine on a long palate; perfect oak. Screwcap. 14° alc. **Rating** 94 **To** 2013 $38

☗☗☗☗☗ **Adelaide Hills Pinot Gris 2007** Distinct pear and lychee aromas, with a light sprinkle of spice; a lively palate with similar flavours, and a long, positive, dry finish. Screwcap. 13° alc. **Rating** 91 **To** 2009 $24

☗☗☗☗ **Adelaide Hills Sauvignon Blanc 2007** Has a somewhat subdued/faintly blurred varietal expression; a soft mix of passionfruit and stone fruit provides plenty to suck on. Screwcap. 13° alc. **Rating** 89 **To** 2009 $18

Devil's Lair   ★★★★★
Rocky Road, Forest Grove via Margaret River, WA 6285 **Region** Margaret River
T (08) 9757 7573 **F** (08) 9757 7533 **www.**devils-lair.com **Open** Not
Winemaker Stuart Pym, Charlotte Newton **Est.** 1981 **Cases** 220 000
Having rapidly carved out a high reputation for itself through a combination of clever packaging and impressive wine quality, Devil's Lair was acquired by Southcorp in 1996. The estate vineyards have been substantially increased since. An exceptionally successful business; production has increased from 40 000 to 220 000 cases. Exports to the UK, the US and other major markets.

☗☗☗☗☗ **Fifth Leg Chardonnay 2006** Sophisticated winemaking, quality grapes and Margaret River come together to make one of the best second-label wines in Australia; seamless white peach tinged with grapefruit and spicy oak. Stunning value. Screwcap. 13° alc. **Rating** 94 **To** 2013 $19.99
Margaret River Chardonnay 2006 Well-balanced and modulated melon, nectarine, white peach and grapefruit, plus quality French oak soars through the finish. Screwcap. 13.5° alc. **Rating** 94 **To** 2015 $44.95
Margaret River 2005 A medium-bodied palate with very good texture, structure, line and length; blackcurrant and black olive notes, with savoury tannins and integrated oak. Screwcap. 14° alc. **Rating** 94 **To** 2025 $60.95

☗☗☗☗☗ **Margaret River 2004** Medium-bodied; understated, classic blend of blackcurrant, earth and olive, with fine but persistent tannins; the length is good, but the wine needs to build a little flesh on the mid-palate; Cabernet Sauvignon/Merlot. Screwcap. 14° alc. **Rating** 91 **To** 2024 $52
Fifth Leg White 2007 A relatively neutral bouquet, but a lively fresh palate untrammelled by oak; gentle grassy notes and a hint of stone fruit from the chardonnay component. Screwcap. 13° alc. **Rating** 90 **To** 2009 $19.99
Fifth Leg Rose 2007 Bright and juicy red fruits with good flavour and a clean, fresh palate; a little grip gives the wine extra interest. Screwcap. 13.5° alc. **Rating** 90 **To** 2011 $20.95

☗☗☗☗ **Margaret River Sauvignon Blanc 2007** Plenty of weight, depth and structure, only the vintage taking the edge off the fruit expression, steering it towards Semillon in character. Screwcap. 13.5° alc. **Rating** 89 **To** 2010 $26.95

🍇 Dexter Wines

210 Foxeys Road, Merricks North, Vic 3926 (postal) **Region** Mornington Peninsula
T (03) 5989 7007 **F** (03) 5989 7009 **www**.dexterwines.com.au **Open** Not
Winemaker Tod Dexter **Est.** 600 **Cases** 2006

Tod Dexter was introduced to wine through a friendship between his parents and then leading Melbourne retailer Doug Crittenden. A skiing trip to the US indirectly led to Tod becoming an apprentice winemaker at Cakebread Cellars, a well-known Napa Valley winery, in 1979. After seven years he returned to Australia and the Mornington Peninsula, and began the establishment of a 7-ha vineyard planted to pinot noir and chardonnay. To keep the wolves from the door he became winemaker at Stonier, and the vineyard was leased to Stonier, the grapes always used in the Stonier Reserve range. Having left Stonier to become Yabby Lake winemaker, and spurred on by turning 50 in 2006 (and at the urging of friends), he and wife Debbie took the decision to establish the Dexter label.

Mornington Peninsula Chardonnay 2006 Very tightly wound and focused; intense melon, stone fruit and grapefruit are intertwined, the oak a bystander. Screwcap. 14° alc. **Rating** 92 **To** 2011

Mornington Peninsula Pinot Noir 2006 Light-bodied; savoury, spicy, brambly, stemmy notes surround the red fruits; a distinctive style, but an uncertain future. Screwcap. 14° alc. **Rating** 89 **To** 2011

di Lusso Wines

Eurunderee Lane, Mudgee, NSW 2850 **Region** Mudgee
T (02) 6373 3125 **F** (02) 6373 3128 **www**.dilusso.com.au **Open** 7 days 10–5
Winemaker Contract **Est.** 1998 **Cases** 5000

Rob Fairall and partner Luanne Hill have brought to fruition their vision to establish an Italian 'enoteca' operation, offering Italian varietal wines and foods. The plantings of 2.5 ha of barbera and 2 ha of sangiovese are supported by 0.5 ha each of nebbiolo, picolit, lagrein and aleatico. The estate also produces olives for olive oil and table olives, and the range of both wine and food will increase over the years. The decision to focus on Italian varieties has been a major success. No samples received; the rating is that of last year.

Di Stasio

Range Road, Coldstream, Vic 3770 **Region** Yarra Valley
T (03) 9525 3999 **F** (03) 9525 3815 **Open** By appt, or at Cafe Di Stasio, St Kilda
Winemaker Rob Dolan, Kate Goodman (Contract) **Est.** 1995 **Cases** 375

Famous Melbourne restaurateur Rinaldo (Ronnie) Di Stasio bought a virgin bushland 32-ha hillside block in the Yarra Valley, adjacent to the Warramate Flora and Fauna Reserve, in 1994. He has established 5.8 ha of vineyards, equally split between pinot noir and chardonnay, put in roads and dams, built a substantial house, and also an Allan Powell–designed Monastery, complete with art gallery and tree-filled courtyard sitting like a church on top of the hill. Production has never been large; the wines are sold through Cafe Di Stasio in St Kilda, a Melbourne icon. Exports to the UK.

Yarra Valley Pinot Noir 2006 Has dark fruits, with hints of stem and spice; a strongly structured savoury palate and finish. Screwcap. 13° alc. **Rating** 88 **To** 2011

Diamond Creek Estate   NR

Diamond Fields Road, Mittagong, NSW 2575 **Region** Southern Highlands
T (02) 4872 3311 **F** (02) 4872 3311 **www**.diamondcreekestate.com.au **Open** By appt
Winemaker Eddy Rossi **Est.** 1997 **Cases** NA

Helen Hale purchased Diamond Creek Estate in late 2002, by which time the chardonnay, sauvignon blanc, riesling, pinot noir and cabernet sauvignon planted in '97 by the prior owner had come into bearing. The vineyard is established at 680 m on rich basalt soil, the north-facing slope being relatively frost-free. Since Helen acquired the property, most of the grapes have been sold to Southern Highlands Winery, but small amounts have been retained for release under the Diamond Creek Estate label: these include Riesling, Sauvignon Blanc, Pinot Noir, Cabernet Sauvignon and a highly successful Noble Diamond Botrytis Chardonnay.

Diamond Island Wines   ★★★★

PO Box 56, Bicheno, Tas 7215 **Region** Northern Tasmania
T 0409 003 988 **Open** Not
Winemaker Winemaking Tasmania (Julian Alcorso) **Est.** 2002 **Cases** 450
Owner Derek Freeman has planted 2 ha of pinot noir, and is the personal full-time viticulturist, helped out during peak periods by a part-time employee. It may not seem much, but successfully growing pinot noir (or any other variety, for that matter) in Tasmania requires an enormous degree of attention to debudding, leaf plucking, wire raising and (in the winter months) pruning. Not surprisingly, Freeman says he has no plans to extend the vineyard at the moment. The wine is made by the immensely experienced Julian Alcorso and the early vintages are full of promise.

Pinot Noir 2005 Holding hue superbly; tight and firm, still to open up and reveal its full potential, which is very considerable. Screwcap. 14.5° alc. **Rating** 93 To 2012 $22

Pinot Noir 2006 Faintly blackish hue; a powerful wine, but seems to have been picked too late, with some shrivel/dead fruit characters. Screwcap. 14.5° alc. **Rating** 87 **To** 2010 $22

Diamond Valley Vineyards   ★★★★★

PO Box 5155, Wonga Park, Vic 3115 **Region** Yarra Valley
T (03) 9722 0840 **F** (03) 9722 2373 **www**.diamondvalley.com.au **Open** Not
Winemaker James Lance **Est.** 1976 **Cases** 7000
One of the Yarra Valley's finest producers of Pinot Noir and an early pacesetter for the variety, making wines of tremendous style and crystal-clear varietal character. They are not cabernet sauvignon lookalikes but true pinot noir, fragrant and intense. The Chardonnays show the same marriage of finesse and intensity, and the Cabernet family wines shine in the warmer vintages. In early 2005 the brand and wine stocks were acquired by Graeme Rathbone (of SpringLane), the Lances continuing to own the vineyard and winery, and make the wine. Exports to the UK.

Reserve Yarra Valley Pinot Noir 2006 Complex aromas, flavours and texture drive a palate with both depth and length; cherry, plum and oriental spices supported by quality French oak; long, lingering finish. Screwcap. 13° alc. **Rating** 95 To 2016 $60
Reserve Yarra Valley Chardonnay 2006 Fragrant nectarine and white peach fruit aromas plus barrel ferment notes lead through to a long palate with identical flavours, tied up with a bow of minerally acidity. Screwcap. 13.5° alc. **Rating** 94 To 2015 $32
Yarra Valley Shiraz Viognier 2005 Succulent and supple, with spice, licorice and tar notes woven through the blackberry fruits; lively finish, and punches above its price weight. Screwcap. 15° alc. **Rating** 94 To 2015 $23
Yarra Valley Shiraz Viognier 2006 Good mouthfeel and balance thanks to controlled alcohol; wild yeast and partial barrel fermentation very well judged, and allowed good varietal expression. Screwcap. 13° alc. **Rating** 94 **To** 2011 $24

Reserve Yarra Valley Shiraz 2005 While only a small percentage of viognier co-fermented, it has had marked effect, adding lift to the spice; however, the wine has fruit flavours which are just too ripe for comfort; not sure where it is headed. Screwcap. 15° alc. **Rating** 92 To 2014 $40
Yarra Valley Pinot Noir 2006 Light colour; stalky/savoury/spicy aromas, the palate down the same track, though with more pinot fruit showing; as ever, has good length. Screwcap. 13° alc. **Rating** 91 **To** 2012 $26

Yarra Valley Chardonnay 2006 Nectarine and melon fruit aromas and flavours in the driver's seat; an easy, smooth style. Screwcap. 13⁰ alc. **Rating** 90 **To** 2010 $23

ΥΥΥΥ **Yarra Valley Viognier 2006** Fresh blossom aromas; gentle fruit, overall lacking varietal intensity, though it is well balanced and has good texture. Screwcap. 13° alc. **Rating** 89 **To** 2009 $26

Diggers Bluff

PO Box 34, Tanunda, SA 5352 **Region** Barossa Valley
T 0419 825 437 **F** (08) 8563 1613 **www**.diggersbluff.com **Open** Not
Winemaker Timothy O'Callaghan **Est.** 1998 **Cases** 1250
Timothy O'Callaghan explains that his family crest is an Irish hound standing under an oak tree; the Diggers Bluff label features his faithful hound Digger, under a Mallee tree. He is a third-generation O'Callaghan winemaker, and – reading his newsletter – it's not too hard to guess who the second generation is represented by. Diggers Bluff has 2.5 ha of grenache, mataro, shiraz, cabernet sauvignon and alicante, all of it old vines. No samples received; the rating is that of last year.

DiGiorgio Family Wines

Riddoch Highway, Coonawarra, SA 5263 **Region** Coonawarra
T (08) 8736 3222 **F** (08) 8736 3233 **www**.digiorgio.com.au **Open** 7 days 10–5
Winemaker Peter Douglas **Est.** 1998 **Cases** 10 000
Stefano DiGiorgio emigrated from Abruzzi, Italy in 1952. Over the years, he and his family gradually expanded their holdings at Lucindale. In 1989 he began planting cabernet sauvignon (99 ha), chardonnay (10 ha), merlot (9 ha), shiraz (6 ha) and pinot noir (2 ha). In 2002 the family purchased the historic Rouge Homme winery, capable of crushing 10 000 tonnes of grapes a year, and its surrounding 13.5 ha of vines, from Southcorp. The enterprise is offering full winemaking services to vignerons in the Limestone Coast Zone. Exports to several major markets.

ΥΥΥΥΥ **Coonawarra Shiraz 2004** Oak dominates the bouquet, with red fruit and a suggestion of mint in the background; quite dark on the palate, and with a long, slightly savoury, finish. Cork. 14° alc. **Rating** 91 **To** 2020 $26
Coonawarra Cabernet Sauvignon 2004 Cassis and cedar aromas supported by well-handled oak; clean and varietal on the long and even finish. Cork. 14.5° alc. **Rating** 90 **To** 2016 $26

ΥΥΥΥ **Lucindale Cabernet Sauvignon 2004** Leafy cabernet aromas are supported by nice cassis flavour on a medium-bodied and balanced palate. Screwcap. 14° alc. **Rating** 88 **To** 2014 $20

Dindima Wines ★★★

Lot 22 Cargo Road, Orange, NSW 2800 **Region** Orange
T (02) 6365 3388 **F** (02) 6365 3096 **www**.dindima.com.au **Open** W'ends & public hols 10–5 or by appt
Winemaker James Bell **Est.** 2002 **Cases** 700
David Bell and family acquired the property known as Osmond Wines in 2002, renaming it Dindima Wines, with the first vintage under the new ownership made in '03 from the 4-ha plantings. It is a retirement occupation for Dave Bell and his wife, but both sons are becoming involved with grapegrowing and winemaking.

ΥΥΥΥ **Semillon 2005** A solid wine; not a lot of expression or movement in the mouth, but (cork permitting) should develop given time; neatly handled French oak. Cork. 12.5° alc. **Rating** 88 **To** 2010 $18

Dinny Goonan Family Estate **NR**

880 Winchelsea–Deans Marsh Road, Bambra, Vic 3241 **Region** Geelong
T 0438 408 420 **F** (03) 5288 7100 **www.**dinnygoonan.com.au **Open** 7 days Jan, w'ends
& public hols Nov–Apr
Winemaker Dinny Goonan **Est.** 2001 **Cases** 1000
The establishment of Dinny Goonan Family Estate dates back to the 1980s when Dinny and
Susan Goonan bought a 20-ha property near Bambra, in the hinterland of the Otway Coast.
Dinny had recently completed a viticulture diploma at CSU, and initially a wide range of
varieties were planted in what is now known as the Nursery block to establish those best
suited to the area. As these came into production Dinny headed back to CSU, where he
completed a wine science degree. In 2001 the decision was taken to focus on the production
of Shiraz and Riesling, with more extensive planting of these varieties. In '07 a 'sticky' block
was added.

Disaster Bay Wines ★★★

133 Oaklands Road, Pambula, NSW 2549 (postal) **Region** South Coast Zone
T (02) 6495 6869 **www.**disasterbaywines.com **Open** Not
Winemaker Dean O'Reilly, Andrew McEwen **Est.** 2000 **Cases** 300
Dean O'Reilly has a 10-year background in the distribution of fine table wines, culminating
in employment by Möet Hennessy Australia. He has accumulated the UK-based WSET
Intermediate and Advanced Certificates, completed various other programs and competitions,
and has been associate judge and judge at various Canberra district events. He has also travelled
through the wine regions of NZ, Champagne, Bordeaux, Chablis, Piedmont and Tuscany. The
wines are made at Kyeema with Andrew McEwen overseeing Dean's apprenticeship; the
grapes come from the 1-ha block owned by Dean adjacent to the Pambula River.

SS Ly-ee-Moon 1886 Semillon Sauvignon Blanc 2007 Very light-bodied;
clever winemaking using small-portion barrel ferment has made up for the
underlying lack of fruit flavour. Screwcap. 11.5° alc. **Rating** 87 **To** 2009

Doctor's Nose Wines ★★★

'Koorooba', Old Racecourse Road, Tenterfield, NSW 2372 **Region** New England
T (02) 6736 3113 **www.**doctorsnosewines.com.au **Open** By appt
Winemaker Mike Hayes (Contract) **Est.** 1997 **Cases** NA
Koorooba has been home to the Reid family since the 1860s, and when the decision was
taken in 1997 to establish a vineyard, three generations were involved: Max, Peter and Ben
Reid. Ben and Janice Reid have since developed the 3.6-ha vineyard planted to sauvignon
blanc, semillon, verdelho, grenache, shiraz, mataro, petit verdot and tempranillo. The slightly
quaint name comes from John Traill, Tenterfield's first doctor, whose nose was apparently
reminiscent of the dominant rocky mountain on the western horizon of the property.

Shiraz 2005 Good colour; bright, fresh, crisp; light- to medium-bodied; needs
more ripe fruit. **Rating** 88 **To** 2010 $17
Tempranillo 2006 Light-bodied; fresh red berry fruits; good length; not
extractive, nor overoaked. **Rating** 88 **To** 2011 $15

DogRidge Vineyard ★★★★

RSD 195 Bagshaws Road, McLaren Flat, SA 5171 **Region** McLaren Vale
T (08) 8383 0140 **F** (08) 8383 0430 **www.**dogridge.com.au **Open** By appt
Winemaker Dave Wright, Jen Wright, Fred Howard, Mike Brown (Consultant)
Est. 1993 **Cases** NA
Dave and Jen Wright had a combined background of dentistry, art and a CSU viticultural
degree when they moved from Adelaide to McLaren Flat to become vignerons. They
inherited vines planted in the early 1940s as a source for Chateau Reynella fortified wines,
and their viticultural empire now has 56 ha of vineyards, ranging from '01 plantings to some
of the oldest vines remaining in the immediate region today. At the McLaren Flat vineyards,

DogRidge has 60+-year-old shiraz, as well as 60-year-old grenache. Part of the grape production is retained, but most is sold to other leading wineries. Exports to the UK, the US, Canada, Singapore and NZ.

ΨΨΨΨΩ **MVP McLaren Vale Shiraz 2004** Good fruit, with strong chocolate married with dark fruits; fleshy and quite juicy on the long, fine finish. Screwcap. 15° alc. **Rating** 91 **To** 2015 $60

The Pup Shiraz 2005 The bouquet and entry to the mouth suggest a touch of reduction, but the back-palate and finish throw off those issues, with good brightness and intensity to the black fruits. Screwcap. 14° alc. **Rating** 90 **To** 2015 $18

Original Plantings McLaren Vale Cabernet Sauvignon 2004 Good fruit definition, with bright blackcurrant/cassis aromas, a hint of cedar, and a long, even palate on the varietal finish. Screwcap. 15° alc. **Rating** 90 **To** 2016 $50

ΨΨΨΨ **WV Chardonnay 2005** Attractive regional chardonnay, ripe, but not hot; flavours of honeydew and peach supported by citrussy acidity and subtle oak. Screwcap. 14° alc. **Rating** 89 **To** 2012 $22

MVP McLaren Vale Shiraz 2003 A tarry tannic and savoury wine with dark fruits as well as a hint of leather and fruitcake. Screwcap. 14° alc. **Rating** 89 **To** 2013 $60

Cadenzia McLaren Vale Grenache 2005 Quite fresh fruits, with good concentration and depth, and some earthy complexity. Screwcap. 14° alc. **Rating** 89 **To** 2014 $21.95

Reserve McLaren Vale Petit Verdot 2005 Good flavour, with some complex sappy aromas, plenty of fragrance and good acid on the vibrant finish. Screwcap. 14° alc. **Rating** 89 **To** 2012 $30

The Pup Sauvignon Blanc 2007 Attractive tropical fruit aromas and flavours, assisted by good acidity, but just a touch short. Screwcap. 11° alc. **Rating** 88 **To** 2009 $18

Original Plantings McLaren Vale Shiraz 2004 A very ripe style, showing a little pruney character; plenty of flavour, but lacks freshness on the finish. Screwcap. 15° alc. **Rating** 88 **To** 2014 $50

Digs Vineyard McLaren Vale Cabernet Sauvignon 2004 A strong palate perhaps lacking a little varietal definition, but has good flavour and brightness on the finish. Screwcap. 14° alc. **Rating** 88 **To** 2014 $30

The Pup Chardonnay 2006 Yellow-green; plenty of honest varietal fruit in a peach spectrum; well balanced. Screwcap. 13.5° alc. **Rating** 87 **To** 2011 $18

MVP McLaren Vale Petit Verdot 2005 Has plenty of oak and some bright red and black fruits beneath, but is very tannic, and just a little short. Will time help? Screwcap. 15° alc. **Rating** 87 **To** 2014 $60

DogRock Winery ★★★★☆

114 De Graves Road, Crowlands, Vic 3377 **Region** Pyrenees
T (03) 5354 9201 www.dogrock.com.au **Open** From October 2006 w'ends 11–5
Winemaker Allen Hart **Est.** 1999 **Cases** 200
This is the micro-venture (but with inbuilt future growth to something slightly larger) of Allen (winemaker) and Andrea (viticulturist) Hart. Having purchased the property in 1998, planting of 6.4 ha of riesling, chardonnay, shiraz, tempranillo and grenache began in 2000. Given Allen Hart's position as research scientist/winemaker with Foster's Wine Estates, the attitude taken to winemaking is utterly unexpected. The estate-grown wines are made in an ultra low-tech fashion, without gas cover or filtration. The one concession to technology, say the Harts, is that 'all wine will be sealed with a screwcap and no DogRock wine will ever be released under natural cork bark'.

ΨΨΨΨΩ **Pyrenees Shiraz 2006** A vibrant, cool wine, with lots of spice, blueberry and blackberry; supple and fine on the finish. Screwcap. 13.5° alc. **Rating** 93 **To** 2016 $25

Pedro's Pyrenees Sparkling Red 2006 Very good fruit base, neither sweet nor oaked; an attractive array of black cherry, mulberry, blackberry and spicy fruits on the palate; will develop excellently; Tempranillo (50%)/Shiraz (40%)/Cabernet Sauvignon (10%). Crown. 13.5° alc. **Rating** 92 **To** 2014 $29

Pyrenees Riesling 2007 A subdued bouquet, but the wine opens up progressively on the palate, with sweet lime juice flavours; has texture and richness. Screwcap. 12° alc. **Rating** 90 **To** 2012 $17

Pyrenees Shiraz 2007 Vibrant hue; a light- to medium-bodied mix of red and black fruits, with a strong line of spicy notes; silky texture. **Rating** 90 **To** 2013

Domain Barossa

25 Murray Street, Tanunda, SA 5352 **Region** Barossa Valley
T (08) 8563 2170 **F** (08) 8563 2164 **www**.domainbarossa.com **Open** 7 days 11–6.30
Winemaker Todd Riethmuller **Est.** 2002 **Cases** 2000

Todd Riethmuller and family are long-term residents of the Barossa Valley, and have the inside running, as it were, when it comes to buying grapes from local growers. Thus they have been able to dispense with the expensive and often frustrating business of having their own winery, yet can make wines of exceptional quality.

Reserve Black Tongue Shiraz 2006 Obvious oak, but also much more compelling dark fruits on offer; a big wine, but quite supple on the finish, with ample tannins. Quite a journey ahead (and higher points). Screwcap. 14.5° alc. **Rating** 93 **To** 2025 $34

Black Tongue Shiraz 2006 Deep garnet; good concentration, flavour and depth of fruit on the finish, but a little one-dimensional. Screwcap. 14.5° alc. **Rating** 88 **To** 2016 $19

Domain Day

24 Queen Street, Williamstown, SA 5351 **Region** Barossa Valley
T (08) 8524 6224 **F** (08) 8524 6229 **www**.domaindaywines.com **Open** By appt
Winemaker Robin Day **Est.** 2000 **Cases** NA

This is a classic case of an old dog learning new tricks, and doing so with panache. Robin Day had a long and distinguished career as winemaker, chief winemaker, then technical director of Orlando; he participated in the management buy-out, and profited substantially from the on-sale to Pernod Ricard. He hastened slowly with the establishment of Domain Day, but there is nothing conservative about his approach in his 15-ha vineyard at Mt Crawford, high in the hills (at 450 m) of the southeastern extremity of the Barossa Valley, two sides of the vineyard bordering the Eden Valley. While the mainstream varieties are merlot, pinot noir and riesling, he has trawled Italy, France and Georgia for the other varieties: viognier, sangiovese, saperavi, lagrein, garganega and sagrantino. Robin Day says, 'Years of writing descriptions for back labels have left me convinced that this energy is more gainfully employed in growing grapes and making wine.' No samples received; the rating is that of last year.

Domaine A

Tee Tree Road, Campania, Tas 7026 **Region** Southern Tasmania
T (03) 6260 4174 **F** (03) 6260 4390 **www**.domaine-a.com.au **Open** Mon–Fri 9–4, w'ends by appt
Winemaker Peter Althaus **Est.** 1973 **Cases** 5000

The striking black label of the premium Domaine A wine, dominated by the single, multicoloured 'A', signified the change of ownership from George Park to Swiss businessman Peter Althaus many years ago. The wines are made without compromise, and reflect the low yields from the immaculately tended vineyards. They represent aspects of both Old World and New World philosophies, techniques and styles. Exports to the UK, Denmark, Switzerland, Germany, France, Belgium, Canada, NZ, China, Japan and Singapore.

♥♥♥♥♥ **Lady A Sauvignon Blanc 2005** A serious wine; extremely complex, with no signs of going vegetal; perfect oak and fruit integration and balance; long and rich. Cork. 13.5° alc. **Rating** 96 **To** 2012 $35

♥♥♥♥♀ **Stoney Vineyard Sauvignon Blanc 2007** Complex texture and structure; herb and grass, with touches of gooseberry and lychee; a rich back-palate. Diam. 13.5° alc. **Rating** 91 **To** 2010 $35

♥♥♥♥ **Stoney Vineyard Pinot Noir 2005** Bright and clear, but quite developed; complex foresty/savoury secondary fruit characters throughout. **Rating** 89 **To** 2010 $35

Domaine Chandon

Green Point, Maroondah Highway, Coldstream, Vic 3770 **Region** Yarra Valley
T (03) 9738 9200 **F** (03) 9738 9201 www.chandon.com.au **Open** 7 days 10.30–4.30
Winemaker Dr Tony Jordan, Matt Steel, Glen Thompson, Andy Santarossa, Adam Keath
Est. 1986 **Cases** 120 000
Wholly owned by Möet et Chandon, and one of the two most important wine facilities in the Yarra Valley, the tasting room has a national and international reputation, having won a number of major tourism awards in recent years. The sparkling wine product range has evolved, and there has been increasing emphasis placed on the table wines. The return of Dr Tony Jordan, the first CEO of Domaine Chandon, has further strengthened both the focus and quality of the brand. As part of a worldwide brand reorganisation, Green Point has been dropped for future releases, and Chandon substituted as brand for both table and sparkling wines. Exports to all major markets.

♥♥♥♥♥ **Green Point Reserve Yarra Valley Chardonnay 2005** Fine and elegant; pure Yarra Valley line and length; relatively low alcohol refines the fruit, and oak doesn't intrude; modern, sotto voce style. Screwcap. 13° alc. **Rating** 95 **To** 2014 $43
Green Point Shiraz 2005 Aromatic spicy red and black fruits lead into an attractive, medium-bodied but long palate, with delicious red fruit flavour, polished tannins and French oak. Heathcote. Screwcap. **Rating** 95 **To** 2025 $31
Green Point Reserve Yarra Valley Shiraz 2005 Bright purple hue; a lifted and highly aromatic wine, with lots of spice permeating the generous palate of red and black fruits; very long, fine and quite silky with ample fruit and a vivacious finish. Screwcap. 14.5° alc. **Rating** 95 **To** 2015 $49
Yarra Valley Vintage Brut 2004 Pale straw, with flicks of green; has ripe, but not heavy, stone fruit with a creamy texture and long finish, which is delicate and fresh; Pinot Noir/Chardonnay/Pinot Meunier; 30 base wines; 30 months; lees contact. Cork. 12.5° alc. **Rating** 95 **To** 2009 $39
Brut Rose Vintage 2004 Pale, clear pink; no doubting the pinot influence, both from added pinot wine and from base components, yet exceptionally delicate and fresh; truly lovely rose. Cork. 12.5° alc. **Rating** 95 **To** 2009 $39
Z*D Vintage Brut 2004 Brilliant green-yellow, with massive mousse; carries the lack of dosage with nonchalant ease, naturally driven by stone fruit and citrus; addictive style. Crown seal. 12.5° alc. **Rating** 94 **To** 2009 $39
Tasmanian Cuvee 2004 A particularly potent and powerful wine, with great richness to the palate; brioche and toast nuances throughout, and a red fruit flavour lift on the finish; Pinot Noir (57%)/Chardonnay (43%); Coal River Valley; 30 months' lees. Cork. 12.5° alc. **Rating** 94 **To** 2009 $39

♥♥♥♥♀ **Brut Rose Non Vintage NV** Bright strawberry-pink; abundant fruit aromas and flavours, with a mix of stone fruit and strawberry; good length and expected balance; Chardonnay/Pinot Noir and a small amount of pinot noir red wine; 18 months' yeast lees. Cork. 12.5° alc. **Rating** 93 **To** 2009 $30
Green Point Yarra Valley Chardonnay 2005 French oak is obvious on both the bouquet and palate; however, the length of the citrus/stone fruit/melon flavours prevail on the finish. Screwcap. 13° alc. **Rating** 93 **To** 2015 $26

Green Point Yarra Valley Chardonnay 2006 Quite tightly wound, with mineral, white pear and a hint of citrus; good concentration, length and complexity. Screwcap. 13° alc. **Rating** 91 **To** 2012 $26

Green Point Pinot Noir Rose 2007 Aromatic strawberry fruit on the bouquet, with spicy elements running through to the bone-dry finish; for classicists. Screwcap. 12.5° alc. **Rating** 90 **To** 2009 $22

ΨΨΨΨ **Green Point Sauvignon Blanc 2007** Has ample texture, substance and weight, partly courtesy of some barrel fermentation in old oak; dry herb and grass flavours; good length. Screwcap. 12° alc. **Rating** 89 **To** 2010 $22

Domaine Epis ★★★★★

812 Black Forest Drive, Woodend, Vic 3442 **Region** Macedon Ranges
T (03) 5427 1204 **F** (03) 5427 1204 **Open** By appt
Winemaker Stuart Anderson **Est.** 1990 **Cases** NA
Three legends are involved in the Domaine Epis and Epis & Williams wines, two of them in their own lifetime. They are long-term Essendon guru and former player Alec Epis, who owns the two quite separate vineyards and brands; Stuart Anderson, who directs winemaking, with Alec doing all the hard work; and the late Laurie Williams, the father of viticulture in the Macedon region and the man who established the Flynn & Williams vineyard in 1976. Alec Epis purchased that vineyard from Laurie Williams in 1999, and as a mark of respect (and with Laurie Williams' approval) continued to use his name in conjunction with his own. The Cabernet Sauvignon comes from this vineyard, the Chardonnay and Pinot Noir from the vineyard at Woodend, where a small winery was built in 2002.

ΨΨΨΨΨ **Macedon Ranges Chardonnay 2006** Rich, textured and complex, with creamy/figgy/nutty characters throughout the palate and bouquet; a powerful, long finish; extraordinary depth for a wine of this alcohol level. Diam. 12.9° alc. **Rating** 94 **To** 2013 $40
The Williams Vineyard 2006 Cassis and blackcurrant, with no green characters despite the relatively low alcohol; a totally delicious medium-bodied wine, with excellent length; Cabernet Sauvignon/Merlot. Cork. 12.9° alc. **Rating** 94 **To** 2016 $35

ΨΨΨΨΨ **Macedon Ranges Pinot Noir 2006** Excellent clarity and limpidity; a classically restrained style with sous bois/savoury undertones to the plum and spice fruit. Diam. 12.9° alc. **Rating** 93 **To** 2014 $60

Domaines Tatiarra ★★★★★

8 Dumblane Street, North Balwyn, Vic 3133 (postal) **Region** Heathcote
T 0411 240 815 **F** (03) 9822 4108 **www.**cambrianshiraz.com **Open** Not
Winemaker Ben Riggs **Est.** 1991 **Cases** 2000
Domaines Tatiarra Limited is an unlisted public company, its core asset being a 60-ha property of Cambrian earth identified and developed by Bill Hepburn, who sold the project to the company in 1991. It will produce only one varietal wine: Shiraz. The majority of the wine will come from the Tatiarra (an Aboriginal word meaning 'beautiful country') property, but the Trademark Shiraz is an equal blend of McLaren Vale and Heathcote wine. The wines are made at the Pettavel Winery in Geelong, with Ben Riggs commuting between McLaren Vale and the winery as required. No new samples received; the rating is that of last year.

Dominic Versace Wines ★★★★☆

Lot 258 Heaslip Road, MacDonald Park, SA 5121 **Region** Adelaide Plains
T (08) 8379 7132 **F** (08) 8338 0979 **www.**dominicversace.com.au **Open** By appt
Winemaker Dominic Versace, Armando Verdiglione **Est.** 2000 **Cases** 3000
Dominic Versace and brother-in-law Armando Verdiglione have a long association with wine, through their families in Italy and in Australia since 1980. In that year Dominic Versace planted 4.5 ha of shiraz, grenache and sangiovese (one of the earliest such plantings in Australia),

selling the grapes until 1999. In 2000 the pair decided to pool their experience and resources, using the near-organically grown grapes from the Versace vineyard, and deliberately rustic winemaking techniques. Exports to Japan, South Korea, China, Indonesia and Singapore.

ŸŸŸŸŸ **Reserve McLaren Vale Shiraz 2006** Healthy bright colour; excellent medium-bodied flavours and texture; supple plum and spice, with just an echo of dark chocolate; has considerable finesse and length; can't be faulted. Cork. 14.5° alc. **Rating** 94 **To** 2020 $50

ŸŸŸŸŸ **Premium McLaren Vale Sparkling Shiraz NV** As often, Dominic Versace surprises; brooding black fruits with unmistakable dark chocolate are left to speak without the usual sugar coating. Serious wine which will age well; unfortunately no vintage or tirage details. Cork. 13.5° alc. **Rating** 92 **To** 2012 $28
Bel Moscato NV This is a really clever wine, much more delicious than normal moscato; ginger, lemon and mandarin; perfectly judged sweetness, more fruit than residual sugar. Cork. 11.5° alc. **Rating** 90 **To** 2009 $20

ŸŸŸŸ **Reserve McLaren Vale Cabernet Sauvignon 2006** The fruit flavour and vanillin oak are too sweet for high-quality cabernet, though the total flavour is more than adequate. Cork. 14.5° alc. **Rating** 88 **To** 2014 $60
Reserve McLaren Vale Unwooded Chardonnay 2007 Reserve unwooded is a vinous oxymoron in both theory and (in this case) reality; a pleasant, generously flavoured drink now white. Screwcap. 13.5° alc. **Rating** 87 **To** 2009 $22
Rossino Adelaide Plains Rose 2007 Bright pink; lively fresh strawberry and red cherry fruit; crisp, clean, dry finish. Screwcap. 11.8° alc. **Rating** 87 **To** 2009 $15

Dominique Portet ★★★★★

870–872 Maroondah Highway, Coldstream, Vic 3770 **Region** Yarra Valley
T (03) 5962 5760 **F** (03) 5962 4938 **www**.dominiqueportet.com **Open** 7 days 10–5
Winemaker Dominique Portet, Scott Baker **Est.** 2000 **Cases** 12 000
Dominique Portet was bred in the purple. He spent his early years at Chateau Lafite (where his father was regisseur) and was one of the very first Flying Winemakers, commuting to Clos du Val in the Napa Valley where his brother is winemaker. Since 1976 he has lived in Australia, spending more than 20 years as managing director of Taltarni, and also developing the Clover Hill Vineyard in Tasmania. After retiring from Taltarni, he moved to the Yarra Valley, a region he had been closely observing since the mid-1980s. In 2001 he found the site he had long looked for, and in a twinkling of an eye built his winery and cellar door, and planted a quixotic mix of viognier, sauvignon blanc and merlot next to the winery; he also undertakes contract winemaking for others. Exports to the UK, the US and other major markets.

ŸŸŸŸŸ **Heathcote Shiraz 2005** Full-bodied; abundant blackberry fruit with touches of bitter chocolate and licorice; ripe tannins and good oak; carries the alcohol without trouble; high-quality cork. 15° alc. **Rating** 94 **To** 2020 $45
Yarra Valley Brut Rose LD NV A totally delicious sparkling wine, bursting with fresh strawberry, cherry and rose petals on a beautifully balanced palate; Pinot Noir/Chardonnay. Cork. 13° alc. **Rating** 94 **To** 2009 $24

ŸŸŸŸŸ **Yarra Valley Sauvignon Blanc 2007** A full-bodied and structured wine with more than a passing nod to white Bordeaux; 15% fermentation in new French oak and lees contact adds weight, and demands food. Screwcap. 13.5° alc. **Rating** 90 **To** 2011 $24
Fontaine Yarra Valley Rose 2007 Has character, with spicy notes to red fruit flavours; light-bodied, of course, but has length and balance; ideal tapas style. Screwcap. 13.5° alc. **Rating** 90 **To** 2009 $20

ŸŸŸŸ **Heathcote Cabernet Sauvignon 2005** Clear-cut varietal character in a ripe spectrum, but persistent and somewhat dry tannins need to resolve and soften. Should improve markedly with extended cellaring. Quality cork. 15° alc. **Rating** 89 **To** 2015 $42

Donaghadee Wines

65 Burrows Road, Lethbridge, Vic 3332 (postal) **Region** Geelong
T (03) 5281 7364 **www**.donaghadeewines.com.au **Open** Not
Winemaker David Warnock **Est.** 2000 **Cases** 200
David and Pam Warnock planted a 0.25-ha plot of shiraz, cabernet and merlot as a hobby,
but with retirement around the corner, and encouragement from their nephew (also a
winemaker), have increased the plantings to 1 ha of chardonnay and 1 ha of shiraz.

ΨΨΨΨΩ **Lighthouse Shiraz 2005** Ripe, dense, blackberry, spice and licorice; very good
tannin and oak management. **Rating** 93 **To** 2016 $25

ΨΨΨΨ **Shiraz 2005** Has fair varietal flavour and good length, though some green notes
do intrude. **Rating** 87 **To** 2011 $20

Dos Rios

PO Box 343, Nyah, Vic 3594 **Region** Swan Hill
T (03) 5030 3005 **F** (03) 5030 3006 **www**.dosrios.com.au **Open** Fri–Mon 9–9
Winemaker Cobaw Ridge (Alan Cooper) **Est.** 2003 **Cases** 1000
Bruce Hall entered the wine business as a small contract grower for McGuigan Simeon
Wines. From this point on, the story goes in reverse: instead of McGuigan Simeon saying it
no longer required the grapes, it purchased the vineyard outright in 2003. In the meantime,
Hall had hand-picked the grapes left at the end of the rows after the mechanical harvester
had passed through, and had the wines made by Alan Cooper of Cobaw Ridge. In 2004 he
purchased a small property northwest of Swan Hill with plantings of 20-year-old shiraz, which
has been extended by small areas of viognier, tempranillo, durif and merlot. Exports to Spain
and Japan.

ΨΨΨΨ **Swan Hill Viognier 2007** Hand-harvested, first crop fruit, whole bunch-pressed;
has nuances of apricot and peach, and the finish is not phenolic. Screwcap. 13° alc.
Rating 87 **To** 2009 $15

Dowie Doole

Cnr McMurtrie Road/Main Road, McLaren Vale, SA 5171 **Region** McLaren Vale
T (08) 8323 8875 **F** (08) 8323 8895 **www**.dowiedoole.com **Open** 7 days 10–5
Winemaker Brian Light (Contract) **Est.** 1996 **Cases** 17 500
Dowie Doole has three vineyards owned by individual partners: California Road in McLaren
Vale, with 25 ha; the so-called Home Block in the Adelaide Hills, with 4.6 ha (sauvignon
blanc); and Tintookie at Blewitt Springs, with 12 ha. Steadily increasing amounts of the grapes
are used for the Dowie Doole wines. Exports to the UK, the US and other major markets.

ΨΨΨΨΨ **McLaren Vale Cabernet Sauvignon 2005** Excellent colour; attractive
medium-bodied palate, with good varietal expression courtesy of the cassis
and blackcurrant fruit; supple and smooth, good length. Diam. 14° alc. **Rating** 94
To 2020 $23

ΨΨΨΨ **McLaren Vale Shiraz 2005** A powerful wine, with quite pervasive tannins
needing to soften and settle down; blackberry with spice and dark chocolate
nuances. Diam. 14.5° alc. **Rating** 89 **To** 2016 $25
McLaren Vale Merlot 2006 A soft, rounded, medium-bodied palate with
appropriate weight and extract; red fruits just a little bland; easy-drinking style.
Diam. 14.5° alc. **Rating** 89 **To** 2011 $23
Hooley Dooley White 2007 A United Nations assemblage of Sauvignon
Blanc/Semillon/Viognier from McLaren Vale/Adelaide Hills just gets over the line.
Screwcap. **Rating** 87 **To** 2010 $15

Downing Estate Vineyard   ★★★★

19 Drummonds Lane, Heathcote, Vic 3523 **Region** Heathcote
T (03) 5433 3387 **F** (03) 5433 3389 **www**.downingestate.com.au **Open** W'ends 11.30–4.30
or by appt
Winemaker Don Lewis **Est.** 1994 **Cases** 1000
Bob and Joy Downing purchased 24 ha of undulating land in 1994, and have since established
a 9.5-ha dry-grown vineyard planted to shiraz (75%), cabernet sauvignon and merlot. At any
one time, a number of vintages of each wine are available for sale. Exports to the UK and
the US.

ŶŶŶŶŶ **Heathcote Cabernet Sauvignon 2005** Full-bodied, with ripe but not jammy
blackcurrant fruit balanced by quite savoury/earthy tannins; has good length and
development potential. Screwcap. 15° alc. **Rating** 90 **To** 2020 $39

ŶŶŶŶ **Heathcote Merlot 2005** Strong colour; very powerful wine, way into cabernet
sauvignon territory; lush blackcurrant fruit will appeal to some as is, and to others
with extended cellaring. Screwcap. 14° alc. **Rating** 89 **To** 2020 $39
Heathcote Shiraz 2005 Slightly hazy colour; no shortage of ripe fruit, but the
texture mirrors the colour; lacking focus. Screwcap. 15° alc. **Rating** 87 **To** 2013 $39

Drayton's Family Wines   ★★★★☆

Oakey Creek Road, Cessnock, NSW 2321 **Region** Lower Hunter Valley
T (02) 4998 7513 **F** (02) 4998 7743 **www**.draytonswines.com.au **Open** Mon–Fri 8–5,
w'ends & public hols 10–5
Winemaker Max Drayton, John Drayton, William Rickard-Bell **Est.** 1853 **Cases** 90 000
This long-established, substantial but low-profile Hunter Valley producer gained national
headlines on 17 Jan 2007 for all the wrong reasons when winemaker Trevor Drayton was
killed in an explosion at the winery, believed to be caused by sparks from welding being
carried out, igniting ethanol in an adjoining room. It was a horrific example of third time
unlucky, following the 1979 death of Barry Drayton, overcome by chlorine in a tank he was
cleaning, and that of Reg and Pam Drayton in the 1994 Seaview air disaster on the way to
Lord Howe Island. Hopefully, the extended Drayton family will regroup, and continue this
quintessential Hunter winery. In the meantime, the entire Hunter Valley wine industry has
joined forces to support the family and winemaking activities. Exports to NZ, the US, Japan,
Singapore, Taiwan, Samoa and Switzerland.

ŶŶŶŶŶ **Susanne Semillon 2005** Rich, ripe flavours verging on stone fruit; has depth
and texture; 100-year-old vines. Deserves better than a cork. 11.5° alc. **Rating** 90
To 2009 $35

ŶŶŶŶ **Hunter Valley Semillon 2007** Firm and long; a minerally backbone with
a touch of grass; classic style; should develop. Screwcap. 11.5° alc. **Rating** 89
To 2014 $16.50
Vineyard Reserve Pokolbin Shiraz 2003 A strongly regional, earthy style;
the dark fruits have a deceptive ability to age; plenty of presence and good tannin
support. Cork. 13° alc. **Rating** 89 **To** 2018 $25
Vineyard Reserve Pokolbin Semillon 2004 The cork scalping is obvious,
stripping aroma and flavour; some minerally acidity. Soggy cork. 10.5° alc.
Rating 87 **To** 2009 $25

Driftwood Estate   ★★★★★

3314 Caves Road, Wilyabrup, WA 6282 **Region** Margaret River
T (08) 9755 6323 **F** (08) 9755 6343 **www**.driftwood-winery.com.au **Open** 7 days 10–5
Winemaker Andrew Spencer-Wright, Hugh Warren **Est.** 1989 **Cases** 25 000
Driftwood Estate is a well-established landmark on the Margaret River scene. Quite apart
from offering a brasserie restaurant capable of seating 200 people (open seven days for
lunch and dinner) and a mock Greek open-air theatre, its wines feature striking and stylish

packaging (even if strongly reminiscent of that of Devil's Lair) and opulent flavours. The winery architecture is, it must be said, opulent rather than stylish. Exports to the UK, the US and Singapore.

ŸŸŸŸŸ **Chardonnay 2006** Great colour; a highly aromatic fusion of fruit and barrel ferment; an elegant yet intense palate; excellent line and length, flowing beautifully through the long finish. **Rating** 95 To 2020
Margaret River Sauvignon Blanc Semillon 2007 Has excellent precision and drive on a long and intense palate offering ripe citrus, grass and herb flavours; a surprise packet. Screwcap. 13.5° alc. **Rating** 94 To 2011 $15.90

ŸŸŸŸŸ **Margaret River Sauvignon Blanc Semillon 2006** A highly perfumed and lifted bouquet, with a fresh herb, grass and lemon palate; clean, vibrant finish. **Rating** 93 To 2014
Margaret River Shiraz Cabernet 2005 Essency dark fruits and serious structure are the key; tannic, but with plenty of fruit in support; it should age very gracefully; good value. Screwcap. 13° alc. **Rating** 91 To 2018 $15.90
Margaret River Shiraz 2004 Brightly coloured and brightly fruited, with a solid core of spicy, savoury fruit on the mid-palate. Cork. 14.5° alc. **Rating** 90 To 2016 $23.90

ŸŸŸŸ **Margaret River Classic White 2007** A lively, light-bodied and zesty mix of stone fruit, citrus, herb and mineral; dry finish. Screwcap. 13° alc. **Rating** 89 To 2010 $15
Reserve Margaret River Shiraz 2000 Showing some development, and drying out a little; good flavour, and displays regional savoury/spicy character. Cork. 14.5° alc. **Rating** 89 To 2010 $50
Margaret River Semillon 2005 Strong varietal aromas of dried and fresh-cut grass; good texture, but seems too hard. Screwcap. 13° alc. **Rating** 87 To 2010 $15.90
Margaret River Cane Cut Semillon 2006 Fresh and clean, barely more than off-dry; for slices of fresh fruit on a summer's day. Screwcap. 11.5° alc. **Rating** 87 To 2009 $19

Dromana Estate ★★★★☆

555 Old Moorooduc Road, Tuerong, Vic 3933 **Region** Mornington Peninsula
T (03) 5974 4400 **F** (03) 5974 1155 **www**.dromanaestate.com.au **Open** Wed–Sun 11–5, 7 days in summer
Winemaker Duncan Buchanan **Est.** 1982 **Cases** 30 000
Since it was established by Garry Crittenden (who exited some years ago), Dromana Estate has always been near or at the cutting edge, both in marketing terms and in terms of development of new varietals, most obviously the Italian range under the 'i' label. The business is now majority-owned by investors; the capital provided has resulted in the Yarra Valley Hills and Mornington Estate wines coming under the Dromana Estate umbrella. Exports to the UK, Canada, Korea, Japan, Singapore and Hong Kong.

ŸŸŸŸŸ **Mornington Peninsula Chardonnay 2005** Developing slowly; elegant and fine, with no hint of elevated alcohol on the long palate, driven by citrus and stone fruit; 18 months in French oak also dealt with easily by the fruit. Screwcap. 14.5° alc. **Rating** 94 To 2012 $33

ŸŸŸŸŸ **Mornington Estate Shiraz Viognier 2005** A very lively, long, incisive and expressive palate, with a pleasing tension between sweet and more savoury/spicy fruit elements. Ready now. Screwcap. 14° alc. **Rating** 93 To 2010 $22

ŸŸŸŸ **Mornington Peninsula Chardonnay 2004** Bottle-developed depth to the ripe nectarine and yellow peach fruit mix; just a little too soft. Screwcap. 14.5° alc. **Rating** 89 To 2009 $33
Mornington Estate Pinot Gris 2007 A fragrant and lively bouquet; a clever play between subliminal sweetness and balancing acidity on the palate, though not much concentration. Screwcap. 13.5° alc. **Rating** 89 To 2009 $20

Mornington Peninsula Pinot Noir 2006 Light-bodied, with spicy overtones to the cherry and strawberry fruit; good length, but not much depth. Screwcap. 13.5° alc. **Rating** 89 **To** 2012 $33

Gary Crittenden i Arneis 2006 Clean, crisp and well made, but at the end of the day it is hard to find positive varietal descriptors; of largely academic interest. Screwcap. 13.5° alc. **Rating** 87 **To** 2009 $20

Drummonds Corrina Vineyard   NR

85 Wintles Road, Leongatha South, Vic 3953 **Region** Gippsland
T (03) 5664 3317 **Open** W'ends 12.30–4.30
Winemaker Bass Phillip **Est.** 1983 **Cases** NA
The Drummond family has 3 ha of vines (1 ha each of pinot noir and sauvignon blanc, and 0.5 ha each of cabernet sauvignon and merlot) which were slowly established without the aid of irrigation. The viticultural methods are those practised by Phillip Jones, who makes the wines for Drummonds: north–south row orientation, leaf plucking on the east side of the rows, low yields, and all fruit picked by hand. Similarly restrained winemaking methods (no pumping, no filters and low SO_2) follow in the winery.

 # Dryridge Estate

The Six Foot Track, Megalong Valley, NSW 2785 **Region** Central Ranges Zone
T (02) 4787 5625 **F** (02) 4787 5626 **www.**dryridge.com.au **Open** Sun & public hols 10.30–3
Winemaker Madrez Wine Services (Chris Derrez, Lucy Maddox) **Est.** 2000 **Cases** NFP
Bob and Barbara Tyrrell (no relation to Tyrrell's of the Hunter Valley) have pioneered commercial viticulture in the Megalong Valley adjacent to the Blue Mountains National Park. They have 1.8 ha of riesling, 1.1 ha of shiraz and 0.9 ha of cabernet sauvignon, and a further 0.9 ha to be planted in due course. The vines are set on typically east-facing rolling hillsides with granitic-derived light, sandy clay loam soils of moderately low fertility. The first of two lodges on the vineyard has been opened, providing accommodation.

▼▼▼▼ **Blue Mountains Rose 2007** Salmon tinges; reflects its cabernet sauvignon base with an attractive spicy/savoury twist to the finish. Screwcap. 12.8° alc. **Rating** 87 **To** 2009 $18

Ducketts Mill

1678, Scotsdale Road, Denmark, WA 6333 **Region** Denmark
T (08) 9840 9844 **F** (08) 9840 9668 **www.**duckettsmillwines.com.au **Open** 7 days 11–5
Winemaker Harewood Estate **Est.** 1997 **Cases** NA
Ducketts Mill is a twin operation with Denmark Farmhouse Cheese, both owned and operated by Ross and Dallas Lewis. They have the only cheese factory in the Great Southern region, and rely on James Kellie (Harewood Estate) to make the wines from the extensive estate plantings. Riesling, chardonnay, merlot, cabernet franc, ruby cabernet and cabernet sauvignon total 7.5 ha; part of the grapes are sold, part made into Riesling, Late Harvest Riesling, Merlot and Three Cabernets under the Ducketts Mill label. The 10 different cheeses make an even wider choice.

▼▼▼▼▼ **Riesling 2006** Very attractive, juicy riesling, with lemon and lime flavours coalescing on a seamless palate. Very long finish. **Rating** 94 **To** 2015 $15

▼▼▼▼ **Shiraz 2006** Distinctly spicy, savoury notes from the bouquet through to the finish; tannins present but in balance. Screwcap. 14° alc. **Rating** 88 **To** 2012 $18

Dudley Wines

Porky Flat Vineyard, Penneshaw, Kangaroo Island, SA 5222 (postal) **Region** Kangaroo Island
T (08) 8553 1509 **F** (08) 8553 1509 **Open** 7 days 11–5
Winemaker Jeff Howard, Brodie Howard **Est.** 1994 **Cases** 5000

Colin Hopkins, Jeff Howard, Alan Willson and Paul Mansfield have formed a partnership to bring together three vineyards on Kangaroo Island's Dudley Peninsula: the Porky Flat Vineyard (5 ha), Hog Bay River (2 ha) and Sawyers (4 ha). It is the quirky vineyard names which give the products their distinctive identities. The partners not only look after viticulture, but also join in the winemaking process. Most of the wines are sold through licensed outlets on Kangaroo Island.

ŸŸŸŸŸ **Shearing Shed Red Kangaroo Island Cabernet Shiraz Merlot 2004** An elegant, well-made medium-bodied wine, with good line, texture and balance to the black fruits, spicy tannins and well-integrated oak; good value. Screwcap. 13.5° alc. **Rating** 91 **To** 2014 $16

Duke's Vineyard   ★★★★★

Porongurup Road, Porongurup, WA 6324 **Region** Porongurup
T (08) 9853 1107 **F** (08) 9853 1107 **www**.dukesvineyard.com **Open** 7 days 10–4.30
Winemaker The Vintage Wineworx (Dr Diane Miller) **Est.** 1998 **Cases** 3000
When Hilde and Ian (Duke) Ranson sold their clothing manufacturing business in 1998, they were able to fulfil a long-held dream of establishing a vineyard in the Porongurup subregion of Great Southern with the acquisition of a 65-ha farm at the foot of the Porongurup Range. They planted 3 ha each of shiraz and cabernet sauvignon and 4 ha of riesling. Hilde Ranson is a successful artist, and it was she who designed the beautiful scalloped, glass-walled cellar door sales area with its mountain blue cladding. In the lead-up to the 2007 vintage the biggest bushfire ever seen in the Porongurup Range led to the loss of the entire vintage due to smoke taint. However, they do have small amounts of earlier vintages available, but the closure of the National Park to tourists through to November 2007 meant almost no cellar door trade right through to Jan '08. Exports to the UK.

Dunelm Wines   ★★★

Lot 509 Scotsdale Road, Denmark WA 6333 **Region** Great Southern
T (08) 9840 9027 **F** (08) 9840 9027 **Open** W'ends, public and school hols 10–4, or by appt
Winemaker Harewood Estate (James Kellie) **Est.** 1999 **Cases** 300
After 35 years as a general practitioner in Fremantle, Graeme Gargett and wife Lesley decided to 'semi-retire' and pursue a career in viticulture. They purchased their beautiful 35-ha property in the Scotsdale Valley in 1997. The north-facing slopes of well-drained karri loam soils were ideal for viticulture, and in 1999 they planted 4 ha of pinot noir, chardonnay, shiraz and cabernet sauvignon. Most of the grapes are sold to Plantagenet, but small quantities have been made each year since 2002, some by Graeme Gargett without the use of preservatives. The Barking Dog label is in honour of the resident bird-scarer, the Gargetts' dachshund Harley.

ŸŸŸŸ **Barking Dog Chardonnay 2006** Melon, yellow peach and a touch of citrus, plus a well-balanced infusion of light oak. Screwcap. 13° alc. **Rating** 87 **To** 2012 $16.50

Dunn's Creek Estate   ★★★

137 McIlroys Road, Red Hill, Vic 3937 **Region** Mornington Peninsula
T 0413 020 467 **F** (03) 5989 2011 **Open** By appt
Winemaker Sandro Mosele (Contract) **Est.** 2001 **Cases** 1270
This is the retirement venture of Roger and Hannah Stuart-Andrews, a former professional couple whose love of Italian and Spanish wines led them to their eclectic choice of varieties. Thus they have planted a total of 2.7 ha of tempranillo, albarino, arneis and barbera in more or less equal quantities.

ŸŸŸŸ **Mornington Peninsula Barbera 2005** A mix of red fruits, pointed acidity and undulating tannins; a strange place for the variety. Diam. 14.5° alc. **Rating** 87 **To** 2010 $25

Dutschke Wines ★★★★★

PO Box 107, Lyndoch, SA 5351 **Region** Barossa Valley
T (08) 8524 5485 **F** (08) 8524 5489 **www.dutschkewines.com Open** Not
Winemaker Wayne Dutschke **Est.** 1998 **Cases** 10 000

Wayne Dutschke spent over 20 years working in Australia and overseas for companies large and small before joining his uncle (and grapegrower) Ken Semmler to form Dutschke Wines. In addition to outstanding table wines, he has a yearly release of fortified wines (doubtless drawing on his time at Baileys of Glenrowan); these sell out overnight, and have received the usual stratospheric points from Robert Parker. Exports to the UK, the US and other major markets.

ŶŶŶŶŶ **Single Barrel Barossa Valley Shiraz 2005** A strong, generously built wine, with opulent and velvety blackberry and plum fruit; hints of licorice, oak and tannins seamlessly woven together. Screwcap. 15° alc. **Rating** 94 To 2025 $55
Oscar Semmler Single Vineyard Reserve Barossa Valley Shiraz 2005 Finely crafted; the wine builds flavour progressively through to the long finish; here gently spicy tannins and quality oak coalesce. Cork. 15° alc. **Rating** 94 To 2025 $52.50
St Jakobi Single Vineyard Barossa Valley Shiraz 2006 Imposing dark fruits on the bouquet, then a deeply complex and full-flavoured palate; plenty of tannin, and good acidity keeps the wine vibrant and fine on the finish; good oak handling. Screwcap. 14.8° alc. **Rating** 94 To 2022 $35

ŶŶŶŶŶ **St Jakobi Single Vineyard Barossa Valley Shiraz 2005** Bright, clear colour; the most savoury of the four shirazs, offering more movement and activity in the mouth; excellent length and balance. Cork. 15° alc. **Rating** 93 To 2019 $35
GHR Four Vineyards Barossa Valley Shiraz 2006 Deeply coloured; very attractive and concentrated bright fruit on the palate; good acidity, with just a hint of fruitcake spice on the finish. Screwcap. 14.8° alc. **Rating** 92 To 2020 $25
SAMI Two Vineyards Barossa Valley Langhorne Creek Cabernet Sauvignon 2006 Super-bright and very focused essency cabernet; full-bodied and full-blooded with plenty of length, and chewy tannin; pushes the limits of ripeness. Screwcap. 14.8° alc. **Rating** 92 To 2018 $30
GHR Four Vineyards Barossa Valley Shiraz 2005 A medium-bodied, supple and fruit-sweet mix of plum, cherry and blackberry; soft tannins and good length. From growers on God's Hill Road. Screwcap. 15° alc. **Rating** 90 To 2015 $25
SAMI Two Vineyards Barossa Valley Langhorne Creek Cabernet Sauvignon 2005 Powerful and focused; against the odds, largely gets away with the alcohol, the blackcurrant fruit ripe but not jammy; fine tannins. Screwcap. 15.5° alc. **Rating** 90 To 2020 $30

ŶŶŶŶ **Willow Bend Barossa Valley Shiraz Merlot Cabernet Sauvignon 2005** An elegant, medium-bodied wine, the varietal components welded together; fine tannins and controlled oak. Screwcap. 15° alc. **Rating** 89 To 2015 $20

Eagle Vale ★★★☆

51 Caves Road, Margaret River, WA 6285 **Region** Margaret River
T (08) 9757 6477 **F** (08) 9757 6199 **www.eaglevalewine.com Open** 7 days 10–5
Winemaker Guy Gallienne **Est.** 1997 **Cases** 10 000

Eagle Vale is a joint venture between the property owners, Steve and Wendy Jacobs, and the operator/winemaking team of Guy, Chantal and Karl Gallienne. It is a united nations team: Steve Jacobs was born in Colorado, and has business interests in Bali. The Galliennes come from the Loire Valley, although Guy secured his winemaking degree at Roseworthy College/Adelaide University. The vineyard, now 11.5 ha, is managed on a low-impact basis, without pesticides (guinea fowls do the work) and with minimal irrigation. All the wines are made from estate-grown grapes. Exports to the UK, the US, Seychelles, Singapore, China and Hong Kong.

Margaret River Chardonnay 2007 Good depth of flavour and character; nice texture, good definition and vibrancy of fruit on the finish. Screwcap. 13.5° alc. **Rating** 91 **To** 2012 $22

Margaret River Shiraz 2004 Cool shiraz with spice and an elegant framework; good weight, and fine tannins on the finish. Screwcap. 14° alc. **Rating** 88 **To** 2009 $36
Margaret River Sauvignon Blanc Fume 2005 Quite toasty and ripe on the bouquet, but still quite fresh; oak dominates a little too much throughout the wine. Screwcap. 14.5° alc. **Rating** 87 **To** 2009 $32

Eaglerange Estate Wines  NR
228 Happy Valley Road, Ovens, Vic 3737 **Region** Alpine Valleys
T (03) 5752 2518 **F** (03) 5752 2548 **www**.happyvalley75.com.au **Open** 7 days 10–5
Winemaker Frank Ivone **Est.** 1995 **Cases** 750
The Eaglerange property has been in the Ivone family for more than three generations, but it was not until 1995 that Frank and Tiziana Ivone began the establishment of their vineyard, initially planting cabernet sauvignon (3 ha), merlot (2 ha) and riesling (1.5 ha). They have since added a hectare of tempranillo and a small amount of viognier. The name of the estate comes from the watchful eagles which have always lived in the area surrounding their home. The family motto of 'Set a stout heart to a steep hill' is particularly appropriate for the property.

Eagles Rise
310 Russells Bridge Road, Russells Bridge (nr Bannockburn), Vic 3331 **Region** Geelong
T (03) 5281 2040 **www**.wildwine.com.au **Open** Wed–Sun 11–5 or by appt
Winemaker David Dillon **Est.** 1996 **Cases** 1000
Erica and David Dillon established Eagles Rise in 1996, on a property 5 km from the township of Bannockburn. In the early years, the grapes were exclusively sold to Southcorp, but (as so often has been the case) that exclusive arrangement no longer continues. Since 2003 Eagles Rise has been making wine in limited but commercial quantities, making Sparkling Pinot Gris, Sparkling Pinot Noir, Pinot Gris, Pinot Noir, Shiraz, Shiraz Cabernet, Cabernet Sauvignon and a Fortified Late Pick Pinot Gris. The winery has had success at the Geelong Wine Show.

Pinot Gris 2007 Aromatic pear and ripe apple bouquet; abundant fruit depth without phenolics; balanced finish. **Rating** 90 **To** 2009 $20

East Arm Vineyard
111 Archers Road, Hillwood, Tas 7250 **Region** Northern Tasmania
T (03) 6334 0266 **F** (03) 6334 1405 **Open** W'ends & public hols, or by appt
Winemaker Bert Sundstrup, Nicholas Butler (Contract) **Est.** 1993 **Cases** 1200
East Arm Vineyard was established by Launceston gastroenterologist Dr John Wettenhall and partner Anita James, who has completed the CSU Diploma in Applied Science (winegrowing). The 2-ha vineyard, which came into full production in 1998, is more or less equally divided among riesling, chardonnay and pinot noir. It is established on a historic block, part of a grant made to retired British soldiers of the Georgetown garrison in 1821, and slopes down to the Tamar River. East Arm has been sold, but details are not available at the time of going to press.

Riesling 2007 Good concentration, the fruit weight and richness carrying the acid well, though falls away a fraction on the finish. **Rating** 89 **To** 2014

Eden Hall
36a Murray Street, Angaston, SA 5353 **Region** Eden Valley
T (08) 8562 4590 **F** (08) 8342 3950 **www**.edenhall.com.au **Open** 7 days 10–5
Winemaker Wine Wise Consultancy **Est.** 2002 **Cases** 1820

David and Mardi Hall purchased the historic Avon Brae property in 1996. The 120-ha property has been planted to 32 ha of cabernet sauvignon (the lion's share), shiraz, merlot, cabernet franc, riesling (over 9 ha) and viognier. The majority of the production is contracted to Yalumba, St Hallett and McGuigan Simeon, with 10% of the best grapes held back for the Eden Hall label. The Riesling, Shiraz Viognier and Cabernet Sauvignon are all excellent, the red wines outstanding. Exports to the UK, the US and Asia.

ŶŶŶŶŶ **Riesling 2007** A powerful bouquet of ripe apple, pear and citrus, but falters fractionally on the palate which, while full-flavoured, doesn't have enough drive for the usual high points for this wine. Screwcap. 12.5° alc. **Rating** 90 **To** 2015 $20

Eden Road Wines

Hamilton Road, Springton, SA 5235 **Region** Eden Valley
T (08) 8568 1766 **F** (08) 8568 1767 **www**.edenroadwines.com.au **Open** By appt
Winemaker Martin Cooper, Hamish Young **Est.** 2006 **Cases** 1100
In 2006, 33-year-old winemaker Martin Cooper and investment banker Chris Coffman acquired the Heritage-listed Stonegarden vineyard and winery at Springton. The original vineyard was planted in 1858, and some time between then and 1871 the winery was built. It is now undergoing a transformation to meet the requirements of modern-day winemaking, while retaining the structure of the building intact and the gravity-fed system. Martin Cooper, former McWilliam's senior winemaker, won the Qantas Medal for Young Winemaker of the Year in 2003, and was an inaugural Len Evans Tutorial Scholar. His talents mesh well with those of Chris Coffman, who has over 25 years of international private equity and investment experience gained in many countries.

ŶŶŶŶŶ **V06 Shiraz 2006** If the weight of the bottle is a guide, then this is worth its price; undoubtedly complex, vibrant and pure, with many layers of its personality opening slowly; the lodestone is the thrust and harmony on the finish, but it will be up to the consumer to judge the price. Screwcap. 15° alc. **Rating** 95 **To** 2025 $220

ŶŶŶŶ **Two Trees Grenache Shiraz 2006** Quite porty bouquet, with masses of red fruits and confit plums on the palate; a bit heavy and thick on the finish. Screwcap. **Rating** 87 **To** 2014 $75

Eden Valley Wines

PO Box 642, Nuriootpa, SA 5355 **Region** Eden Valley
T (08) 8562 4590 **F** (08) 8562 4590 **www**.edenvalleywines.com.au **Open** Not
Winemaker Stephen Henschke, Joanne Irvine (Contract) **Est.** 2003 **Cases** 300
This is one of the more remarkable recent ventures, inspired and owned by Bob Berton, Brian Waples, David Hall, Ian Zander, Jim Irvine, John Dawkins, Jo Irvine, Peter Seppelt, Richard Sheedy, Richard Wiencke, Stephen Henschke and Trevor March, all Eden Valley grapegrowers and/or vignerons, and all self-branded as 'the Saviours'. They have banded their vineyards and skills to protect the Eden Valley wines' reputation, the sole focus being quality rather than volume.

ŶŶŶŶŶ **The Saviours Shiraz 2005** Full-bodied, offering a range of different characteristics ranging from spice and licorice to plum and blackberry, the flavour building progressively through to the back-palate. Screwcap. 14.5° alc. **Rating** 91 **To** 2020 $49.95

ŶŶŶŶ **The Saviours Riesling 2007** Has the depth of citrus flavour common in '07, but lacks the minerally thrust and acidity needed for long life. Screwcap. 12.5° alc. **Rating** 89 **To** 2011 $24.95

Edwards Wines

Cnr Caves Road/Ellensbrook Road, Cowaramup, WA 6284 **Region** Margaret River
T (08) 9755 5999 **F** (08) 9755 5988 **www**.edwardswines.com.au **Open** 7 days 10.30–5
Winemaker Michael Edwards **Est.** 1993 **Cases** 10 000

Edwards Wines is a family-owned and operated winery, with brothers Michael (formerly a winemaker at Voyager Estate) and Christo being the winemaker and viticulturist respectively. There are 25 ha of chardonnay, semillon, sauvignon blanc, shiraz, cabernet sauvignon and merlot. The consistency in the quality of the wines is remarkable. Exports to all major markets.

ΨΨΨΨΨ **Margaret River Semillon Sauvignon Blanc 2007** Some nettle on the bouquet, with quite rich fruit on the palate and considerable persistence to the finish. Screwcap. 13° alc. **Rating** 91 **To** 2012 $21
Margaret River Sauvignon Blanc 2007 Cut-grass and herbaceous aromas; very fresh and lively with good concentration and focus. Screwcap. 13° alc. **Rating** 90 **To** 2012 $21

ΨΨΨΨ **Tiger's Tale Margaret River Semillon Sauvignon Blanc 2007** Good fresh fruit, albeit a little one-dimensional. Screwcap. 13° alc. **Rating** 87 **To** 2010 $16
Tiger's Tale Margaret River Cabernet Merlot 2006 Fresh, crisp, light- to medium-bodied palate with small red fruits and minimal tannins typical of the year; don't delay. Screwcap. 13.5° alc. **Rating** 87 **To** 2010 $18

Eighteen Forty-Seven

PO Box 918, Rowland Flat, SA 5352 **Region** Barossa Valley
T (08) 8524 5328 **F** (08) 8524 5329 **www**.eighteenfortyseven.com **Open** By appt
Winemaker Alex Peel, John Curnow **Est.** 1996 **Cases** 3000
A youthful John Curnow began his career over 30 years ago buying and selling wines from all over the world. He then moved to Coca-Cola, becoming a senior executive or CEO in Hungary, the Czech Republic, NZ, the US and Australia. In 1996 he and wife Sue began the development of Eighteen Forty-Seven, with two vineyards planted to shiraz, semillon, petit verdot and a little sauvignon blanc. The name has a dual source: the original land grant of the Rowland Flat property dates from 1847, and 1–8–47 is John Curnow's birth date. Until 2002 the grapes were sold to other Barossa Valley producers, but in that vintage the first wines were made, and have had much critical acclaim. Exports to the US, Canada, Germany, the Czech Republic and Singapore.

ΨΨΨΨΨ **Home Block Barossa Valley Petit Verdot 2005** Very rich, plush and concentrated black fruits, but in no way over-extracted or overripe; good finish and aftertaste. Screwcap. 14.4° alc. **Rating** 92 **To** 2020 $41.90

ΨΨΨΨ **Pappy's Paddock Barossa Valley Shiraz 2005** Slightly reduced aromas; a medium-bodied palate until the alcohol kicks in on the finish; overall lack of line, though plenty of flavour. Screwcap. 15.2° alc. **Rating** 87 **To** 2012 $41.90

Elderton

3 Tanunda Road, Nuriootpa, SA 5355 **Region** Barossa Valley
T (08) 8568 7878 **F** (08) 8568 7879 **www**.eldertonwines.com.au **Open** Mon–Fri 8.30–5, w'ends, hols 11–4
Winemaker Richard Langford **Est.** 1984 **Cases** 40 000
The wines are based on old, high-quality Barossa floor estate vineyards, but Elderton has moved with the times by moving towards French oak, and is reaping the benefits in quality terms. The Command Shiraz is justifiably regarded as its icon wine; energetic promotion and marketing both in Australia and overseas is paying dividends. Elderton has followed in the footsteps of Cullen by becoming carbon neutral. Exports to all major markets.

ΨΨΨΨΨ **Command Single Vineyard Barossa Shiraz 2003** A complex wine, tangy and spicy, very much a product of a difficult vintage; the wine does have length and mouthfeel, but there must have been some discussion whether it should be released under the Command label. Screwcap. 14.5° alc. **Rating** 90 **To** 2019 $85

ŸŸŸŸ **Ode to Lorraine Barossa Cabernet Sauvignon Shiraz Merlot 2004**
Medium-bodied; distinct cedary/earthy notes run throughout a well-balanced
but not particularly generous palate. Off bottle? Cork. 14.5° alc. **Rating** 89
To 2015 $40
Unoaked Chardonnay 2007 Glowing green-yellow; has enough weight and
flavour to lift it out of the ruck of often boring unoaked chardonnays; good food
style, but don't delay. Screwcap. 13.5° alc. **Rating** 87 **To** 2009 $13.90

Eldredge   ★★★★

Spring Gully Road, Clare, SA 5453 **Region** Clare Valley
T (08) 8842 3086 **F** (08) 8842 3086 **www**.eldredge.com.au **Open** 7 days 11–5
Winemaker Leigh Eldredge **Est.** 1993 **Cases** 6000
Leigh and Karen Eldredge have established their winery and cellar door in the Sevenhill
Ranges at an altitude of 500 m above Watervale. It has a substantial vineyard planted to
shiraz, cabernet sauvignon, merlot, riesling, sangiovese and malbec. Both the Rieslings and
red wines have had considerable success in recent years. Exports to the UK, the US, Canada
and Singapore.

ŸŸŸŸŸ **Blue Chip Shiraz 2005** Generous and full-flavoured; ripe black fruits with a
lavish helping of new American oak (a little less would have been better); should
age well. Screwcap. 14.7° alc. **Rating** 92 **To** 2021 $25
Watervale Riesling 2007 Floral, spicy aromas; a crisp, bright and lively palate,
with attractive lime and lemon flavours; good acidity. Screwcap. 12° alc. **Rating** 91
To 2017 $17
Sangiovese Rose 2006 Complex spicy cherry aromas; a delicious palate, thanks
in no small measure to a precisely calibrated touch of residual sugar. Screwcap.
13.5° alc. **Rating** 90 **To** 2009 $17

ŸŸŸŸ **Clare Valley Cabernet Sauvignon 2004** A powerful wine, with some elements
of sweet and sour, ripe and less-ripe notes; black fruits, mint, dark chocolate and
slightly peaky acidity and dry tannins. Screwcap. 15° alc. **Rating** 89 **To** 2012 $25
Gold Clare Valley Late Harvest Riesling 2007 An interesting attempt at a
Mosel style in a very tough climate to achieve it; balanced and enjoyable, though
doesn't have the velocity and spark of Mosel; will improve. Screwcap. 9° alc.
Rating 89 **To** 2012 $17
Clare Valley Semillon Sauvignon Blanc 2006 A very ripe wine, seemingly
higher in alcohol than it in fact is; the flavours ample, but broad. Screwcap. 12° alc.
Rating 87 **To** 2009 $17

Eldridge Estate of Red Hill   ★★★★★

120 Arthurs Seat Road, Red Hill, Vic 3937 **Region** Mornington Peninsula
T (03) 5989 2644 **www**.eldridge-estate.com.au **Open** Mon–Fri 12–4, w'ends & hols 11–5
Winemaker David Lloyd **Est.** 1985 **Cases** 800
The Eldridge Estate vineyard, with seven varieties included in its 3.5 ha, was purchased by
Wendy and David Lloyd in 1995. Major retrellising work has been undertaken, changing to
Scott Henry, and all the wines are estate-grown and made. David Lloyd has also planted several
Dijon-selected pinot noir clones (114, 115 and 777) which have made their contribution since
2004, likewise the Dijon chardonnay clone 96.

ŸŸŸŸŸ **Chardonnay 2006** A fine bouquet of pear, lemon and a little toast; quite creamy
and fine on the palate, with a long, precise and even finish. Screwcap. 14° alc.
Rating 94 **To** 2014 $40
Clonal Blend Pinot Noir 2006 Ripe red fruit and plums, with a strong spicy
note at the heart; good flavour, and elegantly structured, and nice grip on the
finish. Screwcap. 14° alc. **Rating** 94 **To** 2014 $65

ŶŶŶŶŶ **Single Clone Pinot Noir 2006** Clone MV6; fleshy and fine, with vibrant red berry fruit, plums and an engaging velvety finish. Screwcap. 14° alc. **Rating** 93 To 2014 $40

Gamay 2006 Very serious gamay, with violet and blueberry aromas; fresh and varietal, high acid finish, and quite long; best in Australia. Screwcap. 14° alc. **Rating** 91 To 2012 $30

North Patch Chardonnay 2006 A slightly cooler personality, with subdued citrus fruit and a fine, textured finish. Screwcap. 14° alc. **Rating** 90 To 2012 $30

Pinot Noir 2006 Good flavour; quite angular structure; quite savoury, dry and firm on the finish; needs time. Screwcap. 14° alc. **Rating** 90 To 2012 $48

Eleven Paddocks ★★★★

PO Box 829, Macleod, Vic 3084 **Region** Pyrenees
T (03) 9458 4997 **F** (03) 9458 5075 **www.**elevenpaddocks.com.au **Open** Not
Winemaker Gabriel Horvat, Gary Mills **Est.** 2003 **Cases** 1000
Eleven partners, under the direction of managing partner Danny Gravell, purchased a small vineyard in 2002, in the foothills of the Pyrenees Ranges near Landsborough. The quality of the first vintage was sufficient to encourage the partners to increase planting to 4 ha of shiraz, 2 ha each of chardonnay and cabernet sauvignon and a dash of petit verdot.

ŶŶŶŶŶ **Shiraz 2006** Crimson-purple; elegant wine, the restrained alcohol immediately apparent, and not depriving the well-focused palate of juicy fruit flavours; clean finish. Screwcap. 13° alc. **Rating** 93 To 2016 $22

ŶŶŶŶ **The McKinlay Shiraz 2006** Much riper than the varietal, and, while flavoursome, does not have the same vibrancy and freshness; spice, dark chocolate and prune all make their appearance. Screwcap. 14.4° alc. **Rating** 89 To 2017 $27

Chardonnay 2006 A blend of Pyrenees/Yarra Valley fruit, light-bodied but with some finesse; sensitive use of partial barrel ferment aids the cause. Screwcap. 13.4° alc. **Rating** 87 To 2010 $18

Elgee Park ★★★★

Wallaces Road, RMB 5560, Merricks North, Vic 3926 **Region** Mornington Peninsula
T (03) 5989 7338 **F** (03) 5989 7199 **www.**elgeeparkwines.com.au **Open** 1 day a year –
Sun of Queen's Birthday w'end
Winemaker Contract **Est.** 1972 **Cases** 1600
The pioneer of the Mornington Peninsula in its 20th-century rebirth, owned by Baillieu Myer and family. The wines are made at Stonier and T'Gallant, Elgee Park's own winery having been closed and the overall level of activity having decreased, although the quality has increased.

ŶŶŶŶŶ **Cuvee Brut 2004** Fine and elegant; the long palate offers stone fruit with hints of cream and brioche; a long, balanced finish. Chardonnay (60%)/Pinot Noir (40%); 36 months' lees. Cork. 12.5° alc. **Rating** 93 To 2011 $35

Baillieu Myer Family Reserve Pinot Noir 2005 Some reduction on the bouquet, but has abundant red and black fruits on the palate, with considerable vibrancy and length; clean finish. Screwcap. 14° alc. **Rating** 91 To 2012 $30

ŶŶŶŶ **Cuvee Rouge 2004** Bright, light red; strong strawberry fruit aroma and flavour, with an overall impression of sweetness; Pinot Noir. Cork. 13.5° alc. **Rating** 89 To 2010 $35

Baillieu Myer Family Reserve Riesling 2006 Plenty of apple, pear and citrus flavour on the mid-palate, but falters on the finish. Screwcap. 13.5° alc. **Rating** 88 To 2010 $18

Baillieu Myer Family Reserve Viognier 2005 Gentle, light- to medium-bodied wine with pear and apricot varietal fruit; has good acidity; just a little mild and meek notwithstanding 30-year-old vines. Screwcap. 13.5° alc. **Rating** 88 To 2011 $40

Family Reserve Shiraz Viognier 2005 Light but bright hue; a light-bodied, juicy palate with nice flavours, but lacks structure/depth. Screwcap. 13° alc.
Rating 87 To 2010 $38

Elgo Estate

2020 Upton Road, Upton Hill, via Longwood, Vic 3665 **Region** Strathbogie Ranges
T (03) 5798 5563 **F** (03) 5798 5524 **www.elgoestate.com.au Open** By appt
Winemaker Cameron Atkins, Dennis Clarke **Est.** 1999 **Cases** 7000
The second Australian generation of the Taresch family has an 890-ha grazing property, with 55 ha of vines in three vineyards: Tarcombe Valley Vineyard (the warmest, planted to shiraz and cabernet); Lakeside Vineyard (planted in the 1970s with chardonnay, merlot and riesling); and the highest at Upton Hill (pinot noir and sauvignon blanc), adjacent to the winery built in 2004. Most of the power for the winery comes from a 150 kW wind-powered turbine. Exports to the US.

ⵉⵉⵉⵉⵉ **Strathbogie Ranges Riesling 2004** Attractive bottle-developed lime juice aromas and flavours; excellent length and balance; has developed superbly. Screwcap. **Rating** 94 To 2010 $21

ⵉⵉⵉⵉ **Strathbogie Ranges Sauvignon Blanc Semillon 2005** A 70/30 blend, semillon helping to keep the line of the wine, but also some honeyed characters; fully developed. Screwcap. 12.8° alc. **Rating** 88 To 2009 $17
Allira Sauvignon Blanc 2007 Some mineral and grass aromas and flavours, but lacks the focus for higher points; pleasantly soft finish. Screwcap. 13.1° alc. **Rating** 87 To 2009 $12
Allira Strathbogie Ranges Chardonnay 2006 Quite firm, with some citrussy notes, the acid a fraction hard on the finish; does have length. Screwcap. 14.4° alc. **Rating** 87 To 2010 $12
Allira Strathbogie Ranges Shiraz 2006 Luscious, ripe berry aromas; the slightly rustic palate has lots of spicy, sweet fruit; over-delivers on price. Screwcap. 14° alc. **Rating** 87 To 2009 $12

Ellender Estate

Leura Glen, 260 Green Gully Road, Glenlyon, Vic 3461 **Region** Macedon Ranges
T (03) 5348 7785 **F** (03) 5348 7784 **www.ellenderwines.com Open** W'ends & public hols 11–5, or by appt
Winemaker Graham Ellender **Est.** 1996 **Cases** 1000
The Ellenders have established 4 ha of pinot noir, chardonnay, sauvignon blanc and pinot gris. Wine style is now restricted to those varieties true to the ultra-cool climate of the Macedon Ranges: pinot noir, pinot rose, chardonnay and sparkling. Exports to the UAE.

ⵉⵉⵉⵉⵉ **Macedon Pinot Noir 2006** Light- to medium-bodied; has clear varietal expression in a spicy savoury spectrum; the line, length, texture and balance are all commendable. Screwcap. **Rating** 91 To 2012 $35
Methode Champenoise Pinot Chardonnay NV Distinctly complex; attractive bready brioche yeast lees characters under the fine stone fruit flavours; dry finish, balanced acidity. Cork. 13.5° alc. **Rating** 90 To 2011 $38

ⵉⵉⵉⵉ **Macedon Chardonnay 2006** Unusual floral notes on the bouquet, almost into jasmine, some of which flow through into the citrus-tinged palate. Screwcap. **Rating** 87 To 2011 $25

Elliot Rocke Estate

Craigmoor Road, Mudgee, NSW 2850 **Region** Mudgee
T (02) 6372 7722 **F** (02) 6372 0680 **www.elliotrockeestate.com.au Open** Mon–Fri 9–4, w'ends 10–4
Winemaker Monarch Winemaking Services **Est.** 1999 **Cases** 10 000

Elliot Rocke Estate has 24.2 ha of vineyards dating back to 1987 when the property was known as Seldom Seen. Plantings are made up of 9 ha of semillon, 4.3 ha of shiraz and chardonnay, 2.2 ha of merlot and 2 ha each of cabernet sauvignon and traminer, with 0.5 ha of doradillo. Exports to the US, Korea, Thailand, Singapore and Japan.

♟♟♟♟ **Mudgee Gewurztraminer 2007** Good varietal definition, with floral and lychee on show; just a little phenolic twist on the finish. Screwcap. 12.4° alc. **Rating** 88 **To** 2009 $16.95

Elmswood Estate

75 Monbulk-Seville Road, Wandin East, Vic 3139 **Region** Yarra Valley
T (03) 5964 3015 **F** (03) 5964 3405 **www**.elmswoodestate.com.au **Open** 7 days 10–5
Winemaker Paul Evans **Est.** 1981 **Cases** 3000
Elmswood Estate has 9.5 ha of vineyard, planted in 1981 on the red volcanic soils of the far-southern side of the Yarra Valley. The cellar door offers spectacular views across the Upper Yarra Valley to Mt Donna Buang and Warburton. Exports to China.

♟♟♟♟ **Yarra Valley Merlot 2006** Medium-bodied; good texture and weight to the clear varietal characters, with a mix of cassis, blackcurrant, sage and black olive. Diam. **Rating** 89 **To** 2013 $28
Yarra Valley Cabernet Sauvignon 2006 Diffuse colour; mint and blackcurrant fruit on a light- to medium-bodied palate; happily, fine tannins on the finish are ripe. Diam. **Rating** 88 **To** 2012 $30
Yarra Valley Chardonnay 2006 Light-bodied, with melon and cashew flavours on a minor scale; some oak helps build structure. Diam. **Rating** 87 **To** 2011 $25
Yarra Valley Cabernet Merlot 2006 Has flavour, even if a little mouth-puckering, cassis and green olive, the flavours lingering; could settle down with age in bottle. Diam. **Rating** 87 **To** 2013 $25

Elysium Vineyard ★★★☆

393 Milbrodale Road, Broke, NSW 2330 **Region** Lower Hunter Valley
T 0417 282 746 **F** (02) 9664 2368 **www**.elysiumvineyardcottage.com.au **Open** W'ends 10–5, or by appt
Winemaker Tyrrell's (Nick Paterson) **Est.** 1990 **Cases** 500
Elysium was once part of a much larger vineyard established by John Tulloch. Tulloch (not part of the Tulloch operation previously owned by Southcorp) continues to look after the viticulture, with 1 ha of verdelho. The Elysium Cottage has won a number of tourism awards. Proprietor Victoria Foster, in partnership with Ben Moechtar (then Vice President of the Australian Sommeliers Association), conducts wine education weekends on request, with meals prepared by a chef brought in for the occasion. Very limited quantities of rare back vintages are available. Exports to China.

♟♟♟♟♟ **Limited Release Broke Fordwich Verdelho 2005** Has good intensity, and has been quietly building texture in bottle; has the '05 quality stamp plus good acidity. Screwcap. 12.9° alc. **Rating** 90 **To** 2010 $30

Eppalock Ridge

633 North Redesdale Road, Redesdale, Vic 3444 **Region** Heathcote
T (03) 5443 7841 **www**.eppalockridge.com **Open** By appt
Winemaker Rod Hourigan **Est.** 1979 **Cases** 1500
Sue and Rod Hourigan gave up their careers in fabric design and television production at the ABC in 1976 to chase their passion for fine wine. This took them first to McLaren Vale, Sue working in the celebrated Barn Restaurant, Rod starting at d'Arenberg, and over the next three years both working vintages at Pirramimma and Coriole while undertaking the first short course for winemakers at what is now CSU. After three hectic years they moved to Redesdale in 1979 and established Eppalock Ridge on a basalt hilltop overlooking Lake Eppalock. The 10 ha of shiraz, cabernet sauvignon, cabernet franc and merlot are capable of producing wines of high quality. Exports to the US and Canada.

ŢŢŢŢ **Susan's Selection Heathcote Shiraz Blend 2004** Light-bodied, but does have length and a degree of elegance to the mix of savoury, spicy dark fruits; fine tannins to close. Screwcap. 14° alc. **Rating** 89 **To** 2011 $25

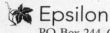 Epsilon ★★★★☆

PO Box 244, Greenock, SA 5360 **Region** Barossa Valley
T (08) 8562 8494 **F** (08) 8562 8597 **www**.epsilonwines.com.au **Open** Not
Winemaker Dan Standish, Jaysen Collins (Contract) **Est.** 2004 **Cases** 2000
Epsilon (the fifth-brightest star in a constellation) takes its name from the five generations of the Kalleske family's involvement in Barossa Valley grapegrowing; Julie Southern is née Kalleske. She and husband Aaron bought back this part of the family farm in 1994, initially selling the grapes but in 2003 joining forces with close friends Dan Standish and Jaysen Collins to produce the Epsilon by Kalleske wine.

ŢŢŢŢŢ **Barossa Valley Tempranillo 2006** Very good crimson; has much more structure and texture than most tempranillos, with spicy/savoury nuances to the deep well of dark fruits; good tannins. Cork. 14° alc. **Rating** 94 **To** 2013 $25

ŢŢŢŢŢ **Barossa Valley Shiraz 2006** Dark colour; soft, velvety mouthfeel to the blackberry and licorice fruit; soft, ripe tannins; good oak. Screwcap. 14.5° alc. **Rating** 93 **To** 2016 $19.50

Ernest Hill Wines NR

307 Wine Country Drive, Nulkaba, NSW 2325 **Region** Lower Hunter Valley
T (02) 4991 4418 **F** (02) 4991 7724 **www**.ernesthillwines.com.au **Open** 7 days 10–5
Winemaker Mark Woods **Est.** 1999 **Cases** 1400
The Wilson family has owned the Ernest Hill property since 1990; the vineyard has 3 ha of semillon, and 1 ha each of chardonnay, traminer and verdelho; an additional hectare of shiraz is leased. The business has had show success with the wines so far released.

`ese Vineyards ★★★★★

1013 Tea Tree Road, Tea Tree, Tas 7017 **Region** Southern Tasmania
T 0417 319 875 **Open** By appt
Winemaker Winemaking Tasmania (Julian Alcorso) **Est.** 1994 **Cases** 3000
Elvio and Natalie Brianese are an architect and graphic designer couple whose extended family has centuries-old viticultural roots in the Veneto region of northern Italy. They have 2.5 ha of bearing vineyard. The Pinot Noir can be outstanding. Exports to China.

ŢŢŢŢŢ **Pinot Noir 2006** Deeply coloured, but brightly fruited; dark cherries and intriguing spices all come to the fore; great concentration and a really slippery palate, and very long and fine on the finish. **Rating** 95 **To** 2014 $25
Pinot Noir 2005 Very bright fruit, with some varietal spice aromas; elegant and fleshy on the palate, with a long finish. **Rating** 94 **To** 2011 $25

ŢŢŢŢŢ **Sauvignon Blanc 2007** Pale colour; ripe fruit with good varietal character, minerally notes framing the ample fruit; clean, fresh and well balanced. **Rating** 90 **To** 2010 $20

ŢŢŢŢ **Pinot Rose 2007** Bright pink; a touch of SO$_2$, but positive mid-palate fruit, and fair length. **Rating** 87 **To** 2009 $18

Eurabbie Estate ★★★★

251 Dawson Road, Avoca, Vic 3467 **Region** Pyrenees
T (03) 5465 3799 **Open** 7 days 10–5
Winemaker John Higgins **Est.** 2000 **Cases** 1500
John and Kerry Higgins have established Eurabbie Estate in an 80-ha forest property overlooking a 4-ha natural lake. Two separate blocks of cabernet sauvignon, shiraz and merlot,

with a dash of pinot noir, give rise to the Eurabbie Estate range. Since 2004 grapes have been purchased from three small Pyrenees growers to produce the Pyrenees Villages range: Percydale Chardonnay, Percydale Cabernet Franc, Amherst Shiraz, Stuart Mill Shiraz and Avoca Cabernet Sauvignon. The wines are made in a mudbrick winery powered by solar energy.

ŸŸŸŸŸ **Ruby Jayne 2006** Crimson-purple; redolent of black fruits, bitter chocolate, licorice and earth; ripe tannins sustain and balance the finish; long life ahead. Screwcap. **Rating** 91 **To** 2026 $27.75
Avoca Pinot Noir 2006 Has remarkable varietal character given region; scores particularly on the long, quite intense palate with notes of black cherry. Screwcap. **Rating** 90 **To** 2012 $19.75
Stephen James Avoca Shiraz 2006 Fragrant and slightly minty bouquet of red fruits, and juicy fruits on the palate; quite long, with a little savoury edge to the finish. Screwcap. 13.5° alc. **Rating** 90 **To** 2014 $22.75

Evans & Tate ★★★★★

Cnr Metricup Road/Caves Road, Wilyabrup, WA 6280 **Region** Margaret River
T (08) 9755 2199 **F** (08) 9755 4362 **www**.evansandtate.com.au **Open** 7 days 10.30–5
Winemaker Richard Rowe **Est.** 1970 **Cases** 450 000
The 38-year history of Evans & Tate has been one of constant change, and, for decades, expansion, moving to acquire substantial wineries in SA and NSW. For a series of reasons having nothing to do with the excellent quality of its Margaret River wines, the empire fell apart in 2005, although it took an interminable time before McWilliam's (together with a syndicate of local growers) finalised its acquisition of Evans & Tate in December '07. Remarkably, wine quality was maintained through the turmoil. Exports to all major markets.

ŸŸŸŸŸ **The Reserve Margaret River Chardonnay 2004** Very fragrant bouquet, still fresh as a daisy; delicious juicy nectarine fruit dominant through the long palate, but with some barrel ferment notes. Screwcap. 14° alc. **Rating** 95 **To** 2016 $29.99
Classic Margaret River Semillon Sauvignon Blanc 2007 A lovely wine, vibrant, with great fruit balance and length, with semillon providing the drive and structure, sauvignon blanc adding a touch of tropical fruit. Screwcap. 13° alc. **Rating** 94 **To** 2011 $18.95

ŸŸŸŸ **X&Y Margaret River Shiraz 2005** Good hue; medium-bodied, with spicy overtones to a mix of red and black fruits; good length and finish. Screwcap. 14.5° alc. **Rating** 89 **To** 2012 $17.95
The Reserve Margaret River Cabernet Sauvignon 2004 Holding hue; a light- to medium-bodied palate with clean blackcurrant fruit plus hints of cedar and spice. Screwcap. 14.5° alc. **Rating** 88 **To** 2014 $29.95

Evelyn County Estate ★★★★☆

55 Eltham-Yarra Glen Road, Kangaroo Ground, Vic 3097 **Region** Yarra Valley
T (03) 9437 2155 **F** (03) 9437 2188 **www**.evelyncountyestate.com.au **Open** Mon–Wed 9–5, Thurs–Sun 9–late
Winemaker Diamond Valley Vineyards (James Lance) **Est.** 1994 **Cases** 2000
The 8-ha Evelyn County Estate has been established by former Coopers & Lybrand managing partner Roger Male and his wife, Robyn, who has completed a degree in Applied Science (wine science) at CSU. An architect-designed cellar door, gallery and restaurant opened in 2001. A small planting of tempranillo bore its first crop in 2004 and this wine is made onsite by Robyn Male. No samples received; the rating is that of last year. Exports to France, Malaysia, Macau, Singapore and Hong Kong.

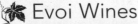 Evoi Wines ★★★★

92 Dunsborough Lakes Drive, Dunsborough, WA 6281 (postal) **Region** Margaret River
T 0407 131 080 **F** (08) 9755 3742 **www**.evoiwines.com **Open** Not
Winemaker Nigel Ludlow **Est.** 2006 **Cases** 450

Nigel Ludlow has been winemaker at Barwick Wines since 2002, having previously been winemaker at Selaks' Marlborough winery in NZ. He had also been a Flying Winemaker, with vintages in Hungary, South Africa and Spain. In 2006 he established Evoi Wines as a small add-on to his major role at Barwick; only two wines will be released, Chardonnay and Cabernet Sauvignon.

ŢŢŢŢŢ **Reserve Margaret River Chardonnay 2007** Very young and oaky, but good concentration; plenty of stone fruits and fruit weight across the creamy palate; a bit raw now, needing bottle age. Screwcap. 14° alc. **Rating** 91 **To** 2013 $49

Eyre Creek   ★★★★

Main North Road, Auburn, SA 5451 **Region** Clare Valley
T 0418 818 400 **F** (08) 8849 2555 **Open** W'ends & public hols 10–5, Mon–Fri as per sign
Winemaker Stephen John **Est.** 1999 **Cases** 1500
John Osborne established Eyre Creek in 1999, with 2 ha of shiraz and 4 ha of grenache, to be joined by viognier, pinot gris and chardonnay at the end of 2008. The tiny output is sold by mail order and through limited wholesale distribution.

ŢŢŢŢŢ **The Brookvale Clare Valley Shiraz 2005** Although the alcohol is lower, this has significantly more polish and fruit richness than the varietal; black and red fruits supported by ripe, fine tannins. Screwcap. 14° alc. **Rating** 93 **To** 2018 $25
Clare Valley Riesling 2007 Fragrant blossom and nettle aromas; bright and lively palate, with balanced acidity adding to the length. Screwcap. 12.5° alc. **Rating** 91 **To** 2014 $18
Semillon Sauvignon Blanc 2007 Delicious tangy light-bodied white, with a mix of tropical sauvignon blanc notes and citrussy/grassy semillon; clean finish. Screwcap. 12.5° alc. **Rating** 90 **To** 2011 $18
Clare Valley Shiraz 2005 Solid medium- to full-bodied black fruits, licorice and earthy fruit, vanilla oak offset by persistent, savoury tannins. Screwcap. 14.3° alc. **Rating** 90 **To** 2015 $20

ŢŢŢŢ **Clare Valley Shiraz 2004** Big, brawny, earthy wine, long on flavour, short on finesse; winter fireside stuff. Screwcap. 13.3° alc. **Rating** 87 **To** 2011 $20
Explorers Clare Valley Grenache 2006 Colour verging on rose, with sweet cherry jam mid-palate flavours to match; however, not sweet on the finish; ready now. Screwcap. 13.5° alc. **Rating** 87 **To** 2009 $15

Faber Vineyard   ★★★★★

233 Haddrill Road, Baskerville, WA 6056 (postal) **Region** Swan Valley
T (08) 9296 0619 **F** (08) 9296 0681 **Open** Not
Winemaker John Griffiths **Est.** 1997 **Cases** 800
Former Houghton winemaker, and now university lecturer and consultant, John Griffiths teamed with wife, Jane Micallef, to found Faber Vineyard. They have established 4 ha of shiraz, chardonnay, verdelho, cabernet sauvignon, petit verdot and brown muscat. Says John, 'It may be somewhat quixotic, but I'm a great fan of traditional warm-area Australia wine styles – those found in areas such as Rutherglen and the Barossa. Wines made in a relatively simple manner that reflect the concentrated ripe flavours one expects in these regions. And when one searches, some of these gems can be found from the Swan Valley.' Possessed of an excellent palate, and with an impeccable winemaking background, the quality of John Griffiths' wines is guaranteed, although the rating is also quixotic.

ŢŢŢŢŢ **Riche Swan Valley Shiraz 2007** Full-bodied, with abundant juicy plum and blackberry flavours, but no hint of dead fruit; perfectly balanced tannins and oak; very good value. Cork. 14.5° alc. **Rating** 94 **To** 2017 $17

ŢŢŢŢ **Swan Valley Petit Verdot 2007** More savoury and elegant than one might expect, for there has been no chase for colour or extract as is often the case; French oak has helped lift the aroma and flavour. Diam. 14° alc. **Rating** 90 **To** 2015 $21

ᵽᵽᵽᵽ **Dwellingup Chardonnay 2007** A vibrant and quite peachy bouquet, and good oak in the background; ripe and juicy on the palate, with balanced persistence on the finish. Screwcap. 13.5° alc. **Rating** 88 **To** 2012 $24

Falls Wines

Belubula Way, Canowindra, NSW 2804 **Region** Cowra
T (02) 6344 1293 **F** (02) 6344 1290 **www.**fallswines.com **Open** 7 days 10–4
Winemaker Madrez Wine Services (Chris Derrez) **Est.** 1997 **Cases** 1500
Peter and Zoe Kennedy have established Falls Vineyard & Retreat (to give it its full name) on the outskirts of Canowindra. They have planted chardonnay, semillon, merlot, cabernet sauvignon and shiraz, with luxury B&B accommodation offering large spa baths, exercise facilities, fishing and a tennis court.

ᵽᵽᵽᵽ **Merlot 2003** A dark and savoury wine, with a little black olive and some spice; plummy, good structure. Screwcap. 13.5° alc. **Rating** 87 **To** 2012 $17

Faraday Ridge Wines

RSD 108 Kennedys Lane, Faraday, Vic 3451 (postal) **Region** Bendigo
T (03) 5473 3354 **F** (03) 5441 1500 **www.**faradayridge.com.au **Open** Not
Winemaker Langanook (Matt Hunter) **Est.** 1979 **Cases** 120
David and Ruth Norris had what they describe as 'a mid-life crisis in their mid-20s', moving to central Vic to grow grapes for the wine industry. They established 1 ha of chardonnay, and 2 ha each of pinot noir and shiraz, which might seem a strange mix for Bendigo, but the vineyard is in fact at the southern end of the region at an altitude of 450 m on the deep, granitic soils of Mt Alexander. Over the years, grapes have been sold to Southcorp, BlackJack, Hanging Rock and Witchmount, but it was not until 2004 that David and Ruth decided to release a Shiraz from that vintage, rewarded with trophies at the Daylesford Wine Show '06, and the Australian Small Winemakers Show '07. Future releases of Chardonnay and Shiraz are in the pipeline, although grape growing (and sales) remains the central part of their business.

Farmer's Daughter Wines

791 Cassilis Road, Mudgee, NSW 2850 **Region** Mudgee
T (02) 6373 3177 **F** (02) 6373 3759 **www.**farmersdaughterwines.com.au
Open Mon–Fri 9–5, Sat 10–5, Sun 10–4
Winemaker Greg Silkman **Est.** 1995 **Cases** 13 0000
The intriguingly named Farmer's Daughter Wines is a family-owned vineyard, run by the daughters of a feed-lot farmer. Much of the production from the substantial vineyard of 20 ha, planted to shiraz (7 ha), merlot (6 ha), chardonnay and cabernet sauvignon (3 ha each), and semillon (1 ha), is sold to other makers, but increasing quantities are made for the Farmer's Daughter label. Exports to Vietnam.

ᵽᵽᵽᵽ **Mudgee Merlot 2006** While light-bodied, does have some olive and herb varietal character along with gently sweet berry fruit; just gets over the line. Screwcap. 14.5° alc. **Rating** 87 **To** 2009 $18
  Mudgee Cabernet Sauvignon 2006 A similar edge of sweetness to all of the '06 Farmer's Daughter reds, offset here by a flick of cabernet tannins. Screwcap. 14.9° alc. **Rating** 87 **To** 2013 $18

Farr Rising ★★★★★

27 Maddens Road, Bannockburn, Vic 3331 **Region** Geelong
T (03) 5281 1733 **F** (03) 5281 1433 **www.**byfarr.com.au **Open** By appt
Winemaker Nicholas Farr **Est.** 2001 **Cases** 2000
Nicholas Farr is the son of Gary Farr, and with encouragement from his father he has launched his own brand with conspicuous success. He learned his winemaking in France and Australia, and has access to some excellent base material, hence the quality of the wines. Exports to Denmark, Hong Kong and Japan.

ŸŸŸŸŸ **Geelong Pinot Noir 2006** Good hue and depth; has abundant plummy fruit and well above-average texture and structure; expands on the long finish and aftertaste. **Rating** 95 **To** 2013

ŸŸŸŸŸ **Geelong Saignee 2006** Light salmon colour; tightly drawn, uncompromising barrel ferment pinot noir style; spicy and savoury more than fruity; bone-dry finish. Cork. **Rating** 90 **To** 2009 $20

Farrawell Wines   ★★★★

60 Whalans Track, Lancefield, Vic 3435 **Region** Macedon Ranges
T (03) 5429 2020 **www.**farrawellwines.com.au **Open** 4th Sat of each month 1–5, or by appt
Winemaker Mount Charlie Wines (Trefor Morgan), Kilchurn Wines (David Cowburn)
Est. 2000 **Cases** 350
Farrawell had a dream start to its commercial life when its 2001 Chardonnay was awarded the trophy for Best Chardonnay at the '03 Macedon Ranges Wine Exhibition. Given that slightly less than 1 ha each of chardonnay and pinot noir are the sole source of wines, production will always be limited. Trefor Morgan is the owner/winemaker of Mount Charlie Winery, but was perhaps better known as a Professor of Physiology at Melbourne University.

ŸŸŸŸŸ **Reserve Macedon Ranges Chardonnay 2005** A complex wine, with the weight and structure only a few other producers in the region attain; stone fruit, fig and melon, with positive but seamless oak and good length. Screwcap. 13.5° alc. **Rating** 93 **To** 2012 $25

ŸŸŸŸ **Macedon Methode Champenoise 2004** A Chardonnay/Pinot Noir blend with several years on lees, but still very fresh and youthful, bright fruit still dominant; controlled dosage. Cork. 12.5° alc. **Rating** 89 **To** 2012 $30

Farrell Estate Wines   NR

PO Box 926, Mildura, Vic 3502 **Region** Murray Darling
T (03) 5022 7066 **F** (03) 5022 7066 **www.**farrellestate.com.au **Open** Not
Winemaker Janel Farrell **Est.** 2000 **Cases** 600
This is an extended family-owned business, dating back to 1982 when John and Janette Carruthers established the vineyard. In 2000 their daughter Janel Farrell and her husband Chad built the winery, and the business moved into its second phase. All have experience in various aspects of the wine industry, from logistics and planning through to wine science and winemaking. Indeed, their combined experience covers every base in the most impressive manner imaginable. The estate vineyards are planted to chardonnay, cabernet sauvignon, sauvignon blanc, sangiovese and viognier.

Feehans Road Vineyard

50 Feehans Road, Mount Duneed, Vic 3216 **Region** Geelong
T (03) 5264 1706 **F** (03) 5264 1307 **www.**feehansroad.com.au **Open** W'ends 10–5
Winemaker Ray Nadeson **Est.** 2000 **Cases** 350
Peter Logan's interest in viticulture dates back to a 10-week course run by Denise Miller (at Dixons Creek in the Yarra Valley) in the early 1990s. This led to further formal studies, and the planting of a 'classroom' vineyard of 500 chardonnay and shiraz vines. A move from Melbourne suburbia to the slopes of Mt Duneed led to the planting of a 1.2-ha vineyard of shiraz in 2000, and, through long-term friend Nicholas Clark of Amietta, to the appointment of Ray Nadeson as winemaker. Plans include the planting of chardonnay and sauvignon blanc to extend the range.

ŸŸŸŸ **Geelong Shiraz 2006** Very deep colour; full, rich and flooded with blackberry, licorice and spice, but (in the view of some) flawed by brett. If true, a huge pity. Screwcap. **Rating** 87 **To** 2015 $23

Feet First Wines ★★★★

32 Parkinson Lane, Kardinya, WA 6163 (postal) **Region** Western Australia
T (08) 9314 7133 **F** (08) 9314 7134 **Open** Not
Winemaker Contract **Est.** 2004 **Cases** 8000

This is the business of Ross and Ronnie (Veronica) Lawrence, who have been fine wine wholesalers in Perth since 1987, handling top-shelf Australian and imported wines. It is a virtual winery, with both grapegrowing and winemaking provided by contract, the aim being to produce easy-drinking, good-value wines under $20; the deliberately limited portfolio includes Semillon Sauvignon Blanc, Cabernets Merlot and Cabernet Merlot.

🍷🍷🍷🍷🍷 **Frankland River Semillon Sauvignon Blanc 2007** Fragrant aromatic display of grassy, citrus and tropical fruits, then an intense and lively palate, breezy and fresh. Screwcap. 13.4° alc. **Rating** 94 **To** 2011 $16.40

🍷🍷🍷🍷 **Geographe Cabernet Merlot 2006** While it shows the limitations of the vintage in flavour terms (leafy, minty notes), has quite good structure, helped by a touch of oak. Screwcap. 13° alc. **Rating** 87 **To** 2011 $16.40

Fenwick Wines ★★★

180 Lings Road, Wallington, Vic 3221 **Region** Geelong
T (03) 5250 1943 **F** (03) 5250 1943 **www**.fenwickwines.com **Open** By appt
Winemaker Scotchmans Hill (Robin Brockett) **Est.** 1997 **Cases** 350

When, in 1988, Madeleine and Dr David Fenwick purchased a 20-ha property between Ocean Grove and Wallington, it was pure chance that it had first been settled by Fairfax Fenwick – no relative. The Fenwicks planted 2 ha of pinot noir in 1997 and have since added 2 ha of chardonnay and 1 ha of shiraz, and increased the pinot noir plantings slightly with three clones (114, 115 and MV6). The first five vintages were contracted to Scotchmans Hill, thereafter split between Scotchmans Hill and Fenwick Wines.

🍷🍷🍷🍷 **Chardonnay 2006** A firm, direct style, with good balance between the stone fruit and melon flavours and oak; good acidity and line. **Rating** 89 **To** 2011 **$25**
Pinot Noir 2006 A distinctive bouquet, then layered fruit with quite good mouthfeel; slight jab of acidity on the finish. **Rating** 88 **To** 2011 **$25**

Fermoy Estate ★★★★☆

Metricup Road, Wilyabrup, WA 6280 **Region** Margaret River
T (08) 9755 6285 **F** (08) 9755 6251 **www**.fermoy.com.au **Open** 7 days 11–4.30
Winemaker Michael Kelly **Est.** 1985 **Cases** 30 000

A long-established estate-based winery with 14 ha of semillon, sauvignon blanc, chardonnay, cabernet sauvignon and merlot. Notwithstanding its substantial production, it is happy to keep a relatively low profile. Exports to the Europe and Asia.

🍷🍷🍷🍷🍷 **Margaret River Semillon 2007** Unusually fine, delicate and long given the usual Margaret River semillon profile; great line and fluid mouthfeel; lemony fruit with a slash of mineral. Screwcap. **Rating** 94 **To** 2015 **$20**

🍷🍷🍷🍷☆ **Margaret River Chardonnay 2007** A very refined wine which goes against normal regional patterns with excellent length and line, but less depth and complexity; should repay cellaring. Screwcap. 13.5° alc. **Rating** 91 **To** 2015 **$28**
Margaret River Sauvignon Blanc 2007 A clean bouquet; positive flavours throughout with a mix of gooseberry and a squeeze of lemony acidity on the finish. Screwcap. 12.5° alc. **Rating** 90 **To** 2010 $18

🍷🍷🍷🍷 **Margaret River Merlot 2005** A wine without any concessions whatsoever, dark and brooding, with tannins through the length of the palate; very difficult to tell where it is headed down the track, but leave it be now. Cork. 13.5° alc. **Rating** 89 **To** 2017 $30

Margaret River Cabernet Sauvignon 2005 Slightly diffuse, hazy colour; a medium-bodied palate, with flavours ranging from herb through to cassis, tannins present throughout. Cork. **Rating** 89 **To** 2020 $30

 # Fernfield Wines

Rushlea Road, Eden Valley, SA 5235 **Region** Eden Valley
T (08) 8564 1041 **F** (08) 8564 1041 **www**.fernfieldwines.com.au **Open** 7 days 10–5
Winemaker Bronwyn Lillecrapp **Est.** 2002 **Cases** 2000

The establishment date of 2002 might, with a little poetic licence, be shown as 1864. Bryce Lillecrapp is the fifth generation of the Lillecrapp family, his great-great-great-grandfather buying land in the Eden Valley in 1864, subdividing it in 1866, establishing the township of Eden Valley and building the first house, Rushlea Homestead. It is this building which was restored by Bryce and opened in 1998 as a bicentennial project, now serving as Fernfield Wines' cellar door. He heads up Fernfield Wines as grapegrower, with his wife Bronwyn chief winemaker, son Shannon cellarhand and assistant winemaker, and daughter Rebecca the wine marketer. While all members of the family have married grapegrowing and winemaking with other vocations, they have moved inexorably back to Fernfield, where they have 24 ha of vines dating back three generations of the family. In 2002 they decided to build a winery, and keep part of the crop for the Fernfield label.

Stompers Eden Valley Shiraz 2004 Potent, powerful savoury/spicy edges to black fruits; all of these wines somewhat rustic and needed more polishing, but the base is there. Cork. 14.8° alc. **Rating** 89 **To** 2015 $30

Pridmore Eden Valley Shiraz 2004 Distinctly richer and riper fruit, the tannins less aggressive, but the finish is very emphatic. Cork. 14.8° alc. **Rating** 88 **To** 2015 $20

Eden Valley Shiraz 2004 A background of blackberry and licorice fruit to rumbling tannins across the mid-palate and finish; needed fining. Screwcap. 14.8° alc. **Rating** 87 **To** 2014 $12.50

Ferngrove

Ferngrove Road, Frankland, WA 6396 **Region** Frankland River
T (08) 9855 2378 **F** (08) 9855 2368 **www**.ferngrove.com.au **Open** 7 days 10–4
Winemaker Kim Horton **Est.** 1997 **Cases** 50 000

After 90 years of family beef and dairy farming heritage, Murray Burton decided in 1997 to venture into premium grapegrowing and winemaking. Today the venture he founded has two large vineyards in Frankland River: one 153 ha, the other 70 ha. The operation centres around the Ferngrove Vineyard, where a large rammed-earth winery and tourist complex was built in 2000. Part of the vineyard production is sold as grapes, part is sold as juice or must, part is sold as finished wine, and the pick of the crop is made under the Ferngrove label. The consistency of its wines across a wide range of price points is wholly admirable. Exports to the UK, the US and other major markets.

Majestic Cabernet Sauvignon 2005 Festooned with trophies and gold medals, and has developed handsomely in the years since release; all the components are now seamlessly welded and balanced. Cork. 15° alc. **Rating** 96 **To** 2029 $26

Leaping Lizard Reserve Chardonnay 2005 Smoky, slightly charry, complex barrel ferment aromas; excellent line and length to the supple, cool-grown nectarine and grapefruit flavours; has movement in the mouth. Screwcap. 14° alc. **Rating** 95 **To** 2015 $22

Cossack Frankland River Riesling 2007 A highly floral, citrus-driven bouquet; very good balance, line and length; continues the tradition. Screwcap. 12.5° alc. **Rating** 94 **To** 2015 $21

Leaping Lizard Reserve Cabernet Sauvignon 2004 A fragrant mix of red and black fruits on the bouquet; a quite tight and firm palate, the tannins on the brink of aggression; needs patience. Cork. 14° alc. **Rating** 93 **To** 2014 $24

Leaping Lizard Semillon Sauvignon Blanc 2007 Aromas of gooseberry and spice, then an unexpectedly powerful and long palate, with grass, asparagus and grapefruit all intermingling. Screwcap. 14° alc. **Rating** 91 **To** 2012 $14.95
Diamond Frankland River Chardonnay 2006 Elegantly structured and composed; subtle, smooth fruit and oak integration; melon and some fig; a wondrous back label describing eight aroma and flavour components. Screwcap. 14° alc. **Rating** 90 **To** 2010 $22
Leaping Lizard Sauvignon Blanc 2007 Clean, bright and fresh; some tropical passionfruit flavours merge with lemony acidity; good length. Screwcap. 13.5° alc. **Rating** 90 **To** 2010 $14.95
Frankland River Chardonnay 2007 Fine, elegant stone fruit aromas, with quite a rich palate, good acidity and a savoury mineral backbone on the finish. Screwcap. 13.5° alc. **Rating** 90 **To** 2012 $18.95
Symbols Frankland River Cabernet Merlot 2005 Medium-bodied; well made, with perfectly ripened, sweet cassis, blackcurrant and spice fruit; minimal tannins and oak. Screwcap. 14° alc. **Rating** 90 **To** 2012 $14.95

ℙℙℙℙ   **Frankland River Shiraz 2005** Bright colour; a touch of reduction on the bouquet, then a lively, fresh, medium-bodied palate, with predominantly red fruits and fine tannins. Screwcap. 14.5° alc. **Rating** 89 **To** 2013 $17.95
Symbols Frankland River Shiraz Viognier 2007 Young, spicy and floral aromas mingle with red fruit, then quite tannic and chewy on the finish. Screwcap. 14° alc. **Rating** 89 **To** 2015 $15.95
Frankland River Sauvignon Blanc 2007 A restrained style throughout; fleeting touches of passionfruit, gooseberry and herbs; a quite firm finish. Screwcap. 14° alc. **Rating** 88 **To** 2009 $18.95
Leaping Lizard Shiraz 2006 A fresh and lively light- to medium-bodied palate, with spice and cherry fruit; minimal contribution from tannins and oak. Screwcap. 13.5° alc. **Rating** 88 **To** 2013 $14.95
Frankland River Merlot 2007 Good colour; hints of black olives accompany the spicy, plummy fruit; a quite savoury, fine and dry finish. Screwcap. 13.5° alc. **Rating** 88 **To** 2012 $18.95
Symbols Frankland River Sauvignon Blanc Semillon 2007 A distinct touch of reduction on the bouquet; a surprisingly fleshy palate, out of the mainstream, though full of flavour. Screwcap. 14° alc. **Rating** 87 **To** 2009 $15.99

Ferraris Estate ★★★★

428 Hermitage Road, Pokolbin, NSW 2321 **Region** Lower Hunter Valley
T (02) 9958 8728 **F** (02) 9958 6724 **www.ferrarisvineyard.com.au Open** 7 days 10–5
Winemaker Rhys Eather **Est.** 2001 **Cases** 550
Claude and Paula Ferraris purchased their property in the Hunter Valley in 2000, guided from the outset by Rhys Eather of Meerea Park. They were also following in the footsteps of their grandparents and parents, who had arrived in Australia at the turn of last century and became pioneers of the sugar industry in Far North Qld. Moving from sugar cane to vines, and to the establishment of 3.6 ha of shiraz on sandy loam with a light clay loam topsoil, has paid dividends.

ℙℙℙℙℙ   **Hunter Valley Shiraz 2006** A savoury, highly perfumed wine, with some whole-bunch characters adding complexity and finesse; very good for the price. Screwcap. 14° alc. **Rating** 92 **To** 2015 $16

Fighting Gully Road ★★★☆

319 Whorouly South Road, Whorouly South, Vic 3735 **Region** Beechworth
T (03) 5727 1434 **F** (03) 5727 1434 **Open** By appt
Winemaker Mark Walpole **Est.** 1997 **Cases** 1000
Mark Walpole (chief viticulturist for Brown Brothers) and partner Carolyn De Poi have begun the development of their Aquila Audax Vineyard, planting the first vines in 1997. It is

situated between 530 and 580 m above sea level: the upper eastern slopes are planted to pinot noir and the warmer western slopes to cabernet sauvignon; there are also small quantities of tempranillo, sangiovese and merlot.

ŢŢŢŢ♀ Tempranillo 2003 Light- to medium-bodied; still retains some freshness and zip to its spicy red fruits, and consequently long finish. Cork. 14° alc. **Rating** 90 To 2012 $40

ŢŢŢŢ Beechworth Cabernet Sauvignon Merlot 2002 Savoury tannins are still leading the way, but there is enough fruit there to provide some balance, and you can't quibble about the length of the palate. Cork. 14° alc. **Rating** 89 To 2012 $40

Fire Gully   ★★★★

Metricup Road, Wilyabrup, WA 6280 **Region** Margaret River
T (08) 9755 6220 **F** (08) 9755 6308 **Open** By appt
Winemaker Dr Michael Peterkin **Est.** 1998 **Cases** 5000
The Fire Gully vineyard has been established on what was first a dairy and then a beef farm. A 6-ha lake created in a gully ravaged by bushfires gave the property its name. In 1998 Mike Peterkin, of Pierro, purchased the property and manages the vineyard in conjunction with former owners Ellis and Margaret Butcher. He regards the Fire Gully wines as entirely separate from those of Pierro, being estate-grown: just under 9 ha is planted to cabernet sauvignon, merlot, shiraz, semillon, sauvignon blanc, chardonnay and viognier. Exports to all major markets.

ŢŢŢŢ♀ Reserve Margaret River Cabernet Sauvignon 2004 Remarkable retention of crimson hue; juicy berry fruit of medium weight complexed by quite firm tannins to provide length; still in its infancy. Cork. **Rating** 91 To 2016 $41.90
Margaret River Chardonnay 2007 A pleasantly complex bouquet and palate, with just a touch of oak adding to the quite intense nectarine and melon fruit; good length. Screwcap. 14° alc. **Rating** 90 To 2015 $25.90

ŢŢŢŢ Reserve Blend 1 Shiraz 2004 Very spicy, leafy, minty, savoury characters surround the light- to medium-bodied blackberry and plum fruit at the core of the wine; a struggle for full ripeness, perhaps. Cork. **Rating** 89 To 2014 $41.90

Fireblock   ★★★★

St Vincent Street, Watervale, SA 5452 **Region** Clare Valley
T 0414 441 925 **F** (02) 9144 1925 **Open** Not
Winemaker O'Leary Walker **Est.** 1926 **Cases** 3000
Fireblock (formerly Old Station Vineyard) is owned by Alastair Gillespie and Bill and Noel Ireland, who purchased the 6-ha, 70-year-old vineyard in 1995. Watervale Riesling, Old Vine Shiraz and Old Vine Grenache are skilfully contract-made, winning trophies and gold medals at capital-city wine shows. Exports to the US, Sweden and Malaysia.

ŢŢŢŢ♀ Clare Valley Old Vine Shiraz 2005 A very complex bouquet and rich palate with a luscious, mouthfilling array of red and black fruits and ripe tannins; fruit sweetness does carry through to the finish; from organically managed vines planted in 1926. Screwcap. 14° alc. **Rating** 93 To 2020 $20

ŢŢŢŢ Clare Valley Old Vine Grenache 2004 A mix of sweet fruit and warm, multi-flavoured spices; you can walk by the prodigious alcohol without going up in flames, but don't delay drinking it; dry-grown vines planted in 1926. Screwcap. 16.5° alc. **Rating** 88 To 2009 $18

 # Firetail   ★★☆

PO Box 791, Margaret River, WA 6285 **Region** Margaret River
T (08) 9757 5156 **F** (08) 9757 5156 **www**.firetail.com.au **Open** Not
Winemaker Contract **Est.** 2002 **Cases** 900

Electrical engineer Jessica Worrall and chemical engineer Rob Glass worked in the oil and gas industry in Australia and the Netherlands for 20 years before making a staged move into grapegrowing and the establishment of Firetail. Their first move was the planting of a small vineyard of merlot in Geographe, which produced its first wine in 2003; the more important move being the acquisition of a mature but somewhat neglected vineyard (and rammed-earth house) in Margaret River. Here the 2 ha of Geographe merlot are supplemented by 1.2 ha of semillon, 1.1 ha of sauvignon blanc and 1 ha of cabernet sauvignon, the Margaret River plantings dating back to 2004. Jessica is studying for a masters degree of viticulture and winemaking at the University of Melbourne, while Rob fills in idle days working part time in the liquefied natural gas industry in London. It comes as no surprise to find that the wines are contract-made.

First Creek Wines

Cnr McDonalds Road/Gillards Road, Pokolbin, NSW 2320 **Region** Lower Hunter Valley
T (02) 4998 7293 **F** (02) 4998 7294 **www**.firstcreekwines.com.au **Open** 7 days 10–4
Winemaker Greg Silkman, Ross Pearson **Est.** 1984 **Cases** 35 000
First Creek is the shop front of Monarch Winemaking Services, which has acquired the former Allanmere wine business and offers a complex range of wines under both the First Creek and the Allanmere labels. Meticulous winemaking results in quality wines both for the contract clients and for the own-business labels. Exports to the UK, the US and Canada.

ŶŶŶŶŶ **Premium Reserve Hunter Valley Shiraz 2006** Good colour; firm, fresh and tightly focused plum and black fruits, sustained by fine tannins; good oak and length; cellaring potential. Screwcap. 13.5° alc. **Rating** 91 **To** 2020 $25

ŶŶŶŶ **Premium Reserve Hunter Valley Chardonnay 2007** Bright green-yellow; abundant white peach fruit with well-integrated and balanced oak; slight warmth on the finish is unexpected at this alcohol. Screwcap. 13.5° alc. **Rating** 89 **To** 2011 $20
Premium Reserve Hunter Valley Verdelho 2007 Accomplished winemaking brings out the best in a workhorse variety; fruit salad on the entry and mid-palate, then a twist of lemony acidity to brighten and lengthen the finish. Screwcap. 13.5° alc. **Rating** 89 **To** 2010 $17

First Drop Wines

PO Box 64, Williamstown, SA 5352 **Region** Barossa Valley
T 0420 971 209 **F** (08) 8563 3110 **www**.firstdropwines.com **Open** Not
Winemaker Matt Gant **Est.** 2005 **Cases** 3500
This is a virtual winery, with no vineyards and no winery of its own. What it does have are two owners with immaculate credentials to produce a diverse range of wines of significantly higher quality than that of many more conventional operations. Matt Gant was in his final year of a geography degree at the University of London in 1995 when lecturer Tim Unwin (a noted wine writer) contrived a course which involved tastings and ultimately a field trip of Burgundy and Champagne. Geography went out the window, and Matt Gant did vintages in NZ, Spain, Italy, Portugal, the US and finally Australia. Working at St Hallett he won the Wine Society's Young Winemaker of the Year Award in 2004, and the Young Gun Wine Award for First Drop in '07. John Retsas has an equally impressive CV, working at St Hallett and Chain of Ponds, and is now general manager of Schild Estate. First Drop's portfolio includes Arneis, Nebbiolo Barbera and Montepulciano (all from the Adelaide Hills), Barossa Albarino and Trincadeira Rose, and then a string of Barossa Shirazs ranging from $24 to $80 a bottle.

ŶŶŶŶŶ **Fat of the Land Seppeltsfield Single Vineyard Barossa Valley Shiraz 2005** Slightly darker fruits and somewhat more compelling; there is a liveliness to this wine that races across the palate, and is brought to its ultimate conclusion with a core of vibrant red fruits; it totally belies the alcohol of 15°. Cork. 15° alc. **Rating** 95 **To** 2020 $65

The Cream Barossa Shiraz 2005 Incredibly dense fruit, and the first wine to show evidence of oak; the fruit beneath is seriously attractive; essency blackberries with brightness at the core; the alcohol is more prominent, but as the wine integrates over time this should reward. Cork. 15° alc. **Rating** 95 **To** 2025 $80

Fat of the Land Ebenezer Single Vineyard Barossa Valley Shiraz 2005 A very impressive wine, with lots of everything; mocha, black fruits, and elements of spice; very correct on the finish, with silky tannins, and well-integrated oak. Cork. 15° alc. **Rating** 94 **To** 2015 $65

ŶŶŶŶ **Bella Coppia Adelaide Hills Arneis 2007** Cool pear fruit bouquet, with tangy acid and a crisp, even finish. Screwcap. 13° alc. **Rating** 89 **To** 2009 $24

Mother's Milk Barossa Shiraz 2006 Pure shiraz fruit, with red and dark berries and a hint of fruitcake spice; rich, yet fresh and quite savoury on the medium-bodied finish. Screwcap. 14.5° alc. **Rating** 89 **To** 2014 $24

Two Percent Barossa Shiraz 2005 Showing a little reduction, but good fruit weight, and more obvious spice than the other wines; fleshy but less serious, and should be enjoyed while the others mature. Screwcap. 14.5° alc. **Rating** 89 **To** 2014 $36

The Matador Barossa Albarino 2006 Quite subdued on the bouquet, the tangy acid provides plenty of life and lift; very fresh, but a bit reticent. Screwcap. 13° alc. **Rating** 88 **To** 2009 $36

5 Blind Mice

PO Box 243, Basket Range, SA 5138 **Region** Adelaide Hills
T (08) 8390 0206 **F** (08) 8390 3693 **www.5blindmice.com.au Open** Not
Winemaker Jodie Armstrong, Hugh Armstrong **Est.** 2004 **Cases** 200
Owners Jodie and Hugh Armstrong say, 'What started out as an idea between friends and family to make something for themselves to drink at home during the week has blossomed into a quest for something to stand proudly on its own.' They purchase pinot noir from three sites in the Adelaide Hills, the vines 15–16 years old. The wine is made in the boutique contract winery Red Heads Studio in McLaren Vale, with Jodie and Hugh making the wine under the eyes of Justin Lane and Adam Hooper, the winemakers at Red Heads.

ŶŶŶŶ **Adelaide Hills Pinot Noir 2006** Deep colour with cherry liqueur aromas and a little savoury spice; quite rich, but not very refined; good flavour. Cork. 15.5° alc. **Rating** 88 **To** 2009 $39

Five Geese

RSD 587 Chapel Hill Road, Blewitt Springs, SA 5171 (postal) **Region** McLaren Vale
T (08) 8383 0576 **F** (08) 8383 0629 **www.fivegeese.com.au Open** Not
Winemaker Boar's Rock (Mike Farmilo) **Est.** 1999 **Cases** 1500
Sue Trott is passionate about her Five Geese wine, which is produced by Hillgrove Wines. The wines come from 32 ha of vines planted in 1927 and '63. The grapes were sold for many years, but in 1999 Sue decided to create her own label and make a strictly limited amount of wine from the pick of the vineyards. Exports to the UK, the US, Canada, Singapore, Hong Kong and China.

ŶŶŶŶŶ **McLaren Vale Shiraz 2005** Abundant and generous blackberry, plum and black cherry fruits; fine tannins and dashes of regional chocolate and spice; American oak well controlled, ditto alcohol. Diam. 14.5° alc. **Rating** 94 **To** 2018 $24

572 Richmond Road

572 Richmond Road, Cambridge, Tas 7170 (postal) **Region** Southern Tasmania
T 0418 889 477 **Open** Not
Winemaker Winemaking Tasmania **Est.** 1994 **Cases** 120
John and Sue Carney have decided not to sell 572 Richmond Road, acknowledging they enjoyed the masochism of owning a vineyard and winery more than they realised. Highly

skilled veteran viticulturist Fred Peacock looks after the 0.75 ha of riesling and 0.37 ha of chardonnay and pinot noir (the last still to come into bearing). However, no wines were produced in 2006 or '07; the rating is for prior vintages.

5 Maddens Lane ★★★☆

PO Box 7001, McMahons Point, NSW 2060 **Region** Yarra Valley
T 0401 145 964 **www**.5maddenslane.com.au **Open** Not
Winemaker Mac Forbes (Contract) **Est.** 2005 **Cases** 1000
5 Maddens Lane has been developed over a number of years. The existing 4 ha of cabernet sauvignon were planted between 1988 and '97, and the 2 ha of sauvignon blanc were planted in '87. Owner Marc de Cure lives in Sydney, and has secured the services of up-and-coming winemaker Mac Forbes as contract maker, and John Evans of Yering Station as vineyard manager. However, de Cure has his own qualifications, with a Master of Wine Quality (with distinction) from the University of Western Sydney.

ΨΨΨΨΩ **Mt Juliet Yarra Valley Sauvignon Blanc 2007** Full-flavoured wine augmented by barrel ferment and 10 months plus lees stirring in barrel; good acidity helps carry the finish. Screwcap. 12° alc. **Rating** 90 **To** 2010 $30

Five Oaks Vineyard NR

60 Aitken Road, Seville, Vic 3139 **Region** Yarra Valley
T (03) 5964 3704 **F** (03) 5964 3064 **www**.fiveoaks.com.au **Open** W'ends & public hols 10–5 & by appt
Winemaker Wally Zuk **Est.** 1997 **Cases** 2000
Wally Zuk and wife Judy run all aspects of Five Oaks – far removed from Wally's background in nuclear physics. He has, however, completed his wine science degree at CSU, and is thus more than qualified to make the Five Oaks wines. Exports to Canada.

Flamebird Wines

Lot 8825 Roberts Road, Pemberton, WA 6260 **Region** Pemberton
T (08) 9776 0083 **F** (08) 9776 0083 **Open** 7 days 10–4
Winemaker Mark Aitken (Contract) **Est.** 2002 **Cases** 350
Owners Wayne Peterson and Lorraine Brinkman have a modestly sized vineyard, with 0.7 ha each of cabernet sauvignon, chardonnay and sauvignon blanc, but had to undergo the labours of Hercules before planting the vineyard. First came the rebuilding of an access bridge, then dealing with mammoth amounts of blackberry to uncover Treen Brook, which runs through the property, and finally removing 30 tonnes of rock turned up by ploughing prior to planting in 2002. Consolation came in the form of a cellar door in 2006, allowing visitors to revel in the natural beauty of the picturesque valley setting. Two-thirds of the grapes are sold, one-third used to make the Flamebird wines.

ΨΨΨΨ **Pemberton Sauvignon Blanc 2006** Abundant passionfruit, gooseberry and citrus aromas and flavours; needs just a touch more acidity. Screwcap. 12.3° alc. **Rating** 89 **To** 2009
Pemberton Rose 2006 Light red fruit flavours, but has unexpected length and freshness. Screwcap. 13° alc. **Rating** 87 **To** 2009

Flaxman Wines

Lot 535 Flaxmans Valley Road, Angaston, SA 5353 **Region** Eden Valley
T 0411 668 949 **F** (08) 8565 3299 **www**.flaxmanwines.com.au **Open** By appt
Winemaker Colin Sheppard **Est.** 2005 **Cases** 500
After visiting the Barossa Valley over a decade, and working during vintage with Andrew Seppelt at Murray Street Vineyards, Melbourne residents Colin and Fiona Sheppard decided on a seachange, and found a small, old vineyard overlooking Flaxmans Valley. It consists of 1 ha of 40+-year-old riesling, 1 ha of 50+-year-old shiraz and a small planting of 40+-year-old semillon. The vines are dry-grown, hand-pruned and hand-picked, and treated – say the

Sheppards – as their garden. Yields are restricted to under 4 tonnes per ha, and small amounts of locally grown grapes are also purchased.

🍷🍷🍷🍷🍷 **The Stranger Barossa Shiraz Cabernet 2006** Bright colour, with essency blackberry fruits; good weight and lively palate, and the luscious fruit pushes through to the finish. Screwcap. 14.5° alc. **Rating** 90 **To** 2014 $35
Barossa Shiraz VP 2006 Great colour with nice definition; a little spice and good spirit; should age with grace. Screwcap. 17.5° alc. **Rating** 90 **To** 2020 $20

🍷🍷🍷🍷 **Eden Valley Riesling 2007** Clean and minerally bouquet; good weight, but lacks a little concentration. Screwcap. 12.5° alc. **Rating** 87 **To** 2015 $25

Flinders Bay   ★★★★☆

Bussell Highway, Metricup, WA 6280 **Region** Margaret River
T (08) 9757 6281 **F** (08) 9757 6353 **Open** 7 days 10–4
Winemaker O'Leary Walker, Flying Fish Cove **Est.** 1995 **Cases** 10 000
A joint venture between Alastair Gillespie and Bill and Noel Ireland, the former a grapegrower and viticultural contractor in the Margaret River region for over 25 years, the latter two Sydney wine retailers for an even longer period. The wines are made from grapes grown on the 50-ha Karridale Vineyard (planted between 1995 and '98), with the exception of a Verdelho, which is purchased from the northern Margaret River. Part of the grape production is sold, and part made under the Flinders Bay and Dunsborough Hills brands. Exports to the UK and the US.

🍷🍷🍷🍷🍷 **Dunsborough Hills Margaret River Sauvignon Blanc Semillon 2007** A clean, crisp, vibrant grassy/minerally bouquet; touches of tropical passionfruit join in on the long palate; good balance. Screwcap. 13.5° alc. **Rating** 92 **To** 2009 $16
Margaret River Chardonnay 2007 A pure and clean bouquet; fruit-driven, with succulent but not heavy nectarine/white peach fruit doing the talking. Screwcap. 13° alc. **Rating** 92 **To** 2011 $18
Dunsborough Hills Sauvignon Blanc 2007 A quite powerful wine, with asparagus and grass flavours, and a degree of structural complexity often associated with a touch of oak somewhere in the mix. Scewcap. 12° alc. **Rating** 90 **To** 2009 $15
Margaret River Sauvignon Blanc Semillon 2007 An aromatic gooseberry/passionfruit/apple bouquet, the fine, fresh palate following suit; good length and balance. Screwcap. 13.5° alc. **Rating** 90 **To** 2009 $18
Margaret River Shiraz 2006 Extremely powerful and concentrated lush blackberry fruits; must have run the gauntlet of a wet autumn; late picking obvious. Screwcap. 15° alc. **Rating** 90 **To** 2013 $20
Dunsborough Hills Reserve Shiraz 2006 Attractive spicy/peppery overtones to the fleshy fruit of the fore-palate, then a firm and long finish. Scewcap. 14° alc. **Rating** 90 **To** 2015 $15

🍷🍷🍷🍷 **Margaret River Verdelho 2007** Fresh, clean and delicately aromatic; has tropical passionfruit flavours without heaviness; lively finish. Screwcap. 13.5° alc. **Rating** 89 **To** 2010 $18
Margaret River Cabernet Sauvignon 2006 Light, clear colour; predominantly red fruit aromas and flavours; light-bodied, hasn't been forced or over-extracted. Screwcap. 13.5° alc. **Rating** 88 **To** 2010 $20

Flint's of Coonawarra   ★★★★☆

PO Box 8, Coonawarra, SA 5263 **Region** Coonawarra
T (08) 8736 5046 **F** (08) 8736 5146 **Open** Not
Winemaker Majella **Est.** 2000 **Cases** 1700
Six generations of the Flint family have lived and worked in Coonawarra since 1840. Damian Flint and his family began the development of 20 ha of cabernet sauvignon, shiraz and merlot in 1989, but it was not until 2000 that they decided to have a small portion of cabernet

sauvignon made at Majella, owned by their lifelong friends the Lynn brothers. The wine had immediate show success; another 10 tonnes were diverted from the 2001 vintage, and the first wines were released in '03. Exports to the UK.

🍷🍷🍷🍷🍷 **Rostrevor Coonawarra Shiraz 2005** Rich, intense blackberry and satsuma plum flavours on the velvety, rich and ripe palate; tannins and oak perfect balance. Trophy Limestone Coast Wine Show '07. Screwcap. **Rating** 95 **To** 2015 $25

🍷🍷🍷🍷🍷 **Gammon's Crossing Cabernet Sauvignon 2005** Excellent depth, structure and texture; powerful blackcurrant and cassis fruit; controlled oak. Cork. **Rating** 93 **To** 2020 $25

Flying Duck Wines

3838 Wangaratta–Whitfield Road, King Valley, Vic 3678 **Region** King Valley
T (03) 9819 7787 **F** (03) 9819 7789 **Open** By appt
Winemaker Trevor Knaggs, Paul Burgoyne, Dennis Clark **Est.** 1998 **Cases** 700
Wayne and Sally Burgoyne, with John and Karen Butler, purchased the three-year-old vineyard in 2001, with 2 ha of shiraz which had been planted by Paul Burgoyne, who continues to be involved with the operation as assistant winemaker. In 2001 2.3 ha of merlot and 1 ha of viognier were planted, with Shiraz Viognier, Merlot and Viognier first made in '05.

Flying Fish Cove

Caves Road, Wilyabrup, WA 6284 **Region** Margaret River
T (08) 9755 6600 **F** (08) 9755 6788 **www**.flyingfishcove.com **Open** 7 days 11–5
Winemaker Damon Eastaugh, Liz Reed, Ryan Aggiss **Est.** 2000 **Cases** 16 000
A group of 20 shareholders acquired the 130-ha property on which the Flying Fish Cove winery was subsequently built. It has two strings to its bow: contract winemaking for others; and the development of three product ranges (Upstream, Prize Catch and Margaret River varietals), partly based on 25 ha of estate plantings, with another 10 ha planned. Exports to the US, Italy, West Indies, Indonesia, Singapore, Japan and Hong Kong.

🍷🍷🍷🍷🍷 **Cuttlefish Classic Margaret River Red 2006** A delicious and fragrant sunburst of red fruits; raspberry, plum, cherry and redcurrant; good length and fine tannins; Cabernet Sauvignon/Merlot. Screwcap. 13.5° alc. **Rating** 92 **To** 2009 $14
Chenin Blanc 2007 WA provides a home away from Loire Valley home for chenin blanc; gentle tropical fruit with seamless flow and line. Screwcap. 13.5° alc. **Rating** 91 **To** 2009 $20
Margaret River Sauvignon Blanc Semillon 2007 A mix of citrus, gooseberry, herb and grass all invisibly sewn together, hence the good balance and mouthfeel. Screwcap. 13° alc. **Rating** 90 **To** 2009 $20
Sparkling Shiraz 2005 Bright red-purple; cherry, plum and spice aromas and flavours; good balance, and not too sweet on the finish; well crafted and should benefit from time on cork. Cork. 13.5° alc. **Rating** 90 **To** 2012 $28

🍷🍷🍷🍷 **Margaret River Shiraz 2006** Dense, almost impenetrable, purple-red; a curious wine; plenty of berry fruit flavours but not much structure. Screwcap. 13.5° alc. **Rating** 89 **To** 2010 $20
Margaret River Cabernet Sauvignon Merlot 2006 Slightly hazy colour; some sweet and sour characters from a mix of red and black fruits, with persistent but balanced tannins. Screwcap. 14° alc. **Rating** 89 **To** 2011 $20
Pinot Noir Chardonnay 2006 Has unexpected intensity and finesse, although inevitably not much yeast autolysis influence. Bottle-fermented. Cork. 12.5° alc. **Rating** 89 **To** 2009 $28
The Italian Job 2007 A slightly reductive bouquet, but has vibrant red berry fruits and a savoury, drying acid finish; quirky, but a good expression of these Italian varietals; Sangiovese/Nebbiolo/Cabernet Sauvignon. Screwcap. 14.5° alc. **Rating** 88 **To** 2012 $22

Flynns Wines

Lot 5 Lewis Road, Heathcote, Vic 3523 **Region** Heathcote
T (03) 5433 6297 **F** (03) 5433 6297 **www**.flynnswines.com **Open** W'ends 11.30–5
Winemaker Greg Flynn, Natala Flynn **Est.** 1999 **Cases** 1500
The Flynn name has a long association with Heathcote. In the 1970s John Flynn and
Laurie Williams established a 2-ha vineyard next door to Mount Ida Vineyard, on the rich,
red Cambrian soil. It produced some spectacular wines before being sold in '83. Greg and
Natala Flynn (no relation to John Flynn) spent 18 months searching for their property,
13 km north of Heathcote on the same red Cambrian soil. They have established 4 ha of
shiraz, sangiovese, cabernet sauvignon, merlot and viognier. Greg Flynn is a Roseworthy
graduate from the marketing course, and has had 22 years working on the coalface of retail
and wholesale businesses, interweaving eight years of vineyard and winemaking experience,
supplemented by the two-year Bendigo TAFE winemaking course. Just for good measure,
wife Natala joined Greg for the last eight years of vineyard and winemaking, and likewise
completed the TAFE course.

ŶŶŶŶŶ **MC Heathcote Shiraz 2005** A vibrantly fresh bouquet of black fruits and gentle
oak leads into a supple, medium-bodied palate finishing with fine tannins. Cork.
14.5° alc. **Rating** 95 **To** 2025 $33

ŶŶŶŶŶ **Irena's Heathcote Verdelho 2007** Has plenty of movement and impact
thanks to lemony acidity surrounding the core of tropical fruit; a hint of oak, too.
Screwcap. 13.6° alc. **Rating** 90 **To** 2012 $25
Heathcote Viognier 2007 A very well-crafted wine; partial barrel ferment
adds a textural dimension to the flavours of apricot, citrus and peach. Screwcap.
13.5° alc. **Rating** 90 **To** 2013 $25
Heathcote Cabernet Merlot 2005 Light- to medium-bodied, showing the
more elegant side of Heathcote; cassis and blackcurrant fruit, with a gentle finish.
Screwcap. 14.5° alc. **Rating** 90 **To** 2012 $29
Heathcote Sangiovese 2005 Shows clear varietal character with spicy red
cherry/sour cherry aromas and flavours; light- to medium-bodied, best sooner
than later. Screwcap. 13.7° alc. **Rating** 90 **To** 2010 $33

Foate's Ridge

241 Fordwich Road, Broke, NSW 2330 (postal) **Region** Lower Hunter Valley
T (02) 6579 1284 **F** (02) 9922 4397 **www**.foate.com.au **Open** By appt
Winemaker Contract **Est.** 1992 **Cases** 400
The Foate family, headed by Tony Foate, planted a total of 10 ha, chardonnay (4 ha) and
verdelho, merlot and cabernet sauvignon (2 ha each), between 1992 and 2001 on the 36-ha
property they purchased in '91. The soils are the typical light alluvial loam of the region,
which promote vigorous vine growth and generous yields, yields which need to be controlled
if quality is to be maximised. Using a Scott Henry trellis, bunch thinning and fewer spur
positions have reduced the 15 tonnes per ha yields to 10 tonnes per ha.

ŶŶŶŶ **Hunter Valley Verdelho 2007** Bright straw colour; quite ripe with good
balance of freshness; plenty of sweet fruit on the mid-palate. Screwcap. 13.2° alc.
Rating 89 **To** 2010 $14.50
Hunter Valley Rose 2007 A big-boned rose with lively red fruits and plenty of
flavour. Screwcap. 13.5° alc. **Rating** 88 **To** 2009 $14.50

Foggo Wines

Lot 21 Foggos Road, McLaren Vale, SA 5171 **Region** McLaren Vale
T (08) 8323 0131 **F** (08) 8323 7626 **www**.foggowines.com.au **Open** Mon–Fri 10.30–4.30,
w'ends & public hols 11–5
Winemaker Herb Van De Wiel **Est.** 1999 **Cases** 3500
Herb and Sandie Van De Wiel have been grapegrowers in McLaren Vale for 16 years, and
in 1999 they were able to purchase the former Curtis winery. They have two vineyards: the

oldest (Foggos Road) is 9 ha of shiraz dating back to 1915; 80-year-old grenache, 45-year-old cinsaut and 20-year-old chardonnay, sauvignon blanc and viognier come from their other vineyard at Blewitt Springs. They have established a formidable reputation for their Shiraz, Grenache, Grenache Shiraz Cinsaut and Cabernet Sauvignon equal to the best. Exports to the US, Canada and Denmark.

ŸŸŸŸ♀ **Hubertus Reserve Shiraz 2005** Medium- to full-bodied; ultra-typical regional style; black fruits, mocha and dark chocolate, supported by balanced tannins; should evolve well. Twin top. **Rating** 91 **To** 2015 $45

ŸŸŸŸ **Old Vine Shiraz 2005** Good concentration, with strong flavours of red and dark fruits, but a little sweet and sour. Cork. 15° alc. **Rating** 88 **To** 2015 $30
Black Myriah Sparkling Shiraz NV Blackberry, licorice, spice and oaky notes, with some sweetness ex dosage; some love this boots-and-all style, which will develop on cork. Cork. 14.5° alc. **Rating** 87 **To** 2010 $30

Fonty's Pool Vineyards ★★★★★

Seven Day Road, Manjimup, WA 6258 **Region** Pemberton
T (08) 9777 0777 **F** (08) 9777 0788 **www**.fontyspoolwines.com.au **Open** 7 days 10–4.30
Winemaker Eloise Jarvis, Melanie Bowater **Est.** 1989 **Cases** 30 000
The Fonty's Pool vineyards are part of the original farm owned by pioneer settler Archie Fontanini, who was granted land by the government in 1907. In the early 1920s a large dam was created to provide water for the intensive vegetable farming which was part of the farming activities. The dam became known as Fonty's Pool, and to this day remains a famous local landmark and recreational facility. The first grapes were planted in 1989, and at 110 ha the vineyard is now one of the region's largest, supplying grapes to a number of leading WA wineries. An increasing amount of the production is used for Fonty's Pool. Exports to all major markets.

ŸŸŸŸŸ **Single Vineyard Pemberton Shiraz 2005** Vibrant, fresh red berry, spice and pepper aromas are repeated on the medium-bodied palate, with appropriately fine tannins and quality oak; enjoy while fresh. Screwcap. 13.5° alc. **Rating** 94 **To** 2011 $22
Single Vineyard Pemberton Shiraz 2006 Very cool-fruited bouquet, with blueberry, spice and a hint of dark plum; medium-bodied with noticeable perfume on the palate, and plentiful fine-grained tannins; surprisingly long. Screwcap. 13° alc. **Rating** 94 **To** 2016 $22

ŸŸŸŸ♀ **Pemberton Sauvignon Blanc Semillon 2007** Clean, fresh, precise fruit aromas and flavours, some tropical notes along with more grassy/snow pea characters; very good finish and aftertaste. Screwcap. 13° alc. **Rating** 93 **To** 2009 $19.50
Single Vineyard Pemberton Viognier 2006 Flowery aromas, and above-average varietal flavour; good texture, wild yeast barrel ferment not overshadowing the fruit. Screwcap. 13° alc. **Rating** 92 **To** 2009 $22
Single Vineyard Pemberton Viognier 2007 Varietal aromas of spiced apricots and just a hint of citrus; the palate is fresh and not heavy, and avoids phenolic bitterness often; a good example. Screwcap. 13.5° alc. **Rating** 91 **To** 2010 $22
Single Vineyard Pemberton Pinot Noir 2006 A fragrant bouquet with cherry and strawberry fruit; silky texture and a long, even finish; just a fraction light-on. **Rating** 90 **To** 2011 $22

ŸŸŸŸ **Pemberton Rose 2007** Pale fuschia; light, delicate and dry; fault-free and eminently drinkable, though not as intense as the best. Screwcap. 14° alc. **Rating** 89 **To** 2009 $17.50
Single Vineyard Pemberton Pinot Noir 2007 Overall, distinctly savoury style, with plenty of personality, though the tannins tremble on the brink; distinctively varietal. Screwcap. 13.5° alc. **Rating** 89 **To** 2011 $22
Single Vineyard Pemberton Cabernet Merlot 2007 Juicy light- to medium-bodied style, with plenty of action and movement on the palate ex both fruit and tannins. Screwcap. 13.5° alc. **Rating** 87 **To** 2011 $17.50

Forest Hill Vineyard ★★★★★

South Coast Highway, Denmark, WA 6333 **Region** Great Southern
T (08) 9848 2199 **F** (08) 9848 3199 **www.**foresthillwines.com.au **Open** 7 days 10–5
Winemaker Clemenc Haselgrove **Est.** 1965 **Cases** 20 000

This family-owned business is one of the oldest 'new' winemaking operations in WA, and was the site for the first grape plantings for Great Southern in 1965. The Forest Hill brand became well known, aided by the fact that a 1975 Riesling made by Sandalford from Forest Hill grapes won nine trophies. In 1997 a program of renovation and expansion of the vineyards commenced; the quality of the wines made from the oldest vines on the property is awesome (released under the numbered vineyard block labels). Exports to the UK, the US and China.

ŸŸŸŸŸ **Block 1 Mount Barker Riesling 2007** Pale and bright, with flowery aromas; an elegant, precisely focused mix of lime, lime zest, spice and mineral; great length and perfect acidity. Screwcap. 12.8° alc. **Rating** 96 **To** 2017 $35
Block 8 Mount Barker Chardonnay 2006 Brilliant colour; intense and penetrating grapefruit, nectarine and melon; very good acidity and oak provide thrust for the long finish; 40-year-old vines, dry-grown, hand-pruned and hand-picked. Screwcap. 13.5° alc. **Rating** 96 **To** 2015 $35
Block 9 Great Southern Shiraz 2005 An elegant fusion of wonderfully focused black cherry and blackberry fruit with quality oak; only medium-bodied, but has effortless length and superfine tannins. Screwcap. 14° alc. **Rating** 96 **To** 2025 $45
Block 5 Great Southern Cabernet Sauvignon 2005 Fine-grained tannins underpin a classically restrained medium-bodied wine, helping its considerable length. Fine, pure blackcurrant fruit, with quality oak in the background. Screwcap. 14° alc. **Rating** 96 **To** 2025 $45
Great Southern Chardonnay 2006 An elegant wine, with some of the intensity of Block 8 to the clearly focused grapefruit and ripe apple flavours; long finish, and has absorbed the oak. Screwcap. 13.8° alc. **Rating** 94 **To** 2013 $23

ŸŸŸŸŸ **Great Southern Sauvignon Blanc Semillon 2007** A slightly closed bouquet, but springs into life on the palate, with intense herb, grass and more tropical fruit accents; dry finish, good length. Screwcap. 13.1° alc. **Rating** 91 **To** 2010 $17

ŸŸŸŸ **Great Southern Riesling 2007** Has as much fruit depth as Block 1, but not the same precision and polish; citrus with a touch of passionfruit, and a good wine by any standards. Screwcap. 12.5° alc. **Rating** 89 **To** 2013 $20

Forester Estate ★★★★

1064 Wildwood Road, Yallingup, WA 6282 **Region** Margaret River
T (08) 9755 2788 **F** (08) 9755 2766 **www.**foresterestate.com.au **Open** By appt
Winemaker Kevin McKay, Michael Langridge **Est.** 2001 **Cases** 20 000

The Forester Estate business partners are Kevin McKay and Redmond Sweeny. Winemaker Michael Langridge has a Bachelor of Arts (Hons) in Psychology and a Bachelor of Applied Science (wine science, CSU). As Kevin McKay says, 'He is the most over-qualified forklift driver in Australia.' They have built and designed a 500-tonne winery, half devoted to contract winemaking, the other half for the Forester label. The estate vineyards are planted to cabernet sauvignon, sauvignon blanc, semillon, chardonnay, shiraz, merlot, malbec, petit verdot and cabernet franc.

ŸŸŸŸŸ **Home Block Margaret River Shiraz 2005** Light- to medium-bodied, relying on length rather than depth or structure; attractive spicy black fruit flavours, and controlled oak. Diam. 14° alc. **Rating** 90 **To** 2013 $31

ŸŸŸŸ **Margaret River Cabernet Sauvignon 2005** Distinctly light-bodied for the region, and in a strongly savoury/earthy mode; length is its strong point. Diam. 14° alc. **Rating** 89 **To** 2015 $29
Margaret River Semillon Sauvignon Blanc 2007 Gentle citrus, tropical, gooseberry and passionfruit melange; easy-access style, though shortens somewhat on the finish. Screwcap. 13° alc. **Rating** 87 **To** 2009 $18.95

Foster's Wine Estates   **NR**

77 Southbank Boulevard, Southbank, Vic 3006 **Region** Various
T 1300 651 650 **F** (03) 9633 2002 **www**.fosters.com.au **Open** Not
Winemaker Chris Hatcher **Est.** 2005 **Cases** 40 million
Foster's Wine Estates has two main streams of brands: those which it had prior to the
amalgamation with Southcorp, and those which came with Southcorp. Alphabetically, in the
former category are: Andrew Garrett, Annie's Lane, Baileys of Glenrowan, Cartwheel, Early
Harvest, Eye Spy, Half Mile Creek, Ingoldby, Jamiesons Run, Maglieri Lambrusco, Maglieri of
McLaren Vale, Metala, Mildara, Mount Ida, Pepperjack, Robertson's Well, Saltram, Shadowood,
St Huberts, T'Gallant, The Rothbury Estate, Wolf Blass, Yarra Ridge and Yellowglen. The
Southcorp originated brands are: Blues Point, Coldstream Hills, Devil's Lair, Edwards & Chaffey,
Fisher's Circle, Glass Mountain, Kaiser Stuhl, Killawarra, Kirralaa, Leo Buring, Lindemans,
Matthew Lang, Minchinbury, Penfolds, Queen Adelaide, Rosemount Estate, Rouge Homme,
Seaview, Seppelt, The Little Penguin, Tollana and Wynns Coonawarra. Those which have
dedicated vineyards wholly or partially within their control and/or have separate winemaking
facilities will be found under their separate entries. Those which are brands without, as it were,
an independent existence are covered within this entry. Exports to all major markets.

Fox Creek Wines   ★★★★☆

Malpas Road, Willunga, SA 5172 **Region** McLaren Vale
T (08) 8556 2403 **F** (08) 8556 2104 **www**.foxcreekwines.com **Open** 7 days 10–5
Winemaker Chris Dix, Scott Zrna **Est.** 1995 **Cases** 35 000
Fox Creek has made a major impact since coming on-stream late in 1995. It is the venture of
the Watts family: Jim (a retired surgeon), wife Helen and son Paul Watts (a viticulturist); and
the Roberts family: John (a retired anaesthetist) and wife Lyn. Kristin McLarty (née Watts) is
marketing manager and Paul Rogers (married to Georgy, née Watts) is general manager. Moves
are afoot to introduce organic practices in the vineyards, with trials of an organically registered
herbicide derived from pine oil for weed control. The wines have enjoyed considerable show
success. Exports to the UK, the US and other major markets.

  ♀♀♀♀♀   **Reserve McLaren Vale Shiraz 2005** Medium- to full-bodied; well balanced
and constructed with blackberry, licorice, dark chocolate and mocha oak; not
overblown or extracted. Screwcap. 14.5° alc. **Rating** 94 **To** 2020 $70

  ♀♀♀♀♀   **Short Row McLaren Vale Shiraz 2006** Strongly regional lush blackberry and
dark chocolate aromas and flavours; soft tannins and controlled oak all make for a
user-friendly style of quality wine. Screwcap. 14.5° alc. **Rating** 93 **To** 2016 $28
Reserve McLaren Vale Cabernet Sauvignon 2005 Yet another powerful
wine; classic blackcurrant fruit dressed with a coat of fine-grained tannins; good
balance, line and length; the first year since '01 in which three Reserve reds have
been produced. Screwcap. 14.5° alc. **Rating** 92 **To** 2020 $36
Reserve McLaren Vale Merlot 2005 The ultimate wannabe cabernet style;
big, luscious black fruits, and a strong fine-grained tannin structure. High points
if varietal character irrelevant, less if relevant. These points are a compromise.
Screwcap. 14.5° alc. **Rating** 90 **To** 2019 $36

  ♀♀♀♀   **McLaren Vale Chardonnay 2007** A solid, well-made wine, the barrel ferment
component in balance with the ripe stone fruit; ready now. Screwcap. 14° alc.
Rating 87 **To** 2010 $17

Fox Gordon   ★★★★★

PO Box 62, Kent Town, SA 5071 **Region** Barossa Valley & Adelaide Hills
T (08) 8361 8136 **F** (08) 8361 9521 **www**.foxgordon.com.au **Open** Not
Winemaker Natasha Mooney **Est.** 2000 **Cases** 3000
This is the venture of three very well-known figures in the wine industry: Jane Gordon, Rachel
Atkins (née Fox) and Natasha Mooney. Natasha Mooney (Tash) has had first-class experience in
the Barossa Valley, particularly during her time as chief winemaker at Barossa Valley Estate. She

and her partners wanted to produce small quantities of high-quality wine which would allow them time to look after their children, the venture planned in the shade of the wisteria tree in Tash's back garden. The grapes come from dry-grown vineyards farmed under biodiversity principles which, says Mooney, makes the winemaker's job easy. Classy packaging adds the final touch. Exports to the UK, the US, Canada, Germany, India and China.

ŶŶŶŶŶ **Hannah's Swing Barossa Valley Shiraz 2006** Dense crimson; even more remarkably rich than Eight Uncles; potent black fruits and licorice; lip-smacking finish. Why, oh why, cork? 13.5° alc. **Rating** 95 **To** 2016 $44.95
Eight Uncles Barossa Valley Shiraz 2006 Very good crimson colour; has excellent texture; medium-bodied, the bright plum and blackberry fruit supported by a fine skein of savoury tannins. Praise be to a wine not driven by alcohol. Screwcap. 13.5° alc. **Rating** 94 **To** 2014 $24.95

ŶŶŶŶŶ **By George Barossa Valley Adelaide Hills Cabernet Tempranillo 2006** Bright purple-crimson; the flavours and textures come together surprisingly well, cassis, blackcurrant and mulberry, with fine, ripe tannins providing the length. Screwcap. 13.5° alc. **Rating** 93 **To** 2016 $19.95
King Louis Barossa Valley Cabernet Sauvignon 2006 Medium-bodied; elegant wine fully reflecting the vintage and early picking; cedary notes, with distinctly savoury tannins; for the purist, even the vinous puritan. Cork. 13.5° alc. **Rating** 90 **To** 2016 $44.95
Abby Viognier 2007 Very good varietal expression, with rounded peach and apricot; has achieved flavour without phenolics, perhaps partly due to repeated hand picking. Adelaide Hills. Screwcap. 13° alc. **Rating** 90 **To** 2012 $19.95

Foxeys Hangout   ★★★★☆

795 White Hill Road, Red Hill, Vic 3937 **Region** Mornington Peninsula
T (03) 5989 2022 **F** (03) 5989 2822 **www.**foxeys-hangout.com.au **Open** W'ends & public hols 11–5
Winemaker Tony Lee, Michael Lee **Est.** 1998 **Cases** 3000
Michael and Tony Lee spent 20 years in the hospitality business, acquiring a considerable knowledge of wine through the selection of wine lists for two decades, then opting for a change of lifestyle and occupation when they planted 4.7 ha of pinot noir, chardonnay and pinot gris on the northeast-facing slopes of an old farm. The name (and the catchy label) stems from the tale of two fox-hunters who began a competition with each other in 1936, hanging their kills on the branches of an ancient eucalypt tree to keep count. The corpses have gone, but not the nickname for the area.

ŶŶŶŶŶ **Reserve Mornington Peninsula Pinot Noir 2005** Shows good development with some game aromas emerging on the bouquet; plenty of flavour on the palate, with silky red fruits; quite spicy, with well-handled oak. Diam. 13.5° alc. **Rating** 92 **To** 2013 $45
Mornington Peninsula Pinot Noir 2006 Very fragrant, with a strong varietal personality of red fruits and a hint of spice; good weight and acidity, and a seamless finish. Diam. 13.5° alc. **Rating** 92 **To** 2014 $25

ŶŶŶŶ **Mornington Peninsula Chardonnay 2006** Restrained style; lively melon and nectarine fruit; slightly thin finish. Screwcap. 13.5° alc. **Rating** 88 **To** 2012 $25
Mornington Peninsula Rose 2007 Dry, crisp style; spice, rose petal and redcurrant fruit. Screwcap. 12.5° alc. **Rating** 87 **To** 2009 $20
Sparkling White NV Youthful, fresh and crisp lemon/lime flavours; low dosage; oysters are the go; bottle-fermented. Cork. 12.5° alc. **Rating** 87 **To** 2012 $25
Sparkling Shiraz 2005 Bottle-fermented; strong flavours, some possibly from oak, but all aggressive; strongly suggest patience and then a cautious approach lest the fox bites. Cork. 13.5° alc. **Rating** 87 **To** 2012 $25

Frankland Estate

Frankland Road, Frankland, WA 6396 **Region** Frankland River
T (08) 9855 1544 **F** (08) 9855 1549 **www.**franklandestate.com.au **Open** Mon–Fri 10–4,
public hols & w'ends by appt
Winemaker Barrie Smith, Judi Cullam **Est.** 1988 **Cases** 15 000
A significant Frankland River operation, situated on a large sheep property owned by Barrie
Smith and Judi Cullam. The 29-ha vineyard has been established progressively since 1988.
The recent introduction of an array of single-vineyard Rieslings has been a highlight. The
venture into the single-vineyard wines is driven by Judi's conviction that terroir is of utmost
importance, and the soils are indeed different. The climate is not, and the difference between
the wines is not as clear-cut as theory might suggest. The Isolation Ridge Vineyard is now
organically grown. Frankland Estate has held several important International Riesling tastings
and seminars over recent years. Exports to the UK, the US and other major markets.

ΨΨΨΨΨ **Isolation Ridge Vineyard Riesling 2007** A quite powerful lemon and lime
bouquet, with touches of spice; an even more powerful and intense palate, with
penetrating citrus and very good length. Screwcap. 12° alc. **Rating** 95 **To** 2017 $27
Poison Hill Vineyard Riesling 2007 More weight and citrus fruits on the very
long and textured mineral finish. Screwcap. 12.5° alc. **Rating** 94 **To** 2016 $27
Isolation Ridge Vineyard Shiraz 2005 The best Isolation Ridge for years;
generous black fruits with a dusting of spice and pepper are supported by fine
tannins and good oak. Screwcap. **Rating** 94 **To** 2025 $27

ΨΨΨΨΨ **Cooladerra Vineyard Riesling 2007** Ripe and full of exotic fruits; quite
minerally and with good texture; long and focused finish. Screwcap. 11° alc.
Rating 92 **To** 2016 $27
Isolation Ridge Vineyard Chardonnay 2006 A savoury style, with grapefruit,
stone fruit and fine acidity; persistent minerality on the finish. Screwcap. 13.5° alc.
Rating 90 **To** 2014 $25
Smith Cullam Shiraz Cabernet 2005 Plenty of concentration, the fruit quite
savoury; full-bodied, with firm, savoury tannins on the finish. Screwcap. 14.5° alc.
Rating 90 **To** 2018 $54
Isolation Ridge Vineyard Cabernet Sauvignon 2005 Powerful black-fruited
cabernet, with pronounced, slightly dry, tannins which need to soften; if left alone
for three-plus years, should come through. Screwcap. **Rating** 90 **To** 2015 $24
Olmo's Reward 2003 A much clearer line and focus than the other estate reds;
a range of red and black fruits balanced by firm tannins; Cabernet Sauvignon/
Merlot/Malbec/Cabernet Franc. Screwcap. 14° alc. **Rating** 90 **To** 2020 $37

ΨΨΨΨ **Rocky Gully Riesling 2007** Firm, direct and utterly correct style, with light
but appealing citrus and mineral flavours; balanced dry finish. Screwcap. 12.5° alc.
Rating 89 **To** 2012 $17
Olmo's Reward 2004 Developed red; a medium-bodied briary/earthy style
with persistent tannins; needs more fruit on the mid-palate. Screwcap. **Rating** 89
To 2012 $38
Isolation Ridge Vineyard Shiraz 2004 Savoury/olive-accented tannins
run through the entire length of the palate, still encircling the underlying fruit.
Screwcap. 14.5° alc. **Rating** 88 **To** 2013 $27
Isolation Ridge Vineyard Cabernet Sauvignon 2004 In typical Frankland
Estate style; savoury, earthy notes surround the blackcurrant fruit; slightly abrasive
texture. Screwcap. 14° alc. **Rating** 88 **To** 2017 $25
Rocky Gully Shiraz Viognier 2006 Powerful and uncompromising, a long
way adrift from usual shiraz viognier style, but has plenty of black fruit flavours.
Screwcap. 13.5° alc. **Rating** 87 **To** 2013 $17

Frankland Grange Wines   ★★★★☆

Lot 71 Frankland/Kojonup Road, Frankland, WA 6396 **Region** Frankland River
T (08) 9388 1288 **F** (08) 9388 1020 **Open** By appt
Winemaker Alkoomi (Michael Staniford) **Est.** 1995 **Cases** 1000
Frank Keet used shiraz cuttings from Alkoomi when he planted 2.5 ha of the variety in 1995, followed by 1.5 ha of chardonnay (also locally sourced) in '98. Given the quality of fruit coming from the Frankland River subregion, it seems highly likely that the number of wine producers will steadily increase in the years ahead.

ΨΨΨΨΨ **Chardonnay 2007** Elegant, intense wine; delicious nectarine and grapefruit
flavours, backed up by balanced acidity on a long finish. **Rating** 94 **To** 2012 $28

 # Fraser Gallop Estate   ★★★☆

547 Metricup Road, Wilyabrup, WA 6280 **Region** Margaret River
T (08) 9755 7553 **F** (08) 9755 7443 **www**.fgewines.com.au **Open** By appt
Winemaker Clive Otto (Contract) **Est.** 1999 **Cases** 7000
Nigel Gallop began the development of the 20-ha vineyard in 1999, planting cabernet sauvignon, cabernet franc, petit verdot and multi-clone chardonnay. The vines are dry-grown with modest yields per ha, followed by kid-glove treatment in the winery. The first vintage was 2002, the wine being contract-made offsite, but with Clive Otto (formerly of Vasse Felix) on board, a 300-tonne winery was built onsite for the '08 vintage; as well as wines under the Fraser Gallop Estate label, limited amounts of contract wine will be made for others.

ΨΨΨΨΨ **Margaret River Cabernet Sauvignon 2005** Multi-layered, deep and complex;
there is a strong mineral, slightly briary, note running through the line, along with
lots of cassis and ripe tannins. Screwcap. 13.9° alc. **Rating** 93 **To** 2016 $25

ΨΨΨΨ **Margaret River Semillon Sauvignon Blanc 2007** Benefits from partial barrel
ferment adding to texture; driven by grassy semillon running through to a quite
long finish. Screwcap. 13° alc. **Rating** 89 **To** 2011 $18.30
Margaret River Chardonnay 2007 Grapefruit and nectarine, with a creamy
touch of toasty oak; quite toasty on the palate, which just breaks the line. Screwcap.
13.7° alc. **Rating** 89 **To** 2012 $25
Margaret River Chardonnay 2006 Light-bodied; gentle stone fruit needing
more intensity, but does have balance and length. Screwcap. 13.5° alc. **Rating** 87
To 2010 $24

Freeman Vineyards   ★★★☆

101 Prunevale Road, Prunevale, NSW 2587 **Region** Hilltops
T (02) 6384 4299 **F** (02) 6384 4299 **www**.freemanvineyards.com.au **Open** By appt
Winemaker Dr Brian Freeman **Est.** 2000 **Cases** 600
Dr Brian Freeman has spent much of his long life in research and education, in the latter role as head of CSU's viticulture and oenology campus. In 2004 he purchased the 30-year-old vineyard previously known as Demondrille. He has also established a vineyard next door, and in all has 14 varieties totalling 40.5 ha; these range from staples such as shiraz, cabernet sauvignon, semillon and riesling through to the more exotic, trendy varieties such as tempranillo, and on to corvina and rondinella. He has had a long academic interest in the effect of partial drying of grapes on the tannins, and, living at Prunevale, was easily able to obtain a prune dehydrator to partially raisin the two varieties.

ΨΨΨΨ **Fortuna 2007** Light-bodied, with a savoury, slatey cast to the improbable blend
of Pinot Gris/Riesling/Sauvignon Blanc/Chardonnay/Aleatico, all from the
Hilltops region; a further surprise that all are from 30-year-old vines. Screwcap.
14° alc. **Rating** 88 **To** 2010 $30

Freycinet ★★★★★

15919 Tasman Highway via Bicheno, Tas 7215 **Region** East Coast Tasmania
T (03) 6257 8574 **F** (03) 6257 8454 **www**.freycinetvineyard.com.au **Open** 7 days 9.30–4.30
Winemaker Claudio Radenti, Lindy Bull **Est.** 1980 **Cases** 5000
The original 9-ha Freycinet vineyards are beautifully situated on the sloping hillsides of a
small valley. The soils are brown dermosol on top of jurassic dolerite, and the combination
of aspect, slope, soil and heat summation produces red grapes with unusual depth of colour
and ripe flavours. One of Australia's foremost producers of Pinot Noir, with a wholly
enviable track record of consistency – rare with such a temperamental variety. The Radenti
(sparkling), Riesling and Chardonnay are also wines of the highest quality. Exports to the
UK and Sweden.

ΨΨΨΨΨ **Chardonnay 2006** A lovely wine, with great tension and line to the nectarine
and melon fruit with fine, bracing but balanced acidity; great length and finesse;
gold at Tas Wine Show '08. Screwcap. 13.8° alc. **Rating** 96 **To** 2015 $34
Radenti Pinot Noir Chardonnay 1999 With 7 years on lees prior to
disgorgement, and further time in bottle, this wine is a masterpiece, bringing
nectarine, grapefruit, white peach, brioche and fine creamy characters together on
the immaculately balanced palate, the flavours flowing and rippling. Cork. 12° alc.
Rating 96 **To** 2010 $48
Riesling 2007 Light, fresh and clean; clear-cut apple blossom and lime aromas,
then vibrant apple and lime juice flavours through the long palate; cleansing finish.
Screwcap. 13° alc. **Rating** 94 **To** 2015 $25
Pinot Noir 2005 Good colour, seems to have gained the complexity it lacked
12 months ago, with a complex plum and spice bouquet, the supple palate very
elegant and long, with a peacock's tail finish. Screwcap. 14° alc. **Rating** 94
To 2015 $70

ΨΨΨΨΨ **Pinot Noir 2006** Less dense in colour than many from the vintage, but that's
no bad thing; has excellent texture and structure, but the fruit flavours show
nuances of spice and forest floor, the tannins ripe and fine, the oak restrained; still
developing. Nov '08 release. Screwcap. **Rating** 93 **To** 2015 $50

ΨΨΨΨ **Louis Pinot Noir 2006** Vibrant and lively, with distinct foresty/savoury nuances
and considerable length; as yet rather severe, but tasted 6 months prior to release
(Nov '08). Screwcap. **Rating** 89 **To** 2012 $27
Cabernet Sauvignon Merlot 2004 Light-bodied, fragrant and vibrant, with
a mix of cassis and blackcurrant fruit; fine, supple, flow and finish. Cabernet
Sauvignon (60%)/Merlot (40%). **Rating** 89 **To** 2012 $38
Louis Pinot Noir 2005 Abundant plummy varietal flavours, but doesn't have
the movement of the top wine; soft, easy access. Screwcap. 13.5° alc. **Rating** 88
To 2010 $27
Louis Unwooded Chardonnay 2006 Fresh and vibrant unoaked wine, a cross
in flavour terms between sauvignon blanc and chardonnay, but none the worse for
that; has length. Screwcap. 13.5° alc. **Rating** 87 **To** 2010 $18

Frog Rock Wines ★★★

Edgell Lane, Mudgee, NSW 2850 **Region** Mudgee
T (02) 6372 2408 **F** (02) 6372 6924 **www**.frogrockwines.com **Open** 7 days 10–5
Winemaker David Lowe, Jane Wilson (Contract) **Est.** 1973 **Cases** 8000
Frog Rock is the former Tallara Vineyard, established over 30 years ago by leading Sydney
chartered accountant Rick Turner. There are now 60 ha of vineyard, with 22 ha each of shiraz
and cabernet sauvignon, and much smaller plantings of chardonnay, semillon, merlot, petit
verdot and chambourcin. Exports to Canada, Singapore, Hong Kong and Fiji.

ΨΨΨΨ **Mudgee Semillon Sauvignon Blanc 2007** Almost entirely driven by grass,
herb and capsicum semillon fruit; has length, and a dry finish. Screwcap. 11° alc.
Rating 88 **To** 2010 $15

Mudgee Chambourcin 2006 Has the intense colour the variety is noted for, and some of the mulberry/blackcurrant fruit; as ever, limited structure. Screwcap. 14.5° alc. **Rating** 88 **To** 2009 $20

Frogmore Creek   ★★★★★

208 Denholms Road, Cambridge, Tas 7170 **Region** Southern Tasmania
T (03) 6248 5844 **F** (03) 6248 5855 **www**.frogmorecreek.com.au **Open** W'ends 10–5
Winemaker Alain Rousseau, Nick Glaetzer, Andrew Hood (Consultant) **Est.** 1997
Cases 18 000
Frogmore Creek is a Pacific Rim joint venture, the owners being Tony Scherer of Tasmania and Jack Kidwiler of California. The partners have developed a substantial organically grown vineyard, and have acquired the Hood/Wellington wine business previously owned by Andrew Hood, who continues his involvement as a consultant. Winemaking has been consolidated at Cambridge, where the Frogmore Creek and 42° South brands are made, as well as a thriving contract winemaking business. Exports to the US, Japan and Korea.

ŸŸŸŸŸ **FGR Riesling 2006** Lime and ripe apple aromas; delicious palate, with lime juice and perfect acidity to offset the 40g residual sugar. Screwcap. 10° alc. **Rating** 95 **To** 2012 $22
Iced Gewurztraminer 2007 Very pale colour; beautifully pure, the freeze concentration technique working miracles for the variety, allowing it to give the full varietal expression so rare in dry versions. Top gold, Tas Wine Show '08. **Rating** 95 **To** 2012 $26
Reserve Chardonnay 2005 High-quality chardonnay, travelling well, with an unctuously rich, round and mouthfilling palate; as always, sustained by good natural acidity. Gold, Tas Wine Show '08. Screwcap. 14° alc. **Rating** 94 **To** 2012 $50
Winemaker's Blend Pinot Noir 2005 Deceptively light colour; an elegant, spicy, savoury pinot with hallmark length; a lovely heart of strawberry and cherry fruit. Screwcap. 14° alc. **Rating** 94 **To** 2012 $32

ŸŸŸŸŸ **42° South Sauvignon Blanc 2007** Fragrant blossom and passionfruit aromas; a lively palate with considerable thrust fuelled by crisp, crunchy, lemony acidity. Screwcap. 12.5° alc. **Rating** 93 **To** 2010 $23.50
Cuvee Evermore 2004 Unusual pungent aromas of spiced red fruits; a brisk, bright, penetrating and long palate with considerable pinot influence; bone-dry finish; bottle-fermented. Cork. 12.1° alc. **Rating** 90 **To** 2009 $34.50

ŸŸŸŸ **Sauvignon Blanc 2007** Fresh, tangy, minerally style, with bright acidity; some asparagus and grass flavours grow on the back-palate and finish. **Rating** 89 **To** 2009 $25
Iced Riesling 2007 Skilfully made, reflecting much experience; tangy lime juice flavours, the juicy sweetness of the mid-palate countered on the finish by acidity; as yet, not particularly complex. Screwcap. 8° alc. **Rating** 89 **To** 2012 $26
Riesling 2007 Some nettle aromas, the fruit is fine and the finish harmonious and long. **Rating** 88 **To** 2014 $24
42° South Riesling 2006 Starting to open up and show its wares; generous citrus flavours, rather than finesse. Screwcap. **Rating** 88 **To** 2014 $22
Pinot Noir 2006 Bright colour; plenty of grip and quite long, with oak a little more evident than the fruit. Screwcap. 14° alc. **Rating** 88 **To** 2012 $36
42° South Sparkling NV Delicate but attractive stone fruit and strawberry and citrus flavours; clean, crisp finish; not particularly complex. Cork. 12.5° alc. **Rating** 87 **To** 2011 $24
Ruby Pinot Noir NV Cinnamon and spice, with a little red fruit in the background; good spirit. A strange decision to go down this path with pinot. Cork. 20° alc. **Rating** 87 **To** 2012 $22

Frogspond

NR

400 Arthurs Seat Road, Red Hill, Vic 3937 **Region** Mornington Peninsula
T (03) 5989 2941 **F** (03) 9826 6264 **www**.frogspond.com.au **Open** By appt
Winemaker Matt Harrop, Kilchurn Wines **Est.** 1994 **Cases** 100
The Nelson family has established 2 ha of chardonnay and pinot noir on an ideal north-facing slope. The low yields, thanks to viticulturist Dean Nelson's meticulous care, produce grapes with intense fruit flavours, but only a tiny amount of wine is made. There are three wines: Chardonnay, Pinot Noir and Sparkling (Chardonnay/Pinot Noir).

Galafrey

Quangellup Road, Mount Barker, WA 6324 **Region** Mount Barker
T (08) 9851 2022 **F** (08) 9851 2324 **www**.galafreywines.com.au **Open** 7 days 10–5
Winemaker Kim Tyrer **Est.** 1977 **Cases** 8000
Relocated to a purpose-built but utilitarian winery after previously inhabiting the exotic surrounds of the old Albany wool store, Galafrey makes wines with plenty of robust, if not rustic, character, drawing grapes in the main from nearly 13 ha of estate plantings. Following the death of husband/father/founder Ian Tyrer, Kim and Linda Tyrer have taken up the reins, announcing, 'There is girl power happening at Galafrey Wines!' There is a cornucopia of back vintages available, some superb and underpriced, at the cellar door. Exports to Singapore and Japan.

ŸŸŸŸŸ **Reserve Cabernet Sauvignon 2000** Tawny colour; ripe fruit and prolonged bottle age provide a harmonious wine, with mocha overtones and a smooth finish; ready right now. Cork. 14° alc. **Rating** 90 **To** 2010 $50

ŸŸŸŸ **The Jovial 2003** Developed red; very firm in the mouth, has length but not so much generosity; Cabernet Sauvignon/Merlot/Cabernet Franc. Screwcap. 13° alc. **Rating** 88 **To** 2012 $40
Mount Barker Riesling 2007 A solid wine with good varietal expression, but as yet lacking mid-palate fruit; a track record of development in bottle. Screwcap. 12.1° alc. **Rating** 87 **To** 2012 $18
Dry Land Riesling 2007 A gentle mix of citrus and talcy mineral flavours; falls away somewhat on the finish. Screwcap. 11.5° alc. **Rating** 87 **To** 2011 $20
Mount Barker Chardonnay 2007 An honest wine, with melon and yellow peach flavours. Screwcap. **Rating** 87 **To** 2010 $16
Frankland River Shiraz 2002 Hanging in there gamely, sustained in part by savoury tannins underpinning the spicy fruit. Screwcap. 13.5° alc. **Rating** 87 **To** 2009 $16

Galah

Tregarthen Road, Ashton, SA 5137 **Region** Adelaide Hills
T (08) 8390 1243 **F** (08) 8390 1243 **Open** At Ashton Hills
Winemaker Stephen George **Est.** 1986 **Cases** 500
Over the years Stephen George has built up a network of contacts across SA from which he gains some very high-quality small parcels of grapes or wine for the Galah label. These are all sold direct at low prices given the quality.

ŸŸŸŸŸ **Clare Valley Shiraz 2002** Very good hue for age; excellent line, length and focus; shows the cool vintage and modest alcohol, but is fully ripe in a black fruit mould; tannins entirely tamed. Cork. 13.5° alc. **Rating** 94 **To** 2017 $25

ŸŸŸŸŸ **Mount Lofty Ranges Shiraz 2003** Generous, ripe black fruits, dark chocolate and licorice, particularly meritorious for the vintage; ripe tannins, and a nice savoury twist on the finish. Screwcap. **Rating** 90 **To** 2023 $25
Clare Valley Cabernet Malbec 2002 Developing slowly but surely; the tannins are still to fully resolve and soften, but there is adequate fruit to tide the wine through. Cork. 13.5° alc. **Rating** 90 **To** 2022 $25

ỶỶỶỶ **Three Sheds Red 2004** Holding hue well; a fresh cascade of lively fruit flavours on a light- to medium-bodied palate; high quality, casual, drink-now style. Merlot/ Cabernet Sauvignon. Screwcap. 13.5° alc. **Rating** 89 **To** 2009 $15

Gallagher Wines ★★★★

2770 Dog Trap Road, Murrumbateman, NSW 2582 **Region** Canberra District
T (02) 6227 0555 **F** (02) 6227 0666 **www**.gallagherwines.com.au **Open** W'ends & public hols 10–5
Winemaker Greg Gallagher **Est.** 1995 **Cases** 3000
Greg Gallagher was senior winemaker at Taltarni for 20 years, working with Dominique Portet. He began planning a change of career at much the same time as did Portet, and started establishing a small vineyard at Murrumbateman in 1995, now planted to 1 ha each of chardonnay and shiraz.

ỶỶỶỶỶ **Sauvignon Blanc 2007** A spotless bouquet, with no sweat or reduction; bright precise fruit; asparagus and gooseberry; firm acidity, good length. **Rating** 91 **To** 2009 $17.95
Shiraz 2005 Medium-bodied; a quite complex wine, with spicy/earthy overtones to the black fruits; soft tannins and controlled oak. Screwcap. 13.8° alc. **Rating** 90 **To** 2012 $22
Blanc de Blancs 2005 Fresh, lively citrus fruit is dominant, with a touch of stone fruit also evident; clean, zesty finish. Crown seal. 13.2° alc. **Rating** 90 **To** 2009 $34.95

ỶỶỶỶ **Canberra District Riesling 2007** Distinct tropical aromas plus orange blossom; a powerful palate, with strong fruit structure broadening slightly on the finish. Difficult vintage. Screwcap. 11.9° alc. **Rating** 89 **To** 2012 $18
Shiraz 2006 Notes of spice and leather through a black fruit, medium-bodied palate; not over-extracted, but the oak does not flatter the wine. Screwcap. 13.6° alc. **Rating** 89 **To** 2012 $22
Sparkling Shiraz 2004 Spicy, juicy shiraz fruit; has length, and the sweetness is within bounds. Bottle-fermented. Crown seal. 13.6° alc. **Rating** 87 **To** 2012 $35

Galli Estate ★★★★☆

1507 Melton Highway, Rockbank, Vic 3335 **Region** Sunbury
T (03) 9747 1444 **F** (03) 9747 1481 **www**.galliestate.com.au **Open** 7 days 11–5
Winemaker Stephen Phillips **Est.** 1997 **Cases** 20 000
Galli Estate may be a relative newcomer to the scene, but it is a substantial one. The late Lorenzo, and Pam, Galli first planted 34.5 ha of vines at Rockbank, the lion's share to cabernet sauvignon and shiraz, but with 1.5–2.5 ha of semillon, sauvignon blanc, pinot grigio, chardonnay, sangiovese and pinot noir. This was followed by an even larger vineyard at Heathcote, with 106 ha of an even more diverse spread once 55 ha had been allotted for shiraz. A large underground cellar has been constructed; already 50 m long, it may be extended in the future. Exports to the US, Canada, Japan, Singapore, China and Hong Kong.

ỶỶỶỶỶ **Artigiano Block Two Heathcote Shiraz 2006** Supple, smooth and fine medium-bodied wine, with spiced black and red fruits; has delicious texture and mouthfeel, fine tannins coming on the finish exactly when they are needed. Screwcap. 14° alc. **Rating** 94 **To** 2020 $26

ỶỶỶỶỶ **Artigiano Sunbury Chardonnay 2006** High-quality winemaking gives a sure touch to the fusion of nectarine and grapefruit flavours with French oak; light- to medium-bodied, good length. Screwcap. 14.1° alc. **Rating** 93 **To** 2012 $19.95
Sunbury Chardonnay 2007 Extremely fine, tight and light, giving no hint about the alcohol; lingering grapefruit and nectarine and bright acidity, the oak absorbed by the fruit; for the long haul. Screwcap. 14.4° alc. **Rating** 93 **To** 2015 $22

Artigiano Block Two Heathcote Shiraz 2005 An attractive, well-structured, medium-bodied palate with blackberries, warm spices and well-tempered French oak all providing length; appropriate tannins. Cork. 14.4° alc. **Rating** 92 **To** 2014 $24.95

Artigiano Heathcote Viognier 2007 Clear-cut varietal fruit on both bouquet and palate; good mouthfeel to the apricot and citrus flavours, which avoid the phenolic trap. Screwcap. 14° alc. **Rating** 91 **To** 2010 $21.95

Artigiano Sunbury Shiraz 2006 Like the Heathcote wine, medium-bodied, but with far more accent on spicy, earthy, savoury notes; has good length and balance, and may surprise with its longevity. Screwcap. 14.1° alc. **Rating** 91 **To** 2015 $22

Heathcote Shiraz Viognier 2006 Bright, clear red-purple; a mix of black cherry, plum, spice and blackberry, viognier doing its work with discretion; good use of oak. Screwcap. 14.2° alc. **Rating** 91 **To** 2011 $15.95

Sunbury Sauvignon Blanc 2007 Clean, lively and clearly articulated varietal flavour; herb, asparagus, citrus, mineral and a touch of spice. Screwcap. 13° alc. **Rating** 90 **To** 2009 $15.95

Artigiano Sunbury Pinot Grigio 2007 Aromatic pear, snow pea and herb aromas, then intense palate flavours which track the bouquet. Screwcap. 14° alc. **Rating** 90 **To** 2009 $19.95

Il Acquario Shiraz Grenache Viognier 2006 The unusual blend works well to produce a lively, light- to medium-bodied red with good length and minimal tannins; ready now. Screwcap. 14.5° alc. **Rating** 90 **To** 2010 $39.95

♥♥♥♥ **Sunbury Cabernet Sauvignon 2006** A slightly contrary mix of sweet cassis fruit and spicy/earthy tannins needing time to marry. Screwcap. 13.9° alc. **Rating** 88 **To** 2014 $16

Heathcote Tempranillo Grenache Mourvedre 2006 Ripe red fruits on entry are immediately challenged by tannins, but there is enough to connect the two parts; best with food. Screwcap. 15° alc. **Rating** 88 **To** 2010 $19.95

Heathcote Sangiovese 2006 Light-bodied in red fruit flavour terms, but with all the attendant savoury tannins. Screwcap. 14° alc. **Rating** 87 **To** 2011 $22

Gapsted ★★★★

Great Alpine Road, Gapsted, Vic 3737 **Region** Alpine Valleys
T (03) 5751 1383 **F** (03) 5751 1368 **www.**gapstedwines.com.au **Open** 7 days 10–5
Winemaker Michael Cope-Williams, Shayne Cunningham **Est.** 1997 **Cases** 150 000
Gapsted is the major brand of the Victorian Alps winery, which started life (and continues) as large-scale contract winemaking facilities. However, the quality of the wines it made for its own brand (Gapsted) has led to the expansion of production not only under that label, but under a raft of cheaper, subsidiary labels including Tobacco Road, Coldstone, Buckland Gap, Snowy Creek, Dividing Range, and doubtless others in the pipeline. Its success can be gauged from the increase in production to 150 000 cases, albeit with a hiccup following the 2007 bushfires. Exports to the UK and other major markets.

♥♥♥♥♡ **Limited Release Strathbogie King Valley Shiraz Viognier 2005** Complex aromas; a supple medium-bodied palate with considerable length to the mix of blackberry, black cherry and spice plus superfine tannins. Screwcap. 14.5° alc. **Rating** 92 **To** 2015 $27

Ballerina Canopy Sauvignon Blanc 2007 A blend of Marlborough (NZ)/ Central Ranges/King Valley, a sign of things to come; undoubtedly driven by the Marlborough component, with nicely balanced gooseberry, apple and citrus fruit. Screwcap. 12.5° alc. **Rating** 90 **To** 2009 $22

Ballerina Canopy Shiraz 2005 Good hue; medium-bodied, with lively, fresh and vibrant spicy red and black fruits; fine tannins, good length. Screwcap. 15.5° alc. **Rating** 90 **To** 2015 $25

Limited Release Barbera 2006 While not especially complex, has more going for it than many, with an array of gently ripe fruit flavours; soft tannins and balanced oak. Zork. 14.5° alc. **Rating** 90 **To** 2013 $27

Ballerina Canopy Durif 2003 Complex plum, choc-mint, blackberry, fruitcake and vanilla aromas and flavours; ripe tannins. Cork. 15.5° alc. Rating 90 To 2013 $30

ŶŶŶŶ   **Limited Release Alpine Valleys King Valley Saperavi 2004** Still youthful colour; a medium-bodied mix of flavours ranging from mint to spice to plum and blackberry; fine tannins. Screwcap. 13.5° alc. Rating 89 To 2014 $27

Tobacco Road Shiraz 2004 Good hue for age; much greater volume of sweet black and red fruits than expected at this price point; enjoyable informal drinking. now or in three years' time. Screwcap. 14° alc. Rating 88 To 2010 $13

Coldstone Brut Cuvee NV Doubtless tank-fermented, but has very good balance and is bright and fresh; simple, but has clear flavour and a dry finish. Tumbarumba/King Valley Pinot Noir/Chardonnay. Cork. 12° alc. Rating 88 To 2009 $13

Victorian Alps Muscato 2006 While a cellar door knockout, with its intense sweet, grapey flavours, it has length and vibrancy; moreover, if you add 50% soda water you will end up with 3.75° alcohol, which means you can drink a whole lot more without endangering health or your driver's licence. Spritzers, as they are called, have gone out of fashion; perhaps they ought to come back in. Screwcap. 7.5° alc. Rating 87 To 2009 $16

Limited Release King Valley Alpine Valleys Petit Manseng 2006 Pleasant wine, with a mix of tropical and citrus flavours augmented by a touch of sweetness; however, the rarity of the grape can't justify the price. Screwcap. 13° alc. Rating 87 To 2010 $27

Coldstone Shiraz Viognier 2006 Probably the cheapest co-fermented shiraz viognier going around; has typical juicy fruit and, even if a little rustic, offers an abundance of flavour at a very good price. Screwcap. 14.5° alc. Rating 87 To 2012 $13

Valley Selection Muscato 2007 Intensely sweet and grapey with overtones of banana; ideal candidate for 50% soda water and ice blocks on a hot day. Screwcap. 6.5° alc. Rating 87 To 2009 $16

Victorian Alps Cabernet Merlot 2004 Medium-bodied; generous, soft, and quite sweet red and black fruit flavours; oak and tannins are bit-players; has balance. Screwcap. 14° alc. Rating 87 To 2010 $16

Victorian Alps Cabernet Merlot 2006 Bright colour; fresh red fruits, direct and simple, but like all in this range, excellent value for money; where the wine goes in the '07 and '08 vintages is anyone's guess. Screwcap. 14° alc. Rating 87 To 2009 $9.95

Ballerina Canopy Cabernet Sauvignon 2005 A trace of reduction; has ripe fruit flavours, though not much finesse; SA/King Valley. Screwcap. 14.5° alc. Rating 87 To 2012 $25

Garbin Estate   NR

209 Toodyay Road, Middle Swan, WA 6056 **Region** Swan Valley
T (08) 9274 1747 **F** (08) 9274 1747 **Open** Tues–Sun & public hols 10.30–5.30
Winemaker Peter Garbin **Est.** 1956 **Cases** 4500
Duje Garbin, winemaker and fisherman from a small island near the Dalmatian coast in the Adriatic Sea, migrated to WA in 1937, and purchased the Middle Swan property on which Garbin Estate stands in 1956. When he retired in the early 1990s, son Peter took over what was a thoroughly traditional and small business, and embarked on a massive transition. A new cellar door and processing area, upgraded major plant and equipment, and the establishment of a vineyard in Gingin all followed. A former design draughtsman, Peter is now full-time winemaker, backed up by assistant winemaker, wife Katrina, and sons Joel and Adam.

Garden Gully

★★★★☆

1477 Western Highway, Great Western, Vic 3377 **Region** Grampians
T (03) 5356 2400 **F** (03) 5356 2405 **www**.gardengully.com.au **Open** 7 days 11–4
Winemaker Contract **Est.** 1987 **Cases** 1200
In late 2004 a team of local families purchased Garden Gully. They have renovated and
reopened the cellar door, selling Garden Gully, Grampians Estate and Westgate Wines, various
olive oils and other local produce. The 50-year-old 5.5-ha vineyard has been reworked and
rejuvenated.

ŶŶŶŶŶ **St Ethel's Grampians Shiraz 2006** Much denser colour than the varietal; rich,
textured and complex, the underlying fruit from 60-year-old vines far superior;
attractive licorice nuances to spicy black fruits; good tannin and oak. Screwcap.
14° alc. **Rating** 94 **To** 2026 $40

ŶŶŶŶ **Grampians Sparkling Shiraz 2005** Has plenty of flavour from 12 months'
maturation in old oak puncheons before tiraging, then 12 months on lees before
disgorgement in June '07. All this was correct, but the dosage was too high – a
pity. Crown seal. 14° alc. **Rating** 88 **To** 2012 $30
Grampians Riesling 2007 Solidly built and structured, with ripe (but not sweet)
fruit; fractionally heavy finish. Screwcap. 13° alc. **Rating** 87 **To** 2011 $19
Grampians Shiraz 2006 Some regional mint, along with touches of spice and
mint, all add up to a light- to medium-bodied savoury stye. Screwcap. 14° alc.
Rating 87 **To** 2013 $24

Gardners Ground

★★★

444 Rivers Road, Canowindra, NSW 2804 **Region** Cowra
T (02) 6344 3135 **F** (02) 6344 3175 **www**.gardnersground.com.au **Open** Not
Winemaker Graeme Kerr, Chris Derrez (Contract) **Est.** 2001 **Cases** 2500
Jenny and Herb Gardner chose their property, situated on the southern bank of the Belubula
River, back in 1996. It was the culmination of an extensive search over southeastern
Australia, meeting the requirements of appropriate soil structure as well as natural beauty. It
was always their intention that the 15-ha vineyard would be run organically, and the use of
chemicals ceased in 1996 before planting began. Chardonnay and Shiraz are made by contract
winemakers Graeme Kerr (at Canowindra) and Chris Derrez (at Orange). Most of the wine,
labelled under the Hawkewind brand, is exported to Japan.

ŶŶŶŶ **Cowra Shiraz 2005** Light- to medium-bodied, but has developed nicely;
predominantly red cherry fruits plus some spice and savoury notes; good overall
balance and value. Screwcap. 13.9° alc. **Rating** 87 **To** 2009 $10
Cowra Merlot 2005 Has surprising varietal expression at the savoury/earthy end
of the spectrum; some red fruits, and fine tannins. Screwcap. 13.9° alc. **Rating** 87
To 2009 $10

Garlands

★★★★☆

Marmion Street, Mount Barker, WA 6324 **Region** Mount Barker
T (08) 9851 2737 **F** (08) 9851 1062 **www**.garlandswines.com.au **Open** 7 days 10.30–
4.30; winter Thurs–Sun 10.30–4.30 or by appt
Winemaker Michael Garland **Est.** 1996 **Cases** 5000
Garlands is a partnership between Michael and Julie Garland and their vigneron neighbours,
Craig and Caroline Drummond and Patrick and Christine Gresswell. Michael Garland came
to grapegrowing and winemaking with a varied background (in biological research, computer
sales and retail clothing) and now has a CSU degree in oenology. The winery has a capacity of
150 tonnes, and will continue contract-making for other small producers in the region as well
as making the wine from the 9.25 ha of estate vineyards (planted to shiraz, riesling, cabernet
sauvignon, cabernet franc, chardonnay, sauvignon blanc and semillon). Cabernet Franc is
the winery speciality. No samples received; the rating is that of last year. Exports to the UK,
Switzerland, Trinidad, Hong Kong and Singapore.

Gartelmann Hunter Estate ★★★★☆

701 Lovedale Road, Lovedale, NSW 2321 **Region** Lower Hunter Valley
T (02) 4930 7113 **F** (02) 4930 7114 **www**.gartelmann.com.au **Open** 7 days 10–5
Winemaker Jorg Gartelmann, Ross Pearson **Est.** 1970 **Cases** 3500
In 1996 Jan and Jorg Gartelmann purchased what was previously the George Hunter Estate
– 16 ha of mature vineyards, most established by Sydney restaurateur Oliver Shaul in '70, the
merlot in '97. A major change in the business model resulted in the sale of the vineyards after
the 2006 vintage, and the grapes are now sourced from other Hunter Valley vineyards, giving
the business the maximum flexibility. Exports to UK and Germany.

ΨΨΨΨΨ **Benjamin Semillon 2007** Excellent focus and pure Hunter expression; lemon
and hints of dried straw on the bouquet, with vibrant, clean fruit and very good
acidity on the palate. Screwcap. 10° alc. **Rating** 94 **To** 2020 $25

ΨΨΨΨΩ **Diedrich Shiraz 2006** Great colour, and a commensurately powerful bouquet
and palate, with abundant black fruits offset by drying tannins. Screwcap. 14° alc.
Rating 91 **To** 2012 $40

ΨΨΨΨ **Jessica Verdelho 2007** Good concentration, with abundant ripe citrus fruits
and a hint of dried straw; fine and focused tropical palate. Screwcap. 13.5° alc.
Rating 89 **To** 2012 $20

 # Geddes Wines ★★★★

PO Box 227, McLaren Vale, SA 5171 **Region** McLaren Vale
T (08) 8556 2447 **F** (08) 8556 2447 **Open** Not
Winemaker Tim Geddes **Est.** 2004 **Cases** 800
Owner/winemaker Tim and wife Amanda, a chef, bring considerable experience to the
venture. Tim's started in Hawke's Bay, New Zealand, with three vintages as a cellar hand,
which directly led to a move to Australia to complete the oenology degree at Adelaide
University. Dual vintages in the Barossa and Hunter Valleys were woven between settling
down in McLaren Vale, where he has been a contract winemaker for a number of clients since
2002. Tim's '07 lease of a 500-tonne winery will mean even greater contract work, while he
slowly builds the basic Seldom Inn range (made every vintage) and the Geddes label, which
will only be made in the best years. The long-term aim is to make 3000 cases, relying on the
selection of small parcels of fruit from a number of selected subregions of McLaren Vale.

ΨΨΨΨΨ **Seldom Inn McLaren Vale Shiraz Grenache 2006** Has excellent depth
and structure, the grenache providing ripe, juicy fruit aromas and flavours, the
shiraz the structure and tannins; a splash of regional chocolate on the finish. Gold,
McLaren Vale Wine Show '07. Screwcap. 15° alc. **Rating** 94 **To** 2014 $20

ΨΨΨΨΩ **Seldom Inn McLaren Vale Cabernet Sauvignon 2006** Attractive,
harmonious, medium-bodied mix of blackcurrant and dark chocolate fruit; ripe
tannins, good oak. Screwcap. 14.5° alc. **Rating** 92 **To** 2014 $20

ΨΨΨΨ **Seldom Inn McLaren Vale Shiraz 2006** Considerable depth to the colour,
flavour and overall body; ripe plum and dark chocolate fruit plus ripe tannins;
flavour rather than finesse. Screwcap. 14.5° alc. **Rating** 89 **To** 2016 $20
Another McLaren Vale Shiraz 2005 A big, full-bodied wine, with black fruits,
dark chocolate and licorice, then quite forceful tannins; cries out for time. Cork.
14.5° alc. **Rating** 89 **To** 2015 $30

 # Gelland Estate ★★★

PO Box 1148, Mudgee, NSW 2850 **Region** Mudgee
T (02) 6373 5411 **F** (02) 6372 6603 **www**.gellandestate.com.au **Open** Not
Winemaker Rhys Eather (Contract) **Est.** 1999 **Cases** 500
Warren and Stephanie Gelland moved from Sydney to Mudgee in 1998 'to start a family with
room to move'. They had no background in viticulture, but friends who had previously made

the same move and established a vineyard suggested that the Gellands follow suit, which they duly did by planting 4 ha of cabernet sauvignon and 2 ha of chardonnay. More recently they have purchased small parcels of shiraz and viognier from Mudgee vineyards to add a Cabernet Shiraz, Viognier Chardonnay and Cabernet Rose to the portfolio from 2008.

ȚȚȚȚ **Mudgee Chardonnay 2006** A clean wine, with nectarine fruits and good texture; a hint of toast on the finish is in complete harmony with the fruit on offer. Screwcap. 13.5° alc. **Rating** 88 **To** 2009 $18

Gembrook Hill   ★★★★★
Launching Place Road, Gembrook, Vic 3783 **Region** Yarra Valley
T (03) 5968 1622 **F** (03) 5968 1699 **www.**gembrookhill.com.au **Open** By appt
Winemaker Timo Mayer **Est.** 1983 **Cases** 2000
The 6-ha Gembrook Hill vineyard (sauvignon blanc, chardonnay, pinot noir and semillon) is situated on rich, red volcanic soils 2 km north of Gembrook in the coolest part of the Yarra Valley. The vines are not irrigated, with consequent natural vigour control, and low yields. Harvest usually spans mid-April, three weeks later than the traditional northern parts of the valley, and the style is consistently elegant. Exports to the UK, Denmark, Japan and Malaysia.

ȚȚȚȚȚ **Yarra Valley Sauvignon Blanc 2006** Fresh, clean and crisp; delicate but vibrant, with a strong citrus line and good acidity running throughout. Screwcap. 13° alc. **Rating** 94 **To** 2009 $30
Yarra Valley Pinot Noir 2006 Light, bright hue; fragrant cherry and strawberry fruit aromas; a graceful and willowy palate, a hint of stem adding to the appeal. Diam. 13° alc. **Rating** 94 **To** 2012 $52

Gemtree Vineyards   ★★★★★
PO Box 164, McLaren Vale, SA 5171 **Region** McLaren Vale
T (08) 8323 8199 **F** (08) 8323 7889 **www.**gemtreevineyards.com.au **Open** 7 days 10–5 at Salopian Inn
Winemaker Mike Brown **Est.** 1998 **Cases** 30 000
The Buttery family, headed by Paul and Jill, and with the active involvement of Melissa as viticulturist, have been grapegrowers in McLaren Vale since 1980, when they purchased their first vineyard. Today the family owns a little over 130 ha of vines. The oldest block, of 25 ha on Tatachilla Road at McLaren Vale, was planted in 1970. Exports to the the UK, the US and other major markets.

ȚȚȚȚȚ **Obsidian Shiraz 2004** Deep, dense colour; an excellent portrait of McLaren Vale shiraz at its bounteous best, flush with blackberry, plum and dark chocolate fruit plus velvety smooth tannins. Only 1% of Gemtree shiraz makes Obsidian. Screwcap. 14.5° alc. **Rating** 96 **To** 2024 $45
Uncut Shiraz 2006 Deep colour; a rich, opulent, but not jammy bouquet and palate; a range of blackberry, licorice and dark chocolate fruit with positive, but not aggressive, oak and ripe tannins. Cork. 14.5° alc. **Rating** 95 **To** 2016 $20
White Lees McLaren Vale Shiraz 2004 Rich, round and supple; strongly regional, high quality shiraz with expressive blackberry and dark chocolate flavours; very good texture and length. At this point, minimal difference between the cork and screwcap versions. Cork/Screwcap. 14.5° alc. **Rating** 95 **To** 2024 $37.50
Tatty Road Cabernet Sauvignon Petit Verdot Merlot Cabernet Franc 2006 A striking and pure array of blackcurrant and redcurrant fruit on a long, silky palate, finishing with superfine tannins. Screwcap. 14.5° alc. **Rating** 94 **To** 2016 $18

ȚȚȚȚȚ **Moonstone McLaren Vale Albarino 2007** An interesting savoury wine, with citrus fruits overlaid by complex skin contact character; very high acidity and very long, best enjoyed with food. Screwcap. 13.5° alc. **Rating** 90 **To** 2009 $28
The Phantom McLaren Vale Petit Verdot 2005 Highly fragrant, with plenty of juicy red fruits on the palate; nice vibrant acidity on the finish, cleans up the fruit profile well. Screwcap. 15° alc. **Rating** 90 **To** 2014 $28

TTTT Bloodstone McLaren Vale Shiraz 2006 Quite oaky and toasty on the bouquet, the fruit shows more on the palate; lively, juicy and generous on the finish. Screwcap. 14.5° alc. **Rating** 89 **To** 2014 $15

Bloodstone McLaren Vale Tempranillo 2006 Warm-fruited, with silky fruit on the palate, and a savoury, slightly earthy note to the finish. Screwcap. 14.5° alc. **Rating** 88 **To** 2009 $25

Citrine McLaren Vale Chardonnay 2007 Gently ripe peachy fruit, with nuances of French oak in the background; easy drinking. Screwcap. 13.5° alc. **Rating** 87 **To** 2009 $15

Tadpole Chardonnay Viognier 2007 A pleasant wine, with ripe stone fruit augmented by 10% viognier, which makes its presence felt on the finish. Screwcap. 13° alc. **Rating** 87 **To** 2009 $15

Geoff Merrill Wines

291 Pimpala Road, Woodcroft, SA 5162 **Region** McLaren Vale
T (08) 8381 6877 **F** (08) 8322 2244 **www**.geoffmerrillwines.com **Open** Mon–Fri 10–5, w'ends 12–5
Winemaker Geoff Merrill, Scott Heidrich **Est.** 1980 **Cases** 75 000
If Geoff Merrill ever loses his impish sense of humour or his zest for life, high and not-so-high, we shall all be the poorer. The product range consists of three tiers: premium (varietal); reserve, being the older (and best) wines, reflecting the desire for elegance and subtlety of this otherwise exuberant winemaker; and, at the top, Henley Shiraz. Mount Hurtle wines are sold exclusively through Vintage Cellars/Liquorland. Exports to all major markets.

TTTTT McLaren Vale Shiraz 2004 Bright red-purple sets the scene for a similarly bright and perfectly focused palate, a wine to be quaffed as much as sipped, already near its 5–10-year plateau of peak drinking. Screwcap. 14.5° alc. **Rating** 94 **To** 2014 $25

McLaren Vale Shiraz Grenache Mourvedre 2004 A delicious medium-bodied wine with affinities to the Southern Rhône; the tighter focus of McLaren Vale grenache contributing to the mouthfeel, but richer shiraz and the tannins of mourvedre also play their part. Screwcap. 14.5° alc. **Rating** 94 **To** 2012 $18.50

Reserve Coonawarra McLaren Vale Cabernet Sauvignon 2001 Fine, silky and smooth, with both two years in barrel, then four in bottle prior to release paying dividends; lovely mocha/cedar overtones to gently ripe fruit. Cork. 14° alc. **Rating** 94 **To** 2012 $35

TTTTY McLaren Vale Merlot 2004 Shows the vintage to good advantage; medium-bodied, with harmonious olive/earth/red berry flavours seamlessly woven with oak and soft tannins. Surprise packet. Screwcap. 14.5° alc. **Rating** 93 **To** 2012 $25

McLaren Vale Grenache Rose 2007 Bright fuschia-pink; raspberry and red cherry fruit, then a long, lingering, dry finish; has attitude. Screwcap. 14° alc. **Rating** 92 **To** 2009 $18.50

TTTT Coonawarra McLaren Vale Cabernet Sauvignon 2004 Marked by utterly atypical (for Geoff Merrill) dry tannins; the fruit is a mix of blackcurrant, leaf and earthy/dark chocolate notes; could settle down with further bottle age. Screwcap. 14.5° alc. **Rating** 89 **To** 2015 $25

Mount Hurtle Grenache Rose 2007 Vivid fuschia; has plenty of red fruit flavour; the finish is dry, but a little tough, a small matter at the price and no issue with brasserie summer food. Screwcap. 13° alc. **Rating** 88 **To** 2009 $8

Geoff Weaver

2 Gilpin Lane, Mitcham, SA 5062 (postal) **Region** Adelaide Hills
T (08) 8272 2105 **F** (08) 8271 0177 **www**.geoffweaver.com.au **Open** Not
Winemaker Geoff Weaver **Est.** 1982 **Cases** 5000

This is the full-time business of former Hardys chief winemaker Geoff Weaver. He draws upon a little over 11 ha of vineyard established between 1982 and '88, and invariably produces immaculate Riesling and Sauvignon Blanc, and one of the longest-lived Chardonnays to be found in Australia, with intense grapefruit and melon flavour. The beauty of the labels ranks supreme with Pipers Brook. Exports to the UK and the US.

ΨΨΨΨΨ **Ferus Lenswood Sauvignon Blanc 2005** A wine that breaks all the rules; barrel-fermented in French oak, 12 months on lees, and has positively flourished in the bottle over the 18 months post bottling. Screwcap. 13° alc. **Rating** 96 To 2009 $35
Lenswood Sauvignon Blanc 2007 The usual Weaver style; spotlessly clean, with nuances of gooseberry, apple, citrus and grass in a minerally web. Screwcap. 13.5° alc. **Rating** 94 To 2009 $24

Ghost Riders Vineyard
535 Hermitage Road, Pokolbin, NSW 2320 **Region** Lower Hunter Valley
T (02) 6574 7171 **F** (02) 6574 7171 **www**.ghostriderswines.com.au **Open** 7 days 10–5
Winemaker Rhys Eather (Contract) **Est.** 1999 **Cases** 500
Head and neck surgeon Ian Kalnins and wife Ildi have established Ghost Riders Vineyard in association with their accommodation business, Hermitage Hideaway (accommodating up to 16 guests). Their 2.5-ha vineyard (shiraz, chardonnay, viognier) produced its first Shiraz in 2002, and following the grafting of some of the shiraz, a Chardonnay has followed, with a Shiraz Viognier released in 2007.

ΨΨΨΨΨ **Hunter Valley Chardonnay 2007** Fine, with plenty of citrus fruits and focused acidity; the finish is quite long and harmonious. Screwcap. 13.5° alc. **Rating** 90 To 2012 $18

ΨΨΨΨ **Hunter Valley Chardonnay 2006** Clean and vibrant, with peach and melon notes; quite toasty on the finish, but clean and with good precision. Screwcap. 13.5° alc. **Rating** 89 To 2011 $18
Hunter Valley Shiraz Viognier 2006 Lifted and spicy; quite fleshy and supple, with nice savoury twist to finish. Screwcap. 13.8° alc. **Rating** 89 To 2012 $20

Ghost Rock Vineyard
PO Box 311, Devonport, Tas 7310 **Region** Northern Tasmania
T (03) 6428 4005 **F** (03) 6428 4330 **www**.ghostrock.com.au **Open** Wed–Sun 11–5
(7 days Jan–Feb)
Winemaker Tamar Ridge **Est.** 2001 **Cases** 600
Cate and Colin Arnold purchased the former Patrick Creek Vineyard (planted in 1989) in '01. They run a printing and design business in Devonport, and were looking for a suitable site to establish a vineyard. The 4-ha vineyard (chardonnay, pinot noir, sauvignon blanc and pinot gris) is planted on a northeasterly aspect on a sheltered slope.

ΨΨΨΨ **Pinot Gris 2007** Good varietal expression with distinct pear fruit; some acidity gives brightness and balance, though not particularly long. Screwcap. 13.5° alc. **Rating** 89 To 2009 $25
Sauvignon Blanc 2007 Clean; light- to medium-bodied, with suppressed varietal character, although early picking has retained some acidity and freshness. Screwcap. 12° alc. **Rating** 87 To 2009 $24
Chardonnay 2006 The bouquet is a fraction funky, though not unpleasant; a dry, minerally palate, with minimal oak, and shortening slightly on the finish. Screwcap. 12.4° alc. **Rating** 87 To 2010 $23
Pinot Noir 2006 Bright and clear fruit, plummy fruit on entry, but tends to thin off with stemmy notes on the finish. Screwcap. 14° alc. **Rating** 87 To 2010 $27

Giaconda ★★★★★

30 McClay Road, Beechworth, Vic 3747 **Region** Beechworth
T (03) 5727 0246 **F** (03) 5727 0246 **www**.giaconda.com.au **Open** By appt
Winemaker Rick Kinzbrunner **Est.** 1985 **Cases** NA
These wines have a super-cult status and, given the tiny production, are extremely difficult to
find; they are sold chiefly through restaurants and by mail order. All have a cosmopolitan edge
befitting Rick Kinzbrunner's international winemaking experience. The Chardonnay and
Pinot Noir are made in contrasting styles: the Chardonnay tight and reserved, the Pinot Noir
more variable, but usually opulent and ripe. Exports to the UK and the US.

ΦΦΦΦΦ **Warner Vineyard Shiraz 2005** Fine and focused black fruits; excellent length,
finish and aftertaste. Screwcap. 13.5° alc. **Rating** 94 **To** 2019 $80

Giant Steps/Innocent Bystander ★★★★★

336 Maroondah Highway, Healesville, Vic 3777 **Region** Yarra Valley
T (03) 5962 6111 **F** (03) 5962 6199 **www**.giant-steps.com.au **Open** Mon–Fri 10–10,
w'ends 8–10
Winemaker Phil Sexton, Steve Flamsteed **Est.** 1997 **Cases** 40 000
Phil Sexton made his first fortune as a pioneer micro-brewer, and invested a substantial part
of that fortune in establishing Devil's Lair. Late in 1996 he sold Devil's Lair to Southcorp,
which had purchased Coldstream Hills earlier that year. Two years later he and Allison Sexton
purchased a hillside property less than 1 km from Coldstream Hills, and sharing the same
geological structure and aspect. The name Giant Steps comes in part from their love of jazz
and John Coltrane's album of that name, and in part from the rise and fall of the property
across a series of ridges ranging from 120 m to 360 m. The 35-ha vineyard is predominantly
planted to pinot noir and chardonnay, but with significant quantities of cabernet sauvignon
and merlot, plus small plantings of cabernet franc and petit verdot. It also leases Tarraford
Vineyard, with 8.5 ha of vines up to 13 years old. Innocent Bystander is a successful second
label. Exports to the UK, the US and other major markets.

ΦΦΦΦΦ **Tarraford Vineyard Yarra Valley Pinot Noir 2006** A complex array of red and
dark fruits, toasty oak and earthy aromas on the bouquet; the palate is rich, yet fine
and offers good structure and plentiful fine tannins to support the abundance of
fruit. Screwcap. 13° alc. **Rating** 95 **To** 2015 $39.95
Sexton Vineyard Yarra Valley Chardonnay 2005 A complex bouquet, with
wild yeast barrel ferment characters carrying through to the powerful and complex
palate; good line and balance. Screwcap. 14° alc. **Rating** 94 **To** 2015 $29.95
Sexton Harry's Monster 2005 Intense flavours, texture and structure all
reflecting the Bordeaux blend; tannins are woven through the blackcurrant and
redcurrant fruit, lengthening the finish. Cabernet Sauvignon/Merlot/Petit Verdot/
Cabernet Franc. Screwcap. 14.5° alc. **Rating** 94 **To** 2025 $44.95
Sexton Harry's Monster 2006 Quite serious cabernet blend, with dark savoury
personality; good fruit concentration and with the oak to accompany; needs time,
but is built for the long haul. Screwcap. 14° alc. **Rating** 94 **To** 2025 $44.95

ΦΦΦΦΟ **Sexton Vineyard Yarra Valley Chardonnay 2006** Pear and nectarine aromas,
with a slight nuttiness and fine cool on the palate; tightly wound, and very long on
the finish. Screwcap. 14.1° alc. **Rating** 93 **To** 2015 $34.95
Giant Steps Sexton Vineyard Yarra Valley Pinot Noir 2006 Bright mid-
garnet; tightly wound red fruits and hints of spice, with lovely focus and energy;
a vibrant core of red fruits on the palate; fine-grained tannins on the very long
finish. Screwcap. 13.5° alc. **Rating** 93 **To** 2014 $34.95
Innocent Bystander Yarra Valley Pinot Noir 2006 Vivid hue; fresh, lively,
cherry, strawberry and plum flavours; linear mouthfeel. Screwcap. 13.5° alc.
Rating 90 **To** 2012 $19.95
Innocent Bystander Bleeding Heart Sangiovese Merlot 2006 Briary
sour cherry varietal aromas; crisp acid and savoury tannins; a good example of
sangiovese. Screwcap. 14.5° alc. **Rating** 90 **To** 2012 $19.95

🍷🍷🍷🍷 **Innocent Bystander Yarra Valley Chardonnay 2006** Pronounced barrel ferment oak impact on both bouquet and palate; long, grainy acidity on the finish and aftertaste; will improve. Screwcap. 14° alc. **Rating** 89 **To** 2012 $19.95

Giant Steps Tarraford Vineyard Yarra Valley Chardonnay 2006 The bouquet has rich fruit, with grapefruit and mineral; weighty on the finish, but lacks finesse. Screwcap. 13.5° alc. **Rating** 89 **To** 2014 $39.95

Giant Steps Sexton Vineyard Yarra Valley Pinot Noir 2005 Light-bodied, surprisingly so; a savoury, foresty style needing more sweet fruit, though does have length and certain degree of finesse. Screwcap. 13.4° alc. **Rating** 89 **To** 2011 $29.95

Innocent Bystander Yarra Valley Shiraz Viognier 2006 Fragrant aromas of spice and red fruits; medium-bodied with good weight and texture; a spicy, savoury finish, with nice balance. Screwcap. 14° alc. **Rating** 89 **To** 2016 $19.95

Innocent Bystander Yarra Valley Pinot Gris 2007 The Upper Yarra components give the wine focus, length and good acidity to the pear, apple and lychee flavours. Screwcap. 13.5° alc. **Rating** 88 **To** 2009 $19.95

Innocent Bystander Rose 2007 A pretty rose; strawberries and cream, with an off-dry finish aimed squarely at the cellar door. Screwcap. 13.9° alc. **Rating** 87 **To** 2009 $15

Gibraltar Rock ★★★★

Woodlands Road, Porongurup, WA 6324 **Region** Porongurup
T (08) 9481 2856 **F** (08) 9481 2857 **www**.gibraltarrockwines.com.au **Open** By appt
Winemaker Forest Hill Vineyard (Shane McKerrow) **Est.** 1979 **Cases** 800

A once-tiny Riesling specialist in the wilds of the Porongurups, forced to change its name from Narang because Lindemans felt it could be confused with its (now defunct) Nyrang Shiraz brand. This beautifully sited vineyard was acquired by Perth orthopaedic surgeon Dr Peter Honey in 2001. The vineyard now has 23 ha of riesling, chardonnay, merlot, pinot noir, sauvignon blanc and shiraz. Most of the grapes are sold, but Dr Honey intends to slowly increase production from the older vines under the Gibraltar Rock label. No samples received. Exports to the UK, China and Japan.

Gibson Barossavale ★★★★★

Willows Road, Light Pass, SA 5355 **Region** Barossa Valley
T (08) 8562 3193 **F** (08) 8562 4490 **www**.barossavale.com **Open** Fri–Mon & public hols 11–5
Winemaker Rob Gibson **Est.** 1996 **Cases** 3500

Rob Gibson spent much of his working life as a senior viticulturist for Penfolds. While at Penfolds he was involved in research tracing the characters that particular parcels of grapes give to a wine, which left him with a passion for identifying and protecting what is left of the original vineyard plantings in wine regions around Australia. This led to the acquisition of an additional 8 ha of old shiraz, mourvedre and grenache, plus some of the oldest chardonnay vines in the Barossa (recent arrivals when compared with shiraz, but planted in 1982). Exports to the UK and Hong Kong.

🍷🍷🍷🍷🍷 **Australian Old Vine Collection Barossa Shiraz 2005** 'Resplendent in its generosity', the late Jack Mann would have said with unmitigated approval; luscious but focused and long, a pure expression of seriously old vine grapes. Cork. 14.5° alc. **Rating** 96 **To** 2025 $96

Australian Old Vine Collection Eden Valley Shiraz 2005 A tremendous volume of flavour, but does show hints of the cooler climate with touches of spice and licorice; again, the flavour thrusts through to the finish and aftertaste. Cork. 14.5° alc. **Rating** 95 **To** 2022 $96

Shiraz 2005 Very powerful, full-bodied regional Shiraz with lots of blackberry, licorice and dark chocolate; built-in tannins and the screwcap underwrite the long future. Screwcap. 14.9° alc. **Rating** 94 **To** 2025 $36

Australian Old Vine Collection McLaren Vale Grenache 2005 Youthful and strong colour; as typical of top McLaren Vale grenache as is possible; here powerful plum, dark chocolate and raspberry seamlessly meld, the finish long and the tannins fine. Cork. 14.5° alc. **Rating** 94 **To** 2015 $96

Reserve Merlot 2005 A fragrant mosaic of aromas and flavours reflecting the painstaking architecture; has great thrust, life and persistence. Screwcap. 14.6° alc. **Rating** 94 **To** 2020 $31.90

ＹＹＹＹＹ **The Dirtman Shiraz 2005** Powerful, rich and complex, and carries its alcohol without demur; has marked intensity to its blackberry, licorice and spice fruit, the tannins ripe, the oak incidental. Screwcap. 14.9° alc. **Rating** 93 **To** 2020 $24.50

Wilfreda Blend 2005 A generous, immediately welcoming style with both red and black fruits at perfect ripeness; has more structure, depth and conviction than other similar Barossa Valley blends. Shiraz/Mourvedre/Grenache. Screwcap. 14.5° alc. **Rating** 92 **To** 2015 $24.50

Loose End Grenache Rose 2007 Vivid puce; excellent combination of Australian technology with traditional southern French rose variety; delicate fruit, perfect balance and finish. Screwcap. 13° alc. **Rating** 90 **To** 2009 $14

ＹＹＹＹ **Loose End Shiraz 2006** Very expressive, albeit with not the usual viognier lift, tending more to savoury black fruits and bitter chocolate. 3.9% Viognier. Screwcap. 14.5° alc. **Rating** 89 **To** 2013 $18

Gibson Estate

57 Tubbarubba Road, Merricks North, Vic 3926 **Region** Mornington Peninsula **T** (03) 5989 7501 **www**.gibsonestate.com.au **Open** By appt
Winemaker Phil Kerney **Est.** 2001 **Cases** 400
Kate and Stuart Gibson say they spent 15 years searching for the perfect site to grow classic pinot noir. They ultimately settled on a north-facing slope of the Red Hill area of Mornington Peninsula. It is 110 m above sea level, and is on a moderate (15°) incline picking up maximum sun interception, which allows them to pick a little earlier than vineyards further up the Red Hill hillsides. The 2.5 ha of pinot noir is planted in three equal blocks of MV6, 114 and 115 clones, two-thirds planted on vigour-reducing rootstocks, thus limiting the yield to 2 tonnes to the acre. No samples received; rating is that of last year.

Gilberts

RMB 438 Albany Highway, Kendenup via Mount Barker, WA 6323 **Region** Mount Barker **T** (08) 9851 4028 **F** (08) 9851 4021 **www**.gilbertwines.com.au **Open** 7 days 10–5
Winemaker Plantagenet **Est.** 1980 **Cases** 4000
A part-time occupation for sheep and beef farmers Jim and Beverly Gilbert, but a very successful one. The mature vineyard, coupled with contract winemaking at Plantagenet, has long produced very high-class Riesling, and now also makes excellent Shiraz. The wines sell out quickly each year. Exports to Hong Kong and Switzerland.

ＹＹＹＹＹ **Mount Barker Riesling 2007** Bone-dry and full of lime juice flavour; a strong mineral heart, and pure focused fruit; vibrant, racy, and fine on the finish. Screwcap. 12° alc. **Rating** 94 **To** 2014 $19

Reserve Mount Barker Shiraz 2005 Multi-layered, with exotic spices, red and dark fruits and silky texture; the finish is very long and very bright, the tannins mouthwatering and refreshing. Screwcap. **Rating** 94 **To** 2016 $28

ＹＹＹＹＹ **Alira 2007** Quite ripe, with tropical elements and a little slate in the background; the sweetness is well balanced by the acid and works well. Screwcap. 12° alc. **Rating** 90 **To** 2012 $16

Three Devils Mount Barker Shiraz 2005 A chewy, savoury wine, with notes of spice, tar and black fruits; a little rustic, but with good flavour. Screwcap. 15° alc. **Rating** 90 **To** 2012 $18

�♥ **Three Devils Mount Barker Chardonnay 2007** Ripe and juicy, heading
towards the tropical spectrum; clean and varietal, and showing the purity of no oak
on the palate. Screwcap. 14° alc. **Rating** 88 **To** 2010 $17

Gilligan ★★★★

PO Box 235, Willunga, SA 5172 **Region** McLaren Vale
T (08) 8323 8379 **F** (08) 8323 8379 **www**.gilligan.com.au **Open** Not
Winemaker Mark Day, Leigh Gilligan **Est.** 2001 **Cases** 1000
Leigh Gilligan is a 20-year marketing veteran, mostly with McLaren Vale wineries (including
Wirra Wirra). The Gilligan family has 6 ha of shiraz and 2 ha of grenache on their Old Rifle
Range Vineyard, and they sell the lion's share. In 2001 they persuaded next-door neighbour
Drew Noon to make a barrel of Shiraz, which they drank and gave away. Realising they
needed more than one barrel, they moved to Maxwell Wines, with help from Maxwell
winemaker Mark Day and have now migrated to Mark's new Koltz Winery at Blewitt Springs.
The longer-term plan is to take all the fruit when the Foster's contract terminates; they have
also planted more grenache, and small parcels of mourvedre, marsanne and roussanne on
another property they have acquired in the heart of McLaren Vale. Exports to the UK, the
US and other major markets.

♥♥♥♥♀ **McLaren Vale Shiraz Grenache Mourvedre 2006** Deep purple-red; richly
robed and fruited in a way only McLaren Vale can achieve; luscious black fruits,
dark chocolate and mocha. Great now or later with a T-bone. Diam. 16.5° alc.
Rating 91 **To** 2014 $23

Gipsie Jack Wine Co ★★★☆

PO Box 128, Langhorne Creek, SA 5255 **Region** Langhorne Creek
T (08) 8537 3029 **F** (08) 8537 3284 **www**.gipsiejack.com **Open** Not
Winemaker John Glaetzer, Ben Potts **Est.** 2004 **Cases** 11 000
One might have thought the partners of Gipsie Jack have enough wine on their plate already,
but some just can't resist the temptation, it seems. The two in question are John Glaetzer
and Ben Potts, who made a little over 500 cases from two growers in their inaugural vintage
in 2004. The 2007 vintage produced 11 000 cases from 15 growers, and the intention is to
increase the number of growers each year. Glaetzer and Potts say, 'We want to make this label
fun, like in the "old days". No pretentiousness, no arrogance, not even a back label. A great
wine at a great price, with no discounting.' Exports to Europe, Canada, Singapore, Hong
Kong and NZ.

♥♥♥♥♀ **Langhorne Creek Petit Verdot 2005** Dense colour; a very powerful wine,
although dipping in the mid-palate like cabernet, then coming again on the
finish, paradoxically without aggressive tannins. Screwcap. 14.5° alc. **Rating** 90
To 2020 $28

♥♥♥♥ **Langhorne Creek Malbec 2005** More juicy berry flavours than the Petit
Verdot, but also dips and wanders on its way through to the finish; plenty of
overall flavour. Screwcap. 14.5° alc. **Rating** 89 **To** 2012 $28
Langhorne Creek Rose 2007 Strawberry and red cherry fruit supported
by neatly balanced residual sugar and acidity. Screwcap. 13.5° alc. **Rating** 87
To 2009 $18

GISA ★★★

Samp Road, McLaren Vale, SA 5171 **Region** South Australia
T (08) 8338 2123 **F** (08) 8338 2123 **www**.gisa.com.au **Open** Not
Winemaker Simon Parker **Est.** 2007 **Cases** 750
Matt and Lisa Henbest have chosen a clever name for their virtual winery – GISA standing
for Geographic Indication South Australia – neatly covering the fact that their grapes come
variously from the Adelaide Hills (Sauvignon Blanc), McLaren Vale (Shiraz Viognier) and
Barossa Valley (Reserve Shiraz). It in turn reflects Matt's long apprenticeship in the wine

industry, as a child living on his parent's vineyard, then working in retail trade while he pursued tertiary qualifications, and thereafter wholesaling wine to the retail and restaurant trade. He then moved to Haselgrove, where he spent five years working closely with the small winemaking team, refining his concept of style, and gaining experience on the other side of the fence of the marketing equation.

ΨΨΨΨ **Adelaide Hills Sauvignon Blanc 2007** Light, fresh and quite crisp nuances of passionfruit, herb, grass and asparagus, though not much depth; an easy style. Screwcap. 12.5° alc. **Rating** 88 **To** 2009 $20

McLaren Vale Shiraz Viognier 2004 Pale colour suggests the varieties were not co-fermented, with brick hues; nonetheless, pleasant, light- to medium-bodied wine for immediate drinking. Screwcap. 13.5° alc. **Rating** 87 **To** 2009 $20

Gisborne Peak ★★★

69 Short Road, Gisborne South, Vic 3437 **Region** Macedon Ranges
T (03) 5428 2228 **F** (03) 5428 4816 **www.**gisbornepeakwines.com.au **Open** 7 days 11–5
Winemaker Hanging Rock (John Ellis) **Est.** 1978 **Cases** 1500
Bob Nixon began the development of Gisborne Peak way back in 1978, planting his dream vineyard row-by-row. (Bob is married to Barbara Nixon, founder of Victoria Winery Tours.) The tasting room has wide shaded verandahs, plenty of windows and sweeping views. The 5-ha vineyard is planted to chardonnay, pinot noir, semillon, riesling and lagrein.

ΨΨΨΨ **Mawarra Vineyard Macedon Ranges Chardonnay 2005** Strongly concentrated fruits, yet a cool personality; rich palate, with good texture, a savoury edge and bracing acidity. Screwcap. 12.1° alc. **Rating** 89 **To** 2016 $25

Glaetzer Wines

34 Barossa Valley Way, Tanunda, SA 5352 (postal) **Region** Barossa Valley
T (08) 8563 0288 **F** (08) 8563 0218 **www.**glaetzer.com **Open** Not
Winemaker Ben Glaetzer **Est.** 1996 **Cases** 15 000
Colin Glaetzer and son Ben are almost as well known in SA wine circles as Wolf Blass winemaker John Glaetzer, Colin's twin brother. Glaetzer Wines purchases all its grapes from the Ebenezer subregion of the Barossa Valley, principally from third- and fourth-generation growers. Its four wines (Amon-Ra Shiraz, Anaperenna Shiraz Cabernet Sauvignon, Bishop Shiraz and Wallace Shiraz Grenache) are all made under contract at Barossa Vintners in what might be termed a somewhat incestuous relationship because of the common links in ownership of the very successful Barossa Vintners business. Exports to all major markets.

ΨΨΨΨΨ **Amon-Ra Unfiltered Shiraz 2006** Impenetrable colour; a full-bodied palate, stacked to the gills with layer-upon-layer of blackberry, prune, licorice and plum fruit, yet the tannin and oak are not overdone, nor is the alcohol. Oh for a screwcap. Cork. 14.5° alc. **Rating** 96 **To** 2021 $90

Bishop Barossa Valley Shiraz 2006 Built in typical luscious Glaetzer style, medium- to full-bodied with blackberry and (unusually) some notes of cassis and raspberry; the tannins are soft and fine, oak in its place; stained cork a worry. Cork. 14.5° alc. **Rating** 94 **To** 2016 $35

Anaperenna 2006 Densely packed blackberry, blackcurrant and plum fruit with ripe, plush tannins woven throughout, plus scoops of vanilla and chocolate. Shiraz/ Cabernet Sauvignon. Cork. 14.5° alc. **Rating** 94 **To** 2021 $50

ΨΨΨΨΨ **Wallace by Ben Glaetzer Barossa Valley Shiraz Grenache 2006** Transcends the cosmetic characters of many Barossa Valley grenache blends, with attractive red cherry and raspberry fruits, then a twist of spice on the finish. Screwcap. 14.5° alc. **Rating** 90 **To** 2012 $20

Glen Eldon Wines

Cnr Koch's Road/Nitschke Road, Krondorf, SA 5235 **Region** Eden & Barossa Valleys
T (08) 8568 2996 **F** (08) 8568 1833 **www**.gleneldonwines.com.au **Open** Mon–Fri
8.30–5, w'ends 11–5
Winemaker Richard Sheedy **Est.** 1997 **Cases** 4000
The Sheedy family – brothers Richard and Andrew, and wives Mary and Sue – have
established their base at the Glen Eldon property in the Eden Valley, which is the home of
Richard and Mary. The riesling is planted here; the shiraz and cabernet sauvignon come
from their vineyards in the Barossa Valley. No samples received; the rating is that of last
year. Exports to the UK, the US and Canada.

Glenalbyn

84 Halls Road, Kingower, Vic 3517 **Region** Bendigo
T (03) 5438 8255 **F** (03) 5438 8255 **Open** Most days 10.30–4.30
Winemaker Leila (Lee) Gillespie **Est.** 1997 **Cases** 500
When Lee Gillespie's great-grandfather applied for his land title in 1856, he had already
established a vineyard on the property (in 1853). A survey plan of 1857 shows the cultivation
paddocks, one marked the Grape Paddock, and a few of the original grapevines have survived
in the garden that abuts the National Trust Heritage homestead. In 1986 Lee and husband
John decided on a modest diversification of their sheep, wool and cereal crop farm, and began
the establishment of 4 ha of vineyards. 2003 commemorated 150 years of family ownership
of the property. Ironically, the '03 drought meant that no grapes were picked; however, things
have improved since.

ΨΨΨΨ **Cabernet Sauvignon 2006** Dominated by forest/briar/earth characters,
the tannins tending green; needed to be riper. Screwcap. 13.9° alc. **Rating** 87
To 2013 $30

GlenAyr

Back Tea Tree Road, Richmond, Tas 7025 **Region** Southern Tasmania
T (03) 6260 2388 **F** (03) 6260 2691 **Open** Mon–Fri 8–5
Winemaker Andrew Hood **Est.** 1975 **Cases** 500
The substantial and now fully mature Tolpuddle Vineyard, managed by Warren Schasser, who
is completing a Bachelor of Applied Science (viticulture) at CSU, provides the grapes that go
to make the GlenAyr wines. The major part of the grape production continues to be sold to
Domaine Chandon and Hardys, with most going to make premium table wine, and a lesser
amount to premium sparkling.

ΨΨΨΨΨ **Pinot Noir 2005** Light and highly aromatic; lovely, silky red berry fruits on
the palate; generous and harmonious on the finish, with fine acidity. **Rating** 92
To 2011 $27
Chardonnay 2006 An abundance of ripe stone fruit woven through quality
French oak; excellent overall balance. **Rating** 90 **To** 2013 $23

Glenguin Estate

Milbrodale Road, Broke, NSW 2330 **Region** Lower Hunter Valley
T (02) 6579 1009 **F** (02) 6579 1009 **www**.glenguinestate.com.au **Open** At Boutique
Wine Centre, Broke Road, Pokolbin
Winemaker Robin Tedder MW, Rhys Eather **Est.** 1993 **Cases** 5000
Glenguin's vineyard has been established along the banks of the Wollombi Brook by Robin
and Rita Tedder; Robin is a grandson of Air Chief Marshal Tedder, made Baron of Glenguin
by King George VI in recognition of his wartime deeds. The Glenguin wines come solely
from the 19 ha of estate plantings at Wollombi, and the Maestro label matches grape varieties
and site climates in regions as diverse as Orange and the Adelaide Hills. Exports to the UK,
Hong Kong, Singapore and NZ.

ㅜㅜㅜㅜㅜ **Aristea Hunter Valley Shiraz 2005** A very complex, medium-bodied wine already showing regional character with some gently earthy, spicy overtones to the black fruits; has outstanding texture and structure; will be a true classic; 150 dozen made; dry-grown vines. Screwcap. 14.5° alc. **Rating** 95 **To** 2025 $60

ㅜㅜㅜㅜㅜ **Protos Chardonnay 2007** Complex and concentrated nectarine and peach fruit, the barrel ferment oak balanced and integrated; very good length and style; whole bunch pressed, 300 cases made. Screwcap. 13.5° alc. **Rating** 93 **To** 2014 $30
Schoolhouse Block Shiraz 2005 Firm structure; very earthy, savoury characters with strong dark chocolate notes along with blackberry fruit; the tannins are obvious, but not dry or aggressive. Screwcap. 14.5° alc. **Rating** 92 **To** 2020 $35
The Old Broke Block Semillon 2007 Bright green-straw; in the mainstream of the unique, high-flavoured style of Hunter semillon from '07; layers of flavour, but did need a touch more acidity. Screwcap. 11° alc. **Rating** 90 **To** 2011 $19
Two Thousand Vines Viognier 2007 Considerable varietal aroma and flavour in an apricot/musk spectrum; full-bodied, and does have the almost inevitable, slightly congested finish. Screwcap. 13.5° alc. **Rating** 90 **To** 2010 $25
Stonybroke Shiraz Tannat 2005 Plenty of dark fruit aromas on the bouquet; plum, blackberry, leather and spice on the medium- to full-bodied palate; should be long-lived; 550 cases. Screwcap. 14° alc. **Rating** 90 **To** 2020 $23

ㅜㅜㅜㅜ **Maestro Pinot Grigio 2007** Tart green fruits on the palate, but fresh and vibrant; a juicy drink-early wine. Screwcap. 13° alc. **Rating** 87 **To** 2009 $23
Ironbark Tannat 2006 The palate has dried leather, tar and a little touch of cassis; very chewy tannins on the finish; needs food for enjoyment. Screwcap. 13.5° alc. **Rating** 87 **To** 2016 $35

Glenholme Vineyards ★★★

White Park Road, Bangor via Wirrabara, SA 5481 **Region** Southern Flinders Ranges
T (08) 8666 5222 **F** (08) 8666 5222 **Open** Fri–Mon 10–5
Winemaker Stephen John Wines, Jeanneret **Est.** 1998 **Cases** 650
David and Margaret Blesing have established an 11.5-ha vineyard, with shiraz (8.3 ha) and cabernet sauvignon (2.3 ha) dominant. The remaining hectares are planted to merlot, nebbiolo, riesling, semillon and chardonnay. All but 5 tonnes of the shiraz is sold to Peter Lehmann Wines, its quality attracting a substantial bonus payment on top of the base contract price. A cellar door opened in 2008, adding to the range of cellar doors now available to visitors to the beautiful Southern Flinders Ranges.

ㅜㅜㅜ **Blesing's Garden Southern Flinders Ranges Shiraz 2006** Deep colour; a very powerful, somewhat extractive wine, with dusty tannins running through the black fruits of the palate; time needed. Screwcap. 13.5° alc. **Rating** 89 **To** 2020 $20
Blesing's Garden Southern Flinders Ranges Cabernet Sauvignon 2004 While slightly rustic, has better texture and line than the '06; blackcurrant, mint and slightly dry, powdery tannins. Screwcap. 14.5° alc. **Rating** 88 **To** 2012 $20
Blesing's Garden Southern Flinders Ranges Shiraz 2004 A very powerful and robust palate, with an impression of sweetness, but not clear whether this comes from the alcohol, the fruit or a touch of residual sugar. Screwcap. 15° alc. **Rating** 87 **To** 2014 $20
Blesing's Garden Southern Flinders Ranges Cabernet Sauvignon 2006 Lower alcohol, but pervasive drying tannins should have been fined before bottling; good quality fruit potential here. Screwcap. 13.5° alc. **Rating** 87 **To** 2012 $20

Glenmar Wines ★★★★☆

PO Box 12, Longwood, Vic 3665 **Region** Goulburn Valley
T (03) 9885 0289 **F** (03) 9885 0247 **www**.glenmar.org **Open** Not
Winemaker Plunkett Fowles (Sam Plunkett, Victor Nash) **Est.** 1998 **Cases** NFP

Mark and Glenys Handley did not rush when establishing Glenmar Wines. Planning of the single-site, 2-ha vineyard began in 1998, and they waited seven years for the first vintage. This was not due to any lack of skill or commitment, for the vineyard is managed (on a part-time basis) by Mark Schultz, with many viticultural fingers in the Goulburn Valley region. The same applies to the winemaking, carried out by Sam Plunkett and Victor Nash in the Strathbogie Ranges winery now known as Plunkett Fowles. Both of the initial releases won medals in important wine shows.

ΨΨΨΨΩ **Shiraz 2005** Lively spicy peppery overtones to the predominantly black fruits of the palate, which has superfine tannins in support, giving length. Screwcap. **Rating** 90 **To** 2014 $29.95

ΨΨΨΨ **Cabernet Sauvignon 2005** Fragrant cassis fruit aromas and flavours suggest a relatively cool vineyard site; good length. Screwcap. **Rating** 89 **To** 2015 $29.95
Shiraz 2004 Complex, with new oak coming through strongly on both bouquet and palate; ample ripe fruit flavour, the twitch of acidity on the finish suggesting late adjustment. Screwcap. 14° alc. **Rating** 88 **To** 2014 $29.95
Cabernet Sauvignon 2004 Plenty of sweet cassis-accented fruit; light- to medium-bodied, with balanced tannins and oak. Screwcap. 14° alc. **Rating** 88 **To** 2015 $29.95

Glenwillow Vineyard

40 McIntyre Street, White Hills, Vic 3550 (postal) **Region** Bendigo
T 0428 461 076 **F** (03) 5434 1340 **www.**glenwillow.com.au **Open** Not
Winemaker Matt Hunter (Contract) **Est.** 1999 **Cases** 350
Peter and Cherryl Fyffe began their vineyard at Yandoit Creek, 10 km south of Newstead, in 1999, planting 2 ha of shiraz and 0.3 ha of cabernet sauvignon, and branching out with 0.6 ha of nebbiolo and 0.2 ha of barbera. The choice of Cyclone Gully for the basic wines (the Reserve wines are not made every year) might be considered a little ghoulish. In Jan 1978 a cyclone moved up Sandon-Yandoit Creek Road, causing much property damage, and killing two elderly travellers pulled from their car by the cyclone.

ΨΨΨΨΩ **Reserve Bendigo Shiraz 2006** Far superior colour hue and depth to the Cyclone Gully; powerful and focused; attractive blackberry fruit supported by fine tannins. Screwcap. 14° alc. **Rating** 92 **To** 2020 $28

ΨΨΨΨ **Cyclone Gully Bendigo Shiraz 2006** Despite the alcohol, light- to medium-bodied; spice and plum, with some French oak influence; ripe tannins. Screwcap. 14.5° alc. **Rating** 87 **To** 2012 $18

Gloucester Ridge Vineyard

Lot 7489, Burma Road, Pemberton, WA 6260 **Region** Pemberton
T (08) 9776 1035 **F** (08) 9776 1390 **www.**gloucester-ridge.com.au **Open** 7 days 10–5
Winemaker West Cape Howe Wines (Gavin Berry) **Est.** 1985 **Cases** 6000
Gloucester Ridge is the only vineyard located within the Pemberton town boundary, and is owned and operated by Don and Sue Hancock. The wines are distributed in three ranges: at the bottom the Back Block range, the Mid-range, and the Premium Estate range.

Gnadenfrei Estate

Seppeltsfield Road, Marananga via Nuriootpa, SA 5355 **Region** Barossa Valley
T (08) 8562 2522 **F** (08) 8562 3470 **www.**treetopsbnb.com.au **Open** Tues–Sun 11–5.30
Winemaker Malcolm Seppelt **Est.** 1979 **Cases** 500
Another branch of the Seppelt family, Malcolm and Joylene planted the shiraz (2 ha) and grenache (0.5 ha) vineyard in 1958. Malcolm studied oenology and viticulture at Roseworthy College from 1959–64, thereafter working at B. Seppelt & Sons for 14 years. He left in 1978 to build the hilltop home and cellar door; he and Joylene had previously designed and built the winery and cellar facilities overlooking St Michael's church in Maranagna. The red wines are from the old estate dry-grown vines, and are not filtered.

ŶŶŶŶ **Twenty Rows Sparkling Red NV** Obvious age in the base material, with a fair amount of oak; some bitterness only just balanced by dosage. Ready now. Cork. 13.3° alc. **Rating** 87 **To** 2009 $30

Goaty Hill Wines

Auburn Road, Kayena, Tas 7270 **Region** Northern Tasmania
T (03) 6344 1119 **F** (03) 6344 1119 **www**.goatyhill.com **Open** Fri–Sun 10–5 Oct–May
Winemaker Fran Austin (Contract) **Est.** 1998 **Cases** 1300
The partners in Goaty Hill are six friends from two families who moved from Victoria to Tasmania and, they say, 'were determined to build something for the future while having fun'. The partners in question are Markus Maislinger, Natasha and Tony Nieuwhof, Kristine Grant, and Margaret and Bruce Grant, and in 1998 they began the planting of 18 ha of pinot noir, riesling and chardonnay. Part of the grapes are sold to Bay of Fires and, in return, the highly talented Bay of Fires winemaker, Fran Austin, makes the Goaty Hill wines from that part of the annual crop retained by the partners. Goaty Hill's first wine show entries have yielded a string of medals.

ŶŶŶŶŶ **Riesling 2007** Tight and fine fruit, with lime and slatey minerality; lovely focus on the palate, with good acidity and fruit weight. Screwcap. 12.6° alc. **Rating** 94 **To** 2017 $19.95

ŶŶŶŶ **Sauvignon Blanc 2007** Attractive gently tropical fruits with gooseberry and passionfruit nuances are supported by adequate but softer than usual acidity – no bad thing for an early-drinking style. Screwcap. 12.4° alc. **Rating** 89 **To** 2009 $22.95
Pinot Noir 2007 Clear and bright colour; relatively light-bodied, but very pure and correct red fruit pinot flavours; so far little complexity, which may build with time. Screwcap. 13.7° alc. **Rating** 89 **To** 2012 $27.95
Chardonnay 2007 Light-bodied, with melon and nectarine fruit, the oak (if any) subdued; pleasant, not earth-shattering. Screwcap. **Rating** 87 **To** 2011 $24.95

God's Hill Wines

Lot 211, Gods Hill Road, Lyndoch, SA 5351 **Region** Barossa Valley
T 0412 836 004 **F** (08) 8331 9895 **www**.godshillwines.com **Open** By appt
Winemaker Charlie Scalzi **Est.** 1998 **Cases** 750
Carmine (Charlie) Scalzi arrived in Australia with his parents in 1960, the family settling in Adelaide. His final education was mechanical engineering, and at the age of 24 he established Monza Motors, specialising in Italian cars such as Ferrari and Alfa Romeo. In 1998, having followed in the footsteps of grandfather and father with home winemaking, he purchased a 40-ha property near Lyndoch, planting 4.5 ha each of shiraz and cabernet sauvignon, 2 ha of merlot and 1 ha of chardonnay. Most of the grapes are taken by Dorrien Estate, with a small amount retained for the God's Hill label. Given that the vines are 10 years old, and that the business is a new one, the prices of the wines are certainly in Ferrari territory.

ŶŶŶŶŶ **Menzel Barossa Valley Shiraz 2004** Rich and sumptuous, with fully ripened fruit at relatively modest alcohol; flavours range through satsuma plum, blackberry and raspberry, the spicy tannins mere peacekeepers. 14° alc. **Rating** 94 **To** 2014 $60

ŶŶŶŶ **Menzel Barossa Valley Shiraz 2005** Fully ripe, sweet blackberry and prune fruit, with a somewhat warm finish. Stained cork. Cork. 15.5° alc. **Rating** 89 **To** 2013 $43
Permanent Arm Barossa Valley Cabernet Sauvignon 2004 Medium-bodied, with earthy secondary fruit notes starting to emerge; nicely ripened, with savoury tannins and controlled oak. Where this price comes from I do not know, nor the description of the pruning on the back label. Cork. 14° alc. **Rating** 89 **To** 2012 $180
III Rows Barossa Valley Chardonnay 2007 Over-delivers, with a very nice tangy quality to the finish adding significantly to the flavour. Screwcap. 13.5° alc. **Rating** 88 **To** 2010 $22

Permanent Arm Barossa Valley Cabernet Sauvignon 2002 Slightly cloudy/hazy and brick hues; shows cool vintage, which heightens savoury/earthy characters; medium-bodied, fair balance and length. Mind-bending price. Cork. 14.5° alc. **Rating** 88 **To** 2012 $350
Permanent Arm Barossa Valley Cabernet Sauvignon 2005 Medium-bodied; pleasant, moderately sweet blackcurrant and cassis fruit, the oak well-balanced, the tannins soft. Cork. 14.5° alc. **Rating** 88 **To** 2013 $43

Golden Ball

1175 Beechworth Wangaratta Road, Beechworth, Vic 3747 **Region** Beechworth
T (03) 5727 0284 **F** (03) 5727 0294 **www**.goldenball.com.au **Open** By appt
Winemaker James McLaurin **Est.** 1996 **Cases** 500
The Golden Ball vineyard is on one of the original land grants in the Beechworth region. The 2.4-ha vineyard was planted by James and Janine McLaurin in 1996, mainly to cabernet sauvignon, shiraz and merlot, with lesser plantings of grenache and malbec. The wines are vinified separately and aged in one-third new French oak, the remainder 2–3 years old. The low yields result in intensely flavoured wines, which are to be found in a who's who of Melbourne's best restaurants and a handful of local and Melbourne retailers, including Randall's at Albert Park. The '05 releases seem below par. Exports to Singapore.

Beechworth Shiraz 2005 Good concentration, but a little bitter and smoky on the palate; quite minty, but good structure and depth. Diam. 14° alc. **Rating** 89 **To** 2012 $45

Golden Grove Estate

Sundown Road, Ballandean, Qld 4382 **Region** Granite Belt
T (07) 4684 1291 **F** (07) 4684 1247 **www**.goldengrovee.com.au **Open** 7 days 9–5
Winemaker Raymond Costanzo **Est.** 1993 **Cases** 3000
Golden Grove Estate was established by Mario and Sebastiana Costanzo in 1946, producing stone fruits and table grapes for the fresh fruit market. The first wine grapes (shiraz) were planted in 1972, but it was not until '85, when ownership passed to son Sam and wife Grace, that the use of the property started to change. In 1993 chardonnay and merlot joined the shiraz, followed by cabernet sauvignon, sauvignon blanc and semillon.

Granite Belt Sauvignon Blanc 2007 Grass, lemon, asparagus; crisp minerally finish; fair length; good acidity. **Rating** 89 **To** 2009 $18
Semillon Sauvignon Blanc 2007 Quite complex and rounded, especially for an '07; will develop quickly. **Rating** 87 **To** 2009 $16

Golders Vineyard

Bridport Road, Pipers Brook, Tas 7254 **Region** Northern Tasmania
T (03) 6395 4142 **F** (03) 6395 4142 **Open** By appt
Winemaker Richard Crabtree **Est.** 1991 **Cases** 400
Richard Crabtree continues to make the Golders Vineyard wines at the Delamere winery as he has in the past. The 2.5-ha vineyard established by Crabtree has in fact been sold, and since 2006, grapes have been purchased from the nearby White Rock Vineyard.

Pinot Noir 2006 Bright colour, and fresh, lively fragrance of cherry blossom; an elegant and precise palate, with great purity and length. Screwcap. 13.8° alc. **Rating** 94 **To** 2013 $27.50

Golding Wines

Western Branch Road, Lobethal, SA 5241 **Region** Adelaide Hills
T (08) 8389 5120 **F** (08) 8389 5290 **www**.goldingwines.com.au **Open** By appt
Winemaker Justin McNamee **Est.** 2002 **Cases** 1500

The Golding family has lived in the Lobethal area of the Adelaide Hills for several generations, and is one of the larger vignerons, owning and operating three separate vineyards with around 40 ha planted to pinot noir, chardonnay, sauvignon blanc, cabernet franc and merlot. In 2002 the Golding Wines brand was created, the owners being Darren and Lucy Golding, together with Darren's parents, Connie and Greg. In 2006 Darren secured some Marlborough sauvignon blanc through his brother-in-law, who happens to be managing director of NZ's largest independent contract winemaking company. This has resulted in three wines: The Local (100% estate-grown); The Tourist (100% Marlborough); and The Leap (51% estate-grown/49% Marlborough).

🍷🍷🍷🍷🍷 **The Leap Lenswood Marlborough Sauvignon Blanc 2007** Very pale; strong nettle aromas with plenty of acid supported by good fruit weight; quite long on the finish. Screwcap. 13.3° alc. **Rating** 92 **To** 2009 $23
Francis John Pinot Noir 2004 Has developed well, with a homogenous blend of plum, black cherry and savoury aromas and flavours; good length and finish. Screwcap. 13.9° alc. **Rating** 90 **To** 2011 $30

🍷🍷🍷🍷 **The Tourist Marlborough Sauvignon Blanc 2007** Dominant nettle aromas with a bit of sweet tomato leaf in the background. A little tart on the finish. Screwcap. 13.4° alc. **Rating** 89 **To** 2009 $20
Billy Goat Hill Chardonnay 2005 Developing slowly but well; soft stone fruit and honeydew melon, the oak integrated. Screwcap. 13.5° alc. **Rating** 89 **To** 2012 $25

Gomersal Wines   ★★★★☆

Lyndoch Road, Gomersal, SA 5352 **Region** Barossa Valley
T (08) 8563 3611 **F** (08) 8563 3776 **www**.gomersalwines.com.au **Open** 7 days 10–5
Winemaker Ben Glaetzer **Est.** 1887 **Cases** 3500
The 1887 establishment date has a degree of poetic licence. In 1887 Friedrich W Fromm planted the Wonganella Vineyards, following that with a winery on the edge of the Gomersal Creek in 1891, which remained in operation for 90 years, finally closing in 1983. In 2000 a group of friends 'with strong credentials in both the making and consumption end of the wine industry' bought the winery and re-established the vineyard, planting 17 ha of shiraz, 2.25 ha of mourvedre and 1 ha of grenache via terraced bush vines. The Riesling comes from purchased grapes, the Grenache Rose, Grenache Shiraz Mataro and Shiraz from the replanted vineyard. Exports to the US and Ireland.

🍷🍷🍷🍷🍷 **Barossa Valley Shiraz 2005** Rich, ripe and generous, with clearly defined dark fruit and fruitcake spice; warm, thick and unctuous, but not heavy, and quite long. Good value. Screwcap. 14.5° alc. **Rating** 94 **To** 2020 $20

🍷🍷🍷🍷🍷 **Eden Valley Riesling 2007** A very tight, lean and minerally wine; quite focused and fine, and appears to be built for ageing. Screwcap. 12° alc. **Rating** 90 **To** 2016 $15

Goombargona Park   ★★★★☆

Near Nug Nug, Vic 3737 (postal) **Region** Alpine Valleys
T (03) 5754 2224 **www**.goombargonapark.com.au **Open** Not
Winemaker Ian Black **Est.** 1996 **Cases** 300
What a tale to tell. Co-owner Ian Black (with wife Clare Leeuwin-Clark) has myriad connections with wine growers (and consumers), including a long-ago family relationship with Francois de Castella, one of the heroes in the development of the Yarra Valley in the 19th century. Since then, the contacts have become rather more direct, firstly through his two sons completing oenology degrees at CSU, and – prior to that time – an on-again, off-again career as an occasional weekend grapegrower. Goombargona Park (with its wonderful address, no fax, no email and only a postcode to direct the delivery of mail) is his third and most serious wine venture. The fortified wines were made by Ian Black, not purchased from others.

♀♀♀♀♀ **Muscadelle NV** High quality, well above Muscat; intense toffee, tea leaf and cake, long palate. Cork. 17.5° alc. **Rating** 94 **To** 2009 $70

♀♀♀♀♀ **Muscat NV** Still with some reddish hues; nicely aged and complex muscat raisin and Christmas pudding. Cork. 18.1° alc. **Rating** 93 **To** 2009 $70

Goona Warra Vineyard

790 Sunbury Road, Sunbury, Vic 3429 **Region** Sunbury
T (03) 9740 7766 **F** (03) 9744 7648 **www.**goonawarra.com.au **Open** 7 days 10–5
Winemaker John Barnier, Tessa Brown **Est.** 1863 **Cases** 3000
A historic stone winery, established under this name by a 19th-century Victorian premier. A brief interlude as part of The Wine Investment Fund in 2001 is over, the Barniers having bought back the farm. Excellent tasting facilities, an outstanding venue for weddings and receptions, and lunch on Sunday. Exports to Canada, China and Korea.

♀♀♀♀♀ **Sunbury Shiraz 2005** A strong savoury mineral core runs through the heart of red fruit; a fragrant, spicy and quite firm and fine palate. Screwcap. 14.5° alc. **Rating** 90 **To** 2016 $30

♀♀♀♀ **Sunbury Pinot Noir 2006** Very ripe deep plum aromas with a hint of spice; quite firm, dry and savoury finish. Screwcap. 13° alc. **Rating** 89 **To** 2014 $25
Sunbury Chardonnay 2006 Cool-grown style; hints of onion skin and lemon fruits on the bouquet with high acidity, slightly austere framework. **Rating** 87 **To** 2011 $25

Goorambath

103 Hooper Road, Goorambat, Vic 3725 **Region** Glenrowan
T (03) 5764 1380 **F** (03) 5764 1320 **www.**goorambath.com.au **Open** By appt
Winemaker Dookie College (David Hodgson) **Est.** 1997 **Cases** 650
Lyn and Geoff Bath have had a long association with the Victorian wine industry. Since 1982 Geoff has been senior lecturer in viticulture with the University of Melbourne at Dookie campus; he and wife Lyn also owned (in conjunction with two other couples) a vineyard at Whitlands for 18 years. In 2000 they sold their interest in that vineyard to focus on their small vineyard at Goorambat, hence the clever name. Planting had begun in 1998 with 0.8 ha of shiraz, subsequently joined by 0.4 ha each of verdelho and pinot gris and 0.2 ha each of orange muscat and tannat. Exports to Canada and Hong Kong.

Gordon Parker Wines

PO Box 109, Cottesloe, WA 6911 **Region** Geographe
T 0439 913 039 **www.**gordonparkerwines.com **Open** Not
Winemaker Gordon Parker **Est.** 2005 **Cases** 2500
In 1992 Gordon 'Gordo' Parker left the retail wine business in Perth, and headed south to gain winemaking experience, working at Plantagenet Wines, Forest Hill Vineyards, Cape Clairault and Amberley Estate, before spreading his wings by working at Coldstream Hills and Domaine Chandon in the Yarra Valley. He added to this a Flying Winemaker stint in 1998 in the south of France. He returned to work as a winemaker in WA before deciding to set up his own business in early 2005. He leases a 3.8-ha vineyard in Geographe, and buys grapes from other vineyards in the Frankland River, Geographe, Margaret River and Mount Barker regions. No samples received; the rating is that of last year.

Gotham ★★★☆

PO Box 343, Mona Vale, NSW 1660 **Region** Langhorne Creek
T 0412 124 811 **F** (02) 9973 3586 **Open** Not
Winemaker Bruce Clugston **Est.** 2004 **Cases** 600
Bruce Clugston, with a long involvement in the wine industry, purchases grapes from various vineyards; the 2005 Shiraz was made from 5 tonnes of premium shiraz from Jon Pfeiffer's

outstanding vineyard at Marananga in the Barossa Valley. Troy Kalleske identified the fruit for Bruce, keeping things within the family, as Pfeiffer is Kalleske's uncle.

ΨΨΨΨΨ **Langhorne Creek McLaren Vale Shiraz 2006** A mélange of red and dark fruit, overlain with a touch of mint; very full on the palate, with distinct chocolate on the finish. Screwcap. 14.5° alc. **Rating** 92 **To** 2016 $20

Goulburn Terrace

340 High Street, Nagambie, Vic 3608 **Region** Nagambie Lakes
T (03) 5794 2828 **F** (03) 5794 1854 **www**.goulburnterrace.com.au **Open** Sat 11–5, Sun & most public hols 12–5
Winemaker Dr Mike Boudry, Greta Moon **Est.** 1993 **Cases** 1000
Dr Mike Boudry and Greta Moon have established their 7-ha vineyard on the west bank of the Goulburn River, 8 km south of Lake Nagambie. Planting began in 1993: chardonnay on the alluvial soils (10 000 years old, adjacent to the river), and cabernet sauvignon on a gravelly rise based on 400-million-year-old Devonian rocks. The wines are made in small volumes, with open fermentation and hand-plunging of the reds; all are basket-pressed. Exports to Canada and Japan.

ΨΨΨΨΨ **Moon Sparkling Marsanne 2002** First tasted with two and a half years on yeast lees, now with five years, adding further to the complexity and creamy notes, but not unduly diminishing the crisp fruit evident when the wine was younger. 13° alc. **Rating** 90 **To** 2010 $35

ΨΨΨΨ **Nagambie Viognier 2004** Clean and supple, shrugging off high alcohol in part due to balanced acidity; crushed pear and peach flavours. Cork. 15° alc. **Rating** 88 **To** 2013 $28
Nagambie Cabernet Sauvignon 2002 Firm, earthy and very austere wine; has all the structure for a long life, but not the fruit; past its best-by date. Cork. 14° alc. **Rating** 87 **To** 2009 $28

Goundrey

Muirs Highway, Mount Barker, WA 6324 **Region** Mount Barker
T (08) 9892 1777 **F** (08) 9851 1997 **www**.goundreywines.com.au **Open** 7 days 10–4.30
Winemaker Peter Dillon **Est.** 1976 **Cases** NFP
Jack Bendat acquired Goundrey when it was on its knees; through significant expenditure on land, vineyards and winery capacity, it became the House that Jack Built. In late 2002 it was acquired by Vincor, Canada's largest wine producer, for a price widely said to be more than $30 million, a sum which would have provided Bendat with a very satisfactory return on his investment. It is now part of Constellation, the world's largest wine group, which acquired Vincor in 2007. Exports to all major markets.

ΨΨΨΨΨ **Shiraz Viognier 2005** Very good colour; supple, smooth, medium-bodied palate with a mix of red and black fruits, and that viognier lift; good texture. Trophy, National Wine Show '07. Screwcap. 14° alc. **Rating** 95 **To** 2015 $21
Sauvignon Blanc Semillon 2007 A charming style, with delicate fruit aromas and flavours; a mix of lemon and more tropical fruit running through to a clean finish. **Rating** 94 **To** 2011 $17.50

ΨΨΨΨΨ **Offspring Riesling 2006** A lovely, rich wine, full of ripe tropical and lime flavours; best now, as it has developed quickly. Screwcap. 13.5° alc. **Rating** 93 **To** 2010 $21.50
Reserve Selection Chardonnay 2006 From Pemberton, giving it a finer profile than Margaret River, though not as much depth; sensitively made, stone fruit, barrel ferment and mlf all working together. Screwcap. 13.5° alc. **Rating** 92 **To** 2013 $36
Reserve Selection Mount Barker Riesling 2005 Is moving towards a long plateau of maturity; a faint hint of pyrazine on the bouquet, then a deep play of citrus and mineral on the palate. Screwcap. 13° alc. **Rating** 90 **To** 2014 $27.50

ȲȲȲȲ **Reserve Selection Shiraz 2005** Medium-bodied; spicy savoury components are the most interesting, the core fruit flavours a little wishy washy. Screwcap. 14.5° alc. **Rating** 88 **To** 2013 $36

Governor Robe Selection

Waterhouse Range Vineyards, Lot 11, Old Naracoorte Road, Robe, SA 5276 **Region** Limestone Coast Zone
T (08) 8768 2083 **F** (08) 8768 2190 **www**.waterhouserange.com.au **Open** At The Attic House, Victoria St, Robe
Winemaker Cape Jaffa Wines (Nigel Westblade) **Est.** 1998 **Cases** 1500
Bill and Mick Quinlan-Watson, supported by a group of investors, began the development of Waterhouse Range Vineyards Pty Ltd in 1995, planting 15 ha of vines, with further plantings over the following few years lifting the total area under vine to just under 60 ha. The majority of the grapes are sold. The name comes from the third Governor of SA, Frederick Holt Robe, who in 1845 selected the site for a port and personally put in the first survey peg at Robe.

Grace Devlin Wines   **NR**

53 Siddles Road, Redesdale, Vic 3444 **Region** Heathcote
T (03) 5425 3101 **Open** By appt
Winemaker Brian Paterson, Lee Paterson **Est.** 1998 **Cases** 300
Brian and Lee Paterson have 2 ha of cabernet sauvignon and 0.5 ha of merlot at Redesdale, one of the most southerly vineyards in the Heathcote region. The name comes from the middle names of Brian Paterson's grandmother, mother and daughters. The small production is available from a number of local outlets.

Gracedale Hills Estate

770 Healesville-Kooweerup Road, Healesville, Vic 3777 **Region** Yarra Valley
T (03) 5967 3403 **F** (03) 5967 3581 **www**.gracedalehills.com.au **Open** Not
Winemaker Gary Mills **Est.** 1996 **Cases** 500
Dr Richard Gutch established 2.2 ha of chardonnay and 1 ha of shiraz at a time when most would be retiring from active business, but it represents the culmination of a lifelong love of fine wine, and Richard has no hard feelings towards me – it was I who encouraged him, in the mid-1990s, to plant vines on the north-facing slopes of his property. Here, too, the grapes have been sold to others, but he now retains sufficient grapes to make around 500 cases a year. In 2007 a purpose-built gravity feed winery was built to reduce the amount of travelling, handling and processing of the fruit for the estate-grown wines.

ȲȲȲȲȲ **Hill Paddock Yarra Valley Shiraz 2006** Highly attractive medium-bodied shiraz, with vibrant cherry and blackberry fruit on the fluid palate and fine finish. Screwcap. 13.5° alc. **Rating** 93 **To** 2016 $30

ȲȲȲȲ **Hill Paddock Yarra Valley Chardonnay 2006** Some funky barrel ferment aromas and flavours on a fairly lean palate. Screwcap. 12.6° alc. **Rating** 87 **To** 2010 $25

Graham Cohen Wines

PO Box 195, Bannockburn, Vic 3331 **Region** Geelong
T (03) 5281 7438 **F** (03) 5281 7387 **Open** Not
Winemaker Contract **Est.** 1985 **Cases** 200
Graham and Jan Cohen have established 1 ha of pinot noir, which produces a sole wine called Captains Birchwood. The unusual name was chosen by the Cohens' four sons, each one in turn House Captain of Birchwood House at their school.

ȲȲȲȲȲ **Captains Birchwood Pinot Noir 2006** Good colour; clear-cut varietal fruit; damson plum with quite firm acidity and good length. Vines planted 1985. Screwcap. 14° alc. **Rating** 90 **To** 2011 $23

Gralyn Estate

★★★★★

4145 Caves Road, Wilyabrup, WA 6280 **Region** Margaret River
T (08) 9755 6245 **F** (08) 9755 6136 **www.**gralyn.com.au **Open** 7 days 10.30–4.30
Winemaker Graham Hutton, Merilyn Hutton, Dr Bradley Hutton **Est.** 1975 **Cases** 3000
Under the eagle eye of Merilyn Hutton, Gralyn Estate has established a high reputation for
its wines. The primary focus is on the full-bodied red wines, which are made in a distinctively
different style than most from Margaret River, with an opulence reminiscent of some of the
bigger wines from McLaren Vale. The age of the vines (30+ years) and the site are significant
factors. Lesser amounts of chardonnay and fortified wines are also made.

ΨΨΨΨΨ   **Reserve Margaret River Shiraz 2005** Complex, rich, supple, round and
generously (but not over-) oaked in typical Gralyn style; medium- to full-bodied;
excellent texture and finish. Screwcap. 14.3° alc. **Rating** 94 **To** 2025 $90
Margaret River Cabernet Sauvignon 2005 A very rich and supple medium-
to full-bodied palate, with layers of black fruits rippling within a framework of
cedary French oak and fine but persistent tannins. Cork. 14.3° alc. **Rating** 94
To 2025 $90

ΨΨΨΨ   **Margaret River Rose 2007** As befits Gralyn, at the big end of town with strong
red fruit flavours; needs food. Screwcap. 12.8° alc. **Rating** 87 **To** 2009 $27

Grampians Estate

★★★★★

366 Mafeking Road, Willaura, Vic 3379 **Region** Grampians
T (03) 5354 6245 **F** (03) 5354 6257 **www.**grampiansestate.com.au **Open** At Garden Gully
Winemaker Hamish Seabrook, Don Rowe, Tom Guthrie **Est.** 1989 **Cases** 1000
Local farmers and graziers Sarah and Tom Guthrie diversified their activities, with 2 ha of
shiraz and 1.2 ha of chardonnay, while continuing to run their fat lamb and wool production.
In 2006, 90% of the vineyard was devastated by bushfire; various wineries from across
Victoria donated grapes and wine, ensuring the production of wine for the year. They have
an exceptional newsletter that helps build fierce loyalty, and as the vineyard recovers, both the
Guthries and their customers will be the winners.

ΨΨΨΨΨ   **Black Sunday Friends Reserve Shiraz 2006** In the genre of the '98
Bannockburn Shiraz; grapes from six Vic cool-climate regions, most from the
Grampians and Pyrenees; a wonderful tapestry of vibrant spices and black fruits;
marvelous thrust to the almost explosive finish. Screwcap. **Rating** 96 **To** 2021 $50
Black Sunday Friends Shiraz 2006 A lovely wine with great colour, loads of
spice, silky mid-palate fruit and a combination of dark and red fruits on offer. Fine
and long on the finish. Screwcap. 14.8° alc. **Rating** 95 **To** 2018 $23
Streeton Reserve Shiraz 2005 Has great vinosity line and length, with
dark spicy fruits and hints of the sap of the vine; complex, dark and intriguing.
Screwcap. 15.3° alc. **Rating** 94 **To** 2020 $55

ΨΨΨΨ   **Mafeking Shiraz 2005** Bright colour, with real juicy blackberry jube personality.
Has good weight, but is a little one-dimensional. Screwcap. 14.2° alc. **Rating** 89
To 2015 $28

Granite Hills

★★★★★

1481 Burke & Wills Track, Baynton, Kyneton, Vic 3444 **Region** Macedon Ranges
T (03) 5423 7264 **F** (03) 5423 7288 **www.**granitehills.com.au **Open** Mon–Sat 10–6,
Sun 1–6
Winemaker Llew Knight, Ian Gunter **Est.** 1970 **Cases** 6000
Granite Hills is one of the enduring classics, pioneering the successful growing of riesling
and shiraz in an uncompromisingly cool climate. It is based on 11 ha of riesling, chardonnay,
shiraz, cabernet sauvignon, merlot and pinot noir (the last also used in its sparkling wine). After
a quiet period in the 1990s, it has been reinvigorated, with its original two icons once again
to the fore. The Rieslings age superbly, and the Shiraz is at the forefront of the cool-climate
school in Australia. Exports to Ireland, Canada, China and NZ.

Granite Range Estate ★★★

183 Wilson Road, Wangandary, Vic 3678 **Region** Glenrowan
T (03) 5725 3292 **F** (03) 5725 3292 **Open** Tues–Sun 10–5
Winemaker Peter Long **Est.** 1998 **Cases** 2000
This is the retirement venture of Peter and Maureen Long, who acquired a 16-ha bare-paddock in 1997, with the Warby Ranges behind and a panoramic view of the Australian Alps. The following year they established 2.3 ha each of shiraz and merlot, and a grape purchase contract with Baileys of Glenrowan. Since 2003, production has been split between sales to other producers, and wine under the Granite Range Estate label. The modern building complex comprises the Longs' house, cellar door, barrel store and self-contained accommodation. Exports to Singapore.

Grant Burge ★★★★★

Jacobs Creek, Barossa Valley, SA 5352 **Region** Barossa Valley
T (08) 8563 3700 **F** (08) 8563 2807 **www**.grantburgewines.com.au **Open** 7 days 10–5
Winemaker Grant Burge, Craig Stansborough **Est.** 1988 **Cases** 400 000
As one might expect, this very experienced industry veteran makes consistently good, full-flavoured and smooth wines chosen from the pick of the crop of his extensive vineyard holdings, which total 440 ha; the immaculately restored/rebuilt stone cellar door sales buildings are another attraction. The provocatively named The Holy Trinity (Grenache/Shiraz/Mourvedre) joins Shadrach and Meshach at the top of the range. In 1999 Grant Burge repurchased the farm from Mildara Blass by acquiring the Krondorf winery in Tanunda (not the brand), in which he made his first fortune. He renamed it Barossa Vines and opened a cellar door offering casual food. A third cellar door (Illaparra) is open at Murray Street, Tanunda. Exports to all major markets.

🍷🍷🍷🍷🍷 **Meshach 2002** A glorious expression of a cool vintage shiraz with small berries and a long growing season; blackberry, spice and licorice, with fine, lingering tannins. Predominantly American oak for two years' maturation; 85-year-old vines. Multi-trophy winner. Cork. 14° alc. **Rating** 96 **To** 2022 $100

Cameron Vale Cabernet Sauvignon 2004 Exceptional colour; delicious but serious cabernet, blackcurrant and cassis offset by savoury tannins and quality French oak. Admirable control of alcohol. Cork. 13.5° alc. **Rating** 95 **To** 2014 $22.98

Shadrach Cabernet Sauvignon 2005 Deeper, though less bright colour than the Cameron Vale; fine texture and structure, and very good varietal fruit profile; fine-grained tannins and quality oak. Cork. **Rating** 95 **To** 2020 $54.90

The Holy Trinity Grenache Shiraz Mourvedre 2004 Although it shouldn't be the case, here both the fruit is more intense and the line is quite seamless, with a lingering finish and aftertaste. Cork. **Rating** 94 **To** 2019 $37.70

🍷🍷🍷🍷 **Miamba Shiraz 2006** Luscious, supple, medium-bodied wine, with appealing spicy fruit nuances, fine tannins and subtle oak; bears testament to the vintage; long finish. Screwcap. **Rating** 93 **To** 2020 $24

Cameron Vale Cabernet Sauvignon 2005 Some herbal overlays to aromas; medium- to full-bodied; strides confidently off towards serious blackcurrant fruit and fine tannins. Screwcap. **Rating** 93 **To** 2020 $24

Summers Eden Valley Adelaide Hills Chardonnay 2006 Developed colour; is obvious, but, particularly on the palate, fine, nectarine fruit comes through strongly, reflecting the regional components. Screwcap. 14° alc. **Rating** 91 **To** 2010 $22.98

Barossa Vines Semillon Viognier 2006 A seemingly quixotic blend, which does, however, work quite well, for it is light on its feet, with citrus/mineral acidity tightening the palate and giving length. Screwcap. 13° alc. **Rating** 90 **To** 2009 $16.25

Meshach 2003 Has managed to largely surmount the challenges of the very difficult vintage, with good colour and an abundance of quality American and French oak helping the cause. Cork. 14.5° alc. **Rating** 90 **To** 2018 $120

Shadrach Cabernet Sauvignon 2004 Ripe blackcurrant fruit verging on outright sweetness; some chocolate and vanilla notes plus supple tannins. Cork. 14° alc. **Rating** 90 **To** 2014 $50

ŢŢŢŢ **Filsell Barossa Valley Shiraz 2005** Suspect colour suggesting elevated pH; a rich chocolate and blackberry mix of fruit, with ripe tannins; needs more focus despite near-century-old vines. Cork. 15° alc. **Rating** 89 **To** 2013 $34.29
Miamba Shiraz 2005 More savoury and chocolatey than the '06, partly vintage and partly more development; fine tannins a plus. Cork. **Rating** 89 **To** 2013 $24
Abednego Grenache Mourvedre Shiraz 2004 Good hue; the fruit and tannin lines are entirely disconnected, the sweet fruit first, then the tannins; the RRP is something to conjure with. Cork. **Rating** 88 **To** 2014 $61.73
Hillcot Merlot 2005 A curate's egg, scrambled into the bargain; has flashes of varietal character, but sweet and sour obstacles stand in the way; overall, plenty of flavour. Screwcap. 14.5° alc. **Rating** 87 **To** 2010 $19.20
Barossa Vines Chardonnay 2006 Developed colour; an honest wine, with plenty of peachy fruit, though not much finesse. Screwcap. 14° alc. **Rating** 87 **To** 2009 $15.50
Barossa Vines Grenache Mourvedre Shiraz 2006 A very typical example of both region and blend, with distinct fruit sweetness despite the low alcohol; technically perfect, but simply not to my personal taste. Screwcap. 13.5° alc. **Rating** 87 **To** 2009 $14.95
Barossa Vines Cabernet Merlot 2005 Developed colour; a mix of herbal savoury/earthy/minty aromas and flavours, with sweet vanilla oak. Screwcap. 14.5° alc. **Rating** 87 **To** 2009 $15.50
Sparkling Shiraz Cabernet NV Relatively speaking, of light- to medium-bodied weight (a surprise); seems needlessly (though perhaps intentionally) sweet. Cork. 14° alc. **Rating** 87 **To** 2009 $30.86

Grassy Point Wines   ★★★★★

Coatsworth Farm, 145 Coatsworth Road, Portarlington, Vic 3223 **Region** Geelong
T 0409 429 608 **www**.grassypointwines.com.au **Open** By appt
Winemaker Provenance (Scott Ireland) **Est.** 1997 **Cases** 800
Partners David Smith, Robert Bennett and Kerry Jones purchased this 32-ha undeveloped grazing property in 1997. Coatsworth Farm now has 6.6 ha of vines (chardonnay, sauvignon blanc, pinot noir, shiraz and cabernet franc), South Devon beef cattle and Perendale/White Suffolk-cross lambs.

ŢŢŢŢŢ **Bellarine Peninsula Pinot Noir 2006** An appealing wine; very good line and length, elegant and precise; lingering finish and aftertaste. **Rating** 94 **To** 2012 $28
Bellarine Peninsula Shiraz 2006 Bright colour; fragrant spicy red cherry, raspberry and cassis fruit on an elegant and perfectly balanced medium-bodied palate; cool-climate shiraz at its early drinking best. Screwcap. 14.1° alc. **Rating** 94 **To** 2012 $20

ŢŢŢŢŢ **Bellarine Peninsula Chardonnay 2006** Smoky bacon barrel ferment inputs; a complex, highly worked style; needed more fruit concentration for top points. **Rating** 90 **To** 2011 $20

Green Valley Vineyard   ★★★

3137 Sebbes Road, Forest Grove, WA 6286 **Region** Margaret River
T (08) 9757 7510 **F** (08) 9757 7510 **www**.greenvalleyvineyard.com.au **Open** 7 days 10–5
Winemaker Ian Bell **Est.** 1980 **Cases** 5000
Major changes are afoot at Green Valley Vineyard, since its acquisition by investment banker and cricket lover Graeme Seed and medical practitioner Dr Helen Thomas. Vineyard management and winemaking are now under the control of Ian Bell (formerly of Moss Wood, and with his own Glenmore venture), with substantial investment in and upgrading of the vineyard. This is planted to shiraz (3 ha), chardonnay and cabernet sauvignon (2 ha each) and

riesling (1 ha), although the latter is being grafted over the chardonnay. Exports to Singapore, Vietnam, Hong Kong and China.

Greenstone Vineyard   ★★★★★

319 Whorouly South Road, Whorouly South, Vic 3735 (postal) **Region** Heathcote
T (03) 5727 1434 **F** (03) 5727 1434 **www.**greenstoneofheathcote.com **Open** Not
Winemaker Sandro Mosele (Contract), Alberto Antonini **Est.** 2002 **Cases** 3500
This is one of the most interesting new ventures to emerge over the past few years, bringing together David Gleave MW, born and educated in Canada, but now a long-term UK resident, managing an imported wine business and writing widely about the wines of Italy; Alberto Antonini, a graduate of the University of Florence, with postgraduate degrees from Bordeaux and University of California (Davis), and Italian Flying Winemaker; and Mark Walpole, a 20-year veteran with Brown Brothers and now manager of their 700 ha of vineyards. The partners have chosen what they consider an outstanding vineyard on the red soil of the Heathcote region, planted to 17 ha of shiraz, and 1 ha each of monastrell (mourvedre), sangiovese and tempranillo. Exports to the UK, the US and other major markets.

♟♟♟♟♟ **Heathcote Shiraz 2006** Grapes picked at optimal ripeness, producing a wine that is stacked with regional black fruits but has no alcohol-derived sweetness; long finish with fine-grained tannins. Screwcap. 13.5° alc. **Rating** 95 **To** 2021 $40

Greg Cooley Wines   ★★★★☆

Lot 2 & 4, Seipelt Lane, Penwortham, SA 5453 (postal) **Region** Clare Valley
T (08) 8843 4284 **F** (08) 8843 4284 **Open** Not
Winemaker Greg Cooley **Est.** 2002 **Cases** 1600
Greg Cooley says, 'I followed the traditional path to winemaking via accountancy, fraud squad, corporate investigations, running a Wendy's Supa Sundaes franchise and then selling residential property. I left the property market in Brisbane just as the boom started in 2001 and moved to the beautiful Clare just about when the wine glut started. Things didn't look overly promising when my first wine entered into the Clare Show in 2003. The Riesling came 97th of a total of 97, a platform on which I have since built, having sought loads of advice from local winemakers and subsequently winning a medal the following year.' He explains, 'All my wines are named after people who have been of influence to me in my 45 years and their influence is as varied as the wine styles – from pizza shop owners, to my greyhound's vet and, indeed, my recently departed greyhound Tigger.' I have to confess that I am taken by Greg Cooley's path to glory because my move through law to wine was punctuated by the part-ownership of two greyhounds that always wanted to run in the opposite direction to the rest of the field.

♟♟♟♟♀ **Bennett & Byrne Reserve Clare Valley Shiraz 2005** A big, soft but chewy Clare style; plush dark fruits, with plenty of oak and ripe tannins all cohabiting without stress. Screwcap. 15° alc. **Rating** 92 **To** 2020 $27
Winna & Toop Clare Valley Cabernet Merlot 2005 Built in similar fashion to the Glyn & Pini Merlot, but with more punch and length courtesy of the cabernet; good balance. Screwcap. 15° alc. **Rating** 91 **To** 2016 $20
Glyn & Pini Clare Valley Merlot 2005 A dense wine in typical Clare Valley mode for the variety; rich, dark fruits with mocha and vanilla softening; not especially varietal, but enjoyable. Screwcap. 15° alc. **Rating** 90 **To** 2014 $20
Rehbein & Ryan Reserve Clare Valley Cabernet 2005 Densely coloured; rich, ripe, luscious black fruits speak more of the region and alcohol than cabernet; earlier picking might have made a better wine. Screwcap. 15° alc. **Rating** 90 **To** 2020 $27

♟♟♟♟ **Monica, Macca & Moo Clare Valley Shiraz 2005** A flavoursome, medium-bodied wine without the plush fruit of Bennett & Byrne; direct blackberry flavours and firm tannins. Screwcap. 15° alc. **Rating** 89 **To** 2013 $20

Grey Sands

Cnr Kerrisons Road/Frankford Highway, Glengarry, Tas 7275 **Region** Northern Tasmania
T (03) 6396 1167 **F** (03) 6396 1153 **www**.greysands.com.au **Open** Last Sun of month
10–5, or by appt
Winemaker Bob Richter **Est.** 1989 **Cases** 800
Bob and Rita Richter began the establishment of Grey Sands in 1989, slowly increasing the
plantings to the present total of 2.5 ha. The ultra-high density of 8900 vines per ha reflects
the experience gained by the Richters during a 3-year stay in England, when they visited
many vineyards across Europe, as well as Bob Richter's graduate diploma from Roseworthy
College.

♀♀♀♀♀ **Merlot 2003** A once schizophrenic wine, with all the components now falling
perfectly into place; a lovely wine, with cassis and redcurrant supported by smooth,
fine tannins on a long finish. Cork. 13.2° alc. **Rating** 93 **To** 2010 $30

Griffin Wines

PO Box 221, Clarendon, SA 5157 **Region** Adelaide Hills
T (08) 8239 2545 **F** (08) 8388 3557 **www**.griffinwines.com **Open** Not
Winemaker Phil Christiansen, Shaw & Smith, Di Fabio Estate **Est.** 1997 **Cases** 2500
The Griffins (Trevor, Tim, Mark and Val) planted 26 ha of pinot noir, chardonnay, sauvignon
blanc, merlot and shiraz in 1997, having owned the property for over 30 years. It is situated
3 km from Kuitpo Hall; its 350 m elevation gives sweeping views over the valley below.

♀♀♀♀♀ **No. 1 Adelaide Hills Shiraz 2005** Deep colour; strong blackberry, licorice and
spice fruit throughout; very nearly carries the elevated alcohol. Screwcap. 15° alc.
Rating 92 **To** 2020 $25
No. 3 Adelaide Hills Pinot Noir 2005 Savoury, spicy, foresty notes run
through the dark fruits of the medium-bodied palate, which finishes with fine
tannins; has length. Screwcap. 14.7° alc. **Rating** 90 **To** 2010 $30

♀♀♀♀ **No. 2 Adelaide Hills Sauvignon Blanc 2007** Clean, fresh and quite crisp,
albeit with somewhat diminished varietal character; nice balance and length.
Screwcap. 13° alc. **Rating** 89 **To** 2010 $19
Adelaide Hills Rose 2007 Quite attractive raspberry and cherry fruit aromas and
flavours, then a slightly tough finish. Screwcap. 13° alc. **Rating** 87 **To** 2009 $17

Groom

28 Langmeil Road, Tanunda, SA 5352 (postal) **Region** Barossa Valley
T (08) 8563 1101 **F** (08) 8563 1102 **www**.groomwines.com **Open** Not
Winemaker Daryl Groom **Est.** 1997 **Cases** 5500
The full name of the business is Marschall Groom Cellars, a venture owned by David and
Jeanette Marschall and their six children, and Daryl and Lisa Groom and their four children.
Daryl Groom was a highly regarded winemaker at Penfolds before he moved to Geyser Peak
in California. Years of discussion between the families came to a head with the purchase of a
35-ha block of bare land near Kalimna, adjacent to Penfolds' 130-year-old Kalimna Vineyard.
Shiraz was planted in 1997, giving its first vintage in '99, the wine blended with the output
from two vineyards, one 100 years old, the other 50 years old. The next acquisition was an
8-ha vineyard at Lenswood in the Adelaide Hills, planted to sauvignon blanc. In 2000, 3.2 ha
of zinfandel was planted on the Kalimna Bush block, with the first vintage in '03. Not
surprisingly, a substantial part of the production is exported to the US.

♀♀♀♀♀ **Barossa Valley Shiraz 2006** Dense purple; rich, focused and powerful
blackberry and licorice fruit, oak in the back stalls; harmonious and complete wine
with great balance and mouthfeel. Cork. 14.3° alc. **Rating** 96 **To** 2016 $48

♀♀♀♀ **Adelaide Hills Sauvignon Blanc 2007** Has considerable weight and texture,
but lacks thrust and finesse. Screwcap. 12.8° alc. **Rating** 87 **To** 2009 $24

Grosset ★★★★★

King Street, Auburn, SA 5451 **Region** Clare Valley
T (08) 8849 2175 **F** (08) 8849 2292 **www**.grosset.com.au **Open** Wed–Sun 10–5 from
Sept for approx 6 weeks
Winemaker Jeffrey Grosset **Est.** 1981 **Cases** 9000
Jeffrey Grosset served part of his apprenticeship at the vast Lindeman Karadoc winery, moving
from the largest to one of the smallest when he established Grosset Wines in its old stone
winery. He crafts the wines with the utmost care from grapes grown to the most exacting
standards; all need a certain amount of time in bottle to achieve their ultimate potential, not
the least the Rieslings and Gaia, which are among Australia's best examples of their kind. He is
also a passionate advocate of the use of screwcaps on all wines. Exports to all major markets.

♀♀♀♀♀ **Gaia 2005** Lovely cabernet, expressive of a more red fruit personality, pure
and quite generous; it would be easy to miss the structure of this wine, given
the abundance of tightly focused fruit, but it is there and will see this wine age
gracefully for a decade to come. Screwcap. 14° alc. **Rating** 95 **To** 2018 $58
Semillon Sauvignon Blanc 2007 Powerful and complex, with barrel ferment
obvious on the bouquet; mouthfilling with abundant flavour; Clare Valley semillon
gives it robust character. Screwcap. 13° alc. **Rating** 94 **To** 2013 $31
Piccadilly Adelaide Hills Chardonnay 2006 Ripe stone fruits, and flashy oak
aromas evident in this complex wine; more citrus comes through on the palate,
and there is great drive through to the ample, yet fine, long and minerally finish.
Screwcap. 14° alc. **Rating** 94 **To** 2013 $53
Adelaide Hills Pinot Noir 2006 Vibrant purple hue; dark plum fruits with
spice and a hint of stem; quite serious palate weight, but follows through with
lightness and typical pinot peacock's tail; very long. Screwcap. 14° alc. **Rating** 94
To 2012 $65

♀♀♀♀♀ **Polish Hill Riesling 2007** A discrete, refined bouquet with a touch of apple
blossom; a firm, linear and precise palate, with line and length; needs time, and will
handsomely repay it. Screwcap. 13° alc. **Rating** 93 **To** 2015 $42
Springvale Vineyard Watervale Riesling 2007 Floral notes of passionfruit
and citrus; more developed, generous and mouthfilling than the usual Grosset style;
ripe citrus and tropical fruit. Screwcap. 13° alc. **Rating** 93 **To** 2015 $35

Grove Estate Wines ★★★★

Murringo Road, Young, NSW 2594 **Region** Hilltops
T (02) 6382 6999 **F** (02) 6382 4527 **www**.groveestate.com.au **Open** W'ends 10–5, or by appt
Winemaker Clonakilla (Tim Kirk) **Est.** 1989 **Cases** 4000
A partnership of Brian Mullany, John Kirkwood and Mark Flanders has established a 31-ha
vineyard planted to semillon, chardonnay, merlot, shiraz, cabernet sauvignon, nebbiolo and
zinfandel. Some of the grapes are sold (principally to Foster's), but an increasing amount
of very good and interesting wine is contract-made for the Grove Estate label. Exports to
the UK.

♀♀♀♀♀ **Hilltops Semillon 2007** Above-average weight and depth for young unwooded
semillon, but not coarse or phenolic; ripe citrus verging on tropical; best drunk
sooner than later. Screwcap. 12.9° alc. **Rating** 90 **To** 2012 $19

♀♀♀♀ **Cellar Block Reserve Shiraz Viognier 2006** Despite the skill of maker Tim
Kirk, I'm not convinced about the wine, which, while having plenty of flavour,
lacks the expected focus and line. Screwcap. 14.5° alc. **Rating** 88 **To** 2012 $36

Growlers Gully ★★★

354 Shaws Road, Merton, Vic 3715 **Region** Upper Goulburn
T (03) 5778 9615 **F** (03) 5778 9615 **Open** W'ends & public hols 11–5, or by appt
Winemaker Les Oates **Est.** 1997 **Cases** NA

Les and Wendy Oates began the establishment of the Growlers Gully vineyard in 1997, extending it in '98 to a total of 4 ha of shiraz and 1 ha of cabernet sauvignon. It sits at an elevation of 375 m on fertile brown clay loam soil. A rammed-earth cellar door sales outlet offers light meals and barbecue facilities.

ŶŶŶŶŶ **Upper Goulburn Shiraz 2006** Strong colour; a full, supple medium- to full-bodied palate with a blend of satsuma plum and blackberry, the tannins soft. A shiraz/pinot noir blend from Growlers Gully could be interesting. Diam. 13.9° alc. **Rating** 90 **To** 2012 $25

Guichen Bay Vineyards ★★★☆

PO Box 582, Newport, NSW 2106 **Region** Mount Benson
T (02) 9997 6677 **F** (02) 9997 6177 www.guichenbay.com.au **Open** At Mount Benson Tourist & Wine Information Centre
Winemaker Cape Jaffa Wines (Derek Hooper), Koltz (Mark Day) **Est.** 2003 **Cases** 850
Guichen Bay Vineyards is one of three adjacent vineyards known collectively as the Mount Benson Community Vineyards. Between 1997 and 2001, 120 ha of vines were planted to chardonnay, sauvignon blanc, shiraz, merlot and cabernet sauvignon. While the major part of the production is sold, the owners have obtained a producer's licence, and a small quantity of grapes is held back and made by local winemakers under the Guichen Bay Vineyards label.

ŶŶŶŶŶ **Mount Benson Reserve Shiraz 2006** Deeply coloured; the bouquet has very good fruit concentration along with oak; full-bodied and full-flavoured with chewy tannins and lots of dark fruits on the finish. Screwcap. 14.8° alc. **Rating** 91 **To** 2018 $27

Haan Wines

Siegersdorf Road, Tanunda, SA 5352 **Region** Barossa Valley
T (08) 8562 4590 **F** (08) 8562 4590 www.haanwines.com.au **Open** Not
Winemaker Mark Jamieson (Contract) **Est.** 1993 **Cases** 4500
Hans and Fransien Haan established their business in 1993 when they acquired a 19-ha vineyard near Tanunda (since extended to 36.7 ha). The primary focus is on merlot, in particular the luxury Merlot Prestige, supported by Semillon, Viognier and Shiraz. These are wines that polarise opinion; the issue is not alcohol, but the amount of oak used, and the way it is used. I think the outcome is very successful, but I would never seek to make wines in this style. Exports to all major markets.

ŶŶŶŶŶ **Merlot Prestige 2005** Has the extra degree of intense varietal fruit and gently opulent oak; has length, and a supple, velvety finish. Cork. 15° alc. **Rating** 95 **To** 2015 $45
Barossa Valley Viognier Prestige 2007 One of the best viogniers going; flowery, aromatic apricot nuances on the bouquet, the palate adding touches of fruit spice and musk; long finish, no phenolics. Screwcap. 14° alc. **Rating** 94 **To** 2011 $35
Barossa Valley Shiraz Prestige 2005 Bright colour courtesy of 5% viognier co-fermented; a sumptuous, velvety wine, with lifted blackberry, dark chocolate and mocha flavours supported by ripe tannins; in the mainstream of Haan style. Cork. 14.5° alc. **Rating** 94 **To** 2020 $47.50
Wilhelmus 2005 Has that hallmark softness of all the Haan reds, finishing fermentation in oak part of the reason; a supple, smooth and round blend of the five Bordeaux varieties. Cork. 15° alc. **Rating** 94 **To** 2015 $49.95

ŶŶŶŶ **Hanenhof Viognier 2006** Mouthfilling and rich, verging on too much so, but giving the character many lack; peach and apricot fruit; slightly congested finish. Screwcap. 14.5° alc. **Rating** 89 **To** 2010 $21.50

Hackersley

Ferguson Road, Dardanup, WA 6236 **Region** Geographe
T (08) 9384 6247 **F** (08) 9383 3364 **www.**hackersley.com.au **Open** Thurs–Sun 10–4
Winemaker Tony Davis (Contract) **Est.** 1997 **Cases** 1200
Hackersley is a partnership between the Ovens, Stacey and Hewitt families, friends since
their university days, and with (so they say) the misguided belief that growing and making
their own wine would be cheaper than buying it. They found a 'little piece of paradise in
the Ferguson Valley just south of Dardanup', and in 1998 they planted a little under 8 ha,
extended since then to 11.5 ha of the mainstream varieties; interestingly, they turned their
back on chardonnay. Most of the crop is sold to Houghton, but a small quantity is made for
the Hackersley label. No samples received; the rating is that of last year.

Hahndorf Hill Winery ★★★★★

Lot 10, Pains Road, Hahndorf, SA 5245 **Region** Adelaide Hills
T (08) 8388 7512 **F** (08) 8388 7618 **www.**hahndorfhillwinery.com.au **Open** 7 days 10–5
Winemaker Geoff Weaver (Consultant) **Est.** 2002 **Cases** 4000
Larry Jacobs and Marc Dobson, both originally from South Africa, purchased Hahndorf
Hill Winery in 2002. Jacobs gave up a career in intensive-care medicine in 1988 when
he purchased an abandoned property in Stellenbosch, and established the near-iconic
Mulderbosch Wines. When Mulderbosch was purchased at the end of 1996, the pair migrated
to Australia and eventually found their way to Hahndorf Hill. In 2006, their investment in the
winery and cellar door was rewarded by induction into the South Australian Great Tourism
Hall of Fame, having won the award for Best Tourism Winery for three consecutive years.
Since 2007 they have begun the process of converting the vineyard to biodynamic status, and
they were one of the first movers in implementing a carbon offset program. Exports to the
UK, the US and Singapore.

ΨΨΨΨΨ **Adelaide Hills Chardonnay 2004** The screwcap and good natural acidity
have combined to give the wine remarkable freshness; strong grapefruit and citrus
flavours, and subtle oak. Screwcap. 13.5° alc. **Rating** 94 **To** 2014 $26
Adelaide Hills Shiraz 2005 Medium-bodied; attractive spicy/savoury nuances
to the plum, black cherry and blackberry fruit; good texture, structure and length.
Cork. 14.5° alc. **Rating** 94 **To** 2015 $28

ΨΨΨΨΨ **Adelaide Hills Sauvignon Blanc 2007** A relatively quiet bouquet, but builds
flavour intensity and complexity on the back-palate and finish, with a contrasting
mix of grassy and tropical passionfruit flavours. Screwcap. 12.5° alc. **Rating** 92
To 2009 $21
Adelaide Hills Pinot Grigio 2007 Has above-average intensity and varietal
character, offering pear, musk, apple and spice, with good acidity and length.
Screwcap. 13° alc. **Rating** 91 **To** 2010 $24

ΨΨΨΨ **Adelaide Hills Rose 2007** A clean, fresh bouquet; light and lively, with citrussy
aspects to the small red fruit flavours. Trollinger/Lemberger, varieties exclusive to
Hahndorf Hill in Australia. Screwcap. 12° alc. **Rating** 87 **To** 2009 $18.50

Halifax Wines

Lot 501, Binney Road, McLaren Vale, Willunga, SA 5172 **Region** McLaren Vale
T 0412 257 149 **F** (08) 8367 0333 **www.**halifaxwines.com.au **Open** Thurs–Mon 10–4
or by appt
Winemaker Peter Butcher **Est.** 2000 **Cases** 1500
Owned and operated by Elizabeth Tasker (background in advertising and marketing) and
Peter Butcher (20+ years in the wine industry, in marketing, sales, distribution, education and
winemaking). A passionate proponent of wine's 'sense of place', Peter has worked with some of
Australia's most well-known winemakers – Jeffrey Grosset, Peter Leske, Mike Farmilo and Peter
Gago – and has also been influenced by visits to France and Italy. Produces a single-vineyard
Shiraz from 4 ha of estate plantings, supplemented by small quantities of grenache (50-year-old
vines) and cabernet sauvignon (40-year-old vines). Exports to the US and Hong Kong.

ƏƏƏƏ **Coach House McLaren Vale Cabernet Sauvignon 2006** A pointed fruit profile, brisk and firm; slightly hazy colour reflects the no fining or filtration policy, but does not impinge on the length of the wine. Screwcap. 14° alc. **Rating** 89 To 2014 $28

Ad Lib 2006 Vibrant hue; very light, more in Barossa than McLaren Vale style, with juicy/jammy red fruits and minimal tannins; enjoy today rather than tomorrow. Grenache/Shiraz/Cabernet Sauvignon. Screwcap. 14.5° alc. **Rating** 87 To 2009 $23

Hamelin Bay   ★★★★

McDonald Road, Karridale, WA 6288 **Region** Margaret River
T (08) 9758 6779 **F** (08) 9758 6779 **www.**hbwines.com.au **Open** 7 days 10–5
Winemaker Julian Scott **Est.** 1992 **Cases** 15 000
The 25-ha Hamelin Bay vineyard was established by the Drake-Brockman family. The initial releases were contract-made, but a winery with cellar door sales facility was opened in 2000; this has enabled an increase in production. Exports to the UK, Canada, Malaysia and Singapore.

ƏƏƏƏƏ **Five Ashes Vineyard Margaret River Semillon Sauvignon Blanc 2007** A lively wine with a mix of herb, grass, lemon and gooseberry; a fine, tight palate. Screwcap. 13° alc. **Rating** 91 To 2011 $20

Five Ashes Vineyard Margaret River Chardonnay 2006 Clear-cut varietal nectarine and grapefruit flavours; good length and finish, oak in the background; low alcohol a plus. Screwcap. 13° alc. **Rating** 91 To 2012 $26

Five Ashes Vineyard Margaret River Sauvignon Blanc 2007 Is in a tight herb/grass/asparagus/mineral flavour spectrum; crisp, dry finish. Screwcap. 13° alc. **Rating** 90 To 2010 $22

ƏƏƏƏ **Rampant White 2007** Light- to medium-bodied; clean, somewhat amorphous fruit, but lengthened and braced by citrussy acidity. Screwcap. 13° alc. **Rating** 87 To 2010 $18

Five Ashes Vineyard Margaret River Rose 2007 Clean, fresh strawberry and raspberry fruit flavours; a crisp, dry finish. Screwcap. 13.5° alc. **Rating** 87 To 2009 $20

Hanging Rock Winery   ★★★★★

88 Jim Road, Newham, Vic 3442 **Region** Macedon Ranges
T (03) 5427 0542 **F** (03) 5427 0310 **www.**hangingrock.com.au **Open** 7 days 10–5
Winemaker John Ellis **Est.** 1982 **Cases** 40 000
The Macedon area has proved very marginal in spots, and the Hanging Rock vineyards, with their lovely vista towards the Rock, are no exception. John Ellis has thus elected to source additional grapes from various parts of Victoria to produce an interesting and diverse range of varietals at different price points. Exports to the UK and other major markets.

ƏƏƏƏƏ **Cambrian Rise Heathcote Shiraz 2004** Deep colour; a powerful wine, full of black fruits and, as yet, formidable tannins; patience will be rewarded, for the wine is in balance. Cork. 14° alc. **Rating** 94 To 2024 $27

Hanson-Tarrahill Vineyard   ★★★☆

49 Cleveland Avenue, Lower Plenty, Vic 3093 (postal) **Region** Yarra Valley
T (03) 9439 7425 **F** (03) 9439 4217 **Open** Not
Winemaker Dr Ian Hanson **Est.** 1983 **Cases** 1000
Dental surgeon Ian Hanson planted his first vines in the late 1960s, close to the junction of the Yarra and Plenty Rivers; in '83 those plantings were extended (with 3000 vines), and in '88 the Tarrahill property at Yarra Glen was established with a further 4 ha. Exports to the UK.

🍷🍷🍷🍷 **Tarra's Block Yarra Valley Cabernet Franc Cabernet Sauvignon Shiraz 2005** The shiraz plays a big part in the wine; cool spice and blackberry dominate the wine; good flavour, but could be fresher for its age. Cork. 15° alc. **Rating** 88 To 2011 $20

Happs ★★★★☆

575 Commonage Road, Dunsborough, WA 6281 **Region** Margaret River
T (08) 9755 3300 **F** (08) 9755 3846 **www**.happs.com.au **Open** 7 days 10–5
Winemaker Erl Happ, Mark Warren **Est.** 1978 **Cases** 20 000
One-time schoolteacher, potter and winemaker Erl Happ is now the patriarch of a three-generation family. More than anything, Erl Happ has been a creator and experimenter, building the self-designed winery from mudbrick, concrete form and timber, and designing and making the first crusher. In 1994 he began an entirely new vineyard at Karridale, planted to no less than 28 different varieties, including some of the earliest plantings in Australia of tempranillo. The Three Hills label is made from varieties grown at the 30-ha Karridale vineyard. Erl passed on to son Myles a love of pottery, and Happs Pottery now has four potters, including Myles.

🍷🍷🍷🍷🍷 **Margaret River Viognier 2006** An opulent wine, with ripe apricot, and a rich and lively palate; good oak handling; a full-flavoured, but not heavy, harmonious finish. Cork. **Rating** 94 To 2009 $18

🍷🍷🍷🍷🍷 **Three Hills Chardonnay 2006** Quite rich and ripe aromas, dominated by toasty oak; good flavour with the fruit coming to the fore on the palate; very fresh acidity, long and fine on the finish. Cork. 14° alc. **Rating** 93 To 2011 $27
Three Hills Eva Marie 2006 Strong oak dominates; quite fresh and very toasty, but quite atypical for the blend; more exotic and complex than a younger fresher style. Semillon/Sauvignon Blanc. Cork. 12.5° alc. **Rating** 90 To 2009 $27

Harbord Wines ★★★☆

PO Box 41, Stockwell, SA 5355 **Region** Barossa Valley
T (08) 8562 2598 **F** (08) 8562 2598 **www**.harbordwines.com.au **Open** Not
Winemaker Roger Harbord **Est.** 2003 **Cases** 1000
Roger Harbord is a well-known and respected Barossa winemaker, with over 20 years' experience, the last 10 as chief winemaker for Cellarmasters Wines, Normans and Ewinexchange. He has set up his own virtual winery as a complementary activity; the grapes are contract-grown, and he leases winery space and equipment to make and mature the wines. Exports to the UK, Canada and Singapore.

🍷🍷🍷🍷 **Adelaide Hills Pinot Noir 2007** Light-bodied, with savoury elements and fair balance, but needs more varietal fruit; the problem's in the vineyard rather than the winery. Screwcap. 14° alc. **Rating** 87 To 2010 $18

Harcourt Valley Vineyards

3339 Calder Highway, Harcourt, Vic 3453 **Region** Bendigo
T (03) 5474 2223 **www**.harcourtvalley.com.au **Open** 7 days 11–5 (11–6 daylight saving)
Winemaker Kye Livingstone, Quinn Livingstone **Est.** 1976 **Cases** 2000
Established by Ray and Barbara Broughton, the vineyard was handed over to John and Barbara Livingstone in 1988. Barbara's Shiraz was created by Barbara Broughton, but with the arrival of the 'new' Barbara it lives on as the flagship of the vineyard. The Livingstones planted a further 2 ha of shiraz on north-facing slopes with the aid of two sons, who, says Barbara, then 'bolted, vowing never to have anything to do with vineyards, but having developed fine palates'. John Livingstone died in mid-2004, but Barbara continues her role of viticulturist; winemaking is now in the hands of Barbara's sons Kye and Quinn (who have returned to the fold).

ŶŶŶŶŶ **Reserve Cabernet Sauvignon 2005** Much riper and richer than the varietal; blackcurrant, with some plum jam notes; surges through to a deeply fruited finish, with malbec and cabernet franc helping. Screwcap. 14.2° alc. **Rating** 92 To 2020 $35

Barbara's Reserve Shiraz 2005 Deeply coloured; medium- to full-bodied; luscious confit plum/plum pudding flavours, with oak making a strong (too strong?) contribution; 22 months in oak. Screwcap. 13.8° alc. **Rating** 91 To 2017 $35

Cabernet Sauvignon 2005 Excellent colour; ripe cassis and blackcurrant fruit with some regional minty overtones; still quite fresh and juicy, though the supporting tannins are there. Screwcap. 13.4° alc. **Rating** 90 To 2018 $25

ŶŶŶŶ **Barbara's Shiraz 2005** No shortage of aromas or flavour; vanilla oak is a major driver behind the savoury black fruits, with more spice and leather than the Reserve. Screwcap. 13.4° alc. **Rating** 89 To 2014 $25

Riesling 2006 Big, broad, high-flavoured tropical pineapple fruit; good acidity. Screwcap. 10.7° alc. **Rating** 87 To 2009 $16

Hardys   ★★★★★

Reynell Road, Reynella, SA 5161 **Region** McLaren Vale
T (08) 8392 2222 **F** (08) 8392 2202 **www**.hardys.com.au **Open** Mon–Fri 10–4.30, Sat 10–4, Sun 11–4, closed public hols
Winemaker Paul Lapsley (Chief) **Est.** 1853 **Cases** NFP
The 1992 merger of Thomas Hardy and the Berri Renmano group may well have had some of the elements of a forced marriage when it took place, but the merged group prospered mightily over the next 10 years. So successful was it that a further marriage followed in early 2003, with Constellation Wines of the US the groom, and BRL Hardy the bride, creating the largest wine group in the world. The Hardys wine brands are many and various, from the lowest price point to the highest, and covering all the major varietals. Exports to all major markets.

ŶŶŶŶŶ **Chateau Reynella Cellar 1 Shiraz 2004** Exceptionally deep and youthful colour; layer-upon-layer of luscious blackberry and dark chocolate fruit, with seamless tannins and quality oak. High-quality cork. 14° alc. **Rating** 96 To 2024 $54

Reynell Basket Pressed Cabernet Sauvignon 2004 Very good colour; without question a vintage that favoured cabernet sauvignon; has effortlessly achieved intensity and length without alcoholic boost; cassis, blackcurrant and cedary French oak flavours. Cork. 13.5° alc. **Rating** 96 To 2019 $47

Starvedog Lane Adelaide Hills Chardonnay 2004 An aromatic, flowery nectarine, white peach and grapefruit bouquet repeated by the intense and seamless palate; just cruising. Screwcap. 12.5° alc. **Rating** 95 To 2014 $24.50

Hardys Tintara Blewitt Shiraz 2005 A complex wine, with very good texture and structure to the black fruits; manages to combine depth and freshness. **Rating** 95 To 2025 $65

Tintara McLaren Flat Shiraz 2005 Marries finesse with intensity, elegance with power; lovely blackberry and licorice fruits, seamless tannins and oak components. Quality cork. 14° alc. **Rating** 95 To 2021 $65

Tintara Reserve Shiraz 2004 A super-intense evocation of region and variety, yet only medium-bodied, allowing the multiple components free reign to express themselves in a richly embroidered tapestry. Cork. 14.5° alc. **Rating** 95 To 2020 $65

Chateau Reynella Basket Press Cabernet Sauvignon 2005 Strong, deep colour; powerful, full-bodied but luscious cabernet, achieved at an astonishing (low) 13.3 alcohol; has exceptional intensity and length, sustained by the expected tannin structure. Stained cork. 13.3° alc. **Rating** 95 To 2021 $54

Oomoo McLaren Vale Shiraz 2006 Yet another success for this label; crammed full of regional black fruits, dark chocolate and a flick of oak; the tannins still pronounced, but are in balance and will soften. Cork. 14° alc. **Rating** 94 To 2017 $16.99

Eileen Hardy Shiraz 2005 Immaculate winemaking; a very pure style, with outstanding fruit and oak balance and integration; long finish with good tannins. **Rating** 94 **To** 2020 $98

Starvedog Lane Shiraz Viognier 2005 Has the perfumed, high-toned bouquet of great shiraz viognier; the palate is plush and textured, with a mix of blueberry and blackberry fruit, and supple tannins to close. **Rating** 94 **To** 2015 $25.50

Sir James Tumbarumba Pinot Noir Chardonnay 2000 A highly aromatic and tangy bouquet, then a very fine and focused palate, seeming much younger than is the case, delicately dry finish. Cork. 13° alc. **Rating** 94 **To** 2013 $35

ȲȲȲȲȲ **Chateau Reynella McLaren Vale Shiraz 2005** Powerful, deep and brooding, with layers of blackberry, licorice and dark chocolate fruit; ripe tannins; needs time to slim down. **Rating** 93 **To** 2020 $54

Tintara McLaren Vale Shiraz 2005 Complete with retro label, archetypal McLaren Vale style except possibly for moderate alcohol; good entry and mid-palate, but picks up pace and thrust on a deliciously spiced finish and aftertaste. Cork. 14° alc. **Rating** 93 **To** 2015 $27

Sir James Vintage 2003 Has a particularly harmonious mouthfeel, and likewise excellent length of flavour; delicate stone fruit and small red berry nuances; perfectly judged finish. Tasmania/Yarra Valley/Pyrenees. Cork. 13° alc. **Rating** 93 **To** 2009 $23.99

Starvedog Lane Adelaide Hills Sauvignon Blanc 2007 Spotlessly clean, bright and fresh aromas, with passionfruit and tropical notes on the bouquet and palate; well above-average for the vintage. **Rating** 92 **To** 2009 $25.50

Tintara McLaren Vale Cabernet Sauvignon 2005 Full of magimix cassis fruit and dark chocolate, with a restrained girdle of French oak to join the tannins in tightening up the finish. Cork. 14° alc. **Rating** 92 **To** 2015 $27

Vintage Port 2001 Black fruit, plum, licorice and dark chocolate, with a savoury twist on the finish; very good spirit; one of the best going around. Cork. 20.5° alc. **Rating** 92 **To** 2026 $34

Sir James Brut de Brut NV Bright pale green-straw; an elegant wine with complexity that most lack at this price point, though fresh, lively citrussy fruit is the driver; quite long, dry finish. Cork. 12° alc. **Rating** 90 **To** 2009 $15.99

Starvedog Lane Adelaide Hills Chardonnay 2005 Complex wine, suggesting the full suite of winemaking techniques used with a strong varietal base. Screwcap. 13° alc. **Rating** 90 **To** 2012 $28.50

Oomoo McLaren Vale Grenache Shiraz Mourvedre 2006 Totally delicious light- to medium-bodied wine, with a spring flower display of a profusion of red fruits, itching to be enjoyed today while the blooms remain fresh and vibrant. Screwcap. 14° alc. **Rating** 90 **To** 2010 $18.50

Starvedog Lane Adelaide Hills Chardonnay Pinot Noir Pinot Meunier 2002 As ever, well-crafted; a stone fruit and citrus mix with plenty of depth and mouthfeel. Cork. 12.5° alc. **Rating** 90 **To** 2011 $26

Sir James Vintage 2004 Four golds at Rutherglen (2), Perth and Brisbane says as much about the shows as the wine. Has good depth of flavour from extended lees contact and requisite balance. Pinot Noir/Chardonnay. Cork. 12.5° alc. **Rating** 90 **To** 2010 $27

ȲȲȲȲ **Nottage Hill Chardonnay 2007** The quality of the wine reflects a buyer's market for chardonnay; far more polish than Banrock Station, with fine nectarine and melon fruit, the smidge of oak barely visible. Value plus. Screwcap. 13° alc. **Rating** 89 **To** 2010 $10.50

Starvedog Lane Adelaide Hills Cabernet Merlot 2005 Serious wine, with bite to the mix of black and red fruits and firm tannins; needs a bit more stroking over the next few years. Screwcap. 14° alc. **Rating** 89 **To** 2015 $25.50

Oomoo Coonawarra Cabernet Sauvignon 2006 Well-defined varietal flavour and structure; bright blackcurrant fruit and enough tannins to provide a structural backbone. Cork. 13.5° alc. **Rating** 89 **To** 2014 $18.50

Starvedog Lane Adelaide Hills Sauvignon Blanc 2006 A light- to medium-bodied, clean and fresh mix of herb, grass and gently tropical fruit; does have good length. Screwcap. 13° alc. **Rating** 88 **To** 2009 $23.95

Starvedog Lane Adelaide Hills Pinot Grigio 2006 No activity on the bouquet, but does have action and movement on the palate, with pear and citrus flavours followed by a lively, well-balanced finish. Screwcap. 13.5° alc. **Rating** 88 **To** 2009 $23.95

Starvedog Lane Ibrido 2005 Grippy tannins run through the length of the palate; will appeal to vino-masochists. Ilbrido is Italian for 'hybrid', which this wine is not; it's simply a blend of Tempranillo/Nebbiolo/Barbera/Sangiovese/Shiraz. Screwcap. 14.4° alc. **Rating** 87 **To** 2013 $24.95

Starvedog Lane Adelaide Hills Pinot Noir 2007 A pretty, light-bodied pinot with strawberry fruit bolstered by fine but evident tannins on the finish. Drink now. Screwcap. 13.4° alc. **Rating** 87 **To** 2010 $28.50

Hare's Chase   ★★★★☆

PO Box 46, Melrose Park, SA 5039 **Region** Barossa Valley
T (08) 8277 3506 **F** (08) 8277 3543 **www**.hareschase.com **Open** Not
Winemaker Peter Taylor **Est.** 1998 **Cases** 5000
Hare's Chase is the creation of two families who own a 100-year-old vineyard in the Marananga Valley area of the Barossa Valley. The simple, functional winery sits at the top of a rocky hill in the centre of the vineyard, which has some of the best red soil available for dry-grown viticulture. The winemaking arm of the partnership is provided by Peter Taylor, now in charge of Foster's vineyards and grape suppliers worldwide. Exports to the US, Canada, Switzerland, Singapore and Malaysia.

�♥ **Barossa Valley Tempranillo 2005** Very fresh and focused on the palate; more Barossa than tempranillo, thanks in part to the generous oak. Screwcap. 13° alc. **Rating** 88 **To** 2011 $20

Harewood Estate   ★★★★★

Scotsdale Road, Denmark, WA 6333 **Region** Denmark
T (08) 9840 9078 **F** (08) 9840 9053 **www**.harewoodestate.com.au **Open** 7 days 10–4
Winemaker James Kellie **Est.** 1988 **Cases** 5000
In 2003 James Kellie, who for many years was a winemaker with Howard Park, and was responsible for the contract making of Harewood Wines since 1998, purchased the estate with his father and sister as partners. Events moved quickly thereafter: a 300-tonne winery was constructed, offering both contract winemaking services for the Great Southern region, and the ability to expand the Harewood range to include subregional wines that showcase the region. Exports to the UK, Hong Kong and Japan.

♥♥♥♥♥ **Denmark Riesling 2007** Delicate but beautifully composed; crystal clear fruit ranging from lime to passionfruit; perfect acidity, long finish. Screwcap. 12.5° alc. **Rating** 94 **To** 2015 $19.50
Frankland River Shiraz 2006 Fragrant and spicy red fruit and licorice aromas and flavours; medium-bodied and unforced, with just enough extract to provide texture. **Rating** 94 **To** 2014 $30

♥♥♥♥♀ **Denmark Semillon Sauvignon Blanc 2007** Has well above-average depth and richness to the palate, with tropical fruit in abundance, and no reliance on residual sugar. Screwcap. 13.5° alc. **Rating** 92 **To** 2009 $19.50

♥♥♥♥ **Denmark Chardonnay 2006** Vibrant colour, and quite a racy palate; plenty of roasted nuts and a bit of grip on the vibrant, high-acid finish. Screwcap. **Rating** 89 **To** 2011 $25

Harmans Ridge Estate

Cnr Bussell Highway/Harmans Mill Road, Wilyabrup, WA 6284 **Region** Margaret River
T (08) 9755 7409 **F** (08) 9755 7400 www.harmansridge.com.au **Open** 7 days 10.30–5
Winemaker Paul Green **Est.** 1999 **Cases** 5000
Harmans Ridge Estate, with a crush capacity of 1600 tonnes, is primarily a contract maker
for larger producers in the Margaret River region, which do not have their own winery/
winemaker. It does, however, have 2 ha of shiraz, and does make wines under the Harmans
Ridge Estate label from grapes grown in Margaret River. Exports to the UK and the US.

 Margaret River Chardonnay 2007 Good depth and length to the palate;
controlled barrel ferment inputs to a stone fruit- and grapefruit-flavoured palate;
more texture than many. **Rating** 92 **To** 2012 $20
Margaret River Chenin Blanc 2007 A highly aromatic and pure example of
chenin blanc; flowery aromas, then an apple, honey and lemon mix on the palate;
good acidity. **Rating** 92 **To** 2011 $20

 Howling Wolves Semillon Sauvignon Blanc 2007 Nicely framed and
balanced wine, with gentle tropical and gooseberry fruit; clean, crisp, dry finish.
Rating 89 **To** 2010 $14
Howling Wolves Shiraz 2006 Savoury, spicy aromas and flavours; light-bodied,
quite firm finish. **Rating** 87 **To** 2009 $14

Harrington Glen Estate

88 Townsend Road, Glen Aplin, Qld 4381 **Region** Granite Belt
T (07) 4683 4388 **F** (07) 4683 4388 **Open** 7 days 10–4, Sat & public hols 10–5
Winemaker Jim Barnes, Stephen Oliver **Est.** 2003 **Cases** 1200
The Ireland family planted 2.8 ha of cabernet sauvignon, shiraz, merlot and verdelho vines in
1997. Red grapes not required for cellar door production are sold to local wine producers, and
some white grapes are purchased from other Granite Belt grape producers.

Harris River Estate

Lot 1293, Harris River Road, Collie, WA 6225 **Region** Geographe
T (08) 9734 1555 **F** (08) 9734 1555 www.harrisriverestate.com **Open** Thurs–Sun 11–4
Winemaker Jane Gilham **Est.** 2001 **Cases** 2500
In 2000 Karl and Lois Hillier (and their six children) purchased the Harris River property to
run cattle and have a farm life for the family. When it was subsequently suggested the soils
were ideal for vineyards, the family quickly diversified into grapegrowing, and even more
quickly formed a company owned by family and friends to fast-track the planting of 27 ha of
viognier, verdelho, chardonnay (4 ha each), shiraz (3 ha), and merlot and cabernet sauvignon
(6 ha each). At the same time a 200-tonne winery, incorporated in a 3-storey winery/cellar
door/restaurant/function centre, swung into action in 2002.

 Verdelho 2007 Has good focus, with tangy aspects to the fruit, good acidity and
a pleasantly dry finish. **Rating** 88 **To** 2009
Chardonnay 2007 Abundant white peach and melon flavour; ripe and fleshy.
Rating 87 **To** 2009

Hartley Estate

260 Chittering Valley Road, Lower Chittering, WA 6084 **Region** Perth Hills
T (08) 9481 4288 **F** (08) 9481 4291 www.hartleyestate.com.au **Open** By appt
Winemaker Western Range Wines (Ryan Sudano) **Est.** 1999 **Cases** 3300
While driving through the Chittering Valley one Sunday with his daughter Angela, and
reminiscing about the times he had spent there with his father Hartley, Bernie Stephens saw a
'For Sale' sign on the property, and later that day the contract for sale was signed. Planting of
17 ha of vines began, with Cabernet Sauvignon and Shiraz released in 2003. They form part
of the Generations Series, recognising the involvement of three generations of the family. The

major part of the crop goes to Western Range Wines; the remainder is made for the Hartley Estate label. Extensive landscaping has been carried out throughout the property, featuring sculptures, bird life, wild flowers and a lake.

ᵧᵧᵧᵧ Chittering Valley Shiraz 2006 Very powerful, imposing wine; strong bouquet and firm palate; blackberry, sage and herb notes. **Rating** 89 **To** 2014 $15
Cabernet Sauvignon Merlot Shiraz 2006 Pleasant spicy overtones to a light-bodied palate, with black fruits and minimal tannins; does have length. **Rating** 89 **To** 2010 $15
Cabernet Merlot 2006 Clean, fresh, fragrant cassis and blackcurrant fruit; does not force the pace, and all the better for that. Screwcap. 14° alc. **Rating** 88 **To** 2012 $15
Chittering Valley Chardonnay 2007 Well made; generous stone fruit balanced by enough citrussy acidity to tighten the finish. Best now. Screwcap. 14° alc. **Rating** 87 **To** 2009 $15
Chittering Valley Shiraz 2005 Light- to medium-bodied, with blackberry, dark chocolate and licorice on the mid-palate; a lively finish which, paradoxically, is a trifle short. Screwcap. 14.5° alc. **Rating** 87 **To** 2010 $15

Hartz Barn Wines

1 Truro Road, Moculta, SA 5353 **Region** Eden Valley
T (08) 8563 9002 **F** (08) 8563 9002 www.hartzbarnwines.com.au **Open** By appt
Winemaker David Barnett **Est.** 1997 **Cases** 2600
Hartz Barn Wines was formed in 1997 by Penny Hart (operations director), David Barnett (winemaker/director), Katrina Barnett (marketing director) and Matthew Barnett (viticulture/cellar director), which may suggest that the operation is rather larger than it in fact is. The business name and label have an unexpectedly complex background, too, involving elements from all the partners. The grapes come from the 11.5-ha Dennistone Vineyard, which is planted to merlot, shiraz, riesling, cabernet sauvignon, chardonnay and lagrein. Exports to Canada, Sweden, Japan and NZ.

ᵧᵧᵧᵧᵧ General Store Barossa Shiraz 2004 More elegant than the previous Hartz Barn style; good line, focus and length, the fruit not suppressed by 24 months in French and American oak. Screwcap. 13.9° alc. **Rating** 93 **To** 2019 $29.95
Carriages Barossa Cabernet Sauvignon 2004 Has the clear varietal expression that the Barossa achieves in vintages such as this, the emphasis on blackcurrant, then fine tannins on the finish. Screwcap. 13.5° alc. **Rating** 90 **To** 2014 $29.95

ᵧᵧᵧᵧ Mail Box Barossa Merlot 2004 An unresolved mix of cosmetic/jujube fruit and more savoury/olive components; needs more structure to sort out the struggle. Screwcap. 13.9° alc. **Rating** 87 **To** 2011 $29.95
Dennistone Eden Valley Lagrein 2005 A touch of reduction evident; deep colour and intense, mouthcoating flavours without over-much structure; not certain what bottle age will achieve. Puzzling price. Screwcap. 13.5° alc. **Rating** 87 **To** 2012 $48

Harvey River Bridge Estate

Third Street, Harvey, WA 6220 **Region** Geographe
T (08) 9729 0600 **F** (08) 9729 2298 www.harveyfresh.com.au **Open** 7 days 10–4
Winemaker Stuart Pierce **Est.** 2000 **Cases** 30 000
This is a highly focused business, which is a division of parent company Harvey Fresh (1994) Ltd, a producer of fruit juice and dairy products exported to more than 12 countries. It has 12 contract growers throughout the Geographe region, with the wines being made in a company-owned winery and juice factory. The current releases are decidedly impressive. Exports to the UK, the US, Canada, Malaysia and Singapore.

♟♟♟♟♟ **Joseph River Estate Reserve Geographe Sauvignon Blanc 2006**
Spotlessly clean; perfectly ripened fruit in the middle range between asparagus, gooseberry and the more tropical notes; fresh finish. **Rating** 94 **To** 2010 $19

♟♟♟♟♟ **Joseph River Estate Reserve Geographe Shiraz 2006** Attractive medium-bodied wine, with bright juicy black cherry and blackberry fruit and a nice sprinkle of spice. Diam. 14.7° alc. **Rating** 91 **To** 2014 $19
Joseph River Estate Reserve Geographe Merlot 2006 Has admirable texture, weight and balance in medium-bodied (not full-bodied as the back label suggests) mode; attractive cassis fruits offset by black olive and briar. Diam. 14.4° alc. **Rating** 90 **To** 2013 $19

♟♟♟♟ **Joseph River Estate Reserve Geographe Sauvignon Blanc 2007**
A touch of sweatiness on the bouquet, but the delicate palate, with a mix of tropical passionfruit and gooseberry, is pleasant. Screwcap. 12.5° alc. **Rating** 88 **To** 2010 $19

Haselgrove Wines ★★★★

150 Main Road, McLaren Vale, SA 5171 **Region** McLaren Vale
T (08) 323 8706 **F** (08) 8323 8049 **www.**haselgrove.com.au **Open** 7 days 11–4
Winemaker Simon Parker **Est.** 1981 **Cases** 54 000
Between Oct 2002 and Feb '08, BankWest took over ownership and management of Haselgrove Wines in an endeavour to recover the substantial loans it had made to the business. That achieved, five investors, all with substantial, long-term involvement either in winemaking or wine marketing, acquired Haselgrove Wines from BankWest in early 2008. The business also includes McLaren Vale Custom Crush, a substantial contract processing, winemaking and storage facility adding $1.4 million of annual turnover to the $3 million of Haselgrove Wines. Wines are released in three ranges: at the top, the Haselgrove Reserve Series (HRS); next the McLaren Vale series (MVS); and at the bottom the Sovereign series. Exports to Europe and Asia.

♟♟♟♟♟ **Vincent's Breeze McLaren Vale Shiraz 2005** Elegant, medium-bodied display of regional varietal fruit in a lively cherry/blackberry/raspberry framework; fine tannins, good length. Screwcap. 14.5° alc. **Rating** 93 **To** 2020 $15
HRS Reserve Adelaide Hills Viognier 2007 Pure viognier, full of apricot and Asian spices; quite light and lively on the palate, with prominent fresh acidity. Screwcap. 13° alc. **Rating** 90 **To** 2009 $24.95
HRS Reserve Coonawarra Cabernet Sauvignon 2006 Good colour; a very ripe cassis fruit bouquet, with some mint and cedar; quite weighty, with fresh and vibrant dark fruit on the finish. Screwcap. 14° alc. **Rating** 90 **To** 2016 $24.95

♟♟♟♟ **Wet Feet Adelaide Hills Semillon Sauvignon Blanc 2007** Crisp, firm mineral/herb/grass flavours; clean finish, good acidity. Screwcap. 12.5° alc. **Rating** 87 **To** 2009 $14.95
Vincent's Breeze Adelaide Hills Viognier Pinot Gris 2007 A quixotic blend that does not speak about either variety, yet has a lively mouthfeel with faint echoes of tropical fruits. Screwcap. 12.5° alc. **Rating** 87 **To** 2009 $15
HRS Reserve McLaren Vale Shiraz 2004 Fractionally dull colour; a soft palate, which needs more focus to its sweet fruit flavours. Screwcap. 14° alc. **Rating** 87 **To** 2011 $24.95
MVS McLaren Vale Cabernet Sauvignon 2004 Fresh, crisp, cabernet fruit flavours just into ripeness spectrum; perhaps a low pH may be at work. Should soften with a little more age. Screwcap. 14° alc. **Rating** 87 **To** 2012 $14.95

Hastwell & Lightfoot ★★★★

Foggos Road, McLaren Vale, SA 5171 (postal) **Region** McLaren Vale
T (08) 8323 8692 **F** (08) 8323 8098 **www.**hastwellandlightfoot.com.au **Open** By appt
Winemaker Goc DiFabio (Contract) **Est.** 1990 **Cases** 3500

Hastwell & Lightfoot is an offshoot of a rather larger grapegrowing business, with the majority of the grapes from the 16 ha of vineyard being sold to others. The vineyard was planted in 1988 to shiraz, cabernet sauvignon, chardonnay, cabernet franc, viognier, tempranillo and barbera. Incidentally, the labels are once seen, never forgotten. Exports to the UK, the US, Canada, Norway, Malaysia, Singapore and NZ.

ㅜㅜㅜㅜㅜ **McLaren Vale Shiraz 2005** Plenty of depth and richness achieved without excess alcohol; intense blackberry, licorice and dark chocolate; built-in tannins, good oak. Screwcap. 14.5° alc. **Rating** 93 **To** 2020 $21.95

ㅜㅜㅜㅜ **McLaren Vale Cabernet Sauvignon 2005** Briar, earth and olive overtones to the blackcurrant fruit, the tannins firm but not oppressive. Screwcap. 14° alc. **Rating** 88 **To** 2013 $21.95
McLaren Vale Tempranillo 2005 A bright, savoury mix of sour cherry and dried citrus flavours; good tannin support. Screwcap. 14.5° alc. **Rating** 88 **To** 2013 $21.95
McLaren Vale Viognier 2007 If nothing else, proves this is not an easy variety; some pear and apricot nuances, but not much excitement. Screwcap. 14° alc. **Rating** 87 **To** 2009 $21.95

Hat Rock Vineyard   ★★★

2330 Portarlington Road, Bellarine, Vic 3221 (postal) **Region** Geelong
T (03) 5259 1386 **F** (03) 9833 1150 **www.**hatrockvineyard.com.au **Open** Not
Winemaker Contract **Est.** 2000 **Cases** NFP
Steven and Vici Funnell began the development of Hat Rock in 2000, planting pinot noir and chardonnay. The vineyard derives its name from a hat-shaped rocky outcrop on the Corio Bay shore, not far from the vineyard, a landmark named by Matthew Flinders when he mapped the southern part of Australia. The wines are available through the website.

ㅜㅜㅜㅜ **Pinot Noir 2006** Good varietal expression to the ripe, not over-ripe plummy fruit; falters fractionally on its way through to the finish. Screwcap. 13.5° alc. **Rating** 89 **To** 2012 $22

Hatherleigh Vineyard   ★★★★

35 Redground Heights Road, Laggan, NSW 2583 **Region** Southern New South Wales
T (02) 6288 3505 **www.**nickbulleid.com/hatherleigh **Open** Not
Winemaker PJ Charteris, Nick Bulleid **Est.** 1996 **Cases** 300
This is the venture of long-term Brokenwood partner and peripatetic wine consultant Nick Bulleid. It has been a slowly, slowly venture, with all sorts of obstacles along the way, with 1 ha of pinot noir planted between 1996 and '99, but part thereafter grafted to a better clone, resulting in a clonal mix of MV6 (predominant) with two rows of clone 777 and a few vines of clone 115. The wines are made at Brokenwood under the joint direction of PJ Charteris and Nick, and are available though the website.

ㅜㅜㅜㅜㅜ **Pinot Noir 2004** Taut and fine structure; a mix of forest and whole bunch notes; considerable length, and holding well. Screwcap. 13.5° alc. **Rating** 91 **To** 2012 $35
Pinot Noir 2005 Follows convincingly on from the '04, with plum and black cherry intertwined with strongly savoury foresty notes; has good length and intensity. Screwcap. 13.8° alc. **Rating** 90 **To** 2012

ㅜㅜㅜㅜ **Pinot Noir 2003** In very similar style to the '04, but overall fractionally greener and more minty. Screwcap. 13.5° alc. **Rating** 89 **To** 2010 $35
Laggan Pinot Noir 2002 In the family, and while having less structure and flavour, is a bargain at the price, the length coming as a bonus. Screwcap. 13.5° alc. **Rating** 87 **To** 2009 $15

Hay Shed Hill Wines   ★★★★★

Harmans Mill Road, Wilyabrup, WA 6280 **Region** Margaret River
T (08) 9755 6046 **F** (08) 9755 6083 **www**.hayshedhill.com.au **Open** 7 days 10.30–5
Winemaker Michael Kerrigan **Est.** 1987 **Cases** 35 000
The changes continue at Hay Shed Hill. Highly regarded former winemaker at Howard Park, Mike Kerrigan has acquired the business (with co-ownership by the West Cape Howe syndicate) and is now the full-time winemaker. He had every confidence he could dramatically lift the quality of the wines, which is precisely what he has done.

ȲȲȲȲȲ **Block 6 Margaret River Chardonnay 2005** Very complex, funky Burgundian aromas; an equally complex palate, tangy and intense; outside the normal square. Screwcap. 13° alc. **Rating** 95 **To** 2015 $35
Block 1 Margaret River Semillon Sauvignon Blanc 2007 Fine, elegant and tightly focused; citrus, mineral and herb flavours seamlessly welded; subliminal oak on a long, dry finish. Screwcap. 12° alc. **Rating** 94 **To** 2011 $25
Margaret River Chardonnay 2006 A good example of Margaret River style; nectarine, melon and grapefruit encased in gently creamy/nutty notes; lingering acidity and subtle oak. Screwcap. 12.8° alc. **Rating** 94 **To** 2016 $25
Block 2 Margaret River Cabernet Sauvignon 2005 Excellent colour and clarity; a powerful, full-bodied palate with perfectly delineated cabernet fruit supported by firm tannins; will richly repay the cellaring it demands. Screwcap. 13.5° alc. **Rating** 94 **To** 2025 $50

ȲȲȲȲȲ **Margaret River Cabernet Sauvignon 2005** Delicious redcurrant/cassis/black-currant fruit on a medium-bodied palate, with balanced tannins running through the long finish, the oak restrained. Screwcap. 14° alc. **Rating** 92 **To** 2020 $25

ȲȲȲȲ **Pitchfork Shiraz 2005** Plenty of flavour and action at this price point, with red and black plum and cherry fruit plus savoury tannins. Screwcap. 14° alc. **Rating** 89 **To** 2012 $16
Margaret River Shiraz Tempranillo 2006 A clean, fresh and fragrant bouquet leads into a light-bodied, lively palate with predominantly red fruits, and an echo of citrus from the tempranillo; drink any time, anywhere. Screwcap. 12.5° alc. **Rating** 89 **To** 2011 $20
Margaret River Sauvignon Blanc Semillon 2007 A whisper of reduction, with sauvignon blanc driving both the bouquet and palate; good mid-palate tropical fruit, but a slightly broken line on the finish. Screwcap. 12.4° alc. **Rating** 88 **To** 2010 $20
Pitchfork Semillon Sauvignon Blanc 2007 No shortage of robust flavour; herb, grass and some mineral; has strength in citrussy acidity on the dry finish. Screwcap. 12° alc. **Rating** 88 **To** 2010 $16
Pitchfork Chardonnay 2007 A straight up and down the line, unoaked style; honeydew melon and nectarine fruit, with ample acidity. Screwcap. 12.5° alc. **Rating** 87 **To** 2011 $16

Hazyblur Wines   ★★★★

Lot 5, Angle Vale Road, Virginia, SA 5120 **Region** Adelaide Plains
T (08) 8380 9307 **F** (08) 8380 8743 **www**.hazyblur.com **Open** By appt
Winemaker Ross Trimboli **Est.** 1998 **Cases** 3700
Robyne and Ross Trimboli hit the jackpot with their 2000 vintage red wines, sourced from various regions in SA, including one described by Robert Parker as 'Barotta, the most northerly region in SA' (it is in fact Baroota, and is not the most northerly), with Parker points ranging between 91 and 95. One of the wines was a Late Harvest Shiraz, tipping the scales at 17° alcohol, and contract-grown at Kangaroo Island. It is here that the Trimbolis have established their own 4.7-ha vineyard, planted principally to cabernet sauvignon and shiraz (first vintage 2004). Exports to the UK, the US and other major markets.

♥♥♥♥♀ **The Invictus Shiraz 2006** Full-bodied; a massive wine in full-on Robert Parker mode, taking flavour impact to a new high, courtesy of very ripe fruit and concomitant alcohol. Cork. **Rating** 92 **To** 2026 $93.50

Barossa Valley Shiraz 2006 Full-frontal Barossa Valley style, with blackberry, leather, licorice and very savoury tannins; a little jumpy early in its life, but should settle down. Cork. **Rating** 90 **To** 2020 $33

♥♥♥♥ **McLaren Vale Shiraz 2006** Very rustic, boots and all; regional dark bitter chocolate plus leather and earth; considerable extract and strong tannins. Cork. **Rating** 89 **To** 2016 $18.50

The Baroota Shiraz 2006 In similar highly extractive style; black fruits, power laden; will likely long outlive its closure. Cork. **Rating** 89 **To** 2020 $18.50

Kangaroo Island Cabernet Sauvignon 2006 Deep colour; good varietal fruit on the bouquet and palate with full ripe cassis and mulberry fruit plus a hint of spice; controlled extract a relief. Cork. **Rating** 89 **To** 2016 $18.50

Heafod Glen Winery   ★★★

8691 West Swan Road, Henley Brook, WA 6055 **Region** Swan Valley
T (08) 9296 3444 **F** (08) 9296 3555 **www**.heafodglenwine.com.au **Open** Wed–Sun 10–5
Winemaker Neil Head **Est.** 1999 **Cases** NFP
A combined vineyard and restaurant business, each sustaining the other. The estate plantings are shiraz (2.5 ha), cabernet sauvignon (1 ha), viognier (0.75 ha) and chenin blanc, chardonnay and verdelho (0.25 ha each). The wines are made by vineyard owner Neil Head. Chesters restaurant, created by Paul Smith (famed for establishing Dear Friends restaurant in Perth), is run by Duncan Head and sister Anna, and is situated in a former stable, which has been restored with all of the tables, cabinet works and feature walls crafted from the original timber.

♥♥♥♥ **Swan Valley Shiraz Viognier 2006** Bright and fragrant, with good acid and length; lacks a little concentration. Screwcap. 12.8° alc. **Rating** 87 **To** 2012 $23

Heartland Wines   ★★★★

229 Greenhill Road, Dulwich, SA 5065 **Region** Langhorne Creek/Limestone Coast Zone
T (08) 8431 4322 **F** (08) 8431 4355 **www**.heartlandwines.com.au **Open** Not
Winemaker Ben Glaetzer **Est.** 2001 **Cases** 80 000
This is a joint venture of five industry veterans: winemakers Ben Glaetzer and Scott Collett, viticulturist Geoff Hardy, General Manager Vicki Arnold and wine industry management specialist Grant Tilbrook. It uses grapes grown in the Limestone Coast and Langhorne Creek, predominantly from vineyards owned by the partners. It currently exports 70% of its make to 38 international markets, and 30% domestic. The wines are principally contract-made at Barossa Vintners and represent excellent value for money. Exports to all major markets.

♥♥♥♥♀ **Director's Cut Shiraz 2006** Supple and luscious red and black fruits, dark chocolate, fine savoury tannins and quality, well-integrated oak; long finish. Cork. 14.5° alc. **Rating** 92 **To** 2016 $30

Langhorne Creek Limestone Coast Cabernet Sauvignon 2006 Flavoursome, well-balanced and long with supple blackcurrant and mulberry fruit on both bouquet and palate; sure handling of fine tannins and a lick of French oak. Screwcap. 14.5° alc. **Rating** 90 **To** 2016 $18

♥♥♥♥ **Langhorne Creek Dolcetto & Lagrein 2006** Possibly the only such blend in the world, and certainly in Australia; flows evenly across the palate with a mix of red and black fruits and a jab of fresh acidity on the finish; Dolcetto (60%)/Lagrein (40%). Screwcap. 14.5° alc. **Rating** 89 **To** 2012 $20

Langhorne Creek Limestone Coast Shiraz 2006 Medium-bodied; clean and smooth, very much a junior, but closely tied, brother to Director's Cut; freshness ex screwcap; fractionally short. Screwcap. 14.5° alc. **Rating** 89 **To** 2013 $18

Stickleback Red 2006 A cheerful array of red fruits in a light- to medium-bodied frame with unexpected length; ready right now. Screwcap. 14° alc. **Rating** 87 **To** 2009 $12

Heathcote Estate

8/1 Milton Parade, Malvern Vic 3144 (postal) **Region** Heathcote
T (03) 9821 0533 **F** (03) 9824 6277 **www**.heathcoteestate.com **Open** Not
Winemaker Tom Carson, Tod Dexter, Larry McKenna (Consultant) **Est.** 1988 **Cases** 9000
Heathcote Estate is a thoroughly professional venture, a partnership between Louis Bialkower, founder of Yarra Ridge, and Robert G. Kirby, owner of Yabby Lake Vineyards, Director of Escarpment Vineyards (NZ) and Chairman of Village Roadshow Ltd. They purchased a prime piece of Heathcote red Cambrian soil in 1999, and have an experienced and skilled winemaking team in the form of Tod Dexter (ex-Stonier) and Larry McKenna (of NZ) as consultant. They have planted 30 ha of vines, 85% shiraz and 15% grenache, the latter an interesting variant on viognier. The wines are matured exclusively in French oak (50% new). The arrival of the hugely talented Tom Carson as Group Winemaker can only add lustre to the winery and its wines. The rating is soley for the shiraz.

Shiraz 2006 Dense purple-crimson; typical mouthfilling array of generously proportioned blackberry, licorice and spice fruit; alcohol, tannins and oak all appropriate. Screwcap. **Rating** 95 **To** 2026 $45

Grenache Noir 2006 Bright but light hue; has an extra degree of conviction to the spicy components in the long, well-balanced palate; nice wine, but I'm not sure why they bother. Screwcap. 14.5° alc. **Rating** 90 **To** 2012 $45

Heathcote II

290 Cornella-Toolleen Road, Toolleen, Vic 3551 **Region** Heathcote
T (03) 5433 6292 **F** (03) 5433 6293 **www**.heathcote2.com **Open** W'ends 10–5
Winemaker Peder Rosdal **Est.** 1995 **Cases** 500
This is the venture of Danish-born, French-trained, Flying Winemaker (California, Spain and Chablis) Peder Rosdal and viticulturist Lionel Flutto. The establishment of the vineyard dates back to 1995, with new plantings in '04 lifting the total to a little over 5 ha of shiraz (with the lion's share of 2.2 ha), cabernet sauvignon, cabernet franc, merlot and tempranillo. The vines are dry-grown on the famed red Cambrian soil, and the wines are made onsite using fermentation, hand-plunging, basket press and (since 2004) French oak maturation. No samples received; the rating is that of last year. Exports to the US, Switzerland, Denmark, Germany, Japan and Singapore.

Heathcote Winery

183-185 High Street, Heathcote, Vic 3523 **Region** Heathcote
T (03) 5433 2595 **F** (03) 5433 3081 **www**.heathcotewinery.com.au **Open** 7 days 10–5
Winemaker Rachel Brooker **Est.** 1978 **Cases** 10 000
The Heathcote Winery was one of the first to be established in the region. The wines are produced predominantly from the 16.65-ha estate vineyard (shiraz, chardonnay and viognier), and some from local and other growers under long-term contracts; the tasting room facilities have been restored and upgraded. Exports to Poland.

Slaughterhouse Paddock Shiraz 2006 A medium-bodied wine with blackberry and plum fruit supported by fine tannins; the American oak not overplayed and the alcohol restrained. Screwcap. 14.8° alc. **Rating** 94 **To** 2021 $40
Mail Coach Shiraz 2006 Despite the lower alcohol, seems more exuberantly fruity than the Curagee, the splash of viognier producing vibrance and lift; subtle oak and ripe tannins sustain the long palate. Screwcap. 14.6° alc. **Rating** 94 **To** 2024 $28.50

ΥΥΥΥΥ Cravens Place Shiraz 2006 Has all the depth of flavour expected of Heathcote; dark plum and blackberry fruits, supple, ripe tannins and vanillin oak. Screwcap. 14.3° alc. **Rating** 92 **To** 2014 $19.50

Curagee Shiraz 2006 While undoubtedly influenced by 3% co-fermentation of viognier, it's no more than medium-bodied, and there's no sign of alcohol or dead fruit, but more spicy and savoury nuances rather than the normal viognier-lifted fruit. Screwcap. 14.8° alc. **Rating** 92 **To** 2020 $55

Heathvale   ★★★☆

Saw Pit Gully Road, via Keyneton, SA 5353 **Region** Eden Valley
T (08) 8564 8248 **F** (08) 8564 8248 **www.**heathvalewines.com.au **Open** By appt
Winemaker Trevor March **Est.** 1987 **Cases** 1200
The origins of Heathvale go back to 1865, when William Heath purchased the property, building the home and establishing 8 ha of vineyard. The property is now 65 ha and has 10 ha of vineyard in production, with future plantings planned. The wine was made in the cellar of the house, which still stands on the property (now occupied by owners Trevor and Faye March). The vineyards were re-established in 1987, and consist of shiraz, cabernet sauvignon, chardonnay and riesling, with a 1000-vine sagrantino trial planted in 2004. The 2008 vintage wines were produced onsite in the newly built winery. Exports to the US.

ΥΥΥΥΥ Eden Valley Barossa Cabernet Sauvignon 2005 Plenty of development; fruitcake and just a hint of cassis; good flavour and weight; pleasing. Screwcap. 13.5° alc. **Rating** 90 **To** 2016 $25

ΥΥΥΥ Eden Valley Barossa Shiraz 2005 A wine in two parts, with slightly minty fruit on the bouquet, and rich fruitcake fruit on the palate; quite bright on the finish. Screwcap. 13.5° alc. **Rating** 87 **To** 2015 $30

Eden Valley Barossa Shiraz Cabernet 2005 Lots of sweet fruit; good weight and texture; just a little one-dimensional. Screwcap. 13.5° alc. **Rating** 87 **To** 2013 $25

Hedberg Hill   ★★★

701 Forbes Road, Orange, NSW 2800 **Region** Orange
T (02) 6365 3428 **F** (02) 6365 3428 **www.**hedberghill.com.au **Open** By appt
Winemaker Simon Gilbert **Est.** 1998 **Cases** NFP
Peter and Lee Hedberg have established their 5.6-ha hilltop vineyard 4 km west of Orange, planted to 0.8 ha each of cabernet sauvignon, merlot, tempranillo, chardonnay, viognier, sauvignon blanc and riesling. It has great views of Mt Canobolas and the surrounding valleys, and visitors are welcome by appointment.

Heggies Vineyard   ★★★★☆

Heggies Range Road, Eden Valley, SA 5235 **Region** Eden Valley
T (08) 8565 3203 **F** (08) 8565 3380 **www.**heggiesvineyard.com **Open** At Yalumba
Winemaker Peter Gambetta **Est.** 1971 **Cases** 13 000
Heggies was the second of the high-altitude (570 m) vineyards established by S Smith & Sons (Yalumba). Plantings on the 120-ha former grazing property began in 1973, and 62 ha are now under vine. Plantings of both chardonnay and viognier were increased in 2002. Exports to all major markets.

ΥΥΥΥΥ Reserve Eden Valley Chardonnay 2005 Immaculately fine; a totally seamless flow of fruit, oak and acidity, and a crystal clear finish and aftertaste. From 1.3 ha of French clones 76, 95 and 96. Screwcap. 14° alc. **Rating** 96 **To** 2013 $34.95

ΥΥΥΥΥ Eden Valley Chardonnay 2006 An elegant, medium-bodied wine, with seamless oak and fruit balance; the flavours range through melon and into more nutty/creamy notes. Screwcap. 13.5° alc. **Rating** 90 **To** 2012 $24.95

∀∀∀∀ Eden Valley Merlot 2006 Strong cedar aromas, with redcurrant and a little
toasty oak; medium-bodied fine and fresh; lacks complexity and a little stuffing.
Cork. 13° alc. **Rating** 87 **To** 2012 $24.95

Heidenreich Estate   NR

PO Box 99, Tanunda, SA 5352 **Region** Barossa Valley
T (08) 8563 2644 **F** (08) 8563 1554 **www.**heidenreichvineyards.com.au **Open** Not
Winemaker Noel Heidenreich **Est.** 1998 **Cases** 2000
The Heidenreich family arrived in the Barossa in 1857, with successive generations growing
grapes ever since, and is now owned and run by Noel and Cheryl Heidenreich. Having
changed the vineyard plantings, and done much work on the soil, they were content to sell the
grapes from the 4.5 ha of shiraz, cabernet sauvignon, cabernet franc, viognier and chardonnay
until 1998, when they and friends crushed a tonne in total of shiraz, cabernet sauvignon and
cabernet franc. Since that time, production has increased to around 1000 cases, most exported
to San Diego in the US, and a little sold locally.

Helen's Hill Estate

16 Ingram Road, Lilydale, Vic 3140 **Region** Yarra Valley
T (03) 9739 1573 **F** (03) 9739 0350 **www.**helenshill.com.au **Open** 7 days 10–5
Winemaker Scott McCarthy **Est.** 1984 **Cases** 3000
Helen's Hill Estate is named after the previous owner of the property, Helen Fraser. Venture
partners, Andrew and Robyn McIntosh and Lewis, Roma and Allan Nalder, combined
childhood farming experience with more recent careers in medicine and finance to establish
and manage the day-to-day operations of the 65-ha estate. There are around 45 ha of
vines, most planted in the mid-1990s, with small plantings of chardonnay and pinot noir
planted in the mid-'80s. The wines are made onsite from estate-grown fruit using traditional
winemaking techniques. The multi-gold medal-winning 2006 Chardonnay was chosen for
Cathay Pacific first class. A new winery and cellar door complex was opened in 2006, with
views of the winemaking facilities and barrel room from the mezzanine floor. The elegant
130-seat restaurant, with a private function room, has commanding views of the Yarra Valley.

∀∀∀∀∀ Yarra Valley Chardonnay 2006 Vibrant colour; good concentration of varietal
chardonnay fruit and fine oak. Good weight and texture with a long even finish.
Very well-made wine. **Rating** 94 **To** 2012 $23.50

∀∀∀∀∀ Yarra Valley Shiraz 2006 A cool-climate shiraz profile with spice and pepper,
but also showing fully ripe fruit in a lush black fruit and licorice spectrum; good
tannin and oak management. Screwcap. 14.9° alc. **Rating** 93 **To** 2021 $25
Single Vineyard Yarra Valley Cabernets 2006 Has good thrust and vibrancy
to the cornucopia of fruit flavours from the five Bordeaux varieties; supple tannins
and integrated oak. Screwcap. 14.5° alc. **Rating** 92 **To** 2017 $28

Helm

Butt's Road, Murrumbateman, NSW 2582 **Region** Canberra District
T (02) 6227 5953 **F** (02) 6227 0207 **www.**helmwines.com.au **Open** Thurs–Mon 10–5
Winemaker Ken Helm **Est.** 1973 **Cases** 3000
Ken Helm is well known as one of the more stormy petrels of the wine industry and is an
energetic promoter of his wines and of the Canberra District generally. His wines have been
workmanlike at the least, but recent vintages have lifted the quality bar substantially.

∀∀∀∀∀ Premium Canberra District Cabernet Sauvignon 2005 Potent and intense,
with strong cedar, earth and spice notes to the blackcurrant fruit; the best Helm
red wine for years; great aftertaste. Screwcap. 14.8° alc. **Rating** 94 **To** 2015 $45

∀∀∀∀∀ Classic Dry Canberra District Riesling 2007 Citrus, herb and spice aromas;
tightly focused, but has lovely lime juice flavours with perfectly balanced acidity;
very good length. Screwcap. 11.8° alc. **Rating** 92 **To** 2017 $25

🍇 Henley Hill Wines ★★★★☆

9 Vernon Street, South Blackburn, Vic 3130 (postal) **Region** Yarra Valley
T 0414 563 439 **F** (03) 9764 3675 **Open** Not
Winemaker Rob Dolan, Travis Bush (Contract) **Est.** 2003 **Cases** 7500
The history of Henley Hill dates back to 1849, when Rowland Hill began growing crops in the Yarra Valley, the home built in the 1860s by David Mitchell, Dame Nellie Melba's father. It was on a property that adjoined Gulf Station, but when that property was sold in the 1930s the home was moved to Henley, and re-erected by Clive and Hilda Hill. Clive then purchased an 80-ha property adjoining Gulf Station, completing a full circle for the origins of the Henley name. In 2003 Debbie Hill (Clive's granddaughter), Errol Campbell (Debbie's father-in-law) and Nick and Andrew Peters planted 12 ha of chardonnay, sauvignon blanc, pinot gris and shiraz, Errol, Nick and Andrew having been long-time partners in various business ventures in the hospitality industry and property development.

🍷🍷🍷🍷♀ **Yarra Valley Sauvignon Blanc 2006** Hints of tropical fruits, but with a strong mineral core and quite fresh acidity; very long and very focused on the finish. Screwcap. 12.5° alc. **Rating** 90 **To** 2009 $17.50

🍷🍷🍷🍷 **Yarra Valley Sauvignon Blanc 2007** A ripe, yet distinctively sauvignon bouquet; hints of tropical fruit, and a little cut grass; quite generous, yet fresh on the finish. Screwcap. 12° alc. **Rating** 88 **To** 2009 $17.50
Limited Release Yarra Valley Shiraz Viognier 2006 Good colour; very oaky bouquet, but backed up by bright red fruits, and a little spice; very high acid on the finish. Screwcap. 13.5° alc. **Rating** 88 **To** 2012 $29.95

🍇 Hennings View Vineyard ★★★★

2562 Heathcote-Rochester Road, Cobinannin, Vic 3559 **Region** Heathcote
T (03) 5432 9266 **F** (03) 5432 9266 **Open** By appt
Winemaker Sergio Carlei (Contract) **Est.** 1998 **Cases** 500
The 14 ha of shiraz is established on part of a family-owned farm founded by Henning Rathjen in 1858. He first planted vines in the 1860s, and award-winning wines were made at the property throughout his lifetime. The vines were removed in the 1920s in favour of broad acre farming, but in 1998 Finlay and Darryl Rathjen (third and fourth generation descendants) replanted vines on the original site, and Henning Rathjen's historic cellar once again houses wine. Most of the grapes are sold, with part made by Sergio Carlei for the Hennings View label.

🍷🍷🍷🍷♀ **Mount Camel Range Shiraz 2004** Deep colour; extremely concentrated blackberry, licorice and dark chocolate fruit, yet surprises with a dip on the back palate and finish. Diam. 14.5° alc. **Rating** 91 **To** 2015 $28
Mount Camel Range Shiraz 2002 Good hue; ripe blackberry and plum fruits, then a lively, spicy finish; good oak contribution. Cork. 14.5° alc. **Rating** 90 **To** 2012 $28

🍷🍷🍷🍷 **Mount Camel Range Shiraz 2003** Unconvincing colour; a lack of focus and intensity suggests drought stress, though there is some sweet fruit and chocolate evident. Cork. 14.5° alc. **Rating** 88 **To** 2012 $28

Henry Holmes Wines ★★★★

Gomersal Road, Tanunda, SA 5352 **Region** Barossa Valley
T (08) 8563 2059 **F** (08) 8563 2581 **www.**woodbridgefarm.com **Open** By appt
Winemaker Robin Day **Est.** 1998 **Cases** 2000
The Holmes family's background dates from Samuel Henry Holmes (whose parents William Henry and Penelope Jane Holmes are co-owners of the property) to Samuel Henry's great-great-grandparents, whose son (and his great-grandfather) Henry Holmes was born en route to Australia from England. A further distinction is that the property owned by the Holmes

family today was first planted by the Henschke family in the 1860s. The label denotes the division of opinion between Bill and Penny (as they are known) on the merits of viticulture on the one hand and White Suffolk sheep on the other; 26.2 ha of shiraz, cabernet sauvignon and grenache are on one side of the property, sheep on the other (held at bay by a fence). Exports to the US.

ΨΨΨΨ **Barossa Riesling 2007** Light-bodied, crisp and lively, the portion from Mt Crawford playing a substantial role; in the end, just a little too light, odd for an '07, may develop well; good value. Screwcap. 12° alc. **Rating** 88 **To** 2013 $15

Henry's Drive Vignerons   ★★★★★

Hodgsons Road, Padthaway, SA 5271 **Region** Padthaway
T (08) 8765 5251 **F** (08) 8765 5180 **www**.henrysdrive.com **Open** 7 days 10–4
Winemaker Kim Jackson, Chris Ringland (Consultant) **Est.** 1998 **Cases** 170 000
The Longbottom families have been farming in Padthaway since the 1940s, with a diverse operation ranging from sheep and cattle to growing onions. In 1992 they decided to plant a few vines, and now have almost 300 ha of vineyard consisting mainly of shiraz and cabernet sauvignon, plus some chardonnay, merlot, verdelho and sauvignon blanc. Henry's Drive is owned and operated by Mark and Kim Longbottom. Exports to the UK, the US and other major markets.

ΨΨΨΨΨ **Pillar Box Reserve 2006** Masses of black fruits, licorice and spice; a very long velvety palate; long future, great value. Gold medal, Limestone Coast Wine Show '07. Shiraz. Screwcap. 15° alc. **Rating** 94 **To** 2021 $18
Reserve Shiraz 2006 A deep, dark and concentrated shiraz; mulberry and fruitcake layered by toasty oak; medium-bodied, vibrant, juicy and fine on the long and ample finish. Cork. 15.5° alc. **Rating** 94 **To** 2020 $55

ΨΨΨΨΨ **Padthaway Shiraz 2006** A suggestion of mint complements the ample levels of black fruit; medium-bodied and quite plush on the finish. Cork. 15° alc. **Rating** 91 **To** 2016 $32
Parson's Flat Padthaway Shiraz Cabernet 2006 Has abundant fruit along with obvious winemaker inputs, including an abundance of oak; gets away with it, and will improve. Cork. 15° alc. **Rating** 91 **To** 2016 $35
Dead Letter Office Shiraz 2006 The bouquet is dominated by oak, but beneath there are ample levels of dark fruit; fruitcake flavour are brought to the fore by the bright Padthaway component. McLaren Vale/Padthaway. Screwcap. 15° alc. **Rating** 90 **To** 2015 $23

ΨΨΨΨ **Padthaway Shiraz 2005** Brighter and clearer than Dead Letter Office; an attractive mix of fresh red and black fruit flavours with a sprinkle of spice; well-handled oak. Lots of coconut vanilla oak. Cork. 15° alc. **Rating** 89 **To** 2013 $32
The Trial of John Montford Cabernet Sauvignon 2006 Light and bright-fruited; cassis and mint with a little toast in the background; fine and elegant. Cork. 14.5° alc. **Rating** 89 **To** 2015 $30
Pillar Box Red 2006 More substance than expected, with all three varieties (Shiraz/Cabernet Sauvignon/Merlot) contributing to the outcome, and to the exceptional value. Screwcap. 15° alc. **Rating** 89 **To** 2011 $12
Dead Letter Office Shiraz 2005 Slightly hazy; a ripe, fruit-forward style, hedonistic, and not for intellectual discussion/deconstruction. Screwcap. 15° alc. **Rating** 88 **To** 2011 $23
Reserve Shiraz 2005 Abundant fruit and oak intermingle, the oak giving an overall impression of sweetness. Crowd pleaser. Cork. 15.7° alc. **Rating** 88 **To** 2012 $55

Henschke

★★★★★

Henschke Road, Keyneton, SA 5353 **Region** Eden Valley
T (08) 8564 8223 **F** (08) 8564 8294 **www**.henschke.com.au **Open** Mon–Fri 9–4.30,
Sat 9–12, public hols 10–3
Winemaker Stephen Henschke **Est.** 1868 **Cases** 50 000
Regarded as the best medium-sized red wine producer in Australia, and has gone from
strength to strength over the past three decades under the guidance of winemaker Stephen
and viticulturist Prue Henschke. The red wines fully capitalise on the very old, low-yielding,
high-quality vines and are superbly made with sensitive but positive use of new small oak: Hill
of Grace is second only to Penfolds Grange as Australia's red wine icon, and from 2005 will
only be sold with a screwcap. Exports to all major markets.

♥♥♥♥♥ **Hill Of Grace 2004** Typically medium-bodied and restrained, showing its class
with its extreme length and great balance. Berry fruits and seductive spicy notes
are in plentiful supply. Screwcap. **Rating** 96 To 2029 $600
Julius Eden Valley Riesling 2007 Has the Henschke riesling stamp on
both bouquet and palate; tighter and more intense than the Lenswood; similar
generosity to the regional lime juice flavours. Screwcap. 12.5° alc. **Rating** 95
To 2016 $27
Louis Eden Valley Semillon 2006 A very attractive mix of grass, lemon juice
and spice; a long, minerally finish; very good balance and line. Screwcap. 13° alc.
Rating 95 To 2013 $28
Tappa Pass Barossa Shiraz 2004 Has the quality expected at this price level;
classic medium-bodied structure, with spicy overtones to cool-grown fruit, and
a long palate finishing with savoury tannins. Screwcap. 14° alc. **Rating** 95
To 2024 $63
Lenswood Abbott's Prayer 2005 Bright, clear colour; excellent texture,
structure and mouthfeel, with a seamless flow of redcurrant and blackcurrant fruit,
plus a hint of black olive. Screwcap. 14.5° alc. **Rating** 95 To 2019 $75
Cyril Henschke Eden Valley Cabernet Sauvignon 2005 High quality wine;
blackcurrant and cassis fruit leads both bouquet and palate; fine tannins and cedary
oak add layers to the mouthfeel. Screwcap. **Rating** 95 To 2025 $120
Green's Hill Lenswood Riesling 2007 In typical full-flavoured, generous style,
though not the least heavy, ripe citrus verging on stone fruit. Screwcap. 12.5° alc.
Rating 94 To 2014 $27
Joseph Hill Eden Valley Gewurztraminer 2007 Quite pronounced lychee
and spice aromas and flavours, with strong varietal presence; achieves the difficult
balance between flavour and finesse. Screwcap. 13° alc. **Rating** 94 To 2011 $35
Coralinga Lenswood Sauvignon Blanc 2007 Clean, fresh aromas of citrus
blossom and passionfruit; builds nicely on the palate and fruit-driven finish.
Screwcap. 12.5° alc. **Rating** 94 To 2009 $25
Eleanor's Cottage Eden Valley Sauvignon Blanc Semillon 2007 Fine,
elegant, fresh and lively; seamless fruit fusion of herbaceous semillon and aromatic,
gently tropical sauvignon blanc. Screwcap. 12.5° alc. **Rating** 94 To 2011 $23
Mount Edelstone 2005 Elegant and medium-bodied, with marked spice,
pepper and savoury components on both bouquet and palate; a core of red and
black fruits, plus silky, fine tannins. Screwcap. 14.5° alc. **Rating** 94 To 2025 $93
Keyneton Estate Euphonium 2005 The Eden Valley gives focus and structure;
a cascade of predominantly red fruits including cherry and raspberry, but resting
on a firm foundation. Shiraz/Cabernet Sauvignon/Merlot. Screwcap. 14.5° alc.
Rating 94 To 2015 $44

♥♥♥♥♡ **Littlehampton Innes Vineyard Adelaide Hills Pinot Gris 2007** Candied
citrus fruits, and plenty of flavour; it also maintains finesse and structure, a feat
many others are unable to achieve. Screwcap. 14° alc. **Rating** 91 To 2012 $33
Peggy's Hill Eden Valley Riesling 2007 Powerful, deep aromas and flavours;
a mix of ripe tropical fruit and an edge of lemony acidity. Screwcap. 12.5° alc.
Rating 91 To 2014 $19.50

Tappa Pass Barossa Shiraz 2005 An oaky bouquet, but with succulent red berry fruits and a cool spicy edge; quite tannic and rich, with a savoury persistence to the finish. Screwcap. **Rating** 91 **To** 2015 $63

Henry's Seven 2006 A lively, approachable, soft and silky blend where all of the parts play a role; right now the viognier dominates with accentuated florals, but over time the more robust character of the other varieties will shine. Shiraz/Grenache/Mourvedre/Viognier. Screwcap. 15° alc. **Rating** 91 **To** 2014 $31

Cranes Eden Valley Chardonnay 2007 A fine linear style, with citrus and pear fruits, strong minerality, and quite succulent fruit flavour; the palate is vibrant, and shows good persistence. Screwcap. 12.5° alc. **Rating** 90 **To** 2009 $31

Johann's Garden 2006 Aromatic and fresh; a light- to medium-bodied array of raspberry, red cherry and plum flavours with fine tannins and minimal oak; early drinking. Screwcap. 15.5° alc. **Rating** 90 **To** 2011 $37

ŶŶŶŶ **Hill Of Grace 2003** The colour is typical of many '03s, slightly blurred, as is the flavour and structure; a puzzling decision to release, and even more the price ($150 above '02 Grange). Cork. 14.5° alc. **Rating** 89 **To** 2013 $660

Tilly's Vineyard 2006 Generously endowed, albeit with a somewhat amorphous fruit profile; for simple enjoyment with food. Screwcap. 13° alc. **Rating** 88 **To** 2009 $18

Giles Lenswood Pinot Noir 2006 Vibrant colour; fresh cherry aromas and a little spice; good flavour, but pulls up a little short. Screwcap. 13.5° alc. **Rating** 88 **To** 2009 $46

Hentley Farm Wines ★★★★★

PO Box 246, Tanunda, SA 5352 **Region** Barossa Valley
T (08) 8562 8427 **F** (08) 8562 8427 **www**.hentleyfarm.com.au **Open** Not
Winemaker Reid Bosward (Contract) **Est.** 1999 **Cases** 2000
Keith and Alison Hentschke purchased the Hentley Farm in 1997, then an old vineyard and mixed farming property. Keith had thoroughly impressive credentials at the time of the purchase, having studied agricultural science at Roseworthy, then studied wine marketing, and obtained an MBA. During the 1990s he had a senior production role with Orlando, before moving on to manage one of Australia's largest vineyard management companies, and from 2002 to '06 he worked with Nepenthe. Just under 15 ha of shiraz, 5 ha of grenache, 2 ha of cabernet sauvignon, 0.8 ha of zinfandel and 0.1 ha of viognier are now in production. The vineyard is situated among rolling hills on the banks of Greenock Creek, with red clay loam soils overlaying shattered limestone, lightly rocked slopes and little top soil. It hardly needs to be said the emphasis is on quality.

ŶŶŶŶŶ **The Beast Barossa Valley Shiraz 2006** Saturated colour; full-bodied, brooding blackberry fruit with notes of licorice, mocha and dark chocolate for good measure; very complex, and shrugs off its alcohol with apparent ease. Cork. 15.5° alc. **Rating** 95 **To** 2021 $80

Barossa Valley Shiraz 2006 Saturated colour, as is the full-bodied palate, with rich blackberry and dark chocolate fruit but – surprisingly – no alcohol heat, nor excessive extract. A long life ahead. Screwcap. 15° alc. **Rating** 94 **To** 2026 $35

The Beauty Barossa Valley Shiraz 2006 Deep hue; at once slightly lighter (medium- to full-bodied) and more savoury than The Beast, no doubt intentionally. Has lots of light and shade to its texture. Pray for the cork. 15° alc. **Rating** 94 **To** 2016 $50

ŶŶŶŶŶ **Fools Bay Dusty's Desire Barossa Valley Shiraz 2006** Utterly belies its alcohol, with a distinctly fresh and lively medium-bodied palate offering black fruits, licorice and some bitter chocolate; good balance and length. Screwcap. 15° alc. **Rating** 91 **To** 2016 $19

ŶŶŶŶ **Barossa Valley Zinfandel 2007** Has the kitchen sink of flavours, in a way only zinfandel can achieve through its multiple levels of berry ripeness in each bunch; endless descriptors can be used before the fires of 16.5° alcohol take hold. Screwcap. 16.5° alc. **Rating** 89 **To** 2012 $28

Fools Bay Beached Barossa Valley Shiraz Cabernet 2006 Light- to medium-bodied; direct red and black fruits run through a relatively long palate; good value. Screwcap. 14.5° alc. **Rating** 89 **To** 2012 $14

The Stray Mongrel Barossa Valley Grenache Blends 2007 Attractively light-bodied, with vibrant fresh cherry, raspberry and plum fruits, best enjoyed in the full flower of its youth, though will live. Screwcap. 14.5° alc. **Rating** 89 **To** 2011 $28

Fools Bay Dirty Bliss Barossa Valley Grenache Shiraz 2006 A tangy, lively, fresh mix of predominantly red fruits; minimal tannins, good length. Screwcap. 14.5° alc. **Rating** 89 **To** 2012 $19

Henty Estate   ★★★★★

657 Hensley Park Road, Hamilton, Vic 3300 (postal) **Region** Henty
T (03) 5572 4446 **F** (03) 5572 4446 **www**.henty-estate.com.au **Open** Not
Winemaker Peter Dixon **Est.** 1991 **Cases** 1000
Peter and Glenys Dixon have hastened slowly with Henty Estate. In 1991 they began the planting of 4.5 ha of shiraz, 1 ha each of cabernet sauvignon and chardonnay, and 0.5 ha of riesling. In their words, 'we avoided the temptation to make wine until the vineyard was mature', establishing the winery in 2003. Encouraged by neighbours John Thomson and Tamara Irish, they have limited the yield to 3–4 tonnes per ha on the VSP-trained, essentially dry-grown vineyard.

ŦŦŦŦŦ **Shiraz 2006** Intense crimson; while only medium-bodied in weight, is packed full of beautifully ripe, lip-smacking spicy black fruits, the tannins and new French oak seamlessly interwoven. What a wine. Screwcap. 14° alc. **Rating** 96 **To** 2026 $22
Cabernet Sauvignon 2006 Bright, light crimson; medium-bodied, classically structured cool-grown cabernet sauvignon without any green or minty characters; very fine tannins add to the length. Screwcap. 14° alc. **Rating** 94 **To** 2015 $24

ŦŦŦŦŶ **Riesling 2007** Voluminous lime and a touch of passionfruit on the bouquet; rich, almost fleshy palate; relatively early developing. Screwcap. 12.8° alc. **Rating** 92 **To** 2013 $20

Herbert Vineyard   ★★★★

Bishop Road, Mount Gambier, SA 5290 **Region** Mount Gambier
T 0408 849 080 **F** (08) 8724 9512 **Open** By appt
Winemaker David Herbert **Est.** 1996 **Cases** 200
David and Trudy Herbert have planted 2 ha of pinot noir, and a total of 0.4 ha of cabernet sauvignon, merlot and pinot gris. The majority of the pinot noir is sold to Foster's for sparkling wine, but the Herberts have built a 2-level (mini) winery, which overlooks a 1600-sq metre maze planted in 2000, and which is reflected in the label logo.

ŦŦŦŦŶ **Barrel Number 1 Mount Gambier Pinot Noir 2006** Spicy, foresty, earthy nuances to the bouquet, then a powerful, ripe palate with considerable depth to the plum fruit; savoury finish. Screwcap. 13.6° alc. **Rating** 93 **To** 2013 $33

ŦŦŦŦ **Mount Gambier Cabernet+ 2006** There are distinct herbal mint overtones to the cabernet, but the shiraz (15%) helps build the fruit profile in a cool-grown style. Screwcap. 12.5° alc. **Rating** 87 **To** 2011 $18

Heritage Wines   ★★★★★

106a Seppeltsfield Road, Marananga, SA 5355 **Region** Barossa Valley
T (08) 8562 2880 **F** (08) 8562 2692 **www**.heritagewinery.com.au **Open** Mon–Fri 10–5, w'ends & public hols 11–5
Winemaker Stephen Hoff **Est.** 1984 **Cases** 5500
A little-known winery that deserves a far wider audience, for veteran owner/winemaker Stephen Hoff is apt to produce some startlingly good wines. At various times the Riesling

(from old Clare Valley vines), Cabernet Sauvignon and Shiraz (now the flag-bearer) have all excelled. Exports to the UK, the US, Hong Kong and Malaysia.

🍷🍷🍷🍷🍷 **Barossa Shiraz 2005** Traditional, full-flavoured Heritage style without excess alcohol; a mix of black fruits, chocolate and vanilla oak supported by ripe tannins, the components in balance. Cork. 14.5° alc. **Rating** 94 **To** 2015 $25
Rossco's Shiraz 2005 Retains good colour and hue; has quite remarkable finesse and structure for this alcohol level, the explanation lying in the superb quality of the old dry-grown grapes (and sensitive winemaking) purchased from Ross Kalleske every year. Cork. 15.2° alc. **Rating** 94 **To** 2015 $41

🍷🍷🍷🍷 **Barossa Semillon 2007** Solid Barossa Valley semillon, looking to the past as much as to the future, but has flavour without phenolics. Screwcap. 12.2° alc. **Rating** 87 **To** 2012 $15

 Herriot Wines ★★★

RMB 36, Graphite Road, Manjimup, WA 6258 **Region** Manjimup
T (08) 9772 1048 **F** (08) 9772 1048 **www.**herriotwines.com.au **Open** Thurs–Sun 10–4
Winemaker John Herriot **Est.** 1997 **Cases** 500
John and Yvonne Herriot have the clearest possible vision statement for their vineyard and winery. The fact that the 13-ha vineyard moved to biodynamic practices in 2000, and was Demeter certified in '05, is but a reflection of their desire to grow grapes and make wine with as little human intervention as possible, consistent with the aim of continuous improvements in the health and vitality of their soil and vines, and the minimisation of additives or processing aids in the winery. It's not an easy road to follow, particularly when there is a positive acceptance of the impact of changing weather from one vintage to the next. If the weather is ideal, all is fine, but it takes a steady hand and a firm commitment to bend to the will of the weather gods.

🍷🍷🍷🍷 **Manjimup Riesling 2006** A quiet bouquet, but there is plenty of ripe apple and citrus flavour on the palate; balanced acidity and a hint of residual sugar. Cork. 11.2° alc. **Rating** 89 **To** 2013 $18.50

Hesketh Wine Company ★★★★

6 Blairgowrie Road, St Georges, SA 5064 **Region** Warehouse
T 0419 003 144 **F** (08) 8344 9429 **www.**heskethwinecompany.com.au **Open** Not
Winemaker Various **Est.** 2006 **Cases** 4000
The Hesketh Wine Company is a New World version of the French Negociant Eleveur, commonly known in Australia as a virtual winery, owned by Jonathon Hesketh and wife Trish, and children. Jonathon spent seven years as the Global Sales & Marketing Manager of Wirra Wirra, two and a half years as General Manager of Distinguished Vineyards in NZ working with the Möet Hennessy wine and champagne portfolio, plus the Petaluma group, and also had significant global responsibility for Mars Corporation over a four-year period. He also happens to be the son of Robert Hesketh, one of the key players in the development of many facets of the SA wine industry in particular. The model for Hesketh Wine Company is to find wines that best express the regions they come from and closely monitor their production, but own neither vineyards nor a winery.

🍷🍷🍷🍷🍷 **Hidden Garden Marlborough Sauvignon Blanc 2006** Spotlessly clean; has that extra intensity of flavour expected from Marlborough, ranging through gooseberry, passionfruit and redcurrant; good balance and length. Screwcap. **Rating** 93 **To** 2009 $25

🍷🍷🍷🍷 **Usual Suspects McLaren Vale Shiraz 2005** Medium-bodied; quite elegant and understated, the relatively low alcohol (by McLaren Vale standards) offset by the viognier lift; not particularly complex or concentrated. Screwcap. 13.5° alc. **Rating** 89 **To** 2012 $25

Hewitson

The Old Dairy Cold Stores, 66 London Road, Mile End, SA 5031 **Region** Southeast
Australia
T (08) 8443 6466 **F** (08) 8443 6866 **www**.hewitson.com.au **Open** By appt
Winemaker Dean Hewitson **Est.** 1996 **Cases** 22 000
Dean Hewitson was a winemaker at Petaluma for 10 years, and during that time managed
to do three vintages in France and one in Oregon as well as undertaking his Masters at
UC Davis, California. It is hardly surprising that the wines are immaculately made from a
technical viewpoint. He has also managed to source 30-year-old riesling from the Eden Valley
and 70-year-old shiraz from McLaren Vale, and makes a Barossa Valley Mourvedre from vines
planted in 1853 at Rowland Flat and a Barossa Valley Shiraz and Grenache from 60-year-old
vines at Tanunda. Exports to the UK, the US and other major markets.

ΨΨΨΨΨ **The Mad Hatter McLaren Vale Shiraz 2005** McLaren Vale at its best; masses
of blackberry, spice and dark chocolate in a cocoon of fine but persistent tannins
and quality French oak; excellent length. Opulent but not corpulent. Screwcap.
14.5° alc. **Rating** 95 **To** 2025 $50
Ned & Henry's Barossa Valley Shiraz 2006 A stylish, medium-bodied wine
with excellent length and balance; fresh plum, black cherry and blackberry fruit
flavours; fine tannins, subtle oak. Screwcap. 14.5° alc. **Rating** 95 **To** 2020 $25
Miss Harry Dry Grown & Ancient 2006 A prime example of the blend
(Grenache/Shiraz/Mourvedre) and the region (McLaren Vale), with spicy earthy
nuances to a vibrant medium-bodied palate with exceptional length. Screwcap.
14.5° alc. **Rating** 94 **To** 2020 $23
Old Garden Barossa Valley Mourvedre 2006 A somewhat idiosyncratic
wine that creeps up on you by progressively building flavour and structure through
the length of the palate with spicy and pleasingly sour (sour cherry perhaps) notes.
Screwcap. 14.5° alc. **Rating** 94 **To** 2016 $50 .

ΨΨΨΨΨ **Gun Metal Eden Valley Riesling 2007** Spotlessly clean and well made; ripe
lime juice bouquet and palate, with splashes of spice and mineral; good length.
Screwcap. 12.5° alc. **Rating** 93 **To** 2015 $23
LuLu Adelaide Hills Sauvignon Blanc 2007 A good wine in the context of
the vintage; gentle apple and gooseberry fruit; crisp, dry finish. Screwcap. 12.5° alc.
Rating 92 **To** 2009 $23
Baby Bush Barossa Valley Mourvedre 2006 Slightly hazy colour; sprightly
savoury/spicy notes to the dark fruits, with ripe but fine tannins providing good
structure. Screwcap. 14.5° alc. **Rating** 90 **To** 2013 $29

ΨΨΨΨ **Private Cellar Basham's Beach Tempranillo 2006** Pleasant light-bodied
wine, with cedary oak and gently spicy red fruits, but I'm not convinced about the
10 years cellaring claim on the label. Screwcap. 14.5° alc. **Rating** 89 **To** 2012 $69

Hickinbotham of Dromana

194 Nepean Highway (near Wallaces Road), Dromana, Vic 3936 **Region** Mornington
Peninsula
T (03) 5981 0355 **F** (03) 5987 0692 **www**.hickinbotham.biz **Open** 7 days 11–5
Winemaker Andrew Hickinbotham **Est.** 1981 **Cases** 3000
After a peripatetic period and a hiatus in winemaking, Hickinbotham established a permanent
vineyard and winery base at Dromana. It now makes only Mornington Peninsula wines,
drawing in part on 6.5 ha of estate vineyards, and in part on contract-grown fruit.

ΨΨΨΨ **David Hickinbotham Sauvignon Blanc 2006** Slightly herbaceous aromas, the
palate with good texture and weight. Screwcap. 13.5° alc. **Rating** 87 **To** 2009 $25

Hidden Creek

Eukey Road, Ballandean, Qld 4382 **Region** Granite Belt
T (07) 4684 1383 **F** (07) 4684 1355 **www**.hiddencreek.com.au **Open** Mon & Fri 11–3,
w'ends 10–4
Winemaker Jim Barnes **Est.** 1997 **Cases** 1200
A beautifully located vineyard and winery on a 1000 m-high ridge overlooking the
Ballandean township and the Severn River Valley. The granite boulder–strewn hills mean
that the 70-ha property only provides a little over 2 ha of vineyard, in turn divided into
six different blocks. The business is owned by a group of Brisbane wine enthusiasts and Jim
Barnes, who also continues a contract winemaking business as well as making the Hidden
Creek wines. The latter in turn has three labels: Hidden Creek, Red Bird and Rooklyn.
Rooklyn is made from Granite Belt grapes, which are either of outstanding quality, unusual
styles, or are emerging varieties, and have had overwhelming success in wine shows. One of
the top wineries in Qld.

ΨΨΨΨ **Rooklyn Granite Belt Shiraz 2006** Lots of flavour, with fresh blackberry and
some plum pudding; rich and vibrant, but a little simple and very oaky. Screwcap.
14.5° alc. **Rating** 88 **To** 2012 $45

Hidden River Estate

Mullineaux Road, Pemberton, WA 6260 **Region** Pemberton
T (08) 9776 1437 **F** (08) 9776 0189 **www**.hiddenriver.com.au **Open** 7 days 9–4
Winemaker Brenden Smith, Phil Goldring **Est.** 1994 **Cases** 2000
Phil and Sandy Goldring spent 10 years operating farm chalets in the Pemberton area before
selling the business and retiring to become grapegrowers, with the intention of selling the
grapes. However, they found old habits hard to kick, so opened a cellar door and restaurant.
A renovated 1901 Kalgoorlie tram (the streetcar named Desire) has been installed to provide
more seating for the award-winning restaurant. I hope the Goldrings did not pay too much
for the tram.

ΨΨΨΨ **Unwooded Chardonnay 2005** Loaded with sweet fruit and oak; good texture
on the palate, and acid cleans the fruit up well. **Rating** 88 **To** 2011 $16.50

High Valley Wines

137 Cassilis Road, Mudgee, NSW 2850 **Region** Mudgee
T (02) 6372 1011 **F** (02) 6372 1033 **www**.highvalley.com.au **Open** 7 days 10–5
Winemaker Ian MacRae, David Lowe (Contract) **Est.** 1995 **Cases** 2000
The Francis family, headed by Ro and Grosvenor Francis, have operated a sheep, wheat and
cattle property at Dunedoo for several generations. When they handed over the property to
their sons in 1995, Ro and Grosvenor subdivided and retained a 40-ha block on which they
have since established 11 ha of shiraz, 6 ha of cabernet sauvignon and 5 ha of chardonnay.

ΨΨΨΨ **Mudgee Shiraz 2001** Has developed well; while medium-bodied at best, has
good length to its gently earthy/savoury black fruits. Cork. 14° alc. **Rating** 88
To 2011 $18
Mudgee Shiraz 2006 Medium-bodied, fresh and lively black and red fruits, a
touch of spice and a firm but not tannic finish. On the evidence of earlier vintages
under cork, should develop impressively. 14° alc. **Rating** 88 **To** 2014 $18
Mudgee Late Harvest 2005 Pleasant; how much better would it have been if
the fermentation was stopped at around 11° baume. Screwcap. 15° alc. **Rating** 87
To 2010 $18
Muscat NV Has plenty of varietal raisin flavour, but is fully priced at $20 per
375 ml. Screwcap. **Rating** 87 **To** 2009 $20

Highland Heritage Estate

Mitchell Highway, Orange, NSW 2800 **Region** Orange
T (02) 6361 3612 **F** (02) 6361 3613 **Open** 7 days 9–5
Winemaker Hunter Wine Services (John Hordern, David Main), Rex D'Aquino
Est. 1984 **Cases** 15 000
The estate plantings have increased from 4 ha to 16 ha, with 1995 and '97 plantings now in full production. The tasting facility is unusual: a converted railway carriage overlooking the vineyard. Exports to all major markets.

♀♀♀♀   **Mount Canobolas Shiraz 1999** Light- to medium-bodied, and obviously fully developed, but has good line to the savoury spicy fruit, the tannins perfectly balanced. Cork. 13° alc. **Rating** 88 **To** 2010 $25
Mount Canobolas Orange Riesling 2006 Fresh aromas; light-bodied citrus and mineral palate, overall a little thin. Screwcap. 13° alc. **Rating** 87 **To** 2012 $20

Hill Smith Estate

Flaxmans Valley Road, Eden Valley, SA 5235 **Region** Eden Valley
T (08) 8561 3200 **F** (08) 8561 3393 **www**.hillsmithestate.com **Open** At Yalumba
Winemaker Kevin Glastonbury **Est.** 1979 **Cases** 5000
Part of the Yalumba stable, drawing upon estate plantings, including 15 ha of sauvignon blanc. Mature vineyards and skilled winemaking have made the estate a model of consistency and quality. No samples received; rating is that of last year.

Hillbillé

Blackwood Valley Estate, Balingup Road, Nannup, WA 6275 **Region** Blackwood Valley
T (08) 9481 0888 **F** (08) 9486 1899 **www**.hillbille.com **Open** W'ends & hols 10–4
Winemaker Woodlands Wines (Stuart Watson) **Est.** 1998 **Cases** 3000
Gary Bettridge has 19 ha of shiraz, cabernet sauvignon, merlot, chardonnay and semillon. The vineyard is situated in the Blackwood Valley between Balingup and Nannup, which the RAC describes as 'the most scenic drive in the southwest of WA'. A significant part of the grape production is sold to other makers, but since 2003, part has been vinified for the Hillbillé label. The following wines were not released when first reviewed, but are now available, and the 2006 wines will appear in the 2010 *Wine Companion*. Exports to Japan and Singapore.

♀♀♀♀♀   **Reserve Shiraz 2005** Brilliant clarity and hue; medium-bodied, clean and fresh, smooth and supple; a seamless fruit/oak/tannin line. Screwcap. 14.4° alc. **Rating** 94 **To** 2015 $35

♀♀♀♀♀   **Signature Series James Brittain 2005** Brilliant purple-red hue; a lively, fresh, brightly flavoured medium-bodied wine; fine tannins and an appropriately firm finish. Shiraz/Viognier. Screwcap. 14° alc. **Rating** 92 **To** 2013 $35

♀♀♀♀   **Reserve Merlot 2005** Light- to medium-bodied, with fresh red berry, green olive and leaf, simply needing more mid-palate presence. Screwcap. 13.7° alc. **Rating** 89 **To** 2013 $35

Hillbrook   **NR**

639 Doust Road, Gearys Gap, NSW 2621 **Region** Canberra District
T (02) 6236 9455 **F** (02) 6236 9455 **Open** W'ends & public hols 10–5
Winemaker Contract **Est.** 1994 **Cases** NA
Adolf and Levina Zanzert began the establishment of 8.5 ha of vines at Gearys Gap in 1994. The wines have retail distribution in the ACT, Bungendore and Cooma, and are also available through the cellar door and via a mailing list.

Hillbrook Wines   NR

Cnr Hillbrook Road/Wheatley Coast Road, Quinninup, WA 6258 **Region** Pemberton
T (08) 9776 7202 **F** (08) 9776 6473 **www**.hillbrookwines.com.au **Open** By appt
Winemaker Castle Rock Estate **Est.** 1996 **Cases** 500
When Brian Eade and partner Anne Walsh left Alice Springs in 1996 to move to Pemberton,
they made (in their words) the ultimate tree change. As well as establishing 3.5 ha of sauvignon
blanc and 1.5 ha of merlot, they have 600 olive trees, and added chardonnay in the vineyard.

Hillcrest Vineyard   ★★★★★

31 Phillip Road, Woori Yallock, Vic 3139 **Region** Yarra Valley
T (03) 5964 6689 **F** (03) 5961 5547 **www**.hillcrestvineyard.com.au **Open** By appt
Winemaker David Bryant, Tanya Bryant, Phillip Jones (Consultant) **Est.** 1971 **Cases** 500
The small, effectively dry-grown vineyard was established by Graeme and Joy Sweet, who
ultimately sold it to David and Tanya Bryant. The pinot noir, chardonnay, semillon and
cabernet sauvignon grown on the property have always been of the highest quality and,
when Coldstream Hills was in its infancy, were particularly important resources for it. The
Bryants have developed the Hillcrest label and, under the guiding hand of Phillip Jones, are
progressively taking control of making these excellent wines.

🍷🍷🍷🍷🍷 **Reserve Pinot Noir 2006** Has very similar characteristics to the Premium,
except that it is even finer and longer, the tannins superfine. Cork. 13° alc.
Rating 95 **To** 2014 $80
Premium Pinot Noir 2006 Similar colour and many other aspects to the Estate;
slightly brighter fruit, with more life and thrust; very good balance to the fruit and
oak. Cork. 13° alc. **Rating** 94 **To** 2013 $50
Estate Yarra Valley Pinot Noir 2006 Slightly cloudy colour, the wine neither
filtered nor fined; concentrated plum and spice; power and length; some slightly
stemmy characters add rather than detract. Cork. 13° alc. **Rating** 94 **To** 2013 $35
Estate Yarra Valley Cabernet Sauvignon 2006 A beautifully poised and
weighted wine, which is no more than medium-bodied, but has lovely fresh cassis
fruit supported to perfection by superfine tannins and integrated French oak; silky
aftertaste. Cork. 13° alc. **Rating** 94 **To** 2016 $35
Premium Yarra Valley Cabernet Sauvignon 2006 Lovely pure varietal
cabernet, with cassis, cigar box and toasty oak; good concentration, but in an
elegant style; patient cellaring needed. Cork. 13° alc. **Rating** 94 **To** 2020 $50

🍷🍷🍷🍷🍷 **Premium Yarra Valley Chardonnay 2006** In very similar style to the Estate,
slightly softer on the mid-palate, but once again finishing with challenging acidity,
which is quite certainly natural, Phillip Jones being the winemaker. Cork. 13° alc.
Rating 90 **To** 2013 $50
Village Yarra Valley Merlot 2006 Good colour; dark plum aromas, and quite
serious structure; not your average merlot, with more depth, weight and tannins.
Cork. 13° alc. **Rating** 90 **To** 2015 $20

🍷🍷🍷🍷 **Estate Yarra Valley Chardonnay 2006** Undeniably complex from start to
finish, with barrel ferment inputs on both bouquet and palate, where they meet
citrussy fruit, finishing with quite pungent lemony acidity. Picked too early? Cork.
13° alc. **Rating** 89 **To** 2012 $35

Hirsch Hill Estate   ★★★☆

2088 Melba Highway, Dixons Creek, Vic 3775 **Region** Yarra Valley
T (03) 8622 0118 **F** (03) 9640 0370 **www**.hirschhill.com **Open** Not
Winemaker Yering Farm (Alan Johns) **Est.** 1998 **Cases** 3500
The Hirsch family has planted a 14.5-ha vineyard to pinot noir (predominantly), cabernet
sauvignon, chardonnay, shiraz, merlot, cabernet franc, sauvignon blanc and viognier. The
vineyard is part of a larger racehorse stud, situated in a mini-valley at the northern end of the
Yarra Valley.

ŶŶŶŶ   **Yarra Valley Shiraz 2005** Very good colour; the flavours and aromas range between mint, plum and prune, overall luscious; drink with the heart, not the head. Screwcap. 14.9° alc. **Rating** 89 **To** 2012 $19
Yarra Valley Cabernet Sauvignon 2005 Medium-bodied; cassis dominates both bouquet and palate but tannins break the line on the back-palate; Gold, International Cool Climate Show '07. Screwcap. 14.3° alc. **Rating** 88 **To** 2014 $19
Yarra Valley Rose 2007 Distinctly spicy/savoury, dry, food style, made from shiraz. Screwcap. 13° alc. **Rating** 87 **To** 2009 $17
Yarra Valley Merlot 2005 Just that little bit overripe and jammy, but the basic character affirms that the Yarra's climate is highly suited to the variety. Screwcap. 14.1° alc. **Rating** 87 **To** 2013 $19

Hochkirch Wines

Hamilton Highway, Tarrington, Vic 3301 **Region** Henty
T (03) 5573 5200 **F** (03) 5573 5200 **Open** 11–5 by appt
Winemaker John Nagorcka **Est.** 1997 **Cases** 2000
Jennifer and John Nagorcka have developed Hochkirch in response to the very cool climate: growing season temperatures are similar to those in Burgundy. A high-density planting pattern was implemented, with a low fruiting wire taking advantage of soil warmth in the growing season, and the focus was placed on pinot noir (4.5 ha), with lesser quantities of riesling, cabernet sauvignon, semillon and shiraz. The vines are not irrigated, and no synthetic fungicides, pesticides or fertilisers are used; the Nagorckas have moved to certified biodynamic viticulture.

ŶŶŶŶŶ   **Shiraz 2005** Luscious, rich and velvety; blackberry and licorice fruit; soft tannins, good oak. Cork. 13.8° alc. **Rating** 94 **To** 2020 $40

Hoddles Creek Estate

505 Gembrook Road, Hoddles Creek, Vic 3139 **Region** Yarra Valley
T (03) 5967 4692 **F** (03) 5967 4692 **www**.hoddlescreekestate.com.au **Open** By appt
Winemaker Franco D'Anna **Est.** 1997 **Cases** 10 000
In 1997, the D'Anna family decided to establish a vineyard on the property that had been in the family since 1960. There are now two vineyard blocks totalling 24.75 ha, which are hand-pruned and hand-harvested. A 300-tonne, split-level winery was completed in 2003. Son Franco D'Anna is the viticulturist and winemaker, having started to work in the family liquor store at 13, graduating to chief wine buyer by the time he was 21, then completing a Bachelor of Commerce degree at Melbourne University before studying viticulture at CSU. A vintage at Coldstream Hills, then consulting help from Peter Dredge of Red Edge and Mario Marson (ex Mount Mary), has put an old head on young shoulders. Together with his uncle Bruno and one other worker, he is solely responsible for the vineyard and winery. Exports to South Africa.

ŶŶŶŶŶ   **Yarra Valley Chardonnay 2006** Typical Yarra Valley chardonnay; has great length and harmony, with nectarine and melon fruit; fine quality French oak is well balanced and integrated. Screwcap. 13.2° alc. **Rating** 94 **To** 2013 $18

ŶŶŶŶ   **Yarra Valley Pinot Gris 2007** Clean with hints of pears and a little onion skin; good acid and texture; well made. Screwcap. 13° alc. **Rating** 89 **To** 2011 $18.95
Yarra Valley Pinot Noir 2006 Fragrant and spicy; stemmy tannins are evident on the palate, needing more fruit flesh to surround them; does, however, have hallmark pinot noir length. Screwcap. 13.2° alc. **Rating** 88 **To** 2012 $19.95

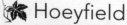 Hoeyfield

PO Box 156, Woodbridge, Tas 7162 **Region** Southern Tasmania
T (03) 6267 4149 **F** (03) 6267 4249 **Open** Not
Winemaker Hood Wines (Andrew Hood) **Est.** 1995 **Cases** 100

Richard and Jill Pringle-Jones run a postage stamp–size vineyard of 0.25 ha each of pinot noir and chardonnay, planted on a vine-by-vine basis. When they purchased Hoeyfield in 2004, plantings of chardonnay and pinot noir had spread over '98, '00, and '02; Richard and Jill added more pinot noir (the new Dijon clone 777), planting in '04 and '05. It is very much a weekend and holiday occupation, Richard's real job being with ABN AMRO Morgans Limited.

ŢŢŢŢŢ **Pinot Noir 2005** Very concentrated, with dark plums and spice and even a hint of mocha; bright acid, and good flavour on the finish. **Rating** 90 **To** 2011

ŢŢŢŢ **Pinot Noir 2006** Good colour; bright red fruits with just a little spice; straightforward, but good flavour; if the '05 is any guide, will develop well. **Rating** 87 **To** 2010

Hoffmann's

Ingoldby Road, McLaren Flat, SA 5171 **Region** McLaren Vale
T (08) 8383 0232 **F** (08) 8383 0232 **www**.hoffmannswine.com.au **Open** 7 days 11–5
Winemaker Hamish McGuire (Consultant) **Est.** 1996 **Cases** 2500
Peter and Anthea Hoffmann have been growing grapes at their property since 1978, and Peter Hoffmann has worked at various wineries in McLaren Vale since '79. Both he and Anthea have undertaken courses at the Regency TAFE Institute in Adelaide, and (in Peter's words), 'in 1996 we decided that we knew a little about winemaking and opened a small cellar door'. Exports to the UK, the US, Germany and Singapore.

ŢŢŢŢŢ **McLaren Vale Shiraz Cabernet 2006** Very ripe black fruit aromas, but the cabernet freshens up the palate with fine fruit running through to the finish. Screwcap. 14.5° alc. **Rating** 90 **To** 2014 $24

ŢŢŢŢ **McLaren Vale Shiraz 2006** Plenty of punch to the bouquet, with regional chocolate to go with the blackberry fruit; a toasty palate, just a little heavy on the finish. Screwcap. 14.5° alc. **Rating** 88 **To** 2015 $24
McLaren Vale Cabernet Sauvignon 2006 Loaded with sweet ultra-ripe fruits on the bouquet, but fresher and more vibrant dark fruits on the palate. Screwcap. 14.5° alc. **Rating** 87 **To** 2012 $24

Holley Hill

140 Ronalds Road, Willung, Vic 3847 **Region** Gippsland
T (03) 5198 2205 **F** (03) 5198 2205 **Open** By appt
Winemaker David Packham **Est.** 1998 **Cases** 300
David Packham has used his background as a research scientist to plan the establishment of Holley Hill. He served his apprenticeship with Sergio Carlei at the Green Vineyards for two years before acquiring the then-two-year-old vineyard. The 1.7-ha vineyard is planted to chardonnay, sauvignon blanc and pinot noir, supplemented by purchased grapes. Due to frost and smoke taint, no vintage was produced in 2007.

ŢŢŢŢ **Merton Shiraz 2006** Strongly herbal/spicy components somewhat at odds with the alcohol; there is an angularity to the wine, which needs to soften. Diam. 15° alc. **Rating** 87 **To** 2014 $22

Hollick

Riddoch Highway, Coonawarra, SA 5263 **Region** Coonawarra
T (08) 8737 2318 **F** (08) 8737 2952 **www**.hollick.com **Open** 7 days 9–5
Winemaker Ian Hollick, Matthew Caldersmith **Est.** 1983 **Cases** 40 000
A family business owned by Ian and Wendy Hollick, and winner of many trophies (including the most famous of all, the Jimmy Watson), its wines are well crafted and competitively priced. A $1 million cellar door and restaurant complex opened in 2002. The Hollicks have progressively expanded their vineyard holdings: the first is the 12-ha Neilson's Block vineyard, one of the original John Riddoch selections, but used as a dairy farm between 1910 and '75;

the Hollicks planted cabernet sauvignon and merlot in '75. The second is the 80-plus ha Wilgha vineyard, purchased in '87 with already established dry grown cabernet sauvignon and shiraz; total area under vine is 45 ha. The last is the Red Ridge vineyard in Wrattonbully, where 24 ha have been planted, including trial plantings of tempranillo and sangiovese. Exports to most major markets.

ҮҮҮҮҮ **Sauvignon Blanc Semillon 2007** A fragrant bouquet; a delicate but flavoursome palate, with passionfruit and gooseberry flavour; dry finish, good acidity. Mount Benson/Coonawarra. Screwcap. 13° alc. **Rating** 91 **To** 2009 $19
Wilgha Coonawarra Shiraz 2005 Good concentration, with a seductive core of red fruits and interesting fruitcake flavours; long fleshy and ample; an attractive example of Coonawarra shiraz. Cork. 14.5° alc. **Rating** 90 **To** 2016 $45

ҮҮҮҮ **Wrattonbully Shiraz 2005** A massive wine; great depth to the array of black fruits, but is slightly extractive. Will improve. **Rating** 89 **To** 2015 $23
Wrattonbully Tempranillo 2006 Good colour and flavour; quite aromatic and defined with red fruits and a little savoury edge; soft and fleshy finish. Screwcap. 12.6° alc. **Rating** 89 **To** 2012 $22
Reserve Coonawarra Chardonnay 2006 Partial mlf makes a major impact, providing a creamy texture, albeit with diminished fruit intensity; the oak is balanced. Screwcap. 14° alc. **Rating** 88 **To** 2012 $23
Coonawarra Sparkling Merlot 2006 Bright in colour, with plum and spice and a dry savoury finish. Crown Seal. 13.5° alc. **Rating** 88 **To** 2012 $28
Pinot Noir 2006 Cherry and plum fruit in distinct varietal mode; fresh, but lacks texture. Possibly wholly or partly from Mount Gambier. Screwcap. 13.5° alc. **Rating** 87 **To** 2010 $19
Ravenswood Coonawarra Cabernet Sauvignon 2005 An elegant, light- to medium-bodied palate, with clear fruit and varietal character, but not enough depth or texture for higher points. Cork. 14° alc. **Rating** 87 **To** 2012 $78

Holm Oak   ★★★☆

11 West Bay Road, Rowella, Tas 7270 **Region** Northern Tasmania
T (03) 6394 7577 **F** (03) 6394 7350 **www**.holmoakvineyards.com.au **Open** 7 days 10–5
Winemaker Rebecca Wilson **Est.** 1983 **Cases** 2000
Holm Oak takes its name from its grove of oak trees, planted around the beginning of the 20th century, and originally intended for the making of tennis racquets. In 2004 Ian and Robyn Wilson purchased the property. The 7-ha vineyard is planted to pinot noir, cabernet sauvignon, riesling and sauvignon blanc (the latter not yet bearing), with small quantities of merlot and cabernet franc. In 2006 the Wilson's daughter Rebecca (with extensive winemaking experience both in Australia and California) became winemaker, and partner Tim Duffy (a viticultural agronomist) has taken over management of the vineyard. A winery was completed just in time for the 2007 vintage, and the vineyard has been increased to 8.5 ha (with additional pinot gris, chardonnay and arneis), with another 1.5 ha of sauvignon blanc and new pinot clones in the pipeline.

ҮҮҮҮ **Pinot Noir 2006** A bright and fresh array of cherry, plum and strawberry fruit, but finishes with a touch of green acidity. **Rating** 89 **To** 2012 $30
Cabernet Sauvignon 2006 Firm, blackcurrant fruit then those inevitably green tannins make their appearance; controlled oak a plus. **Rating** 88 **To** 2012 $30

Home Hill

38 Nairn Street, Ranelagh, Tas 7109 **Region** Southern Tasmania
T (03) 6264 1200 **F** (03) 6264 1069 **www**.homehillwines.com.au **Open** 7 days 10–5
Winemaker Peter Dunbavan **Est.** 1994 **Cases** 3000
Terry and Rosemary Bennett planted their first 0.5 ha of vines in 1994 on gentle slopes in the beautiful Huon Valley. Between 1994 and '99 the plantings were increased to 3 ha of pinot noir, 1.5 ha chardonnay and 0.5 ha sylvaner. Home Hill has had great success with its exemplary Pinot Noir, winning the pinot noir trophy in the Tri Nations '07 challenge between Australia, NZ and South Africa, but this is by no means the only success.

♟♟♟♟♟ **Pinot Noir 2006** Deep colour; very powerful and concentrated, with dark briary, plummy fruit; carries through to the long finish, with none of the green acid uncertainty of other wines. Screwcap. 14° alc. **Rating** 95 **To** 2013 $30

♟♟♟♟♟ **Kelly's Reserve Chardonnay 2006** Ripe stone fruit and melon flavour, with good texture, a squeeze of citrus on the finish adds length and some flavour complexity. Screwcap. **Rating** 90 **To** 2012 $25

♟♟♟♟ **Kelly's Reserve Pinot Noir 2006** A highly fragrant bouquet, and a lively palate, with a mix of red and black fruits before the firm acidity of the '06 vintage closes off the finish; may well resolve with time. Screwcap. **Rating** 89 **To** 2013 $35

Honeytree Estate

16 Gillards Road, Pokolbin, NSW 2321 **Region** Lower Hunter Valley
T (02) 4998 7693 **F** (02) 4998 7693 **www**.honeytreewines.com **Open** Wed–Fri 11–4, w'ends 10–5
Winemaker Monarch Winemaking Services **Est.** 1970 **Cases** 2400
The Honeytree Estate vineyard was first planted in 1970, and for a period of time wines were produced. It then disappeared, but the vineyard has since been revived by Dutch-born Henk Strengers and family. Its 10 ha of vines are of shiraz, cabernet sauvignon, semillon and a little clairette, known in the Hunter Valley as blanquette, a variety which has been in existence there for well over a century. Jancis Robinson comments that the wine 'tends to be very high in alcohol, a little low in acid and to oxidise dangerously fast', but in a sign of the times, the first Honeytree Clairette sold out so quickly (in four weeks) that 2.2 ha of vineyard has been grafted over to additional clairette. Exports to the Netherlands.

Hope Estate

2213 Broke Road, Pokolbin, NSW 2320 **Region** Lower Hunter Valley
T (02) 4993 3555 **F** (02) 4993 3556 **www**.hopeestate.com.au **Open** 7 days 10–5
Winemaker James Campkin **Est.** 1996 **Cases** 40 000
Hope Estate has, in the manner of a hermit crab, cast off its older, smaller shell, and moved into a resplendent new home. New in the sense for Hope Estate, for it is in fact the former Rothbury Estate winery. The timing was serendipitous; the giant miner Xstrata found a rich coal seam under the Saxonvale winery previously owned by Michael Hope, and made an offer he couldn't refuse. It will be interesting to watch the future development of Hope Estate, made more complex by the acquisition of quality vineyards in WA. Exports to the UK, the US and other major markets.

♟♟♟♟ **Michael Hope Semillon 2006** Quite precise, with good flavour; lemon and straw with good focus; pulls up a little quickly for a young wine. Cork. 11.5° alc. **Rating** 88 **To** 2012 $35
Hunter Valley Shiraz 2006 Redcurrant and a little briary note; medium-bodied and quite tannic on the finish. Needs time. Cork. 13.5° alc. **Rating** 87 **To** 2014 $18

Horndale

41–45 Fraser Avenue, Happy Valley, SA 5159 **Region** McLaren Vale
T (08) 8387 0033 **F** (08) 8387 0033 **Open** Mon–Sat 9–5, Sun & public hols 10–5.30
Winemaker Phil Albrecht, Bleasdale, Patritti **Est.** 1896 **Cases** 1270
Established in 1896 and has remained continuously in production in one way or another since that time, though with a number of changes of ownership and direction; 0.4 ha of 100-year-old estate shiraz is a link with the winery's origins. My father used to buy Horndale Brandy 70 years ago, but it no longer appears on the extensive price list. Horndale still has a significant business selling fortified wine in bulk.

♟♟♟♟♟ **Old Horndale Cabernet Merlot Shiraz 2006** Bright and juicy; hints of spice, cassis and a little leather; vibrant finish. Screwcap. 14.6° alc. **Rating** 90 **To** 2016 $12.90

ΥΥΥΥ   Old Horndale Shiraz Grenache 2006 Bright and juicy red fruits, with good flavour and depth, and an even finish. Screwcap. 15° alc. **Rating** 87 **To** 2015 $13.90

Horvat Estate

2444 Ararat-St Arnaud Rd, Landsborough, Vic 3384 **Region** Pyrenees
T (03) 5356 9208 **F** (03) 5356 9208 **Open** 7 days 10–5
Winemaker Andrew Horvat, Gabriel Horvat **Est.** 1995 **Cases** 1500
The Horvat family (including Janet, Andrew and Gabriel) began developing their 5-ha vineyard of shiraz in 1995, supplementing production with contract-grown grapes. The wines are made using traditional methods and ideas, deriving in part from the family's Croatian background.

ΥΥΥΥΥ   Gabriel Horvat Grampians Shiraz 2005 Bright, deep colour; a complex array of aromas, spice, mint and dark fruits; lovely depth on the palate, with focused acid and tannins on the very long finish. Cork. 15° alc. **Rating** 94 **To** 2018 $35

ΥΥΥΥΥ   Native Youth Cabernet Shiraz 2005 Very minty, but supported by some dark cabernet fruit on the mid- and back palate. Quite long and very supple, almost silky. Cork. 14.2° alc. **Rating** 90 **To** 2016 $30

ΥΥΥΥ   Family Reserve Pyrenees Shiraz 2005 Lifted red and dark fruits accompanied by mint on the bouquet; plenty of stuffing and flavour, and the palate is quite long. Cork. 14.5° alc. **Rating** 89 **To** 2015 $30

Houghton

Dale Road, Middle Swan, WA 6065 **Region** Swan Valley
T (08) 9274 9540 **F** (08) 9274 5372 **www.**houghton-wines.com.au **Open** 7 days 10–5
Winemaker Robert Bowen **Est.** 1836 **Cases** NFP
The 5-star rating was once partially justified by Houghton White Burgundy (now called White Classic), one of Australia's largest selling white wines: it was almost entirely consumed within days of purchase, but is superlative with seven or so years' bottle age. The Jack Mann, Gladstones Shiraz, Houghton Reserve Shiraz, the Margaret River reds and Frankland Riesling are all of the highest quality, and simply serve to reinforce the rating. To borrow a saying of the late Jack Mann, 'There are no bad wines here.' Exports to all major markets.

ΥΥΥΥΥ   Gladstones Margaret River Cabernet Sauvignon 2002 Has needed five years to bring all the components together; very stylish, with cedary oak and warm, soft tannins supporting, not threatening, the blackcurrant and plum fruit. Cork. 14.5° alc. **Rating** 96 **To** 2015 $60
Jack Mann 2004 A beautiful wine in every respect; purity of classic varietal fruit; texture, structure and length all perfect; fine tannins and integrated oak. **Rating** 96 **To** 2024 $98
Pemberton Chardonnay 2006 Glorious green-yellow colour; intense line and length, with cool-grown grapefruit and nectarine flavours; fine acidity, oak a support role. **Rating** 95 **To** 2015 $31
Jack Mann 2001 First tasted in Mar '05 and given a towering 96 points. Still a massive wine; disconcertingly, tannins give the impression they will outlive the fruit, however much of the latter is there. Quite possibly going through a dip in its development curve. Cork. 14.5° alc. **Rating** 94 **To** 2021 $100
Margaret River Cabernet Sauvignon 2002 Finely crafted and balanced, restraint valued more than flamboyance; pure blackcurrant cabernet is king, oak and tannins hand maidens. Cork. 14° alc. **Rating** 94 **To** 2017 $32
Pemberton Chardonnay Pinot Noir 2002 Bright straw-green; fine bead; has an extra dimension of power, flavour and length; intense stone fruit and yeasty/creamy notes throughout the length of the palate; four years on lees. Cork. 13° alc. **Rating** 94 **To** 2009 $27.99

♥♥♥♥♡ **Crofters Cabernet Merlot 2005** The juicy malbec component is obvious, but in the same flavour spectrum as the cabernet, or is it? Black fruits morph into red on retasting, and the palate lengthens. Cabernet Sauvignon/Malbec. Cork. 14° alc. **Rating** 93 **To** 2018 $30

♥♥♥♥ **Crofters Sauvignon Blanc Semillon 2005** Has faltered somewhat with bottle development; slight vegetal aromas; the palate has length, but drink soon. Screwcap. 13° alc. **Rating** 89 **To** 2009 $21.50
Chardonnay Verdelho 2007 Fresh, lively and juicy fruit salad with extra portions of stone fruit and citrus; lovely flavour, but slightly short. Twin top. 13.5° alc. **Rating** 88 **To** 2011 $14

Howard Park (Denmark) ★★★★★

Scotsdale Road, Denmark, WA 6333 **Region** Great Southern
T (08) 9848 2345 **F** (08) 9848 2064 **www**.howardparkwines.com.au **Open** 7 days 10–4
Winemaker Tony Davis, Andy Browning **Est.** 1986 **Cases** NFP
All the Howard Park wines are made here at the large modern winery. There are three groups of wines: those sourced from either Great Southern or Margaret River; the icon Howard Park Riesling and Cabernet Sauvignon Merlot; and the multi-regional MadFish range. All are very impressive. Exports to all major markets.

♥♥♥♥♥ **Riesling 2007** Pale straw-green; superfine, flawless riesling on bouquet and palate; apple blossom and lime, with a long and pure finish. Outstanding development potential. Screwcap. 12.5° alc. **Rating** 96 **To** 2020 $25
Sauvignon Blanc 2007 Combines elegance and delicacy with great length, and a lingering finish; passionfruit and citrus drive a vivid wine; shows up the eastern states vintage. Screwcap. 12.5° alc. **Rating** 95 **To** 2010 $25
Chardonnay 2006 A refined, restrained style; remarkable how grapefruit and nectarine fruit has swallowed the oak (60% new, 12 months); a long, clean finish. Screwcap. 13° alc. **Rating** 95 **To** 2013 $38
Scotsdale Great Southern Shiraz 2005 A very powerful wine with abundant extract and tannins; licorice, spice and blackberry fruit is sufficiently strong to carry the tannins, but patience is needed. Screwcap. 14.5° alc. **Rating** 94 **To** 2025 $40
Scotsdale Great Southern Cabernet Sauvignon 2004 Classically proportioned, medium-bodied cabernet; blackcurrant and cassis; supple tannins and quality French oak; full flavour at a modest alcohol level. Screwcap. 13.5° alc. **Rating** 94 **To** 2024 $40

♥♥♥♥ **Scotsdale Great Southern Cabernet Sauvignon 2005** Very youthful indeed; the varietal fruit is there, but here the tannins needed more polishing prior to bottling. Screwcap. 14.5° alc. **Rating** 89 **To** 2020 $40

Howard Park (Margaret River) ★★★★★

Miamup Road, Cowaramup, WA 6284 **Region** Margaret River
T (08) 9756 5200 **F** (08) 9756 5222 **www**.howardparkwines.com.au **Open** 7 days 10–5
Winemaker Tony Davis, Genevieve Stols **Est.** 1986 **Cases** NFP
In the wake of its acquisition by the Burch family, and the construction of a large state-of-the-art winery at Denmark, a capacious cellar door (incorporating Feng Shui principles) has opened in the Margaret River, where there are also significant estate plantings. The Margaret River flagships are the Leston Shiraz and Leston Cabernet Sauvignon, but the Margaret River vineyards routinely contribute to all the wines in the range, from MadFish at the bottom, to the icon Cabernet Sauvignon Merlot at the top. Exports to all major markets.

♥♥♥♥♥ **Leston Margaret River Cabernet Sauvignon 2004** Wonderfully pure cabernet sauvignon varietal character; vibrant blackcurrant and cassis; fine tannins and quality oak help support the long finish. Screwcap. 14.5° alc. **Rating** 96 **To** 2024 $40

Leston Margaret River Shiraz 2005 Markedly different weight and structure compared to the Denmark Scotsdale, the tannins are finer, the cherry and plum fruit more spicy; long finish. Screwcap. 14.5° alc. **Rating** 95 **To** 2020 $40

MadFish Chardonnay 2006 Fresh, fragrant and lively; nectarine and grapefruit flavours, the touch of oak adding as much to texture as flavour; bright finish. Screwcap. 13.5° alc. **Rating** 94 **To** 2012 $25

Cabernet Sauvignon Merlot 2005 Medium-bodied but intense and long in the mouth; blackcurrant and cassis supported by fine tannins and high quality French oak. Screwcap. **Rating** 94 **To** 2020 $85

Leston Margaret River Cabernet Sauvignon 2005 The fragrant bouquet shows the 18 months in French oak, leading into a bold, full-bodied wine on the palate; here, fruit, oak and tannins are in balance; the future is assured, but patience needed. Screwcap. 14.5° alc. **Rating** 94 **To** 2025 $40

🍷🍷🍷🍷🍷 **MadFish Riesling 2007** Has the usual verve and crisp focus of MadFish, with a framework of minerally acidity; however, lacks mid-palate fruit for higher points. Screwcap. 13° alc. **Rating** 90 **To** 2013 $17

MadFish Gold Turtle Frankland River Shiraz 2005 Much more power and depth than prior vintages, taking it out of early drinking territory; indeed demands patience. The touch of viognier hasn't softened the wine. Screwcap. 14° alc. **Rating** 90 **To** 2012 $23.95

🍷🍷🍷🍷 **MadFish Sauvignon Blanc Semillon 2007** An abundance of tropical fruit on both bouquet and palate, plus a subliminal touch of sweetness; crowd pleaser style. Screwcap. 13° alc. **Rating** 89 **To** 2009 $19

MadFish Premium White 2007 Plenty of generous stone fruit flavours flanked by minerally/citrussy acidity; good length. Screwcap. 13.5° alc. **Rating** 89 **To** 2010 $19

MadFish Premium Red 2005 A distinctly firm structure courtesy of persistent Italianate tannins, slightly at odds with the normal come-hither early-drinking style of MadFish. Screwcap. 14.5° alc. **Rating** 89 **To** 2012 $19

MadFish Carnelian 2005 Unexpected depth of character to the black fruits, dark chocolate and spice; the tannins just a little aggressive; should repay cellaring. Screwcap. 14° alc. **Rating** 89 **To** 2015 $25

MadFish Pinot Noir 2006 Modest cherry and plum varietal fruit; a direct, simple, no frills style, but pinot nonetheless. Screwcap. 13.5° alc. **Rating** 88 **To** 2010 $19

Howards Lane Vineyard ★★★☆

Howards Lane, Welby, Mittagong, NSW 2575 **Region** Southern Highlands
T (02) 4872 1971 www.howardslane.com.au **Open** 7 days 10–5
Winemaker Michelle Crockett (Contract) **Est.** 1991 **Cases** 1250
Tony and Mary Betteridge migrated to Australia in 2002 with the dual objectives of finding an attractive place to live and a worthwhile occupation for their retirement. They say 'The beautiful view we chose came with the vineyard, thus determining our occupation. Within a year we had mastered the tractor, pruned our first vines, chosen a name, logo and label ... planted a second vineyard, built a rustic cellar door, and added considerably more knowledge of wine culture to our limited experience of simply enjoying Cape (South African) wines.'

Hugh Hamilton ★★★★

McMurtrie Road, McLaren Vale, SA 5171 **Region** McLaren Vale
T (08) 8323 8689 **F** (08) 8323 9488 www.hughhamiltonwines.com.au **Open** Mon–Fri 10–5.30, w'ends & public hols 11–5.30
Winemaker Hugh Hamilton **Est.** 1991 **Cases** 30 000
Hugh Hamilton is the fifth generation of the famous Hamilton family, who first planted vineyards at Glenelg in 1837. A self-confessed black sheep of the family, Hugh embraces non-mainstream varieties such as sangiovese, tempranillo, petit verdot and viognier, and is one of

only a few growing saperavi. Production comes from 29 ha of estate plantings, which includes the original Church Block, home to McLaren Vale's oldest chardonnay vines, and a vineyard in Blewitt Springs with 85-year-old shiraz and 65-year-old cabernet sauvignon. The irreverent black sheep packaging was the inspiration of daughter Mary (newly appointed CEO). The cellar door is lined with the original jarrah from Vat 15 from the historic Hamilton's Ewell winery, the largest wooden vat ever built in the southern hemisphere. Exports to the UK, the US, and other major markets.

ΨΨΨΨΨ **The Ratbag McLaren Vale Merlot 2005** Strong olive, blackcurrant and earth varietal flavours; fine tannin structure aids the length; impressive example. Screwcap. 14.5° alc. **Rating** 92 **To** 2018 $19.50
The Nutter McLaren Vale Petit Verdot 2005 Firm, earthy, foresty black fruits, with a near-citrus tang; the tannins are present, but not overwhelming, although some may think the price is. Screwcap. 14° alc. **Rating** 90 **To** 2015 $34.50

ΨΨΨΨ **The Mongrel 2006** Sweet and sour cherry aromas and flavours do most of the talking; fine structure and balance. Sangiovese/Merlot/Tempranillo. Screwcap. 14.5° alc. **Rating** 88 **To** 2012 $19.50

Hugo ★★★★

Elliott Road, McLaren Flat, SA 5171 **Region** McLaren Vale
T (08) 8383 0098 **F** (08) 8383 0446 **www**.hugowines.com.au **Open** Mon–Fri 9.30–5, Sat 12–5, Sun 10.30–5
Winemaker John Hugo **Est.** 1982 **Cases** 12 000
A winery that came from relative obscurity to prominence in the late 1980s with some lovely ripe, sweet reds, which, while strongly American oak-influenced, were quite outstanding. Has picked up the pace again after a dull period in the mid-1990s. There are 32 ha of estate plantings, with part of the grape production sold to others. Exports to the UK, the US and Canada.

ΨΨΨΨΨ **McLaren Vale Shiraz 2005** A dense, richly textured palate suggesting juice concentration given the controlled alcohol; soft, velvety black fruits and bitter chocolate; will be long lived. Screwcap. 14.5° alc. **Rating** 91 **To** 2020 $22.50
Reserve McLaren Vale Shiraz 2005 Savoury/spicy/earthy overtones to the black fruits; medium-bodied, with length rather than depth, elegance rather than opulence. Screwcap. 14.5° alc. **Rating** 91 **To** 2015 $35

ΨΨΨΨ **McLaren Vale Grenache Shiraz 2006** A fragrant, elegant, light- to medium-bodied palate, with juicy red berry fruits and soft tannins. Enjoy now. Vines 55 years old. Screwcap. 15° alc. **Rating** 89 **To** 2009 $19
McLaren Vale Cabernet Sauvignon 2005 A firm, medium- to full-bodied palate, tightly structured, with strong olive and leaf components; mimics cool-grown fruit. Screwcap. 14.5° alc. **Rating** 88 **To** 2014 $21.50

Humbug Reach Vineyard ★★★☆

72 Nobelius Drive, Legana, Tas, 7277 **Region** Northern Tasmania
T (03) 6330 2875 **F** (03) 6330 2739 **www**.humbugreach.com.au **Open** Not
Winemaker Winemaking Tasmania (Julian Alcorso) **Est.** 1988 **Cases** 450
The Humbug Reach Vineyard was established in the late 1980s on the banks of the Tamar River, with plantings of pinot noir; riesling and chardonnay followed thereafter. It has been owned by Paul and Sally McShane since 1999, who proudly tend the 5000 or so vines on the property. Frost entirely decimated the 2007 vintage, but the '06 Pinot Noir is available, and the '06 Chardonnay may still be available in small quantities.

ΨΨΨΨ **Pinot Noir 2006** Bright colour; plenty of flavour and texture, with touches of mint and spice, and oak in support. Screwcap. 13.9° alc. **Rating** 89 **To** 2012 $32
Chardonnay 2006 Apple, pear and stone fruit flavours; has length, though not overmuch intensity. Screwcap. 13° alc. **Rating** 87 **To** 2008 $21

Hundred Tree Hill

Redbank Winery, 1 Sally's Lane, Redbank, Vic 3478 **Region** Pyrenees
T (03) 5467 7255 **F** (03) 5467 7248 **www**.sallyspaddock.com.au **Open** Mon–Sat 9–5,
Sun 10–5
Winemaker Scott Hutton, Sasha Robb **Est.** 1973 **Cases** 3000
The next generation of the Robb family (Emily, Huw and Sasha) have established their
own vineyard, with 6 ha each of shiraz, cabernet sauvignon and cabernet franc, plus 2 ha
of pinot noir. Hundred Tree Hill was so named to commemorate the 100 trees that went
into the building of the Hundred Tree Homestead. Exports to the US, Canada, Germany
and Philippines.

ŸŸŸŸ **Pyrenees Shiraz 2005** Retains good colour; fresh, light- to medium-bodied
wine with a tangy, slightly green finish a plus as much as a minus. Cork. 13.5° alc.
Rating 87 **To** 2012 $14.50

Hungerford Hill

1 Broke Road, Pokolbin, NSW 2320 **Region** Lower Hunter Valley
T 1800 187 666 **F** (02) 4998 7375 **www**.hungerfordhill.com.au **Open** 7 days 10–5
Winemaker Phillip John, Andrew Thomas, Michael Hatcher **Est.** 1967 **Cases** 50 000
Hungerford Hill, sold by Southcorp to the Kirby family in 2002, has emerged with its home
base at the impressive winery previously known as One Broke Road. The development of
the One Broke Road complex proved wildly uneconomic, and the rationalisation process
has resulted in Hungerford Hill becoming the sole owner. The quality of the wines has
seen production soar from 20 000 cases to 50 000 cases, reversing the pattern under prior
Southcorp ownership. Lack of tasting of current wines has led to a nominal rating. Exports
to all major markets.

ŸŸŸŸ **Hunter Valley Semillon 2007** A vivid, striking green colour; full of flavour;
very unusual for young semillon, but not so unusual in the context of the vintage.
Screwcap. 11.5° alc. **Rating** 88 **To** 2014 $25

Huntington Estate

NR

Cassilis Road, Mudgee, NSW 2850 **Region** Mudgee
T (02) 6373 3825 **F** (02) 6373 3730 **www**.huntingtonestate.com.au **Open** Mon–Sat
10–5, Sun & public hols 10–4
Winemaker Tim Stevens **Est.** 1969 **Cases** 20 000
Bob and Wendy Roberts invested a lifetime in Huntington Estate, joined in more recent
years by daughter Susie as winemaker. When the time came to sell, it was to next door
neighbour Tim Stevens of Abercorn. The sale included the 2003–05 vintages, which are
being progressively released over '08 and '09. Stevens has deliberately remained faithful to the
slightly rustic, traditional ageing style of Huntington, picking up from the '06 vintage. Another
element of continuity is the music festival held at the winery each November. The transition
has been rocky from a wine quality viewpoint, making it impossible to give a meaningful
winery rating, hence NR.

Hurley Vineyard

101 Balnarring Road, Balnarring, Vic 3926 **Region** Mornington Peninsula
T (03) 5931 3000 **F** (03) 5931 3200 **www**.hurleyvineyard.com.au **Open** By appt
Winemaker Kevin Bell **Est.** 1998 **Cases** 600
It's never as easy as it seems. Though Kevin Bell is now a Victorian Supreme Court
judge, and his wife Tricia Byrnes has a busy legal life as a family law specialist in a small
Melbourne law firm, they have done most of the hard work in establishing Hurley
Vineyard themselves, with family and friends. Most conspicuously, Kevin Bell has
completed the Applied Science (Wine Science) degree at CSU, and has drawn on Nat
White for consultancy advice, and occasionally from Phillip Jones of Bass Phillip, and
Domaine Fourrier in Gevrey Chambertin.

ΨΨΨΨΨ Harcourt Mornington Peninsula Pinot Noir 2006 Has a little more thrust and verve than the Estate, yet not more weight; long palate with dark plum flavours and a long, peacock's tail finish. Diam. 13.5° alc. **Rating** 96 **To** 2014 $49
Estate Mornington Peninsula Pinot Noir 2006 Supple, velvety and seductive mouthfeel and flavours; perfectly ripened plum and black cherry fruit; silky tannins and balanced oak. Diam. 13.5° alc. **Rating** 95 **To** 2013 $40

Hutton Vale Vineyard

Stone Jar Road, Angaston, SA 5353 **Region** Eden Valley
T (08) 8564 8270 **F** (08) 8564 8385 **www.**huttonvale.com **Open** By appt
Winemaker Torbreck Vintners, Rockford **Est.** 1960 **Cases** 700
John Howard Angas (who arrived in SA in 1843, aged 19, charged with the responsibility of looking after the affairs of his father, George Fife Angas) named part of the family estate Hutton Vale. It is here that John Angas, John Howard's great-great-grandson, and wife Jan tend a little over 26 ha of vines. Almost all the grapes are sold, but a tiny quantity has been made by the who's who of the Barossa Valley, notably David Powell of Torbreck and Chris Ringland of Rockford. Exports to Singapore and NZ.

ΨΨΨΨΨ Eden Valley Cabernet Sauvignon 2005 Considerable depth, power and thrust to the voluminous redcurrant, blackcurrant and mulberry fruit; still very youthful, leave alone for 3–5 years. Screwcap. 14° alc. **Rating** 92 **To** 2025 $29
Eden Valley Riesling 2006 Has texture and framework with a good minerally backbone; finesse and delicacy rather than power. Screwcap. 12° alc. **Rating** 91 **To** 2013 $19

Hutton Wines **NR**

Caves Road, Wilyabrup, WA 6280 (postal) **Region** Margaret River
T 0417 923 126 **F** (08) 9759 1246 **Open** Not
Winemaker Dr Bradley Hutton **Est.** 2006 **Cases** 375
This is another venture of the Hutton family of Gralyn fame, with brothers (and sons) Bradley and Michael Hutton doing their own thing. Bradley Hutton became winemaker at Gralyn in 2001 following the completion of postgraduate studies in oenology at the University of Adelaide, so this is a busman's holiday. Cabernet sauvignon, shiraz and chardonnay are made from grapes purchased from the family vineyard and other growers in the surrounding area.

Idavue Estate ★★★★

470 Northern Highway, Heathcote, Vic 3523 **Region** Heathcote
T (03) 5433 3464 **F** (03) 5433 3049 **www.**idavueestate.com **Open** W'ends & public hols 10.30–5
Winemaker Andrew Whytcross, Sandra Whytcross **Est.** 2000 **Cases** NA
Owners and winemakers Andrew and Sandra Whytcross both undertook a two-year wine-making course through the Bendigo TAFE; with assistance from son Marty, they also look after the 5.7-ha vineyard, planted to 3 ha of shiraz, 1.9 ha of cabernet sauvignon, and 0.4 ha each of semillon and chardonnay. So far, only red wines have been released, made in typical small-batch fashion with hand-picked fruit, hand-plunged fermenters and a basket press.

ΨΨΨΨΨ Heathcote Shiraz 2006 Full-bodied; dark and brooding with good levels of spice and ample fruit weight on the palate; long and luscious, with a savoury twist on the finish. Diam. 15° alc. **Rating** 91 **To** 2016 $25
Heathcote Shiraz 2005 A fresh wine with prominent red fruits and a bit of spice; vibrant and juicy, but just beginning to show some developing softness. Diam. 13.5° alc. **Rating** 90 **To** 2015 $25

ΨΨΨΨ Blue Note Heathcote Shiraz 2006 Good colour; a very oaky wine with vanilla essence aromas and flavours; rich and ripe, with a little spice and red and dark berries. Diam. 15° alc. **Rating** 89 **To** 2014 $32

Heathcote Cabernet Sauvignon 2006 Vibrant purple hue; lifted mineral and blueberry aromas, with an element of cassis beneath; medium bodied and fleshy on the finish. Diam. 13.5° alc. **Rating** 89 **To** 2015 $25

Heathcote Shiraz Cabernet 2006 Plenty of dark fruits, with some leather and spice; fine and firm on the palate, but pulls up a little short on fruit. Diam. 14° alc. **Rating** 88 **To** 2014 $25

Ilnam Estate

750 Carool Road, Carool, NSW 2486 **Region** Northern Rivers Zone
T (07) 5590 7703 **F** (07) 5590 7922 www.ilnam.com.au **Open** Mon–Fri 11–4, w'ends 10–5
Winemaker Mark Quinn, Lachlan Quinn **Est.** 1998 **Cases** 2000
This is the first vineyard and winery to be established in the Tweed Valley, 30 mins from the Gold Coast. There are 2 ha each of chardonnay, cabernet sauvignon and shiraz, plus a small planting of chambourcin. In addition, Ilnam Estate has a number of growers in the Stanthorpe area who supply grapes. Ione, Lachlan, Nathan, Andrew and Mark Quinn are all involved in the family business.

Indigo Ridge ★★★

719 Icely Road, Orange, NSW 2800 **Region** Orange
T (02) 6362 1851 **F** (02) 6362 1851 www.indigowines.com.au **Open** W'ends & public hols 12–5
Winemaker Contract **Est.** 1994 **Cases** 2000
Paul Bridge and Trish McPherson describe themselves as the owners, labourers and viticulturists at Indigo Ridge; they planted and tend every vine on the 5-ha vineyard. The plantings are of cabernet sauvignon, sauvignon blanc, merlot and a few riesling vines. Exports to the UK, Malaysia and Singapore.

Indigo Wine Company

1221 Beechworth–Wangaratta Road, Everton Upper, Vic 3678 **Region** Beechworth
T (03) 5727 0233 **Open** By appt
Winemaker Brokenwood (Iain Riggs, PJ Charteris) **Est.** 1999 **Cases** 1900
Indigo Wine Company has a little over 46 ha of vineyards planted to 11 varieties incorporating the top French and Italian grapes. The business was and is primarily directed to growing grapes for sale to Brokenwood, but since 2004 small parcels of grapes have been vinified for the Indigo label. The somewhat incestuous nature of the whole business sees the Indigo wines being made at Brokenwood by Brokenwood CEO Iain Riggs and senior winemaker PJ Charteris.

TTTTT **Cabernet Sauvignon Merlot Petit Verdot 2004** Satisfyingly complex earthy/savoury/spicy flavours suggesting the region is more suited to later-ripening varieties than pinot noir; has length. Screwcap. 13.5° alc. **Rating** 90 **To** 2012 $39

TTTT **Chardonnay 2005** Pleasing wine, with the focus on gently mouthfilling fruit, winemaking inputs to the white peach and melon flavours restrained; maturing nicely. Screwcap. 13.6° alc. **Rating** 88 **To** 2011 $27

Inghams Skilly Ridge Wines

Gillentown Road, Sevenhill via Clare, SA 5453 **Region** Clare Valley
T (08) 8843 4330 **F** (08) 8843 4330 **Open** W'ends 10–5, or by appt tel 0418 423 998
Winemaker Clark Ingham, O'Leary Walker **Est.** 1994 **Cases** 3000
Clark Ingham has established a substantial 25-ha vineyard of shiraz, cabernet sauvignon, merlot, chardonnay, riesling and tempranillo. Part of the production is made by contract winemaker David O'Leary (with input from Clark Ingham); the remaining grape production is sold. Exports to the UK, Germany and China.

ㅟㅟㅟㅟ **Para River Barossa Valley Shiraz 2005** Attractive medium-bodied wine, with black cherry and plum fruit lengthened by controlled American oak and surprisingly lively, fine, tannins. Screwcap. 14.5° alc. **Rating** 90 **To** 2015 $22

ㅟㅟㅟ **Clare Valley Riesling 2007** Ripe, full-flavoured but broad and quite soft; typical '07; ready now. Screwcap. **Rating** 87 **To** 2010 $21

Ingoldby ★★★★

GPO Box 753, Melbourne, Vic 3001 **Region** McLaren Vale
T 1300 651 650 **F** (08) 8383 0790 **www**.ingoldby.com.au **Open** Not
Winemaker Matt O'Leary **Est.** 1983 **Cases** 170 000
Part of the Foster's group, with the wines now having a sole McLaren Vale source. Over the years, Ingoldby has produced some excellent wines, which provide great value for money.

ㅟㅟㅟㅟ **Reserve McLaren Vale Shiraz 2004** Dense colour, great for age; a voluptuous and dense amalgam of black fruits, dark chocolate, cedary French oak and ripe tannins; pity about cork choice. 14.5° alc. **Rating** 93 **To** 2019 $42.95

ㅟㅟㅟ **McLaren Vale Shiraz 2005** A stained and pockmarked cork is not an ideal introduction, nor is 15° alcohol, but the medium-bodied palate of black fruits, spice and dark chocolate is quite fair. 15° alc. **Rating** 87 **To** 2012 $18.95

Iron Gate Estate NR

Oakey Creek Road, Pokolbin, NSW 2320 **Region** Lower Hunter Valley
T (02) 4998 6570 **F** (02) 4998 6571 **www**.iron-gate-estate.com.au **Open** 7 days 10–4
Winemaker Roger Lilliott, Craig Perry **Est.** 2001 **Cases** 6000
Iron Gate Estate would not be out of place in the Napa Valley, which favours bold architectural statements made without regard to cost. No expense has been spared in equipping the winery, or on the lavish cellar door facilities. The wines are made from 10 ha of estate plantings of semillon, verdelho, chardonnay, cabernet sauvignon and shiraz, and include such exotic offerings as a sweet shiraz and a chardonnay made in the style of a fino sherry. Exports to the UK.

Iron Pot Bay Wines ★★★

766 Deviot Road, Deviot, Tas 7275 **Region** Northern Tasmania
T (03) 6394 7320 **F** (03) 6394 7346 **www**.ironpotbay.com.au **Open** Thurs–Sun 11–5
Sept–May, June–Aug by appt
Winemaker Andrew Pirie **Est.** 1988 **Cases** 2100
Iron Pot Bay is now part of the syndicate that established Rosevears Estate, with its large, state-of-the-art winery on the banks of the Tamar. The vineyard takes its name from a bay on the Tamar River (now called West Bay) and is strongly maritime-influenced, producing delicate but intensely flavoured unwooded white wines. It has 4.58 ha of vines, over half being chardonnay, the remainder semillon, sauvignon blanc, pinot gris, gewurztraminer and riesling.

ㅟㅟㅟ **Pinot Grigio 2007** Some stone fruit flavours, with moderate intensity across the palate; good length. **Rating** 87 **To** 2009 $27

Ironbark Hill Estate

694 Hermitage Road, Pokolbin, NSW 2321 **Region** Lower Hunter Valley
T (02) 6574 7085 **F** (02) 6574 7089 **www**.ironbarkhill.com.au **Open** 7 days 10–5
Winemaker Trevor Drayton **Est.** 1990 **Cases** 5000
Ironbark Hill Estate is owned by Peter Drayton and his accountant, Michael Dillon. His father Max Drayton, and brothers John and Greg, run Drayton's Family Wines. There are 14 ha of estate plantings of semillon, chardonnay, verdelho, shiraz, cabernet sauvignon, merlot and tyrian. Peter Drayton is a commercial/industrial builder, and constructing the cellar door was

a busman's holiday. The hope is that the striking building and landscape surrounds will bring more wine tourists to the Hermitage Road end of Pokolbin. The quality of the wines, too, is commendable. No samples received; the rating is that of last year.

Ironwood Estate

RMB 1288, Porongurup, WA 6234 **Region** Porongurup
T (08) 9853 1126 **F** (08) 9853 1172 **Open** By appt (closed Tues)
Winemaker The Vintage Wineworx (Dr Diane Miller), Bill Crappsley (Consultant), Mick Perkins **Est.** 1996 **Cases** 2500

Ironwood Estate was established in 1996; the first wines were made from purchased grapes. In the same year, chardonnay, shiraz and cabernet sauvignon were planted on a northern slope of the Porongurup Range. The first estate-grown grapes are now vinified at The Vintage Wineworx winery, co-owned with Jingalla, Chatsfield and Montgomery's Hill.

ŸŸŸŸ   **Porongurup Classic Red Blend 2005** Lifted spice notes complement elements of cassis and briar; good depth and weight across the palate. Cabernet Sauvignon/Shiraz/Merlot. Screwcap. 13.1° alc. **Rating** 89 **To** 2009 $16
Porongurup Cabernet Sauvignon 2004 Clean and varietal, with cassis fruit and medium-bodied weight; fine and even on the finish. Cork. 13.4° alc. **Rating** 88 **To** 2012 $20
Sauvignon Blanc 2007 A varietal sauvignon bouquet, with pungent herbaceous notes, and a hint of tropical on the finish. Screwcap. 14.3° alc. **Rating** 87 **To** 2009 $16
Rocky Rose 2006 Quite sweet, but with nice fruit flavour and good definition; needs to be very well chilled. Screwcap. 13.1° alc. **Rating** 87 **To** 2009 $14
Porongurup Cabernet Merlot 2006 Fresh, vibrant and full of red fruits; a fraction simple, but with good flavour. Screwcap. 12.6° alc. **Rating** 87 **To** 2010 $18

Irvine

PO Box 308, Angaston, SA 5353 **Region** Eden Valley
T (08) 8564 1046 **F** (08) 8564 1314 **www.**irvinewines.com.au **Open** At Eden Valley Hotel
Winemaker James Irvine, Joanne Irvine **Est.** 1980 **Cases** 8000

Industry veteran Jim Irvine, who has successfully guided the destiny of so many SA wineries, quietly introduced his own label in 1991. The vineyard from which the wines are sourced was planted in 1983 and now comprises a patchwork quilt of 10 ha of vines. The flagship is the rich Grand Merlot. Exports to all major markets.

ŸŸŸŸŸ   **James Irvine Grand Merlot 2002** Holding hue well – no brick starting to appear; developing with assurance, retaining all the positives of the varietal fruit, oak and tannins precisely positioned on the long palate. Cork. 14.5° alc. **Rating** 95 **To** 2014 $100

ŸŸŸŸŸ   **Merlot Cabernet Franc 2004** Showing distinct signs of development, but this does not detract from the pleasure of the wine; cedar, plum and red cherry flavours rest on a bed of gently warm tannins. Screwcap. 14.5° alc. **Rating** 93 **To** 2014 $25
The Baroness 2005 A blend of Merlot/Cabernet Franc/Cabernet Sauvignon from Eden Valley/Barossa Valley; has considerable intensity and authority of flavour without excessive tannins, though the oak is, as always, present; good length. Screwcap. 14.5° alc. **Rating** 93 **To** 2015 $45
Barossa Albarino 2007 Exotic aromas of ginger, clove and spice continue into the palate, joined there by sweet citrus flavours; a striking wine; one of the first examples of this Spanish variety. Screwcap. 12° alc. **Rating** 90 **To** 2009 $25

ŸŸŸŸ   **Springhill Barossa Merlot 2006** Powerful medium- to full-bodied example, the varietal fruit rich and a mix of cassis and plum, the tannins savoury and there for the long haul. Good value. Screwcap. 14.5° alc. **Rating** 89 **To** 2014 $18
Reserve Eden Valley Zinfandel 2005 Light- to medium-bodied; red fruits (cherry, raspberry) have a sprinkle of spices around them, soft barrel ferment oak a frame. Screwcap. 15° alc. **Rating** 88 **To** 2012 $35

Ivanhoe Wines   ★★★★

Marrowbone Road, Pokolbin, NSW 2320 **Region** Lower Hunter Valley
T (02) 4998 7325 **F** (02) 4998 7848 **www**.ivanhoewines.com.au **Open** 7 days 10–5
Winemaker Stephen Drayton **Est.** 1995 **Cases** 10 000
Stephen Drayton is the son of the late Reg Drayton and, with wife Tracy, is the third branch
of the family to be actively involved in winemaking in the Hunter Valley. The property on
which the vineyard is situated has been called Ivanhoe for over 140 years, and 25 ha of
30-year-old vines provide high-quality fruit for the label. The plans are to build a replica
of the old homestead (burnt down, along with much of the winery, in the 1968 bushfires)
to operate as a sales area.

ΨΨΨΨΨ **TLD Semillon 2007** Outstanding green-straw colour; fine, long and penetrating;
lime, lemon and lemon zest. Screwcap. 10.5° alc. **Rating** 93 **To** 2017 $22
Hunter Valley Traminer 2007 Strong exotic traminer fruits, with aromas of rose
petals and hints of talc; plenty of flavour and richness on the palate, but cleans up
well and finishes light. Diam. 14.8° alc. **Rating** 90 **To** 2011 $23
Premium Reserve Shiraz 2003 A medium-bodied wine, with plenty of
structure and depth, though does shorten slightly on the finish. Cork. 14.1° alc.
Rating 90 **To** 2013 $60

ΨΨΨΨ **Hunter Valley Chardonnay 2006** Waxy, citrus fruit on the bouquet, with fine
acid and stone fruits on the palate; good persistence on the finish. Screwcap.
12.5° alc. **Rating** 88 **To** 2012 $23
Hunter Valley Verdelho 2007 Hints of grapefruit and spice on the palate; a bit
of grip on the fresh finish; ready to go. Screwcap. 13.3° alc. **Rating** 87 **To** 2011 $23
Premium Reserve Shiraz 2005 A deceptively elegant, light-bodied wine,
presently hiding its light under a bottle. 14.1° alc. **Rating** 87 **To** 2013 $40

Jackson's Hill Vineyard   ★★★

Mount View Road, Mount View, NSW 2321 **Region** Lower Hunter Valley
T 1300 720 098 **F** 1300 130 220 **www**.jacksonshill.com.au **Open** By appt
Winemaker Christian Gaffey **Est.** 1983 **Cases** 1500
One of the low-profile operations on the spectacularly scenic Mount View Road, making
small quantities of estate-grown (3 ha) wine sold exclusively through the cellar door and
Australian Wine Selectors.

ΨΨΨΨ **The Underblock Semillon 2007** An intense mix of citrus and grass; long and
penetrating; on the big side and looks as if it will develop very quickly. Screwcap.
11° alc. **Rating** 88 **To** 2011 $25

Jacob's Creek   ★★★★☆

Jacob's Creek Visitor Centre, Barossa Valley Way, Rowland Flat, SA 5352 **Region** Barossa Valley
T (08) 8521 3000 **F** (08) 8521 3003 **www**.jacobscreek.com **Open** 7 days 10–5
Winemaker Philip Laffer, Bernard Hicken **Est.** 1973 **Cases** NFP
Jacob's Creek is one of the largest selling brands in the world and is almost exclusively
responsible for driving the fortunes of this French-owned (Pernod Ricard) company. A
colossus in the export game, chiefly to the UK and Europe, but also to the US and Asia.
Wine quality across the full spectrum from Jacob's Creek upwards has been exemplary,
driven by the production skills of Philip Laffer. The global success of the basic Jacob's Creek
range has had the perverse effect of prejudicing many critics and wine writers who fail (so
it seems) to objectively look behind the label and taste what is in fact in the glass. Jacob's
Creek now has four ranges, with all the wines having a connection, direct or indirect, with
Johann Gramp, who built his tiny stone winery on the banks of the creek in 1847. The 4-tier
range consists of Icon (Johann Shiraz Cabernet); then Heritage (Steingarten Riesling, Reeves
Point Chardonnay, Centenary Hill Barossa Shiraz and St Hugo Coonawarra Cabernet); then
Reserve (all of the major varietals); and finally Traditional (ditto).

ŶŶŶŶŶ **Limited Release 35th Anniversary Shiraz 2005** Dense, rich, layered texture; abundant plum, blackberry and licorice fruit, which, despite the depth, is not extractive; persistent tannins in balance. **Rating** 94 **To** 2020

ŶŶŶŶ♀ **Reserve Riesling 2007** Plenty of lime juice flavours and slatey minerality; good concentration and weight for the vintage; will be best enjoyed in its youth. Screwcap. 13.5° alc. **Rating** 91 **To** 2012 $16.95
Three Vines Semillon Sauvignon Blanc Viognier 2007 A lively and unexpectedly intense array of tangy, citrussy fruit flavours; lingering finish; very good wine at the price. Screwcap. 13° alc. **Rating** 91 **To** 2009 $14.95
St Hugo Coonawarra Cabernet Sauvignon 2004 An elegant medium-bodied wine with classic blackcurrant flavours plus touches of mint and earth typical of the region; fine tannins, good oak. Cork. 14.5° alc. **Rating** 91 **To** 2015 $41.95
Centenary Hill Barossa Valley Shiraz 2003 Good outcome for the vintage; sweet black and red fruits, chocolate and vanilla, soft tannins and gentle oak. Cork. 14.5° alc. **Rating** 90 **To** 2014 $41.95
Reserve Shiraz 2005 Solid dark-berried shiraz; clean and soft, with lots of flavour, and no winemaking excess to get in the way. Screwcap. 14.5° alc. **Rating** 90 **To** 2015 $16.95
Three Vines Shiraz Cabernet Tempranillo 2007 Abundant fruit; the skilled use of modern technology to make a wine with depth of flavour, ready to drink within six months of vintage. Screwcap. 12.5° alc. **Rating** 90 **To** 2010 $14.95
Jacaranda Ridge Coonawarra Cabernet Sauvignon 2003 Good wine, particularly within the constraints of the vintage, but doesn't quite have the verve of the best wines under this label; its main strength is back-palate finesse. Cork. 14.5° alc. **Rating** 90 **To** 2013 $59.99

ŶŶŶŶ **Shiraz 2006** Given the price, a remarkably complete wine with plenty of varietal fruit in a soft plummy frame, before finishing with good acidity and a tickle of spice. Screwcap. 14° alc. **Rating** 89 **To** 2009 $10
Reserve Chardonnay 2006 Clean and correct with melon and hints of dried fig; well-integrated oak. Screwcap. 13.5° alc. **Rating** 89 **To** 2012 $16.95
Reserve Sauvignon Blanc 2007 Very austere and certainly bone dry; not particularly varietal, but clean and well made. Screwcap. 13.5° alc. **Rating** 88 **To** 2009 $16.95
Merlot 2006 Has considerable varietal presence at this price point; savoury olive nuances alongside small red fruits; the palate has surprising length. Screwcap. 13.5° alc. **Rating** 88 **To** 2009 $10.99
Three Vines Shiraz Grenache Sangiovese 2007 Fresh, delicate and dry, but with some genuine character coming from the three varieties in question. Screwcap. 13° alc. **Rating** 87 **To** 2009 $14.95

JAG Wines   ★★★

72 William Street, Norwood, SA 5067 (postal) **Region** Warehouse
T (08) 8364 4497 **F** (08) 8364 4497 **www**.jagwines.com **Open** By appt
Winemaker Grant Anthony White **Est.** 2001 **Cases** 700
The name is doubtless derived from that of owners Julie and Grant White, but might cause raised eyebrows in clothing circles. The project developed from their lifelong love of wine; it started with a hobby vineyard (along with friends) in the Adelaide Hills, then more formal wine studies, then highly successful amateur winemaking. The Whites obtained their producers' licence (and trade-mark) in 2001, purchasing grapes from the major SA regions, bringing them to their suburban house to be fermented and pressed, and then storing the wine offsite in French and American oak until ready for bottling and sale.

Jamabro Wines

PO Box 434, Tanunda, SA 5352 **Region** Barossa Valley
T 0417 890 563 **F** (08) 8563 3837 **www.**jamabro.com.au **Open** Not
Winemaker David Heinze **Est.** 2003 **Cases** 750

Sixth-generation grapegrower David Heinze and wife Juli moved into winemaking in 2003 as many of the major companies taking Barossa grapes reduced their intakes, leaving a potential surplus to rot on the vine. With a little over 21 ha of vines planted to eight varieties, they were able to start with a full suite of wines, using estate-grown grapes and carrying out all the winemaking (other than bottling) onsite. There's some real marketing skill involved with the labelling (Jamabro is taken from a combination of family names), but it is the back labels that catch the eye. The Semillon takes the name of daughter Madison who, having just had her hair straightened for a school photograph, was doused in semillon when a bung came out unexpectedly, requiring lengthy and messy re-straightening (and an aversion to the winery); and Mum's Spade Shiraz celebrates the spade given to Juli by her husband when she turned 21. 'Wherever Mum went, so did her spade…When there was something to dig, out of the car boot came the spade. We lost Mum in 2006. Mum's Spade Shiraz is our tribute to Mum and all the other great Australian farming women, often the quiet achievers.'

ΦΦΦΦΦ **The PT Barossa Valley Shiraz 2005** So crammed with ultra-ripe fruit it's almost syrupy; despite this, has a certain appeal, and strangely there is good texture on the finish; a wine full of secrets and contradictions. Screwcap. 16° alc. **Rating** 91 **To** 2025 $40

Mum's Spade Barossa Valley Shiraz 2005 Very powerful full-bodied prune, blackberry and plum fruit, the alcohol tending to mask or strip the texture of the wine to a degree. Screwcap. 15.7° alc. **Rating** 90 **To** 2020 $25

ΦΦΦΦ **Bush Vine Barossa Valley Grenache 2005** Archetypal juicy jammy berry fruit flavours, at this alcohol hardly surprising, but doesn't burst into flames on the finish. Screwcap. 15.9° alc. **Rating** 89 **To** 2012 $25

Madison Barossa Valley Semillon 2006 Hilarious back label lets slip the barrel fermentation (old oak?) of this generously flavoured but rather short wine. Screwcap. 12.6° alc. **Rating** 87 **To** 2009 $15

Cabulous Barossa Valley Cabernet 2005 The structure and texture are good, but the alcohol and oak choice do not sit well with cabernet sauvignon, here turning it into something else, which is nice enough, but… Screwcap. 15.8° alc. **Rating** 87 **To** 2014 $30

James Haselgrove Wines

PO Box 271, McLaren Vale, SA 5171 **Region** McLaren Vale
T (08) 8383 0886 **F** (08) 8383 0887 **www.**haselgrovevignerons.com **Open** Not
Winemaker James Haselgrove **Est.** 1981 **Cases** 300

While in one sense this is now a virtual winery, Nick Haselgrove is quick to point out that it has access to substantial vineyards and winemaking resources. He and James Haselgrove (who founded this winery) are reluctant to see the business disappear, and intend to continue making and releasing wines under the James Haselgrove label. In terms of both price and style they will differ from Blackbilly (see separate entry). Exports to the US, Canada and Singapore.

ΦΦΦΦΦ **Futures McLaren Vale Shiraz 2005** Classy, strongly regional style; medium-bodied black fruits and dark chocolate; quality French oak and ripe tannins easily carry alcohol; 70-year-old vines. Screwcap. 14.9° alc. **Rating** 94 **To** 2025 $49.95

ΦΦΦΦ **Futures McLaren Vale Shiraz 2006** Plenty of flavour and character, but does struggle in vain under its load of alcohol. Screwcap. 14.9° alc. **Rating** 87 **To** 2013 $49.95

Jamiesons Run

Coonawarra Wine Gallery, Riddoch Highway, Penola, SA 5277 **Region** Coonawarra
T (08) 8737 3250 www.jamiesonsrun.com.au **Open** 7 days 10–5
Winemaker Andrew Hales **Est.** 1987 **Cases** 135 000
The wheel has turned a full 360° for Jamiesons Run. It started out as a single-label, mid-market, high-volume brand developed by Ray King during his time as CEO of Mildara. It grew and grew until the point where Mildara, having many years since been merged with Wolf Blass, decided to rename the Mildara Coonawarra winery as Jamiesons Run, with the Mildara label just one of a number falling under the Jamiesons Run umbrella. Now the Jamiesons Run winery is no more, Foster's has sold it, but retained the brand, the cellar door moving to shared accommodation at the Coonawarra Wine Gallery. Exports to the UK.

ŸŸŸŸŸ **Mildara Coonawarra Cabernet Sauvignon 2006** Dark cabernet fruit, full of cassis and touches of cedar; long and complex, with the oak supporting the abundant fruit very well. Screwcap. 15° alc. **Rating** 93 **To** 2020 $25.95

ŸŸŸŸ **Limestone Coast Chardonnay 2006** Aromatic stone fruit and citrus mix on bouquet and palate; plenty of fruit flavour in a peach spectrum; subtle oak. Sophisticated winemaking at the price. Screwcap. 14.4° alc. **Rating** 89 **To** 2010 $16.95
Sauvignon Blanc Semillon 2007 Abundant flavour and generosity, with the suggestion of some oak; not much finesse. **Rating** 87 **To** 2009 $17.95
Limestone Coast Sauvignon Blanc Semillon 2007 Enough overall flavour to satisfy, with grassy lemony notes running through a longer than expected palate. Screwcap. 11.5° alc. **Rating** 87 **To** 2010 $17.95
Coonawarra Shiraz 2005 Bright and clear colour; has a clean bouquet and palate with precise black and red fruits, albeit without much texture or complexity at present. Screwcap. 14.5° alc. **Rating** 87 **To** 2015 $17.95
Coonawarra Merlot 2005 Light- to medium-bodied; savoury olive and earth nuances are a fair manifestation of one aspect of merlot varietal character. **Rating** 87 **To** 2012 $17.95

Jamsheed

157 Faraday Street, Carlton, Vic 3053 (postal) **Region** Yarra Valley
T 0409 540 414 **F** (03) 5967 3581 www.jamsheed.com.au **Open** Not
Winemaker Gary Mills **Est.** 2003 **Cases** 200
Jamsheed is the venture of Gary Mills, proprietor of Simpatico Wine Services, a boutique contract winemaking company established at the Hill Paddock Winery in Healesville. The wines are sourced from a 30-year-old, low-yielding vineyard, and are made using indigenous/wild yeasts and minimal handling techniques. For the short-term future the business will focus on old vine sites in the Yarra Valley, but plans are to include a Grampians and Heathcote Shiraz along with a Strathbogie Gewurztraminer. The name, incidentally, is that of a Persian king recorded in the Annals of Gilgamesh.

ŸŸŸŸŸ **Great Western Shiraz 2006** Bright colour; a savoury wine with ironstone elements supporting the red fruits; tightly wound, with strong mineral notes and plenty of grip on the finish. Diam. 14.5° alc. **Rating** 92 **To** 2014 $35
Yarra Valley Shiraz 2006 A truly spicy, cool-climate wine; white pepper, red fruits and little toast from oak; classic supple Yarra Valley fruit on the palate, and very fine on the finish. Diam. 13.5° alc. **Rating** 91 **To** 2014 $35

ŸŸŸŸ **Heathcote Shiraz 2006** More aromatic, but not quite as focused as the Great Western; red fruits are lifted by a little volatility; pulls up a a fraction short on the finish; good flavour. Diam. 13.5° alc. **Rating** 87 **To** 2012 $35

Jane Brook Estate

229 Toodyay Road, Middle Swan, WA 6056 **Region** Swan Valley
T (08) 9274 1432 **F** (08) 9274 1211 www.janebrook.com.au **Open** Mon–Fri 10–5,
w'ends & public hols 12–5
Winemaker Julie Smith, Rob Mathews **Est.** 1972 **Cases** 25 000
Beverley and David Atkinson have worked tirelessly to build up the Jane Brook Estate wine
business over the past 30-plus years. The most important changes during that time have been
the establishment of a Margaret River vineyard, and sourcing grapes from other southern
wine regions in WA. Exports to the UK, the US and other major markets.

ŸŸŸŸ **Back Block Shiraz 2006** Big, rich, round, bold full-bodied Swan Valley shiraz in
an unashamedly traditional style, tannins supporting the potent blackberry fruits;
should be long lived. Screwcap. 14.5° alc. **Rating** 89 **To** 2016 $24.50
Shovelgate Vineyard Margaret River Cabernet Sauvignon 2006
Medium-bodied, with touches of leaf and mint to the blackcurrant fruit doubtless
a memento of a difficult, cool vintage. Screwcap. 13.7° alc. **Rating** 88 **To** 2014
$24.50
Pemberton Sauvignon Blanc Semillon 2007 None of the sweatiness of the
'07 Sauvignon Blanc; positive aromas and flavours in the grassy/herbal spectrum;
shortens slightly on the finish. Screwcap. 13.1° alc. **Rating** 87 **To** 2010 $20.50
Plain Jane Cabernet Shiraz 2005 Offers more than the Plain Jane white, the
regional blend (Swan Valley/Margaret River) working synergistically in a light-
to medium-bodied wine suited to a wide range of foods. Screwcap. 13.2° alc.
Rating 87 **To** 2012 $14.50

Jansz Tasmania

1216b Pipers Brook Road, Pipers Brook, Tas 7254 **Region** Northern Tasmania
T (03) 6382 7066 **F** (03) 6382 7088 www.jansztas.com **Open** 7 days 10–5
Winemaker Natalie Fryar **Est.** 1985 **Cases** 35 000
Jansz is part of the S Smith & Son/Yalumba group, and was one of the early sparkling wine
labels in Tasmania, stemming from a short-lived relationship between Heemskerk and Louis
Roederer. Its 15 ha of chardonnay, 12 ha of pinot noir and 3 ha of pinot meunier correspond
almost exactly to the blend composition of the Jansz wines. It is the only Tasmanian winery
entirely devoted to the production of sparkling wine, which is of high quality. Exports to all
major markets.

ŸŸŸŸŸ **Premium Rose NV** A different flavour profile to the standard, with pinot noir
contribution quite evident; flowery, strawberry blossom aromas; bready, toasty notes
and a long, dry finish. Similar background to the Premium Cuvee NV. Cork.
12.5° alc. **Rating** 94 **To** 2009 $22.95
Premium Vintage Rose 2004 Pale pink; has very good texture and weight; rich
fruit, with the ever-present suggestion of strawberries; a long, cleansing acid finish.
Rating 94 **To** 2012 $24.95

ŸŸŸŸŸ **Premium Cuvee NV** Combines delicacy with intensity and length; tangy fruit
flavour with some bready notes, then a clean, zesty finish. Extended lees contact;
several vintages; 100% Tasmania. Cork. 12.5° alc. **Rating** 93 **To** 2009 $22.95
Late Disgorged Vintage Cuvee 2000 A bigger brother of the Vintage Cuvee,
with some spice and caramel characters together with brioche; a big, mouthfilling
food style. **Rating** 92 **To** 2010 $49.95
Premium Vintage Cuvee 2003 An unusual bouquet, complex, and showing
immediate autolysis characters, and perhaps a touch of oak; a similarly complex,
slightly grippy palate. Cork. 12.5° alc. **Rating** 90 **To** 2009 $36.95

Jardine Wines ★★★★☆

1 Mugsies Road, Moonambel, Vic 3478 **Region** Pyrenees
T (03) 5467 2376 **F** (03) 5467 2378 **www**.jardinewines.com.au **Open** W'ends &
public hols 11–5
Winemaker Col Jardine **Est.** 1999 **Cases** 600
Colin and Cynthia Jardine began the development of their 8.5-ha vineyard in 1999, planting
4 ha of shiraz, 3 ha of cabernet sauvignon and 1.5 ha of pinot noir. Col Jardine, who doubles
up as viticulturist and winemaker, uses sustainable management practices, and limits the yield
to no more than 2 tonnes to the acre. No samples received; the rating is that of last year.

Jarrah Ridge Winery ★★★

651 Great Northern Highway, Herne Hill, WA 6056 **Region** Perth Hills
T (08) 9296 6337 **F** (08) 9403 0800 **www**.jarrahridge.com.au **Open** 7 days 10–5
Winemaker Rob Marshall (Contract) **Est.** 1998 **Cases** 9000
Syd and Julie Pond have established a 20.5-ha vineyard with shiraz the most important, the
remainder chenin blanc, chardonnay, cabernet sauvignon, verdelho, viognier and merlot.
Children Michael and Lisa are also involved in the business. Most of the wines have a degree
of sweetness, which will doubtless appeal to cellar door and restaurant customers. Exports to
Canada and Hong Kong.

ŸŸŸŸ **Viognier 2005** Despite a hint of reduction, is developing nicely, and building
varietal flavour; does toughen slightly on the finish, as often happens. Screwcap.
12.6° alc. **Rating** 87 **To** 2009 $16

Jarvis Estate ★★★★

Lot 13, Wirring Road, Margaret River, WA 6285 **Region** Margaret River
T (08) 9758 7526 **F** (08) 9758 8017 **www**.jarvisestate.com.au **Open** By appt
Winemaker Naturaliste Vintners (Bruce Dukes) **Est.** 1995 **Cases** 3000
Matt and Jackie Jarvis carefully researched the Margaret River region, and in particular
the Bramley locality, before purchasing their property, where they now live. It is planted to
cabernet sauvignon, shiraz, merlot, chardonnay and cabernet franc (8.4 ha). Exports to Taiwan,
Greece and Ireland.

ŸŸŸŸŸ **Margaret River Cabernet Sauvignon 2005** Excellent hue and clarity; classic
Margaret River cabernet, with very fine but persistent tannins on the long palate;
good oak balance. Cork. 13.5° alc. **Rating** 92 **To** 2014 $24
Margaret River Shiraz 2005 An elegantly framed, medium-bodied palate, with
a mix of red and black cherry, blackberry and spice; fine tannins, good oak. Twin
top. 14° alc. **Rating** 90 **To** 2015 $24

ŸŸŸŸ **Margaret River Merlot 2005** Medium-bodied; distinct olive/savoury/briary
nuances throughout; a lively finish, with fractionally drying herbal notes. Twin top.
14.5° alc. **Rating** 88 **To** 2012 $24

Jasper Hill ★★★★★

Drummonds Lane, Heathcote, Vic 3523 **Region** Heathcote
T (03) 5433 2528 **F** (03) 5433 3143 **www**.jasperhill.com **Open** By appt
Winemaker Ron Laughton, Emily Laughton **Est.** 1975 **Cases** 3500
The red wines of Jasper Hill are highly regarded and much sought after, invariably selling
out at the cellar door and through the mailing list within a short time of release. These are
wonderful wines in admittedly Leviathan mould, reflecting the very low yields and the care
and attention given to them by Ron Laughton. The oak is not overdone, and the fruit flavours
show Heathcote at its best. Exports to the UK, the US and other major markets.

ŸŸŸŸŸ **2006 Georgia's Paddock Heathcote Shiraz** Slightly brighter hue than
Emily's; a full-bodied wine that carries its alcohol with ease, the savoury, spicy,
earthy elements to the dark fruit background providing both texture and balance.
Cork. **Rating** 95 **To** 2020 $70

2006 Emily's Paddock Heathcote Shiraz Cabernet Franc Has added elements of mint and herb on both bouquet and palate; overall, distinctly savoury, verging on the austere; extremely interesting style and outcome. Cork. **Rating** 94 **To** 2016 $85

jb Wines ★★★

PO Box 530, Tanunda, SA 5352 **Region** Barossa Valley
T (08) 8563 0291 **F** (08) 8379 4359 **www.**jbwines.com **Open** At Mt Jagged Wines
Winemaker Joe Barritt, Tim Geddes **Est.** 2005 **Cases** 260
The Barritt family has been growing grapes in the Barossa since the 1850s, but this particular venture was established in 2005 by Lenore, Joe and Greg Barritt. It is based on 17.7 ha of shiraz, cabernet sauvignon and chardonnay (with tiny amounts of zinfandel, pinot blanc and clairette) planted between 1972 and 2003. Greg Barritt runs all the vineyard operations, and Joe Barritt, with a bachelor of agricultural science degree from Adelaide University, followed by 10 years of winemaking in Australia, France and the US, is now the winemaker together with Tim Geddes at McLaren Vale, where the wines are made.

Chardonnay 2007 Well-crafted from hand-pruned and hand-picked fruit, the relatively low alcohol providing the wine with more finesse and elegance than most Barossa Valley chardonnays; a mix of nectarine and citrus. Screwcap. 12.5° alc. **Rating** 89 **To** 2013 $20
Clairette 2007 A neutral bouquet, but there is quite unexpected green apple fruit flavour on the palate balanced by a subliminal touch of sweetness on the finish. Screwcap. 12.5° alc. **Rating** 88 **To** 2012 $20
Pinot Blanc 2007 Not as interesting as the Clairette, perhaps due to the need for a cool climate for this variety to shine, but the twist of acidity on the finish makes the wine worth a look. Screwcap. 12.5° alc. **Rating** 87 **To** 2009 $20

Jean Pauls Vineyard ★★★★

RMB 6173, Yea, Vic 3717 (postal) **Region** Upper Goulburn
T (03) 5797 2235 **www.**jeanpaulsvineyard.com.au **Open** Not
Winemaker William de Castella **Est.** 1995 **Cases** 200
This is a cameo exercise, with all the detail portrayed in finest detail. It is owned by William and Heather de Castella, a direct descendant of the famous de Castella family of the Yarra Valley. Hubert de Castella established St Huberts, while brother Paul had the even larger Yering Vineyard in his care. The full name of today's vigneron is William Jean Paul de Castella, hence the indirect reference to William's distinguished forebears. His 3-ha vineyard (shiraz, cabernet sauvignon) has been run on full biodynamic principles since the first 0.5 ha of shiraz was planted in 1994–95. The vineyard is NASAA Certified Organic/Biodynamic and uses minimal irrigation. Even though copper and sulphur sprays are permitted, they have never been used, and the yields are tiny. To add a further degree of difficulty to an already difficult project, no sulphur dioxide is added to the wine either during fermentation or prior to bottling.

Shiraz 2005 Very good texture, structure and length are the mainstays of a quality wine, with spicy blackberry and plum fruit supported by positive oak and fine tannins; no need to wait but will cellar. Cork. 14.5° alc. **Rating** 94 **To** 2015 $25

Bold Colonial Red Cabernet Sauvignon 2005 Good colour; medium-bodied; cassis, mint and leaf nuances along with persistent tannins; needed a touch more ripeness. Cork. 13° alc. **Rating** 88 **To** 2015 $25

Jeanneret Wines ★★★★

Jeanneret Road, Sevenhill, SA 5453 **Region** Clare Valley
T (08) 8843 4308 **F** (08) 8843 4251 **www.**jeanneretwines.com **Open** Mon–Fri 9.30–5, w'ends & public hols 10–5
Winemaker Ben Jeanneret **Est.** 1992 **Cases** 12 000

Jeanneret's winery has a most attractive outdoor tasting area and equally attractive picnic facilities, on the edge of a small lake surrounded by bushland. While the business did not open until 1994, its first wine was in fact made in '92 (Shiraz) and it had already established a loyal following. Ben Jeanneret is the youngest winemaker/winery owner in the Clare Valley. Exports to the US, Canada and Japan.

ITTTI **Doozie 2007** Very intense and full-flavoured, with rich tropical overtones throughout; good now or later. Riesling. Vino-Lok. 12° alc. **Rating** 92 **To** 2015 $40
Denis 2004 As full-bodied and uncompromisingly powerful as the alcohol would suggest, exuding black fruits from every pore; 10 years plus 30-day air-dried beef. Shiraz. Screwcap. 15° alc. **Rating** 92 **To** 2024 $60
Curly Red 2005 Deep colour; full-bodied, and lusciously ripe black and red fruits basically tracking the cabernet and cabernet franc components, but malbec also evident; soft ripe tannins. Screwcap. 15° alc. **Rating** 91 **To** 2020 $22

ITTT **Big Fine Girl Clare Valley Riesling 2007** Solidly built and structured – well named in fact; overall, plenty of flavour and less finesse. Screwcap. 12.5° alc. **Rating** 89 **To** 2012 $18
Hummer 2005 Very ripe and rich, with dense black fruits and touches of mocha; full-on flavour, low on varietal character. Merlot. Vino-Lok. 14.7° alc. **Rating** 89 **To** 2018 $40
Rank and File Clare Valley Shiraz 2005 Massive and full-bodied, the bouquet shows unmistakable dead fruit characters, which (admittedly) do appeal to some. Screwcap. 15.5° alc. **Rating** 87 **To** 2015 $22

Jeir Creek   ★★★★

122 Bluebell Lane, Murrumbateman, NSW 2582 **Region** Canberra District
T (02) 6227 5999 **F** (02) 6227 5900 www.jeircreekwines.com.au **Open** Thurs–Mon & public hols 10–5
Winemaker Rob Howell **Est.** 1984 **Cases** 4500
Rob Howell came to part-time winemaking through a love of drinking fine wine, and is intent on improving both the quality and the consistency of his wines. It is now a substantial (and still growing) business, with the vineyard plantings increased to 11 ha by the establishment of more cabernet sauvignon, shiraz, merlot and viognier.

ITTTI **Canberra District Shiraz Viognier 2005** Better colour and flavour than the '06, showing more of the impact of the viognier, with rich blackberry and spice fruit plus the thrust of the viognier. Screwcap. 13.6° alc. **Rating** 90 **To** 2014 $25
Canberra District Sparkling Shiraz Viognier 2005 Good base material evident; attractive fine fruit eliminates the need for high dosage; will go on developing in bottle. Crown Seal. 14.5° alc. **Rating** 90 **To** 2015 $28

ITTT **Canberra District Botrytis Semillon Sauvignon Blanc 2005** Complex; slightly better acidity and life than the '06 and will live longer, but not by much. Screwcap. 13° alc. **Rating** 89 **To** 2010 $25
Canberra District Botrytis Semillon Sauvignon Blanc 2006 Deep gold; traditional style, marmalade and cumquat with some barrel ferment inputs; classic. Screwcap. 12.5° alc. **Rating** 88 **To** 2009 $25
Canberra District Cabernet Merlot 2006 Powerful and somewhat extractive, with strongly earthy savoury characters demanding time. Screwcap. 14.5° alc. **Rating** 87 **To** 2014 $23

Jenke Vineyards   ★★★★☆

Barossa Valley Way, Rowland Flat, SA 5352 **Region** Barossa Valley
T (08) 8524 4154 **F** (08) 8524 5044 **Open** 7 days 11–5
Winemaker Kym Jenke **Est.** 1989 **Cases** 8500
The Jenke family have been vignerons in the Barossa since 1854 and have over 45 ha of vineyards; a small part of the production is now made and marketed through a charming restored stone cottage cellar door. Exports to the US.

ＹＹＹＹＹ Reserve Barossa Shiraz 2004 Very good colour; distinctly earthy, savoury overtones to medium- to full-bodied blackberry and plum fruit, vanillin oak wrapping up the parcel. Screwcap. 14.3° alc. **Rating** 90 **To** 2019 $45

ＹＹＹＹ Barossa Shiraz 2006 The extreme alcohol seems to take away from rather than augment the varietal fruit flavour and structure; good oak handling helps redeem. Screwcap. 16° alc. **Rating** 87 **To** 2017 $30

Jerusalem Hollow

6b Glyde Street, East Fremantle, WA 6158 (postal) **Region** Margaret River
T (08) 9339 6879 **F** (08) 9339 5192 **www**.jerusalemhollowwines.com.au **Open** Not
Winemaker Clive Otto (Contract) **Est.** 2000 **Cases** 500
Perth eye surgeon Bill Ward, wife (and former nurse) Louise and family began planting their 5.8-ha vineyard in 2000. Bill, a long term admirer of Champagne, was inspired by an article by Max Allen in the *Weekend Australian Magazine* in which Californian sparkling winemaker Harold Osborne (maker of Pelorus for Cloudy Bay in NZ) expressed the view that Margaret River was a good region for sparkling wine. This remains the main thrust of the business, with a side bet on Cabernet Sauvignon and a small amount of Roussanne Chardonnay to follow in due course. The name, incidentally, is a local one, but it so happens that Bill worked at the St John's eye hospital in Jerusalem as a surgical fellow in the late 1980s to early '90s.

ＹＹＹＹ Methode Traditionnelle Margaret River Chardonnay 2005 Fine, fresh citrus, stone fruit and apple; good length and balance; 24 months on lees. Cork. 12.5° alc. **Rating** 88 **To** 2011 $21.40

Jester Hill Wines

292 Mount Stirling Road, Glen Aplin, Qld 4381 **Region** Granite Belt
T (07) 4683 4380 **F** (07) 4683 4396 **www**.jesterhillwines.com.au **Open** 7 days 9–5
Winemaker James Janda **Est.** 1993 **Cases** 1050
A family-run vineyard situated in the pretty valley of Glen Aplin in the Granite Belt. The owners, John and Genevieve Ashwell, aim to concentrate on small quantities of premium-quality wines reflecting the full-bodied style of the region. Believing that good wine is made in the vineyard, John and Genevieve spent the first seven years establishing healthy, strong vines on well-drained soil.

ＹＹＹＹ Touchstone Granite Belt Verdelho 2007 Smooth and supple; light- to medium-bodied with a surprising range of tropical and other fruits. Screwcap. 13.5° alc. **Rating** 87 **To** 2009 $16
Granite Belt Sparkling Shiraz 2004 Quite complex leather, spice and black fruit flavours, the sweetness within bounds; better than many sparkling reds. Cork. 12.5° alc. **Rating** 87 **To** 2010 $22

Jim Barry Wines

Craig's Hill Road, Clare, SA 5453 **Region** Clare Valley
T (08) 8842 2261 **F** (08) 8842 3752 **Open** Mon–Fri 9–5 & w'ends & public hols 9–4
Winemaker Peter Barry **Est.** 1959 **Cases** 80 000
The patriarch of this highly successful wine business, Jim Barry, died in 2004, but the business continues under the active management of several of his many children. There is a full range of wine styles across most varietals, but with special emphasis on Riesling, Shiraz and Cabernet Sauvignon. The ultra-premium release is The Armagh Shiraz, with the McCrae Wood red wines not far behind. Jim Barry Wines is able to draw upon over 200 ha of mature Clare Valley vineyards, plus a small holding in Coonawarra. Exports to all major markets.

ＹＹＹＹＹ The Armagh Shiraz 2005 A dark multi-layered shiraz, with layers of fruit, minerals and a slightly briary savoury edge; has marked nervosity, power and depth; opens slowly, but has a long story to tell. Cork. **Rating** 95 **To** 2030 $220

Watervale Riesling 2007 Is particularly well-balanced in a generous mode; lime and tropical fruit in abundance; good length. Screwcap. 13° alc. Rating 94 To 2017 $14.95

The McCrae Wood Shiraz 2005 Deep vibrant colour; lush blackberry, licorice, mocha/vanilla flavours all coalesce on the medium- to full-bodied palate; well-balanced oak and tannins; long finish. Cork. **Rating** 94 **To** 2025 $55

♟♟♟♟♟ **First Eleven Coonawarra Cabernet Sauvignon 2005** Seductively sweet fruit in a cassis, raspberry range; ripe tannins and good oak; creeps up on you. Cork. 15° alc. **Rating** 93 **To** 2015 $60

The Benbournie Cabernet Sauvignon 2002 Deep colour and equally deep-flavoured wine, with blackcurrant fruit at the extremely ripe end of the scale, the tannins and oak well-handled. Cork. 15° alc.**Rating** 91 **To** 2017 $85

The Cover Drive Cabernet Sauvignon 2006 Good varietal cabernet with plenty of cassis and a mere suggestion of mint; quite fleshy, supple and long on the finish. Screwcap. 15° alc. **Rating** 90 **To** 2014 $19.95

♟♟♟♟ **The Lodge Hill Riesling 2007** Some lime and nettle aromas; abundant flavour and depth at the riper end of the spectrum, but lacks thrust on the finish. Screwcap. 13° alc. **Rating** 89 **To** 2011 $19.50

The Florita Clare Valley Riesling 2007 Shows a more mineral personality than most Clare rieslings; quite rich and textured, with a little grip on the finish; plenty of flavour and very long. Screwcap. 13° alc. **Rating** 89 **To** 2014 $45

The Lodge Hill Shiraz 2006 Very concentrated, almost essency/luscious blackberry fruit with a light briny edge; highly polished and quite chewy on the finish. Value. Screwcap. 15° alc. **Rating** 89 **To** 2015 $19.95

Three Little Pigs Clare Valley Shiraz Cabernet Malbec 2004 Ripe, luscious mouthfilling fruit, with the influence of malbec (though only a small percentage) quite obvious; some sweetness. Screwcap. 14.5° alc. **Rating** 89 **To** 2012 $19.50

Silly Mid On Sauvignon Blanc Semillon 2007 Clean, fresh and lively; a little chalky on the palate, but harmonious and pleasant on the finish. Screwcap. 12° alc. **Rating** 87 **To** 2009 $19.95

Jimbour Wines ★★★

86 Jimbour Station Road, Jimbour, Qld 4406 **Region** Queensland Zone
T (07) 3236 2100 **F** (07) 3236 0110 www.jimbourwines.com.au **Open** 7 days 10–4.30
Winemaker Peter Scudamore-Smith MW (Consultant) **Est.** 2000 **Cases** 15 000
Jimbour Station was one of the first properties opened in the Darling Downs and the heritage-listed homestead was built in 1876. The property has been owned by the Russell family since 1923, which has diversified by establishing a 22-ha vineyard and opening a cellar door on the property in a renovated water tower built in 1870. Increasing production is an indication of its role as one of Qld's major wine producers. Exports to Japan, Taiwan, Hong Kong and China.

♟♟♟♟ **Jimbour Station Verdelho 2007** Highly aromatic with exotic fruit character; vibrant and refreshing acidity on the finish; enjoy while young and juicy. Screwcap. 13.5° alc. **Rating** 88 **To** 2009 $14.95

Ludwig Leichhardt Reserve Pinot Noir Chardonnay 2005 A little toasty nuance, lifted by fresh citrus fruits; nice texture. Cork. 12.5° alc. **Rating** 87 **To** 2009 $27.95

Jindalee Estate ★★★★☆

265 Ballan Road, Moorabool, North Geelong, Vic 3221 **Region** Geelong
T (03) 5276 1280 **F** (03) 5276 1537 www.jindaleewines.com.au **Open** 7 days 10–5
Winemaker Chris Sargeant **Est.** 1997 **Cases** 700 000
Jindalee is part of the Littore Group, which currently has 1200 ha of premium wine grapes in production and under development in the Riverland. Corporate offices are now at the former Idyll Vineyard, acquired by Jindalee in 1997. Here 16 ha of estate vineyards have

been re-trellised and upgraded, and produce the Fettlers Rest range. The Jindalee Estate Chardonnay can offer spectacular value. Exports to all major markets.

ŢŢŢŢŢ Littore Idyll Vineyard Gewurztraminer 2006 Bright yellow-green; abundant varietal character, but achieved at the expense of a slightly phenolic finish; starting to building some toasty characters. Screwcap. 12.5° alc. **Rating** 90 **To** 2009 $26.95

ŢŢŢŢ Circle Collection Chardonnay 2006 In typical Jindalee style, has an abundance of peachy fruit, bolstered by good citrussy acidity and a hint of oak. Screwcap. 13.5° alc. **Rating** 88 **To** 2009 $8.95
Circle Collection Shiraz 2006 Fresh red and black cherry fruits; has good tannin structure at the price, and is well balanced. Screwcap. 14° alc. **Rating** 88 **To** 2009 $8.95

Jingalla ★★★
49 Bolganup Dam Road, Porongurup, WA 6324 **Region** Porongurup
T (08) 9853 1103 **F** (08) 9853 1023 www.jingallawines.com.au **Open** 7 days 10.30–5
Winemaker The Vintage Wineworx (Dr Diane Miller, Greg Jones), Bill Crappsley (Consultant) **Est.** 1979 **Cases** 4000
Jingalla is a family business, owned and run by Geoff and Nita Clarke and Barry and Shelley Coad, the latter the ever-energetic wine marketer of the business. The 9 ha of hillside vineyards are low-yielding, with the white wines succeeding best, but they also produce some lovely red wines. A partner in The Vintage Wineworx winery, which means it no longer has to rely on contract winemaking.

Jinglers Creek Vineyard ★★★★☆
288 Relbia Road, Relbia, Tas 7258 (postal) **Region** Northern Tasmania
T (03) 6344 3966 **F** (03) 6344 3966 www.jinglerscreekvineyard.com.au
Open Thurs–Sun 11–5
Winemaker Tamar Ridge (Michael Fogarty, Andrew Pirie) **Est.** 1998 **Cases** 150
Irving Fong came to grapegrowing later in life, undertaking the viticulture course at Launceston TAFE when he was 67 years old (where he also met his second wife). They have 1.8 ha of pinot noir, with small plantings of pinot gris, sauvignon blanc and chardonnay. The 2007 vintage was decimated by frost.

Jinks Creek Winery ★★★★☆
Tonimbuk Road, Tonimbuk, Vic 3815 **Region** Gippsland
T (03) 5629 8502 **F** (03) 5629 8551 www.jinkscreekwinery.com.au **Open** By appt
Winemaker Andrew Clarke **Est.** 1981 **Cases** 1000
Jinks Creek Winery is situated between Gembrook and Bunyip, bordering the evocatively named Bunyip State Park. While the winery was not built until 1992, planting of the 3.64-ha vineyard started back in 1981 and all the wines are estate-grown. The 'sold out' sign goes up each year. No samples received; the rating is that of last year. Exports to the UK, the US and France.

John Duval Wines ★★★★★
9 Park Street, Tanunda, SA 5352 (postal) **Region** Barossa Valley
T (08) 8563 2591 **F** (08) 8563 0372 www.johnduvalwines.com **Open** Not
Winemaker John Duval **Est.** 2003 **Cases** 5200
John Duval is an internationally recognised winemaker, having been the custodian of Penfolds Grange for almost 30 years as part of his role as chief red winemaker at Penfolds. He remains involved with Penfolds as a consultant, but these days is concentrating on establishing his own brand, and providing consultancy services to other clients in various parts of the world. On the principle 'if not broken, don't fix', he is basing his business on shiraz and shiraz blends from old-vine vineyards in the Barossa Valley. The brand name Plexus, incidentally, denotes a network in an animal body that combines elements into a coherent structure. Exports to the UK, the US and other major markets.

ΥΥΥΥΥ **Entity Barossa Valley Shiraz 2006** Saturated crimson-purple; has achieved the density of fruit to guarantee a 30-year life without the least hint of overripe fruit or alcohol heat; perfect balance and integration of fruit, oak and tannins; the work of a master. Screwcap. 14.5° alc. **Rating** 96 **To** 2036 $45
Eligo Barossa Valley Shiraz 2005 Has great concentration and structure and, above all, length to its panoply of red and black berry fruit; both oak and tannins positive, but nonetheless in a support role. Cork. **Rating** 96 **To** 2020 $100
Plexus Barossa Valley Shiraz Grenache Mourvedre 2006 Crimson-purple; a beautifully balanced and utterly seamless array of red and black fruits, without a scintilla of confection character; lovely now or in 10 years. Bargain. Screwcap. 14.5° alc. **Rating** 95 **To** 2016 $35

John Gehrig Wines

Oxley-Milawa Road, Oxley, Vic 3678 **Region** King Valley
T (03) 5727 3395 **F** (03) 5727 3699 **www.**johngehrigwines.com.au **Open** 7 days 9–5
Winemaker Ross Gehrig **Est.** 1976 **Cases** 5600
In the manner of Burgundian wineries, where many are owned by families with identical or similar family names, so is the case with Gehrig in Northeast Victoria. Or, at least, that is my excuse. Ross Gehrig has taken over management of John Gehrig Wines from his parents, John and Elizabeth, and the business has nothing to do with Gehrig Estate at Barnawartha, owned and managed by Ross's uncle Bernard. Having got that off my chest, I will not complicate the matter further about individual wine entries in prior vintages.

ΥΥΥΥΥ **Pinot Noir 2005** Sensitive winemaking has gone very close to making a silk purse out of a sow's ear; delicate red cherry and spicy elements drive the light-bodied but balanced palate. Best King Valley pinot noir? Screwcap. 13.8° alc. **Rating** 90 **To** 2011 $25

ΥΥΥΥ **King Valley Merlot 2006** Good hue; slightly too much sweet fruit and not quite enough olive, but will appeal to those looking for a soft, medium-bodied red. Screwcap. 14° alc. **Rating** 87 **To** 2011 $25
Elizabeth's Block 2006 Red fruits encased by ripe but persistently savoury tannins; good balance. Screwcap. 14° alc. **Rating** 87 **To** 2012 $30

John Kosovich Wines

Cnr Memorial Avenue/Great Northern Highway, Baskerville, WA 6056 **Region** Swan Valley
T (08) 9296 4356 **F** (08) 9296 4356 **www.**johnkosovichwines.com.au **Open** 7 days 10–5.30
Winemaker Anthony Kosovich **Est.** 1922 **Cases** 4000
The name change from Westfield to John Kosovich Wines does not signify any change in either philosophy or direction for this much-admired producer of a surprisingly elegant and complex Chardonnay; the other wines are more variable, but from time to time there have been attractive Verdelho and excellent Cabernet Sauvignon. Since 1998, wines partly or wholly from the family's planting at Pemberton have been made, the Swan/Pemberton blends released under the Bronze Wing label. Exports to Singapore.

ΥΥΥΥΥ **Limited Release Liqueur Muscat NV** Age immediately obvious from olive-rimmed mahogany; very complex rich plum pudding/Christmas cake mix plus some toffee apple; luscious mid-palate, then classic drying finish. Cork. 18.5° alc. **Rating** 95 **To** 2009 $65

ΥΥΥΥΥ **Limited Release Liqueur Verdelho NV** Brown-gold; complex, with some volatile lift (perfectly acceptable) to the tea leaf and butterscotch flavours; long palate. Cork. **Rating** 93 **To** 2009 $55
Pemberton Chardonnay 2007 An elegant wine, with length and intensity to its mix of grapefruit and nectarine, and barrel ferment oak; well-balanced and integrated. Screwcap. **Rating** 91 **To** 2012 $26

ŸŸŸŸ   **Swan Valley Cabernet Sauvignon 2006** Interesting example of the move to earlier picking in some regions, happy to trade off luscious ripeness in return for brighter fruit flavours. Diam. 13.5° alc. **Rating** 87 **To** 2014 $26

John Siding Vintners   ★★★☆

Barker Road, Mount Barker, SA 6324 **Region** Adelaide Hills
T 0418 713 947 **F** (08) 8398 2927 **Open** By appt
Winemaker John Gilbert **Est.** 1996 **Cases** 12 000
John Gilbert has a number of brands led by Gilberts Siding with a flagship Erebus Shiraz and Earhart Cabernet from McLaren Vale, supported by Sangiovese Shiraz and a Grenache Shiraz. His Jardim do Bomfim wines come from the Thunderbird Vineyard at Middleton (Fleurieu Peninsula), Ironstone Ridge Vineyard in the Adelaide Hills (planted to Italian varieties, including a direct importation of a Sicilian white grillo brought in after the 2001 vintage), and the dry-grown XR-65 Vineyard at Langhorne Creek.

ŸŸŸŸŸ   **Jardim do Bomfim Shiraz 2005** Has an unusual but pleasing array of spice, milk chocolate and warm black fruit flavours, with very good texture courtesy of fine tannins and French oak. Screwcap. 14.5° alc. **Rating** 90 **To** 2015

ŸŸŸŸ   **Jardim do Bomfim Chardonnay 2005** A somewhat hard fruit profile, with citrus rind and some mineral; slow developing, particularly given cork; possibly late-bottled. Cork. 13.2° alc. **Rating** 88 **To** 2012
Jardim do Bomfim Thunderbird Vineyard Cabernet Sauvignon 2005 Cool-grown, with notes of olive and earth; 22 months in oak too long for the volume of primary fruit, but does have length. Screwcap. 14.2° alc. **Rating** 87 **To** 2014

John's Blend   ★★★★★

18 Neil Avenue, Nuriootpa, SA 5355 (postal) **Region** Langhorne Creek
T (08) 8562 1820 **F** (08) 8562 4050 www.johnsblend.com.au **Open** Not
Winemaker John Glaetzer **Est.** 1974 **Cases** 2500
John Glaetzer was Wolf Blass' right-hand man almost from the word go, the power behind the throne of the three Jimmy Watson trophies awarded to Wolf Blass Wines in 1974, '75 and '76, and a small matter of 11 Montgomery trophies for the Best Red Wine at the Adelaide Wine Show. This has always been a personal venture on the side, as it were, by John and wife Margarete Glaetzer, officially sanctioned of course, but really needing little marketing effort. Exports to the UK, the US and other major markets.

ŸŸŸŸŸ   **Margarete's Shiraz 2005** Rich, round and supple; while vanilla American oak is obvious, the barrel fermentation has ensured integration with the black fruits, dark chocolate and spice. Cork. 14.5° alc. **Rating** 94 **To** 2015 $35
Individual Selection Langhorne Creek Cabernet Sauvignon 2004 No. 31. Unsurprisingly, fruit, oak and tannins all seamlessly woven together on the medium- to full-bodied, vibrantly juicy palate; good length and aftertaste; 36 months in French and American oak. Cork. 14.5° alc. **Rating** 94 **To** 2017 $35

Johnston Oakbank   ★★★☆

18 Oakwood Road, Oakbank, SA 5243 **Region** Adelaide Hills
T (08) 8388 4263 **F** (08) 8388 4278 www.johnston-oakbank.com.au **Open** Mon–Fri 8–5
Winemaker David O'Leary (Contract), Geoff Johnston **Est.** 1843 **Cases** 5500
The origins of this business, owned by the Johnston Group, date back to 1839, making it the oldest family-owned business in SA. The vineyard at Oakbank is substantial, with 49 ha chardonnay, pinot noir, sauvignon blanc, shiraz, merlot and cabernet sauvignon.

ŸŸŸŸ   **Adelaide Hills Sauvignon Blanc 2007** A gentle gooseberry/tropical fruit mix on an even palate with good mouthfeel, albeit with the diminished fruit intensity of the vintage. Screwcap. 12° alc. **Rating** 89 **To** 2009 $17.95

Adelaide Hills Cabernet Sauvignon 2004 Briary, earthy, savoury, foresty notes amid black fruits; persistent tannins; overall, austere but in old-time classic mould. Screwcap. 14° alc. **Rating** 89 **To** 2012 $20

Christina Adelaide Hills Pinot Noir Chardonnay 2004 Good focus and intensity to the mix of citrus, stone fruit and strawberry flavours, with some nutty lees complexity; has length. Cork. 12.5° alc. **Rating** 89 **To** 2010 $24.95

Adelaide Hills Unwooded Chardonnay 2007 Has some finesse and a lively, brisk finish, with a touch of grapefruit along the way. Screwcap. 13° alc. **Rating** 87 **To** 2010 $17.95

Jones Road

133 Jones Road, Somerville, Vic 3912 (postal) **Region** Mornington Peninsula
T (03) 5977 7795 **F** (03) 5977 9695 **www.**jonesroad.com.au **Open** Not
Winemaker Sticks (Rob Dolan) **Est.** 1998 **Cases** 5000
It's a long story, but after establishing a very large and very successful herb-producing business in the UK, Rob Frewer and family migrated to Australia in 1997. By a circuitous route they ended up with a property on the Mornington Peninsula, promptly planting pinot noir and chardonnay, then pinot gris, sauvignon blanc and merlot, and have since leased another vineyard at Mt Eliza, and purchased Ermes Estate in 2007. Production is set to increase significantly from its already substantial level. Exports to the UK.

ΨΨΨΨΨ **Mornington Peninsula Chardonnay 2006** A complex style with lemon fruits, hints of toasty oak and a core of minerality; good texture and fresh acidity on the savoury, dry finish. Screwcap. 13.5° alc. **Rating** 91 **To** 2015 $22

ΨΨΨΨ **JR Jones Mornington Peninsula Chardonnay 2006** Good concentration, with grapefruit and melon on the bouquet; nutty complexity on the palate, and fine acidity and texture on the finish. Screwcap. 13.6° alc. **Rating** 89 **To** 2014 $18

Mornington Peninsula Sauvignon Blanc 2007 Dried grass aromas and good varietal intensity on the bouquet; good texture and weight, and quite racy on the finish. Screwcap. 12.5° alc. **Rating** 88 **To** 2009 $18

Mornington Peninsula Pinot Gris 2007 Ripe candied fruits on the bouquet; good flavour and weight; a very user-friendly style. Screwcap. 13.5° alc. **Rating** 87 **To** 2009 $22

Jones Winery & Vineyard

Jones Road, Rutherglen, Vic 3685 **Region** Rutherglen
T (02) 6032 8496 **F** (02) 6032 8495 **www.**joneswinery.com **Open** Mon, Tues, Fri 11–4, w'ends & public hols 10–5
Winemaker Mandy Jones **Est.** 1864 **Cases** 2000
Late in 1998 the winery was purchased from Les Jones by Leanne Schoen and Mandy and Arthur Jones (nieces and nephew of Les). The cellar door sales area is in a building from the 1860s, still with the original bark ceiling and walls made of handmade bricks fired onsite. Wines released under the Jones Winery & Vineyard label are estate-grown, while the Jones the Winemaker label sources grapes from local growers. Exports to Finland.

ΨΨΨΨΨ **LJ Rutherglen Shiraz 2005** Clear, bright colour; distinct touches of earth, spice and leather, but has an elegant drive to the palate unusual in the region. ProCork. 14.8° alc. **Rating** 92 **To** 2015 $45

ΨΨΨΨ **The Winemaker Chardonnay 2007** Apple, melon and grapefruit courtesy of Tumbarumba origin; restrained oak and grainy/minerally finish; not intense. Screwcap. 13.3° alc. **Rating** 89 **To** 2011 $25

The Winemaker Rutherglen Marsanne 2007 Delicate wine, with a mix of chalky and honeysuckle aromas and flavours; demands time in bottle and should richly reward. Screwcap. 12° alc. **Rating** 89 **To** 2015 $20

Rutherglen Shiraz 2005 While the junior brother to the LJ, it shares the same lightness of foot linked to the spicy savoury black fruits. ProCork. 14.8° alc. **Rating** 89 **To** 2012 $28

Josef Chromy Wines   ★★★★☆

370 Relbia Road, Relbia, Tas 7258 **Region** Northern Tasmania
T (03) 6335 8700 **F** (03) 6335 8777 www.josefchromy.com.au **Open** 7 days 10–5
Winemaker Jeremy Dineen **Est.** 2004 **Cases** 5500
Joe Chromy just refuses to lie down and admit the wine industry in Tasmania is akin to a
financial black hole. Since escaping from Czechoslovakia in 1950, establishing Blue Ribbon
Meats, using the proceeds of sale of his shares in that large company to buy Rochecombe and
Heemskerk Vineyards, then selling those and establishing Tamar Ridge before it, too, was sold,
Joe Chromy is at it again, this time investing $40 million in a wine-based but multifaceted
business. If this were not remarkable enough, Joe Chromy is in his late 70s, and spent much of
2006 recovering from a major stroke. Foundation of the new business was the purchase of the
large Old Stornoway Vineyard at a receivership sale in 2003; in all, there are 60 ha of 10-year-
old vines, the lion's share to pinot noir and chardonnay. He has retained Jeremy Dineen (for
many years winemaker at Hood/Wellington) as winemaker, the winery completed prior to
the '07 vintage. Chromy's grandson Dean Cocker is guiding the development of a restaurant,
function and equestrian centre, the latter on a scale sufficient to accommodate the Magic
Millions yearling sales.

ŶŶŶŶŶ **Sparkling 2004** Very lively and fresh, with excellent yeast autolysis giving a
creamy texture and fine mousse on the palate; lots of movement and drive through
to the finish. **Rating** 95 **To** 2012 $35

ŶŶŶŶŶ **Pinot Noir 2006** A wine with plenty of cherry and raspberry on both bouquet
and palate, yet retains eloquence and a supple texture. **Rating** 92 **To** 2012 $29
PEPIK Pinot Noir 2006 Has slightly more drive than the '05, with clearly
expressed varietal fruit on both bouquet and palate. Screwcap. **Rating** 91
To 2011 $19
Riesling 2007 Lime blossom, apple and mineral aromas and flavours; low alcohol
a real plus, accentuating the freshness and velocity in the mouth. Does need time,
however. Screwcap. 11° alc. **Rating** 90 **To** 2017 $25
Sauvignon Blanc 2007 Spotlessly clean; good varietal fruit with gooseberry,
lychee and herb flavours; long finish with typical Tasmanian acidity. Screwcap.
12.9° alc. **Rating** 90 **To** 2010 $24
Chardonnay 2006 A complex wine with abundant fruit and equally abundant
oak running through both the bouquet and palate. Screwcap. 13.9° alc. **Rating** 90
To 2013 $27
PEPIK Pinot Noir 2005 Fresh cherry and strawberry fruit; good texture and
structure, with minimal oak influence (9 months in old oak); 450 cases. Good
value. 13.9° alc. **Rating** 90 **To** 2010 $18

ŶŶŶŶ **Chardonnay 2004** Strong structure and flavour, with grapefruit, nectarine and
citrus, plus a lot of oak and acidity. Screwcap. 13.5° alc. **Rating** 89 **To** 2014 $26

Journeys End Vineyards   ★★★★★

248 Flinders Street, Adelaide, SA 5000 (postal) **Region** Southeast Australia
T 0431 709 305 www.journeysendvineyards.com.au **Open** Not
Winemaker Ben Riggs (Contract) **Est.** 2001 **Cases** 8000
A particularly interesting business in the virtual winery category, which, while focused on
McLaren Vale shiraz, also has contracts for other varieties in the Adelaide Hills and Langhorne
Creek. The shiraz comes in four levels, and, for good measure, uses five different clones of
shiraz to amplify the complexity that comes from having grapegrowers in many different parts
of McLaren Vale. Exports to the UK, the US and other major markets.

ŶŶŶŶŶ **Arrival McLaren Vale Shiraz 2005** Strongly regional and powerful, with a
seamless array of black fruits, dark chocolate, oak and ripe tannins. Five shiraz
clones. Cork. 14.5° alc. **Rating** 95 **To** 2025 $45
Ascent McLaren Vale Shiraz 2005 In similar style to Arrival, but slightly
less powerful; no bad thing perhaps; the components are still in balance. Cork.
14.5° alc. **Rating** 94 **To** 2020 $30

ΥΥΥΥΥ Embarkment Shiraz 2005 Ripest fruit flavours, bordering overripe, though not reflected in the alcohol; solid black fruits, dark chocolate and ripe tannins. Cork. 14.5° alc. **Rating** 92 **To** 2020 $22.50

ΥΥΥΥ **Three Brothers Reunited Shiraz 2006** Reflects the surplus grapes in a very good vintage; has good varietal flavour and depth, simply less oak than the Bobby Dazzler. Bargain by any standards. Screwcap. 14.5° alc. **Rating** 88 **To** 2012 $11
Bobby Dazzler Shiraz 2006 Has considerable flavour, no small part from American oak; easy access medium-bodied style, which does pick up nicely on the finish; more class than the label? Screwcap. 15° alc. **Rating** 88 **To** 2013 $16

Judds Warby Range Estate   ★★★

Jones Road, Taminick via Glenrowan, Vic 3675 **Region** Glenrowan
T (03) 5765 2314 **www**.warbyrange-estate.com.au **Open** 7 days 9–5
Winemaker Ralph Judd **Est.** 1989 **Cases** 500
Ralph and Margaret Judd began the development of their vineyard in 1989 as contract growers. They have gradually expanded the plantings to 4 ha of shiraz and 0.5 ha of durif; they also have 100 vines each of zinfandel, ruby cabernet, cabernet sauvignon, petit verdot, nebbiolo, tempranillo and sangiovese for evaluation. Until 1995, all the grapes were fermented and then sent by tanker to Southcorp, but in '96 the Judds made their first barrel of wine. They have now opened a small cellar door sales area. The wines are monumental in flavour and depth, in best Glenrowan tradition, and will richly repay extended cellaring.

ΥΥΥΥ Glenrowan Durif 2005 The colour is deeper than the Shiraz, and more within expectations; massive black fruits with concomitant savoury tannins, the components in balance. Screwcap. 13.5° alc. **Rating** 89 **To** 2020 $15

Juniper Estate

Harmans Road South, Cowaramup, WA 6284 **Region** Margaret River
T (08) 9755 9000 **F** (08) 9755 9100 **www**.juniperestate.com.au **Open** 7 days 10–5
Winemaker Mark Messenger **Est.** 1973 **Cases** 16 000
When Roger Hill and his wife purchased the Wrights vineyard in 1998, the 10-ha vineyard was already 25 years old, but in need of re-trellising and a certain amount of nursing to bring it back to health. All of that has happened, along with the planting of an additional 1.5 ha of shiraz and cabernet sauvignon. The Juniper Crossing wines use a mix of estate-grown and purchased grapes from other Margaret River vineyards. The Juniper Estate releases are made only from the 28-year-old estate plantings. In late 2006 the Hills purchased Higher Plane Wines, adding 14 ha of vineyard (planted 1997 and '04) together with the Higher Plane brand, and its own second label, South by Southwest. The Higher Plane label is sourced exclusively from the estate plantings (a mirror image of Juniper), the South by Southwest from contract growers. Exports to the UK, the US, Denmark, Indonesia and Taiwan.

ΥΥΥΥΥ Margaret River Shiraz 2005 Fresh, vibrant and quite spicy, with hints of clove supporting the ample red fruits; medium-bodied with lovely silky texture, finesse and focus. Screwcap. 14° alc. **Rating** 93 **To** 2014 $30
Juniper Crossing Margaret River Semillon Sauvignon Blanc 2007 Highly aromatic passionfruit, citrus, lychee and ripe apple aromas; a delicate but long palate; clean finish. Screwcap. 13° alc. **Rating** 92 **To** 2010 $18.95
Margaret River Chardonnay 2007 A harmonious wine from first sniff to finish and aftertaste, all the components precisely where they should be; has a polish to the mouthfeel and texture; long finish. Screwcap. **Rating** 92 **To** 2014 $32
Higher Plane Margaret River Cabernet Sauvignon 2004 Good hue; tightly focused blackcurrant and redcurrant fruit, with fine tannins woven throughout; well-balanced, good length. Screwcap. 13.5° alc. **Rating** 92 **To** 2015
Higher Plane Margaret River Chardonnay 2007 Light and refined compared to the normally richly textured wines of the region; brisk citrus and stone fruit flavours, good acidity and balanced oak. Will develop. Screwcap. 13.5° alc.
Rating 90 **To** 2013 $32

South by Southwest Margaret River Shiraz 2007 Attractive wine, co-fermentation with a little viognier brightening the colour and the spray of red and black fruits; good level of overall extract. Screwcap. 14° alc. **Rating** 90 To 2012 $22

ƤƤƤƤ **Margaret River Semillon 2006** A fine, approachable wine, with elements of cut grass and some juicy tropical fruits across the mid-palate. Screwcap. 12.5° alc. **Rating** 89 To 2009 $25

Margaret River Cabernet Sauvignon 2005 Vibrant colour; nice essency cabernet fruit, with a savoury black olive aspect in the background; quite fleshy, but a little short on the finish. Screwcap. 13.5° alc. **Rating** 89 To 2012 $39

Juniper Crossing Margaret River Geographe Chardonnay 2006 Quite ripe and brassy with grapefruit and elements of straw; quite fleshy on the mid-palate, but is essentially one-dimensional. Screwcap. 13.5° alc. **Rating** 88 To 2009 $22

Juniper Crossing Margaret River Rose 2007 The blend of Cabernet Sauvignon/Shiraz/Merlot works well; relatively intense and fruity, with a clean finish. Screwcap. 13.5° alc. **Rating** 88 To 2009 $18

South by Southwest Margaret River Cabernet Merlot 2006 Fresh red berry/cassis fruit is made more complex by unexpected fine, ripe tannins on the finish; at its best now. Screwcap. 13.5° alc. **Rating** 88 To 2010 $22

South by Southwest Margaret River Semillon Sauvignon Blanc 2007 Semillon (79%) drives the herbaceous aroma and flavour, also providing the backbone; a firm finish, and needing to soften. Screwcap. 13° alc. **Rating** 87 To 2012

Juniper Crossing Margaret River Shiraz 2005 Red fruits and honey/mead aromas; showing some development, but quite fleshy in a medium-bodied style. Screwcap. 13.5° alc. **Rating** 87 To 2009 $18

Just Red Wines ★★★☆

2370 Eukey Road, Ballandean, Qld 4382 **Region** Granite Belt
T (07) 4684 1322 **F** (07) 4684 1381 **www.**justred.com.au **Open** W'ends & public hols 10–5, or by appt
Winemaker Michael Hassall **Est.** 1998 **Cases** 1500
Tony, Julia and Michael Hassall have planted 2 ha of shiraz and 1 ha of merlot at an altitude of just under 900 m in the Granite Belt. They run the vineyard minimising the use of chemicals wherever possible, but do not hesitate to protect the grapes if weather conditions threaten an outbreak of mildew or botrytis. The Hassalls' daughter Nikki was very much involved in the creation of the vineyard, and was driving back from university to be there for the first day of picking. By the ultimate cruel finger of fate, the car crashed and she was killed. The Hassalls went on to pick the grapes 'with our hearts broken'; hopefully the quality of the wines has provided some solace.

ƤƤƤƤ **Granite Belt Merlot 2005** Light- to medium-bodied; clean, bright and fresh; uncomplicated, but has considerable charm in a clear varietal frame; excellent value. Screwcap. 12.5° alc. **Rating** 89 To 2009 $13.95

Nikki's Vineyard Granite Belt Syrah 2005 The style is similar to Daily Red, but with a little more cherry and mint fruit; well made, not over-extracted. Screwcap. 12.5° alc. **Rating** 89 To 2012 $19.95

Daily Red Granite Belt Shiraz 2005 Light-bodied, fresh and lively; does show low alcohol, but isn't green; best served slightly chilled in summer. Screwcap. 12.5° alc. **Rating** 87 To 2009 $11.95

K1 by Geoff Hardy

Tynan Road, Kuitpo, SA 5172 **Region** Adelaide Hills
T (08) 8388 3700 **F** (08) 8388 3564 **www.**k1.com.au **Open** W'ends & public hols 11–5
Winemaker Geoff Hardy, Ben Riggs **Est.** 1980 **Cases** 3500

The ultra-cool Kuitpo vineyard in the Adelaide Hills was begun in 1987 and now supplies leading makers such as Foster's and Petaluma. Geoff Hardy wines come from 20 ha of vines, with a large percentage of the grape production being sold to other makers. The premium K1 range is impressive in both quality and value. Exports to the UK, the US and other major markets.

ŦŦŦŦŦ **Adelaide Hills Shiraz 2006** Crimson; an intriguing mix of spice and chocolate overtones to the blackberry fruits, one foot in the Adelaide Hills, one in McLaren Vale; overall, has excellent mouthfeel and length, ripe tannins and oak supporting the fruit. Outstanding value. Screwcap. 14.5° alc. **Rating** 95 **To** 2021 $28
Adelaide Hills Cabernet Sauvignon 2006 Strong crimson-red, deep but bright; high quality wine, right in the mainstream of classic cabernet flavour profile, and with the structure and length to boot. ProCork. 14.5° alc. **Rating** 94 **To** 2020 $28
Tzimmukin 2005 Good colour; as might be expected from air-dried raisined grapes used variously by the Greeks and two centuries later the Italians, has a core of ripe fruit flavours but is not jammy or hot; nice spicy components. The bottle is almost as big as an amphora, the cork stained. 15° alc. **Rating** 94 **To** 2015 $75

ŦŦŦŦ♀ **Handcrafted Shiraz Viognier 2005** Complex licorice and leather overtones to spicy black fruits, partly the interaction with viognier; a substantial but juicy palate (definitely viognier) and subtle tannins. Screwcap. 14° alc. **Rating** 92 **To** 2011 $18
Adelaide Hills Sauvignon Blanc 2007 Clean, crisp and correct in both varietal and regional terms; a delicate mix of gooseberry and citrus; bright finish. Screwcap. 13° alc. **Rating** 91 **To** 2009 $20
Silver Label Shiraz Viognier 2006 Plenty of bang for the buck with this brightly red fruit-flavoured wine, fine but persistent tannins extending the palate neatly. Screwcap. 14.5° alc. **Rating** 90 **To** 2013 $18

ŦŦŦŦ **Adelaide Hills Chardonnay 2006** Melon and stone fruit, with nutty oak and some creamy nuances. Screwcap. 13° alc. **Rating** 89 **To** 2010 $28
Adelaide Hills Merlot 2005 One of those wannabe cabernet styles, replete with blackcurrant fruit and strong tannin support; this is a good medium- to full-bodied dry red, not a good merlot. Screwcap. 14.5° alc. **Rating** 88 **To** 2015 $28
Silver Label Cabernet Tempranillo 2005 More savoury than fruity, the cabernet rather than the tempranillo driving the agenda; needs a year or two. Screwcap. 14.5° alc. **Rating** 87 **To** 2011 $18

Kabminye Wines ★★★★

Krondorf Road, Tanunda, SA 5352 **Region** Barossa Valley
T (08) 8563 0889 **F** (08) 8563 3828 **www**.kabminye.com **Open** 7 days 11–5
Winemaker Rick Glastonbury **Est.** 2001 **Cases** 3500
Richard and Ingrid Glastonbury's cellar door is on land settled in the 1880s by Ingrid's ancestor Johann Christian Henschke. Kabminye is an Aboriginal word meaning 'morning star', and was given to the hamlet of Krondorf as a result of the anti-German sentiment during the Second World War (since changed back to the original Krondorf). The cellar door and café opened in 2003; SA Tourism has since used the building as a sustainable tourism case study. Rick makes the wines using 100% Barossa fruit, and has planted some unusual grape varieties, including kerner, clairette, zinfandel and pinot blanc. Exports to the UK and Malaysia.

ŦŦŦŦ♀ **Zinfandel 2006** Light, bright colour; has varietal character in a red cherry/ morello cherry/red plum/raspberry spectrum; minimal tannins, and the oak not overdone. Screwcap. 16° alc. **Rating** 93 **To** 2012 $35
Kahl Vineyard Shiraz 2005 Deep colour; more richness and weight than Barritt, and one of those curious instances where the alcohol does not unduly sweeten the palate or heat the finish. Screwcap. 16° alc. **Rating** 91 **To** 2015 $28
Barritt Vineyard Shiraz 2005 Medium-bodied; attractive fragrant savoury/spicy overtones to the blackberry fruits, and an overall degree of elegance; patience not required. Screwcap. 14° alc. **Rating** 90 **To** 2011 $25

ŢŢŢŢ **Schliebs Block 2005** Spicy, chocolatey mocha overtones to the fruit; fine tannins and good length. Screwcap. 14° alc. **Rating** 89 **To** 2015 $27.50
Hubert Barossa Valley Shiraz 2003 Full-flavoured plummy fruit, but has those slightly decadent/confiture characters of the '03 vintage, even though the alcohol is restrained. Cork. 14.5° alc. **Rating** 88 **To** 2012 $33.75
Barossa Valley Cabernet Sauvignon 2005 While a little sweet, does have clear cassis/blackcurrant varietal fruit, tannins in support; it's just that cabernet and Barossa Valley only combine to produce top cabernet every few years. Screwcap. 14° alc. **Rating** 88 **To** 2015 $27

Kaesler Wines   ★★★★★

Barossa Valley Way, Nuriootpa, SA 5355 **Region** Barossa Valley
T (08) 8562 4488 **F** (08) 8562 4499 **www.**kaesler.com.au **Open** Mon–Sat 10–5, Sun & public hols 11.30–4
Winemaker Reid Bosward **Est.** 1990 **Cases** 22 000
The Kaesler name dates back to 1845, when the first members of the family settled in the Barossa Valley. The Kaesler vineyards date back to 1893, but the Kaesler ownership ended in 1968. After several changes, the present (much-expanded) Kaesler Wines was acquired by a Swiss banking family in conjunction with former Flying Winemaker Reid Bosward and wife Bindy. Bosward's experience shows through in the wines, which now come from 37 ha of estate vineyards, two-thirds adjacent to the winery, and one-third in the Marananga area. The latter includes shiraz planted in 1899, with both blocks seeing plantings in the 1930s, '60s, then each decade through to the present. Exports to all major markets.

ŢŢŢŢŢ **Old Vine Barossa Valley Shiraz 2006** Great colour; incredible depth of fruit, blackberry, mocha, plum and spicy oak; the palate is massively proportioned, but belies the 16° alcohol, with a fresh, vibrant and focused finish. Not for the faint of heart. Cork. **Rating** 95 **To** 2025 $60
Alte Reben 2006 Incredibly deep colour; plenty of oak, with exceptional fruit concentration; layers of flavour, with lots of everything: tannins, fruit, oak and more. A monster! Shiraz. Cork. 16° alc. **Rating** 94 **To** 2030 $120
The Bogan 2006 Another full-bodied wine, but again the quality of the fruit and the concentration is beyond question; the flavour is quite astounding and persistent, driven by alcohol. Shiraz. Cork. 16° alc. **Rating** 94 **To** 2020 $50
WOMS Shiraz Cabernet 2006 A deep and dark full-bodied combination of cassis and blackberry; super-ripe and very rich, with plenty of oak; exceptional and amazing concentration; the acid on the finish is vibrant and fresh. Cork. 15.5° alc. **Rating** 94 **To** 2020 $70

ŢŢŢŢŢ **Old Vine Barossa Valley Semillon 2006** The new Barossa style of semillon with finesse and grace; still very pale in colour, and likewise fresh and delicate grass and lemon flavours. Sure to develop. Screwcap. 12° alc. **Rating** 93 **To** 2020 $17
Barossa Valley Cabernet Sauvignon 2006 A rich, voluptuous medium- to full-bodied wine saying more about the region and the high quality vintage than the variety, but the French oak is well-handled. Cork. 15° alc. **Rating** 92 **To** 2015 $25
Patel 2006 A wine of epic proportions, with a hint of mint in evidence; coats the palate and does not let go without a struggle, but the quality of the fruit is beyond question. A matter of balance? Cork. 16° alc. **Rating** 91 **To** 2025 $120
Stonehorse Barossa Valley Grenache Shiraz Mourvedre 2006 Almost entirely fruit-driven, with a supple and synergistic blend of the varieties, each contributing its part to the palate. Screwcap. 15.5° alc. **Rating** 90 **To** 2011 $18

ŢŢŢŢ **Avignon 2006** Bright fruits but a little green on the bouquet; firm and tannic on the palate, this wine has plenty of flavour and grip. Grenache/Shiraz/Mourvedre. Cork. 16° alc. **Rating** 89 **To** 2015 $30

Kalari Wines

120 Carro Park Road, Cowra, NSW 2794 **Region** Cowra
T (02) 6342 1465 **F** (02) 6342 1465 www.kalariwines.com.au **Open** Fri–Mon &
public hols 10–5
Winemaker Madrez Wine Services (Chris Derrez) **Est.** 1995 **Cases** NA
The name Kalari was that given by the Wiradjuri people for the nearby Lachlan River before
white settlement. The family-owned vineyard saw chardonnay, verdelho and shiraz planted
in 1995, followed by cabernet sauvignon, merlot and semillon in '97, with a total of 14 ha
planted. Unusually, Kalari produces four different styles of wine from verdelho: a light, dry
wine; a semi-sweet table wine; Fortello, the first fortified wine from the region; and, most
recently, a dessert wine (Semillon/Verdelho).

ΨΨΨΨ   **Cowra Verdelho 2006** An extra 12 months in bottle has helped build some
interest on the palate; fruit salad and ripe pear flavours; good balance. Diam. 13° alc.
Rating 88 **To** 2010 $15
Cowra Late Picked Verdelho 2006 Well made, with good acidity to balance
the slightly sweet fruit; just rather simple. Diam. 12.5° alc. **Rating** 87 **To** 2010 $15

Kalgan River Wines

PO Box 5559, Albany, WA 6332 **Region** Albany
T (08) 9841 4413 **F** (08) 9841 6471 www.kalganriverwines.com.au **Open** Not
Winemaker Garlands (Mike Garland) **Est.** 2000 **Cases** 2300
John and Dianne Ciprian have brought different backgrounds to their substantial Kalgan
River property. John is a descendent of two generations of grapegrowers, grandfather on the
Dalmatian Coast of the Adriatic, and father in the Swan Valley. However, it was his success as
a jeweller that provided the wherewithal for Kalgan River; Dianne started as a mathematics
teacher, and then became a jewellery valuer, both occupations requiring intellectual rigour.
Thanks to what they describe as 'hard yakka', they have established 20 ha of shiraz, cabernet
sauvignon, riesling, chardonnay and viognier.

ΨΨΨΨΨ   **Great Southern Riesling 2007** Above-average depth of flavour; rich, soft
tropical fruit with good overall flavour, but early developing. Screwcap. 12.7° alc.
Rating 90 **To** 2010 $19.95

ΨΨΨΨ   **Great Southern Chardonnay 2006** Nicely made; good balance of nectarine
and citrus fruit and oak; carries its alcohol with ease. Screwcap. 14.5° alc. **Rating**
89 **To** 2011 $24.95
Great Southern Riesling 2006 A clean bouquet leads into a palate with a firm,
minerally profile, and slatey finish; needs just a little more flesh. Screwcap. 12.7° alc.
Rating 88 **To** 2010 $19.95

Kalleske

Vinegrove Road, Greenock, SA 5360 **Region** Barossa Valley
T 0403 811 433 **F** (08) 8562 8118 www.kalleske.com **Open** Not
Winemaker Troy Kalleske **Est.** 1999 **Cases** 7000
The Kalleske family has been growing and selling grapes on a mixed farming property at
Greenock for over 100 years. Fifth-generation John and Lorraine Kalleske embarked on a
trial vintage for a fraction of the grapes in 1999. It was an immediate success, and led to the
construction of a small winery with son Troy Kalleske as winemaker. The vineyards, with
an average age of 50 years, see no chemical fertilisers or pesticides; some blocks are certified
organic. The density of the flavour of the Shiraz and Grenache is awesome. Pirathon is the
first wine to come from other growers, hence Pirathon Shiraz by Kalleske. Exports to all
major markets.

ΨΨΨΨΨ   **Johann Georg Old Vine Barossa Valley Shiraz 2005** Despite the alcohol,
only medium-bodied; has that 100+-year-old vine stamp; deceptively moderate
weight, yet a great array of licorice, blackberry and black cherry fruit; harmonious
oak. Vines planted 1875. Cork. 15.5° alc. **Rating** 95 **To** 2025 $100

Pirathon by Kalleske Barossa Valley Shiraz 2005 A wonderfully complex wine that lives up to its War & Peace back label description of the vineyard sources and winemaking techniques; luscious, velvety, sweet black fruits, chocolate and mocha; plush tannins; great value. Cork. 15° alc. **Rating** 95 **To** 2015 $23
Greenock Barossa Valley Shiraz 2006 Deep magenta; deep fruited with great concentration and red and black fruits in abundance; hints of spice and a core of bright fruits lead to a long, full and harmonious finish. Cork. 15.5° alc. **Rating** 94 **To** 2018 $40

ΨΨΨΨΨ **JMK Barossa Valley Shiraz VP (375 ml) 2005** A stylish fortified wine, with quality spirit; spicy black fruits, licorice and plum, the relatively low baume a distinct plus. Will mature quickly in its small, uniquely shaped bottle. Cork. 18° alc. **Rating** 92 **To** 2015 $24
Old Vine Barossa Valley Grenache 2005 A supple, light- to medium-bodied mix of the sweet and more savoury sides of grenache; next to no tannins, but good mouthfeel and length. Cork. 15.5° alc. **Rating** 91 **To** 2012 $45
Clarry's Barossa Valley Red 2006 Good colour; great wine at the price; super-abundant blackberry, licorice and cherry fruit supported by soft tannins and incidental oak. Estate-grown Grenache (65%)/Shiraz (35%). Screwcap. 14° alc. **Rating** 91 **To** 2011 $19

ΨΨΨΨ **Clarry's Semillon Chenin Blanc 2007** Clean, bright and fresh; definitely the modern style of Barossa Valley winemaking for varieties other than riesling; does diminish slightly on the finish. Screwcap. 12° alc. **Rating** 88 **To** 2009 $15

Kamberra

Cnr Northbourne Avenue/Flemington Road, Lyneham, ACT 2602 **Region** Canberra District
T (02) 6262 2333 **F** (02) 6262 2300 **www**.kamberra.com.au **Open** 7 days 10–5
Winemaker Alex McKay **Est.** 2000 **Cases** 18 000
Kamberra was part of the Hardys group, established in 2000 with the planting of 40 ha of vines and a winery in the ACT, only a few hundred metres from the showground facilities where the National Wine Show is held every year. Riesling and Shiraz are fully estate-grown, and most of the wines have a Kamberra component. In March '07 Kamberra was sold to a Canberra company, part of the Elvin Group, leaving the business intact. No samples received; the rating is that of last year.

Kangarilla Road Vineyard

Kangarilla Road, McLaren Vale, SA 5171 **Region** McLaren Vale
T (08) 8383 0533 **F** (08) 8383 0044 **www**.kangarillaroad.com.au **Open** Mon–Fri 9–5, w'ends 11–5
Winemaker Kevin O'Brien **Est.** 1997 **Cases** 40 000
Kangarilla Road was formerly known as Stevens Cambrai. Long-time industry identity Kevin O'Brien and wife Helen purchased the property in 1997, soon establishing the strikingly labelled Kangarilla Road brand. They have access to 14 ha of estate vineyards, intake supplemented by purchases from other vineyards in the region. Exports to the UK, the US and other major markets.

ΨΨΨΨΨ **McLaren Vale Cabernet Sauvignon 2006** Immediately proclaims its regional origin with dark chocolate overtones to quite luscious black and redcurrant fruit; lovely mouthfeel; great value. Screwcap. 14.5° alc. **Rating** 94 **To** 2018 $19

ΨΨΨΨΨ **McLaren Vale Shiraz 2006** Vibrant and full of juicy dark fruits, with a telltale sign of chocolate in the background; always terrific value. Screwcap. **Rating** 91 **To** 2012 $19
McLaren Vale Shiraz Viognier 2006 Dense chewy fruit, with a distinct floral lift from the viognier; fleshy, ample and fine on the finish. Screwcap. 15° alc. **Rating** 91 **To** 2014 $25

Kangderaar Vineyard

288 Wehla–Kingower Road, Rheola, Vic 3517 **Region** Bendigo
T (03) 5438 8292 **F** (03) 5438 8292 **Open** 7 days 10–5
Winemaker James Nealy **Est.** 1980 **Cases** 600
The 4.5-ha vineyard is near the Melville Caves, said to have been the hideout of the bushranger Captain Melville in the 1850s, and surrounded by the Kooyoora State Park. It is owned by James and Christine Nealy.

ΨΨΨΨ   **Riesling Traminer 2006** A surprise packet, achieving juicy citrussy flavours without a sweet finish; standout for Chinese food, low alcohol a plus. Screwcap. 11.4° alc. **Rating** 88 **To** 2009 $13
Cabernet 2005 Very rustic texture, but has a bottomless pit of blackcurrant and cassis fruit, and should settle down given time. Screwcap. 14° alc. **Rating** 87 **To** 2015 $20

Kara Kara Vineyard

99 Edelsten Road, St Arnaud, Vic 3478 **Region** Pyrenees
T (03) 5496 3294 **F** (03) 5496 3294 **www**.karakarawines.com.au **Open** Mon–Fri 10.30–6, w'ends 9–6
Winemaker Steve Zsigmond, Hanging Rock Winery **Est.** 1977 **Cases** 1000
Hungarian-born Steve Zsigmond comes from a long line of vignerons and sees Kara Kara as the eventual retirement occupation for himself and wife Marlene. He is a graduate of the Adelaide University (Roseworthy) wine marketing course, and worked for Yalumba and Negociants as a sales manager in Adelaide and Perth. He looks after sales and marketing from the Melbourne premises of Kara Kara, and the wine is made at Hanging Rock, with consistent results. Draws upon 9 ha of estate plantings.

ΨΨΨΨΨ   **Estate Pyrenees Shiraz 2005** Dense colour; intense and dense from go to whoa; dried prune, blackberry and licorice fruit, ample tannins and oak. Rape, not seduction, but patience should reward. Screwcap. 14.9° alc. **Rating** 91 **To** 2025 $35

ΨΨΨΨ   **Estate Pyrenees Rose 2007** A bone-dry, spicy, savoury style with some vague overtones of Southern Rhône Rose. Screwcap. 13° alc. **Rating** 87 **To** 2009 $18

Karatta Wine

43/22 Liberman Close, Adelaide, SA 5000 (postal) **Region** Robe
T (08) 8215 0250 **F** (08) 8215 0450 **www**.karattawines.com.au **Open** By appt (08) 8735 7255
Winemaker Patrick Tocaciu **Est.** 1994 **Cases** 1720
The vineyards include the former Anthony Dale vineyard, planted to 12 ha of shiraz, cabernet sauvignon, pinot noir, malbec and, more recently, sauvignon blanc and chardonnay. It is owned by Karatta Wine Company in association with the Tenison Vineyard. Since the change of ownership, the volume and weight of flavour in the wines has increased dramatically, due in part to low yields.

ΨΨΨΨ   **12 Mile Vineyard Robe Shiraz 2006** Deeply coloured, and packed full of dark fruits; fruitcake and chewy fruits; a bit heavy on the finish, but quite promising. Screwcap. 14.5° alc. **Rating** 89 **To** 2015 $18
12 Mile Vineyard Shiraz Cabernet Sauvignon 2006 An intriguing European feel to the fruit; the cassis comes to the fore, with a slightly savoury, black olive drying finish. Screwcap. 14.5° alc. **Rating** 89 **To** 2014 $18

Karina Vineyard ★★★★

35 Harrisons Road, Dromana, Vic 3936 **Region** Mornington Peninsula
T (03) 5981 0137 **F** (03) 5981 0137 **Open** W'ends 11–5, 7 days in January
Winemaker Gerard Terpstra **Est.** 1984 **Cases** 2000

A typical family-owned (Gerard and Joy Terpstra) Mornington Peninsula vineyard, situated in the Dromana/Red Hill area on rising, north-facing slopes, just 3 km from the shores of Port Phillip Bay, immaculately tended and with picturesque garden surrounds. Fragrant Riesling and cashew-accented Chardonnay are usually its best wines. Retail distribution in Victoria; exports to Canada and Japan.

ϙϙϙϙϙ **Terroir Mornington Peninsula Cabernet Merlot 2006** Great colour; cabernet fruit, with nice texture and weight; quite supple and juicy with fine acidity. Screwcap. 14° alc. **Rating** 90 **To** 2018 $25

Karra Yerta Wines ★★★★

Lot 534, Flaxman's Valley Road, Wilton, SA 5353 **Region** Eden Valley
T 0438 870 178 **www.**karrayertawines.com.au **Open** By appt
Winemaker James Linke, Peter Gajewski, Peter Schell **Est.** 2006 **Cases** 350
The name Karra Yerta is derived from the local Aboriginal language, 'karra' the name for the majestic red gum trees, and 'yerta' meaning country or ground. The landscape has changed little (other than the patches of vineyard) since the ancestors of James and Marie Linke arrived (separately) in SA in 1847. Both James and Marie were born in Angaston, but moved to the Flaxmans Valley in 1985, and in '87 purchased one of the old stone cottages in the region. Much time has been spent in reviving the vineyard, which provides most of their grapes; the 2 ha of riesling, shiraz and semillon had been largely abandoned. While most of the grapes were sold, they indulged in home winemaking for many years, but have now moved into commercial winemaking on a micro scale. Exports to the UK.

ϙϙϙϙϙ **Limited Release Eden Valley Riesling 2007** Pale straw-green; a gently perfumed bouquet leads into a light-bodied palate with apple and lime fruit, with a touch of minerality on the finish. A success for '07. Screwcap. 12° alc. **Rating** 90 **To** 2012 $25
Limited Release Barossa Shiraz 2005 Both oak and alcohol evident throughout, but so are the red and black fruits; needs time to come together. Screwcap. 14.6° alc. **Rating** 90 **To** 2015 $35
Bullfrog Flat Eden Valley Shiraz 2005 An aromatic, slightly minty bouquet, with good focus and a light floral background of red fruits; quite high levels of acid, works well with the fruit. Screwcap. 14.5° alc. **Rating** 90 **To** 2016 $30

Kassebaum Wines ★★★★☆

Nitschke Road, Marananga, SA 5355 **Region** Barossa Valley
T (08) 8562 2731 **F** (08) 8562 4751 **Open** By appt
Winemaker Rod Chapman (Contract) **Est.** 2003 **Cases** 400
David and Dianne Kassebaum are third-generation grapegrowers. David has been involved in the wine industry for 20 years, working first with Penfolds in bottling, microbiology and maturation laboratories, and most recently in the Vinpac International laboratory. They have 6.9 ha of shiraz on two separate vineyards, most of the production being sold. Yields vary from 1 to 1.5 tonnes per acre. The small amount of shiraz retained for the Kassebaum Magdalena label is matured in new French and American oak for 12 months. Exports to the US.

ϙϙϙϙϙ **Magdalena Barossa Valley Shiraz 2006** Dense colour; rich blackberry, plum and dark chocolate fruit; good oak support, and soft tannins. Cork. 15.9° alc. **Rating** 90 **To** 2014 $30

Katnook Estate

Riddoch Highway, Coonawarra, SA 5263 **Region** Coonawarra
T (08) 8737 2394 **F** (08) 8737 2397 **www.**katnookestate.com.au **Open** Mon–Sat 10–5, Sun 11–4
Winemaker Wayne Stehbens **Est.** 1979 **Cases** 125 000

One of the largest contract grapegrowers and suppliers in Coonawarra, selling more than half its grape production to others. The historic stone wool shed in which the second vintage in Coonawarra (1896) was made, and which has served Katnook since 1980, is being restored. The Odyssey Cabernet Sauvignon and Prodigy Shiraz are the icon duo at the top of a multi-tiered production. Freixenet, the Spanish Cava producer, owns 60% of the business. Exports to all major markets.

♀♀♀♀♀ **Prodigy Coonawarra Shiraz 2004** An aromatic, cedary, spicy bouquet, then an intense and long palate, showing extended maturation in French and American oak; typical Prodigy style. Cork. 14.5° alc. **Rating** 94 **To** 2024 $100

♀♀♀♀♀ **Founder's Block Shiraz 2005** Quite fragrant and spicy red and black fruits accompanied by some cedary/savoury/spicy notes on the palate; overall, an attractive light- to medium-bodied wine. Screwcap. 14° alc. **Rating** 92· **To** 2014 $19.99
Coonawarra Shiraz 2005 Lovely clean blackberry fruit, with just a little spice; good flavour, and sure oak treatment; bright fruit on the medium-bodied palate; long and fine finish. Cork. 14° alc. **Rating** 92 **To** 2018 $40
Coonawarra Merlot 2005 Medium-bodied, but has complex aromas, flavours and texture; redcurrant, plum, cedar and spice are all surrounded by gentle, soft tannins running through to the finish. Cork. 14.5° alc. **Rating** 92 **To** 2015 $40
Odyssey Coonawarra Cabernet Sauvignon 2003 Silky texture and sweet cabernet fruit, but submerged in oak after 38 months in new French and American barrels; 12 months less surely would have made a better and less expensive wine. Cork. 14.5° alc. **Rating** 91 **To** 2015 $100

♀♀♀♀ **Founder's Block Chardonnay 2005** Clean, well made and balanced; gentle stone fruit and equally gentle oak; easy style. Screwcap. 14.5° alc. **Rating** 89 **To** 2009 $19.99
Founder's Block Coonawarra Cabernet Sauvignon 2005 Cedary/spicy/earthy overtones to medium-bodied blackcurrant fruit; ripe but soft tannins. Screwcap. 14.5° alc. **Rating** 89 **To** 2011 $19.99
Founder's Block Coonawarra Sauvignon Blanc 2007 Has some varietal fragrance and fruit a mix of gentle tropical flavours and well-balanced acidity; better than many '07s. Screwcap. 13° alc. **Rating** 88 **To** 2009 $20
Coonawarra Sauvignon Blanc 2007 Not as ripe as other vintages, showing a little fresh-cut grass on the bouquet, and the tropical notes in the background. Screwcap. 13.5° alc. **Rating** 88 **To** 2009 $27
Riddoch Coonawarra Shiraz 2004 Retains good freshness and focus; likewise length and balance to the black cherry, plum and mulberry fruit. Screwcap. 13.5° alc. **Rating** 88 **To** 2012 $16.99
Riddoch Cabernet Shiraz 2004 Light- to medium-bodied; cedary/earthy/minty flavours; overall quite bright and fresh, if somewhat simple. Screwcap. 13.5° alc. **Rating** 87 **To** 2009 $16.99
Chardonnay Brut 2006 A good example of blanc de blanc style, with lots of citrus, and quite creamy mouthfeel; a little simple, but nice flavour. Cork. 12.5° alc. **Rating** 87 **To** 2011 $32

Kay Bros Amery   ★★★★★

Kay Road, McLaren Vale, SA 5171 **Region** McLaren Vale
T (08) 8323 8211 **F** (08) 8323 9199 **www**.kaybrothersamerywines.com **Open** Mon–Fri 9–5, w'ends & public hols 12–5
Winemaker Colin Kay **Est.** 1890 **Cases** 14 000
A traditional winery with a rich history and nearly 20 ha of priceless old vines; while the white wines have been variable, the red wines and fortified wines can be very good. Of particular interest is Block 6 Shiraz, made from 100-year-old vines; both vines and wines are going from strength to strength. Exports to the UK, the US and other major markets.

ŢŢŢŢŢ **Hillside Shiraz 2004** Bright red and dark fruits on the bouquet, with a little savoury edge of dried leather and spice; the finish is long, pure and even. Screwcap. 14.5° alc. **Rating** 94 **To** 2018 $40
Hillside Shiraz 2005 Bright red fruits, particularly fresh and vibrant on the bouquet; deeply fruited and long, with fresh acidity on the finish. Screwcap. 15.5° alc. **Rating** 94 **To** 2020 $40

ŢŢŢŢŢ **Block 6 Shiraz 2005** Big, rich and ripe, but not a hint of shrivel; full-bodied with plenty of oak to go with the mocha, fruitcake and intense varietal shiraz. Screwcap. 16° alc. **Rating** 92 **To** 2020 $50
McLaren Vale Cabernet Sauvignon 2004 Ripe varietal cabernet fruit aromas, with essency cassis and a little cedar; plenty of concentration on the fine, full and quite supple palate. Screwcap. 14° alc. **Rating** 92 **To** 2014 $22

ŢŢŢŢ **McLaren Vale Shiraz 2005** Good fruit weight and depth. Plenty of tannin and certainly very ripe. Screwcap. 15.5° alc. **Rating** 89 **To** 2016 $22
McLaren Vale Shiraz 2004 Good bouquet and plenty of flavour, with typical chocolate and fruitcake fruits on the palate; a touch blocky and one-dimensional. Screwcap. 14° alc. **Rating** 89 **To** 2018 $22
McLaren Vale Merlot 2005 Plenty of bright red fruits on the bouquet, with good concentration and plenty of flavour at the finish; a little one-dimensional. Screwcap. 15.5° alc. **Rating** 88 **To** 2012 $22

Keith Tulloch Wine

Hunter Ridge Winery, Hermitage Road, Pokolbin, NSW 2320 **Region** Lower Hunter Valley
T (02) 4998 7500 **F** (02) 4998 7211 www.keithtullochwine.com.au **Open** Wed–Sun 10–4, or by appt
Winemaker Keith Tulloch **Est.** 1997 **Cases** 11 500
Keith Tulloch is, of course, a member of the Tulloch family, which has played such a lead role in the Hunter Valley for over a century. Formerly a winemaker at Lindemans and then Rothbury Estate, he has developed his own label since 1997. There is the same almost obsessive attention to detail, the same almost ascetic intellectual approach, the same refusal to accept anything but the best as that of Jeffrey Grosset. Exports to the UK, the US, Canada, Sweden and Singapore.

ŢŢŢŢŢ **Hunter Valley Semillon 2007** Pure Hunter, with good concentration and an abundance of tightly wound lemon fruit; will go the distance. Screwcap. 11° alc. **Rating** 94 **To** 2020 $26
Kester Hunter Valley Shiraz 2005 Has much greater weight and complexity than the '05 Shiraz Viognier; a layered texture, with earth and spice nuances to the core of black fruits; persistent but fine tannins, and positive oak contribution. Screwcap. 14.5° alc. **Rating** 94 **To** 2020 $50
Hunter Valley Botrytis Semillon 2006 Cleverly crafted, with good levels of botrytis showing as crème brulee and hints of fresh apricots; quite sweet, but well-balanced acidity. Screwcap. 11.5° alc. **Rating** 94 **To** 2016 $35

ŢŢŢŢŢ **Hunter Valley Chardonnay 2007** Tight citrus and stone fruit, with fresh racy acidity on the palate; very long and very fine. Screwcap. 13° alc. **Rating** 93 **To** 2014 $26

Kellybrook

Fulford Road, Wonga Park, Vic 3115 **Region** Yarra Valley
T (03) 9722 1304 **F** (03) 9722 2092 www.kellybrookwinery.com.au **Open** Mon 11–5, Tues–Sat 10–5, Sun 11–5
Winemaker Philip Kelly, Darren Kelly **Est.** 1960 **Cases** 3000
The 8.5-ha vineyard is at Wonga Park, one of the gateways to the Yarra Valley, and has a picnic area and a full-scale restaurant. A very competent producer of both cider and apple

brandy (in Calvados style) as well as table wine. When it received its winery licence in 1960, it became the first winery in the Yarra Valley to open its doors in the 20th century, a distinction often ignored or forgotten (by this author as well as others). Exports to the UK and Denmark.

ŸŸŸŸŸ **Yarra Valley Shiraz 2006** Excellent cool-grown shiraz; predominantly spiced red fruits on a long, silky palate; good acidity and a fresh finish. Diam. 13.5° alc. **Rating** 94 **To** 2016 $27

ŸŸŸŸ **Pinot Noir Chardonnay Brut 2005** Well made; nicely balanced strawberry and stone fruit flavours; good length and a pleasingly dry finish. Cork. 12.6° alc. **Rating** 89 **To** 2011 $30
Yarra Valley Riesling 2006 An array of juicy fruit flavours ranging from citrus to tropical to stone fruit; accessible now. Screwcap. 12° alc. **Rating** 88 **To** 2011 $19
Yarra Valley Chardonnay 2006 Some funky fruit aromas, possibly partly ex oak; brisk, bright, citrus flavours, verging on green; interesting low alcohol style. Screwcap. 12° alc. **Rating** 87 **To** 2011 $24

Kelman Vineyards   ★★★

Cnr Oakey Creek Road/Mount View Road, Pokolbin, NSW 2320 **Region** Lower Hunter Valley
T (02) 4991 5456 **F** (02) 4991 7555 **www.**kelmanwines.com.au **Open** 7 days 10–4.30
Winemaker Tower Estate **Est.** 1999 **Cases** 3000
Kelman Vineyards is a California-type development on the outskirts of Cessnock. A 40-ha property has been subdivided into 80 residential development lots, but with 9 ha of vines wending between the lots, which are under common ownership. Part of the chardonnay has already been grafted across to shiraz before coming into full production, and the vineyard has the potential to produce 8000 cases a year. In the meantime, each owner receives 12 cases of wine a year.

Kelvedon   ★★★★

PO Box 126, Swansea, Tas 7190 **Region** Southern Tasmania
T (03) 6257 8283 **F** (03) 6257 8179 **Open** Not
Winemaker Winemaking Tasmania (Julian Alcorso) **Est.** 1998 **Cases** 550
Jack and Gill Cotton began the development of Kelvedon by planting 1 ha of pinot noir in 1998. The plantings were extended in 2000/01 by an additional 5 ha, half to pinot noir and half to chardonnay; the production from this is under contract to Hardys. The Pinot Noir can be of excellent quality.

ŸŸŸŸŶ **Pinot Noir 2006** An elegant style, with good focus and length to the clear-cut cherry and plum fruit on the fore-palate, but finishing with that slightly green/tangy acidity of '06. Screwcap. 13.5° alc. **Rating** 92 **To** 2013 $26

Kersbrook Hill   ★★★★

Lot 102, Bagshaw Road, Kersbrook, SA 5231 **Region** Adelaide Hills
T 0419 570 005 **www.**kersbrookhill.com.au **Open** By appt
Winemaker Ben Jeanneret **Est.** 1998 **Cases** 1500
Paul Clark purchased what is now the Kersbrook Hill property, then grazing land, in 1997, planting 0.4 ha of shiraz on a reality check basis. Encouraged by the results, two years later he lifted the plantings to 3 ha of shiraz and 1 ha of riesling. Mark Whisson is consultant viticulturist (Whisson has been growing grapes in the Adelaide Hills for 20 years) and Ben Jeanneret was chosen as winemaker because of his experience with riesling. Exports to the US, China, Hong Kong and NZ.

ŸŸŸŸŶ **Adelaide Hills Riesling 2007** A tangy, almost tropical wine; quite precise, but lacks depth on the finish; a very pleasant flavour profile though. Screwcap. 12.5° alc. **Rating** 93 **To** 2015 $27

Adelaide Hills Shiraz 2006 Distinctive cool-grown licorice and spice elements to the black fruits; attractive thrust and extension to the back-palate and finish. Screwcap. **Rating** 91 **To** 2016 $28

Kidman Coonawarra Wines

66 Sydenham Road, Norwood, SA 5067 (postal) **Region** Coonawarra
T 0417 800 035 **F** (08) 8363 3242 **www**.kcwines.com.au **Open** Not
Winemaker Peter Douglas (Contract) **Est.** 2003 **Cases** 4000
Branches of the Kidman family have been part of Coonawarra viticulture since 1970, and long before that one of the great names in the Australian cattle industry. Tim, Philip and Mardi Kidman (brothers and sister) run a separate business to that of cousin Sid Kidman, with 40.2 ha of cabernet sauvignon, 14.3 ha of shiraz, 1.5 ha of merlot and 1 ha of viognier, planting the first 2 ha of shiraz in 1970, and moving into wine production in 2003, albeit still selling the major part of the grape production. The first wine (a Cabernet Sauvignon) was made in 2004, labelled Roy the Cattleman, a tribute to their paternal grandfather who worked as a stockman for his uncle Sir Sidney Kidman. Other labels of Cabernet Sauvignon and Viognier have since followed.

🍷🍷🍷🍷🍷 **Roy the Cattleman Cabernet Sauvignon 2004** Ripe, vibrant and full of very precise cassis fruit, with good concentration and nice depth to the long, even and lively finish. Screwcap. 13.6° alc. **Rating** 92 **To** 2016 $38
Wombat Dig Cabernet Sauvignon 2005 Lovely fine and focused cabernet fruit; super-bright on the palate, and really fresh on the finish. Screwcap. 13.4° alc. **Rating** 92 **To** 2014 $19
Adelaide Hills Sauvignon Blanc 2007 Attractive wine, with some of the passionfruit missing from so many in this vintage; gentle, well-balanced and totally enjoyable. Screwcap. 13° alc. **Rating** 90 **To** 2009 $18

🍷🍷🍷🍷 **Shiraz 2004** Attractive light- to medium-bodied wine with blackberry, cherry and plum fruit, fine, spicy tannins, and a splash of vanillin oak. ProCork. 14° alc. **Rating** 89 **To** 2012 $18
Cabernet Sauvignon 2004 Has good depth of flavour to the blackcurrant and cassis fruit, in turn typical of good Coonawarra cabernet; no frills, perhaps, but doesn't need them. Cork. 14° alc. **Rating** 89 **To** 2014 $20

Kies Family Wines

Barossa Valley Way, Lyndoch, SA 5381 **Region** Barossa Valley
T (08) 8524 4110 **F** (08) 8524 4544 **www**.kieswines.com.au **Open** 7 days 9.30–4.30
Winemaker Wine Wise Consultancy **Est.** 1969 **Cases** 3000
The Kies family has been resident in the Barossa Valley since 1857, with the present generation of winemakers being the fifth, their children the sixth. Until 1969 the family sold almost all the grapes to others, but in that year they launched their own brand, Karrawirra. The coexistence of Killawarra forced a name change in 1983 to Redgum Vineyard; this business was subsequently sold. Later still, Kies Family Wines opened for business, drawing upon vineyards (up to 100 years old) that had remained in the family throughout the changes, offering a wide range of wines through the 1880 cellar door. The absence of tasting notes is due to a system failure at my end; wines were submitted before the deadline. Exports to the UK, China, Singapore and Japan.

Kilgour Estate

85 McAdams Lane, Bellarine, Vic 3223 **Region** Geelong
T (03) 5251 2223 **F** (03) 5251 2223 **www**.kilgourestate.com.au **Open** Tues–Sun 10.30–6, 7 days in Jan
Winemaker Alister Timms **Est.** 1989 **Cases** 3500
Kilgour Estate is a family-owned venture, with just over 10 ha of vines. The beautifully situated cellar door has a restaurant and barbecue facilities. The consistency of the quality of the large portfolio of wines is commendable.

ȲȲȲȲȲ **Bellarine Peninsula Cabernet Sauvignon 2005** Medium-bodied and elegant; blackcurrant, cassis and an unusual hint of citrus on the long, fruit-driven palate; fine tannins and controlled oak. Diam. 13.8° alc. **Rating** 90 **To** 2018 $25

ȲȲȲȲ **Oaked Bellarine Peninsula Chardonnay 2006** Stone fruit and citrus aromas and flavours, French oak present, but not dominant; good length. Diam. 13.3° alc. **Rating** 89 **To** 2012 $35

Shiraz 2005 Light- to medium-bodied; fresh red and black cherry fruit, spice and a hint of licorice; lively and fresh; fine-grained tannins. Diam. 13.8° alc. **Rating** 89 **To** 2015 $25

Methode Traditionale Pinot Noir 2005 Pale pink-salmon; citrus-tinged strawberry fruit, then a surprisingly firm and dry finish. Cork. 12.5° alc. **Rating** 87 **To** 2010 $30

Kilikanoon   ★★★★★

Penna Lane, Penwortham, SA 5453 **Region** Clare Valley
T (08) 8843 4377 **F** (08) 8843 4246 **www**.kilikanoon.com.au **Open** Thurs–Sun & public hols 11–5, or by appt
Winemaker Kevin Mitchell **Est.** 1997 **Cases** 40 000
Kilikanoon has over 300 ha of vineyards, predominantly in the Clare Valley, but spreading to all regions around Adelaide and the Barossa Valley. It had the once-in-a-lifetime experience of winning five of the six trophies awarded at the Clare Valley Wine Show '02, spanning Riesling, Shiraz and Cabernet, and including Best Wine of Show. In August 2007 it purchased the iconic Seppeltsfield in the Barossa Valley (see separate entry). Exports to all major markets.

ȲȲȲȲȲ **Oracle Clare Valley Shiraz 2005** A powerful, concentrated wine reflecting all the vineyard and winery inputs; focused and rich, retaining supple mouthfeel and good balance. Low yield, French oak, no filtration. Cork. 15° alc. **Rating** 95 **To** 2020 $79

Parable McLaren Vale Shiraz 2005 Immediately proclaims its region of origin; dark chocolate, mocha and black fruits coalesce with tannins and oak; long finish. Screwcap. 15° alc. **Rating** 95 **To** 2020 $40

M McLaren Vale Shiraz 2005 Dense crimson; extremely powerful, dense and rich, sumptuous rather than aggressive; dark chocolate comes through strongly, and the wine has a certain finesse on the finish. Cork. 15° alc. **Rating** 95 **To** 2016 $79

Covenant Clare Valley Shiraz 2005 Rich and luscious, as much Barossa in style as Clare Valley, the fruit flavours almost juicy; controlled oak and fine tannins. Screwcap. 15° alc. **Rating** 94 **To** 2025 $40

Greens Vineyard Barossa Valley Shiraz 2005 As ever, deeply coloured; spicy/earthy nuances to go with the black fruits of the palate, where tannins distinguish a very good wine, with considerable length and balance. Cork. 15° alc. **Rating** 94 **To** 2015 $79

Blocks Road Clare Valley Cabernet Sauvignon 2005 A generously ripe blackcurrant and dark chocolate fruit melange; good supporting oak and tannins; quality in vineyard and winery inputs. Screwcap. 14.5° alc. **Rating** 94 **To** 2015 $30

ȲȲȲȲȲ **Baroota Reserve Southern Flinders Shiraz 2005** Has that richness and density that Kilikanoon achieves with all its reds; lush plum, prune and blackberry; good oak and tannin management. Cork. 15° alc. **Rating** 93 **To** 2015 $30

The Duke Clare Valley Grenache 2005 Certainly has far more weight and structure than any other Clare Valley grenache, the rich raspberry, rhubarb and cherry fruit a coherent whole. Cork. 15° alc. **Rating** 93 **To** 2012 $69

Mort's Block Riesling 2007 Stacked to the gills with citrus-based aromas and flavours; deep palate, and good length, though less finesse. Screwcap. 12.5° alc. **Rating** 92 **To** 2017 $20

Testament Barossa Valley Shiraz 2005 A generous, full-bodied palate; the flavours reflect the alcohol, but there is no excessive heat, with a mix of spice, vanilla and blackberry; soft tannins. Screwcap. 15° alc. **Rating** 92 **To** 2021 $40

Mort's Reserve Watervale Riesling 2007 Opens quietly on the bouquet, then progressively builds through the length of the palate and finish, with strong citrus and punchy acidity. Screwcap. 12.5° alc. **Rating** 91 **To** 2017 $30

Killerman's Run Shiraz 2006 Medium-bodied, with all the components in balance; ripe plum fruit, with a dab of dark chocolate; oak and tannins sufficient for the task; good value. Screwcap. 14.5° alc. **Rating** 90 **To** 2013 $19

ΨΨΨΨ **The Medley GSM 2005** A pleasant, medium-bodied quaffing wine, with spicy/ earthy/savoury characters to the fore; unconvincing colour. Screwcap. 15° alc. **Rating** 89 **To** 2010 $25

Prodigal Clare Valley Grenache 2005 Strongly varietal and regional, with confit fruit and inbuilt sweetness; all a question of style. Screwcap. 15° alc. **Rating** 88 **To** 2013 $27

Killerman's Run Cabernet Sauvignon 2006 A reflection of the very good SA vintage, even at this level, soft blackcurrant fruit with nicely balanced tannins. Screwcap. 14.5° alc. **Rating** 88 **To** 2013 $19

Second Fiddle Clare Valley Rose 2007 Juicy strawberry, plum and cherry fruit, with a commercially targeted touch of sweetness on the finish. Screwcap. 13.5° alc. **Rating** 87 **To** 2009 $19

Killara Estate ★★★★★

773 Warburton Highway, Seville East, Vic 3139 **Region** Yarra Valley
T (03) 5961 5877 **F** (03) 5961 5629 **www**.killaraestate.com.au **Open** 7 days 11–5
Winemaker David Bicknell **Est.** 1997 **Cases** 7000
The Palazzo family moved to extend its already substantial investment in the Yarra Valley (dating from 1997) by purchasing an additional established vineyard on the corner of Warburton Highway and Sunnyside Road in late 2005. This 40-ha property had 35 ha planted, but also provided an excellent location for the cellar door, which was built and opened in mid-2007. With over 90 ha of vineyards on the two properties, Killara Estate is a major supplier of grapes to other Yarra Valley producers, retaining sufficient grapes for a 7000-case production, and has the flexibility to increase this should demand grow. Exports to the UK.

ΨΨΨΨΨ **Reserve Yarra Valley Chardonnay 2006** Complex pear and melon, grilled nuts and layers of toast; the vibrant palate packs plenty of punch, and builds to a long, fine, quite grippy crescendo. Screwcap. 12.6° alc. **Rating** 94 **To** 2012 $35

Yarra Valley Chardonnay 2006 Lovely ripe melon fruit, with lively citrus aromas in the background; quite toasty, and very creamy on the palate, the wine has precision, depth and finesse. Screwcap. 13.5° alc. **Rating** 94 **To** 2013 $25

Yarra Valley Shiraz 2006 Lifted blueberry and red fruit aromas mingle with toasty oak; the medium-bodied palate delivers hints of spice, earth and tar, and the finish is chewy but not heavy. Screwcap. 14° alc. **Rating** 94 **To** 2018 $20

ΨΨΨΨ♀ **Yarra Valley Pinot Noir 2006** Deep and darkly fruited, with game and spice in the background; quite tannic and dry, but the palate is long and even; time will see it soften and open up. Screwcap. 13.5° alc. **Rating** 93 **To** 2014 $25

Yarra Valley Sparkling Cuvee 2005 A closed bouquet, but has a creamy leesy texture, with some chalky complexity, and a fresh lemon finish; a nice aperitif style. Diam. 12° alc. **Rating** 91 **To** 2009 $30

ΨΨΨΨ **Racers & Rascals Yarra Valley Chardonnay 2006** Ripe pear flesh, and just a hint of toast on the bouquet; a fine wine, with precise acidity, and a little mineral core supporting the fruit. Screwcap. 13.5° alc. **Rating** 89 **To** 2009 $17

Racers & Rascals Yarra Valley Shiraz Viognier 2006 Juicy, spicy and with a little funky edge; a drink early, café-style, for those with fun on their minds. Screwcap. 14° alc. **Rating** 89 **To** 2012 $17

Racers & Rascals Yarra Valley Pinot Noir 2006 Very deep colour; raspberry fruits, stem and a hint of earth; very tannic and a little too much extract leaves the silk out of this wine. Screwcap. 13.5° alc. **Rating** 88 **To** 2010 $15

Killerby ★★★★

Caves Road, Wilyabrup, WA 6280 **Region** Margaret River
T 1800 655 722 **F** 1800 679 578 www.killerby.com.au **Open** Not
Winemaker Simon Ding **Est.** 1973 **Cases** 15 000
Killerby has moved from Geographe to Margaret River following the acquisition of a vineyard
with 25-year-old chardonnay vines on Caves Road. It has kept its substantial mature vineyards
in Geographe, where the wines are still made. The property was listed for sale by Gaetjens
Langley (www.wineryforsale.com.au) in November 2007, and in April '08 was still waiting
for a buyer. Exports to the US and Denmark.

ΨΨΨΨΨ **Semillon 2007** A voluminous herb and grass bouquet; elegant, intense and long
palate; oak influence subtle yet important. Part barrel-fermented in new French
oak plus lees contact. Screwcap. 13° alc. **Rating** 92 **To** 2015 $20
Chardonnay 2005 Youthful colour, with vibrant grapefruit aromas supported
by discreet oak. A fine persistent palate; long and harmonious. Screwcap. 13.7° alc.
Rating 90 **To** 2012 $30
Chardonnay 2006 A tight, lean and minerally style, showing good texture
and concentration; long and fine on the finish. Screwcap. 13.6° alc. **Rating** 90·
To 2012 $30

ΨΨΨΨ **Sauvignon Blanc 2007** A bright and lively palate in a citrus/capsicum/kiwi fruit
spectrum; partial barrel ferment new French oak. Screwcap. 12.5° alc. **Rating** 89
To 2009 $20
Shiraz 2005 Attractive medium-bodied wine, with vanillin oak and black fruits
seamlessly interwoven, each contributing to the overall flavour; from vines planted
1973. Screwcap. 14.5° alc. **Rating** 89 **To** 2015 $25
Shiraz 2004 Good colour; bright varietal fruit; juicy and straightforward; good
weight and balance; a little simple. Screwcap. 13.6° alc. **Rating** 88 **To** 2012 $25

Killibinbin Wines ★★★★☆

PO Box 108, Crafers, SA 5152 **Region** McLaren Vale
T (08) 8339 8664 **F** (08) 8339 8664 www.killibinbin.com.au **Open** Not
Winemaker Rolf Binder, Kym Teusner, Phil Christiansen, Justin Lane **Est.** 1998 **Cases** 4000
Business partners Liz Blanks and Wayne Anderson embarked on their virtual winery (with,
they say, 'no money, no winemaker, no vineyard and no winery') with the inaugural 1997
Langhorne Creek Shiraz. Robert Parker promptly gave it 92 points, which meant that all of
the production, and all of the subsequent growth, went to the US. A challenging set of new
labels straight from the early 1940s have gained (and will gain) much attention. No samples
received; the rating is that of last year.

Kiltynane Estate ★★★☆

Cnr School Lane/Yarra Glen–Healesville Road, Tarrawarra, Vic 3775 **Region** Yarra Valley
T 0418 339 555 **F** (03) 5962 1897 www.kiltynane.com.au **Open** W'ends 11–4 or by appt
Winemaker Kate Kirkhope **Est.** 2000 **Cases** 500
Kate Kirkhope has owned and run Kiltynane Estate since 1994. Having completed a local
viticulture course in 1997, she began the development of the 3.8-ha vineyard, planted to seven
clones of pinot noir, in 2000. Her son's education at a Rudolf Steiner School had given her
an interest in biodynamics, and biodynamic practices are followed wherever possible: the vines
are not irrigated, and no pesticides are used. Exports to Denmark.

ΨΨΨΨ **Preliminaire Blanc de Noir 2007** Clean, dry and fresh, with a hint of
herbaceousness providing cut and focus on the finish; table wine, not sparkling.
Diam. 12.5° alc. **Rating** 87 **To** 2009 $40

Kimbarra Wines

422 Barkly Street, Ararat, Vic 3377 **Region** Grampians
T (03) 5352 2238 **F** (03) 5342 1950 **www**.kimbarrawines.com.au **Open** Mon–Fri 9–4.30
or by appt
Winemaker Peter Leeke, Ian MacKenzie **Est.** 1990 **Cases** 900
Jim, Peter and David Leeke have established 12 ha of riesling, shiraz and cabernet sauvignon,
varieties that have proved best suited to the Grampians region. The particularly well-made,
estate-grown wines deserve a wider audience.

ΨΨΨΨΩ **Great Western Shiraz 2005** Vibrant red fruits and quite a bit of spice;
finely textured, and good acidity on the finish. Screwcap. 12.9° alc. **Rating** 91
To 2014 $24
Great Western Riesling 2007 Very ripe fruit flavours moving towards the
tropical, but generous texture on the palate, and fine lingering acidity. Screwcap.
13° alc. **Rating** 90 To 2014 $14
Great Western Cabernet Sauvignon 2005 Vibrant blackcurrant fruit, with
a slight savoury note; firm and full on the finish. Screwcap. 13.4° alc. **Rating** 90
To 2014 $22

Kindred Spirit Wines ★★★

PO Box 90, Coldstream, Vic 3770 **Region** Yarra Valley/Strathbogie Ranges
T 0400 662 224 **F** (03) 9739 1277 **Open** Not
Winemaker Keith Salter **Est.** 2006 **Cases** 900
Owner and winemaker Keith Salter had 29 years' experience working in the wine industry
when he established Kindred Spirit Wines in 2006. That experience was gained in Tasmania,
Geelong, Swan Hill and 'even a stint in the UK teaching a motley group of wine students
the finer points of winemaking', says Salter. These days he not only operates the Bianchet
winery and vineyard, but is a partner in Small Batch Winemakers, a contract winemaking
business also located at Bianchet. He buys grapes from various parts of the Yarra Valley for
Kindred Spirit's Steel Breeze label, but the frost of 2007 severely cut production; drought and
frost permitting, the range of Sauvignon Blanc and Rose (from the Yarra Valley) and Viognier
(Strathbogie Ranges) will be completed by the addition of a Yarra Valley Shiraz.

ΨΨΨΨ **Steel Breeze Viognier 2007** Lively and fresh; an apricot and citrus mix with a
bright, crisp finish. Screwcap. 13° alc. **Rating** 88 To 2009 $22

King River Estate

3556 Wangaratta-Whitfield Road, Wangaratta, Vic 3678 **Region** King Valley
T (03) 5729 3689 **F** (03) 5729 3688 **www**.kingriverestate.com.au **Open** W'ends, or by appt
Winemaker Trevor Knaggs **Est.** 1996 **Cases** 6000
Trevor Knaggs, with the assistance of his father Collin, began the establishment of King
River Estate in 1990, making the first wines in '96. The initial plantings were 3.3 ha each
of chardonnay and cabernet sauvignon, followed by 8 ha of merlot and 3 ha of shiraz.
More recent plantings have extended the varietal range with verdelho, viognier, barbera and
sangiovese, lifting the total plantings to a substantial 24 ha. Exports to Canada.

ΨΨΨΨΩ **King Valley Sangiovese 2006** Has more colour, flavour, weight and structure
than many, with a mix of sweet and sour cherries and ripe tannins. Diam. 14° alc.
Rating 90 To 2012 $22

ΨΨΨΨ **King Valley Barbera 2005** Considerable development brings a seamless joining
of black and red cherry, Asian spices and cedary French oak, the tannins in a
relaxed support role. Diam. 14.6° alc. **Rating** 89 To 2012 $22
Reserve King Valley Merlot 2005 Spicy earthy leafy minty components all
intermingle along with blackcurrant; whence now? Diam. 15° alc. **Rating** 88
To 2012 $45

King Valley Cabernet Sauvignon 2006 Full-bodied; the fruit flavour is very ripe, and overall extract of tannins and oak in the same ball park. Diam. 14.5° alc. **Rating 88 To** 2015 $22

Reserve Viognier 2005 Undeniably powerful and, to a slightly lesser degree, varietal; the problem comes with the alcohol necessary to achieve all this. Diam. 15° alc. **Rating 87 To** 2013 $45

Kings Creek Vineyard ★★★★

237 Myers Road, Bittern, Vic 3918 **Region** Mornington Peninsula
T (03) 5983 1802 **F** (03) 5983 1802 **Open** W'ends 11–5
Winemaker Sandro Mosele (Contract) **Est.** 1980 **Cases** 600
In the wake of the implosion of the original Kings Creek winery, Graham and Dorothy Turner purchased the name Kings Creek, and acquired the original home vineyard block, taking the decision to radically change the trellis system from lyre to vertical spur. The vines have taken time to recover (as is normal in such circumstances), and winemaker Sandro Mosele forecast at the time that it would take until 2006 for the vines to regain balance and produce their best fruit.

ΨΨΨΨΨ **Chardonnay 2006** Bright colour, with clean varietal fruits, and cool hints of lemon. Good flavour and a fine harmonious finish. Diam. 13° alc. **Rating 90 To** 2011 $20

Mornington Peninsula Pinot Noir 2006 The bouquet has bright red fruits, with serious but fine structure in support, and just the merest hint of mint on the finish; good flavour. Cork. 13.3° alc. **Rating 90 To** 2013 $25

Kingsdale Wines

745 Crookwell Road, Goulburn, NSW 2580 **Region** Southern New South Wales Zone
T (02) 4822 4880 **F** (02) 4822 4881 **www**.kingsdale.com.au **Open** W'ends & public hols 10–5
Winemaker Howard Spark **Est.** 2001 **Cases** 1000
Howard and Elly Spark have established their 2.5-ha vineyard south of the burgeoning Southern Highlands region, falling in the Southern NSW Zone. It sits at 700 m above sea level on deep red soils with iron rich sediments (doubtless causing the colour) and limestone. The limestone-clad cellar door overlooks the substantial Lake Sooley, 7 mins drive from Goulburn.

ΨΨΨΨ **Semillon Chardonnay Sauvignon Blanc 2005** Unoaked, and the screwcap has retained freshness to a light-bodied palate with grass, herb and citrus components. Screwcap. 12.5° alc. **Rating 87 To** 2009 $18

Merlot Malbec 2005 Light- to medium-bodied; a very sweet fruit profile with malbec making a statement; minimum tannins; good overall feel. Screwcap. 14° alc. **Rating 87 To** 2010 $30

Kingston Estate ★★★☆

Sturt Highway, Kingston-on-Murray, SA 5331 **Region** Southeast Australia
T (08) 8130 4500 **F** (08) 8130 4511 **www**.kingstonestatewines.com **Open** By appt
Winemaker Bill Moularadellis **Est.** 1979 **Cases** 2.5 million
Kingston Estate, under the direction of Bill Moularadellis, has its production roots in the Riverland region, but it has also set up long-term purchase contracts with growers in the Clare Valley, the Adelaide Hills, Coonawarra, Langhorne Creek and Mount Benson. It has also spread its net to take in a wide range of varietals, mainstream and exotic, under a number of different brands at various price points. Exports to Europe.

ΨΨΨΨ **Echelon Cabernet Sauvignon 2005** Distinctly earthy overtones to a firm, somewhat austere palate with good length, the alcohol folded within the fruit and tannins. Screwcap. 15° alc. **Rating 89 To** 2015 $21.95

Shiraz 2006 Abundant, ripe blackberry fruit, with good depth; a suggestion of sweetness somewhere in the mix. Cork. 14.5° alc. **Rating 88 To** 2012

Merlot 2006 Unusually clear varietal characters at this price point, courtesy of an olivaceous twist on the finish of the extended palate. Great value. Cork. 14° alc. **Rating** 88 **To** 2011 $12.50

Echelon Petit Verdot 2005 Full-bodied and robust, with masses of extract of fruit and tannins; great at a night barbecue. Screwcap. 14.5° alc. **Rating** 88 **To** 2011 $21.95

Echelon Chardonnay 2006 Full-bodied; ripe, peachy fruit and integrated oak; a slightly hot finish; curious gold medal from Rutherglen Wine Show. Screwcap. 13.5° alc. **Rating** 87 **To** 2009 $21.95

Echelon Shiraz 2005 Powerful, earthy wine with dried prune and blackberry flavours all attesting to the impact of alcohol; time may or may not tame it. Screwcap. 15° alc. **Rating** 87 **To** 2016 $21.95

Kinloch Wines

'Kainui', 221 Wairere Road, Booroolite, Vic 3723 **Region** Upper Goulburn
T (03) 5777 3447 **F** (03) 5777 3449 **www**.kinlochwines.com.au **Open** 7 days 10–4
Winemaker Al Fencaros (Contract) **Est.** 1996 **Cases** 2000
In 1996 Susan and Malcolm Kinloch began the development of their vineyard, at an altitude of 400 m on the northern slopes of the Great Dividing Range, 15 mins from Mansfield. One of the unusual varieties in the portfolio is Pinot Meunier. The grapes are hand-picked and taken to the Yarra Valley for contract making.

ŢŢŢŢŢ **Mary Friend 2005** Good hue; tangy/savoury/minty nuances to the core of sweet red and black fruits; gentle tannins. Cabernet Sauvignon/Cabernet Franc/Merlot. Twin top. 14° alc. **Rating** 90 **To** 2014 $50

ŢŢŢŢ **Sauvignon Blanc 2007** Aromatic herb and lemongrass; a bright, firm palate in a clearly focused grassy/mineral frame. Screwcap. 12.5° alc. **Rating** 89 **To** 2009 $22

Don Kinloch Chardonnay Pinot Noir Pinot Meunier 2006 Good fruit flavours, simple and direct; deserves longer on lees to build complexity. Cork. 11.8° alc. **Rating** 87 **To** 2010 $28

Kiola

'Abbey Ridge', Delaneys Road, Cowra, NSW 2794 (postal) **Region** Hilltops
T (02) 6385 8325 **F** (02) 6385 8325 **www**.kiolavineyard.com.au **Open** Not
Winemaker Roger Harris **Est.** 1996 **Cases** NFP
Mark and Louisa Sims have two vineyards, one with 1 ha of shiraz on their property in Cowra, the other of 4 ha in shiraz the Hilltops region. Mark Sims has been a vineyard manager and viticulturist for 25 years after graduating from CSU (as it is now called) in 1983; from an early career managing vineyards in Germany, he came back to Australia and to the Hunter Valley and Cowra at various times. As a quite separate venture to Kiola, in 2002 he formed a partnership to develop 100 ha of vineyards in the Canowindra area.

ŢŢŢŢ **Shiraz 2005** Light- to medium-bodied; cool-grown spicy/peppery/savoury overtones to the black fruits, but needs a touch more flesh to carry those characters. Screwcap. 13.4° alc. **Rating** 87 **To** 2010 $19

Kirrihill Wines

Wendouree Road, Clare, SA 5453 **Region** Clare Valley
T (08) 8842 4087 **F** (08) 8842 4089 **www**.kirrihillwines.com.au **Open** 7 days 10–4
Winemaker Donna Stephens, Julian Midwinter **Est.** 1998 **Cases** 30 000
A large development, with an 8000-tonne, $12 million winery making and marketing its own range of wines, also acting as a contract maker for several producers. Focused on Clare Valley and the Adelaide Hills, grapes are sourced from specially selected parcels of Kirribilly's 1300 ha of managed vineyards as well as the Edwards and Stanway families' properties in these regions. The quality of the wines is thus no surprise. The Companions range comprises blends of both regions, while the Single Vineyard Series aims to elicit a sense of place from the chosen vineyards. Exports to all major markets.

ŢŢŢŢŶ **Adelaide Hills Chardonnay 2005** Has developed very well, with layers of nectarine and white peach, the oak very well integrated and balanced on the long palate. Screwcap. 14° alc. **Rating** 93 **To** 2013 $20

Single Vineyard Series Tulach Mor Clare Valley Shiraz 2005 An immediately appealing wine; plum, blackberry and black cherry are intertwined with fine, ripe tannins and quality oak. Screwcap. 14° alc. **Rating** 93 **To** 2013 $19.95

Single Vineyard Series Cuasin Na Sleine Riesling 2007 A faint hint of reduction along with some spicy characters on the bouquet; a tight, minerally palate with crisp acidity. Screwcap. 12° alc. **Rating** 91 **To** 2012 $19.95

Single Vineyard Series Serendipity Pinot Grigio 2007 Lively and flavoursome, with pear, apple and musk all combining; long palate, dry finish. Impressive example. Screwcap. 13.5° alc. **Rating** 90 **To** 2009 $19.95

Single Vineyard Series Baile An Gharrai Clare Valley Shiraz Mourvedre Grenache 2006 A strongly varietal mix with a range of flavours at the sweet end of the spectrum; has weight, and is not jammy; in a particular style. Screwcap. 14.5° alc. **Rating** 90 **To** 2012 $19.95

ŢŢŢŢ **Langhorne Creek Shiraz 2005** Supple medium-bodied palate, with the soft black and red fruits and some choc-mint, which are all typical characters of Langhorne Creek. Screwcap. 14° alc. **Rating** 89 **To** 2011 $20

Single Vineyard Series Tulach Mor Clare Valley Cabernet Sauvignon 2005 A powerful wine, the oak very evident on the bouquet, the tannins on the palate; cassis and blackcurrant fruit the third man. Screwcap. 14° alc. **Rating** 89 **To** 2013 $19.95

Companions Adelaide Hills Clare Valley Tempranillo Garnacha 2007 A joyous celebration of fresh, vibrant red fruits, demanding to be opened and consumed today while it keeps its youth and vivacity. Screwcap. 14.5° alc. **Rating** 88 **To** 2009 $15

Companions Clare Valley Adelaide Hills Riesling Pinot Gris 2007 I'm not entirely sure why they do this, but it is cleverly made, with citrussy/limey riesling the dominant partner; a touch of residual sugar on the finish; points for lateral approach. Screwcap. 12° alc. **Rating** 87 **To** 2009 $14.95

Companions Clare Valley Adelaide Hills Shiraz Viognier 2006 Bright colour; fresh red fruits dominate, with just a dusting of tannins to add structure. Screwcap. 14.5° alc. **Rating** 87 **To** 2011 $15

Kladis Estate

NR

Princes Highway, Wandandian, NSW 2540 **Region** Shoalhaven Coast
T (02) 4443 5606 **F** (02) 4443 6485 **www**.kladisestatewines.com.au **Open** 7 days 10–5
Winemaker Steve Dodd **Est.** 1996 **Cases** 10 000
Jim and Niki Kladis have developed 11 ha of shiraz, cabernet sauvignon, grenache, verdelho, merlot and muscadelle at their Shoalhaven property, and 4 ha of gewurztraminer and cabernet sauvignon in the Hunter Valley. Additional grapes are also sourced from the Adelaide Hills. The inspiration has been the medium-bodied red wines Jim Kladis grew up with on the Greek island of Zante. The winery has recently had a $1.5 million upgrade to include a conference centre, restaurant and cellar door. Exports to China, Japan, Fiji and Vanuatu.

Knappstein

★★★★☆

2 Pioneer Avenue, Clare, SA 5453 **Region** Clare Valley
T (08) 8841 2100 **F** (08) 8841 2101 **www**.knappstein.com.au **Open** Mon–Fri 9–5, Sat 11–5, Sun & public hols 11–4
Winemaker Paul Smith **Est.** 1969 **Cases** 35 000
Knappstein's full name is Knappstein Enterprise Winery & Brewery, reflecting its history before being acquired by Petaluma, and since then part of Lion Nathan's stable, with Paul Smith having taken over from Andrew Hardy, who has returned to Petaluma headquarters. The 115 ha of mature estate vineyards in prime locations supply grapes both for the

Knappstein brand and for wider Petaluma use. Despite making seriously good wines, Knappstein can't get across the line to greatness. Exports to all major markets.

🍷🍷🍷🍷🍷 **Enterprise Vineyard Clare Valley Cabernet Sauvignon 2005** Deep colour; full-bodied, dense and concentrated, with luscious but dark fruits that have soaked up both tannins and oak. Will repay extended cellaring; high-quality cork. 14.5° alc. **Rating** 94 **To** 2020 $40.95

🍷🍷🍷🍷🍷 **Clare Valley Sparkling Shiraz 1998** Fine and elegant, with an obviously long time on lees shaping the palate; just a touch needlessly sweet on the finish. Deserves further time in bottle. Cork. 14° alc. **Rating** 91 **To** 2015 $45
Ackland Vineyard Watervale Riesling 2007 Restrained bouquet and entry to the mouth, but comes alive on the back palate and finish with notes of honey, passionfruit and lime; clean aftertaste. Screwcap. 13° alc. **Rating** 90 **To** 2013 $29.95
Clare Valley Shiraz 2005 Fragrant medium-bodied wine with plum, dark cherry and some blackberry; fine tannins and subtle oak. Screwcap. 14.5° alc. **Rating** 90 **To** 2013 $20.95

🍷🍷🍷🍷 **Hand Picked Clare Valley Riesling 2007** A relatively subdued bouquet, the palate with good structure and classic Clare riesling flavours, but held in check by the vintage. Screwcap. 13.5° alc. **Rating** 89 **To** 2012 $20.95
Clare Valley Cabernet Merlot 2005 Medium- to full-bodied; undeniably at the ripe end of the spectrum, but not dead fruit or jammy; a mix of blackcurrant and cassis, with soft tannins. Screwcap. 14.5° alc. **Rating** 89 **To** 2012 $20.95
Thr3e Clare Valley Gewurztraminer Riesling Pinot Gris 2007 A successful ploy to cover the lack of varietal character with Clare gewurztraminer; nice citrus lime fruit and a dusting of spice. Screwcap. 13.5° alc. **Rating** 88 **To** 2012 $21.95

Knots Wines

A8 Shurans Lane, Heathcote, Vic 3552 **Region** Heathcote
T (03) 5441 5429 **F** (03) 5441 5429 **www**.thebridgevineyard.com.au **Open** Select w'ends, or by appt
Winemaker Lindsay Ross **Est.** 1997 **Cases** 1000
This is the venture of former Balgownie winemaker Lindsay Ross and wife Noeline, and is part of a broader business known as Winedrops, which acts as a wine production and distribution network for the Bendigo wine industry. The Knots wines are sourced from long-established Heathcote and Bendigo vineyards, providing 0.5 ha each of semillon and chardonnay, and 4 ha each of shiraz and cabernets. The viticultural accent is on low-cropping vineyards with concentrated flavours, the winemaking emphasis on flavour, finesse and varietal expression.

🍷🍷🍷🍷🍷 **The Bridge Heathcote Shiraz 2005** A massive wine in what I used to describe as Henry VIII style, yet the alcohol doesn't heat the palate as much as one might imagine; fine tannins and good length. Diam. 15.5° alc. **Rating** 92 **To** 2020 $50

🍷🍷🍷🍷 **Lark's Head Bendigo Cabernet Sauvignon Merlot Cabernet Franc 2004** Markedly earthy with notes of briar and bracken; texture and structure revolve around firm but not abrasive tannins. Diam. 14.5° alc. **Rating** 88 **To** 2013 $25

Knotting Hill Vineyard

247 Carter Road, Wilyabrup WA 6280 **Region** Margaret River
T (08) 9755 3377 **F** (08) 9755 7744 **www**.knottinghill.com.au **Open** 7 days 11–4
Winemaker Flying Fish Cove (Elizabeth Reed) **Est.** 1997 **Cases** 3000
The Gould family has been farming in WA since 1907, and still owns the land and grant taken up on their arrival from Scotland. In 1997 the two generations of the family who now own Knotting Hill decided to diversify, and acquired their Wilyabrup property in the Margaret River. In 2002 they leased the wheat farm, and have devoted all their time to Knotting Hill. In 1998 they propagated 56 000 cuttings by hand and planted them on an onsite nursery, using

their extensive farming background to supervise plantings, create a 5.5-ha dam, and build the 45 m bridge entry to the local limestone cellar door, which opened in '05. The spectacular 37-ha vineyard setting is established on a natural amphitheatre, with the lake at the bottom.

ŢŢŢŢŢ **Margaret River Cabernet Merlot 2005** A complex, medium-bodied wine; blackcurrant and spice with an array of tannins and quality French oak in support. Trophy, WA Wine Show '07. Screwcap. 13.6° alc. **Rating** 94 **To** 2015 $25

ŢŢŢŢŢ **Margaret River Cabernet Sauvignon 2005** Fragrant blackcurrant aromas, then a medium-bodied palate with bright varietal fruit, supported by quite firm tannins; has a dash of cabernet franc and French oak. Screwcap. 13.6° alc. **Rating** 91 **To** 2020 $25

ŢŢŢŢ **Reef Knot Red 2006** Light- to medium-bodied; attractive cassis/redcurrant fruit with fine tannins in support. An achievement for the '06 vintage. Screwcap. 13.1° alc. **Rating** 89 **To** 2009 $16
Semillon Sauvignon Blanc 2007 Abundant passionfruit, gooseberry and tropical fruit on both bouquet and palate; a touch of spritz adds life. Screwcap. 13.1° alc. **Rating** 88 **To** 2010 $18
Verdelho 2007 Fresh and clean; fairly low fruit profile, but has good length and crisp acidity to close. Screwcap. 13.1° alc. **Rating** 87 **To** 2009 $18
Reef Knot White 2007 Water white; juicy and fresh, with plenty of stone fruit and citrus flavours; summer's day picnic wine. Chardonnay/Semillon/Verdelho/Sauvignon Blanc. Screwcap. 13° alc. **Rating** 87 **To** 2009 $16

Kominos Wines   ★★★★

27145 New England Highway, Severnlea, Qld 4352 **Region** Granite Belt
T (07) 4683 4311 **F** (07) 4683 4291 **www**.kominoswines.com **Open** 7 days 9–5
Winemaker Tony Comino **Est.** 1976 **Cases** 5000
Tony Comino is a dedicated viticulturist and winemaker and, with wife Mary, took over ownership of the winery from his parents on its 21st vintage. Comino is proud of the estate-grown, -made and -bottled heritage of the winery and is content to keep a relatively low profile, although the proud show record of the wines might suggest otherwise. Another Queensland producer to make seriously good wines, capable of holding their own against all-comers from the south (as Queenslanders refer to anyone not born in the state). Exports to the US, Taiwan, Hong Kong and Singapore.

ŢŢŢŢŢ **Botrytis Semillon 2004** Surprise packet; still delicious and fresh, the clear botrytis influence and consequent lusciousness balanced by cleansing lemony acidity; has uncommon elegance; enjoy now. Twin top. 11° alc. **Rating** 92 **To** 2011 $16
Estate Cabernet Sauvignon 2006 Clean medium-bodied wine with good varietal fruit expression through blackcurrant and black olive flavours; good texture and structure. Diam. 13.5° alc. **Rating** 90 **To** 2016 $24

ŢŢŢŢ **Vin Doux 2006** As the name suggests this blend of Sauvignon Blanc/Muscat is off-dry, and has nothing to do with sauvignon blanc as such; serve fully chilled. Diam. 12° alc. **Rating** 87 **To** 2009 $15
Estate Merlot 2006 Savoury earth and black olive characters dominate a somewhat severe wine, which, however, will flourish with red meats. Diam. 13° alc. **Rating** 87 **To** 2011 $25

Koonara   ★★★★

44 Main Street, Penola, SA 5277 **Region** Coonawarra
T (08) 8737 3222 **F** (08) 8737 3220 **www**.koonara.com **Open** By appt
Winemaker Dru Reschke, Peter Douglas (Consultant) **Est.** 1988 **Cases** 3000
Koonara is a sister, or, more appropriately, brother company to Reschke Wines. The latter is run by Burke Reschke, Koonara by his brother Dru. Both are sons of Trevor Reschke, who planted the first vines on the Koonara property in 1988. The initial planting was of cabernet sauvignon, followed by shiraz in 1993 and additional cabernet sauvignon in '98.

Peter Douglas, formerly Wynns' chief winemaker before moving overseas for some years, has returned to the district and is consultant winemaker. Exports to the US, Taiwan and China.

ŶŶŶŶŶ **Sofiel's Gift Coonawarra Riesling 2005** Has developed very well since first tasted Oct '05; a toasty bouquet with a touch of traditional kerosene, then a palate stacked with juicy lime fruit. Ready now. Screwcap. 12.5° alc. **Rating** 90 To 2010 $16

ŶŶŶŶ **Angel's Peak Coonawarra Shiraz 2005** Some development in colour; a supple and round mix of red and black fruit flavours, the oak and tannins in restraint. Screwcap. 14.5° alc. **Rating** 89 To 2012 $15.95
Angel's Footsteps Adelaide Hills Sauvignon Blanc 2007 Typically subdued aromas of the vintage; has plenty of presence and length on the palate, before toughening slightly on the finish. Screwcap. 12° alc. **Rating** 87 To 2009 $20
The Seductress Coonawarra Shiraz 2004 Light- to medium-bodied; very savoury/earthy style, moving quickly towards its best-by date, though in no danger of collapse; French oak appropriate. Diam. 13.9° alc. **Rating** 87 To 2011 $15.95
The Temptress Coonawarra Cabernet Sauvignon 2004 Light- to medium-bodied, suggesting relatively high-yielding vines; cassis, leaf and earth; minimal tannins. Diam. 13.9° alc. **Rating** 87 To 2011 $15.95

Koonowla Wines   ★★★★

PO Box 45, Auburn, SA 5451 **Region** Clare Valley
T (08) 8849 2080 **F** (08) 8849 2293 **www**.koonowla.com **Open** Not
Winemaker O'Leary Walker Wines **Est.** 1997 **Cases** 3500
It's not often that a light as large as this can be hidden under a bushel. Koonowla is a historic Clare Valley property; situated just east of Auburn, it was first planted with vines in the 1890s, and by the early 1900s was producing 60 000 litres of wine annually. A disastrous fire in 1926 destroyed the winery and wine stocks, and the property was converted to grain and wool production. Replanting of vines began in 1985, and accelerated after Andrew and Booie Michael purchased the property in '91; there are now 40 ha of cabernet sauvignon, 36 ha riesling, 20 ha of shiraz, and 2 ha each of merlot and semillon. In an all too familiar story, the grapes were sold until falling prices forced a change in strategy, and now part of the grapes are vinified by the infinitely experienced David O'Leary and Nick Walker, with the remainder sold. Most of the wines are exported (the UK, the US and NZ).

ŶŶŶŶŶ **Clare Valley Shiraz 2005** A slightly oaky bouquet, but fresh blackberry fruit and fine, savoury tannins on the finish. Screwcap. 14.5° alc. **Rating** 90 To 2015 $18

ŶŶŶŶ **The Ringmaster Shiraz 2004** Not entirely clear, suggesting no filtration; sweet confit fruit at odds with the moderate alcohol; finishes with soft tannins. Screwcap. 14.5° alc. **Rating** 89 To 2011 $10
Clare Valley Riesling 2007 Good intensity, with plenty of minerals, floral touches and good flavour; just a little bitter on the finish. Screwcap. 12.5° alc. **Rating** 88 To 2012 $15
The Ringmaster Cabernet Rose 2007 Bright pale rose; nice varietal aroma, with good flavour and not too much sugar; very clean. Screwcap. 12.3° alc. **Rating** 87 To 2009 $12
The Ringmaster Cabernet Sauvignon 2005 Again, not bright; a powerful wine, with lots of earthy tannins in a savoury style; rump steak and patience recommended. Screwcap. 13.5° alc. **Rating** 87 To 2014 $10
Clare Valley Cabernet Sauvignon 2005 Good varietal cabernet; hint of black olive and plenty of fruit weight; lacks a little freshness, but has good flavour. Screwcap. 15° alc. **Rating** 87 To 2012 $18

Kooroomba Vineyards   ★★★☆

168 FM Bells Road, Mount Alford via Boonah, Qld 4310 **Region** Queensland Zone
T (07) 5463 0022 **F** (07) 5463 0441 **www.kooroomba.com.au Open** Wed–Sun &
public hols 10–5
Winemaker Ballandean Estate **Est.** 1998 **Cases** NA
Kooroomba Vineyards is little more than an hour's drive from the Brisbane CBD, and
offers cellar door wine tasting and sales, a vineyard restaurant and a lavender farm. The 6-ha
vineyard is planted to chardonnay, verdelho, marsanne, shiraz, cabernet merlot, vermentino
and viognier.

♀♀♀♀♀ **Chardonnay 2006** A bright wine, with well defined chardonnay fruit on the
bouquet; good use of oak frames some dried fig flavours; a good example of a
warmer style. Screwcap. 13.2° alc. **Rating** 90 **To** 2012 $25

Kooyong   ★★★★★

PO Box 153, Red Hill South, Vic 3937 **Region** Mornington Peninsula
T (03) 5989 7355 **F** (03) 5989 7677 **www.**kooyong.com **Open** At Port Phillip Estate
Winemaker Sandro Mosele **Est.** 1996 **Cases** 5000
Kooyong, owned by Giorgio and Dianne Gjergja, released its first wines in 2001. The 34-ha
vineyard is planted to pinot noir and chardonnay. Winemaker Sandro Mosele is a graduate
of CSU, having previously gained a science degree, and has a deservedly high reputation. He
also provides contract winemaking services for others. Exports to the UK, the US, Canada,
Sweden, Korea, Japan and Singapore.

♀♀♀♀♀ **Single Vineyard Selection Faultline Chardonnay 2006** Mineral notes,
and tightly wound on the palate; great texture, with silkiness and beautiful focus,
complexed by nuances of cashew and toast; fine and complete. Cork. 13.5° alc.
Rating 95 **To** 2016 $52
Single Vineyard Selection Ferrous Pinot Noir 2006 Plenty of dark fruits,
and concentrated, almost impenetrable, personality; backward at the moment, but
with layers of flavour on the full, rich and bright-fruited finish. Cork. 14° alc.
Rating 95 **To** 2017 $60
Single Vineyard Selection Farrago Chardonnay 2006 Riper than the Estate,
with cashew and grapefruit aromas; a little backward on the palate, but with good
flavour persistence; the key is the texture, quite grippy and savoury, yet fine. Cork.
13.5° alc. **Rating** 94 **To** 2016 $52
Single Vineyard Selection Meres Pinot Noir 2006 A combination of the
Ferrous and Haven; shows a combination of red fruits, spice and sweet fruit on the
bouquet and palate; quite firm, with good flavour and a dark, chewy finish. Cork.
13.5° alc. **Rating** 94 **To** 2017 $52
Single Vineyard Selection Haven Pinot Noir 2006 An essay of bright and
concentrated Mornington pinot; lots of cherry aromas and flavours, with good
acid and quite a firm palate; the ample, sweet core of fruit is the key. Cork.
13° alc. **Rating** 94 **To** 2015 $60

♀♀♀♀♀ **Estate Mornington Peninsula Pinot Noir 2006** Pure varietal pinot with hints
of spice, red cherries and well-handled toasty oak; a fine and tightly wound palate,
with a savoury, slightly tannic twist to the pure red fruit core; long and fine. Cork.
13.5° alc. **Rating** 93 **To** 2015 $40
Estate Mornington Peninsula Chardonnay 2006 Complex and elegant with
citrus-accented fruit supported by grilled nuts and a lick of spicy oak; the palate is
light and fresh, with a very long finish. Cork. 13° alc. **Rating** 92 **To** 2014 $36
Clonale Mornington Peninsula Chardonnay 2007 Citrus fruit with
minerally/savoury nuances on the bouquet; vibrant, almost racy acidity on the
palate; good texture and persistence. Cork. 13° alc. **Rating** 90 **To** 2014 $25

Kopparossa Wines   ★★★★

PO Box 26, Coonawarra, SA 5263 **Region** Coonawarra
T (08) 8736 3268 **F** (08) 8736 3363 **Open** By appt
Winemaker Gavin Hogg, Mike Press **Est.** 1996 **Cases** 5000
Of the many complicated stories, this is one of the most complicated of all. It was founded
by Gavin Hogg and Mike Press in 1996, based on an 80-ha vineyard in the Wrattonbully
region, and the Kopparossa label was born in '00. The vineyard was sold in 2002, and
Mike Press retired to pursue separate interests in his Adelaide Hills family vineyard. Various
wine releases and events occurred until 2005 when a joint venture between Stentiford Pty
Ltd (Kopparossa's parent company) and Estate Licensing Pty Ltd (Olivia Newton John's
wine-naming rights company) was entered into. Says Gavin Hogg's newsletter, 'Put simply,
Stentiford produces and packages wine for the Olivia Label, which is then marketed and
sold by Estate Licensing'. Reading on, we are told there are also Kopparossa wines and the
possibility of a premium platinum release in the future under the Olivia banner. Please don't
ask me to explain this any further. Exports to the UK, the US, Canada, China and Korea.

ΨΨΨΨΨ Coonawarra Unwooded Chardonnay 2006 Citrus-tinged melon fruit
aromas and flavours; quite bright focus; good length. Screwcap. 13.5° alc.
Rating 90 **To** 2011 $16

ΨΨΨΨ Olivia's Wrattonbully Sauvignon Blanc 2007 Aromatic passionfruit and
tropical aromas, then a soft, luscious palate – perhaps a little too soft. Screwcap.
12° alc. **Rating** 89 **To** 2009 $16

Kouark Vineyard   ★★★

300 Thompson Road, Drouin South, Vic 3818 **Region** Gippsland
T (03) 5627 6337 **F** (03) 5627 6337 **www.**gourmetgippsland.com **Open** W'ends 12–5
Winemaker Phil Gray **Est.** 1997 **Cases** 800
Dairy farmers Phil and Jane Gray decided to diversify with the establishment of a 4-ha
vineyard on part of their farm. They have planted 1.3 ha each of chardonnay and pinot noir,
and 0.7 ha each of shiraz and cabernet sauvignon (and a few pinot gris and viognier vines) on
a northeasterly slope, bordered on the east by a 2.4-ha lake. As well as their general farming
background, they have undertaken various CSU grape and wine production courses, and
similar short courses from other education facilities. A simple but appropriately equipped
winery has been established, and the wines are sold through local stores and cafés. The name
is believed to be the word for kookaburra in the language of the local Kurnai people.

Krinklewood Biodynamic Vineyard   ★★★★

712 Wollombi Road, Broke, NSW 2330 **Region** Lower Hunter Valley
T (02) 6579 1322 **F** (02) 9968 2154 **www.**krinklewood.com **Open** W'ends &
public hols 10–5 & by appt
Winemaker Monarch Winemaking Services **Est.** 1981 **Cases** 5000
A boutique, family-owned biodynamic vineyard, Krinklewood produces 100% estate-grown
wines reflecting the terroir of the Broke-Fordwich area of the Hunter Valley. The cellar door
is set amongst Provencal-style gardens that overlook the vineyard, with the Wollombi Brook
and Brokenback range providing a spectacular backdrop.

ΨΨΨΨΨ Biodynamic Vineyard Hunter Valley Chardonnay 2006 Tight and focused,
with cashew and citrus fruit; has toast and generosity on the finish; the savoury
element works very well. Screwcap. 13.2° alc. **Rating** 93 **To** 2013 $28
Biodynamic Vineyard Shiraz 2006 Bright colour; plenty of red fruits, with
good concentration and medium-bodied palate weight on the finish; vibrant and
lively, with good acidity. Screwcap. 13.4° alc. **Rating** 91 **To** 2018 $28
Biodynamic Vineyard Hunter Valley Chardonnay 2004 Big and rich with
ripe Hunter fruit; big flavour and dried figs on the toasty finish; retains freshness.
Screwcap. 13.5° alc. **Rating** 90 **To** 2012 $22

ΨΨΨΨ **Hunter Valley Semillon 2007** Clear-cut grassy, herbal semillon varietal character; good balance, line and length; best years to come, perhaps. Screwcap. **Rating** 89 **To** 2014 $20
Biodynamic Vineyard Hunter Valley Verdelho 2007 A citrussy bouquet with a hint of dried straw; very high acid, but the fruit weight handles it quite well; good flavour concentration. Screwcap. 13.5° alc. **Rating** 87 **To** 2012 $22
Wild White 2007 Has that extra level of fruit weight and expression of the vintage, bolstered by cleverly adjusted acidity. Verdelho (95%)/Chardonnay (5%). Screwcap. 13.5° alc. **Rating** 87 **To** 2009 $15

 # KT & The Falcon

PO Box 99, Watervale, SA 5452 **Region** Clare Valley
T (08) 8843 0040 **F** (08) 8843 0040 www.ktandthefalcon.com.au **Open** Not
Winemaker Kerri Thompson **Est.** 2006 **Cases** 850
KT is winemaker Kerri Thompson and the Falcon is viticulturist Stephen Farrugia. Kerri graduated with a degree in oenology from Roseworthy Agricultural College in 1993, and thereafter made wine in McLaren Vale, Tuscany, Beaujolais and the Clare Valley, becoming well known as the Leasingham winemaker in the Clare. Steve Farrugia managed vineyards in McLaren Vale and the Clare Valley before establishing the 7-ha estate vineyard of KT & The Falcon. Despite her former role within a very large winemaking organisation, the two have unhesitatingly moved into biodynamic management of their own vineyard (planted chiefly to riesling, but with some shiraz) and one of the vineyards they manage (moving to biodynamic farming in 2003). Kerri Thompson resigned from Hardys/Leasingham in 2006 after seven years at the helm, making the first official KT & The Falcon wines the following year, but with trial batches of 200 dozen made (in very different styles) in '04 and '05. She makes these wines at Crabtree, where she is the winemaker.

ΨΨΨΨΨ **Watervale Single Vineyard Riesling 2007** Particularly fine and focused aromas and flavours given the vintage; delicately framed apple and citrus flavours, fluidly gliding across the tongue; impeccable balance; 350 cases. Screwcap. 12.5° alc. **Rating** 94 **To** 2015 $35

ΨΨΨΨΨ **Watervale Riesling 2005** A complex aromatic bouquet, then a rich palate, with the deliberate retention of 19 grams per litre of sugar; a soft and gentle finish. Screwcap. 13° alc. **Rating** 90 **To** 2015 $28
Clare Valley Shiraz Rose 2007 Just when you cynically think this may be just getting on the gravy train at a high price, the length and precision of the palate, with delicately sweet red fruits, followed by a dry finish, teaches you otherwise. Screwcap. 12.5° alc. **Rating** 90 **To** 2010 $25

Kurabana

580 Hendy Main Road, Mt Moriac, Vic 3240 **Region** Geelong
T 0438 661 273 **F** (03) 5266 1116 www.kurabana.com **Open** Not
Winemaker Ray Nadeson, Lee Evans **Est.** 1987 **Cases** 2000
The development of the quite extensive Kurabana Vineyard, west of Geelong in the foothills of Mt Moriac, began in 1987. Pinot noir (7.5 ha) is the largest portion, followed by (in descending order) shiraz, chardonnay, sauvignon blanc and pinot gris. While some of the grapes are sold, there are also limited purchases from the Geelong area.

ΨΨΨΨΨ **Blanc de Noir 2004** Has developed remarkably well since first tasted; it is dominated by its pinot base, the high acidity providing balance and considerable length. 13.5° alc. **Rating** 91 **To** 2009 $25.95

ΨΨΨΨ **Reserve Chardonnay 2006** Pale green-straw; very much in Chablis style, with grassy, minerally acidity. May open up with age. **Rating** 87 **To** 2012
Chardonnay 2006 Fresh, clean, firm citrussy fruit; slightly hard finish. Could surprise with bottle age. **Rating** 87 **To** 2012 $19.95

Kurrajong Downs

Casino Road, Tenterfield, NSW 2372 **Region** New England
T (02) 6736 4590 **F** (02) 6736 1983 **www.**kurrajongdownswines.com
Open Thurs–Mon 9–4
Winemaker Ravens Croft Wines (Mark Ravenscroft), Symphony Hill (Mike Hayes)
Est. 2000 **Cases** 2400
Jonus Rhodes arrived at Tenterfield in 1858, lured by the gold he mined for the next 40 years, until his death in 1898. He was evidently successful, for the family now runs a 2800-ha cattle grazing property on which Lynton and Sue Rhodes have planted a 5-ha vineyard at an altitude of 850 m. Development of the vineyard started in the spring of 1996, and continued the following year.

ŸŸŸŸ   **All Nations Tenterfield Pinot Noir 2006** Bright, light crimson; fresh and crisp; pH too low/acidity too high for required mouthfeel and higher points. Diam. 13° alc. **Rating** 87 **To** 2010 $22

Kurtz Family Vineyards   ★★★★

PO Box 460, Nuriootpa, SA 5355 **Region** Barossa Valley
T 0418 810 982 **F** (08) 8564 3217 **www.**kurtzfamilyvineyards.com.au **Open** Not
Winemaker Steve Kurtz **Est.** 1996 **Cases** 4000
The Kurtz family has 18 ha of vineyard at Light Pass, with 10 ha of shiraz, the remainder planted to cabernet sauvignon, petit verdot, chardonnay, semillon, sauvignon blanc, mataro and malbec. Steve Kurtz has followed in the footsteps of his great-grandfather Ben Kurtz, who first grew grapes at Light Pass in the 1930s. After a career working first at Saltram and then Foster's until 2006, Steve has gained invaluable experience with Nigel Dolan, Caroline Dunn and John Glaetzer among others. Exports to the US, Canada, Macau, Korea, Singapore and Hong Kong.

ŸŸŸŸŸ   **Boundary Row Barossa Valley Shiraz 2005** Spicy aromas, then a delicious medium- to medium-full-bodied palate, smooth and supple; red and black fruits, discreet oak and fine, ripe tannins. Screwcap. 14.5° alc. **Rating** 91 **To** 2015 $22
Boundary Row Barossa Valley Shiraz 2004 Retains good fragrance; abundant flavour to the mid-palate, with blackberry and damson plum; good control of extract and oak, all this at 13.5° alc. Screwcap. 13.5° alc. **Rating** 90 **To** 2015 $22

ŸŸŸŸ   **Boundary Row Barossa Valley Grenache Shiraz Mataro 2005**
Unconvincing colour; typical Barossa jammy/juicy bouquet and palate, with savoury tannins. Cork. 15° alc. **Rating** 87 **To** 2010 $18
Seven Sleepers Siebenschlafer 2005 Firm, savoury black fruits supported by ripe tannins; moderate length. Cabernet Sauvignon/Shiraz/Petit Verdot; a complicated legend behind the name. Screwcap. 14° alc. **Rating** 87 **To** 2010 $15

Kyeema Estate

43 Shumack Street, Weetangera, ACT 2614 (postal) **Region** Canberra District
T 0407 913 912 **www.**kyeemawines.com.au **Open** Not
Winemaker Andrew McEwin **Est.** 1986 **Cases** 900
Part-time winemaker, part-time wine critic (with *Winewise* magazine), Andrew McEwin produces wines full of flavour and character; every wine released under the Kyeema Estate label has won a show award of some description. The vineyard has 1.9 ha shiraz, 1.2 ha chardonnay, 0.6 ha merlot, and smaller amounts of tempranillo, cabernet franc and viognier, with 1.1 ha of cabernet sauvignon being removed in 2007. Andrew McEwin also provides contract winemaking services for regional wineries, crushing 50-60 tonnes for those clients.

ŸŸŸŸ   **Canberra District Shiraz 2006** Light- to medium-bodied; relatively quick-developing style; a mix of spice, earth and black fruits; finishes short. Screwcap. 13.7° alc. **Rating** 87 **To** 2012 $25

Canberra District Merlot 2005 The varietal character is undoubted, but the level of briar, olive and earth may be disconcerting for some. Screwcap. 13.7° alc. **Rating** 87 **To** 2012 $25

Canberra District Late Picked Riesling 2007 Nicely balanced light-bodied offer of lime juice with a gentle cut of acidity; a few years in bottle will add a touch of complexity. Screwcap. 10.5° alc. **Rating** 87 **To** 2012 $18

La Colline Wines ★★★☆

42 Lake Canoboloas Road, Nashdale via Orange, NSW 2800 **Region** Orange
T (02) 6365 3275 **F** (02) 6365 3275 **Open** Wed–Sun 10–5
Winemaker Madrez Wine Services **Est.** 1999 **Cases** 640
Aline and Philippe Prudhomme combine a 14-ha vineyard (selling most of the grapes, but having some contract-made for La Colline) and a 70-seat licensed restaurant featuring the French provincial cuisine from the land of their birth. The cellar door and restaurant are 6 km from the township, with views of the Towac Valley.

ŢŢŢŢŢ **Orange Riesling 2006** Verging on spatlese sweetness, but has plenty of fruit flavour, and balancing acidity; should appeal to Mosel lovers. Screwcap. 11.8° alc. **Rating** 90 **To** 2013 $21

ŢŢŢŢ **Orange Riesling 2007** Bright, clean, fresh and crisp; muted citrus and mineral flavours; dry finish. Screwcap. 12.4° alc. **Rating** 89 **To** 2012 $21

Orange Pinot Noir 2005 Authentic pinot noir in a distinctly stemmy/foresty style; has good length, though it doesn't swell or open on the finish. Cork. 13.5° alc. **Rating** 88 **To** 2010 $22

Orange Merlot 2003 Quite fragrant, with a mix of pretty red fruits, snow pea and olive; minimal tannins. Screwcap. 13.9° alc. **Rating** 87 **To** 2011 $22

La Curio ★★★★☆

11 Sextant Avenue, Seaford, SA 5169 (postal) **Region** McLaren Vale
T (08) 8327 1442 **F** (08) 8327 1442 **www**.lacuriowines.com **Open** Not
Winemaker Adam Hooper, Elena Golakova **Est.** 2003 **Cases** 700
La Curio has been established by Adam Hooper and partner Elena Golakova, who purchase small parcels of grapes from five vineyards in McLaren Vale with an average age of 40 years, the oldest 80 years. They make the wines at Redheads Studio, a boutique winery in McLaren Vale, which caters for a number of small producers. The manacles depicted on the striking label are those of Harry Houdini, and the brand proposition is very cleverly worked through. Winemaking techniques, too, are avant-garde, and highly successful. Exports to the UK, the US, Canada and Hong Kong.

ŢŢŢŢŢ **Reserve McLaren Vale Shiraz 2006** Super-rich, multi-layered, ultra-typical expression of terroir; blackberry, plum, prune and dark chocolate; tannins and oak an afterthought. Stained cork. Cork. 15° alc. **Rating** 94 **To** 2016 $28

ŢŢŢŢŢ **Reserve Bush Vine McLaren Vale Grenache 2006** Vibrant, fresh raspberry and red cherry flavours; strangely, alcohol is not the least hot, though the wine is slightly atypical for McLaren Vale. Cork. 15° alc. **Rating** 90 **To** 2012 $24

ŢŢŢŢ **The Nubile McLaren Vale Grenache Shiraz 2006** Very good colour; ripe, red fruits ex grenache given structure by the shiraz; some ripe tannins to close. Cork. 15° alc. **Rating** 89 **To** 2014 $19

La Fontaine ★★★

295 Manks Road, Fiveways, Vic 3977 **Region** Gippsland
T (03) 5998 1133 **F** (03) 5998 1144 **Open** By appt
Winemaker Wild Dog (Mal Stewart) **Est.** 2004 **Cases** 800
Brett Glover has established 6 ha of vines, and had a dream start when he entered the first vintage wines at the Gippsland Wine Show '07. The wines are available at local establishments in Cranbourne and Berwick, with the cellar door and restaurant opened in late 2007.

ΨΨΨΨ **Pinot Rose 2007** Spiced strawberries on a light, dry, crisp palate; pleasant style. Screwcap. **Rating** 87 **To** 2009 $24

Pinot Sparkling 2004 Fresh and lively, even if surprisingly simple 4 years since vintage; slight lemon tang to the finish. Cork. 13° alc. **Rating** 87 **To** 2010 $24

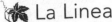 La Linea ★★★

36 Shipsters Road, Kensington Park, SA 5068 (postal) **Region** Adelaide Hills
T (08) 8431 3556 **www**.lalinea.com.au **Open** Not
Winemaker Peter Leske **Est.** 2007 **Cases** 1000
Partners Peter Leske and Jason Quin bring vast experience to this venture. After a number of years with the Australian Wine Research Institute, interacting with many wine businesses, large and small, Peter Leske became chief winemaker at Nepenthe for the better part of a decade. Jason Quin spent years at T'Gallant, one of the pioneers of pinot gris. Working exclusively with tempranillo to produce a serious Rose from a cooler part of the Adelaide Hills, and a dry red (tempranillo) from a separately owned vineyard in the warmer and drier northern end of the Hills, marks the start of the business. La Linea, Spanish for 'the line', reflects the partners' aim to hold the line in style and quality.

ΨΨΨΨ **Alito 2007** Very pale pink; light-bodied, with crisp spice, citrus and cherry flavours; a lively, dry finish. Tempranillo. Screwcap. 13° alc. **Rating** 87 **To** 2009 $21.95

La Pleiade ★★★★★

c/- Jasper Hill, Drummonds Lane, Heathcote, Vic 3523 **Region** Heathcote
T (03) 5433 2528 **F** (03) 5433 3143 **Open** By appt
Winemaker Ron Laughton, Michel Chapoutier **Est.** 1998 **Cases** NFP
This is the joint venture of Michel and Corinne Chapoutier and Ron and Elva Laughton. In the spring of 1998 a vineyard using Australian shiraz clones and imported French clones was planted. The vineyard is run biodynamically, and the winemaking is deliberately designed to place maximum emphasis on the fruit quality.

ΨΨΨΨΨ **Heathcote Shiraz 2006** Saturated, dense purple red; incredibly concentrated flavours of plum, Christmas cake, licorice, spice and dark chocolate; alcohol, oak and tannins all submerged in the fruit; prototype for a 100-year wine; 55 mm cork. **Rating** 95 **To** 2036 $65

Laanecoorie ★★★★

4834 Bendigo/Maryborough Road, Betley, Vic 3472 **Region** Bendigo
T (03) 5468 7260 **F** (03) 5468 7388 **Open** W'ends & public hols 11–5, Mon–Fri by appt
Winemaker Graeme Jukes, John Ellis (Contract) **Est.** 1982 **Cases** 1000
John McQuilten's 7.5-ha vineyard produces grapes of high quality, and competent contract-winemaking has done the rest.

ΨΨΨΨΨ **McQuilten's Reserve Shiraz 2006** Powerful and concentrated black fruits, licorice and leather, with appropriate tannins; carries alcohol with only a small protest. Diam. 15° alc. **Rating** 93 **To** 2021 $39.50

ΨΨΨΨ **Cabernet Sauvignon Cabernet Franc Merlot 2005** Has a broken line between the cassis fruits of the fore-palate and the green tannins of the finish, with an overtone of mint; curate's egg. Screwcap. 13° alc. **Rating** 87 **To** 2012 $23

Labyrinth ★★★★★

PO Box 7372, Shepparton, Vic 3632 **Region** Yarra Valley
T 0438 312 793 **F** (03) 5831 2982 **www**.labyrinthwine.com **Open** Not
Winemaker Rick Hill **Est.** 2000 **Cases** 8500
Rick Hill is running a unique wine business, the name Labyrinth being well chosen. While it is a Pinot Noir-only specialist, one is produced in the southern hemisphere (from the Yarra Valley) and one from the northern hemisphere (Santa Barbara, California) each year. The wines

come from individual vineyards: the Bien Nacido Vineyard has a deserved reputation as one of the best sources of pinot noir in California. Rick Hill uses leased space in California and at Long Gully Estate to make the wines, and also has active consultancy work in California.

♟♟♟♟ **Viggers Vineyard Yarra Valley Pinot Noir 2005** Very different to the Valley Farm; more complex in both flavour and texture; darker fruit flavours, and more savoury tannins, but still has the rigour and discipline for a long life. Cork. 14° alc. **Rating** 95 **To** 2015 $43

Valley Farm Vineyard Yarra Valley Pinot Noir 2005 Youthful colour; bright, firm, tightly focused style; pure line and length, similar to a young, unembellished Burgundy; and with time to grow. Cork. 13.3° alc. **Rating** 94 **To** 2013 $39

Lady Bay Vineyard   ★★★☆

Cnr Vine Drive and Willis Drive, Lady Bay, SA 5204 **Region** Southern Fleurieu
T 0413 185 771 **F** (08) 8445 1561 **www.ladybay.com.au Open** At Links Lady Bay Hotel
Winemaker Ben Riggs, Mike Brown (Contract) **Est.** 1996 **Cases** 1000
Lady Bay has 9.4 ha of viognier, pinot gris, cabernet sauvignon and shiraz a mere 500 m from the waters of the Gulf of St Vincent. On the inland side it is protected by the Great Gorge, part of the southern Mount Lofty Ranges. Cool days and warm nights provide good ripening conditions, even for varieties such as cabernet sauvignon.

♟♟♟♟♟ **Southern Fleurieu Shiraz 2003** Quite fresh for its age; tarry and full of dark fruit, with a long, chewy finish. Screwcap. 14.5° alc. **Rating** 90 **To** 2018 $30

♟♟♟♟ **Yankalilla Southern Fleurieu Viognier 2007** Clean and pure apricot aromas; very fresh, vibrant and clean on the finish. Screwcap. 13.5° alc. **Rating** 89 **To** 2009 $26

Yankalilla Southern Fleurieu Cabernet Rose 2007 A very dry, savoury rose; clean and varietal on the finish; tapas/antipasto friend. Screwcap. 13.5° alc. **Rating** 87 **To** 2009 $22

Southern Fleurieu Cabernet Sauvignon 2003 Clean and focused, with essency cassis fruit, and a hint of olive to close. Screwcap. 13.5° alc. **Rating** 87 **To** 2012 $28

Lake Barrington Estate   ★★★★☆

1133–1136 West Kentish Road, West Kentish, Tas 7306 **Region** Northern Tasmania
T (03) 6491 1249 **F** (03) 9662 9553 **www.lbv.com.au Open** Wed–Sun 10–5 (Nov–Apr)
Winemaker Steve Lubiana (Sparkling), Andrew Hood (Table) **Est.** 1986 **Cases** 400
Charles and Jill Macek purchased the vineyard from founder Maree Tayler in 2005. Charles Macek is a very distinguished company director (Telstra, Wesfarmers). Lake Barrington's primary focus is on high-quality sparkling wine, which has won many trophies and gold medals over the years at the Tasmanian Wine Show, with lesser quantities of high-quality chardonnay and pinot noir. There are picnic facilities at the vineyard and, needless to say, the scenery is very beautiful.

♟♟♟♟♟ **Alexandra 1999** Complex creamy/bready/yeasty autolysis characters at the outer end of the development phase; plenty of length and good balance. **Rating** 93 **To** 2009 $34.65

Lake Breeze Wines   ★★★★☆

Step Road, Langhorne Creek, SA 5255 **Region** Langhorne Creek
T (08) 8537 3017 **F** (08) 8537 3267 **www.lakebreeze.com.au Open** 7 days 10–5
Winemaker Greg Follett **Est.** 1987 **Cases** 15 000
The Folletts have been farmers at Langhorne Creek since 1880, grapegrowers since the 1930s. Since 1987, increasing amounts of their grapes have been made into wine. The quality of the releases has been exemplary, with the red wines particularly appealing. Lake Breeze also owns and makes the False Cape wines from Kangaroo Island. Exports to the UK, the US and other major markets.

ŶŶŶŶŶ **Arthur's Reserve Cabernet Sauvignon Petit Verdot Malbec 2004** A very complex full-bodied wine; big, rich and mouthfilling, with excellent flavour and persistence right across the palate; vibrant acidity draws out the harmonious finish. Cork. 14.5° alc. **Rating** 95 **To** 2025 $32

ŶŶŶŶŶ **Bernoota Langhorne Creek Shiraz Cabernet 2005** Medium-bodied, but with firm structure provided by the cabernet, which also introduces some attractive savoury/earthy nuances to the blackcurrant fruit, and a pleasingly dry finish. Screwcap. 14.5° alc. **Rating** 92 **To** 2017 $22

False Cape The Captain Cabernet Sauvignon 2005 An abundance of blackcurrant fruit on the medium-bodied palate; a little black olive savoury edge on the finish adds to the complexity. Screwcap. 14° alc. **Rating** 92 **To** 2016 $28

Winemaker's Selection Shiraz 2005 Bright hue; an elegant style, no more than medium-bodied, but with intensity and focus to the gently spicy black fruits; has very good length and balance, the tannins – as always – soft. Cork. **Rating** 91 **To** 2015 $40

Langhorne Creek Cabernet Sauvignon 2005 Vibrant redcurrant and cassis fruit, with good acid and plentiful fine-grained tannins; long and juicy on the finish. Screwcap. 14.5° alc. **Rating** 91 **To** 2020 $24

ŶŶŶŶ **False Cape Unknown Sailor Cabernet Merlot 2005** Good colour; toasty oak and bright red fruits; good flavour; a fraction simple. Screwcap. 14° alc. **Rating** 87 **To** 2013 $18

Lake Cairn Curran Vineyard ★★★☆

'Park Hill', Lethbridge Road, Welshman's Reef, Vic 3462 **Region** Bendigo
T (03) 5476 2523 **F** (03) 5476 2523 **www.**lakecairncurranvineyard.com.au **Open** By appt
Winemaker Sarah Ferguson, Rick McIntyre, David Cowburn (Contract) **Est.** 1987
Cases 800
When Ross and Sarah Ferguson purchased what is now known as Lake Cairn Curran Vineyard in 1999, they acquired not only 4.5 ha of chardonnay, pinot noir and shiraz, but also a slice of history, evoked by the beautiful labels. The Park Hill homestead dates back to the establishment of the Tarrengower Run in the 1840s, and the mudbrick cellar door is located adjacent to the homestead, overlooking the Cairn Curran Reservoir and Loddon River Valley. Notwithstanding that Sarah has almost completed a wine science (oenology) degree at CSU, and husband Ross has invested much time in training his palate, winemaking duties are spread around specialists in handling the various varieties.

ŶŶŶŶŶ **Wild Yeast Chardonnay 2006** Bright green-yellow; powerful wine, with stone fruit and some citrus elements; complex oak and a firm finish. Screwcap. **Rating** 90 **To** 2012 $19

ŶŶŶŶ **Chardonnay 2005** Tightly wound and still youthful; citrus elements to the core of stone fruit; subtle oak; will never be flashy or opulent, but well made. Screwcap. 13.5° alc. **Rating** 89 **To** 2012 $19

Shiraz 2006 Dense inky colour, but less extract (and texture) on the palate than expected; dark fruits and some oak; may open up more with time. Screwcap. **Rating** 89 **To** 2016 $20

Pinot Noir 2006 Far superior to the '05, with strong savoury forest floor and bramble components; has some plum and black cherry, but should be consumed asap. Screwcap. **Rating** 88 **To** 2011 $23

Blanc de Blanc 2006 Despite very limited time on lees, has good length of lemony citrussy flavour balanced by dosage designed to please. Cork. 13° alc. **Rating** 87 **To** 2010 $25

Lake Cooper Estate ★★★☆

1608 Midland Highway, Corop, Vic 316 **Region** Heathcote
T (03) 9397 7781 **F** (03) 9397 8502 **www**.lakecooperestate.com.au **Open** W'ends &
public hols 11–5
Winemaker Peter Kelliher, Donald Risstrom **Est.** 1998 **Cases** 900
Lake Cooper Estate is another substantial venture in the burgeoning Heathcote region, set on
the side of Mt Camel Range, with panoramic views of Lake Cooper, Greens Lake and the
Corop township. Planting began in 1998 with 12 ha of shiraz, and has since been extended
to 18 ha of shiraz, 10 ha of cabernet sauvignon and small plantings of merlot and chardonnay;
additional small blocks of more exotic varieties will follow.

♟♟♟♟ **Reserve Heathcote Shiraz 2006** Even riper than the varietal, with colour
suggesting a relatively high pH; within a particular style, which will appeal to some
but not others. Screwcap. 14.3° alc. **Rating** 89 **To** 2015 $30
Heathcote Cabernet Merlot 2006 Unexpectedly savoury/earthy; also some
dark chocolate undertones to blackcurrant fruit; medium-bodied and has good
texture and structure. Screwcap. 14.2° alc. **Rating** 89 **To** 2014 $20
Heathcote Shiraz 2006 Developed colour; unusual wine, even by Heathcote
standards; thick and bordering soupy, and with an abundance of ripe fruit; for a
barbecue T-bone. Screwcap. 14.2° alc. **Rating** 88 **To** 2014 $20

Lake Moodemere Vineyards ★★★☆

McDonalds Road, Rutherglen, Vic 3685 **Region** Rutherglen
T (02) 6032 9449 **F** (02) 6032 7002 **www**.moodemerewines.com.au **Open** Mon, Thurs,
Fri, Sun 10–4, Sat & public hols 10–5
Winemaker Michael Chambers **Est.** 1995 **Cases** 2500
Michael, Belinda, Peter and Helen Chambers are members of the famous Chambers family
of Rutherglen. They have 22 ha of vineyards (tended by Peter), with the Italian grape variety
biancone a vineyard speciality, made in a light-bodied late-harvest style. The cellar door sits
high above Lake Moodemere, and gourmet hampers can be arranged with 24 hours' notice.

♟♟♟♟♟ **Rutherglen Moodemere Muscat NV** Good muscat, with lifted red fruit florals
and good levels of sweetness; a fresher style for everyday drinking. Cork. 17.5° alc.
Rating 90 **To** 2009 $28

Lake's Folly ★★★★★

Broke Road, Pokolbin, NSW 2320 **Region** Lower Hunter Valley
T (02) 4998 7507 **F** (02) 4998 7322 **www**.lakesfolly.com.au **Open** 7 days 10–4 while
wine available
Winemaker Rodney Kempe **Est.** 1963 **Cases** 4500
The first of the weekend wineries to produce wines for commercial sale, long revered for its
Cabernet Sauvignon and nowadays its Chardonnay. Very properly, terroir and climate produce
a distinct regional influence and thereby a distinctive wine style. The winery continues to
enjoy an incredibly loyal clientele, with much of each year's wine selling out quickly by mail
order. Lake's Folly no longer has any connection with the Lake family, having been acquired
some years ago by Perth businessman Peter Fogarty. Peter's family company previously
established the Millbrook Winery in the Perth Hills, so is no stranger to the joys and agonies
of running a small winery.

♟♟♟♟♟ **Hunter Valley Chardonnay 2006** Bright green-yellow; the usual excellent
balance and structure; melon and nectarine fruit, barrel ferment oak inputs
perfectly judged. Cork. 13.5° alc **Rating** 94 **To** 2015 $50
Hunter Valley Cabernets 2006 Not a great vintage for red wines in the
Hunter, but this wine rises above expectations, the medium-bodied palate with
focused blackcurrant, raspberry and mulberry fruit, and a long, silky finish. Cork.
Rating 94 **To** 2016

Lambert Vineyards   ★★★★

810 Norton Road, Wamboin, NSW 2620 **Region** Canberra District
T (02) 6238 3866 **F** (02) 6238 3855 **Open** Thurs–Sun 10–5, or by appt
Winemaker Steve Lambert, Ruth Lambert **Est.** 1998 **Cases** 6000
Ruth and Steve Lambert have established 8 ha of riesling, chardonnay, pinot gris, pinot noir, cabernet sauvignon, merlot and shiraz. Steve Lambert makes the many wines onsite, and does so with skill and sensitivity. Definitely a winery to watch.

♀♀♀♀♀ **Reserve Canberra District Shiraz 2005** Shares most of the flavour characteristics of the varietal, but on a more intense level, both spending 22 months in French oak. Screwcap. 14.5° alc. **Rating** 93 **To** 2020 $40
Canberra District Shiraz 2005 Lively, very tangy plum, cherry and spice aromas and flavours run through a long palate, finish and aftertaste. Screwcap. 14.5° alc. **Rating** 90 **To** 2015 $25

♀♀♀♀ **Canberra District Riesling 2007** Has ripe topical fruit aromas and flavours; a fairly broad and soft palate reflecting the vintage; drink soon. Screwcap. 13° alc. **Rating** 87 **To** 2013 $18
Canberra District Chardonnay 2005 100% barrel ferment and 18 months in oak has left too strong a mark on soft, ripe melon fruit; some will like the style. Screwcap. 14.1° alc. **Rating** 87 **To** 2010 $20
Canberra District Pinot Gris 2006 Ripe, slightly grainy, apple, pear and musk flavours; a touch grippy on the finish. Screwcap. 13.1° alc. **Rating** 87 **To** 2009 $20

Lamont's Winery   ★★★★☆

85 Bisdee Road, Millendon, WA 6056 **Region** Swan Valley
T (08) 9296 4485 **F** (08) 9296 1663 **www.**lamonts.com.au **Open** W'ends & public hols 10–5
Winemaker Digby Leddin **Est.** 1978 **Cases** 10 000
Corin Lamont is the daughter of the late Jack Mann, and oversees the making of wines in a style that would have pleased her father. Lamont's also boasts a superb restaurant run by granddaughter Kate Lamont. The wines are going from strength to strength, utilising both estate-grown and contract-grown (from southern regions) grapes. There are two cellar doors, the second (open 7 days) in the Margaret River at Gunyulgup Valley Drive, Yallingup.

♀♀♀♀♀ **Family Reserve 2005** Strong colour; as usual, a multi-regional blend of the best parcels from the vintage; a luscious but not jammy mix of red and black fruits, tannins and oak assisting the very good length and balance of the wine. Cabernet Sauvignon/Shiraz. Screwcap. 14.3° alc. **Rating** 93 **To** 2020 $40
Margaret River Cabernet Sauvignon 2005 Retains excellent crimson hue; classic medium-bodied cabernet characters, with blackcurrant and cassis fruit and fine tannins; needs more mid-palate depth. Screwcap. 14° alc. **Rating** 92 **To** 2018 $35
Semillon 2006 Barrel-fermented in new French oak plus lees stirring for five months, but is neither heavy nor excessively oaky; controlled alcohol may be the answer; quality Swan Valley wine. Screwcap. 12.5° alc. **Rating** 90 **To** 2013 $30
Viognier 2007 Sophisticated handling of Chittering-sourced viognier, whole bunch-pressed and barrel-fermented in new French oak; seamless and harmonious, with peach and apricot fruit keeping its head above water. Screwcap. 13.8° alc. **Rating** 90 **To** 2011 $30
Shiraz 2005 Medium-bodied, but with excellent drive and thrust through the long, well-focused palate, easily disposing of the alcohol, with its attractively earthy/spicy fruit and savoury tannins. Screwcap. 15° alc. **Rating** 90 **To** 2020 $30
Navera NV A luscious blend of Pedro Ximenez/Frontignac, with a totally delicious mix of spice, candied fruits, toffee and butterscotch. Cork. 19° alc. **Rating** 90 **To** 2009 $30

♀♀♀♀   **Semillon Sauvignon Blanc 2007** Potent, strongly herbaceous fruit from start to finish; great with fish and chips. Screwcap. 13.5° alc. **Rating** 88 **To** 2010 $20
Chardonnay 2006 Well made, with positive fruit and oak contributions; the origin of the grapes is not shown and not easy to recognise – perhaps no bad thing. Screwcap. 13.5° alc. **Rating** 88 **To** 2011 $28

Landsborough Valley Estate

850 Landsborough-Elmhurst Road, Landsborough, Vic 3385 **Region** Pyrenees
T (03) 5356 9390 **F** (03) 5356 9130 **Open** Mon–Fri 10–4, w'ends by appt
Winemaker Walter Henning, Vicki Henning **Est.** 1996 **Cases** 6000
LVE (for short) originated in 1963, when civil engineering contractor Wal Henning was engaged to undertake work at Chateau Remy (now Blue Pyrenees). He was so impressed with the potential of the region for viticulture that he began an aerial search for sites with close friend Geoff Oliver. Their first choice was not available; they chose a site (which is now Taltarni), developing 40 ha. Taltarni was then sold, and the pair (with Geoff's brother Max) moved on to establish Warrenmang Vineyard. When it, too, was sold the pair was left without a vineyard, but in 1996 they were finally able to purchase the property they had identified 33 years previously, which is now partly given over to LVE and partly to the giant Glen Kara vineyard. They have established 20 ha on LVE, the lion's share to shiraz, with lesser amounts of cabernet sauvignon, pinot noir, chardonnay and riesling.

♀♀♀♀♀   **Geoff Oliver Classic Shiraz 2002** A medium-bodied strongly spicy savoury wine reflecting the cool vintage, with considerable show success. Has flourished over the four and a half years since previously tasted, its length and persistence of flavour admirable. Cork. 14° alc. **Rating** 92 **To** 2015
Pyrenees Ranges Cabernet Merlot 2005 Quite lifted and vibrant blueberry and cassis character; generous usage of oak complements the fruit, and regional mint on the finish is in tune with the wine. Screwcap. 14.5° alc. **Rating** 90 **To** 2014 $22

Landscape Wines

383 Prossers Road, Richmond, Tas 7025 **Region** Southern Tasmania
T (03) 6260 4216 **F** (03) 6260 4016 **Open** By appt
Winemaker Andrew Hood, Jeremy Direen, Alain Rousseau (Contract) **Est.** 1998 **Cases** 120
Knowles and Elizabeth Kerry run the Wondoomarook mixed farming and irrigation property in the heart of the Coal River Valley. In 1998–99 they decided to undertake a small scale diversification, planting 0.5 ha each of riesling and pinot noir. The labels, depicting Antarctic scenes by Jenni Mitchell, hark back to the Kerrys' original occupation in Antarctic scientific research.

♀♀♀♀   **Riesling 2007** Crisp bracing wine, light in body, but with length thanks to Tasmanian acidity; touches of passionfruit add to the appeal. Screwcap. 13.5° alc.
Rating 88 **To** 2014 $18

Lane's End Vineyard ★★★☆

885 Mount William Road, Lancefield, Vic 3435 **Region** Macedon Ranges
T (03) 5429 1760 **F** (03) 5429 1760 **www.**lanesend.com.au **Open** By appt
Winemaker Howard Matthews **Est.** 1985 **Cases** 450
Pharmacist Howard Matthews and family purchased the former Woodend Winery in 2000, with 1.8 ha of chardonnay and pinot noir (and a small amount of cabernet franc) dating back to the mid-1980s. Subsequently, the cabernet franc has been grafted over to pinot noir (with a mix of four clones), and the chardonnay now totals 1 ha. After working with next-door neighbour Ken Murchison of Portree Wines for two years gaining winemaking experience, Howard made the first wines in 2003. The 2005 Chardonnay received four significant awards in '07.

♥♥♥♥ **Macedon Ranges Chardonnay 2006** Light straw-green; has a fine, tight, minerally palate with subtle barrel ferment inputs; picks up on the finish and aftertaste; may develop. Screwcap. 13.5° alc. **Rating** 88 **To** 2013 $28

Langanook Wines ★★★★

91 McKittericks Road, Sutton Grange, Vic 3448 **Region** Bendigo
T (03) 5474 8250 **F** (03) 5474 8250 www.langanookwines.com.au **Open** W'ends & public hols 11–5, or by appt
Winemaker Matt Hunter **Est.** 1985 **Cases** 1500
When Matt Hunter was looking for a lifestyle change he left his position as Dean, Faculty of Business, Swinburne University, and searched for land around the cool, granite soil, apple-growing district of Harcourt. He planted vines in 1985 and kept the vineyard small enough so that he could personally control both the vineyard and winemaking (with help from the wine science course at CSU). Exports to Canada.

♥♥♥♥♥ **Bendigo Heathcote Syrah 2006** Vibrant colour; bright and focused with plenty of spice and blackberry fruit; lovely texture and lifted aromas, supported by fresh acidity and fine oak flavour. Screwcap. 15° alc. **Rating** 92 **To** 2014 $30

♥♥♥♥ **Reserve Bendigo Cabernet Sauvignon 2005** Some development with cassis joined by leather and tar; fleshy and rich across the palate, then a little bitter twist to the finish. Screwcap. 15.9° alc. **Rating** 88 **To** 2014 $30
Bendigo Sparkling Shiraz Cabernet 2006 Has some spice and verve, which gives it some of the personality normally only obtained through longer time on lees. Cork. 13.5° alc. **Rating** 87 **To** 2012 $26

Langmeil Winery ★★★★★

Cnr Para Road/Langmeil Road, Tanunda, SA 5352 **Region** Barossa Valley
T (08) 8563 2595 **F** (08) 8563 3622 www.langmeilwinery.com.au **Open** 7 days 10.30–4.30
Winemaker Paul Lindner **Est.** 1996 **Cases** 35 000
Vines were first planted at Langmeil (which possesses the oldest block in Australia) in the 1840s, and the first winery on the site, known as Paradale Wines, opened in 1932. In '96, cousins Carl and Richard Lindner with brother-in-law Chris Bitter formed a partnership to acquire and refurbish the winery and its 5-ha vineyard (planted to shiraz, and including 2 ha planted in 1846). Another vineyard was acquired in 1998, taking total plantings to 14.5 ha and including cabernet sauvignon and grenache. Exports to the UK, the US and other major markets.

♥♥♥♥♥ **The 1843 Freedom Barossa Valley Shiraz 2005** The extreme age of the vines (oldest in SA) manifests itself as much in the length as the depth of the wine, but also manages to carry the alcohol; medium–bodied, and highly polished tannins after two years in 70% new French oak. Cork. 15.5° alc. **Rating** 95 **To** 2020 $100
Barossa Old Vine Company Shiraz 2005 Full-bodied, but supple, round and plush, the sheer density of the black fruits from 100+-year-old vines submerging the alcohol and absorbing 60% new French oak; soft velvety tannins. Diam please. Cork. 15.5° alc. **Rating** 95 **To** 2020 $100
Valley Floor Barossa Valley Shiraz 2006 Deep colour; medium-bodied, but is rich and generous in flavour, the tannins and oak supporting the perfectly ripened plum and blackberry fruit. Cork. 14.5° alc. **Rating** 94 **To** 2020 $24.95
Jackaman's Barossa Valley Cabernet 2005 Achieves considerable intensity and length at a (relatively) modest alcohol; blackcurrant and cassis fruit backed up by positive, but balanced tannins. Screwcap. 14° alc. **Rating** 94 **To** 2025 $50

♥♥♥♥♥ **Orphan Bank Barossa Valley Shiraz 2005** The rich and opulent palate is no surprise given the alcohol; blackberry, plum and prune fruit, with soft tannins, and surprisingly little impact from that alcohol; 140-year-old transplanted vines fit somewhere in the picture. Screwcap. 15.5° alc. **Rating** 93 **To** 2025 $50

Hangin' Snakes Barossa Valley Shiraz Viognier 2006 Abundant red and black fruits lifted by viognier and supported by oak; supple and silky mouthfeel; good length. Screwcap. 14.5° alc. **Rating** 92 **To** 2012 $19.95

Barossa Eden Valley Riesling 2007 Unusually tight and minerally for the vintage; apple skin and slate; clean, dry finish. Screwcap. 12.5° alc. **Rating** 91 **To** 2012 $19.95

Earthworks Barossa Valley Shiraz 2006 A vibrant and fresh palate with red cherry, plum and some blackberry fruit; fine, ripe tannins; controlled oak. Screwcap. 14.5° alc. **Rating** 91 **To** 2013 $14.95

Barossa Valley Sparkling Shiraz NV Shows complexity both from mature base material then 24 months on yeast lees; flavoursome and balanced, neither too oaky or too sweet. Cork. 13.5° alc. **Rating** 90 **To** 2013 $35

Fifth Wave Barossa Valley Grenache 2005 Juicy berry flavours in a red spectrum, but not cosmetic/lollyish; good light- to medium-bodied structure, supported by soft tannins. Cork. 16° alc. **Rating** 90 **To** 2013 $30

♟♟♟♟ **Earthworks Barossa Valley Cabernet Sauvignon 2006** Abundant cassis and blackcurrant fruit on the medium-bodied palate; good tannins and gentle oak. Screwcap. 14.5° alc. **Rating** 89 **To** 2013 $14.95

Three Gardens Barossa Valley Shiraz Grenache Mourvedre 2006 Light colour; fresh juicy berry with some confection ex grenache; café style, drink soon. Screwcap. 14.5° alc. **Rating** 87 **To** 2010 $19.95

Lankeys Creek Wines ★★★★

River Road, Walwa, Vic 3709 **Region** North East Victoria Zone
T (02) 6037 1577 **www.**lankeyscreekwines.com.au **Open** 7 days 11–4
Winemaker Steve Thompson **Est.** 2002 **Cases** 2000
Lankeys Creek is the former Upper Murray Estate crushing 70 tonnes a year, making wine both for its own label and for other growers in the Tumbarumba region, from which most of the Lankeys Creek grapes come. Estate plantings are 3 ha each of shiraz, cabernet sauvignon and merlot, plus 2 ha of chardonnay and 1 ha of riesling. The white wines are made in Flexitank plastic bags, which winemaker Steve Thompson believes prevent oxidation and enhance flavour components, particularly with small batches.

♟♟♟♟♟ **Riesling 2006** High-flavoured and rich; good length and depth, perhaps a little too much of the latter. Screwcap. 11.5° alc. **Rating** 90 **To** 2010 $18

Riesling 2007 A tropical citrus bouquet then a palate bursting with rich, high-flavoured tropical fruit; ready right now. Tumbarumba flourishing in the warm vintage. Screwcap. 11.5° alc. **Rating** 90 **To** 2010 $18

Sauvignon Blanc 2007 Good passionfruit and tropical aromas and flavours; no smoke taint; despite the alcohol, has intense, citrussy acidity on the finish. Screwcap. 13° alc. **Rating** 90 **To** 2009 $20

♟♟♟♟ **Chardonnay 2004** Fully developed colour; a big wine, with some stone fruit and citrus; finishes short. Screwcap. 12.5° alc. **Rating** 87 **To** 2009 $18

LanzThomson Vineyard ★★★☆

Lot 1, Rosedale Scenic Road, Lyndoch, SA 5351 **Region** Barossa Valley
T (08) 8524 9227 **F** (08) 8524 9269 **www.**lanzthomson.com **Open** By appt
Winemaker Jamieson's Wine Consulting (Mark Jamieson) **Est.** 1998 **Cases** 1300
The friendship of the Lanz and Thomson families stretches back 30 years, although it was the two (future) wives who first became friends through Rotary International in the 1970s. In their words 'Brian and Thomas came on the scene over the next few years, sharing stories and bottles of wine'. One thing led to another, and in 1998 they began the establishment of the 15-ha Outlook Vineyard and the 16.5-ha Moolanda Vineyard, each planted predominantly to shiraz, each with around 2 ha of mourvedre and viognier, splitting only with grenache (1.44 ha) on Outlook and cabernet (3.25 ha) on Moolanda. The lion's share of the grapes is sold.

ΨΨΨΨ **Shattered Rock Four Friends 2006** An extremely lifted and fragrant bouquet; the light-bodied palate has exuberant juicy fruit, but needs more structure. Grenache/Shiraz/Mourvedre/Viognier. Screwcap. 14° alc. **Rating** 87 **To** 2009 $22
Shattered Rock Barossa Valley Cabernet Sauvignon 2006 Developed colour, suggesting elevated pH; soft black fruits, with mocha, dark chocolate and vanilla; gentle tannins. Screwcap. 15° alc. **Rating** 87 **To** 2009 $24

Lark Hill   ★★★★☆

521 Bungendore Road, Bungendore, NSW 2621 **Region** Canberra District
T (02) 6238 1393 **F** (02) 6238 1393 **www**.larkhillwine.com.au **Open** Wed–Mon 10–5
Winemaker Dr David Carpenter, Sue Carpenter, Chris Carpenter **Est.** 1978 **Cases** 4000
The 7-ha Lark Hill vineyard is situated at an altitude of 860 m, level with the observation deck on Black Mountain Tower, and offers splendid views of the Lake George escarpment. The Carpenters have made wines of real quality, style and elegance from the start, but have defied all the odds (and conventional thinking) with the quality of their Pinot Noirs in favourable vintages. Significant changes have come in the wake of son Christopher gaining three degrees, including a double in wine science and viticulture through CSU, the progression towards biodynamic certification of the vineyard, and the opening of a restaurant in 2007. In common with many vineyards, 2006 and '07 were marked by frost, hail, grasshoppers and drought decimating production, and because the business is biodynamic, the Carpenters were unable to make up the shortfall with grapes grown elsewhere.

ΨΨΨΨΨ **Riesling 2003** A museum reserve of this wine won the riesling trophy at the Canberra (regional) Wine Show '07 and, as the Carpenters say, is developing beautifully. **Rating** 94 **To** 2010 $30

ΨΨΨΨ **Canberra District Chardonnay 2006** A concentrated style, with fresh lemons, and hints of cashews; the palate is quite sweet and brings the conclusion to a heavy end; plenty of flavour though. Screwcap. 13.5° alc. **Rating** 89 **To** 2010 $35

Larry Cherubino Wines   ★★★★★

PO Box 570, West Perth, WA 6872 **Region** South West Australia Zone
T 0417 848 399 **www**.larrycherubino.com **Open** Not
Winemaker Larry Cherubino **Est.** 2005 **Cases** 2000
Larry Cherubino has had a particularly distinguished winemaking career, first at Hardys Tintara, then Houghton, and thereafter as consultant/Flying Winemaker in Australia, NZ, South Africa, the US and Italy. In 2005 he started Larry Cherubino Wines, and has since developed three ranges: at the top Cherubino (Riesling, Sauvignon Blanc, Shiraz and Cabernet Sauvignon); next The Yard, five single vineyard wines from WA; and at the bottom another five wines under the Ad Hoc label, all single region wines. As expected, the quality is exemplary. Exports to the UK, the US and Canada.

ΨΨΨΨΨ **Riesling 2007** Apple and citrus aromas lead into a palate of good intensity and length, with no sunburnt fruit characters to the lime and mineral flavours; good acidity. Top outcome. Screwcap. 11.5° alc. **Rating** 94 **To** 2015 $35
The Yard Riesling 2007 Tight and refined from the word go; intertwined lime juice and mineral run through the long palate; very good acid balance. From Whispering Hill Vineyard. Screwcap. 11.7° alc. **Rating** 94 **To** 2016 $31.50
Sauvignon Blanc 2007 A powerful expression of sauvignon, with the texture augmented by fermentation in 100% new French oak, and 5% semillon; nuances of apple and passionfruit. Screwcap. 12.5° alc. **Rating** 94 **To** 2009 $35

ΨΨΨΨΨ **Ad Hoc Straw Man Sauvignon Blanc Semillon 2007** Good structure, line and length; a firm, herbal core with some passionfruit and gooseberry; 10% oak invisible; pleasingly dry finish. Screwcap. 12.5° alc. **Rating** 92 **To** 2012 $23.50
Ad Hoc Wallflower Riesling 2007 A spotless apple blossom bouquet; a delicate and fine palate with apple, lime and pear flavours, seemingly early picked. Screwcap. 11.5° alc. **Rating** 91 **To** 2015 $23.50

The Yard Semillon Sauvignon Blanc 2007 Very tight and controlled, the flavours still largely locked up but all in a herbaceous spectrum with some barrel ferment oak in the background; hard to judge so early (January '08). Screwcap. 12.5° alc. **Rating** 90 **To** 2013 $31.50

ŶŶŶŶ **Ad Hoc Middle of Everywhere Shiraz 2005** Bright colour; very pure aromas and flavours in a predominantly red fruit spectrum, but not quite enough texture/structure. Screwcap. 13.5° alc. **Rating** 89 **To** 2013 $23.50

Lashmar ★★★☆

c/- 24 Lindsay Terrace, Belair, SA 5052 **Region** Kangaroo Island
T (08) 8278 3669 **F** (08) 8278 3998 **www.**lashmarwines.com **Open** Not
Winemaker Colin Cooter **Est.** 1996 **Cases** 1000
Colin and Bronwyn Cooter (who are also part of the Lengs & Cooter business) are the driving force behind Antechamber Bay Wines. The wines are in fact labelled and branded Lashmar; the Kangaroo Island Cabernet Sauvignon comes from vines planted in 1991 on the Lashmar family property, which is on the extreme eastern end of Kangaroo Island overlooking Antechamber Bay. The Three Valleys and Sisters wines (from other regions including McLaren Vale and Adelaide Hills) give the business added volume. Exports to the US, Canada, Singapore and Japan.

ŶŶŶŶ **Kangaroo Island Cabernet 2004** Complex aromas and flavours, running from herbal/spicy/savoury through to blackcurrant; 30 months in French and American oak has taken the freshness of the fruit. Screwcap. **Rating** 89 **To** 2013 $26

Latitude 35° South Wines ★★★☆

PO Box 812, Denmark, WA 6333 **Region** Great Southern
T (08) 9848 2081 **F** (08) 9848 2081 **www.**latitude35south.com.au **Open** By appt
Winemaker Harewood Estate (James Kellie) **Est.** 1998 **Cases** 1350
While from a farming background, Bob and Karen Cybula spent much of their working lives owning and operating supermarkets. When they sold their last Perth store in 2007, they decided to go back to their farming roots but with a difference: when they purchased an 80-ha property on Mt Shadforth, they decided to replace cows and kangaroos with vines. In 1998 they began the planting of 2.5 ha each of shiraz, chardonnay and merlot, 2 ha of pinot noir, and 1 ha each of semillon, sauvignon blanc and cabernet franc. Between 2001 and '03 the grapes were sold, but in '04 the first Latitude 35° South wines were made. In the meantime son Matthew (with a significant career as a chef) and wife Tamara (whose parents own Somerset Hill Winery, where Tamara formerly worked) took over management of the vineyards and supervision of the completion of the cellar door, which opened in 2008. Exports to China.

ŶŶŶŶŶ **Denmark Shiraz 2004** A truly spicy/peppery cool-climate shiraz; good array of leather and red fruits on the medium-bodied palate. Screwcap. 13.5° alc. **Rating** 90 **To** 2013 $27

Laughing Jack ★★★★★

Cnr Parbs Road/Boundry Road, Greenock, SA 5360 **Region** Barossa Valley
T 0427 396 928 **F** (08) 8562 3878 **www.**laughingjackwines.com **Open** By appt
Winemaker Mick Schroeter, Shawn Kalleske **Est.** 1999 **Cases** 1500
The Kalleske family has many branches in the Barossa Valley. Laughing Jack is owned by Shawn, Nathan and Helen, Ian and Carol Kalleske, and Mick and Linda Schroeter. They have just under 35 ha of vines, the lion's share to shiraz (22 ha), with lesser amounts of semillon, chardonnay, riesling and grenache. Vine age varies considerably, with old dry-grown shiraz the jewel in the crown. A small part of the shiraz production is taken for the Laughing Jack Shiraz. As any Australian knows, the kookaburra is also called the laughing jackass, and there is a resident flock of kookaburras in the stands of blue and red gum eucalypts surrounding the vineyards.

ŶŶŶŶŶ Limited Three Old Vine Moppa Barossa Valley Grenache 2005 Far more substance, both in fruit flavour and structure, than most Barossa Valley grenache; juicy black fruits with multi-spices and controlled tannins; 1920s planting, 1 tonne per acre. Cork. 16° alc. **Rating** 95 **To** 2020 $45
Limited Two Barossa Valley Shiraz 2004 Concentrated black fruits plus touches of licorice and dark chocolate; the cork quality does not inspire confidence, but the intensity of the fruit does; manages to carry the alcohol, the drinking span giving the cork the benefit of the doubt; 60 dozen made ex two barrels. 16° alc. **Rating** 94 **To** 2021 $85

ŶŶŶŶŶ Barossa Valley Shiraz 2005 Medium- to full-bodied; lusciously rich, but not jammy or over-ripe flavours of blackberry, licorice and dark chocolate; good structure. Cork. 14.5° alc. **Rating** 93 **To** 2015 $36

Laurance of Margaret River

3518 Caves Road, Wilyabrup, WA 6280 **Region** Margaret River
T (08) 9321 8015 **F** (08) 9321 8211 **www**.laurancewines.com **Open** 7 days 10–5
Winemaker Naturaliste Vintners (Bruce Dukes) **Est.** 2001 **Cases** 5000
Dianne Laurance is the driving force of this family business, with husband Peter and son Brendon (and wife Kerrianne) also involved. Brendon is vineyard manager, living on the property with his family. The 40-ha property had 22 ha planted when it was purchased, and since its acquisition it has been turned into a showplace, with a rose garden to put that of Voyager Estate to shame. While the wine is made offsite, a substantial wine storage facility has been built. But it is the tenpin bowling-shaped bottles that will gain the most attention – and doubtless secondary use as lamp stands. The way-out packaging does tend to obscure the quality of the wines in the eyes of intolerant geriatrics such as myself. Exports to Singapore, Hong Kong, Malaysia, Thailand and Japan.

ŶŶŶŶŶ White 2007 Strong varietal sauvignon blanc aromas, with nettles and riper fruits too; good texture and weight, with fresh acidity on the clean finish. Cork. 13° alc. **Rating** 90 **To** 2010 $28

ŶŶŶŶ Chardonnay 2006 A well-made, serious wine in an anything-but-serious bottle; restrained fruit with the suggestion of some scalping (flavour stripping) due to the cork. Good structure. 13.5° alc. **Rating** 89 **To** 2009 $30

Laurel Bank

130 Black Snake Lane, Granton, Tas 7030 **Region** Southern Tasmania
T (03) 6263 5977 **F** (03) 6263 3117 **www**.laurelbankwines.com.au **Open** By appt
Winemaker Winemaking Tasmania (Julian Alcorso) **Est.** 1987 **Cases** 900
Laurel (hence Laurel Bank) and Kerry Carland began planting their 3-ha vineyard in 1986. They delayed the first release of their wines for some years and (by virtue of the number of entries they were able to make) won the trophy for Most Successful Exhibitor at the Hobart Wine Show '95. Things have settled down since; wine quality is solid and reliable.

ŶŶŶŶŶ Pinot Noir 2006 Very good colour; has deliciously juicy, fresh and vibrant plum and cherry running through an even palate and finish; has excellent balance and mouthfeel. Screwcap. 13.3° alc. **Rating** 94 **To** 2013 $24

ŶŶŶŶ Cabernet Sauvignon Merlot 2006 Deep colour; in typical Tasmanian severe mould, but the briary blackcurrant fruit and firm tannin structure demand respect; does need time to soften and open up. Screwcap. 13.1° alc. **Rating** 89 **To** 2013 $28
Sauvignon Blanc 2007 Firm, straight-laced, mouth-puckering style, ideal for fresh seafood; does have presence and personality. Screwcap. 12.2° alc. **Rating** 88 **To** 2010 $20

Lawrence Victor Estate

Riddoch Highway, Nangwarry, SA 5277 **Region** Coonawarra
T (08) 8739 7276 **F** (08) 8739 7344 **www**.lawrencevictorestate.com.au **Open** Not
Winemaker Contract **Est.** 1994 **Cases** 1500
Lawrence Victor Estate is part of a large South Australian company principally engaged in harvesting and transport of plantation softwood. The company was established by Lawrence Victor Dohnt in 1932, and the estate has been named in his honour by the third generation of the family. Though a small part of the group's activities, the plantings are substantial, with 11 ha of shiraz and 20 ha of cabernet sauvignon established between 1994 and '99. An additional 12 ha of cabernet sauvignon and 6 ha of pinot noir were planted in 2000.

♀♀♀♀♀ **Cabernet Sauvignon 2005** Supple, round and smooth; well-integrated cassis and blackcurrant fruit, with high quality oak. Cork. 14.3° alc. **Rating** 93 **To** 2018 $20

Lazy Ballerina ★★★★☆

Woodgate Hill Road, Kuitpo, SA 5172 **Region** McLaren Vale
T (08) 8556 8753 **F** (08) 8556 8753 **www**.lazyballerina.com **Open** Fri–Sun &
public hols 10–5
Winemaker James Hook **Est.** 2004 **Cases** 800
James Hook, a leading viticulturist, and father Paul have set up a small – perhaps very small is a better description – winery in a converted McLaren Vale garage. The equipment extends to shovels, buckets, open fermenters and a small basket press, and enough French and American oak barrels to allow 20 months maturation. The grapes come from micro-selections from a number of vineyards in McLaren Vale, obviously chosen with great skill. Exports to the UK, the US, Canada and Singapore.

♀♀♀♀♀ **McLaren Vale Shiraz 2006** Very concentrated, with mulberry aromas and hints of fruitcake; thickly textured and quite chewy on the finish. Cork. 15° alc. **Rating** 92 **To** 2014 $25

Lazy River Estate NR

29R Old Dubbo Road, Dubbo, NSW 2830 **Region** Western Plains Zone
T (02) 6882 2111 **F** (02) 6882 0644 **www**.lazyriverestate.com.au **Open** By appt Wed–Sun
Winemaker Briar Ridge, Pieter van Gent **Est.** 1997 **Cases** 3000
The Scott family has planted 3 ha each of chardonnay and semillon, 1 ha of merlot, and 1.5 ha each of petit verdot and cabernet sauvignon. The vineyard has been established on rich loamy soil on the banks of the Macquarie River, 6 km from Dubbo.

Le 'Mins Winery NR

40 Lemins Road, Waurn Ponds, Vic 3216 (postal) **Region** Geelong
T (03) 5241 8168 **Open** Not
Winemaker Steve Jones **Est.** 1994 **Cases** 200
Steve Jones presides over 0.5 ha of pinot noir planted in 1998 to the MV6 clone, and 0.25 ha of the same variety planted four years earlier to Burgundy clone 114. The tiny production was made for Le 'Mins at Prince Albert Vineyard, and the wine is basically sold by word of mouth.

Le Poidevin

11 Elizabeth Street, Evandale, SA 5069 (postal) **Region** Mount Lofty Ranges Zone
T (08) 8363 3991 **F** (08) 8363 0905 **www**.sublimewines.net **Open** Not
Winemaker Kellermeister (Trevor Jones, Matt Reynolds) **Est.** 2005 **Cases** 2000
The name Le Poidevin is derived from the French, literally meaning the weight of wine. Greg Le Poidevin's great-great-grandfather Daniel Le Poidevin emigrated from Guernsey, arriving in Adelaide in 1850; various generations of the family retained links to the wine industry, with Greg manifesting his as a devoted consumer during his 35 years as a lawyer. Just as I

divorced my wife (law) and made my mistress (wine) my new wife, so did Greg Le Poidevin in 2005 when he obtained his producer's licence and severely curtailed his legal practice. He has established a virtual winery, sourcing the grapes for his white wine from the Adelaide Hills and the red wines from dry-grown vineyards in the Barossa Valley. A lifelong friendship with Barossa winemaker Trevor Jones has not only secured contract red winemaking of the highest standard, but also assisted in ferreting out small parcels of high quality fruit. In the outcome, the price of the wines has a most unlawyerly ring of modesty.

ΨΨΨΨΨ **Barossa Cabernet Merlot Shiraz 2006** Each of the varieties contributes to the super abundance of blackcurrant, plum, spice and licorice, all competing to be heard first; a modestly priced cellar special. Screwcap. 14.5° alc. **Rating** 90 **To** 2020 $19

ΨΨΨΨ **Adelaide Hills Sauvignon Blanc 2007** Clean bouquet with a mix of tropical and herbaceous characters; delicate palate without much drive. Screwcap. 12° alc. **Rating** 87 **To** 2009 $19
Adelaide Hills Unwooded Chardonnay 2007 Has more punch and life than many; honeydew melon and a squeeze of lemon juice; fresh finish. Screwcap. 13° alc. **Rating** 87 **To** 2010 $19

Leabrook Estate

4/3 Rochester Street, Leabrook, SA 5068 (postal) **Region** Adelaide Hills
T (08) 8331 7150 **F** (08) 8364 1520 **www.leabrookestate.com Open** W'ends 11–5
Winemaker Colin Best **Est.** 1998 **Cases** 5000
With a background as an engineer, and having dabbled in home winemaking for 30 years, Colin Best took the plunge and moved into commercial winemaking in 1998. His wines are found in a who's who of restaurants, and in some of the best independent wine retailers on the east coast. Best says, 'I consider that my success is primarily due to the quality of my grapes, since they have been planted on a 1.2 x 1.2 m spacing and very low yields.' I won't argue with that; he has also done a fine job in converting the grapes into wine. Exports to the UK, Ireland and Singapore.

ΨΨΨΨΨ **Adelaide Hills Sauvignon Blanc 2007** A subdued bouquet, then a powerful palate takes control, rich and seamless; has good length, but '07 has robbed it of the finesse it might otherwise have had. Screwcap. 13° alc. **Rating** 93 **To** 2010 $22
Reserve Adelaide Hills Pinot Noir 2005 While relatively light-bodied, has good focus and even better length as the wine unfolds in the mouth; spice and stems with red fruits; probably best sooner than later. Screwcap. 14° alc. **Rating** 93 **To** 2013 $33
Adelaide Hills Merlot 2005 Unusually strong colour foreshadows a merlot with more flavour and extract than most, yet retains varietal character in a dark-fruited, black olive spectrum. Screwcap. 14.5° alc. **Rating** 91 **To** 2015 $28

ΨΨΨΨ **Adelaide Hills Gewurztraminer 2007** Some spicy/peppery aromas along with rose petals; the residual sugar on the palate makes a seductive drink, but obscures the varietal character somewhat. Screwcap. 12° alc. **Rating** 89 **To** 2014 $25
Adelaide Hills Pinot Gris 2007 Strong ripe pear flesh flavours, with sweet fruit, then a balanced, dry finish. Screwcap. 12.6° alc. **Rating** 88 **To** 2010 $26

Leaky Door ★★★☆

61 Jones Avenue, Mt Clear, Vic 3350 **Region** Ballarat
T (03) 5330 1611 **F** (03) 5330 1851 **Open** By appt
Winemaker Michael Unwin (Contract) **Est.** 1999 **Cases** 200
John Weinrich, a local GP, doubtless shares much of the cost of running the vineyard, but it is wife Jay Mitchell (having completed a viticultural course with the South East Institute of TAFE in SA) who calls the shots and runs the vineyard. Their then teenage children helped the development of the vineyard, which has been a hands-on affair from start to finish. Currently a winery building is nearing completion; the widespread frost of 2006 meant no vintage in '07; thus the first real vintage came in '08. The vineyard is close-planted, primarily

to 2.5 ha of chardonnay and 0.5 ha of pinot noir, and is a favourite haunt of birds, wallabies and foxes, most of which pay little attention to the netting put on two months before vintage.

ϘϘϘϘ **Ballarat Chardonnay 2006** Very firm, austere wine reflecting the cold climate; has length, but needs to soften and open up. Screwcap. 13° alc. **Rating** 87 **To** 2012 $33

Leasingham ★★★★★

7 Dominic Street, Clare, SA 5453 **Region** Clare Valley
T (08) 8842 2555 **F** (08) 8842 3293 www.leasingham-wines.com.au **Open** Mon–Fri 8.30–5.30, w'ends 10–4
Winemaker Simon Osicka **Est.** 1893 **Cases** NFP

Successive big-company ownerships and various peregrinations in labelling and branding have not resulted in any permanent loss of identity or quality. With a core of high-quality, aged vineyards to draw on, Leasingham is in fact going from strength to strength under Constellation's direction. The stentorian red wines take no prisoners, compacting densely rich fruit and layer upon layer of oak into every long-lived bottle; the Bin 7 Riesling often excels. Exports to all major markets.

ϘϘϘϘϘ **Single Vineyard Release Provis Shiraz 2006** A super-saturated wine from go to whoa, the difference from Classic Clare primarily in the fine quality tannins, which provide immaculate texture and structure to the cavalcade of black fruits. Cork. 14° alc. **Rating** 96 **To** 2021 $120

Single Vineyard Release Schobers Cabernet Sauvignon 2005 This wine must come from a very special site in the Clare Valley, given its extreme purity and elegance; it has outstanding length, yet the tannins are more a consequence than a cause; high quality French oak, too. 14° alc. **Rating** 96 **To** 2021 $120

Bin 61 Clare Valley Shiraz 2005 Vivid, deep purple red; powerful, focused and perfectly balanced, with dark berry fruits and fine tannins; a great example of a classic label. Screwcap. 13.5° alc. **Rating** 95 **To** 2020 $24

Classic Clare Riesling 2005 Fragrant and elegant, still mainly in primary phase, apple, citrus and mineral all intermingling on the palate; a very different style to the '04. Screwcap. 12.9° alc. **Rating** 94 **To** 2016 $30

Classic Clare Riesling 2004 More developed and more powerful than the '05, with considerable grip to the long palate; very good fruit/acid balance; still has years of peak drinking. Screwcap. 12.5° alc. **Rating** 94 **To** 2014 $38.50

Classic Clare Shiraz 2006 Crimson; a surprisingly refined though intense and long palate driven by blackberry fruit; the tannins and oak support vehicles, the cork a potential roadside bomb. 14° alc. **Rating** 94 **To** 2016 $55

Classic Clare Cabernet Sauvignon 2004 Mainstream Clare cabernet with unapologetically trenchant black fruits, earth, herb and chocolate, with the sound and fury on entry softening marginally on the back-palate. Cork. 14° alc. **Rating** 94 **To** 2019 $55

Bin 56 Cabernet Sauvignon Malbec 2005 Powerful, youthful but perfectly balanced fruit, oak and tannins; the long history of the wine (1971 great) helps assure the long-term future. Screwcap. 13.5° alc. **Rating** 94 **To** 2029 $24

ϘϘϘϘϘ **Bin 7 Clare Valley Riesling 2007** Full-flavoured and very juicy lemon and lime fruit, braced by a distinct minerally core. Screwcap. 12.5° alc. **Rating** 93 **To** 2017 $23

Classic Clare Sparkling Shiraz 1997 Unmistakable and consistent style; deliberate introduction of oak balanced by high dosage appeals greatly to many, though not myself. Matured in puncheons for 31 months, then 2 years on lees with subsequent time on cork. 14.5° alc. **Rating** 92 **To** 2009 $51.99

Exclusive Release Clare Valley Riesling 2007 Released solely through cellar door, and made in the Mosel style suddenly appearing all over the place; has sexy, sweet lime pineapple juice on the mid-palate, but doesn't dry out quite enough on the finish. Screwcap. 9.5° alc. **Rating** 90 **To** 2015 $23

Bin 56 Cabernet Sauvignon Malbec 2006 Lively fresh wine, unusually so for the normally more robust Clare style, although there certainly is a background of tannins to the cassis fruit. Screwcap. 14° alc. **Rating** 90 **To** 2016 $26

♥♥♥♥ **Magnus Clare Valley Riesling 2007** As with all the Magnus wines, over-delivers, with abundant fruit and a good twist on the aftertaste. Screwcap. 12.5° alc. **Rating** 89 **To** 2013 $16.50

 # Leayton Estate
PO Box 325, Healesville, Vic 3777 **Region** Yarra Valley
T (03) 5962 3042 **F** (03) 5962 4674 **Open** Not
Winemaker Graham Stephens **Est.** 1997 **Cases** 200
Yet another partnership between medicine and winemaking: Dr Graham Stephens is a GP in Healesville, and together with wife Lynda, has established a 1.8 ha vineyard and a supplementary olive plantation on a 12 ha property west of Healesville. Two-thirds of the grapes are sold to Sergio Carlei, and one-third retained for the Leayton Estate label. Graham Stephens is still working full-time as a doctor, but intends to gradually wind back his medical hours and spend more time in the vineyard and winemaking.

♥♥♥♥ **Yarra Valley Chardonnay 2005** Bright colour; significantly more intensity and length than the '06; a linear style, and not particularly complex; minimal oak. Screwcap. 13° alc. **Rating** 89 **To** 2012 $22
Yarra Valley Chardonnay 2006 Clean, fresh, light-bodied melon and stone fruit; well made, though not intense; some development potential. Screwcap. 13° alc. **Rating** 87 **To** 2011 $23

Leconfield
Riddoch Highway, Coonawarra, SA 5263 **Region** Coonawarra
T (08) 8737 2326 **F** (08) 8737 2285 **www.**leconfieldwines.com **Open** Mon–Fri 9–5, w'ends & public hols 10–4.30
Winemaker Paul Gordon, Tim Bailey (Assistant) **Est.** 1974 **Cases** 18 000
A distinguished estate with a proud history. Long renowned for its Cabernet Sauvignon, its repertoire has steadily grown with the emphasis on single-variety wines. The style overall is fruit- rather than oak-driven. Exports to the UK, the US and other major markets.

♥♥♥♥♥ **Old Vines Coonawarra Riesling 2006** Floral apple blossom aromas; a bright and lively palate, with juicy fruit and a crisp finish. Dry-grown vines 30+ years old. Screwcap. 12.5° alc. **Rating** 94 **To** 2015 $19.95
McLaren Vale Shiraz 2006 Deeply coloured; dense and dark fruit aromas, with hints of chocolate and mocha; the palate is rich and chewy, but the flavour is vibrant and lively; very long, and quite tannic; patience required. Screwcap. 14° alc. **Rating** 94 **To** 2021 $30.95
Coonawarra Merlot 2005 Quite firm, clear-cut varietal character, with plum and redcurrant fruit running through a long palate and extended finish; good management of extract. Screwcap. 14° alc. **Rating** 94 **To** 2015 $24.95

♥♥♥♥♡ **Coonawarra Cabernet Sauvignon 2005** Masses of activity the moment the wine enters the mouth; sweet blackcurrant fruit swirling around savoury, but ripe tannins; good oak. Screwcap. 14° alc. **Rating** 92 **To** 2017 $30.95

♥♥♥♥ **Coonawarra Chardonnay 2006** Melon and stone fruit merge with barrel fermentation and six months' maturation in French oak for two-thirds of the wine, the remainder unoaked; a somewhat short finish. Screwcap. 13° alc. **Rating** 89 **To** 2012 $19.95

LedaSwan Organic ★★★

179 Memorial Avenue, Baskerville, WA 6065 **Region** Swan Valley
T (08) 9296 0216 **www**.ledaswan.com.au **Open** 7 days 11–4.30
Winemaker Duncan Harris **Est.** 1998 **Cases** 400
Owners Duncan and Deb Harris say LedaSwan is the only organic winery in the Swan Valley (certified as such in September 2006). All of its wines are made from the 2 ha of estate vineyards, producing organic table wines and preservative-free dessert wines.

Leeuwin Estate ★★★★★

Stevens Road, Margaret River, WA 6285 **Region** Margaret River
T (08) 9759 0000 **F** (08) 9759 0001 **www**.leeuwinestate.com.au **Open** 7 days 10–4:30
Winemaker Paul Atwood **Est.** 1974 **Cases** 60 000
Leeuwin Estate's Chardonnay is, in my opinion, Australia's finest example, based on the wines of the last 20-odd vintages, and it is this wine alone that demands a 5-star rating for the winery. The Cabernet Sauvignon can be an excellent wine with great style and character in warmer vintages, and Shiraz made an auspicious debut. Almost inevitably, the other wines in the portfolio are not in the same Olympian class, although the Prelude Chardonnay and Siblings Sauvignon Blanc are impressive at their lower price level. Exports to all major markets.

♟♟♟♟♟ **Art Series Margaret River Chardonnay 2005** Awesome power, grace, depth and finesse; pure grapefruit, nectarine and peach flesh aromas are framed by complex, toasty, grilled nuts; the palate is amazingly concentrated, yet portrays a lightness that is completely beguiling and incredibly long. Screwcap. 14.5° alc. **Rating** 97 **To** 2020 $96
Art Series Margaret River Cabernet Sauvignon 2003 Great colour, really vibrant; pure focused cabernet fruit bouquet, with a typical savoury edge of black olive and cedar; more cassis on the palate and the oak comes through with ample fine tannins in support. Cork. 13.5° alc. **Rating** 94 **To** 2020 $55.50

Lengs & Cooter ★★★★☆

24 Lindsay Terrace, Belair, SA 5042 **Region** Southeast Australia
T (08) 8278 3998 **F** (08) 8278 3998 **www**.lengscooter.com.au **Open** Not
Winemaker Contract **Est.** 1993 **Cases** 8000
Karel Lengs and Colin Cooter began making wine as a hobby in the early 1980s. Each had (and has) a full-time occupation outside the wine industry, and it was all strictly for fun. One thing has led to another, and although they still possess neither vineyards nor what might truly be described as a winery, the wines have graduated to big-boy status, winning gold medals at national wine shows and receiving critical acclaim from writers across Australia. Exports to the UK, Canada, Singapore and Malaysia.

♟♟♟♟♟ **Swinton McLaren Vale Cabernet Sauvignon 2004** Great hue; the full-bodied palate speaks eloquently of both variety and place, with a ripe tapestry of blackcurrant fruit and dark chocolate; how the wine has handled 3 years in new French hogsheads is amazing. Screwcap. 14.5° alc. **Rating** 94 **To** 2020 $25

♟♟♟♟♟ **Reserve McLaren Vale Shiraz 2004** Deep colour; very powerful, with oak in abundance, but then so are the black fruit and dark chocolate flavours, all sustained by ripe tannins. Built to last. Screwcap. **Rating** 93 **To** 2020 $50
The Victor McLaren Vale Shiraz 2006 Has more finesse and elegance than is common in McLaren Vale; spice and mocha overtones to the fruit, with particularly fine tannins. Good value. Screwcap. 14.5° alc. **Rating** 90 **To** 2016 $19
Old Vines Clare Valley Shiraz 2004 Supple and smooth, reflecting 30 months in French oak; quite sweet (not jammy) fruit on the medium-bodied palate, and a soft finish. Screwcap. 14.5° alc. **Rating** 90 **To** 2013 $30

Lenton Brae Wines ★★★★★

Wilyabrup Valley, Margaret River, WA 6285 **Region** Margaret River
T (08) 9755 6255 **F** (08) 9755 6268 **www.**lentonbrae.com **Open** 7 days 10–6
Winemaker Edward Tomlinson **Est.** 1983 **Cases** NFP
Former architect and town planner Bruce Tomlinson built a strikingly beautiful winery
(now heritage listed by the Shire of Busselton), which is now in the hands of winemaker son
Edward, who consistently makes elegant wines in classic Margaret River style. Exports to the
UK, Canada, Singapore and Vietnam.

ŸŸŸŸŸ **Margaret River Chardonnay 2005** Has tremendous length and intensity of
flavour, nectarine fruit and oak seamlessly woven together. A beautifully restrained
style developing slowly but surely. Screwcap. 13.6° alc. **Rating** 96 **To** 2015 $40
Wilyabrup Semillon Sauvignon Blanc 2007 In typical Lenton Brae style, with
immaculate line, length and balance, the French oak perfectly integrated with the
mix of citrus, gooseberry and herbs. A special 100-case release through cellar door.
Screwcap. 13° alc. **Rating** 94 **To** 2012 $30

ŸŸŸŸŸ **Margaret River Chardonnay 2006** An exercise in restraint from vineyard to
bottle; tightly focused nectarine, white peach and citrussy acidity are framed by a
fine bead of oak; will be long lived. Screwcap. 13.6° alc. **Rating** 93 **To** 2020 $40
Margaret River Semillon Sauvignon Blanc 2007 Rich and ample lemon,
herb and lime flavours; overall freshness and brightness; good length. **Rating** 92
To 2010 $20
Southside Vineyard Margaret River Chardonnay 2005 A junior sister,
perhaps, but also striking for its length (though not depth) of flavour, and the
elegance from the low alcohol; great summer's day chardonnay. Screwcap. 13° alc.
Rating 91 **To** 2011 $24
Margaret River Cabernet Sauvignon 2004 Medium- to full-bodied; regional
tannins make themselves felt from the first sip through to the end of the palate;
the fruit flavours are, however, correct; it all adds up to food required. Screwcap.
14° alc. **Rating** 90 **To** 2015 $45

ŸŸŸŸ **Cabernet Merlot 2005** Light- to medium-bodied; overall plenty of backwards
glimpses of Bordeaux; tangy, savoury notes to the blackcurrant fruit. Screwcap.
13.5° alc. **Rating** 89 **To** 2015 $22
Cabernet Merlot 2006 Good hue; medium-bodied; notes of mint and green leaf
run through the length of the palate. Screwcap. 13.2° alc. **Rating** 87 **To** 2010 $22

Leo Buring ★★★★★

GPO Box 753, Melbourne, Vic 3001 **Region** Barossa Valley
T 1300 651 650 **www.**leoburing.com.au **Open** Not
Winemaker Oliver Crawford **Est.** 1931 **Cases** 15 000
Australia's foremost producer of Rieslings over a 35-year period, with a rich legacy left by
former winemaker John Vickery. After veering away from its core business with other varietal
wines, it has now been refocused as a specialist Riesling producer. The top of the range is the
Leonay Eden Valley Riesling under a changing DW bin no. (DWI for 2005, DWJ for '06, etc),
supported by a Clare Valley Riesling and Eden Valley Riesling at significantly lower prices, and
expanding its wings to Tasmania and WA.

ŸŸŸŸŸ **Leonay Eden Valley Riesling 2007** DWK17. Lime blossom and touches of
spice; elegant, fine, intense regional lime juice, with lovely structure and length;
dances in the mouth with lively acidity; great achievement for the vintage.
Screwcap. 11.5° alc. **Rating** 96 **To** 2027 $36.95
Maturation Reserve Clare Valley Riesling 2005 Light straw-green; a
delicious wine, but still very delicate and with many years in front of it. Screwcap.
12° alc. **Rating** 94 **To** 2017 $49.95
Eden Valley Riesling 2007 Lime blossom aromas; lovely regional fruit
characters of lime juice; lively; and lots of finesse. Screwcap. 12.5° alc. **Rating** 94
To 2020 $18.95

Leopold Riesling 2006 DW J45. Wonderfully fine structure and length; strong mineral/slate streak along with apple and citrus in the background; perfect acid for long life. Tas/WA. Screwcap. 12.5° alc. **Rating** 94 **To** 2017 $39.95

ΨΨΨΨΨ **Leopold Riesling 2007** DW K20. Pale colour; bone-dry, crisp and tightly focused; some florals, but lime and slate linger on the palate; long future. Tasmania. Screwcap. 12° alc. **Rating** 93 **To** 2017 $39.95

ΨΨΨΨ **Clare Valley Riesling 2007** Lime, toast, lemon blossom and spice aromas; rich and full-flavoured; good balance, though not particularly long. Screwcap. 12.5° alc. **Rating** 89 **To** 2015 $18.95

Lerida Estate

The Vineyards, Old Federal Highway, Lake George, NSW 2581 **Region** Canberra District
T (02) 6295 6640 **F** (02) 6295 6676 **www**.leridaestate.com **Open** 7 days 10–5
Winemaker Malcolm Burdett **Est.** 1999 **Cases** 3500
Lerida Estate continues the planting of vineyards along the escarpment sloping down to Lake George. It is immediately to the south of the Lake George vineyard established by Edgar Riek 36 years ago. Inspired by Edgar Riek's success with pinot noir, Lerida founder Jim Lumbers planted 3.75 ha of pinot noir together with lesser amounts of pinot gris, chardonnay, shiraz, merlot, viognier and cabernet franc (7.4 ha total). The Glenn Murcutt–designed winery, barrel room, cellar door and café complex has spectacular views over Lake George.

ΨΨΨΨΨ **Lake George Shiraz 2005** Juicy, very ripe, red cherry, plum and blackberry fruits, with a sprinkle of spice, run through the palate, the tannins and oak neatly controlled but adding to the total. Screwcap. 15° alc. **Rating** 91 **To** 2020 $49.50
Lake George Botrytis Pinot Gris 2007 A muffled bouquet, but utterly remarkable richness and intensity, with layers of cumquat marmalade; citrussy acidity gives length and balance. Screwcap. 9.3° alc. **Rating** 90 **To** 2010 $30

ΨΨΨΨ **Lake George Shiraz Viognier 2006** Has the typical viognier lift to both bouquet and palate, but suffers from fractionally edgy oak. Has good length, and may settle down. Screwcap. 15.7° alc. **Rating** 89 **To** 2014 $59.50
Lake George Chardonnay 2006 Has tangy citrussy/minerally nuances to the core of melon fruit; the oak, however, is not entirely convincing. Screwcap. 14° alc. **Rating** 88 **To** 2011 $29.50
Lake George Merlot 2005 Extremely earthy savoury and extractive; finding the right place and the right way to make merlot in Australia continues to be as difficult as ever. Screwcap. 14.9° alc. **Rating** 87 **To** 2014 $39.50

Lethbridge Wines

74 Burrows Road, Lethbridge, Vic 3222 **Region** Geelong
T (03) 5281 7279 **F** (03) 5281 7221 **www**.lethbridgewines.com **Open** Thurs–Sun & public hols 10.30–5, or by appt
Winemaker Ray Nadeson, Maree Collis **Est.** 1996 **Cases** 2500
Lethbridge was founded by scientists Ray Nadeson, Maree Collis and Adrian Thomas. In Ray Nadeson's words, 'Our belief is that the best wines express the unique character of special places'. As well as understanding the importance of terroir, the partners have built a unique straw-bale winery, designed for its ability to recreate the controlled environment of cellars and caves in Europe. Winemaking is no less ecological: hand-picking, indigenous yeast fermentations, small open fermenters, pigeage (foot-stamping) and minimal handling of the wines throughout the maturation process are all part and parcel of the highly successful Lethbridge approach. Nadeson also has a special touch with Chardonnay, and has a successful contract winemaking limb to the business.

ΨΨΨΨΨ **Allegra Chardonnay 2005** Vibrant green-yellow; rich, supple, ripe nectarine and white peach supported by gentle French oak; line, length and balance. Screwcap. 13° alc. **Rating** 94 **To** 2012 $55

ㅸㅸㅸㅸㅸ **Chardonnay 2006** An intense, fruit-driven wine, the sweet fruit counterbalanced by lingering acidity. Screwcap. 13.5° alc. **Rating** 90 **To** 2011 $35
Geelong Pinot Noir 2006 Good colour; smooth and precise pinot flavours on entry, but with a faintly herbal finish; oak in the background. Diam. 13.5° alc. **Rating** 90 **To** 2013 $35

ㅸㅸㅸㅸ **Menage a Noir Geelong Pinot Noir 2006** Fresh, distinctly lighter-bodied than the varietal; red fruits and touches of mint; sweet and sour; ready now. Clever name. Screwcap. 13.5° alc. **Rating** 88 **To** 2009 $25

Leura Park Estate   NR

1400 Portarlington Road, Curlewis, Vic 3222 **Region** Geelong
T (03) 5253 3180 **F** (03) 5251 5199 **www.**leuraparkestate.com.au **Open** W'ends & public hols 10.30–5, 7 days Jan
Winemaker De Bortoli (Steve Webber) **Est.** 1995 **Cases** 600
Stephen and Lisa Cross gained fame as restaurateurs in the 1990s, first at Touché and then at the outstanding Saltwater at Noosa Heads. They have established a substantial 15-ha vineyard, planted to chardonnay, pinot noir, pinot gris, sauvignon blanc and shiraz. Most of the production is sold.

Liebich Wein   ★★★★

Steingarten Road, Rowland Flat, SA 5352 **Region** Barossa Valley
T (08) 8524 4543 **F** (08) 8524 4543 **www.**liebichwein.com.au **Open** Wed–Mon 11–5
Winemaker Ron Liebich **Est.** 1992 **Cases** 2500
Liebich Wein is Barossa Deutsch for 'Love I wine'. The Liebich family have been grapegrowers and winemakers at Rowland Flat since 1919, with CW 'Darkie' Liebich one of the great local characters. His nephew Ron began making wine in 1969, but it was not until '92 that he and wife Janet began selling wine under the Liebich Wein label. Exports to the UK, Mexico, Germany, Switzerland, Malaysia and Singapore.

Lienert of Mecklenburg   ★★★★

Box 5, Lienert Road, She Oak Log, SA 5371 **Region** Barossa Valley
T (08) 8524 9062 **F** (08) 8524 9208 **Open** Not
Winemaker Charles Cimicky (Contract) **Est.** 2001 **Cases** 530
The 21.5-ha shiraz vineyard owned by John and Cheryl Lienert is planted on land purchased by John's great-grandfather Conrad Lienert in 1880. The Mecklenburg area within the Barossa Valley was given that name in 1854 by émigrés from the Grand Duchy of Mecklenburg, part of the wave of settlers who left what is now Germany to gain religious freedom. John Lienert obtained a diploma of agricultural administration from Marcus Oldham College, Geelong, in 2000 and has overseen the establishment and ongoing management of the vineyard.

ㅸㅸㅸㅸㅸ **Reserve Sauvignon Blanc 2005** Densely coloured; dark fruitcake and a little mocha on the mid-palate, heavy, rich fruit on the finish. Cork. 14.5° alc. **Rating** 90 **To** 2020 $40

Light's View Wines/Pure Vision

PO Box 258, Virginia, SA 5120 **Region** Adelaide Plains
T 0412 800 875 **F** (08) 8380 9501 **www.**purevisionwines.com.au **Open** Not
Winemaker David Norman, Jim Irvine, Ken Carypidis **Est.** 2001 **Cases** 23 000
The Carypidis family runs two brands: Pure Vision has 15 ha of certified organically grown grapes, and there's a much larger Light's View planting of 54 ha of conventionally grown grapes. If you are going to grow grapes under a certified organic regime, it makes the task much easier if the region is warm to hot and dry, conditions unsuitable for botrytis and downy mildew. You are still left with weed growth (no herbicides are allowed) and powdery mildew (sulphur sprays are permitted) but the overall task is a much easier one. The Adelaide

Plains, where Pure Vision's vineyard is situated, is such a region, and owner Ken Carypidis has been clever enough to secure the services of Jim Irvine as co-winemaker. Light's View wines are exported to the US, Canada, China and Papua New Guinea, and the Pure Vision wines to the US.

ΨΨΨΨ **Pure Vision Organic Merlot 2005** An attractive, medium-bodied wine with clearly expressed varietal fruit, the savoury/olive notes balanced by sweeter redcurrant fruit. A triumph for the region. Screwcap. 14.5° alc. **Rating** 89 To 2012 $22.50

Light's View The Virginian Adelaide Plains Shiraz 2004 Lively, fresh red and black fruits in a light- to medium-bodied frame with good length – and good winemaking. Screwcap. 14.5° alc. **Rating** 88 To 2010 $13.50

Pure Vision Organic Shiraz 2005 Bright and clear; light- to medium-bodied, with blackberry and licorice fruit, fine tannins and good balance; brasserie style. Screwcap. 14.5° alc. **Rating** 88 To 2009 $22.50

Light's View The Virginian Adelaide Plains Merlot 2004 Amazing that the region can produce a merlot with so much varietal character; olive, black fruits, savoury but fine tannins, and good length. Screwcap. 14.7° alc. **Rating** 88 To 2011 $13.50

Pure Vision Organic Sauvignon Blanc 2007 Herb, grass and mineral aromas and flavours; bone-dry, and just a fraction grippy. Screwcap. 10.5° alc. **Rating** 87 To 2009 $17.50

Light's View The Virginian Adelaide Plains Merlot 2005 Defies the logic that merlot should adapt to the heat of the Adelaide Plains climate; is lighter-bodied than the '04, but has similar varietal character. Screwcap. 15° alc. **Rating** 87 To 2010 $13.50

Lilac Hill Estate ★★★★

55 Benara Road, Caversham, WA 6055 **Region** Swan Valley
T (08) 9378 9945 **F** (08) 9378 9946 **www.**lilachillestate.com.au **Open** Tues–Sun 10.30–5
Winemaker Stephen Murfit **Est.** 1998 **Cases** 15 000
Lilac Hill Estate is part of the renaissance that is sweeping the Swan Valley. Just when it seemed it would die a lingering death, supported only by Houghton, Sandalford and the remnants of the once Yugoslav-dominated cellar door trade, wine tourism has changed the entire scene. Lilac Hill Estate, drawing in part upon 4 ha of estate vineyards, has built a substantial business; considerable contract winemaking fleshes out the business even further.

ΨΨΨΨΨ **Swan Valley Verdelho 2007** Clear-cut fruit salad aroma and flavour; good mouthfeel, the fruit accented by citrussy acidity on a long finish. Screwcap. 13° alc. **Rating** 90 To 2010 $18

Cape White 2007 Fragrant fruit salad aromas and flavours, with plenty of character; the slightly sweet palate and finish is commercially desirable. Screwcap. 13.8° alc. **Rating** 90 To 2010 $18

Lillian ★★★★

Box 174, Pemberton, WA 6260 **Region** Pemberton
T (08) 9776 0193 **F** (08) 9776 0193 **Open** Not
Winemaker John Brocksopp **Est.** 1993 **Cases** 400
Long-serving (and continuing consultant) viticulturist to Leeuwin Estate, John Brocksopp established 3 ha of the Rhône trio of marsanne, roussanne and viognier and the South of France duo of shiraz and mourvedre. The varietal mix may seem à la mode, but it in fact comes from John's early experience working for Seppelt at Barooga in NSW, and his formative years in the Barossa Valley. Exports to the UK and Japan.

ΨΨΨΨΨ **Lefroy Brook Pemberton Chardonnay 2006** Grapefruit and pear, with a healthy dose of toasty oak; vibrant, and clean, the oak dominates now, but the creamy palate points to a healthy future. Screwcap. 13.5° alc. **Rating** 91 To 2012 $35

Pemberton Marsanne Roussanne 2006 A fine example of the blend, with hints of honeysuckle and dried straw; good flavour and depth, and a rich nutty finish. Screwcap. 14° alc. **Rating** 90 **To** 2012 $21

Lillico Wines ★★★

297 Copelands Road, Warragul, Vic 3820 **Region** Gippsland
T (03) 5623 4231 **F** (03) 5623 4231 **www**.lillicowines.com.au **Open** Thurs–Sun & public hols 10–6, or by appt
Winemaker Marie Young **Est.** 1998 **Cases** 1000
Cattle farmer Robert and senior nurse Marie Young impulsively planted 2 ha of cabernet sauvignon on their property in 1998. Two years later they added 1 ha of pinot noir, and in the meantime Marie had completed a diploma of horticulture, specialising in viticulture, at Dookie College. The first commercial vintage of cabernet was sold, and encouraged by the quality of the wine made from their grapes, Marie and Rob decided to produce some of their own wine. Marie promptly enrolled in the diploma of wine technology course, and now makes the wines. The vineyard is run on a no-pesticide and non-residual chemical regime, and the vines are not irrigated.

ŸŸŸŸ Gippsland Unwooded Chardonnay 2007 Ripe nectarine and lemon juice aromas; quite cool and minerally, with nice persistence of citrus flavour on the finish. Screwcap. 13° alc. **Rating** 89 **To** 2009 $17

Lillydale Estate

45 Davross Court, Seville, Vic 3139 **Region** Yarra Valley
T (03) 5964 2016 **F** (03) 5964 3009 **www**.mcwilliams.com.au **Open** 7 days 11–5
Winemaker Jim Brayne, Max McWilliam **Est.** 1975 **Cases** NFP
Lillydale Estate was acquired by McWilliam's in 1994. The major part of the production comes from the two estate vineyards, Morning Light and Sunnyside, planted in 1976. The names have been given by McWilliam's: the former is that of the ship that brought Samuel McWilliam from Ireland to Melbourne in 1857, and Sunnyside is the name of the first winery and vineyard he established at Corowa in NSW in 1877. The estate production is bolstered by contract-grown fruit from other growers in the Valley.

ŸŸŸŸŸ Yarra Valley Sauvignon Blanc 2006 Vibrantly crisp and fresh, lively acidity underpinning the gooseberry, passionfruit and lime flavours. Screwcap. 11.5° alc. **Rating** 92 **To** 2009 $19.95
Yarra Valley Pinot Noir 2006 Strong colour; red cherry, plum and rhubarb aromas and flavours; good length, balance and overall mouthfeel. Screwcap. 14.5° alc. **Rating** 90 **To** 2013 $26
Yarra Valley Chardonnay 2006 Very much in the understated estate style; fresh melon and nectarine fruit, oak a whisper in the background. Great length, and is certain to improve. Screwcap. 13° alc. **Rating** 90 **To** 2013 $19.95

Lillypilly Estate

Lillypilly Road, Leeton, NSW 2705 **Region** Riverina
T (02) 6953 4069 **F** (02) 6953 4980 **www**.lillypilly.com **Open** Mon–Sat 10–5.30, Sun by appt
Winemaker Robert Fiumara **Est.** 1982 **Cases** 18 000
Botrytised white wines are by far the best from Lillypilly, with the Noble Muscat of Alexandria unique to the winery; these wines have both style and intensity of flavour and can age well. However, table wine quality is always steady. Exports to the UK, the US and Canada.

ŸŸŸŸŸ Noble Blend 2006 Has fruit complexity as well as abundant sweetness; acidity nicely judged, the botrytis influence present but not overwhelming. Screwcap. 11° alc. **Rating** 90 **To** 2009 $24.50

ŸŸŸŸ VP Fortified Cabernet 1976 Has length and is not too sweet; but what style is it intended to be? Good clean spirit. Screwcap. 17.5° alc. **Rating** 88 **To** 2009 $55

Fratelli 7 Domenic Blend NV A tawny style, with an average age of over 20 years; has life and vivacity in a style not noted for such qualities. Screwcap. 19.5⁶ alc. **Rating** 88 **To** 2009 $23.50

VP 1998 As the bottle suggests, more a tawny than a vintage port; not bottle aged, actually has no Australian parallel. Screwcap. 20.5° alc. **Rating** 87 **To** 2010 $17.50

Limbic

NR

295 Morrison Road, Pakenham Upper, Vic 3810 **Region** Port Phillip Zone
T (03) 5942 7723 **F** (03) 5942 7723 **www**.limbicwines.com.au **Open** By appt
Winemaker Michael Pullar **Est.** 1997 **Cases** 600

Jennifer and Michael Pullar have established a vineyard on the hills between Yarra Valley and Gippsland, overlooking the Mornington Peninsula and Westernport Bay (thus entitled only to the Port Phillip Zone GI). They have planted 3.1 ha of pinot noir, 1.8 ha of chardonnay and 1.3 ha of sauvignon blanc, increasingly using organic and thereafter biodynamic practices. Trial vintages under the Limbic label commenced in 2001, followed by the first commercial releases in '03. 'Limbic' is the word for a network of neural pathways in the brain that link smell, taste and emotion.

Linda Domas Wines

★★★★★

PO Box 1988, McLaren Flat, SA 5171 **Region** McLaren Vale
T (08) 8383 0195 **F** (08) 8383 0178 **www**.ldwines.com.au **Open** Not
Winemaker Linda Domas **Est.** 2003 **Cases** 5000

Linda Domas, Steve Brunato and Markus Domas have their fingers in many vinous pies in many parts of the world. The venture came into being in 2001, made by Linda Domas and Steve Brunato while they were holidaying in Australia. At that time both were employed by Casa Vinicola Calatrasi in Sicily, Linda in charge of winemaking and Steve head viticulturist for the company's vineyards in Tunisia, Sicily and Puglia. After three vintages with Calatrasi, they decided to head home to McLaren Vale to start their own label, making both the Linda Domas wines and other contract-made wines in leased space at Daringa Cellars. To keep them in touch with the rest of the world, they say, they have done both winemaking and viticulture work in Slovenia, Bulgaria, and are currently undertaking a project with Sula Wines in Nashik, India. It can safely be said they are very busy. Exports to the UK, the US, Canada, Chile, China and Singapore.

ŸŸŸŸŸ **Salience Southern Fleurieu Sauvignon Blanc 2007** Bright and fresh; considerable thrust to the progression from gentle tropical/passionfruit aromas to a grassy palate, and citrussy acid on the finish. Screwcap. 11.5° alc. **Rating** 94 **To** 2010 $20

Egidio McLaren Vale Shiraz 2005 A lovely style, lively and spicy, with far more velocity than higher alcohol McLaren Vale wines possess; bright red fruits on the finish. Ready now. Screwcap. 13.5° alc. **Rating** 94 **To** 2012 $28

Shot Bull Southern Fleurieu Shiraz 2005 Great colour; more depth and structure than Egidio, with fine, savoury tannins interwoven with black fruits. Screwcap. 13.5° alc. **Rating** 94 **To** 2017 $25

ŸŸŸŸŸ **Shot Bull Southern Fleurieu Rose 2007** Salmon-pink; has interesting flavour and texture highlights in a spicy/savoury range; a dry, long finish. Screwcap. 13° alc. **Rating** 90 **To** 2009 $16

ŸŸŸŸ **Vis a Vis Southern Fleurieu Viognier Chardonnay 2007** Stone fruit and grapefruit are the dominant flavours deriving from the chardonnay component, unsullied by oak; fresh crisp finish. Screwcap. 12.5° alc. **Rating** 88 **To** 2010 $20

Our Souls Southern Fleurieu Semillon Sauvignon Blanc Viognier 2007 Early picking accentuates the freshness and acidity, with grass and mineral flavours dominant; good length. Screwcap. 11° alc. **Rating** 88 **To** 2010 $16

Alchemy McLaren Vale Shiraz Grenache 2006 Juicy, spicy and lively red and black fruits on a light- to medium-bodied palate. Screwcap. 14.5° alc. **Rating** 88 **To** 2012 $20

Boycat McLaren Vale Merlot 2006 Borders on overripe flavours for merlot, but there are some herb and olive notes to give varietal balance. Screwcap. 13.5° alc. **Rating** 88 **To** 2011 $25

Top Hat McLaren Vale Grenache 2006 Light but clear juicy/jammy grenache varietal fruit; drink-me-quick style; lighter than most McLaren Vale grenaches. Screwcap. 14° alc. **Rating** 87 **To** 2009 $25

Lindemans (Coonawarra/Padthaway)　★★★★★

Coonawarra Wine Gallery, Riddoch Highway, Coonawarra, SA 5263 **Region** Coonawarra
T (08) 8737 3250 **F** (08) 8737 3231 **www**.lindemans.com **Open** 7 days 10–5
Winemaker Brett Sharpe **Est.** 1908 **Cases** 7 million
Lindemans' Limestone Coast vineyards are of increasing significance because of the move towards regional identity in the all-important export markets, which has led to the emergence of a range of regional/varietal labels. After a quiet period, the wines are on the march again. Exports to the UK, the US, Canada and NZ.

🍷🍷🍷🍷🍷 **Pyrus 2005** Medium-bodied and elegant; a supple, well-balanced palate with blackcurrant backed by ripe tannins and good oak. Trophy, Limestone Coast Wine Show '07. **Rating** 95 **To** 2018 $54.95
Reserve Padthaway Shiraz 2005 Rich, ripe blackberry, plum and prune fruit, teetering on the edge of excessive ripeness, but not extractive; considerable presence. Top gold, National Wine Show '07. Screwcap. 14° alc. **Rating** 94 **To** 2015 $13.95

🍷🍷🍷🍷🍷 **Limestone Ridge 2005** Continues the return to form for the Lindemans stable; solid, quite chunky, fruit, with pleasant savoury tannins. **Rating** 90 **To** 2018 $54.95
Rouge Homme Cabernet Sauvignon 2005 Subtle, smooth medium-bodied palate; mulberry and blackcurrant fruit, with balanced oak and ripe tannins. Screwcap. **Rating** 90 **To** 2015 $16.95
St George Coonawarra Cabernet Sauvignon 2005 Light- to medium-bodied; elegant wine with blackcurrant fruit interwoven with powdery tannins; was it picked a little too early? Screwcap. 13° alc. **Rating** 90 **To** 2015 $54.95

🍷🍷🍷🍷 **Reserve Merlot 2005** The wine does have good texture and structure, with attractive savoury tannins, although the oak is not convincing. **Rating** 87 **To** 2011 $13.95

Lindemans (Hunter Valley)　★★★★

McDonalds Road, Pokolbin, NSW 2320 **Region** Lower Hunter Valley
T (02) 4998 7684 **F** (02) 4998 7324 **www**.lindemans.com.au **Open** 7 days 10–5
Winemaker Matthew Johnson **Est.** 1843 **Cases** 7 million
One way or another, I have intersected with the Hunter Valley in general and Lindemans in particular for over 50 years. The wines are no longer made in the Lower Hunter, and the once mighty Semillon is a mere shadow of its former self. However, the refurbished historic Ben Ean winery (while no longer making wine) is a must-see for the wine tourist. Exports to the UK, the US and other major markets.

🍷🍷🍷🍷🍷 **Limited Release Hunter River Semillon 2007** Bin 0755. Good mouthfeel, line and length; pure semillon fruit flavours, the accent on lemon, herb and lanolin; from several vineyards up to 80 years old. Screwcap. 11° alc. **Rating** 91 **To** 2015
Limited Release Hunter River Shiraz 2006 Bin 0603. Elegant medium-bodied wine from 35-year-old vines on red soil; some earthy notes attest to the region; subtle French oak. Screwcap. 14° alc. **Rating** 90 **To** 2020

Lindemans (Karadoc)　★★★

John's Way, Karadoc via Red Cliffs, Vic 3496 **Region** Murray Darling
T (03) 5051 3285 **F** (03) 5051 3390 **www**.lindemans.com **Open** 7 days 10–4.30
Winemaker Hayden Donohue **Est.** 1974 **Cases** 7 million

Now the production centre for all the Lindemans and Leo Buring wines, with the exception of special lines made in Coonawarra. The very large winery allows all-important economies of scale, and is the major processing centre for Foster's beverage wine sector (casks, flagons and low-priced bottles). Exports to all major markets.

Bin 50 Shiraz 2007 Generous, round and smooth light- to medium-bodied blackberry flavours; ready now, and outperforms its price. Screwcap. 13.5° alc. Rating 88 To 2012 $10.95
Early Harvest Semillon Sauvignon Blanc 2007 A brave attempt, though the low alcohol strips the flavour; an honorary 87 points for the sake of interest, and a 30% reduction in calories. Screwcap. 8.5° alc. Rating 87 To 2009 $13.95
Bin 65 Chardonnay 2007 An important wine for Australia, even after donating its market share in the US to yellowtail; clean, bright, quite fresh, with balanced peachy/stone fruit; oak irrelevant, and isn't obviously sweet. Screwcap. 13.5° alc. Rating 87 To 2009 $10.95
Bin 95 Sauvignon Blanc 2007 A clean bouquet; a light but quite bright palate with echoes of passionfruit and stone fruit; good value. Screwcap. 11.5° alc. Rating 87 To 2009 $10.95
Early Harvest Crisp Dry White 2007 A subliminal hint of sweetness gives the wine slightly more mouthfeel without compromising the freshness. Screwcap. 8.5° alc. Rating 87 To 2009 $13.95

Linfield Road Wines

65 Victoria Terrace, Williamstown, SA 5351 **Region** Barossa Valley
T (08) 8524 6140 **F** (08) 8524 6427 **www**.linfieldroadwines.com **Open** 7 days 10–5
Winemaker David Norman **Est.** 2002 **Cases** 10 000
The Wilson family has been growing grapes at their estate vineyard for over 100 years; Steve and Deb Wilson are fourth-generation vignerons. The vineyard is in one of the coolest parts of the Barossa Valley, in an elevated position near the Adelaide Hills boundary. The estate's 19 ha are planted to riesling, cabernet sauvignon, semillon, shiraz, merlot, grenache and chardonnay. In 2002 the Wilsons decided to vinify part of the production. Within 12 months of the first release, the wines had accumulated three trophies and five gold medals. An (as ever) delayed ambition to open a cellar door finally came to pass in mid-2008.

Edmund Major Reserve Shiraz 2005 The 100-year-old vines impart thrust and authority on the back-palate and finish of the wine, after a relatively quiet and slow start on the palate; will surely gain with extended cellaring. Screwcap. 14.5° alc. Rating 90 To 2025 $65

Lirralirra Estate

15 Paynes Road, Chirnside Park, Vic 3116 **Region** Yarra Valley
T (03) 9735 0224 **F** (03) 9735 0224 **www**.lirralirraestate.com.au **Open** W'ends & hols 10–6
Winemaker Alan Smith **Est.** 1981 **Cases** 400
Alan Smith started Lirralirra with the intention of specialising in a Sauternes-style blend of botrytised semillon and sauvignon blanc. It seemed a good idea – in a sense it still does on paper – but it simply didn't work. He has changed direction to a more conventional mix with dignity and humour, challenged by the mysterious removal of winery direction signs in 2006, and by the combination of drought and frost, which meant no grapes at all in '07.

Pinot Noir 2006 Solid wine, strong structure for the ripe plummy fruit; oak and tannins needing time to settle down. Screwcap. Rating 89 To 2013 $30
Cabernets 2006 Unequivocally cool-grown (despite warm vintage) with overtones of spice, leaf, olive and mint to the cornerstones of black fruits and firm acidity on the finish; good future. Screwcap. Rating 88 To 2015 $25
Cabernets 2005 Bottled on the same day as the '06, and shows a softer, juicier profile, with seemingly more oak influence; more in a drink-soon style. Screwcap. Rating 88 To 2011 $25

Little Brampton Wines

PO Box 61, Clare, SA 5453 **Region** Clare Valley
T (08) 8843 4201 **www**.littlebramptonwines.com.au **Open** By appt
Winemaker Contract **Est.** 2001 **Cases** 800
Little Brampton Wines is a boutique, family-owned business operated by Alan and Pamela Schwarz. They purchased their 24-ha property in the heart of the Clare Valley in the early 1990s (Alan graduated from Roseworthy in 1981). The property has produced grapes since the 1860s, but the vineyard had been removed during the Vine Pull Scheme of the 1980s. The Schwarzes have replanted 10 ha to riesling, shiraz and cabernet sauvignon on northwest slopes at 520 m; a small proportion of the production is vinified for the Little Brampton label.

ŸŸŸŸ **Clare Valley Cabernet Sauvignon 2005** Soft and varietal with a whisp of mint; bright and juicy on the finish. Screwcap. 14.9° alc. **Rating** 87 **To** 2010 $19

Little Bridge ★★★

PO Box 499, Bungendore, NSW 2621 **Region** Canberra District
T (02) 6226 6620 **F** (02) 6226 6842 **www**.littlebridgewines.com.au **Open** Not
Winemaker Canberra Winemakers (Greg Gallagher, Rob Howell), Mallaluka
Winemakers (John Leyshon) **Est.** 1996 **Cases** 1000
Little Bridge is a partnership between long-term friends John Leyshon, Rowland Clark, John Jeffrey and Steve Dowton. Two ha of chardonnay, pinot noir, riesling and merlot were planted on Rowland Clark's property at Butmaroo, near Bungendore, at an altitude of 860 m. In 2004 a further 2.5 ha of shiraz, cabernet sauvignon, sangiovese, grenache and gamay were planted on John Leyshon's property near Yass (560 m). Canberra Winemakers makes the white wines, and the reds are made at Bungendore.

ŸŸŸŸ **Canberra District Cabernet Sauvignon 2005** Light- to medium-bodied mix of red and blackcurrant fruit, with nuances of mint and spice, the tannins at maximum level for the fruit. Screwcap. 13.5° alc. **Rating** 87 **To** 2013 $20

Littles ★★★

Cnr Palmers Lane/McDonalds Road, Pokolbin, NSW 2321 **Region** Lower Hunter Valley
T (02) 4998 7626 **F** (02) 4998 7867 **www**.littleswinery.com.au **Open** Fri–Mon 10–4.30
Winemaker Peter Orr (Contract) **Est.** 1984 **Cases** 2000
Littles is managed by the Kindred family, the ownership involving a number of investors. The winery has mature vineyards planted to shiraz (6 ha), semillon (7.2 ha), chardonnay (5.7 ha), pinot noir (1.4 ha), cabernet sauvignon (1.8 ha) and marsanne (0.7 ha). Exports to Germany, Taiwan and Japan.

ŸŸŸŸ **Premium Cuvee Pinot Noir Chardonnay 2005** Clean citrus fruit, with a vibrant mousse and good flavour. Cork. 13° alc. **Rating** 87 **To** 2010 $23

Llangibby Estate

off Old Mount Barker Road, Echunga, SA 5153 **Region** Adelaide Hills
T (08) 8398 5505 **F** (08) 8398 5505 **www**.llangibbyestate.com **Open** By appt
Winemaker Chris Addams Williams, John Williamson, James Hastwell **Est.** 1998
Cases 1200
Chris Addams Williams and John Williamson have established a substantial vineyard cresting a ridge close to Echunga, at an altitude of 360 m. The vineyard plantings have morphed since the outset; there are now 7.09 ha of sauvignon blanc, 4.67 ha pinot gris, 1.95 tempranillo and 0.17 ha pinot noir, with most of the grapes sold to other producers. Exports to the UK.

ŸŸŸŸŸ **Adelaide Hills Tempranillo Shiraz Cabernet Sauvignon 2005** Light-bodied, vibrant and fresh, with no reduction to the predominantly red fruits; fine tannins, minimal oak. Great bargain. Screwcap. 14.5° alc. **Rating** 90 **To** 2009 $10

Lloyd Brothers

34 Warners Road, McLaren Vale, SA 5171 **Region** McLaren Vale
T (08) 8323 8792 **F** (08) 8323 8833 **www.**lloydbrothers.com.au **Open** 7 days 10–5
Winemaker Sam Temme **Est.** 2002 **Cases** 2500
The business is owned by David Lloyd (nephew of Mark Lloyd, and son of the late Guy Lloyd of Lloyd Aviation). It has 12 ha of shiraz planted 10–12 years ago, and shares a property with a planting of old olive trees, which produces high-quality table olives and extra-virgin olive oil sold through The Olive Grove at McLaren Vale. Lloyd Brothers sells a significant part of its grape production (inter alia to d'Arenberg) and sells the entire crop in years where the standard is not considered high enough to warrant an estate release. Lloyd Brothers also has an Adelaide Hills vineyard planted to 5 ha of chardonnay, verdelho, pinot noir and sauvignon blanc; their Adelaide Hills cellar door is at 94 Main St, Hahndorf.

ΨΨΨΨΨ **McLaren Vale Shiraz 2005** A very attractive bouquet of pure varietal fruit and subtle oak; ample weight on the palate, with a long fleshy finish; lovely purity throughout. Screwcap. 14.5° alc. **Rating** 94 **To** 2018 $19

ΨΨΨΨΨ **White Chalk McLaren Vale Shiraz 2006** Slightly reduced, and more tannin and savoury fruits in evidence; roasted meats and briar accompany a healthy use of oak; needs time, but should reward. Screwcap. 15° alc. **Rating** 93 **To** 2025 $38
McLaren Vale Shiraz 2006 Abundant dark fruits, with mocha and fruitcake on the bouquet and palate; rich and full on the ample full-fruited finish. Screwcap. 14.5° alc. **Rating** 92 **To** 2018 $19
Bonvale Adelaide Hills Chardonnay 2007 Aromas of melon and grapefruit on the bouquet; good flavour, and cleansing acidity on the finish. Screwcap. 13.2° alc. **Rating** 90 **To** 2012 $19

ΨΨΨΨ **Bonvale Adelaide Hills Chardonnay 2006** Pale lemon; a ripe and brassy bouquet, with good acid to clean the palate and finish. Screwcap. 13.5° alc. **Rating** 88 **To** 2012 $17

Lobethal Road Wines

PO Box 367, Mount Torrens, SA 5244 **Region** Adelaide Hills
T 0439 894 595 **F** (08) 8389 4595 **www.**lobethalroad.com **Open** Not
Winemaker Michael Sykes (Contract) **Est.** 1998 **Cases** 1400
Dave Neyle and Inga Lidums bring diverse but very relevant experience to the 5-ha Lobethal Road vineyard, which has 2 ha of chardonnay, 1.5 ha of shiraz, 0.9 ha of sauvignon blanc and 0.6 ha of riesling. Dave Neyle has been in vineyard development and management in SA and Tasmania since 1990, and is currently managing 60 ha in the Adelaide Hills. Inga Lidums brings 25 years' experience in marketing and graphic design in both Australia and overseas, with a focus on the wine and food industries. The property is managed with minimal chemical input, and the use of solar and biodiesel-generated power in the pursuit of an environmentally sustainable product and lifestyle.

ΨΨΨΨΨ **Adelaide Hills Sauvignon Blanc 2007** Good structure and depth to an array of gooseberry and passionfruit flavours before a faintly grassy/minerally finish. Screwcap. 12.5° alc. **Rating** 92 **To** 2009 $20
Adelaide Hills Shiraz 2004 Supple and smooth mouthfeel; black fruits, spice and licorice flavours on the medium-bodied palate, then ripe tannins adding to the spicy notes. Screwcap. 14° alc. **Rating** 92 **To** 2019 $20
Adelaide Hills Riesling 2006 Apple and lime blossom aromas; abundant fruit with a touch of sweetness; an all-purpose crowd pleaser. Screwcap. 12.5° alc. **Rating** 91 **To** 2013 $20

Loch-Lea Vineyard

PO Box 1144, Legana, Tas 7277 **Region** Northern Tasmania
T (03) 6330 1444 **F** (03) 6330 2190 **Open** Not
Winemaker Dr Richard Richardson (Consultant) **Est.** 1984 **Cases** 200

Loch-Lea Vineyard is owned by John and Luba Richards, and is one of the oldest in the Tamar Valley. The original plantings extended to 2.7 ha of pinot noir, chardonnay and cabernet sauvignon, the wines being sold through a restaurant onsite. The restaurant is no more, nor are the chardonnay and cabernet sauvignon; the pinot noir block of 1000 vines, now over 20 years old, produces the sole wine.

▼▼▼▼▽ **Pinot Noir 2006** A light style, but with plenty of flavour and finesse; ripe cherries, fine acid and nice persistence on the finish. Screwcap. **Rating** 90 **To** 2009 $25

Lochmoore ★★★

PO Box 430, Trafalgar, Vic 3824 **Region** Gippsland
T 0402 216 622 **Open** Not
Winemaker Lyre Bird Hill, Narkoojee **Est.** 1997 **Cases** 300
The 2 ha of chardonnay, pinot noir, pinot gris and shiraz at Lochmoore are tended by one of the most highly qualified viticulturists one is ever likely to meet. Sue Hasthorpe grew up in Trafalgar, and went on to obtain a Bachelor of Science (Hons) and Doctor of Philosophy in Physiology at the University of Melbourne; she then worked and travelled as a medical research scientist in Australia, the UK, the US and Europe, and after returning to Australia studied viticulture via the University of Melbourne, Dookie College campus (distance education). If this were not enough, she has now completed a Masters of Agribusiness at the University of Melbourne.

▼▼▼▼ **Trafalgar Gippsland Pinot Noir 2006** Sweet red cherries offset with earthy personality; good acid on the finish, fresh and ready to go. Screwcap. **Rating** 89 **To** 2011 $20

Logan Wines ★★★★

Castlereagh Highway, Apple Tree Flat, Mudgee, NSW 2850 **Region** Mudgee
T (02) 6373 1333 **F** (02) 6373 1390 **www**.loganwines.com.au **Open** 7 days 10–5
Winemaker Peter Logan, Andrew Ling **Est.** 1997 **Cases** 42 000
Logan is a family-owned and operated business with emphasis on cool-climate wines from Orange and Mudgee. The business is run by husband and wife team Peter (winemaker) and Hannah (sales and marketing). Wines are released from three ranges: Logan (from Orange), Weemala and Apple Tree Flat. Exports to the UK, the US and other major markets.

▼▼▼▼▽ **Orange Shiraz 2005** Medium-bodied; fresh and well-balanced, with good line and flow to the black and red cherry fruit, plus touches of spice and licorice; fine tannins to close. Cork. 14.5° alc. **Rating** 91 **To** 2015 $25
Vintage M Orange Cuvee 2005 Has length and intensity to its mix of nectarine, strawberry and citrus fruit, the finish long and dry; 24 months on lees. Duck for cover when removing the cork. 12.5° alc. **Rating** 90 **To** 2012 $35
Orange Pinot Noir 2006 Quite intense spicy, stemmy notes to the varietal fruit; good texture and length, again with a stemmy cut on the finish, adding rather than subtracting. Screwcap. 14.5° alc. **Rating** 90 **To** 2012 $35

▼▼▼▼ **Orange Sauvignon Blanc 2007** A clean and fresh wine tending towards grassy/minerally flavours; good length to the palate. Screwcap. 13° alc. **Rating** 89 **To** 2011 $20
Orange Chardonnay 2006 Delicate, but quite complex; some smoky aromas, and has above-average length; crisp finish. Screwcap. 14.5° alc. **Rating** 89 **To** 2012 $25
Orange Cabernet Merlot 2005 Ripe cassis, mint and blackcurrant fruit on entry, moving through to a more savoury finish. Cork. 15° alc. **Rating** 89 **To** 2012 $25
Orange Cabernet Merlot 2006 Dark and quite savoury, with real extract and plenty of vibrant fruit on the finish. Cork. **Rating** 89 **To** 2015 $25
Vintage M Orange Cuvee 2006 Salmon colour; potent aromas, and an equally full-flavoured palate; 18 months on lees has added to quality pinot noir/chardonnay/pinot meunier base wine. Cork. 12.5° alc. **Rating** 89 **To** 2012 $35

Weemala Brut NV Light, but surprisingly fruity and flavoursome, with a strawberry-accented palate; good length and acidity. Cork. 12º alc. **Rating** 88 **To** 2009 $22

Apple Tree Flat Merlot 2006 I'm not sure how this came about at this price; it's not a great wine, but is aromatic, and has vibrant sweet fruits and touches of snow pea; carefree drinking. Screwcap. 14.5° alc. **Rating** 87 **To** 2009 $11

Weemala Orange Pinot Gris 2007 Delicate and crisp, with elements of pear, green apple and mineral; uncluttered, dry finish. Screwcap. 13.5° alc. **Rating** 87 **To** 2009 $16

Hannah Orange Rose 2007 A fresh crisp and dry style; small red fruits and balanced acidity, but the strange decision to use a cork makes it highly probable the wine will be past its best by 2009. 14.5° alc. **Rating** 87 **To** 2008 $20

Weemala Orange Pinot Noir 2007 Has the correct texture and mouthfeel, also foresty notes, but the varietal fruit conviction isn't there. Screwcap. 13.5° alc. **Rating** 87 **To** 2010 $16

Weemala Central Ranges Shiraz Viognier 2006 Fresh, lively, plum and spice aromas and flavours; just the right amount of tannins to provide texture. Screwcap. 13.5° alc. **Rating** 87 **To** 2011 $16

Weemala Central Ranges Merlot 2006 Not bad by half; light- to medium-bodied savoury black olive and herbal fruit, but not bitter or excessively green. Screwcap. 14.5° alc. **Rating** 87 **To** 2010 $16

Lone Crow Wines   NR

RSM 343, Busselton, WA 6280 (postal) **Region** Geographe
T (08) 9753 3023 **F** (08) 9753 3032 **Open** Not
Winemaker Mark Messenger (Contract) **Est.** 1996 **Cases** 600
The Kennedy (David and Michelle) and Espinos (Kim and Jodie) families progressively established 14 ha of sauvignon blanc, semillon, shiraz, merlot and cabernet sauvignon between 1996 and '99 in the foothills of the Whicher Ranges, 15 km inland from Busselton. Most of the grapes are sold, principally to Evans & Tate; limited quantities are made under the Lone Crow label.

Long Gully Estate   ★★★★

Long Gully Road, Healesville, Vic 3777 **Region** Yarra Valley
T (03) 9510 5798 **F** (03) 9510 9859 **www.**longgullyestate.com **Open** 7 days 11–5
Winemaker Luke Houlihan **Est.** 1982 **Cases** 12 000
Owned by Reiner and Irma Klapp, this is one of the larger Yarra Valley producers to have successfully established a number of export markets, doubtless due to its core of mature vineyards, which have grown from 2.2 ha to nearly 30 ha, underlining its commercial success. Long-term winemaker Peter Florance retired in 2004, and was replaced by the very experienced and well-regarded Yarra winemaker Luke Houlihan. Exports to the UK, Switzerland and Singapore.

ççççç **Irma's Yarra Valley Cabernet 1998** Has travelled best of all of the three re-release Irma's Cabernets, with attractive cedary notes to back up the blackcurrant fruit; good tannin structure. Re-release, magnum. **Rating** 93 **To** 2009 $120

Yarra Valley Sauvignon Blanc 2007 Deliberately made to maximise complexity in both texture and flavour, with a 40% wild ferment in older puncheons; sweet tropical fruit, grassy and more nutty flavours combine; bold try, though slightly phenolic. Screwcap. 13.7° alc. **Rating** 90 **To** 2010 $25

Majors Creek Heathcote Shiraz 2005 Lighter in colour and body than most Heathcote shirazs, possibly due to earlier picking; elegant and fine black and red cherry flavours; balanced extract and oak. Diam. **Rating** 90 **To** 2015 $30

Reserve Yarra Valley Merlot 2005 Light- to medium–bodied palate, with clear varietal character in a mix of cassis, black olive and spice, the tannins fine and soft, the oak not oppressive. Diam. **Rating** 90 **To** 2013 $30

Irma's Yarra Valley Cabernet 1999 Retains good structure; nicely developed blackcurrant fruit, with a sweet fruit edge and fine tannins. Re-release, magnum. **Rating** 90 **To** 2009 $120

♥♥♥♥ **Cattleyard Yarra Valley Cabernet Merlot 2005** A mix of cassis and blackcurrant with considerable mocha oak contribution; works well, with gently ripe tannins in support. Deluxe packaging. Diam. **Rating** 89 **To** 2015 $30
Irma's Yarra Valley Cabernet 2000 Savoury, minty, leafy notes with redcurrant fruit; not powerful, but has length. Re-release, magnum. **Rating** 89 **To** 2009 $120
Yarra Valley Riesling 2007 A generous style, with tropical fruit overtones before a slight dip in the mid-palate; finishes with good acidity. Screwcap. 13.4° alc. **Rating** 87 **To** 2013 $30

Longview Creek Vineyard ★★★☆

150 Palmer Road, Sunbury, Vic 3429 **Region** Sunbury
T (03) 9740 2448 **F** (03) 9740 2495 **www**.longviewcreek.com.au **Open** W'ends & public hols 11–5, or by appt
Winemaker Roland Kaval (Contract) **Est.** 1988 **Cases** 900
Bill and Karen Ashby purchased the Longview Creek Vineyard from founders Dr Ron and Joan Parker in 2003. It is situated on the brink of the spectacular Longview Gorge, the bulk of the plantings of chardonnay (0.8 ha), pinot noir (0.6 ha) and chenin blanc (0.4 ha) being made between 1988 and '90. Thereafter a little cabernet franc (0.3 ha) and riesling (0.1 ha) were planted. Simon Glover oversees viticulture, and Roland Kaval the winemaking. Spring frosts in October 2006 spelt the end of the '07 vintage, with the next new releases to follow in November '08.

Longview Vineyard ★★★★★

Pound Road, Macclesfield, SA 5153 **Region** Adelaide Hills
T (08) 8388 9694 **F** (08) 8388 9693 **www**.longviewvineyard.com.au **Open** Sun–Fri 11–5
Winemaker Shaw & Smith, Kangarilla Road, O'Leary Walker **Est.** 1995 **Cases** 15 000
In a strange twist of fate, Longview Vineyard came to be through the success of Two Dogs, the lemon-flavoured alcoholic drink created by Duncan MacGillivray and sold in 1995 to the Pernod Ricard Group (also the owners of Orlando). Over 60 ha have been planted: shiraz and cabernet sauvignon account for a little over half, and there are significant plantings of chardonnay and merlot, and smaller plantings of viognier, semillon, riesling, sauvignon blanc, zinfandel and nebbiolo. The majority of the production is sold, but $1.2 million has been invested in a cellar door and function area, barrel rooms and an administration centre for the group's activities. All the buildings have a spectacular view over the Coorong and Lake Alexandrina. In February 2008 the newsletter of *Wine Business Monthly* disclosed that the property had been sold to Adelaide retailer Leon Saturno. Exports to the UK, the US and Canada.

♥♥♥♥♥ **Yakka Adelaide Hills Shiraz 2006** A totally harmonious, medium-bodied wine, both bouquet and palate with perfect blackberry, licorice and spice aromas and flavours. Immaculate tannin and oak backup. Gold, National Wine Show '07. Screwcap. 14.5° alc. **Rating** 95 **To** 2026 $38
Devils Elbow Adelaide Hills Cabernet Sauvignon 2006 More power and depth than the colour suggests; clear-cut, varietal cassis berry fruit, and fine, savoury, persistent tannins. Grows on retasting. Screwcap. 14.2° alc. **Rating** 94 **To** 2020 $32

♥♥♥♥♡ **Whippet Adelaide Hills Sauvignon Blanc 2007** A clean but closed bouquet; the palate opens quietly, then squeaky lemony acidity on the finish lifts the wine significantly. Screwcap. 13° alc. **Rating** 90 **To** 2010 $19.95

♥♥♥♥ **My Fat Goose Adelaide Hills Semillon Sauvignon Blanc 2007** Very much driven by the grassy, stony semillon component, gaining texture ex some old oak maturation; a food style for all seasons. Screwcap. 12.6° alc. **Rating** 88 **To** 2010 $19.95

Red Bucket Shiraz Cabernet 2006 A light- to medium-bodied, fresh and expressive mix of cherry, blackberry and blackcurrant fruit; direct flavour and minimal texture. Screwcap. 14.8° alc. **Rating** 88 **To** 2013 $14.95

Loom Wine ★★★★

PO Box 162, McLaren Vale, SA 5171 **Region** McLaren Vale
T (08) 8323 8623 **F** (08) 8323 8694 **www**.loomwine.com **Open** Not
Winemaker Steve Grimley **Est.** 2005 **Cases** 120 000
Steve Grimley runs a substantial offsite winemaking business, which includes the Loom Wine and Willundry Road brands of Shiraz, and contract winemaking services for others. The estate vineyards comprise 10 ha of shiraz in McLaren Vale; other varieties are contract-grown. Exports to the UK, the US and other major markets.

ΨΨΨΨΩ **t = 0 Shiraz 2006** Quite luscious sweet fruit on the medium-bodied palate, the restrained alcohol giving a sheen of elegance; single vineyard at Blewitt Springs, the wine matured in puncheons for 18 months. Cork. 14° alc. **Rating** 91 **To** 2015 $40
Single Vineyard Blewitt Springs Shiraz 2006 An elegant, medium-bodied palate, unusually fine for McLaren Vale; spicy nuances to a core of black cherry and plum fruit; good balance and length. Value. Screwcap. 14° alc. **Rating** 90 **To** 2013 $15

ΨΨΨΨ **Soaring Kite Limestone Coast McLaren Vale Cabernet Shiraz 2006** Has a touch of class; both the flavours of black and red fruits and the textures of the components knit together well; value. Screwcap. 14° alc. **Rating** 89 **To** 2013 $15
Single Vineyard Eden Valley Riesling 2007 A clean bouquet; the palate is fresh, well-balanced, but not particularly intense, concluding with some lemony acidity; 60-year-old vines. Screwcap. 12.5° alc. **Rating** 89 **To** 2012 $15
t = 0 Riesling Viognier 2007 Much more texture and weight (barrel ferment?), bizarrely with the viognier here in the driver's seat; 'curiouser and curiouser', said Alice. Screwcap. 13° alc. **Rating** 88 **To** 2011 $25
Single Vineyard Adelaide Hills Viognier 2007 Quite fragrant and clear apricot/pastille varietal aromas; has avoided phenolics, but the palate lacks the intensity promised by the bouquet. Screwcap. 13° alc. **Rating** 88 **To** 2010 $15
Soaring Kite Adelaide Hills Eden Valley Viognier Riesling 2007 A thoroughly left field blend, with one-third riesling making the major statement via citrussy fruit; quite fresh and lively. Screwcap. 12.5° alc. **Rating** 87 **To** 2010 $15

Lost Lake ★★★

Lot 3, Vasse Highway, Pemberton, WA 6260 **Region** Pemberton
T (08) 9776 1251 **F** (08) 9776 1919 **www**.lostlake.com.au **Open** 7 days 10–4
Winemaker Mark Aitken **Est.** 1990 **Cases** 3000
Previously known as Eastbrook Estate, its origins go back to 1990, to the acquisition of an 80-ha farming property, which was subdivided into three portions: 16 ha, now known as Picardy, were acquired by Dr Bill Pannell, 18 ha became the base for Lost Lake, and the remainder was sold. The initial plantings in 1990 were of pinot noir and chardonnay, followed by shiraz, sauvignon blanc, merlot and cabernet sauvignon; 9 ha are now planted. A jarrah and cedar winery with a crush capacity of 150 tonnes was built in 1995, together with a large restaurant. Steve and Karen Masters acquired the property in 2006, and moved from Perth to live full-time at the property.

ΨΨΨΨ **Sauvignon Blanc 2006** Thoroughly attractive fruit in the middle of the tropical spectrum; retains freshness through to a long, clean finish. Screwcap. **Rating** 89 **To** 2009 $15
Classic White 2007 Fragrant and very fruity, with uncompromising residual sugar aimed at cellar door and those who look for sweetness in their wines. Sauvignon Blanc/Chardonnay/Semillon. Screwcap. **Rating** 87 **To** 2009 $17

Lost Valley Winery   ★★★

PO Box 4123, Wishart, Vic 3189 **Region** Upper Goulburn
T (03) 9592 3531 **F** (03) 9551 7470 **www.**lostvalleywinery.com **Open** Not
Winemaker Alex White (Contract) **Est.** 1995 **Cases** 5000
Dr Robert Ippaso planted the Lost Valley vineyard at an elevation of 450 m on the slopes of
Mt Tallarook, with 13 ha of merlot, shiraz, cortese and sauvignon blanc. This cortese is the only
planting in Australia. It pays homage to Dr Ippaso's birthplace: Savoie, in the Franco-Italian
Alps, where cortese flourishes. Exports to the US, Canada, Hong Kong and Indonesia.

♀♀♀♀   **Thousand Hills Upper Goulburn Shiraz 2005** Very earthy, savoury overtones
        to quite sombre, albeit spicy, black fruits; medium-bodied and not over-extracted,
        with good length. Cork. 13.5° alc. **Rating** 89 **To** 2014 $34
        Cortese 2007 A variety that always seems determined to reveal as little about
        itself as possible other than its attractive mouthfeel and balance; a vinous Mona
        Lisa. Screwcap. 13.5° alc. **Rating** 88 **To** 2011 $30

Lou Miranda Estate   ★★★☆

Barossa Valley Way, Rowland Flat, SA 5352 **Region** Barossa Valley
T (08) 8524 4537 **F** (08) 8524 4066 **www.**loumirandaestate.com.au **Open** Mon–Fri 10–4,
w'ends 11–4
Winemaker Lou Miranda **Est.** 2005 **Cases** 15 000
Lou Miranda's daughters Lisa and Victoria are the driving force behind the estate, albeit
with continuing hands-on involvement from Lou. Thirty ha of predominantly shiraz (14 ha,
including 5 ha of old vines), cabernet sauvignon (7 ha), merlot (6 ha), with lesser amounts of
chardonnay, pinot grigio, mataro and a small patch of old vine grenache, provide the grapes
for the venture. The cellar door works on the principle that there should be a wine for every
conceivable taste. Exports to Germany, Austria, Russia, Singapore, Taiwan and Japan.

♀♀♀♀   **Individual Vineyard Old Vine Barossa Valley Shiraz 2005** From a single
        block of 100-year-old vines, medium-bodied (as is often the case) but with too
        much vanilla oak; good texture and mouthfeel, but loses on the flavour issue. Cork.
        14.5° alc. **Rating** 89 **To** 2014 $25.95
        Individual Vineyard Cordon Cut Barossa Valley Shiraz 2005 No question
        some Italian Amarone overtones, but is this necessary or desirable? Beauty in the
        eye of the beholder, perhaps. Cork. 15° alc. **Rating** 88 **To** 2012 $29.95
        Angel's Vineyard Old Vine Barossa Valley Shiraz Mourvedre 2005 A
        thick fruit texture and flavour in a particular Barossa Valley genre, which seems
        riper than the alcohol would suggest. Cork. 14.5° alc. **Rating** 88 **To** 2012 $29.95
        Leone Adelaide Hills Sauvignon Blanc 2007 Clean, but extremely light, with
        twitches of passionfruit offset by some herbal notes. Screwcap. 12.5° alc. **Rating** 87
        To 2009 $16.95

Lowe Family Wines   ★★★☆

Tinja Lane, Mudgee, NSW 2850 **Region** Mudgee
T (02) 6372 0800 **F** (02) 6372 0811 **www.**lowewine.com.au **Open** Fri–Mon 10–5,
or by appt
Winemaker David Lowe, Jane Wilson **Est.** 1987 **Cases** 6000
Business partners David Lowe and Jane Wilson have consolidated their operations in Mudgee,
moving back from their cellar door in the Hunter Valley. They have started a new Mudgee
business, Mudgee Growers, at the historic Fairview winery. The main business is here, and
they have spread their wings, successfully introducing less well-known varieties, and looking to
other regions more suited for both mainstream styles (e.g. Orange for pinot gris and sauvignon
blanc) and outre varieties (e.g. Orange roussanne). Since 2006, all wines are classified as
organic. Exports to the UK, Japan and Denmark.

♀♀♀♀   **Reserve Mudgee Shiraz 2006** Brighter colour and a clear step up from the
        varietal; more concentration and complexity, with licorice evident, supporting the
        juicy dark fruits. Cork. 13.5° alc. **Rating** 89 **To** 2014 $45

Reserve Merlot 2006 Slightly better focus than the varietal; more red berry fruits and some savoury black olive notes, plump on the medium-bodied finish Cork. 14° alc. **Rating** 89 **To** 2011 $45

Reserve Zinfandel 2006 Ripe and almost syrupy, the fruit shows the riper spectrum of zinfandel personality; very succulent and very varietal. Cork. 14.8° alc. **Rating** 88 **To** 2011 $45

Tinja Orange Sauvignon Blanc 2007 A ripe wine, with rich texture; lacks varietal punch, but has good flavour. Screwcap. 13° alc. **Rating** 87 **To** 2009 $20

Tinja Orange Pinot Gris 2007 Hints of citrus and a little apple blossom; weighty texture with a very fragrant finish. Screwcap. 13.4° alc. **Rating** 87 **To** 2009 $20

Mudgee Merlot 2006 Sweet and ripe with good fruit concentration, nice texture and palate weight; a little simple, but with good flavour. Cork. 13.5° alc. **Rating** 87 **To** 2010 $28

Lucas Estate

329 Donges Road, Severnlea, Qld 4352 **Region** Granite Belt
T (07) 4683 6365 **F** (07) 4683 6356 **www**.lucasestate.com.au **Open** 7 days 10–5
Winemaker Colin Sellers, Louise Samuel **Est.** 1999 **Cases** 1500
Louise Samuel and husband Colin Sellers purchased Lucas Estate in 2003. The wines are made from the 2.5-ha estate vineyard (at an altitude of 825 m), which is planted to chardonnay, verdelho, cabernet sauvignon, shiraz, merlot and muscat, and also from purchased grapes. A new winery was completed in time for the 2008 vintage, with a pneumatic press for the white wines, leaving the basket press for reds.

ŸŸŸŸŸ **Cabernet Sauvignon 2006** Substantial wine; strong, rather austere varietal character; blackcurrant, firm tannins. **Rating** 91 **To** 2014 $25

The Partners Granite Belt Cabernet Sauvignon Merlot 2006 Fresh and vibrant, with red fruits and a hint of cassis; the palate is fresh and focused, with thrust on the medium-bodied finish. Cork. 13.7° alc. **Rating** 90 **To** 2012 $35

ŸŸŸŸ **Harry's Block Shiraz 2006** Strong red-purple; considerable oak; vanilla, coconut, plum and black cherry; fine tannins, fraction green. **Rating** 89 **To** 2013 $20

Classic Dry Rose 2007 Cleverly made; very light bright colour; fresh flavour; citrussy acidity, and some sweetness. **Rating** 87 **To** 2009 $19

Luke Lambert Wines

PO Box 403, Yarra Glen, Vic 3775 (postal) **Region** Yarra Valley
T 0448 349 323 **www**.lukelambertwines.com.au **Open** By appt
Winemaker Luke Lambert **Est.** 2003 **Cases** 500
Luke Lambert graduated from CSU's wine science course in 2002, aged 23, cramming in winemaking experience at Mount Pleasant, Coldstream Hills, Mount Prior, Poet's Corner, Palliser Estate in Martinborough, and Badia di Morrona in Chianti. With this background he has established a virtual winery, purchasing grapes from quality-conscious growers in the Yarra Valley and Heathcote. After several trial vintages, the first wines were released from the 2005 vintage. In 2006 he and his partner moved to Piedmont, Italy for an extended stay, with intermittent trips back to the Yarra Valley for the winemaking, sales and continuation of the Luke Lambert wines and the monitoring of a 0.8 ha block of nebbiolo in Heathcote and a 0.8 ha block of shiraz in the Yarra Valley.

ŸŸŸŸŸ **Yarra Valley Syrah 2006** A wine that seems to draw inspiration from the Northern Rhône; medium-bodied, savoury, with a fine palate showing stems, savoury meats, gently toasty oak, and plentiful fine-grained tannins. Diam. 12.8° alc. **Rating** 94 **To** 2016 $33

LynneVale Estate

83 Cahills Road, Mandurang, Vic 3551 **Region** Bendigo
T (03) 5439 3635 **F** (03) 5439 3635 **www.**lynnevale.com.au **Open** W'ends &
public hols 11–5
Winemaker Wes Vine, Shane Colbert **Est.** 1999 **Cases** 1000
Shane and Lynne Colbert have planted 1.4 ha of shiraz and 0.6 ha of cabernet sauvignon for
their estate-grown red wines, extending the range with Chardonnay and Verdelho made from
contract-grown grapes. The cellar door overlooks the vineyard and the Mandurang Valley
below, and has been expanded to create a conference/function facility, a restaurant and B&B.
They also offer day tours of local wineries, including lunch.

▽▽▽▽ **Verdelho 2007** Good flavour with honeysuckle and lemon; fresh and bright on
the finish. Screwcap. 13° alc. **Rating** 87 **To** 2009 $15

Lyre Bird Hill

370 Inverloch Road, Koonwarra, Vic 3954 **Region** Gippsland
T (03) 5664 3204 **F** (03) 5664 3206 **www.**lyrebirdhill.com.au **Open** Wed–Mon 10–5
Winemaker Owen Schmidt **Est.** 1986 **Cases** 2400
Former Melbourne professionals Owen and Robyn Schmidt make small quantities of estate-
grown wine (the vineyard is 2.4 ha). Various weather-related viticulture problems have seen
the Schmidts supplement their estate-grown intake with grapes from contract growers in
Gippsland and the Yarra Valley, and also provide contract winemaking services for others.

▽▽▽▽▽ **Gewurztraminer 2005** Bright straw with green tinges; vibrant and full of musk
and rose petals; strongly varietal and fresh with quite rich texture. Screwcap. 12° alc.
Rating 90 **To** 2012 $15

▽▽▽▽ **South Gippsland Shiraz 2002** Very fresh for its age; a true cool-climate shiraz
with plenty of spice, framed by red fruits and prominent acidity. Cork. 12.9° alc.
Rating 88 **To** 2015 $18

Mabrook Estate

258 Inlet Road, Bulga, NSW 2330 **Region** Lower Hunter Valley
T (02) 9971 9994 **F** (02) 9971 9924 **Open** W'ends 10–4
Winemaker Larissa Kalt, Michale McManus **Est.** 1996 **Cases** 500
The Swiss-born Kalt family began the establishment of Mabrook Estate in 1996, planting 3 ha
of semillon, 2 ha of shiraz and 1 ha of verdelho. Parents Mona and Tony Kalt decided to use
organic growing methods from the word go, but the vineyard is not certified. Daughter Larissa,
having obtained an Honours degree in Medical Science at the University of Sydney, decided
to pursue winemaking by working as a 'lab rat' and cellar hand at a local winery, and visited
Switzerland and Italy to observe small-scale family winemaking in those countries. The red
wines are all very light in structure and extract, which may be intentional.

▽▽▽▽▽ **2nd Conspiracy Semillon 2004** Still vibrantly fresh and lively, with some juicy
flavours emerging, honey and toast still to come (but will). Value. Screwcap. 11° alc.
Rating 92 **To** 2014 $14

▽▽▽▽ **2nd Conspiracy Rose 2007** Deep colour; abounds with red berry fruits, and
just a hint of sweetness on the finish; good cellar door style; cabernet sauvignon
base. Screwcap. 13.5° alc. **Rating** 87 **To** 2009 $18

McAdams Lane

90 McAdams Lane, Bellarine, Vic 3223 (postal) **Region** Geelong
T 1300 651 485 **F** (03) 5251 1009 **www.**mcadamslane.com.au **Open** Not
Winemaker Anthony Brain, James Rimmer **Est.** 2003 **Cases** 1000
Retired quantity surveyor Peter Slattery bought the 48-ha property in 2001, intending
to plant the vineyard, make wine and develop a restaurant. He has in fact achieved all of

this (with help from others, of course), planting shiraz (6.5 ha), pinot noir (1.8 ha), pinot gris (1 ha), picolit (0.6 ha), chardonnay (0.4 ha) and zinfandel (0.3 ha). Picolit is the most interesting, a highly regarded grape in northern Italy, where it makes small quantities of high quality sweet wine. It has proved to be very temperamental here, as in Italy, with very unreliable fruitset. The restaurant has been built, and will open in the latter part of 2008.

ίίίίί **Bellarine Peninsula Pinot Noir 2006** A real find! Bright and focused red berry fruits, with elements of spice; the silky texture of the wine is drawn through to a long, even and surprisingly complex finish; very good pinot for under $20. Cork. 13.5° alc. **Rating** 93 **To** 2012 $18

ίίίί **Terindah Estate Bellarine Peninsula Chardonnay 2006** Green and grassy, with hints of figs and plenty of toast; good depth and weight; a brassy style. Cork. 13° alc. **Rating** 88 **To** 2010 $18

Terindah Estate Bellarine Peninsula Pinot Gris 2006 Good flavour; pear drop bouquet with nice weight, and a rich, almost nutty finish. Screwcap. 13.2° alc. **Rating** 88 **To** 2009 $16

Macaw Creek Wines   NR

Macaw Creek Road, Riverton, SA 5412 **Region** Mount Lofty Ranges Zone
T (08) 8847 2237 **F** (08) 8847 2237 www.macawcreekwines.com.au **Open** Sun & public hols 11–4
Winemaker Rodney Hooper **Est.** 1992 **Cases** 5000
The property on which Macaw Creek Wines is established has been owned by the Hooper family since the 1850s, but development of the estate vineyards did not begin until 1995 (30 ha have since been planted). The Macaw Creek brand was established in 1992 with wines made from grapes from other regions, including the Preservative-Free Yoolang Cabernet Shiraz. Rodney Hooper is a highly qualified and skilled winemaker with experience in many parts of Australia and in Germany, France and the US. Exports to the UK, the US, Canada, Denmark and China.

McCrae Mist Wines   ★★★★

21 Bass Street, McCrae, Vic 3938 (postal) **Region** Mornington Peninsula
T 0416 008 630 **F** (03) 5986 6973 **Open** Not
Winemaker Brien Cole **Est.** 2003 **Cases** 1000
The McCrae Mist vineyard was acquired by Dr Stephen Smith after the Kings Creek business was broken up' in 2003. He thus inherited 15.5 ha of pinot grigio, pinot noir, shiraz and sangiovese, adding another 4 ha of chardonnay in 2005.

ίίίί **Mornington Peninsula Pinot Noir 2005** A little developed, but good varietal definition and a little complex game/undergrowth character; vibrant acidity. Screwcap. 13.4° alc. **Rating** 88 **To** 2009 $19.50

macforbes   ★★★★☆

c/– Sticks, Glenview Road, Yarra Glen, Vic 3775 **Region** Yarra Valley
T (03) 9818 8099 **F** (03) 9818 8299 www.macforbes.com **Open** Not
Winemaker Mac Forbes **Est.** 2004 **Cases** 3000
Mac Forbes cut his vinous teeth at Mount Mary, where he was winemaker for several years before heading overseas in 2002. He spent two years in London working for Southcorp in a marketing liaison role, before heading to Portugal and Austria to gain further winemaking experience. He returned to the Yarra Valley prior to the 2005 vintage, purchasing grapes for the 2-tier portfolio: first, the Victorian range (employing unusual varieties or unusual winemaking techniques) and, second, the Yarra Valley range of multiple terroir-based offerings of Chardonnay and Pinot Noir.

ίίίίί **RS31 Strathbogie Ranges Riesling 2007** Lovely vibrant and fresh aromas and flavours; great balance akin to Mosel Kabinett; lime juice balanced by zesty acidity. Screwcap. 10.5° alc. **Rating** 94 **To** 2016 $24

♥♥♥♥♀ **Woori Yallock Pinot Noir 2006** Brighter colour than the Coldstream, with good concentration; a strong mineral undercurrent to the fruit and quite savoury and firm on the finish; a seductive sweet core is the essence of this wine. Screwcap. 13° alc. **Rating** 92 **To** 2013 $46

Woori Yallock Chardonnay 2006 A tightly wound cool wine, with a strong mineral core, and plenty of lemon fruits on the palate; quite toasty and rich finish. Screwcap. 13° alc. **Rating** 90 **To** 2012 $32

Yarra Valley Pinot Noir 2006 A fine, elegant wine with lots of spice and earthy tones; nice weight and texture, and certainly light-bodied; long and savoury on the finish. Screwcap. 12.5° alc. **Rating** 90 **To** 2009 $28

♥♥♥♥ **Coldstream Pinot Noir 2006** A bit cloudy; a savoury wine with red cherry fruits, a little spice; quite fine and firm on the finish. Screwcap. 13.5° alc. **Rating** 88 **To** 2012 $38

Barbera 2005 Has the somewhat broken line for which the variety is known in Australia; a mix of red fruits and slightly rough tannins; good bistro wine. King Valley. Screwcap. 14° alc. **Rating** 87 **To** 2009 $26

McGlashan's Wallington Estate

225 Swan Bay Road, Wallington, Vic 3221 **Region** Geelong
T (03) 5250 5760 **F** (03) 5250 5760 **Open** By appt
Winemaker Robin Brockett (Contract) **Est.** 1996 **Cases** 1500
Russell and Jan McGlashan began the establishment of their 10-ha vineyard in 1996. Chardonnay and pinot noir make up the bulk of the plantings, with the remainder shiraz and pinot gris, and the wines are made by Robin Brockett, with his usual skill and attention to detail. Local restaurants around Geelong and the Bellarine Peninsula take much of the wine.

McGuigan Wines

Cnr Broke Road/McDonald Road, Pokolbin, NSW 2321 **Region** Lower Hunter Valley
T (02) 4998 7400 **F** (02) 4998 7401 **www.**mcguiganwines.com.au **Open** 7 days 9.30–5
Winemaker Peter Hall **Est.** 1992 **Cases** 1.4 million
A public-listed company, which was the ultimate logical expression of Brian McGuigan's marketing drive and vision, on a par with that of Wolf Blass in his heyday; has been particularly active in export markets, notably the US and more recently China. The overall size of the company has been measurably increased by the acquisition of Simeon Wines; Yaldara and Miranda are now also part of the business, which in 2006 made wine industry headlines when it terminated a large number of grape purchase contracts, a decision likely to cost it dearly in the 2008 and '09 vintages. In 2007 McGuigan Simeon acquired Nepenthe Vineyards, a move that surprised many. In 2008 the group was renamed Australian Vintage Limited, a slightly curious moniker. Exports to all major markets.

♥♥♥♥♥ **Genus 4 Semillon 2007** Stacked full of flavour, with sweet fruit balanced by very good acidity; very complex. **Rating** 94 **To** 2017 $18.95

♥♥♥♥♀ **Bin 9000 Hunter Valley Semillon 2007** Floral, scented and fine; lemon blossom aromas; lovely mouthfeel and length. Yet another outstanding Bin 9000. Screwcap. 11° alc. **Rating** 93 **To** 2017 $14.95

Bin 9000 Hunter Valley Semillon 2006 Still very youthful, but has fine lemon juice fruit with touches of herb; gives every indication of a prosperous future. Screwcap. 11° alc. **Rating** 92 **To** 2016 $14.95

The Short List Barossa Valley Shiraz 2006 Medium- to full-bodied juicy black and red fruits; supple texture and good structure; Barossa style; has a nicely tightened finish. Screwcap. **Rating** 92 **To** 2018 $26.95

The Short List Coonawarra Cabernet Sauvignon 2006 Very concentrated blackcurrant fruit, with a hint of TCA-like aroma, presumably from the oak; a curate's egg, most extremely good. Screwcap. **Rating** 92 **To** 2026 $26.95

The Short List Adelaide Hills Chardonnay 2007 Shows typical Adelaide Hills terroir; controlled stone fruit and citrus fruit, integrated oak and balanced acidity; thins out fractionally on the finish. Screwcap. **Rating** 90 **To** 2013 $26.95

Personal Reserve Vanessa Vale Shiraz 2006 Typical Hunter (Vanessa Vale is a vineyard) medium-bodied wine, verging on light-bodied, with black cherry fruit, fine tannins; good now or in 20 years. Diam. 14° alc. **Rating** 90 **To** 2026 $45

ŦŦŦŦ **Hunter Valley Semillon 2005** Very fresh and vibrant, with a little lemon sherbet on the bouquet; clean fruit on the palate and good focus, but needing a little more concentration. Screwcap. 10.5° alc. **Rating** 89 **To** 2020 $14.95

Genus 4 Old Vine Hunter Valley Shiraz 2005 Has a degree of thrust and life to the palate not expected after a so-so colour and bouquet, but the claim by McGuigan to be the best wine of the millennium seems somewhat premature. Diam. 13.5° alc. **Rating** 88 **To** 2020 $18.95

Genus 4 Old Vine Hunter Valley Chardonnay 2006 Has abundant white and yellow peach fruit, and supporting oak; however, thins out on the mid- to back-palate. Screwcap. 13.5° alc. **Rating** 88 **To** 2011 $18.95

Earth's Portrait Eden Valley Riesling 2003 Strong mineral and citrus aromas; good flavour on the palate, but pulls up a little short. Screwcap. 12° alc. **Rating** 87 **To** 2011 $18.95

McHenry Hohnen Vintners ★★★★★

PO Box 1480, Margaret River, WA 6285 **Region** Margaret River
T (08) 9757 7600 **F** (08) 9757 7999 **www**.mchv.com.au **Open** Not
Winemaker David Hohnen, Freya Hohnen, Ryan Walsh **Est.** 2004 **Cases** 6500
McHenry Hohnen is a substantial business owned by the McHenry and Hohnen families, sourcing grapes from four vineyards owned by various members of the families. In all, 120 ha of vines have been established on the McHenry's, Calgardup Brook, Rocky Road and McLeod Creek properties. A significant part of the grape production is sold to others (including Cape Mentelle) but McHenry Hohnen have 18 varieties to choose from in fashioning their wines. The family members with direct executive responsibilities are leading Perth retailer Murray McHenry, Cape Mentelle founder and former long-term winemaker David Hohnen, and Freya Hohnen, who shares the winemaking duties with father David. In 2007 David Hohnen received the inaugural Len Evans Award for Leadership. Exports to the UK, Canada and NZ.

ŦŦŦŦŦ **Calgardup Brook Margaret River Chardonnay 2006** An intense, fruit-driven melon, stone fruit and grapefruit mix; crisp, crunchy acidity; long finish. Screwcap. 12.5° alc. **Rating** 94 **To** 2013 $37

3 Amigos Margaret River Marsanne Chardonnay Roussanne 2006 Fragrant and fresh, with very good mouthfeel and length; wild yeast barrel ferment treatment gives the wine a lovely silky texture. Screwcap. 13.5° alc. **Rating** 94 **To** 2011 $25

ŦŦŦŦŦ **3 Amigos Margaret River Shiraz Grenache Mataro 2006** You could never mistake this for a Barossa Valley blend of the same varieties; it is lighter-bodied, but has a sharper focus to the delicious red fruits, and more length. Screwcap. 14° alc. **Rating** 93 **To** 2016 $25

Margaret River Semillon Sauvignon Blanc 2007 Good complexity, texture and weight, and a prominent mineral line across the palate; surprisingly long on the finish. Screwcap. 12.5° alc. **Rating** 91 **To** 2014 $22

Tiger Country Tempranillo Petit Verdot Cabernet Sauvignon 2005 A medium-bodied but firm structure to a basket of black fruit flavours, not as schizophrenic as the conjunction of varieties might suggest; fine, ripe tannins help. Cork. 14° alc. **Rating** 90 **To** 2015 $32

McIvor Estate

80 Tooborac-Baynton Road, Tooborac, Vic 3522 **Region** Heathcote
T (03) 5433 5266 **F** (03) 5433 5358 **www.**mcivorestate.com.au **Open** W'ends &
public hols 10–5, or by appt
Winemaker Various contract **Est.** 1997 **Cases** 2000
McIvor Estate is situated at the base of the Tooborac Hills, at the southern end of the
Heathcote wine region, 5 km southwest of Tooborac. Gary and Cynthia Harbor have planted
5.3 ha of marsanne, roussanne, shiraz, cabernet sauvignon, merlot, nebbiolo and sangiovese.

ＴＴＴＴＴ **Shiraz 2005** Bright, deep purple-red; succulent blackberry, plum and bitter
chocolate flavours; good tannin structure and balance, likewise oak; great future.
Diam. **Rating** 94 **To** 2025 $30

ＴＴＴＴＴ **Sangiovese 2005** Light- to medium-bodied, but quite intense black cherry/sour
cherry/briar flavours, and good length; has clear varietal character, but also stands
on its own feet as a wine regardless of its variety. Diam. **Rating** 90 **To** 2012 $35

ＴＴＴＴ **Marsanne Roussanne 2006** Has already begun to develop the honeyed aromas
and flavours that will drive the wine in 5 years time, the only question being its
diminished length; well worth following. Diam. **Rating** 89 **To** 2013 $22
Merlot Cabernet Sauvignon 2005 Medium- to full-bodied; although the
cabernet is only 40% of the blend, it provides much of the structure and flavour,
dominated by blackcurrant; well-balanced but firm tannins round the wine off.
Diam. **Rating** 89 **To** 2015 $25

McKellar Ridge Wines

Point of View Vineyard, 2 Euroka Avenue, Murrumbateman, NSW 2582
Region Canberra District
T (02) 6258 1556 **F** (02) 6258 9770 **www.**mckellarridgewines.com.au **Open** Sun 12–5
or by appt Sept–Jun
Winemaker Dr Brian Johnston **Est.** 2000 **Cases** 500
Dr Brian Johnston and his wife Janet are the partners in McKellar Ridge Wines. Brian has
been undertaking a postgraduate diploma in science at CSU, focusing on wine science and
wine production techniques. The wines come from 3.7 ha of low-yielding, mature vines and
have had significant show success. They are made using a combination of traditional and new
winemaking techniques, the emphasis being on fruit-driven styles.

ＴＴＴＴＴ **Canberra District Cabernet Sauvignon Cabernet Franc 2006** An attractive
medium-bodied palate, with soft fleshy fruit, and very good persistence. Screwcap.
14° alc. **Rating** 90 **To** 2017 $24

McKinnon Estate   NR

'Parkside' 308 Parks Road, Lancefield, Vic 3435 **Region** Macedon Ranges
T (03) 5429 1787 **F** (03) 5429 1739 **Open** By appt
Winemaker Lachlan McKinnon, Brian Wilson **Est.** 2006 **Cases** 500
Lachlan and Gerda McKinnon purchased Parkside in 2004; the 65-ha property was primarily
used for thoroughbred agistment, but included a rundown 2-ha vineyard. It also had a grand,
fully restored 120-year-old house, now home to the McKinnons. The first year was spent
rehabilitating the vineyard, the second converting the dairy on the property into a winery
under the direction of winemaker Brian Wilson. The sauvignon blanc, chardonnay and pinot
noir all show considerable promise, but the McKinnons would be the first to admit they are
on a sharp learning curve, with much more to show in the future.

McLaren Ridge Estate

Whitings Road, McLaren Vale, SA 5171 **Region** McLaren Vale
T (08) 8383 0504 **F** (08) 8383 0504 **www.**mclarenridge.com **Open** 7 days 11–5
Winemaker Brian Light **Est.** 1997 **Cases** 5000

Peter and Heather Oliver have 5 ha of shiraz and 1 ha of grenache, planted over 50 years ago on the ridge that now gives their estate its name. The cellar door opened in 2007, and luxury vineyard accommodation is available. Exports to the UK and Canada.

🍷🍷🍷🍷🍷 **Cabernet Sauvignon 2005** A surprisingly powerful expression of varietal fruit; intense blackcurrant supported by very well pitched tannins and good oak. Diam. 14° alc. **Rating** 93 **To** 2020 $18.50

🍷🍷🍷🍷 **Shiraz Cabernet Franc Merlot 2005** The blend works quite well; medium-bodied, supple red and black fruits, ripe tannins, and some dusting of regional chocolate. ProCork. 14.5° alc. **Rating** 89 **To** 2013 $18.50

McLaren Vale Shiraz 2005 Light- to medium-bodied; well-balanced and not forced; gentle blackberry, earth and dark chocolate flavours supported by balanced tannins. Cork. 14.5° alc. **Rating** 88 **To** 2012 $18.50

McLaren Vale III Associates ★★★★

130 Main Road, McLaren Vale, SA 5171 **Region** McLaren Vale
T 1800 501 513 **F** (08) 8323 7422 **www.**associates.com.au **Open** Mon–Fri 9–5, tasting by appt
Winemaker Brian Light **Est.** 1999 **Cases** 14 000
The three associates in question all have a decade or more of wine industry experience; Mary Greer is managing partner, Reginald Wymond chairing partner, and Christopher Fox partner. The partnership owns 34 ha of vines spanning two vineyards, one owned by Mary and John Greer, the other by Reg and Sue Wymond. An impressive portfolio of affordable quality wines has been the outcome, precisely as the partners wished. Exports to the US, Canada, Germany and Singapore.

🍷🍷🍷🍷🍷 **Squid Ink Reserve Shiraz 2006** Very good colour, bright and not black; a vibrant fresh mix of black and red fruits, chocolate and vanilla; fine but persistent tannins, balanced American oak. Cork. 14.5° alc. **Rating** 94 **To** 2012 $45

🍷🍷🍷🍷 **Charisma Cabernet Viognier 2006** This flavoursome wine will undoubtedly attract because of its novelty; a dreadful pity if the tentacles of viognier reach into all reds. Screwcap. 14.5° alc. **Rating** 89 **To** 2012 $25.90

Squid Ink Sparkling Shiraz NV Quite complex, with abundant fruit and not too much sweetness on the finish; some oak doesn't intrude. Cork. 14.5° alc. **Rating** 88 **To** 2012 $45

Sabbatical Semillon Sauvignon Blanc 2007 A powerful wine, with a particularly long and firm finish; not much finesse, best with hearty food. Screwcap. 13° alc. **Rating** 87 **To** 2009 $17.90

Renaissance Merlot Cabernet Petit Verdot 2006 Brisk notes of forest, olive and earth surround the black fruits; fine tannins; not an easy wine to come to terms with. Screwcap. 14° alc. **Rating** 87 **To** 2011 $22.90

McLaren Wines ★★★★

PO Box 488, McLaren Vale, SA 5171 **Region** McLaren Vale
T 0408 575 200 **F** (08) 8557 4363 **www.**mclarenwines.com **Open** Not
Winemaker Matthew Rechner **Est.** 2001 **Cases** 2000
Matt Rechner entered the wine industry in 1988, spending most of the intervening years at Tatachilla Winery in McLaren Vale, starting as laboratory technician and finishing as operations manager. Frustrated by the constraints of large winery practice, he decided to strike out on his own in 2001 via the virtual winery option. His long experience has meant he is able to buy grapes from high-quality producers. The success of McLaren Wines in the Great Australian Shiraz Challenge '06 was testimony enough to the quality of the wines.

🍷🍷🍷🍷 **2 Mates Shiraz 2005** In no-holds-barred McLaren Vale style with alcohol-warmed red and black fruits; soft tannins. Screwcap. 15.2° alc. **Rating** 89 **To** 2014 $28.95

McLean's Farm

barr-Eden Vineyard, Menglers Hill Road, Tanunda, SA 5352 **Region** Barossa Valley
T (08) 8564 3340 **F** (08) 8564 3340 **www**.mcleansfarm.com **Open** W'ends 10–5 or by appt
Winemaker Bob McLean **Est.** 2001 **Cases** 2500

At various times known as the Jolly Green Giant and Sir Lunchalot, Bob McLean has gone perilously close to being a marketing legend in his own lifetime, moving from Orlando to Petaluma and then St Hallett. The farm shed on the home property houses the winery which handles the estate-grown red grapes, which amount to 30 tonnes (or less) a year. Production has been 'downsized' in the wake of a decision to only use estate-grown grapes. Exports to the UK and US.

barr-Eden Riesling 2007 Attractive lemon/lime blossom aromas; quite delicate palate, crisply focused, and has thrust. Impressive. Screwcap. **Rating** 91 **To** 2014 $18
barr-Eden Shiraz Cabernet 2003 Strong overtones of mocha and chocolate and spice enliven both bouquet and palate, countering the usual effects of the vintage; good length and balance. Cork. 14.5° alc. **Rating** 90 **To** 2013 $40
barr-Eden GSM 2006 Crimson-purple; has an abundance of ripe fruit without cosmetic or confit characters, and is supported by fine tannins; a touch of alcohol heat is the Achilles Heel. Screwcap. 15° alc. **Rating** 90 **To** 2016 $35

McLeish Estate

462 De Beyers Road, Pokolbin, NSW 2320 **Region** Lower Hunter Valley
T (02) 4998 7754 **F** (02) 4998 7754 **www**.mcleishhunterwines.com.au **Open** 7 days 10–5, or by appt
Winemaker Andrew Thomas **Est.** 1985 **Cases** 5000

Bob and Maryanne McLeish began planting their vineyard in 1985, and now have 14 ha (semillon, chardonnay, verdelho, shiraz, merlot and cabernet sauvignon). They have also opened their cellar door, having accumulated a number of gold medals for their wines. Exports to the UK, the US, Japan, Singapore and NZ.

Hunter Valley Semillon 2007 Brilliant green-yellow; intensely aromatic lemon and grass aromas; a delicious and expressive palate with vibrant fruit; '07 at its best; relatively early drinking. Screwcap. 11.8° alc. **Rating** 95 **To** 2012 $18

Hunter Valley Semillon Sauvignon Blanc 2007 Unsurprisingly, the 60% lemony semillon component is the dominant player in a fresh, zesty, crisp wine; particularly good length and finish; 100% Hunter a surprise. Screwcap. 12° alc. **Rating** 92 **To** 2009 $15
Reserve Cabernet Sauvignon 2006 Skilled winemaking for a variety not suited to the region; firm blackcurrant fruit, balanced tannins and oak promise development over the medium term. Cork. 13.4° alc. **Rating** 90 **To** 2016 $35

Hunter Valley Shiraz 2006 Good fruit concentration, if a little one-dimensional; plenty of flavour, and quite rich finish. Screwcap. 13.8° alc. **Rating** 88 **To** 2015 $20
Hunter Valley Verdelho 2007 Well made; a clean but sedate wine for inconspicuous consumption with salads and so forth. Screwcap. 13.9° alc. **Rating** 87 **To** 2009 $16

McPherson Wines

PO Box 767, Hawthorn, Vic 3122 **Region** Nagambie Lakes
T (03) 9832 1700 **F** (03) 9832 1750 **www**.mcphersonwines.com **Open** Not
Winemaker Andrew McPherson, Geoff Thompson **Est.** 1993 **Cases** 400 000

McPherson Wines is not well known in Australia but is, by any standards, a substantial business. Its wines are largely produced for the export market, with some sales in Australia. The wines are made at various locations from 250 ha of estate vineyards, supplemented with contract-grown grapes, and represent very good value. For the record, McPherson Wines is a joint venture between Andrew McPherson and Alister Purbrick (Tahbilk), both of whom have had a lifetime of experience in the industry. Exports to all major markets.

ŸŸŸŸŸ Cabernet Sauvignon 2007 Great value; strong varietal characters, and cedar to balance out the cassis; well made. Exceptional value. Screwcap. 14° alc. Rating 90 To 2014 $10.95

ŸŸŸŸ Shiraz 2007 Good colour; bright fruits on the bouquet supported by a lick of oak and a little spice. Good value. Screwcap. 14° alc. Rating 88 To 2012 $10.95
Basilisk Shiraz Mourvedre 2006 Chewy, meaty and dark, with leather, spice and blackberries on the finish; the strength of the mourvedre shines through. Screwcap. 14° alc. Rating 88 To 2014 $17.95
Verdelho 2007 Fruit-laden, with fresh acid and good flavour. Screwcap. 13° alc. Rating 87 To 2009 $10.95
Cabernet Rose 2007 Red fruit aromas with a hint of spice; clean and well-made, but still well worth the price. Screwcap. 13° alc. Rating 87 To 2009 $10.95

Macquarie Grove Vineyards  ★★☆

120 Eumungerie Road, Narromine, NSW 2821 **Region** Western Plains Zone
T (02) 6889 4968 **F** (02) 6889 2500 **Open** Mon–Sat 10–5
Winemaker Red Earth Estate (Ken Borchardt) **Est.** 2001 **Cases** 3000
This business has very interesting parentage. Dianne and David Cliffe started the business as seedling growers in Narromine before establishing a vine propagation nursery via a sister company (which they also own). Here they have 33 varieties collected from various parts of Australia, mainly from very old vines, but also including carmenere (sourced from Chile some years ago), barbera, tempranillo, viognier, sangiovese, shiraz and chardonnay. As the collection has aged, so has it grown, moving into grapegrowing and winemaking as a further arm of the business. Ken Borchardt of Red Earth Estate is the contract maker for this and many other businesses in the region.

Macquariedale Estate ★★★

170 Sweetwater Road, Rothbury, NSW 2335 **Region** Lower Hunter Valley
T (02) 6574 7012 **F** (02) 6574 7013 **www**.macquariedale.com.au **Open** Fri–Mon, school & public hols 10–5
Winemaker Ross McDonald **Est.** 1993 **Cases** 4000
Macquariedale is an acorn to oak story, beginning with a small hobby vineyard in Branxton many years ago, and now extending to three certified organic (in conversion) vineyards around the Lower Hunter with a total 13 ha of semillon, chardonnay, pinot noir, shiraz, merlot, mataro and cabernet sauvignon. This has led to Ross McDonald (and his family) leaving a busy Sydney life to be full-time grapegrower and winemaker. Exports to Canada, Japan and China.

ŸŸŸŸ Hunter Valley Chardonnay 2007 Ripe and brassy chardonnay fruit, with peaches and a slight waxy note; good flavour depth and the finish is fine. Screwcap. 12.5° alc. Rating 87 To 2009 $20

McWilliam's ★★★★★

Jack McWilliam Road, Hanwood, NSW 2680 **Region** Riverina
T (02) 6963 0001 **F** (02) 6963 0002 **www**.mcwilliams.com.au **Open** Mon–Sat 9–5
Winemaker Jim Brayne, Russell Cody **Est.** 1916 **Cases** NFP
The best wines to emanate from the Hanwood winery are from other regions, notably the Barwang Vineyard at Hilltops (see separate entry), Coonawarra (Brand's Laira), Yarra Valley (Lillydale Estate) and Eden Valley. As McWilliam's viticultural resources have expanded, they have been able to produce regional blends from across Australia in the last few years and these have been startlingly good value. The 2006 sale of McWilliam's Yenda winery to Casella has led to a major upgrade in both the size and equipment at the Hanwood winery, now the nerve centre for the business. Exports to all major markets via a major distribution joint venture with Gallo.

ppppp Catching Thieves Margaret River Semillon Sauvignon Blanc 2007 Fresh
fruit aromas and flavours with a tropical and gooseberry mix; falters slightly on the
drive to the finish. Screwcap. 13° alc. Rating 90 To 2009 $16.99
Catching Thieves Margaret River Chardonnay 2006 Lively nectarine and
stone fruit; understated elegance; a long, clean finish. A new brand for McWilliam's
with much to commend it. Screwcap. 13° alc. Rating 90 To 2012 $15.95

pppp Inheritance Semillon Sauvignon Blanc 2007 Utterly impossible to beat at
this price; while not having the depth of its Hanwood big brother, makes up for it
with its delicate freshness. Screwcap. 12° alc. Rating 89 To 2009 $6.99
Hanwood Estate Shiraz 2005 Well made, with a seamless fusion of plummy
fruit, oak and tannins in a light- to medium-bodied frame; has a degree of finesse
not common in wines at this price. Screwcap. 13.5° alc. Rating 89 To 2010 $11.99
Catching Thieves Margaret River Cabernet Merlot 2005 Fruit-forward
flavours ranging through cherry, raspberry, cassis and blackcurrant; minimal tannins
and structure. Screwcap. 13.5° alc. Rating 89 To 2011 $15.95
Catching Thieves Margaret River Semillon Sauvignon Blanc 2006
Spotlessly clean; aromatic passionfruit and more herbal/asparagus notes; good
mouthfeel, line and length. Screwcap. 12° alc. Rating 89 To 2010 $15.95
Catching Thieves Margaret River Cabernet Merlot 2006 A medium-
bodied mix of red and black fruits supported by tannins which are a little
assertive. Gold medal, Melbourne Wine Show '07. Screwcap. 13.5° alc. Rating 89
To 2010 $15.95
Hanwood Estate Semillon Sauvignon Blanc 2007 Abundant flavour that
doesn't rely on residual sugar; a mix of lemon, herb and ripe tropical fruit, the
semillon a major component. Screwcap. 12° alc. Rating 88 To 2009 $11.99
Hanwood Estate Chardonnay 2006 Very well made, middle of the road
Chardonnay; melon and stone fruit with a whisk of oak. Gold medal, Rutherglen
Wine Show '06 surprising. Value. Screwcap. 13° alc. Rating 88 To 2009 $12
Hanwood Cabernet Sauvignon 2006 Unforced and perhaps a little simple,
but has good varietal fruit and balance; tip top value. Rating 88 To 2012 $12.95
Inheritance Cabernet Merlot 2006 Hard to imagine how more could be
expected at this price; light- to medium-bodied, with vibrant raspberry and cassis
fruit, and not without structure. Screwcap. 14° alc. Rating 87 To 2009 $6.99
Catching Thieves Margaret River Rose 2006 Does have the flavours of
watermelon (as claimed on the back label, and which I have never liked) but
touches of strawberry and cherry come to the rescue. Screwcap. 13.5° alc.
Rating 87 To 2009 $15.95
Hanwood Estate Shiraz 2006 Right in the typical Hanwood style, unforced
but supremely honest and ready to drink right now. Rating 87 To 2009 $12.95
Inheritance Shiraz Cabernet 2006 Fresh, lively, uncompromisingly light-
bodied; juicy fruit, but minimal structure. Top gold, Early Drinking Red, Qld Wine
Show '06, still fresh 18 months later. Screwcap. 13.5° alc. Rating 87 To 2009 $6.99

McWilliam's Mount Pleasant ★★★★★

Marrowbone Road, Pokolbin, NSW 2320 **Region** Lower Hunter Valley
T (02) 4998 7505 **F** (02) 4998 7761 **www**.mountpleasantwines.com.au **Open** 7 days 10–5
Winemaker Phillip Ryan, Andrew Leembruggen **Est.** 1921 **Cases** NFP
McWilliam's Elizabeth and the glorious Lovedale Semillon are generally commercially
available with 4–5 years of bottle age and are undervalued treasures with a consistently superb
show record. The individual vineyard wines, together with the Maurice O'Shea memorial
wines, add to the lustre of this proud name. Exports to many countries, the most important
being the UK, the US, Germany and NZ.

ppppp Lovedale Limited Release Hunter Valley Semillon 2002 Glowing yellow-
green; starting to build complexity around a pure and fragrant core of grass and
citrus fruit. Cork. Rating 95 To 2015 $49.95

Elizabeth Semillon 2003 Developing superbly; still vibrant and lemony, with the first hints of toast starting to appear. **Rating** 95 **To** 2018 $37

Museum Release Elizabeth Semillon 1999 Deep yellow-green; fully mature, with generous honey and citrus fruit, then a crisp finish. A trace oxidised? Cork. **Rating** 94 **To** 2012 $37

Mad Dog Wines

7a Murray Street, Tanunda, SA 5352 (postal) **Region** Barossa Valley
T (08) 8563 1551 **F** (08) 8563 0754 **Open** Not
Winemaker Jeremy Holmes **Est.** 1999 **Cases** 500
Geoff (aka Mad Dog) Munzberg is a third-generation grapegrower who has joined with Jeremy and Heidi Holmes, Aaron and Kirsty Brasher and son Matthew to create Mad Dog Wines. The principal wine, Shiraz, comes from 5 ha of vines with an average age of 35 years. Most of the grapes are sold, with the best kept for the Mad Dog label. The acquisition of a neighbouring vineyard in 2006 has led to the inclusion of some 100-year-old vine fruit, and the range will be slightly extended with small amounts of Moscato and Sangiovese. Exports to the UK and US.

Barossa Valley Shiraz 2005 Clear crimson-red; medium- to full-bodied, full and round texture and flavours, French oak undoubtedly helping to keep the mad dog in check, and lengthen the finish. Cork. 14.5° alc. **Rating** 93 **To** 2015 $30

Maglieri of McLaren Vale

GPO Box 753, Melbourne, Vic 3001 **Region** McLaren Vale
T 1300 651 650 **Open** Not
Winemaker Alex Mackenzie **Est.** 1972 **Cases** 10 000
Was one of the better-kept secrets among the wine cognoscenti, but not among the many customers who drink thousands of cases of white and red Lambrusco every year, an example of niche marketing at its profitable best. It was a formula that proved irresistible to Beringer Blass, which acquired Maglieri in 1999. Its dry red wines are generously proportioned and full of character, the Shiraz particularly so.

Cabernet Sauvignon 2005 Generous richly fruited palate with flavours of blackcurrant and a wraparound of dark chocolate and a dash of French oak. Cork. 14.5° alc. **Rating** 90 **To** 2015 $21.95

Shiraz 2006 Full-bodied, and far from ready to drink; strong black fruits and bitter chocolate, but yet to build mid-palate vinosity; indifferent cork. 14.5° alc. **Rating** 89 **To** 2015 $20.95

Magpie Estate   ★★★★☆

PO Box 126, Tanunda, SA 5352 **Region** Barossa Valley
T (08) 8562 3300 **F** (08) 8562 1177 **Open** Not
Winemaker Rolf Binder, Noel Young **Est.** 1993 **Cases** 6500
This is a partnership between Rolf Binder and Cambridge (England) wine merchant Noel Young. It came about in 1993 when there was limited demand for or understanding of Southern Rhône–style blends based on shiraz, grenache and mourvedre. Initially a small, export-only brand, the quality of the wines was such that it has grown substantially over the years, although the intention is to limit production. The majority of the wines are very reasonably priced, the super-premiums more expensive. Exports to the UK, the US, Canada, Austria and Singapore.

The Malcolm Barossa Valley Shiraz 2005 An epic wine; super-ripe and concentrated, with a hedonistic personality of almost, but not quite, pruney fruit; supported by an adequate use of oak for such intensity; not for the faint of heart. **Rating** 94 **To** 2030 $150

♟♟♟♟♟ **The Election Barossa Valley Shiraz 2005** Dark-fruited and slightly briny; concentrated and deep, with an almost meat/savoury character; dense, thick and chewy on the finish. Screwcap. 14.5° alc. **Rating** 92 **To** 2025 $60
The Schnell Shiraz Grenache 2006 Clean and fleshy, and a pure expression of the fruit; a fragrant and gently savoury finish. Screwcap. 14.5° alc. **Rating** 90 **To** 2012 $20

♟♟♟♟ **The Sack Barossa Valley Shiraz 2005** Clean and lively, with dark fruit on offer; a little fruitcake on the mid-palate carried through to the finish. Cork. 15.5° alc. **Rating** 89 **To** 2018 $30
The Wit & Shanker Barossa Valley Cabernet Sauvignon 2005 Quite essency fruit, almost jubey; good flavour though, and a fresh and vibrant finish. Screwcap. 14.5° alc. **Rating** 89 **To** 2015 $30

Magpie Springs ★★★★☆

RSD 1790 Meadows Road, Hope Forest, SA 5172 **Region** Adelaide Hills
T (08) 8556 7351 **F** (08) 8556 7351 **www**.magpiesprings.com.au **Open** Fri–Sun & public hols 10–5
Winemaker James Hastwell, Reg Wilkinson **Est.** 1991 **Cases** 1000
Stuart Brown and Rosemary (Roe) Gartelmann purchased the property on which Magpie Springs is now established in 1983, growing flowers commercially and grazing cattle. Chardonnay was planted experimentally, and were among the earliest vines in the area. In 1991 the commencement of the vineyard proper led to the planting of a little over 16 ha of semillon, chardonnay, sauvignon blanc, riesling, shiraz, pinot noir and merlot. Roe Gartelmann began painting professionally from the Magpie Springs studio in the late 1980s, and many classes and workshops have been held over the years. Her studio can be visited during cellar door hours.

♟♟♟♟♟ **Lenore Adelaide Hills Chardonnay 2005** Attractive wine; nectarine, white peach and grapefruit; perfectly integrated oak; developing very well indeed. Screwcap. 13.2° alc. **Rating** 94 **To** 2012 $22

♟♟♟♟♟ **Adelaide Hills Shiraz 2006** Lively, slightly estery, spicy black fruit aromas; the light- to medium-bodied palate has good thrust, with spicy/peppery nuances, the alcohol well hidden. Screwcap. 15° alc. **Rating** 90 **To** 2013 $18

♟♟♟♟ **Adelaide Hills Riesling 2005** Out of the same nest as the '06, but is smoother and drier; plenty of fruit in a tropical spectrum; good acidity. Screwcap. **Rating** 89 **To** 2011 $18
The Sweet Spot 2006 Unusual honeyed aromas and some apricot; also a suggestion of some less than noble rot. Botrytis Chardonnay. Screwcap. 12.9° alc. **Rating** 88 **To** 2009 $28
Adelaide Hills Riesling 2006 Some toast and pyrozine aromas starting to build on the bouquet; abundant flavour with some sweetness, and does show alcohol. Screwcap. 13° alc. **Rating** 87 **To** 2010 $18

Main Ridge Estate ★★★★★

80 William Road, Red Hill, Vic 3937 **Region** Mornington Peninsula
T (03) 5989 2686 **F** (03) 5931 0000 **www**.mre.com.au **Open** Mon–Fri 12–4, w'ends 12–5
Winemaker Nat White **Est.** 1975 **Cases** 1200
Nat White gives meticulous attention to every aspect of his viticulture and winemaking, doing annual battle with one of the coolest sites on the Peninsula. The same attention to detail extends to the winery and the winemaking. Despite such minuscule production, exports to Singapore.

♟♟♟♟♟ **Mornington Peninsula Chardonnay 2006** Right in the mainstream of the Main Ridge style, wonderfully rich, deep and already complete, the fruit carrying all the winemaker inputs. Screwcap. **Rating** 94 **To** 2013 $50

ＴＴＴＴＴ Half Acre Mornington Peninsula Pinot Noir 2005 Bright and lively, fresh cherry fruit with lots of spice and forest, has unexpected length and persistence, the mark of all good pinots, but needs a little more body weight. Screwcap. 14° alc. **Rating** 92 **To** 2011 $55

Majella ★★★★★

Lynn Road, Coonawarra, SA 5263 **Region** Coonawarra
T (08) 8736 3055 **F** (08) 8736 3057 www.majellawines.com.au **Open** 7 days 10–4.30
Winemaker Bruce Gregory **Est.** 1969 **Cases** 15 000
Majella is one of the foremost grapegrowers in Coonawarra, with 61 ha of vineyard, principally shiraz and cabernet sauvignon, and with a little riesling and merlot. The Malleea is one of Coonawarra's greatest wines, The Musician one of Australia's most outstanding red wines selling for less than $20. Exports to the UK, the US and other major markets.

ＴＴＴＴＴ Coonawarra Merlot 2005 Excellent varietal character in the bouquet and palate; made without ostentation, but attention to detail; redcurrant, spicy flavours run through to a lingering finish. Screwcap. 14° alc. **Rating** 95 **To** 2015 $28
Coonawarra Cabernet Sauvignon 2005 Seductive and sumptuous cassis and blackcurrant fruit with ripe, silky tannins giving great mouthfeel; French oak is exactly where it should be. Screwcap. 14.5° alc. **Rating** 95 **To** 2025 $30
The Musician Coonawarra Cabernet Shiraz 2006 A lively wine; has vibrancy and great texture; a mix of red and black fruits run through to the long finish. Superlative value. Gold medal, Limestone Coast Wine Show '07. Screwcap. 14.5° alc. **Rating** 95 **To** 2016 $18
The Malleea 2004 The finest and most elegant of the Majella wines with lower alcohol, though this is partly a function of the season. Undoubtedly a wine for the purist; watch for the '05. Cork. 14° alc. **Rating** 94 **To** 2024 $70

ＴＴＴＴＴ Coonawarra Shiraz 2005 As always, an attractive wine; gentle plum and blackberry fruit with fine, ripe tannins driving the medium-bodied palate; controlled oak. Screwcap. 14.5° alc. **Rating** 90 **To** 2015 $30

ＴＴＴＴ Sparkling Shiraz 2005 Full-bodied, complex and rich; ripe fruit, and definitely needs food. Disgorged '06. Crown seal. 14° alc. **Rating** 89 **To** 2009 $28

Majors Lane Wines ★★★☆

64 Majors Lane, Lovedale, NSW 2320 **Region** Lower Hunter Valley
T (02) 4930 7328 **F** (02) 4930 7023 www.majorslane.com **Open** Thurs–Mon 10–5
Winemaker Alasdair Sutherland (white), David Hook (red) **Est.** 1987 **Cases** 650
Sydney lawyers Ivan and Susan Judd, specialising in contract and industrial law, purchased the Majors Lane vineyard in 2001. Fourteen years earlier Alan and Rosemary MacMillan had planted 3 ha each of semillon, chardonnay and shiraz, plus 1 ha of chambourcin, adding 700 olive trees a decade later. Susan Judd has retired from legal practice to run the cellar door and help in the restaurant, with husband Ivan commuting to and from Sydney.

ＴＴＴＴ Llewellyn Chardonnay 2006 Smoky, slightly funky, barrel ferment aromas; medium-bodied stone fruit and fig flavours, again with a background of that oak. Screwcap. 14° alc. **Rating** 89 **To** 2013 $23

Malcolm Creek Vineyard ★★★★

Bonython Road, Kersbrook, SA 5231 **Region** Adelaide Hills
T (08) 8389 3619 **F** (08) 8389 3542 www.malcolmcreekwines.com.au **Open** W'ends & public hols 11–5, or by appt
Winemaker Reg Tolley (Consultant) **Est.** 1982 **Cases** 700
Malcolm Creek was set up as the retirement venture of Reg Tolley, who decided to upgrade his retirement by selling the venture to Bitten and Karsten Pedersen in 2007. They intend to continue making the wines in the same ageworthy style, with Reg Tolley overseeing

winemaking. The wines are invariably well made and develop gracefully; they are worth seeking out, and are usually available with some extra bottle age at a very modest price. Exports to the UK, the US and Denmark.

♟♟♟♟♟ Adelaide Hills Cabernet Sauvignon 2005 Strong tones of herb and earth run alongside the blackcurrant fruit; 20 months in French oak and a further 2 years in bottle before release in mid-2009 have, or will, soften those tones appropriately. Cork. 14.3° alc. **Rating** 91 **To** 2018 $25

Mandalay Estate
Mandalay Road, Mumballup, WA 6010 **Region** Geographe
T (08) 9372 2006 **F** (08) 9372 3006 **www**.mandalayestate.com.au **Open** 7 days 10–5
Winemaker Contract **Est.** 1997 **Cases** NA
Tony and Bernice O'Connell have established 6 ha of chardonnay, shiraz, cabernet sauvignon and zinfandel on their 40-ha property, previously owned by Bunnings Tree Farms and abounding with tree stumps. The tasting room has been established in an old plant shed on the property. Most of the grapes are sold.

♟♟♟♟♟ Mandalay Road Sauvignon Blanc Semillon 2007 Fresh and breezy citrus, grass and herb mix, picking up velocity on the tingling, citrussy finish; good value. Screwcap. 13° alc. **Rating** 90 **To** 2010 $14
Mandalay Road Chardonnay 2007 Light straw-green; lively, fresh and tangy grapefruit-accented palate, with good length. Value. Screwcap. 12.8° alc. **Rating** 90 **To** 2010 $14

♟♟♟♟ Mandalay Road Zinfandel 2006 Very attractive, juicy wine, with clear cut varietal character; spice, rose petal and small red fruits. Screwcap. **Rating** 89 **To** 2011 $19
Mandalay Road Shiraz 2006 A light-bodied, fresh and bright mix of spice and predominantly red fruits; hasn't been forced or over-extracted, and alcohol barely registers. Screwcap. 14.5° alc. **Rating** 88 **To** 2011 $16

Mandurang Valley Wines
77 Fadersons Lane, Mandurang, Vic 3551 **Region** Bendigo
T (03) 5439 5367 **F** (03) 5439 3850 **www**.mandurangvalleywines.com.au
Open Fri–Tues 11–5
Winemaker Wes Vine, Steve Vine **Est.** 1994 **Cases** 2500
Wes and Pamela Vine planted their first vineyard at Mandurang in 1976 and started making wine as a hobby. Commercial production began in 1993, and an additional vineyard was established in '97. Wes (a former school principal) has been full-time winemaker since 1999, with son Steve becoming more involved each vintage, the two now forming a formidable marketing team. Exports to China.

Mansfield Wines
204 Eurunderee Lane, Mudgee, NSW 2850 **Region** Mudgee
T (02) 6373 3871 **F** (02) 6373 3708 **www**.mansfieldwines.com.au **Open** Thurs–Tues & public hols 10–5, or by appt
Winemaker Bob Heslop **Est.** 1975 **Cases** 2000
Family-owned Mansfield Wines has moved with the times, moving the emphasis from fortified wines to table wines (though still offering some fortifieds) and expanding the product range to take in new generation reds such as Touriga and Zinfandel.

♟♟♟♟ Tinto Cao 2006 Light-bodied, but has persistent fruit covering a wide spectrum of flavours from cherry to raspberry and a background of spice; ready now. Cork. 12.5° alc. **Rating** 87 **To** 2010 $18

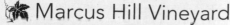 ## Marcus Hill Vineyard   ★★★★

560 Banks Road, Marcus Hill, Vic 3222 (postal) **Region** Geelong
T (03) 5222 5764 **Open** Not
Winemaker Darren Burke, Justyn Baker (Contract) **Est.** 2000 **Cases** NFP
In 2000, Richard and Margot Harrison, together with 'gang pressed friends', planted 2 ha of
pinot noir, overlooking Port Lonsdale, Queenscliffe and Ocean Grove, a few kilometres from
Bass Strait and Port Phillip Bay. Between 2001 and '04, 0.5 ha of chardonnay and 0.2 ha each
of shiraz and pinot gris were added. The vineyard is run with minimal sprays, and the aim is
to produce elegant wines, which truly express the maritime site.

🍷🍷🍷🍷⟨🍷⟩ **Chardonnay 2006** Bright green-yellow; a stylish wine with very good balance
of fruit, oak and mlf inputs; long finish. **Rating** 92 **To** 2013

Margan Family   ★★★★★

1238 Milbrodale Road, Broke, NSW 2330 **Region** Lower Hunter Valley
T (02) 6579 1317 **F** (02) 6579 1267 **www**.margan.com.au **Open** 7 days 10–5
Winemaker Andrew Margan **Est.** 1997 **Cases** 30 000
Andrew Margan followed in his father's footsteps by entering the wine industry over 20 years
ago and has covered a great deal of territory since, working as a Flying Winemaker in Europe,
then for Tyrrell's. Andrew and wife Lisa now have over 80 ha of fully yielding vines at their
Ceres Hill property at Broke, and lease the nearby Vere Vineyard. Wine quality is consistently
good. The rammed earth cellar door and restaurant are highly recommended. Exports to the
UK, the US and other major markets.

🍷🍷🍷🍷🍷 **Limited Release Shiraz 2005** A complex wine with exceptional balance
from start to finish; blackberry fruit, spice, fine French oak and ripe tannins are
seamlessly interwoven; perfect line. Screwcap. 14° alc. **Rating** 94 **To** 2020 $30
Limited Release Shiraz Mourvedre 2005 A rich, sumptuous palate, with ripe
black fruits, the shiraz utterly dominant; very good texture, structure and activity in
the mouth. Screwcap. 14.5° alc. **Rating** 94 **To** 2020 $30

🍷🍷🍷🍷⟨🍷⟩ **Hunter Valley Botrytis Semillon 2007** As ever, extremely sweet and
unctuously rich; lemon preserve fruit flavours, with citrussy acidity offsetting the
sweetness; half a tonne to the acre. Screwcap. 9.5° alc. **Rating** 92 **To** 2012 $30
Limited Release Semillon 2006 Despite the screwcap, has developed quite
rapidly, but not to its cost; has generous, sweet lemon fruit with touches of lightly
browned toast. Screwcap. 11° alc. **Rating** 92 **To** 2013 $30
Limited Release Shiraz 2006 Strong colour; abundant black fruits ranging
through blackberry, prune and plum; earthy regional characters lurk underneath,
and will develop with time. Screwcap. 14° alc. **Rating** 91 **To** 2015 $30
Limited Release Cabernet Merlot 2005 A potent wine, the blackcurrant and
cassis fruit backed by strong earthy/savoury tannins; patience should be rewarded.
Screwcap. 14° alc. **Rating** 90 **To** 2025 $30

🍷🍷🍷🍷 **Hunter Valley Shiraz 2005** A hint of reduction on the bouquet; medium- to
full-bodied, with ripe blackberry fruit; gentle, ripe tannins and balanced French
oak. Screwcap. 13.5° alc. **Rating** 89 **To** 2015 $20
Hunter Valley Merlot 2005 Abundant flavour in a soft, cushioned envelope
style; sweet red fruits offset by slightly savoury, regional tannins. Screwcap. 13.5° alc.
Rating 88 **To** 2010 $20

Maritime Estate   ★★★★☆

Tucks Road, Red Hill, Vic 3937 **Region** Mornington Peninsula
T (03) 9848 2926 **F** (03) 9848 2926 **Open** W'ends & public hols 11–5,
7 days Dec 27–Jan 26
Winemaker Sandro Mosele **Est.** 1988 **Cases** 1000

John and Linda Ruljancich and Kevin Ruljancich have enjoyed great success since their first vintage in 1994, no doubt due in part to skilled winemaking but also to the situation of their vineyard, looking across the hills and valleys of the Red Hill subregion. No samples received; the rating is that of last year.

Marius Wines

PO Box 545, Willunga, SA 5172 **Region** McLaren Vale
T 0402 344 340 **F** (08) 8556 4839 **www**.mariuswines.com.au **Open** Not
Winemaker Roger Pike, James Hastwell **Est.** 1994 **Cases** 800
Roger Pike says he has loved wine for over 30 years; that for 15 years he has had the desire to add a little bit to the world of wine; and that over a decade ago he decided to do something about it, ripping the front paddock and planting 1.8 ha of shiraz in 1994. He sold the grapes from the 1997–99 vintages, but when the '98 vintage became a single-vineyard wine (made by the purchaser of the grapes) selling in the US at $40, the temptation to have his own wine became irresistible. Exports to the US and Denmark.

♀♀♀♀♀ **Symposium McLaren Vale Shiraz Mourvedre 2006** A luscious, but not jammy array of black fruits interwoven with dark chocolate and ripe tannins; good line, texture and length; impressive blend. Screwcap. 14.7° alc. **Rating** 94 **To** 2021 $29

♀♀♀♀♀ **Symphony Single Vineyard McLaren Vale Shiraz 2005** More density, ripeness and richness than the Symphony; power rather than seduction; will take much longer to reach its peak. Screwcap. 15° alc. **Rating** 91 **To** 2017 $35
Simpatico Single Vineyard McLaren Vale Shiraz 2005 Medium-bodied; flush with cherry, raspberry and redcurrant fruit and a sweet, silky texture to the fine tannins. Screwcap. 14.5° alc. **Rating** 91 **To** 2012 $24

Marlargo Wines

PO Box 371, Glenside, SA 5065 **Region** Warehouse
T 0438 987 255 **F** (08) 8379 0596 **www**.marlargowines.com **Open** Not
Winemaker Various contract **Est.** 2003 **Cases** 3000
This is the ultimate virtual winery, with virtual homes in Yarra Glen, McLaren Vale, Adelaide Hills and the Clare Valley. Each of the garishly labelled wines is contract-made by a different winemaker at a different winery, and the range is being extended further. The partners in the venture are Simon Austerberry, a sixth-generation farmer in the Pyrenees, and Mark Gibbs, a financial adviser from Melbourne. I'm far from convinced by the labels and purple prose (the Latina Cabernet said 'be seduced … sultry, seductive, sensual' and assured us the wine is matured in 'charismatic oak'). Both prices and production volume aspirations have been significantly – and sensibly – reduced. Exports to the US, Canada and Singapore.

♀♀♀♀♀ **McLaren Vale Shiraz 2006** A far more serious wine than the label would suggest; classic regional black fruits and dark chocolate, but a particularly lively palate in medium-bodied mode. Screwcap. 15° alc. **Rating** 90 **To** 2014 $25

♀♀♀♀ **Clare Valley Riesling 2007** A closed bouquet, and a light-bodied palate in the slate/mineral/herb spectrum. Has development potential. Screwcap. 12.5° alc. **Rating** 87 **To** 2012 $20
Adelaide Hills Pinot Grigio 2006 Has an attractive mix of citrus, pear and stone fruit, though the structure is simple; has resisted the easy fix of sweetness. Screwcap. 14° alc. **Rating** 87 **To** 2009 $20
Fingers Crossed Red 2006 Neatly balanced predominantly red fruits, the 13% Petit Verdot helping the colour and structure of the 87% Shiraz; ready to roll right now. Screwcap. 14.5° alc. **Rating** 87 **To** 2010 $15
Heathcote Cabernet 2006 Medium-bodied at best, with quite juicy blackcurrant flavours; easy style, without the usual authority of Heathcote, suggesting young vines or high yield. Screwcap. 14.5° alc. **Rating** 87 **To** 2011 $25

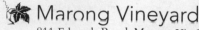 **Marong Vineyard**

811 Edwards Road, Marong, Vic 3515 **Region** Bendigo
T (03) 5435 2473 **Open** By appt
Winemaker Richard Verkuylen **Est.** 1994 **Cases** 100
Richard and Sally Verkuylen have planted 2 ha of shiraz on the flats of Bullock Creek on the outskirts of Bendigo. The vines are very low-yielding, and the wine is entirely estate-grown, hand-picked and made onsite. At any given point, up to three vintages are available at thoroughly old-fashioned prices.

Marri Wood Park

Cnr Caves Road/Whittle Road, Yallingup, WA 6282 **Region** Margaret River
T 0438 525 580 **F** (08) 9755 2343 **www**.margaretriver.com **Open** Thurs–Sun 11–5
Winemaker Clive Otto, Ian Bell, Bob Cartwright **Est.** 1993 **Cases** 1800
With plantings commencing in 1993, Marri Wood Park has 7 ha of vineyards: 1.6 ha semillon and 1.7 each of sauvignon blanc and cabernet sauvignon; part of the grape production is sold to other makers. The budget-priced Guinea Run range takes its name from the guinea fowl, which are permanent vineyard residents, busily eating the grasshoppers, weevils and bugs that cluster around the base of the vines, thus reducing the need for pesticides. The premium Marri Wood Park range takes its name from the giant Marri gum tree depicted on the label. Exports to Japan.

ƒƒƒƒ **Reserve Margaret River Chenin Blanc 2006** Early picking invests the wine with citrus and grass components more often found in sauvignon blanc; this is oyster country. Screwcap. 12.2° alc. **Rating** 87 **To** 2010 $25

Marsh Estate

Deasy's Road, Pokolbin, NSW 2321 **Region** Lower Hunter Valley
T (02) 4998 7587 **F** (02) 4998 7884 **Open** Mon–Fri 10–4.30, w'ends 10–5
Winemaker Andrew Marsh **Est.** 1971 **Cases** 6000
Through sheer consistency, value for money and unrelenting hard work, the Marsh family has built up a sufficiently loyal cellar door and mailing list clientele to allow all the production to be sold direct. Wine style is always direct, with oak playing a minimal role, and prolonged cellaring paying handsome dividends.

ƒƒƒƒƒ **Vat S Hunter Valley Shiraz 2006** A very different bouquet to Vat R, with earthy/savoury characters; a long palate with a mix of those earthy notes, and quite sweet plum and blackberry fruit. Cork. 13° alc. **Rating** 93 **To** 2016 $27.50
Vat R Hunter Valley Shiraz 2006 A supple, medium-bodied palate with blackberry and vanilla flavours, regional nuances of earth still to come. Stained cork. 13° alc. **Rating** 92 **To** 2016 $27.50
Holly's Block Hunter Valley Semillon 2007 Bright green-straw; a ripe style, rich and focused; lemon/lemon tart flavours on a long, high-flavoured palate. Cork. 11.5° alc. **Rating** 91 **To** 2012 $27.50

ƒƒƒƒ **Hunter Valley Semillon 2007** A powerful wine, punching above its alcohol weight; big and somewhat broad; ready now. Cork. 11° alc. **Rating** 87 **To** 2010 $19.50

Martins Hill Wines NR

1179 Castlereagh Highway, Mudgee, NSW 2850 **Region** Mudgee
T (02) 6373 1248 **F** (02) 6373 1248 **www**.martinshillwines.com.au **Open** Not
Winemaker Pieter Van Gent (Contract) **Est.** 1985 **Cases** 600
Janette Kenworthy and Michael Sweeny are committed organic grapegrowers and are members of the Organic Vignerons Association. Theirs is a tiny operation at the moment, with 0.5 ha each of sauvignon blanc and pinot noir, 1 ha each of cabernet sauvignon and shiraz in production. The vineyard is carbon neutral, with solar electricity and plantings of native trees and shrubs. Organic vineyard tours and talks can be arranged by appointment.

Mason Wines

27850 New England Highway, Glen Aplin, Qld 4381 **Region** Granite Belt
T (07) 4684 1341 **www**.masonwines.com.au **Open** 7 days 11–4
Winemaker Jim Barnes **Est.** 1998 **Cases** 3500
Robert and Kim Mason set strict criteria when searching for land suited to viticulture: a long history of commercial stone fruit production with well-drained, deep soil. The first property was purchased in 1997, the vines planted thereafter. A second orchard was purchased in 2000, and a cellar door was constructed. They have planted 25 ha of chardonnay, verdelho, sauvignon blanc, viognier, semillon, cabernet sauvignon, shiraz, merlot and petit verdot. Yet another Queenslander on the ascent. Exports to South Korea.

ΨΨΨΨΨ **Granite Belt Verdelho 2007** Lifted and varietal peach flesh bouquet; good weight, and clean vibrant acidity on the finish. Impressive for the region. Screwcap. 14° alc. **Rating** 90 **To** 2011 $16

ΨΨΨΨ **Granite Belt Viognier 2006** Clean and vibrant, with some apricot and spice; a thickly textured palate that cleans up nicely with good acidity; slightly nutty finish. Screwcap. 13.8° alc. **Rating** 89 **To** 2009 $16
Rees Road Granite Belt Shiraz 2006 Ripe and juicy; lots of leather and spice on the chewy finish. Screwcap. 14.5° alc. **Rating** 88 **To** 2012 $20
Granite Belt Cabernet Sauvignon 2006 Vibrant colour, and loads of primary fruit; almost jammy, but not quite; quite supple, and there is good flavour to enjoy on the finish. Screwcap. 14.5° alc. **Rating** 88 **To** 2010 $18

Massena Vineyards

PO Box 54, Tanunda, SA 5352 **Region** Barossa Valley
T (08) 8564 3037 **F** (08) 8564 3038 **www**.massena.com.au **Open** By appt
Winemaker Dan Standish, Jaysen Collins **Est.** 2000 **Cases** 5000
Massena Vineyards draws upon 4 ha of mataro (mourvere), saperavi, primitivo (petite syrah) and tannat at Nuriootpa. It is an export-oriented business although the wines can be purchased by mail order, which, given both the quality and innovative nature of the wines, seems more than ordinarily worthwhile. Exports to the UK, the US and other major markets.

ΨΨΨΨΨ **The Eleventh Hour Barossa Valley Shiraz 2005** An intense, complex and supple array of flavours with black fruits, licorice and quality oak; very good structure, balance and length. Cork. 14.5° alc. **Rating** 94 **To** 2018 $32
The Howling Dog Barossa Valley Durif 2005 Deep colour and hue; savoury aspects to a powerful foundation of black fruits; tannins present but balanced. Good example of the variety. Cork. 14.5° alc. **Rating** 94 **To** 2020 $35

ΨΨΨΨΨ **The Moonlight Run 2005** An appropriately complex wine, with spicy/savoury notes in authentic Southern Rhône style running through to a long finish. Grenache/Shiraz/Mataro/Cinsault. Cork. 14.5° alc. **Rating** 93 **To** 2011 $25

ΨΨΨΨ **The Surly Muse Barossa Valley Viognier 2007** Peach flesh and hints of pepper on the bouquet, and plenty of texture on the palate. Screwcap. 13.5° alc. **Rating** 88 **To** 2011 $25

Matilda's Estate

★★★★

18 Hamilton Road, Denmark, WA 6333 **Region** Denmark
T (08) 9848 1951 **F** (08) 9848 1957 **www**.matildasestate.com **Open** Tues–Sun 10–5, 7 days during school hols
Winemaker Gavin Berry, Dave Cleary **Est.** 1990 **Cases** 4500
In 2003 the founders of Matilda's Meadow (as it was then known), Don Turnbull and Pamela Meldrum, sold the business to former citizen of the world Steve Hall. It is a thriving business based on 10 ha of estate plantings of chardonnay, semillon, sauvignon blanc, pinot noir, cabernet sauvignon, cabernet franc, merlot and shiraz.

ŸŸŸŸŸ **Chardonnay 2006** A complex mix of melon, peach and grapefruit plus creamy/ nutty flavours; has good length and well-handled oak. Screwcap. 13.6° alc. Rating 93 To 2013 $25

Semillon Sauvignon Blanc 2006 Good weight and mouthfeel, the fruit seeming far riper than the low alcohol would suggest; tingling, lemony acidity drives the finish. Screwcap. 11.4° alc. **Rating** 92 To 2013 $17

Sauvignon Blanc 2007 Attractive, clean passionfruit/tropical aromas; bright, fresh and lively citrussy acidity drives the palate. Screwcap. 12.5° alc. **Rating** 91 To 2010 $20

Pinot Noir 2005 Fresh and lively despite the bottle age; quite pure red cherry, strawberry and lemony acidity; has length. Screwcap. 14.5° alc. **Rating** 91 To 2012 $28

Sauvignon Blanc 2006 Has more drive and length than the '07, but the fruit aromas are less exuberant, the palate with a mix of white peach and lemon zest. Screwcap. 12.4° alc. **Rating** 90 To 2010 $20

Semillon Sauvignon Blanc 2007 Quite tightly constructed, with herb, grass, gooseberry and mineral flavours; crisp finish. Screwcap. 12.3° alc. **Rating** 90 To 2012 $17

ŸŸŸŸ **Unwooded Chardonnay 2007** Has some positive white peach and grapefruit flavours, with good movement in the mouth. Screwcap. 13.3° alc. **Rating** 88 To 2011 $17

Cabernet Merlot 2004 Light- to medium-bodied; savoury/minty overtones to cassis fruit; minimal tannin structure. Screwcap. 13.1° alc. **Rating** 87 To 2011 $25

🍇 Maverick Wines   ★★★★★

Lot 141, Light Pass Road, Vine Vale, Moorooroo, SA 5352 **Region** Barossa Valley
T (08) 8563 3551 **F** (08) 8563 3554 **www.**maverickwines.com.au **Open** By appt
Winemaker Christopher Taylor, Ronald Brown **Est.** 2004 **Cases** 7250
A new but ambitious venture of Ronald Brown, Jeremy Vogler, Adrian Bell and Christopher Taylor. Taking advantage of (likely short-lived) excess grape production in Australia, the partners have acquired four vineyards in key areas of the Eden Valley and Barossa Valley. There are a little over 30 ha planted, with vines ranging in age from 40 to over 100 years. Although production in 2008 was over 7000 cases, the wines are all made in small batches in tanks of half a tonne to 3-tonne capacity, and are then matured in French oak. For a relatively new kid on the block – and a strong emphasis on export to countries ranging from Japan to the UK, the US and Russia – Maverick has already achieved celebrity listings in top restaurants and fine wine retailers such as Tetsuya's and Ultimo Wine Centre in Sydney, a dazzling array of hotels and restaurants in Tokyo, and the Hilton Hotel in Osaka.

ŸŸŸŸŸ **Trial Hill Eden Valley Shiraz 2005** Has great density and depth without any jammy, overripe characters; delicious blackberry, licorice, spice and plum fruit; perfectly weighted tannins and oak. Cork. 14.5° alc. **Rating** 96 To 2025 $60

Trial Hill Eden Valley Riesling 2007 Lemon, lime, mineral and spice aromas; a very intense and long palate of ripe apple and citrus; fresh citrussy acidity. Screwcap. 12.5° alc. **Rating** 94 To 2017 $33

Trial Hill Eden Valley Chardonnay 2006 Very skilfully made; seamless nectarine and white peach fruit and oak; citrussy acidity. Screwcap. 14° alc. Rating 94 To 2012 $35

Greenock Rise Barossa Valley GSM 2006 Fragrant, flowery red fruits on the bouquet; a silky smooth palate with lovely line and flow; flavours of raspberry, redcurrant and blackberry. Part 110-year-old bush vine grenache. Cork. 15.2° alc. Rating 94 To 2016 $35

ŸŸŸŸŸ **Twins Barossa Valley Cabernet Sauvignon Merlot Petit Verdot Cabernet Franc 2006** Luscious, but not jammy red fruits; cassis, redcurrant, raspberry and mulberry; very good oak and tannin management; fresh finish. Screwcap. 14.5° alc. Rating 92 To 2015 $25

Trial Hill Eden Valley Riesling 2006 Has developed weight and richness; perhaps also the vintage effect. No hint of reduction, but doesn't have as much vibrancy as the '07; possibly going through a dumb phase. Screwcap. 12.5° alc. **Rating** 91 **To** 2016 $25

Twins Barossa Valley Shiraz 2006 A supple, smooth, medium-bodied palate, with perfectly ripened black fruit supported by fine, savoury tannins and appropriate oak. Screwcap. 14.5° alc. **Rating** 91 **To** 2016 $25

Twins Barossa Valley GSM 2006 Fragrant spicy, juicy berry aromas and flavours; attractive, but without the authority of the Greenock Rise. Cork. 15° alc. **Rating** 91 **To** 2011 $30

Maxwell Wines

Olivers Road, McLaren Vale, SA 5171 **Region** McLaren Vale
T (08) 8323 8200 **F** (08) 8323 8900 **www.**maxwellwines.com.au **Open** 7 days 10–5
Winemaker Mark Maxwell, Maria de Una **Est.** 1979 **Cases** 15 000
Maxwell Wines has come a long way since opening for business in 1979 using an amazing array of Heath Robinson equipment in cramped surroundings. A state-of-the-art and much larger winery was built in 1997. The brand has produced some excellent white and red wines in recent years; it is also sourcing grapes from Kangaroo Island. Exports to all major markets.

ŸŸŸŸŸ **Minatour Reserve Shiraz 2005** The quality of the fruit shines through on bouquet and palate with luscious plum and blackberry flavours; good acidity, 2 years in oak no problem for balance. Cork. 15° alc. **Rating** 95 **To** 2020 $80
Ellen Street McLaren Vale Shiraz 2004 Full-bodied; ultra-classic McLaren Vale style, with lashings of blackberry fruit wrapped in dark chocolate, oak and tannins merely providing a stage for the fruit. Cork. 15° alc. **Rating** 94 **To** 2029 $33
Lime Cave McLaren Vale Cabernet 2005 Concentrated, rich and deep; very good cabernet blackcurrant fruit, quality French oak and precisely judged tannins make an exemplary wine. Cork. 14.5° alc. **Rating** 94 **To** 2020 $32.95

ŸŸŸŸŸ **Lime Cave McLaren Vale Cabernet 2004** Medium-bodied; tightly knit blackcurrant fruit with fine tannins and quality oak; a long, cleansing finish. Cork. 14.5° alc. **Rating** 92 **To** 2024 $33
Little Demon McLaren Vale Cabernet Merlot 2005 Appealing cassis and plum fruits on the bouquet; good weight and flesh; medium-bodied, with bright acid and fine tannins on the finish. Screwcap. 14.5° alc. **Rating** 90 **To** 2014 $16.95

ŸŸŸŸ **Ellen Street McLaren Vale Shiraz 2005** Tangy medium-bodied wine with earthy/tangy/chocolatey flavours on a neatly structured and balanced palate. Cork. 15° alc. **Rating** 89 **To** 2014 $32.95
Silver Hammer Shiraz 2005 Soft, relatively developed, mocha, chocolate and vanilla alongside light- to medium-bodied dark fruits; soft tannins. Screwcap. 14.5° alc. **Rating** 88 **To** 2010 $19.99

Mayer ★★★★★

66 Miller Road, Healesville, Vic 3777 **Region** Yarra Valley
T (03) 5967 3779 **www.**timomayer.com.au **Open** By appt
Winemaker Timo Mayer **Est.** 1999 **Cases** 600
Timo Mayer, also winemaker at Gembrook Hill Vineyard, teamed with partner Rhonda Ferguson to establish Mayer Vineyard on the slopes of Mt Toolebewoong, 8 km south of Healesville. The steepness of those slopes is presumably self-apparent from the name given to the wines (Bloody Hill). There is just under 2.5 ha of vineyard, the lion's share to pinot noir, and smaller amounts of shiraz and chardonnay – all high-density plantings. Mayer's winemaking credo is minimal interference and handling, and no filtration.

ŸŸŸŸŸ **Close Planted Yarra Valley Pinot Noir 2006** A complex pinot with damson plum, hints of exotic spices and a touch of stem; has seductive mouthfeel and expands across the palate; the label may be fun, but the wine is definitely serious. Cork. 13.5° alc. **Rating** 95 **To** 2014 $50

Bloody Hill Yarra Valley Chardonnay 2006 A truly cool expression of chardonnay; pure lemon flavour and aromas, with vibrant, almost piercing acidity drawing out the strong mineral elements; should have a long and interesting journey ahead. Cork. 13.2° alc. **Rating** 94 **To** 2014 $27

ŸŸŸŸŸ **Bloody Hill Yarra Valley Pinot Noir 2006** Cool, spicy and full of light red berry fruits; the palate is quite silky and fine and, while not a big wine, offers length and focus right through to the finish. Cork. 13.2° alc. **Rating** 91 **To** 2009 $27
Big Betty Yarra Valley Shiraz 2006 Quite reductive, but also alluring; roasted meats, blackberry and tar all mingle together on the medium-bodied palate; very good acid line to the finish; needs time. Cork. 14.2° alc. **Rating** 91 **To** 2016 $30

Mayfield Vineyard   ★★★★☆

Icely Road, Orange, NSW 2800 **Region** Orange
T (02) 6365 9292 **F** (02) 6365 9281 **www**.mayfieldvineyard.com **Open** Thurs–Sun 10–5, or by appt
Winemaker Jon Reynolds (Contract) **Est.** 1998 **Cases** 10 000
The property – including the house in which owners Richard and Kathy Thomas now live, and its surrounding arboretum – has a rich history as a leading Suffolk sheep stud, founded upon the vast fortune accumulated by the Crawford family via its biscuit business in the UK. The Thomases planted the 37-ha vineyard in 1998, with merlot (15.3 ha) leading the way, followed (in descending order) by cabernet sauvignon, sauvignon blanc, chardonnay, pinot noir, riesling and sangiovese. The wines are marketed under the Mayfield Vineyard and Icely Road brands. Exports to the UK, the US and Sweden.

ŸŸŸŸŸ **Single Vineyard Orange Riesling 2007** Ripe, almost exotic, fruits on the bouquet; good flavour depth, and fruit sweetness on the finish; long and focused. Screwcap. 12° alc. **Rating** 91 **To** 2016 $28
Single Vineyard Orange Cabernet Merlot 2005 Deep colour; generous blackcurrant fruit on the mid-palate, then a twitch of (possibly adjusted) acidity unsettles the line; the good parts of the curate's egg are in the majority. Screwcap. 14.2° alc. **Rating** 90 **To** 2015 $28

ŸŸŸŸ **Icely Road Orange Riesling 2007** A minerally, quite dry palate; good flavour and clean citrus fruits on the finish. Screwcap. 12.5° alc. **Rating** 88 **To** 2014 $21.50
Icely Road Orange Chardonnay 2006 Good flavour, with some grapefruit and melon on the bouquet; ripe yet quite fine on the finish. Screwcap. 13.5° alc. **Rating** 88 **To** 2013 $21.50
Icely Road Orange Rose 2007 A fine style, with red fruits and quite a dry but complex finish. Screwcap. 12.5° alc. **Rating** 88 **To** 2009 $19.50
Icely Road Orange Merlot 2006 Quite cool and focused; dark plum fruits and just a little spice. Screwcap. 14.5° alc. **Rating** 87 **To** 2012 $21.50

Maygars Hill Winery   ★★★★★

53 Longwood–Mansfield Road, Longwood, Vic 3665 **Region** Strathbogie Ranges
T (03) 5798 5417 **F** (03) 5798 5457 **www**.strathbogieboutiquewines.com **Open** By appt
Winemaker Plunkett Wines (Sam Plunkett) **Est.** 1997 **Cases** 1200
Jenny Houghton purchased this 8-ha property in 1994, planting 3.4 ha of shiraz and cabernet sauvignon, and has established a stylish B&B cottage. The name comes from Lieutenant Colonel Maygar, who fought with outstanding bravery in the Boer War in South Africa in 1901, where he won the Victoria Cross. In World War I he rose to command the 8th Light Horse Regiment, winning yet further medals for bravery. He died on 1 November 1917.

ŸŸŸŸŸ **Shiraz 2006** Superb colour; an exotic array of rich blackberry, plum, aniseed and licorice aromas and flavours; quality oak and ripe tannins round off a lovely wine. **Rating** 95 **To** 2016

Reserve Shiraz 2006 Bright and vibrant, with redcurrant and blackberry fruit; the palate is fresh, with good acidity and plenty of spice offering real interest on the long, firm finish. Screwcap. **Rating** 94 **To** 2020 $34
Cabernet Sauvignon 2006 Medium-bodied, with ripe cassis and blackcurrant fruit; skilled oak handling, and gentle tannin extract. **Rating** 94 **To** 2016

ϙϙϙϙϙ **Reserve Shiraz 2005** A complex bouquet and palate, with leather, chocolate and hints of tar in amongst the dark fruits; good weight, and quite spicy on the finish. Screwcap. 14.5° alc. **Rating** 90 **To** 2012 $34

ϙϙϙϙ **Cabernet Sauvignon 2005** Developed colour, but the palate has sweet blackcurrant fruit along with some pleasantly minty notes, finishing with soft tannins. **Rating** 89 **To** 2013 $20

Meadowbank Estate

699 Richmond Road, Cambridge, Tas 7170 **Region** Southern Tasmania
T (03) 6248 4484 **F** (03) 6248 4485 **www.**meadowbankwines.com.au **Open** 7 days 10–5
Winemaker Hood Wines (Andrew Hood) **Est.** 1974 **Cases** 6000
An important part of the Ellis family business on what was once a large grazing property on the banks of the Derwent. Increased plantings are under contract to Hardys, and a splendid winery has been built to handle the increased production. The winery has expansive entertainment and function facilities, capable of handling up to 1000 people, and offering an arts and music program, plus a large restaurant. Exports to Germany, Sweden, the Netherlands and Hong Kong.

ϙϙϙϙϙ **FGR Riesling 2007** Elegant and fine, with tangy lemon and herb flavours; very good balance and finish; fresh, and it is extraordinary how the 40g residual sugar is not obvious. **Rating** 94 **To** 2015 $25

ϙϙϙϙϙ **Mardi 2005** Has abundant flavour, with sweet strawberry and stone fruit/biscuity notes from 18 months on lees flowing through on the palate. Cork. 12° alc. **Rating** 90 **To** 2013 $39

ϙϙϙϙ **Riesling 2006** Still restrained and tightly wound, with a core of herb and lime fruit, and a long finish. Has potential to go further. Screwcap. **Rating** 88 **To** 2014 $25
Pinot Noir 2006 Bright colour, with quite a silky palate and textured finish; slightly pencilly oak. Screwcap. 13.5° alc. **Rating** 88 **To** 2013 $30
Henry James Pinot Noir 2006 Clear but developed colour; dark fruits with stem and herb notes on both the bouquet and firm palate; needs more sweet fruit. Screwcap. 14° alc. **Rating** 88 **To** 2012 $43
Pinot Gris 2007 Slightly left-field aromas, veering towards apricot rather than pear, the palate down the same track; far from unpleasant. Screwcap. 13.4° alc. **Rating** 87 **To** 2010 $29.50

Medhurst

24–26 Medhurst Road, Gruyere, Vic 3770 **Region** Yarra Valley
T (03) 5964 9022 **F** (03) 5964 9033 **www.**medhurstwines.com.au **Open** Fri–Mon 10–5
Winemaker Dominique Portet **Est.** 2000 **Cases** 2500
The wheel has come full circle for Ross and Robyn Wilson; in the course of a very distinguished corporate career, Ross Wilson was CEO of Southcorp during the time it brought the Penfolds, Lindemans and Wynns businesses under the Southcorp banner. For her part, Robyn spent her childhood in the Yarra Valley, her parents living less than a kilometre away as the crow flies from Medhurst. Immaculately sited and tended vineyard blocks, most on steep, north-facing slopes, promise much for the future. In all, there are 13 ha planted to sauvignon blanc, chardonnay, pinot noir, cabernet sauvignon and shiraz, all run on a low-yield basis. Red Shed is the newly introduced second label, taking its name from the recently opened café.

ŶŶŶŶ♀ **Yarra Valley Chardonnay 2006** Light-bodied but lively white peach and grapefruit, has all the Yarra hallmark of length one could wish for. Screwcap 14° alc. **Rating** 90 To 2013 $20

ŶŶŶŶ **Yarra Valley Shiraz 2005** Fresh, lively, light- to medium-bodied wine, with gently spicy overtones to the blackberry fruit; fine tannins; no need for cellaring. Cork. 14.2° alc. **Rating** 88 To 2010 $25
Yarra Valley Rose 2007 Delicate dry crisp style; some light touches of strawberries; good dry finish. Screwcap. 13.5° alc. **Rating** 87 To 2009 $16
Yarra Valley Cabernet Sauvignon 2004 Briary cedary earthy characters starting to emerge from the light-bodied palate; young vines are evident. ProCork. 13.5° alc. **Rating** 87 To 2012 $25

Meerea Park   ★★★★★

188 Palmers Lane, Pokolbin, NSW 2320 **Region** Lower Hunter Valley
T (02) 4998 7474 **F** (02) 4998 7974 **www.**meereapark.com.au **Open** At The Boutique Wine Centre, Pokolbin
Winemaker Rhys Eather **Est.** 1991 **Cases** 10 000
All the wines are produced from grapes purchased from growers, primarily in the Pokolbin area, but also from the Upper Hunter, and as far afield as Young. It is the brainchild of Rhys Eather, a great-grandson of Alexander Munro, a leading vigneron in the mid-19th century; he makes the wine at the former Little's Winery at Palmers Lane in Pokolbin, which was purchased in 2007 and is now named Meerea Park. Exports to the UK, the Netherlands, Germany, Canada and Singapore.

ŶŶŶŶŶ **Alexander Munro Individual Vineyard Hunter Valley Semillon 2002** A lovely, pure semillon, with just the right amount of development; long and seamless, with an array of flavours that really persist. Cork. 10.5° alc. **Rating** 95 To 2018 $35
Terracotta Semillon 2003 Has less depth than Alexander Munro, but more drive and intensity to the more focused lemon and mineral flavours, and pronounced citrussy acidity. Screwcap. 11° alc. **Rating** 94 To 2013 $30
Hell Hole Hunter Valley Shiraz 2005 A silky, fluid mouthfeel, with undulations of red fruits and supple tannins; though only light- to medium-bodied, has all the flavour one could wish for. Screwcap. 13.5° alc. **Rating** 94 To 2020 $55
Aged Release Alexander Munro Individual Vineyard Hunter Valley Shiraz 1998 Now shows all the classic Hunter aromas and flavours of mature shiraz, with leather and warm earth along with black fruits; the tannins are fine, but sufficient to sustain it for another decade or two, and underpin its great length. Cork. 13.5° alc. **Rating** 94 To 2018 $100

ŶŶŶŶ♀ **Alexander Munro Individual Vineyard Hunter Valley Semillon 2003** Glowing yellow-green; doesn't quite deliver on the promise of the colour; an attractive citrus/honey/toast/mineral melange, but not quite enough drive on the finish. Screwcap. 11° alc. **Rating** 92 To 2012 $35
Alexander Munro Individual Vineyard Chardonnay 2007 Impressive Hunter chardonnay; melon and white peach fruit; good line and length, the oak well-balanced and integrated. Screwcap. 14° alc. **Rating** 92 To 2013 $30
Alexander Munro Individual Vineyard Hunter Valley Shiraz 2005 Classic regional style; a seamless fusion of dark fruits, spice and earth underpinned by fine, savoury tannins. A challenging price even if from 40-year-old vines. Screwcap. 14.5° alc. **Rating** 91 To 2020 $60

ŶŶŶŶ **Hell Hole Semillon 2007** Clever winemaking; a touch of sweetness balanced by acidity; good length. Screwcap. 11° alc. **Rating** 89 To 2015 $25

Melaleuca Grove

8 Melaleuca Court, Rowville, Vic 3178 (postal) **Region** Yarra Valley
T (03) 9752 7928 **F** (03) 9752 7928 **www.**melaleucawines.com.au **Open** Not
Winemaker Jeff Wright **Est.** 1999 **Cases** 500
Jeff and Anne Wright are both Honours graduates in biochemistry who have succumbed to the lure of winemaking after lengthy careers elsewhere; in the case of Jeff, 20 years in research and hospital science. He commenced his winemaking apprenticeship in 1997 at Green Vineyards, backed up by vintage work in '99 and 2000 at Bianchet and Yarra Valley Hills, both in the Yarra Valley. At the same time he began the external Bachelor of Applied Science (Wine Science) course at CSU, while still working in biochemistry in the public hospital system. They purchase grapes from various cool-climate regions, including the Yarra Valley and Yea. Exports to Canada.

Yarra Valley Marsanne 2005 Good varietal character; a firm mix of mineral and honeysuckle; good structure and texture to the herb and grass flavours; pleasingly dry finish. Screwcap. 14° alc. **Rating** 90 **To** 2012 $18

Yarra Valley Pinot Noir 2006 Attractive spicy/savoury nuances on the bouquet; plenty of red fruit in support on the light- to medium-bodied palate. Screwcap. 13.5° alc. **Rating** 89 **To** 2010 $25

Melville Hill Estate Wines

PO Box 1247, Tamworth, NSW 2340 **Region** New England
T (02) 6760 9309 **F** (02) 6760 9306 **www.**melvillehill.com.au **Open** Not
Winemaker Poole's Rock (Patrick Auld, Usher Tinkler) **Est.** 2000 **Cases** 18 750
This is one of the larger vineyard developments in New England, established by Rajesh and Geeta Upadhyaya. They have planted chardonnay (10 ha), shiraz (7 ha), verdelho and tempranillo (4 ha each). The grapes from the estate plantings are supplemented by pinot noir, semillon, sauvignon blanc, riesling, merlot and cabernet sauvignon, giving rise to 20 wines on the price list. Much of the wine is sold through a wine club.

Mermerus Vineyard

60 Soho Road, Drysdale, Vic 3222 **Region** Geelong
T (03) 5253 2718 **F** (03) 5251 1555 **www.**mermerus.com.au **Open** Sun 11–4
Winemaker Paul Champion **Est.** 2000 **Cases** 250
Paul Champion has established 1.5 ha of pinot noir, 1 ha of chardonnay and 0.2 ha of riesling at Mermerus since 1996. The wines are made from the small but very neat winery on the property, with small batch handling and wild yeast fermentation playing a major part in the winemaking, oak taking a back seat. He also acts as contract winemaker for small growers in the region.

Shiraz 2006 Bright colour; elegant light- to medium-bodied cool-grown style, which makes light of 15° alcohol; spice and black fruits on a quite silky palate. Diam. 15° alc. **Rating** 90 **To** 2015 $20

Pinot Noir 2006 Light- to medium-bodied; a pretty wine, with a mix of red and black fruits, though not so much structure and texture; some green tinges. **Rating** 89 **To** 2011 $20

Merops Wines

5992 Caves Road, Margaret River, WA 6825 **Region** Margaret River
T (08) 9757 9195 **F** (08) 9757 3193 **www.**meropswines.com.au **Open** By appt
Winemaker Flying Fish Cove (Damon Eastough, Elizabeth Reed) **Est.** 2000 **Cases** 3000
Jim and Yvonne Ross have been involved in horticulture for over 25 years, in production, retail nurseries and viticulture. They established a nursery and irrigation business in the

Margaret River township in 1985 on a 3-ha property before establishing a rootstock nursery. In 2000 they removed the nursery and planted 6.3 ha of cabernet sauvignon, cabernet franc, merlot and shiraz on the laterite gravel over clay soils. They use the practices developed by Professor William Albrecht in the US 50 years ago, providing mineral balance and thus eliminating the need for insecticides and toxic sprays. Organic pre-certification was completed in July 2007, which resulted in the '08 vintage being certified organic. Exports to the US and Indonesia.

ȚȚȚȚ **Ornatus 2006** Light-bodied; fresh red fruits with some olive and citrus nuances; fair length. Merlot/Cabernet Sauvignon/Shiraz/Cabernet Franc. Screwcap. 13° alc. **Rating** 87 **To** 2010 $22

Merricks Creek Wines   ★★★★★

44 Merricks Road, Merricks, Vic 3916 **Region** Mornington Peninsula
T (03) 5989 8868 **F** (03) 5989 9070 **www.**pinot.com.au **Open** By appt
Winemaker Nick Farr **Est.** 1998 **Cases** 650

Peter and Georgina Parker retained Gary Farr as viticultural consultant before they began establishing their 2-ha pinot noir vineyard. They say, 'He has been an extraordinarily helpful and stern taskmaster. He advised on clonal selection, trellis design and planting density, and visits the vineyard regularly to monitor canopy management.' (Son Nick completes the circle as contract winemaker.) The vineyard is planted to a sophisticated collection of pinot noir clones, and is planted at ultra-high density of 500 mm spacing. Exports to the UK, the US and Canada.

ȚȚȚȚȚ **Mornington Peninsula Pinot Noir 2006** A fragrant mix of cherry, plum and spice on the bouquet and palate; very good balance and length, and has considerable thrust. Diam. 13.5° alc. **Rating** 94 **To** 2013 $46

Merricks Estate   ★★★★☆

Thompsons Lane, Merricks, Vic 3916 **Region** Mornington Peninsula
T (03) 5989 8416 **F** (03) 9613 4242 **www.**merricksestate.com.au **Open** 1st w'end of month, each w'end in Jan & public hol w'ends 12–5
Winemaker Paul Evans **Est.** 1977 **Cases** 750

Melbourne solicitor George Kefford, with wife Jacquie, runs Merricks Estate as a weekend and holiday enterprise. Right from the outset it has produced distinctive, spicy, cool-climate Shiraz, which has accumulated an impressive array of show trophies and gold medals. For some inexplicable reason, no Shiraz was tasted for this edition.

ȚȚȚȚȚ **Cabernet Sauvignon 2001** Flies in the face of (my) accepted wisdom that Mornington can't ripen cabernet; cedary but pure (age accepted) with ripe cabernet fruit, minimal tannins. Atrociously stained cork. 13.5° alc. **Rating** 90 **To** 2010 $25

Metier Wines   ★★★★☆

Tarraford Vineyard, 440 Healesville Road, Yarra Glen, Vic 3775 (postal) **Region** Yarra Valley
T 0419 678 918 **F** (03) 0816 3474 **www.**metierwines.com.au **Open** Not
Winemaker Martin Williams MW **Est.** 1995 **Cases** 2000

Metier is the French word for craft, trade or profession; the business is that of Yarra Valley–based Martin Williams, who has notched up an array of degrees and had winemaking stints in France, California and Australia, which are, not to put too fine a word on it, extraordinary. The focus of Metier is individual vineyard wines, initially based on grapes from the Tarraford and Schoolhouse Vineyards. Exports to the UK, the US and Hong Kong.

ȚȚȚȚȚ **Schoolhouse Vineyard Yarra Valley Chardonnay 2003** Complex aroma and texture; cashew, fig and cream all interwoven; still cruising after four years; lovely mouthfeel and length. Screwcap. 14° alc. **Rating** 94 **To** 2013 $29.95

YYYYY Tarraford Vineyard Yarra Valley Chardonnay 2003 A classic, tight structure reflecting unusually low alcohol, taking the wine in a Chablis direction; contrasting cashew and minerally acidity. Screwcap. 12.5° alc. **Rating** 93 **To** 2013 $29.95

YYYY Milkwood Yarra Valley Pinot Noir 2004 Fully mature, with spicy/savoury/earthy characters now leading the way; ready now, and don't delay. Screwcap. 13° alc. **Rating** 87 **To** 2009 $19.50

Meure's Wines

16 Fleurtys Lane, Birchs Bay, Tas 7162 **Region** Southern Tasmania
T (03) 6267 4483 **F** (03) 6267 4483 **www.**dmeure.com.au **Open** Not
Winemaker Dirk Meure **Est.** 1991 **Cases** 300
Dirk Meure has established 1 ha of vineyard on the shores of D'Entrecasteaux Channel, overlooking Bruny Island. He says he has been heavily influenced by his mentors, Steve and Monique Lubiana. The philosophy is to produce low yields and to interfere as little as possible in the winemaking and maturation process. The vines are planted with an ultra-high density of 8000 vines per ha, and are dry-farmed. No chemicals are used in the viticulture or winemaking, and the wines are bottled without fining or filtering. This is the ultimate challenge.

YYYYY d'Meure Special Reserve Pinot Noir 2005 More varietal fruits than the standard, and a little development, but lashings of oak mask it a little; massively proportioned, has been made for the long haul. Diam. 13.4° alc. **Rating** 90 **To** 2014 $90

YYYY d'Meure Pinot Noir 2005 Deeply coloured and incredibly oaky; no doubt about the intensity, but for now the winemaking dominates the fruit. Diam. 13.4° alc. **Rating** 88 **To** 2014 $75

Miceli

60 Main Creek Road, Arthurs Seat, Vic 3936 **Region** Mornington Peninsula
T (03) 5989 2755 **F** (03) 5989 2755 **Open** 1st w'end month 12–5, public hols, & every w'end & by appt in Jan
Winemaker Anthony Miceli **Est.** 1991 **Cases** 3500
This may be a part-time labour of love for general practitioner Dr Anthony Miceli, but that hasn't prevented him taking the whole venture very seriously. He acquired the property in 1989 specifically to establish a vineyard, planting 1.8 ha in 1991, followed by a further ha of pinot gris in '97. Between '91 and '97 Dr Miceli completed the Wine Science course at CSU and now manages both vineyard and winery. One of the top producers of sparkling wine on the Peninsula.

YYYYY Rose Methode Champenoise 2001 Strawberry and spice aromas and flavours; still lively and well-balanced; has improved with three extra years on cork since first tasted in March '04. **Rating** 92 **To** 2010 $40
Michael Mornington Peninsula Methode Champenoise 2003 Delicate, almost fairy floss territory; pear, citrus and strawberry all haunt the back-palate. Chardonnay/Pinot Noir/Pinot Gris. Cork. 11.5° alc. **Rating** 90 **To** 2010 $32
Iolanda Mornington Peninsula Pinot Grigio 2007 Very cool lime juice bouquet, with hints of dried straw in the background; very zesty on the palate, with good concentration; acid is just a little tart. Screwcap. 13.5° alc. **Rating** 90 **To** 2009 $22

Michael Unwin Wines

2 Racecourse Road (Western Highway), Beaufort, Vic 3373 **Region** Grampians
T (03) 5349 2021 **F** (03) 5349 2032 **www.**michaelunwinwines.com.au **Open** Mon–Fri 8.30–5, w'ends 11–4.30
Winemaker Michael Unwin **Est.** 2000 **Cases** 2000

Established by winemaker Michael Unwin and wife and business partner Catherine Clark. His track record as a winemaker spans 27 years, and includes extended winemaking experience in France, NZ and Australia; he has also found time to obtain a postgraduate degree in oenology and viticulture at Lincoln University, Canterbury, NZ. The winery location was chosen because it is the geographical centre of the best viticultural areas in Western Victoria. The grapes are either estate- or contract-grown in up to six mature vineyards, all with different site climates. In all, approximately 2 ha of shiraz and 1 ha each of cabernet sauvignon, sangiovese, barbera, durif, riesling and chardonnay are grown or contracted.

ŸŸŸŸŸ **Acrobat Umbrella Man Chardonnay 2006** Lively aromas and flavours of grapefruit and nectarine allied with barrel ferment inputs; crisp acidity to close; early picking a bonus. Screwcap. 13° alc. **Rating** 91 **To** 2012 $25
Tattooed Lady Shiraz 2003 Rich, ripe, concentrated black fruits with some spice and licorice, a touch of sweetness somewhere in the mix; also the impact of drought; 200 cases made. Screwcap. 14° alc. **Rating** 90 **To** 2015 $45

ŸŸŸŸ **Acrobat Umbrella Man Durif 2005** Typical strong colour and deep, dark berry, licorice and dark chocolate fruit; gentle tannins. Screwcap. 14° alc. **Rating** 88 **To** 2011 $25
Acrobat Umbrella Man Riesling 2007 A generously flavoured tropical lime mix; relatively soft finish and early developing. Screwcap. 12° alc. **Rating** 87 **To** 2010 $19
Acrobat Umbrella Man Barbera 2005 Spiced plum flavours on a basically sweet, light- to medium-bodied palate are enough to satisfy; ready now. Screwcap. 14° alc. **Rating** 87 **To** 2009 $19

Michelini Wines   ★★★☆

Great Alpine Road, Myrtleford, Vic 3737 **Region** Alpine Valleys
T (03) 5751 1990 **F** (03) 5751 1410 **www**.micheliniwines.com.au **Open** 7 days 10–5
Winemaker Greg O'Keefe **Est.** 1982 **Cases** 19 000
The Michelini family are among the best known grapegrowers in the Buckland Valley of Northeast Victoria. Having migrated from Italy in 1949, the Michelinis originally grew tobacco, diversifying into vineyards in 1982. They now have a little over 34 ha of vineyard on terra rossa soil at an altitude of 300 m, mostly with frontage to the Buckland River. A previous grape supply agreement with Orlando has expired, but given the likely shortages of grapes for the remainder of this decade, Michelini will be able to decide whether to sell grapes, juice or wine. The winery has the capacity to handle 1000 tonnes of fruit, which eliminates the problem of moving grapes out of a declared phylloxera area.

ŸŸŸŸŸ **Unwooded Chardonnay 2007** Particularly impressive for the vintage and style; has considerable thrust and length to its mix of grapefruit, citrus and nectarine flavours; some sauvignon blanc notes. Screwcap. 13.5° alc. **Rating** 90 **To** 2010 $15

ŸŸŸŸ **Chardonnay Pinot Cuvee NV** Fresh and lively; not complex, but the fruit flavours of citrus, stone fruit and apple are appealing. Cork. 12.5° alc. **Rating** 88 **To** 2010 $20
Sangiovese 2006 Light-bodied; clear varietal character with a mix of sour cherry, red cherry, herbs and spice. Cork. 13.5° alc. **Rating** 87 **To** 2011 $18.50

Midhill Vineyard   ★★★★

PO Box 30, Romsey, Vic 3434 **Region** Macedon Ranges
T (03) 5429 5565 **Open** Not
Winemaker Contract **Est.** 1993 **Cases** 200
The Richards family has been breeding Angus cattle for the past 35 years, and diversified into grapegrowing in 1993. The vineyard has been planted on a northeast-facing slope on red volcanic clay loam, which is free-draining and moderately fertile. There are 2 ha of chardonnay and 0.5 ha each of pinot noir and gewurztraminer.

🍷🍷🍷🍷🍷 **Macedon Blanc de Blancs 2004** A very fine but clear fruit profile in a lemon, nectarine and grapefruit range; a long, delicately lingering, dry finish; three years on lees. Cork. 12° alc. **Rating** 92 **To** 2013

Mike Press Wines

PO Box 224, Lobethal, SA 5241 **Region** Adelaide Hills
T (08) 8389 5546 **F** (08) 8389 5546 **www**.mikepresswines.com.au **Open** Not
Winemaker Mike Press **Est.** 1998 **Cases** 8000
Mike and Judy Press established their Kenton Valley Vineyards in 1998, when they purchased 34 ha of land in the Adelaide Hills at an elevation of 500 m. Over the next 2 years they planted 24 ha of mainstream, cool-climate varieties intending to sell the grapes to other wine producers. Even an illustrious 42-year career in the wine industry did not prepare Mike for the downturn in grape prices that followed, and that led to the development of the Mike Press wine label. They produce Sauvignon Blanc, Chardonnay, Pinot Noir, Merlot, Shiraz, Cabernet Merlot and Cabernet Sauvignon, which, despite accumulating gold medals and trophies, are sold at an average price of $10 per bottle.

Milhinch Wines ★★★★☆

PO Box 655, Greenock, SA 5360 **Region** Barossa Valley
T (08) 8563 4003 **F** (08) 8563 4003 **www**.seizetheday.net.au **Open** At Barossa Small Winemakers, Chateau Tanunda
Winemaker Contract **Est.** 2003 **Cases** 1200
Peter Milhinch and Sharyn Rogers have established 2 ha each of shiraz and cabernet sauvignon, the first vintages made by big name Barossa Valley boutique winemakers. The current releases are particularly impressive.

🍷🍷🍷🍷🍷 **Seize the Day Single Vineyard Barossa Valley Cabernet Sauvignon 2006** Serious cabernet with complex aromas of violets, cedar, cassis and a touch of black olive; wonderfully pure on the palate, with great depth to the full-bodied fruit. Screwcap. 14.5° alc. **Rating** 94 **To** 2018 $38

🍷🍷🍷🍷🍷 **Seize the Day Single Vineyard Barossa Valley Shiraz 2006** Deep colour; slightly savoury notes, with red fruits and hints of mocha; good weight with bright acidity, and good persistence of dark fruits on the finish. Screwcap. 14.9° alc. **Rating** 91 **To** 2018 $38
Seize the Day Single Vineyard Barossa Valley Shiraz 2005 Densely packed, with fruit ripeness on the cusp of dead fruit; blackberry, prune and licorice flavours; has dealt with 21 months in oak. Screwcap. 14.8° alc. **Rating** 90 **To** 2020 $38

🍷🍷🍷🍷 **Seize the Day Single Vineyard Barossa Valley Cabernet Sauvignon 2005** Fully ripe, warm-grown cabernet palate; blackberry and dark chocolate; sweet edges to the fruit (not residual sugar) blur the line. Screwcap. 14.3° alc. **Rating** 89 **To** 2018 $38
Seize the Day Barossa Valley Rose 2007 Vibrant fuschia colour; abundant red fruit/cassis flavours, the sweetness on the finish not needed. Cabernet Sauvignon. Screwcap. 12.5° alc. **Rating** 87 **To** 2009 $21

Millamolong Estate ★★★★☆

Millamolong Road, Mandurama, NSW 2792 **Region** Orange
T 0429 635 191 **F** (02) 6367 4088 **www**.millamolong.com **Open** 7 days 9–4
Winemaker Madrez Wine Services, Lowe Family Wines **Est.** 2000 **Cases** 1000
This is a book about wine, not polo, but it so happens that Millamolong Estate has been the centrepiece of Australian polo for over 80 years. For an even longer period, generations of James Ashton (differentiated by their middle Christian name) have been at the forefront of a dynasty to make *Rawhide* or *McLeod's Daughters* seem tame. In the context of this, 28 ha of chardonnay, riesling, cabernet, shiraz and merlot may seem incidental, but it happens to add to the luxury accommodation at the main homestead, which caters for up to 18 guests.

ΨΨΨΨΨ **56 Miles Orange Shiraz 2006** An aromatic black fruit bouquet; plum, blackberry and spice fill a well-focused palate; fine tannins and subtle oak. Diam. 14.5° alc. **Rating** 94 **To** 2016 $20

ΨΨΨΨΩ **26 Ponies Orange Chardonnay 2006** An elegant, fresh grapefruit and stone fruit mix with good acidity and minimal oak. Screwcap. 14° alc. **Rating** 90 **To** 2012 $20

Millbrook Winery   ★★★★★

Old Chestnut Lane, Jarrahdale, WA 6124 **Region** Perth Hills
T (08) 9525 5796 **F** (08) 9525 5672 www.millbrookwinery.com.au **Open** 7 days 10–5
Winemaker Damian Hutton, Marius Mencel **Est.** 1996 **Cases** 20 000
The strikingly situated Millbrook Winery is owned by the highly successful Perth-based entrepreneur Peter Fogarty and wife Lee. They also own Lake's Folly in the Hunter Valley, and Deep Woods Estate in Margaret River, and have made a major commitment to the quality end of Australian wine. Millbrook draws on 7.5 ha of vineyards in the Perth Hills, planted to sauvignon blanc, semillon, chardonnay, viognier, cabernet sauvignon, merlot, shiraz and petit verdot. The wines (Millbrook and Barking Owl) are of consistently high quality. Exports to the UK, Belgium, Germany, Denmark, Russia, Malaysia, Hong Kong and Japan.

ΨΨΨΨΨ **Sauvignon Blanc 2007** Delicate and fresh blossom aromas; a delicious balance of passionfruit, gooseberry and more herbal notes; long, clean finish. Gold, Adelaide Wine Show '07. Screwcap. 12.5° alc. **Rating** 94 **To** 2010 $19.95
Estate Shiraz Viognier 2005 Strong purple-crimson; medium- to full-bodied with abundant black fruits, licorice, spice and tannins, the 5% viognier providing that special lift to the fruit profile; good length; will be long lived. Screwcap. 14.5° alc. **Rating** 94 **To** 2020 $35

ΨΨΨΨΩ **Limited Release Shiraz Cabernet 2006** Has distinct touches of herb and spice in the mix of blackberry and cassis; the palate has an almost angular thrust, which will abate with time. Screwcap. 14.5° alc. **Rating** 92 **To** 2021 $45
Limited Release Chardonnay 2006 Medium- to full-bodied; ripe melon, peach and a touch of grapefruit finishing with refreshing acidity; good oak integration and balance. Geographe. Screwcap. 14.5° alc. **Rating** 91 **To** 2012 $35
Limited Release Chardonnay 2007 From 100% Geographe fruit reflected in the fine melon and stone fruit flavour and structure; controlled barrel ferment inputs; accelerates on the finish and aftertaste. Screwcap. 14° alc. **Rating** 90 **To** 2014 $35

ΨΨΨΨ **Estate Viognier 2007** Has sufficient varietal character on both bouquet and palate to satisfy, but seems needlessly sweet. **Rating** 88 **To** 2012 $35
Limited Release Viognier 2007 Abundant varietal fruit achieved at the expense of some phenolics; a catch 22 variety, if there ever was one. **Rating** 88 **To** 2009 $35
Estate Viognier 2007 The winemakers have endeavoured to give textural interest (barrel ferment, etc) but the fruit definition isn't really there, just the alcohol, numbered bottled notwithstanding. Screwcap. 14.5° alc. **Rating** 88 **To** 2009 $35
Barking Owl Rose 2007 Vivid pale fuschia tells of the cornucopia of red fruits on the palate, though not so much the slight congestion on the finish. Screwcap. 13° alc. **Rating** 87 **To** 2009 $16.95
Barking Owl Shiraz Viognier 2005 Light- to medium-bodied at best, but the palate is still zesty and fresh, with pleasant small berry fruits; good everyday wine. Screwcap. 14.5° alc. **Rating** 87 **To** 2012 $16.95

Miller's Dixons Creek Estate

1620 Melba Highway, Dixons Creek, Vic 3775 **Region** Yarra Valley
T (03) 5965 2553 **F** (03) 5965 2320 **www**.graememillerwines.com.au **Open** 7 days 10–5
Winemaker Graeme Miller **Est.** 2004 **Cases** 5000
Graeme Miller is a Yarra Valley legend in his own lifetime, having established Chateau Yarrinya
(now De Bortoli) in 1971, and as a virtual unknown winning the Jimmy Watson Trophy in '78
with the '77 Chateau Yarrinya Cabernet Sauvignon. He sold Chateau Yarrinya in 1986 and,
together with wife Bernadette, established a vineyard, which has steadily grown to over 30 ha
with chardonnay, cabernet sauvignon, pinot noir, shiraz, sauvignon blanc, petit verdot, pinot
gris and merlot. A significant part of the production is sold, but the opening of the winery in
2004, and a cellar door thereafter, has seen production increase.

 🍷🍷🍷🍷 **Yarra Valley Petit Verdot 2005** Has a plentiful volume of red fruit flavours,
though strong minty overtones suggest the fruit was not fully ripe; good tannin
control a plus. Cork. 13.5° alc. **Rating** 87 **To** 2014 $25

Milton Vineyard

14635 Tasman Highway, Cranbrook, Tas 7190 **Region** Southern Tasmania
T (03) 6257 8298 **F** (03) 6257 8297 **www**.miltonvineyard.com.au **Open** 7 days 10–5
Winemaker Winemaking Tasmania (Julian Alcorso) **Est.** 1992 **Cases** 1000
Michael and Kerry Dunbabin have one of the most historic properties in Tasmania, dating
back to 1826. The property is 1800 ha, meaning the 2.7 ha of pinot noir and 1 ha each of
riesling and pinot gris (and a touch of traminer) have plenty of room for expansion. Michael
Dunbabin says, 'I've planted some of the newer pinot clones in 2001, but have yet to plant
what I reckon will prove to be some of the best vineyard sites on the property.' Initially the
grapes were sold to Hardys, but since 2005 much of the production has been retained for the
Milton Vineyard label.

 🍷🍷🍷🍷🍷 **Freycinet Coast Pinot Noir 2006** Bright colour; a complex wine with good
flavour and excellent texture; also good structure on the long and fine finish.
Rating 94 **To** 2013 $28

 🍷🍷🍷🍷 **Freycinet Coast Riesling 2007** Has some faintly grassy aromas, but the palate
moves firmly to lime and lemon fruit; long finish with typical Tasmanian acidity.
Screwcap. 11° alc. **Rating** 89 **To** 2013 $22

Milvine Estate Wines

108 Warren Road, Heathcote, Vic 3523 **Region** Heathcote
T (03) 5433 2772 **F** (03) 5433 2769 **Open** W'ends & public hols 11–5
Winemaker Graeme Millard **Est.** 2002 **Cases** 300
Jo and Graeme Millard planted 2 ha of clonally selected shiraz in 1995, picking their first
grapes in '98; in that and the ensuing four vintages the grapes were sold to Heathcote
Winery, but in '03 part of the production was vinified by Heathcote Winery for the Millards.
Production will increase in the years ahead, and the Millards have a carefully thought-out
business plan to market the wine.

 🍷🍷🍷🍷🍷 **Heathcote Shiraz 2005** Full-bodied, with intense, very ripe fruit but not soupy;
lively mix of black flavours with spice, licorice and vanillin oak contributing;
however, heats up on the finish. Diam. 15° alc. **Rating** 90 **To** 2020 $29.50

Minko Wines

13 High Street, Willunga, SA 5172 **Region** Southern Fleurieu
T (08) 8556 4987 **F** (08) 8556 2688 **www**.minkowines.com **Open** Wed–Sun 11–5
Winemaker Hawkers Gate (James Hastwell), Mark Day (Consultant) **Est.** 1997 **Cases** 2000
Mike Boerema (veterinarian) and Margo Kellet (ceramic artist) established the Minko
vineyard on their cattle property at Mt Compass. The 10.5-ha vineyard is planted to pinot
noir, merlot, cabernet sauvignon, chardonnay and pinot gris, and managed using sustainable
eco-agriculture; 60 ha of the 160-ha property is heritage listed. Exports to the UK.

ŶŶŶŶŶ **Mount Compass Reserve Cabernet Sauvignon 2005** Dense, deep purple-red; rich, layered folds of blackcurrant fruit, and echoes of licorice; superfine tannins could be a little more forceful. Screwcap. 14° alc. **Rating** 94 **To** 2025 $28

ŶŶŶŶŶ **Mount Compass Southern Fleurieu Pinot Grigio 2007** Firm, bright, tangy, minerally wine, reflecting the suitability of the climate and terroir; good depth. Screwcap. 13.5° alc. **Rating** 90 **To** 2009 $18.50
Mount Compass Pinot Noir 2005 Spicy/herbal nuances to the bouquet, but the palate has good length and clear varietal character; impressive for a new pinot noir region. Screwcap. 14° alc. **Rating** 90 **To** 2012 $25

Minnow Creek ★★★★

5 Hillside Road, Blackwood, SA 5051 (postal) **Region** McLaren Vale
T 0404 288 108 **F** (08) 8278 8248 **www.**minnowcreekwines.com.au **Open** Not
Winemaker Tony Walker **Est.** 2005 **Cases** 1200
Former Fox Creek winemaker Tony Walker has set up Minnow Creek in partnership with William Neubauer, the grapes grown by Don Lopresti at vineyards just to the west of Willunga. The name of the venture reflects the intention of the partners to keep the business focused on quality rather than quantity, and to self-distribute much of the wine through the large number of highly regarded Adelaide restaurants.

ŶŶŶŶŶ **McLaren Vale Shiraz 2005** Medium-bodied, with clear varietal and regional definition; a mix of blackberry, spice, plum and dark chocolate; persistent, but fine and ripe tannins. Screwcap. 14.5° alc. **Rating** 93 **To** 2014 $25
McLaren Vale Rose 2007 Has more complexity and length than most; spicy overtones to cherry, raspberry and cassis fruit; a dry, balanced finish. Serious rose. Part barrel ferment, wild yeast. Cabernet Sauvignon (85%)/Sangiovese (15%). Screwcap. 13.5° alc. **Rating** 92 **To** 2009 $17.50

ŶŶŶŶ **The Black Minnow McLaren Vale Sangiovese Cabernet Sauvignon Malbec 2006** Has some of the elements of a wine designed by a committee; savoury/sour cherry elements from sangiovese, with some structural support from the other components. 65%/25%/10% Screwcap. 13.5° alc. **Rating** 87 **To** 2010 $18.50

Minot Vineyard ★★★★

Lot 4, Harrington Road, Margaret River, WA 6285 **Region** Margaret River
T (08) 9757 3579 **F** (08) 9757 2361 **www.**minotwines.com.au **Open** By appt 10–5
Winemaker Harmans Estate (Paul Green) **Est.** 1986 **Cases** 3000
Minot, which takes its name from a small chateau in the Loire Valley in France, is the husband and wife venture of the Miles family, and produces just two wines from the 4.2-ha plantings of semillon, sauvignon blanc and cabernet sauvignon. Exports to the UK and Singapore.

ŶŶŶŶŶ **Margaret River Sauvignon Blanc Semillon 2007** A good example of this very popular blend; varietal and with a hint of herbaceous and tropical fruit; quite long; good value. Screwcap. 13.1° alc. **Rating** 90 **To** 2009 $15.50

Mintaro Wines ★★★★

Leasingham Road, Mintaro, SA 5415 **Region** Clare Valley
T (08) 8843 9150 **F** (08) 8843 9050 **Open** 7 days 10–4.30
Winemaker Peter Houldsworth **Est.** 1984 **Cases** 5000
Has produced some very good Riesling over the years, developing well in bottle. The red wines, too, have improved significantly. The labelling is nothing if not interesting, from the depiction of a fish drinking like a fish, not to mention the statuesque belles femmes. Exports to Singapore.

♟♟♟♟ Belles Femmes 2005 Ripe, luscious fruit in a blackberry and prune spectrum, the alcohol investing the wine with some sweetness; well made, and will have particular appeal to some (as will the label). Shiraz. Screwcap. 15° alc. **Rating** 89 To 2015 $28

Clare Valley Shiraz 2005 More developed and more robust than the Belles Femmes, with added touches of earth and bark; again, some sweetness. Screwcap. 15° alc. **Rating** 87 **To** 2011 $23

Miramar   ★★★★☆

Henry Lawson Drive, Mudgee, NSW 2850 **Region** Mudgee
T (02) 6373 3874 **F** (02) 6373 3854 **www**.miramarwines.com.au **Open** 7 days 9–5
Winemaker Ian MacRae **Est.** 1977 **Cases** 6000
Industry veteran Ian MacRae has demonstrated his skill with every type of wine over the decades, ranging from Rose to Chardonnay to full-bodied reds. All have shone under the Miramar label at one time or another; in 2005 there was a marked swing to white wines, with which Ian MacRae has always had a special empathy. The majority of the production from the 35 ha of estate vineyard is sold to others, the best being retained for Miramar's own use. No samples received; the rating is that of last year.

Mistletoe Wines   ★★★★★

771 Hermitage Road, Pokolbin, NSW 2320 **Region** Lower Hunter Valley
T (02) 4998 7770 **F** (02) 4998 7792 **www**.mistletoewines.com **Open** 7 days 10–6
Winemaker Nick Paterson **Est.** 1989 **Cases** 5000
Mistletoe Wines, owned by Ken and Gwen Sloan, can trace its history back to 1909, when a substantial vineyard was planted on what was then called Mistletoe Farm. The Mistletoe Farm brand made a brief appearance in the late 1970s. The wines are made onsite by Nick Paterson, who has had significant experience in the Hunter Valley. The quality, and the consistency of these wines is irreproachable, as is their price.

♟♟♟♟♟ Home Vineyard Hunter Valley Semillon 2007 Fragrant and pronounced herb, grass and lanolin aromas; a long, vibrant palate with a lingering finish introducing a note of lemon juice. Screwcap. 10° alc. **Rating** 94 **To** 2017 $17

Hunter Valley Shiraz 2006 Has well above-average drive and intensity to the tangy black fruits; long palate and finish; very good quality and even better value. Drink this, cellar the Reserve. Screwcap. 13.5° alc. **Rating** 94 **To** 2014 $20

Reserve Hunter Valley Shiraz 2006 Deep colour; new French oak adds a structure though not a flavour dimension, with slightly more tannins and texture on the long finish. Screwcap. 13.5° alc. **Rating** 94 **To** 2021 $28

♟♟♟♟♟ Reserve Hunter Valley Semillon 2007 Spotlessly clean; clean, crisp and very long in the mouth; great medium-term development potential. Screwcap. 10° alc. Rating 93 To 2013 $22

Reserve Hunter Valley Chardonnay 2007 Has greater elegance and focus than the varietal, more white peach and nectarine; good length and well-integrated new and used French oak; 260 cases. Screwcap. 13° alc. **Rating** 91 To 2012 $24

♟♟♟♟ Hunter Valley Chardonnay 2007 Whole bunch-pressed; plenty of fleshy yellow and white peach fruit; barrel-fermented in old French oak, adding to the texture and structure. Screwcap. 13.5° alc. **Rating** 89 **To** 2010 $20

Barrel Fermented Hunter Valley Rose 2007 Youthful crimson; plenty of black cherry flavour, well-balanced and dry. Screwcap. 12.5° alc. **Rating** 88 To 2009 $20

Hunter Valley Mozcato 2007 Manages something different, with tangy lemon zest aromas; from estate-grown muscat à petit grains; 375 ml bottle. Screwcap. 7.5° alc. **Rating** 87 **To** 2009 $15

Mitchell ★★★★★

Hughes Park Road, Sevenhill via Clare, SA 5453 **Region** Clare Valley
T (08) 8843 4258 **F** (08) 8843 4340 **www**.mitchellwines.com **Open** 7 days 10–4
Winemaker Andrew Mitchell **Est.** 1975 **Cases** 30 000
One of the stalwarts of the Clare Valley, producing long-lived Rieslings and Cabernet
Sauvignons in classic regional style. The range now includes very creditable Semillon,
Grenache and Shiraz. A lovely old stone apple shed provides the cellar door and upper section
of the compact winery. Exports to the US.

ɅɅɅɅɅ **McNicol Clare Valley Riesling 2006** Abundant minerally edges to the bouquet
and palate, providing structure and texture; has a particularly long palate with a
core of lime fruit. Screwcap. **Rating** 94 **To** 2016 $32
Clare Valley Semillon 2006 Given complexity and structure by barrel ferment
in French oak (mainly old) without compromising the grassy varietal fruit or
delicacy; good line and length. Screwcap. 13° alc. **Rating** 94 **To** 2016 $21

ɅɅɅɅɅ **Peppertree Vineyard Shiraz 2005** A restrained approach invests the wine with
elegance and length; fine, supple mouthfeel; fine tannins, good length, controlled
oak. Screwcap. 14.5° alc. **Rating** 93 **To** 2020 $26
Sparkling Peppertree NV Light but bright red hue; nicely balanced, with a
delicacy and freshness often lacking; plenty of spicy black fruits before a pleasingly
dry finish. Multi-vintage, 4 years on lees; disgorged May '06. Cork. **Rating** 93
To 2010 $31
McNicol Clare Valley Shiraz 2000 Medium-bodied, showing the expected
development one would expect, the flavours moving into an earthy, secondary
spectrum, supported by savoury tannins. Now or in 5 years. Screwcap. **Rating** 91
To 2013 $45
Sevenhill Vineyard Clare Valley Cabernet Sauvignon 2004 Youthful wine,
with the cassis and blackcurrant of the bouquet and fore-palate still to mesh with
the tannins; will likely be long lived. Screwcap. **Rating** 91 **To** 2024 $26

ɅɅɅɅ **Watervale Riesling 2007** Intense bouquet of herb, lime and mineral is repeated
on the powerful palate; has quite grainy structure. Screwcap. 13.5° alc. **Rating** 89
To 2013 $21
Clare Valley Grenache Sangiovese Mourvedre 2004 Good colour; in
typical Clare style, with strong spicy notes to the cherry fruits and lingering
tannins; creeps up on you. Screwcap. **Rating** 89 **To** 2012 $21

Mitchelton ★★★★☆

Mitchellstown via Nagambie, Vic 3608 **Region** Nagambie Lakes
T (03) 5736 2222 **F** (03) 5736 2266 **www**.mitchelton.com.au **Open** 7 days 10–5
Winemaker Ben Haines **Est.** 1969 **Cases** 220 000
Acquired by Petaluma in 1994 (both now part of Lion Nathan), having already put the
runs on the board in no uncertain fashion with gifted winemaker Don Lewis (who retired
in '04). Boasts an array of wines across a broad spectrum of style and price, each carefully
aimed at a market niche. No samples received; the rating is that of last year. Exports to all
major markets.

Mitolo Wines ★★★★★

PO Box 520, Virginia, SA 5120 **Region** McLaren Vale
T (08) 8282 9012 **F** (08) 8282 9062 **www**.mitolowines.com.au **Open** Not
Winemaker Ben Glaetzer **Est.** 1999 **Cases** 20 000
Frank Mitolo began making wine in 1995 as a hobby, and soon progressed to undertaking
formal studies in winemaking. His interest grew year by year, but it was not until 2000 that
he took the plunge into the commercial end of the business, retaining Ben Glaetzer to make
the wines for him. Since that time, a remarkably good series of wines have been released.
Imitation being the sincerest form of flattery, part of the complicated story behind each label

name is pure Torbreck, but Mitolo then adds a Latin proverb or saying to the name. Exports to all major markets.

ƳƳƳƳƳ Savitar McLaren Vale Shiraz 2006 A monster! Showing a little reduction from more oak, the fruit weight of this wine is staggering; layers of fruit strip away as you let it hang around on your palate for a seriously long time; the strong core of dark minerality shows just how complex it is. Cork. 14.5° alc. **Rating** 96 **To** 2025 $80
G.A.M. McLaren Vale Shiraz 2006 Pristine, powerful and purple fruit; blue and blackberries, loads of spice and a restrained use of oak for such powerful fruit; very pure and bright on the vibrant finish. Screwcap. 14.5° alc. **Rating** 95 **To** 2020 $58
Reiver Barossa Valley Shiraz 2006 A muscular wine, of great depth and power; the secret here is the delicacy of the oak handling for the fruit; the dark fruits are matched by red ones, and the core is intense and chewy, very long and surprisingly supple. Screwcap. 14.5° alc. **Rating** 95 **To** 2020 $58
Jester McLaren Vale Shiraz 2006 Power and intensity achieved without reliance on elevated alcohol; blackberry and a whisper of regional dark chocolate, the tannins fine, the oak controlled. Screwcap. 14.5° alc. **Rating** 94 **To** 2019 $28

ƳƳƳƳ Jester McLaren Vale Sangiovese Rose 2007 Pale salmon-pink; initially light-bodied, but increases its impact with a spicy/cherry back palate and dry finish. Screwcap. 14° alc. **Rating** 89 **To** 2009 $23
Jester McLaren Vale Cabernet Sauvignon 2006 Signs of adolescent confusion; slightly jammy fruit, a solid slab of chocolate and vanilla oak, then a slightly short finish. May improve with time. Screwcap. 14.5° alc. **Rating** 89 **To** 2012 $28

Mollydooker Wines ★★★★

8/938 South Road, Edwardstown, SA 5039 (postal) **Region** South Australia
T (08) 8179 6500 **F** (08) 8179 6555 **www.**mollydookerwines.com.au **Open** By appt
Winemaker Sarah Marquis, Sparky Marquis **Est.** 2005 **Cases** 70 000
As Sarah and Sparky Marquis wound their way through Fox Creek, Henry's Drive, Parsons Flat, Marquis Philips and Shirvington, they left a vivid trail of high-flavoured, medal-winning wines in their wake. After 10 years they took the final step, launching Mollydooker Wines, with Robert Parker their number one ticket holder. Everything about their wines and their business is larger than life, with a 70 000-case virtual winery having no credible challenge from within Australia. They draw grapes from McLaren Vale, Padthaway and Langhorne Creek, restricting themselves to verdelho, merlot, cabernet sauvignon and – most importantly, of course – shiraz. Oh, and incidentally, 'mollydooker' is Australian slang for left-handed, an attribute shared by Sarah, Sparky and Robert Parker. As the tasting notes will make clear, the primary market for the wines will be the US, and that market should add five points to each of my scores. The 2007 acquisition of Classic McLaren Wines gives them a real base, and underwrites the future of the business. Exports to the US, the UK and other major markets.

ƳƳƳƳƳ Enchanted Path Shiraz Cabernet 2006 Dense colour; a plush, rich and deep amalgam of black fruits, dark chocolate, licorice and vanilla; carries its alcohol better than the others. Screwcap. 16° alc. **Rating** 92 **To** 2026 $80

ƳƳƳƳ Carnival of Love Shiraz 2006 A very complex and intense lifted bouquet; massive flavour achieved through the alcohol; time and barbecue rump steak might work wonders. Screwcap. 16° alc. **Rating** 89 **To** 2021 $80
Two Left Feet 2006 Juicy, predominantly plum and black cherry fruit, with some notes of redcurrant; manages to carry the alcohol quite well, but needs food. Shiraz/Merlot/Cabernet Sauvignon. Screwcap. 16° alc. **Rating** 89 **To** 2016 $23
Blue Eyed Boy Shiraz 2006 Powerful black fruits, but the alcohol really makes the head snap back; others in other places value such characters more than I do. Screwcap. 16° alc. **Rating** 88 **To** 2016 $50
Gigglepot Cabernet Sauvignon 2006 Massively powerful and fiery, saying much about winemakers' philosophy and region of origin, but nothing about variety. Screwcap. 16° alc. **Rating** 87 **To** 2016 $50

Monbulk Winery   NR

Macclesfield Road, Monbulk, Vic 3793 **Region** Yarra Valley
T (03) 9756 6965 **F** (03) 9756 6965 **www**.monbulkwinery.com **Open** W'ends &
public hols 12–5, or by appt
Winemaker Marian Berry, John Berry **Est.** 1984 **Cases** 500
Originally concentrated on kiwifruit wines but now extending to table wines; the very cool
Monbulk area should be capable of producing wines of distinctive style, but the table wines
are not of the same standard as the kiwifruit wines, which are quite delicious.

Mongrel Creek Vineyard   NR

109 Hayes Road, Yallingup Siding, WA 6281 **Region** Margaret River
T 0417 991 065 **F** (08) 9755 5708 **Open** W'ends, school & public hols 10–5
Winemaker Tony Davis, Genevieve Stols **Est.** 1996 **Cases** 900
Larry and Shirley Schoppe both have other occupations, Larry as vineyard supervisor at
Howard Park's Leston Vineyard, Shirley as a full-time nurse. Thus the 2.8-ha vineyard, planted
to shiraz, semillon and sauvignon blanc in 1996, is still a weekend and holiday business. Given
the viticultural and winemaking expertise of those involved, it is hardly surprising that the
wines have been consistent show medal winners.

Montalto Vineyards   ★★★★★

33 Shoreham Road, Red Hill South, Vic 3937 **Region** Mornington Peninsula
T (03) 5989 8412 **F** (03) 5989 8417 **www**.montalto.com.au **Open** 7 days 11–5
Winemaker Robin Brockett **Est.** 1998 **Cases** 4500
John Mitchell and family established Montalto Vineyards in 1998, but the core of the vineyard
goes back to '86. There are 5.6 ha pinot noir, 3 ha chardonnay, 1 ha pinot gris, and 0.5 ha each
of semillon, riesling and pinot meunier. Intensive vineyard work opens up the canopy, with
yields ranging between 1.5 and 2.5 tonnes per acre. Wines are released under two labels, the
flagship Montalto and Pennon, the latter a lower-priced, second label. All offer good value.

 \u2641\u2641\u2641\u2641\u2641 **Mornington Peninsula Chardonnay 2006** Has finesse and restraint; melon and
nectarine fruit, creamy mlf and quality French oak inputs all coalesce. Screwcap.
13.1° alc. **Rating** 94 **To** 2012 $32
Mornington Peninsula Pinot Noir 2006 Very pure pinot aroma and flavour,
ranging through predominantly spicy red fruit notes to touches of plum; lively,
fresh finish. Screwcap. 13.2° alc. **Rating** 94 **To** 2012 $39
Pennon Hill Shiraz 2006 A fragrant, almost floral, bouquet of red berries and
spices; free-flowing medium-bodied palate with a lingering, silky finish; totally
delicious, no patience required. Screwcap. 13.5° alc. **Rating** 94 **To** 2014 $25

\u2641\u2641\u2641\u2641\u2641 **Cuvee One 2004** Pale straw-green; abundant fruit ranging through stone fruit,
citrus and strawberry; enjoyable style, clean, dry finish. Chardonnay/Pinot Noir/
Pinot Meunier; bottle-fermented. Cork. 12.5° alc. **Rating** 92 **To** 2009 $30
Pennon Hill Pinot Noir 2006 A fragrant cherry and strawberry bouquet; light-
to medium-bodied silky finish; attractive early-drinking style. Screwcap. 13.2° alc.
Rating 91 **To** 2011 $25

\u2641\u2641\u2641\u2641 **Pennon Hill Pinot Grigio 2007** Relatively crisp and with just enough fruit
expression, but definitely won't frighten the horses, seemingly the first duty of the
variety. Screwcap. 13.5° alc. **Rating** 87 **To** 2009 $23

Montara   ★★★

76 Chalambar Road, Ararat, Vic 3377 **Region** Grampians
T (03) 5352 3868 **F** (03) 5352 4968 **www**.montara.com.au **Open** 7 days 11–4
Winemaker Leigh Clarnette **Est.** 1970 **Cases** 3500
Achieved considerable attention for its Pinot Noirs during the 1980s, and continues to
produce wines of distinctive style. One of the most engaging promotions in the entire wine

industry is the annual Montara Scarecrow Competition held in the vineyard at the end of April. Even Cirque du Soleil might gain inspiration. I hope the Stapleton family, who have purchased the winery from the founding McRae family, will not evict the scarecrows. Exports to the UK, Switzerland, Canada and Hong Kong.

♀♀♀♀♀ Sauvignon Blanc 2007 A mineral face of sauvignon, with good flavour depth and weight; very even finish. Screwcap. 12° alc. **Rating** 90 **To** 2012 $17

Montgomery's Hill   ★★★★

South Coast Highway, Upper Kalgan, Albany, WA 6330 **Region** Albany
T (08) 9844 3715 **F** (08) 9844 3819 **www**.montgomeryshill.com.au **Open** 7 days 11–5
Winemaker The Vintage Wineworx (Dr Diane Miller), Bill Crappsley (Consultant)
Est. 1996 **Cases** 6000
Montgomery's Hill is 16 km northeast of Albany on a north-facing slope on the banks of the Kalgan River. Previously used as an apple orchard; it is a diversification for the third generation of the Montgomery family. Chardonnay, cabernet sauvignon, cabernet franc, sauvignon blanc, shiraz and merlot were planted in 1996–97. The wines are made with a gentle touch.

♀♀♀♀♀ Albany Chardonnay 2007 Tangy grapefruit and nectarine fruit with well-balanced and integrated gently spicy oak; has length. Screwcap. 13.5° alc. **Rating** 90 **To** 2012 $21
The Mulberry Block Reserve Albany Chardonnay 2007 The fresh bouquet doesn't foretell the delicious white peach, fig and cashew flavours of the palate; with more acidity would merit top points. Screwcap. 13.5° alc. **Rating** 90 **To** 2012 $29

♀♀♀♀ Albany Unwooded Chardonnay 2007 Shows (as ever) unwooded chardonnay performs best in cool climates; tangy grapefruit and melon, a soft version of sauvignon blanc. Screwcap. 13.5° alc. **Rating** 87 **To** 2010 $17
Albany Shiraz 2006 Pleasant, but very light-bodied wine, with juicy cherry and strawberry fruits; could be substituted for rose on a hot day. Screwcap. 14° alc. **Rating** 87 **To** 2010 $21

Montvalley   ★★★☆

150 Mitchells Road, Mount View, NSW 2325 (postal) **Region** Lower Hunter Valley
T (02) 4991 1936 **F** (02) 4991 7994 **www**.montvalley.com.au **Open** Not
Winemaker Monarch Winemaking Services **Est.** 1998 **Cases** 2000
Having looked at dozens of properties over the previous decade, John and Deirdre Colvin purchased their 80-ha property in 1998. They chose the name Montvalley in part because it reflects the beautiful valley in the Brokenback Ranges of which the property forms part, and in part because the name Colvin originates from France, 'col' meaning valley and 'vin' meaning vines. They have planted 5.7 ha of vines, the lion's share to shiraz, with lesser amounts of chardonnay and semillon.

♀♀♀♀ Hunter Valley Semillon 2007 Pure lemon juice bouquet, with a touch of herb; good flavour, but the line breaks a little on the finish. Screwcap. 9.7° alc. **Rating** 88 **To** 2015 $18.75

Monument Vineyard   ★★★★

Cnr Escort Way/Manildra Road, Cudal, NSW 2864 **Region** Central Ranges Zone
T (02) 6364 2294 **F** (02) 4268 6925 **www**.monumentvineyard.com.au **Open** At
Underwood Lane Wines (02) 6365 2221
Winemaker Alison Eisermann **Est.** 1998 **Cases** 1500
In the early 1990s five mature-age students at CSU, successful in their own professions, decided to form a partnership to develop a substantial vineyard and winery. After a lengthy search, a large property at Cudal was identified, with ideal terra rossa basalt-derived soil over a limestone base. The property has 110 ha under vine, planted in 1998 and '99.

Moody's Wines ★★☆

'Fontenay', Stagecoach Road, Orange, NSW 2800 **Region** Orange
T (02) 6365 9117 **F** (02) 6391 3650 **Open** W'ends 10–5 or by appt
Winemaker Madrez Wine Services (Chris Derrez) **Est.** 2000 **Cases** 75
Tony Moody's great-grandfather started a retail chain of shops in Merseyside, England, under
the banner Moody's Wines. The business was ultimately sold to a brewery in 1965 seeking to
minimise off-licence competition. Tony Moody planted 1 ha of shiraz 'in a promising sheep
paddock' in 2000, and has subsequently added 1 ha of sauvignon blanc (water shortages
meaning the first vintage of that sauvignon blanc will not be until '09 at the earliest).

Moombaki Wines ★★★★☆

341 Parker Road, Kentdale via Denmark, WA 6333 **Region** Denmark
T (08) 9840 8006 **F** (08) 9840 8006 **www**.moombaki.com **Open** Thurs–Mon 11–5,
7 days summer & school hols, or by appt
Winemaker Harewood Estate (James Kellie) **Est.** 1997 **Cases** 1200
David Britten and Melissa Boughey (with three young sons in tow) established 2 ha of vines
on a north-facing gravel hillside with a picturesque Kent River frontage. Not content with
establishing the vineyard, they put in significant mixed tree plantings to increase wildlife
habitats. It is against this background that they chose Moombaki as their vineyard name: a local
Aboriginal word meaning 'where the river meets the sky'. Exports to the UK, Switzerland,
Malaysia, Japan and Singapore.

ŸŸŸŸŸ **Reserve 2005** Good colour; very fine and no less focused and intense;
blackcurrant, cassis, mint and cedar; very long palate and finish; long future.
Cabernet Sauvignon/Shiraz/Cabernet Franc/Malbec. Bottle 94 of 840 produced.
Screwcap. 14° alc. **Rating** 95 **To** 2030 $55

ŸŸŸŸ **Chardonnay 2006** Very tight and closed, still to open up; demands time, for the
fruit and French oak are perfectly integrated and balanced; try in 2 years time, and
likely higher points. Screwcap. 13.5° alc. **Rating** 87 **To** 2014 $28

Moondah Brook ★★★★

Dale Road, Middle Swan, WA 6056 **Region** Swan Valley
T (08) 9274 5172 **F** (08) 9274 5372 **www**.moondahbrook.com.au **Open** At Houghton
Winemaker Courtney Treacher **Est.** 1968 **Cases** NFP
Part of the Constellation wine group, which has its own special character, as it draws part
of its fruit from the large Gingin vineyard, 70 km north of the Swan Valley, and part from
the Margaret River and Great Southern. From time to time it has excelled even its own
reputation for reliability with some quite lovely wines, in particular honeyed, aged Chenin
Blanc, generous Shiraz and finely structured Cabernet Sauvignon. Exports to the UK and
other major markets.

ŸŸŸŸŸ **Chardonnay 2006** Wholly satisfying fruit flavours in the middle of the varietal
spectrum, reflecting cool and warm-grown inputs; sure barrel ferment oak
component adds to the appeal. Screwcap. 13.5° alc. **Rating** 93 **To** 2011 $14.99
Chenin Blanc 2006 As a young wine shows why this label can age so well; has
an extra grip to the palate, yet retains clarity and finesse; not unlike a souped-up
semillon. Screwcap. 12.5° alc. **Rating** 90 **To** 2011 $14.99
Rose 2007 Abundant colour, aroma and flavour, almost crossing the line from
rose to light dry red; food style. **Rating** 90 **To** 2009 $17.50

ŸŸŸŸ **Chenin Blanc 2007** Lively, clean and positive fruit runs through the length of
the palate; easy to see how the rich, honeyed flavours will develop over 5 years.
Screwcap. 13.5° alc. **Rating** 89 **To** 2013 $18

Moondarra

Browns Road, Moondarra, Vic 3825 (postal) **Region** Gippsland
T (03) 9598 3049 **F** (03) 9598 0677 **Open** Not
Winemaker Neil Prentice **Est.** 1991 **Cases** 3200
In 1991 Neil Prentice and family established their Moondarra Vineyard in Gippsland, eventually focusing on the 2 ha of low-yielding pinot noir. Subsequently, they began planting their Holly's Garden vineyard at Whitlands in the King Valley, where they have 4 ha of pinot gris and 3 ha of pinot noir. It is from this vineyard that all but 200 cases of their wines come, sold under the Holly's Garden label. Bushfires prevented the making of the Moondara wines in 2006 and '07. Exports to the US and Japan.

Moonrise Estate

47 Clark Lane, Stanthorpe, Qld 4380 **Region** Granite Belt
T (07) 4683 6203 **F** (07) 4683 6203 **www**.moonriseestate.com.au **Open** 7 days 10–5
Winemaker Grant Casley (Contract) **Est.** 2005 **Cases** 800
Former Victorians Trevor and Carol Sharp acquired a 29-ha property at Severnlea after moving to Queensland. They have planted 1.5 ha each of shiraz and black muscat, 0.75 ha of chardonnay, 0.25 ha of merlot, and a few vines of cabernet sauvignon; all of the vines are dry-grown. The cellar door has great views of the surrounding country, and complements the stone B&B accommodation.

♟♟♟♟♟ **Shiraz 2006** Clear varietal character, with ripe blackberry and satsuma plum fruit with spicy elements; a medium-bodied surprise packet with soft tannins. Diam. **Rating** 90 **To** 2013 $22

♟♟♟♟ **JRP Blend 2006** Substantial wine; high-toned mix of ripe/unripe, sweet/sour but enough fruit to gain points. Cabernet Sauvignon/Shiraz/Merlot. Cork. **Rating** 89 **To** 2013 $24
JRP Reserve Cabernet Shiraz Merlot 2006 A light- to medium-bodied mix of red and black fruits, supported by savoury tannins. Stained Diam. 13.5° alc. **Rating** 87 **To** 2011 $24

Moorabool Estate

45 Dog Rocks Road, Batesford, Vic 3221 (postal) **Region** Geelong
T (03) 5276 1536 **F** (03) 5276 1665 **Open** Not
Winemaker Graham Bonney, Doug Neal **Est.** 1988 **Cases** 1000
Moorabool Estate is established on the site of the original Paradise Vineyard planted in 1848 by Swiss vigneron Jean Henri Dardel, and now owned by Ruth and Graham Bonney. Moorabool Estate re-established grapegrowing in the Moorabool Valley in 1988 with plantings of 0.75 ha each of chardonnay, shiraz and cabernet sauvignon. Doug Neal is a fanatical wine lover, with fingers in many vinicultural pies, and is a particular lover of Burgundy and the Rhône Valley.

♟♟♟♟ **Shiraz 2005** Quite sweet fruit, but lacks varietal intensity; that said, not over-extracted. Diam. 13.5° alc. **Rating** 87 **To** 2011 $15

Moorabool Ridge

23 Spiller Road, Lethbridge, Vic 3332 **Region** Geelong
T (03) 5281 9240 **F** (03) 5281 9240 **Open** W'ends & public hols 11–5
Winemaker Peter Flewellyn, Ray Nadeson **Est.** 1991 **Cases** 250
Tim Harrop and Katarina Romanov-Harrop planted their first vines in 1990, and the first olive trees in 2001 (the latter now extended to 800 trees and a commercial olive oil and olive business). Despite the name, the vines are planted on the floor of the Moorabool Valley on the bank of Moorabool River; there are 2 ha of shiraz and 1 ha each of semillon, chardonnay, cabernet sauvignon, cabernet franc and merlot. For the first 10 years the grapes were sold, but thereafter part of the production was retained for the Moorabool Ridge label, sold through the cellar door situated in the historic Sheppard's Hut dating from 1856.

🍷🍷🍷🍷🍷 **Sofia Reserve Shiraz 2006** Cool spice, red fruits and lifted bouquet of violets; medium-bodied, with fine tannins and fresh acidity; elegance with poise and power. Screwcap. 14° alc. **Rating** 91 **To** 2015 $20

Moores Hill Estate

3343 West Tamar Highway, Sidmouth, Tas 7270 **Region** Northern Tasmania
T (03) 6394 7649 **F** (03) 6394 7649 **www**.mooreshill.com.au **Open** Oct–June
Wed–Sun 10–5
Winemaker Tamar Ridge **Est.** 1997 **Cases** 3000
Rod and Karen Thorpe established Moores Hill Estate in 1997 on the gentle slopes of the West Tamar Valley. The vineyard has 4.9 ha of riesling, chardonnay, pinot noir, merlot and cabernet sauvignon. The vineyard represents a full circle for the Thorpes, who bought the farm nearly 30 years ago and ripped out a small vineyard. The Wine Centre (built in 2002 mainly from timber found on the property) overlooks the vineyard.

Moorilla Estate ★★★★☆

655 Main Road, Berriedale, Tas 7011 **Region** Southern Tasmania
T (03) 6277 9900 **F** (03) 6249 4093 **www**.moorilla.com.au **Open** 7 days 10–5
Winemaker Alan Ferry **Est.** 1958 **Cases** 16 000
Moorilla Estate is an icon in the Tasmanian wine industry and is thriving. Wine quality continues to be unimpeachable, and the opening of the museum in the marvellous Alcorso House designed by Sir Roy Grounds adds even more attraction for visitors to the estate, which is a mere 15–20 mins from Hobart. Five-star self-contained chalets are available, with a stylish, high-quality restaurant open for lunch 7 days. A microbrewery, fastidiously equipped and surgically clean, also operates onsite. Exports to the US and Singapore.

🍷🍷🍷🍷🍷 **Praxis Chardonnay 2007** A complex style, full of cashews, charcuterie and citrus; some charry complexity, but not too much; long and fine on the finish. **Rating** 92 **To** 2013 $19.50
Muse Pinot Noir 2006 Exceptional colour; spiced plum on entry, then a more savoury/stalky/foresty finish. **Rating** 91 **To** 2013 $40
Muse Riesling 2007 Some herb and flower blossom aromas, tight palate, fine, long, reserved; dry finish. Time to go. Screwcap. 13° alc. **Rating** 90 **To** 2016 $30
Muse Chardonnay 2006 Elegant and tight mineral/citrus/stone fruit belying its alcohol; very good line and flow and controlled oak; Tasmanian acidity very evident. Screwcap. 14° alc. **Rating** 90 **To** 2014 $40

🍷🍷🍷🍷 **Muse Sauvignon Blanc 2007** Exotic varietal fruits with good focus, texture and weight. **Rating** 88 **To** 2009 $25
Muse Cabernet Merlot 2006 A bit of mintiness, but quite ripe fruit; good weight and freshness. **Rating** 87 **To** 2011 $30
Muse Brut 2003 Vibrant colour; a complex wine with some aldehydic components evident. **Rating** 87 **To** 2009 $35
Muse Brut Rose 2004 Deep pink; good flavour assisted by relatively high dosage balancing the acidity; could have broad consumer appeal. **Rating** 87 **To** 2009 $25

Moorooduc Estate ★★★★★

501 Derril Road, Moorooduc, Vic 3936 **Region** Mornington Peninsula
T (03) 5971 8506 **F** (03) 5971 8550 **www**.moorooducestate.com.au **Open** W'ends 11–5,
7 days in Jan
Winemaker Dr Richard McIntyre **Est.** 1983 **Cases** 2500
Richard McIntyre has taken Moorooduc Estate to new heights as he has completely mastered the difficult art of gaining maximum results from wild yeast fermentations. While the Chardonnays remain the jewels in the crown, the Pinot Noirs are also very impressive. Exports to Hong Kong and Singapore.

The Moorooduc Pinot Noir 2006 Brilliantly clear; a highly perfumed bouquet of wild strawberry and hints of forest floor foreshadows a supremely elegant palate with great intensity; has arresting length and aftertaste. Screwcap. 14°alc. **Rating** 95 To 2014 $55

Chardonnay 2006 A complex bouquet has nuances of nectarine, cashew and beeswax leading into a palate with excellent thrust, progressively building tightly focused flavours through to the long, lingering finish. Screwcap. 13.5°alc. **Rating** 94 **To** 2013 $35

Pinot Noir 2006 Has great structure and power, plus quite exceptional length; layers of dark berry flavours are supported by superfine tannins and good oak. Screwcap. 14°alc. **Rating** 94 **To** 2012 $35

Moothi Estate ★★★☆

85 Rocky Waterhole Road, Mudgee, NSW 2850 (postal) **Region** Mudgee
T (02) 9868 6014 **F** (02) 9868 6017 **www**.moothiestate.com.au **Open** W'ends &
public hols 10.30–4.30
Winemaker Michael Slater **Est.** 1995 **Cases** NA
Phil and Susan Moore purchased a property on the northwest-facing slopes of Mt Frome, at an elevation of 550 m, in 1995. The site has reddish-brown clay with limestone, quartz and ironstone gibber soil, well suited to the chardonnay, shiraz, merlot and cabernet sauvignon established on the property, 24 ha in all. The names for the wines are derived from the Koori name for Mudgee, which is Moothi; 'Moothi Mud' is said to be local slang for Mudgee's full-bodied reds.

 Moothi Mud Very Special Selection Shiraz 2002 Still very youthful, so much so you have to wonder whether it will ever change much – but then it doesn't need to, as its red fruits are riper, the tannins soft, the finish long. **Rating** 90 **To** 2012 $20

 Very Special Selection Shiraz 2003 Quite fragrant and fresh, the sweet fruits of its youth still very much in evidence, with a savoury twist to conclude. **Rating** 88 **To** 2012 $18

Moothi Waters Chardonnay 2006 Very light-bodied stone fruit and citrus flavours, which get out of jail just when the wine kicks again to lengthen the finish. Screwcap. 12.8° alc. **Rating** 87 **To** 2011 $18

🥀 Mopeta Wines ★★☆

Box 31, Port Germein, SA 5495 **Region** Southern Flinders Ranges
T (08) 8634 6031 **F** (08) 8631 6096 **www**.mopetawines.com.au **Open** Not
Winemaker Paracombe Wines (Paul Drogemuller) **Est.** 1997 **Cases** 500
The Dennis family has farmed at Mopeta (an Aboriginal word meaning 'running water') since the 1920s. In 1997, Robert, Michelle, Peter and Bev Dennis began plantings of shiraz, cabernet sauvignon and merlot, followed by further shiraz in '98 and 2001, lifting total plantings to a little over 20 ha. Most of the grapes are sold, but a small amount is retained for the Bridal Track label. The name is a play on words; the real bridle track (a 4WD track over the Flinders Ranges) has a story from the early 1900s of a bridegroom taking his new wife to their new home over the ranges via horseback on their wedding night.

Morambro Creek Wines ★★★★

PMB 98, Naracoorte, SA 5271 (postal) **Region** Padthaway
T (08) 8765 6043 **F** (08) 8765 6011 **www**.morambrocreek.com.au **Open** Not
Winemaker Ben Riggs **Est.** 1994 **Cases** 30 000
The Bryson family has been involved in agriculture for more than a century, moving to Padthaway in 1955 as farmers and graziers. Starting in the early 1990s, they have progressively established 170 ha of shiraz, cabernet sauvignon and chardonnay, lifting production from 6000 cases, and establishing export markets, including the UK and the US. The wines have been consistent winners of bronze and silver medals.

♀♀♀♀♀ Jip Jip Rocks Shiraz 2006 Replete with fully ripe blackberry and plum fruit; a flavour bomb, though not so much structure. **Rating** 90 **To** 2014 $14.95

Moranghurk Vineyard   ★★★☆

1516 Sturt Street, Ballarat, Vic 3350 (postal) **Region** Geelong
T (03) 5331 2105 **F** (03) 5332 9244 **Open** Not
Winemaker Dan Buckle (Contract) **Est.** 1996 **Cases** 340
Ross and Liz Wilkie have established a tiny vineyard on the historic Moranghurk property, which was first settled in 1840. They have planted 0.6 ha of clonally selected pinot noir and 0.5 ha of chardonnay on volcanic soil overlying shale and clay. The vineyard is mulched, and is in the course of being converted to organic, with yields of less than 5 tonnes per ha.

♀♀♀♀♀ Moorabool Valley Pinot Noir 2006 Attractive wine; silky, spicy fruit, with good length and line; ageing nicely. Screwcap. 12.5° alc. **Rating** 92 **To** 2012 $25

♀♀♀♀ Moorabool Valley Chardonnay 2006 In a very different style to the '05 with strong oak and mlf inputs providing richness, somewhat beyond the capacity of the fruit to handle it. Screwcap. 12.3° alc. **Rating** 87 **To** 2011 $25

Morgan Simpson   ★★★★

PO Box 39, Kensington Park, SA 5068 **Region** McLaren Vale
T 0417 843 118 **F** (08) 8364 3645 **www**.morgansimpson.com.au **Open** Not
Winemaker Richard Simpson **Est.** 1998 **Cases** 1200
Morgan Simpson was founded by South Australian businessman George Morgan (since retired) and winemaker Richard Simpson, who is a graduate of CSU. The grapes are sourced from the Clos Robert Vineyard (where the wine is made), established by Robert Allen Simpson in 1972. The aim is to provide drinkable wines at a reasonable price; it succeeds admirably.

♀♀♀♀♀ Row 42 McLaren Vale Cabernet Sauvignon 2004 Good colour; nice poise with redcurrant and black olive, supported by a little cedar; bright, fleshy and fine on the quite long finish. As always, value. Cork. 13.7° alc. **Rating** 91 **To** 2014 $19
McLaren Vale Chardonnay 2004 Clearly shows early picking can hold the wine together, giving brightness to the grapefruit and melon fruit flavours; gentle oak, great value. Screwcap. 12.9° alc. **Rating** 90 **To** 2009 $15

♀♀♀♀ Basket Press McLaren Vale Shiraz 2005 Amazingly, largely gets away with the grotesque alcohol; the black fruits and dark chocolate are thinned, rather than exaggerated, by that alcohol. Screwcap. 16.7° alc. **Rating** 89 **To** 2015 $23.50
Two Clowns McLaren Vale Chardonnay 2005 For a light-bodied Chardonnay, has developed well; still fresh, with understated but nonetheless clear fruit and a well-integrated touch of oak. Screwcap. 13.6° alc. **Rating** 88 **To** 2010 $15

MorganField   ★★★★☆

104 Ashworths Road, Lancefield, Vic 3435 **Region** Macedon Ranges
T (03) 5429 1157 **www**.morganfield.com.au **Open** W'ends & public hols 11–5 or by appt
Winemaker John Ellis (Contract) **Est.** 2003 **Cases** 1000
The vineyard (then known as Ashworths Hill) was first planted in 1980 to pinot noir, shiraz, pinot meunier and cabernet sauvignon. When purchased by Mark and Gina Morgan, additional pinot noir and chardonnay plantings increased the area under vine to 4 ha. The wines are deliberately made in a light-bodied, easy-access fashion.

♀♀♀♀♀ Macedon Ranges Chardonnay 2005 Intense grapefruit and melon aromas and flavours; subtle oak infusion; very long palate. Screwcap. 13.9° alc. **Rating** 94 **To** 2015 $25

♀♀♀♀♀ Macedon Ranges Unwooded Chardonnay 2006 Clean, brisk and brightly fruited, with grapefruit and stone fruit flavours; long finish. Very good example of the style. Screwcap. 12.5° alc. **Rating** 90 **To** 2011 $18

ΨΨΨΨ   **Macedon Ranges Pinot Noir 2005** Light-bodied, but has length and intensity
to flavours ranging from red fruits through to an almost lemony finish; needs more
richness. Screwcap. 12.5° alc. **Rating** 89 **To** 2012 $25

Morning Sun Vineyard   ★★★★☆

337 Main Creek Road, Main Ridge, Vic 3928 **Region** Mornington Peninsula
T (03) 5989 6571 **www.**morningsunvineyard.com.au **Open** Fri–Sun 10–5
Winemaker Owen Goodwin **Est.** 1995 **Cases** 1500
When Mario Toniolo retired, aged 70, and purchased a property on the hills of Main Ridge,
he had ideas of a yabby farm and a few cattle on what was an abandoned apple orchard. His
Italian blood got the better of him, and he now has 2 ha of pinot noir, 1.5 ha each of pinot
grigio and chardonnay, and a 1.8-ha olive grove. In 2005 he employed Owen Goodwin as
viticultural manager, who had worked at Yarra Yarra while studying wine science at CSU,
and thereafter worked vintages overseas. His first vintage at Morning Sun in 2006 resulted in
gold medals for both the Chardonnay and Pinot Noir and a silver medal for the Pinot Grigio
(never easy to gain).

ΨΨΨΨΨ   **Chardonnay 2006** Bright green; tight and minerally, with lemon and flint;
fine acid and good line with a long persistent finish. Screwcap. 14° alc. **Rating** 94
To 2012 $29

ΨΨΨΨ   **Mornington Peninsula Pinot Grigio 2006** A clean and fresh bouquet; flavours
of ripe apple and pear enrich the palate, but do catch slightly on the finish.
Screwcap. 14° alc. **Rating** 89 **To** 2009 $25
Mornington Peninsula Pinot Noir 2006 Quite fragrant; a delicate palate
with a mix of minty/leafy and riper fruit notes. Screwcap. 14.2° alc. **Rating** 88
To 2011 $33

Morningside Vineyard   ★★★★

711 Middle Tea Tree Road, Tea Tree, Tas 7017 **Region** Southern Tasmania
T (03) 6268 1748 **F** (03) 6268 1748 **www.**morningsidevineyard.com.au **Open** By appt
Winemaker Peter Bosworth **Est.** 1980 **Cases** 600
The name Morningside was given to the old property on which the vineyard stands because
it gets the morning sun first; the property on the other side of the valley was known as
Eveningside. Consistent with the observation of the early settlers, the Morningside grapes
achieve full maturity with good colour and varietal flavour. Production will increase as the
2.9-ha vineyard matures, and as recent additions of clonally selected pinot noir (including
8104, 115 and 777) come into bearing. The Bosworth family, headed by Peter and wife
Brenda, do all the vineyard and winery work, with conspicuous attention to detail.

ΨΨΨΨ♀   **Riesling 2007** Herb, lime and apple aromas; a fresh and lively lime juice and
mineral palate; tight and lively on the finish. **Rating** 92 **To** 2017 $20
Pinot Noir 2006 Excellent, clear colour; fragrant, spiced cherry fruit on the fresh
and vibrant palate; a twist of green herb on the finish; 200 cases. Diam. 13.5° alc.
Rating 92 **To** 2013 $34

Morris   ★★★★★

Mia Mia Road, Rutherglen, Vic 3685 **Region** Rutherglen
T (02) 6026 7303 **F** (02) 6026 7445 **www.**morriswines.com **Open** Mon–Sat 9–5, Sun 10–5
Winemaker David Morris **Est.** 1859 **Cases** 100 000
One of the greatest of the fortified winemakers, ranking with Chambers Rosewood. Just
to confuse matters a little, Morris has decided to move away from the 4-tier classification
structure used by other Rutherglen winemakers (other than Chambers, that is) and simply
have two levels: varietal and Old Premium. The oldest components of the Old Premium
are entered in a handful of shows, but the trophies and stratospheric gold medal points they
receive are not claimed for the Old Premium wines. The art of all of these wines lies in the
blending of very old and much younger material. They have no equivalent in any other part

of the world. Despite this, owner Orlando has put the property on the market, but is evidently in no hurry to sell.

ＹＹＹＹＹ Old Premium Liqueur Tokay NV Much deeper aged olive-brown colour; the wine viscous when poured; while rich and lusciously mouthfilling, the richness is balanced to perfection by nutty/smoky rancio characters highlighting the array of spices, burnt toffee and tea-leaf; exceptional length. A national treasure. Cork. 18° alc. **Rating** 97 **To** 2009 $62

Old Premium Liqueur Muscat NV Deep olive-brown, coating the sides of the glass briefly when it is swirled; needless to say, is exceptionally rich and luscious, but – even more – complex, with a dense array of oriental sweet spices, dried raisins, and (for me) childhood memories of mother's Christmas pudding laced with brandy. And, yes, this really does go with dark, bitter chocolate in any form. Cork. 17.5° alc. **Rating** 97 **To** 2009 $62

Old Premium Rare Rutherglen Muscat NV Deep olive brown; dense spice, plum pudding and raisin aromas; utterly exceptional intensity and length; altogether in another dimension; while based upon some very old wine, is as fresh as a daisy. Cork. 17.5° alc. **Rating** 97 **To** 2009 $69.95

Old Premium Tawny Port NV Medium depth to the colour, true tawny and not liqueur; a vibrant palate, with rich and luscious fruit, then extreme rancio provides perfect balance, the acidity neither biting nor volatile. Great texture. Cork. 18° alc. **Rating** 96 **To** 2009 $42

Grand Rutherglen Tokay NV Very rich, very complex tea leaf, spice and Christmas cake aromas, some honey and butterscotch lurking; floods the mouth, intense and long, with a pronounced rancio cut, yet not sharp nor volatile. Cork. 17.5° alc. **Rating** 95 **To** 2009 $30

Rutherglen Durif 2004 Old vines and decades of experience result in a full-throated yet supple and satisfying wine, a benchmark for the variety. Cork. 14° alc. **Rating** 94 **To** 2020 $20.99

Liqueur Tokay NV Pale golden-brown; classic toffee (dominant), tea-leaf, honey, butterscotch and cake run through the long palate; good spirit is, as ever, beautifully balanced and composed. Marvellous aftertaste and pricing. Screwcap. 18° alc. **Rating** 94 **To** 2009 $15.50

Liqueur Muscat NV More touches of red-brown than the Liqueur Tokay, precisely as it should be; fragrant raisin varietal fruit luring you into the second glass; perfect balance. Screwcap. 18° alc. **Rating** 94 **To** 2009 $15.50

Grand Rutherglen Muscat NV Full olive brown, green rim. A powerful and intense bouquet, rancio, spice and raisin; while less unctuous than some of its peers, the palate has outstanding texture, intensity and length. Cork. 17.5° alc. **Rating** 94 **To** 2009 $30

ＹＹＹＹＹ Blue Imperial Cinsaut 2004 Bright, clear colour; a lively mix of red and black fruits plus spice; overall has a certain delicacy. Screwcap. 13.5° alc. **Rating** 90 **To** 2009 $18.99

ＹＹＹＹ Old Premium Amontillado Sherry NV Golden brown; a crystal clear nutty rancio bouquet with clean, fresh spirit; the palate shows lots of nutty rancio flavour through to the finish, but has a very biscuity aftertaste which I see as a distraction. **Rating** 87 **To** 2009 $42

Morrisons Riverview Winery   ★★★☆

Lot 2, Merool Lane, Moama, NSW 2731 **Region** Perricoota
T (03) 5480 0126 **F** (03) 5480 7144 **www**.morrisons.net.au **Open** 7 days 10–5
Winemaker John Ellis **Est.** 1996 **Cases** 5000

Alistair and Leslie Morrison purchased this historic piece of land in 1995. Plantings began in 1996 with shiraz and cabernet sauvignon, followed in '97 by sauvignon blanc, frontignac and grenache in '98, totalling 6 ha. Its restaurant has received an award for Restaurant of the Year for southern NSW.

ΨΨΨΨΨ **Reserve Cabernet 2005** Very good colour for age and region; attractive cassis and blackcurrant fruit; adjusted acidity is the Achilles Heel of the wine, but nonetheless impressive. Screwcap. 15° alc. **Rating** 93 To 2015 $25

ΨΨΨΨ **Pink Fronti 2006** A cellar door special; crammed with red fruits and sweetness; alcohol and acidity provide balance. Screwcap. 10.5° alc. **Rating** 87 To 2009 $18

Mosquito Hill Wines   ★★★☆

18 Trinity Street, College Park, SA 5069 (postal) **Region** Southern Fleurieu
T 0411 661 149 **F** (08) 8222 5896 **Open** Not
Winemaker Glyn Jamieson, Peter Leske **Est.** 2004 **Cases** 1700
In 1994, Glyn and Elizabeth Jamieson bought their small property on Mosquito Hill Road at Mt Jagged on the Fleurieu Peninsula. Glyn Jamieson is yet another of the innumerable tribe of doctors who combine two professions; he just happens to be the prestigious Dorothy Mortlock Professor and Chairman of the Department of Surgery of the University of Adelaide. He and wife Elizabeth's interest in wine goes back for decades, and in 1990 they lived in France for a year where he received both vinous and medical recognition. In 1994 Glyn commenced the part-time (distance) degree at CSU and says that while he never failed an exam, it did take him 11 years to complete the course. His year in France directed him to Burgundy, rather than Bordeaux, hence the planting of 2.2 ha of chardonnay and 1.6 ha pinot noir and a small plot of pinot blanc on the slopes of Mt Jagged. Drought stress meant that no wine was made in 2007. Exports to China.

ΨΨΨΨΨ **Southern Fleurieu Chardonnay 2006** Clean and balanced fruit and French oak, the wine coming alive on the back palate and finish, with citrussy components and acidity. Screwcap. 12.9° alc. **Rating** 90 To 2013 $17.90

Moss Brothers   ★★★★

3857 Caves Road, Wilyabrup, WA 6280 **Region** Margaret River
T (08) 9755 6270 **F** (08) 9755 6298 **www**.mossbrothers.com.au **Open** 7 days 10–5
Winemaker Navneet Singh, David Moss (Consultant) **Est.** 1984 **Cases** 16 000
Established by long-term viticulturist Jeff Moss and his family, notably sons Peter and David and Roseworthy graduate daughter Jane. A 100-tonne rammed-earth winery was constructed in 1992 and draws upon both estate-grown and purchased grapes. Exports to Canada, Germany, Hong Kong and Singapore.

ΨΨΨΨΨ **Jane Moss Margaret River Cabernet Merlot 2004** An elegant, fine and long wine, with cassis, blackcurrant and raspberry fruit, fine tannins and ready to roll. Screwcap. 14.5° alc. **Rating** 91 To 2012 $22
Margaret River Shiraz 2004 Medium-bodied, but firm and well-focused; blackberry with touches of plum and black cherry; good tannin and oak balance. Cork. 14.5° alc. **Rating** 90 To 2015 $30

ΨΨΨΨ **Margaret River Sauvignon Blanc 2007** A fractionally blurred bouquet falling short of outright reduction; crisp, bright grass/asparagus/gooseberry flavours; good length. Screwcap. 13° alc. **Rating** 89 To 2009 $24
Single Vineyard Margaret River Chardonnay 2006 Light- to medium-bodied; clean stone fruit and melon flavours, with some creamy/nutty notes, but little or no oak influence. Screwcap. 13° alc. **Rating** 89 To 2012 $30
Jane Moss Margaret River Semillon Sauvignon Blanc 2007 Curiously, has more tropical fruit than the Sauvignon Blanc, and shows no sign of reduction; does shorten slightly. Screwcap. 13° alc. **Rating** 88 To 2009 $22

Moses Rock Margaret River Shiraz 2005 Light- to medium-bodied; spice and earth overtones to the black fruits, with gently savoury tannins; moderate length. Screwcap. 14° alc. **Rating** 88 **To** 2013 $18

Moses Rock Margaret River Sauvignon Blanc Semillon 2007 Light- to medium-bodied; a clean mix of herb, grass and some tropical fruit notes; minerally acidity is balanced by subliminal sweetness. Screwcap. 13° alc. **Rating** 87 **To** 2009 $18

Margaret River Cabernet Sauvignon 2004 A light- to medium-bodied mix of savoury notes, black fruits, and some sweetness courtesy of the alcohol. Screwcap. 15° alc. **Rating** 87 **To** 2012 $22

Moss Wood

Metricup Road, Wilyabrup, WA 6284 **Region** Margaret River
T (08) 9755 6266 **F** (08) 9755 6303 **www**.mosswood.com.au **Open** By appt
Winemaker Keith Mugford, Josh Bahen, Amanda Shepherdson **Est.** 1969 **Cases** 15 000
Widely regarded as one of the best wineries in the region, capable of producing glorious Semillon in both oaked and unoaked forms, unctuous Chardonnay and elegant, gently herbaceous, superfine Cabernet Sauvignon, which lives for many years. In 2000 Moss Wood acquired the Ribbon Vale Estate; the Ribbon Vale wines are now treated as vineyard-designated within the Moss Wood umbrella. Exports to all major markets.

ΨΨΨΨΨ **Margaret River Cabernet Sauvignon 2004** Classic, austere regional/varietal expression; curiously, the grip is more evident on entry than on the finish and aftertaste, thanks to superfine tannins. Screwcap. 14.5° alc. **Rating** 95 **To** 2025 $100

Margaret River Chardonnay 2007 Strong colour; typically rich and powerful palate, with ripe stone fruit and melon augmented by toasty cashew notes; insistent finish. Screwcap. **Rating** 94 **To** 2015

Margaret River Chardonnay 2006 Finely sculptured; restrained oak is perfectly balanced and integrated with the nectarine, grapefruit and melon fruit; long finish. Screwcap. 14.5° alc. **Rating** 94 **To** 2013 $55

Ribbon Vale Vineyard Margaret River Cabernet Sauvignon Merlot 2005 Medium-bodied; a nice tension between sweet redcurrant and more savoury blackcurrant notes; fine, ripe tannins; good oak handling. Screwcap. 14° alc. **Rating** 94 **To** 2020 $37

ΨΨΨΨΨ **Ribbon Vale Vineyard Semillon Sauvignon Blanc 2007** A powerful, intense bouquet, predominantly driven by herbaceous semillon, plus touches of gooseberry and asparagus. A supple and smooth palate, but lightens off slightly on the finish. Screwcap. 13.5° alc. **Rating** 93 **To** 2011 $25

Margaret River Semillon 2007 Complex and focused, a light year away from Hunter Valley style; no oak, and certainly doesn't need it; will develop into a rich, food style. Screwcap. 14° alc. **Rating** 92 **To** 2014 $30

Ribbon Vale Vineyard Margaret River Merlot 2005 Crystal clear varietal/ regional expression; olives, black fruits and wild herbs; medium-bodied, as it should be; oak simply a vehicle. Screwcap. 13.5° alc. **Rating** 92 **To** 2018 $37

Ribbon Vale Vineyard Margaret River Merlot 2006 Bright colour; a fragrant and flowery burst of black and red berries, a touch of snow pea, cedary French oak and gossamer tannins; good wine from a challenging vintage. Screwcap. **Rating** 91 **To** 2015

Ribbon Vale Vineyard Margaret River Cabernet Sauvignon Merlot 2006 Light colour and light- to medium-bodied; strongly savoury notes and touches of herb and olive; in vineyard style, but I prefer the Merlot (contrary to Keith Mugford). Screwcap. **Rating** 90 **To** 2014

ΨΨΨΨ **Amy's Margaret River Cabernet Sauvignon 2006** Light colour doesn't convince; light- to medium-bodied, with briar/bracken notes running alongside red and blackcurrant fruit. Screwcap. 13.5° alc. **Rating** 89 **To** 2012 $27

Motton Terraces   NR

119 Purtons Road, North Motton, Tas 7315 **Region** Northern Tasmania
T (03) 6425 2317 **www**.cradlecoastwines.info/ **Open** W'ends 10–5, or by appt
Winemaker Flemming Aaberg **Est.** 1990 **Cases** NA
Another of the micro-vineyards which seem to be a Tasmanian speciality; Flemming and
Jenny Aaberg planted slightly less than 0.5 ha of chardonnay and riesling in 1990, and are only
now increasing that to 1 ha with more riesling and some sauvignon blanc. The exercise in
miniature is emphasised by the permanent canopy netting to ward off possums and birds.

Mount Appallan Vineyards   NR

239 Mitchell Road, Biggenden, Qld 4621 **Region** Queensland Coastal
T (07) 4127 1390 **F** (07) 4127 1090 **www**.mtappallan.com.au **Open** At Rosehill on the
River, Tinana
Winemaker Rod MacPherson, Syd Goodchild **Est.** 1998 **Cases** NA
The Goodchild family settled on the Draycot property in 1912, successive generations
carrying on first wool growing and thereafter dairying. The 160-ha farm is 75 km west
of Maryborough, in what is known locally as the Wide Bay–Burnett area, where the rich
volcanic soils and semi-maritime mild climate is not very different from that of South
Burnett. The family has established 7.6 ha of vineyards planted to verdelho, shiraz, merlot,
cabernet sauvignon, petit verdot and viognier, with a small amount each of grenache and
mourvedre. Third-generation Syd Goodchild returned as a mature-age student to study
viticulture at Adelaide University (adding a fourth academic degree), and fourth-generation
Bernie Wixon manages the property, including the dairy side.

 ## Mount Ashby Estate   NR

RMB 403 Nowra Road, Moss Vale, NSW 2577 **Region** Southern Highlands
T (02) 4869 3736 **F** (02) 4869 4792 **www**.mountashby.com.au **Open** Fri–Sun &
public hols 10–5
Winemaker High Range Vintners **Est.** 1999 **Cases** 600
Chris Harvey and wife Sally Beresford purchased the Mirrabooka property in 1999, part of
one of the earliest dairy farms established in the Southern Highlands in the 19th century.
They run one of the few remaining Holstein cattle studs in the region, but also planted
1 ha each of merlot and pinot gris. The cellar door is a replica of the original dairy, but also
includes the relocated barrel produce store (circa 1918) used to restore provincial antique
furniture for sale in Sally Beresford's antique shops (and the cellar door, of course).

Mount Avoca   ★★★☆

Moates Lane, Avoca, Vic 3467 **Region** Pyrenees
T (03) 5465 3282 **F** (03) 5465 3544 **www**.mountavoca.com **Open** 7 days 10–5
Winemaker Matthew Barry **Est.** 1970 **Cases** 20 000
A substantial winery which has long been one of the stalwarts of the Pyrenees region, and
is steadily growing, with 23.7 ha of vineyards. There has been a significant refinement in the
style and flavour of the red wines over the past few years. I suspect a lot of worthwhile work
has gone into barrel selection and maintenance. Reverted to family ownership in 2003 after a
short period as part of the ill-fated Barrington Estates group. Exports to Asia.

 Shiraz 2004 Clear and bright; supple, smooth, fresh medium-bodied shiraz;
good line and length. ProCork. 14° alc. **Rating** 90 **To** 2013 $23.50

Chardonnay 2004 Makes a major statement from the oak and bottle
development, and not from the alcohol; ageing slowly but surely; striking new
label design. Screwcap. 12.5° alc. **Rating** 89 **To** 2011 $23.50

Mount Beckworth ★★★

RMB 915, Learmonth Road, Tourello via Ballarat, Vic 3363 **Region** Ballarat
T (03) 5343 4207 **F** (03) 5343 4207 **www**.ballarat.com/beckworthwines **Open** W'ends
10–6 & by appt
Winemaker Paul Lesock **Est.** 1984 **Cases** 1000
The 4-ha Mount Beckworth vineyard was planted between 1984 and '85, but it was not
until '95 that the full range of wines under the Mount Beckworth label appeared. Until that
time much of the production was sold to Seppelt (Great Western) for sparkling wine use. It is
owned and managed by Paul Lesock, who studied viticulture at CSU, and his wife Jane. The
wines usually reflect the very cool climate. A second cellar door has been opened in Clunes.

ŢŢŢŢ   **Ballarat Pinot Noir 2005** Remarkably deep colour; the power of the palate
suggests a very slow, long ripening period, and some fruit desiccation; does shorten
on the finish. Screwcap. 13.5° alc. **Rating** 88 **To** 2012 $18
Ballarat Shiraz 2005 Medium-bodied, and strongly spicy/peppery, but is ripe
and has good mouthfeel and length, tannins and oak incidental. Screwcap. 14° alc.
Rating 88 **To** 2012 $20
Ballarat Chardonnay 2005 Attractive fruit, although the high natural acidity
seems to be offset by a touch of sweetness on the finish; developing slowly, the oak
input minimal. Screwcap. 13.5° alc. **Rating** 87 **To** 2011 $18

Mt Bera Vineyards ★★★★☆

PO Box 372, Gumeracha, SA 5233 **Region** Adelaide Hills
T (08) 8389 2433 **F** (08) 8389 2433 **www**.mtberavineyards.com.au **Open** Not
Winemaker Jeanneret Wines **Est.** 1997 **Cases** 600
Louise Warner began the development of Mt Bera Vineyards in 1997 with her late partner
Peter Hall, who died after a short illness in 2003. The temptation to give up and leave was
more than offset by the beauty of the vineyard and quality of the grapes, which had already
been found by Peter Gago, senior Penfolds red winemaker. These grapes come from 12 ha of
merlot, cabernet sauvignon and pinot noir. Most of the grapes continue to be sold, with the
Clare Valley's Ben Jeanneret taking over as contract winemaker in 2005. Exports to the UK.

ŢŢŢŢŢ   **3.13 Adelaide Hills Pinot Noir 2006** Spicy, tangy aromas; good texture and
structure, and equally good black cherry, plum, spice and forest flavours; has
elegance; 3.13 ha of pinot planted. Screwcap. 13.5° alc. **Rating** 94 **To** 2012 $25

ŢŢŢŢŷ   **4.23 Reserve Adelaide Hills Merlot 2005** An elegant medium-bodied wine
with exemplary structure and varietal flavour; a mix of olive, spice and redcurrant;
tannins and oak perfectly judged. Screwcap. 13.5° alc. **Rating** 92 **To** 2011 $19.20

ŢŢŢŢ   **4.19 Adelaide Hills Cabernet Sauvignon 2005** A light- to medium-bodied
savoury mix of earth, leaf, mint and berry; fine tannins and almost lemony acidity
on a long finish. Screwcap. 15.5° alc. **Rating** 89 **To** 2012 $25

Mt Billy ★★★★★

18 Victoria Street, Victor Harbor, SA 5211 (postal) **Region** Southern Fleurieu
T 0416 227 100 **F** (08) 8552 8333 **www**.mtbillywines.com.au **Open** Not
Winemaker Dan Standish, Peter Schell **Est.** 2000 **Cases** 1800
Having been an avid wine collector and consumer since 1973, John Edwards (a dentist) and
wife Pauline purchased a 3.75-ha property on the hills behind Victor Harbor, planting 1.2 ha
each of chardonnay and pinot meunier. The original intention was to sell the grapes, but low
yields quickly persuaded Edwards that making and selling a bottle-fermented sparkling wine
was the way to go. Additionally, in 1999 1 tonne each of grenache and shiraz were purchased
in the Barossa Valley, and David Powell of Torbreck agreed to make the wine. Mt Billy was
born. Exports to the UK, the US, Canada, Japan and Hong Kong.

ŸŸŸŸŸ **Antiquity Shiraz 2006** Extremely dense and intense flavours, yet no more than medium- to full-bodied thanks to controlled alcohol and extract; has exceptional thrust and movement on the mid- to back-palate, with licorice and spice joining black fruits. Screwcap. 14.5° alc. **Rating** 96 **To** 2021 $45
Circe Shiraz Viognier 2006 Crimson-purple; very fragrant blackberry and raspberry bouquet, the palate following logically but with intensity through to a long finish. 15.2° alc. **Rating** 94 **To** 2021 $25

Mount Broke Wines ★★★

130 Adams Peak Road, Broke, NSW 2330 **Region** Lower Hunter Valley
T (02) 6579 1314 **F** (02) 6579 1314 **www**.mtbrokewines.com.au **Open** W'ends 12–3
Winemaker First Creek Winemaking Services **Est.** 1997 **Cases** 900
Phil McNamara began planting the 9.6-ha vineyard to shiraz, merlot, verdelho, barbera, semillon, chardonnay and cabernet sauvignon in 1997 on the west side of Wollombi Brook. Over the years since coming into production, the wines have been prolific medal winners in regional and boutique wine shows. Most of the grapes are sold, with limited production under the Mount Broke label.

ŸŸŸŸ **Quince Tree Paddock Hunter Valley Semillon 2007** Somewhat broad, though has ripe fruit and stacks of flavour. Screwcap. 10.5° alc. **Rating** 87 **To** 2009 $18

Mt Buffalo Vineyard ★★★★☆

6300 Great Alpine Road, Eurobin, Vic 3739 **Region** Alpine Valleys
T (03) 5756 2523 **F** (03) 5756 2523 **Open** 7 days 9–5
Winemaker Cyril Ciavarella **Est.** 1998 **Cases** 450
Colin and Lorraine Leita have a substantial horticultural property (Bright Berry Farms) in the foothills of Mt Buffalo. They have diversified into viticulture with 1 ha each of viognier, shiraz and cabernet sauvignon, and 4 ha of merlot. The Great Alpine Road provides a steady stream of visitors to the cellar door. Due to the combination of drought and bushfire, no wine was made in 2007.

Mount Burrumboot Estate ★★★★

3332 Heathcote-Rochester Road, Colbinabbin, Vic 3559 **Region** Heathcote
T (03) 5432 9238 **F** (03) 5432 9238 **www**.burrumboot.com **Open** W'ends & public hols 11–5, or by appt
Winemaker Cathy Branson **Est.** 1999 **Cases** 1500
To quote, 'Mount Burrumboot Estate was born in 1999, when Andrew and Cathy Branson planted vines on the Home Block of the Branson family farm, Donore, on the slopes of Mt Burrumboot, on the Mt Camel Range, above Colbinabbin. Originally the vineyard was just another diversification of an already diverse farming enterprise. However, the wine bug soon bit Andrew and Cathy, and so a winery was established. The first wine was made in 2001 by contract – however, 2002 vintage saw the first wine made by Cathy in the machinery shed, surrounded by headers and tractors. Very primitive, and the appearance of the new 50-tonne winery in 2002 was greeted with great enthusiasm!' And then you taste the wines. Amazing. The original plantings of a little over 11 ha of shiraz and merlot have since been expanded to take in lesser amounts of petit verdot, sangiovese, tempranillo, gamay, marsanne and viognier. There is no intention to expand the business further.

ŸŸŸŸŸ **Heathcote Viognier 2007** Bright colour; medium–bodied, with clear varietal character in a musk, apricot and pear spectrum on both bouquet and palate. Screwcap. 14° alc. **Rating** 90 **To** 2012 $25
Mad Uncle Jack's Heathcote Petit Verdot 2005 A big, brooding wine with deep blackcurrant and leather fruit; slightly abrasive tannins are evident, but balanced. Diam. 14.2° alc. **Rating** 90 **To** 2015 $28

ỴỴỴỴ   **Heathcote Gamay 2005** Retains good hue; well-made gentle plum fruit with a core of acidity providing length. Screwcap. 13° alc. **Rating** 89 **To** 2010 $35
Heathcote Merlot 2005 The distinctly foresty, savoury elements are within the varietal spectrum; good texture and mouthfeel; touches of black olive and gentle tannins. Diam. 14.5° alc. **Rating** 89 **To** 2012 $28
Heathcote Marsanne Viognier 2006 Green pear, chalk and apple aromas and flavours, with a firm finish, all led by the marsanne. Screwcap. 13° alc. **Rating** 88 **To** 2011 $22
Heathcote Shiraz 2005 Slightly weak colour; a light- to medium-bodied palate with some suggestions of stressed vines; a spicy, savoury finish, but overall lack of depth. Diam. 14.2° alc. **Rating** 88 **To** 2014 $30
Elle Rougit 2006 Pale salmon; light-bodied spicy/savoury blend of Tempranillo/Sangiovese/Shiraz; some length to the finish. Cork. 12.8° alc. **Rating** 87 **To** 2009 $18
Heathcote Sangiovese 2005 Light colour; a light-bodied wine with some authentic spicy/sour cherry fruit; for devotees of Sangiovese. Diam. 14° alc. **Rating** 87 **To** 2009 $25

Mount Camel Ridge Estate   ★★★★★

473 Heathcote-Rochester Road, Heathcote, Vic 3523 **Region** Heathcote
T (03) 5433 2343 **www.**mountcamelridgeestate.com **Open** By appt
Winemaker Ian Langford, Gwenda Langford **Est.** 1999 **Cases** 350
Commencing in 1999, Ian and Gwenda Langford planted 18 ha of vines, the majority to shiraz (8.5 ha), cabernet sauvignon (3.8 ha) and merlot (3 ha), with a little over 0.5 ha each of petit verdot, viognier and mourvedre. The land has been developed using organic principles, using composted chicken manure every three years, the application of seaweed fertiliser and mulching of the prunings. The vineyard is dry-grown, and no copper, lime or sulphur fungicide has been used. The Langfords say, 'As a result, worms have reappeared, and there is now an extensive frog population, ladybirds and other invertebrates and a range of beautiful spiders.' Scientists from Melbourne University have commenced a survey in the vineyard to establish the connection between the health of the vines and the resident invertebrate population. The very attractive red wines are made in open half-tonne vats, basket-pressed and matured in French oak.

ỴỴỴỴỴ   **Heathcote Shiraz 2006** Dense red-purple; rich, concentrated blackberry, dark plum and licorice, with a subtle background of French oak; not over-extracted nor is it overripe; stained Diam a worry. 14.4° alc. **Rating** 94 **To** 2021 $45

ỴỴỴỴ   **Heathcote Cabernet Sauvignon 2006** Colour lacks depth; a mix of leaf, mint and earth overtones to berry fruit; picked too early. Diam. 12.4° alc. **Rating** 87 **To** 2012 $45

Mount Cathedral Vineyards

125 Knafl Road, Taggerty, Vic 3714 **Region** Upper Goulburn
T 0409 354 069 **F** (03) 9374 4286 **www.**mtcathedralvineyards.com **Open** By appt
Winemaker Oscar Rosa, Nick Arena **Est.** 1995 **Cases** NA
The Rosa and Arena families established Mount Cathedral Vineyards in 1995, at an elevation of 300 m on the north face of Mt Cathedral. The first plantings were of 1.2 ha of merlot and 0.8 ha of chardonnay, followed by 2.5 ha of cabernet sauvignon and 0.5 ha of cabernet franc in 1996. Oscar Rosa, chief winemaker, has completed two TAFE courses in viticulture and winemaking, and completed a Bachelor of Wine Science course at CSU in 2002. He gained practical experience working at Yering Station during 1998 and '99.

ΨΨΨΨΨ **Reserve Merlot 2004** Excellent example of the variety, full of life and thrust to the mix of cassis, olive and spice; fine tannins on a lingering finish. Diam. 14° alc. **Rating** 94 **To** 2017 $35

ΨΨΨΨΩ **Reserve Merlot 2005** Riper, richer and fuller than the varietal, but not necessarily better; more flavour but slightly less verve; for the longer haul, perhaps. Diam. **Rating** 90 **To** 2016 $35
Cabernet Merlot 2003 A powerful mix of cassis and blackcurrant fruit; medium- to full-bodied, supple and mouthcoating; soft tannins, complementary oak. Diam. 13.9° alc. **Rating** 90 **To** 2015 $20

ΨΨΨΨ **Chardonnay 2004** Fractionally softer and lighter, more oaky than the '05, a different face from the same vineyard and winemaking philosophy due to higher crop levels. Screwcap. 14° alc. **Rating** 89 **To** 2011 $20
Chardonnay 2005 Firm, tightly focused fruit revolves around grapefruit and nectarine; a lingering, slightly green finish. Screwcap. 14.5° alc. **Rating** 89 **To** 2012 $20
Merlot 2005 Light- to medium-bodied; good varietal character expression with a mix of cassis and black olive plus spicy nuances. Diam. **Rating** 89 **To** 2014 $20
Chardonnay 2006 A powerful wine, driven by tight fruit and firm acidity; needs much patience if it is to soften and open up. Screwcap. **Rating** 87 **To** 2015 $20
Upper Goulburn Cabernet 2005 Dense colour; extremely potent and powerful, still coming to terms with itself; difficult to gauge precisely how it will develop, needs 5 years to provide an answer. Diam. **Rating** 87 **To** 2018 $20

Mount Charlie Winery ★★★

228 Mount Charlie Road, Riddells Creek, Vic 3431 **Region** Macedon Ranges
T (03) 5428 6946 **F** (03) 5428 6946 **www**.mountcharlie.com.au **Open** Most w'ends 11–3 or by appt
Winemaker Trefor Morgan **Est.** 1991 **Cases** 800
Mount Charlie's wines are sold principally by mail order and through selected restaurants. A futures program encourages mailing list sales with a discount of over 25% on the release price. Owner/winemaker Trefor Morgan is perhaps better known as Professor of Physiology at Melbourne University. He also acts as a contract maker for others in the region.

Mount Coghill Vineyard ★★★

Cnr Pickfords Road/Coghills Creek Road, Coghills Creek, Vic 3364 **Region** Ballarat
T (03) 5343 4329 **F** (03) 5343 4329 **Open** W'ends 10–5
Winemaker Darren Latta **Est.** 1993 **Cases** 250
Ian (an award-winning photographer) and Margaret Pym began planting their tiny vineyard in 1995 with 1280 pinot noir rootlings, and added 450 chardonnay rootlings the next year. Since 2001 the wine has been made and released under the Mount Coghill Vineyard label.

Mount Cole Wineworks ★★★★

197 Mount Cole Road, Warrail, Vic 3377 **Region** Grampians
T (03) 5352 2311 **F** (03) 5354 3279 **www**.mountcolewineworks.com.au **Open** By appt
Winemaker Dr Graeme Bertuch **Est.** 1998 **Cases** 520
Dr Graeme Bertuch's involvement in grapegrowing and winemaking goes back far further than the establishment of Mount Cole Wineworks. In 1977 he established Cathcart Ridge, but found the time demands on a rural doctor-cum-vigneron were too much. He sold Cathcart Ridge in '93, but did not sell the itch to grow grapes and make wine. In '98 he and wife Carolyn purchased a property at the foot of Mt Cole State Forest and began planting 3.5 ha of shiraz, adding 1 ha of viognier and 0.5 ha each of nebbiolo and riesling by 2004, the same year that he made his first wine. In '07 he purchased the Mt Chalambar Vineyard owned by Trevor Mast, with 2.5 ha of riesling and 2 ha chardonnay planted more than 20 years ago.

ŸŸŸŸŸ **Fenix Rising Grampians Shiraz 2005** Deep colour; rich, ripe confit fruit, with a distinct overlay of sweetness, perhaps from the alcohol; soft tannins, and lashings of flavour. Screwcap. 15° alc. **Rating** 90 **To** 2015 $37

ŸŸŸŸ **Off the Beaten Track Grampians Shiraz 2005** Lighter and more lively than Fenix Rising, but doesn't have the same compelling richness; slightly edgy acidity. Screwcap. 15° alc. **Rating** 88 **To** 2012 $25

Mount Eyre Vineyards

173 Gillards Road, Pokolbin, NSW 2321 **Region** Lower Hunter Valley
T 0438 683 973 **F** (02) 6842 4513 **www.**mounteyre.com **Open** Tues–Sun 11–5
Winemaker Stephen Hagan, Aniello Iannuzzi **Est.** 1970 **Cases** 5000
Mount Eyre draws on two vineyards, the first a 24-ha estate at Broke, planted to semillon, chardonnay, shiraz, chambourcin, cabernet franc and cabernet sauvignon, and the second, Holman Estate, in Gillards Road, Pokolbin, with 4 ha of shiraz and 1.8 ha of merlot. Exports to Canada, Mexico and Asia.

ŸŸŸŸŸ **Holman Shiraz 2006** An elegant, medium-bodied wine, with a mix of red and black fruits on both bouquet and palate; lovely supple texture and silky finish. Diam. 13.5° alc. **Rating** 94 **To** 2016 $45

ŸŸŸŸŸ **Shiraz 2006** Denser colour than the Holman, and a total contrast in style, with robust black fruits on a full-bodied palate; ripe tannins. Value. Screwcap. 14° alc. **Rating** 90 **To** 2020 $14.95

ŸŸŸŸ **Three Ponds Chardonnay 2006** Medium-bodied tropical peach fruit; soft mouthfeel to an early-drinking style. Screwcap. **Rating** 87 **To** 2009 $22.95

Mt Franklin Estate

2 Whybrow Street, Franklinford, Vic 3461 **Region** Macedon Ranges
T (03) 5476 4475 **F** (03) 5476 4473 **www.**mtfranklinwines.com.au **Open** By appt
Winemaker Scott McGillivray, Colin Mitchell, Graeme Leith (Contract) **Est.** 2000
Cases 380
Owner Lesley McGillivray was well ahead of her time when, in 1988, she planted two test rows of Italian varieties on rich volcanic soil situated near the foothills of Mt Franklin. The varieties to succeed best were dolcetto and pinot gris, and with family and friends they planted the first third of their 4-ha vineyard with dolcetto and pinot gris in 2000. Since then, the vineyard has been completed with more dolcetto, pinot gris and a little nebbiolo.

ŸŸŸŸ **Dolcetto 2006** Sweet fruited with blueberries and a hint of spice; quite savoury and drying on the finish; should be enjoyed in its youth. Screwcap. 13° alc. **Rating** 88 **To** 2009 $22

Mount Gisborne Wines

83 Waterson Road, Gisborne, Vic 3437 **Region** Macedon Ranges
T (03) 5428 2834 **F** (03) 5428 2834 **www.**mountgisbornewines.com.au
Open Wed–Sun 10–6
Winemaker David Ell, Stuart Anderson **Est.** 1986 **Cases** 1500
David and Mary Ell planted 2.8 ha of pinot noir and chardonnay between 1986 and '90. The first wines were made in '91, signalling a partnership with the veteran Stuart Anderson, who is now theoretically in retirement. Exports to Canada, Singapore and Malaysia.

ŸŸŸŸŸ **Macedon Ranges Pinot Noir 2006** Excellent depth, texture and structure; plum and blackberry fruit; very good line and length. Diam. 14° alc. **Rating** 94 **To** 2013 $32

♀♀♀♀ Macedon Ranges Chardonnay 2006 Colour more developed than the wine; light- to medium-bodied reflecting modest alcohol; a citrussy/nutty/minerally palate with marked acidity. Diam. 13° alc. **Rating** 89 **To** 2011 $28

Mount Horrocks ★★★★★

The Old Railway Station, Curling Street, Auburn, SA 5451 **Region** Clare Valley
T (08) 8849 2243 **F** (08) 8849 2265 **www**.mounthorrocks.com **Open** W'ends & public hols 10–5
Winemaker Stephanie Toole **Est.** 1982 **Cases** 4500
Mount Horrocks has well and truly established its own identity in recent years, aided by positive marketing and, equally importantly, wine quality, which has resulted in both show success and critical acclaim. Stephanie Toole has worked long and hard to achieve this, and I strongly advise you (or anyone else) not to get in her way. Exports to the UK, the US and other major markets.

♀♀♀♀♀ Watervale Shiraz 2005 A highly aromatic and fragrant bouquet; rich, perfectly ripened shiraz with round, mouthfilling blackberry flavours plus bitter chocolate and ripe tannins; controlled alcohol. Screwcap. 14° alc. **Rating** 95 **To** 2025 $35
Semillon 2006 As always, no reduction; herb, grass and beautifully integrated French oak providing another layer of flavour, though without the penalty of phenolics. Screwcap. 13.5° alc. **Rating** 94 **To** 2012 $27

♀♀♀♀♀ Cordon Cut 2007 Glowing yellow-green; a delicious, moderately sweet wine with concentration, but no botrytis cut. Riesling. Screwcap. 11° alc. **Rating** 92 **To** 2015 $35
Clare Valley Cabernet Sauvignon 2005 A bouquet of leafy red and blackcurrant; quite intense fruit, with good structure, and ample fine-grained tannins on the long and supple finish. Screwcap. 14° alc. **Rating** 91 **To** 2018 $35
Watervale Riesling 2007 Some colour development; a full palate of ripe fruit, ranging from apple to more tropical; crisp acidity. Screwcap. 13° alc. **Rating** 90 **To** 2012 $28

Mt Jagged Wines ★★★★

Main Victor Harbor Road, Mt Jagged, SA 5211 **Region** Southern Fleurieu
T (08) 8554 9532 **F** (08) 8340 7633 **www**.mtjaggedwines.com.au **Open** Oct–May 7 days 10–5, June–Sept by appt
Winemaker Stephen Pannell, Tom White **Est.** 1989 **Cases** 7000
Mt Jagged's vineyard was established in 1989 by the White family, with close-planted merlot, cabernet sauvignon, shiraz, chardonnay and semillon. The vineyard sits at 350 m above sea level on a diversity of soils ranging from ironstone/clay for the red varieties to sandy loam/clay for the whites. The cool-climate vineyard (altitude and proximity to the ocean) produces fresh, crisp, zingy white wines and medium-bodied savoury reds of complexity and depth. The vineyard has good rainfall and natural spring water in abundance, and is currently in the process of conversion to organic/biodynamic viticulture principles. Exports to the US and Canada.

♀♀♀♀♀ Single Vineyard Reserve Shiraz 2005 Spicy aromas flow into the medium-bodied palate, joining bright plum and blackberry fruit; good tannin and French oak management; 250 cases. Adelaide Hills. Screwcap. 14° alc. **Rating** 93 **To** 2018 $35

♀♀♀♀ Single Vineyard Southern Fleurieu Adelaide Hills Shiraz 2005 From the Southern Fleurieu estate vineyard and Adelaide Hills, with 2% viognier; overall light- to medium-bodied, with spicy, tangy flavours; unequivocal cool-grown wine. Screwcap. 14° alc. **Rating** 88 **To** 2012 $20

Mount Langi Ghiran Vineyards   ★★★★★

Warrak Road, Buangor, Vic 3375 **Region** Grampians
T (03) 5354 3207 **F** (03) 5354 3277 **www.**langi.com.au **Open** Mon–Fri 9–5, w'ends 10–5
Winemaker Dan Buckle, Kate Petering **Est.** 1969 **Cases** 60 000
A maker of outstanding cool-climate peppery Shiraz, crammed with flavour and vinosity, and very good Cabernet Sauvignon. The Shiraz points the way for cool-climate examples of the variety. The business was acquired by the Rathbone family group in 2002, and hence the marketing has been integrated with the Yering Station, Parker Coonawarra and Xanadu Estate wines, a synergistic mix with no overlap. Exports to all major markets.

♀♀♀♀♀ **Langi Shiraz 2006** A vibrant, medium-bodied wine, with spice, pepper and plum in classic cool-grown mode; superfine tannins and exceptional length. **Rating** 95 **To** 2016 $55
Riesling 2007 Distinctly finer and more intense than the basic Cliff Edge; bright citrus flavours build progressively through the long palate and finish. Screwcap. 13° alc. **Rating** 94 **To** 2016 $30
Nowhere Creek Vineyard Shiraz 2006 Strong crimson-purple; abundant and seriously rich black fruits run through a velvety palate, spice, tannins and oak providing textural embroidery. Screwcap. 14.5° alc. **Rating** 94 **To** 2026 $25
Cliff Edge Shiraz 2006 Similar in many ways to Billi Billi, but with a riper fruit spectrum and much more juicy plum and spice fruit on the finish; controlled oak too. Screwcap. 14.5° alc. **Rating** 94 **To** 2021 $25

♀♀♀♀♀ **Moyston Hills Vineyard Shiraz 2006** Lighter coloured, and more fragrant, with spicy cherry and raspberry fruit flavours; fine tannins complete an elegant light- to medium-bodied wine. Screwcap. 13.5° alc. **Rating** 93 **To** 2016 $25
Cliff Edge Riesling No. 2 2006 A rich, spatlese style, the sweetness evident from the word go; supple and smooth in wannabe Mosel style, but needed a touch more acidity; 60-year-old vines. Will develop. Screwcap. 9° alc. **Rating** 92 **To** 2016 $20
Billi Billi Shiraz 2006 Light- to medium-bodied; a spotlessly clean bouquet, with seductively fresh plum, cherry and spice fruit running through to the palate and finish. Bargain. Drink now or in a few years. Screwcap. 14° alc. **Rating** 90 **To** 2012 $15

♀♀♀♀ **Cliff Edge Riesling 2007** Bright straw-green; has good depth to the flavour, with ripe apple and some tropical components; enough to build on. Screwcap. 12° alc. **Rating** 89 **To** 2011 $20
Cliff Edge Pinot Gris 2007 Clean, fresh pear, apple and musk varietal fruit; good length, dry finish. Screwcap. 12.5° alc. **Rating** 89 **To** 2009 $20
The Gap Passito Riesling 2006 Fresh, lively and excellently balanced, the sweetness partly hidden by acidity; will grow in bottle. Grapes partly dried on the vine. Screwcap. 9.5° alc. **Rating** 89 **To** 2013 $22

Mt Lofty Ranges Vineyard   ★★★★

Harris Road, Lenswood, SA 5240 **Region** Adelaide Hills
T (08) 8389 8339 **F** (08) 8389 8349 **Open** W'ends 11–5, or by appt Aug–May
Winemaker Various contract **Est.** 1992 **Cases** 800
Owners Alan Herath and Jan Reed developed and operate the 4.5-ha vineyard and cellar door. Skilled contract winemaking by Nepenthe, Neville Falkenerg and Adelaide Hills Fine Wine Centre has brought rewards and recognition to the vineyard. Distributed in SA by Domaine Wine Shippers.

♀♀♀♀♀ **Chardonnay 2006** A very complex, aromatic bouquet with some pleasing funky notes; the palate also complex and intense, ranging through grapefruit and ripe apple; great value. Screwcap. 14° alc. **Rating** 93 **To** 2012 $16

♀♀♀♀ **Sauvignon Blanc 2007** A relatively subdued but clean bouquet, the palate fresh and firm, the acidity good despite relatively high alcohol; good length. Screwcap. 13.5° alc. **Rating** 89 **To** 2009 $18

Five Vines Riesling 2007 A clean but subdued bouquet; has raw-boned flavour showing the full impact of the '07 growing season. Screwcap. 12° alc. **Rating** 87 To 2009 $16

Old Pump Shed Pinot Noir 2006 Despite the high alcohol, relatively light-bodied strawberry and cherry fruit in a direct style; however, the finish and aftertaste do heat up. Screwcap. 15° alc. **Rating** 87 **To** 2009 $20

Mount Macedon Winery ★★★

433 Bawden Road, Mount Macedon, Vic 3441 **Region** Macedon Ranges
T (03) 5427 2735 **F** (03) 5427 1071 **www**.mountmacedonwinery.com.au **Open** Mon–Fri 12–4, w'ends & public hols 11–5
Winemaker Kilchurn Wines (David Cowburn) **Est.** 1989 **Cases** 4300
The property on which Mount Macedon Winery is situated was purchased by David and Ronda Collins in 2003. The 32-ha property, at an altitude of 680 m, has 7.3 ha of chardonnay, pinot noir and gewurztraminer.

ΨΨΨΨ **Gewurztraminer 2007** A subdued bouquet, but rose petal/spice/lychee comes through on the palate, the elevated alcohol pushing the Alsace style connection. Screwcap. 14.7° alc. **Rating** 87 **To** 2012 $30

Mount Majura Vineyard

RMB 314 Majura Road, Majura, ACT 2609 (postal) **Region** Canberra District
T (02) 6262 3070 **F** (02) 6262 4288 **www**.mountmajura.com.au **Open** Thurs–Mon 10–5
Winemaker Dr Frank van de Loo **Est.** 1988 **Cases** 3000
The first vines were planted in 1988 by Dinny Killen on a site on her family property, which had been especially recommended by Dr Edgar Riek; its attractions were red soil of volcanic origin over limestone, with reasonably steep east and northeast slopes providing an element of frost protection. The 1-ha vineyard was planted to pinot noir, chardonnay and merlot in equal quantities. The syndicate that purchased the property in 1999 has extended the plantings and built a new winery and cellar door.

ΨΨΨΨΨ **Canberra District Riesling 2007** Fragrant apple, herb and lime aromas; very good length and intensity, with citrussy fruit and fine, minerally acidity. Low alcohol a plus. Screwcap. 11.1° alc. **Rating** 94 **To** 2017 $16

ΨΨΨΨΨ **Canberra Chardonnay 2005** Controlled intensity of citrus, stone fruit, melon and mineral flavours, oak a background whisper; developing with grace. Screwcap. 12.7° alc. **Rating** 91 **To** 2011 $20
Canberra District Shiraz 2006 Light- to medium-bodied, with spice and red fruits; needs a little more conviction from the vineyard (rather than the winery). Screwcap. 14.1° alc. **Rating** 90 **To** 2016 $25

ΨΨΨΨ **Canberra District Rose 2007** Vivid colour; the expectation/fear that it may be sweet, but is not; lively cherry and strawberry fruit; good length and balance. Screwcap. 11.9° alc. **Rating** 89 **To** 2009 $16
Canberra District Tempranillo 2006 A light- to medium-bodied mix of small red fruits intermingling with persistent tannins; still needs deciphering. Screwcap. 13.2° alc. **Rating** 88 **To** 2011 $25
Canberra District Merlot 2005 As always, clear though not entirely comfortable varietal expression; savoury earth and green olive characters; drying finish. Screwcap. 13.5° alc. **Rating** 87 **To** 2010 $16

Mount Mary ★★★★★

Coldstream West Road, Lilydale, Vic 3140 **Region** Yarra Valley
T (03) 9739 1761 **F** (03) 9739 0137 **www**.mountmary.net **Open** Not
Winemaker Rob Hall **Est.** 1971 **Cases** 3500

Superbly refined, elegant and intense Cabernets and usually outstanding and long-lived Pinot Noirs fully justify Mount Mary's exalted reputation. The Triolet blend is very good; more recent vintages of Chardonnay are even better. Founder and long-term winemaker, the late Dr John Middleton, was one of the great, and truly original, figures in the Australian wine industry. He liked nothing more than to tilt at windmills, and would do so with passion. His annual newsletter grew longer as each year passed, although the paper size did not. The only change necessary was a reduction in font size, and ultimately very strong light or a magnifying glass (or both) to fully appreciate the barbed wit and incisive mind of this great character. The determination of the family to continue the business is simply wonderful, even if the 2007 vintage was severely reduced by frost. Limited quantities of the wines are sold through the wholesale/retail distribution system in Victoria, New South Wales, Queensland and South Australia.

♀♀♀♀♀ **Yarra Valley Chardonnay 2006** A complex bouquet, with some barrel ferment oak inputs leading the way; the palate is tightly focused, pure and very long, the accent entirely on the stone fruit and citrus fruit; lean and lissom. Diam. 13.5° alc. **Rating** 95 **To** 2015 $70

Quintet 2005 Supremely graceful and fine in typical Mount Mary style; the long and silky palate has a tapestry of red and black fruit flavours, the finish long and satisfying, the aftertaste lingering for minutes. Cork. 13° alc. **Rating** 95 **To** 2020 $100

Yarra Valley Pinot Noir 2005 Super-elgant and super-refined; the long track record of prior releases guarantees this wine will build on the long, linear fruit base it was born with; easily overlooked, perhaps. Cork. 13° alc. **Rating** 94 **To** 2018 $100

♀♀♀♀♀ **Triolet 2006** Restrained aromas, to a degree, flavours, as the three varieties (Sauvignon Blanc/Semillon/Muscadelle) each exert their influence, largely untroubled by oak; the acidity is good, and the wine will flourish with time. Cork. 12.5° alc. **Rating** 93 **To** 2016 $70

Mount Moliagul   ★★★★☆

Clay Gully Lane, Moliagul, Vic 3472 **Region** Bendigo
T (03) 9809 2113 **www.**mountmoliagulwines.com.au **Open** By appt 0427 221 641
Winemaker Terry Flora **Est.** 1991 **Cases** 400
Terry and Bozenka Flora began their tiny vineyard in 1991, gradually planting 0.5 ha each of shiraz and cabernet sauvignon, and 0.2 ha of chardonnay. Terry Flora has completed two winemaking courses, one with Winery Supplies and the other at Dookie College, and has learnt his craft very well.

Mount Pierrepoint Estate   ★★★★☆

271 Pierrepoint Road, Tarrington, Vic 3301 (postal) **Region** Henty
T (03) 5572 5558 **F** (03) 5572 5558 **www.**mountpierrepoint.com **Open** Not
Winemaker Jennifer Lacey **Est.** 1997 **Cases** 400
Mount Pierrepoint Estate was established by Andrew and Jennifer Lacey on the foothills of Mt Pierrepoint between Hamilton and Tarrington. The initial planting of pinot noir in 1998 was followed by plantings of pinot gris in '99, chardonnay in 2003 and further plantings of pinot gris in '05. No samples received; the rating is that of last year.

Mount Prior Vineyard   ★★★☆

1194 Gooramadda Road, Rutherglen, Vic 3685 **Region** Rutherglen
T (02) 6026 5591 **F** (02) 6026 5590 **www.**rutherglenvic.com **Open** 7 days 10–5
Winemaker Brian Devitt **Est.** 1860 **Cases** 5000
A full-scale tourist facility, with yet more in the pipeline. It has full accommodation packages at the historic Mount Prior House; a restaurant operating weekends; picnic and barbecue facilities; and a California-style gift shop. The 112 ha of vineyards were expanded in 1998 by

a further 5 ha of durif, a mark both of the success of Mount Prior and of interest in durif. Exports to the US and Japan.

ŶŶŶŶ **Black Label Durif 2004** Massively dense and full-bodied dark fruits and strong tannins; back label says 10–100 years cellaring, future generations will tell. Screwcap. 15° alc. **Rating** 89 **To** 2019 $27

Rutherglen Shiraz 2005 Blackberry and plum offset by abundant vanilla/mocha oak; soft tannins, good length. Screwcap. 14° alc. **Rating** 89 **To** 2015 $23

Reserve Museum Release Port NV Tawny gold, obvious age; fairly potent spirit; more tokay sweet white than port. **Rating** 89 **To** 2009 $25

Cabernet Merlot 2004 Has more sweet, small berry fruit than the varietal Merlot, with notes of dark chocolate, tannins swooping in on the finish; Cabernet/ Merlot. Cork. 13.5° alc. **Rating** 87 **To** 2010 $19.50

Rutherglen Sparkling Shiraz Durif 2005 Despite the base blend, is far more elegant than most, with light spicy notes, the hint of sweetness no issue for devotees of the style. Cork. 13° alc. **Rating** 87 **To** 2012 $27

Noble Gold 2006 Lusciously sweet wine; vanilla and peach; needs time, not complex; over ice cream. Screwcap. 11.5° alc. **Rating** 87 **To** 2010 $19.50

Limited Cellar Pack Release Vintage Port 2005 Potent wine; distinct black chocolate characters have not much to do with vintage port; however, may develop. Screwcap. 18° alc. **Rating** 87 **To** 2015 $20

Director's Selection Muscat NV Some age evident in colour; powerful, very sweet wine not as much varietal character as the Tokay. **Rating** 87 **To** 2009 $20

Mt Samaria Vineyard ★★★☆

3231 Midland Highway, Lima South, Vic 3673 **Region** Upper Goulburn
T (03) 5768 2550 **www**.mtsamaria.com.au **Open** By appt
Winemaker Roger Cowan, Delatite, Auldstone Cellars **Est.** 1992 **Cases** 600
The 3-ha Mt Samaria Vineyard, with shiraz (1.7 ha) and tempranillo (0.8 ha) having the lion's share, accompanied by a little cabernet and pinot gris, is owned and operated by Judy and Roger Cowan. Plantings took place over an 8-year period, and in the early days the grapes were sold to Delatite until the Cowans ventured into wine production in 1999. Striking labels are a distinct plus, although wombats are not normally welcome visitors in vineyards.

ŶŶŶŶ **Tempranillo 2006** Typical tangy, savoury, lemony twist to the relatively shy red and black fruits; does accelerate on the finish and aftertaste. Screwcap. 14.5° alc. **Rating** 88 **To** 2011 $25

Mount Stapylton Vineyard ★★★★

1212 Northern Grampians Road, Laharum, Vic 3401 (postal) **Region** Grampians
T (03) 9824 6680 **www**.mtsv.com.au **Open** Not
Winemaker Don McRae **Est.** 2002 **Cases** 60
The Mount Stapylton Vineyard forms part of the historic Goonwinnow Homestead farming property on the northwest side of the Grampians in front of Mt Stapylton. Owners Howard and Samantha Staehr began the development of the 1-ha shiraz vineyard (two-thirds Great Western Old Block clone and one-third clone 1654) in 2002, and the vines have already produced four highly acclaimed vintages; expansion of the vineyard will follow over the next few years. Winemaker Don McRae is a busy man: he has been involved to a minor degree in the Vic wine industry since undertaking a vine propagation and vineyard establishment course at Wangaratta TAFE in 1987, following this with a wine science degree at CSU in Wagga, finishing in 2000, while also involved in hospital work and studies.

ŶŶŶŶŶ **Grampians Shiraz 2006** Dense purple-red; masses of correspondingly dense blackberry, plum, licorice and spice fruit, all achieved at a modest alcohol level. Lots of potential poor cork permitting. 14° alc. **Rating** 92 **To** 2013 $40

Mt Surmon Wines

Scarlattis Cellar Door Gallery, Basham Road, Stanley Flat, SA 5453 **Region** Clare Valley
T (08) 8842 1250 **www.mtsurmon.com.au Open** 7 days 10–5
Winemaker Various contract **Est.** 1995 **Cases** 800
The Surmon family has established just under 20 ha of vineyard, half to shiraz, the remainder
to cabernet sauvignon, nebbiolo, chardonnay, pinot gris and viognier. Most of the grapes are
sold to other wineries, but small quantities are contract-made and sold through Scarlattis
Gallery Function Centre and a few local hotels.

Clare Valley Shiraz 2006 A powerful, concentrated wine; the extract tends to
sit on top of blackberry, licorice and plum fruit, but will soften with bottle age.
Screwcap. 14° alc. **Rating** 90 **To** 2016 $25

Clare Valley Cabernet Sauvignon 2006 Ripe, though not jammy, cassis and
blackcurrant varietal flavours, with persistent and slightly dry tannins; a slight dip
on the mid- to back palate. Screwcap. 14° alc. **Rating** 89 **To** 2014 $25
Clare Valley Nebbiolo 2006 This is such a difficult variety; the colour is good,
but the savoury, green characters are decidedly challenging. Screwcap. 13° alc.
Rating 87 **To** 2011 $25

Mount Tamborine Winery ★★★

128 Long Road, Eagle Heights, Qld, 4271 **Region** Granite Belt
T (07) 5545 3506 **F** (07) 5545 3068 **www.mttamborinewinery.com Open** 7 days 10–4
Winemaker Jim Barnes **Est.** 1990 **Cases** NA
The Mount Tamborine name has caused no small degree of confusion over the years between
several wineries in that region. This venture had its birthplace in the Tamborine region, but
has now migrated to the Granite Belt, where its vineyard and winery are located. Here there is
8 ha of shiraz, 4.8 ha each of chardonnay and cabernet sauvignon, and 3.2 ha merlot.

Black Shiraz 2006 Rich, ripe and a little spicy; well-flavoured across the palate,
with a little toastiness from the oak on the finish. Cork. 14.8° alc. **Rating** 88
To 2014 $33
Tehembrin Merlot 2005 Some whole bunch evident, with a stemmy profile;
interesting flavour and good depth to the fruit. Cork. 13° alc. **Rating** 87
To 2012 $25

Mount Torrens Vineyards ★★★★★

PO Box 1679, Mt Torrens, SA 5244 **Region** Adelaide Hills
T (08) 8389 4229 **Open** Not
Winemaker Torbreck (David Powell) **Est.** 1996 **Cases** 1000
Mount Torrens Vineyards has 2.5 ha of shiraz and viognier, and the distinguished team of
Mark Whisson as viticulturist and David Powell as contract winemaker. The excellent wines
are available by mail order, but are chiefly exported to the UK and the US.

Solstice Adelaide Hills Shiraz 2004 As expected, no less firm than the Shiraz
Viognier; excellent texture, structure and balance in a medium- to full-bodied
frame; restrained oak, quality savoury tannins and very good length. Screwcap.
14.4° alc. **Rating** 94 **To** 2018 $35
Solstice Adelaide Hills Shiraz Viognier 2004 Very complex, paradoxically
with more grip and structure than often encountered with shiraz viognier
notwithstanding the very high (10%) viognier component; black fruits, spice and
licorice; fine, savoury tannins. Screwcap. 14.2° alc. **Rating** 94 **To** 2017 $35

Mount Towrong ★★★

10 Taylors Road, Mount Macedon, Vic 3441 (postal) **Region** Macedon Ranges
T (03) 5426 3050 **F** (03) 5426 3050 **Open** Not
Winemaker David Cowburn **Est.** 1996 **Cases** 250

When George and Deirdre Cremasco commenced the establishment of their 1.8 ha vineyard (chardonnay, nebbiolo and prosecco), they did so with the help of George's father and grandfather. Strongly influenced by their Italian heritage, the vineyard has been terraced, with Chardonnay the first wine in production, followed by a wine simply called Rosso (a blend of pinot purchased from the region and nebbiolo), and the first vintage of prosecco following in 2008.

♀♀♀♀ **Macedon Ranges Chardonnay 2005** Fig, melon and peach flavours uncommon in the region; perhaps a reflection of vintage more than the region, but also hinting at a touch of oxidation. Screwcap. 13.5° alc. **Rating** 87 To 2015 $18

Mount Trio Vineyard ★★★★☆

2534 Porongurup Road, Mount Barker WA 6324 **Region** Porongurup
T (08) 9853 1136 **F** (08) 9853 1120 **www**.mounttriowines.com.au **Open** By appt
Winemaker Gavin Berry **Est.** 1989 **Cases** 7000
Mount Trio was established by Gavin Berry and Gill Graham shortly after they moved to the Mount Barker district in late 1988. They have slowly built up the Mount Trio business, based in part on estate plantings of 2 ha of pinot noir and 0.5 ha of chardonnay and in part on purchased grapes. An additional 6 ha was planted in the spring of 1999. Exports to the UK, Denmark and Singapore.

♀♀♀♀♀ **Gravel Pit Porongurup Riesling 2007** Arresting exotic fruit aromas, with a mix of tropical and lemon juice on the bouquet and palate; has excellent line and minerality on the finish. Screwcap. 11° alc. **Rating** 92 To 2018 $19.50
Great Southern Chardonnay 2007 Clean citrus fruits, with a splash of green apple at the core; a fresh and mineral edge to the fruit; fine, lightly wooded wine. Screwcap. 13° alc. **Rating** 90 To 2014 $16

♀♀♀♀ **Gravel Pit Porongurup Pinot Noir 2006** Light-bodied, but absolutely correct varietal character; flavours of cherry, strawberry and plum; not forced. Screwcap. 13° alc. **Rating** 89 To 2010 $19.95
Great Southern Cabernet Merlot 2006 Cedar prominent against the cassis on the bouquet; medium-bodied, with plenty of blackcurrant fruit; best drunk early. Screwcap. 13.5° alc. **Rating** 89 To 2012 $16
Great Southern Sauvignon Blanc 2007 Shows the faintest touch of reduction; tightly bound herb, gooseberry and mineral flavours; needs to loosen its bonds. Screwcap. 12.5° alc. **Rating** 88 To 2009 $15.95

Mount View Estate ★★★★

Mount View Road, Mount View, NSW 2325 **Region** Lower Hunter Valley
T (02) 4990 3307 **F** (02) 4991 1289 **www**.mtviewestate.com.au **Open** Sat, Mon, Tues 10–5, Wed, Thurs, Fri, Sun 10–4
Winemaker Janelle Zerk **Est.** 1971 **Cases** 4000
John and Polly Burgess became the owners of Mount View Estate in 2000, and in '04 purchased the adjoining Limestone Creek Vineyard; planted in '82, it fits seamlessly into the Mount View Estate production.

♀♀♀♀♀ **Reserve Semillon 2007** Pale straw; good concentration with lemon sherbet fruit and hints of minerals; perhaps a little soft for a young Hunter semillon. Screwcap. 13.6° alc. **Rating** 90 To 2020 $19

♀♀♀♀ **Special Reserve Liqueur Muscat NV** A dry style with plenty of rancio and good acid; savoury and nutty on the finish, quite long. Cork. 18.5° alc. **Rating** 89 To 2012 $25
Limestone Creek Vineyard Semillon Sauvignon Blanc 2006 Pale straw-green; strong aromas of dried straw as the semillon dominates; a rich palate, if a little short. Screwcap. 11.9° alc. **Rating** 88 To 2010 $25
Reserve Verdelho 2007 Good flavour with fresh acid, lemony fruit and nice texture. Screwcap. 14.4° alc. **Rating** 88 To 2011 $17

Mt Vincent Estate

1139 Leggetts Drive, Mount Vincent, NSW 2323 **Region** Lower Hunter Valley
T 1300 791 139 **F** (02) 4938 0048 **www**.1300shiraz.com **Open** By appt
Winemaker Monarch Winemaking Services **Est.** 1999 **Cases** 5000
If you drive from Sydney to the Hunter Valley by the most conventional and quickest route,
Mt Vincent Estate is the first vineyard you will come to, at the foot of Mt Vincent in the
Mulbring Valley. The 50-ha property includes a 2-ha lake stocked with fish and yabbies, a
5-bedroom accommodation retreat, and a sign that normally says closed. The range of wines
had extended from Orange to the Hunter Valley to Tasmania, the common factor contract
winemaking of the highest order.

♀♀♀♀ **Watagan Semillon Verdelho 2004** Faint reduction on the bouquet; the
palate has developed considerable toasty, honeyed richness. Screwcap. 12.5° alc.
Rating 88 **To** 2009 $18.75

Mount William Winery

Mount William Road, Tantaraboo, Vic 3764 **Region** Macedon Ranges
T (03) 5429 1595 **F** (03) 5429 1998 **www**.mtwilliamwinery.com.au **Open** 7 days 11–5
Winemaker Kilchurn Wines (David Cowburn) **Est.** 1987 **Cases** 3000
Adrienne and Murray Cousins established 7.5 ha of vineyards, planted to pinot noir, cabernet
franc, merlot and chardonnay, between 1987 and '99. The wines are sold through a stone cellar
door, and through a number of fine wine retailers around Melbourne. No samples received;
the rating is that of last year.

Mountadam

High Eden Road, Eden Valley, SA 5235 **Region** Eden Valley
T (08) 8564 1900 **F** (08) 8564 1999 **www**.mountadam.com.au **Open** By appt
Winemaker Con Moshos **Est.** 1972 **Cases** 30 000
Founded by the late David Wynn for the benefit of winemaker son Adam, Mountadam was
(somewhat surprisingly) purchased by Cape Mentelle (doubtless under the direction of Möet
Hennessy Wine Estates) in 2000. Rather less surprising has been its sale in '05 to Adelaide
businessman David Brown, who has extensive interests in the Padthaway region. The arrival
of Con Moshos (long-serving senior winemaker at Petaluma) has already made a significant
impact in lifting the quality of the wines. Exports to the UK, the US, Poland and Japan.

♀♀♀♀♀ **High Eden Estate Chardonnay 2006** An elegant wine; nectarine, melon
and grapefruit are all there; 100% mlf has not stripped the fruit flavour; quality oak
and good length; synergy from four clones. Screwcap. 13.5° alc. **Rating** 95
To 2014 $45

♀♀♀♀♀ **Eden Valley Pinot Gris 2007** Plenty of candied fruits and a touch of exotic
quince and spice on the palate; rich and not the least bit heavy; very well made.
Screwcap. 13.8° alc. **Rating** 90 **To** 2009 $25

♀♀♀♀ **Eden Valley Shiraz Viognier 2006** Lifted and fragrant, with a delicate touch
of spice; medium-bodied, with good acidity and line; slightly one-dimensional.
Screwcap. 13.8° alc. **Rating** 89 **To** 2012 $25

Eden Valley Unoaked Chardonnay 2006 The melon and stone fruit flavour
has considerable impact at 13°; however, not enough zest for higher points.
Screwcap. 13° alc. **Rating** 88 **To** 2011 $18

Barossa Chardonnay 2007 A well-made wine with generous peach fruits,
good toasty oak, and a fresh and vibrant finish, if a little simple. Screwcap. 13.5° alc.
Rating 88 **To** 2009 $18

Barossa Cabernet Merlot 2006 Clean, fresh, varietal and focused; lacks concentration, but the flavour is correct. Screwcap. 13.2° alc. **Rating** 87 **To** 2011 $20

Mountain X Wine Co ★★★★

6864 Great Alpine Road, Porepunkah, Vic 3740 (postal) **Region** Hunter Valley/Yarra Valley
T (02) 9492 4140 **F** (02) 9492 4199 **www**.mountainx.com.au **Open** Not
Winemaker Rhys Eather, Franco d'Anna (Contract) **Est.** 2006 **Cases** 150
Mountain X Wine Co is a modest and loose partnership between part-time wine writer
Gary Walsh and friend and full-time wine writer Campbell Mattinson. It is more or less
the direct outcome of Campbell's research for and writing of *The Wine Hunter*, the story of
Maurice O'Shea of Mt Pleasant. Says Campbell, 'It's no secret that during the research and
writing of the Maurice O'Shea story I came not only to love the man, the land he worked
on and his wines, but Hunter Valley reds fullstop.' Discussions over appropriate glasses of
wine with Gary Walsh made them wonder why shiraz pinot blends were so rarely made, and
the only rational conclusion was that they should have wines made for them to their own
specifications: the best possible grapes, large format French puncheons (only 25% new) and
a percentage of pinot, which could only be obtained outside the Hunter Valley. This in turn
has led to the idea of a Yarra Valley Shiraz Pinot Noir to join the 2006 and '07 Mountain X
Hunter Valley Shiraz Pinots ('08 lost in the ever-present rain of that vintage).

ΨΨΨΨΨ **Hunter Shiraz 2006** Deeply coloured; densely packed wine with dark fruits and
plenty of leather; a long, tannic and drying finish; needs time to fully integrate.
Diam. 13.5° alc. **Rating** 90 **To** 2016 $35

Mountford NR

Bamess Road, West Pemberton, WA 6260 **Region** Pemberton
T (08) 9776 1345 **F** (08) 9776 1345 **www**.mountfordwines.com.au **Open** 7 days 10–4
Winemaker Andrew Mountford, Saxon Mountford **Est.** 1987 **Cases** NA
English-born and trained Andrew Mountford and wife Sue migrated to Australia in 1983, and
were one of the early movers to select Pemberton for their vineyard. The cool climate and
spectacular forested countryside were important considerations in the move. Their strikingly
packaged wines are produced from 6 ha of permanently netted, dry-grown vineyards. Exports
to the UK.

Mr Riggs Wine Company ★★★★★

Main Road, McLaren Vale, SA 5171 **Region** McLaren Vale
T (08) 8556 4460 **F** (08) 8556 4462 **www**.mrriggs.com.au **Open** 7 days 10–5
Winemaker Ben Riggs **Est.** 2001 **Cases** 20 000
After 14 years as winemaker at Wirra Wirra, and another six at various Australian wineries
as well as numerous northern hemisphere vintages, Ben Riggs established his own business.
His major activity is as consultant winemaker to Penny's Hill, Pertaringa, Coriole, Geoff
Hardy and others, offering a 'grape-to-plate' service, plus keeping his hand in consulting
for Cazal Viel in the south of France. He also makes wine for his Mr Riggs label, initially
buying select parcels of grapes from old vines in McLaren Vale, but also using grapes from
his own vineyard at Piebald Gully, where he has planted shiraz, viognier and petit verdot.
Exports to the UK, the US and other major markets.

ΨΨΨΨΨ **McLaren Vale Shiraz 2006** Medium- to full-bodied, rich and mouthfilling;
lashings of blackberry and dark chocolate, the tannins ripe and the oak well-
integrated. Deserves better than a cork. 14.5° alc. **Rating** 95 **To** 2020 $55
Adelaide Shiraz Viognier 2006 Undeniably rich and opulent, but squarely
raises the question 'can there be too much of a good thing?' Crammed to the gills
with flavour and the texture is good; half an ox might be the best food match.
Screwcap. 14° alc. **Rating** 94 **To** 2026 $30
Yacca Paddock Adelaide Hills Tempranillo 2005 Bright colour; fragrant
red fruit aromas, and similar juicy red fruits on the long palate; fine tannin finish.
Screwcap. 15° alc. **Rating** 94 **To** 2013 $27

🍷🍷🍷🍷♀ **Watervale Riesling 2007** A more conventional wine than the VOR-GS; good citrus, mineral and apple aromas and flavours, firm, dry finish. Screwcap. 13° alc. **Rating** 92 **To** 2016 $24

The Gaffer McLaren Vale Shiraz 2006 A solid, sturdy wine, simultaneously proclaiming its regionality and varietal base on both bouquet and palate. Screwcap. 15° alc. **Rating** 92 **To** 2016 $25

Sticky End McLaren Vale Viognier 2006 Very good flavour, and in particular good texture and freshness on the finish; moderately sweet, not for the die-hard sugar fan. Screwcap. 12° alc. **Rating** 92 **To** 2014 $22

Adelaide Hills Riesling VOR-GS 2007 An interesting wine; some Germanic riesling sweetness throughout the palate, finish and aftertaste; in the style of Germany's Rheingau, not Mosel. Screwcap. 11.5° alc. **Rating** 91 **To** 2015 $24

Yacca Paddock Adelaide Hills Tempranillo 2006 Very aromatic, with some barrel ferment/charry notes; good flavour, crisp acidity and chewy tannins on the spicy finish. Screwcap. 15° alc. **Rating** 90 **To** 2012 $25

🍷🍷🍷🍷 **Sticky End McLaren Vale Viognier 2007** A good level of sweetness, with ripe and clean fleshy fruit; a hint of botrytis, but fresh acid keeps the finish clean. Screwcap. 12° alc. **Rating** 89 **To** 2010 $22

Adelaide Viognier 2007 Multiple winemaker inputs (barrel fermentation, partial mlf, ditto wild yeast, prolonged lees contact) overshadow the varietal fruit character and flavour; possibly may build in bottle. Screwcap. 13.5° alc. **Rating** 88 **To** 2010 $27

Mulyan ★★★★

North Logan Road, Cowra, NSW 2794 **Region** Cowra
T (02) 6342 1336 **F** (02) 6341 1015 **Open** W'ends & public hols 10–5, or by appt
Winemaker Contract **Est.** 1994 **Cases** 2000
Mulyan is a 1350-ha grazing property purchased by the Fagan family in 1886 from Dr William Redfern, a leading 19th-century figure in Australian history. The current-generation owners, Peter and Jenni Fagan, began planting in 1994, and intend the vineyard area to be 100 ha in all. Presently there are 29 ha of shiraz, 14.5 ha of chardonnay, and 4.6 ha each of merlot and viognier. The label features a statue of the Roman god Mercury, which has stood in the homestead garden since being brought back from Italy in 1912 by Peter Fagan's grandmother. Exports to the UK and China.

🍷🍷🍷🍷♀ **Block 7 Cowra Chardonnay 2006** No question, does have far more finesse and intensity than normal in Cowra, the stone fruit and oak perfectly balanced, the acidity on the finish likewise. Screwcap. 13.6° alc. **Rating** 93 **To** 2013 $25

Cowra Chardonnay 2006 Elegant and well-balanced, above the normal standard, but not the same intensity as Block 7; both wines hark back to the glory days of Cowra in the early '80s. Screwcap. 13.6° alc. **Rating** 90 **To** 2012 $20

🍷🍷🍷🍷 **Cowra Viognier 2006** The vintage was very kind to Mulyan; here peach and apricot provide a supple palate, aided by barrel ferment in older oak. Another surprise. Screwcap. 14.2° alc. **Rating** 89 **To** 2010 $20

Munari Wines

Ladys Creek Vineyard, 1129 Northern Highway, Heathcote, Vic 3523 **Region** Heathcote
T (03) 5433 3366 **F** (03) 5433 3905 **www**.munariwines.com **Open** Tues–Sun 11–5
Winemaker Adrian Munari, Deborah Munari **Est.** 1993 **Cases** 2500
Adrian and Deborah Munari made a singularly impressive entry into the winemaking scene, with both their initial vintages winning an impressive array of show medals, and have carried on in similar vein since then. With a little under 8 ha of estate vines, production is limited, but the wines are well worth seeking out. Exports to France and Switzerland.

★★★★★ **Ladys Pass Heathcote Shiraz 2005** Full-bodied, with real concentration of dark fruits and plenty of oak; very fresh on the palate, with good persistence, and a lightness to the finish that is quite appealing. Cork. 14° alc. **Rating** 94 **To** 2015 $45
Heathcote Late Harvest Viognier Marsanne 2005 Interesting wine, with dried straw character, a la Rhône Valley; nice level of sweetness, and a little phenolic twist for freshness on the finish. Screwcap. 12.5° alc. **Rating** 94 **To** 2012 $25

★★★★★ **The Ridge Shiraz 2005** Big, rich and ripe style with more dark fruits and a little spice; the concentration is there, but is less complex; good flavour. Screwcap. **Rating** 90 **To** 2014 $25

★★★★ **India Red Heathcote Cabernet Sauvignon 2005** An uncompromisingly full-bodied wine, with abundant fruit, alcohol, oak and tannins; needs time. Cork. **Rating** 89 **To** 2014 $35
Malbec Shiraz 2005 Very concentrated, but with curious bonox/cold tea edge to the bouquet; the palate is more lively and fresh, and the oak is less obvious. Screwcap. **Rating** 89 **To** 2014 $30

Mundoonen

1457 Yass River Road, Yass, NSW 2582 **Region** Canberra District
T (02) 6227 1353 **F** (02) 6227 1453 **www**.mundoonen.com.au **Open** W'ends & public hols 11–5 or by appt
Winemaker Terry O'Donnell **Est.** 2003 **Cases** 700
Jenny and Terry O'Donnell released their first wines in 2003. The winery is situated beside the Yass River, behind one of the oldest settlers' cottages in the Yass River Valley, dating back to 1858. Estate plantings of shiraz and viognier are supplemented by contract-grown riesling, sauvignon blanc and cabernet sauvignon. The barrel shed has been created by refurbishing and insulating a 140-year-old building on the property. No wines were produced in 2007 due to frost.

Murchison Wines

105 Old Weir Road, Murchison, Vic 3610 **Region** Goulburn Valley
T (03) 5826 2294 **F** (03) 5826 2510 **www**.murchisonwines.com.au **Open** Fri–Mon & most public hols 10–5, or by appt
Winemaker Guido Vazzoler **Est.** 1975 **Cases** 4000
Sandra (ex kindergarten teacher turned cheesemaker) and Guido Vazzoler (ex Brown Brothers) acquired the long-established Longleat Estate vineyard in 2003 (renaming it Murchison Wines), having lived on the property (as tenants) for some years. The mature vineyard comprises 2.8 ha shiraz, 1.8 ha cabernet sauvignon, 0.6 ha each of semillon, sauvignon blanc and chardonnay, and 0.2 ha petit verdot. No samples received; the rating is that of last year. Exports to Hong Kong.

Murdoch Hill

Mappinga Road, Woodside, SA 5244 **Region** Adelaide Hills
T (08) 8389 7081 **F** (08) 8389 7991 **www**.murdochhill.com.au **Open** By appt
Winemaker Brian Light (Contract), Michael Downer **Est.** 1998 **Cases** 2600
A little over 21 ha of vines were established on the undulating, gum-studded countryside of Charlie and Julie Downer's 60-year-old Erinka property, 4 km east of Oakbank. In descending order of importance, the varieties established are sauvignon blanc, shiraz, cabernet sauvignon and chardonnay. Ten years on, son Michael Downer, with a recently gained Bachelor of Oenology degree from Adelaide University, joined Brian Light as assistant winemaker.

★★★★★ **Adelaide Hills Shiraz 2006** Crimson-red; very lively, with a juicy spicy array of red and black fruits on the medium-bodied palate; good focus, line and exceptional length. Ticks all the boxes; super value. Screwcap. 14° alc. **Rating** 94 **To** 2016 $19

ŸŸŸŸŸ **Adelaide Hills Sauvignon Blanc 2007** Feisty asparagus, herb, citrus and mineral flavours run through the palate, which has good length and intensity. Screwcap. 13° alc. **Rating** 91 **To** 2009 $19

Adelaide Hills Cabernet Sauvignon 2004 Has cool-grown characters, but not too green; structure and mouthfeel are good, with nice tension between cassis blackcurrant fruit and fine tannins. Screwcap. 13.5° alc. **Rating** 90 **To** 2014 $18

Murdock   ★★★★★

Riddoch Highway, Coonawarra, SA 5263 **Region** Coonawarra
T (08) 8737 3700 **F** (08) 8737 2107 **www**.murdockwines.com **Open** By appt
Winemaker Balnaves **Est.** 1998 **Cases** 4000
The Murdock family has established 10.4 ha of cabernet sauvignon, 2 ha of shiraz, 1 ha of merlot, and 0.5 ha each of chardonnay and riesling, and produces small quantities of an outstanding Cabernet Sauvignon, contract-made by Pete Bissell. A second vineyard has been added in the Barossa Valley, with 5.8 ha of shiraz and 2.1 ha each of semillon and cabernet sauvignon. The labels, incidentally, are ultra-minimalist; there's no flood of propaganda here. The Barossa Valley cellar door is now open 7 days 10–5 (Magnolia Road, Vine Vale). Exports to the US, Canada and Asia.

ŸŸŸŸŸ **The Editorial 2004** This is a really interesting exercise in hand-making, rearing and hand-packaging 980 bottles of an exceptionally intense and long wine, with cassis, blackcurrant and blackberry in a silky cocoon of finely tempered tannins and oak; a vinous Matthew Hayden. Cork. 15° alc. **Rating** 95 **To** 2015 $140

Barossa Shiraz 2005 Medium- to full-bodied; has very good structure and texture to its blackberry and plum fruit, both tannins and oak adding to the mouthfeel and length; not alcohol dependent. ProCork. 14.5° alc. **Rating** 94 **To** 2025 $40

Coonawarra Cabernet Sauvignon 2003 Has very pure cabernet fruit on both bouquet and palate, speaking of both variety and terroir; cedary/earthy/dusty notes seamlessly interwoven with black fruits and oak. Cork. 14° alc. **Rating** 94 **To** 2018 $42

ŸŸŸŸŸ **The Merger 2005** Has a supple and seductive array of red and black fruits on the medium-bodied palate; tannins and oak in a support role. Coonawarra Cabernet/Barossa Shiraz. Screwcap. 15° alc. **Rating** 92 **To** 2015 $18.50

ŸŸŸŸ **Dos Trios 2006** Complex; its spicy savoury make-up causing it to look more mature than its vintage suggests; perhaps just a touch of sunny Spain. Grenache/Tempranillo/Shiraz. Screwcap. 15° alc. **Rating** 89 **To** 2010 $20

Coonawarra Merlot 2005 A powerful, potent wine with lots of structure, and good ageing potential; is in the wannabe cabernet class. **Rating** 88 **To** 2015 $23

Murdup Wines

Southern Ports Highway, Mount Benson, SA 5275 **Region** Mount Benson
T (08) 8768 6190 **F** (08) 8768 6190 **www**.murdupwines.com.au **Open** 7 days 10–4 (Spring–Autumn)
Winemaker Neil Doddridge **Est.** 1996 **Cases** 2000
Andy and Melinda Murdock purchased Murdup in 1996, retaining the name of the property which was first settled for grazing in the 1860s. They began by planting 10.5 ha of vineyard, the lion's share going to cabernet sauvignon and shiraz, with smaller patches of chardonnay and sauvignon blanc, most of the wine going to the UK. Ten years later they dramatically upped the ante by purchasing the Mildara Black Wattle Vineyard across the road, lifting their vineyards to 65 ha. The also commenced reworking portions of the newly acquired vineyard, removing 6 ha of poorly performing shiraz, replacing it with equal quantities of sauvignon blanc and pinot gris. They have also substantially upped their wine marketing, and introduced a second label, Soaring Kite. Exports to the UK.

ΥΥΥΥ   **Sauvignon Blanc 2007** A clean, firm, minerally/grassy style, in sharp contrast to many from the vintage. **Rating** 87 **To** 2009 $17

Murphy Wines ★★★★☆

PO Box 1418, Nagambie, Vic 3608 **Region** Strathbogie Ranges
T 0438 557 801 **F** (03) 5796 2719 **www**.murphywines.com **Open** Not
Winemaker Arran Murphy **Est.** 2004 **Cases** 200

The story of Arran Murphy has a fairy tale ring to it. He began as an unqualified cellarhand at Tahbilk in 2000, and in '03 was offered the opportunity of a traineeship at Plunkett Wines. He began studying wine production, and in '04 received a scholarship under the umbrella of Taste of Victoria, which enabled him to do a harvest in the Sonoma Valley. He found this to be a great experience, and also opened his eyes to the potential of export markets. Since 2000 he had been making small batches of wine collecting grapes from the end of rows picked by mechanical harvesters (the end posts always prevent collection of the fruit from the last vine or so), using chicken wire as a destemmer, and using a three-generation-old basket press. In '04 he decided to purchase a few tonnes of grapes and make his first commercial wine, which he has done every year since. With next to no capital, he was unable to afford any new oak, so experimented with inner staves, chips and oak cubes (all in fact widely used throughout the industry). This resulted in three batches of wine in '04, which he called Hazel Shiraz, honouring his late grandmother Hazel Murphy who had constantly encouraged him to strive to better himself and aim high. With some trepidation he entered the 2004 Hazel Shiraz in the '07 Strathbogie Ranges Wine Show (of which I was Chairman), at which point he takes up (and ends) the story, 'when I received a gold medal I couldn't believe it!'

ΥΥΥΥΥ   **Hazel Shiraz 2004** Full-bodied, with rich blackberry and plum fruit doing the talking, rather than oak and/or tannins; stained cork a worry for the long-term cellaring the wine deserves. **Rating** 93 **To** 2014 $50

Murray Street Vineyard ★★★★★

Lot 723, Murray Street, Greenock, SA 5360 **Region** Barossa Valley
T (08) 8562 8373 **F** (08) 8562 8414 **Open** 7 days 10–4.30
Winemaker Andrew Seppelt **Est.** 2001 **Cases** 10 000

Andrew Seppelt has moved with a degree of caution in setting up Murray Street Vineyard, possibly because of inherited wisdom and the business acumen of partner Bill Jahnke, a successful investment banker with Wells Fargo. Andrew is a direct descendant of Benno and Sophia Seppelt, who built Seppeltsfield and set the family company bearing their name on its path to fame. The partnership has 46 ha of vineyards, one block at Gomersal, the other at Greenock, with the lion's share going to shiraz, followed by grenache, mourvedre, viognier, marsanne, semillon and zinfandel. Most of the grapes are sold, with a small (but hopefully increasing) amount retained for the Murray Street Vineyard brand. The Benno (shiraz mataro) is the icon tribute on the masculine side; the Sophia (shiraz) the feminine icon. Unusually good point of sale/propaganda material. Exports to the UK, the US, Canada and Denmark.

ΥΥΥΥΥ   **Sophia 2005** Bright purple; a densely proportioned shiraz, which, nonetheless, shows real finesse and a bright personality thanks to the lifted red fruits giving it a suppleness that belies the weight; excellent flavour on the finish, and very long. Cork. 14° alc. **Rating** 95 **To** 2020 $75

Greenock 2006 A big-boned shiraz, but with a dark mineral streak to the fruit; savoury and chewy and a little lighter on the finish, which lingers for a very long time, and the oak sits in the background; should go the distance. Screwcap. 15° alc. **Rating** 95 **To** 2030 $50

Benno 2005 Great colour; lots of very good oak frames lashings of dark fruits, mocha and cassis; very long, fine, focused and particularly generous finish. Cork. 15° alc. **Rating** 94 **To** 2020 $75

ΥΥΥΥΥ   **Gomersal 2006** A bruising shiraz with extravagant levels of fruit and oak; massively proportioned, deeply tannic, highly alcoholic and completely hedonistic; not for the faint of heart. Screwcap. 15.5° alc. **Rating** 93 **To** 2025 $50

The Barossa 2006 Complex fragrant aromas point to the blend (Shiraz/ Grenache/Mataro/Cinsault), medium-bodied, but with good structure to carry the multiplicity of flavours, spice and herb framing a solid core of black and red fruits. Screwcap. 15° alc. **Rating** 93 **To** 2020 $30

Barossa Valley Shiraz 2006 Big, bold and succulent Barossa shiraz, with blackberry, dark chocolate and mocha filling the mouth, aided by ripe tannins and oak. Will improve. Screwcap. 15° alc. **Rating** 92 **To** 2016 $30

ƱƱƱƱ   **Shiraz Zinfandel 2005** Super-ripe and super-rich; almost fortified in style, but plenty of flavour in this wine; a brute! Screwcap. 15° alc. **Rating** 89 **To** 2009 $40

Barossa Valley Viognier Marsanne 2007 Good fruit definition, and a good example of exotic fruit character; rich, full and clean, it should be enjoyed in its youth. Screwcap. 14° alc. **Rating** 88 **To** 2009 $25

Murrindindi Vineyards

30 Cummins Lane, Murrindindi, Vic 3717 **Region** Upper Goulburn
T (03) 5797 8448 **F** (03) 5797 8448 **www**.murrindindivineyards.com
Open At Marmalades Café, Yea
Winemaker Alan Cuthbertson **Est.** 1979 **Cases** 5000

Situated in an unequivocally cool climate, which means that special care has to be taken with the viticulture to produce ripe fruit flavours. In more recent vintages, Murrindindi has by and large succeeded in so doing.

ƱƱƱƱ   **Don't Tell Dad Shiraz 2006** Light- to medium-bodied; a mix of spice and sweet red and black fruits; good length, but will develop quickly. Screwcap. **Rating** 89 **To** 2012 $18

Chardonnay 2006 Smoky/charry oak elements evident in both bouquet and palate, intensifying the green notes of the fruit; nonetheless has good length. Screwcap. **Rating** 88 **To** 2012 $17

Family Reserve Cabernet 2005 Bright, clear colour; has a mix of cassis and mint in a light- to medium-bodied frame, earthy tannins underneath. Screwcap. **Rating** 88 **To** 2014 $38

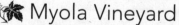 Myalup Wines

NR

Pead Road, Myalup, WA 6220 **Region** Geographe
T (08) 9797 1764 **F** (08) 9797 1764 **www**.myalupvines.com **Open** Fri–Mon 10–4.30
Winemaker Trevor Hutchinson **Est.** 1994 **Cases** NA

What started as a weekend hobby for Trevor and Carmel Hutchinson has grown into a winery, cellar door, picnic and barbecue facilities, and function centre for summer concerts and events. They have 2.5 ha of shiraz, chardonnay and chenin blanc, which they tend by hand from pruning, to shoot and leaf thinning, netting and ultimately picking. Most of the wines are unwooded, including one of two Shirazs.

Myola Vineyard

137 Griffins Road, Coghills Creek, Vic 3364 (postal) **Region** Ballarat
T (03) 5343 4368 **F** (03) 5343 4369 **Open** Not
Winemaker Eastern Peake (Norman Latta) **Est.** 1996 **Cases** 72

Cheryl Hines and Anthony Fergusson purchased Conihfer Park in 2003. It is part agistment farm and part vineyard, with 1.5 ha of pinot noir and 1 ha of chardonnay planted in 1996. The vines were in full bearing, and the grapes were sold to other wineries in the region. One tonne of pinot was retained and vinified for Myola Vineyard in 2005, followed by another small make in '07. The partners hope to eventually make some pinot each year, with chardonnay part of the mix. Finally, they have made a sparkling wine for their daughter's wedding, and intend to follow this up with limited releases in the years to come.

ŢŢŢŢ♀ **Pinot Noir 2005** Good colour and hue; plum and cherry fruit with spicy nuances; silky smooth, with just a touch of mint/green on the finish. Screwcap. 13° alc. **Rating** 90 **To** 2012 $20

ŢŢŢŢ **Sparkling Pinot Noir Blanc NV** Pale salmon-pink; not much intensity to the strawberry-accented fruit, but has good balance. Cork. 12.5° alc. **Rating** 87 **To** 2009 $20

Myrtaceae

53 Main Creek Road, Main Ridge, Vic 3928 **Region** Mornington Peninsula
T (03) 5989 2045 **F** (03) 5989 2845 **Open** 1st w'end of month, public hols & Jan w'ends
Winemaker Julie Trueman **Est.** 1985 **Cases** 250
The development of the Myrtaceae vineyard began with the planting of 0.7 ha of cabernet sauvignon, cabernet franc and merlot intended for a Bordeaux-style red blend. It became evident that these late-ripening varieties were not well suited to the site, so the vineyard was converted to 0.5 ha each of pinot noir and chardonnay. John Trueman (viticulturist) and Julie Trueman (winemaker) are the proprietors. Part of the property is devoted to the Land for Wildlife Scheme.

Myrtle Vale Vineyard

7626 Maroondah Highway, Kanumbra, Vic 3719 **Region** Upper Goulburn
T (03) 5773 4310 **F** (03) 5773 4312 **Open** By appt
Winemaker Peter Beckingham (Contract) **Est.** 1990 **Cases** 300
Robyn Dickens and Leigh Coleman have established Myrtle Vale Vineyard on a property between Yea and Mansfield at 330 m. The name comes from a sheep station selected in the mid-1800s, of which the vineyard now forms a small part. Cabernet sauvignon (2 ha), chardonnay (1 ha) and a tiny patch of viognier are used to make the wines, while surplus grape production is sold.

ŢŢŢŢ **Cabernet Sauvignon 2005** Light- to medium-bodied; clear-cut cassis varietal fruit; not over-extracted or over-oaked. Cork. 14.4° alc. **Rating** 88 **To** 2012 $19.50

Naked Range Wines

125 Rifle Range Road, Smiths Gully, Vic 3760 **Region** Yarra Valley
T (03) 9710 1575 **F** (03) 9710 1655 **www**.nakedrangewines.com **Open** By appt
Winemaker Simon Wightwick (Contract) **Est.** 1996 **Cases** 2500
Mike Jansz has established 6.2 ha of vineyard on a steep and rocky site, one-third sauvignon blanc, a small patch of pinot noir and the remainder cabernet sauvignon (predominant), merlot and chardonnay. The wines are made at Punt Road and marketed under the striking Naked Range label, with a second label, Duet, using grapes from other Victorian regions and exported to Asia.

Nalbra Estate Wines

225 Whitcombes Road, Drysdale, Vic 3222 **Region** Geelong
T (03) 5253 2654 **F** (03) 5253 2414 **Open** By appt
Winemaker Dick Simonsen, Ray Nadeson, Maree Collis (Contract) **Est.** 2001 **Cases** NA
Terri and Leigh Robinson began the establishment of their vineyard, perched on Mt Bellarine overlooking Port Phillip Bay, in 2001. Shiraz and pinot gris were planted in that year, followed by sauvignon blanc and viognier in '03. In all, there are 2.8 ha under vine, and the Robinsons are progressively moving from being grapegrowers to wine producers.

Nangwarry Station

PO Box 1, Nangwarry, SA 5277 **Region** Mount Gambier
T (08) 8739 7274 **F** (08) 8739 7009 **www**.nangwarrystation.com.au **Open** Not
Winemaker Peter Douglas **Est.** 1999 **Cases** 2000

Nangwarry Station was purchased by Ian McLachlan in 1964, variously a former high profile President of the National Farmers Federation and Federal Minister of Defence. The property is now managed by Ian's son Dugald and wife Sophie, ardent supporters of the family's philosophy of long-term sustainability. One example is the wetlands and conservation areas which have created natural habitats for over 100 species of birds. In what is a large business, the establishment of 9 ha of vineyard (4 ha of cabernet sauvignon, 3 ha of pinot noir and 1 ha each of chardonnay and sauvignon blanc) is a small diversification, but it has been a very successful one. The immensely experienced (and equally likeable) Peter Douglas, for many years a winemaker in Coonawarra, has produced some lovely wines, which hold promise for the future as the vines mature.

🍷🍷🍷🍷 **Mount Gambier Sauvignon Blanc 2006** Some gentle, tropical fruit, holding nicely onto life without any compost characters. **Rating** 87 **To** 2009 $15
Cabernet Sauvignon 2005 Light- to medium-bodied; not surprisingly, some slightly stemmy notes; this is a very cool region for cabernet sauvignon. Thanks to the '05 vintage, enough sweet fruit to give the wine mouth appeal. An investment in climate change, perhaps. Screwcap. 13° alc. **Rating** 87 **To** 2011 $22

Nardone Baker Wines ★★★☆

PO Box 386, McLaren Vale, SA 5171 **Region** McLaren Vale
T (08) 8445 8100 **F** (08) 8445 8200 **www**.nardonebaker.com **Open** Not
Winemaker Brian Light (Contract) **Est.** 1999 **Cases** 23 000
Italian-born Joe Nardone and English-born John Baker were brought together by the marriage of Joe's daughter and John's son. Both were already in the wine industry, John studying at Roseworthy Agricultural College and establishing a vineyard. The second generation of Frank Nardone and Patrick Baker, the latter having also studied at Roseworthy, now run what is a significant virtual winery, sourcing grapes from all over SA, with contract winemaking by Brian Light at the Boar's Rock winemaking facility. There are five ranges, headed by The Wara Manta Reserve, followed by the Nardone Baker, Blaxland's Legacy, Treeview Selection and Wara Manta (non-reserve). Exports to various markets including the UK and the US.

🍷🍷🍷🍷🍷 **The Wara Manta Reserve McLaren Vale Shiraz 2002** Fully developed with plenty of dark fruit, moving towards savoury, leather and game; quite fine and lively, despite development. Cork. 14.5° alc. **Rating** 91 **To** 2014 $78

🍷🍷🍷🍷 **Sparkling Shiraz NV** A nice balance of shiraz fruit with sugar; finish is quite dry and savoury. Cork. 13.5° alc. **Rating** 87 **To** 2009 $17.95

Narkoojee ★★★★☆

170 Francis Road, Glengarry, Vic 3854 **Region** Gippsland
T (03) 5192 4257 **F** (03) 5192 4257 **www**.narkoojee.com **Open** 7 days 10.30–4.30
Winemaker Harry Friend, Axel Friend **Est.** 1981 **Cases** 3000
Narkoojee Vineyard (originally a dairy farm owned by the Friend family) is within easy reach of the old gold mining town of Walhalla and looks out over the Strzelecki Ranges. The wines are produced from a little over 10 ha of estate vineyards, with chardonnay accounting for half the total. Former lecturer in civil engineering and extremely successful winemaker Harry Friend changed horses in 1994 to take control of the family vineyard and winery, and hasn't missed a beat since; his skills show through with all the wines, none more so than the Chardonnay. Exports to Canada, Ireland, Maldives, Japan, Hong Kong and Singapore.

🍷🍷🍷🍷🍷 **Gippsland Pinot Noir 2006** Deep colour; powerful and solidly built, with clear varietal character in a dark berry/plum/spice spectrum; cries out for another year or two in bottle. Diam. 14.5° alc. **Rating** 93 **To** 2015 $24
Isaac Gippsland Shiraz 2006 Quite European in style, with red fruits, Asian spices and fine acidity; plenty of fine-grained tannins, and savoury roasted meat flavours across the finish. Cork. 14° alc. **Rating** 93 **To** 2016 $28

Reserve Gippsland Chardonnay 2006 More complex and lively than the Lily Grace, with a savoury twist, a little grip and rich toasty oak on the finish. Diam. **Rating** 92 **To** 2013 $32

Gippsland Cabernet Sauvignon 2005 Vibrant purple hue; slightly waxy, essency cassis fruit aromas; fine acid and tannin on the palate lead to a long and harmonious finish. Cork. 14.5° alc. **Rating** 92 **To** 2016 $28

Reserve Gippsland Chardonnay 2005 Bright colour; good peach, nectarine and melon fruit on both bouquet and palate; a slightly hard finish is the Achilles Heel of an otherwise very good wine. Diam. **Rating** 90 **To** 2011 $32

Lily Grace Gippsland Chardonnay 2006 A fresh yet soft wine, with good concentration, roasted cashew and lemon curd, and lively acid on the soft, yet long, finish. Diam. 13.5° alc. **Rating** 90 **To** 2011 $20

Nashwauk

PO Box 852, Nuriootpa, SA 5355 **Region** McLaren Vale
T (08) 8562 4488 **F** (08) 8562 4499 **www.**nashwaukvineyards.com.au **Open** Not
Winemaker Reid Bosward, Stephen Dew **Est.** 2005 **Cases** 5000
This is an estate-based venture, with 18 ha of shiraz and 1 ha each of cabernet and tempranillo, all except the tempranillo between 12 and 40 years old. It is a stand-alone business of the Kaesler family, and the first time it has extended beyond the Barossa Valley. The striking label comes from satellite photos of the vineyard, showing the contour planting; the name Nashwauk comes from Canada's Algonquin indigenous language meaning 'land between'. The property is situated in the (unofficial) Seaview subregion, with Kays, Chapel Hill and Coriole as its neighbours, which all benefit from sea breezes and cooler nights.

McLaren Vale Shiraz 2006 Densely coloured; rich, concentrated black fruits and bitter chocolate provide abundant flavour; somewhat hot finish ex the alcohol. Cork. 15.5° alc. **Rating** 91 **To** 2016 $25

Wrecked McLaren Vale Shiraz 2006 Higher alcohol and pH than the varietal; powerful with dense black fruit and regional dark chocolate, but the higher alcohol tends to slightly thin out the fruit line. Cork. 16° alc. **Rating** 90 **To** 2016 $70

McLaren Vale Cabernet Sauvignon 2006 Good varietal fruit subverted by high alcohol, this even less suited to cabernet sauvignon than shiraz. Nonetheless, will appeal greatly to some. Cork. 16° alc. **Rating** 88 **To** 2016 $25

McLaren Vale Tempranillo 2006 A very consistent house/maker imprint and philosophy; however, in my view, too ripe for varietal expression. Cork. 15.5° alc. **Rating** 87 **To** 2010 $25

Nazaaray

266 Meakins Road, Flinders, Vic 3929 **Region** Mornington Peninsula
T (03) 5989 0126 **F** (03) 5989 0495 **www.**nazaaray.com.au **Open** 1st weekend of each month, or by appt
Winemaker Paramdeep Ghumman **Est.** 1996 **Cases** 900
Paramdeep Ghumman is, as far as I am aware, the only Indian-born winery proprietor and winemaker in Australia. He and his wife migrated from India over 20 years ago, and purchased the Nazaaray vineyard property in 1991. An initial trial planting of 400 vines in 1996 was gradually expanded to the present level of 1.6 ha of pinot noir, 0.4 ha of pinot gris and 0.15 ha of chardonnay. Notwithstanding the micro size of the estate, all the wines are made and bottled onsite. Exports to Singapore.

Mornington Peninsula Pinot Gris 2007 A lovely example of pinot gris with flavour; candied fruits, and hints of citrus with very good focus and vibrant acidity on the finish; very long. Screwcap. 14.5° alc. **Rating** 93 **To** 2009 $25

Mornington Peninsula Shiraz 2007 Abounds with satsuma plum and blackberry fruit on the medium- to full-bodied but supple and smooth palate; oak and tannins in balance; well-priced. Screwcap. 14.2° alc. **Rating** 93 **To** 2020 $25

ŸŸŸŸ   **Mornington Peninsula Sauvignon Blanc 2007** A powerful wine with a long and intense palate; its Achilles Heel is a somewhat reduced/sweaty bouquet, to which I am very sensitive. Screwcap. 13.2° alc. **Rating** 88 **To** 2010 $25

Neagles Rock Vineyards   ★★★★★

Lot 1 & 2, Main North Road, Clare, SA 5453 **Region** Clare Valley
T (08) 8843 4020 **F** (08) 8843 4021 www.neaglesrock.com **Open** Mon–Sat 10–5, Sun 11–4
Winemaker Steve Wiblin, John Trotter & Ang Meany (Consultant) **Est.** 1997 **Cases** 11 000
Owner-partners Jane Willson and Steve Wiblin have taken the plunge in a major way, simultaneously raising a young family, resuscitating two old vineyards, and – for good measure – stripping a dilapidated house to the barest of bones and turning it into a first-rate, airy restaurant–cum–cellar door. They bring decades of industry experience, gained at all levels of the wine industry, to Neagles Rock, and built upon this by the 2003 acquisition of the outstanding and mature vineyards of Duncan Estate, adding another level of quality to their wines, which now draw on a total of 19 ha. Exports to the UK, the US and other major markets.

ŸŸŸŸŸ **Misery Clare Valley Grenache Shiraz 2006** Much more tension and focus than most Clare Valley grenache/shiraz blends; attractive red fruits, and a long finish with particularly good acidity holding the palate together. Screwcap. 14.5° alc. **Rating** 94 **To** 2010 $20
       Clare Valley Cabernet Sauvignon 2005 Medium- to full-bodied; a strongly built cabernet sauvignon with blackcurrant and blackberry fruit; the tannins appropriately powerful, providing both length and balance. Screwcap. 14.5° alc. **Rating** 94 **To** 2020 $25

ŸŸŸŸŸ **One Black Dog Reserve Clare Valley Cabernet Shiraz 2005** An attractive array of blackberry, blackcurrant and black cherry; fine tannin structure and generous oak round the dog off. ProCork. **Rating** 92 **To** 2020 $60
       Clare Valley Riesling 2007 A dry minerally classic Clare riesling; lime juice, talc and florals and prominent acidity; quite long. Screwcap. 12.5° alc. **Rating** 90 **To** 2014 $19

ŸŸŸŸ   **Clare Valley Semillon Sauvignon Blanc 2007** Plenty of honest, if somewhat four-square, flavour augmented by partial barrel fermentation of the semillon component. Screwcap. 13° alc. **Rating** 89 **To** 2009 $19

Ned's Vineyard   ★★★★

RMB 1404, Ararat, Vic 3377 (postal) **Region** Pyrenees
T (03) 5356 9337 **F** (03) 5356 9337 www.nedsvineyard.com.au **Open** Not
Winemaker Mount Langi Ghiran Vineyards **Est.** 1995 **Cases** 250
In 1994 Michael (Mick) Hobson purchased his property situated in the foothills of the Pyrenees on the southern boundary of the region. Planting of shiraz (4 ha) began the following year with advice from Southcorp viticulturists Kym Ludvigsen and Stuart McNab. The first few years' production was sold to Southcorp, and since 2002 to Mount Langi Ghiran. Most of the grapes are still sold, but the ultimate aim is to use all of the grapes for the Ned's Vineyard label.

ŸŸŸŸŸ **Pyrenees Shiraz 2006** Light- to medium-bodied; vibrant plum, cherry and spice fruit with superfine tannins and a nice touch of oak. An elegant Pyrenees Shiraz, not common. Screwcap. 14° alc. **Rating** 92 **To** 2016 $31.60

Neilson Estate Wines   ★★★☆

63 Logue Road, Millendon, WA 6056 **Region** Swan Valley
T (08) 9296 4849 **F** (08) 9296 4849 www.neilsonestate.com.au **Open** By appt
Winemaker John Griffiths, Jim Neilson **Est.** 1998 **Cases** 275

Jim and Jenny Neilson planted their 2-ha vineyard of shiraz and merlot in 1998. Jim has completed two years of the 3-year viticulture and oenology degree course at Curtin University, but handed the winemaking reins to John Griffiths at Faber Wines for the 2006 vintage, an arrangement that will continue into the future. The aim is to produce the highest possible quality Swan Valley wines using regulated deficit irrigation and concentration techniques in the winemaking.

ŸŸŸŸŸ **Titan's Trail Verdelho 2007** Trophy at the Swan Valley Wine Show '07, the traditional heartland of WA verdelho; quite buttery and nutty; despite the screwcap, best now. Screwcap. 13.5° alc. **Rating** 90 **To** 2009 $18

ŸŸŸŸ **Titan's Trail Swan Valley Shiraz 2007** Good colour; robust, full-bodied, traditional Swan Valley style; blackberry fruit with plenty of structure without excessive tannins. Diam. 14° alc. **Rating** 88 **To** 2017 $18

Nelwood Wines

PO Box 196, Paringa, SA 5340 **Region** Riverland
T (08) 8595 8042 **F** (08) 8595 8182 **www**.nelwood.com **Open** By appt
Winemaker Boar's Rock (Mike Farmilo) **Est.** 2002 **Cases** 5000
The wines (released under the Red Mud label) come from 45-ha plantings of shiraz, chardonnay, petit verdot and cabernet sauvignon near Nelwood, 32 km east of Renmark near the South Australian border. The grapegrowers who are shareholders in the company have been growing grapes for up to three generations in the Riverland. Exports to the US.

Nepenthe

Jones Road, Balhannah, SA 5242 **Region** Adelaide Hills
T (08) 8398 8888 **F** (08) 8388 1100 **www**.nepenthe.com.au **Open** 7 days 10–4
Winemaker Michael Fogarty, Andre Bandar **Est.** 1994 **Cases** 100 000
The Tweddell family has established a little over 110 ha of close-planted vineyards in the Adelaide Hills since 1994, with an exotic array of varieties. In late 1996 it obtained the second licence to build a winery in the Adelaide Hills (Petaluma was the only prior successful applicant, back in '78). Nepenthe quickly established its reputation as a substantial producer of high-quality wines. Founder Ed Tweddell died unexpectedly in 2006; in March '07 son James announced that McGuigan Simeon had purchased the winery, and caused many industry observers to scratch their heads. Exports to all major markets.

ŸŸŸŸŸ **Ithaca Adelaide Hills Chardonnay 2004** Developing slowly but surely; a full array of fruit, oak and malolactic characters are seamlessly welded leading through to a long, clean finish. Screwcap. 13.5° alc. **Rating** 94 **To** 2013 $40

ŸŸŸŸŸ **The Good Doctor Adelaide Hills Pinot Noir 2005** Has abundant dark plum fruit in a smooth framework, gaining velocity on the back-palate, finish and aftertaste in classic pinot mould. Screwcap. 14° alc. **Rating** 93 **To** 2012 $40
Adelaide Hills Pinot Gris 2007 Crisp fresh pear and apple aromas and flavours; good line and length, and a bright finish. Screwcap. 14° alc. **Rating** 90 **To** 2010 $23
The Good Doctor Adelaide Hills Pinot Noir 2004 A distinctly foresty/ spicy/savoury style; shows development in both colour and flavour and best drunk sooner than later. Screwcap. 14° alc. **Rating** 90 **To** 2009 $40
The Fugue 2003 Medium-bodied, classic briary/cedar/cigar box characters over a blackcurrant base; good balance, fine tannins and a long finish. Cabernet Sauvignon/Malbec/Merlot/Franc. Screwcap. 14.5° alc. **Rating** 90 **To** 2013 $30
The Fugue 2004 Impressive medium-bodied Bordeaux style, with a briary savoury herbal twist to the base of blackcurrant and redcurrant fruit; good length. Cabernet Sauvignon/Merlot/Malbec. Screwcap. 14° alc. **Rating** 90 **To** 2015 $30
Adelaide Hills Zinfandel 2005 Has strong affinities with warm-grown Californian zinfandel; rich essency jammy fruits flood the mouth and do all the talking; a Robert Parker special. Screwcap. 15.5° alc. **Rating** 90 **To** 2013 $38

ŶŶŶŶ   **Adelaide Hills Sauvignon Blanc 2007** Well made, with good balance, line and length; the vintage has suppressed full varietal fruit expression; worth a year or two. Screwcap. 14° alc. **Rating** 89 **To** 2009 $23

Adelaide Hills Unoaked Chardonnay 2007 Quite fragrant, and has lift and thrust thanks to citrussy flavours and acidity; may be too close to sauvignon blanc for some. Screwcap. 13° alc. **Rating** 88 **To** 2009 $19.50

Tryst Adelaide Hills Sauvignon Blanc Semillon Pinot Gris 2007 Bright, lively, zesty lemony flavours; cleverly made and blended; 68/27/5. Screwcap. 13° alc. **Rating** 88 **To** 2010 $16.95

Charleston Adelaide Hills Pinot Noir 2006 A light but fragrant mix of black cherry, spice, mint and leaf; early developing. Screwcap. 13.5° alc. **Rating** 88 **To** 2010 $23

Tryst Adelaide Hills Cabernet Sauvignon Tempranillo Zinfandel 2006 One suspects a shotgun marriage in the first place, but now has a track record of light- to medium-bodied bright blackcurrant fruit plus some extra fragrance and spice. Screwcap. 14° alc. **Rating** 88 **To** 2012 $17

Tryst Cabernet Sauvignon Rose 2007 Clean, delicate and fresh cassis fruit without much depth, but does have quite good length. Screwcap. 13.5° alc. **Rating** 87 **To** 2009 $16.95

Charleston Adelaide Hills Pinot Noir 2005 A very big wine, with distinct confit fruit characters of stewed plum and spice. Screwcap. 14° alc. **Rating** 87 **To** 2009 $23

Neqtar Wines   ★★★

Campbell Avenue, Irymple, Vic 3498 **Region** Murray Darling
T (03) 5024 5704 **F** (03) 5024 6605 www.neqtarwines.com.au **Open** Mon–Sat 10–4.30
Winemaker Donna Stephens, Marnie Roberts **Est.** 1998 **Cases** 400 000
This is yet another Australian–UK joint venture in similar vein to Willunga 100 Wines. The UK end is distributor HwCg, while the Australian components include the former Evans & Tate–owned Salisbury Winery at Irymple, and Roberts Estate at Merbein. A $2 million upgrade of the Salisbury Winery was completed prior to the 2007 vintage. The wines come in three price levels: at the bottom under the Roberts Estate brand (sub $10 in Australia); the Commissioner's Block next (sub $14) and, at the top, Calder Grove (sub $15). Exports to the UK, the US and other major markets.

ŶŶŶŶ   **Calder Grove Shiraz 2006** Light- to medium-bodied; pleasant red and black fruits; not over-extracted or forced. Screwcap. 14° alc. **Rating** 87 **To** 2010 $14.95

New England Estate   ★★★★

Delungra, NSW 2403 **Region** New England
T (02) 6724 8508 **F** (02) 6724 8507 **Open** 7 days 10–5
Winemaker John Cassegrain (Contract) **Est.** 1997 **Cases** NA
New England Estate is 33 km west of Inverell; Ross Thomas has established a very substantial vineyard of 36 ha planted to chardonnay, cabernet sauvignon, merlot and shiraz. The cellar door has barbecue and picnic facilities; there is also a museum and accommodation available.

ŶŶŶŶŶ   **Chardonnay 2006** Plenty of clearly articulated varietal fruit; nectarine, peach, some grapefruit; well handled oak; good line and length. **Rating** 94 **To** 2010

ŶŶŶŶ   **Tawny Port NV** Cellar door special; a little too sweet, but quite supple and spicy. **Rating** 87 **To** 2009

New Era Vineyards   ★★★★★

PO Box 391, Woodside SA 5244 **Region** Adelaide Hills
T (08) 8389 7715 **F** (08) 8389 7715 www.neweravineyards.com.au **Open** Not
Winemaker Robert Baxter, Reg Wilkinson **Est.** 1988 **Cases** 700

The New Era vineyard is situated over a gold reef, which was mined for 60 years until all recoverable gold had been extracted and mining ceased in 1940. The 12.5-ha vineyard was originally planted to chardonnay, shiraz, cabernet sauvignon, merlot and sauvignon, mostly contracted to Foster's. Recently, the 2 ha of cabernet sauvignon has been replaced with sauvignon blanc. The small amount of wines made has been the subject of favourable reviews, and it's not hard to see why.

ɯɯɯɯɯ **Basket Pressed Adelaide Hills Shiraz 2002** Great colour, still crimson; a Peter Pan style, still with a youthful flush of intense blackberry and spice shiraz fruit; very good oak and tannin management. Cork. 13.5° alc. **Rating** 94 **To** 2027 $18
Basket Pressed Adelaide Hills Cabernet Sauvignon Merlot 2002 Shares with the Shiraz a remarkable freshness and intensity for a 6-year-old wine, with clear blackcurrant fruit to the fore picked at perfect ripeness; has absorbed the quixotic choice of American oak. Cork. 13.5° alc. **Rating** 94 **To** 2017 $18

Newtons Ridge   ★★★☆

1170 Cooriemungle Road, Timboon, Vic 3268 **Region** Geelong
T (03) 5598 7394 **F** (03) 5598 7396 **www.**newtonsridge.com.au **Open** 7 days 11–5 Nov–Apr, or by appt
Winemaker David Newton **Est.** 1998 **Cases** 1200
David and Dot Newton say that after milking cows for 18 years, they decided to investigate the possibility of planting a northeast-facing block of land which they also owned. Their self-diagnosed mid-life crisis also stemmed from a lifelong interest in wine. They planted 2 ha of chardonnay and pinot noir in 1998, and another 2 ha of pinot gris, pinot noir and sauvignon blanc the following year. Having done a short winemaking course at Melbourne University (Dookie campus), the Newtons completed a small winery in 2003. Originally called Heytesbury Ridge, the winery had a speedy name change to Newtons Ridge after a large legal stick was waved in their direction.

ɯɯɯɯɯ **Pinot Noir 2006** Bright and clear hue; refined pinot with considerable intensity and length; a small quibble with fractionally green finish should not detract. Screwcap. 12.9° alc. **Rating** 92 **To** 2013 $22

ɯɯɯɯ **Chardonnay 2007** Crisp minerally texture, the fruit in a grapefruit/citrus spectrum; well-integrated touch of French oak. Screwcap. 13.3° alc. **Rating** 88 **To** 2012 $25

Ngeringa   ★★★★★

91 Williams Road, Mount Barker, SA 5251 **Region** Adelaide Hills
T (08) 8398 2667 **F** (08) 8398 2867 **www.**ngeringa.com **Open** By appt
Winemaker Erinn Klein **Est.** 2001 **Cases** 2500
Erinn and Janet Klein say 'As fervent practitioners of biodynamic wine growing, we respect biodynamics as a sensitivity to the rhythms of nature, the health of the soil and the connection between plant, animal and cosmos. It is a pragmatic solution to farming without the use of chemicals and a necessary acknowledgement that the farm unit is part of a great whole.' It is not an easy solution, and the Kleins have increased the immensity of the challenge by using ultra-close vine spacing of 1.5 x 1 m, necessitating a large amount of hand training of the vines plus a tiny crawler tractor. Lest it be thought they have stumbled onto biodynamic growing without understanding wine science, they teamed up while both studying oenology (Erinn) and viticulture/wine marketing (Janet) at Adelaide University in 2000, and then spent time looking at the great viticultural regions of the old world, with a particular emphasis on biodynamics. The thick straw-bale walls of the winery result in a constant temperature throughout the year. The JE label is used for the basic wines, Ngeringa only for the very best.

ɯɯɯɯɯ **Adelaide Hills Syrah 2005** Lovely texture, weight and mouthfeel; a cascade of fruit at perfect ripeness, long finish, superfine tannins. Screwcap. 14° alc.
Rating 96 **To** 2025 $40

ΨΨΨΨΨ **JE Adelaide Hills Pinot Noir 2005** Complex aromas and flavours; some forest and animal notes to black cherry and spice fruit; very long finish. Screwcap. 13° alc. **Rating** 93 **To** 2012 $25
JE McLaren Vale Shiraz 2004 Earthy/savoury/spicy flavours but has similarly fine texture and structure to the Adelaide Hills Syrah '05, some sweeter fruit appearing on the back palate. Screwcap. 13.5° alc. **Rating** 91 **To** 2017 $20
JE Adelaide Hills Chardonnay 2005 Vibrant, fresh, lively citrus and nectarine fruit; good length to the finish; just a little too fine. Screwcap. 13° alc. **Rating** 90 **To** 2015 $25
Adelaide Hills Syrah 2006 Full of spices and cracked pepper on the light-to medium-bodied palate, with subliminal touches of mint and leaf; good length. Screwcap. 14° alc. **Rating** 90 **To** 2015 $50

ΨΨΨΨ **JE Adelaide Hills Pinot Noir 2006** Unambiguously at the earthy/forest floor end of the spectrum; the fruit is light-bodied, its supports stronger; may evolve. Screwcap. **Rating** 87 **To** 2011 $50

Nicholson River

57 Liddells Road, Nicholson, Vic 3882 **Region** Gippsland
T (03) 5156 8241 **F** (03) 5156 8433 **www**.nicholsonriverwinery.com.au **Open** 7 days 10–4
Winemaker Ken Eckersley **Est.** 1978 **Cases** 2000
The fierce commitment to quality in the face of the temperamental Gippsland climate and frustratingly small production has been handsomely repaid by some massive Chardonnays and impressive red wines (from 6 ha of estate plantings). Ken Eckersley refers to his Chardonnays not as white wines but as gold wines, and lists them accordingly in his newsletter. Exports to the US.

ΨΨΨΨΨ **Pinot Noir 2005** Distinct colour development; spicy, savoury, foresty characters; while light-bodied, does have good length and persistence. ProCork. 13° alc. **Rating** 91 **To** 2010 $35
Syrah 2004 Light- to medium-bodied; elegant spicy, savoury notes run throughout the flavours of blackberry and bitter chocolate; fine tannins. ProCork. 13° alc. **Rating** 90 **To** 2014 $35

ΨΨΨΨ **Unwooded Chardonnay 2006** A rich, powerful wine, seemingly with some skin contact to bolster the flavour and texture; in many ways, traditional Australian. ProCork. 13° alc. **Rating** 87 **To** 2009 $19

Nillahcootie Estate

3630 Midland Highway, Lima South, Vic 3673 **Region** Upper Goulburn
T (03) 5768 2685 **F** (03) 5768 2678 **www**.nillahcootieestate.com.au **Open** Mon–Thurs by appt, Fri 12–4, Sat 11–11, Sun 12–5
Winemaker Plunkett Wines (Sam Plunkett), Kilchurn Wines (David Cowburn), Victor Nash **Est.** 1988 **Cases** 1200
Karen Davy and Michael White decided to diversify their primary business of beef cattle production on their 280-ha property in 1988. Between then and 2001 they planted a little over 8 ha of grapes, initially content to sell the production to other local wineries, but in '01 they retained a small proportion of the grapes for winemaking, increasing in the following year to its current level. In '01 they also purchased a 20-ha property overlooking Lake Nillahcootie, on which they have built a strikingly designed restaurant and cellar door.

Nintingbool

56 Wongerer Lane, Smythes Creek, Vic 3351 (postal) **Region** Ballarat
T (03) 5342 4393 **F** (03) 5342 4393 **www**.nintingbool.com **Open** Not
Winemaker Peter Bothe **Est.** 1998 **Cases** 70

Peter and Jill Bothe purchased the Nintingbool property in 1982, building the home in which they now live in '84, using old bluestone dating back to the goldrush period. They established an extensive Australian native garden and home orchard, but in '98 diversified with the planting of pinot noir, a further planting the following year lifting the total to 2 ha; a small amount of property remains to be planted with pinot gris. This is one of the coolest mainland regions, and demands absolute attention to detail (and a warm growing season) for success. In 2002 and '03 the grapes were sold to Ian Watson, the wine made and released under the Tomboy Hill label, but with the Nintingbool Vineyard shown on the label (the '02 was quite a beautiful wine). In '04 they decided to make the wines themselves, the opening vintage producing a tiny 44 cases.

ΨΨΨΨΨ **Ballarat Pinot Noir 2006** Bright, light crystal clear colour; light-bodied, but has great life and thrust to the red cherry and strawberry fruit; minimal tannin and oak involvement. Screwcap. 13.9° alc. **Rating** 92 **To** 2011 $37

No Regrets Vineyard
40 Dillons Hill Road, Glaziers Bay, Tas 7109 **Region** Southern Tasmania
T (03) 6295 1509 **F** (03) 6295 1509 **Open** By appt, also at Salamanca Market (Hobart) most Saturdays
Winemaker Hood Wines **Est.** 2000 **Cases** 350
Having sold Elsewhere Vineyard, Eric and Jette Phillips have planted the former flower gardens around the old Elsewhere homestead, where they still live, exclusively to pinot noir, and renamed this 1-ha 'retirement' vineyard No Regrets.

ΨΨΨΨ **Pinot Noir 2006** Seems quite developed for its age, with notes of stem and toasty oak; overall has elegance, and good intensity, but is best drunk sooner rather than later. Screwcap. 13.9° alc. **Rating** 89 **To** 2010 $30

 # Nocton Park ★★★★☆
373 Colebrook Road, Richmond, Tas 7025 **Region** Southern Tasmania
T (03) 6260 2088 **F** (03) 6260 2880 **Open** By appt
Winemaker Winemaking Tasmania (Julian Alcorso) **Est.** 1998 **Cases** 8000
Nocton Park is part of a corporate group, which aims to become a major supplier of Tasmanian wine and selected gourmet food to the Chinese market. It will thus not only distribute its own wines, but those of Domaine A and Panorama Vineyard. The connection with Domaine A is fundamental, because it was Peter Althaus of Domaine A who, in 1995, showed Nocton Park executive Chris Ellis a 100-ha site which he (Althaus) described as the best vineyard land in the Coal River Valley. Today that site has 19 ha of pinot noir, 5 ha of chardonnay, 3.9 ha of merlot and 3.7 ha of sauvignon blanc. Unfortunately the venture hit financial rocks in late 2007 and its future is not known at the time of going to press.

ΨΨΨΨΨ **Chardonnay 2006** A perfectly proportioned wine, with supple and smooth nectarine and melon fruit, and a long, silky, balanced finish. Diam. **Rating** 94 **To** 2014

ΨΨΨΨΨ **Pinot Noir 2006** Very good hue; good mouthfeel, balance and line; pure black cherry and plum fruit; silky and long, but just a tiny twist of green on the finish. Diam. **Rating** 93 **To** 2014
Pinot Noir 2005 Richer and more oaky and more velvety than the '06; ripe plum and black cherry fruit, with ripe tannins and good length. Zork. 14.2° alc. **Rating** 93 **To** 2012 $18.50
Sauvignon Blanc 2007 Attractive aromas and flavours of abundant passionfruit and other tropical fruits; good line and mouthfeel. **Rating** 90 **To** 2010

ΨΨΨΨ **Chardonnay 2005** Developed melon and peach fruit, with integrated oak; good mouthfilling texture and flavour. Zork. 14.3° alc. **Rating** 89 **To** 2010 $18.50
Benson's Block Merlot 2006 More red fruit on entry to the mouth than the '05, but a fairly nippy finish, the acidity obvious. Diam. 14.5° alc. **Rating** 87 **To** 2012 $18.50

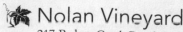 # Nolan Vineyard

217 Badger Creek Road, Badger Creek, Vic 3777 **Region** Yarra Valley
T (03) 5962 3435 **Open** Wed–Sun & public hols 10–5
Winemaker Paul Evans (Contract) **Est.** 2000 **Cases** 250
John and Myrtle Nolan have established 2 ha of low-yielding, non-irrigated clones 114, 115 and MV6 pinot noir. Myrtle had worked in Yarra Valley vineyards for 10 years across all sectors of the Valley, and (one assumes it is Myrtle who says) 'John is a faithful supporter of the vineyard endeavours and is highly valued at picking time because of his large and extended family.' The vineyard, incidentally, is very close to the Healesville Sanctuary.

Noorinbee Selection Vineyards

53 Monaro Highway, Cann River, Vic 3890 **Region** Gippsland
T (03) 5158 6500 **Open** Wed–Sun & public hols 10.30–5
Winemaker Ronald Luhrs **Est.** 1992 **Cases** 400
Ronald and Elaine Luhrs have 2.7 ha of vines, mostly planted back in 1992. The principal varieties are cabernet sauvignon, merlot, malbec, cabernet franc and petit verdot (hence their wines modelled on those of the Medoc in Bordeaux) with a little pinot noir and shiraz. In 2006 they made two interesting blends: a Harslevelu Sauvignon Blanc, and a Mammolo Merlot. They have built a mudbrick cellar door, restaurant and gallery complex.

ΨΨΨΨ **Harslevelu Sauvignon Blanc 2007** Has an interesting profile, moving backwards and forwards between quite tart citrussy acidity, then more fleshy fruit with distinct sauvignon blanc characters; fermentation in old oak; well made. ProCork. 12.7° alc. **Rating** 88 **To** 2011

Norfolk Rise Vineyard

Limestone Coast Road, Mount Benson, SA 5265 **Region** Mount Benson
T (08) 8768 5080 **F** (08) 8768 5083 **www**.norfolkrise.com.au **Open** Mon–Fri 9–5
Winemaker Kristen McGann **Est.** 2000 **Cases** 85 000
This is by far the largest and most important development in the Mount Benson region. It is ultimately owned by a privately held Belgian company, G & C Kreglinger, established in 1797. In early 2002 it acquired Pipers Brook Vineyard; it will maintain the separate brands of the two ventures. The Mount Benson development commenced in 2000, with a 160-ha vineyard and a 2000-tonne winery, primarily aimed at the export market. Exports to the UK, the US and other major markets.

ΨΨΨΨ **Mount Benson Shiraz 2006** Developed colour; light- to medium-bodied spicy black fruits and fine tannins; has quite good length. Screwcap. 14.5° alc. **Rating** 88 **To** 2011 $16

Normanby Wines **NR**

Rose-Lea Vineyard, 178 Dunns Avenue, Harrisville, Qld 4307 **Region** Queensland Zone
T (07) 5467 1214 **F** (07) 5467 1021 **www**.normanbywines.com.au **Open** 7 days Winter 10–5, Summer 10–7
Winemaker Golden Grove Estate (Ray Costanzo) **Est.** 1999 **Cases** 700
Normanby Wines, about 50 km due south of Ipswich, fills in more of the Qld viticultural jigsaw puzzle. The vineyard has just under 3 ha planted to verdelho, shiraz, merlot, viognier, chambourcin, durif and grenache.

Norton Estate

758 Plush Hannans Road, Lower Norton, Vic 3401 **Region** Western Victoria Zone
T (03) 5384 8235 **F** (03) 5384 8235 **www**.nortonestate.com.au **Open** Wed–Sun 10–5
Winemaker Best's Wines **Est.** 1997 **Cases** 1300
In 1996 the Spence family purchased a run-down farm at Lower Norton and, rather than farming the traditional wool, meat and wheat, trusted their instincts and planted vines on

the elevated frost-free buckshot rises. The surprising vigour of the initial planting of shiraz prompted further plantings of shiraz, cabernet sauvignon and sauvignon blanc. The vineyard is halfway between the Grampians and Mt Arapiles, 6 km northwest of the Grampians GI and will have to be content with the Western Victoria Zone, but the wines show traditional Grampians character and style. A traditional Wimmera ripple iron barn has been converted into a cellar door.

🍷🍷🍷🍷🍷 **Spence's Arapiles Run Shiraz 2006** Supple and round, with plenty of movement to the perfectly ripened array of cherry, plum and licorice fruit, oak in the background. Screwcap. 13.5° alc. **Rating** 93 **To** 2021 $35

🍷🍷🍷🍷 **Spence's Sauvignon Blanc 2007** Big, rich mouthfilling style; very ripe tropical flavours, saved by the clean finish. **Rating** 89 **To** 2009 $16.50
Spence's Cabernet Sauvignon 2005 Light, bright colour; a medium-bodied array of fresh minty, leafy, red berry fruits, with just sufficient tannins. Screwcap. 13.5° alc. **Rating** 87 **To** 2011 $22

Nova Vita Wines

GPO Box 1352, Adelaide, SA 5001 **Region** Adelaide Hills
T (08) 8356 0454 **F** (08) 8356 1472 **www**.novavitawines.com.au **Open** Not
Winemaker Mark Kozned, Peter Leske **Est.** 2005 **Cases** 2500
Mark and Jo Kozned spent months of painstaking research before locating the property on which they have now established their substantial vineyard. Situated 4 km outside of Gumeracha, it has gentle slopes, plenty of water and, importantly, moderately fertile soils. The vineyard has 25.6 ha of chardonnay, 3.8 ha of sauvignon blanc and 0.7 ha of shiraz. The name Nova Vita reflects the beginning of the Kozneds' new life, the firebird on the label coming from the Kozneds' Russian ancestry. It is a Russian myth that only a happy or lucky person may see the bird or hear its song.

🍷🍷🍷🍷🍷 **Firebird Adelaide Hills Sauvignon Blanc 2007** A clean varietal bouquet, with a little pungency supporting the dominant tropical aromas; good flavour for the vintage. Screwcap. 13° alc. **Rating** 90 **To** 2009 $20

Nugan Estate

60 Banna Avenue, Griffith, NSW 2680 **Region** Riverina
T (02) 6962 1822 **F** (02) 6962 6392 **www**.nuganestate.com.au **Open** Mon–Fri 9–5
Winemaker Darren Owers **Est.** 1999 **Cases** 400 000
Nugan Estate arrived on the scene like a whirlwind. It is an offshoot of the Nugan Group headed by Michelle Nugan, inter alia the recipient of an Export Hero Award in 2000. In the mid-1990s the company began developing vineyards, and is now a veritable giant, with 310 ha at Darlington Point, 52 ha at Hanwood and 120 ha at Hillston (all in NSW), 100 ha in the King Valley, and 10 ha in McLaren Vale. In addition, it has contracts in place to buy 1000 tonnes of grapes per year from Coonawarra. It sells part of the production as grapes, part as bulk wine and part under the Cookoothama and Nugan Estate labels. Both brands are having considerable success in wine shows, large and small. Exports to the UK, the US and other major markets.

🍷🍷🍷🍷🍷 **Cookoothama Darlington Point Botrytis Semillon 2006** Terrific levels of botrytis and unctuous texture on the palate; long, almost treacly, but with a twist of orange rind freshness on the finish. Cork. 11° alc. **Rating** 94 **To** 2015 $22.95

🍷🍷🍷🍷🍷 **Frasca's Lane Vineyard King Valley Chardonnay 2006** A well-balanced, full-flavoured wine, rich, but not phenolic; 14 months in French oak has not gone over the top. Screwcap. 13.8° alc. **Rating** 93 **To** 2011 $18.95

🍷🍷🍷🍷 **Frasca's Lane King Valley Pinot Grigio 2007** Lemon and dried straw, with real life to the acidity; certainly grigio in style and with nice persistence and freshness. Screwcap. 13.5° alc. **Rating** 89 **To** 2009 $19.95

Manuka Grove Vineyard Durif 2005 Big, rich and ripe, with chocolate cake and confiture blackberries on the palate. Well-made big style. Screwcap. 14.5° alc. Rating 88 To 2014 $22.95

Margaret River Sauvignon Blanc 2007 Typically subdued bouquet, but has good flavour in a ripe tropical spectrum on the mid-palate, broadening out on the finish. Screwcap. 13° alc. Rating 87 To 2009 $19.95

Nursery Ridge Estate　★★★

8514 Calder Highway, Red Cliffs, Vic 3496 **Region** Murray Darling
T (03) 5024 3311 **F** (03) 5024 3114 **Open** Thurs–Sun, school & public hols 10–4.30
Winemaker Bob Shields **Est.** 1999 **Cases** 2000
The estate takes its name from the fact that it is situated on the site of the original vine nursery at Red Cliffs. It is a family-owned and operated affair, with shiraz, cabernet sauvignon, chardonnay, petit verdot and viognier. The well-priced wines are usually well made, with greater richness and depth of fruit flavour than most other wines from the region.

♀♀♀♀　Old Vine Reserve Shiraz 2005 Deeper and darker than the Cassia, with more oak evident and plenty of flavour. Cork. 15° alc. Rating 88 To 2014 $30

Nyora Vineyard & Winery　NR

Cnr Peacock Road/Williams Road, The Gurdies, Vic 3984 **Region** Gippsland
T (03) 5997 6205 **Open** Wed–Mon 10–6
Winemaker Klaus Griese, Denise Griese **Est.** 1995 **Cases** 600
Klaus and Denise Griese have established a Joseph's coat of varieties since 1995; in descending order shiraz, chardonnay, cabernet sauvignon, sauvignon blanc, colombard, semillon, pinot noir, pinot gris, merlot, riesling and verdelho totalling a little under 5 ha in all. The vineyard is planted on a northeast slope near the top of the ridge overlooking the Bass River Valley, and a 3-storey winery (the bottom floor underground) has been built. All of the wines are, to a lesser or greater degree, sweet, and aimed at the cellar door.

O'Leary Walker Wines　★★★★★

Main Road, Leasingham, SA 5452 (PO Box 49, Watervale, SA 5452) **Region** Clare Valley
T (08) 8843 0022 **F** (08) 8843 0156 **www**.olearywalkerwines.com **Open** Mon–Fri 10–7, w'ends by appt
Winemaker David O'Leary, Nick Walker **Est.** 2001 **Cases** 16 000
David O'Leary and Nick Walker together have more than 30 years' experience as winemakers working for some of the biggest Australian wine groups. They then took the plunge, and backed themselves to establish their own winery and brand. Their main vineyard is at Watervale in the Clare Valley, with over 36 ha of riesling, shiraz, cabernet sauvignon, merlot and semillon. In the Adelaide Hills they have established 14 ha of chardonnay, cabernet sauvignon, pinot noir, shiraz, sauvignon blanc and merlot. Exports to the UK, Ireland and Singapore.

♀♀♀♀♀　Claire Reserve Shiraz 2004 Refined concentration and power immediately obvious; a delicious array of blackberry, plum and cherry fruit; fine tannins, balanced oak; great length. From 100-year-old vines yielding 1 tonne per acre; 200 cases made. Screwcap. 14.5° alc. Rating 96 To 2029 $90

Adelaide Hills Sauvignon Blanc 2007 A fragrant and expressive bouquet of gooseberry, stone fruit and passionfruit is precisely reflected on the long, perfectly balanced palate. Screwcap. 12.5° alc. Rating 95 To 2009 $18.50

Adelaide Hills Chardonnay 2005 Delicious, mouthfilling nectarine, white peach and melon fruit; mlf has added texture without diminishing the fruit profile; oak perfectly integrated. Bargain. Screwcap. 13.5° alc. Rating 95 To 2013 $22.50

Watervale Riesling 2007 Similar depth of colour to the Polish Hill, though no hint of browning; a complex mix of tropical fruit, spice and citrussy acidity; has length and drive through the finish. Screwcap. 12.5° alc. Rating 94 To 2017 $17.50

ŶŶŶŶŶ **Clare Valley McLaren Vale Shiraz 2005** Slightly dull colour; a complex pattern of flavours accentuating the dark chocolate underlay; blackberry, mocha and ripe tannins; supple mouthfeel. Screwcap. 14.5° alc. **Rating** 93 **To** 2018 $22.50
Blue Cutting Road Sauvignon Blanc Semillon 2007 The combination of WA (60%)/Clare Valley (40%) fruit works well; a seamless flow of line and length, and overall generosity. Screwcap. 12.5° alc. **Rating** 91 **To** 2009 $14
Adelaide Hills Pinot Noir 2006 Plenty of presence and character; predominantly dark plum and dark cherry flavours; depth without over-extraction. Screwcap. 14° alc. **Rating** 91 **To** 2013 $22.50
Clare Valley Cabernet Sauvignon 2005 Pleasant blackcurrant fruit with splashes of cassis and chocolate on the medium-bodied palate; soft tannins and gentle oak. Screwcap. 14.5° alc. **Rating** 90 **To** 2015 $22.50

ŶŶŶŶ **Polish Hill River Riesling 2007** Developed colour, though bright; plenty of flavour, but lacks the usual penetration and punch of this wine. Screwcap. 12.5° alc. **Rating** 88 **To** 2012 $17.50

O'Reilly's Canungra Valley Vineyards   NR

Lamington National Park Road, Canungra Valley, Qld 4275 **Region** Queensland Coastal
T (07) 5543 4011 **F** (07) 5543 4162 **www**.oreillys.com.au/cvv **Open** 7 days 10–4.30
Winemaker Symphony Hill (Mike Hayes), Clovely Estate (Luke Fitzgerald) **Est.** 1997
Cases 7000
Canungra Valley Vineyards has been established in the hinterland of the Gold Coast with a clear focus on broad-based tourism. Vines (8 ha) have been established around the 19th-century homestead (relocated to the site from its original location in Warwick), but these provide only a small part of the wine offered for sale. In deference to the climate, 70% of the estate planting is chambourcin, the rain and mildew-resistant hybrid; the remainder is semillon.

Oakdene Vineyards   ★★★★☆

255 Grubb Road, Wallington, Vic 3221 **Region** Geelong
T (03) 5256 3886 **F** (03) 5256 3881 **www**.oakdene.com.au **Open** Wed–Sun 12–9.30
Winemaker Ray Nadeson, Robin Brockett (Contract) **Est.** 2001 **Cases** 1500
Bernard and Elizabeth Hooley purchased Oakdene in 2001. Bernard focused on planting 5.4 ha of shiraz, chardonnay and pinot noir in that year, followed by 2.4 ha of sauvignon blanc in '02, while his wife worked to restore the 1920s homestead. In 2004 they opened the Oakdene restaurant, through which much of the wine is sold. Ray Nadeson of Lethbridge Wines makes Chardonnay, Pinot Noir and Shiraz; Robin Brockett of Scotchmans Hill makes the Sauvignon Blanc.

ŶŶŶŶŶ **Chardonnay 2006** A complex, smoky, tangy bouquet leads into an elegant palate; grapefruit and nectarine are dominant, oak subservient; very long finish. Trophy, Geelong Wine Show '07. **Rating** 95 **To** 2012 $21

ŶŶŶŶŶ **Shiraz 2006** In typical winery fashion, with abundant blackberry and plum fruit; splashes of spice, and integrated oak. Screwcap. 13.5° alc. **Rating** 93 **To** 2020 $26
Elizabeth Chardonnay 2006 Abundant weight, flavour and texture; ripe yellow peach and other stone fruit flavours; the power comes from concentration, not alcohol. Screwcap. 13° alc. **Rating** 91 **To** 2012 $29
Pinot Noir 2006 Strong purple-red; dense, plum and cherry fruit; needs time to evolve, but has everything it needs to do so, moving to higher points in the future. Screwcap. 13.5° alc. **Rating** 90 **To** 2014 $28

Oakridge   ★★★★★

864 Maroondah Highway, Coldstream, Vic 3770 **Region** Yarra Valley
T (03) 9739 1920 **F** (03) 9739 1923 **www**.oakridgeestate.com.au **Open** 7 days 10–5
Winemaker David Bicknell **Est.** 1978 **Cases** 15 000

The long, dark shadow of Evans & Tate's ownership is now totally dispelled. Life is never easy, but winemaker (and now CEO) David Bicknell has proved his worth time and again as an extremely talented winemaker. At the top of the brand tier is 864, all Yarra Valley vineyard selections, and only released in the best years (Chardonnay, Shiraz, Cabernet Sauvignon, Riesling); next is the Oakridge core label (the Chardonnay, Pinot Noir and Sauvignon Blanc come from the cooler Upper Yarra Valley, the Shiraz, Cabernet Sauvignon and Viognier from the Lower Yarra); and the Over the Shoulder range, drawn from all of the sources available to Oakridge (Sauvignon Blanc, Pinot Grigio, Pinot Noir, Shiraz Viognier, Cabernet Sauvignon). Exports to the UK and Asia.

ΨΨΨΨΨ **864 Yarra Valley Chardonnay 2006** A brilliant successor to the equally good '05; fermented in large French oak barrels with wild and inoculated yeast; the finesse and intensity of Upper Yarra fruit an ideal blend mate for a superbly built wine. Screwcap. 13.5° alc. **Rating** 96 **To** 2015 $49

Fume Blanc 2007 Highly sophisticated and successful winemaking; barrel ferment has built excellent texture and complexity around positive gooseberry and passionfruit flavours. Screwcap. 11.5° alc. **Rating** 95 **To** 2010 $29

864 Yarra Valley Shiraz 2005 A sprightly wine, medium-bodied, but with very good line and length as red fruits and a throng of spices emerge through to the finish; from a single, dry-grown vineyard. Deserves the 864 label. Screwcap. 14.5° alc. **Rating** 94 **To** 2020 $50

Limited Release Blanc de Blanc 2004 Excellent focus and style, with crisp nectarine and citrus, then a lingering finish; 3 years on yeast lees has added both texture and flavour. Cork. 12° alc. **Rating** 94 **To** 2010 $35

ΨΨΨΨΨ **Yarra Valley Cabernet Sauvignon 2006** Classic, cool-grown, medium-bodied cabernet, with fine tannins built in through the length of the cedary palate, with some echoes of Bordeaux. Screwcap. 13.5° alc. **Rating** 92 **To** 2020 $30

Over the Shoulder Sauvignon Blanc 2007 A spotlessly clean bouquet; a crisp, fresh palate with flavours of asparagus, grass and lemon juice; long finish. Screwcap. 11.5° alc. **Rating** 91 **To** 2009 $18.99

Limited Release Yarra Valley Viognier 2007 Has very good texture, balance and line, whole bunch-pressed, wild indigenous yeast and fermentation in used French puncheons; doesn't show overmuch varietal expression. Screwcap. 13° alc. **Rating** 90 **To** 2012 $30

Yarra Valley Shiraz 2006 Light- to medium-bodied; fresh spicy red and black fruits; good line and length, plus well-integrated oak. Screwcap. 13.5° alc. **Rating** 90 **To** 2012 $30

ΨΨΨΨ **Over the Shoulder Yarra Valley Chardonnay 2007** Very crisp, fresh and lively, with light-bodied citrus and grapefruit components coming from early picking; an airbrush of oak. Screwcap. 12° alc. **Rating** 89 **To** 2011 $18

Over the Shoulder Yarra Valley Cabernet Merlot 2006 Clear-cut varietal expression, ranging through blackcurrant, redcurrant black olive and bramble, all in a medium-bodied frame. Screwcap. 13.5° alc. **Rating** 89 **To** 2013 $18

Over the Shoulder Yarra Valley Pinot Grigio 2007 Brightened and given character by citrussy acidity surrounding core flavours of pear and apple. Screwcap. 12.5° alc. **Rating** 88 **To** 2009 $18.95

Over the Shoulder Yarra Valley Pinot Noir 2007 Spicy, savoury and fresh; light-bodied red fruits; perhaps a little too light, but the other side of the coin makes for a light-hearted café drink. Screwcap. 12° alc. **Rating** 88 **To** 2010 $18

Oakvale   ★★★★★

Broke Road, Pokolbin, NSW 2320 **Region** Lower Hunter Valley
T (02) 4998 7088 **F** (02) 4998 7077 **www**.oakvalewines.com.au **Open** 7 days 10–5
Winemaker Steve Hagan **Est.** 1893 **Cases** 10 000
Richard and Mary Owens purchased the historic winery and vineyard in 1999, for three quarters of a century in the ownership of the founding Elliot family, whose original slab hut

homestead is now a museum. One of the 'must see' destinations in the Hunter. Exports to the US and Mexico.

ᵀᵀᵀᵀ **Elliott's Well Semillon 2003** Very youthful colour; super expressive Hunter Semillon; toasty and rich on the one hand, tight and fine on the other; long and generous with quite silky texture. Cork. 10.5° alc. **Rating** 94 **To** 2012 $24.50
Peppercorn Shiraz 2006 An elegant, supple and smooth medium-bodied wine, with plum and blackberry fruit supported by exceptionally fine, faintly spicy tannins. Screwcap. 14° alc. **Rating** 94 **To** 2026 $29.50

ᵀᵀᵀᵀᵀ **Gold Rock Semillon 2007** Has plenty of fruit in a ripe lemon spectrum, rounded off by good acidity. Screwcap. 11.5° alc. **Rating** 92 **To** 2014 $17.50
Gold Rock Shiraz 2006 Has great power, especially for the price; bright red fruits are framed by leather and a little tobacco; there is a strong mineral element, and the finish is quite fresh and lively. Screwcap. 14° alc. **Rating** 90 **To** 2014 $17.50
Sparkling Shiraz 2005 Quite a deep red, with a little leather and spice playing with the red fruits; quite dry on the finish, but with good balance. Cork. 13.5° alc. **Rating** 90 **To** 2016 $39

ᵀᵀᵀᵀ **Gold Rock Shiraz Rose 2007** Well made; attractive red cherry and plum fruit; dry, balanced finish. Screwcap. 13.5° alc. **Rating** 89 **To** 2009 $17.50
Block 37 Verdelho 2007 Has an abundance of ripe fruit in the tropical spectrum on both bouquet and palate; avoids the phenolic trap. Screwcap. 13.5° alc. **Rating** 88 **To** 2010 $19.50

Oakway Estate   ★★★

575 Farley Road, Donnybrook, WA 6239 **Region** Geographe
T (08) 9731 7141 **F** (08) 9731 7190 **www**.oakwayestate.com.au **Open** By appt
Winemaker Sharna Kowalczuk **Est.** 1998 **Cases** 1500
Ria and Wayne Hammond run a vineyard, beef cattle and sustainable blue gum plantation in undulating country on the Capel River in the southwest of WA. The grapes are grown on 2 ha of light gravel and loam soils that provide good drainage, situated high above the river, giving even sun exposure to the fruit and minimising the effects of frost. Varieties include shiraz, merlot, cabernet sauvignon and chardonnay, and have won a number of medals at wine shows.

 # Oatley Estate   ★★★

9A Kitchener Street, Oatley, NSW 2223 (postal) **Region** Lower Hunter Valley
T 0419 402 989 **F** (02) 9580 7002 **Open** Not
Winemaker Contract **Est.** 1989 **Cases** 5000
Graeme and Margaret Staas have lived in Oatley for 33 years and registered the name Oatley Estate wines in 1989. They also own a 40-ha block which forms part of the famous Sunshine Estate once owned by Lindemans, and which produced many of the great Lindemans wines through to the early 1970s. Here they have planted 8 ha of shiraz, semillon, chardonnay and traminer, producing around 50 to 60 tonnes per year. Most of the grapes have been sold over the years to other producers, but from 2003 they reserved part for wines to be released under the Oatley Estate (and Sunshine) labels. The Staas' connection with the wine industry is a long one, as they founded and owned a major label printing business, Assta Label House. Needless to say, the Oatley family is less than impressed, but there is no suggestion the registration of the Oatley Estate name is anything other than entirely legitimate.

ᵀᵀᵀᵀ **Semillon 2006** Pale straw-green; a clean bouquet, and has plenty of fruit in a citrus/grass/lemon tart spectrum; fair length. Great value. Screwcap. 11° alc. **Rating** 88 **To** 2011 $8.30
Chardonnay 2006 Light green-straw; crisp, fresh, citrus and stone fruit; very early picking, perfect for an unwooded style. Screwcap. 12° alc. **Rating** 88 **To** 2009 $8.30

Semillon Chardonnay 2006 Direct, fresh light bodied palate, with nice tension between the two components; good value. Screwcap. 11.5° alc. **Rating** 87 **To** 2010 $8.30

Oatley Wines

Craigmoor Road, Mudgee, NSW 2850 **Region** Mudgee
T (02) 6372 2208 **F** (02) 9433 0456 **www**.oatleywines.com.au **Open** 7 days 10–4
Winemaker James Manners **Est.** 2006 **Cases** NFP
Oatley Wines, with Wild Oats its main brand, is the latest venture of the Oatley family, previously best known as the owners of Rosemount Estate until it was sold to Southcorp. The founder of both businesses is chairman Bob Oatley, and the new venture is run by son Sandy, with considerable hitting power added by deputy executive chairman Chris Hancock. Wild Oats, as anyone with the remotest interest in yachting and the Sydney–Hobart Yacht Race will know, has been the name of Bob Oatley's racing yachts. The family has long owned vineyards in Mudgee, but the new business has been rapidly expanded by the acquisition of the Montrose winery, the Craigmoor cellar door and restaurant, and seven vineyards (totalling 465 ha) spread across the Mudgee region. The family has recently completed a $10 million upgrade for the Montrose winery.

005 **Wild Oats Sauvignon Blanc Semillon 2007** A lively wine, with strong varietal definition, and a nice balance between flavour and texture; quite long on the finish. Screwcap. 12.2° alc. **Rating** 90 **To** 2010 $18.95

004 **Wild Oats Pinot Grigio 2007** Dried straw and and a little broad; clean and fleshy on the palate; a good example of the grigio style. Screwcap. 13.5° alc. **Rating** 88 **To** 2009 $18.95
Wild Oats Shiraz Viognier 2006 Soft, fleshy and varietal; plenty of flavour, and nice texture, but ultimately a little one-dimensional. Screwcap. 14.1° alc. **Rating** 88 **To** 2012 $18.95
Wild Oats Chardonnay 2007 Melon and fig, and lots of toast on the bouquet; clean fruit, but lacks excitement and precision. Screwcap. 12.8° alc. **Rating** 87 **To** 2010 $18.95
Wild Oats Rose 2007 Very pale pink; wild strawberry aromas and a hint of sweetness on the finish; commercial style. Screwcap. 12.5° alc. **Rating** 87 **To** 2009 $18.95

Observatory Hill Vineyard

107 Centauri Drive, Mt Rumney, Tas 7170 **Region** Southern Tasmania
T (03) 6248 5380 **Open** By appt
Winemaker Andrew Hood, Alain Rousseau **Est.** 1991 **Cases** 600
Glenn and Chris Richardson's Observatory Hill Vineyard has been developing since 1991 when Glenn and his late father-in-law Jim Ramsey planted the first of the 8500 vines that now make up the estate. Together with the adjoining property owned by Chris' brother Wayne Ramsey and his wife Stephanie, the vineyard now covers 3 ha, with new plantings having been made each year. The name 'Observatory Hill' comes from the state's oldest observatory, which is perched on the hill above the vineyard.

005 **Chardonnay 2006** Has emerged from its chrysalis over the last 12 months, developing seamless flavours of melon, citrus, slate and high quality oak; a palate of great length and style. Gold, Tas Wine Show '08. Screwcap. 13.5° alc. **Rating** 95 **To** 2014 $22

Occam's Razor

c/– Jasper Hill, Drummonds Lane, Heathcote, Vic 3523 **Region** Heathcote
T (03) 5433 2528 **F** (03) 5433 3143 **Open** By appt
Winemaker Emily Laughton **Est.** 2001 **Cases** 400

Emily Laughton has decided to follow in her parents' footsteps after first seeing the world and having a range of casual jobs. Having grown up at Jasper Hill, winemaking was far from strange, but she decided to find her own way, buying the grapes from a small vineyard owned by Jasper Hill employee Andrew Conforti and his wife Melissa. She then made the wine 'with guidance and inspiration from my father'. The name comes from William of Ockham – also spelt Occam – (1285–1349), a theologian and philosopher responsible for many sayings, including that appearing on the back label of the wine: 'what can be done with fewer is done in vain with more'. Exports to the US, Canada and Singapore.

ΨΨΨΨΨ **Shiraz 2006** Has very good weight and mouthfeel; full-bodied, supple and rich, and — remarkably at this alcohol — no dead fruit or porty characters, just blackberry and plum; the twitch on the finish (ex alcohol) is acceptable. Cork. **Rating** 94 **To** 2018 $38

Oceanview Estates   NR
2557 Mt Mee Road, Ocean View, Qld 4521 **Region** Queensland Coastal
T (07) 3425 3900 **F** (07) 3425 3800 **www**.oceaniewestates.com.au **Open** Thurs–Sat 10–late, Sun 8.30am–9pm
Winemaker Thomas Honnef **Est.** 1998 **Cases** 2100
The Oceanview property was purchased in 1993 by Rosemary and Calvin Irons; in '96 Kate and Thomas Honnef joined as partners, with Thomas Honnef responsible both for the vineyard establishment (which commenced in '98) and for the onsite winery, which was erected prior to the 2003 vintage. All of the wines are estate-grown and made onsite, initially with guidance from consultant winemaker Brian Wilson. Most recently a substantial restaurant (and cellar door), together with two vineyard cottages, have opened, with weddings specially catered for.

Oddfellows Wines
PO Box 88, Langhorne Creek, SA 5255 **Region** Langhorne Creek
T (08) 8537 3326 **F** (08) 8537 3319 **www**.oddfellowswines.com.au **Open** At Bremer Place, Langhorne Creek 7 days 11–5
Winemaker David Knight **Est.** 1997 **Cases** 2000
Oddfellows is the name taken by a group of five individuals who decided to put their expertise, energy and investments into making premium wine. Langhorne Creek vignerons David and Cathy Knight were two of the original members, and in 2007 took over ownership and running of the venture. David had worked with Greg Follett from Lake Breeze to produce the wines, gradually taking over more responsibility, and is now both winemaker and viticulturist for the estate's 40-ha vineyard in Langhorne Creek. This vineyard also produces the Winners Tank label (in conjunction with Reid Bosward of Kaesler Wines in the Barossa), the first two vintages made for export only (US and Canada) but with limited domestic distribution of the '06 vintage. Exports to the UK, the US, Canada, Singapore, Indonesia and China.

ΨΨΨΨΨ **Langhorne Creek Shiraz 2004** More structure and weight to this wine; savoury black fruits and a twist of licorice; long finish and aftertaste. Cork. **Rating** 90 **To** 2014 $25

ΨΨΨΨ **Svengali Langhorne Creek Shiraz Cabernet Sauvignon 2005** An abundant forthcoming array of red and black fruits with soft tannins, and a gold medal from the Adelaide Wine Show '06 under its belt. Cork. 15° alc. **Rating** 89 **To** 2012 $20
The Winner's Tank Eskadale Langhorne Creek Shiraz 2006 Typical succulent Langhorne fruit, with an abundance of flavour though less structure; as ready now as it ever will be. Screwcap. 14.5° alc. **Rating** 88 **To** 2010 $14

Old Kent River

1114 Turpin Road, Rocky Gully, WA 6397 **Region** Frankland River
T (08) 9855 1589 **F** (08) 9855 1660 **www**.oldkentriver.com.au **Open** At Kent River, Denmark
Winemaker Alkoomi (Contract), Michael Staniford **Est.** 1985 **Cases** 3000
Mark and Debbie Noack have earned much respect from their neighbours and from the other producers to whom they sell more than half the production from the 16.5-ha vineyard on their sheep property. The quality of their wines has gone from strength to strength, Mark having worked particularly hard with his Pinot Noir. Regrettably, no Pinot Noir tasted this year. Exports to the UK, the US, Hong Kong, Malaysia and Singapore.

ΨΨΨΨΨ **Backtrack Frankland River Chardonnay 2007** Fine structure and focus; a mix of citrus, stone fruit and mineral; good length. **Rating** 90 **To** 2013 $16.20

 ## Old Mill Estate Wines

Lot 102, Saltmarsh Road, Langhorne Creek, SA 5255 (postal) **Region** Langhorne Creek
T (08) 8537 3006 **F** (08) 8537 3006 **www**.oldmillestatewines.com **Open** Not
Winemaker Contract **Est.** 2003 **Cases** 2500
Peter and Vicki Widdop have planted 10 ha of cabernet sauvignon, 6 ha of touriga nacional and 2 ha of shiraz by the banks of the Bremer River, near the shores of Lake Alexandrina. In earlier days the property was the home of a mill, which produced chaff from lucerne grown on the estate. The bulk of the grape production is sold, but a useful amount is made under the Old Mill Estate label.

Old Plains ★★★★

6 Winser Avenue, Seaton, SA 5023 (postal) **Region** Adelaide Plains
T 0407 605 601 **F** (08) 8355 3603 **www**.oldplains.com **Open** Not
Winemaker Domenic Torzi, Tim Freeland **Est.** 2003 **Cases** 2000
Old Plains is a partnership between Tim Freeland and Domenic Torzi who have located small parcels of old vine grenache, shiraz and cabernet sauvignon in the Adelaide Plains region. A large portion of the consistently high-quality wines, sold under the Old Plains and Longhop labels, are exported to the US, Denmark, Hong Kong and NZ.

ΨΨΨΨΨ **Longhop Adelaide Plains Shiraz 2006** Dense purple; layers of blackberry and blackcurrant fruit with tannins in appropriate support; not much finesse, but so what? Over-delivers on its price. Screwcap. 14.5° alc. **Rating** 90 **To** 2015 $15

ΨΨΨΨ **Longhop Old Vine Adelaide Plains Grenache 2006** Light- to medium-bodied; clear varietal character in a slightly jammy mode; needs more structure. Screwcap. 14.5° alc. **Rating** 87 **To** 2010 $20

Olivers Taranga Vineyards

Seaview Road, McLaren Vale, SA 5171 **Region** McLaren Vale
T (08) 8323 8498 **F** (08) 8323 7498 **www**.oliverstaranga.com **Open** 7 days 10–4
Winemaker Corrina Rayment **Est.** 1841 **Cases** 4000
William and Elizabeth Oliver arrived from Scotland in 1839 to settle at McLaren Vale. Six generations later, members of the family are still living on the Whitehill and Taranga farms. The Taranga property has 12 varieties planted on 99 ha; grapes from the property have been sold, but since 1994 some of the old vine shiraz has been made under the Olivers Taranga label. Since 2000 the wine has been made by Corrina Rayment (the Oliver family's first winemaker and a sixth-generation family member). Exports to Sweden, Belgium, Singapore, Thailand and Hong Kong.

ΨΨΨΨΨ **HJ Reserve Shiraz 2004** Strong colour; very complex, with abundant savoury aromas and dark fruits aplenty; lovely texture and weight, and a very long and bright finish. Cork. 14.5° alc. **Rating** 95 **To** 2020 $45

Corrina's Shiraz Cabernet Sauvignon 2005 Deep crimson-purple; quite lifted and focused red fruits on the bouquet; full-bodied, the palate is full of rich, bright fruits and is surprisingly long. Screwcap. 15° alc. **Rating** 94 **To** 2018 $28

ΤΤΤΤΥ **McLaren Vale Shiraz 2005** Good colour; good concentration with fruitcake aromas and dark fruits; the full-bodied palate has plenty of punch on the chewy finish. Cork. 15° alc. **Rating** 92 **To** 2018 $28
Cadenzia McLaren Vale Grenache 2006 Raspberry fruit and hints of dried herbs on the bouquet and palate; good flavour on the finish, with plenty of fruit and nice chewy tannins. Screwcap. 14.5° alc. **Rating** 90 **To** 2014 $28

Olsen   ★★★★

RMB 252, Osmington Road, Osmington, WA 6285 **Region** Margaret River
T (08) 9757 4536 **F** (08) 9757 4114 **www**.olsen.com.au **Open** By appt
Winemaker Bernard Abbott, Jarrad Olsen **Est.** 1986 **Cases** 3000
Steve and AnnMarie Olsen have planted 10.5 ha of cabernet sauvignon, shiraz, merlot, verdelho, shiraz, semillon and chardonnay, which they tend with the help of their four children. It was the desire to raise their children in a healthy country environment that prompted the move to establish the vineyard, coupled with a long-standing dream to make their own wine. Not to be confused with Olsen Wines in Melbourne. Exports to Canada and Singapore.

ΤΤΤΤΥ **Margaret River Cabernet Sauvignon 2005** Good varietal cabernet; cassis and blackcurrant with cedary oak and fine concentration; good tannin structure; fine and fresh acidity. Cork. 13.5° alc. **Rating** 92 **To** 2016 $20

ΤΤΤΤ **Margaret River Semillon Sauvignon Blanc 2007** Riper and more exotic style than most from the Margaret River; good flavour, with hints of tropical fruits, and an even, generous finish. Screwcap. 12.9° alc. **Rating** 89 **To** 2010 $20
Margaret River Merlot 2005 Soft and fleshy, with good flavour and quite silky dark fruit on the finish. Screwcap. 13.5° alc. **Rating** 89 **To** 2012 $20

Olsen Wines Victoria   ★★★★☆

131 Koornang Road, Carnegie, Vic 3163 **Region** Port Phillip Zone
T (03) 9569 2188 **F** (03) 9563 5038 **www**.vin888.com **Open** Mon–Thurs 10.30–8, Fri–Sat 10.30–9
Winemaker Glenn Olsen **Est.** 1991 **Cases** 55 000
Glenn Olsen, a science and engineering graduate of the University of Melbourne, has been involved in the wine industry since 1975, initially importing wines and spirits from Europe, then moving into retailing. In 1991, he started Olsen Wines, claiming to be Melbourne's first inner suburban winery. Several others may dispute this claim, but that is perhaps neither here nor there. Most of the wines come either from grapes grown on the Murray River in Northeast Victoria, or from the Yarra Valley. Exports to the US, Canada, Japan, China and Hong Kong.

ΤΤΤΤΤ **Personal Reserve Yarra Valley Cabernet Sauvignon 2005** Medium-bodied and graceful, with perfectly ripened blackcurrant and spice cabernet fruit, the tannins and French oak seamlessly integrated. Trophies for Best Cabernet Sauvignon at both Victoria and Yarra Valley wine shows '07. Cork. 14.3° alc. **Rating** 95 **To** 2020 $38

ΤΤΤΤΥ **The Old Bailey 15 Year Old Tawny NV** Some good aged material judiciously blended with some fresher; good rancio and length. Screwcap. 18° alc. **Rating** 91 **To** 2009 $25.95
Yarra Valley Verdelho 2006 Shows what magic the Yarra Valley can produce, for this has a seldom encountered (with Verdelho) vibrancy and intensity on the mid-palate and finish. Will develop. Screwcap. 14.9° alc. **Rating** 90 **To** 2014 $19

Personal Reserve The Old Bailey 15 Year Old Madeira NV A name about to disappear from Australian labels (Madeira), but this does have some true Madeira character, on the dry/sercial side of the fence. Screwcap. 18.5° alc. **Rating** 90 **To** 2009 $25.95

🍷🍷🍷🍷 **Preservative Free Yarra Valley Cabernet Sauvignon 2006** Screwcap is the only closure for preservative-free wines; here, the colour is bright and the ripe fruit is showing no signs of collapse; adjusted acidity important. Screwcap. 14.9° alc. **Rating** 88 **To** 2010 $20

Big Fella Cabernet Sauvignon 2004 A populist style of cabernet, if there is such a thing; medium-bodied fruit, blackcurrant sweetened by some oak, and the tannins tamed. Screwcap. 13.7° alc. **Rating** 88 **To** 2013 $20

Yarra Valley Shiraz 2005 A pleasant mix of leaf, spice, sweet berry fruit and light tannins, all pointing to early consumption. Screwcap. 14.9° alc. **Rating** 87 **To** 2010 $22

Big Fella Cabernet Merlot 2004 Medium-bodied; quite firm blackcurrant fruit, with a rustic edge to the tannin structure. Screwcap. 14.5° alc. **Rating** 87 **To** 2012 $19.95

Olssen ★★★★★

Sollys Hill Road, Watervale, SA 5452 **Region** Clare Valley
T (08) 8843 0065 **F** (08) 8843 0065 **Open** Thurs–Sun & public hols 11–5, or by appt
Winemaker Kevin Olssen, Julian Midwinter **Est.** 1994 **Cases** 4000

Kevin and Helen Olssen first visited the Clare Valley in 1986. Within two weeks they and their family decided to sell their Adelaide home and purchased a property in a small, isolated valley 3 km north of the township of Watervale. As a result of the acquisition of the Bass Hill Vineyard, estate plantings have risen to more than 32 ha, including unusual varieties such as carmenere and primitivo di Gioia. The Bass Hill project is a joint venture between parents Kevin and Helen and children David and Jane Olssen. Exports to the UK, the US, Norway and Canada.

🍷🍷🍷🍷🍷 **The Olssen Six 2005** A super-intense wine with great thrust to the long palate, with notes of cedar, spice, blackcurrant and earth, fine tannins adding to the length. Cabernet Sauvignon/Merlot/Cabernet Franc/Carmenere/Malbec/Petit Verdot. Screwcap. 15° alc. **Rating** 94 **To** 2019 $65

Bass Hill Vineyard MMS 2005 Full-bodied; very complex aromas and flavours with licorice, plum, blackberry and spice all supported by ripe tannins, the blend seamless and synergistic; long finish. Mataro/Malbec/Shiraz. Screwcap. 13.5° alc. **Rating** 94 **To** 2025 $35

🍷🍷🍷🍷½ **Clare Valley Shiraz 2005** Medium- to full-bodied; a rich amalgam of blackberry, mocha, chocolate and licorice, the texture supple and smooth, oak and tannins controlled; destined for a long life. Screwcap. 14° alc. **Rating** 93 **To** 2025 $25

Bass Hill Vineyard Clare Valley Carmenere 2006 Has more richness to the fruit than expected, quite sweet but not jammy, with an attractive foresty savoury twist to the finish. Screwcap. 13.5° alc. **Rating** 90 **To** 2013 $35

🍷🍷🍷🍷 **Bass Hill Vineyard Clare Valley Primitivo 2006** Lively multifaceted spicy aroma and flavour; light- to medium-bodied, but has good thrust and attack to the flavour and mouthfeel. Screwcap. 14.5° alc. **Rating** 89 **To** 2012 $35

Clare Valley Riesling 2007 A voluminous mix of tropical and citrus aromas leads into a full-flavoured, forward style for early drinking. Screwcap. 11.5° alc. **Rating** 88 **To** 2011 $20

Orange Mountain Wines ★★★

Cnr Forbes Road/Radnedge Lane, Orange, NSW 2800 **Region** Orange
T (02) 6365 2626 **www**.orangemountain.com.au **Open** W'ends & public hols 9–5
Winemaker Terry Dolle **Est.** 1997 **Cases** 3000

Terry Dolle has a total of 5.5 ha of vineyards, part at Manildra (established 1997) and the remainder at Orange (in 2001). The Manildra climate is distinctly warmer than that of Orange, and the plantings reflect the climatic difference, with pinot noir and sauvignon blanc at Orange, shiraz, cabernet sauvignon, merlot and viognier at Manildra.

 TTTT **Manildra Shiraz Viognier 2006** A spicy wine with pronounced acidity, and a long, tannic, slightly chewy finish; plenty of vibrant red fruits on offer. Screwcap. 14.9° alc. **Rating** 89 **To** 2014 $25
Manildra Pinot Noir 2006 Well made; light- to medium plum fruit, with distinct savoury, foresty nuances adding to structure and complexity. Screwcap. **Rating** 88 **To** 2011 $25
Manildra Shiraz Viognier 2005 A fleshy, medium-bodied wine with real lift on the palate; falls away a little on the finish. Screwcap. 14.5° alc. **Rating** 87 **To** 2010 $25

Oranje Tractor ★★★★

198 Link Road, Albany, WA 6330 **Region** Albany
T (08) 9842 5175 **F** (08) 9842 5175 **www**.oranjetractor.com **Open** W'ends & hols and by appt 12–5 Oct–June
Winemaker Rob Diletti, Mike Garland (Contract) **Est.** 1998 **Cases** 1000
The name celebrates the 1964 vintage, orange-coloured, Fiat tractor, acquired when Murray Gomm and Pamela Lincoln began the establishment of the vineyard. Murray was born next door, but moved to Perth to work in physical education and health promotion. Here he met nutritionist Pamela, who completed the wine science degree at CSU in 2000, before being awarded a Churchill Fellowship to study organic grape and wine production in the US and Europe. When the partners established their 3-ha vineyard, they went down the organic path.

TTTTT **Reverse Riesling 2007** A clean but subdued bouquet; in a Mosel Kabinett style, stacked with sweet lime juice fruit; the clever name may go through to the keeper for some. Screwcap. 10° alc. **Rating** 92 **To** 2013 $17
Albany Sauvignon Blanc 2006 A classic herbaceous style without sweatiness or coarseness; has velocity on the palate and finish, with appealing citrussy acidity. Excellent for the vintage. Screwcap. 11.5° alc. **Rating** 91 **To** 2009 $19

TTTT **Busted Clutch Shiraz 2005** Light- to medium-bodied; savoury spicy earthy palate; quite good length, fine tannins. Why cork? 12.5° alc. **Rating** 88 **To** 2012 $18
Albany Rose 2007 Fresh, bright, zesty red berry style, with good acidity and length. Screwcap. 12.5° alc. **Rating** 87 **To** 2009 $17.50

Organic Vignerons Australia ★★★☆

Section 395 Derrick Road, Loxton North, SA 5333 **Region** South Australia
T (03) 9467 0015 **F** (03) 9646 8383 **www**.ova.com.au **Open** Not
Winemaker David Bruer **Est.** 2002 **Cases** 9000
Organic Vignerons Australia is a very interesting winemaking business. It consists of the owners of five certified organic SA properties: Claire and Kevin Hansen at Padthaway, Bruce and Sue Armstrong at Waikerie, Brett and Melissa Munchenberg at Loxton, Terry Markou at Adelaide Plains and David and Barbara Bruer at Langhorne Creek. The wines are made by David Bruer at Temple Bruer, which is itself a certified organic producer. The company went into liquidation, but by early 2008 had commenced trading again. Exports to the UK, Germany, Hong Kong, Taiwan, Singapore, Philippines and NZ.

Orlando ★★★★★

Jacob's Creek Visitor Centre, Barossa Valley Way, Rowland Flat, SA 5352
Region Barossa Valley
T (08) 8521 3000 **F** (08) 8521 3003 **www**.orlandowines.com **Open** 7 days 10–5
Winemaker Philip Laffer, Bernard Hicken **Est.** 1847 **Cases** NFP

Orlando is the parent who has been divorced by its child, Jacob's Creek (see separate entry). Orlando is 160 years old, Jacob's Creek little more than 34 years. For what are doubtless sound marketing reasons, Orlando aided and abetted the divorce, but the average consumer is unlikely to understand the logic, and – if truth be known – care about it even less.

ŸŸŸŸŸ St Helga Eden Valley Riesling 2006 Spotlessly clean, lively and fresh; delicate purity and length to the lime-accented fruit; great track record. Screwcap. 12.5° alc. **Rating** 95 **To** 2016 $17.99

St Hilary Padthaway Chardonnay 2006 Good intensity, focus and length to the nectarine fruit; drives through to the finish and aftertaste, supported by good oak. Gold medal, Limestone Coast Wine Show '07. **Rating** 94 **To** 2014

Lawson's Padthaway Shiraz 2002 Cool vintage fruit with a layer of mint, and redcurrant fruits on the bouquet; very bright fruit, and the vibrant acidity draws out the long finish. Trophy, Sydney Wine Show '08. Cork. 14.5° alc. **Rating** 94 **To** 2016 $59.95

ŸŸŸŸ Trilogy Cuvee Brut NV Good bead; mouthfilling flavours of stone fruit; quite rich overall, dry finish. Cork. 12.5° alc. **Rating** 89 **To** 2009 $15.99

Trilogy Rose Sparkling NV Takes the blush rose to another level, though still retains delicacy while adding fruit flavours in a citrus and strawberry spectrum; dry finish. Cork. 12° alc. **Rating** 89 **To** 2009 $15.95

St Hilary Padthaway Chardonnay 2005 Spotlessly clean and well-balanced, but still very subdued, and on the light side; not certain it will ever gain personality. Screwcap. **Rating** 88 **To** 2010 $17.99

Chardonnay Pinot Brut Cuvee NV Pale straw-green with plenty of mousse; quite fresh and delicate, with a balanced, largely dry finish; well made. Cork. 12° alc. **Rating** 88 **To** 2009 $13.99

Carrington Blush Special Cuvee NV Pale salmon-pink; a touch of red fruit flavours and a light, dry finish; very good at the price, given an extra point in recognition. Cork. 11.5° alc. **Rating** 87 **To** 2009 $7.95

Otway Estate ★★★

20 Hoveys Road, Barongarook, Vic 3249 **Region** Geelong
T (03) 5233 8400 **F** (03) 5233 8343 www.otwayestate.com.au **Open** Mon–Fri 11–4.30, w'ends 10–5
Winemaker Ian Deacon **Est.** 1983 **Cases** 3000
The history of Otway Estate dates back to 1983, when the first vines were planted by Stuart and Eileen Walker. The current group of six family and friends, including winemaker Ian Deacon, have substantially expanded the scope of the business: there are now 6 ha of vineyard, planted primarily to chardonnay (3 ha) and pinot noir (2 ha) with small patches of riesling, semillon, sauvignon blanc and cabernet making up the remainder. The wines made from these plantings are sold under the Otway Estate label; wines made from contract-grown grapes in the region are marketed under the Yahoo Creek label. Exports to Canada.

ŸŸŸŸ Pinot Noir 2006 Savoury foresty stemmy aromas and flavours; light-bodied, but has length and persistence; overcomes poor colour. **Rating** 87 **To** 2009 $20

Outlook Hill

97 School Lane, Tarrawarra, Vic 3777 **Region** Yarra Valley
T (03) 5962 2890 **F** (03) 5962 2890 www.outlookhill.com.au **Open** Fri–Sun 11–4.45
Winemaker Al Fencaros, Peter Snow **Est.** 2000 **Cases** 2300
After several years overseas, former Melbourne professionals Peter and Lydia Snow returned in 1997 planning to open a wine tourism business in the Hunter Valley. However, they had second thoughts, and in 2000 returned to the Yarra Valley, where they have now established three tourist B&B cottages, 5.3 ha of vineyard, a terrace restaurant and adjacent cellar door outlet, backed by a constant temperature wine storage cool room. Exports to Denmark and Japan.

Padthaway Estate

Riddoch Highway, Padthaway, SA 5271 **Region** Padthaway
T (08) 8734 3148 **F** (08) 8734 3188 **www**.padthawayestate.com **Open** 7 days 10–4
Winemaker Ulrich Grey-Smith **Est.** 1980 **Cases** 6000
For many years, until the opening of Stonehaven, this was the only functioning winery in
Padthaway, set in the superb grounds of the estate in a large and gracious old stone wool shed;
the homestead is in the Relais et Chateaux mould, offering luxurious accommodation and
fine food. Sparkling wines are the speciality. Padthaway Estate also acts as a tasting centre for
other Padthaway-region wines.

ΨΨΨΨΨ **Eliza Pinot Noir Chardonnay 2004** Pale bronze; great balance from the
dosage provides excellent mouthfeel accompanied by nice nutty biscuity/brioche
characters. Cork. 12.5° alc. **Rating** 93 **To** 2012 $25
Eliza Sparkling Rose 2004 Bright pink; plenty of citrus and strawberry fruit;
lively; controlled dosage. Pinot Noir/Pinot Meunier. Cork. 12.5° alc. **Rating** 93
To 2012 $35
Eliza Sparkling Shiraz 2004 Has abundant cherry fruit without excessive
dosage or oak; good balance and length. Cork. 13° alc. **Rating** 90 **To** 2012 $35

Palandri Wines

Bussell Highway, Cowaramup, WA 6284 **Region** Margaret River
T (08) 9755 5711 **F** (08) 9755 5722 **www**.palandri.com.au **Open** 7 days 10–5
Winemaker Ben Roodhouse **Est.** 1999 **Cases** 250 000
When Palandri went into voluntary administration in February 2008, some industry
observers simply asked why had it taken so long to happen. There were eerie echoes of
the collapse of Adelaide Steamship's byzantine corporate structure, for five Palandri group
companies followed the sixth (Palandri Finance Pty Ltd), which had gone into administration
a little under two weeks earlier. The group has substantial winemaking assets, including a
2500-tonne winery and a fraction under 500 ha of vineyards. Exports to all major markets.

ΨΨΨΨΨ **Great Southern Margaret River Sauvignon Blanc 2006** Clean, with good
structure; gooseberry, citrus, passionfruit, grass and mineral are all there, yet not
overly intense. Screwcap. 12.5° alc. **Rating** 90 **To** 2009 $19.95

ΨΨΨΨ **Vita Novus Margaret River Great Southern Shiraz 2004** Medium-bodied;
has a soft range of red and black fruits, all making for early drinking. Screwcap.
14.5° alc. **Rating** 87 **To** 2012 $23.50
Vita Novus Margaret River Cabernet Sauvignon 2005 Slightly leafy
character offset by cassis and a little cedar; full-bodied, with firm, drying tannins
on the finish. Screwcap. 14° alc. **Rating** 87 **To** 2014 $23.50

Palmer Wines

1271 Caves Road, Dunsborough, WA 6281 **Region** Margaret River
T (08) 9756 7388 **F** (08) 9756 7399 **Open** 7 days 10–5
Winemaker Mark Warren **Est.** 1977 **Cases** 6000
Stephen and Helen Palmer planted their first hectare of vines way back in 1977, but a series
of events (including a cyclone and grasshopper plagues) caused them to lose interest and
instead turn to thoroughbred horses. But with encouragement from Dr Michael Peterkin of
Pierro, and after a gap of almost 10 years, they again turned to viticulture and now have 60 ha
planted to the classic varieties. The 2006 Chardonnay had an outstanding show career in '07,
winning gold medals at the WA Wine Show, Margaret River, Small Winemakers and Perth.
Exports to Indonesia.

ΨΨΨΨΨ **Margaret River Chardonnay 2006** Vibrant grapefruit and melon offset by
some creamy cashew malolactic notes; oak well-balanced and integrated. Screwcap.
Rating 94 **To** 2019 $25

ŸŸŸŸ   Margaret River Sauvignon Blanc 2006 Very fresh bouquet, with strong nettle character, and vibrant, quite racy fruit. Screwcap. 12.5° alc. **Rating** 87 **To** 2009 $15

Pankhurst

'Old Woodgrove', Woodgrove Road, Hall, NSW 2618 **Region** Canberra District
T (02) 6230 2592 **F** (02) 6230 2592 **www**.pankhurstwines.com.au **Open** W'ends, public hols, or by appt
Winemaker Lark Hill (Dr David Carpenter, Sue Carpenter), Brindabella Hills (Dr Roger Harris) **Est.** 1986 **Cases** 4000
Agricultural scientist and consultant Allan Pankhurst and wife Christine (with a degree in pharmaceutical science) have established a 5.7-ha split-canopy vineyard. The first wines produced showed considerable promise. In recent years Pankhurst has shared success with Lark Hill in the production of good Pinot Noir. Says Christine Pankhurst, 'the result of good viticulture here and great winemaking at Lark Hill', and she may well be right.

ŸŸŸŸŸ   Canberra District Chardonnay 2006 Generous and rich tropical/stone fruit flavours with balanced oak; seems much riper than the alcohol suggests, but is not flabby. Screwcap. 13.4° alc. **Rating** 90 **To** 2011 $20

ŸŸŸŸ   Canberra District Pinot Noir 2006 Briary savoury/stemmy/foresty notes, take your pick; rather less red fruits, but does have length. Screwcap. 13.2° alc. **Rating** 88 **To** 2011 $28

Panorama

1848 Cygnet Coast Road, Cradoc, Tas 7109 **Region** Southern Tasmania
T (03) 6266 3409 **F** (03) 6266 3482 **www**.panoramavineyard.com.au **Open** Wed–Mon 10–5
Winemaker Michael Vishacki **Est.** 1974 **Cases** 5500
Michael and Sharon Vishacki purchased Panorama from Steve Ferencz in 1997, and have since spent considerable sums in building a more modern winery and an attractive cellar door sales outlet, and in trebling the vineyard size (7 ha pinot noir, 3 ha chardonnay and 1 ha sauvignon blanc). Exports to Canada, Singapore and China.

ŸŸŸŸŸ   Estate Chardonnay 2006 Elegant, intense, finely chiselled citrus and nectarine fruit, pushed and pulled by slightly austere Tasmanian acidity giving considerable length. Screwcap. **Rating** 90 **To** 2014 $32
Reserve Chardonnay 2005 Lots of vanilla on the bouquet, and the oak dominates the palate too; good flavour and persistence though, and still fresh and youthful. Twin top. 13.5° alc. **Rating** 90 **To** 2010 $60

ŸŸŸŸ   Tom Bordeaux Blend 2005 Attractive and quite ripe red fruit flavours, and plenty of oak in support; worth following. Screwcap. 13° alc. **Rating** 88 **To** 2012 $35

Panton Hill Winery

145 Manuka Road, Panton Hill, Vic 3759 **Region** Yarra Valley
T (03) 9719 7342 **F** (03) 9719 7362 **www**.pantonhillwinery.com.au **Open** W'ends & public hols 11–5, or by appt
Winemaker Dr Teunis AP Kwak **Est.** 1988 **Cases** 1500
Melbourne academic Dr Teunis Kwak and wife Dorothy have a 4-ha fully mature vineyard, part planted in 1976, the remainder in '88. The deliberately low-yielding vineyard was established on a fairly steep, picturesque, undulating hillside. Over the years the Kwaks have built four major, and a couple of lesser, stone buildings on the property, all built from sandstone sourced onsite or from their neighbour's paddocks. A number of left-field wines are made, including a Vintage Pinot Port, a Chardonnay Liqueur and a Sparkling Cabernet Franc, and the Kwaks cheerfully admit that even their table wines are calculated to please their cellar door customers rather than wine show judges.

ҮҮҮҮҮ Yarra Valley Chardonnay 2005 Bright green-yellow; plenty of varietal fruit depth and power, with layers of ripe stone fruit and melon; appropriate oak. Diam. 13° alc. **Rating** 90 **To** 2011 $25

Paracombe Wines ★★★★★

Main Road, Paracombe, SA 5132 **Region** Adelaide Hills
T (08) 8380 5058 **F** (08) 8380 5488 **www.**paracombewines.com **Open** By appt
Winemaker Paul Drogemuller **Est.** 1983 **Cases** 7700
Paul and Kathy Drogemuller established Paracombe following the devastating Ash Wednesday bushfires in 1983. It has become a very successful business, producing a range of wines from the 15-ha vineyard that are never less than good, often very good. The wines are made onsite in the 250-tonne winery with every part of the production process through to distribution handled from the winery. Exports to Canada, Sweden, Switzerland, Singapore, Taiwan and India.

ҮҮҮҮҮ Holland Creek Adelaide Hills Riesling 2007 Lime and passionfruit aromas and flavours; has excellent mouthfeel, with intense yet refined fruit running through to the finish; outstanding for the vintage. Screwcap. 12.5° alc. **Rating** 94 **To** 2015 $19
Adelaide Hills Sauvignon Blanc 2007 Intense aromas of thyme and wild flowers, the palate stacked with gooseberry and citrus fruit; has velocity and length; striking wine. Screwcap. 12.5° alc. **Rating** 94 **To** 2010 $21

ҮҮҮҮҮ Somerville Adelaide Hills Shiraz 2004 Higher pH (and alcohol) than the varietal evident in the colour; rich and powerful, the sheer density of the fruit helping to carry the alcohol; flavours of blackberry, dark chocolate and licorice before a spike of acidity on the finish. Cork. 16° alc. **Rating** 92 **To** 2018 $69
Adelaide Hills Cabernet Sauvignon 2004 Good hue; fresh red and black-currant fruit on both bouquet and the medium-bodied, lively palate; Paracombe does tend to keep one guessing. Screwcap. 14.5° alc. **Rating** 92 **To** 2016 $21
The Reuben 2004 Good hue; does show its alcohol, but there is a large volume of predominantly blackcurrant fruit, with the added complexity of an amazing blend of 6 clones of Cabernet Sauvignon (60%)/Merlot (14%)/Cabernet Franc (12%)/Malbec (8%)/Shiraz (6%). Screwcap. 15° alc. **Rating** 90 **To** 2019 $21
Adelaide Hills Cabernet Franc 2005 Retains excellent hue; a wine jumping around, with cassis, then tannins and finally acidity all coming through on the palate; could age well. Screwcap. 14° alc. **Rating** 90 **To** 2015 $27

ҮҮҮҮ Adelaide Hills Pinot Gris 2007 Pear, musk and spice aromas, then a touch of sweet citrus fruit on the palate; dry finish. Screwcap. 13° alc. **Rating** 89 **To** 2009 $19
Adelaide Hills Shiraz 2004 Does have a hard jab of alcohol, which disrupts the flow of the fruit line; flavours of blackberry and licorice. Screwcap. 15.5° alc. **Rating** 88 **To** 2014 $21
Adelaide Hills Shiraz Viognier 2005 Deep colour, a very powerful wine, but the alcohol fights with the influence of the co-fermented viognier and the French oak; a pity. Screwcap. 16° alc. **Rating** 88 **To** 2013 $21

Paradigm Hill ★★★★☆

26 Merricks Road, Merricks, Vic 3916 **Region** Mornington Peninsula
T (03) 5989 9000 **F** (03) 5989 8555 **www.**paradigmhill.com.au **Open** 1st w'end of month, public hols or by appt
Winemaker Dr George Mihaly **Est.** 1999 **Cases** 1200
Dr George Mihaly (with a background in medical research, then biotech and pharmaceutical industries) and wife Ruth (a former chef and caterer) have realised a 30-year dream of establishing their own vineyard and winery, abandoning their previous careers to do so. George had all the necessary scientific qualifications, and built on those by making the 2001

Merricks Creek wines, moving to home base at Paradigm Hill for the '02 vintage, all along receiving guidance and advice from Nat White from Main Ridge Estate. The vineyard, under Ruth's control with advice from Shane Strange, is planted to 2.1 ha of pinot noir, 1 ha of shiraz, 0.9 ha of riesling and 0.4 ha of pinot gris. Exports to the UK, Canada, China and Singapore.

ŸŸŸŸŸ **Col's Block Mornington Peninsula Shiraz 2006** Zesty red fruits and spices supported by good oak; a lovely example of cool-climate Shiraz with vibrant, juicy fruits on the fine, silky finish. Diam. 14° alc. **Rating** 94 **To** 2018 $38

ŸŸŸŸŸ **Mornington Peninsula Pinot Gris 2007** Ripe exotic fruits with tangerine and pear flesh; good flavour and complexity. Screwcap. 13.9° alc. **Rating** 90 **To** 2011 $39

L'ami Sage Mornington Peninsula Pinot Noir 2006 Generous red fruits at the core, plus plenty of spice; nice weight and texture, and an even finish. Diam. 14° alc. **Rating** 90 **To** 2012 $45

Paramoor Wines

439 Three Chain Road, Carlsruhe via Woodend, Vic 3442 **Region** Macedon Ranges
T (03) 5427 1057 **F** (03) 5427 3927 **www**.paramoor.com.au **Open** 7 days 10–5
Winemaker William Fraser **Est.** 2003 **Cases** 700
Paramoor Wines is the retirement venture of Will Fraser, formerly Managing Director of Kodak Australasia. To be strictly correct, he is Dr Will Fraser, armed with a PhD in chemistry from the Adelaide University. Very much later he added a Diploma of wine technology from the University of Melbourne, Dookie Campus, to his degrees. Paramoor's winery is set on 17 ha of beautiful country not far from Hanging Rock, originally a working Clydesdale horse farm, with a magnificent heritage-style barn now used for cellar door sales and functions. Will has planted 0.8 ha each of pinot noir and pinot gris, and intends to supplement the product range by purchasing varieties more suited to warmer climates than the chilly hills of the Macedon Ranges. He shares the winery with Keith Brien of Silver Wings Winemaking.

ŸŸŸŸŸ **The Fraser Shiraz Cabernet Sauvignon Merlot 2006** Absolutely seductive and delicious wine, with a panoply of luscious blackberry and blackcurrant fruit flavours; fine tannins give a silky mouthfeel. Outstanding value. Diam. 14.4° alc. **Rating** 96 **To** 2020 $22

ŸŸŸŸŸ **Joan Picton Pinot Noir 2006** Well-constructed pinot, all the parts in place: colour, flavour, texture, length and balance. Enjoyable now, but will build more complexity with time. Screwcap. 13° alc. **Rating** 92 **To** 2012 $22

Macedon Ranges Botrytis Riesling 2007 Kabinett level sweetness, but with lovely citrus fruit and overall thrust through to the finish. Cork. 11.5° alc. **Rating** 90 **To** 2012 $18

Paringa Estate

44 Paringa Road, Red Hill South, Vic 3937 **Region** Mornington Peninsula
T (03) 5989 2669 **F** (03) 5931 0135 **www**.paringaestate.com.au **Open** 7 days 11–5
Winemaker Lindsay McCall **Est.** 1985 **Cases** 12 000
Schoolteacher-turned-winemaker Lindsay McCall has shown an absolutely exceptional gift for winemaking across a range of styles, but with immensely complex Pinot Noir and Shiraz leading the way. The wines have an unmatched level of success in the wine shows and competitions Paringa Estate is able to enter, the limitation being the relatively small size of the production of the top wines in the portfolio. His skills are no less evident in contract winemaking for others. Exports to the UK, Denmark, Korea, Singapore and Hong Kong.

ŸŸŸŸŸ **Reserve Special Barrel Selection Shiraz 2006** Saturated colour; significantly greater volume of flavour than the Estate, even though alcohol is similar; all share the elements of spice and cracked pepper that make these wines so special. Screwcap. 14° alc. **Rating** 96 **To** 2026 $80

Estate Pinot Noir 2006 Fragrant aromas of cherry, plum and spice, then a lively, fresh palate, with pure varietal fruit expression; delicious now, or in 5–6 years time. Screwcap. 14.5° alc. **Rating** 95 **To** 2012 $60

Reserve Special Barrel Selection Pinot Noir 2006 A more complex bouquet than the Estate, and a correspondingly more complex palate, with deeper, darker fruit flavours; cellaring special. Screwcap. 14.5° alc. **Rating** 95 **To** 2016 $90

Estate Shiraz 2006 Vivid crimson; bright, fresh, highly spiced, peppery red fruits on a medium-bodied but very long palate, the tannins silky and fine. Outstanding cool-climate shiraz. Screwcap. 14° alc. **Rating** 95 **To** 2021 $50

Estate Chardonnay 2006 Still quite pale, but bright; intense nectarine and grapefruit flavours have subsumed the French oak; very good length. Screwcap. 14.5° alc. **Rating** 94 **To** 2013 $35

Estate Pinot Gris 2007 A super-fragrant and flowery bouquet, the palate providing intense support in a citrus/pear/apple spectrum; long, bone-dry finish. Equal to Seppelt Coborra. Screwcap. 14.5° alc. **Rating** 94 **To** 2009 $25

ＰＰＰＰＰ **Peninsula Shiraz 2006** Riper than the Estate, with more black fruit components, and slightly more tannin weight. Screwcap. 14.5° alc. **Rating** 93 **To** 2016 $25

Peninsula Chardonnay 2006 Lively, fragrant, fruit-driven style, with considerable length to the bright stone fruit flavours; good acidity. Screwcap. 14.5° alc. **Rating** 90 **To** 2011 $20

ＰＰＰＰ **Estate Riesling 2007** Full-flavoured; ripe lime with a touch of tropical fruit; not the usual finesse, but ready now. Screwcap. 14° alc. **Rating** 89 **To** 2011 $15

Parker Coonawarra Estate ★★★★★

Riddoch Highway, Coonawarra, SA 5263 **Region** Coonawarra
T (08) 8737 3525 **F** (08) 8737 3527 www.parkercoonawarraestate.com.au **Open** 7 days 10–4
Winemaker Peter Bissell (Contract) **Est.** 1985 **Cases** 7000
Parker Coonawarra Estate is at the southern end of Coonawarra, on rich terra rossa soil over limestone. Cabernet sauvignon is the predominant variety (17.45 ha), with minor plantings of merlot and petit verdot. Acquired by the Rathbone family in 2004. Exports to all major markets.

ＰＰＰＰＰ **Terra Rossa Cabernet Sauvignon 2005** Rich and generous, full of expressive cassis and blackcurrant fruit; silky tannins and quality oak; very long finish. Screwcap. 15° alc. **Rating** 95 **To** 2030 $34.95

Terra Rossa Merlot 2005 Strong varietal character, right from the first sniff through to the finish and aftertaste; a mix of redcurrant and snow pea, with a hint of olive; good structure and texture. Screwcap. 15° alc. **Rating** 94 **To** 2020 $39.50

Terra Rossa First Growth 2004 Cedar and earth aromas showing the first sign of developing; an austere style, with lurking tannins, but in the end all comes together very well. For classicists. Cork. 14.5° alc. **Rating** 94 **To** 2020 $79.95

ＰＰＰＰＰ **Terra Rossa First Growth 2005** Glorious deep purple-red; a complex bouquet, with fruit and oak both evident; the grippy tannins on the palate come as a shock; puzzling why they were not fined more. Screwcap. 15° alc. **Rating** 93 **To** 2025 $79.95

Parri Estate

Sneyd Road, Mount Compass, SA 5210 **Region** Southern Fleurieu/McLaren Vale
T (08) 8554 9660 **F** (08) 8554 9694 www.parriestate.com.au **Open** 7 days 11–5
Winemaker Linda Domas **Est.** 1998 **Cases** 10 000
Alice, Peter and John Phillips have established a substantial business with a clear marketing plan and an obvious commitment to quality. The 33-ha vineyard is planted to chardonnay, viognier, sauvignon blanc, semillon, pinot noir, cabernet sauvignon and shiraz, using modern trellis and

irrigation systems. In 2004 a 9-ha property on Ingoldby Road, McLaren Vale was acquired, with a modern warehouse and shiraz, grenache and cabernet sauvignon up to 60 years old. Exports to the UK, the US and other major markets.

ŸŸŸŸŸ **Pangkarra Southern Fleurieu Cabernet Sauvignon 2005** Bright colour; more blackberry than blackcurrant, but good flavour intensity; slightly one-dimensional on the finish, but quite long. Cork. 13.5° alc. **Rating** 90 **To** 2015 $24

ŸŸŸŸ **McLaren Vale Cabernet Sauvignon 2006** Quite concentrated with good flavour, plenty of cedar and some red berry fruits. Cork. 14° alc. **Rating** 89 **To** 2015 $20

Passing Clouds ★★★★

RMB 440 Kurting Road, Kingower, Vic 3517 **Region** Bendigo
T (03) 5438 8257 **F** (03) 5438 8246 **www**.passingclouds.com.au **Open** W'ends 12–5, Mon–Fri by appt
Winemaker Graeme Leith, Cameron Leith **Est.** 1974 **Cases** 4000
In 1974, Graeme Leith and Sue Mackinnon planted the first vines at Passing Clouds, 60 km northwest of Bendigo. Graeme Leith is one of the great personalities of the wine industry, with a superb sense of humour, and makes lovely regional reds with cassis, berry and mint fruit. Sheltered by hills of ironbark forest, the valley offers an ideal growing climate for premium red wine. The main varieties planted on the 6-ha vineyard are shiraz, cabernet sauvignon and pinot noir. With the passing of years (and clouds), Graeme is gradually handing over winemaking responsibilities to son Cameron. Wines from the Three Wise Men joint venture are also available (see separate entry). Exports to the UK and the US.

ŸŸŸŸŸ **The Angel Cabernet Sauvignon 2005** A fragrant mix of blackcurrant and mint fruit aromas; a medium-bodied palate, with silky texture and good length, pleasantly savoury tannins making a contribution. Diam. **Rating** 91 **To** 2015 $30
Pinot Noir 2006 A powerful palate; abundant dark plum/black cherry fruit, and fine but persistent tannins; needs 3+ years to fully open up. Diam. 14° alc. **Rating** 90 **To** 2013 $23

ŸŸŸŸ **Reserve Bendigo Shiraz 2006** A smooth medium-bodied wine, with gently ripe blackberry fruit and mocha/vanillin notes on the relatively soft finish; no need for cellaring. Diam. **Rating** 89 **To** 2015 $35
Zonnebeke Shiraz 2006 Full-bodied, and dominated by tannins that run through the length of the palate; needs time, but it is not certain it will come into balance. Diam. 13.6° alc. **Rating** 88 **To** 2016 $30

Patina

109 Summerhill Lane, Orange, NSW 2800 **Region** Orange
T (02) 6362 8336 **F** (02) 6361 2949 **www**.patinawines.com.au **Open** By appt
Winemaker Gerald Naef **Est.** 1999 **Cases** NFP
Gerald Naef's family home in Woodbridge in the Central Valley of California was surrounded by the vast vineyard and winery operations of Gallo and Robert Mondavi. It would be hard to imagine a more different environment than that provided by Orange. Gerald Naef and wife Angie left California in 1981, initially establishing an irrigation farm in the northwest of NSW, but 20 years later moved to Orange, and by 2006 Gerald Naef was a final-year student of wine science at CSU. He set up a micro-winery at the Orange Cool Stores, and his first wine was a 2003 Chardonnay, made from vines planted by him in '99. At its first show entry it won the trophy for Best White Wine of Show at the Orange Wine Show '06, of which I was Chairman. Dream starts seldom come better than this. No samples received; the rating is that of last year.

Patrick T Wines

Cnr Ravenswood Lane/Riddoch Highway, Coonawarra, SA 5263 **Region** Coonawarra
T (08) 8737 3687 **F** (08) 8737 3689 **www**.patricktwines.com **Open** 7 days 10–5
Winemaker Pat Tocaciu **Est.** 1996 **Cases** 10 000
Patrick Tocaciu is a district veteran, setting up Patrick T Winemaking Services after prior careers at Heathfield Ridge Winery and Hollick Wines. He and his partners have almost 55 ha of vines at Wrattonbully, and another 2 ha of cabernet sauvignon in Coonawarra. The Wrattonbully plantings cover all the major varieties, while the Coonawarra plantings give rise to the Home Block Cabernet Sauvignon. Also carries out contract winemaking for others. Exports to Chile and Korea.

ŶŶŶŶ   **Wrattonbully Sauvignon Blanc 2007** A spotlessly clean, crisp bouquet and palate; light fruit mainly in the snow pea/grass spectrum; nice dry finish. Screwcap. 12° alc. **Rating** 88 **To** 2010 $18

Patritti Wines

13–23 Clacton Road, Dover Gardens, SA 5048 **Region** Adelaide Zone
T (08) 8296 8261 **F** (08) 8296 5088 **www**.patritti.com.au **Open** Mon–Sat 9–5
Winemaker G Patritti, J Mungall, B Heide **Est.** 1926 **Cases** 150 000
A traditional, family-owned business offering wines at modest prices, but with impressive vineyard holdings of 10 ha of shiraz in Blewitt Springs and 6 ha of grenache at Aldinga North. The surging production (which increased from 100 000 cases to 150 000 cases in 2007) points to success in export markets, and also to the utilisation of contract-grown grapes as well as estate-grown. Exports to the US and other major markets.

Paul Bettio Wines

34 Simpsons Lane, Moyhu, Vic 3732 **Region** King Valley
T (03) 5727 9308 **F** (03) 5727 9344 **www**.paulbettiowines.com.au **Open** 7 days 10–5
Winemaker Damien Star **Est.** 1995 **Cases** 7000
The Bettio family, with Paul and Daniel at the helm, have established 27 ha of vines in the King Valley. The plantings are of sauvignon blanc, chardonnay, merlot and cabernet sauvignon, and the wines, including a range of back vintages, are chiefly sold through the cellar door. A new cellar door and café are being constructed on King Valley Road.

ŶŶŶŶ   **Cabernet Merlot 2007** Nice fleshy, forward cabernet fruit, with hints of cassis and quite good structure; a good wine considering the drama of the vintage. Screwcap. 13.8° alc. **Rating** 87 **To** 2012 $11

Paul Conti Wines

529 Wanneroo Road, Woodvale, WA 6026 **Region** Greater Perth Zone
T (08) 9409 9160 **F** (08) 9309 1634 **www**.paulcontiwines.com.au **Open** Mon–Sat 10–5,
Sun by appt
Winemaker Paul Conti, Jason Conti **Est.** 1948 **Cases** 6000
Third-generation winemaker Jason Conti has now assumed control of winemaking, although father Paul (who succeeded his father in 1968) remains interested and involved in the business. Over the years Paul Conti challenged and redefined industry perceptions and standards; the challenge for Jason Conti was to achieve the same degree of success in a relentlessly and increasingly competitive market environment, and he is doing just that. Plantings at the Carabooda Vineyard have been expanded with 1 ha of tempranillo, petit verdot and viognier, and both pinot noir and merlot are purchased from Manjimup. Exports to the UK, Indonesia and Japan.

ŶŶŶŶŶ   **The Tuarts Chenin Blanc 2007** Nice clean fruit with hints of fresh green apple and lively acidity; fine and dry on the flavoursome finish. Screwcap. 13.5° alc. **Rating** 91 **To** 2012 $16

Mariginiup Shiraz 2005 Bright fruits with a savoury edge; good flavour and depth if just a little short. Cork. 15° alc. Rating 90 To 2015 $28

ŶŶŶŶ Medici Ridge Shiraz 2006 Abundant, concentrated and sweet, ripe fruit with plenty of vanilla oak. Cork. 14.5° alc. Rating 89 To 2014 $14
Old Vine Grenache Shiraz 2006 Charry oak dominates the bouquet, but good fruit concentration pushes through on the palate and delivers plenty of red berry flavours, and a long, firm finish. Screwcap. 14.5° alc. Rating 89 To 2013 $16
Late Harvest Muscat Fronti 2007 Clean, fresh, vibrant and full of grapey aromatics. A nice example of an off-dry style. Screwcap. 11° alc. Rating 88 To 2011 $16

Paul Osicka ★★★★

Majors Creek Vineyard at Graytown, Vic 3608 **Region** Heathcote
T (03) 5794 9235 **F** (03) 5794 9288 **Open** By appt
Winemaker Paul Osicka **Est.** 1955 **Cases** NA
A frustratingly low-profile producer but reliable, particularly when it comes to its smooth but rich Shiraz. Exports to Ireland, Hong Kong and Japan.

ŶŶŶŶŶ Majors Creek Vineyard Heathcote Shiraz 2005 Deep colour; very rich, ripe, concentrated and luscious prune and black fruit flavours from the oldest vines in the region; tannins controlled, oak likewise. Cork. 15.5° alc. Rating 93 To 2020 $36

Paulett ★★★★★

Polish Hill Road, Polish Hill River, SA 5453 **Region** Clare Valley
T (08) 8843 4328 **F** (08) 8843 4202 **www**.paulettwines.com.au **Open** 7 days 10–5
Winemaker Neil Paulett **Est.** 1983 **Cases** 13 000
The Paulett story is a saga of Australian perseverance, commencing with the 1982 purchase of a property with 1 ha of vines and a house, promptly destroyed by the terrible Ash Wednesday bushfires of the following year. Son Matthew has joined Neil and Alison Paulett as a partner in the business, responsible for viticulture, and the plantings now total 25 ha on a much-expanded property holding of 147 ha. The winery and cellar door have wonderful views over the Polish Hill River region, and the memories of the bushfires are long gone. Exports to the UK, NZ and Hong Kong.

ŶŶŶŶŶ Antonina Riesling 2006 Less colour development than the '07 varietal; a super-elegant wine, with perfectly fused apple, citrus and slate flavours, then squeaky, lemony acidity on the finish. Screwcap. 12° alc. Rating 96 To 2019 $38
Andreas 2004 Sweet black cherry, blackberry, mocha and vanilla aromas and flavours; fine-grained tannins, and considerable length. Shiraz. Screwcap. 14° alc. Rating 94 To 2024 $42

ŶŶŶŶŶ Polish Hill River Riesling 2007 Full green-yellow; an early-developing, full-flavoured, ripe pineapple and tropical mix; redeeming acidity. Screwcap. 12.5° alc. Rating 90 To 2012 $20

ŶŶŶŶ Polish Hill River Shiraz 2004 Slightly sawdusty oak impinges on ripe fruit; some choc mint plus vanilla flavours. Screwcap. 14° alc. Rating 89 To 2014 $22
Polish Hill River Cabernet Merlot 2004 A medium-bodied mix of spicy, savoury, cedary notes alongside redcurrant and blackcurrant fruit. Screwcap. 14° alc. Rating 88 To 2014 $22

Paulmara Estate ★★★★

47 Park Avenue, Rosslyn Park, SA 5072 (postal) **Region** Barossa Valley
T 0417 895 138 **F** (08) 8364 3019 **www**.paulmara.com.au **Open** Not
Winemaker Paul Georgiadis, Neil Pike **Est.** 1999 **Cases** 250

Born to an immigrant Greek family, Paul Georgiadis grew up in Waikerie, where his family had vineyards and orchards. His parents worked sufficiently hard to send him first to St Peters College in Adelaide and then to do a marketing degree at Adelaide University. He became the whirlwind grower relations manager for Southcorp, and one of the best known faces in the Barossa Valley. Paul and wife Mara established a 12-ha vineyard in 1995, planted to semillon, shiraz, sangiovese, merlot and cabernet sauvignon. Part of the production is sold, and the best shiraz makes the Syna Shiraz ('syna' being Greek for together). Exports to the UK and the US.

ΨΨΨΨΨ **Syna Barossa Valley Shiraz 2006** Old-fashioned style; sweet fruit with sweet oak to complement, but the depth of flavour is undeniable; the real question is how tannic this wine is, and the answer is very. Cork. 15.4° alc. **Rating** 91 To 2020 $80

Paxton ★★★★★

Wheaton Road, McLaren Vale, SA 5171 **Region** McLaren Vale
T (08) 8323 8645 **F** (08) 8323 8903 **www**.paxtonvineyards.com **Open** Thurs–Sun 10–5, public hols by appt
Winemaker Michael Paxton **Est.** 1979 **Cases** 14 000
David Paxton is one of Australia's best known viticulturists and consultants. He founded Paxton Vineyards in McLaren Vale with his family in 1979, and has since been involved in various capacities in the establishment and management of vineyards in several leading regions across the country. Former Flying Winemaker, son Michael (with 14 years' experience in Spain, South America, France and Australia) is responsible for making the wines. There are five vineyards in the 67.87-ha family holdings: the Thomas Block, the Jones Block, Quandong Farm and Landcross Farm Settlement and Homestead. Here an underground barrel store has been completed and a cellar door opened in the original shearing shed. Paxton has become the first member of 1% For The Planet (www.onepercentfortheplanet.org). By 2006 all of the five vineyards were managed using full biodynamic principles. Exports to the UK, the US, Canada, Denmark and Sweden.

ΨΨΨΨΨ **Elizabeth Jean 100 Year McLaren Vale Shiraz 2005** A fitting tribute to the 100th birthday of David Paxton's mother and Michael Paxton's grandmother; the vines are also 100 years old. An effortless spectrum of blackberry, plum, cherry and spice; silky tannins and great mouthfeel. Cork. 14.5° alc. **Rating** 96 To 2030 $85
McLaren Vale Chardonnay 2007 Outstanding McLaren Vale chardonnay; an aromatic stone fruit and grapefruit bouquet leads into a palate with quality French barrel ferment notes enshrining the fruit; very good texture and length. Screwcap. 13.5° alc. **Rating** 94 To 2013 $29
Jones Block McLaren Vale Shiraz 2004 Full of lively, sweet but not jammy, red and black fruits supported by fine, ripe tannins and well-balanced oak on a long palate. Lingering finish. Cork. 14.5° alc. **Rating** 94 To 2019 $39
AAA McLaren Vale Shiraz Grenache 2006 Attractive medium-bodied wine, with considerable drive and movement; spiced black fruits, fine tannins and no cosmetic notes from the grenache. Screwcap. 14.2° alc. **Rating** 94 To 2014 $23

ΨΨΨΨΨ **Quandong Farm McLaren Vale Shiraz 2006** With more elegance than many McLaren Vale shirazs, yet is strongly regional with dark chocolate wrapping around black fruits and controlled oak. Screwcap. 14.5° alc. **Rating** 92 To 2016 $30
McLaren Vale Chardonnay 2006 A fractionally oaky bouquet, but then a streamlined, fine and long palate, nectarine and melon fruit leading the way. Screwcap. 13.5° alc. **Rating** 91 To 2010 $29

ΨΨΨΨ **McLaren Vale Pinot Gris 2007** A complex bouquet and palate, unusual for this variety; lemon and pear, with a crisp finish; 230 cases made. Screwcap. 14° alc. **Rating** 89 To 2009 $23

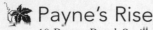 Payne's Rise   ★★★

10 Paynes Road, Seville, Vic 3139 **Region** Yarra Valley
T 0408 618 346 **F** (03) 5961 9383 **www**.paynesrise.com.au **Open** By appt
Winemaker Jeff Wright, Keith Salter (Contract) **Est.** 1998 **Cases** 500
Tim and Narelle Cullen have progressively established 2 ha of cabernet sauvignon and 1 ha each of shiraz and sauvignon blanc since 1998, supplemented by chardonnay and pinot noir purchased from local growers. They carry out all the vineyard work in parallel with full-time employment elsewhere, Tim as a viticulturist for a local agribusiness, and Narelle as a hairdresser. The contract-made wines have won several awards at the Victorian Wine Show.

🍷🍷🍷 **Yarra Valley Cabernet Sauvignon 2004** Light- to medium-bodied; a mix of mint, leaf and red berry fruit; not much texture or structure, but the overall flavour is fresh. Close-planted vines. Cork. 13.8° alc. **Rating** 87 **To** 2010 $22

Peacock Hill Vineyard   ★★★

29 Palmers Lane, Pokolbin, NSW 2320 **Region** Lower Hunter Valley
T (02) 4998 7661 **F** (02) 4998 7661 **www**.peacockhill.com.au **Open** Thurs–Mon, public & school hols 10–5, or by appt
Winemaker George Tsiros, Bill Sneddon, Rod Russell, Steve Langham (Contract)
Est. 1969 **Cases** 1500
The Peacock Hill Vineyard was first planted in 1969 as part of the Rothbury Estate, originally owned by a separate syndicate but then moving under the direct control and ownership of Rothbury. After several further changes of ownership as Rothbury sold many of its vineyards, George Tsiros and Silvi Laumets acquired the 8-ha property in 1995.

🍷🍷🍷 **A Great Life 2006** Ripe black cherry and blackcurrant fruit, more so than alcohol might suggest; needs time to shed some of its weight. Cork. 14° alc. **Rating** 89 **To** 2016 $45

Pearson Vineyards   ★★★

Main North Road, Penwortham, SA 5453 **Region** Clare Valley
T (08) 8843 4234 **F** (08) 8843 4141 **Open** As per roadside sign
Winemaker Jim Pearson **Est.** 1993 **Cases** 500
Jim Pearson makes the Pearson Vineyard wines at Mintaro Cellars. The 1.5-ha estate vineyards surround the beautiful little stone house, which acts as a cellar door – and which appears on the cover of my book, *The Wines, The History, The Vignerons of the Clare Valley*. Exports to the US.

🍷🍷🍷 **Clare Valley Cabernet Franc 2006** Spicy/leafy/minty red fruits in a light- to medium-bodied frame; some Chinon aspects; for the adventurous. Screwcap. 14° alc. **Rating** 87 **To** 2012 $20

Pearwood Wines Piccadilly   NR

4 Lampert Road, Piccadilly, SA 5151 **Region** Adelaide Hills
T (08) 8339 1749 **Open** By appt
Winemaker Simon Greenleaf (Contract) **Est.** 2007 **Cases** NFP
This is the venture of the Swaly family (Bernard, Sandra and Andrew), which has a longer history than the year of establishment would suggest. When Bernard Swaly was working for the CSIRO Land and Water Division, he grew raspberries on what had previously been a vegetable market garden, but changed to vines after the 1983 bushfires, planting chardonnay which was sold to Petaluma. In 1999 Yalumba took over the purchase agreement, and supplied the high-quality Burgundy clone 76 and 95, now part of the 2.1 ha plantings. Senior Yalumba winemaker Louisa Rose believes the character of the chardonnay is quite similar to that of Tasmania thanks to the cool, quite wet site climate of Pearwood. In 2005 the grape surplus led to a small-volume production for home consumption, but as from '07 the quantities (while limited) are of commercial size.

Peel Estate ★★★★

Fletcher Road, Baldivis, WA 6171 **Region** Peel
T (08) 9524 1221 **F** (08) 9524 1625 **www**.peelwine.com.au **Open** 7 days 10–5
Winemaker Will Nairn, Mark Morton **Est.** 1974 **Cases** 6500
The icon wine is the Shiraz, a wine of considerable finesse and with a remarkably consistent track record. Every year Will Nairn holds a Great Shiraz Tasting for 6-year-old Australian Shirazs, and pits Peel Estate (in a blind tasting attended by 100 or so people) against Australia's best. It is never disgraced. The wood-matured Chenin Blanc is another winery speciality, although not achieving the excellence of the Shiraz. Exports to the UK, the US, Malaysia, Japan and Singapore.

 Chardonnay 2005 Well made; grapefruit, melon and plenty of toasty oak; the creamy texture is cleaned up with vibrant acidity, and the finish is complex, nutty and long. Screwcap. 13.5° alc. **Rating** 92 **To** 2012 $20

Peerick Vineyard ★★★★

Wild Dog Track, Moonambel, Vic 3478 **Region** Pyrenees
T (03) 5467 2207 **F** (03) 5467 2207 **www**.peerick.com.au **Open** W'ends & public hols 11–4
Winemaker Chris Jessup, Mount Langhi Ghiran (Dan Buckle) **Est.** 1990 **Cases** 2000
Peerick is the venture of Chris Jessup and wife Meryl. They have mildly trimmed their Joseph's coat vineyard by increasing the plantings to 5.6 ha and eliminating the malbec and semillon, but still grow cabernet sauvignon, shiraz, cabernet franc, merlot, sauvignon blanc and viognier. Quality has improved as the vines have reached maturity. Exports to NZ.

 Pyrenees Shiraz 2005 Medium-bodied, but with a coruscating display of ripe fruits on the one hand, and cinnamon, spice and licorice on the other, the tannins fine and ripe, oak appropriate. Screwcap. 13.5° alc. **Rating** 92 **To** 2015
Pyrenees Merlot 2005 At the upper end of good merlot in terms of ripeness and weight, but retains good varietal character in a redcurrant mode; tannins under control. Screwcap. 14° alc. **Rating** 91 **To** 2016

YYYY **Pyrenees Viognier 2007** Has plenty of varietal fruit, but pays the penalty of a somewhat touchy, phenolic finish. This is a difficult variety, period. Screwcap. 13° alc. **Rating** 87 **To** 2011

✿ Pemberley Farms ★★★

Box 107, Pemberton, WA 6260 **Region** Pemberton
T (08) 9776 1373 **F** (08) 9776 1373 **www**.pemberleyfarms.com.au **Open** Not
Winemaker Willow Bridge Estate (David Crawford) **Est.** 1995 **Cases** 1000
Pemberley Farms is owned by David and Monica Radomiljac. Known as Rado for short, David has been a vineyard manager in Pemberton for several decades. As well as 14 ha of vineyards owned by Pemberley Farms, Rado manages a 35-ha vineyard at Forest View, with all of the grapes sold to Houghton and Willow Bridge Estate, and a 60-ha vineyard at Big Tree contracted to Goundrey and Houghton. The Big Tree Vineyard was awarded the Best New Vineyard Development at the WA Wine Industry Awards 2005. The focused marketing in Broome of the relatively small amount of Pemberley Farms wines made by David Crawford (at Willow Bridge) is interesting: it is called the Broome Wine Collection, because David and Monica realised the wines being offered to these major tourist destinations had no link whatsoever with the regions. Since you can't grow grapes and make wine in Broome or the Kimberleys, they have done the next best thing through wine names and label designs.

YYYY **Sauvignon Blanc 2007** A quiet, clean bouquet, then a zesty palate with some lemon sherbet and cut grass flavours; strong acid to close. Screwcap. 13° alc. **Rating** 89 **To** 2010 $19
Cable Beach Sunset Sauvignon Blanc Semillon 2007 Firm, crisp and well-balanced, with mineral, citrus and grass elements neatly fused; particularly good value. Screwcap. 12.5° alc. **Rating** 88 **To** 2010 $12

Kimberley Dawn Rose 2007 Considerable red fruit fragrance and mid-palate fruit flavour; the feared off-dry finish doesn't materialise. Good value. Screwcap. 13° alc. **Rating** 88 **To** 2009 $11

Pemberley Pearl Chardonnay 2007 Light-bodied white peach and other stone fruits; unembellished and fresh. Value. Screwcap. 13° alc. **Rating** 87 **To** 2009 $12

Pindan Shiraz 2004 Brilliantly clear colour; likewise flavours, which are untrammelled by any tannins or oak to speak of. For a summer's day in Broome. Screwcap. 14.5° alc. **Rating** 87 **To** 2010 $16

Penfolds   ★★★★★

Tanunda Road, Nuriootpa, SA 5355 **Region** Barossa Valley
T (08) 8568 9389 **F** (08) 8568 9489 **www.**penfolds.com.au **Open** Mon–Fri 10–5, w'ends & public hols 11–5
Winemaker Peter Gago **Est.** 1844 **Cases** 1.4 million

Senior among the numerous wine companies or stand-alone brands of Foster's and undoubtedly one of the top wine companies in the world in terms of quality, product range and exports. The consistency of the quality of the red wines and their value for money has long been recognised worldwide; the white wines, headed by the ultra-premium Yattarna Chardonnay, are now on a par with the red wines. Exports to the UK and the US.

ҮҮҮҮҮ Great Grandfather Rare Old Liqueur Tawny NV Rich, but by no means heavy; great balance rancio and fruit; long and very fine; superbly balanced. Cork. 19° alc. **Rating** 96 **To** 2009 $349.95

Yattarna Chardonnay 2005 Remarkably pale and bright colour; apple, nectarine and melon; new oak especially apparent after '04, but is balanced and will settle down as wine ages over next six months; very long finish. Screwcap. 13.5° alc. **Rating** 95 **To** 2015 $129.99

Grange 2003 Deep and bright colour; major surprise along the lines of the '00, albeit in very different style; here there is density and structure; the fruit is rich, but not spongy or dead. Ultra careful selection. **Rating** 95 **To** 2028 $550

Bin 389 Cabernet Shiraz 2005 Super luscious, voluptuous black fruits, with an underlay of red; rippling velvety tannins; almost too much sweet fruit, but likely it's just puppy fat waiting to be shed. **Rating** 95 **To** 2029 $57.99

Bin 51 Eden Valley Riesling 2007 High-toned effusive aromas mix blossom and spice; the palate follows precisely in footsteps of bouquet; won't be especially long-lived, but will always charm. Screwcap. 12.4° alc. **Rating** 94 **To** 2012 $31.99

Thomas Hyland Chardonnay 2006 A restrained, cool-climate style, with good line, length and balance; the Robe component (49%) drives the style and flavour every bit as much as the Adelaide Hills component (55%); Fleurieu (6%). Controlled barrel ferment/wild yeast adds complexity. Screwcap. 13° alc. **Rating** 94 **To** 2010 $20.95

Kalimna Bin 28 Shiraz 2005 Excellent hue and depth; abundant flavour, depth and structure; luscious blackberry, licorice fruit; firm, balanced tannins. **Rating** 94 **To** 2025 $31.99

Bin 128 Coonawarra Shiraz 2006 A gorgeous mouthful of fruit bursting with flavour; great texture and structure; potentially the best ever. **Rating** 94 **To** 2020 $32.99

RWT Barossa Shiraz 2005 Good red-purple; fragrant aromas of black cherry, plum and blackberry; utterly delicious mouthfeel and seductive fruit; will live, but extreme patience not needed. **Rating** 94 **To** 2020 $159.99

Grandfather Fine Old Liqueur Tawny NV The colour almost indistinguishable from Great Grandfather, but on the one hand has more power, yet on the other, less of the silky smoothness of the older wine. Cork. 19.5° alc. **Rating** 94 **To** 2009 $99.95

ҮҮҮҮҮ Reserve Bin Chardonnay 2006 Bin 06A. Despite lower alcohol, a mouthfilling wine developing more quickly than the '04 or '05. 13.1° alc. **Rating** 93 **To** 2010 $89.99

St Henri 2004 Really interesting; is true to St Henri style, even with all on offer from the vintage; for a fleeting moment it seemed it could be best yet under this label, but the finish said otherwise. Very, very good wine, but not great. **Rating** 93 **To** 2019 $89.99

ŢŢŢŢ **Thomas Hyland Chardonnay 2007** Elegant wine, aromatic and fine, with citrussy elements to the stone fruit, the oak well-balanced. Screwcap. 13° alc. **Rating** 89 **To** 2011 $20.95
Koonunga Hill Cabernet Sauvignon 2006 Medium-bodied; good varietal expression, with blackcurrant fruit rather than tannins or oak doing the talking, but has adequate structure. Screwcap. 13.5° alc. **Rating** 89 **To** 2015 $15.95
Rawson's Retreat Chardonnay 2007 Has plenty of flavour, a trade-off with the purer fruit of Lindemans Bin 65, oak slightly more evident in Penfolds style. Screwcap. 13.5° alc. **Rating** 87 **To** 2010 $11.95
Koonunga Hill Shiraz 2006 Light- to medium-bodied; moderately savoury/earthy overtones to the black fruits; balanced oak and tannins; slightly disappointing given the vintage. Screwcap. 13.5° alc. **Rating** 87 **To** 2013 $15.95
Koonunga Hill Cabernet Merlot 2006 Light- to medium-bodied; well made at this price point; gentle cassis and berry fruit; modest length. Screwcap. 13.5° alc. **Rating** 87 **To** 2010 $15.95

Penfolds Magill Estate ★★★★☆
78 Penfold Road, Magill, SA 5072 **Region** Adelaide Zone
T (08) 8301 5400 **F** (08) 8301 5544 **www**.penfolds.com **Open** 7 days 10.30–4.30
Winemaker Peter Gago **Est.** 1844 **Cases** 3 million
This is the birthplace of Penfolds, established by Dr Christopher Rawson Penfold in 1844, his house still part of the immaculately maintained property. It includes 5.2 ha of precious shiraz used to make Magill Estate; the original and subsequent winery buildings, most still in operation or in museum condition; and the much-acclaimed Magill Restaurant, with panoramic views of the city, a great wine list and fine dining. All this is a 20-min drive from Adelaide's CBD.

ŢŢŢŢŢ **Shiraz 2005** Intense hue; an interesting wine, with a mix of sweet fruit and more herbal characters; good, but at this stage not in the class of the '04. **Rating** 93 **To** 2025 $99.99

Penley Estate ★★★★☆
McLeans Road, Coonawarra, SA 5263 **Region** Coonawarra
T (08) 8736 3211 **F** (08) 8736 3124 **www**.penley.com.au **Open** 7 days 10–4
Winemaker Kym Tolley **Est.** 1988 **Cases** 40 000
Owner winemaker Kym Tolley describes himself as a fifth-generation winemaker, the family tree involving both the Penfolds and the Tolleys. He worked 17 years in the industry before establishing Penley Estate and has made every post a winner since, producing a succession of rich, complex, full-bodied red wines and stylish Chardonnays. These are made from 111 precious ha of estate plantings. Exports to all major markets.

ŢŢŢŢŢ **Special Select Coonawarra Shiraz 2005** Great colour; a very oaky bouquet, but an abundance of ripe, dark fruits and even a little fruitcake spice; full-bodied and tannic, and should age gracefully. Cork. 15° alc. **Rating** 94 **To** 2012 $50.50

ŢŢŢŢŢ **Reserve Coonawarra Cabernet Sauvignon 2005** Full-bodied, with supple tannins and layers of dark fruits; has good line and length, but does show some heat from the 15° alcohol. Cork. 15° alc. **Rating** 90 **To** 2018 $50.50

ŢŢŢŢ **Condor Shiraz Cabernet 2006** Very firm, and as yet rather callow; nice flavour, but needs time to soften and open up. **Rating** 89 **To** 2015 $18.95
Gryphon Coonawarra Merlot 2006 Good concentration, with nice depth of fruit to the bouquet and flavour to match, but somewhat one-dimensional. Screwcap. 15° alc. **Rating** 88 **To** 2013 $18.95

Phoenix Coonawarra Cabernet Sauvignon 2006 Good cabernet character and quite juicy and forward; plenty of fruit, and made to be enjoyed as a young wine. Screwcap. 15° alc. **Rating** 88 **To** 2014 $18.95

Penmara   ★★★★

Suite 42, 5–13 Larkin Street, Camperdown, NSW 2050 (postal) **Region** Upper Hunter Valley/Orange
T (02) 9517 4429 **F** (02) 9517 4439 **www**.penmarawines.com.au **Open** Not
Winemaker Hunter Wine Services (John Horden) **Est.** 2000 **Cases** 25 000
Penmara was formed with the banner 'Five Families: One Vision', pooling most of their grapes, with a central processing facility, and marketing focused exclusively on exports. The six sites are Lilyvale Vineyards, in the Northern Slopes Zone near Tenterfield; Tangaratta Vineyards at Tamworth; Birnam Wood, Rothbury Ridge and Martindale Vineyards in the Hunter Valley; and Highland Heritage at Orange. In all, these vineyards give Penmara access to 128 ha of shiraz, chardonnay, cabernet sauvignon, semillon, verdelho and merlot, mainly from the Hunter Valley and Orange. Exports to the UK, the US and other major markets.

♥♥♥♥♀ **Reserve Orange Sauvignon Blanc 2007** An aromatic, gently tropical bouquet; has the required intensity and thrust of good sauvignon blanc to its mix of tropical and more citrussy/minerally fruit. Screwcap. 11° alc. **Rating** 93 **To** 2010 $19.95
Five Families Riesling 2005 More weight than the '06, partly bottle-developed, partly vintage impact; excellent length thanks to a citrus backbone. Screwcap. 13.5° alc. **Rating** 92 **To** 2015 $15.95

♥♥♥♥ **Five Families Riesling 2006** Clean, clear-cut riesling flavours with a distinctly minerally structure. Orange. Screwcap. 13.5° alc. **Rating** 89 **To** 2013 $15.95
Reserve Orange Shiraz 2006 As with all the current release Penmara wines, spinning screwcap lifts straight off; wine still has primary spicy savoury black fruits, but should be drunk asap. Screwcap. 13.5° alc. **Rating** 87 **To** 2009 $19.95
Reserve MCP 2006 Extraordinary; as the back label suggests, there are peachy undertones to the bouquet; the palate is juicy, here with touches of mint and lemon; loose screwcap a real worry. Merlot/Cabernet Franc/Petit Verdot. Screwcap. 13.5° alc. **Rating** 87 **To** 2009 $19.95

Penna Lane Wines   ★★★★☆

Lot 51, Penna Lane, Penwortham via Clare, SA 5453 **Region** Clare Valley
T (08) 8843 4364 **F** (08) 8843 4349 **www**.pennalanewines.com.au **Open** Thurs–Sun & public hols 11–5, or by appt
Winemaker Ray Klavins, Paulett Wines **Est.** 1998 **Cases** 3500
A seachange brought Ray Klavins and Stephen Stafford-Brookes together. Ray ran a landscaping business in Adelaide and Stephen was a sales rep in the UK. Both decided to get into wine production and, with enormous support from their wives, began studying oenology and viticulture at Roseworthy College in 1991. Ray and wife Lynette purchased their 14-ha property in the Skilly Hills in '93; it was covered with rubbish, Salvation Jane, a derelict dairy and tumbledown piggery. They spent all their spare time clearing up the property, living in a tent and the old shearing shed, and planted the first vines in '94. In '98 the Klavins and Stafford-Brookes families formed a partnership to produce and sell wine under the Penna Lane label. Exports to the US and Hong Kong.

♥♥♥♥♀ **Clare Valley Sauvignon Blanc Semillon 2007** Surprising varietal expression; gooseberry and passionfruit offset with mineral and herb notes from the semillon; has balance and length. Screwcap. 12.5° alc. **Rating** 92 **To** 2011 $18
Clare Valley Riesling 2007 Some blossom aromas; a rich, ripe, tropical/citrus mix, with the weight typical of '07, but also the lack of finesse. Screwcap. 12.6° alc. **Rating** 90 **To** 2012 $20
Clare Valley Cabernet Sauvignon 2005 Firm, blackcurrant fruit with some earthy, pencil shaving characters, which in fact meld quite well. Screwcap. 14° alc. **Rating** 90 **To** 2015 $24

♟♟♟♟ Clare Valley Shiraz 2005 A powerful wine, suggesting riper fruit and higher
alcohol than is the case, the palate dense, with some sweet fruit notes; needs a
touch more focus. Screwcap. 14.3° alc. **Rating** 89 **To** 2013 $24
Clare Valley Rambling Rose 2007 Abundant flavours of raspberry and black
cherry fruit; a full finish, the touch of sweetness balanced by acidity. Screwcap.
13.5° alc. **Rating** 87 **To** 2010 $18

Penny's Hill ★★★★★

Main Road, McLaren Vale, SA 5171 **Region** McLaren Vale
T (08) 8556 4460 **F** (08) 8556 4462 **www**.pennyshill.com.au **Open** 7 days 10–5
Winemaker Ben Riggs **Est.** 1988 **Cases** 9000
Penny's Hill is owned by Adelaide advertising agency businessman Tony Parkinson and wife
Susie. The vineyard is 43.5 ha and, unusually for McLaren Vale, is close-planted with a thin
vertical trellis/thin vertical canopy, the work of consultant viticulturist David Paxton. The
innovative red dot packaging was the inspiration of Tony Parkinson, recalling the red dot 'sold'
sign on pictures and giving rise to the Red Dot Art Gallery at Penny's Hill. The restaurant was
officially named as Australia's Best Restaurant in a Winery for 2007/08. Exports to all major
markets, particularly via the Woop Woop joint venture between Ben Riggs and Penny's Hill.

♟♟♟♟♟ McLaren Vale Shiraz 2006 Dark chocolate aromas; mulberry and flamboyant
oak aromas; thickly textured and full-bodied on the palate; rich and expansive on
the finish. Cork. 14.5° alc. **Rating** 94 **To** 2020 $27
Footprint McLaren Vale Shiraz 2005 Ultra-regional, with dark chocolate
framing the core of quite juicy blackberry fruit, the tannins and oak completing
the picture. Cork. 14.5° alc. **Rating** 94 **To** 2015 $50

♟♟♟♟♟ Specialized McLaren Vale Shiraz Cabernet Merlot 2006 Obvious toasty
oak, but with very good fruit concentration and a long, almost luscious finish.
Cork. 15° alc. **Rating** 91 **To** 2018 $22
Red Dot Shiraz Viognier 2006 Achieves the synergy expected of the blend;
soft, plush mouthfeel, with lifted berry aromas and flavours; easy drinking style.
Screwcap. 15° alc. **Rating** 90 **To** 2014 $14.95

♟♟♟♟ The Black Chook Shiraz Viognier 2006 Curiously, despite the lower alcohol
than the Red Dot, seems riper and more brutish, with strong savoury/spicy notes;
the hue, too, is less vivid. Screwcap. 14.5° alc. **Rating** 89 **To** 2013 $17.95
Malpas Road McLaren Vale Merlot 2006 Correct light- to medium-bodied
weight and texture; some black olive/savoury overtones; has length. Cork. 15° alc.
Rating 89 **To** 2014 $22
The Black Chook VMR 2007 Plenty of action on the palate, with viognier
to the fore, but the 20% marsanne and roussanne adding to the authority of the
finish. Screwcap. 14° alc. **Rating** 88 **To** 2011 $17.95
Woop Woop Chardonnay 2007 Lively, fresh grapefruit and stone fruit; simple,
but has length and freshness. Screwcap. 13.5° alc. **Rating** 87 **To** 2009 $12.95
Red Dot Rose 2007 A very friendly wine with plenty of sweetness on the
palate; clean and surprisingly long on the finish. Screwcap. 12.5° alc. **Rating** 87
To 2010 $15
Specialized McLaren Vale Shiraz Cabernet Merlot 2005 A robust wine
which presently lacks line and precision; may knit together with time. Cork.
15° alc. **Rating** 87 **To** 2012 $22
Woop Woop Cabernet 2006 Pleasant red fruits on entry, moving towards
darker flavours on the back-palate; minimal tannins. Screwcap. 15° alc. **Rating** 87
To 2010 $12.95

Pennyweight Winery

Pennyweight Lane, Beechworth, Vic 3747 **Region** Beechworth
T (03) 5728 1747 **F** (03) 5728 1704 **www**.pennyweight.com.au **Open** 7 days 10–5
Winemaker Stephen Newton Morris, Stephen MG Morris, Frederick Morris **Est.** 1982
Cases 1400
Pennyweight was established by Stephen Morris, great-grandson of GF Morris, founder of
Morris Wines. The 3.5 ha of vines at Beechworth and 1.5 ha at Rutherglen are not irrigated
and are organically grown. The business is run by Stephen, together with his wife Elizabeth
and assisted by their three sons; Elizabeth Morris says, 'It's a perfect world', suggesting that
Pennyweight is more than happy with its lot in life.

ΨΨΨΨΩ **Beechworth Pinot Noir 2006** Fresh, lively and clear varietal character in a
light-bodied frame, with attractive cherry and plum fruit; not over-elaborated.
Heavily stained cork. Cork. **Rating** 90 **To** 2011 $35

Peos Estate

Graphite Road, Manjimup, WA 6258 **Region** Manjimup
T (08) 9772 1378 **F** (08) 9772 1372 **www**.peosestate.com.au **Open** 7 days 10–4
Winemaker Forest Hill Vineyard **Est.** 1996 **Cases** 4000
The Peos family has farmed the West Manjimup district for over 50 years, the third generation
of four brothers commencing the development of a substantial vineyard in 1996; there is a
little over 33 ha of vines, with shiraz (10 ha), merlot (7 ha), chardonnay (6.5 ha), cabernet
sauvignon (4 ha) and pinot noir, sauvignon blanc and verdelho (2 ha each). Exports to the
UK, Canada and Denmark.

ΨΨΨΨΩ **Four Aces Chardonnay 2005** Developing slowly but surely; tightly focused
apple and citrus fruit; oak present, but nicely balanced. Screwcap. 14° alc.
Rating 92 **To** 2012 $25

ΨΨΨΨ **Four Aces Shiraz 2005** Bright colour and hue; lively and brisk red and black
fruits, though slightly green tannins on the finish. Diam. 14° alc. **Rating** 89
To 2015 $30
Manjimup Pinot Noir 2006 A mix of plum, spice and some savoury/foresty
notes; falters a little on the finish. Screwcap. 12.5° alc. **Rating** 88 **To** 2011 $21

Pepper Tree Wines

Halls Road, Pokolbin, NSW 2321 **Region** Lower Hunter Valley
T (02) 4998 7539 **F** (02) 4998 7746 **www**.peppertreewines.com.au **Open** Mon–Fri 9–5,
w'ends 9.30–5
Winemaker Jim Chatto **Est.** 1993 **Cases** 50 000
The Pepper Tree winery is part of a complex that also contains The Convent guest house
and Roberts Restaurant. In 2002 it was acquired by a company controlled by Dr John Davis,
who owns 50% of Briar Ridge. The appointment of Jim Chatto as chief winemaker in March
2007 brought the talents of the best young wine judge on the Australian wine show circuit,
with winemaking talents to match. It sources the majority of its Hunter Valley fruit from its
Tallavera Grove vineyard at Mt View, but also has premium vineyards at Orange, Coonawarra
and Wrattonbully, which provide its Grand Reserve and Reserve (single region) wines. The
arrival of Jim Chatto as winemaker should bring further improvement (vintage conditions
accepted). Exports to the US, Canada, Switzerland, Indonesia, Singapore, China and NZ.

ΨΨΨΨΩ **Reserve Hunter Valley Semillon 2006** Tightly wound lemon curd and hints
of dried straw; a classic wine, with real persistence and precision; will reward bottle
age. Screwcap. 11° alc. **Rating** 92 **To** 2020 $25
Grand Reserve Wrattonbully Cabernet Sauvignon 2004 Quite deep and
dark fruited with a slight vegetal edge that adds to the bouquet; very concentrated,
and very rich and ripe on the finish. Cork. 14.5° alc. **Rating** 92 **To** 2015 $55

ΨΨΨΨ **Grand Reserve Wrattonbully Tannat 2005** Dark and savoury bouquet, with
high levels of the tannins for which the variety is known; fresh and vibrant finish,
but a very big mouthful of flavour. Cork. 14.7° alc. **Rating** 88 **To** 2016 $60

Semillon Sauvignon Blanc 2007 Fresh and vibrant, with plenty of sweet fruit on the mid-palate; slightly one-dimensional, but clean and fine. Screwcap. 12.5° alc. **Rating** 87 **To** 2009 $18

Pepperilly Estate Wines

18 Langham Street, Nedlands, WA 6009 (postal) **Region** Geographe
T 0401 860 891 **F** (08) 9389 6444 **www**.pepperilly.com **Open** Not
Winemaker The Vintage Wineworx (Dr Diane Miller) **Est.** 1999 **Cases** 2500
Partners Geoff and Karyn Cross, and Warwick Lavis, planted their substantial 10-ha vineyard in 1991 with cabernet sauvignon, shiraz, semillon, sauvignon blanc, chardonnay, viognier, merlot and grenache. The vineyard has views across the Ferguson Valley to the ocean, with sea breezes providing good ventilation.

Sauvignon Blanc Semillon 2007 Highly aromatic bouquet; lively with citrus through to tropical fruit flavours; very good balance and mouthfeel. Semillon a minor component. Screwcap. 12° alc. **Rating** 93 **To** 2009 $17
Geographe Shiraz 2006 Spicy, tarry, licorice fruit; very good flavour, and toasty on the finish. Screwcap. **Rating** 90 **To** 2014 $22

Cabernet Merlot 2006 Quite essency young blueberry and cassis fruits; juicy, focused and fine, if a little one-dimensional. Screwcap. **Rating** 88 **To** 2009 $17

 # Peregrine Ridge

19 Carlyle Street, Moonee Ponds, Vic 3039 (postal) **Region** Heathcote
T 0411 741 772 **F** (03) 9326 2885 **www**.peregrineridge.com.au **Open** Not
Winemaker Graeme Quigley, Sue Kerrison **Est.** 2001 **Cases** 900
Graeme Quigley and Sue Kerrison purchased a property high on the Mt Camel Range (the name comes from the peregrine falcons that co-habit the vineyard) and planted 4.4 ha of shiraz. Irrigation is used sparingly, with the yields restricted to 2.5 to 3.5 tonnes per ha; the grapes are hand-picked and made in small batches.

Limited Release Heathcote Shiraz 2005 Remarkable how different the wine is to the American Oak Blend, both in structure and flavour terms; this is tighter and longer, although the fruit base is presumably identical; will live longer. Screwcap. 14.7° alc. **Rating** 94 **To** 2020 $35

American Oak Blend Heathcote Shiraz 2005 Good colour, focus and concentration; plum, blackberry and licorice fruit is not overwhelmed by the oak; ripe tannins on the lifted finish. Screwcap. 14.7° alc. **Rating** 93 **To** 2015 $35

Heathcote Sparkling Shiraz 2004 Intense plum and black cherry fruit plus spice; elegant; could develop well. Cork. 13.8° alc. **Rating** 89 **To** 2013 $55

Pertaringa

Cnr Hunt Road/Rifle Range Road, McLaren Vale, SA 5171 **Region** McLaren Vale
T (08) 8323 8125 **www**.pertaringa.com.au **Open** Mon–Fri 10–5, w'ends & public hols 11–5
Winemaker Ben Riggs **Est.** 1980 **Cases** 20 000
While Pertaringa remains closely associated with the Geoff Hardy business, it is in fact a separate entity, with separate owners (Geoff Hardy and Ian Leask) and has a separate address. Hence a Siamese twin operation has taken place, and Pertaringa now stands on its own. Exports to the UK and other major markets.

Rifle & Hunt McLaren Vale Cabernet Sauvignon 2006 Firm, medium- to full-bodied, with tightly focused varietal character; excellent length and integration of new French oak plus fine tannins. McLaren Vale cabernet at its best. ProCork. 15° alc. **Rating** 95 **To** 2021 $35

Over The Top McLaren Vale Shiraz 2006 Luscious ripe blackberry fruit in a coating of dark chocolate and a slather of oak. ProCork. 15° alc. **Rating** 93 **To** 2026 $39

The Full Fronti NV Interesting Asian spices, considerable length; average age 20 years. Bargain. Cork. 18.5° alc. **Rating** 92 **To** 2009 $24

Stage Left Adelaide Merlot 2006 Apart from the fact merlot is the dominant variety on the right bank (of Bordeaux) not the left bank (the genesis of the name), this is a very handy wine, with just the right balance between cassis and snow pea flavours. Screwcap. 15° alc. **Rating** 90 **To** 2011 $20

 PPPP   Two Gentlemens McLaren Vale Grenache 2006 You are either a Mr or an Esq, but not both, and there should be an apostrophe before the s; the wine? Light, spicy, savoury and enjoyable. Screwcap. 15° alc. **Rating** 89 **To** 2011 $20

Bonfire Block Adelaide Semillon 2007 Mainly from an estate vineyard in McLaren Vale, the remainder from the K1 vineyard in the Adelaide Hills; plenty of life and lemony flavours. Screwcap. 13.5° alc. **Rating** 89 **To** 2012 $18

Scarecrow Adelaide Sauvignon Blanc 2007 A clean fresh bouquet, the palate following logically; some grass and herb, and good length, but not exciting. Screwcap. 13° alc. **Rating** 88 **To** 2009 $18

Undercover McLaren Vale Shiraz 2006 More spice, herb and earth and mint than the Over the Top, notwithstanding the same alcohol; fine tannins reign in the finish. Screwcap. 15° alc. **Rating** 88 **To** 2014 $20

Understudy McLaren Vale Cabernet Petit Verdot 2006 Full-flavoured rustic wine best not overanalysed, simply drink with barbecued T-bone. Screwcap. 15° alc. **Rating** 87 **To** 2012 $18

Petaluma   ★★★★★

Spring Gully Road, Piccadilly, SA 5151 **Region** Adelaide Hills
T (08) 8339 9300 **F** (08) 8339 9301 **www**.petaluma.com.au **Open** At Bridgewater Mill, Bridgewater
Winemaker Andrew Hardy **Est.** 1976 **Cases** 50 000

The Lion Nathan group comprises Petaluma, Knappstein, Mitchelton, Stonier and Smithbrook. The Petaluma range has been expanded beyond the core group of Croser Sparkling, Clare Valley Riesling, Piccadilly Chardonnay and Coonawarra (Cabernet Sauvignon/Merlot). Newer arrivals of note include Adelaide Hills Viognier and Adelaide Hills Shiraz. Bridgewater Mill is the second label, which consistently provides wines most makers would love to have as their top label. The Sotuh Australian plantings in the Clare Valley, Coonawarra and Adelaide Hills now total 186 ha, providing a more than sufficient source of estate-grown grapes and wines. Exports to all major markets.

PPPPP   Piccadilly Vineyard Chardonnay 2006 Toasty and complex, with grilled nuts, grapefruit and floral notes; very elegantly structured, with fine acid and fruit, and the flavour builds across the palate to a long, harmonious and fresh finish. Screwcap. 13.5° alc. **Rating** 95 **To** 2015 $45

Adelaide Hills Viognier 2006 Apple, apricot and nougat aromas; an altogether superior palate; has depth of flavour without oily phenolics, the oak barely intruding. Screwcap. 14.5° alc. **Rating** 95 **To** 2011 $42

Adelaide Hills Shiraz 2005 A voluminous bouquet speaks both for the 7% viognier co-fermented, and the 18 months in 100% new French oak, characters faithfully reflected by the palate. Screwcap. 14.5° alc. **Rating** 95 **To** 2020 $48

Hanlin Hill Clare Valley Riesling 2007 Mouthfilling, pure and long, with a linear profile; citrus fruit with relatively soft acidity; early developing. Screwcap. 13° alc. **Rating** 94 **To** 2011 $25

Piccadilly Vineyard Chardonnay 2005 A sophisticated wine, with a range of precisely judged inputs leaving only a faint imprint on the varietal fruit; minerally finish. Pity about the cork. 13.5° alc. **Rating** 94 **To** 2012 $45

Bridgewater Mill Adelaide Hills Shiraz 2005 Rippling with fruit-sweet blackberry, chocolate, spice and licorice flavours; fine tannins, good line and length. Screwcap. 14.5° alc. **Rating** 94 **To** 2020 $24.95

Coonawarra 2004 In the tradition of Petaluma Coonawarra, relies on stealth rather than outright power; will stand the test of time, but will never scale the ultimate heights. Cork. 14.5° alc. **Rating** 94 **To** 2019 $60

Coonawarra 2005 Youthful hue; vibrant, blueberry fruit is slightly dominated by lavish levels of new wood; however, beneath there are ample levels of fruit, with an almost velvety texture and slightly chewy tannins; very long finish. Cork. 13.5° alc. **Rating** 94 **To** 2020 $60

ΨΨΨΨΨ **Bridgewater Mill Adelaide Hills Chardonnay 2006** Gentle melon and stone fruit aromas, but is unexpectedly lively and intense on the palate and finish. Screwcap. 14° alc. **Rating** 92 **To** 2013 $24.95
Adelaide Hills Viognier 2007 Apricot, spice and even a little honey; good flavour depth, and very clean and high levels of acidity keep the wine fresh and vibrant. Screwcap. 13° alc. **Rating** 91 **To** 2009 $42
Bridgewater Mill Adelaide Hills Rose 2007 Vivid fuschia; a greater fruit depth than many, ranging through cherry, plum and raspberry; good balance and a dry finish. Screwcap. 12.5° alc. **Rating** 91 **To** 2009 $22.95
Coonawarra Merlot 2004 Has good depth of flavour, with some black olive notes, but the oak dominates now; seriously structured, with ample fine-grained tannins; needs time to integrate. Cork. 14.5° alc. **Rating** 91 **To** 2018 $60
Bridgewater Mill Adelaide Hills Pinot Grigio 2007 A clean, correct bouquet, then fresh mouthfeel and flavours of nashi pear and lemon rind; dry finish. Screwcap. 13.5° alc. **Rating** 90 **To** 2009 $22.95

ΨΨΨΨ **Bridgewater Mill Adelaide Hills Sauvignon Blanc 2007** A clean, correct bouquet and palate; the varietal character in diminuendo, but crisp minerally notes on the finish help. Screwcap. 13° alc. **Rating** 89 **To** 2010 $22.95
Bridgewater Mill Adelaide Hills Viognier 2007 A clean, fresh bouquet lacking the varietal character that comes through to a degree on a zesty palate; should develop. Screwcap. 14° alc. **Rating** 88 **To** 2010 $24.95

Peter Douglas Wines ★★★★☆

c/- Cnr Ingles Street/Anderson Street, Port Melbourne, Vic 3207 (postal)
Region Coonawarra
T (03) 9647 0015 **F** (03) 9646 8383 **www**.peterdouglaswines.com.au **Open** Not
Winemaker Peter Douglas **Est.** 2007 **Cases** NFP
Peter Douglas made a name for himself while working as a senior winemaker with Wynns Coonawarra Estate in the 1980s. For various reasons, he and his medical practitioner wife headed overseas, briefly in the US, and thereafter Sicily. The wheel has now turned full circle with the Douglases once again living in Coonawarra, Peter both making wine under his own label, and running an extensive winemaking consultancy business. He makes two cabernets: Chime Hoop, matured in American oak, and designed for early drinking; and Bulge Hoop, matured in French oak, with greater depth and richness, and a longer life.

ΨΨΨΨΨ **Bulge Hoop Coonawarra Cabernet Sauvignon 2004** Good purple-red; medium- to full-bodied; classic blackcurrant cabernet fruit on both bouquet and palate, the French oak providing perfectly judged support; long finish and aftertaste. Screwcap. 14.4° alc. **Rating** 94 **To** 2019 $44.95

ΨΨΨΨΨ **Chime Hoop Coonawarra Cabernet Sauvignon 2004** Good texture; very different to the Bulge Hoop due to less new oak (American); has juicy red fruits alongside blackcurrant, plus touches of vanilla mocha. Screwcap. 14.2° alc. **Rating** 90 **To** 2014 $24.95

Peter Howland Wines ★★★★☆

2/14 Portside Crescent, Wickham, NSW 2293 **Region** Lower Hunter Valley
T 0412 622 223 **F** (02) 4920 2699 **www**.peterhowlandwines.com **Open** By appt
Winemaker Peter Howland **Est.** 2001 **Cases** 3000
Peter Howland graduated from Adelaide University in 1997 with a first-class Honours degree in oenology. He has worked in the Hunter Valley, Margaret River, Hastings Valley, Macedon Ranges and Puglia in Italy. Newcastle may seem a strange place for a winery cellar door, but

this is where his insulated and refrigerated barrel shed is located. From 2004 he has fermented his wines at Serenella Estate, where he also acts as contract winemaker. His wines are sourced from both sides of the continent: Great Southern and the Hunter Valley. Exports to the US, Canada, Hong Kong, Singapore and Japan.

ΨΨΨΨΩ **Maxwell Vineyard Hunter Valley Chardonnay 2005** Rich and ripe, with dried figs and lots of toasted nuts; still fresh and vibrant, but certainly at its best now. Screwcap. 13.9° alc. **Rating** 90 **To** 2009 $30

ΨΨΨΨ **Parsons Vineyard Frankland River Shiraz 2005** Deeply coloured; very concentrated and deep, but the flavours are extremely earthy, verging on bitter, and the wine needs to soften. Screwcap. **Rating** 88 **To** 2009 $40
Langley Vineyard Donnybrook Shiraz 2005 At this juncture, oak-dominated on both bouquet and palate; there is blackcurrant fruit underneath, but it is uncertain whether it will fight free of the oak. **Rating** 88 **To** 2015 $30

Peter Lehmann

Para Road, Tanunda, SA 5352 **Region** Barossa Valley
T (08) 8563 2100 **F** (08) 8563 3402 **www.**peterlehmannwines.com **Open** Mon–Fri 9.30–5, w'ends & public hols 10.30–4.30
Winemaker Andrew Wigan, Leonie Lange, Ian Hongell, Kerry Morrison, Phil Lehmann **Est.** 1979 **Cases** 200 000
Under the benevolent ownership of the Swiss/Californian Hess Group, Peter Lehmann has continued to flourish, making wines from all the major varieties at multiple price points, the common link being over-delivery against expectations. Its record with its Reserve Eden Valley Riesling (usually released when 5 years old) is second to none, and it has refined and refined its semillons to the point where it can take on the Hunter Valley at its own game with 5-year-old releases, exemplified by the 2002 Reserve Semillon. At the base level, the Semillon is the largest seller in that category in the country. Yet it is as a red winemaker that Peter Lehmann is best known in both domestic and export markets, again with some outstanding wines leading the charge. Exports to all major markets.

ΨΨΨΨΨ **Reserve Riesling 2002** Rich and complex, mouthcoating yet still fresh and very intense; ageing slowly but surely through to a long, lingering finish. **Rating** 96 **To** 2015 $40
Reserve Margaret Semillon 2002 Marvellously intense and long, with a mix of citrus and mineral, toast yet to come. Richly deserved trophy for Best Semillon Sydney Wine Show '08. Screwcap. 12° alc. **Rating** 96 **To** 2012 $28
The 1885 Shiraz 2005 Densely coloured; excellent intensity, balance and focus; redolent with blackberry, plum, mint and spice; very good texture and structure thanks to fine, ripe, but persistent, tannins. From a vineyard planted in 1885, and tended by six generations of the Schrapel family. Screwcap. 14.5° alc. **Rating** 96 **To** 2030 $55
The Futures Shiraz 2004 Right in the slot of the current Peter Lehmann style; high quality fruit in the first place, then sensitive but positive winemaking; blackberry fruits, fine, ripe tannins and seamlessly welded French oak. Cork. 14.5° alc. **Rating** 95 **To** 2020 $28.50

ΨΨΨΨΩ **Ruediger Cabernet Sauvignon 2005** Medium-bodied; quite distinctive varietal character, structure and mouthfeel; blackcurrant plus nuances of earth, leaf and olive. Screwcap. 14° alc. **Rating** 92 **To** 2022 $30
Eden Valley Riesling 2007 Floral, spicy aromas with a touch of passionfruit; quite rich and (relatively speaking) full-bodied; early-drinking style; good length. Screwcap. 12° alc. **Rating** 91 **To** 2010 $15
Burdon Greenock Shiraz 2005 A medium-bodied, elegant, unforced wine; blackberry, mocha, touches of earth and spice all fused together. From a single 45-year-old vineyard. Screwcap. 14.5° alc. **Rating** 91 **To** 2020 $30

ΨΨΨΨ **Barossa Rose 2007** Clever winemaking; juxtaposition of a hint of sweetness and crisp acidity lifts the cherry and raspberry flavours; has length. Screwcap. 11° alc. **Rating** 89 **To** 2009 $15
Barossa Tempranillo 2006 An interesting example of the variety; has more structure and texture than most, but the fruit flavours are not particularly distinctive; probably young vines. Screwcap. 14.5° alc. **Rating** 88 **To** 2009 $18
Barossa Shiraz 2005 A pleasant light- to medium-bodied palate, but needs more fruit focus to gain attention at this price. Screwcap. 14.5° alc. **Rating** 87 **To** 2009 $18

Petersons   NR
Mount View Road, Mount View, NSW 2325 **Region** Lower Hunter Valley
T (02) 4990 1704 **F** (02) 4991 1344 **www**.petersonswines.com.au **Open** Mon–Sat 9–5, Sun 10–5
Winemaker Colin Peterson, Gary Reed **Est.** 1971 **Cases** 15 000
Ian and Shirley Peterson were among the early followers in the footsteps of Max Lake, contributing to the Hunter Valley renaissance which has continued to this day. Grapegrowers since 1971 and winemakers since '81, the second generation of the family, headed by Colin Peterson, now manages the business. It has been significantly expanded to include 16 ha at Mount View, a 42-ha vineyard in Mudgee (Glenesk), and an 8-ha vineyard near Armidale (Palmerston), each with its own cellar door.

Pettavel   ★★★★☆
65 Pettavel Road, Waurn Ponds, Vic 3216 **Region** Geelong
T (03) 5266 1120 **F** (03) 5266 1140 **www**.pettavel.com **Open** 7 days 10–5.30
Winemaker Peter Flewellyn **Est.** 2000 **Cases** 15 000
This is a major landmark in the Geelong region. Mike and wife Sandi Fitzpatrick sold their large Riverland winery and vineyards, and moved to Geelong, where, in 1990, they began developing vineyards at Sutherlands Creek. Here they have been joined by daughter Robyn (who has overseas management of the business) and son Reece (who coordinates the viticultural resources). A striking and substantial winery/restaurant complex was opened in 2002. Exports to the UK, the US, and other major markets.

ΨΨΨΨΨ **Evening Star Geelong Chardonnay 1999** Not surprisingly shows considerable development and complexity; good balance of tangy fruit and barrel ferment inputs; toasty cashew also from bottle age. Screwcap. 13.5° alc. **Rating** 93 **To** 2010 $18
Evening Star Geelong Chardonnay 2006 Very ripe, with melon and fig, and a rich texture; the finish is even and fine. Screwcap. 13.5° alc. **Rating** 91 **To** 2012 $18
Southern Emigre Geelong Shiraz Viognier 2004 Spice, cedar, pine needle and blackberry aromas; a particularly robust style, with lingering tannins. Screwcap. 14.5° alc. **Rating** 91 **To** 2015 $42
Southern Emigre Geelong Shiraz Viognier 2005 Its silky texture sees the wine glide across the tongue unveiling its array of exotic spices and black fruits through to the fine tannins of the finish. Screwcap. 14.5° alc. **Rating** 91 **To** 2015 $42

ΨΨΨΨ **Platina Geelong Viognier 2007** Neatly treads the middle path for viognier, avoiding oily phenolics, and accumulating fruit flavours of peach and apricot. Screwcap. 13.5° alc. **Rating** 89 **To** 2011 $27
Evening Star Geelong Shiraz 2006 Strong savoury herbal spice aromas and flavours reflecting the cool region; fine-grained tannins. Screwcap. 14° alc. **Rating** 89 **To** 2014 $18
Evening Star Late Harvest Riesling 2007 Has some bottle age potential; certainly rich, though not especially complex. Possibly freeze-concentrated. **Rating** 87 **To** 2011 $18

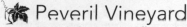 Peveril Vineyard ★★★

3360 Colac-Lavers Hill Road, Ferguron, Vic 3237 **Region** Geelong
T (03) 5235 9201 **F** (03) 5235 9201 **www**.greatoceanroad.com.au/peverilvineyard
Open W'ends, public & school hols 10–6
Winemaker Provenance Wines (Scott Ireland) **Est.** 2002 **Cases** 300
In 1999, Bruce and Marg Rossiter (in their words) 'left home in the city to begin a second career in the country'. By 2001 they found their property in the Otway Ranges, built a house and planted their first vines, completing the plantings of 3 ha of pinot noir, sauvignon blanc and riesling over the ensuing years. They also grow blueberries, and operate in a chemical-free environment to the maximum extent possible. The name, incidentally, is a tribute to Marg's three aunts, Peggie, Vera and Lil, and the berries are available from January to March each year.

ŸŸŸŸ   **Pinot Noir 2005** Light-bodied; savoury/minty/leafy flavours needing more fruit, but has balance and length. **Rating** 89 **To** 2009 $22
Pinot Noir 2006 Light- to medium-bodied, elegant, with nicely ripened fruit; good line and length. **Rating** 88 **To** 2010 $25
Sauvignon Blanc 2006 Has a fair volume of varietal fruit, gained in part at the expense of a slightly phenolic finish. **Rating** 87 **To** 2009 $20

Pewsey Vale ★★★★★

Browns Road, Eden Valley, SA 5353 (postal) **Region** Eden Valley
T (08) 8561 3200 **F** (08) 8561 3393 **www**.pewseyvale.com **Open** At Yalumba
Winemaker Louisa Rose **Est.** 1847 **Cases** 20 000
Pewsey Vale was a famous vineyard established in 1847 by Joseph Gilbert, and it was appropriate that when S Smith & Son (Yalumba) began the renaissance of the Adelaide Hills plantings in 1961, they should do so by purchasing Pewsey Vale and establishing 40 ha of riesling and 2 ha each of gewurztraminer and pinot gris. The Riesling has also finally benefited from being the first wine to be bottled with a Stelvin screwcap in 1977. While public reaction forced the abandonment of the initiative for almost 20 years, Yalumba/Pewsey Vale never lost faith in the technical advantages of the closure. A quick taste (or better, a share of a bottle) of 5–7-year-old Contours Riesling will tell you why. Exports to all major markets.

ŸŸŸŸŸ   **The Contours Eden Valley Riesling 2002** Glorious complexity and intensity; has fulfilled all the promises it showed as a gold medal winner at the National Wine Show '04; beautiful line and balance to the lime/citrus fruit, and a lingering finish. Screwcap. **Rating** 96 **To** 2015 $27.95
Prima Eden Valley Riesling 2007 The highly successful outcome of several years experimentation, modelled on the Mosel (Germany) pattern; bright and intense lime juice flavours on the mid-palate yield to the crisp acidity of the finish, leaving the mouth fresh and thirsting for more. Screwcap. 9.5° alc. **Rating** 96 **To** 2012 $24.95

ŸŸŸŸŸ   **Individual Vineyard Selection Eden Valley Pinot Gris 2007** Pear blossom aromas; pear and citrus flavours on the lingering palate and finish. Screwcap. 13° alc. **Rating** 93 **To** 2009 $22.95
Individual Vineyard Selection Eden Valley Riesling 2007 As one would expect, good balance and structure; quite fluid in the mouth, with good line to the mix of citrus, apple and mineral fruit. Screwcap. 13° alc. **Rating** 91 **To** 2014 $17.95
Individual Vineyard Eden Valley Gewurztraminer 2007 An attractive, aromatic wine with good balance and length, although the varietal character is not particularly pronounced; the old dilemma. Screwcap. 13.5° alc. **Rating** 91 **To** 2010 $22.95

Pfeiffer Wines

167 Distillery Road, Wahgunyah, Vic 3687 **Region** Rutherglen
T (02) 6033 2805 **F** (02) 6033 3158 **www.**pfeifferwines.com.au **Open** Mon–Sat 9–5,
Sun 10–5
Winemaker Christopher Pfeiffer, Jen Pfeiffer **Est.** 1984 **Cases** 20 000
Ex-Lindeman fortified winemaker Chris Pfeiffer occupies one of the historic wineries (built
1880) which abound in Northeast Victoria, and which is worth a visit on this score alone. The
fortified wines are good, and the table wines have improved considerably over recent vintages,
drawing upon 28 ha of estate plantings. Exports to the UK, the US and other major markets
(under the Carlyle and Three Chimneys labels).

⍾⍾⍾⍾⍾ **Gamay 2007** Fragrant, spiced plum aromas and flavours; good balance, and an
unexpected result for the region and vintage; good acidity. Screwcap. 13.5° alc.
Rating 90 **To** 2009 $16.50

Pfitzner

PO Box 1098, North Adelaide, SA 5006 **Region** Adelaide Hills
T (08) 8390 0188 **Open** Not
Winemaker Petaluma **Est.** 1996 **Cases** 1500
The subtitle to the Pfitzner name is Eric's Vineyard. The late Eric Pfitzner purchased and
aggregated a number of small, subdivided farmlets to protect the beauty of the Piccadilly Valley
from ugly rural development. His three sons inherited the vision, with a little under 6 ha of
vineyard planted principally to chardonnay and pinot noir, plus small amounts of sauvignon
blanc and merlot. Half the total property has been planted, the remainder preserving the
natural eucalypt forest. Roughly half the production is sold in the UK, no surprise given the
bargain basement prices asked for these lovely wines.

⍾⍾⍾⍾⍾ **Eric's Vineyard Piccadilly Valley Chardonnay 2005** Very complex, very tight
and very long, barrel ferment and high-toned nectarine fruit woven through each
other; effortless quality. Screwcap. 13.5° alc. **Rating** 94 **To** 2012 $28

⍾⍾⍾⍾ **Piccadilly Valley Sauvignon Blanc 2007** Lively, fresh and very crisp; snow pea/
grass/gooseberry; long finish. Screwcap. 12.5° alc. **Rating** 89 **To** 2010 $15

Phaedrus Estate

220 Mornington-Tyabb Road, Moorooduc, Vic 3933 **Region** Mornington Peninsula
T (03) 5978 8134 **F** (03) 5978 8134 **www.**phaedrus.com.au **Open** W'ends &
public hols 11–5
Winemaker Ewan Campbell, Maitena Zantvoort **Est.** 1997 **Cases** 2000
Ewan Campbell and Maitena Zantvoort established Phaedrus Estate in 1997. At that time
both had already had winemaking experience with large wine companies, and were at the
point of finishing their wine science degrees at Adelaide University. They decided they
wished to (in their words) 'produce ultra-premium wine with distinctive and unique varietal
flavours, which offer serious (and light-hearted) wine drinkers an alternative to mainstream
commercial styles'. Campbell and Zantvoort believe that quality wines involve both art and
science, and I don't have any argument with that. Exports to Hong Kong.

⍾⍾⍾⍾⍾ **Mornington Peninsula Chardonnay 2007** Elegant and expressive; quite
intense stone fruit flavours complexed by sophisticated fermentation techniques
and astute oak use. Screwcap. 13.9° alc. **Rating** 92 **To** 2012 $22
Reserve Pinot Noir 2005 Fragrant, tangy/smoky aromas, the palate with
considerable velocity thanks to savoury, foresty characters coming through strongly.
Has developed very well. Screwcap. 13.9° alc. **Rating** 91 **To** 2012 $45

⍾⍾⍾⍾ **Mornington Peninsula Pinot Noir 2006** A generous wine; spiced plum
fruit on the upper edge of ripeness; solid finish. Screwcap. 13.9° alc. **Rating** 89
To 2012 $23

Mornington Peninsula Shiraz 2006 Despite relatively light colour, has plenty of life and thrust to the mix of red and black fruits and sundry spicy notes. Screwcap. 13.9° alc. **Rating** 89 **To** 2012 $24
Mornington Peninsula Pinot Gris 2007 Gentle spice, pear and apple fruit; wanders along on the way to the finish. Screwcap. 14.3° alc. **Rating** 87 **To** 2009 $20

PHI ★★★★★

Lusatia Park Vineyard, Owens Road, Woori Yallock, Vic 3139 **Region** Yarra Valley
T (03) 5964 6070 **www**.phiwines.com **Open** By appt
Winemaker Steve Webber **Est.** 1985 **Cases** NFP
This is a joint venture between two very influential wine families: that of De Bortoli and Shelmerdine. The key executives are Stephen Shelmerdine and Steve Webber (and their respective wives). It has a sole viticultural base: the Lusatia Park vineyard of the Shelmerdine family. Unusually, however, it is of specific rows of vines, not even blocks, although the rows are continuous. They are pruned and managed quite differently to the rest of the block, with the deliberate aim of strictly controlled yields. While the joint venture was only entered into in 2005, De Bortoli has been buying grapes from the vineyard since '02, and has had the opportunity to test the limits of the grapes. The outcome has been wines of the highest quality, and a joint venture that will last for many years. The name, incidentally, is derived from the 21st letter of the ancient Greek alphabet, symbolising perfect balance and harmony. It's courageous pricing for a new kid on the block, but reflects the confidence the families have in the wines. Exports to the UK.

�♥♥♥♥ **Lusatia Park Vineyard Yarra Valley Sauvignon 2007** High quality from a challenging vintage; highly aromatic, and a brilliantly clear varietal fruit profile; top mouthfeel, line and length. Screwcap. 12° alc. **Rating** 95 **To** 2010 $42
Lusatia Park Vineyard Yarra Valley Pinot Noir 2006 Great mouthfeel and line to the palate, with an array of black cherry, plum and spice fruit flavours; oak has added its voice, though quietly. Screwcap. 13.5° alc. **Rating** 94 **To** 2013 $54

♥♥♥♥♀ **Lusatia Park Vineyard Yarra Valley Chardonnay 2006** Complex barrel ferment aromas; a strongly structured palate, with apple, nuts and some grapefruit, the oak now in the background. Screwcap. 13° alc. **Rating** 92 **To** 2016 $48

Philip Shaw Wines ★★★★

Koomooloo Vineyard, Caldwell Lane, Orange, NSW 2800 **Region** Orange
T (02) 6365 2334 **F** (02) 6365 2449 **www**.philipshaw.com.au **Open** W'ends 12–5, or by appt
Winemaker Philip Shaw **Est.** 1989 **Cases** 8000
Philip Shaw, former chief winemaker of Rosemount Estate and then Southcorp Wines, first became interested in the Orange region in 1985. In 1988 he purchased the Koomooloo Vineyard, and began the planting of 43 ha sauvignon blanc, chardonnay, shiraz, merlot, cabernet franc and cabernet sauvignon. Exports to the UK, the US and other major markets.

♥♥♥♥♀ **No. 11 Orange Chardonnay 2006** Pure, clean varietal chardonnay, with good fruit intensity, well-handled oak; harmonious persistent finish. **Rating** 93 **To** 2010 $29.95
No. 89 Orange Shiraz Viognier 2006 Good colour; attractive, tangy, spicy medium-bodied palate, with the black and red fruits given the usual lift by the viognier; fine tannins. Screwcap. 13.9° alc. **Rating** 92 **To** 2020 $44.95
No. 89 Orange Shiraz Viognier 2005 Abundant depth and concentration of flavour; blackberry, spice and just a hint of viognier lift to the aroma and flavour. Screwcap. **Rating** 91 **To** 2020 $44.95
No. 8 Orange Pinot Noir 2006 Opens up as a pretty wine, with light, fresh red cherry and raspberry fruit flavours; does have good length and texture on the back-palate and finish. Ready now. Screwcap. 13.9° alc. **Rating** 90 **To** 2011 $39.95

No. 17 Orange Merlot Cabernet Sauvignon Cabernet Franc 2006 Attractive bouquet and palate, with fresh blackcurrant and cassis fruit supported by fine tannins on a juicy finish. Screwcap. 13.8° alc. **Rating** 90 **To** 2014 $26.95

ȲȲȲȲ **No. 19 Orange Sauvignon Blanc 2007** Well made, although the varietal expression on both the bouquet and palate is muted; the balance and dry finish are good. Screwcap. 13.8° alc. **Rating** 87 **To** 2009 $23.95

Phillip Island Vineyard ★★★★★

Berrys Beach Road, Phillip Island, Vic 3922 **Region** Gippsland
T (03) 5956 8465 **F** (03) 5956 8465 **www.**phillipislandwines.com.au **Open** 7 days 11–5
Winemaker David Lance, James Lance **Est.** 1993 **Cases** 3000
The first harvest from the 2.5 ha of the Phillip Island Vineyard was marked in 1997, and the vineyard is totally enclosed in the permanent silon net which acts both as a windbreak and protection against birds. The quality of the wines across the board make it clear that this is definitely not a tourist-trap cellar door; it is a serious producer of quality wine. Exports to Indonesia.

ȲȲȲȲȲ **Chardonnay 2006** Pale colour; really fine fruit on the bouquet, with lemon and mineral on the finish; long and satisfying. Screwcap. 13.5° alc. **Rating** 94 **To** 2014 $28
Pinot Noir 2006 Deeply coloured, with lavish amounts of toasty oak and dark cherry and plum fruits in abundance; quite rich and chewy for pinot, but maintains lovely varietal integrity and precision on the finish. Screwcap. 14° alc. **Rating** 94 **To** 2012 $50

ȲȲȲȲȲ **The Pinnacles Sauvignon Blanc 2007** Pungent gooseberry fruit and good weight and texture; hints of nettle on the surprisingly long finish. Screwcap. 13° alc. **Rating** 90 **To** 2009 $28
Rose 2007 A little salmon in the colour; savoury bouquet and dry palate, with good line of acid and minerals on the finish. Sophisticated winemaking. Screwcap. 13° alc. **Rating** 90 **To** 2011 $22
The Pinnacles Botrytis Riesling 2007 Aromas and flavours of cumquat and lime; in the style of Mosel, and would make a lively aperitif. Screwcap. 10° alc. **Rating** 90 **To** 2014 $22

Phillips Brook Estate ★★★☆

118 Redmond-Hay River Road, Redmond, WA 6332 **Region** Albany
T (08) 9845 3124 **www.**phillipsbrook.com.au **Open** Wed–Sun 12–4
Winemaker Harewood Estate (James Kellie) **Est.** 1975 **Cases** NA
Bronwen and David Newbury first became viticulturists near the thoroughly unlikely town of Bourke, in western NSW, but in 2001 they moved back to the Great Southern region. The name comes from the adjoining Phillips Brook Nature Reserve, and the permanent creek on their property. Riesling and cabernet sauvignon (4.5 ha in all) had been planted in 1975, but thoroughly neglected. The Newburys have rehabilitated the old plantings, and have added 7.5 ha of chardonnay, merlot, cabernet franc and sauvignon blanc.

ȲȲȲȲȲ **Albany Riesling 2007** Lime and tangerine aromas; more to tropical fruit on the flavoursome, soft palate. Screwcap. 11.5° alc. **Rating** 90 **To** 2012 $16.20

ȲȲȲȲ **Albany Sauvignon Blanc 2007** Grass, herb and nettle aromas; gooseberry and some stone fruit on the palate; like the Riesling, quite soft. Screwcap. 13° alc. **Rating** 89 **To** 2010 $14.30
Albany Cabernet Sauvignon 2005 Clear, bright colour; relatively light-bodied, but is fragrant, and has appealing cassis and spice fruit on the unforced palate. Attractive, drink-now style. Screwcap. 13° alc. **Rating** 89 **To** 2011 $18

Pialligo Estate ★★★☆

18 Kallaroo Road, Pialligo, ACT 2609 **Region** Canberra District
T (02) 6247 6060 **F** (02) 6262 6074 www.pialligoestate.com.au **Open** 7 days 10–5
Winemaker Andrew McEwin, Frank Van de Loo (Contract) **Est.** 1999 **Cases** 1500
Sally Milner and John Nutt planted their 4-ha vineyard (0.6 ha of merlot, 1.5 ha riesling,
0.4 ha sangiovese, and 0.5 ha each of shiraz, cabernet sauvignon and pinot gris) in 1999. The
newly extended and renovated cellar door and café has views of Mt Ainslie, Mt Pleasant,
Duntroon, the Telstra Tower, Parliament House and the Brindabella Ranges beyond. The
property, which has a 1-km frontage to the Molonglo River, is only a 5-min drive from the
centre of Canberra.

ΨΨΨΨΨ **Pinot Grigio 2007** Despite (or thanks to?) relatively low alcohol, has good
intensity and length, with clean pear and quince flavours. Screwcap. 12° alc.
Rating 90 **To** 2009 $22

ΨΨΨΨ **Sangiovese 2006** Light- to medium-bodied; bright fresh red cherry fruit, then
savoury tannins cut in somewhat abruptly, plus brisk acidity; should settle down
by the end of '08. Screwcap. 13.1° alc. **Rating** 89 **To** 2012 $25
Riesling 2007 A clean bouquet; the palate is solid, with ripe fruit partially offset
by minerally acidity; honest wine. Screwcap. 11.5° alc. **Rating** 88 **To** 2012 $20
Chardonnay 2007 Light-bodied, clean and correct; minimal depth to the
nectarine fruit, but does have a twist of grapefruity acidity to give length.
Screwcap. 13.5° alc. **Rating** 88 **To** 2009 $20
Shiraz 2005 Light- to medium-bodied; savoury, spicy overtones to blackberry
fruit run through the length of the palate; good texture. Screwcap. 13.7° alc.
Rating 88 **To** 2012 $20
Merlot 2005 Strongly accented varietal earth, olive and spice; no compromise;
has length, but needed more sweet fruit on the mid-palate. Screwcap. 14° alc.
Rating 88 **To** 2012 $20
Rose 2007 Crafted from four unspecified varieties; strawberry and cherry
fruits plus zesty acidity, and a clean, dry finish. Screwcap. 13.2° alc. **Rating** 87
To 2009 $20

Piano Gully ★★★

Piano Gully Road, Manjimup, WA 6258 **Region** Manjimup
T (08) 9772 3140 **F** (08) 9316 0336 www.pianogully.com.au **Open** By appt
Winemaker Ashley Lewkowski **Est.** 1987 **Cases** 4000
The 5-ha vineyard was established in 1987 on rich Karri loam, 10 km south of Manjimup,
with the first wine made from the '91 vintage. The name of the road (and the winery)
commemorates the shipping of a piano from England by one of the first settlers in the region.
The horse and cart carrying the piano on the last leg of the long journey were within sight
of their destination when the piano fell from the cart and was destroyed.

Picardy ★★★★★

Cnr Vasse Highway/Eastbrook Road, Pemberton, WA 6260 **Region** Pemberton
T (08) 9776 0036 **F** (08) 9776 0245 www.picardy.com.au **Open** By appt
Winemaker Bill Pannell, Dan Pannell **Est.** 1993 **Cases** 7000
Picardy is owned by Dr Bill Pannell, wife Sandra and son Daniel; Bill and Sandra founded
Moss Wood winery in Margaret River in 1969. Picardy initially reflected Bill Pannell's
view that the Pemberton area was one of the best regions in Australia for Pinot Noir and
Chardonnay, but it is now clear Pemberton has as much Rhône and Bordeaux as Burgundy
in its veins. The Pannell Family wines are a separate venture to Picardy. Exports to the UK,
the US and other major markets.

ΨΨΨΨΨ **Pemberton Merlot Cabernet Sauvignon Cabernet Franc 2005** Very
aromatic, and a delicious palate with perfect fruit/oak/tannin balance; lush redcurrant fruit and silky mouthfeel and thrust. Cork. 14° alc. **Rating** 95 **To** 2020 $25

Pemberton Chardonnay 2006 Sophisticated winemaking; complex barrel ferment, creamy/nutty overtones to the core of grapefruit and nectarine; very long finish. Cork. 13° alc. **Rating** 94 **To** 2011 $40

♟♟♟♟♟ Pannell Family Trial Batch Pemberton Sauvignon Blanc 2007 Batch No. 2. Highly aromatic passionfruit that flows through to the palate and lingering finish; all in all, an emphatic varietal statement. Cork. 13° alc. **Rating** 93 **To** 2009 $14
Pemberton Shiraz 2005 An elegant, medium-bodied palate, with spicy/savoury tannins running throughout its length, supporting the plummy black fruit flavours. Cork. 14° alc. **Rating** 91 **To** 2015 $20

Pierro ★★★★★

Caves Road, Wilyabrup via Cowaramup, WA 6284 **Region** Margaret River
T (08) 9755 6220 **F** (08) 9755 6308 **www.**pierro.com.au **Open** 7 days 10–5
Winemaker Dr Michael Peterkin **Est.** 1979 **Cases** 10 000
Dr Michael Peterkin is another of the legion of Margaret River medical practitioners; for good measure, he married into the Cullen family. Pierro is renowned for its stylish white wines, which often exhibit tremendous complexity; the Chardonnay can be monumental in its weight and texture. That said, its red wines from good vintages can be every bit as good. Exports to the UK, the US, Japan and Indonesia.

♟♟♟♟♟ Reserve Margaret River Cabernet Sauvignon Merlot 2004 A beautiful wine, intriguingly more elegant than the Cabernet Sauvignon Merlot LTCf, with a silky fragrance and mouthfeel, the accent on a rainbow of red fruits, the tannins exceptionally fine. Cork. 13° alc. **Rating** 96 **To** 2024 $62.90
Margaret River Cabernet Sauvignon Merlot LTCf 2005 Not only has a touch of cabernet franc, but also petit verdot and malbec. It is a great example of regional Cabernet Merlot in the fullest and best style of the Margaret River, marrying intensity with grace; almost lilting red and black fruits, and very fine tannins on the long finish. Great value. Cork. 14.5° alc. **Rating** 95 **To** 2020 $32.90
Margaret River Semillon Sauvignon Blanc LTC 2007 A tried and true formula; semillon is the foundation and framework around which the wine is built, plus minerally acidity on the finish. Screwcap. 14.5° alc. **Rating** 94 **To** 2012 $28
Margaret River Chardonnay 2006 Restrained, finely crafted wine, with seamless stone fruit and oak; long, balanced acidity on the finish. Screwcap. 13.5° alc. **Rating** 94 **To** 2013 $69.90

Piggs Peake ★★★★★

697 Hermitage Road, Pokolbin, NSW 2321 **Region** Lower Hunter Valley
T (02) 6574 7000 **F** (02) 6574 7070 **www.**piggspeake.com **Open** 7 days 10–5
Winemaker Steve Langham, Michael Partridge **Est.** 1998 **Cases** 4000
The derivation of the name remains a mystery to me; if it is a local landmark, I have not heard of it. It sources its grapes from a wide variety of places, to make a range of wines that are well outside the straight and narrow. Piggs Peake has secured listings at a number of leading Sydney metropolitan and NSW country restaurants. The arrival of Steve Langham (having previously worked four vintages at Allandale) has seen a marked increase in quality. The winery and rating remain intact, notwithstanding the absence of tasting notes; all of the first-tier wines have sold out, but will reappear in the future.

Pike & Joyce ★★★★★

PO Box 54, Sevenhill, SA 5453 **Region** Adelaide Hills
T (08) 8843 4370 **F** (08) 8843 4353 **www.**pikeandjoyce.com.au **Open** Not
Winemaker Neil Pike, John Trotter **Est.** 1998 **Cases** 45 000
This is a partnership between the Pike family (of Clare Valley fame) and the Joyce family, related to Andrew Pike's wife, Cathy. The Joyce family have been orchardists at Lenswood for over 100 years, but also have extensive operations in the Riverland. Together with Andrew

Pike they have established 1 ha of vines; the lion's share to pinot noir, sauvignon blanc and chardonnay, followed by merlot, pinot gris and semillon. The wines are made at Pikes Clare Valley winery. Exports to the UK, the US, Canada, Singapore and Japan.

ΨΨΨΨΨ **Adelaide Hills Chardonnay 2005** A quality wine; nectarine, melon and grapefruit are seamlessly woven through French oak; long finish. Screwcap. 14° alc. **Rating** 94 **To** 2013 $30
Adelaide Hills Chardonnay 2006 An elegant wine; beautifully integrated and balanced fruit and oak; melon and nectarine on the long palate; good acidity; ageing slowly and surely. Screwcap. 13.5° alc. **Rating** 94 **To** 2012 $32

ΨΨΨΨ♀ **Adelaide Hills Pinot Noir 2006** Tangy and lively, with considerable velocity in the mouth; dark fruits, foresty/stemmy nuances a definite plus; good length. Screwcap. 13° alc. **Rating** 93 **To** 2012 $32
Adelaide Hills Pinot Noir 2005 Light red cherry/cherry stone/spicy/ strawberry aromas and flavours. A pretty wine, best enjoyed right now. Screwcap. 13.5° alc. **Rating** 90 **To** 2009 $30

ΨΨΨΨ **The Bleedings Adelaide Hills Pinot Noir Rose 2007** Light, but has spicy complexity to the strawberry fruit; crisp, dry finish. Screwcap. 13.5° alc. **Rating** 89 **To** 2009 $20
Adelaide Hills Sauvignon Blanc 2007 Clean, well made and balanced; pleasant apple, citrus and herb aromas, and some gooseberry; lacks velocity in the mouth. Screwcap. 13° alc. **Rating** 88 **To** 2009 $22
Adelaide Hills Pinot Gris 2007 Has a range of aromas and flavours spanning stone fruit and pear, which do, however, dip slightly on the finish. Screwcap. 13° alc. **Rating** 88 **To** 2009 $22

Pikes   ★★★★★

Polish Hill River Road, Sevenhill, SA 5453 **Region** Clare Valley
T (08) 8843 4370 **F** (08) 8843 4353 www.pikeswines.com.au **Open** 7 days 10–4
Winemaker Neil Pike, John Trotter **Est.** 1984 **Cases** 35 000
Owned by the Pike brothers: Andrew was for many years the senior viticulturist with Southcorp, Neil was a winemaker at Mitchell. Pikes now has its own winery, with Neil Pike presiding. In most vintages its white wines, led by Riesling, are the most impressive. Planting of the vineyards has been an ongoing affair, with a panoply of varietals, new and traditional, reflected in the 2007 plantings of an additional 4.3 ha of riesling (26 ha in total), 3.5 ha shiraz (lifting the total to 13.5 ha) and a first-up planting of 1.24 ha of albarino. These take the estate vineyards to over 65 ha. Exports to the UK, the US and other major markets.

ΨΨΨΨΨ **The EWP Reserve Clare Valley Shiraz 2005** Medium- to full-bodied, intense, long and focused; blackberry fruit with quality oak and fleeting hints of choc mint all work very well in the mouth; fine tannins on the finish. In honour of founder Edgar Walter Pike. Screwcap. 14.5° alc. **Rating** 95 **To** 2030 $65
Traditionale Clare Valley Riesling 2007 Classy riesling; good intensity without heaviness to the lime and tropical fruit flavours; good balance and length. Screwcap. 12° alc. **Rating** 94 **To** 2015 $24.95
Luccio Sangiovese Merlot Cabernet Sauvignon 2006 A sangiovese (80%) that really sings, its display of cherry fruits beautifully backed by slightly savoury tannins of the other blend components; a bargain which should be on every Italian restaurant wine list in Australia. Screwcap. 14.5° alc. **Rating** 94 **To** 2011 $17

ΨΨΨΨ♀ **The Hill Block Clare Valley Cabernet 2005** In common with the other '05 releases, a lively and attractive wine; blackcurrant, spice and a touch of black olive; good mouthfeel and length. Screwcap. 14.5° alc. **Rating** 92 **To** 2025 $22
The Dogwalk Clare Valley Cabernet Merlot 2005 An attractive medium-bodied wine, all the components in balance; blackcurrant, cassis and fine tannins. Screwcap. 14.5° alc. **Rating** 91 **To** 2020 $18

The Red Mullet 2005 Complex dark fruit aromas; the light- to medium-bodied palate has juicy fruit flavours on entry, then savoury tannins on the finish. Shiraz/Mourvedre/Tempranillo/Grenache. Screwcap. 14.5° alc. **Rating** 90 **To** 2012 $15

The Dogwalk Clare Valley Cabernet Merlot 2006 The olive and spice of the merlot is woven through stronger, riper cabernet fruit with notes of redcurrant; fine tannins and balanced oak. Screwcap. 14.5° alc. **Rating** 90 **To** 2014 $19

ΨΨΨΨ **Luccio Pinot Gris Sauvignon Blanc Semillon 2007** A more cohesive blend than expected; early picking pays dividends, with seamless citrussy/lemony flavours; vibrant, fresh finish; 50/37/13. Screwcap. 11.5° alc. **Rating** 89 **To** 2009 $17

Eastside Clare Valley Shiraz 2005 A medium-bodied, unforced wine, with black and red cherry, blackberry fruit providing gentle mouthfeel; subtle oak. Screwcap. 14.5° alc. **Rating** 89 **To** 2015 $22

Valley's End Clare Valley Sauvignon Blanc Semillon 2007 A faintly blurred bouquet; a firm palate, with good length, though the sauvignon blanc component is muted. Screwcap. 12° alc. **Rating** 88 **To** 2009 $19

Gill's Farm Clare Valley Viognier 2006 Has good weight and some textural interest, but the varietal expression is limited; more time in bottle may help, as may older vines. Screwcap. 12° alc. **Rating** 88 **To** 2011 $22

Valley's End Clare Valley Sauvignon Blanc Semillon 2006 Well-made, but doesn't have the life and precision expected, and certainly less than the '05. Screwcap. 13° alc. **Rating** 87 **To** 2009 $18

Luccio Clare Valley Sangiovese Rose 2007 Delicate cherry and spice fruit aromas and flavours; clean, dry finish. Screwcap. 11.5° alc. **Rating** 87 **To** 2009 $15

The Hill Block Clare Valley Cabernet 2006 Light- to medium-bodied; a strongly savoury/earthy wine, needing more conviction about its mid-palate fruit. Screwcap. 14.5° alc. **Rating** 87 **To** 2010 $30

Pindarie ★★★★

PO Box 341, Tanunda, SA 5352 **Region** Barossa Valley
T (08) 8524 9019 **F** (08) 8524 9090 **www**.pindarie.com.au **Open** Not
Winemaker Mark Jamieson **Est.** 2005 **Cases** 1500
Owners Tony Brooks and Wendy Allan met while studying at Roseworthy College in 1985, but had very different family backgrounds. Tony Brooks was the sixth generation of farmers in SA and WA, and was studying agriculture, while NZ-born Wendy Allan was studying viticulture. On graduation Tony worked overseas managing sheep feedlots in Saudi Arabia, Turkey and Jordan, while Wendy worked for the next 12 years with Penfolds, commencing as a grower liaison officer and working her way up to become a senior viticulturist. She also found time to study viticulture in California, Israel, Italy, Germany, France, Portugal, Spain and Chile, working vintages and assessing vineyards for wine projects. In 2001 she completed a graduate diploma in wine business. Today they are renovating the original bluestone homestead and outbuildings, while managing the vineyards, mixed farm enterprises, a wine business and raising three children. Small wonder they have retained Mark Jamieson as executive winemaker. Exports to Canada and Hong Kong.

ΨΨΨΨΨ **Shiraz 2006** Concentrated and rich, but without any sign of dead fruit; plum, blackberry and a hint of spice, and has absorbed the oak; soft tannins. Screwcap. 14.5° alc. **Rating** 91 **To** 2016 $23

Bar Rossa Tempranillo Sangiovese Shiraz 2007 Bright colour; light-bodied, but a very attractive, fresh array of juicy cherry/red berry fruits; minimal tannins; drink soon. Screwcap. 14° alc. **Rating** 90 **To** 2009 $23

Pipers Brook Vineyard ★★★★☆

1216 Pipers Brook Road, Pipers Brook, Tas 7254 **Region** Northern Tasmania
T (03) 6382 7527 **F** (03) 6382 7226 **www**.pipersbrook.com **Open** 7 days 10–5
Winemaker Rene Bezemer **Est.** 1974 **Cases** 90 000

The Pipers Brook Tasmanian empire has over 185 ha of vineyard supporting the Pipers Brook and Ninth Island labels, with the major focus, of course, being on Pipers Brook. Fastidious viticulture and winemaking, immaculate packaging and enterprising marketing create a potent and effective blend. Pipers Brook operates two cellar door outlets, one at headquarters, the other at Strathlyn. In 2001 it became yet another company to fall prey to a takeover, in this instance by Belgian-owned sheepskin business Kreglinger, which has also established a large winery and vineyard at Mount Benson in SA. Exports to all major markets.

ΨΨΨΨΨ **Kreglinger Vintage Brut 2000** Very neatly balanced; ripe nectarine and apple with typical Tasmanian minerally acidity; long and fluid in the mouth. Cork. 12.5° alc. **Rating** 94 **To** 2009 $48

ΨΨΨΨΨ **Estate Riesling 2007** An ever-so-faintly reduced bouquet, but a lively light-bodied palate with great thrust; lime and passionfruit flavours, with balanced acidity. Screwcap. 13.5° alc. **Rating** 93 **To** 2017 $21.50
Ninth Island Pinot Noir 2006 Some minty notes to the bouquet over a substrate of red fruits; plenty of substance and structure to the palate, with plum, spice and cherry fruit, excellent value. Screwcap. 13.5° alc. **Rating** 93 **To** 2012 $25
Estate Pinot Gris 2007 A clean but quiet bouquet and entry to the mouth, then fruit progressively rising to a crescendo on the finish; very impressive. Screwcap. 13.5° alc. **Rating** 92 **To** 2011 $21.50
Kreglinger Vintage Brut 2001 Fine mousse; a very refined wine with obvious bready autolysis on a fine, stoney/minerally base; a long, dry finish. Cork. 12.5° alc. **Rating** 91 **To** 2013 $46.50
Estate Pinot Noir 2006 Strong barrel character, with roast meat, oak and dark fruits on offer; quite full on the palate, there are plenty of tannins and squeaky acidity on the long and ample finish. Screwcap. 13.5° alc. **Rating** 90 **To** 2011 $41.50
The Lyre Single Site Pinot Noir 2004 Retains remarkable purple hues; very intense, savoury and very long, drawn out by high acidity (and low pH), which explain the colour; for the aesthetes. Cork. 13.5° alc. **Rating** 90 **To** 2014 $95

ΨΨΨΨ **Reserve Pinot Noir 2004** Light red; light, spicy, verging on lemony aromas; the palate has a strongly savoury foresty edge; the primary fruit is fading. Cork. 13.5° alc. **Rating** 89 **To** 2009 $65
Ninth Island Sauvignon Blanc 2007 Quite exotic tropical fruits, with some pungency on the bouquet and palate. Screwcap. 13.5° alc. **Rating** 88 **To** 2012 $21.50
Estate Gewurztraminer 2007 Well-proportioned, flavoured and balanced, but there is a notable overall lack of varietal character and thrust. Screwcap. 13.5° alc. **Rating** 87 **To** 2012 $21.50

Pirie Estate   ★★★★★

17 High Street, Launceston, Tas 7250 (postal) **Region** Northern Tasmania
T (03) 6334 7772 **F** (03) 6334 7773 **Open** Not
Winemaker Andrew Pirie **Est.** 2004 **Cases** 8000
After a relatively short break, Andrew Pirie has re-established his winemaking activities in Tasmania. He has leased the Rosevears winery, where he will oversee the production of wines for the Rosevears group, for his own brands, and for others on a contract basis. His main responsibility, however, is now his role as CEO of Tamar Ridge, where he will also oversee winemaking.

ΨΨΨΨΨ **Pirie South Riesling 2007** Delicate blossom aromas; a mix of lime, mineral and green apple; fine finish. Screwcap. 12.8° alc. **Rating** 94 **To** 2015 $20
Chardonnay 2006 Opens very well with elegant stone fruit and melon; some cashew adds complexity; excellent length. Screwcap. 14° alc. **Rating** 94 **To** 2012 $38

ỌỌỌỌỌ Pinot Noir 2006 Bright, deep hue; a lively, fresh palate with good weight and good length. Screwcap. 13.5° alc. **Rating** 90 **To** 2013 $38

ỌỌỌỌ South Sauvignon Blanc 2007 Clean, crisp aromas; the palate has the natural acidity denied most mainland regions in '07; an attractive mix of gooseberry and more tropical fruit; clean, but slightly short. Screwcap. 13° alc. **Rating** 89 **To** 2010 $22.50
South Pinot Gris 2006 Well made; notes of apple, spice and spearmint; a long, dry, balanced finish. Screwcap. 13.5° alc. **Rating** 89 **To** 2009 $22.50
South Pinot Gris 2007 Pale bronze-pink; a ripe style with bruised pear, spice and a hint of red fruits; slightly loose texture. Screwcap. 13.5° alc. **Rating** 88 **To** 2010 $23
Pirie South Pinot Noir 2007 Made in early developing style, but with good fruit concentration and weight, with a little bit of forest to add interest. Screwcap. 13.5° alc. **Rating** 88 **To** 2012 $25

Pirramimma

Johnston Road, McLaren Vale, SA 5171 **Region** McLaren Vale
T (08) 8323 8205 **F** (08) 8323 9224 **www**.pirramimma.com.au **Open** Mon–Fri 9–5,
Sat 11–5, Sun, public hols 11.30–4
Winemaker Geoff Johnston **Est.** 1892 **Cases** 50 000
A long-established, family-owned company with outstanding vineyard resources. It is using those resources to full effect, with a series of intense old-vine varietals including Semillon, Sauvignon Blanc, Chardonnay, Shiraz, Grenache, Cabernet Sauvignon and Petit Verdot, all fashioned without over-embellishment. There are two quality tiers, both offering excellent value, the packaging significantly upgraded recently. Exports to the UK, the US and other major markets.

ỌỌỌỌỌ ACJ 2004 Dense red-purple; a strongly regional, rich, black-fruited Bordeaux blend with very good texture and structure; will be long-lived. Honours founder Alexander Campbell Johnston. Cork. 14.5° alc. **Rating** 95 **To** 2029 $55
McLaren Vale Cabernet Sauvignon 2004 Perfect expression of the marriage of region and variety, dark chocolate wrapped around the blackcurrant fruit; good extract of tannin and oak. Cork. 14° alc. **Rating** 94 **To** 2019 $26.50

ỌỌỌỌỌ Digby McLaren Vale Old Tawny Port NV Obvious aged rancio characters; a refreshing, complex Tawny, with some Portuguese echoes thanks to the low baume; has length and class. Cork. 18.5° alc. **Rating** 92 **To** 2009 $37
McLaren Vale Shiraz 2005 Good colour retention; strongly regional in character, with spices and dark chocolate wrapped around the core of blackberry and plum fruit; good length and tannin support. Cork. 14° alc. **Rating** 90 **To** 2015 $26.50

ỌỌỌỌ Old Bush Vine McLaren Vale Grenache 2004 Shows spicy, earthy bottled-developed characters; distinct Southern Rhône notes, the tannins balanced. Vines planted in 1944. Screwcap. 14° alc. **Rating** 89 **To** 2011 $18
McLaren Vale Shiraz 2003 Medium-bodied; an earthy, spicy mix with riper plum, prune and chocolate flavours; the '03s aren't getting any better with age. Cork. 14° alc. **Rating** 88 **To** 2010 $26.50
Stock's Hill McLaren Vale Semillon Sauvignon Blanc 2007 Clean fresh and well made; a short-term proposition. Screwcap. 12.5° alc. **Rating** 87 **To** 2010 $15

Pizzini

Lano-Trento Vineyard, 175 King Valley Road, Whitfield, Vic 3768 **Region** King Valley
T (03) 5729 8278 **F** (03) 5729 8495 **www**.pizzini.com.au **Open** 7 days 10–5
Winemaker Alfred Pizzini, Joel Pizzini **Est.** 1980 **Cases** 14 000
Fred and Katrina Pizzini have been grapegrowers in the King Valley for over 25 years, with more than 50 ha of vineyard. Originally much of the grape production was sold, but today 80% is retained for the Pizzini brand, and the focus is on winemaking, which has been

particularly successful. Their wines rank high among the many King Valley producers. It is not surprising that their wines should span both Italian and traditional varieties, and I can personally vouch for their Italian cooking skills. Exports to Japan.

ΨΨΨΨΨ **Il Barone 2003** Still very youthful and slightly rough around the edges; abundant black fruits and spices suggest patience will be well-rewarded. Cabernet Sauvignon/Shiraz/Sangiovese/Nebbiolo. Cork. 14.2° alc. **Rating** 90 **To** 2018 $45
Rubacuori King Valley Sangiovese 2003 This is a very good sangiovese by Australian standards, but the price is breathtaking; silky tannins and sour cherries do provide genuine varietal character. Cork. 14.2° alc. **Rating** 90 **To** 2015 $110
King Valley Nebbiolo 2002 Tobacco, cigar box, leaf, earth, spice and cherry all make their appearance; finishes with fine tannins. Ambitious price, although this is a superb nebbiolo. Cork. 14° alc. **Rating** 90 **To** 2012 $55

ΨΨΨΨ **King Valley Barbera 2005** Clear-cut varietal character, both in its strength (red fruit flavours) and its weakness (slightly disjointed tannins); the good parts do prevail. Screwcap. 14.2° alc. **Rating** 88 **To** 2011 $36
Sauvignon Blanc 2007 Crisp and fresh; driven to the Yarra Valley by smoke taint problems in the King Valley, but does not entirely escape its clutches; is bright and lively, with good length and acidity. Screwcap. 12° alc. **Rating** 87 **To** 2009 $17

Plan B   ★★★☆

PO Box 139, Cowaramup, WA 6284 **Region** Margaret River
T 0413 759 030 **F** (08) 9755 6267 **www**.planbwines.com **Open** By appt
Winemaker Bill Crappsley, Garry Gosatti **Est.** 2005 **Cases** 6000
This is a joint venture between Bill Crappsley, a 43-year veteran winemaker/consultant; Martin Miles, with a wine distribution business in the southwestern part of the state; Gary Gosatti, of Arlewood Estate; and Terry Chellappah, wine consultant and now also in partnership with Gary Gosatti. The shiraz is sourced from Bill Crappsley's Calgardup Vineyard, the remaining wines from Arlewood and all are single-vineyard releases. Exports to the UK, the US, Switzerland, Singapore, Hong Kong and Malaysia.

ΨΨΨΨ **Margaret River Shiraz 2006** Really peppery style, with lively acid and good oak; lacks fruit on the mid-palate though. Screwcap. 14° alc. **Rating** 89 **To** 2014 $19

Plantagenet   ★★★★☆

Albany Highway, Mount Barker, WA 6324 **Region** Mount Barker
T (08) 9851 3111 **F** (08) 9851 1839 **www**.plantagenetwines.com **Open** 7 days 9–5
Winemaker John Durham, Andries Mostert **Est.** 1974 **Cases** 90 000
The senior winery in the Mount Barker region, making superb wines across the full spectrum of variety and style: highly aromatic Riesling, tangy citrus-tinged Chardonnay, glorious Rhône-style Shiraz and ultra-stylish Cabernet Sauvignon. Exports to all major markets.

ΨΨΨΨΨ **Great Southern Shiraz 2005** Shows the good vintage to full effect; a tapestry of black fruit flavours, spices and pepper, augmented by quality oak and ripe tannins; great line and length. Screwcap. 14.5° alc. **Rating** 96 **To** 2020 $40

ΨΨΨΨΨ **Great Southern Riesling 2007** Delicate, crisp, floral apple and lime aromas flow through to the palate, likewise fresh and lively; good length. Screwcap. 12° alc. **Rating** 92 **To** 2017 $19
Hazard Hill Semillon Sauvignon Blanc 2007 A spotless bouquet with fragrant passionfruit aromas, then a lively palate with lemony/citrussy semillon coming through; has the crisp delicacy so important to the style; great value. Screwcap. 13° alc. **Rating** 91 **To** 2009 $12
Omrah Unoaked Chardonnay 2007 Has abundant varietal fruit, retaining cool-grown grapefruit and nectarine flavours notwithstanding the vintage; plenty of character and style. Screwcap. 14° alc. **Rating** 90 **To** 2011 $18

ᵠᵠᵠᵠ Eros 2006 A light, crisp, quite spicy wine, with plenty of intensity and good length; with or without food. Rose. Screwcap. 13.5° alc. **Rating** 89 **To** 2009 $16.50
Lioness Great Southern Shiraz Viognier 2005 Has that typical viognier lift to the bouquet, introducing hints of wild flowers and spice; light- to medium-bodied, with good balance, although the finish is not entirely convincing. Screwcap. 14.5° alc. **Rating** 89 **To** 2012 $25
Hazard Hill Shiraz 2005 Bright and spicy with redcurrant and blackberry on the bouquet and palate; a drink-early accessible style. Screwcap. 14.5° alc. **Rating** 87 **To** 2014 $12

Platypus Lane Wines   ★★★

PO Box 1140, Midland, WA 6936 **Region** Swan District
T (08) 9250 1655 **F** (08) 9274 3045 **Open** Not
Winemaker Brenden Smith (Contract) **Est.** 1996 **Cases** NA
Platypus Lane, with a core of 2.5 ha of chardonnay, shiraz and muscat, gained much publicity for owner Ian Gibson when its Shiraz won the inaugural John Gladstones Trophy at the Qantas WA Wine Show for the wine showing greatest regional and varietal typicity. Much of the credit can no doubt go to winemaker Brenden Smith, who handles significant quantities of grapes brought in from other producers as well as from the core vineyards. Exports to the UK and the US.

ᵠᵠᵠᵠ Unwooded Chardonnay 2006 Abundant soft stone fruit on both bouquet and fore-palate, tightening up nicely with crisp acidity on the finish. **Rating** 88 **To** 2009

Plum Hill Vineyard   ★★★★

45 Coldstream West Road, Chirnside Park, Vic 3116 **Region** Yarra Valley
T (03) 9735 0985 **F** (03) 9735 4109 **Open** By appt
Winemaker Contract **Est.** 1998 **Cases** 2000
Ian and June Delbridge had been breeding cattle on their 36-ha property since the early 1970s, before deciding to establish a vineyard in '98 on the advice of the late Dr John Middleton. They planted a little over 7 ha of merlot, pinot noir, cabernet sauvignon and shiraz, in the distinguished neighbourhood of Mount Mary, Bianchet and Yarra Edge. Grapes from the first two vintages were sold, but in 2003 the decision was taken to make and bottle the wines under the Plum Hill Vineyard label.

ᵠᵠᵠᵠᵠ Yarra Valley Merlot 2006 Quite expressive merlot fruit on both the bouquet and light- to medium-bodied palate; spicy, savoury notes, but not quite enough small berry fruit on the mid-palate. Screwcap. 13.4° alc. **Rating** 90 **To** 2013 $20
Yarra Valley Cabernet 2006 Deeply coloured; ripe blackcurrant and cassis, with plenty of depth to the structure; matching ripe tannins, and gentle oak. Screwcap. 14.1° alc. **Rating** 90 **To** 2015 $20

ᵠᵠᵠᵠ Yarra Valley Shiraz 2006 Medium-bodied; an elegant fusion of black cherry fruit and soft oak, fine tannins; needs a little more conviction. Screwcap. 14.1° alc. **Rating** 89 **To** 2012 $20

Plunkett Fowles   ★★★★☆

Cnr Hume Highway/Lambing Gully Road, Avenel, Vic 3664 **Region** Strathbogie Ranges
T (03) 5796 2150 **F** (03) 5796 2147 **www**.plunkettfowles.com.au **Open** 7 days 9–5
Winemaker Sam Plunkett, Victor Nash, Lindsay Brown, Michael Clayden **Est.** 1968
Cases 20 000
Plunkett Fowles is the new face for two families committed to building a prominent international wine business. The co-managers, Sam Plunkett and Matt Fowles, are in their late 30s and late 20s, with both winemaking and business skills. They profess to be committed to a strategy of selling wine that exceeds the expectations for any given price point, and see shiraz as one of the key varietals for this strategy (but they're also exploring alternative varieties). Exports to the UK, the US and other major markets.

ŢŢŢŢŢ **Plunkett Reserve Strathbogie Ranges Shiraz 2005** Loaded with vibrant red fruits, lots of spice and a savoury minerality at its core, this wine displays a long rich and complex array of flavours on the finish. Screwcap. 15° alc. **Rating** 94 To 2016 $39.95

ŢŢŢŢŢ **Plunkett Strathbogie Ranges Riesling 2007** Generous and rich fruit in a citrus/pineapple/tropical spectrum; clean, with good texture, but needed a touch more acidity. Screwcap. 12° alc. **Rating** 90 To 2013 $18.95
Plunkett Strathbogie Ranges Chardonnay 2006 Well made; clearly defined varietal honeydew melon and nectarine fruit; a nice touch of cashew oak. Screwcap. 14° alc. **Rating** 90 To 2015 $19.95
Plunkett Reserve The Exception Cabernet Sauvignon 2004 A fragrant bouquet, then a lively palate, with touches of mint to the cassis-accented fruit; cedary French oak. Screwcap. 14.5° alc. **Rating** 90 To 2019 $39.95

ŢŢŢŢ **Blackwood Ridge Unwooded Chardonnay 2007** Light- to medium-bodied; an attractive unwooded style with direct nectarine and melon fruit; good acidity and length. Screwcap. 14° alc. **Rating** 89 To 2010 $16.95
Blackwood Ridge Traminer Riesling 2007 Prominent traminer florals on the bouquet, and the palate is really quite sweet; good flavour, and thoroughly enjoyable served chilled. Screwcap. 12° alc. **Rating** 89 To 2009 $16.95
Blackwood Ridge Shiraz 2005 A bit of pine resin aroma, with black fruits and a slightly savoury edge; good weight and texture, with a rush of red fruits on the finish. Screwcap. 15° alc. **Rating** 89 To 2012 $16.95
Plunkett Strathbogie Ranges Gewurztraminer 2007 A somewhat muted varietal character; faint touches of lychee and rose petal; good balance and line, simply needing more varietal definition. Screwcap. 13.5° alc. **Rating** 88 To 2010 $18.95
Blackwood Ridge Pinot Noir 2006 Simple light cherry and strawberry aromas; a little spice on the palate, with nice intensity, length and bright fruit on the finish. Screwcap. 13° alc. **Rating** 87 To 2011 $16.95

Poacher's Ridge Vineyard ★★★★

1630 Spencer Road, Narrikup, WA 6326 **Region** Mount Barker
T (08) 9387 5003 **F** (08) 9387 5503 **www**.prv.com.au **Open** Fri–Sun 10–4 or by appt
Winemaker Robert Diletti (Contract) **Est.** 2000 **Cases** 1600
Alex and Janet Taylor purchased the Poacher's Ridge property in 1999; before then it had been used for cattle grazing. In 2000, 7 ha of vineyard (shiraz, cabernet sauvignon, merlot, riesling, marsanne and viognier) were planted. The first small crop came in '03, a larger one in '04, together making an auspicious debut. However, winning the Tri Nations merlot class against the might of Australia, NZ and South Africa in '07 with its 2005 Louis' Block Great Southern Merlot was a dream com true. Exports to the US and Canada.

ŢŢŢŢŢ **Louis' Block Great Southern Riesling 2007** Highly aromatic, with lifted citrus blossom aromas; long citrus, mineral and green pea palate with good acidity to close. **Rating** 94 To 2013

ŢŢŢŢ **Louis' Block Great Southern Merlot 2006** Tangy, spicy, savoury characters provide clear varietal definition, but without the depth of the outstanding '05s; fine-grained tannins. Cork. 14° alc. **Rating** 89 To 2013 $23.95
Sophie's Yard Great Southern Shiraz 2006 Light but bright hue; perfumed, and light- to medium-bodied, with spicy/peppery overtones to the red fruits; minimal tannins. ProCork. 14° alc. **Rating** 88 To 2014 $23.95
Louis' Block Great Southern Cabernet Sauvignon 2006 Fresh, lively, light-bodied redcurrant fruit; picked early in response to vintage rain; ready now. Cork. 13.6° alc. **Rating** 88 To 2009 $19.95

Point Leo Road Vineyard

214 Point Leo Road, Red Hill South, Vic 3937 **Region** Mornington Peninsula
T 0406 610 815 **F** (03) 9882 0327 **www**.pointleoroad.com.au **Open** By appt
Winemaker Phillip Kittle, Andrew Thomson, David Cowburn **Est.** 1996 **Cases** 1000
John Law and family planted 2 ha of pinot noir and 1.6 ha of chardonnay in 1996 as
contract growers for several leading Mornington Peninsula wineries. They subsequently
planted 1 ha of pinot gris and 0.6 ha of lagrein. These have in turn been followed by 1.4 ha
of gewurztraminer and sauvignon blanc, lifting total plantings to 6.6 ha, although the latest
additions will not come into bearing until 2008. They have decided to have part of the
grapes contract-made, and now have two labels: Point Leo Road for premium wines, and
Point Break the second label.

♀♀♀♀♀ **Mornington Peninsula Pinot Noir 2006** Bright red fruits with a briary edge;
quite firm on the palate with some toasty oak poking through at the end; quite
long on the finish. Screwcap. 13.5° alc. **Rating** 92 **To** 2011 $30

Pokolbin Estate

McDonalds Road, Pokolbin, NSW 2321 **Region** Lower Hunter Valley
T (02) 4998 7524 **F** (02) 4998 7765 **www**.pokolbinestate.com.au **Open** 7 days 9–5
Winemaker Andrew Thomas (Contract) **Est.** 1980 **Cases** 3500
If you go to the lengths that Pokolbin Estate has done to hide its light under a bushel, you
end up with something like seven vintages of Semillon, six of Riesling, eight of Shiraz, three
of Tempranillo, three each of Nebbiolo and Sangiovese and sundry other wines adding up
to more than 40 in total. Between 1998 and 2000 Neil McGuigan and Gary Reid shared
the winemaking tasks; since '01 Andrew Thomas has skilfully made the wines from vineyards
planted between 1960 and the early '70s.

♀♀♀♀♀ **Reserve Hunter Valley Shiraz 2006** Has lovely fruit concentration and a
bright core of red fruits; quite firm and drying, but ample fruit weight to handle
the lavish use of oak. Screwcap. 14.3° alc. **Rating** 94 **To** 2018 $50

♀♀♀♀♀ **Hunter Valley Semillon 2000** Strong toasty aromas with hints of freshly
buttered toast and lemon curd; lots of flavour and quite long. Cork. 12.3° alc.
Rating 91 **To** 2012 $25
Belebula Hunter Valley Tempranillo 2006 Very oaky bouquet, but backed
up by ripe, fleshy fruit; good concentration and length with good tannins on the
finish. Screwcap. 14.5° alc. **Rating** 91 **To** 2014 $32
Hunter Valley Semillon 2007 Layer upon layer of sweet citrus fruit; deep and
vigorous; why wait? Screwcap. 12° alc. **Rating** 90 **To** 2009 $20
George's Hunter Valley Tawny Port (500 ml) NV Genuine tawny style,
with nutty rancio character, and no real bitterness; finish is quite dry, long and
endearing. Cork. 18.5° alc. **Rating** 90 **To** 2016 $50

♀♀♀♀ **Hunter Valley Shiraz Viognier 2006** More lifted than the varietal, but a
bit short on the palate; nice weight. Screwcap. 14° alc. **Rating** 87 **To** 2012 $22
Belebula Hunter Valley Sangiovese 2006 Savoury red fruits; very dry, but
a quite varietal and focused finish. Screwcap. 13.5° alc. **Rating** 87 **To** 2012 $25
Belebula Hunter Valley Nebbiolo 2006 Quite good flavour, with a little
leather and lifted fruit; tannic, but with a red fruit core that persists on the finish.
Screwcap. 13.8° alc. **Rating** 87 **To** 2014 $25

Polin & Polin Wines ★★★★

Mistletoe Lane, Pokolbin, NSW 2230 **Region** Upper Hunter Valley
T (02) 9969 9914 **F** (02) 9969 9665 **www**.polinwines.com.au **Open** W'ends &
public hols 11–4
Winemaker Peter Orr, Patrick Auld **Est.** 1997 **Cases** 2000

The 6-ha vineyard was established by Lexie and Michael Polin (and family) in 1997. It is not named for them, as one might expect, but to honour Peter and Thomas Polin, who migrated from Ireland in 1860, operating a general store in Coonamble. Limb of Addy has a distinctly Irish twist to it, but is in fact a hill immediately to the east of the vineyard.

⟨⟨⟨⟨⟨ **Tudor Hunter Valley Chardonnay 2005** Excellent colour; particularly well-made, still tight and elegant; gentle stone fruit and carefully crafted oak inputs to a slow-developing wine. Screwcap. 13.9° alc. **Rating** 92 **To** 2012 $20
Limb of Addy Hunter Valley Shiraz 2005 Earthy, spicy aromas are distinctly regional, as is the palate, medium-bodied but complex; good tannin and oak. Screwcap. 13° alc. **Rating** 91 **To** 2018 $26

Politini Wines   NR

65 Upper King River Road, Cheshunt, Vic 3678 **Region** King Valley
T (03) 5729 8277 **F** (03) 5729 8373 **www**.politiniwines.com.au **Open** 7 days 11–5
Winemaker Luis Simian **Est.** 1989 **Cases** 2000
The Politini family have been grapegrowers in the King Valley supplying major local wineries since 1989, selling to Brown Brothers, Miranda and the Victorian Alps Winery. In 2000 they decided to withhold 20 tonnes per year for the Politini Wines label.

Polleters   ★★★★★

80 Polleters Road, Moonambel, Vic 3478 **Region** Pyrenees
T (03) 9569 5030 **www**.polleters.com **Open** W'ends 10–5
Winemaker Mark Summerfield **Est.** 1994 **Cases** 1500
Pauline and Peter Bicknell purchased the 60-ha property on which their vineyard now stands in 1993, at which time it was part of a larger grazing property. The first vines were planted in '94, and there are now 6 ha of shiraz, cabernet sauvignon, cabernet franc and merlot. In the first few years the grapes were sold, but since 2001 part of the production has been used to produce the impressively rich and powerful wines. The grapes are hand-picked, fermented in open vats with hand-plunging, and matured for 18 months in American oak. The '05 wines are still available from cellar door; the '06s are due for release late '09.

⟨⟨⟨⟨⟨ **Pyrenees Cabernet Sauvignon 2005** Full purple-red; serious cabernet sauvignon, with pristine blackcurrant aromas and flavours; perfect alcohol and extract, oak likewise; fine tannins. Screwcap. 13.5° alc. **Rating** 96 **To** 2030 $25
Morgans Choice 2005 Has the same succulent, fine, lingering palate structure as the other Polleter '05 wines; a mix of all black fruits imaginable; needs time. Screwcap. 14.5° alc. **Rating** 94 **To** 2025 $25

⟨⟨⟨⟨⟨ **Pyrenees Merlot 2005** A complex, ultra-concentrated wine; smooth and supple, and will be very long-lived. As ever, varietal expression is muted. Screwcap. 14.5° alc. **Rating** 93 **To** 2020 $25
Moonambel Shiraz 2005 Bright purple-red; a full-bodied mix of blackberry, plum and nuances of mocha and spice; good balance and structure; simply needs time. Screwcap. 15° alc. **Rating** 92 **To** 2020 $25

Ponda Estate   ★★★

150 Rhinds Road, Wallington, Vic 3221 **Region** Geelong
T (03) 5250 5300 **F** (03) 5250 5300 **Open** W'ends & public hols 10–5, or by appt
Winemaker St Regis (Peter Nicol) **Est.** 2000 **Cases** 300
Each year owners Greg Blair and Helen Gannon are joined by friends and family to help pick the grapes from the 1.4 ha of pinot noir they have planted and carefully tend, only using irrigation where absolutely necessary. They also source a small amount of chardonnay from local growers.

Pondalowie Vineyards ★★★★★

6 Main Street, Bridgewater-on-Loddon, Vic 3516 **Region** Bendigo
T (03) 5437 3332 **F** (03) 5437 3332 **www.**pondalowie.com.au **Open** W'ends 12–5, or
by appt
Winemaker Dominic Morris, Krystina Morris **Est.** 1997 **Cases** 2500
Dominic and Krystina Morris both have strong winemaking backgrounds, gained from
working in Australia, Portugal and France. Dominic has worked alternate vintages in Australia
and Portugal since 1995, and Krystina has also worked at St Hallett, and at Boar's Rock. They
have established 5.5 ha of shiraz, 2 ha each of tempranillo and cabernet sauvignon, and a little
viognier and malbec. Incidentally, the illustration on the Pondalowie label is not a piece of
barbed wire, but a very abstract representation of the winery kelpie dog. Exports to the UK,
Singapore and Japan.

ŶŶŶŶŶ **Shiraz Viognier 2006** Deeply coloured, with high levels of dark berry fruits,
hints of minerals and a robust personality; good concentration, with good
structure; should go the distance. Screwcap. 14.5° alc. **Rating** 94 **To** 2020 $30
Special Release Cabernet Malbec 2005 Lavish levels of fruit, but with a
savoury undercurrent; full-bodied with a core of bright red fruits coming through
on the rich but fine finish. Screwcap. 14° alc. **Rating** 94 **To** 2015 $40

ŶŶŶŶŶ **Shiraz 2006** Bright-fruited, with blueberries and a hint of spice; a little
savoury, but soft and supple on the finish; restrained elegance. Screwcap.
14.5° alc. **Rating** 90 **To** 2014 $25
Heathcote Tempranillo 2007 Very ripe fruit, moving in to a kirsch liqueur
bouquet; sweet and supple fruit on the palate, with a dry, slightly dusty finish.
Screwcap. 13.5° alc. **Rating** 90 **To** 2012 $22

Poole's Rock/Cockfighter's Ghost ★★★★☆

DeBeyers Road, Pokolbin, NSW 2321 **Region** Lower Hunter Valley
T (02) 4998 7356 **F** (02) 4998 6866 **www.**poolesrock.com.au **Open** 7 days 9.30–5
Winemaker Patrick Auld, Usher Tinkler **Est.** 1988 **Cases** NFP
Sydney merchant banker David Clarke has had a long involvement with the wine industry.
The 18-ha Poole's Rock vineyard, planted purely to chardonnay, is his personal venture; it
was initially bolstered by the acquisition of the larger, adjoining Simon Whitlam Vineyard.
However, the purchase of the 74-ha Glen Elgin Estate, upon which the 2500-tonne former
Tulloch winery is situated, takes Poole's Rock (and its associated brands, Cockfighter's Ghost
and Firestick) into another dimension. Exports to all major markets.

ŶŶŶŶŶ **Poole's Rock Hunter Valley Semillon 2005** No surprise that it accumulated
an important trophy at the Hunter Valley Wine Show '06; still in its infancy, but
has that extra dimension of lemony fruit of the '05 Hunter vintage; long finish.
Screwcap. 11.9° alc. **Rating** 95 **To** 2017 $24.95

ŶŶŶŶŶ **Cockfighter's Ghost Tasmania Pinot Noir 2005** Powerful, intense and
focused; black cherry and spice with touches of briar and forest floor; will
continue to develop well; fully priced. Screwcap. **Rating** 92 **To** 2012 $34.95
Poole's Rock Hunter Valley Chardonnay 2006 More refined than the
Cockfighter's Ghost, but also has very good length, and an attractive touch
of minerality on the finish, not common in the Hunter. Screwcap. 13.1° alc.
Rating 92 **To** 2014 $31.95
Cockfighter's Ghost Hunter Valley Semillon 2007 A strong mix of citrus
and grass aromas; fresh and long in the mouth; less opulent than some, but no bad
thing. Screwcap. 11.6° alc. **Rating** 90 **To** 2017 $17.50
Cockfighter's Ghost Hunter Valley Chardonnay 2006 Well made, the small
portion of barrel-ferment lying behind the considerable intensity and length of the
nectarine, citrus and melon palate. Surprise packet. Screwcap. 13.2° alc. **Rating** 90
To 2012 $19.95

Poole's Rock Hunter Valley Shiraz 2005 Bright clear colour; in the mainstream of Hunter Valley style, with medium-bodied black and red fruits, silky tannins and yet to develop the more earthy characters that will come with age. Screwcap. 13.5° alc. **Rating** 90 **To** 2020 $36.95

ŦŦŦŦ **Cockfighter's Ghost Tasmania Pinot Noir 2006** Well-articulated plum and black cherry varietal fruit; has length; needs more mid-palate vinosity for higher points in a good Tasmanian vintage. Screwcap. 14° alc. **Rating** 89 **To** 2012 $39.95
Poole's Rock Hunter Valley Shiraz 2003 Lively, fresh red fruits; gives the impression of late acid adjustment, but, nonetheless, will be long-lived, and grow in bottle. Screwcap. 13° alc. **Rating** 89 **To** 2018 $34.95
Cockfighter's Ghost Clare Valley Riesling 2007 A clean, though still closed bouquet; attractive mid-palate fruit, but finishes short. Screwcap. 13.2° alc. **Rating** 88 **To** 2012 $21.95
Cockfighter's Ghost Hunter Valley Verdelho 2007 Above-average concentration and length to ripe fruit salad flavours; does thicken slightly on the finish. Screwcap. 13.2° alc. **Rating** 88 **To** 2010 $18.95
Firestick Semillon Sauvignon Blanc 2007 The blend incorporates a little viognier, though it is the passionfruit sauvignon blanc component that gets this light but fresh wine over the line. Screwcap. 12° alc. **Rating** 87 **To** 2009 $14.95

Pooley Wines   ★★★★★

Cooinda Vale Vineyard, Barton Vale Road, Campania, Tas 7026 **Region** Southern Tasmania
T (03) 6260 2895 **F** (03) 6260 2895 **www**.pooleywines.com.au **Open** 7 days 10–5
Winemaker Matt Pooley, Andrew Hood (Contract) **Est.** 1985 **Cases** 2600
Three generations of the Pooley family have been involved in the development of Pooley Wines, although the winery was previously known as Cooinda Vale. Plantings have now reached 6.4 ha in a region that is substantially warmer and drier than most people realise. In 2003 the family planted 1 ha of pinot noir at Richmond on a heritage property with an 1830s Georgian home (and 28 ha in all), which will be known as the Belmont Vineyard, and will have a cellar door in an old sandstone barn on the property.

ŦŦŦŦŦ **Coal River Late Harvest Riesling 2007** Pure aromas of lime and green apple, the level of sweetness perfectly balanced by acidity; cleansing finish of the highest quality. Gold, Tas Wine Show '08. **Rating** 95 **To** 2017 $28
Nellies Nest Riesling 2007 Fine and focused bouquet; an attractive, complex palate, full of lime, citrus and minerals; very pure, with a slatey backbone, and racy acidity. Screwcap. **Rating** 94 **To** 2018 $16

ŦŦŦŦ **Butchers Hill Pinot Noir 2006** Bright and clear colour; a fresh, lively and bright wine, but a little too stemmy/briary, needing more sweet fruit. Screwcap. 13.1° alc. **Rating** 89 **To** 2010 $30
Coal River Riesling 2007 A relatively subdued bouquet, then a pure, very fine palate at this stage dominated by acidity; will flourish. **Rating** 87 **To** 2017 $22

Poonawatta Estate   ★★★★★

PO Box 340, Angaston, SA 5353 **Region** Eden Valley
T (08) 8565 3248 **F** (08) 8565 3248 **www**.poonawatta.com **Open** Not
Winemaker Reid Bosward, Jo Irvine, Andrew Holt **Est.** 1880 **Cases** 600
The Poonawatta Estate story is complex, stemming from 1.8 ha of shiraz planted in 1880. When Andrew Holt's parents purchased the Poonawatta property, the vineyard had suffered decades of neglect, and a slow process of restoration began. While that was underway, the strongest canes available from the winter pruning of the 1880s block were slowly and progressively dug into the stony soil of the site. It took seven years to establish the matching 1.8 ha, and the yield is even lower than that of the 1880s block. In 2004 Andrew and wife Michelle were greeted with the same high yields that were obtained right across South Eastern Australia, and this led to declassification of part of the production, giving rise to a

second label, Monties Block, which sits underneath The Cuttings (from the 'new' vines) and, at the top, The 1880. In 2005 a Riesling was introduced, produced from a single vineyard of 2 ha hand-planted by the Holt family in the 1970s. The 2007 drought and frosts mean there will be no Riesling from that year, a Ratafia from '06 filling the gap. Exports to the US, France, Singapore and Hong Kong.

ŶŶŶŶŶ **The 1880 Eden Valley Shiraz 2006** Dark, complex and multi-layered; plenty of good oak in evidence, but the very fine, yet powerful fruit will engulf it easily with time; rich and savoury on the finish; lively, fresh and surprisingly supple given its weight and power. Cork. 14.5° alc. **Rating** 95 **To** 2025 $80
Monties Block Eden Valley Shiraz 2006 Savoury mineral notes complement the bright red fruits; medium-bodied, vibrant and focused on the long and even finish. Screwcap. 15° alc. **Rating** 94 **To** 2018 $29

ŶŶŶŶŶ **The Cuttings Eden Valley Shiraz 2006** Fine and distinctly savoury medium-bodied wine, with a long, spicy palate and finish; utterly belies its alcohol. Cork. 15° alc. **Rating** 92 **To** 2014 $49

Port Phillip Estate ★★★★★

261 Red Hill Road, Red Hill, Vic 3937 **Region** Mornington Peninsula
T (03) 5989 2708 **F** (03) 5989 3017 **www**.portphillip.net **Open** W'ends & public hols 11–5
Winemaker Sandro Mosele **Est.** 1987 **Cases** 4000
Established by Melbourne QC Jeffrey Sher, who sold the estate to Giorgio and Dianne Gjergja in 2000. The Gjergjas were rightly more than content with the quality and style of the wines; the main changes are enhanced cellar door facilities and redesigned labels. The ability of the site (enhanced, it is true, by the skills of Sandro Mosele) to produce outstanding Syrah, Pinot Noir, Chardonnay, and very good Sauvignon Blanc, is something special. Whence climate change? Quite possibly the estate may have answers for decades to come. A futuristic, multimillion-dollar restaurant, cellar door and winery complex is under construction. Exports to the UK, Canada and Singapore.

ŶŶŶŶŶ **Morillon Tete De Cuvee Mornington Peninsula Pinot Noir 2005** Brilliantly clear but strong colour; a mix of spice, stalk and fruit straddling black and red berry spectrums; fine, lingering tannins. Diam. 14° alc. **Rating** 95 **To** 2012 $46
Mornington Peninsula Chardonnay 2006 Super tight; in Chablis mode, with abundant mineral and tight lemon fruits on the palate; very fresh, very long and racy. Cork. 13.5° alc. **Rating** 94 **To** 2018 $27
Mornington Peninsula Pinot Noir 2006 Brilliant hue and clarity; intense, highly focused, vibrant cherry and plum fruit; a long, lingering finish. Diam. 13.5° alc. **Rating** 94 **To** 2015 $37
Morillon Tete De Cuvee Mornington Peninsula Pinot Noir 2006 Quite backward and subdued on the bouquet; highly aromatic and elegant fruit style, almost a Volnay personality; savoury and red-fruited, with a firm mineral edge to the finish. Cork. 13.5° alc. **Rating** 94 **To** 2016 $42

ŶŶŶŶŶ **Mornington Peninsula Sauvignon Blanc 2007** The small barrel ferment portion shows up immediately on the bouquet, but less so on the palate, no bad thing; has good mouthfeel and length. Diam. 13° alc. **Rating** 93 **To** 2009 $25
Rimage Tete de Cuvee Mornington Peninsula Syrah 2006 A very savoury bouquet full of roasted meats and spices; a medium-bodied palate with pronounced acidity and plentiful ingrained tannins; needs a little time, but will reward. Cork. 13.5° alc. **Rating** 92 **To** 2020 $38
Quartier Mornington Peninsula Sauvignon Blanc 2007 Nicely composed and balanced; fresh gooseberry fruit is offset by spicy acidity; clean, long finish. Screwcap. 13° alc. **Rating** 90 **To** 2009 $21
Quartier Mornington Peninsula Barbera 2005 A tangy, spicy, savoury wine, with lots of activity and movement in the mouth; fully reflects the cool growing conditions. Diam. 14° alc. **Rating** 90 **To** 2017 $26

TTTT **Quartier Mornington Peninsula Arneis 2006** Clean, fresh, delicate cinnamon and apple flavours; not much depth, but, then, no phenolics either. Screwcap. 13.5° alc. **Rating** 87 **To** 2010 $25

Portree

72 Powells Track via Mount William Road, Lancefield, Vic 3455 **Region** Macedon Ranges
T (03) 5429 1422 **F** (03) 5429 2205 **www**.portreevineyard.com.au **Open** W'ends & public hols 11–5
Winemaker Ken Murchison **Est.** 1983 **Cases** 1500
Owner Ken Murchison selected his 5-ha Macedon vineyard after studying viticulture at CSU and being strongly influenced by Dr Andrew Pirie's doctoral thesis. All the wines show distinct cool-climate characteristics, the Quarry Red having clear similarities to the wines of Chinon in the Loire Valley. However, Portree has done best with Chardonnay, its principal wine (in terms of volume). Exports to China and Vanuatu.

TTTTT **Quarry Red Macedon Ranges Cabernet Franc 2003** As always, light colour; has developed exceedingly well, cherry fruit adorned with spicy, cedary, tobacco leaf overtones; fine tannins. Best yet. Screwcap. 13° alc. **Rating** 90 **To** 2012 $28

Portsea Estate

PO Box 3148, Bellevue Hill, NSW 2023 **Region** Mornington Peninsula
T (02) 9328 6359 **F** (02) 9326 1984 **www**.portseaestate.com **Open** Not
Winemaker Paringa Estate (Lindsay McCall) **Est.** 2000 **Cases** 700
Warwick Ross and sister – and silent partner – Caron Wilson-Hawley may be relative newcomers to the Mornington Peninsula (the first vintage was 2004), but they have had exceptional success with their Pinot Noir, the '05 winning top gold medal at the Ballarat Wine Show '07, and the '06 taking Champion Wine of the Show of the National Cool Climate Wine Show '07 (against all varietal comers). The vines are planted on calcareous sand and limestone (the chardonnay is in fact on the site of a 19th-century limestone quarry) only 700 m from the ocean. Warwick Ross has been a very successful film producer and says 'I'm not sure if that makes me a film-maker with a passion for wine, or a vigneron with a passion for film. Either way, I'm very happy with the collision of the two.'

TTTTT **Mornington Peninsula Pinot Noir 2006** A focused wine with lots of spice, earth and red fruits on display; dense on the bouquet, but with pure pinot lightness across the expansive palate. Cork. 13.6° alc. **Rating** 92 **To** 2012 $32

Possums Vineyard

31 Thornber Street, Unley Park, SA 5061 (postal) **Region** McLaren Vale
T (08) 8272 3406 **F** (08) 8272 3406 **www**.possumswines.com.au **Open** Not
Winemaker Mariana Ranftl **Est.** 2000 **Cases** 8000
Possums Vineyard is owned by Dr John Possingham and Carol Summers. They have 22 ha of shiraz, 17 ha of cabernet sauvignon, 18 ha of chardonnay, 1 ha of viognier and 0.5 ha of grenache established in two vineyards (at Blewitt Springs and Willunga). In 2007 they completed construction of a 500-tonne winery at Blewitt Springs and will sell both bottled and bulk wine. Exports to the US, the UK and other markets.

TTTTT **Willunga Shiraz 2006** A lovely, harmonious mix of perfectly ripened red and black fruits; fine, soft tannins, with oak in support; outstanding bargain. Screwcap. 14.5° alc. **Rating** 95 **To** 2016 $15
McLaren Vale Shiraz 2005 Makes a strong regional and varietal expression without resorting to excessive alcohol; blood plum, blackberry and bitter chocolate fruit supported by fine, ripe tannins; has absorbed 22 months in French and American oak. Screwcap. 14.5° alc. **Rating** 94 **To** 2020 $25

ŶŶŶŶŶ **Blewitt Springs Viognier 2007** Overall, shows varietal character in both flavour and texture; ample mouthfeel without phenolics to the ripe peach and apricot flavours. Screwcap. 14° alc. **Rating** 90 **To** 2011 $19

ŶŶŶŶ **McLaren Vale Grenache 2006** Very light-bodied; marzipan and raspberry varietal character not in doubt, but lacks the strength of most McLaren Vale grenache. Screwcap. 14° alc. **Rating** 87 **To** 2009 $16

 # Postcode Wines   NR
PO Box 769, Cessnock, NSW 2325 **Region** Warehouse
T (02) 4998 7474 **F** (02) 4998 7974 **www**.postcodewines.com.au **Open** At The Boutique Wine Centre, Pokolbin
Winemaker Rhys Eather **Est.** 2004 **Cases** 1000
This is a new and separate venture for Rhys and Garth Eather (of Meerea Park) taking as its raison d'etre wines that clearly show their postcode by exhibiting true regional character. The initial releases were two Shirazs from the Hunter Valley [2320] with a Cabernet Sauvignon from Hilltops [2587], and with several white wines in the future mix.

Poverty Hill Wines
PO Box 76, Springton, SA 5235 **Region** Eden Valley
T (08) 8568 2220 **F** (08) 8568 2220 **www**.povertyhillwines.com.au **Open** Fri–Mon 10–5
Winemaker John Eckert, Colin Forbes **Est.** 2002 **Cases** 4000
I'm not sure whether there is a slight note of irony in the name, but Poverty Hill Wines brings together four men who have had a long connection with the Eden Valley. Colin Forbes has been making wine there for over 30 years, establishing Craneford Wines at the end of the 1970s, though having long sold that particular business. Robert Buck owns a small vineyard on the ancient volcanic soils east of Springton, producing both Shiraz and Cabernet Sauvignon. Next is Stuart Woodman, who owns the vineyard that supplied Craneford Wines with the riesling that produced glorious wines in the early 1990s, and also has high-quality, mature-vine cabernet sauvignon. Finally, there is John Eckert, who worked with Colin Forbes at Saltram, and followed him to Craneford. He not only works as assistant winemaker at Poverty Hill, but manages Rob Buck's vineyard and his own small block of young riesling in the Highlands of Springton.

ŶŶŶŶŶ **Shiraz Grenache 2006** Unusually rich and powerful, the grenache component seamlessly welded with the shiraz; blackberry, plum and a touch of cherry; fine, ripe tannins. Screwcap. **Rating** 92 **To** 2021 $60
Eden Valley Riesling 2007 A voluminous bouquet full of sweet citrus fruit; backs off slightly on the palate, but should fill out with more time in bottle. Screwcap. 12° alc. **Rating** 91 **To** 2017 $18
Eden Valley Merlot 2006 Clean and expressive varietal aromas flow into the palate with plenty of cassis, redcurrant and black olive nuances; tannins barely visible, the oak neatly marshalled. Screwcap. 14.5° alc. **Rating** 91 **To** 2014 $20
Eden Valley Shiraz 2005 Abundant bright red fruits and hints of spice and mint; although slightly dry on the finish, has good overall flavour. Screwcap. **Rating** 90 **To** 2016 $28
20 Year Old Tawny Port NV Some tawny; pronounced rancio; biscuit and Christmas cake; long finish. **Rating** 90 **To** 2009 $45

Prancing Horse Estate
39 Paringa Road, Red Hill South, Vic 3937 **Region** Mornington Peninsula
T (03) 5989 2602 **F** (03) 9827 1231 **www**.prancinghorseestate.com **Open** By appt
Winemaker Sergio Carlei, Pascal Marchand **Est.** 1990 **Cases** 600
Anthony and Catherine Hancy acquired the Lavender Bay Vineyard in early 2002, renaming it the Prancing Horse Estate, and embarking on an increase in the estate vineyards to 4.5 ha,

with 2 ha each of chardonnay and pinot noir, and 0.5 ha of pinot gris. The Hancys avoid the use of pesticides, herbicides and fungicides. They appointed Sergio Carlei as winemaker, and the following year became joint owners with Sergio in Carlei Wines. Exports to the US, Sweden and France.

ŶŶŶŶŶ **Mornington Peninsula Chardonnay 2006** Very lively, intense and fresh; one assumes the back label assertion of 'whole berries fermented in open vats' was written for pinot, for this wine shows none of the rampant phenolics that would result from such treatment, just lovely citrus and stone fruit. Screwcap. 13.5° alc. **Rating** 95 **To** 2016 $58
Mornington Peninsula Pinot Noir 2006 Bright and clear colour; fresh, lively and pure pinot, with great elegance; made for maximum enjoyment over the next few years. Diam. 13.5° alc. **Rating** 94 **To** 2011 $45

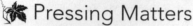

Pressing Matters ★★★★☆

PO Box 2119, Lower Sandy Bay Road, Tas 7005 **Region** Southern Tasmania
T 0439 022 988 **Open** Not
Winemaker Winemaking Tasmania (Julian Alcorso) **Est.** 2002 **Cases** NFP
Greg Melick simultaneously wears more hats than most people manage in a lifetime. He is a top-level barrister (Senior Counsel), a Major General (thus the highest ranking officer in the Australian Army Reserve) and has presided over a number of headline special commissions and enquiries into subjects as diverse as Sharne Warne's drug-taking to the Beaconsfield mine collapse. Yet, if asked, he would probably nominate wine as his major focus in life. Having built up an exceptional cellar of the great wines of Europe, he has turned his attention to grapegrowing and winemaking, having planted a 6-ha riesling and pinot noir vineyard on Middle Tea Tree Road in the Coal River Valley. It is a perfect north-facing slope, and the early wines promise much for the future, the Mosel-style Rieslings jumping out of the box.

ŶŶŶŶŶ **Riesling 9 2007** Good residual sugar (9g) and acid balance, the sweetness all but hidden, more tactile than flavour impact; good length; modern evocation of riesling. **Rating** 90 **To** 2014 $39

ŶŶŶŶ **Riesling 139 2007** The high level of residual sugar (139g) is neatly balanced by acidity; the wine still needs time in bottle to come together over a minimum 5-year period. **Rating** 89 **To** 2016

Preston Peak ★★★

31 Preston Peak Lane, Toowoomba, Qld 4352 **Region** Darling Downs
T (07) 4630 9499 **F** (07) 4630 9499 **www**.prestonpeak.com **Open** Wed–Sun 10–5
Winemaker Rod MacPherson **Est.** 1994 **Cases** 5000
Dentist owners Ashley Smith and Kym Thumpkin have a substantial tourism business. The large, modern cellar door can accommodate functions of up to 150 people, and is often used for weddings and other events. It is situated less than 10 mins drive from the Toowoomba city centre, with views of Table Top Mountain, the Lockyer Valley and the Darling Downs.

ŶŶŶŶ **Reserve Semillon 2005** Some colour development; a complex wine, with oak driving both the aroma and palate, and not quite enough fruit to justify this level of oak. Screwcap. 13° alc. **Rating** 87 **To** 2011 $28
Reserve Shiraz 2005 Sophisticated winemaking techniques used, but the American oak does threaten to overwhelm the fruit; however, many will have no problems with the oak. Screwcap. 14° alc. **Rating** 87 **To** 2010 $28

Pretty Sally Estate ★★★★

PO Box 549, Kilmore East, Vic 3764 **Region** Central Victoria Zone
T (03) 5783 3082 **F** (03) 5783 2027 **www**.prettysally.com **Open** Not
Winemaker Hanging Rock **Est.** 1996 **Cases** 1000

The McKay, Davies and Cornew families have joined to create the Pretty Sally business. It is based on estate plantings of 11.7 ha of shiraz, 23.8 ha of cabernet sauvignon and a splash of sauvignon blanc. The wines are chiefly exported to the US, where Pretty Sally has an office.

ΨΨΨΨΩ **Sauvignon Blanc 2007** A particularly lively palate, with zesty acidity under-pinning an apple, passionfruit and herb fruit mix; fresh finish. Screwcap. 12.5° alc. **Rating** 91 **To** 2010 $19.90

Preveli Wines

Bessell Road, Rosa Brook, Margaret River, WA 6285 **Region** Margaret River
T (08) 9757 2374 **F** (08) 9757 2790 **www**.preveliwines.com.au **Open** At Prevelly General Store, 7 days 10–8
Winemaker John Durham (Consultant), Sharna Kowalczuk **Est.** 1998 **Cases** 5000
Andrew and Greg Home have turned a small business into a substantial one, with 15 ha of vineyards at Rosabrook (supplemented by contracts with local growers), and winemaking spread among a number of contract makers. The wines are of consistently impressive quality. The Prevelly General Store (owned by the Homes) is the main local outlet.

ΨΨΨΨΨ **Margaret River Cabernet Merlot 2005** Good varietal intensity; cassis and cedar, and fine-grained tannins; quite fresh and lively on the finish, with understated elegant texture. Screwcap. 14° alc. **Rating** 94 **To** 2014 $24.95

ΨΨΨΨΩ **Margaret River Cabernet Shiraz 2005** Strong toasty bouquet, with cassis and blackberry in the background; fleshy and quite dense finish. Screwcap. 13.7° alc. **Rating** 90 **To** 2015 $17.95

Primo Estate

McMurtie Road, McLaren Vale, SA 5171 **Region** McLaren Vale
T (08) 8323 6800 **F** (08) 8323 6888 **www**.primoestate.com.au **Open** 7 days 11–4
Winemaker Joseph Grilli **Est.** 1979 **Cases** NFP
One-time Roseworthy dux Joe Grilli has always produced innovative and excellent wines. The biennial release of the Joseph Sparkling Red (in its tall Italian glass bottle) is eagerly awaited, the wine immediately selling out. Also unusual and highly regarded are the vintage-dated extra virgin olive oils. However, the core lies with the La Biondina, the Il Briccone Shiraz Sangiovese and the Joseph Cabernet Merlot. The business has expanded to take in both McLaren Vale and Clarendon, with 36.3 ha of cabernet sauvignon, colombard, shiraz, merlot, riesling, nebbiolo, sangiovese, riesling, sauvignon blanc and pinot grigio. Exports to all major markets.

ΨΨΨΨΨ **Shale Stone Shiraz 2005** A refined yet intense wine with outstanding texture and mouthfeel, more in an Old World than typical New World cast; fine black fruits and equally fine, savoury tannins. Cork. 14.5° alc. **Rating** 96 **To** 2020 $32
Joseph McLaren Vale Cabernet Sauvignon Merlot 2004
An elegant, medium-bodied palate with blackcurrant, a dash of cassis and hints of olive and bitter chocolate; fine tannins, long finish. Cork. 15° alc. **Rating** 95 **To** 2019 $55
Joseph Pinot Grigio d'Elena 2007 A powerful bouquet and rich palate with abundant spice, pear and musk; a real wine. Screwcap. 13° alc. **Rating** 94 **To** 2010 $25
Il Briccone Shiraz Sangiovese 2006 Delivers precisely what was intended, a very fine medium-bodied cherry-accented palate which fuses the ripe fruit of the shiraz with the savoury fruit tannins of the sangiovese; an all-too-rare wine that demands a second glass (or more). Screwcap. 14° alc. **Rating** 94 **To** 2012 $22
Joseph McLaren Vale Cabernet Sauvignon Merlot 2005 Very powerful, showing great depth of fruit, and a succulent edge that is unique for the blend; dark mocha flavours dominate, but the varietal cabernet sings through on the finish; savoury and very long. Cork. 15° alc. **Rating** 94 **To** 2018 $55

ȲȲȲȲȲ **Joseph Nebbiolo 2005** Nebbiolo is a very difficult horse to ride, but Joe Grilli understands the nature of the beast. Think of pinot noir with a tannin saddle, and then focus on the extreme length of the stride, and you may also understand the wine. Cork. 13.5° alc. **Rating** 93 **To** 2015 $75
Il Briccone Shiraz Sangiovese 2005 Lively, fresh and vibrant red fruits and spice, and with just the right structure to restrain the fruity exuberance. Screwcap. 14.5° alc. **Rating** 92 **To** 2011 $22
Zamberlan Cabernet Sauvignon Sangiovese 2004 Interesting wine; has considerable texture, length and finesse, though the impact of the Ripasso technique (re-ferment on skins) not obvious. Screwcap. 14° alc. **Rating** 92 **To** 2012 $28
Primo & Co The Tuscan Shiraz Sangiovese Toscana 2006 A fascinating comparison to Il Briccone, slightly lighter in body and slightly more firm and savoury overall, but these are definitely brothers. Grown and bottled in Italy. ProCork. 13° alc. **Rating** 91 **To** 2012 $25
La Biondina Colombard Sauvignon Blanc 2007 Despite the low alcohol, has more richness to the flavours than prior vintages; good balance and length to a pleasing, ready-to-roll white. Screwcap. 12° alc. **Rating** 90 **To** 2009 $15

Prince Albert ★★★

100 Lemins Road, Waurn Ponds, Vic 3216 **Region** Geelong
T (03) 5241 8091 **F** (03) 5241 8091 **Open** By appt
Winemaker Bruce Hyett **Est.** 1975 **Cases** 400
In 2007 Dr David Yates, with a background based on a university degree in chemistry, purchased the pinot noir–only Prince Albert vineyard from founder Bruce Hyett. David's plans are to spend 6-12 months running the vineyard and winery exactly as it has been, with advice from Bruce on winemaking, and Steve Jones in the vineyard. So far as the latter is concerned, Yates is firmly committed to retaining the certified organic status for Prince Albert, and at this juncture sees no reason to change the style of the wine, which he has always loved.

ȲȲȲȲ **Geelong Pinot Noir 2006** Good depth to colour; has plenty of mouthfilling fruit on the mid-palate, but falters on the back palate and finish. Cork. 14.5° alc. **Rating** 89 **To** 2013 $30

Prince Hill Wines ★★★★☆

1220 Sydney Road, Mudgee, NSW 2850 **Region** Mudgee
T (02) 6373 1245 **F** (02) 6373 1350 **www**.princehillwines.com **Open** Mon–Sat 9–5, Sun 10–4
Winemaker Roger Harbord **Est.** 1993 **Cases** 35 000
Prince Hill Wines has become the new name and identity for Simon Gilbert Wines, following several years of financial travail by the ASX-listed company. It is now associated with the Watson Wine Group, which has the difficult task of returning the business to profit. One might have thought the large, well-designed winery was well placed to take grapes from the various regions along the western side of the Great Dividing Range of NSW, but observers have questioned whether this can become a reality. Indeed, winemaking has now been relocated to the Cassegrain winery, with the Mudgee winery on the market.

ȲȲȲȲȲ **Eighty Links Reserve Mudgee Chardonnay 2006** Has a clever balance between barrel ferment and stainless steel fermentation; has abundant nectarine fruit, good mouthfeel and good length. Screwcap. 14° alc. **Rating** 90 **To** 2012 $25

ȲȲȲȲ **Card Collection Sangiovese Barbera 2005** Light- to medium-bodied; spicy, sour and red cherry fruits deliver more than might be expected at this price point; good length. Screwcap. 13° alc. **Rating** 88 **To** 2012 $14.50
Mudgee Chardonnay 2006 Gentle stone fruit and melon, with some creamy notes; mineral oak impact. Screwcap. 14° alc. **Rating** 87 **To** 2011 $18.50

Mudgee Shiraz 2006 Dubious colour; plum, prune, blackberry and lots of vanillin oak give an overall impression of sweetness; crowd pleaser style. Screwcap. 14.5° alc. **Rating** 87 **To** 2012 $18.50

Mudgee Sangiovese 2006 Light but bright hue; a mix of sweet red and sour cherry fruit, and silky tannins; just needs a touch more depth. Screwcap. 14.5° alc. **Rating** 87 **To** 2012 $18.50

Principia   ★★★★☆

139 Main Creek Road, Red Hill, Vic 3937 (postal) **Region** Mornington Peninsula
T (03) 5931 0010 **www**.principiawines.com.au **Open** Not
Winemaker Darrin Gaffy **Est.** 1995 **Cases** 450
Darren and Rebecca Gaffy spent their honeymoon in SA, and awakened their love of wines. In due course they gravitated to Burgundy, and began the search in Australia for a suitable cool-climate site to grow pinot noir and chardonnay. In 1995 they began to develop their vineyard, with 2.5 ha of pinot noir, and 0.8 ha of chardonnay. Darren continues to work full-time as a toolmaker (and in the vineyard on weekends and holidays); while Rebecca's career as a nurse took second place to the Bachelor of Applied Science (Wine Science) course at CSU, graduating in 2002. Along the way she worked at Red Hill Estate, Bass Phillip, Virgin Hills and Tuck's Ridge, and as winemaker at Massoni Homes. A cellar door is planned.

ΨΨΨΨΨ **Mornington Peninsula Chardonnay 2006** Has terrific concentration and poise; grilled nuts and preserved lemon interplay on the palate, which has precision and persistence; shows strong European influence. Cork. 14° alc. **Rating** 95 **To** 2013 $32

ΨΨΨΨΨ **Mornington Peninsula Pinot Noir 2006** Strongly spicy savoury components, but also quite lush red fruits, already showing signs of coming together. Diam. 13.5° alc. **Rating** 91 **To** 2013 $35

Printhie Wines   ★★★★★

489 Yuranigh Road, Molong, NSW 2866 **Region** Orange
T (02) 6366 8422 **F** (02) 6366 9328 **www**.printhiewines.com.au **Open** Mon–Sat 10–4
Winemaker Drew Tuckwell **Est.** 1996 **Cases** 18 000
Jim and Ruth Swift have planted 33 ha of shiraz, cabernet sauvignon, merlot, pinot gris and viognier, and built the largest winery in the region, with sons David and Ed now assuming much of the business responsibility. Winemaking passed from Robert Black to Drew Tuckwell in late 2007, having achieved exceptional results for the multiple trophy-winning red wines from '06. Notwithstanding its substantial estate vineyards, Printhie also purchases grapes from growers in the Orange region. The wines are modestly priced, and will gain further weight as the vines age. Printhie can fairly claim to be the premier winery in the Orange region. Exports to the US and Denmark.

ΨΨΨΨΨ **Orange Cabernet Merlot 2006** An attractive gently savoury medium-bodied palate with delicious blackcurrant fruit dominant, fine, ripe tannins and a touch of oak completing the impressive picture. Great value. Screwcap. 13.5° alc. **Rating** 94 **To** 2016 $16.95

Swift Family Heritage Cabernet Sauvignon 2005 Pure cassis and blackcurrant fruit on the bouquet, flowing through logically to the palate, with fine-grained tannins firming up the finish. Yet another very good wine from Printhie. Screwcap. **Rating** 94 **To** 2025 $32

ΨΨΨΨΨ **Orange Chardonnay 2007** Pale and bright colour; lively grapefruit and nectarine flavours drive through the long, clean palate; any oak is incidental. Screwcap. 13.5° alc. **Rating** 90 **To** 2014 $16.95

Orange Pinot Noir 2007 Attractive red cherry, plum and strawberry fruit; pure and unadorned, but none the worse for that; drink sooner rather than later. Screwcap. 13.5° alc. **Rating** 90 **To** 2011 $21.95

Orange Shiraz Viognier 2007 Lively and fresh, the accent entirely on the fragrant sweet red fruit rather than the structure, although there are fine tannins present. Screwcap. 13.5° alc. **Rating** 90 **To** 2013 $21.95

Orange Shiraz Cabernet 2006 Shiraz leads the pack with ripe plum and blackberry fruit, the cabernet adding subtle touches of choc-mint; another well-made and balanced wine. Screwcap. 13.5° alc. **Rating** 90 **To** 2016 $16.95

Orange Merlot 2006 Generous style, with ripe cassis and some blackcurrant; medium-bodied, as it should be, and with soft tannins. Screwcap. 13.5° alc. **Rating** 90 **To** 2014 $16.95

ŢŢŢŢ Orange Shiraz 2006 Very more-ish juicy red and black fruits with a sprinkle of spice; only light- to medium-bodied, the tannins fine, the oak subtle. Ready to roll, but will hold. Screwcap. 13.5° alc. **Rating** 89 **To** 2015 $16.95

 # Protero Wines ★★★★

PO Box 2082, Magill North, SA 5072 **Region** Adelaide Hills
T (08) 8337 6308 **F** (08) 8337 6308 **www**.proterowines.com.au **Open** Not
Winemaker Paul Drougemuller, Steven Pannell (Contract) **Est.** 1998 **Cases** 5000
This is one of the more carefully thought out new wine ventures. Frank and Rosemary Baldasso purchased the property in 1998, and spent two years researching the lie of the land, the most suitable varieties, and (from a commercial viewpoint) the most appropriate wines. Between 2000 and '01 they planted 3 ha each of chardonnay and viognier, 2.1 ha of merlot, 1.8 ha of nebbiolo, 1.6 ha of pinot noir and 1.2 ha of cabernet sauvignon, and are headed towards organic certification, having had chemical-free viticulture for the past three vintages. Exports to the US, UK, Japan, Singapore and Malaysia are in place, and the plan is to increase production in line with demand, not in front of it.

ŢŢŢŢŢ Gumeracha Adelaide Hills Viognier 2007 Very well made; marries good apricot and peach varietal character with an almost silky finish, rare with viognier. Screwcap. 14° alc. **Rating** 90 **To** 2012 $29

Gumeracha Adelaide Hills Merlot 2006 Attractive medium-bodied red berry fruits with attendant light, spicy tannins; good length and balance. Screwcap. 14.5° alc. **Rating** 90 **To** 2013 $29

ŢŢŢŢ Gumeracha Adelaide Hills Nebbiolo 2005 It's a hard and unforgiving mistress, is nebbiolo, and expensive into the bargain. I will politely allow others to explore this arcane world. Cork. 14.5° alc. **Rating** 87 **To** 2015 $60

Gumeracha Adelaide Hills Red Blend 2005 Cedary savoury earthy foresty notes are the key drivers, lacking enough red fruits for the passengers' comfort. Cork. 14.5° alc. **Rating** 87 **To** 2012 $25

Provenance Wines ★★★★☆

870 Steiglitz Road, Sutherlands Creek, Vic 3331 **Region** Geelong
T (03) 5281 2230 **F** (03) 5281 2205 **www**.provenancewines.com.au **Open** By appt
Winemaker Scott Ireland, Kirilly Gordon, Sam Vogel **Est.** 1995 **Cases** 2000
Scott Ireland and his partner Jen Lilburn established Provenance Wines in 1997 as a natural extension of Scott's years of winemaking experience, both here and abroad. Located in the Moorabool Valley, the winery team of Scott, Kirilly Gordon and Sam Vogel focus on the classics in a cool climate sense – Pinot Gris, Chardonnay, Pinot Noir in particular, as well as Shiraz. Fruit is sourced both locally within the Geelong region and further afield (when the fruit warrants selection). They are also major players in contract making for the Geelong region. Exports to the UK.

ŢŢŢŢŢ Geelong Chardonnay 2006 An elegant and highly focused wine, with stone fruit and grapefruit flavours, the oak perfectly balanced and integrated; long finish. Screwcap. 13.5° alc. **Rating** 94 **To** 2013 $29

ŢŢŢŢŢ Geelong Pinot Noir 2006 Good colour and hue; supple and silky texture, with attractive red fruits, then a pure line running through from the mid-palate to the finish. Screwcap. 13.5° alc. **Rating** 92 **To** 2012 $30

Geelong Shiraz 2006 Complex medium-bodied wine, with notes of mocha and spice along with the black and red fruits; the long palate is sustained by fine, gently savoury tannins. Screwcap. 13.5° alc. **Rating** 92 **To** 2018 $30

Providence Vineyards

236 Lalla Road, Lalla, Tas 7267 **Region** Northern Tasmania
T (03) 6395 1290 **F** (03) 6395 2088 **www**.providence.com.au **Open** 7 days 10–5
Winemaker Hood Wines (Andrew Hood, Alain Rousseau), Riverview Wines (Guy Wagner) **Est.** 1956 **Cases** 1000
Providence incorporates the pioneer vineyard of Frenchman Jean Miguet, now owned by the Bryce family, who purchased it in 1980. The original 1.3-ha vineyard has been expanded to a little over 3 ha, and unsuitable grenache and cabernet (left from the original plantings) have been grafted over to chardonnay, pinot noir and semillon. Miguet called the vineyard 'La Provence', reminding him of the part of France he came from, but after 40 years the French authorities forced a name change. The cellar door offers 70 different Tasmanian wines.

Puddleduck Vineyard ★★★★★

992 Richmond Road, Richmond, Tas 7025 **Region** Southern Tasmania
T (03) 6260 2301 **F** (03) 6260 2301 **www**.puddleduckvineyard.com.au **Open** 7 days 10–5
Winemaker Hood Wines (Andrew Hood) **Est.** 1997 **Cases** 890
After working the majority of their adult lives at vineyards in southern Tasmania, Darren and Jackie Brown bought land in 1996 with the dream of one day having their own label and cellar door. The dream is now reality, and the next step is a small cheesery making cheese from their small goat herd to complement the wines, which are sold exclusively through the cellar door.

ℙℙℙℙℙ Riesling 2006 Has fulfilled all and more of the promise of a year ago; great finesse, purity of line and length to the polished lime juice flavour; great finish. Screwcap. 12.8° alc. **Rating** 94 **To** 2015 $26
Chardonnay 2007 Ripe, pure and focused; very intense across the palate, and vibrant on the finish; outstanding length and finesse. **Rating** 94 **To** 2014 $28

ℙℙℙℙℙ Sauvignon Blanc 2007 A herbal, grassy bouquet, opening up on the palate with gentle tropical stone fruit and lychee flavours. Screwcap. 13° alc. **Rating** 91 **To** 2010 $26

ℙℙℙℙ Pinot Noir 2006 Very good colour; light-bodied, vibrant and fresh red fruits, then a slightly green acid finish still to resolve itself. **Rating** 89 **To** 2013 $32
Bubbleduck 2006 Pale and bright; fine bead, focused and zesty, with good concentration; very clean and pure but a little simple. **Rating** 89 **To** 2009 $42
Riesling 2007 Pure lime juice, with notes of talc and the abundant acid of the vintage; needs time. **Rating** 88 **To** 2017 $26

Pulpit Rock

172 Forbes Street, Woolloomooloo, NSW 2011 (postal) **Region** Southern Highlands
T 0418 242 045 **F** (02) 9356 4571 **www**.pulpitrockestate.com.au **Open** Not
Winemaker Rhys Eather (Contract) **Est.** 1998 **Cases** 400
Pulpit Rock brings together a team of professionals covering the field from grape to glass. Dr Richard Smart was the consultant viticulturist to give the venture his blessing; the wine is made by well-known Hunter Valley winemaker Rhys Eather; it is distributed by co-owner Carol-Ann Martin, with more than 20 years experience as owner of a fine wine distribution business; and the wine is consumed wherever possible by her architect husband Philip Martin. The 2 ha each of chardonnay and pinot noir are managed on a minimal intervention basis, never easy in the Southern Highlands climate, but with obvious success.

ℙℙℙℙℙ Southern Highlands Chardonnay 2004 Glowing yellow-green; a complex wine with nectarine and peach fruit; excellent drive and length. Screwcap. 13.8° alc. **Rating** 94 **To** 2011 $35

ŸŸŸŸ♀ **Southern Highlands Chardonnay 2002** Aromas and flavours still fresh and bright; some toasty notes starting to develop; overall striking consistency of quality and style; very good length and finesse. Screwcap. 13° alc. **Rating** 93 **To** 2010 $35
Southern Highlands Chardonnay 2003 Still very youthful, validating the decision to give bottle age prior to release; spotlessly clean and fresh, with some similarities to the '05. Screwcap. 13° alc. **Rating** 92 **To** 2010 $35
Southern Highlands Chardonnay 2005 Supple, smooth peach, melon and stone fruit flavours; good oak handling and good length. Screwcap. 13° alc. **Rating** 91 **To** 2013

Punch   ★★★★★

2130 Kinglake Road, St Andrews, Vic 3761 (postal) **Region** Yarra Valley
T (03) 9710 1155 **F** (03) 9710 1369 **www**.punched.com.au **Open** Not
Winemaker James Lance **Est.** 2004 **Cases** 600
In the wake of Graeme Rathbone taking over the brand (but not the real estate) of Diamond Valley, the Lances' son James and his wife Claire leased the vineyard and winery from David and Catherine Lance including the 0.25-ha block of close-planted pinot noir. In all, Punch has 2.25 ha of pinot noir (including the close planted), 0.8 ha of chardonnay and 0.4 ha of cabernet sauvignon.

ŸŸŸŸŸ **Lance's Vineyard Yarra Valley Chardonnay 2006** Refined, elegant, but intense grapefruit, nectarine and melon flavours, with well-integrated barrel ferment oak; excellent length. Screwcap. 13° alc. **Rating** 94 **To** 2013 $40
Lance's Vineyard Yarra Valley Cabernet Sauvignon 2006 Classic cool-grown cabernet fruit; strong blackcurrant, cassis and a touch of mint; medium-bodied, with fine tannins. Screwcap. 13° alc. **Rating** 94 **To** 2016 $40

Punt Road   ★★★★

10 St Huberts Road, Coldstream, Vic 3770 **Region** Yarra Valley
T (03) 9739 0666 **F** (03) 9739 0633 **www**.puntroadwines.com.au **Open** 7 days 10–5
Winemaker Kate Goodman **Est.** 2000 **Cases** 15 000
Punt Road was originally known as The Yarra Hill, a name abandoned because of the proliferation of wineries with the word 'Yarra' as part of their name. The wines are made from the best parcels of fruit grown on the 100-ha Yarra Hill Vineyard owned by the Napoleone family, long-standing orchardists in the Yarra Valley, who planted their first vines in 1987. The winery produces the Punt Road wines, as well as undertaking substantial contract winemaking for others. Exports to the UK, the US and other major markets.

ŸŸŸŸ♀ **Botrytis Semillon 2006** Brilliant green-yellow; cumquat, honey, mandarin and butterscotch; very good acid balance to a seductive wine. The front label incorrectly shows Yarra Valley as the region, the back label acknowledging Riverina. Cork. 11.5° alc. **Rating** 92 **To** 2011 $31.95
Yarra Valley Chardonnay 2006 Light-bodied, but well-balanced; melon, apple and some nectarine with controlled oak, and a fresh finish. Screwcap. 13° alc. **Rating** 90 **To** 2012 $22
MVN Yarra Valley Cabernet Sauvignon 2005 Bright, clean and fresh; light- to medium-bodied red and blackcurrant fruit; finely polished tannins, oak in diminuendo. Screwcap. **Rating** 90 **To** 2015 $48

ŸŸŸŸ **MVN Yarra Valley Pinot Noir 2006** An elegant, light-bodied, unforced style, true to variety, but without the intensity and length needed for higher points. Screwcap. **Rating** 89 **To** 2012 $48
Yarra Valley Shiraz 2005 A trace of reduction on the bouquet; spicy red and black fruits on the light- to medium-bodied palate, plus a flick of oak and gentle tannins. Screwcap. 14° alc. **Rating** 89 **To** 2015 $24.95
Yarra Valley Sauvignon Blanc 2007 A quiet bouquet, but does have a lively palate with notes of citrus and passionfruit; good acidity on the finish. Screwcap. 12.5° alc. **Rating** 88 **To** 2009 $20

Little Rebel Yarra Valley Cabernet Merlot 2005 More to the palate than the developed colour suggests, with savoury/olivaceous overtones to blackcurrant fruit; balanced tannins, minimal oak. Screwcap. 14° alc. **Rating** 88 **To** 2012 $18

Yarra Valley Cabernet Sauvignon 2005 Slightly hazy colour; plenty of full-flavoured ripe blackcurrant fruit; fair length and structure. Screwcap. 14° alc. **Rating** 88 **To** 2013 $24.95

Little Rebel Yarra Valley Chardonnay 2006 Straightforward style; light-bodied and fruit-driven with gentle melon and stone fruit flavours. Screwcap. 13° alc. **Rating** 87 **To** 2009 $18

Yarra Valley Pinot Gris 2007 Light, crisp, pear, apple and spice aromas, the flavours down the same track, then a dry finish. Screwcap. 13.5° alc. **Rating** 87 **To** 2009 $22

Yarra Valley Pinot Noir 2006 Has developed quickly; in a spicy, foresty, stemmy fruit spectrum; needs more flesh. Screwcap. 13.5° alc. **Rating** 87 **To** 2009 $25

Punters Corner

Cnr Riddoch Highway/Racecourse Road, Coonawarra, SA 5263 **Region** Coonawarra
T (08) 8737 2007 **F** (08) 8737 3138 **www**.punterscorner.com.au **Open** 7 days 10–5
Winemaker Balnaves (Peter Bissell) **Est.** 1988 **Cases** 8000

Punters Corner started its life in 1975 as James Haselgrove, but in '92 was acquired by a group of investors who evidently had few delusions about the uncertainties of viticulture and winemaking, even in a district as distinguished as Coonawarra. The arrival of Peter Bissell as winemaker at Balnaves paid immediate (and continuing) dividends. Sophisticated packaging and label design add to the appeal of the wines. Exports to Canada, the Netherlands, Malaysia, Singapore, Japan and China.

ΨΨΨΨΨ **Spartacus Reserve Shiraz 2005** Rich black fruits with plenty of depth and length; balanced oak and tannins. **Rating** 94 **To** 2018 $59.50

Sovereign Reserve Cabernet Sauvignon 2005 Mocha and blackcurrant aromas; complex and a touch of mint on the palate; very long, and quite fleshy on the finish. Cork. 15.5° alc. **Rating** 94 **To** 2016 $59.50

ΨΨΨΨΨ **Coonawarra Cabernet Sauvignon 2005** A powerful, medium- to full-bodied palate, with a mix of dusty and riper blackcurrant fruit supported by positive oak. **Rating** 92 **To** 2018 $30

Single Vineyard Coonawarra Chardonnay 2006 A rich and ripe bouquet with melon and fig; good flavour on the palate with oak evident on the finish. Screwcap. 14° alc. **Rating** 90 **To** 2012 $26

Coonawarra Shiraz 2005 Lively fruits, ranging from red cherry and plum through to blackberry; has freshness and elegance. **Rating** 90 **To** 2015 $20

ΨΨΨΨ **Triple Crown 2005** A light- to medium-bodied palate, with a lively mix of red fruits, mint and leaf; fine tannins; early maturing style. Cabernet Sauvignon/Shiraz/Merlot. Screwcap. 15.5° alc. **Rating** 88 **To** 2012 $24

Pycnantha Hill Estate

Benbournie Road, Clare, SA 5453 (postal) **Region** Clare Valley
T (08) 8842 2137 **F** (08) 8842 2137 **www**.pycnanthahill.com.au **Open** Not
Winemaker Jim Howarth **Est.** 1997 **Cases** 800

The Howarth family progressively established 2.4 ha of vineyard from 1987, and made its first commercial vintage in '97. *Acacia pycnantha* is the botanical name for the golden wattle that grows wild over the hills of the Howarth farm, and they say it was 'a natural choice to name our vineyards Pycnantha Hill'. I am not too sure that marketing gurus would agree, but there we go.

ΨΨΨΨΨ **Clare Valley Shiraz 2005** Rich, flashy and full-bodied in good regional style with abundant blackberry fruit, a splash of dark chocolate, and good overall extract. Screwcap. 15° alc. **Rating** 92 **To** 2020 $18

Pyramid Hill Wines

194 Martindale Road, Denman, NSW 2328 **Region** Upper Hunter Valley
T (02) 6547 2755 **F** (02) 6547 2735 **www**.pyramidhillwines.com **Open** 7 days 10–5
Winemaker First Creek Winemaking Services **Est.** 2002 **Cases** 5000
Pyramid Hill is a partnership between the Adler and Hilder families. Richard Hilder is a veteran viticulturist who oversaw the establishment of many of the Rosemount vineyards. Nicholas Adler and Caroline Sherwood made their mark in the international film industry before moving to Pyramid Hill in 1997. There are now 71.5 ha of chardonnay, semillon, verdelho, shiraz, merlot, cabernet sauvignon and ruby cabernet, with a computer-controlled irrigation system backed up by a network of radio-linked weather and soil moisture sensors, which constantly relay data detailing the amount of available moisture at different soil depths to a central computer, thus avoiding excess irrigation and preventing stress. Most of the grapes are sold, but part has been vinified, with cautious expansion planned. Exports to the UK, Canada, Japan and Singapore.

ΨΨΨΨΨ **Hunter Valley Verdelho 2007** Unusual depth of flavour, heading into chardonnay territory, with stone fruit and citrus as much as fruit salad; long finish. Screwcap. 13° alc. **Rating** 92 **To** 2011 $16.95
Semillon 2007 Brilliant green-straw; a big, rich and complex wine with layered fruit, but avoids phenolics. Screwcap. 11° alc. **Rating** 90 **To** 2014 $17

ΨΨΨΨ **Hunter Valley Shiraz 2005** Light- to medium-bodied; distinctly earthy/savoury regional characters; has deceptive length. Cork. 13° alc. **Rating** 88 **To** 2012 $21.95

Pyramids Road Wines

Pyramids Road, Wyberba via Ballandean, Qld 4382 **Region** Granite Belt
T (07) 4684 5151 **F** (07) 4684 5151 **www**.pyramidsroad.com.au **Open** Thurs–Mon, school & public hols 10–4.30
Winemaker Warren Smith **Est.** 1999 **Cases** 900
Warren Smith and partner Sue moved to the Granite Belt region in 1999. With encouragement and assistance from the team at Ballandean Estate, the first vines were planted in '99, and the first vintage following in 2002. The current vineyard area is just 2 ha (shiraz, cabernet sauvignon, merlot, mourvedre and muscat); further plantings are planned but will not exceed 4 ha. All wines are made onsite; the production area can be viewed from the cellar door. The 2005 Shiraz is outstanding, a reflection of a top vintage in the region.

ΨΨΨΨΨ **Granite Belt Shiraz 2005** Good colour; excellent varietal fruit, blackberry and licorice; ripe, soft tannins; good oak, lovely wine. **Rating** 96 **To** 2015 $30

ΨΨΨΨ **Granite Belt Cabernet Merlot 2005** Fresh red berry fruit aromas; delicate, unforced style; good mouthfeel; very slightly green. **Rating** 89 **To** 2012 $22
Granite Belt Bernie's Blend 2005 Fairly austere wine; does have structure and length. Cabernet Sauvignon/Shiraz/Mourvedre. **Rating** 87 **To** 2010 $30

Pyren Vineyard

22 Errard Street North, Ballarat, Vic 3350 (postal) **Region** Pyrenees
T (03) 5467 2352 **F** (03) 5021 0804 **www**.pyrenvineyard.com **Open** By appt
Winemaker Mount Avoca Winery, Pyrenees Ridge **Est.** 1999 **Cases** 4500
This is a substantial venture. Martin and Kevyn Joy have planted 25 ha of shiraz, 3 ha each of cabernet sauvignon and viognier, 1 ha of durif and 2 ha comprising cabernet franc, malbec and petit verdot on the slopes of the Warrenmang Valley near Moonambel. The initial releases in 2005 were of Shiraz, a Cabernet blend followed in '06, and Durif and Viognier will follow in the future as the vines mature. Yield is restricted to between 1.5 and 2.5 tonnes per acre.

ΨΨΨΨΨ **Block E Pyrenees Shiraz 2006** A very fine Shiraz, with pure red fruit focus and a lovely line of linear acidity through the palate; very fine tannins and quite supple on the finish. Screwcap. **Rating** 94 **To** 2015 $26

🍷🍷🍷🍷🍷 **Broken Quartz Pyrenees Cabernet Sauvignon 2006** Strong minerality to the dark and red fruits in this wine; very nice line and length, with a real sense of purpose to the fine-grained tannin finish. Screwcap. **Rating** 91 **To** 2014 **$**16

Broken Quartz Pyrenees Shiraz 2006 Vibrant colour; supple and smooth blackberry and plum fruits, with a juicy mid- and back-palate; has structure, but delicious early-drinking style. Value. Screwcap. **Rating** 90 **To** 2011 **$**16

Pyrenees Ridge Winery ★★★★☆

532 Caralulup Road, Lamplough via Avoca, Vic 3467 **Region** Pyrenees
T (03) 5465 3710 **F** (03) 5465 3320 **www**.pyreneesridge.com.au **Open** Thurs–Mon & public hols 10–5
Winemaker Graeme Jukes **Est.** 1998 **Cases** 3000

Notwithstanding the quite extensive winemaking experience (and formal training) of Graeme Jukes, this started life as small-scale winemaking in the raw version of the French garagiste approach. Graeme and his wife Sally-Ann now have another 10 ha of shiraz, cabernet sauvignon and chardonnay; the grape intake is supplemented by purchases from other growers in the region. After a fire in Sept 2007, which destroyed the winery and cellar door, the facility has been rebuilt, bigger and better than before. Exports to the US, Canada, Japan, China and Hong Kong.

🍷🍷🍷🍷🍷 **Cabernet Sauvignon 2006** Good concentration of dark, powerful fruit; full-bodied with black olives and a little eucalypt on the finish. Diam. 14° alc. **Rating** 94 **To** 2015 **$**27

🍷🍷🍷🍷🍷 **Shiraz 2006** Fresh and vibrant, with prominent raspberry fruits, and a touch of mint; nice weight and chewy texture on the finish. Diam. 14.5° alc. **Rating** 90 **To** 2015 **$**28

Quarisa Wines ★★★★

743 Slopes Road, Tharbogang, NSW 2680 (postal) **Region** Warehouse
T (02) 6963 6222 **F** (02) 6963 6473 **www**.quarisa.com.au **Open** Not
Winemaker John Quarisa **Est.** 2005 **Cases** 5000

Quarisa Wines was established by John and Josephine Quarisa (plus their three young children). John Quarisa has had a distinguished career as a winemaker spanning 22 years, working for some of Australia's largest wineries including McWilliam's, Casella and Nugan Estate. He was also chiefly responsible for winning the Jimmy Watson Trophy in 2004 (Melbourne) and the Stodart Trophy (Adelaide). In a busman's holiday venture, they have set up a small family business using grapes from various parts of Australia and made in leased space. After a slightly uncertain start, the current releases offer exemplary value for money, and it is no surprise that one of the leading national distributors, Domaine Wine Shippers, has taken on the brand. Exports to Canada and Sweden.

🍷🍷🍷🍷🍷 **Treasures Coonawarra Cabernet Merlot 2005** Bright colour; abundant cassis and cedar aromas, and a hint of mint; plenty of ripe tannins and a long finish; very good value. Screwcap. 14.5° alc. **Rating** 93 **To** 2013 **$**14.95

Treasures Langhorne Creek Shiraz 2004 Good colour; vibrant blackberry fruits and a little spice; good value for the money, and very fresh for age. Screwcap. 14.5° alc. **Rating** 90 **To** 2015 **$**14.95

🍷🍷🍷🍷 **Treasures Coonawarra Merlot 2005** Clean and vibrant, with red fruits and hints of plum and spice; good structure and the flavour persists well for the variety. Screwcap. 14.5° alc. **Rating** 89 **To** 2013 **$**14.95

Treasures Coonawarra Cabernet Sauvignon 2004 Good fruit, especially for the money; good concentration and depth on the medium-bodied palate. Screwcap. 14.5° alc. **Rating** 89 **To** 2014 **$**14.95

Treasures Padthaway Chardonnay 2006 Nectarine and hints of toast on the palate; good weight and texture on the finish, made for early consumption. Screwcap. 13.5° alc. **Rating** 87 **To** 2010 **$**14.95

Johnny Q Shiraz 2006 Quite lifted and aromatic; tarry on the palate, with red fruits and plenty of chewy tannins on the finish. Well priced. Screwcap. 14.5° alc. Rating 87 To 2012 $11.95

Johnny Q Shiraz Viognier 2006 Spicy and lifted red fruit shiraz, but the strong oak on the palate cuts the fruit a little short; good flavour and freshness. Screwcap. 14.5° alc. Rating 87 To 2012 $11.95

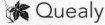 Quealy ★★★★

Balnarring Vineyard, 62 Bittern-Dromana Road, Balnarring, Vic 3926
Region Mornington Peninsula
T (03) 5983 2483 **www**.quealy.com.au **Open** 7 days 11–5
Winemaker Kathleen Quealy **Est.** 1982 **Cases** 3000
Kathleen Quealy and husband Kevin McCarthy lost no time after their ties with T'Gallant (purchased from them by Foster's in 2003) were finally severed. As they were fully entitled to do, they already had their ducks set up in a row, and in short order acquired Balnarring Estate winery (now to be significantly upgraded) and 8-ha vineyard, leased Earl's Ridge Vineyard near Flinders, and Mary's Vineyard at Main Ridge. In a move reminiscent of Janice McDonald at Stella Bella and Suckfizzle in the Margaret River, they launched their business with Pobblebonk (a blended white wine) and Rageous (a red blend), plus a Pinot Noir and a Pinot Gris with a passing nod to convention. Kathleen (with five children) is a human dynamo; this is a business sure to succeed.

🍷🍷🍷🍷🍷 Rageous 2006 A bright, light-bodied wine, with red berry fruit flavours and a clean, zesty, long finish. Sangiovese/Shiraz/Pinot Noir/Merlot co-fermented. Screwcap. 13.5° alc. Rating 90 To 2009 $30

🍷🍷🍷🍷 Pobblebonk 2006 Flinty texture and mouthfeel, with mineral and citrus flavours; pinot gris a likely major component (four unspecified varieties); pleasing dry finish. Diam. 13° alc. Rating 89 To 2009 $25

Racecourse Lane Wines ★★★

PO Box 215, Balgowlah, NSW 2093 **Region** Lower Hunter Valley
T 0408 242 490 **F** (02) 9949 7185 **www**.racecourselane.com.au **Open** Not
Winemaker David Fatches (Contract) **Est.** 1998 **Cases** 1000
Mike and Helen McGorman purchased their 15-ha property in 1998. They have established 5.2 ha of shiraz, sangiovese, semillon, verdelho and viognier. Consultancy viticultural advice from Brian Hubbard, and winemaking by David Fatches (a long-term Hunter Valley winemaker, who also makes wine in France each year), has paid dividends. Exports to the UK.

🍷🍷🍷🍷 Hunter Valley Sangiovese 2006 Light colour, already brick hued; savoury tobacco leaf and sour cherry nuances are varietal; for sangio lovers. Screwcap. 12.5° alc. Rating 87 To 2009 $19

Radford Wines ★★★★☆

RSD 355, Eden Valley, SA 5235 (postal) **Region** Eden Valley
T (08) 8565 3256 **F** (08) 8565 3244 **www**.radfordwines.com **Open** Not
Winemaker Gill Radford, Ben Radford **Est.** 2003 **Cases** 900
I first met Ben Radford when he was working as a head winemaker at the Longridge/ Winecorp group in Stellenbosch, South Africa. A bevy of international journalists grilled Ben, a French winemaker and a South African about the wines they were producing for the group. The others refused to admit there were any shortcomings in the wines they had made (there were), while Ben took the opposite tack, criticising his own wines even though they were clearly the best. He and Gill Radford are now the proud owners of a 4-ha vineyard in the Eden Valley, with 1.2 ha of riesling planted in 1930, 1.1 ha planted in '70, and 1.7 ha of shiraz planted in 2000. Ben also acts as a contract winemaker for a number of other Barossa Zone businesses. Following Ben's appointment as winemaker at Rockford in '07, executive

winemaking responsibilities are now Gill's, who says 'I get to have a play outside the kitchen', adding 'he gets to boss me around a bit'. Exports to the UK, the US, Denmark, Sweden and Malaysia.

♀♀♀♀♀ **Barossa Eden Valley Shiraz 2005** Complex flavours; a medium-bodied mix of licorice, multi-spice and mocha to the background of black fruits; the tannins are silky and ripe, the oak restrained. Cork. 14.5° alc. **Rating** 93 **To** 2015 $32.50

Rahona Valley Vineyard
PO Box 256, Red Hill South, Vic 3937 **Region** Mornington Peninsula
T (03) 5989 2924 **F** (03) 5989 2924 **www.**rahonavalley.com.au **Open** Not
Winemaker John Salmons, Rebecca Gaffy (Consultant) **Est.** 1991 **Cases** 200
John and Leonie Salmons have one of the older and more interesting small vineyards on the Mornington Peninsula, on a steep north-facing slope of a small valley in the Red Hill area. The area takes its name from the ancient red basalt soils. In all there are 1.2 ha of pinot noir planted to five different clones and a few hundred vines each of pinot meunier and pinot gris.

Ralph Fowler Wines ★★★★
Limestone Coast Road, Mount Benson, SA 5275 **Region** Mount Benson
T (08) 8768 5000 **F** (08) 8768 5008 **www.**ralphfowlerwines.com.au **Open** 7 days 10–5
Winemaker Ralph Fowler **Est.** 1999 **Cases** 5000
Established in 1999 by the Fowler family, headed by well-known winemaker Ralph Fowler, with wife Deborah and children Sarah (Squires) and James all involved in the 40-ha property. Ralph Fowler began his winemaking career at Tyrrell's, rising to the position of chief winemaker before heading off to various wineries. In 2005 he passed on the operation of the business to Sarah. Exports to Canada, the Netherlands, China and Singapore.

♀♀♀♀♀ **Cabernet Sauvignon 2005** Good colour; a firm, well-focused palate with particularly good line to the blackcurrant; polished tannins. Screwcap. 14.5° alc. **Rating** 91 **To** 2020 $25
Merlot 2005 Savoury, spicy varietal aromas and flavours; the olive notes do not lead to green vegetal characters, perhaps because of alcohol; good oak and tannins. Screwcap. 15° alc. **Rating** 90 **To** 2013 $25

♀♀♀♀ **Mount Benson Shiraz 2005** Quite developed; strong spice and mocha overtones to predominantly black fruits, with some sweeter red notes; good balance. Cork. 14.5° alc. **Rating** 89 **To** 2012 $25
Viognier 2006 Has developed some complexity to apricot and stone fruit flavours; good balance, and not phenolic. Screwcap. 13° alc. **Rating** 88 **To** 2009 $25
Shiraz Viognier 2005 The impact of viognier is very marked on both bouquet and palate, giving some slight confection character to the dark fruits. Cork. 14.5° alc. **Rating** 87 **To** 2011 $25
Sticky 2004 Some jujube/pastille/apricot fruit; pleasing mouthfeel and balance, but not particularly complex or intense. Cork. 13° alc. **Rating** 87 **To** 2011 $25

Random Valley Organic Wines
410 Brockman Highway, Karridale, WA 6288 **Region** Margaret River
T (08) 9758 6707 **F** (08) 9758 6743 **www.**randomvalley.com **Open** 7 days 10–5
Winemaker Naturaliste Vintners (Bruce Dukes) **Est.** 1995 **Cases** 1000
The Little family has established 7 ha of sauvignon blanc, semillon, shiraz and cabernet sauvignon, with a certified organic grapegrowing program. No chemical-based fertilisers, pesticides or herbicides are used in the vineyard, building humus and biological activity in the soil. Given that the 7 ha produce 50 tonnes per year, it is evident that the approach has worked well. The cellar door (opened December 2007) has a unique air-conditioning system provided by 13 750 recycled wine bottles filled with water, producing a cooling effect in summer, and a warming effect in winter.

ŸŸŸŸ   **Margaret River Shiraz 2006** Strongly spicy/peppery fruit which is, however, slightly thin; has some length. Rating 87 To 2012 $19.50
Margaret River Shiraz 2004 Light, very savoury/leafy/spicy wine, its main market appeal being its organic status. Screwcap. 13.5° alc. **Rating** 87 To 2010 $25

Rangemore Estate   NR

366 Malling-Boundary Road, Maclagan, Qld 4352 **Region** Darling Downs
T (07) 4692 1338 **F** (07) 4692 1338 **www**.rangemoreestate.com.au **Open** Fri–Sun 10–5
Winemaker Ravens Croft Wines **Est.** 1999 **Cases** 700
The 4.5-ha vineyard of Rangemore Estate, planted to verdelho, shiraz, cabernet and merlot, is high in the southern foothills of the Bunya Mountains. The soil is a sandy loam over sandstone, and the low-yielding vines are grown with little or no irrigation. The founding Allen family operates a cellar door and café, with B&B accommodation, offering spectacular views of the Bunya Mountains.

Ravens Croft Wines

274 Spring Creek Road, Stanthorpe, Qld 4380 **Region** Granite Belt
T (07) 4683 3252 **www**.ravenscroftwines.com.au **Open** Fri–Sun 10–4.30 or by appt
Winemaker Mark Ravenscroft **Est.** 2002 **Cases** 600
Mark Ravenscroft was born in South Africa, and studied oenology there. He moved to Australia in the early 1990s, and in '94 became an Australian citizen. He makes 500 cases of wine under the Ravens Croft label, with limited quantities of grapes purchased from other growers in the Granite Belt to supplement the estate-grown fruit. In addition to his winemaking for Robert Channon, he makes wines for other clients.

ŸŸŸŸŸ   **Verdelho 2007** Well made in emphatic style; the palate has depth to ripe fruit salad flavours. Screwcap. 13.5° alc. **Rating** 90 To 2010 $18
Petit Verdot 2006 Big black fruit flavours and even bigger tannins; needs time, but should come together well. Screwcap. 14° alc. **Rating** 90 To 2016 $25

ŸŸŸŸ   **Reserve Cabernet Sauvignon 2005** A very savoury wine, with some dark chocolate and blackcurrant fruit within encircling, rather dry tannins; will improve with time. Cork. 14.5° alc. **Rating** 88 To 2014 $35

Ravensworth

312 Patemans Lane, Murrumbateman, ACT 2582 **Region** Canberra District
T (02) 6226 8368 **F** (02) 6262 2161 **www**.ravensworthwines.com.au **Open** Not
Winemaker Bryan Martin **Est.** 2000 **Cases** 1600
Winemaker, vineyard manager and partner Bryan Martin (with dual wine science and winegrowing degrees from CSU) has a background of wine retail, food and beverage in the hospitality industry, and teaches part-time in that field. He is also assistant winemaker to Tim Kirk at Clonakilla, after seven years at Jeir Creek. Judging at wine shows is another string to his bow. Ravensworth has 7.5 ha of vineyards spread over two sites: Rosehill planted in 1998 to cabernet sauvignon, merlot and sauvignon blanc, and Martin Block (planted 2000–01) to shiraz, viognier, marsanne and sangiovese.

ŸŸŸŸŸ   **Canberra District Hunter Valley Sauvignon Blanc Semillon 2007** Complexity is delivered by the varietal blend and wild yeast barrel fermentation of the sauvignon blanc; good weight and length; crisp acidity adds to the length and fresh finish. Screwcap. 11.5° alc. **Rating** 92 To 2010 $20
Canberra District Marsanne 2006 Elegantly balanced; gentle honeysuckle, fig and apricot flavours provide excellent mouthfeel, balanced by chalky acidity on the finish. Screwcap. 13.8° alc. **Rating** 92 To 2013 $22
Canberra District Riesling 2006 A spotlessly clean bouquet; light citrus and passionfruit flavours with a fractionally sweet finish. Either more or less sweetness might have been a better option. Screwcap. 12° alc. **Rating** 90 To 2014 $20

Hunter Valley Semillon 2007 Herb, grass and mineral aromas; the palate tight and crisp, finishing with lemony acidity; good balance. Screwcap. 10° alc. **Rating** 90 **To** 2015 $20

Canberra District Viognier 2006 Has more expression and character than many young viogniers with apricot, peach and musk on a lively palate with good mouthfeel. Screwcap. 14° alc. **Rating** 90 **To** 2011 $26

ҭҭҭҭ   **Canberra District Shiraz Viognier 2006** Medium-bodied; black cherry, plum and blackberry, the viognier impact partially masked by the tannins on the finish. Screwcap. 14° alc. **Rating** 89 **To** 2016 $28

Canberra District Sangiovese 2006 A spicy mix of sour and red cherries, tobacco and spices; positively demands Italian food. Screwcap. 14° alc. **Rating** 89 To 2011 $20

Red Earth Estate Vineyard

18L Camp Road, Dubbo, NSW 2830 **Region** Western Plains Zone
T (02) 6885 6676 **F** (02) 6882 8297 **www**.redearthestate.com.au **Open** Thurs–Tues 10–5
Winemaker Ken Borchardt **Est.** 2000 **Cases** 2500
Ken and Christine Borchardt look set to be the focal point of winegrowing and making in the future Macquarie Valley region of the Western Plains Zone. They have planted 1.3 ha each of riesling, verdelho, frontignac, grenache, shiraz and cabernet sauvignon plus 0.5 ha of torrentes. The winery has a capacity of 14 000 cases, and the Borchardts also contract winemaking facilities for others in the region.

ҭҭҭҭ   **Reserve Shiraz 2006** Dense, impenetrable colour; massive, heavily extracted and tannic; the opposite end of the universe to the thin varietal '06. Screwcap. 13.9° alc. **Rating** 87 **To** 2021 $32

Red Edge

Golden Gully Road, Heathcote, Vic 3523 **Region** Heathcote
T (03) 9337 5695 **F** (03) 9337 7550 **Open** By appt
Winemaker Peter Dredge, Judy Dredge **Est.** 1971 **Cases** 1500
Red Edge is a relatively new name on the scene, but the vineyard dates back to 1971, and the renaissance of the Victorian wine industry. In the early 1980s it produced the wonderful wines of Flynn & Williams and has now been rehabilitated by Peter and Judy Dredge, producing two quite lovely wines in their inaugural vintage and continuing that form in succeeding vintages. They now have a little under 15 ha under vine. Exports to the UK, the US and Canada.

ҭҭҭҭҭ   **Heathcote Shiraz 2006** In the mainstream of Heathcote style, with an abundance of black fruits and savoury tannins; carries its alcohol well, the oak merely a backdrop. Screwcap. 14.6° alc. **Rating** 94 **To** 2021 $45

ҭҭҭҭ꙳   **Degree Heathcote Shiraz 2006** Interesting wine, with more elegance and complexity than usual, perhaps due to the Mourvedre (6%)/Riesling (3%) components; the texture is firm, verging on crisp, the finish long but not the least extractive. Screwcap. 14.5° alc. **Rating** 91 **To** 2013 $25

Heathcote Tempranillo Monastrell 2006 Unusual blend, pointing the way for other reds in Heathcote; lively spicy tones to the fruit flavours ranging from red to dark; fine tannins and balanced oak. Screwcap. 14.2° alc. **Rating** 90 **To** 2012 $30

Red Hill Estate

53 Shoreham Road, Red Hill South, Vic 3937 **Region** Mornington Peninsula
T (03) 5989 2838 **F** (03) 5931 0143 **www**.redhillestate.com.au **Open** 7 days 11–5
Winemaker Michael Kyberd, Luke Curry **Est.** 1989 **Cases** 35 000
Red Hill Estate was established by Sir Peter Derham and family, and has three vineyard sites: Range Road, with a little over 31 ha, Red Hill Estate (the home vineyard) with 10 ha, and

The Briars with 2 ha. Taken together, the vineyards make Red Hill Estate one of the larger producers of Mornington Peninsula wines. The tasting room and ever busy restaurant have a superb view across the vineyard to Westernport Bay and Phillip Island. In 2007 it (surprisingly) merged with Arrowfield Estate in the Hunter Valley; one can only assume marketing synergies are expected to drive the new InWine Group Australia. Exports to the UK, the US, Canada, Sweden, Norway, Denmark, Hong Kong, Singapore and Japan.

ŶŶŶŶŶ **Classic Release Chardonnay 2005** Developing slowly and with great assurance; grapefruit nectarine fruit with a fine skein of French oak. Diam. **Rating** 94 **To** 2015 $32
Mornington Peninsula Pinot Noir 2006 Lively and complex; spicy/foresty notes accompany sweet, small berry fruits, the palate with very good drive and length. Value. Screwcap. 13.5° alc. **Rating** 94 **To** 2012 $22

ŶŶŶŶŶ **Mornington Peninsula Chardonnay 2006** Complex aromas and flavours, with cleverly balanced use of barrel ferment and mlf; predominantly melon and cashew flavours; good length. Screwcap. 13° alc. **Rating** 90 **To** 2013 $22
Mornington Peninsula Shiraz 2005 Proclaims its cool-climate origins, with bursts of spice and pepper through its red and black fruits on a medium-bodied palate; good length. Screwcap. **Rating** 90 **To** 2013 $22

ŶŶŶŶ **Mornington Peninsula Pinot Grigio 2007** Has undoubted varietal fruit in an apple and pear spectrum; less drive than some. Screwcap. 12.5° alc. **Rating** 88 **To** 2010 $22

Red Nectar Wines   ★★★★☆

Stonewell Road, Marananga, SA 5355 **Region** Barossa Valley
T 0409 547 478 **F** (08) 8563 3624 **www.**rednectar.com.au **Open** By appt
Winemaker Troy Kalleske **Est.** 1997 **Cases** 800
Tammy Pfeiffer may be a sixth-generation grapegrower, but she was only 19 when she purchased the 27-ha property now known as Red Nectar Estate in 1997. At that time there were 2.4 ha shiraz plantings, the remainder grazing land with a beautiful view towards the Seppeltsfield palm avenue. The existing shiraz had been sourced from 80-year-old vines grown in the Moppa district, and Tammy has since established another 5.3 ha of shiraz and 2 ha of cabernet sauvignon. She carries out much of the work on the vineyards herself, using sustainable vineyard practices wherever possible. The Stonewell area, in which the vineyard is situated, is well-known for its high-quality shiraz fruit. The winemaking is done by her good friend and cousin Troy Kalleske. No samples received; the rating is that of last year. Exports to the UK, the US and other major markets.

Redbank Victoria   ★★★☆

Whitfield Road, King Valley, Vic 3678 **Region** King Valley
T (03) 5729 3604 **F** (08) 8561 3411 **www.**redbankwines.com **Open** Fri–Mon 11–11
Winemaker Nigel Blieschke, Kevin Glastonbury **Est.** 2005 **Cases** 75 000
The Redbank brand was for decades the umbrella for Neill and Sally Robb's Sally's Paddock. In 2005 long-term distributor of Redbank, the Yalumba Wine Group, acquired the Redbank brand from the Robbs, leaving them with the Redbank Winery and Sally's Paddock. Yalumba is most unhappy with the continued designation of the winery as Redbank, while the Robbs say it is simply the name of the winery as shown in district maps, district signposts and at the gate, but is in no sense a brand. Redbank Victoria now draws almost all its grapes from the King Valley, purchasing viognier from the Taylor's vineyard, and pinot gris from the Cavedon Vineyard.

ŶŶŶŶŶ **The Widow Jones King Valley Viognier 2006** Nicely framed musk and apricot aromas and flavours; plenty of presence without phenolics. Screwcap. 14.5° alc. **Rating** 91 **To** 2010 $22.95

ioio The Long Paddock Sauvignon Blanc 2007 Has fair overall balance and length in a crisp, minerally mode, finishing with grassy/lemony acidity. Good value. Screwcap. 12° alc. **Rating** 88 **To** 2009 $12.95
Sunday Morning King Valley Pinot Gris 2006 A pleasant wine unlikely to frighten the horses; gentle citrus and pear by-play; relatively dry finish. Screwcap. 14.5° alc. **Rating** 87 **To** 2009 $22.95
The Long Paddock Shiraz 2005 Clear, deep colour; light- to medium-bodied, with plenty of ripe red and black fruit flavours; minimal tannins and oak, but enough. Screwcap. 14.5° alc. **Rating** 87 **To** 2009 $12.95

Redbox Vineyard & Winery ★★★

2 Ness Lane, Kangaroo Ground, Vic 3097 **Region** Yarra Valley
T (03) 9712 0440 **F** (03) 9712 0422 **www**.redboxvineyard.com.au **Open** W'ends & public hols 11–6, or by appt
Winemaker Phil Kelly (Contract) **Est.** 2004 **Cases** 2000
Colin and Clayton Spencer have moved quickly since establishing their business, with a kaleidoscopic array of wines, partly from the Yarra Valley, and partly from the Perricoota region north of the Murray River. The wines are released under the Redbox, Wildfell Estate and Murray Flyer labels, with all of the red wines (other than Pinot Noir) coming from Perricoota. Their estate plantings in the Yarra comprise 1.7 ha of cabernet sauvignon, 0.6 ha of chardonnay and 0.4 ha of riesling; they also purchase pinot gris from the Yarra Valley region.

ioio **Perricoota Shiraz 2005** Lifted red fruits, with a distinctly briary edge; a little simple, but quite juicy and fleshy on the palate. Screwcap. 14.5° alc. **Rating** 88 **To** 2009 $18
Private Reserve Yarra Valley Cabernet Merlot 2006 Good colour, with vibrant red fruits and a little cedary complexity to the medium-bodied palate. Cork. 13.7° alc. **Rating** 87 **To** 2012 $24

Redden Bridge Wines ★★★

PMB 147, Naracoorte, SA 5271 (postal) **Region** Wrattonbully
T (08) 8764 7494 **F** (08) 8764 7501 **www**.reddenbridge.com **Open** Not
Winemaker Robin Moody (Contract) **Est.** 2002 **Cases** 800
This is the venture of Greg and Emma Koch, Greg with a quarter-century of viticultural experience, first in Coonawarra (17 years) and thereafter turning his attention to Wrattonbully, buying land there in 1995 and setting up Terra Rossa Viticultural Management to assist growers across the Limestone Coast. Greg and Emma now have 24 ha of cabernet sauvignon and 22 ha of shiraz, and in 2002 retained the services of the immensely experienced Robin Moody to oversee the making of the Redden Bridge wines at Cape Jaffa Estate.

ioio **Gully Wrattonbully Shiraz 2004** Medium-bodied; very savoury earthy overtones to the blackberry fruit, which thins out somewhat on the finish. Screwcap. 14.4° alc. **Rating** 87 **To** 2013 $28

Redesdale Estate Wines ★★★★☆

North Redesdale Road, Redesdale, Vic 3444 **Region** Heathcote
T (03) 5425 3236 **F** (03) 5425 3122 **www**.redesdale.com **Open** By appt
Winemaker Tobias Ansted (Contract) **Est.** 1982 **Cases** 900
Planting of the Redesdale Estate vines began in 1982 on the northeast slopes of a 25-ha grazing property, fronting the Campaspe River on one side. The rocky quartz and granite soil meant the vines had to struggle, and when Peter Williams and wife Suzanne Arnall-Williams purchased the property in 1988 the vineyard was in a state of disrepair. They have rejuvenated the vineyard, planted an olive grove, and, more recently, erected a 2-storey cottage surrounded by a garden, which is part of the Victorian Open Garden Scheme (and cross-linked to a villa in Tuscany). No samples received; the rating is that of last year.

Redgate ★★★★★

Boodjidup Road, Margaret River, WA 6285 **Region** Margaret River
T (08) 9757 6488 **F** (08) 9757 6308 **www**.redgatewines.com.au **Open** 7 days 10–5
Winemaker Simon Keall **Est.** 1977 **Cases** 10 000
Founder and owner of Redgate, Bill Ullinger, chose the name not simply because of the nearby eponymous beach, but also because – so it is said – a local farmer (with a prominent red gate at his property) had run an illegal spirit still 100 or so years ago, and its patrons would come to the property and ask whether there was any 'red gate' available. True or not, Ullinger was one of the early movers in the Margaret River, and there is now a little over 21 ha of mature estate plantings (the majority to sauvignon blanc, semillon, cabernet sauvignon, cabernet franc, shiraz and chardonnay). Exports to the US, Switzerland, Denmark, Japan and Singapore.

ⵍⵍⵍⵍⵍ **OFS Semillon 2007** Has soared above the limitations of the vintage; a bright, crisp and clear delineation of semillon, offering herb, grass and touches of passionfruit and citrus; very good finish. Screwcap. 12.5° alc. **Rating** 95 **To** 2014 $25
Cabernet Franc 2005 Supports the idea that Margaret River has a superior clone of cabernet franc to any in the east, or is it terroir? Either way, has fragrant red fruits, spices and fine, silky tannins. Screwcap. **Rating** 94 **To** 2015 $40

ⵍⵍⵍⵍⵎ **Shiraz 2006** Light but bright hue; light- to medium-bodied, lively and fresh; both red and black fruits plus lots of spice; good length and restrained oak; delicious early-drinking style. Screwcap. **Rating** 92 **To** 2011 $25
Bin 588 2005 Very well-constructed, with good texture and structure; savoury black fruits, but no green characters whatsoever; good length. Screwcap. **Rating** 91 **To** 2015 $22.50
Margaret River Chardonnay 2006 A faint touch of reduction; highly focused, with tight green apple, melon and citrus fruit, the oak restrained. Screwcap. 13° alc. **Rating** 90 **To** 2013 $35

ⵍⵍⵍⵍ **Margaret River Chardonnay 2007** Like the Sauvignon Blanc, very pale; very light and crisp, seemingly early picked; does have length and development potential; citrussy tang. Screwcap. **Rating** 89 **To** 2015 $35
WW Ullinger Reserve Margaret River Cabernet Merlot 2005 Unconvincing colour; spicy/savoury/foresty flavours on a medium-bodied palate; needs more fruit at its core. Screwcap. 13° alc. **Rating** 89 **To** 2013 $45
Reserve Margaret River Sauvignon Blanc 2007 Water white, bottled Dec '07; remarkably light and crisp for the vintage, in the end too much so, needing more varietal fruit. Screwcap. **Rating** 87 **To** 2010 $27
Rose 2007 Pleasant red fruits; faintly sweet, but balanced; any time, anywhere style. Screwcap. 13.5° alc. **Rating** 87 **To** 2009 $17
Cabernet Sauvignon 2005 Diffuse colour; spicy blackcurrant aroma and forepalate, then tannins cut in forcefully; the tannins need to soften before the fruit fades. Screwcap. 13° alc. **Rating** 87 **To** 2013 $30
William 2004 Spicy; quite dry and long, with good varietal character although here the spirit is a little aggressive. Shiraz port style. Screwcap. 17.5° alc. **Rating** 87 **To** 2012 $22.50
Ezabella 2007 Cleverly made for cellar door; the light spirit has quite good balance; said to be a white port style. Screwcap. 16.5° alc. **Rating** 87 **To** 2009 $22.50

Redman ★★★☆

Main Road, Coonawarra, SA 5263 **Region** Coonawarra
T (08) 8736 3331 **F** (08) 8736 3013 **www**.redman.com.au **Open** Mon–Fri 9–5, w'ends 10–4
Winemaker Bruce Redman, Malcolm Redman, Daniel Redman **Est.** 1966 **Cases** NFP
In March 2008 the Redman family celebrated 100 years of winemaking in Coonawarra. The 2008 vintage also marked the arrival of Daniel as the fourth-generation Redman winemaker.

Daniel gained winemaking experience in Central Victoria, the Barossa Valley and the US before taking up his new position. It was felicitous timing, for the 2004 Cabernet Sauvignon and '04 Cabernet Merlot were each awarded a gold medal from the national wine show circuit in '07, the first such accolades for a considerable time.

ΨΨΨΨΨ **Coonawarra Cabernet Sauvignon 2004** Rich and powerful ripe redcurrant and blackcurrant fruit, the tannins just a fraction dusty/furry. Gold medal, National Wine Show '07. Cork. 13.5° alc. **Rating** 93 **To** 2014 $31

ΨΨΨΨ **Premium Blend 2005** Medium-bodied, but quite firm, thanks to forceful, grainy tannins; on the other side, has plenty of black fruits and length. **Rating** 88 **To** 2016 $36.50
Coonawarra Cabernet Sauvignon 2005 A quite robust palate, which lacks polish, but does have plenty of black fruit flavours. **Rating** 87 **To** 2015 $33

Reedy Creek Vineyard   NR

Reedy Creek, via Tenterfield, NSW 2372 **Region** New England
T (02) 6737 5221 **F** (02) 6737 5200 **www**.reedycreekwines.com.au **Open** 7 days 9–5
Winemaker Nick De Stefani **Est.** 1971 **Cases** NA
Like so many Italian settlers in the Australian countryside, the De Stefani family has been growing grapes and making wine for its own consumption for over 30 years at its Reedy Creek property in the far north of NSW. What is more, like their compatriots in the King Valley, the family's principal activity until 1993 was growing tobacco, but the continued rationalisation of the tobacco industry prompted the De Stefanis to turn a hobby into a commercial exercise. The vineyard has now been expanded to 8 ha, and an onsite winery has been completed.

Reilly's Wines   ★★★★

Cnr Hill Street/Burra Street, Mintaro, SA 5415 **Region** Clare Valley
T (08) 8843 9013 **F** (08) 8843 9013 **www**.reillyswines.com **Open** 7 days 10–4
Winemaker Justin Ardill **Est.** 1994 **Cases** 25 000
Cardiologist Justin and Julie Ardill are no longer newcomers in the Clare Valley, with 10 or so vintages under their belt. An unusual sideline of Reilly's Cottage is the production of extra virgin olive oil, made from wild olives found in the Mintaro district of the Clare Valley. Justin Ardill also does some contract making for others. Reilly's has a second cellar door in Adelaide, which also holds wine classes. Exports to the US, Ireland, Malaysia, China and Singapore.

ΨΨΨΨΨ **Watervale Riesling 2007** Has everything that the Barking Mad lacks; fine, juicy, lime-accented fruit and excellent line and length; by far the best value of the two. Screwcap. 13° alc. **Rating** 93 **To** 2015 $19

ΨΨΨΨ **Barking Mad Clare Valley Shiraz 2006** Has a superabundance of blackberry and licorice fruit, partly reflected in the alcohol perhaps; great value, unbeatable as a barbecue red on a cool night. Screwcap. 15° alc. **Rating** 88 **To** 2014 $15
Barking Mad Watervale Riesling 2007 At this price, hard to be overly critical; has varietal fruit, just a little thin, and a slightly tough finish, presumably pressings. Screwcap. 12° alc. **Rating** 87 **To** 2012 $12

Remarkable View Wines   ★★★

Main North Road, Murray Town, SA 5481 **Region** Southern Flinders Ranges
T (08) 8667 2223 **F** (08) 8667 2165 **www**.remarkableview.com.au **Open** W'ends & public hols 11–4.30, or by appt (closed Jan)
Winemaker Contract **Est.** 1997 **Cases** 320
Karen and the late Malcolm Orrock (and their family) began the establishment of the vineyard in 1997, and over the next four years planted shiraz, cabernet sauvignon, sangiovese, grenache, tempranillo and petit verdot. There are now a little under 20 ha of vines, the bulk of the

production being sold to Peter Lehmann Wines, with limited amounts made for sale under the Remarkable View brand label.

ΨΨΨΨ   **Southern Flinders Ranges Petit Verdot 2005** Deep colour; strong black fruits and bitter chocolate speak loudly of the variety, the tannins firm but not over the top. A little brutal now, needing time. Screwcap. 14° alc. **Rating** 89 **To** 2013 $20

Southern Flinders Ranges Shiraz 2004 Mainstream blackberry aroma, which flows through to the palate, there meeting touches of dark chocolate, mocha and vanilla, with savoury tannins to close. Screwcap. 14.8° alc. **Rating** 88 **To** 2012 $20

Southern Flinders Ranges Cabernet Sauvignon 2004 Holding hue; light- to medium-bodied, and has been cunningly made, with astute use of oak to paper over the cracks in the underlying fruit, and to enhance the length. Screwcap. 13.8° alc. **Rating** 87 **To** 2012 $20

Southern Flinders Ranges Tempranillo 2005 Tangy, spicy and zesty, very much in the Australian rendition of this variety; more flavour than structure, perhaps. Screwcap. 14° alc. **Rating** 87 **To** 2010 $20

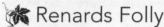 # Renards Folly   ★★★

PO Box 499, McLaren Vale, SA 5171 **Region** McLaren Vale
T (08) 8556 2404 **F** (08) 8556 2404 **Open** Not
Winemaker Tony Walker **Est.** 2005 **Cases** 1000
The dancing foxes on the label, one with a red tail, give a subliminal hint that this is a virtual winery, owned by Linda Kemp (who looks after the marketing and sales) and Mark Dimberline, who has spent 16 years in the wine industry. Aided by friend and winemaker Tony Walker, they source the shiraz for their single wine from the McLaren Vale sub-district, and allow the Vale to express itself without too much elaboration, the alcohol nicely controlled. Exports to the US, the UK and elsewhere.

ΨΨΨΨ   **McLaren Vale Shiraz 2005** An unforced, well-balanced, medium-bodied wine; blackberry, dark chocolate and mocha flavours supported by fine but ripe tannins. Screwcap. 14.5° alc. **Rating** 89 **To** 2015 $20

McLaren Vale Shiraz 2006 Ripe blackberry, blackcurrant and confit plum fruit; an overall impression of some sweetness on the rich palate. Screwcap. 14.5° alc. **Rating** 88 **To** 2013 $19.95

McLaren Vale Sangiovese Cabernet 2006 Has plenty of red fruit flavour, but the tannins build with disconcerting swiftness; absolutely demands food, and vigorous decanting. Screwcap. 14° alc. **Rating** 88 **To** 2013 $16.95

Renewan Murray Gold Wines   ★★★

Murray Valley Highway, Piangil, Vic 3597 **Region** Swan Hill
T (03) 5030 5525 **F** (03) 5030 5695 **Open** 7 days 9–5
Winemaker Hanging Rock **Est.** 1989 **Cases** 220
In 1990 former senior executive at Nylex Corporation in Melbourne, Jim Lewis, and artist wife Marg, retired to what is now Renewan, set on the banks of the Murray River. It is a small business, based on 2 ha of estate plantings.

Reschke Wines   ★★★★☆

Level 1, 183 Melbourne Street, North Adelaide, SA 5006 (postal) **Region** Coonawarra
T (08) 8239 0500 **F** (08) 8239 0522 **www.**reschke.com.au **Open** Not
Winemaker Peter Douglas (Contract) **Est.** 1998 **Cases** 10 000
It's not often that the first release from a new winery is priced at $100 per bottle, but that was precisely what Reschke Wines achieved with its 1998 Cabernet Sauvignon. The family has been a landholder in the Coonawarra region for 100 years, with a large landholding which is partly terra rossa, part woodland. There are 15.5 ha of merlot, 105 ha of cabernet sauvignon, 0.5 ha of cabernet franc and 2.5 ha of shiraz in production, with a further 26 ha planted in 2001 to shiraz, and a little petit verdot. Exports to the US, the UK and other major markets.

♀♀♀♀♀ **Bull Trader Coonawarra Cabernet Merlot 2004** Some development, with floral varietal cassis aromas and some complex cedar notes; fresh, lively and silky on the finish; ready now. Value plus. Screwcap. 14° alc. **Rating** 93 **To** 2012 $18

♀♀♀♀ **Vitulus 2004** Good fruit and focus; slightly simple and essency cassis and blackcurrant, but with good flavour and length. Cabernet Sauvignon. Cork. **Rating** 89 **To** 2015 $25
Coonawarra Fume Sauvignon Blanc 2007 Hints of sweet oak support the generous fruit; a little smoky and quite full-flavoured; a good example of the fume style. Vino-Lok. 13° alc. **Rating** 87 **To** 2010 $18

Restif   ★★★★
64 Parker Road, Wandin East, Vic 3139 (postal) **Region** Yarra Valley
T (03) 5964 2341 **F** (03) 5964 3651 **Open** Not
Winemaker Gary Mills **Est.** 1990 **Cases** 700
Val Diamond and Professor John Funder (of Prince Henrys Institute at the Monash Medical Centre) purchased the vineyard in 2003, when the chardonnay vines were already 13 years old. They also planted cabernet sauvignon, which has now come into bearing. Thus, both the 2005 and 2006 Restif Chardonnay came off the Front Block (as it is known). The first Cabernet Sauvignon (from younger plantings) to merit the label will be the 2006, not to be released for some time. Exports to the US and Hong Kong.

♀♀♀♀♀ **Cabernet Sauvignon 2006** Vibrant colour, with slightly savoury red berry fruit aromas; the palate is fine, linear and focused, with ample fine-grained tannins on the finish. Cork. 13.7° alc. **Rating** 90 **To** 2014 $27.50

♀♀♀♀ **Yarra Valley Chardonnay 2007** Quite complex, with cool citrus aromas, and slatey minerality; a little waxy on the palate, but good depth and concentration. Screwcap. 13° alc. **Rating** 87 **To** 2009 $27.50

Richard Hamilton
Cnr Main Road/Johnstone Road, Willunga, SA 5172 **Region** McLaren Vale
T (08) 8323 8830 **F** (08) 8323 8881 **www.**leconfieldwines.com **Open** Mon–Fri 10–5, w'ends & public hols 11–5
Winemaker Paul Gordon, Tim Bailey (Assistant) **Est.** 1972 **Cases** 25 000
Richard Hamilton has outstanding estate vineyards, some of great age, all fully mature. The arrival (in 2001) of former Rouge Homme winemaker Paul Gordon has allowed the full potential of those vineyards to be expressed. His move to lower alcohol wines (without sacrificing flavour) is to be commended. Exports to the UK, the US and other major markets.

♀♀♀♀♀ **Hamilton Centurion Old Vine Shiraz 2005** Very deep colour; layers of chocolate fruit and fruitcake sweetness on the bouquet; chewy and dense full-bodied palate, with lots of tannin and an ample amount of dark berry fruit on the finish; 113-year-old vines. Cork. 14.5° alc. **Rating** 94 **To** 2025 $59.95
Cadenzia Burton's Vineyard Old Bush Vine Grenache Shiraz 2003 Serious wine, with a powerfully structured and long palate offering red fruit flavours, ranging through raspberry to plum and to blackberry. Cork. 14.5° alc. **Rating** 94 **To** 2013 $25.95

♀♀♀♀♀ **Hut Block McLaren Vale Cabernet Sauvignon 2006** Good colour; essency cassis with cedar and a hint of black olives; plenty of oak, but the fruit concentration carries it well. Screwcap. 14° alc. **Rating** 91 **To** 2018 $17.95
Lot 148 McLaren Vale Merlot 2006 Aromatic berry and olive aromas, and similar flavours on the long palate; perfectly judged tannins. 14° alc. **Rating** 90 **To** 2014 $17.95

♀♀♀♀ **Slate Quarry McLaren Vale Riesling 2007** Good focus, with plenty of mineral slate on the bouquet; hints of lime juice and prominent acidity on the palate; excellent for region and vintage. Screwcap. 12.5° alc. **Rating** 89 **To** 2012 $13.95

Almond Grove McLaren Vale Chardonnay 2006 Light-bodied; clean, fresh stone fruit and melon aromas and flavours, with a neatly judged touch of oak. Drink sooner rather than later. Screwcap. 13.5° alc. **Rating** 89 **To** 2009 $19.95

Gida's McLaren Vale Rose 2007 Plenty of small berry red/strawberry grenache fruit; some length, and a balanced finish. Screwcap. 13° alc. **Rating** 88 **To** 2009 $13.95

Almond Grove McLaren Vale Chardonnay 2007 Clean, vibrant and juicy with plenty of melony chardonnay fruit on board; made for early drinking. Screwcap. 13.5° alc. **Rating** 87 **To** 2009 $13.95

Jette's Viognier 2007 The barrel ferment component is quite obvious, and increases texture and complexity; good for richer fish and white meat dishes. Screwcap. 13.5° alc. **Rating** 87 **To** 2010 $17.95

Richfield Estate ★★★★

Bonshaw Road, Tenterfield, NSW 2372 **Region** New England
T (02) 6737 5488 **F** (02) 6737 5598 **www.**richfieldvineyard.com.au **Open** By appt 10–4
Winemaker John Cassegrain **Est.** 1997 **Cases** 6000
Singapore resident Bernard Forey is the Chairman and majority shareholder of Richfield Estate. The 500-ha property, at an altitude of 720 m, was selected after an intensive survey by soil specialists. Just under 30 ha of shiraz, cabernet sauvignon, merlot, semillon, chardonnay and verdelho were planted, the first vintage coming in 2000. Winemaker John Cassegrain is a shareholder in the venture, and much of the wine is exported to Thailand and Malaysia.

 New England Chardonnay 2006 Clean, crisp, citrussy tang to stone fruit and green apple flavours; good balance and length; some malolactic influence. **Rating** 90 **To** 2011 $12.90

 New England Verdelho 2006 Well made; plenty of juicy fruit salad varietal character; not phenolic, but a little yeasty. **Rating** 90 **To** 2009 $12.90

Richmond Grove ★★★★

Para Road, Tanunda, SA 5352 **Region** Barossa Valley
T (08) 8563 7303 **F** (08) 8563 7330 **www.**richmondgrovewines.com **Open** 7 days 10.30–4.30
Winemaker Steve Clarkson, John Vickery (Consultant) **Est.** 1983 **Cases** 150 000
Richmond Grove, owned by Orlando Wyndham, draws its grapes from diverse sources. The Richmond Grove Barossa Valley and Watervale Rieslings made by the team directed by consultant winemaker John Vickery represent excellent value for money (for Riesling) year in, year out. Exports to the UK.

 Coonawarra Cabernet Sauvignon 2002 Considerable depth and concentration to blackcurrant and mulberry fruit, and achieves full ripeness in a cool vintage; good length and balance. Gold medal, Limestone Coast Wine Show '06. Cork. 14.2° alc. **Rating** 93 **To** 2015 $19.95

Limited Release Barossa Vineyards Shiraz 2003 A powerful wine, with fully ripe black fruits that rise above the challenges of the vintage; spice, chocolate and bramble notes on the finish. Cork. 15° alc. **Rating** 91 **To** 2013 $19.95

 Chardonnay Pinot Noir NV Pale green-straw, with good mousse; has some finesse and length, though not particularly complex; citrus and stone fruit flavours with a balanced finish. Cork. 12° alc. **Rating** 88 **To** 2009 $14.99

Limited Release Watervale Riesling 2007 A powerful wine reflecting the relatively high alcohol; solid ripe apple flavour, and some minerally notes. Screwcap. 13.5° alc. **Rating** 87 **To** 2014 $19.99

Limited Release Adelaide Hills Vineyards Pinot Grigio 2007 Good mouthfeel to fluid pear, apple and musk flavours, finishing with crisp acidity. Screwcap. 12.5° alc. **Rating** 87 **To** 2010 $19.95

Richmond Park Vineyard

Logie Road, Richmond, Tas 7025 (postal) **Region** Southern Tasmania
T (03) 6265 2949 **F** (03) 6265 3166 **Open** Not
Winemaker Hood Wines (Andrew Hood) **Est.** 1989 **Cases** NA
A small vineyard owned by Tony Park, which gives the clue to the clever name. It is 20 mins'
drive from Hobart; a particular (and uncommon) attraction for mailing list clients is the
availability of 375 ml bottles.

ΨΨΨΨ   **Chardonnay Pinot Noir 2004** Deep colour; a dry style, with plenty of lemon
fruit and hints of toastiness; good flavour until a slightly bitter twist on the finish.
Rating 87 **To** 2009

Rickety Gate

1949 Scotsdale Road, Denmark, WA 6333 **Region** Great Southern
T (08) 9840 9504 **F** (08) 9840 9502 **www.**ricketygate.com.au **Open** Fri–Mon & hols 11–4
Winemaker John Wade **Est.** 2000 **Cases** 2600
The 3-ha vineyard of Rickety Gate is situated on north-facing slopes of the Bennet Ranges,
in an area specifically identified by Dr John Gladstones as highly suited to cool-climate
viticulture. The property was purchased by Russell and Linda Hubbard at the end of 1999,
and 1.8 ha of merlot, 0.8 ha of riesling and 0.5 ha of chardonnay and pinot noir were planted
in 2000. John Wade contract-makes the wines at the small onsite winery.

ΨΨΨΨΨ   **Denmark Shiraz 2005** Elegant and focused cool-grown shiraz; medium-bodied,
with red fruits and lively spicy notes supported by fine tannins and integrated
French oak. Screwcap. 14° alc. **Rating** 94 **To** 2017 $22

ΨΨΨΨΨ   **Denmark Merlot 2005** Fragrant and silky light- to medium-bodied wine,
with clear varietal fruit; touches of black olive and spice; fine tannins. Screwcap.
Rating 90 **To** 2012 $24.50
Denmark Cabernet Merlot 2005 Very good hue, still with crimson hues;
elegant palate, very fresh in a low-pH, slow-developing style. Screwcap. **Rating** 90
To 2020 $22

ΨΨΨΨ   **Denmark Riesling 2007** Very youthful, tightly structured, with minerally acidity
running the length of the palate and finish; still in its cocoon, no shimmering
butterfly yet. Screwcap. **Rating** 89 **To** 2015 $22.50
Late Harvest Riesling 2007 Really not one thing or the other; crisp, fresh
and barely sweet; needed to go further, leaving less alcohol and more sweet fruit.
Screwcap. 11.9° alc. **Rating** 87 **To** 2010 $16.50

Ridgemill Estate

218 Donges Road, Severnlea, Qld 4352 **Region** Granite Belt
T (07) 4683 5211 **F** (07) 4683 5211 **www.**ridgemillestate.com **Open** Thurs–Mon 10–5
Winemaker Martin Cooper, Peter McGlashan, Jim Barnes (Consultant) **Est.** 1998
Cases 800
Martin Cooper and Dianne Maddison acquired what was then known as Emerald Hill
Winery in 2004. In '05 they expanded the existing 2 ha of vineyard (planted to chardonnay,
tempranillo, shiraz, merlot and cabernet sauvignon) by adding 0.2 ha each of saperavi, lagrein
and viognier, firmly setting a course down the alternative variety road. The 2005 Chardonnay
was the first Qld wine to win an international gold medal (at the International Chardonnay
Challenge '05 in Gisborne, NZ). Its best wines are part of the Qld charge to recognition
against all-comers.

ΨΨΨΨ   **Rhone Ranger Shiraz Viognier 2006** High-toned, fragrant viognier lift;
fresh, light-bodied, crisp; early-drinking style. Screwcap. 13.5° alc. **Rating** 89
To 2010 $18
Vintage Fortified 2006 Clean spirit, with vibrant and fresh fruit; good flavour,
should develop well. Cork. 18.5° alc. **Rating** 89 **To** 2020 $35

First Press Rose 2007 Bright fuchsia-crimson; distinctly sweet but does have some fresh fruit and balancing acidity. Shiraz **Rating** 88 **To** 2009 $18

RidgeView Wines

273 Sweetwater Road, Rothbury, NSW 2335 **Region** Lower Hunter Valley
T 0419 475 221 **F** (02) 9534 5468 **www.**ridgeview.com.au **Open** Fri–Sun 10–5
Winemaker Cameron Webster, Darren Scott, Gary MacLean **Est.** 2000 **Cases** 2500
Darren and Tracey Scott (plus their four children and extended family) have transformed a 40-ha timbered farm into a 10-ha vineyard together with self-contained accommodation and cellar door. The lion's share of the plantings are 4.5 ha of shiraz, with cabernet sauvignon, chambourcin, merlot, pinot gris, viognier and traminer making up a somewhat eclectic selection of varieties. Exports to Japan.

ȲȲȲȲ **Generations Reserve Hunter Valley Shiraz 2006** Good concentration of fruit, with a distinct leather note to the palate, and plenty of oak; a chewy and quite full-bodied finish. Screwcap. 15° alc. **Rating** 89 **To** 2014 $40
Semillon 2007 Shows less varietal fruit than many of its vintage, but is well enough balanced. Screwcap. 12.5° alc. **Rating** 87 **To** 2010 $17
Hunter Valley Shiraz 2006 Quite juicy, with red fruits, licorice and a little leather in the background; not as deep as the reserve, but has good flavour. Screwcap. 13.5° alc. **Rating** 87 **To** 2012 $20

Rimfire Vineyards

Bismarck Street, Maclagan, Qld 4352 **Region** Darling Downs
T (07) 4692 1129 **F** (07) 4692 1260 **www.**rimfirewinery.com.au **Open** 7 days 10–5
Winemaker Louise Connellan **Est.** 1991 **Cases** 6000
The Connellan family (Margaret and Tony and children Michelle, Peter and Louise) began planting the 8-ha, seven-variety Rimfire Vineyards in 1991 as a means of diversification of their large cattle stud in the foothills of the Bunya Mountains, northeast of Toowoomba. The vineyard is planted to shiraz, cabernet sauvignon, ruby cabernet, cabernet franc, sangiovese, touriga nacional and graciano, all between 1 ha and 1.5 ha. The wine simply called 1893 is made from a vine brought to the property by a German settler in about 1893; the vineyard ceased production in the early 1900s, but a single vine remained, and DNA testing has established that the vine does not correspond to any vine cultivar currently known in Australia. Rimfire propagated cuttings, and a small quantity is made each year.

ȲȲȲȲȲ **Reserve Chardonnay 2006** Well above the average Qld chardonnay; luscious stone fruit flavours balanced by citrussy acidity and quality oak; 4 barrels made. Screwcap. 13.5° alc. **Rating** 90 **To** 2012 $25

ȲȲȲȲ **Shiraz 2006** Light- to medium-bodied; savoury, spicy, earthy nuances to the core of blackberry fruit; good control of extract and oak. Screwcap. **Rating** 89 **To** 2013 $19.80
Touriga Nacional 2006 Has a tangy, almost citrussy edge to the black fruit flavours; not as tannic as expected, and has length. Screwcap. **Rating** 87 **To** 2012 $22

Riposte ★★★★☆

PO Box 256, Lobethal, SA 5241 **Region** Adelaide Hills
T (08) 8389 8149 **F** (08) 8389 8178 **Open** Not
Winemaker Tim Knappstein **Est.** 2006 **Cases** 3000
It's never too late to teach an old dog new tricks when the old dog in question is Tim Knappstein. With 40 years of winemaking and more than 500 wine show awards under his belt, Tim has started yet another new wine life with Riposte, a subtle response to the various vicissitudes he has suffered in recent years. While neither he nor his former wife, Annie, have any continuing financial interest in the Lenswood Vineyards they established so many years ago, Tim is sourcing the grapes for Riposte from that Lenswood Vineyard. Exports to the UK and Canada.

🍷🍷🍷🍷🍷 **The Foil Adelaide Hills Sauvignon Blanc 2007** A clean and expressive bouquet reflecting the abundant gooseberry/passionfruit/tropical flavours of the palate; crisp acidity to close. Screwcap. 13° alc. **Rating** 94 **To** 2009 $19

🍷🍷🍷🍷🍷 **The Sabre Adelaide Hills Pinot Noir 2006** Highly aromatic strawberry, cherry and spice aromas; good texture on the palate with some whole bunch/stalk/forest characters; has length. Screwcap. 13.5° alc. **Rating** 93 **To** 2013 $27
The Rapier Adelaide Hills Traminer 2007 Clean, crisp with gentle spice and lychee flavours; no phenolics, won't frighten the horses, but well made. Screwcap. 13° alc. **Rating** 90 **To** 2012 $19

Riseborough Estate ★★★

Lot 21, Petersen Rise, off Mooliabeenee Road, Gingin, WA 6503 **Region** Swan District
T (08) 9575 1211 **F** (08) 9575 1211 **Open** Wed–Sun 10–4
Winemaker Flying Fish Cove, Oakover Wines **Est.** 1998 **Cases** NA
Don Riseborough and Susan Lamp began developing their 8.7-ha vineyard, a stone's throw from Moondah Brook, in 1998. They have planted shiraz, cabernet sauvignon, merlot, cabernet franc and grenache; the grapes take the slightly unusual trip south to Margaret River where the red wines are made by Flying Fish Cove. A small selection of non-estate white wines (Chenin Blanc, Chardonnay and Verdelho, all with a small amount of residual sweetness) are made by Rob Marshall in the Swan Valley.

🍷🍷🍷🍷 **Merlot Cabernet Franc 2004** An interesting wine, given the hot region and high alcohol; has managed to hold onto varietal character and good colour, with supple red fruits. Screwcap. 15.4° alc. **Rating** 87 **To** 2011 $14
Cabernet Sauvignon 2004 Light- to medium-bodied; a pleasantly savoury twist to the finish adds authenticity to the varietal expression. Screwcap. 14.6° alc. **Rating** 87 **To** 2012 $14

Rising Dust Wines ★★★

PO Box 163, Gol Gol, NSW 2735 **Region** Murray Darling
T 0400 790 309 **F** (03) 5021 4235 **www.**risingdustwines.com.au **Open** Not
Winemaker Bob Shields **Est.** 2005 **Cases** 2000
Richard Mills is a member of the family that has farmed in the region for over 50 years. Born in 1976, he was in his 20s when he realised that he wanted to establish a long-term wine business founded on estate-grown grapes. He planted 40 ha of chardonnay, sauvignon blanc and shiraz, and the business was underway. He retained the services of Bob Shields, arguably the most experienced winemaker in the region, and the first wines were made in 2005. As well as Australian distribution, Rising Dust is exported to Canada, and there are ample grapes available to increase production if the demand for the wines grows.

🍷🍷🍷🍷 **Chardonnay 2006** Clever winemaking (and grapegrowing); not particularly complex, but is fresh and unforced, with good balance. Screwcap. 13° alc. **Rating** 88 **To** 2010 $14
Sauvignon Blanc 2007 A flowery, aromatic bouquet; particularly well made, transcending the limitations of the hot climate; distinct varietal character, even though the finish is short. Screwcap. 12.5° alc. **Rating** 87 **To** 2009 $14
Shiraz 2006 As with the white wines, consistently delivers more than expected; light- to medium-bodied cherry, plum and a dash of oak. Disciplined winemaking. Screwcap. 13.5° alc. **Rating** 87 **To** 2011 $14

Rivergate Wines ★★★

580 Goornong Road, Axedale, Vic 3551 **Region** Bendigo
T (03) 5439 7367 **F** (03) 5439 7366 **www.**rivergatewines.com.au **Open** By appt
Winemaker Greg Dedman, Geoff Kerr **Est.** 1999 **Cases** 700

Geoff and Ann Kerr have lived in the Campaspe River Valley, north of Axedale, for 25 years. It was not until the late 1990s that they took the decision to plant 2 ha of shiraz; while the vines were establishing themselves, Geoff Kerr completed the viticulture and winemaking courses at Bendigo TAFE, studying successively under Vince Lakey, Mal Steward and Lindsay Ross. Rivergate continues to use the contract winemaking facilities of the TAFE to crush, ferment and press the grapes, bringing the fermented juice back to Rivergate for barrel maturation, bottling and packaging. When conditions permit (2002, '03, '04), a small amount of Reserve is made, spending two years in oak, rather than the 12 months for the standard Shiraz.

Robert Channon Wines ★★★★

32 Bradley Lane, Stanthorpe, Qld 4380 **Region** Granite Belt
T (07) 4683 3260 **F** (07) 4683 3109 **www**.robertchannonwines.com **Open** Mon–Fri 11–4, w'ends & public hols 10–5
Winemaker Mark Ravenscroft **Est.** 1998 **Cases** 3500
Peggy and Robert Channon have established 8 ha of chardonnay, verdelho, shiraz, merlot and cabernet sauvignon under permanent bird protection netting. The initial cost of installing permanent netting is high, but in the long term it is well worth it: it excludes birds and protects the grapes,, against hail damage. Also, there is no pressure to pick the grapes before they are fully ripe. The winery has established a particular reputation for its Verdelho.

♆♆♆♆♆ **Pinot Gris 2007** First vintage from grafted vines, and within the limitations of pinot gris, an impressive start; authentic varietal pear, apple and citrus flavours, and a long, dry finish. Screwcap. 13° alc. **Rating** 90 **To** 2010 $22.50
Verdelho 2007 Has an abundance of ripe, even sweet, tropical fruit salad on the mid-palate, but finishes dry and quite firm. Screwcap. 13.5° alc. **Rating** 90 **To** 2012 $24.50

♆♆♆♆ **Merlot 2005** Slightly lighter colour than the Reserve, still bright; a similarly finer, more fluid mouthfeel, the tannins less obvious, making the wine more pleasing now. Screwcap. 14° alc. **Rating** 89 **To** 2011 $20
Reserve Merlot 2005 Bright colour; very savoury wine, with earthy tannins running through the length of the medium-bodied palate; designed to age, but the fruit may not outlive those tannins. Screwcap. 14° alc. **Rating** 89 **To** 2015 $29.50
Reserve Cabernet Sauvignon 2005 Good colour; ripe blackcurrant fruit; medium-bodied; soft tannins; does shorten slightly; very oaky. **Rating** 88 **To** 2011 $29.50
Chardonnay 2007 A light-bodied, low intensity wine which has been sensitively made and not forced, the oak appropriately subtle, the fruit fresh. Screwcap. 12.5° alc. **Rating** 87 **To** 2010 $18
Cabernet Sauvignon 2005 Light-bodied and fault-free; some savoury/earthy black fruits with an appropriate dusting of tannins and oak. Screwcap. 14° alc. **Rating** 87 **To** 2011 $20

Robert Johnson Vineyards ★★★★☆

PO Box 6708 Halifax Street, Adelaide, SA 5000 **Region** Eden Valley
T (08) 8227 2800 **F** (08) 8227 2833 **Open** Not
Winemaker Robert Johnson **Est.** 1997 **Cases** 2500
The home base for Robert Johnson is a 12-ha vineyard and olive grove purchased in 1996, with 0.4 ha of merlot and 5 ha of dilapidated olive trees. The olive grove has been rehabilitated, and 2.1 ha of shiraz, 1.2 ha of merlot and a small patch of viognier have been established. Wines made from the estate-grown grapes are released under the Robert Johnson label; these are supplemented by Alan & Veitch wines purchased from the Sam Virgara vineyard in the Adelaide Hills, and named after Robert Johnson's parents.

♆♆♆♆♆ **Eden Valley Merlot 2005** Abundant blackcurrant and black olive fruit, mouthfilling but not overripe; good structure and tannins; prime varietal example. Cork. 14.5° alc. **Rating** 94 **To** 2015

ΨΨΨΨΨ **Eden Valley Shiraz 2005** Medium-bodied; pleasing black and red cherry, plum and blackberry fruit; fine, ripe tannins; good length. Screwcap. 14.8° alc. **Rating** 93 To 2018

ΨΨΨΨ **Eden Valley Riesling 2006** The bouquet is still to evolve and express itself, but there is plenty of citrussy fruit on the palate, and good length; time to build further. Screwcap. 12° alc. **Rating** 89 To 2015
Alan & Veitch Adelaide Hills Sauvignon Blanc 2006 Bright green-straw; has some bottle-developed flavours as much akin to riesling as sauvignon blanc, with a tropical overlay. Screwcap. 12.5° alc. **Rating** 88 To 2009

Robert Stein Vineyard ★★★

Pipeclay Lane, Mudgee, NSW 2850 **Region** Mudgee
T (02) 6373 3991 **F** (02) 6373 3709 **www**.robertstein.com.au **Open** 7 days 10–4.30
Winemaker Michael Slater, Andrew Stein **Est.** 1976 **Cases** 10 000
The sweeping panorama from the winery is its own reward for cellar door visitors. Right from the outset this has been a substantial operation but has managed to sell the greater part of its production direct from the winery by mail order and cellar door, with retail distribution in Sydney, Vic and SA. Wine quality, once variable (albeit with top wines from time to time) has become much more consistent. Exports to the Germany and Hong Kong.

ΨΨΨΨ **Reserve Mudgee Shiraz 2003** Radically different to the varietal, more brambly, savoury and spicy, reflecting its lower alcohol; medium-bodied and quite supple. Cork. 13.6° alc. **Rating** 88 To 2011 $30
Reserve Mudgee Shiraz 2005 Some development showing; strong spice, herb and earth elements, with an almost lemony finish. Vino-Lok. 13.5° alc. **Rating** 88 To 2012 $35
Reserve Mudgee Cabernet Sauvignon 2003 Earthy, savoury cedary notes have developed with oncoming maturity; a nice touch of cassis on the back-palate, the tannins controlled. Cork. 13.2° alc. **Rating** 88 To 2013 $30
Mudgee Shiraz 2003 No shortage of blackberry and confit plum fruit on the mid-palate, but shortens significantly. Cork. 14° alc. **Rating** 87 To 2010 $20

Robertson of Clare Wines

Suite 8, Level 1, 694 Pacific Highway, Killara, NSW 2071 (postal) **Region** Clare Valley
T (02) 9499 6002 **F** (02) 9449 8001 **www**.rocwines.com.au **Open** Not
Winemaker Simon Gilbert, Leigh Eldredge **Est.** 2004 **Cases** 1800
This is a venture of Simon Gilbert, established after he ceased to have an executive position with Simon Gilbert Wines in Mudgee. He has joined with Clare Valley vigneron Leigh Eldredge to produce limited quantities of Clare Valley wines. The first release, MAX V, was sourced from three growers in the Clare Valley, utilising the five grapes of Bordeaux: cabernet sauvignon, cabernet franc, merlot, malbec and petit verdot. The wine was made by conducting the entire primary fermentation and malolactic fermentation in French barrels from a range of forests and coopers at Sevenhill Cellars. Exports to the UK, the US and other major markets.

ΨΨΨΨΨ **Angus Block 8 Shiraz 2005** Two vineyard sources (one 90-year-old vines) have had the winemaking book thrown at them, with fermentation in new 400-l 'vinification integral' barrels before 24 months in new Francois Freres and new Demptos American oak French-coopered barrels with toasted heads; impossible to rationally point. Streaky stained cork. 15° alc. **Rating** 92 To 2035 $75

Robinsons Family Vineyards

Curtin Road, Ballandean, Qld 4382 **Region** Granite Belt
T (07) 4684 1216 **F** (07) 4684 1216 **www**.robinsonswines.com.au **Open** Sat–Wed 10–5, Thurs & Fri by appt
Winemaker Craig Robinson **Est.** 1969 **Cases** 2000

One of the pioneers of the Granite Belt, with the second generation of the family Robinson now in control. One thing has not changed: the strongly held belief of the Robinsons that the Granite Belt should be regarded as a cool, rather than warm, climate. It is a tricky debate, because some climatic measurements point one way, others the opposite. Embedded in all this are semantic arguments about the meaning of 'cool' and 'warm'. Suffice it to say that shiraz and (conspicuously) cabernet sauvignon are the most suitable red varieties for the region; semillon, verdelho and chardonnay are the best white varieties.

ŸŸŸŸ **Granite Belt Chardonnay 2005** Medium- to full straw-gold; strongly influenced by barrel ferment throughout; old vine (early '70s) fruit struggles to express itself, but ample overall flavour. Diam. 14° alc. **Rating** 88 **To** 2011 $21.95

Robinvale ★★★

Sea Lake Road, Robinvale, Vic 3549 **Region** Murray Darling
T (03) 5026 3955 **F** (03) 5026 1123 www.organicwines.com.au **Open** 7 days 9–5
Winemaker Bill Caracatsanoudis **Est.** 1976 **Cases** 13 500
Robinvale was one of the first Australian wineries to be fully accredited with the Biodynamic Agricultural Association of Australia. Most, but not all, of the wines are produced from organically grown grapes, with some made preservative-free. Production has grown dramatically, no doubt reflecting the interest in organic and biodynamic viticulture and winemaking. At the Australian Alternative Varieties Wine Show '07 the 2002 Kerner was awarded a rare gold medal, while the '07 Late Harvest Lexia and '05 Zoe Dimitra Cabernet Sauvignon won bronze medals at both the Australian Inland Wine Show '07 and highly competitive Australian Small Winemakers Show '07. Exports to the UK, the US, Canada, Belgium, Korea, Vietnam and NZ.

Robyn Drayton Wines ★★★

Cnr Pokolbin Mountain Road/McDonalds Road, Pokolbin, NSW 2321
Region Lower Hunter Valley
T (02) 4998 7523 **F** (02) 4998 7523 www.robyndraytonwines.com.au **Open** 7 days 10–5
Winemaker Robyn Drayton, Andrew Spanazi **Est.** 1989 **Cases** 5000
Reg and Pam Drayton were among the victims of the Seaview/Lord Howe Island air crash in 1984, having established Reg Drayton Wines after selling their interest in the long-established Drayton Family Winery. Their daughter Robyn (a fifth-generation Drayton and billed as the Hunter's first female vigneron) and husband Craig have significantly expanded the business (under the Robyn Drayton name) with an additional 6 ha of vineyard plantings and a much-expanded cellar door and café.

Roche Wines ★★★

Broke Road, Pokolbin, NSW 2320 **Region** Lower Hunter Valley
T (02) 4998 7600 **F** (02) 4998 7706 www.hvg.com.au **Open** 7 days 10–5
Winemaker Tempus Two Wines **Est.** 1999 **Cases** 10 000
Roche Wines, with its 45 ha of semillon, shiraz and chardonnay (plus a few bits and pieces), is but the tip of the iceberg of the massive investment made by Bill Roche in the Pokolbin subregion. He has transformed the old Hungerford Hill on the corner of Broke and McDonalds roads, and built a luxurious resort hotel with extensive gardens and an Irish pub on the old Tallawanta Vineyard, as well as resuscitating the vines on Tallawanta. The wines are all sold through the various outlets in the overall development; excess grapes are sold to other makers.

Rochford Wines ★★★★☆

Cnr Maroondah Highway/Hill Road, Coldstream, Vic 3770 **Region** Yarra Valley
T (03) 5962 2119 **F** (03) 5962 5319 www.rochfordwines.com **Open** 7 days 10–5
Winemaker David Creed **Est.** 1988 **Cases** 30 000

Following the acquisition of the former Eyton-on-Yarra by Helmut and Yvonne Konecsny, major changes have occurred. Most obvious is the renaming of the winery and brand, slightly less so the move of the winemaking operations of Rochford to the Yarra Valley. The large restaurant is open 7 days for lunch and Rochford is well-known for the numerous concerts it stages in its lakeside amphitheatre. Exports to the UK, Canada, Singapore, Hong Kong and China.

ΨΨΨΨΨ **Macedon Ranges Chardonnay 2006** Very fine and focused, the high level of natural acidity providing backbone to the grapefruit and apple flavours, the oak subtle. Screwcap. 14° alc. **Rating** 93 **To** 2012 $27

Yarra Valley Chardonnay 2006 A well-made, subtle wine, with melon and nectarine fruit set within a light framework of French oak, good length. Screwcap. 13.5° alc. **Rating** 92 **To** 2012 $25

Yarra Valley Sauvignon Blanc 2007 At the herbal/mineral end of the spectrum, but does have some more tropical fruit on the mid-palate; a three-vineyard blend works well. Screwcap. 12.5° alc. **Rating** 90 **To** 2009 $25

Macedon Ranges Pinot Gris 2007 Spicy edges to the primary pear fruit lift the wine on bouquet and palate; good mouthfeel and length. Screwcap. 13° alc. **Rating** 90 **To** 2010 $27

ΨΨΨΨ **Yarra Valley Pinot Noir 2006** Hmmm; a very potent and quite aggressive wine, crying out for time in bottle; certainly has the requisite length. Screwcap. 14° alc. **Rating** 89 **To** 2013 $30

Yarra Valley Shiraz 2005 Some colour development; light- to medium-bodied, supple and smooth, the level of French oak very obvious and suggesting 24 months in oak too long for what was in any event ripe fruit. Screwcap. 15° alc. **Rating** 89 **To** 2014 $27

Reserve Macedon Ranges Pinot Noir 2006 Developed, light colour; uncompromisingly foresty/briary/savoury/earthy style, varietal but lacking enough sweet fruit for balance. Diam. 13.5° alc. **Rating** 88 **To** 2011 $54

RockBare   ★★★★☆

PO Box 63, Mt Torrens, SA 5244 **Region** McLaren Vale
T (08) 8389 5192 **F** (08) 8389 5193 **www**.rockbare.com.au **Open** Not
Winemaker Tim Burvill **Est.** 2000 **Cases** 30 000
A native of WA, Tim Burvill moved to SA in 1993 to do the winemaking course at the Adelaide University Roseworthy campus. Having completed an Honours degree in oenology, he was recruited by Southcorp, and quickly found himself in a senior winemaking position, with responsibility for super-premium whites including Penfolds Yattarna. He makes the RockBare wines under lend-lease arrangements with other wineries. No samples received; the rating is that of last year. Exports to all major markets.

Rockfield Estate   ★★★★★

Rosa Glen Road, Margaret River, WA 6285 **Region** Margaret River
T (08) 9757 5006 **F** (08) 9757 5006 **www**.rockfield.com.au **Open** Wed–Sun & hols 11–5, or by appt
Winemaker Andrew Gaman Jr, John Durham (Consultant) **Est.** 1997 **Cases** 8000
Rockfield Estate Vineyard is very much a family affair. Dr Andrew Gaman wears the hats of chief executive officer, assistant winemaker and co-marketing manager; wife Anne Gaman is a director; Alex Gaman is the viticulturist; Andrew Gaman Jr is winemaker; and Anna Walter (née Gaman) helps with the marketing. Chapman Brook meanders through the property, the vines running from its banks up to the wooded slopes above the valley floor. Exports to the UK.

ΨΨΨΨΨ **Reserve Margaret River Chardonnay 2006** Notable for its purity and line; all the focus on nectarine and melon fruit; oak plays a pure support role. Screwcap. 14° alc. **Rating** 95 **To** 2014 $30

Semillon 2007 A complex array of aromas from cut grass to a touch of citrus; a powerful palate reflecting the bouquet; has depth and length. Screwcap. 13° alc. Rating 94 To 2012 $22

Reserve Margaret River Cabernet Sauvignon 2005 Abundant, supple and silky blackcurrant fruit, perfectly ripened, supported by ripe but fine tannins and quality, cedary French oak. Screwcap. 14° alc. Rating 94 To 2020 $39

ȲȲȲȲȲ **Semillon Sauvignon Blanc 2007** Partial barrel ferment in no way takes away from the aromaticity or fruit freshness, simply adding mouthfeel to the passionfruit and tropical flavours. Screwcap. 13° alc. Rating 92 To 2009 $17

Reserve Margaret River Chardonnay 2005 Striking pale green; still very fresh and tight with flavours in a grapefruit and stone fruit spectrum; may never fully soften and open up. Screwcap. 13.5° alc. Rating 92 To 2015 $35

Margaret River Merlot 2006 Attractive red fruits; picked at perfect ripeness for varietal expression of cassis, the tannins present but not needed to balance any sweet meat fruit — there is none. Screwcap. 14° alc. Rating 90 To 2013 $24

ȲȲȲȲ **Chardonnay 2007** Entirely fruit-driven, with sweet, ripe nectarine and peach fruit; crowd pleaser. Screwcap. 13.5° alc. Rating 88 To 2009 $18

Margaret River Cabernet Merlot 2005 Solid regional expression; blackcurrant and cassis fruit offset by moderately firm, slightly drying tannins. Screwcap. 14° alc. Rating 88 To 2014 $24

Rockford
★★★★★

Krondorf Road, Tanunda, SA 5352 **Region** Barossa Valley
T (08) 8563 2720 **F** (08) 8563 3787 **Open** 7 days 11–5
Winemaker Robert O'Callaghan, Ben Radford **Est.** 1984 **Cases** NFP
Rockford can only be described as an icon, no matter how overused that word may be. It has a devoted band of customers who buy most of the wine through the cellar door or mail order (Rocky O'Callaghan's entrancing annual newsletter is like no other.) Some wine is sold through restaurants, and there are two retailers in Sydney, and one each in Melbourne, Brisbane and Perth. Whether they will have the Basket Press Shiraz available is another matter; it is as scarce as Henschke Hill of Grace (and less expensive). Exports to the UK, Canada, Switzerland, Singapore, Vietnam and NZ.

ȲȲȲȲȲ **Handpicked Eden Valley Riesling 2005** Quality lime/lemon aromas; tightly structured and powerful, with good acidity giving thrust; has brushed aside the challenge of the cork. 12.5° alc. Rating 94 To 2012 $18.50

Black Shiraz NV Lively, but slightly lighter than some prior releases, though I am not sure why; regardless, impeccable balance and length, with indefinite ageing. Disgorged Sept '07. 13.5° alc. Rating 94 To 2015 $55

ȲȲȲȲȲ **Moppa Springs Barossa Valley Grenache Mataro Shiraz 2003** Very developed colour, but has good intensity, velocity and length to the tangy, earthy fruit. Outstanding achievement from '03. Cork. 14.5° alc. Rating 92 To 2010 $23

Basket Press Barossa Valley Shiraz 2005 Mid-garnet; surprisingly elegant and light-bodied; has good flavour and length, but seems a fraction under-ripe; better than the other extreme. Cork. 14.5° alc. Rating 90 To 2015 $49

Rifle Range Barossa Valley Cabernet Sauvignon 2005 Strong varietal cabernet, but just a little leafy and green on the bouquet; quite long and supple on the finish, and the tannins refreshing. Cork. 14.5° alc. Rating 90 To 2014 $35

ȲȲȲȲ **Barossa Valley White Frontignac 2007** Gently flowery/grapey/spicy aromas; a lively, fresh palate with juicy fruit, and residual sugar balanced by acidity. Top Chinese restaurant drop. Screwcap. 10.5° alc. Rating 89 To 2009 $15

Local Growers Barossa Valley Semillon 2004 Very developed colour; full-bodied traditional style, with lemony, buttery flavours and just enough acidity for the weight. Cork. 11.5° alc. Rating 88 To 2010 $18

Alicante Bouchet 2007 Typical vivid purple-red of the variety; you can sense a touch of sweetness to the plummy fruit even on the bouquet; a trifle short on the finish. Screwcap. 10° alc. **Rating** 87 **To** 2009 $17

Rocky Passes Estate ★★★★☆

1590 Highlands Road, Seymour, Vic 3660 **Region** Upper Goulburn
T (03) 5796 9366 **F** (03) 5796 9366 **www**.rockypassesestate.com.au **Open** W'ends 10–5
Winemaker Vitto Oles **Est.** 2000 **Cases** 7800
Vitto Oles and Candida Westney run this tiny, cool-climate vineyard situated at the southern end of the Strathbogie Ranges, which in fact falls in the Upper Goulburn region. They have planted 1.6 ha of shiraz and 0.4 ha of viognier, growing the vines with minimal irrigation and preferring organic and biodynamic soil treatments. Vitto Oles is also a fine furniture designer and maker, with a studio at Rocky Passes.

Rocland Estate ★★★★

PO Box 679, Nuriootpa, SA 5355 **Region** Barossa Valley
T (08) 8562 2142 **F** (08) 8562 2182 **www**.roclandwinery.com.au **Open** By appt
Winemaker Peter Gajewski **Est.** 2000 **Cases** 3000
Rocland Wines is primarily a bulk winemaking facility for contract work, but Frank Rocca does have 6 ha of shiraz which is used to make Rocland Wines, largely destined for export markets (the US, Singapore and Malaysia), but with retail distribution in Adelaide.

 Lot 147 Barossa Valley Shiraz 2005 A big, generously endowed wine offering black fruits, dark chocolate, plum and mocha oak; soft and round mouthfeel and finish; 600 cases made. Screwcap. 14.5° alc. **Rating** 93 **To** 2020 $28
Kilroy Was Here Barossa Valley Shiraz 2006 Full-on Barossa Valley style, with considerable intensity and length to the array of black fruits, a touch of dark chocolate and oak. Screwcap. 14.5° alc. **Rating** 91 **To** 2021 $20

 Kilroy Was Here Barossa Valley Cabernet Sauvignon 2006 Bright, breezy cassis and raspberry fruit, light tannins and good balance. Screwcap. 14.5° alc. **Rating** 89 **To** 2011 $20
Lot 147 Barossa Valley Shiraz 2006 Strongly perfumed sweet shiraz fruit; juicy and almost jubey on the palate, the toasty oak comes through and and tidies up the finish. Screwcap. 15° alc. **Rating** 88 **To** 2014 $22
Kilroy Was Here Barossa Valley Sparkling Shiraz 2006 Vibrant purple hue; clean as a whistle, clearly varietal and with nice texture from start to finish. Cork. 13° alc. **Rating** 88 **To** 2014 $25

Rogues Lane Vineyard ★★★★

370 Lower Plenty Road, Viewbank, Vic 3084 (postal) **Region** Heathcote
T 0409 202 103 **F** (03) 9457 2811 **www**.rogueslane.com.au **Open** Not
Winemaker Hanging Rock (John Ellis) **Est.** 1998 **Cases** 500
Pauline and Eric Dowker have planted 4 ha of shiraz (including a smattering of malbec), the first vintage coming in 1998. 'Dowker' is an ancient word meaning 'herder of ducks and geese', making the location of the vineyard on Wild Duck Creek doubly appropriate.

♟♟♟♟♟ **Heathcote Shiraz Malbec 2004** Impenetrable colour; massive, mouthcoating fruit, and some juicy notes from the malbec; the tannins are largely obscured, the power coming from the hyper-ripe grapes rather than extraction in the winery. Cork. 16° alc. **Rating** 92 **To** 2024 $75
Heathcote Shiraz 2004 A huge wine with black fruits, dark chocolate, prune, and again the extract and tannins are controlled – or just hidden, like the oak? Diam. 16° alc. **Rating** 91 **To** 2029 $70
Heathcote Shiraz 2005 Dense, impenetrable colour; huge blackberry, prune and plum fruit, with alcohol warmth. Curiously not tannic, and has absorbed 22 months in oak. For Robert Parker disciples. Diam. 15.5° alc. **Rating** 90 **To** 2020 $70

Rohrlach Family Wines

PO Box 864, Nuriootpa, SA 5355 **Region** Barossa Valley
T (08) 8562 4121 **F** (08) 8562 4202 **www.**rohrlachfamilywines.com.au **Open** Not
Winemaker Dan Standish (Contract) **Est.** 2000 **Cases** 1000

Brothers Kevin, Graham and Wayne Rohrlach, with wives Lyn, Lynette and Kaylene, are third-generation owners of 95 ha of prime vineyard land, the first plantings made back in 1930 by their paternal grandfather. Until 2000 the grapes were sold to two leading Barossa wineries, but (in a common story) in that year some of the grapes were retained to make the first vintage of what became Rohrlach Family Wines. In '03 the family received the ultimate local accolade when the Barons of the Barossa gave them the title of 'Vignerons of the Year'.

Barossa Shiraz 2005 Slightly unconvincing colour, but does have an interesting range of flavours from blackberry to spicy/herbal/savoury; a wine that grows on retasting, as its exceptional length becomes obvious. High-quality cork. 14.8° alc. **Rating** 94 **To** 2015 $18

Barossa Shiraz 2002 A great example of a very cool low-yielding year; has great focus, concentration and thrust through the length of the palate; spicy notes accompany black fruits, the tannins fine. Cork. 14.5° alc. **Rating** 94 **To** 2013 $18

Barossa Cabernet Merlot 2005 Savoury minty earthy nuances to the black-currant fruit on the medium-bodied palate; very fine tannins. Cork. 14.5° alc. **Rating** 88 **To** 2013 $18

Rojo Wines   NR

34 Breese Street, Brunswick, Vic 3056 **Region** Port Phillip Zone
T (03) 9386 5688 **F** (03) 9386 5699 **Open** W'ends 10–6
Winemaker Graeme Rojo **Est.** 1999 **Cases** 600

Rojo Wines is part of Melbourne's urban winery at Brunswick. Core production is cool-climate wines from the Strathbogie Ranges (Sauvignon Blanc, Chardonnay, Shiraz and Merlot). Fruit is also sourced from various regions in Victoria. Production is low, allowing maximum time to be spent with each wine through its development.

Rokewood Junction   ★★★★☆

123 Georges Road, Cambrian Hill, Vic 3352 (postal) **Region** Ballarat
T (03) 5342 0307 **F** (03) 5342 0307 **Open** Not
Winemaker Graham Jacobsson **Est.** 1995 **Cases** 200

Western District farmer Graham Jacobsson planted 0.5 ha of pinot noir on a steep north-facing slope in 1995. There are vertical slabs of shaley rock both under and on the surface, and the roots of the vines penetrate the fissures. With no top soil and a very windy, exposed site, the vineyard is basically devoid of diseases, and minimal vineyard intervention is needed. For a period of time, Jacobsson sold his grapes to Tomboy Hill, but since 2005 has made wine under his own label. No samples received; the rating is that of last year.

Rolf Binder Veritas Winery   ★★★★★

Cnr Seppeltsfield Road/Stelzer Road, Tanunda, SA 5352 **Region** Barossa Valley
T (08) 8562 3300 **F** (08) 8562 1177 **www.**rolfbinder.com **Open** Mon–Sat 10–4.30
Winemaker Rolf Binder, Christa Deans **Est.** 1955 **Cases** 30 000

The change of accent from Veritas to Rolf Binder came with the 50th anniversary of the winery, established by the parents of Rolf and sister Christa Deans. The growth in production and sales is due to the quality of the wines rather than the (hitherto) rather laid-back approach to marketing. The winery produces a full range of all the main white and red wines sourced from the Barossa and Eden Valleys. It has had conspicuous success with semillon at the Barossa Valley Wine Show, but the red wines are equally commendable. Exports to the UK, the US and other major markets.

ΨΨΨΨΨ **Hanisch Barossa Valley Shiraz 2005** Rich, wonderfully, hedonistically luscious, but not jammy; perfect tannin support (and oak) provides the magic to a very particular wine. Oh for a screwcap. Cork. 14.5° alc. **Rating** 96 **To** 2015 $95
Heysen Barossa Valley Shiraz 2005 High quality shiraz, again avoiding the overripe fruit trap, and with excellent flavour and texture complexity, but not that last drop of elixir of the Hanisch. Cork. 14.5° alc. **Rating** 94 **To** 2015 $60

ΨΨΨΨΨ **Binder's Bull's Blood Shiraz Mataro Pressings 2005** Complete with full-on retro label; blackberry and plum fruitcake flavours, the tannins far from oppressive; good length and aftertaste. Cork. 14.5° alc. **Rating** 93 **To** 2015 $50
Christa Rolf Barossa Valley Semillon 2007 Glowing yellow-green; skilled winemaking adding a light touch of French oak to a framework of lemongrass and mineral; good length and value. Screwcap. 12.5° alc. **Rating** 92 **To** 2012 $17
Heinrich Barossa Valley Shiraz Mataro Grenache 2006 Medium- to full-bodied; a powerful wine with distinctly savoury elements from the mataro (mourvedre), plus red fruits from the grenache; needs time to show its best. Screwcap. 14.5° alc. **Rating** 92 **To** 2021 $35
Christa Rolf Barossa Valley Shiraz Grenache 2005 Attractive, restrained medium-bodied wine, with fine-grained tannins supporting black cherry, plum and spice fruit; has fine, supple mouthfeel. Value. Now or in 10 years. Screwcap. 14° alc. **Rating** 91 **To** 2015 $20
Eden Valley Riesling 2007 Even and fluid in the mouth; classic lime/lime blossom, plus nuances of apple and pear. Screwcap. 12.5° alc. **Rating** 90 **To** 2012 $17
Barossa Valley Shiraz 2006 Combines elegance with regional expression; blackberry, blueberry and notes of mocha are supported by fine, ripe tannins. Screwcap. 14.5° alc. **Rating** 90 **To** 2016 $18

Romney Park Wines   ★★★★★

Lot 100, Johnson Road, Balhannah, SA 5242 **Region** Adelaide Hills
T (08) 8398 0698 **F** (08) 8398 0698 **Open** By appt
Winemaker Rod Short, Rachel Short **Est.** 1997 **Cases** 1000
Rod and Rachel Short began the planting of shiraz (3 ha), chardonnay (2ha), merlot (1.5 ha) and pinot noir (1 ha) in 1997. The first vintage was in 2002, made from 100% estate-grown grapes. Yields are limited to 1.5-2 tonnes per acre for the red wines, and 2-3 tonnes for the chardonnay. The vineyard is managed organically, with guinea fowl cleaning up the insects. Most of the grapes are sold; the limited production is sold by mail order. The property, incidentally, was previously known as Balhannah Estate. Exports to Germany.

ΨΨΨΨΨ **Reserve Adelaide Hills Pinot Noir 2006** Good hue; light-bodied, but with clear varietal fruit in a spicy/foresty spectrum; fine, long finish. Trophy Best Pinot, Adelaide Hills Wine Show '07. Cork. 14° alc. **Rating** 94 **To** 2013 $36
Reserve Adelaide Hills Shiraz 2006 Bright crimson; light- to medium-bodied, but has considerable intensity and length on the mix of black fruits and spice; fine tannins, oak a mere whisper. Diam. 14.8° alc. **Rating** 94 **To** 2016 $34
Reserve Adelaide Hills Shiraz 2005 Slightly cloudy, but good hue; powerful and intense spiced black fruits, supported by fine tannins and oak through to the long finish and aftertaste. Diam. 14.8° alc. **Rating** 94 **To** 2020 $34

ΨΨΨΨΨ **Adelaide Hills Blanc de Blancs 2004** Whole bunch-pressed (in a basket press!), barrel fermentation and taken through mlf, tiraged Sept '04; disgorged to order, this on 20/11/07; strong citrus nectarine chardonnay with bright acidity unaffected by mlf. Crown Seal. 12.5° alc. **Rating** 90 **To** 2015 $28

ΨΨΨΨ **Adelaide Hills Merlot 2005** Sweet red berry/cassis fruit, ripe tannins with a savoury twist on the aftertaste. Diam. 14.5° alc. **Rating** 87 **To** 2011 $19

Rookery Wines

PO Box 132, Kingscote, Kangaroo Island, SA 5223 **Region** Kangaroo Island
T (08) 8553 9099 **F** (08) 8553 9201 **www**.rookerywines.com.au **Open** By appt
Winemaker Garry Lovering, Geoff Weaver (Consultant) **Est.** 1999 **Cases** 2000
Garry and Gael Lovering have established a total of 8.4 ha of vines, with 3.2 ha of cabernet
sauvignon and 1.6 ha of shiraz, the remainder divided between sauvignon blanc, tempranillo,
saperavi, sangiovese, chardonnay, merlot, petit verdot and riesling. The wines are made under
the watchful eye of Geoff Weaver, as experienced as he is skilled.

Kangaroo Island Shiraz 2005 Distinct aromas of charry meat and dark fruits,
with a healthy dose of toasty oak; lovely vibrancy on the palate, and the tannins are
silky and supple. Screwcap. 14.8° alc. **Rating** 94 **To** 2016 $30.75

Kangaroo Island Cabernet Sauvignon 2005 Quite a brambly, slightly
European style, with succulent dark fruits, and quite fine-grained tannins on the
light and fresh finish. Screwcap. 14° alc. **Rating** 92 **To** 2015 $19.40
Halls Road Kangaroo Island Cabernet Sauvignon 2004 Fresh varietal
cabernet, with cassis toasty oak and a lifted perfume; good weight and flavour;
fresh acidity on the finish. Screwcap. 14.5° alc. **Rating** 90 **To** 2012 $23.65

Rosby

122 Strikes Lane, Mudgee, NSW 2850 **Region** Mudgee
T (02) 6373 3856 **F** (02) 6373 3109 **www**.rosby.com.au **Open** By appt
Winemaker Tim Stevens **Est.** 1997 **Cases** 700
Gerald and Kaye Norton-Knight have 4 ha of shiraz and 2 ha of cabernet sauvignon
established on what is truly a unique site in Mudgee. Many new vignerons like to think that
their vineyard has special qualities, but in this instance the belief is well-based. It is situated in
a small valley, with unusual red basalt over a quartz gravel structure, encouraging deep root
growth, and making the use of water far less critical than normal. Tim Stevens of Abercorn
and Huntington Estate has purchased much of the production, and has no hesitation in
saying it is of the highest quality (it formed an important part of his multi-trophy winning
A Reserve range).

Mudgee Shiraz 2005 Good concentration and depth of fruit; blackberries are
framed by leather and tar; chewy and a little juicy on the finish. Screwcap.
13.6° alc. **Rating** 87 **To** 2012 $20

 # Rose Hill Estate Wines

1400 Oxley Flats Road, Milawa, Vic 3678 **Region** King Valley
T (03) 5727 3930 **F** (03) 5727 3930 **www**.rosehillestatewines.com.au **Open** Fri–Mon 10–6
Winemaker Jo Hale **Est.** 1996 **Cases** 350
The Rose Hill vineyard, winery and house are all the work of Milawa cabinet-maker Stan
Stafford (and friends). The house, using 150-year-old bricks from a former chapel at Everton,
came first, almost 30 years ago. Then came the vineyard, with merlot planted in 1987,
and durif planted in 2002 to fill in the gaps where merlot had died. It's a strange mix of
bedfellows, but it's easy to tell which is which. In '04, after many sleepless nights weighing up
the pros and cons, Jo Hale and Kevin de Henin purchased the estate from Stan. They knew
what they were doing: Jo had helped Stan in both vineyard and winery in the last few years
while studying wine science at CSU, and working for Brown Brothers, Gapsted Wines and
Sam Miranda, while Kevin had also worked at many regional vineyards and wineries.

King Valley Merlot 2005 Clear-cut varietal character, with red fruits offset by
black olive and savoury tannins on a light- to medium-bodied palate; good length.
Screwcap. 14° alc. **Rating** 91 **To** 2014 $18

Rosebrook Estate

1092 Maitlandvale Road, Rosebrook, NSW 2320 **Region** Lower Hunter Valley
T (02) 4930 6961 **F** (02) 4930 6963 **www**.rosebrookestatewines.com.au
Open At Morpeth Wine Cellar (02) 4933 2612
Winemaker Graeme Levick **Est.** 2000 **Cases** 2000
Graeme and Tania Levick run Rosebrook Estate and Hunter River Retreat as parallel operations. They include self-contained cottages, horse-riding, tennis, canoeing, swimming, bushwalking, fishing, riverside picnic area, recreation room and minibus for winery tours and transport to functions or events in the area. Somewhere in the middle of all this they have established 2.5 ha each of chardonnay and verdelho, purchasing shiraz and muscat to complete the product range.

ΨΨΨΨΩ **River Bank Hunter Valley Shiraz 2005** Has clear but pleasing leathery earthy nuances on the bouquet; red and black fruits drive the palate, which is long and uncluttered; delicious aftertaste. Diam. 13.5° alc. **Rating** 90 **To** 2015 $18

ΨΨΨΨ **Hunter Valley Chardonnay 2006** Plenty of sweet peachy fruit and just a little oak to sustain the fruit; no fuss, drink now. Screwcap. 13° alc. **Rating** 87 **To** 2009 $15

Rosemount Estate (Hunter Valley)

Rosemount Road, Denman, NSW 2328 **Region** Upper Hunter Valley
T (02) 6549 6400 **F** (02) 6549 6499 **www**.rosemountestates.com **Open** 7 days 10–4
Winemaker Matthew Koch **Est.** 1969 **Cases** 3 million
Rosemount Estate achieved a miraculous balancing act, maintaining wine quality while presiding over an ever-expanding empire and dramatically increasing production. The wines were consistently of excellent value; all had real character and individuality, and more than a few were startlingly good. The outcome was the merger with Southcorp in 2001; what seemed to be a powerful and synergistic merger turned out to be little short of a disaster. Southcorp lost more than its market capitalisation and more than half of its most effective and talented employees. Now part of Foster's. Exports to all major markets.

ΨΨΨΨΩ **Show Reserve Western Australia Semillon Sauvignon Blanc 2007** Light-bodied; a fresh, delicate and lively mix of grass, herb, gooseberry and passionfruit, then a bright, crisp finish. Screwcap. 13° alc. **Rating** 91 **To** 2010 $20.95
Show Reserve Marlborough Sauvignon Blanc 2007 Curious labelling as Show Reserve, eligible only for a few Australian shows; nonetheless, well in Marlborough style with plenty of gooseberry fruit; long finish, good acidity. Screwcap. 13° alc. **Rating** 90 **To** 2009 $20.95
Diamond Label Sauvignon Blanc 2007 Well made with more varietal expression and intensity than many at its price point; a mix of tropical and lemon citrus fruit; good aftertaste. Screwcap. 12.5° alc. **Rating** 90 **To** 2009 $15.95
Roxburgh Chardonnay 2004 Glowing yellow-green; early-picked fruit helps tighten the flavours with a mix of stone fruit, melon and citrus, but has some stillborn aspects. Cork. 13° alc. **Rating** 90 **To** 2012 $38.95

ΨΨΨΨ **Show Reserve Chardonnay 2006** Plenty of ripe peachy fruit and even more oak; fruity, but not sweet. Screwcap. 13.5° alc. **Rating** 89 **To** 2009 $20.95
Diamond Label Pinot Noir 2007 Obvious that Foster's fruit resources now see pinot from cool regions in this deep-coloured plummy wine which has enough varietal flavour to satisfy, even though somewhat short. Screwcap. 13.5° alc. **Rating** 88 **To** 2012 $15.95
Diamond Label Shiraz 2006 Light- to medium-bodied; supple and smooth, with black cherry, plum and some blackberry fruit. Screwcap. 13.5° alc. **Rating** 88 **To** 2010 $15.95
Diamond Cellars Traminer Riesling 2007 Specifically designed for Chinese food, with juicy fruit in a lime pastille spectrum and restrained sweetness on the finish. Screwcap. 11° alc. **Rating** 87 **To** 2009 $11.95

Rosemount Estate (McLaren Vale)   ★★★★

Chaffeys Road, McLaren Vale, SA 5171 **Region** McLaren Vale
T (08) 8323 8250 **F** (08) 8323 9308 **www**.rosemountestate.com.au **Open** Mon–Sat 10–5,
Sun & public hols 11–4
Winemaker Charles Whish **Est.** 1888 **Cases** 3 million
The specialist red wine arm of Rosemount Estate, responsible for its prestigious Balmoral
Syrah, Show Reserve Shiraz and GSM, as well as most of the other McLaren Vale–based
Rosemount brands. These wines come in large measure from 325 ha of estate plantings.
Exports to all major markets.

ŸŸŸŸŸ   **Grenache Shiraz Mourvedre 2004** Manages to combine fragrance and
elegance with depth and power to the complex array of red and black fruits; soft
tannins, minimal oak. **Rating** 93 **To** 2014 $20.95
Show Reserve GSM 2004 As ever, McLaren Vale grenache has no lolly/sweet
notes, rather more to dark fruits, spices and touches of regional chocolate; good
balance and structure. Screwcap. 14.5° alc. **Rating** 92 **To** 2014 $20.95
Show Reserve Shiraz 2004 A pleasant, medium-bodied wine, with an easy mix
of red and black fruits plus touches of chocolate and vanilla. Screwcap. 14.5° alc.
Rating 90 **To** 2012 $20.95
Show Reserve Traditional 2004 Medium- to full-bodied; a powerful wine,
with cassis and blackcurrant plus contrasting notes of black olive and a dash of
chocolate; plenty of structure and depth. Cabernet Sauvignon/Merlot/Petit Verdot.
Screwcap. 14° alc. **Rating** 90 **To** 2019 $20.95

ŸŸŸŸ   **Show Reserve Coonawarra Cabernet Sauvignon 2005** Medium-bodied;
blackcurrant, with notes of spice, earth and olive; quite oaky and falters slightly on
the finish. Screwcap. 14° alc. **Rating** 89 **To** 2013 $20.95

Rosenthal Wines   ★★★☆

PO Box Y3110, East St Georges Terrace, Perth, WA 6832 **Region** Blackwood Valley
T 0407 773 966 **F** (08) 9368 6445 **www**.rosenthalwines.com.au **Open** Not
Winemaker The Vintage Wineworx (Dr Diane Miller) **Est.** 1997 **Cases** 800
Perth medical specialist Dr John Rosenthal heads Rosenthal Wines, which is a small part
of the much larger 180-ha Springfield Park cattle stud situated between Bridgetown and
Manjimup. He acquired the property from Gerald and Marjorie Richings, who in 1997 had
planted a small vineyard as a minor diversification. The Rosenthals extended the vineyard to
just under 5 ha, equally divided between shiraz, cabernet sauvignon and cabernet franc. The
wines, especially the Sparkling Shiraz, have had significant show success.

ŸŸŸŸŸ   **Cabernet Shiraz 2005** A pleasant array of redcurrant, cassis and cherry fruit on
the medium-bodied palate; silky, savoury tannins and spice; good length. Cabernet
Sauvignon/Cabernet Franc/Shiraz. Screwcap. 13° alc. **Rating** 90 **To** 2014 $25

ŸŸŸŸ   **Richings Shiraz 2005** An understated, light- to medium-bodied palate, with
gently sweet red and black fruits plus touches of spice; restrained oak and tannins;
easy access. Screwcap. 13° alc. **Rating** 89 **To** 2013 $18.50
Sparkling Shiraz 2005 A cheerful, red-fruited sparkling wine, the sweetness
within the parameters of the style; needs years on cork to grow complexity.
13.4° alc. **Rating** 87 **To** 2012 $35

Rosenvale Wines   ★★★★☆

Lot 385, Railway Terrace, Nuriootpa, SA 5355 **Region** Barossa Valley
T 0407 390 788 **F** (08) 8565 7206 **www**.rosenvale.com.au **Open** By appt
Winemaker James Rosenzweig, Mark Jamieson **Est.** 2000 **Cases** 3500
The Rosenzweig family has 80 ha of vineyards, some old and some new, planted to riesling,
semillon, pinot noir, grenache, shiraz and cabernet sauvignon. Most of the grapes are sold to
other producers, but since 1999 select parcels have been retained and vinified for release under
the Rosenvale label. Exports to the UK, the US and other major markets.

ŸŸŸŸỌ **Reserve Barossa Valley Cabernet Sauvignon 2005** Deep colour; pronounced mocha oak aromas, but very ripe and quite focused fruit; full-bodied and long, needing time for the oak to integrate. Cork. **Rating** 93 **To** 2018 $33
Estate Barossa Valley Grenache 2006 Quite complex, with elements of spice, raspberries and a hint of dark plums; good weight on the palate, with plenty of flavour. Cork. **Rating** 90 **To** 2014 $22

Rosevears Estate ★★★

1a Waldhorn Drive, Rosevears, Tas 7277 **Region** Northern Tasmania
T (03) 6330 1800 **F** (03) 6330 1810 **Open** 7 days 9–5
Winemaker Andrew Pirie **Est.** 1999 **Cases** NA
Rosevears Estate has had a turbulent track record since being established in 1999. It has now passed into the ownership of Tamar Ridge, but the brand will remain (as will Notley Gorge), and the beautifully situated winery and cellar door will showcase not only the Rosevears and Notley Gorge wines, but also the Pirie Tasmania portfolio.

ŸŸŸŸ **Gewurztraminer 2007** Good texture; ripe, full and fleshy varietal fruit, then a clean and vibrant finish. **Rating** 88 **To** 2011

Rosily Vineyard ★★★★☆

Yelveton Road, Wilyabrup, WA 6284 **Region** Margaret River
T (08) 9755 6336 **F** (08) 9221 3309 **www**.rosily.com.au **Open** W'ends 10–5,
7 days over Christmas
Winemaker Mike Lemmes, Dan Pannell (Consultant) **Est.** 1994 **Cases** 6500
The partnership of Mike and Barb Scott and Ken and Dot Allan acquired the Rosily Vineyard site in 1994. Under the direction of consultant Dan Pannell (of the Pannell family), 12 ha of vineyard were planted over the next three years: sauvignon blanc, semillon, chardonnay, cabernet sauvignon, merlot, shiraz and a little grenache and cabernet franc. The first crops were sold to other makers in the region, but in 1999 Rosily built a winery with 120-tonne capacity, and is now moving to fully utilise that capacity. Exports to the UK, Hong Kong and Singapore.

ŸŸŸŸỌ **Margaret River Merlot 2005** Good hue; clear-cut varietal expression; redcurrant and snow pea fruit with great support from fine but persistent tannins. Margaret River at work. Screwcap. 13.9° alc. **Rating** 91 **To** 2012 $20
The Cartographer 2004 Medium-bodied; the elegant Bordeaux blend works very well, no surprise given the region; juicy berry fruits lift on the finish, effectively replacing tannins. Good oak. Screwcap. 14° alc. **Rating** 91 **To** 2012 $22
Margaret River Sauvignon Blanc 2007 A clean, fresh bouquet; considerable intensity to the palate, ranging from grass and asparagus through to more tropical flavours; persistent finish. Screwcap. 13.5° alc. **Rating** 90 **To** 2009 $16
Margaret River Semillon Sauvignon Blanc 2007 A stout wine with considerable textural complexity, partly from herbal semillon fruit and part oak maturation; has grip and length; will improve. Screwcap. 13.9° alc. **Rating** 90 **To** 2012 $18
Margaret River Chardonnay 2006 Elegant and intense, with seamless line and balance of fruit, oak and acidity; just needs a little more punch. Screwcap. 13.7° alc. **Rating** 90 **To** 2013 $22

Rosnay Organic Wines ★★★

Rivers Road, Canowindra, NSW 2804 **Region** Cowra
T (02) 6344 3215 **F** (02) 6344 3229 **www**.organicfarms.com.au **Open** By appt
Winemaker Various contract **Est.** 2002 **Cases** 3000
Organic Wines is an interesting business venture of the Statham family, which moved onto the property in 1995. There are 30 ha of vineyard on the 140-ha property, part of which has been divided into 12 blocks along with 10 housing blocks, each of 5000 m². The viticulture

is organic, and the management company provides active growers or absentee investors with a range of specialist organic farming machinery and contract management. Winemaking is split between John Cassegrain of Cassegrain Wines, Kevin Karstrom of Botobolar and Rodney Hooper, each one of whom has expertise in organic grapegrowing and organic winemaking.

ΨΨΨΨ **Cowra Semillon 2004** A clean bouquet; developing slowly and still gaining weight, necessary given the light body. Screwcap. 12° alc. **Rating** 87 **To** 2011 $18
Cowra Unwooded Chardonnay Semillon 2003 Semillon and the screwcap combine to keep the wine fresh, albeit a little reduced; first tasted Dec '03, and is now a far better wine, although still light-bodied. **Rating** 87 **To** 2009 $18

Ross Estate Wines   ★★★★

Barossa Valley Way, Lyndoch, SA 5351 **Region** Barossa Valley
T (08) 8524 4033 **F** (08) 8524 4533 **www**.rossestate.com.au **Open** 7 days 10–4
Winemaker Neville Falkenberg, Alex Peel **Est.** 1999 **Cases** 18 000
Darius and Pauline Ross laid the foundation for Ross Estate Wines when they purchased 43 ha of vines which included two blocks of 75- and 90-year-old grenache. Also included were blocks of 30-year-old riesling and semillon, and 13-year-old merlot. Chardonnay, sauvignon blanc, cabernet sauvignon, cabernet franc and shiraz followed. Neville Falkenberg has moved to Ross Estate from Chain of Ponds to take the place of Rod Chapman, who has retired. Exports to the UK, the US and other major markets.

ΨΨΨΨΨ **Estate Barossa Valley Riesling 2007** Considerable depth to the flavour, and has strong structure, holding the fruit together; very impressive show record, but drink soon. Screwcap. 13° alc. **Rating** 91 **To** 2012 $16
Estate Barossa Valley Shiraz 2005 Smooth and supple medium- to full-bodied wine; abundant blackberry fruit supported by mocha/vanilla oak and ripe tannins. ProCork. 14.5° alc. **Rating** 91 **To** 2017 $26
Single Vineyard Old Vine Barossa Valley Grenache 2006 Attractive medium-bodied wine, the 96-year-old vines doing the talking through fresh red fruits and silky tannins; no confection fruit. Bargain. Screwcap. 14.5° alc. **Rating** 91 **To** 2014 $19
ROSS Barossa Valley Shiraz 2006 Mainstream medium-bodied Barossa Valley shiraz; clear-cut blackberry fruit with overtones of chocolate and mocha; rounded mouthfeel, ripe tannins. Screwcap. 14.5° alc. **Rating** 90 **To** 2016 $18

ΨΨΨΨ **Estate Barossa Valley Cabernet Sauvignon 2004** Strong, verging on rustic structure and flavours; black fruits, earth and tannins interwoven; heavily stained cork ominous. 14° alc. **Rating** 89 **To** 2013 $25
Lynedoch 2005 Light- to medium-bodied; savoury earthy minty overtones, but the mouthfeel is supple and the finish not green; catches up on you. Cork. 14° alc. **Rating** 89 **To** 2013 $25
Barossa Valley Chardonnay 2007 Lively lemony acidity lifts the wine out of the ruck, especially commendable in the warm vintage; stone fruit flavours supported by subtle oak. Screwcap. 14° alc. **Rating** 88 **To** 2011 $16

Ross Hill Vineyard   ★★★★

62 Griffin Road, Orange, NSW 2800 **Region** Orange
T (02) 6360 0175 **F** (02) 6363 1674 **www**.rosshillwines.com.au **Open** Sat 11–5 or by appt
Winemaker David Lowe (Contract) **Est.** 1994 **Cases** 4000
Peter and Terri Robson began planting 10 ha of vines in 1994. Chardonnay, sauvignon blanc, merlot, cabernet sauvignon, shiraz and cabernet franc have been established on north-facing, gentle slopes at an elevation of 800 m. No insecticides are used in the vineyard, the grapes are hand-picked and the vines are hand-pruned. Ross Hill also has an olive grove with Italian and Spanish varieties.

♀♀♀♀♀ Isabelle Orange Cabernet Franc Merlot 2006 Abundant flavour, with a seamless mix of red and black fruits running through a long palate; a rare blend which seldom succeeds as well as this. Screwcap. 13.5° alc. **Rating** 93 **To** 2016 **$25**
Jack's Lot Limited Release Orange Cabernet Franc 2006 Spicy cedary red berry aromas and flavours; medium-bodied, with good length and focus; a difficult variety, here dry-grown on a high, rocky east-facing slope to produce a wine full of interest. Cork. 15° alc. **Rating** 92 **To** 2016 **$40**
Orange Cabernet Sauvignon 2006 A powerful wine by any standards; flush with ripe blackcurrant fruit balanced by ripe tannins and oak; stained cork a worry. 15° alc. **Rating** 91 **To** 2016 **$28**

♀♀♀♀ Orange Merlot 2006 Crimson-purple; ripe blackcurrant and cassis; full-blooded wannabe cabernet, but will appeal to many for its generous fruit, and will develop. Screwcap. **Rating** 88 **To** 2016 **$22**

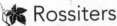# Rossiters

PO Box 25, Toorak, Vic 3142 **Region** Murray Darling
T (03) 5024 0455 **F** (03) 5024 0455 **Open** Not
Winemaker Karl Feddern **Est.** 1997 **Cases** NFP
Karl and Sue Feddern established a 10-ha vineyard near Red Cliffs, giving substance to a love of wine gained during their years as successful restaurateurs. They have planted 4.65 ha of shiraz, 2.8 ha of colombard and 2 ha of cabernet sauvignon, with small amounts of lagrein, barbera and vermentino. Most of the grapes are sold, a small amount retained for the Rossiters label.

♀♀♀♀ Lagrein 2002 Remarkable colour retention, and likewise red cherry, strawberry and plum fruit; a relative lack of structure, but extraordinary how the variety has prospered in a climate theoretically far too warm. Stained cork. 13° alc. **Rating** 88 **To** 2011 **$19.50**
Cabernet Sauvignon 2006 Good outcome for the region; light- to medium-bodied, with juicy cassis and raspberry fruit; fresh finish. Screwcap. 13.5° alc. **Rating** 87 **To** 2009 **$14**

Roundstone Winery & Vineyard

54 Willow Bend Drive, Yarra Glen, Vic 3775 **Region** Yarra Valley
T (03) 9730 1181 **F** (03) 9730 1151 **www.**roundstonewine.com.au **Open** Wed–Sun & public hols 10–5, or by appt
Winemaker John Derwin **Est.** 1998 **Cases** 5000
John and Lynne Derwin have moved quickly since establishing Roundstone, planting 8 ha of vineyard (half to pinot noir with a mix of the best clones), building a small winery and opening a cellar door and restaurant. The Derwins tend the vineyard, enlisting the aid of friends to pick the grapes; John makes the wine with advice from Rob Dolan; Lynne is the chef and sommelier. Her pride and joy is a shearer's stove which was used at the Yarra Glen Grand Hotel for 100 years before being abandoned. The restaurant has established itself as one of the best winery restaurants in the valley. Exports to Ireland.

♀♀♀♀♀ Yarra Valley Basket Pressed Viognier 2006 A pure example of viognier; apricots and spice, with a fleshy, yet focused and vibrant palate. Screwcap. 13° alc. **Rating** 90 **To** 2009 **$28**
Yarra Valley Cabernet Merlot 2005 Light- to medium-bodied; a fresh array of red and black fruits in a cassis spectrum; fine tannins and supple finish; attractive wine. Screwcap. 13° alc. **Rating** 90 **To** 2014 **$22**

♀♀♀♀ Lynette Pinot Noir 2006 Soft and clean, with a little beet and spice personality; soft and ample on the finish. Screwcap. 13° alc. **Rating** 87 **To** 2009 **$20**

Rowans Lane Wines

★★★

10 Farnham Road, Dennington, Vic 3280 **Region** Henty
T (03) 5565 1586 **F** (03) 5565 1586 **www**.rowanslanewines.com.au **Open** W'ends & public hols 10.30–5 or by appt
Winemaker Ted Rafferty **Est.** 2003 **Cases** 500

Ted and Judy Rafferty expanded their lifetime interest in wine by establishing an experimental 0.8-ha vineyard at their Rowans Lane property in 1999, making their first Pinot Noir in 2003. This encouraged them to expand their plantings to 3.6 ha at a second site at Dennington, on the banks of the Merri River. To supplement their own production, they have purchased grapes from other leading Henty grapegrowers, each with an impressive track record.

Botrytis Chardonnay 2007 Dried quince, candied fruit and fresh lemons are on show; a quite sweet mid-palate, but the finish is surprisingly light and dry. Cork. 14.3° alc. **Rating** 88 **To** 2012 **$18**

Rowanston on the Track

★★★★

2710 Burke & Wills Track, Glenhope, Vic 3444 **Region** Macedon Ranges
T (03) 5425 5492 **F** (03) 5425 5493 **Open** Fri–Sun 9–5, or by appt
Winemaker John Frederiksen **Est.** 2003 **Cases** 800

John (a social worker) and Marilyn (a former teacher turned viticulturist) Frederiksen are no strangers to grapegrowing and winemaking in the Macedon Ranges. They founded Metcalfe Valley Vineyard in 1995, planting 5.6 ha of shiraz, going on to win gold medals at local wine shows. They sold the vineyard in early 2003, moving to their new property in the same year, which has 4 ha of shiraz, 2 ha of merlot (planted between 1998 and 2000), and 2 ha of pinot noir and 1.3 ha of riesling (planted between '00 and '02).

Rubicon

★★★☆

186 Blue Range Road, Rubicon, Vic 3172 **Region** Upper Goulburn
T (03) 9802 2174 **F** (03) 9803 2844 **Open** By appt
Winemaker Robert Zagar **Est.** 2004 **Cases** 800

Douglas Gordan and wife Lillian purchased Rubicon in 2004, intending to expand their cattle enterprise. The property included a 6-ha vineyard planted in 1992 to chardonnay, pinot noir and cabernet sauvignon by the original owners. When the sale of the grapes fell through, Douglas Gordan decided to have the wines made. Douglas is studying viticulture/wine production at Swinburne TAFE, and manages the vineyard using minimal intervention techniques with the help of his family.

Lorna's Vintage Upper Goulburn Chardonnay 2006 Light crisp mix of citrus, stone fruit and mineral, oak appropriately restrained; the length does grow on retasting; twin top a pity. 13.5° alc. **Rating** 88 **To** 2010

Russell Wines

★★★★★

45 Murray Street, Angaston, SA 5353 **Region** Barossa Valley
T (08) 8564 2511 **F** (08) 8564 2533 **www**.russellwines.com.au **Open** By appt
Winemaker Shawn Kalleske (Contract) **Est.** 2001 **Cases** 3000

John Russell (and wife Rosalind) came to the Barossa in 1990 to create the Barossa Music Festival. The winemaking bug soon bit, and in '94 they planted 14 ha of vines at Krondorf, expanded over the years to 32 ha on three vineyards (St Vincent, Augusta and Greenock Farm), which in turn give rise to the three labels. The cellar door is situated in the old Angaston Court House, where wine, food, music and art exhibitions are all on offer. Shawn Kalleske not only makes the wine, but oversees both his and Russell Wines' vineyards; a substantial part of the production from the latter is sold to other Barossa wineries.

♟♟♟♟♟ **The Victor Greenock Farm Barossa Valley Shiraz 2005** An ultra-rich, ripe and velvety array of plum, prune and blackberry fruits plus a touch of licorice manages to carry the formidable alcohol well. Cork. 15.5° alc. **Rating** 94 **To** 2020 $85

St Vincent Barossa Valley Shiraz 2004 Deep purple-red; a dense and rich wine, with masses of black fruits, earth and licorice; powerful but balanced tannins, good oak. Cork. 14.9° alc. **Rating** 94 **To** 2019 $45

♟♟♟♟♀ **St Vincent Barossa Valley Chardonnay 2005** Still fresh, and with uncommon ·line and drive to the grapefruit and nectarine flavours; must be a very cool site in the Valley. Screwcap. 13.8° alc. **Rating** 93 **To** 2014 $20

Augusta Shiraz 2001 Strongly oaked, but vibrant and fresh; nice weight and good fruit concentration; ripe tannins on the full-fruited finish. Cork. 14.3° alc. **Rating** 91 **To** 2016 $30

Augusta Barossa Valley Shiraz Cabernet 2004 Very good colour; a dense and powerful array of blackberry fruits, plus strands of licorice, dark chocolate and mocha; good balance and length. Cork. 14.8° alc. **Rating** 91 **To** 2014 $25

Greenock Farm The Fenceline 2005 Grenache/Shiraz/Mourvedre/Semillon/ Riesling/Red Frontignac/White Frontignac/Tokay; where is the viognier? Just when you think the white components are miniscule, the influence of the frontis comes in; this is a weirdo of gargantuan proportions. Cork. 15.5° alc. **Rating** 90 **To** 2015 $85

Augusta Shiraz 2005 Exceedingly oaky, but very good fruit beneath; needs time to fully integrate, but certainly a powerful wine. Cork. 14.5° alc. **Rating** 90 **To** 2018 $25

♟♟♟♟ **St Vincent Barossa Valley Cabernet Sauvignon 2005** Slightly hazy hue; a firm mix of black and redcurrant fruit, with a slight prickle of CO_2; has length, needs time. Cork. 14° alc. **Rating** 88 **To** 2015 $30

Rusticana ★★★★☆

Lake Plains Road, Langhorne Creek, SA 5255 **Region** Langhorne Creek
T (08) 8537 3086 **F** (08) 8537 3220 **www**.rusticanawines.com.au **Open** 7 days 10–5
Winemaker Bremerton Wines **Est.** 1998 **Cases** 2400
Brian and Anne Meakins are also owners of Newman's Horseradish, which has been on the SA market for over 80 years. Increasing demand for the horseradish forced them to move from Tea Tree Gully to Langhorne Creek in 1985. It wasn't until 1997 that they succumbed to the urging of neighbours and planted 5 ha each of shiraz and cabernet, adding 1 ha each of durif and zinfandel several years later. In a slightly unusual arrangement, the premium Black Label wines are made at Bremerton, the White Label range at the Langhorne Creek winery. No samples received, the rating is that of last year.

Rutherglen Estates

Cnr Great Northern Road/Murray Valley Highway, Rutherglen, Vic 3685 **Region** Rutherglen
T (02) 6032 7999 **F** (02) 6032 7998 **www**.rutherglenestates.com.au **Open** At Tuileries Building, Rutherglen 7 days 10–6
Winemaker Nicole Esdaile, Ricky James **Est.** 2000 **Cases** 50 000
Rutherglen Estates is an offshoot of a far larger contract crush-and-make business, with a winery capacity of 4000 tonnes (roughly equivalent to 280 000 cases). Rutherglen is in a declared phylloxera region, which means all the grapes grown within that region have to be vinified within it, itself a guarantee of business for ventures such as Rutherglen Estates. It also means that some of the best available material can be allocated for the brand, with an interesting mix of varieties. Smart, upgraded, packaging is yet another part of the marketing mix. Exports to the UK, the US and other major markets.

ﾏﾏﾏﾏﾏ **Shiraz 2006** Developed, but has real finesse and life, an achievement given the region, long and soft in the mouth. **Rating** 92 **To** 2013 $19.95
Renaissance Petit Sirah 2005 Concentrated, focused, earthy black fruits, licorice and earth flavours; not over-extracted, and has good length; will develop slowly but well. Screwcap. 14.5° alc. **Rating** 91 **To** 2015 $39.95
Renaissance Viognier Roussanne Marsanne 2006 Well-constructed and balanced, with a range of yellow peach, apricot and honey flavours starting to build, sustained by good acidity. Screwcap. 14° alc. **Rating** 90 **To** 2014 $30.95
Renaissance Zinfandel 2006 Bright colour, and bright aromas and flavours; black and red cherry, raspberry and a twist of lemon zest; good finish. Screwcap. 14.5° alc. **Rating** 90 **To** 2014 $34.95

Rymill Coonawarra ★★★★☆

Riddoch Highway, Coonawarra, SA 5263 **Region** Coonawarra
T (08) 8736 5001 **F** (08) 8736 5040 **www**.rymill.com.au **Open** 7 days 10–5
Winemaker John Innes, Sandrine Gimon **Est.** 1974 **Cases** 50 000
The Rymills are descendants of John Riddoch and have long owned some of the finest Coonawarra soil, upon which they have grown grapes since 1970; present plantings are 150 ha. The output from the modern winery is substantial, the quality dependable rather than exciting. Quite why this should be so is an interesting question without an obvious answer. Exports to all major markets.

ﾏﾏﾏﾏﾏ **Sauvignon Blanc 2007** Grass, herb and asparagus aromas; an intense and vibrant palate with excellent line and citrus-accented fruit plus a few tropical notes. Trophy Limestone Coast Wine Show '07. **Rating** 94 **To** 2010 $17

ﾏﾏﾏﾏﾏ **The Yearling Cabernet Sauvignon 2006** Excellent value; fresh and vibrant, with no compromise on varietal fruit in classic blackcurrant mulberry earth Coonawarra fashion; no oak apparent. Diam. 13.5° alc. **Rating** 90 **To** 2010 $13
Cabernet Sauvignon 2005 Blackcurrant, mulberry and spicy fruit; good integration of French oak builds the flavour; fine tannins and good length. Cork. 13.5° alc. **Rating** 90 **To** 2015 $28.50

ﾏﾏﾏﾏ **MC2 Cabernet Sauvignon Merlot Cabernet Franc 2005** Nicely balanced and weighted, with cassis, blackcurrant and mint fruit; good oak integration. **Rating** 89 **To** 2014 $17
Shiraz 2004 Bright colour and an equally bright and fresh light- to medium-bodied palate with red and black fruits, and a quite tangy finish. Diam. 14° alc. **Rating** 88 **To** 2012 $23

Saddlers Creek ★★★☆

Marrowbone Road, Pokolbin, NSW 2320 **Region** Lower Hunter Valley
T (02) 4991 1770 **F** (02) 4991 2482 **www**.saddlerscreekwines.com.au **Open** 7 days 9–5
Winemaker John Johnstone **Est.** 1989 **Cases** 20 000
Made an impressive entrance to the district with full-flavoured and rich wines, and has continued on in much the same vein, with good wines across the spectrum. Exports to Canada, NZ and Mauritius.

Sailors Falls Estate

1073 Telegraph Road, Sailors Falls, Vic 3460 **Region** Macedon Ranges
T (03) 5438 6626 **F** (03) 9370 8813 **www**.sailorsfallsestate.com.au **Open** W'ends & public hols 11–5 or by appt
Winemaker Eastern Peake (Norman Latta) **Est.** 1999 **Cases** 100
Robert and Margaret McDonald run a combined luxury B&B operation in tandem with a little under 2 ha of vineyard planted to pinot gris, pinot noir, chardonnay, gewurztraminer and a touch of gamay. The accommodation is set at the end of the vineyard, with up to six people accommodated in two luxury villa units. A forest trail leads from the vineyard to the Sailors Falls waterfalls and many other attractions typical of the beautiful Daylesford area.

ŶŶŶŶ Pinot Noir 2005 Retains good hue; surprising power for age and region; dark fruits and some spice; stalls a little on the finish; nonetheless, good effort. Screwcap. 13° alc. **Rating** 87 **To** 2011 $22

Salet Wines   NR

PO Box 19, Currarong, NSW 2540 **Region** Warehouse
T (02) 4448 3999 **F** (02) 4448 3999 **www**.salet.com.au **Open** By appt
Winemaker Michael Salecich **Est.** 2002 **Cases** 700
Michael Salecich hails from Croatia, where his family has made wine for many generations. His winemaking methods are strongly influenced by the practices of his Croatian family, who he visits each year. He buys his grapes from SA, bringing them to his onsite winery in refrigerated trucks. Here the wines are crushed and fermented, and then matured in shaved hogsheads for three and a half years, in the style of Barolo made the traditional way. Difficult to judge by normal standards.

Salitage

Vasse Highway, Pemberton, WA 6260 **Region** Pemberton
T (08) 9776 1771 **F** (08) 9776 1772 **www**.salitage.com.au **Open** 7 days 10–4
Winemaker Patrick Coutts, Greg Kelly **Est.** 1989 **Cases** 20 000
Salitage is the showpiece of Pemberton. If it had failed to live up to expectations, it is a fair bet the same fate would have befallen the whole of the Pemberton region. The quality and style of Salitage did once vary substantially, presumably in response to vintage conditions and yields, but since 1999 has found its way, with a succession of attractive wines. Exports to the UK, the US and other major markets.

ŶŶŶŶŶ Sauvignon Blanc 2007 A fragrant and floral bouquet of passionfruit blossom and honeysuckle, then a lively, crisp palate, long and quite intense; very good outcome for the vintage; well made. Screwcap. 13° alc. **Rating** 93 **To** 2010 $24
Chardonnay 2006 Crisp, clean and lively, reflecting its relatively low alcohol; stone fruit and citrus, pronounced acidity on the finish; restrained oak. Screwcap. 12.5° alc. **Rating** 92 **To** 2011 $37
Pinot Noir 2005 A complex bouquet with a whisper of reduction/stalky notes; relatively light-bodied, but has length to the firm mix of spicy, savoury fruit promised by the bouquet. Screwcap. 14° alc. **Rating** 92 **To** 2011 $42
Treehouse Chardonnay Verdelho 2007 An interesting blend, and – even more interesting – freshness and life at this alcohol level; an attractive tropical and citrus mix. Screwcap. 14.5° alc. **Rating** 90 **To** 2010 $17

ŶŶŶŶ Treehouse Sauvignon Blanc 2007 Elegant and quite delicate; more minerally and spicy than the more expensive version; nicely balanced, and a crisp, dry finish. Screwcap. 13.5° alc. **Rating** 89 **To** 2009 $20
Pemberton Unwooded Chardonnay 2007 Clean, fresh and crisp; light melon and stone fruit; shortens slightly. Screwcap. 13.5° alc. **Rating** 88 **To** 2009 $21
Treehouse Chardonnay 2007 A somewhat reduced bouquet almost immediately offset by very ripe peachy fruit; plenty of overall flavour. Screwcap. 14° alc. **Rating** 87 **To** 2009 $17
Pinot Noir 2006 Shows early-picked characters throughout, with herbal green aspects to both the bouquet and palate; does have length and might possibly soften and open up a little. Screwcap. 12.5° alc. **Rating** 87 **To** 2011 $40

Sally's Paddock

Redbank Winery, 1 Sally's Lane, Redbank, Vic 3478 **Region** Pyrenees
T (03) 5467 7255 **F** (03) 5467 3478 **www**.sallyspaddock.com.au **Open** Mon–Sat 9–5, Sun 10–5
Winemaker Neill Robb **Est.** 1973 **Cases** 6400

The Redbank brand and stocks (Long Paddock, etc) were acquired by the Hill Smith Family Vineyards (aka Yalumba) several years ago. The winery and surrounding vineyard which produces Sally's Paddock were retained by Neill and Sally Robb, and continue to produce (and sell) this single-vineyard, multi-varietal red wine and the Sally's Hill range. There is some disagreement on the use of the Redbank Winery name (see Redbank Victoria entry), but there is no dispute about Sally's Paddock. Exports to the US, Germany and Asia.

ŸŸŸŸŸ **Sally's Paddock 2005** Fragrant and lighter-bodied than Sally's Hill; lively earthy tones to the Bordeaux blend of this wine; rough edges on the finish need to settle down. Diam. 13.5° alc. **Rating** 91 **To** 2015 $57.80
Sally's Hill Cabernet 2005 Powerful, concentrated, earthy wine, with classic, slightly severe, cabernet fruit, finishing with firm tannins; demands patience. Diam. 13.5° alc. **Rating** 90 **To** 2015 $21.90

ŸŸŸŸ **Sally's Hill Chardonnay 2006** Plenty of flavour to the ripe stone fruit of the mid-palate, a touch of oak also present; somewhat static in the mouth. Diam. 13.5° alc. **Rating** 88 **To** 2011 $21.90

Salomon Estate   ★★★★★

PO Box 829, McLaren Vale, SA 5171 **Region** Southern Fleurieu
T 0417 808 243 **F** (08) 8323 8668 **www**.salomonwines.com **Open** Not
Winemaker Bert Salomon, Simon White, Boar's Rock (Mike Farmilo) **Est.** 1997 **Cases** 7000
Bert Salomon is an Austrian winemaker with a long-established family winery in the Kremstal region, not far from Vienna. He became acquainted with Australia during his time with import company Schlumberger in Vienna; he was the first to import Australian wines (Penfolds) into Austria in the mid-1980s, and later became head of the Austrian Wine Bureau. He was so taken by Adelaide that he moved his family there for the first few months each year, sending his young children to school and setting in place an Australian red winemaking venture. He retired from the Bureau, and now is a full-time travelling winemaker, running the family winery in the northern hemisphere vintage, and overseeing the making of the Salomon Estate wines at Boar's Rock in the first half of the year. The circle closes as Mike Farmilo, former Penfolds chief red winemaker, now makes Salomon Estate wines. Exports to the UK, the US, and other major markets.

ŸŸŸŸŸ **Finniss River Shiraz 2005** Rich, ripe, bold and oaky, a tale of varied styles; distinctly warm fruited and Australian, but with a tarry, almost chewy European edge which speaks volumes of its heritage. Cork. 14.5° alc. **Rating** 94 **To** 2015 $40
Bin 4 Baan Shiraz & Company 2006 Elegant, distinctly spicy/savoury wine; medium-bodied, but has length to the blackberry fruit and a twist of cassis; true finesse. Shiraz and a touch of Merlot. Twin top. 14.5° alc. **Rating** 94 **To** 2014 $23
Altus Red 2001 Fully mature, but with lovely texture, weight and ample flesh on the slightly salty, leathery finish; a truly savoury wine that delivers what it has set out to achieve. Cork. 14.5° alc. **Rating** 94 **To** 2010 $110 $26

ŸŸŸŸŸ **Norwood Shiraz Cabernet Merlot 2006** A synergistic blend harmoniously bringing together plum, blackberry, blackcurrant and dark chocolate; finishes with ripe tannins and mocha oak. Cork. 14° alc. **Rating** 91 **To** 2016 $26

Salt Collins   ★★★

Locked Mail Bag No 6, Sydney, NSW 2000 **Region** Warehouse
T (02) 9958 3373 **F** (02) 9958 3373 **www**.saltcollins.com.au **Open** Not
Winemaker Various contract **Est.** 2005 **Cases** NA
This is a full-blown virtual winery, owning neither vineyards nor winery. Gary Collins is a 22-year veteran of the wine industry in Sydney, and CEO Peter Salt, who works in the recruitment industry, has turned a consumer's love of wine into a business enterprise. The partners seek out premium parcels of grapes, and then employ winemakers such as James Kellie (in Great Southern, WA) to make the wines.

ȚȚȚȚ **Tranquility Sauvignon Blanc 2005** A mix of gently tropical fruit and lemony/ citrussy acidity, the latter holding the wine together nicely. Screwcap. **Rating** 88 **To** 2009 $20

Saltram ★★★★★

Nuriootpa Road, Angaston, SA 5355 **Region** Barossa Valley
T (08) 8561 0200 **F** (08) 8561 0232 **www**.saltramwines.com.au **Open** Mon–Fri 9–5, w'ends & public hols 10–5
Winemaker Caroline Dunn **Est.** 1859 **Cases** 150 000
There is no doubt that Saltram has taken giant strides towards regaining the reputation it held 30 or so years ago. Under Nigel Dolan's stewardship, grape sourcing has come back to the Barossa Valley for the flagship wines, a fact of which he is rightly proud. The red wines, in particular, have enjoyed great show success over the past few years, with No. 1 Shiraz, Mamre Brook and Metala leading the charge. Nigel Dolan retired in late 2007, taking with him the best wishes of all in the industry who knew him. Exports to the UK, the US and other major markets.

ȚȚȚȚȚ **Metala Original Plantings Langhorne Creek Shiraz 2004** A beautifully framed and focused wine, the fruit at once intense yet delicately fine, with a shimmering mix of plum, blackberry and warm spice. Cork. 14° alc. **Rating** 96 **To** 2019 $56.95
Mamre Brook Barossa Shiraz 2005 Deep colour; unashamedly full-bodied with masses of blackberry fruit and firm but ripe tannins; good oak and great length. Cork. 15° alc. **Rating** 94 **To** 2020 $26.95
The Eighth Maker Barossa Shiraz 2004 Exemplifies the strengths of the '04 vintage, the wines getting better and better as they go through the first years of development; fluid black fruits, silky tannins and very good oak. Cork. **Rating** 94 **To** 2019 $199.95
Pepperjack Barossa Shiraz Viognier 2006 Full-on shiraz viognier, with a major impact from the viognier on the rich and mouthfilling palate. Gold, National Wine Show '07. **Rating** 94 **To** 2014 $23.95

ȚȚȚȚȚ **Mamre Brook Eden Valley Riesling 2007** Lemon and lime fruit aromas and flavours; quite penetrating acidity running through the long finish. Screwcap. 11° alc. **Rating** 93 **To** 2015 $26.95
No. 1 Barossa Shiraz 2005 In typical No. 1 style, with rich, multiple layers of black fruits swathed in oak; good mouthfeel and length. **Rating** 93 **To** 2025 $69.95
Mamre Brook Barossa Cabernet Sauvignon 2005 A powerful, intense, full-bodied palate with blackcurrant and mulberry varietal character; stout tannins and oak underline the structure. Cork. 15° alc. **Rating** 93 **To** 2020 $26.95
Shadowood Eden Valley Chardonnay 2007 Attractively smooth mouthfeel to melon and white peach fruit; perfectly integrated oak; punches above its weight. Screwcap. 13.5° alc. **Rating** 90 **To** 2012 $24.95
Pepperjack Barossa Shiraz 2006 Deep colour; full-bodied, powerful palate with blackberry, prune, plum and some savoury notes; should repay extended cellaring. Screwcap. 15° alc. **Rating** 90 **To** 2020 $25.95

ȚȚȚȚ **Shadowood Barossa Semillon 2007** Joins the rush to emulate the Hunter Valley in the Barossa; tight, crisp and lemony, with good acidity; has development potential. Screwcap. 11.5° alc. **Rating** 89 **To** 2014 $24.95
Metala Original Plantings Langhorne Creek Shiraz 2002 Expected colour development; strong savoury aspects to both bouquet and palate; has length, but not much flesh. Cork. 14° alc. **Rating** 89 **To** 2012 $45
Pepperjack Barossa Cabernet Sauvignon 2006 A solid medium- to full-bodied wine, with plenty of blackberry fruit and sustained tannins; overall, rather butch. Cork. 14.5° alc. **Rating** 89 **To** 2014 $25.95

Pepperjack Barossa Grenache Rose 2007 Vivid fuschia; has an abundance of raspberry fruit suggesting an off-dry finish is coming, but it is in fact dry. Screwcap. 14.5° alc. **Rating** 87 **To** 2009 $23.95

Pepperjack Barossa Cabernet Sauvignon 2005 A pleasant, medium-bodied wine with enough blackcurrant and plum fruit to satisfy, but not to enthral. Cork. 15° alc. **Rating** 87 **To** 2012 $22.95

Sam Miranda of King Valley ★★★☆

1019 Snow Road, Oxley, Vic 3678 **Region** King Valley
T (03) 5727 3888 **F** (03) 5727 3853 **www**.sammiranda.com.au **Open** 7 days 10–5
Winemaker Sam Miranda **Est.** 2004 **Cases** 14 000

Sam Miranda, grandson of Francesco Miranda, joined the family business in 1991, striking out on his own in '04 after Miranda Wines was purchased by McGuigan Simeon. The High Plains Vineyard is in the Upper King Valley at an altitude of 450 m; 12 ha of vines are supplemented by some purchased grapes. In 2005 Sam Miranda purchased the Symphonia Wines business, and intends to keep its identity intact and separate from the Sam Miranda brand. Rewarded with gold medals for its 2006 Saperavi and '06 Las Triadas Tempranillo.

ΥΥΥΥΥ **Girls Block Cabernet Sauvignon Petit Verdot 2004** Crimson hue; as fresh as the colour suggests, and has absorbed 15 months in new French oak; bright juicy red and black fruits; low pH style. Cork. 14° alc. **Rating** 90 **To** 2014 $34

ΥΥΥΥ **High Plains Chardonnay 2005** A lively, crisp, firm style with focused stone fruit and citrus flavours; good length, and has developed well. Screwcap. 13.2° alc. **Rating** 88 **To** 2009 $16

High Plains Cabernet Sauvignon 2006 Light- to medium-bodied; good texture and structure, likewise varietal fruit definition in cassis blackcurrant spectrum; good tannins and French oak. Screwcap. 14° alc. **Rating** 88 **To** 2013 $17

Limited Release Late Harvest Petit Manseng 2006 An extremely rare wine; some lime, pear and nectarine fruit characters; not complex, but has good balance and may repay short-term cellaring. Screwcap. 13° alc. **Rating** 88 **To** 2011 $35

High Plains Merlot 2006 Good colour; impressively robust, albeit with a structure outside the normal varietal range; aggressive tannins. Screwcap. 13.8° alc. **Rating** 87 **To** 2012 $17

High Plains Durif 2005 Smooth, relatively low key version of the variety; both alcohol and tannin extract well-controlled on the supple, medium-bodied palate. Screwcap. 14.5° alc. **Rating** 87 **To** 2009 $17

Sparkling Shiraz Durif 2004 Full-bodied style; the dosage doesn't cover phenolics sufficiently, but prolonged cork age could see the wine soften. Cork. 14° alc. **Rating** 87 **To** 2014 $30

Samuel's Gorge ★★★★★

Lot 10 Chaffeys Road, McLaren, SA 5171 **Region** McLaren Vale
T (08) 8323 8651 **F** (08) 8323 8673 **www**.gorge.com.au **Open** First w'end of spring until sold out, or by appt
Winemaker Justin McNamee **Est.** 2003 **Cases** 1250

After a wandering winemaking career in various parts of the world, Justin McNamee became a winemaker at Tatachilla in 1996, where he remained until 2003, leaving to found Samuel's Gorge. He has established his winery in a barn built in 1853, part of a historic property known as the old Seaview Homestead. The property was owned by Sir Samuel Way, variously Chief Justice of the South Australian Supreme Court and Lieutenant Governor of the State. The grapes come from small contract growers spread across the ever-changing (unofficial) subregions of McLaren Vale, and are basket-pressed and fermented in old open slate fermenters lined with beeswax – with impressive results.

ΥΥΥΥΥ **McLaren Vale Shiraz 2005** Complex aromas of blackberry, bitter chocolate and a touch of earth; a very powerful and equally long palate reflects the same characters right through to the finish. Cork. 14.5° alc. **Rating** 95 **To** 2020 $40

McLaren Vale Grenache 2005 A rich, utterly persuasive wine, simultaneously highlighting the region (via depth and that dash of chocolate) and variety (courtesy of strong red fruit). Cork. 14.5° alc. **Rating** 94 **To** 2015 $40

McLaren Vale Tempranillo 2006 Abundant colour; more richness, depth of flavour and structure than the vast majority of Australian tempranillos; complete and satisfying; will cellar well. Cork. 14.5° alc. **Rating** 94 **To** 2015 $40

Sandalford ★★★★★

3210 West Swan Road, Caversham, WA 6055 **Region** Margaret River
T (08) 9374 9374 **F** (08) 9274 2154 **www**.sandalford.com **Open** 7 days 10–5
Winemaker Paul Boulden, Hope Metcalf **Est.** 1840 **Cases** 100 000

Some years ago the upgrading of the winery and the appointment of Paul Boulden as chief winemaker resulted in far greater consistency in quality, and the proper utilisation of the excellent vineyard resources of the 96-ha vineyard planted in 1970. Things have continued on an even keel since, with the entry level Element range (from various parts of WA), Protege (from Margaret River) at the mid-level, and Single Vineyard Estate (Margaret River) at the top level. Exports to all major markets.

ΨΨΨΨΨ **Prendiville Reserve Margaret River Cabernet Sauvignon 2005** Shows the additional oak impact of 24 months in new French oak, but also the superior fruit; classic cassis and blackcurrant fruit plus balanced and fully integrated tannins. Screwcap. 14.5° alc. **Rating** 96 **To** 2025 $90

Estate Reserve Sauvignon Blanc Semillon 2007 A delicious wine; lovely flow and feel to the citrus, gooseberry and passionfruit flavours; tight acidity balances a hint of sweetness. Gold medal, National Wine Show '07. Screwcap. 12.5° alc. **Rating** 94 **To** 2010 $19.95

Estate Reserve Margaret River Shiraz 2004 A fresh and vibrant wine, with an array of red and black fruits; barrel ferment adds to spicy flavours and the harmony of the oak. Screwcap. 14.5° alc. **Rating** 94 **To** 2024 $33.95

Estate Reserve Cabernet Sauvignon 2005 Elegant, medium-bodied, with clear cassis and blackcurrant fruit; has completely absorbed 18 months in French oak. Screwcap. 14.5° alc. **Rating** 94 **To** 2015 $33.95

ΨΨΨΨΨ **Sandalera (375 ml) NV** Lots of rancio nuttiness, with good fruit concentration and quite fresh for the style; the old material contributes to complexity. Cork. 18° alc. **Rating** 92 **To** 2020 $55

Margaret River Chardonnay 2005 Glowing yellow-green; a high-toned wine, with a curious touch of iodine on the bouquet; stone fruit and citrus flavours with judicious barrel ferment inputs. Screwcap. 13.5° alc. **Rating** 90 **To** 2011 $24.95

Margaret River Verdelho 2007 Bright straw-green; appealing fruit salad flavours, with citrus overtones giving brightness and length to the palate. Screwcap. 14° alc. **Rating** 90 **To** 2010 $22.95

Estate Reserve Margaret River Verdelho 2007 Some candied fruit and plenty of citrus on the bouquet; fruit-sweet on the palate, and quite long, with good texture on the finish. Screwcap. 14° alc. **Rating** 90 **To** 2012 $22.95

ΨΨΨΨ **Estate Reserve Riesling 2007** An aromatic, floral bouquet, then a fresh and lively palate with crisp citrus and green apple flavours; long finish. Screwcap. 12° alc. **Rating** 89 **To** 2015 $19.95

Protege Chardonnay 2006 Clever winemaking keeps light fruit, oak and a touch of sweetness in a balanced circle, albeit without the usual Margaret River depth. Screwcap. 13° alc. **Rating** 89 **To** 2010 $17.99

Protege Premium Classic White 2006 Quite aromatic and lively, with zesty light fruit flavours on the palate; good length and balance. Screwcap. 12.5° alc. **Rating** 88 **To** 2009 $17.99

Protege Rose 2007 Has plenty of red fruit flavours, augmented by some residual sugar on the finish; no forewarning of the sweetness. Screwcap. 11.5° alc. **Rating** 88 **To** 2009 $17.99

Element Merlot 2006 Quite attractive small berry fruit flavours, with touches of olive and herb on a more savoury finish. Screwcap. 14° alc. **Rating** 87 **To** 2009 $12.99

Sandhurst Ridge

156 Forest Drive, Marong, Vic 3515 **Region** Bendigo
T (03) 5435 2534 **F** (03) 5435 2548 **www**.sandhurstridge.com.au **Open** 7 days 11–5
Winemaker Paul Greblo, George Greblo **Est.** 1990 **Cases** 3000
The Greblo brothers (Paul and George), with combined experience in business, agriculture, science and construction and development, began the establishment of Sandhurst Ridge in 1990 with the planting of the first 2 ha of shiraz and cabernet sauvignon. Plantings have now been increased to over 7 ha, principally cabernet and shiraz, but also a little merlot and nebbiolo. As the business has grown, the Greblos have supplemented their crush with grapes grown in the region. Exports to Canada, Taiwan and Hong Kong.

ΨΨΨΨΨ **Bendigo Shiraz 2006** Light- to medium-bodied, much lighter (and more elegant) than the usual Sandhurst Ridge blockbuster; has good length and balance, with fresh acidity on the finish. Diam. 13.5° alc. **Rating** 94 **To** 2015 $28

ΨΨΨΨΩ **Bendigo Merlot 2006** Fresh cassis fruit on the bouquet and palate; a silky mouthfeel thanks to tightly controlled alcohol and extract. Screwcap. 13.5° alc. **Rating** 92 **To** 2013 $28
Reserve Bendigo Shiraz 2005 Full-bodied; no-holds-barred style, with masses of ripe fruit, and a warm coat of alcohol adding to the impression of sweetness. Time may tame it. Diam. 15° alc. **Rating** 90 **To** 2025 $42

ΨΨΨΨ **Fringe Bendigo Shiraz 2006** Medium-bodied; carries American oak and alcohol quite well to provide a user friendly palate with ample flavour and soft extract. Screwcap. 15° alc. **Rating** 89 **To** 2013 $22

Sanguine Estate

77 Shurans Lane, Heathcote, Vic 3523 **Region** Heathcote
T (03) 9646 6661 **F** (03) 9646 1746 **www**.sanguinewines.com.au **Open** By appt
Winemaker Mark Hunter, Ben Riggs (Consultant) **Est.** 1997 **Cases** 7500
The Hunter family, with parents Linda and Tony at the head, and their children, Mark and Jodi, with their respective partners Melissa and Brett, began establishing the vineyard in 1997. It has grown to 20 ha of shiraz, and 2 ha of eight different varieties, including chardonnay, viognier, merlot, tempranillo, zinfandel, petit verdot, cabernet sauvignon, merlot and cabernet franc. Low-yielding vines and the magic of the Heathcote region have produced Shiraz of exceptional intensity, which has received rave reviews in the US, and led to the 'sold out' sign being posted almost immediately upon release. With the ever-expanding vineyard, Mark Hunter has become full-time vigneron, and Jodi Marsh part-time marketer and business developer. Exports to the UK, the US, Canada, Singapore and Hong Kong.

ΨΨΨΨΨ **Heathcote Shiraz 2006** Showing strong elements of minerals and earth, but framed by well-defined fruit; almost luscious on the palate, the finish tightens up and delivers a strong sense of minerality and longevity. Screwcap. 14.8° alc. **Rating** 94 **To** 2020 $35

ΨΨΨΨΩ **Heathcote Cabernet Sauvignon 2006** A deep wine, with mulberry and cassis, and a little ironstone personality; fleshy on the mid-palate, but quite firm on the finish. Screwcap. 14.5° alc. **Rating** 90 **To** 2015 $29
Heathcote Tempranillo 2006 Quite a rich tempranillo, with ample levels of red and dark fruits and a little edge of lifted florals; sweet and succulent, there is a nice twang of acidity on the finish. Screwcap. 14.5° alc. **Rating** 90 **To** 2012 $29

ΨΨΨΨ **Progeny Heathcote Shiraz 2005** Has a slight green edge, but underneath there is good fruit, and plenty of richness; just pulls up a little short. Screwcap. 14.7° alc. **Rating** 88 **To** 2014 $19

Heathcote Chardonnay 2006 Good concentration and depth; a bit one-dimensional, but with nice freshness on the finish. Screwcap. 12.7° alc. **Rating** 87 To 2009 $25

Saracen Estates

3517 Caves Road, Wilyabrup, WA 6280 **Region** Margaret River
T (08) 9221 4955 **F** (08) 9221 4966 **www**.saracenestates.com.au **Open** 7 days 10–6
Winemaker Naturaliste Vintners (Bruce Dukes), Bob Cartwright (Consultant) **Est.** 1998
Cases 7000
Luke and Maree Saraceni have 17 ha of vines on their 80-ha property, with a striking restaurant and cellar door opened in 2007. This was followed by a visitor facility in 2008 incorporating a craft brewery, a beer garden, and restaurant. Exports to the UK, Singapore, Malaysia, Hong Kong, India and Denmark.

ŸŸŸŸŸ **Margaret River Chardonnay 2006** Bright and vibrant, with nectarine fruit and a subtle lick of oak; bright and fresh on the finish, with lively acidity prominent. Screwcap. 13.5° alc. **Rating** 94 **To** 2014 $30

ŸŸŸŸŸ **Margaret River Sauvignon Blanc 2007** Fresh and lively varietal aromas of cut grass and hints of tropical fruits; good texture and very fresh. Screwcap. 13.5° alc. **Rating** 90 **To** 2009 $22

Sarsfield Estate

345 Duncan Road, Sarsfield, Vic 3875 **Region** Gippsland
T (03) 5156 8962 **F** (03) 5156 8970 **www**.sarsfieldestate.com.au **Open** By appt
Winemaker Dr Suzanne Rutschmann **Est.** 1995 **Cases** 1200
Owned by Suzanne Rutschmann, who has a PhD in Chemistry, a Diploma in Horticulture and a BSc (Wine Science) from CSU, and Swiss-born Peter Albrecht, a civil and structural engineer who has also undertaken various courses in agriculture and viticulture. For a part-time occupation, these are exceptionally impressive credentials. Their 2-ha vineyard was planted between 1991 and '98. Sarsfield Pinot Noir has enjoyed conspicuous success in both domestic and international wine shows over the past few years. No insecticides are used in the vineyard, the winery using solar and wind energy, and relying entirely on rain water. Exports to Ireland.

ŸŸŸŸŸ **Pinot Noir 2006** Vibrant cherry and plum fruits with some stem evident; nice weight and serious texture, and very fine acid balance on the very long finish. ProCork. 14° alc. **Rating** 94 **To** 2012 $25

ŸŸŸŸ **Cabernets Shiraz Merlot 2006** Vibrant purple hue; firm acid frames the dark, spicy fruits; cinnamon and cloves are evident, and there is plenty of grip on the finish. ProCork. **Rating** 89 **To** 2009 $21

SC Pannell

14 Davenport Terrace, Wayville, SA 5034 (postal) **Region** McLaren Vale
T (08) 8299 9256 **F** (08) 8299 9274 **Open** Not
Winemaker Stephen Pannell **Est.** 2004 **Cases** 2500
The only surprising piece of background is that it took (an admittedly still reasonably youthful) Stephen Pannell (and wife Fiona) so long to cut the painter from Constellation/Hardys and establish their own winemaking and consulting business. Steve Pannell radiates intensity, and extended experience backed by equally long experimentation and thought has resulted in wines of the highest quality right from the first vintage. At present the focus of their virtual winery (they own neither vineyards nor winery) is grenache and shiraz grown in McLaren Vale. This is a label which is well on its way to icon status.

ŸŸŸŸŸ **McLaren Vale Shiraz 2005** A fine wine from the first whiff through to the finish and aftertaste; has intense black and red fruit flavours with no alcohol heat; perfectly integrated and balanced French oak. Screwcap. 14.5° alc. **Rating** 96 **To** 2025 $60

Adelaide Hills Sauvignon Blanc 2007 Potent aromas of tropical fruits and gooseberry flow through to the positive palate; picked at exactly the right time. Screwcap. 12.5° alc. **Rating** 95 **To** 2009 $25

McLaren Vale Shiraz Grenache 2005 A supple and smooth ride from start to finish; has lovely red, perfumed fruit along with a dash of chocolate; fine-grained tannins and quality French oak. Screwcap. 14.5° alc. **Rating** 95 **To** 2020 $50

McLaren Vale Grenache 2006 This is amazing grenache; bright red fruits, a hint of garrigue, and jam-packed with silky fruits right across the palate; deeply complex with serious tannins and the finish is incredibly bright and long. Screwcap. 14.5° alc. **Rating** 95 **To** 2016 $50

McLaren Vale Grenache Rose 2007 Bright purple-fuschia; a rose with attitude and impressive complexity; cherry and raspberry fruit runs through the palate; the back label description of Turkish Delight is spot-on. Screwcap. 12.5° alc. **Rating** 94 **To** 2009 $22

McLaren Vale Shiraz 2006 Really essency McLaren fruit, with chocolate and blackberries aplenty; there is a generous amount of toasty oak; the wine is quite tannic, but the fruit will soak the tannins up with time. Screwcap. 14.5° alc. **Rating** 94 **To** 2018 $60

McLaren Vale Shiraz Grenache 2006 Vibrant colour; juicy raspberry fruits from the grenache supported by spice and dark fruits of the shiraz; hints of mocha on the finish, which is long and quite slippery. Screwcap. 14.5° alc. **Rating** 94 **To** 2014 $50

ΨΨΨΨΨ **Pronto Red 2006** Fragrant red berry aromas, then a vibrant, juicy, light-bodied palate in a drink-me-quick mode; clever winemaking, wide appeal. Grenache/Shiraz/Touriga. Screwcap. 14° alc. **Rating** 92 **To** 2009 $25

Nebbiolo 2005 More spicy and red fruit aromas than many, though the palate is dominated by nebbiolo tannins. Not to be undertaken lightly; bistecca fiorentina needed. Screwcap. 14.5° alc. **Rating** 91 **To** 2015 $50

Scaffidi Wines   ★★★★☆

Talunga Cellars, Adelaide-Mannum Road, Gumeracha, SA 5233 **Region** Adelaide Zone
T (08) 8389 1222 **F** (08) 8389 1233 **www**.talunga.com.au **Open** Wed–Sun & public hols 10.30–5
Winemaker Vince Scaffidi **Est.** 1994 **Cases** 2000
Owners Vince and Tina Scaffidi have a one-third share of the 80-ha Gumeracha Vineyards, and it is from these vineyards that the wines are sourced. The cellar door and restaurant is named Talunga Cellars. The wines are exceptionally well-priced given their quality. No samples received, the rating is that of last year.

 # Scalawag Wines   ★★★☆

PO Box 743, West Perth, WA 6872 **Region** Great Southern
T (08) 9302 6591 **F** (08) 9302 6594 **www**.scalawag.com.au **Open** Not
Winemaker Harewood Estate (James Kellie), Garlands (Mike Garland) **Est.** 1998 **Cases** 8000
Peter Hodge, Laurence Huck, Kevin Tangney and Alf Baker are the owners of Scalawag Wines, and have made a substantial investment in the large estate vineyard, planted to riesling (4.6 ha), chardonnay (12 ha), sauvignon blanc (4 ha), merlot (7.3 ha), shiraz (24.9 ha) and cabernet sauvignon (19.5 ha). The planting material came from the Forest Hill Vineyard, the oldest in the Mount Barker region. The Scalawag property has well-known vineyards on three sides, the Hay River and Yamballup Creek forming the southern boundary of the vineyard. The emphasis in the vineyard is on organic products, and minimum chemical use. The first releases promise much for the future.

Scarborough Wine Co

179 Gillards Road, Pokolbin, NSW 2320 **Region** Lower Hunter Valley
T (02) 4998 7563 **F** (02) 4998 7786 **www**.scarboroughwine.com.au **Open** 7 days 9–5
Winemaker Ian Scarborough, Jerome Scarborough, Aaron Mercer **Est.** 1985 **Cases** 15 000
Ian Scarborough honed his white winemaking skills during his years as a consultant, and has brought all those skills to his own label. He makes three different styles of Chardonnay: the Blue Label in a light, elegant, Chablis style for the export market and a richer barrel-fermented wine (Yellow Label) primarily directed to the Australian market; the third is the White Label, a cellar door-only wine made in the best vintages. However, the real excitement for the future lies with the portion of the old Lindemans Sunshine Vineyard which he has purchased (after it lay fallow for 30 years) and planted with semillon and (quixotically) pinot noir. The first vintage from the legendary Sunshine Vineyard was made in 2004. Exports to the UK and the US.

ΨΨΨΨΨ **White Label Hunter Valley Semillon 2007** Has all the attributes of very good young semillon; grass, herb and a touch of lemon on the bouquet, then an intense and focused palate with excellent citrussy/lemony fruit; bright acidity on the finish; classic in 5 years. Screwcap. 10° alc. **Rating** 94 **To** 2017 $22
Late Harvest Semillon 2007 Brilliant green-yellow; totally delicious, almost a pure grape and lime juice mix; great balance; no need to delay; for a fresh fruit platter on a sunny day. Screwcap. 9.5° alc. **Rating** 94 **To** 2009 $18

ΨΨΨΨΨ **Blue Label Chardonnay 2006** Pink Ribbon Release. Very well-crafted wine; attractive white peach and melon fruit, with good oak integration and balance; long, fresh finish. Screwcap. 13° alc. **Rating** 92 **To** 2011 $21
White Label Hunter Valley Chardonnay 2006 Abounds with white peach/nectarine fruit in a mouthfilling supple palate, achieving richness without phenolics; oak a bit-player. Screwcap. 13° alc. **Rating** 92 **To** 2012 $30

Scarpantoni Estate

Scarpantoni Drive, McLaren Flat, SA 5171 **Region** McLaren Vale
T (08) 8383 0186 **F** (08) 8383 0490 **www**.scarpantoni-wines.com **Open** Mon–Fri 9–5, w'ends & public hols 11–5
Winemaker Michael Scarpantoni, Filippo Scarpantoni **Est.** 1979 **Cases** 30 000
With 20 ha of shiraz, 11 ha of cabernet sauvignon, 3 ha each of chardonnay and sauvignon blanc, 1 ha each of merlot and gamay, and 0.5 ha of petit verdot, Scarpantoni has come a long way since Domenico Scarpantoni purchased his first property in 1958. He was working for Thomas Hardy at its Tintara winery; he subsequently became vineyard manager for Seaview Wines. In 1979 his sons Michael and Filippo built the winery, which has now been extended to enable all the grapes from the estate plantings to be used to make wine under the Scarpantoni label. As the vines have matured, quality has improved. Exports to the US, the UK and other major markets.

ΨΨΨΨΨ **Estate Reserve 2005** Medium-bodied; smooth and elegant, easily handling the alcohol; a mix of blackberry, blackcurrant, plum and dark chocolate; soft tannins. Shiraz/Cabernet Sauvignon. Screwcap. 15° alc. **Rating** 94 **To** 2020 $36

ΨΨΨΨ **Black Tempest NV** Very youthful black fruits; has length and has avoided the distressingly common sweetness from excessive dosage. **Rating** 89 **To** 2012 $28

Schild Estate Wines

Cnr Barossa Valley Way/Lyndoch Valley Road, Lyndoch, SA 5351 **Region** Barossa Valley
T (08) 8524 5560 **F** (08) 8524 4333 **www**.schildestate.com.au **Open** 7 days 10–5
Winemaker Wine Wise (Jo Irvine) **Est.** 1998 **Cases** 35 000
Ed Schild is a Barossa Valley grapegrower who first planted a small vineyard at Rowland Flat in 1952, steadily increasing his vineyard holdings over the next 50 years to their present 150 ha. Currently 12% of the production from these vineyards (now managed by son Michael Schild)

is used to produce Schild Estate Wines, and the plan is to increase this percentage. The flagship wine is made from 150-year-old shiraz vines on the Moorooroo Block. The cellar door is in the old ANZ Bank at Lyndoch, and provides the sort of ambience which can only be found in the Barossa Valley. Exports to the UK, the US and other major markets.

ႛႛႛႛ **Barossa Semillon Sauvignon Blanc 2007** Grassy, minerally semillon does most of the talking; the palate gains strength on the long finish; sensible alcohol. Screwcap. 12° alc. **Rating** 89 **To** 2009 $15

Barossa Riesling 2007 Big, broad, generous, tropical fruit; soft finish, and ready now. Screwcap. 12° alc. **Rating** 87 **To** 2009 $15

Schiller Vineyards ★★★★

Light Pass Road, Light Pass, SA 5355 **Region** Barossa Valley
T (08) 8562 1258 **F** (08) 8562 2560 **www.**schillervineyards.com.au **Open** By appt
Winemaker Neville Falkenberg (Contract) **Est.** 1864 **Cases** 450

How can it be that a business established in 1864 is a new entry in the *Wine Companion*? The answer is simple: Carl Freidrich Schiller arrived in SA in 1855, purchasing his first property in 1864 at Light Pass and soon thereafter establishing the first vines for the Schiller family. For six generations the Schiller family has been producing premium grapes for the best wineries of the Barossa; very few wineries in Bordeaux, Burgundy or California can claim to have had six generations of continuous viticulture under the same family name (a point often missed by distinguished wine writers from other parts of the world). To ram the point home, the underground cellar for the Schiller wines is situated below the original 1860 Schiller homestead (built on leased land in 1855). Only a tiny quantity of the 65 ha of estate vineyards (chardonnay, riesling, semillon, shiraz, merlot, mourvedre, grenache and cabernet sauvignon) is vinified under the Schiller Vineyards label.

ႛႛႛႛႛ **The Race Course Barossa Shiraz Grenache 2003** Medium-bodied; slightly more weight and complexity, with some blackberry fruit notes; balanced and harmonious. A triumph for the vintage. Screwcap. 14.5° alc. **Rating** 90 **To** 2012 $19

Stone Train Barossa Shiraz Cabernet Sauvignon 2002 Good colour; in the ripe flavour spectrum of Schiller, but with more finesse and length than most; good back-palate structure. Cork. 14.5° alc. **Rating** 90 **To** 2015 $35

ႛႛႛႛ **Stone Train Barossa Shiraz Cabernet Sauvignon 2004** Medium-bodied; a ripe array of black fruits supported by soft tannins; supple mouthfeel to an early-drinking style. Cork. **Rating** 89 **To** 2011 $35

The Race Course Barossa Shiraz Grenache 2004 Light- to medium-bodied; in very similar style to the '05, with a near identical flavour profile. Screwcap. 14° alc. **Rating** 88 **To** 2012 $19

The Race Course Barossa Shiraz Grenache 2005 Light- to medium-bodied; sweet confit fruit characters, with gentle tannins and a whisk of vanillin oak. Screwcap. 14° alc. **Rating** 88 **To** 2013 $19

Stone Train Barossa Shiraz Cabernet Sauvignon 2003 Distinct dried fruit/prune characters, the alcohol seeming higher than it is; all in all, shows the problems of '03. Cork. 14.5° alc. **Rating** 87 **To** 2011 $35

Stone Train Barossa Shiraz Cabernet Sauvignon 2001 Ripe confit fruits, riper than the alcohol suggests; the palate is assisted by gentle, ripe tannins on the finish. Cork. 14° alc. **Rating** 87 **To** 2012 $35

Schindler Northway Downs ★★★

437 Stumpy Gully Road, Balnarring, Vic 3926 **Region** Mornington Peninsula
T (03) 5983 1945 **F** (03) 5983 1987 **www.**northwaydowns.com.au **Open** First w'end of month
Winemaker Tammy Schindler-Hands **Est.** 1996 **Cases** 250

The Schindler family planted the first 2 ha of pinot noir and chardonnay in 1996. A further 4 ha of pinot noir was planted on an ideal north-facing slope in 1999, and the first vintage followed in 2000. The cellar door offers Austrian food and live Austrian music on Sundays.

ŶŶŶŶ **Mornington Peninsula Pinot Noir 2006** Despite the alcohol, light-bodied, with no dead fruit characters, rather a mix of cherry, spice and stemmy flavours, finishes with some corrected acidity. Diam. 14.8° alc. **Rating** 88 **To** 2011 $24

Schubert Estate ★★★★★

Roennfeldt Road, Marananga, SA 5355 **Region** Barossa Valley
T (08) 8562 3375 **F** (08) 8562 4338 **www**.schubertestate.com.au **Open** Not
Winemaker Steve Schubert **Est.** 2000 **Cases** 500
Steve and Cecilia Schubert are primarily grapegrowers, with 13 ha of shiraz and 2 ha of viognier. They purchased the 25-ha property in 1986, when it was in such a derelict state that there was no point trying to save the old vines. Both were working in other areas, so it was some years before they began replanting, at a little under 2 ha per year. Almost all the production is sold to Torbreck. In 2000 they decided to keep enough grapes to make a barrique of wine for their own (and friends') consumption. They were sufficiently encouraged by the outcome to venture into the dizzy heights of two hogsheads a year (since increased to four or so). The wine is made with wild yeast, open fermentation, basket pressing and bottling without filtration. Exports to the US and other major markets.

ŶŶŶŶŶ **Goose-yard Block Barossa Valley Shiraz 2006** Deep red, some crimson; medium- to full-bodied, and particularly intense; perfectly ripened fruit gives blackberry and bitter chocolate flavours without a scintilla of overripe/dead fruit characters; great length. Cork. 14.5° alc. **Rating** 96 **To** 2021 $60
The Gander Reserve Barossa Valley Shiraz 2004 A single French barrel was used, and has added significantly to the flavour tapestry of the wine and its texture, all in the black fruits range. The hand-inserted, stained and deformed cork is little short of a travesty for such a lovely wine. 14.5° alc. **Rating** 95 **To** 2012 $68

ŶŶŶŶŶ **The Gosling Barossa Valley Shiraz 2006** Because the fruit is less dense than Goose-yard, the excellent texture and structure is more evident in a wine with quality blackberry fruit, weight and length. Screwcap. 14.5° alc. **Rating** 92 **To** 2016 $22
The Lone Goose Barossa Valley Shiraz 2006 The 3% viognier (which can't be shown on the front label) certainly adds to the expression of the vibrant red fruits; light- to medium-bodied, and won't fade away, but at its best over the next year or so. Screwcap. 14.5° alc. **Rating** 90 **To** 2010 $22

ŶŶŶŶ **The Lone Goose Barossa Valley Shiraz 2005** Exotic aromas and flavours, more to dark plum/blackberry/Christmas cake and only ultimately spice, but has very good length. Great value. Screwcap. 14.5° alc. **Rating** 89 **To** 2010 $15

Schulz Vignerons ★★★★

PO Box 121, Nuriootpa, SA 5355 **Region** Barossa Valley
T (08) 8565 6257 **F** (08) 8565 6257 **Open** By appt
Winemaker David Powell (Contract) **Est.** 2003 **Cases** 1450
Marcus and Roslyn Schulz are the fifth generation of one of the best known wine families (or, rather, extended families) in the Barossa Valley. Four generations of grapegrowing and winemaking precede them, but they went down a new path by initiating biological farming in 2002. They have moved from irrigation and extensive spraying to the situation where the vines are now virtually dry-grown, producing generous yields of high-quality grapes, using natural nitrogen created by the active soil biology, and minimal chemical input. They have a 58-ha vineyard with 12 varieties planted, shiraz, mourvedre, grenache and cabernet sauvignon leading the band. They are also actively involved in a local co-operative campaign to protect blocks of native vegetation to encourage biodiversity. As might be imagined, the lion's share of the grapes are sold to other producers (some finding its way to Torbreck).

ȲȲȲȲȲ Benjamin Barossa Valley Shiraz 2005 Rich, mouthfilling blackberry and plum
fruit with hints of vanilla and mocha; the fully ripe tannins are soft, the oak good;
will live. Screwcap. 14.5° alc. **Rating** 92 To 2020 $25
Marcus Barossa Valley Old Shiraz 2004 A concentrated array of black fruits,
with cornerstones of vanilla oak and ripe tannins; needs time to loosen up. From
vines over 50 years old. Screwcap. 15° alc. **Rating** 92 To 2024 $70

ȲȲȲȲ Julius Barossa Valley Merlot 2005 A well-balanced and constructed medium-
bodied dry red, the only thing lacking being obvious merlot varietal character.
Screwcap. 13.5° alc. **Rating** 88 To 2012 $25
Anthony Barossa Valley Cabernet Sauvignon 2005 Medium-bodied;
some varietal fruit in a fairly loose-knit frame; pleasant, early access style. Screwcap.
14° alc. **Rating** 87 To 2011 $20
Johann Barossa Valley Zinfandel 2005 An aromatic, scented bouquet, then
strawberry jam fruit on the palate; a little over the top, as is the lingering sweetness.
Screwcap. 14.5° alc. **Rating** 87 To 2009 $20

Schwarz Wine Company   ★★★★☆

PO Box 182, Tanunda, SA 5352 **Region** Barossa Valley
T 0417 881 923 **F** (08) 8562 3534 **www**.schwarzwineco.com.au **Open** By appt
Winemaker Jason Schwarz **Est.** 2001 **Cases** 1300
The economical name is appropriate for a business which started with 1 tonne of grapes
making two hogsheads of wine in 2001. The shiraz was purchased from Jason Schwarz's
parents' vineyard in Bethany; the following year half a tonne of grenache was added, once
again purchased from the parents, the vines planted 60 years ago. Production remained static
until 2005, when the grape sale agreements to another (larger) winery were terminated,
freeing up 1.8 ha of shiraz, and 0.8 ha of grenache. From this point on things moved a little
more quickly: in 2006 Jason Schwarz worked with Peter Schell of Spinifex, which led to
the formation of a partnership (Biscay Road Vintners) with Peter Schell giving each total
control over production. Using grapes purchased from other growers, Jason Schwarz hopes to
eventually increase production to 3000–4000 cases. Exports to the UK, the US, Canada, the
Netherlands, Denmark, Singapore and Hong Kong.

ȲȲȲȲȲ Nitschke Block Barossa Valley Shiraz 2006 A heady wine, with confit black
fruit and licorice; terrific concentration, and a full throttle whack of fruit on the
finish. Screwcap. 15° alc. **Rating** 94 To 2015 $32

ȲȲȲȲȲ The Dust Kicker 2006 Super-ripe fruit, yet vibrant, with plenty of richness
across the palate. Screwcap. 14.7° alc. **Rating** 90 To 2011 $20

Scion Vineyard & Winery   ★★★★

74 Slaughterhouse Road, Rutherglen, Vic 3685 **Region** Rutherglen
T (02) 6032 8844 **www**.scionvineyard.com **Open** W'ends & public hols 10–5
Winemaker Jan Milhinch, Mandy Jones, Howard Anderson (Contract) **Est.** 2002 **Cases** 1200
Former audiologist Jan Milhinch is a great-great-granddaughter of GF Morris, founder
of the most famous Rutherglen wine family. She was in her 50s and at the height of her
professional career when she decided to take what she describes as a 'vine change', moving
from Melbourne to establish a little over 3 ha of durif, grenache, orange muscat, brown
muscat and viognier on a quartz-laden red clay slope planted in 2002, but with a viticultural
history stretching back to 1890 before phylloxera struck and the vineyard was abandoned.
Jan makes the wines in conjunction with Mandy Jones, and occasional additional help from
Howard Anderson, both veteran winemakers in the region, with a particular and somewhat
unexpected aim to lower the alcohol levels in the durif.

ȲȲȲȲȲ Durif 2006 Very good durif, with bright red fruits complementing the richness
of the dark fruits; good acid provides balance and length. Cork. **Rating** 92
To 2014 $32

Sweet Durif 2006 Not overly sweet, but very clean and focused with nice tannin on the finish; great with the right sort of cheese. Cork. 18.5° alc. **Rating** 90 **To** 2016 $24

♟♟♟♟ **Durif 2005** A somewhat rough-hewn wine, even by the standards of durif; does have masses of flavour; great with a T-bone steak from a wood-fired barbecue. ProCork. 13.7° alc. **Rating** 88 **To** 2012 $29

Scorpiiion ★★★★☆

32 Waverley Ridge Road, Crafers, SA 5152 (postal) **Region** Warehouse
T 0409 551 110 **F** (08) 8353 1562 **www**.scorpiiionwines.com.au **Open** Not
Winemaker Spinifex (Peter Schell) **Est.** 2002 **Cases** 1200
Scorpiiion Wines was the concept of Mark Herbertt who decided to buy a small quantity of McLaren Vale and Barossa grapes in 2002 and have the wine made for himself, friends and family. In 2004 Paddy Phillips and Michael Szwarcbord, like Mark Herbertt sharing the Scorpio birth sign, joined the partnership. It is a virtual winery, with the grapes purchased, and the wines contract-made by the brilliant Peter Schell. They say 'We share a number of likes and dislikes in relation to Australian red wines – apart from that, we don't really agree on anything ... We aim for a fruit-driven style with elegant oak, rather than a big, oak-driven style.' Oh, and they are united in their insistence on using screwcaps rather than corks. As a postscript, the poor 2007 vintage, low in yield and quality, means only one wine (Grenache Shiraz Mataro) is likely to be released.

♟♟♟♟♀ **Barossa Valley Shiraz 2005** Very good colour; generous, rich and well-balanced; a medium- to full-bodied array of black fruits and a deft touch of French and American oak; carries alcohol well. Screwcap. 14.8° alc. **Rating** 92 **To** 2017 $27
Barossa Valley Grenache Shiraz Mataro 2006 Fragrant, juicy berry aromas and flavours in mainstream of French at its best; main inputs from Grenache (45%) and Shiraz (42%). Screwcap. 15° alc. **Rating** 91 **To** 2012 $22
Barossa Valley McLaren Flat Cabernet Sauvignon 2006 A scented, exotic bouquet leads into a full-frontal, luxuriant and lusciously ripe palate in bold Aussie 'love me or leave me' style. Screwcap. 14.5° alc. **Rating** 90 **To** 2016 $32

Scorpo Wines ★★★★★

23 Old Bittern-Dromana Road, Merricks North, Vic 3926 **Region** Mornington Peninsula
T (03) 5989 7697 **F** (03) 9813 3371 **www**.scorpowines.com.au **Open** By appt
Winemaker Paul Scorpo, Sandro Mosele (Contract) **Est.** 1997 **Cases** 2600
Paul Scorpo has a 27-year background as a horticulturist/landscape architect, and has worked on major projects ranging from private gardens to golf courses in Australia, Europe and Asia. His family has a love of food, wine and gardens, all of which led to them buying a derelict apple and cherry orchard on gentle rolling hills between Port Phillip and Westernport Bay. Part of a ridge system which climbs up to Red Hill, it offers north and northeast-facing slopes on red-brown, clay loam soils. They have established 6 ha of pinot noir, chardonnay, pinot gris and shiraz. Exports to Canada.

♟♟♟♟♟ **Mornington Peninsula Pinot Noir 2005** Supple and round on entry to the mouth, then progressively expands across the mid-palate to the finish; well-handled oak and extract. Diam. 14° alc. **Rating** 95 **To** 2015 $39
Aubaine Mornington Peninsula Chardonnay 2006 Quite delicate, yet intense, long and well-balanced; nectarine and grapefruit flavours, subtle oak, and a lingering finish. Enticing price. Diam. 14° alc. **Rating** 94 **To** 2013 $27
Aubaine Mornington Peninsula Chardonnay 2007 The cool climate shapes this intense and long wine from start to finish, with grapefruit leading nectarine, the oak integrated, the acidity excellent. Diam. 13.5° alc. **Rating** 94 **To** 2015 $30
Mornington Peninsula Chardonnay 2006 Similar to the Aubaine in terms of weight and structure, the fruit slightly more intense, and driving the palate, oak a background bit-player; developing slowly. Diam. 14° alc. **Rating** 94 **To** 2016 $38

Noirien Mornington Peninsula Pinot Noir 2006 Aromatic, clean and fresh; abuzz with an array of red fruits, cherry, strawberry and rhubarb; good mouthfeel and finish; delicious right now. Diam. 14° alc. **Rating** 94 **To** 2009 $27

Mornington Peninsula Pinot Noir 2006 Much more savour and more foresty than the '07 Noirien, and more red fruit flavours; has good length and expands delicately on the long finish; for the purist, perhaps. Diam. 13.5° alc. **Rating** 94 **To** 2013 $40

Mornington Peninsula Shiraz 2006 Like a perfect, sunlit spring day, this wine is all about freshness and life, its sparkling red fruits with enough tannins and oak to provide the basic structure, but not impinging on the fruit. Diam. 13.5° alc. **Rating** 94 **To** 2016 $40

ŸŸŸŸŸ **Mornington Peninsula Chardonnay 2005** A powerful wine with some bottle development showing more weight and slightly less fruit finesse than the '06; stone fruit and melon, nicely restrained oak. Diam. 14° alc. **Rating** 93 **To** 2012 $36

Noirien Mornington Peninsula Pinot Noir 2007 Noirien was used in Burgundy from 1325; this wine shows great crimson colour; rich plum and spice aromas and flavours towards the big end of town but not over the top; just a millimetre short; time needed. Diam. 13° alc. **Rating** 93 **To** 2015 $30

Mornington Peninsula Pinot Gris 2006 An almost startling depth of flavours of ripe pear, musk and apple; stacked with fruit and no reliance on residual sugar. Diam. 13.5° alc. **Rating** 91 **To** 2009 $30

Mornington Peninsula Pinot Gris 2007 A fresh, lively, minerally wine, with pear, apple and musk offset by lemony acidity on the dry finish; in the upper echelon. Diam. 13.5° alc. **Rating** 90 **To** 2010 $34

Mornington Peninsula Shiraz 2005 A light-bodied, vibrant wine with spicy black fruits, fine tannins and subtle oak. Diam. 14° alc. **Rating** 90 **To** 2013 $39

Scotchmans Hill ★★★★★

190 Scotchmans Road, Drysdale, Vic 3222 **Region** Geelong
T (03) 5251 3176 **F** (03) 5253 1743 **www.**scotchmanshill.com.au **Open** 7 days 10.30–5.30
Winemaker Robin Brockett, Marcus Holt **Est.** 1982 **Cases** 70 000
Situated on the Bellarine Peninsula, southeast of Geelong, with a well-equipped winery and first-class vineyards. It is a consistent performer with its Pinot Noir and has a strong following in Melbourne and Sydney for its astutely priced, competently made wines. The second label, Swan Bay, has been joined at the other end of the spectrum with top-end individual vineyard wines. Exports to the UK and other major markets.

ŸŸŸŸŸ **Cornelius Sauvignon 2006** A powerful wine, all about texture, structure and length; has style links to white Bordeaux courtesy of barrel ferment in old French oak and lees contact. Screwcap. 13.5° alc. **Rating** 94 **To** 2010 $35

Geelong Chardonnay 2006 Disciplined winemaking; quite sweet stone fruit, melon and citrus flavours do the talking; oak in a support role. Screwcap. 13.5° alc. **Rating** 94 **To** 2011 $28

ŸŸŸŸŸ **Swan Bay Chardonnay 2006** A wholly stylish second label, with crystal clear cool-grown fruit expression of stone fruit, melon and citrus, the oak in restraint. Screwcap. 14° alc. **Rating** 91 **To** 2012 $19

Cornelius Pinot Gris 2006 Similar winemaking to Cornelius Sauvignon; barrel fermentation in old oak has worked well to provide structure and length; a lingering, dry finish. Screwcap. 13.5° alc. **Rating** 91 **To** 2010 $35

Geelong Shiraz 2006 Spicy red fruit aromas, with quite a succulent and juicy palate; medium-bodied and focused on the finish. Screwcap. 14.5° alc. **Rating** 91 **To** 2014 $29.50

Geelong Sauvignon Blanc 2007 Pale colour; good fruit intensity, with a little savoury edge; varietal on the palate and quite fresh, with good texture on the finish. Screwcap. 14° alc. **Rating** 90 **To** 2011 $24

Geelong Pinot Noir 2006 Good colour and concentrated fruit, but a little one-dimensional; slightly paddy on the finish, but the flavour is good. Screwcap. 14° alc. **Rating** 89 **To** 2012 $29.50

Swan Bay Pinot Noir 2007 Plum and spice, with a savoury edge to the palate; quite firm and dry on the finish. Screwcap. 14° alc. **Rating** 89 **To** 2012 $19

Cornelius Syrah 2005 Developed colour; not up to the other Cornelius wines, despite Rolls-Royce treatment in the winery; not enough fruit power to build on despite the alcohol. Screwcap. 15° alc. **Rating** 89 **To** 2013 $45

Geelong Cabernet Sauvignon 2006 Cassis and leafy notes on the bouquet; medium-bodied, with good persistence and clean fruit on the finish. Screwcap. 14° alc. **Rating** 89 **To** 2014 $29.50

Swan Bay Geelong Late Harvest Riesling 2007 Lightly sweet, with green apple and quince flavours; fine and even on the finish. Screwcap. 9° alc. **Rating** 89 **To** 2014 $19

Seabrook Wines ★★★★☆

Lot 350 Light Pass Road, Tanunda, SA 5352 **Region** Barossa Valley
T 0427 224 353 **F** (08) 8563 1210 **Open** By appt
Winemaker Hamish Seabrook **Est.** 2004 **Cases** 400

Hamish Seabrook is the youngest generation of a proud Melbourne wine family once involved in wholesale and retail distribution, and as leading show judges of their respective generations. Hamish, too, is a wine show judge, but was the first to venture into winemaking, working with Best's and Brown Brothers in Vic before moving to SA with wife Joanne. Here they have a small planting of shiraz (recently joined by viognier) but also continue to source small amounts of shiraz from the Pyrenees and Grampians. In February 2008 Hamish Seabrook set up his own winery located on the family property in Vine Vale, having previously made the wines at Dorrien Estate and elsewhere.

 Pyrenees Shiraz 2005 A delicious medium- to full-bodied palate; lots of spicy/juicy/succulent red berry fruits, fine tannins and a correspondingly lively finish. Screwcap. 14° alc. **Rating** 94 **To** 2020 $38

Seaforth Estate ★★★★☆

520 Arthurs Seat Road, Red Hill, Vic 3937 **Region** Mornington Peninsula
T (03) 5989 2362 **F** (03) 5989 2506 **www.**seaforthwines.com.au **Open** Spring & summer w'ends 11–5
Winemaker Phillip Kittle (Contract) **Est.** 1994 **Cases** 1800

Andrew and Venetia Adamson planted their 3.6 ha vineyard to chardonnay (2.2 ha), pinot noir (1 ha) and pinot gris (0.4 ha) in 1994. At 300 m, it is one of the highest on the Mornington Peninsula, and is always amongst the last to pick. The wines are 100% estate-grown, and all of the standard vineyard operations are carried out personally by Andrew and Venetia, with only picking requiring outside help.

Secret Garden Wines ★★★★☆

251 Henry Lawson Drive, Mudgee, NSW 2850 **Region** Mudgee
T (02) 6373 3874 **F** (02) 6373 3854 **Open** Fri–Sun & public hols 9–5
Winemaker Ian MacRae **Est.** 2000 **Cases** NA

Secret Garden Wines is owned by Ian and Carol MacRae, and is a sister operation to their main business, Miramar Wines. Estate plantings consist of 10 ha of shiraz and around 2 ha each of cabernet sauvignon and chardonnay. The wines are made at Miramar, the cellar door is at Secret Garden. The property is only 5 km from Mudgee, and also fronts Craigmoor Road, giving it a prime position in the so-called 'golden triangle'. No samples received, the rating is that of last year.

Sedona Estate   ★★★★

182 Shannons Road, Murrindindi, Vic 3717 **Region** Upper Goulburn
T (03) 9730 2883 **F** (03) 9730 2583 **Open** By appt
Winemaker Paul Evans **Est.** 1998 **Cases** 1500
The Sedona Estate vineyard was chosen by Paul and Sonja Evans after a long search for what they considered to be the perfect site. Situated on north-facing and gently undulating slopes, with gravelly black soils, it is planted (in descending order) to 4 ha of shiraz, cabernet sauvignon, merlot and sangiovese. Paul Evans (former Oakridge winemaker) also contract-makes wines for a number of other small Yarra Valley producers.

ΨΨΨΨΩ **Yea Valley Shiraz 2006** A savoury bouquet with nuances of blackberry, earth, brine and licorice and a hint of oak; medium-bodied with good flavour on the finish. Cork. 14° alc. **Rating** 90 **To** 2012 $20.90

See Saw   ★★★★

PO Box 611, Manly, NSW 1655 **Region** Lower Hunter Valley
T (02) 8966 9020 **F** (02) 8966 9021 www.seesawwine.com **Open** Not
Winemaker Hamish MacGowan, Andrew Margan, Sarah-Kate Dineen **Est.** 2006 **Cases** 6000
This is another venture of Hamish MacGowan, the winemaker-cum-marketer who was responsible for Angus the Bull. While working in the Hunter Valley he met Andrew Margan and Sarah-Kate Dineen, then winemaker at Tempus Two. She has now returned to NZ (with winemaker husband Dan Dineen) to make sauvignon blanc, and Andrew Margan remains in the Hunter with his own substantial winery and business. See Saw is a blend of 85% Hunter Valley Semillon and 15% Marlborough Sauvignon Blanc.

ΨΨΨΨΩ **Hunter Valley Marlborough Semillon Sauvignon Blanc 2007** A truly synergistic blend of varieties and regions, each component obvious but balanced; lemon, gooseberry, grass and herb; good length and finish. Screwcap. 12.5° alc. **Rating** 92 **To** 2010 $18.95

 ## Seplin Estate Wines   ★★★

36 Chifley Road, Wee Waa, NSW 2388 **Region** Western Plains Zone
T (02) 6795 3636 **F** (02) 6795 3636 www.seplinestatewines.com.au **Open** 7 days 10–10
Winemaker James Estate (Peter Orr) **Est.** 1998 **Cases** 6000
Seplin Estate was established by the late Seppi Widauer and wife Lindy. It was the culmination of a long-held ambition to have their own wines and their own cellar door. When Seppi died suddenly in March 2004 his wife and children (Jamie and Simon) decided to continue the project, opening the cellar door and function centre in April '06. It is situated in a 70-year-old building overlooking the nearby lagoon and gum trees. Most of the wine comes from 5.2 ha of shiraz and 4.6 ha of chardonnay, supplemented by some purchases of cabernet sauvignon.

ΨΨΨΨ **Unwooded Chardonnay 2005** Glowing yellow-gold; generous ripe peachy fruit; has length. **Rating** 89 **To** 2009
Reserve Chardonnay 2004 Obvious oak; ripe stone fruit; has aged respectably. **Rating** 87 **To** 2009 $18

Seppelt   ★★★★★

Moyston Road, Great Western, Vic 3377 **Region** Grampians
T (03) 5361 2239 **F** (03) 5361 2328 www.seppeltwines.com.au **Open** 7 days 10–5
Winemaker Emma Wood **Est.** 1908 **Cases** 150 000
Australia's best known producer of sparkling wine, always immaculate in its given price range but also producing excellent Great Western-sourced table wines, especially long-lived Shiraz and Australia's best Sparkling Shirazs. The glitzy labels of the past have rightly been consigned to the rubbish bin, and the product range has been significantly rationalised and improved. Following the sale of Seppeltsfield to Kilikanoon, this is the sole operating arm of Seppelt under Foster's ownership. Exports to the UK, the US and other major markets.

Drumborg Riesling 2007 An aromatic floral blossom bouquet leads into a beautiful palate, with fine lime, lemon and passionfruit flavours, tied off by perfect acidity. Screwcap. 13° alc. **Rating** 96 **To** 2027 $34.95

St Peters Grampians Shiraz 2005 In the new St Peters style, focusing more on line, length and balance in a medium-bodied framework; lovely blackberry fruit with spice and licorice, finishing with soft tannins and quality French oak. Meritorious alcohol. Screwcap. 13.5° alc. **Rating** 95 **To** 2025 $69.95

Jaluka Drumborg Vineyard Chardonnay 2007 Cool-climate chardonnay of a high order; very tight, long and focused, with a minerally streak through nectarine and grapefruit flavours; immaculate oak. Gold, Sydney Wine Show '08. Screwcap. 13° alc. **Rating** 94 **To** 2015 $26.95

Coborra Drumborg Vineyard Pinot Gris 2007 Has more intensity and thrust than any other mainstream gris or grigio; pear, apple and a fabulous web of citrus; long, dry finish. Screwcap. 14° alc. **Rating** 94 **To** 2012 $25

Mt Ida Vineyard Shiraz 2005 Rich boots-and-all Heathcote style; masses of blackberry and blood plum fruit with supporting new oak and ripe tannins. **Rating** 94 **To** 2025 $55

Benno Bendigo Shiraz 2005 An elegant, medium-bodied palate with particularly good balance of fruit, oak and tannins; black and red cherry f lavours run through to a long finish; quality oak. Screwcap. 13.5° alc. **Rating** 94 **To** 2020 $54.95

Chalambar Bendigo Grampians Shiraz 2006 Strong red-purple; sophisticated winemaking produces a medium-bodied palate with a silky smooth texture to the plum and blackberry fruits and fine tannins; modern-day classic of this great label. Screwcap. 14° alc. **Rating** 94 **To** 2016 $26.95

Grampians Cabernet Sauvignon 2005 Medium-bodied, with supple mouthfeel from perfectly ripened blackcurrant fruit; ripe but fine tannins and well-balanced oak. Value plus. Screwcap. 14° alc. **Rating** 93 **To** 2015 $18.95

Silverband Grampians Sparkling Shiraz NV A very good example of the style; does not hit you over the head with a mallet; the shiraz varietal character is certainly there; the '07 release had an average age of six years on tirage. Crown seal. 13° alc. **Rating** 92 **To** 2015 $35

Victorian Shiraz 2005 Scented notes of spice and herb; not particularly rich, but has length; oak and tannins in balance. 14° alc. **Rating** 91 **To** 2014 $17.95

Silverband Grampians Shiraz 2005 Light- to medium-bodied; a distinctly savoury style with good texture and structure, but needing more sweet fruit on the mid-palate. Screwcap. 14° alc. **Rating** 90 **To** 2017 $35

Grampians Moyston Cabernet Sauvignon 2006 Definitely for those who like a touch of vino-sadism in their cabernet, with uncompromising slightly dry tannins running through the length of the palate; some echoes of older-style Bordeauxs. Screwcap. 14° alc. **Rating** 89 **To** 2016 $25.95

Salinger 2004 Crisp, lively and long, with citrussy characters; lacks complexity. Neither region nor varieties specified. Cork. 12.5° alc. **Rating** 89 **To** 2011 $30

Fleur de Lys Pinot Noir Chardonnay Pinot Meunier 2004 Strawberry and other red fruit characters from the pinot noir and pinot meunier components; finishes with crisp, crunchy acidity. Cork. 12° alc. **Rating** 89 **To** 2011 $21.95

Seppeltsfield   ★★★★★

1 Seppeltsfield Road, Seppeltsfield via Nuriootpa, SA 5355 **Region** Barossa Valley **T** (08) 8568 6217 **F** (08) 8562 8333 **www**.seppelt.com.au **Open** Mon–Fri 10–5, w'ends & public hols 11–5
Winemaker James Godfrey **Est.** 1851 **Cases** 150 000
In August 2007 this historic property and its treasure trove of great fortified wines dating back to 1878 was purchased by the Kilikanoon group. There was a series of complicated lease-back arrangements, and supply agreements entered into between Kilikanoon and vendor Foster's,

further complicated by Foster's keeping the Seppelt brand for table and sparkling wines (mostly produced at Great Western, Vic, see separate entry) but the Seppelt brand for fortified wines vesting in purchaser Kilikanoon. The winery was fully recommissioned for the 2008 vintage, including the gravity flow system designed by Benno Seppelt in 1878.

ŸŸŸŸŸ **100 Year Old Para Liqueur 1907** The usual honey, treacle consistency, the olive-green/brown wine staining the sides of the glass as it is swirled; offers cinnamon stick, every spice known to man, grandma's Christmas pudding and a hundred other things; the senses almost go into free-fall, so intense and complex is the wine. The length is extraordinary, and all the components (including volatile acidity) are exactly as they should be. In prior years I have given the wine 98 points, which is clearly wrong. This is the one and only 100-point wine made in Australia. Cork. 23°alc. **Rating** 100 **To** 2100 $1000

Rare Tawny DP90 NV By common consent, the greatest Australian tawny, but with no similarity whatsoever to Para Liqueur. Superb, scintillating length, balance and harmony; so much finesse with so much flavour. 500 ml. 20.5° alc. **Rating** 97 **To** 2009 $65.95

Rare Rutherglen Tokay DP59 NV Wave-upon-wave of gloriously complex flavours; luscious tea leaf, butterscotch and spiced cake; mouthfilling, lingering, thrilling. 17.5° alc. **Rating** 97 **To** 2009 $65.95

Amontillado DP116 NV Marvellous balance and intensity of nutty rancio with penetrating acidity; flavour-packed, fleetingly sweet and nutty, then a dry finish. Screwcap. 22° alc. **Rating** 96 **To** 2009 $21.95

Rare Rutherglen Muscat GR113 NV Deep mahogany-brown; olive rim; a mix of almond, smoke, spice, rose petal and raisin; a Joseph's coat of flavours; wonderful life and style, the finish lasting forever. 500 ml. 17.5° alc. **Rating** 96 **To** 2009 $67.95

Oloroso DP38 NV Mid-brown, with a hint of green on the rim; nutty rancio complexity, with just a touch of sweetness; finely balanced with a constant interplay between nutty, honeyed sweetness and drier, rancio characters. The finish lingers in the mouth for minutes, without any hint of alcohol heat. Screwcap. 21° alc. **Rating** 95 **To** 2008 $21.95

Oloroso Sherry DP118 NV Golden brown; a very complex bouquet of nuts, dried fruits and rancio; the palate is intense, complex and very long, with acidity counterbalancing the sweetness, and outstanding rancio character preventing any chance of the wine cloying. **Rating** 95 **To** 2009 $21.95

Grand Rutherglen Muscat DP63 NV Glowing olive-brown; intense but very supple, with spicy plum pudding and caramel flavours; a fine and lingering finish. **Rating** 94 **To** 2009 $29.95

ŸŸŸŸŸ **Fino DP117 NV** The alcohol is less than many Barossa Valley red wines; finesse and grace so well-constructed you do not think it is dry until the aftertaste, which is as clear as a spring day. Along the way you meet cut green apple and nutty characters, adding to a wine which comes second only to freshly imported Spanish manzanilla. Screwcap. 15.5° alc. **Rating** 93 **To** 2009 $21.95

Rutherglen Tokay DP37 NV Pale, bright golden-brown; rich, tea leaf, honey and malt aromas; the palate with a more complex structure and weight than the other wines in its class. Serve fully chilled in summer and at cellar temperature in winter. **Rating** 90 **To** 2009 $17.95

Rutherglen Muscat DP33 NV Bright tawny-gold; fresh, floral fruit aromatics with splashes of spice; clean spirit. Lively, grapey/raisiny fruit perfectly balanced by acidity and the thrust of the spirit. **Rating** 90 **To** 2009 $17.95

Serafino Wines   ★★★★★

McLarens on the Lake, Kangarilla Road, McLaren Vale, SA 5171 **Region** McLaren Vale
T (08) 8323 0157 **F** (08) 8323 0158 **Open** Mon–Fri 10–5, w'ends & public hols 10–4.30
Winemaker Scott Rawlinson **Est.** 2000 **Cases** 20 000

In the wake of the sale of Maglieri Wines to Beringer Blass in 1998, Maglieri founder Steve Maglieri acquired the McLarens on the Lake complex originally established by Andrew Garrett. The accommodation has been upgraded and a larger winery was commissioned in 2002. The operation draws upon 40 ha each of shiraz and cabernet sauvignon, 7 ha of chardonnay, 2 ha each of merlot, semillon, barbera, nebbiolo and sangiovese, and 1 ha of grenache. Part of the grape production is sold. Exports to the UK, the US and other major markets.

♀♀♀♀♀ **Sharktooth Wild Ferment McLaren Vale Chardonnay 2006** Has unusual intensity for McLaren Vale; lovely nectarine and grapefruit aromas and flavours; quality oak; delicate finish. Screwcap. 13.5° alc. **Rating** 95 **To** 2011 $28

Sharktooth McLaren Vale Shiraz 2006 Very concentrated colour and bouquet; lashings of oak, mocha, fruitcake and dark berry fruits; thick and unctuous across the palate, but with good acidity for the silky textured finish. Cork. 15° alc. **Rating** 94 **To** 2025 $50

♀♀♀♀♀ **McLaren Vale Cabernet Sauvignon 2006** Medium-bodied; good line, length and balance; fruit, oak and tannins all seamless. **Rating** 91 **To** 2016 $24

McLaren Vale Shiraz 2005 A supple and smooth palate, with deliciously ripe black cherry, plum and blackberry fruit, plus the omnipresent dark chocolate; however, the oak level is too high. Cork. 14.5° alc. **Rating** 90 **To** 2018 $25

Sorrento McLaren Vale Cabernet Sauvignon Cabernet Franc Merlot 2005 Plenty of sweet dark fruit, and even a little chocolate; a soft, fleshy and ample finish. Screwcap. 14.5° alc. **Rating** 90 **To** 2016 $15

Grenache Tempranillo Shiraz 2006 Aromatic bouquet; appealing soft, fresh fruit, with well-balanced oak, finishing with soft tannins; ready now. Screwcap. 15° alc. **Rating** 90 **To** 2010 $20

♀♀♀♀ **Goose Island Semillon Sauvignon Blanc 2007** A delicate gooseberry/tropical citrus mix on the palate, with a subliminal touch of sweetness on the finish. Screwcap. 12.5° alc. **Rating** 89 **To** 2009 $14

Reserve McLaren Vale Chardonnay 2006 A wine of considerable weight; stone fruit and melon flavours with 100% barrel ferment in French oak. Screwcap. 13.5° alc. **Rating** 89 **To** 2011 $19

Sharktooth Wild Ferment McLaren Vale Chardonnay 2007 Deep colour; a very nutty wine, with high levels of oak, juicy grapefruit and vibrant acidity on the very toasty finish. Screwcap. 13.5° alc. **Rating** 89 **To** 2009 $30

Reserve McLaren Vale Chardonnay 2007 Appealing aromas of toasty oak, bright stone fruits and some roasted nuts for good measure; clean and vibrant on the finish. Screwcap. **Rating** 89 **To** 2009 $18

McLaren Vale Shiraz 2006 Good concentration, but there is a dryness to the bitter chocolate finish that breaks the line; maybe time is the answer. Cork. 14.5° alc. **Rating** 89 **To** 2015 $24

McLaren Vale Cabernet Sauvignon 2005 Earthy/chocolatey overtones to ripe plum and blackberry fruit; pleasant wine for easy drinking. Cork. 14.5° alc. **Rating** 89 **To** 2011 $25

Goose Island McLaren Vale Shiraz 2005 A bit reductive, but lovely bright red fruits and savoury spices; quite fine and firm on the finish, which is quite long and harmonious. Screwcap. 14.5° alc. **Rating** 88 **To** 2012 $13

Goose Island McLaren Vale Cabernet Merlot 2004 Clean, fresh, spicy black and red fruits; minimal tannins and oak; ready to roll right now. Screwcap. 14° alc. **Rating** 88 **To** 2009 $14

Goose Island McLaren Vale Chardonnay 2007 Rich, ripe and almost tropical fruits; good weight, and quite textural; self contradictory. Screwcap. 13° alc. **Rating** 87 **To** 2009 $13

Goose Island McLaren Vale Rose 2007 Fine and focused red fruit, with just a little spice and refreshing acidity. Screwcap. 12° alc. **Rating** 87 **To** 2009 $13

Serrat ★★★★☆

PO Box 478, Yarra Glen, Vic 3775 **Region** Yarra Valley
T (03) 9730 1439 **F** (03) 9730 1579 **www.serrat.com.au Open** Not
Winemaker Tom Carson **Est.** 2001 **Cases** 400
Serrat is the family business of Tom Carson (after a 12-year reign at Yering Station, now running Yabby Lake and Heathcote Estate for the Kirby family) and partner Nadege Suné. They have close-planted (at 8800 vines per ha) 0.8 ha each of pinot noir and chardonnay, 0.42 ha shiraz, and a sprinkling of viognier. Exports to Singapore.

ŸŸŸŸŸ **Yarra Valley Chardonnay 2006** Pale straw-green; super-elegant style, with seamless fusion and balance of nectarine/melon fruit, controlled oak and acidity. Has a long life ahead. Screwcap. 13.5° alc. **Rating** 94 **To** 2015 $28.50

ŸŸŸŸŸ **Yarra Valley Pinot Noir 2006** Brilliantly clear colour; disciplined winemaking has not tried to force a clearly defined but light pinot into something it is not; delicate, silky farewell. Screwcap. 13.5° alc. **Rating** 92 **To** 2011 $28.50

Serventy Organic Wines ★★★☆

Rocky Road, Forest Grove, WA 6286 **Region** Margaret River
T (08) 9757 7534 **F** (08) 9757 7272 **www.serventy.com.au Open** 7 days 10–5
Winemaker Andrew Gaman **Est.** 1984 **Cases** 2000
In 2003 a small group of wine enthusiasts from Perth acquired the business from the famous naturalist Serventy family (one of the early movers in organic viticulture and winemaking). Substantial investments have been made to both vineyard and winery, and the house on the property has been restored for short-term holiday stays. The quality of the wines has improved significantly, without losing the original identity. Exports to the UK.

ŸŸŸŸŸ **Purely Organic Margaret River Chardonnay 2005** A soft wine, with white peaches and creamy mouthfeel; still vibrant and fresh; one of the better examples of organic wines around. Cork. 13.5° alc. **Rating** 90 **To** 2009 $29

ŸŸŸŸ **Purely Organic Solstice 2007** A fresh wine with red fruits and good flavour; a little sweetness here, but with quite a dry finish; clean and well made. Good value organic red. Screwcap. 12.5° alc. **Rating** 88 **To** 2009 $18
Purely Organic Margaret River Shiraz 2005 A spicy wine, with redcurrant fruits, and a little herbaceous undertone; medium-bodied and quite fresh. Cork. 14° alc. **Rating** 88 **To** 2009 $29
Purely Organic Margaret River Sparkling Pinot Noir 2006 Bright pale pink, with good acidity, and a dry, slightly savoury, finish. Cork. 13° alc. **Rating** 88 **To** 2012 $29
Pinot Noir Merlot Rose 2007 Fresh red fruit flavours in a light frame; just a touch of sweetness on the finish, largely balanced by acidity. **Rating** 87 **To** 2009 $18

Setanta Wines ★★★★★

RSD 43 Williamstown Road, Forreston, SA 5233 (postal) **Region** Adelaide Hills
T (08) 8380 5516 **F** (08) 8380 5516 **www.setantawines.com.au Open** Not
Winemaker Rod Chapman, Rebecca Wilson **Est.** 1997 **Cases** 5000
Setanta is a family-owned operation involving Sheilagh Sullivan, her husband Tony, and brother Bernard; the latter is the viticulturist, while Tony and Sheilagh manage marketing, administration and so forth. Of Irish parentage (they are first-generation Australians), they chose Setanta, Ireland's most famous mythological hero, as the brand name. The beautiful and striking labels tell the individual stories which give rise to the names of the wines. Exports to Ireland, of course; also to the UK, Dubai, Singapore, Hong Kong and Japan.

ŸŸŸŸŸ **Emer Adelaide Hills Chardonnay 2007** An elegant wine with stone fruit and a light touch of toasty oak; the flavour builds across the palate, and the finish is long and harmonious. Screwcap. 13.3° alc. **Rating** 94 **To** 2012 $22

Black Sanglain Adelaide Hills Cabernet Sauvignon 2006 This is a seriously opulent cabernet, with violets, cassis and cedar, and even mineral notes; the palate is really fleshy, but the structure is there to gobble up the fruit; very long and very fine and generous. Cork. 14.5° alc. **Rating** 94 **To** 2018 $29

Settlement Wines

Lot 101 Seaview Road, McLaren Vale, SA 5171 **Region** McLaren Vale
T (08) 8323 7344 **F** (08) 8323 7355 **www**.settlementwines.com.au **Open** Mon–Fri 10–5, w'ends & public hols 11–5
Winemaker Vincenzo Berlingieri **Est.** 1992 **Cases** 3500
Vincenzo Berlingieri is a bigger than life graduate of Perugia University, Italy. He arrived in Melbourne with beard flowing and arms waving (his words) in 1964 as a research scientist to work in plant genetics. He subsequently moved to SA, and gained considerable publicity for the winery he then owned, and for his larger than life wines. There is nothing new in the reincarnated Settlement Wines, still with big table wines, but with specialties in liqueurs and fortified wines.

ŢŢŢŢŢ **Black Pedro Ximinex NV** Dark chocolate and raisin plum pudding; mouthcoating and an extremely rich and luscious finish. Cork. 18° alc. **Rating** 93 **To** 2020 $30
Langhorne Creek Tinta Negra 1997 Interesting rancio, roasted walnut aromas and flavours; a good line of acid and freshness to the finish maintains the intrigue; quite dry on the finish. Cork. 18.5° alc. **Rating** 90 **To** 2016 $30

ŢŢŢŢ **Muscat Liqueur NV** Strong rancio, nutty aromas really pushing the envelope to quite a dry and savoury, raisined finish. Cork. 18.5° alc. **Rating** 87 **To** 2015 $30
White Pedro NV Quite fresh and lively, with a dry nutty rancio character, which gives a hint of bitterness to the finish. Unique style. Cork. 18.5° alc. **Rating** 87 **To** 2015 $30

Settlers Rise Montville

249 Western Avenue, Montville, Qld 4560 **Region** Queensland Coastal
T (07) 5478 5558 **F** (07) 5478 5655 **www**.settlersrise.com.au **Open** 7 days 10–5
Winemaker Peter Scudamore-Smith MW (Contract) **Est.** 1998 **Cases** 3500
Settlers Rise is located in the beautiful highlands of the Blackall Range, a 75-min drive north of Brisbane and 20 mins from the Sunshine Coast. A little over 1 ha of chardonnay, verdelho, shiraz and cabernet sauvignon have been planted at an elevation of 450 m on the deep basalt soils of the property. First settled in 1887, Montville has gradually become a tourist destination, with a substantial local arts and crafts industry and a flourishing B&B and lodge accommodation. In December 2007 there was a change of ownership, but no change to the operations.

ŢŢŢŢ **Queensland Classic Sauvignon Semillon 2007** Misleading label, as Orange provided the sauvignon blanc, and did so handsomely in flavour terms, semillon providing the structure. Screwcap. 12° alc. **Rating** 88 **To** 2010 $18.50

Seven Ochres Vineyard   NR

PO Box 202, Dunsborough, WA 6281 **Region** Margaret River
T (08) 9755 2030 **F** (08) 9755 2030 **www**.sevenochres.com.au **Open** Not
Winemaker Chris Harding **Est.** 1998 **Cases** 150
Chris and Alice Harding have taken a roundabout route to the Margaret River, Chris' interest in wine blossoming while working at the Royal Sydney Yacht Squadron in the late 1970s, before moving to Scotland. He and wife Alice returned to Australia in 1994, immediately settling in the Margaret River with their young family. They established the Viticlone Supplies Grapevine Nursery, and now have 60 grape varieties and over 120 clones available. Some of the more exotic varieties in propagation are vermentino, fiano, mondeuse, lagrein, sagrantino, cilliegiolo and sangiovese brunello di montalcino. They have established 1 ha of

viognier, encouraged by the early results from this variety. They have also purchased cabernet sauvignon, petit verdot and merlot from a single-vineyard site in the northern part of the Margaret River.

Sevenhill Cellars

College Road, Sevenhill, SA 5453 **Region** Clare Valley
T (08) 8843 4222 **F** (08) 8843 4382 **www**.sevenhillcellars.com.au **Open** Mon–Fri 9–5, w'ends & public hols 10–5
Winemaker Liz Heidenreich **Est.** 1851 **Cases** 35 000
One of the historical treasures of Australia; the oft-photographed stone wine cellars are the oldest in the Clare Valley, and winemaking is still carried out under the direction of the Jesuitical Manresa Society. Quality is very good, particularly of the powerful Shiraz; all the wines reflect the estate-grown grapes from old vines. Exports to the UK, Switzerland, Norway and NZ.

Brother John May Reserve Shiraz 2004 Richly robed, luscious dark fruits; ripe tannins and complementary oak; cork permitting, will be long-lived; 50 dozen made. Cork. **Rating** 93 **To** 2019 $50

Lost Boot Rose 2007 Has enough structure to please those drinking the wine with food, and enough sweetness for those who just want a quaff. Screwcap. 14° alc. **Rating** 87 **To** 2009 $14

Seville Estate

65 Linwood Road, Seville, Vic 3139 **Region** Yarra Valley
T (03) 5964 2622 **F** (03) 5964 2633 **www**.sevilleestate.com.au **Open** 7 days 10–5
Winemaker Dylan McMahon **Est.** 1970 **Cases** 3500
Dr Peter McMahon and wife Margaret commenced planting Seville Estate in 1972 as part of the resurgence of the Yarra Valley. Peter and Margaret retired in 1997, selling to Brokenwood. Graham and Margaret Van Der Meulen acquired the property in '05, bringing it back into family ownership. Graham and Margaret are hands-on in the vineyard and winery, working closely with winemaker Dylan McMahon who is the grandson of Peter and Margaret. The philosophy is to capture the fruit expression of the vineyard in styles that reflect the cool climate.

Reserve Yarra Valley Chardonnay 2005 A bright bouquet, with plenty of pear flesh and toasty oak; lively palate, with good texture and a very fresh finish; has harmony and balance. Screwcap. 14.5° alc. **Rating** 94 **To** 2016 $40

The Barber Yarra Valley Chardonnay 2006 The initial impression is of delicacy and freshness to the grapefruit/melon flavours, but the wine gains power and intensity on the back-palate and finish. Screwcap. 14° alc. **Rating** 92 **To** 2013 $19
Yarra Valley Shiraz 2005 Brighter fruit than the Old Vine Reserve; plenty of spice on the bouquet and palate; generous flavour profile. Screwcap. 14.5° alc. **Rating** 90 **To** 2018 $27

The Barber Yarra Valley Shiraz Cabernet 2005 A mix of blackberry, blackcurrant, pepper and spice; evenly distributed tannins give length. Screwcap. 14.5° alc. **Rating** 89 **To** 2012 $19
Reserve Old Vine Yarra Valley Shiraz 2005 Quite cool and spicy aromas; herbs and medium-bodied red fruits on the palate; quite fine, but lacks flavour despite level of alcohol. Screwcap. 14.5° alc. **Rating** 87 **To** 2016 $60

Seville Hill

8 Paynes Road, Seville, Vic 3139 **Region** Yarra Valley
T (03) 5964 3284 **F** (03) 5964 2142 **www**.sevillehill.com.au **Open** 7 days 10–6
Winemaker Dominic Bucci, John D'Aloisio **Est.** 1991 **Cases** 3000

John and Josie D'Aloisio have had a long-term involvement in the agricultural industry, which ultimately led to the establishment of the Seville Hill vineyard in 1991. There they have 2.4 ha of cabernet sauvignon and 1.3 ha each of merlot, shiraz and chardonnay. John D'Aloisio makes the wines with Dominic Bucci, a long-time Yarra resident and winemaker.

ŸŸŸŸŸ **Yarra Valley Cabernet Shiraz Merlot 2005** Good balance and flow to the mix of black and red fruits, the tannins fine and ripe, the oak subtle; by far the best of the current range. Diam. 14.5° alc. **Rating** 90 **To** 2014 $20

ŸŸŸŸ **Yarra Valley Pinot Noir 2005** Very rich and ripe, with some dried plum characters, but no shortage of flavour; will live, and satisfy pinot critics. Diam. 14° alc. **Rating** 89 **To** 2013 $30
Reserve Yarra Valley Shiraz 2005 Strong colour; obviously, a decision to produce the ripest possible wines from the Yarra Valley in a style which should appeal to Robert Parker Jnr. Diam. 15.6° alc. **Rating** 89 **To** 2015 $30

Shadowfax

K Road, Werribee, Vic 3030 **Region** Geelong
T (03) 9731 4420 **F** (03) 9731 4421 **www.**shadowfax.com.au **Open** 7 days 11–5
Winemaker Matt Harrop **Est.** 2000 **Cases** 15 000
Shadowfax is part of an awesome development at Werribee Park, a mere 20 mins from Melbourne. The truly striking winery, designed by Wood Marsh architects, built in 2000, is adjacent to the extraordinary 60-room private home built in the 1880s by the Chirnside family and known as The Mansion. It was then the centrepiece of a 40 000-ha pastoral empire, and the appropriately magnificent gardens were part of the reason why the property was acquired by Parks Victoria in the early 1970s. The Mansion is now The Mansion Hotel, with 92 rooms and suites. Exports to the UK, Japan, NZ and Singapore.

ŸŸŸŸŸ **One Eye Heathcote Shiraz 2005** A lovely bright and focused example, with red and dark fruits, plush texture, fine-grained tannins and focused acidity; long, fine and complex, will age gracefully. Screwcap. 14.4° alc. **Rating** 95 **To** 2018 $65
Chardonnay 2006 Immaculate winemaking brings together Geelong/Macedon/Beechworth/Cardinia Ranges components into a coherent and convincing whole; stone fruit, cashew and creamy touches all combining. Screwcap. 13.5° alc. **Rating** 94 **To** 2012 $28
Macedon Ranges Chardonnay 2006 A wine of understated power; prominent citrus fruit is framed by complex mineral flavours and cool acidity; very long and fine on the finish. Screwcap. 13° alc. **Rating** 94 **To** 2015 $45
Pink Cliffs Heathcote Shiraz 2005 Richer and warmer than the One Eye, and nearly as compelling; dark fruits and a little fruitcake spice; sweet and ample, with a chewy, fruitful finish. Screwcap. 14.3° alc. **Rating** 94 **To** 2018 $65

ŸŸŸŸŸ **Viognier 2007** Quite complex, with a strong savoury spicy personality; lovely texture and a little grip on the finish. Goulburn Valley/Yarra Valley. Screwcap. 13° alc. **Rating** 90 **To** 2009 $28

ŸŸŸŸ **Pinot Noir 2005** A savoury wine, with minerals, red fruits and a quite rich and firm palate; long and velvety texture on the finish. Screwcap. 13.5° alc. **Rating** 89 **To** 2009 $29
Landscape Shiraz 2005 Bright red fruits are framed by a little mint; medium-bodied and with silky texture; quite spicy and fine on the finish. Screwcap. 14° alc. **Rating** 89 **To** 2014 $29
Adelaide Hills Sauvignon Blanc 2007 Dominated by minerals on the bouquet, with quite rich texture and a strong savoury, mineral edge on the finish. Screwcap. 12.5° alc. **Rating** 88 **To** 2009 $18
Adelaide Hills Pinot Gris 2007 A good example of gris style, with candied orange fruits, ample flesh and a clean finish. Screwcap. 13° alc. **Rating** 87 **To** 2009 $22

Shantell

1974 Melba Highway, Dixons Creek, Vic 3775 **Region** Yarra Valley
T (03) 5965 2155 **F** (03) 5965 2331 **www**.shantellvineyard.com.au **Open** 7 days 10.30–5
Winemaker Shan Shanmugam, Turid Shanmugam **Est.** 1980 **Cases** 1800
The substantial and fully mature Shantell vineyards provide the winery with a high-quality
fruit source; part is sold to other Yarra Valley makers, the remainder vinified at Shantell.
Chardonnay, Semillon and Cabernet Sauvignon are its benchmark wines, sturdily reliable,
sometimes outstanding. Exports to the UK and Singapore.

ŢŢŢŢŢ **Yarra Valley Chardonnay 2005** Quite a savoury wine, with hints of dried straw,
grapefruit and grilled nuts; good texture on the palate, with a little amaro twist.
Cork. 13.5° alc. **Rating** 91 **To** 2012 $28
Yarra Valley Cabernet Sauvignon 2003 Pure cassis on the bouquet, with a
little Yarra edge; good flavour and weight; quite soft and supple, and a long finish.
Cork. **Rating** 91 **To** 2015 $28

Sharmans ★★★

Glenbothy, 175 Glenwood Road, Relbia, Tas 7258 **Region** Northern Tasmania
T (03) 6343 0773 **F** (03) 6343 0773 **www**.sharmanswines.com **Open** W'ends 10–5
Winemaker Tamar Ridge (Andrew Pirie) **Est.** 1987 **Cases** 1000
Mike Sharman pioneered one of the more interesting wine regions of Tasmania, not far south
of Launceston but with a distinctly warmer climate than (say) Pipers Brook. Ideal north-facing
slopes are home to a vineyard now approaching 4 ha. This additional warmth gives the red
wines greater body than most Tasmanian counterparts.

ŢŢŢŢ **Pinot Noir 2006** Bright and lively colour, likewise aromas; overall good flavour,
though could do with a touch more thrust on the finish. Screwcap. 13.9° alc.
Rating 87 **To** 2011
Cabernet Merlot 2006 A very savoury wine, with black olive and ample
tannins; the fruit is tightly wound, but may open with time. Screwcap. 13° alc.
Rating 87 **To** 2012
Shaman 2004 Generous flavour and depth, with a combination of fruit and
toasty lees development. Diam. 12.5° alc. **Rating** 87 **To** 2010

Shaw & Smith

Lot 4 Jones Road, Balhannah, SA 5242 **Region** Adelaide Hills
T (08) 8398 0500 **F** (08) 8398 0600 **www**.shawandsmith.com **Open** W'ends 11–4
Winemaker Martin Shaw, Darryl Catlin **Est.** 1989 **Cases** 35 000
Has progressively moved from a contract grape-grown base to estate production with the
development of a 51.5-ha vineyard at Balhannah, followed in 2000 by a state-of-the-art,
beautifully designed and executed winery, which ended the long period of tenancy at
Petaluma. From a single wine (Sauvignon Blanc) operation, now makes three benchmark
wines (Sauvignon Blanc, M3 Chardonnay and Shiraz) and smaller quantities of cellar door
specialities (Riesling and Pinot Noir), all of the highest quality. Exports to all major markets.

ŢŢŢŢŢ **M3 Vineyard Adelaide Hills Chardonnay 2006** Superfine and elegant, all the
components seamlessly married; whole bunch pressing, wild yeast and partial mlf;
nectarine and citrus fruit, quality oak, and a lingering finish. Beautiful wine, near
the very top of the Australian tree. Screwcap. 13.5° alc. **Rating** 97 **To** 2013 $38
Adelaide Hills Riesling 2007 A beautifully poised and calibrated wine; has
a delicacy not often encountered in the '07s, with all the requirements for
development in bottle. Screwcap. 13° alc. **Rating** 95 **To** 2012 $21
Adelaide Hills Sauvignon Blanc 2007 Spotlessly clean herb, spice and mineral
aromas; excellent balance, line and length building lemony flavour through to the
finish. Screwcap. 13° alc. **Rating** 95 **To** 2009 $25

Shaw Vineyard Estate ★★★★

34 Isabel Drive, Murrumbateman, NSW 2582 **Region** Canberra District
T (02) 6227 5827 **F** (02) 6227 5865 **www**.shawvineyards.com.au **Open** Wed–Sun &
public hols 10–5
Winemaker Bryan Currie, Graeme Shaw **Est.** 1999 **Cases** 3000
Graeme and Michael Shaw established a 33-ha vineyard (semillon, riesling, shiraz, merlot and
cabernet sauvignon) in 1998 on a 280-ha fine wool-producing property established in the
mid-1800s known as Olleyville. Production has grown; quality is up in leaps and bounds, as
reflected by numerous wine awards. Exports to Singapore and Macau.

ΨΨΨΨΨ **Murrumbateman Riesling 2007** Bright green-straw; has sweet lime juice
flavours throughout, with a core of well-balanced acidity, and good length.
Screwcap. 11.8° alc. **Rating** 90 **To** 2013 $22
Murrumbateman Shiraz Cabernet 2006 Attractive medium-bodied wine,
with a juicy blend of predominantly black fruits on a supple, verging silky, palate
almost entirely driven by fruit. Screwcap. 14° alc. **Rating** 90 **To** 2014 $22
Murrumbateman Cabernet Merlot 2006 Good colour; a fresh, quite
juicy mix of blackcurrant, cassis and a savoury twist of black olive; fine tannins.
Screwcap. 14° alc. **Rating** 90 **To** 2016 $22

ΨΨΨΨ **Murrumbateman Shiraz 2006** A medium- to full-bodied wine with an
abundance of ripe, rounded blackberry and plum fruit; slightly blurred line
and mouthfeel. Screwcap. 14° alc. **Rating** 89 **To** 2014 $22
Murrumbateman Cabernet Sauvignon 2006 Fresh and lively cassis and
blackcurrant aromas and flavours, with tannins appropriate for the variety; still
a little simple, but should develop. Screwcap. 14° alc. **Rating** 89 **To** 2016 $22

Shays Flat Estate ★★★★

482 Shays Flat-Malakoff Road, Landsborough, Vic 3384 **Region** Pyrenees
T 0417 589 136 **F** (03) 9826 6191 **www**.shaysflat.com **Open** Not
Winemaker Michael Unwin Wines **Est.** 1999 **Cases** 1400
With advice from leading viticultural consultant Di Davidson, Rob and Isabella Burns
have planted 11 ha of shiraz, 3.5 ha of cabernet sauvignon, 3.1 ha of merlot and 0.9 ha of
sangiovese on the western slopes of the Pyrenees Ranges. Since the arrival of Glenlofty
Vineyard in 1995, almost 1000 ha of vines have been planted in the valley. The Shays Flat soil
has a thin layer of loam over a red-orange duplex clay heavily dispersed with quartz particles,
the quartz providing favourable water holding and draining properties. At an altitude of
300–330 m on gently rising ridges, the property is situated at the end of the Great Dividing
Range, and is slightly warmer than most of the Pyrenees and Grampians vineyards. Exports
to Hong Kong and Singapore.

ΨΨΨΨΨ **Pyrenees Sangiovese 2005** Bright clear red; very lively and fresh, with
vibrancy and thrust, even though the palate is only light- to medium-bodied;
thoroughly impressive. Screwcap. 13.5° alc. **Rating** 92 **To** 2011 $20
Jack's View Pyrenees Shiraz 2006 Dark purple; medium- to full-bodied,
with licorice, prune, plum and blackberry fruit which does not go into overripe
territory; good balance and length. Screwcap. 14.2° alc. **Rating** 90 **To** 2013 $24

ΨΨΨΨ **Pyrenees Cabernet Sauvignon 2006** Medium-bodied; low alcohol does
throw up some mint and leaf notes, but the wine has good life and freshness to its
cassis fruit and superfine tannins. Screwcap. 13° alc. **Rating** 89 **To** 2013 $18
Pyrenees Merlot 2006 Has the appropriate weight and texture to the bramble,
olive and red fruits, but 18 months in barrel seems to have been too long, stripping
away some of the fruit on the finish. Screwcap. 14° alc. **Rating** 87 **To** 2011 $18

She-Oak Hill Vineyard

82 Hope Street, South Yarra, Vic 3141 (postal) **Region** Heathcote
T (03) 9866 7890 **www**.sheoakhill.com.au **Open** Not
Winemaker Hanging Rock (John Ellis) **Est.** 1995 **Cases** 800
Gordon, Judith and Julian Leckie selected a vineyard site on the east side of She-Oak Hill, lying between Jasper Hill Emily's Paddock and Mount Ida, sharing the same Cambrian red soil and an immaculate address pedigree. They opted for a dry-grown vineyard, but years of drought meant the establishment phase was prolonged, and it was not until 2001 (six years after the vines were planted) that the first commercial crop was obtained. The vines now have a deep root system and are producing well without any supplementary water. They have 4 ha of shiraz and 0.5 ha of chardonnay, producing around 400–600 cases of Shiraz and 200–300 cases of Chardonnay, with yearly variation depending on the growing conditions. Lower than usual alcohol levels is a feature of the wines.

Heathcote Shiraz Reserve 2005 Strong crimson-purple; a full-bodied palate, with blackberry, licorice and spice surrounded by dense but ripe tannins; needs at least 10 years. Cork. 14° alc. **Rating** 94 **To** 2025 $31.90

Heathcote Shiraz 2005 Good colour and lively dark fruit aromas; a little simple on the palate but well made. **Rating** 90 **To** 2012 $25

Sheep's Back

PO Box 441, South Melbourne, Vic 3205 **Region** Barossa Valley
T (03) 9696 7018 **F** (03) 9686 4015 **Open** Not
Winemaker Dean Hewitson **Est.** 2001 **Cases** 3000
Sheep's Back is a joint venture between Neil Empson (with 30 years' experience as an exporter to Australia and elsewhere of Italian wines) and Dean Hewitson. They decided to produce a single estate-grown shiraz after an extensive search found a 6-ha vineyard of 75-year-old vines. Exports to the US and Canada. No samples received; the rating is that of last year.

Shelmerdine Vineyards

Merindoc Vineyard, Lancefield Road, Tooborac, Vic 3522 **Region** Heathcote
T (03) 5433 5188 **F** (03) 5433 5118 **www**.shelmerdine.com.au **Open** 7 days 10–5
Winemaker De Bortoli (Yarra Valley) **Est.** 1989 **Cases** 10 000
Stephen Shelmerdine has been a major figure in the wine industry for well over 20 years, like his family (who founded Mitchelton Winery) before him, and has been honoured for his many services to the industry. The venture has 130 ha of vineyards spread over three sites: Lusatia Park in the Yarra Valley and Merindoc Vineyard and Willoughby Bridge in the Heathcote region. Substantial quantities of the grapes produced are sold to others; a small amount of high-quality wine is contract-made. Exports to the UK.

Yarra Valley Chardonnay 2006 A fragrant, complex bouquet offering barrel ferment notes and nectarine and melon fruit which flows onto the palate; has a long, tangy but bone-dry finish. Screwcap. 13.5° alc. **Rating** 94 **To** 2013 $28

Yarra Valley Pinot Noir 2007 Very good hue; remarkable depth to the cherry and plum fruit given (deliberately) low alcohol; touches of spice and oak, and good acidity; overall elegance. Screwcap. **Rating** 94 **To** 2012

Yarra Valley Pinot Noir 2006 An elegant, finely drawn and structured pinot in a sotto voce style; fruit forward, but with sufficient silky tannins to sustain it. Screwcap. 13.5° alc. **Rating** 94 **To** 2013 $30

Heathcote Shiraz 2006 Medium-bodied; outstanding texture and structure are the drivers of the wine, with appealing red and black fruits filling the mid-palate. Screwcap. 14° alc. **Rating** 94 **To** 2016 $31

Heathcote Cabernet Sauvignon 2006 Bright crimson; robust but correct cabernet flavours (blackcurrant, earth and cedar) and structure (firm tannins); good length; a little severe at the moment. Screwcap. 14° alc. **Rating** 93 **To** 2021 $32

Yarra Valley Rose 2007 Pale salmon; a distinct European cast to spicy red fruits; complex texture, and good length. Whole bunch-pressed pinot fermented in old oak. Screwcap. 13.5° alc. **Rating** 90 **To** 2010 $18

 **Yarra Valley Sauvignon Blanc 2007** Quiescent bouquet; firm herb, stone, grass and asparagus palate; long finish. Screwcap. 12.5° alc. **Rating** 89 **To** 2009 $22
Heathcote Viognier 2007 A powerful bouquet and palate leave no space for introspection; strong apricot and dried fruit characters, the dry finish a boon. Screwcap. 14.5° alc. **Rating** 89 **To** 2012 $28
Merindoc Vineyard Heathcote Shiraz 2005 Developed colour, not entirely bright; a complex palate, though the fruit does struggle to sustain the oak. Screwcap. 14.5° alc. **Rating** 89 **To** 2015 $55
Heathcote Merlot 2006 An initially attractive and authentic merlot, opening with sweet cassis fruit, then into more olive/savoury notes, and finally tannins, which are unfortunately too dry. Screwcap. 14° alc. **Rating** 89 **To** 2016 $28
Heathcote Riesling 2007 Developed colour; rich, broad, citrus and toast characters; a struggle with the vintage (and, perhaps, the region). Screwcap. 13.5° alc. **Rating** 87 **To** 2012 $22
Red Hat Shiraz Merlot Cabernet Sauvignon 2004 A light-bodied, early-drinking style, with gently sweet fruit, but not much structure. Screwcap. 14.5° alc. **Rating** 87 **To** 2009 $18

Shenton Ridge ★★☆

PO Box 129, Brunswick Junction, WA 6224 **Region** Margaret River
T (08) 9726 1284 **F** (08) 9726 1575 **www.**shentonridge.com.au **Open** Not
Winemaker John Durham (Contract) **Est.** 2002 **Cases** 6400
The Catalano family purchased the Shenton Ridge property in the Jindong area of Margaret River in 2002. The choice lay between extracting the gravel-rich soils, or planting a vineyard; the coin came down on the side of a vineyard, and 10 ha of vines (predominantly shiraz and chardonnay) were planted. Andrea Catalano is now the sole owner and manager of the vineyard.

Shepherd's Hut ★★★

PO Box 194, Darlington, WA 6070 **Region** Porongurup
T (08) 9299 6700 **F** (08) 9299 6703 **www.**shepherdshutwines.com **Open** Not
Winemaker Rob Diletti, Tony Davis **Est.** 1996 **Cases** 2000
The shepherd's hut which appears on the wine label was one of four stone huts used in the 1850s to house shepherds tending large flocks of sheep. When WA pathologist Dr Michael Wishart (and family) purchased the property in 1996, the hut was in a state of extreme disrepair. It has since been restored, and still features the honey-coloured Mount Barker stone. A total of 15.5 ha of riesling, chardonnay, sauvignon blanc, shiraz and cabernet sauvignon have been established; the daily running of the vineyard is the responsibility of son Philip, who also runs a large farm of mainly cattle; son William helps with marketing and sales. Most of the grapes are sold to other makers in the region. Exports to the UK.

 Porongurup Sauvignon Blanc 2007 Quite aromatic; rich tropical fruit, ever so faintly reduced; good length. **Rating** 88 **To** 2009 $18
Porongurup Shiraz 2004 Despite the alcohol, light- to medium-bodied and developing quickly; spicy berry fruit just holding for the short term. Stained cork. Cork. 14.8° alc. **Rating** 87 **To** 2009 $19

Shepherd's Moon ★★★☆

1 Barwang Road, Young, NSW 2594 **Region** Hilltops
T (02) 6382 6363 **F** (02) 6382 6363 **Open** By appt
Winemaker Canberra Winemakers (Greg Gallagher) **Est.** 1979 **Cases** 1000

Rick and Julie Hobba purchased the Hansen Hilltops property in 2002. They have since engaged in an extensive rehabilitation program in the vineyard, which is starting to pay dividends. The plantings are 2 ha of cabernet sauvignon, 1.5 ha riesling, and 1 ha each of chardonnay, shiraz and semillon.

ŸŸŸŸ⅋ **Shiraz 2006** Some mint, herb and spice aromas, the palate with intense blackberry fruit, the other notes still to come back into focus; firm and long, demands cellaring. Screwcap. 14.6° alc. **Rating** 90 **To** 2016 $22

ŸŸŸŸ **Cabernet Sauvignon 2006** Crimson-purple; firm, cool-grown cabernet aromas and flavours; strong tannin structure, oak largely incidental; should age well. Screwcap. 14.3° alc. **Rating** 89 **To** 2020 $22

Shingleback ★★★★★

1 Main Road, McLaren Vale, SA 5171 **Region** McLaren Vale
T (08) 8323 7388 **F** (08) 8323 7336 **www.**shingleback.com.au **Open** 7 days 10–4
Winemaker John Davey, Dan Hills **Est.** 1995 **Cases** 100 000
Shingleback has 100 ha of vineyards in McLaren Vale, all of which is vinified for the Shingleback labels. Originally a specialist export business, but now the wines are also available in Australia. Quality has risen greatly, as has total production. Which is the chicken, which is the egg? It doesn't really matter, is the best answer. Exports to the UK, the US, and other major markets.

ŸŸŸŸŸ **The Gate McLaren Vale Shiraz 2005** An attractive and lively, slightly left field, reflection of the region; medium-bodied, with a range of red and black fruits, spice and dark chocolate, and no alcohol impact. Cork. **Rating** 94 **To** 2015 $34.95
D Block Reserve McLaren Vale Shiraz 2005 A lusciously velvety melange of black fruits, dark chocolate, oak and ripe tannins; hard to resist if it is flavour you are after. Cork. 14.5° alc. **Rating** 94 **To** 2020 $59.95

ŸŸŸŸ⅋ **D Block Reserve McLaren Vale Cabernet Sauvignon 2005** Good colour; floods the mouth with intense blackcurrant varietal fruit; good texture, structure and length; despite cork, cellar-worthy. 14° alc. **Rating** 93 **To** 2020 $59.95
McLaren Vale Shiraz 2005 If nothing else, goes to prove the quality of the Reserve, for this too is typical McLaren Vale with all the components at a medium-bodied level; good finish. Cork. 14.5° alc. **Rating** 90 **To** 2015 $24.95

ŸŸŸŸ **McLaren Vale Cabernet Sauvignon 2005** Shows more regional dark chocolate than the Reserve, perhaps because a little riper; very savoury finish. Cork. 14.5° alc. **Rating** 89 **To** 2014 $24.95
Red Knot McLaren Vale Chardonnay 2006 Ripe, rich and quite fruity on the bouquet; nice weight and good flavour, especially for the price. Screwcap. 13.5° alc. **Rating** 87 **To** 2009 $14.95
Red Knot McLaren Vale Shiraz 2006 Brightly coloured with a little reduction on the bouquet; plenty of fleshy fruits on the palate in a drink-early, albeit full-bodied style. Screwcap. 14° alc. **Rating** 87 **To** 2013 $14.95
Cellar Door McLaren Vale Shiraz 2006 True regional expression, with black fruits and dark chocolate running through a medium-bodied palate; uncomplicated drink-soon style. Screwcap. 14° alc. **Rating** 87 **To** 2013 $17.95

Shottesbrooke ★★★★☆

Bagshaws Road, McLaren Flat, SA 5171 **Region** McLaren Vale
T (08) 8383 0002 **F** (08) 8383 0222 **www.**shottesbrooke.com.au **Open** Mon–Fri 10–4.30, w'ends & public hols 11–5
Winemaker Nick Holmes, Hamish Maguire **Est.** 1984 **Cases** 12 000
For many years now the full-time business of former Ryecroft winemaker Nick Holmes (now with stepson Hamish Maguire), drawing primarily on estate-grown grapes at his Myoponga vineyard. He has always stood out for the finesse and elegance of his wines compared with

the dam-buster, high-alcohol reds for which McLaren Vale has become famous (or infamous, depending on one's point of view). Now the wheel has started to turn full circle, and finesse and elegance are much more appreciated. Exports to all major markets.

ΨΨΨΨΨ **Eliza McLaren Vale Shiraz 2005** Ultimate regional style, with dark chocolate running alongside black cherry and blackberry fruit from start to finish; fine, soft tannins; good oak. Screwcap. 14.5° alc. **Rating** 94 **To** 2019 $38

ΨΨΨΨΨ **Adelaide Hills Sauvignon Blanc 2007** A clean, fresh bouquet, the palate ranging from herb and grass through to gentle tropical fruit; crisp finish. Screwcap. 13.5° alc. **Rating** 90 **To** 2009 $19.95

ΨΨΨΨ **McLaren Vale Merlot 2005** A scented bouquet with some varietal olivaceous overtones; light- to medium-bodied, but well-structured nonetheless. Screwcap. 14° alc. **Rating** 89 **To** 2011 $18
Merlette McLaren Vale Merlot Rose 2007 A cross between conventional rose and light dry red; attractive cassis fruit notes; dry finish. Screwcap. 13° alc. **Rating** 88 **To** 2009 $14.95
McLaren Vale Chardonnay 2007 Well made, particularly in a vintage not suited to more delicate styles such as those of Shottesbrooke. A hint of French oak and marginal fruit. Screwcap. 14° alc. **Rating** 87 **To** 2009 $19.95

Sieber Road Wines
Sieber Road, Tanunda, SA 5352 **Region** Barossa Valley
T (08) 8562 8038 **F** (08) 8562 8681 **www.**sieberwines.com **Open** 7 days 11–4
Winemaker Tim Geddes **Est.** 1999 **Cases** 4500
Richard and Val Sieber are the third generation to run Redlands, the family property, traditionally a cropping/grazing farm. They have diversified into viticulture with a total of 18 ha of vines, shiraz (14 ha) with the lion's share, the remainder viognier, grenache and mourvedre. Son Ben Sieber is a viticulturist.

ΨΨΨΨΨ **Special Release Barossa Valley Shiraz 2006** Similar diffuse colour to Ernest, but has deeper and apparently riper blackberry and licorice fruit despite the same alcohol; tannins and oak in balance. Screwcap. 15.5° alc. **Rating** 92 **To** 2021 $28
Barossa Valley Viognier 2007 Complex winemaking; whole bunch pressing, then 80% wild yeast fermentation with 80% matured in old oak; very good mid-palate flavour, but a slightly short finish. Screwcap. 14.5° alc. **Rating** 90 **To** 2012
Barossa Valley Grenache Shiraz Mourvedre 2006 Good depth and structure to the 45/30/25 estate-grown blend; considerable synergy between the components, the alcohol a positive rather than a negative. Major surprise. Screwcap. 15.5° alc. **Rating** 90 **To** 2015 $18

ΨΨΨΨ **Ernest Barossa Valley Shiraz 2006** High alcohol plays tricks with the wine, diminishing the flavour impact of the mid-palate, yet not making the overall flavour jammy, nor the finish hot. Screwcap. 15.5° alc. **Rating** 89 **To** 2016 $20
Barossa Valley Shiraz Viognier 2006 Usual vivid colour and perfumed bouquet, but the palate seems overworked/extracted, the oak too obvious; the net result is plenty of flavour, less finesse. Screwcap. 14.5° alc. **Rating** 87 **To** 2014 $18

Sienna Estate
Canal Rocks Road, Yallingup, WA 6282 **Region** Margaret River
T (08) 9755 2028 **F** (08) 9755 2101 **www.**siennaestate.com.au **Open** W'ends & hols 10–5
Winemaker Egidijus Rusilas, Sharna Kowalczuk, Siobhan Lynch **Est.** 1978 **Cases** 2000
The 3.7-ha vineyard, planted to semillon, sauvignon blanc, riesling and cabernet sauvignon, was established by David Hunt in 1978. It has now passed into the ownership of the Rusilas family, which has significantly enhanced its legacy. Exports to Lithuania and Singapore.

ⵧⵧⵧⵧⵧ **Momentum of Passion Semillon Sauvignon Blanc 2007** A bright, lively, zesty array of aromas and flavours circling between passionfruit and citrus; triumph for the year and the price. Screwcap. **Rating** 93 **To** 2010 $15

Momentum of Youth Semillon 2007 Top value; has the intensity and thrust of high quality wine, with positive flavours verging on grapefruit and stone fruit; does stumble fractionally on the finish. Screwcap. **Rating** 91 **To** 2012 $12

ⵧⵧⵧⵧ **Momentum of Freedom Chardonnay 2007** Pale straw-green; light-bodied, with a mix of stone fruit and apple aromas; clean, dry finish. Screwcap. **Rating** 87 **To** 2012 $15

Sigismondi Estate Wines ★★★

Main Road, Lyrup, SA 5343 **Region** Riverland
T (08) 8583 8203 **F** (08) 8583 8365 www.southernsecret.com.au **Open** 1 day (see below)
Winemaker Dino Sigismondi **Est.** 2003 **Cases** 2000
While the establishment date of the winery is given as 2003, Dino and Veronica Sigismondi purchased their first 12-ha vineyard in 1989, and have progressively increased to the present level of 75 ha of chardonnay, shiraz, cabernet sauvignon, merlot and petit verdot. They have two labels: Southern Secret, which is made onsite from start to finish, and a second label, Kuali Cliff, using estate grapes but contract-made offsite. The Southern Secret Petit Verdot has had great success, winning gold medals at successive Riverland wine shows (with successive vintages) and numerous enthusiastic press reviews. They have had several overseas marketing trips which has taught them the hazards and difficulties of exporting, but without dimming their hopes and expectations. It is open once a year from 8 am to 12 pm for the 'Around the Region' festival day.

ⵧⵧⵧⵧ **Southern Secret Shiraz 2005** Good colour and hue; commendable depth to blackberry and chocolate fruit; the sweetness on the finish will appeal to its market niche. Screwcap. 15.5° alc. **Rating** 88 **To** 2009 $12

Silk Hill ★★★★☆

324 Motor Road, Deviot, Tas 7275 **Region** Northern Tasmania
T (03) 6394 7385 **F** (03) 6394 7392 **Open** By appt
Winemaker Gavin Scott **Est.** 1989 **Cases** 500
Pharmacist Gavin Scott has been a weekend and holiday viticulturist for many years, having established the Glengarry Vineyard, which he sold, and then establishing the 1.5-ha Silk Hill (formerly Silkwood Vineyard) in 1989, planted exclusively to pinot noir.

Silver Wings Winemaking ★★★★★

28 Munster Terrace, North Melbourne, Vic 3051 **Region** Central Victoria Zone
T (03) 5429 2444 **F** (03) 5429 2442 **Open** By appt
Winemaker Keith Brien **Est.** 2003 **Cases** 1500
This is the venture of Keith Brien, formerly of Cleveland. After a brief shared occupation with Goona Warra Winery in Sunbury, he has moved Silver Wings to a small winery at Carlsruhe, near Lancefield. Here he offers contract winemaking and export consulting, as well as making the Silver Wings wines from 4 ha of contract-grown grapes (3 ha of mourvedre, 1 ha of shiraz) coming from 50-year-old vines. The cellar door, which also runs wine education programs and social events, has now moved to North Melbourne.

ⵧⵧⵧⵧⵧ **Macedon Ranges Brut NV** #98. Bright green-straw; superfine but intense citrus and stone fruit flavours, immaculate balance and minimal dosage; 78% from '98; 30% reserve wines from '90–'95. Chardonnay (75%)/Pinot Noir (25%). Cork. 11.8° alc. **Rating** 94 **To** 2011 $30

#2 Macedon Ranges Brut Rose NV Salmon-pink; very elegant, with fragrant, small red fruits and a lovely citrussy, juicy finish; 53% pinot noir from '98 vintage; remainder reserve wines from '90 and '95; 4 years on lees, disgorged '04. Cork. 12.6° alc. **Rating** 94 **To** 2011 $25

ŢŢŢŢ♀ **Vincenzo O.V. Mourvedre Shiraz 2005** Has good richness and supple texture, coming from old vines near Shepparton; black fruits are dominant, plus splashes of licorice and spice; 60/40. Diam. 13.5° alc. **Rating** 90 **To** 2012 $25

Silverstream Wines ★★★

2365 Scotsdale Road, Denmark, WA 6333 **Region** Great Southern
T (08) 9840 9119 **F** (08) 9384 5657 **www**.silverstreamwines.com **Open** W'ends &
public hols 11–4
Winemaker John Wade (Contract) **Est.** 1999 **Cases** 500
Tony and Felicity Ruse have 9 ha of chardonnay, merlot and cabernet franc in their vineyard 23 km from Denmark. The wines are contract-made, and after some hesitation, the Ruses decided their very pretty garden and orchard more than justified their recently opened cellar door, a decision supported by the quality on offer at very reasonable prices.

ŢŢŢŢ **Denmark Cabernet Franc Rose 2007** Slight salmon tinge; a mix of raspberries and cold tea; quite dry finish. Screwcap. 13° alc. **Rating** 87 **To** 2009 $17

Silverwaters Vineyard ★★★★

PO Box 41, San Remo, Vic 3925 **Region** Gippsland
T (03) 5678 5230 **F** (03) 5678 5989 **Open** Not
Winemaker Paul Evans (Contract) **Est.** 1995 **Cases** 1000
Lyn and Lionel Hahn planted 0.5 ha each of chardonnay, pinot gris, pinot noir, shiraz and cabernet sauvignon in 1995. The first commercial vintage followed five years later, and the wines have gone from strength to strength, the 2003 Pinot Noir winning the trophy and gold medal for Pinot Noir at the International Cool Climate Wine Show '05.

ŢŢŢŢ♀ **Pinot Gris 2007** Apple, pear and citrus flavours illuminate the long, intense and dry palate; well above average. Diam. 13.5° alc. **Rating** 90 **To** 2010 $21
Shiraz 2006 Considerable depth and richness to the dark chocolate and blackberry fruit, a slightly savoury twist to the tannins adding both flavour and textural interest. Diam. 14.5° alc. **Rating** 90 **To** 2016 $24
Cabernet Sauvignon 2006 Concentrated and ripe, far more so than the cool region would suggest; velvety texture to blackberry and dark chocolate fruit; ripe tannins. Diam. 14° alc. **Rating** 90 **To** 2020 $24

ŢŢŢŢ **Pinot Noir 2006** Finishes slightly short, but does have gently ripe plum fruit and well-handled oak adding texture. Diam. 13.5° alc. **Rating** 88 **To** 2011 $26

Silverwood Wines ★★★★

66 Bittern-Dromana Road, Balnarring, Vic 3926 **Region** Mornington Peninsula
T 0419 890 317 **F** (03) 8317 6642 **www**.silverwoodwines.com.au **Open** Not
Winemaker Paul Dennis, Phillip Kittle **Est.** 1997 **Cases** 700
Paul and Denise Dennis were inspired to establish Silverwood by living in France for a year. They, with members of their family, did much of the establishment work on the vineyard, which is meticulously maintained. All of the grapes are now used for Silverwood (in earlier years some were sold), not surprising given that the 2005 Pinot Noir topped the class of 48 '05 pinots at the strictly judged Winewise Small Vignerons Awards '06 in Canberra.

ŢŢŢŢ♀ **Marque d'Argent Special Release Mornington Peninsula Pinot Noir 2005** A lifted bouquet of red fruit, spice and a little game; ample and fine on the palate, the finish long and savoury. Cork. 13.9° alc. **Rating** 91 **To** 2014 $39
Mornington Peninsula Chardonnay 2006 Ripe nectarine and a little toast; fresh and vibrant, with linear acidity, and good texture on the finish. Screwcap. 13.9° alc. **Rating** 90 **To** 2012 $26

Simon Hackett

Budgens Road, McLaren Vale, SA 5171 **Region** McLaren Vale
T (08) 8323 7712 **F** (08) 8323 7713 **Open** Wed–Sun 11–5
Winemaker Simon Hackett **Est.** 1981 **Cases** 12 000
In 1998 Simon Hackett acquired the former Taranga winery in McLaren Vale, which has made his winemaking life a great deal easier. He has 8 ha of estate vines, and has contract growers in McLaren Vale and the Barossa Valley, with another 32 ha of vines. Exports to the UK, the US, Germany, the Netherlands, Russia, Oman and Hong Kong.

ŸŸŸŸŸ **Old Vine McLaren Vale Grenache 2005** Quite lifted fruit, but dark and quite serious on the palate; rich and thickly textured, and chewy on the medium-bodied finish. Screwcap. 14° alc. **Rating** 90 **To** 2014 $15

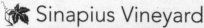 ## Sinapius Vineyard

111 Archers Road, Hillwood, Tas 7252 (postal) **Region** Northern Tasmania
T 0417 341 764 **F** (03) 6336 1073 **Open** Not
Winemaker Vaughn Dell **Est.** 2005 **Cases** 300
When Vaughn Dell and Linda Morice purchased the former Golders Vineyard from Richard Crabtree in 2005, both were only 24. Both were originally from Tasmania, but between '01 and '05 worked in various parts of Australia, Linda to complete a university degree in occupational therapy and Vaughn working at wineries in the Hunter Valley, Yarra Valley (at Wedgetail Estate) and Margaret River (Barwick Estates) before returning to Tasmania to undertake vintage at Tamar Ridge in '05. The vineyard had 1 ha of mature pinot noir and 0.5 ha of mature chardonnay, which are now being expanded with new clones, and they have planted a high-density pinot block on a 1 m-by-1.3 m spacing. Vaughn made the 2007 Pinot Noir and Chardonnay at Holm Oak under the guidance of Rebecca Wilson, and a small winery and cellar door are planned; until the winery is completed future wines will be made at nearby Delamere.

ŸŸŸŸŸ **Pipers Brook Pinot Noir 2006** Deep colour; plenty of concentration of fruit and oak; a fresh palate with good flavour depth and length. Screwcap. 13.5° alc. **Rating** 90 **To** 2012 $34

Sinclair of Scotsburn

256 Wiggins Road, Scotsburn, Vic 3352 **Region** Ballarat
T 0419 885 717 **F** (03) 8699 7550 **www**.sinclairofscotsburn.com.au **Open** By appt
Winemaker Scott Ireland **Est.** 1997 **Cases** 200
David and Barbara Sinclair purchased their property in 2001. At that time 1.2 ha of chardonnay and 0.8 ha of pinot noir had been planted, but had struggled, the pinot noir yielding less than 0.25 tonnes in '02. With the aid of limited drip irrigation, cane pruning, low crop levels and bird netting, limited quantities of high-quality chardonnay and pinot have since been produced. Half the annual production is sold to Tomboy Hill, the other half made for the Sinclair of Scotsburn label.

ŸŸŸŸ **Manor House Pinot Noir 2006** Light, bright colour; a fresh, brisk palate, with red cherry, strawberry and spice fruit; not complex, but the flavours are correct. Screwcap. 13.5° alc. **Rating** 89 **To** 2012 $21
Wallijak Chardonnay 2006 Has reached full ripeness; a complex palate with almond meal, fig and some peach; more weight (and less finesse) than expected. Screwcap. 13.5° alc. **Rating** 88 **To** 2010 $21

Sinclair Wines ★★★★☆

Graphite Road, Glenoran, WA 6258 **Region** Manjimup
T (08) 9335 6318 **F** (08) 9433 5489 **www**.sinclairwines.com.au **Open** By appt
Winemaker Elizabeth Reed (Contract), Bill Crappsley (Consultant) **Est.** 1994 **Cases** 4000

Sinclair Wines is the child of Darelle Sinclair, a science teacher, wine educator and graduate viticulturist from CSU, and John Healy, a lawyer, traditional jazz musician and graduate wine marketing student of Adelaide University, Roseworthy campus. The 5 ha of estate plantings underpin high-quality wines at mouthwatering prices. Looking at the range as a whole, one cannot help but wonder how anyone thought that pinot noir would be the most suitable variety for this part of the world. Exports to the UK, Canada, the Netherlands and Japan.

ŶŶŶŶŶ **Jezebel Manjimup Cabernet Merlot 2005** Despite its modest alcohol has all the weight and flesh one could wish for; seductive cassis and blackcurrant fruit runs the full length of the palate; fine tannins and oak. Great value. Screwcap. 13° alc. **Rating** 94 **To** 2020 $20

ŶŶŶŶŶ **Ricardo Shiraz 2005** Fragrant and lively aromas; excellent cool-grown bright cherry, spice and cracked pepper aromas and flavours; fine tannins, good length. Screwcap. 14.5° alc. **Rating** 92 **To** 2017 $25
Giovanni Manjimup Cabernet Sauvignon 2005 Curiously lighter in flavour impact than the Shiraz or Cabernet Merlot; pretty cassis/redcurrant flavours; does have length, though. Screwcap. 13° alc. **Rating** 90 **To** 2013 $20
Jeremy Cabernet Shiraz 2006 Softer than the Cabernet Sauvignon, but has many of the same red fruit characters, and the fruit is allowed to express itself without being pumped up by oak; appealing light- to medium-bodied wine. Screwcap. 13° alc. **Rating** 90 **To** 2012 $10

ŶŶŶŶ **Swallow Hill Manjimup Sauvignon Blanc 2007** Light touches of cut grass and some tropical fruit; good palate weight and texture. Screwcap. 13.5° alc. **Rating** 88 **To** 2009 $16
Lady Claire Manjimup Chardonnay 2005 Clever, restrained use of 25% barrel fermentation gives both texture and the impression of more nectarine fruit sweetness to the unwooded version. Screwcap. 13° alc. **Rating** 88 **To** 2008 $18
Rose of Glenoran 2007 Deeply coloured and with lots of flavour; hints of spice frame the red fruit. Screwcap. 12.5° alc. **Rating** 87 **To** 2009 $16

Sinclair's Gully   ★★★☆

Lot 3 Colonial Drive, Norton Summit, SA 5136 **Region** Adelaide Hills
T (08) 8390 1995 **www.**sinclairsgully.com **Open** Wed–Sun 12–4 Aug–May or by appt
Winemaker Contract **Est.** 1998 **Cases** 600
Sue and Sean Delaney purchased their 10.5 ha property at Norton Summit in 1997. The property had a significant stand of remnant native vegetation, with a State Conservation Rating, and since acquiring the property much energy has been spent in restoring 8 ha of pristine bushland, home to 130 species of native plants and 66 species of native birds, some recorded as threatened or rare. It has been a DIY venture for the Delaneys (supported by family and friends) with Sue Delaney hand-pruning the 0.4 ha each of chardonnay and sauvignon blanc planted in 1998. The progressive adoption of biodynamic viticulture has coincided with numerous awards for the protection of the natural environment, and most recently, the Rural Landholder Award '07 for the Protection of a Threatened Species or Ecosystem.

ŶŶŶŶ **Adelaide Hills Sauvignon Blanc 2007** A clean but relatively inexpressive bouquet; firm asparagus, grass and mineral flavours, the palate finishing with crisp, citrussy acidity. Screwcap. 12.6° alc. **Rating** 89 **To** 2010 $22
Family Reserve Barossa Shiraz 2005 Significant colour development indicative of elevated alcohol and pH; soft confit black fruits and mocha ex oak. Screwcap. 15.5° alc. **Rating** 87 **To** 2010 $25

Sirromet Wines   ★★★★

850–938 Mount Cotton Road, Mount Cotton, Qld 4165 **Region** Queensland Coastal
T (07) 3206 2999 **F** (07) 3206 0900 **www.**sirromet.com **Open** 7 days 10–5
Winemaker Adam Chapman, Velten Tiemann **Est.** 1998 **Cases** 100 000

This was an unambiguously ambitious venture, which has succeeded in its aim of creating Qld's premier winery. The founding Morris family retained a leading architect to design the striking state-of-the-art winery with an 80 000-case production capacity; the state's foremost viticultural consultant to plant the four major vineyards (in the Granite Belt) which total over 100 ha; and the most skilled winemaker practising in Qld, Adam Chapman, to make the wine. It has a 200-seat restaurant, a wine club offering all sorts of benefits to its members, and is firmly aimed at the domestic and international tourist market, taking advantage of its situation, halfway between Brisbane and the Gold Coast. Exports to the Netherlands, Malaysia, Taiwan, Singapore, Japan and China.

ŸŸŸŸŸ **Seven Scenes Granite Belt Merlot 2005** Medium-bodied, quality merlot, balancing savoury/olive characters with gently sweet red berry fruits; snow pea and cassis. Screwcap. 14° alc. **Rating** 91 **To** 2014 $21.95
Seven Scenes Granite Belt Chardonnay 2005 Has nectarine and melon fruit woven together with oak and notes of cashew; deceptively well-balanced. Like the Merlot, puts Qld well and truly on the quality map. Screwcap. 12.8° alc. **Rating** 90 **To** 2012 $21.95
Seven Scenes Cabernet Sauvignon 2005 Some colour development; a mix of cedar, earth and black fruits in a medium-bodied frame; savoury but balanced tannins, and good oak. Screwcap. 14° alc. **Rating** 90 **To** 2013 $24.99

ŸŸŸŸ **820 Above Pinot Gris 2006** Straw-bronze; has plenty of flavour, building progressively through the palate to the finish, which is clear and crisp. Screwcap. 12.7° alc. **Rating** 89 **To** 2009 $14.99
Seven Scenes Chardonnay Pinot Noir 2005 Pale pink-salmon; notwithstanding the chardonnay dominance in the blend, the pinot noir contribution is obvious throughout; a delicate, nicely crisp and well-balanced wine; dry finish. Cork. 11.9° alc. **Rating** 89 **To** 2009 $25
Viognier 2006 Well made; gentle apricot, pear and citrus flavours; a fresh, clean finish. Screwcap. 13° alc. **Rating** 88 **To** 2010 $18.99
820 Above Cabernet Merlot 2005 A pleasant, light- to medium-bodied mix of small dark berry fruits plus notes of herb, sage and earth; appropriate tannin and oak support. Screwcap. 14.3° alc. **Rating** 88 **To** 2010 $14.99
820 Above Pinot Gris 2007 Attractive aromas and flavours on the mid-palate before sliding away somewhat on the finish; at least not propped up by sugar. Screwcap. 12° alc. **Rating** 87 **To** 2009 $15
TM Granite Belt Viognier 2006 Ripe exotic fruit aromas; good weight on the palate, and still quite fresh, with a spicy finish. Screwcap. 13° alc. **Rating** 87 **To** 2011 $20

Sittella Wines   ★★★★

100 Barrett Street, Herne Hill, WA 6056 **Region** Swan Valley
T (08) 9296 2600 **F** (08) 9296 0237 **www.**sittella.com.au **Open** Tues–Sun & public hols 11–5
Winemaker Matthew Bowness **Est.** 1998 **Cases** 7000
Perth couple Simon and Maaike Berns acquired a 7-ha block (with 5 ha of vines) at Herne Hill, making the first wine in 1998 and opening a most attractive cellar door facility later in the year. They also own the 10-ha Wildberry Springs Estate vineyard in the Margaret River region. Consistent and significant wine show success has brought well-deserved recognition for the wines.

ŸŸŸŸŸ **Margaret River Chardonnay 2006** Bright pale straw-green; well made, with positive supple stone fruit flavours and quality barrel ferment oak inputs in support. Good value. Screwcap. 13.5° alc. **Rating** 91 **To** 2012 $22
Margaret River Semillon 2007 Fresh and lively; the small proportion matured in oak has added to the structure without diminishing the fruit; nice herb and grass flavours. Screwcap. 13.4° alc. **Rating** 90 **To** 2012 $19.50

Margaret River Merlot 2006 Light crimson; complex aromas and flavours within a medium-bodied context, with blackcurrant cassis and oriental spices plus a touch of oak; enjoy it for its freshness. Screwcap. 13.7° alc. **Rating** 90 To 2012 $19.95

Show Reserve Liqueur Verdelho NV Is as complex as the blend of liqueur Verdelho/Pedro Ximinez/Muscat would suggest, the two minor components much older, the verdelho with nice toffee/Christmas cake characters. Cork. 18.5° alc. **Rating** 90 To 2009 $45

♀♀♀♀ **Margaret River Cabernet Sauvignon 2006** Some slightly minty, herbal aromas, but has good mouthfeel and length to the cassis and blackcurrant of the palate; well-integrated French oak. Screwcap. 14° alc. **Rating** 89 To 2014 $23

Skillogalee ★★★★

Off Hughes Park Road, Sevenhill via Clare, SA 5453 **Region** Clare Valley
T (08) 8843 4311 **F** (08) 8843 4343 **www**.skillogalee.com.au **Open** 7 days 10–5
Winemaker Dave Palmer, Daniel Palmer **Est.** 1970 **Cases** 10 000
David and Diana Palmer purchased the small hillside stone winery from the George family at the end of the 1980s and have fully capitalised on the exceptional fruit quality of the Skillogalee vineyards. All the wines are generous and full-flavoured, particularly the reds. In 2002 the Palmers purchased next-door neighbour Waninga Vineyards, with 30 ha of 30-year-old vines, allowing a substantial increase in production without any change in quality or style. Exports to the UK, Switzerland, the US, Malaysia and Hong Kong.

♀♀♀♀♀ **Clare Valley Cabernet Sauvignon Cabernet Franc Malbec 2004** Excellent colour clarity; strong blackcurrant, cassis and mulberry fruit picked at perfect ripeness; generous but not heavy or jammy; good oak and tannin management. Screwcap. 14.5° alc. **Rating** 94 To 2024 $28.50

♀♀♀♀♀ **Single Vineyard Clare Valley Riesling 2007** A substantial and powerful wine, with pineapple and citrus fruit; a flavour dip on the back-palate, but comes again on the aftertaste. Screwcap. 13° alc. **Rating** 91 To 2012 $22.50

Smallfry Wines ★★★★☆

13 Murray Street, Angaston, SA 5353 **Region** Barossa Valley
T (08) 8564 2182 **F** (08) 8564 2182 **www**.smallfrywines.com.au **Open** By appt
tel 0412 153 243
Winemaker Wayne Ahrens, Colin Forbes, Tim Smith **Est.** 2005 **Cases** 1200
The engagingly-named Smallfry Wines is the venture of Wayne Ahrens and partner Suzi Hilder. Wayne comes from a fifth-generation Barossa family, Suzi is the daughter of well-known Upper Hunter viticulturist Richard Hilder and wife Del, partners in Pyramid Hill Wines. Both have degrees from CSU, and both have extensive experience – Suzi as a senior viticulturist for Foster's, and Wayne's track record includes seven vintages as a cellar hand at Orlando Wyndham and other smaller Barossa wineries. They have 5.5 ha of cabernet sauvignon, 2.3 ha of riesling, 1.5 ha of shiraz and a few vines of mataro, plus an additional 18 ha of recently purchased old vine vineyard in the Vine Vale subregion. Most of the fruit from this vineyard is sold to other Barossa wineries, but a small amount will be held back to add to the Smallfry range.

♀♀♀♀♀ **Barossa Shiraz 2006** Medium-bodied, with excellent balance, structure and length; fully ripe flavours with moderate alcohol an achievement in itself; oak a subtle backwash. Screwcap. 14° alc. **Rating** 94 To 2016 $28

♀♀♀♀♀ **Barossa Grenache Shiraz Mataro 2006** Good colour; altogether more satisfying, with more fruit complexity and more structure than the Grenache; has balanced tannins and good length. Screwcap. 15° alc. **Rating** 92 To 2013 $28

♀♀♀♀ **Barossa Grenache 2006** Bright colour; in many ways, utterly belies its alcohol; whatever view one takes of Barossa Valley grenache, this is best drunk sooner rather than later. Screwcap. 16° alc. **Rating** 89 To 2009 $28

Barossa Tempranillo Grenache 2007 Young and juicy red fruit bouquet; vibrant and lively palate, with plenty of fruit. Screwcap. **Rating** 88 **To** 2012 $28
Cabernet Grenache Rose 2007 Not a lot of fruit depth, but a neat tension between acidity and sweetness achieved in the winery. Eden Valley. Screwcap. 11° alc. **Rating** 87 **To** 2009 $18

Smidge Wines   ★★★★

62 Austral Terrace, Malvern, SA 5061 (postal) **Region** Southeast Australia
T (08) 8272 0369 **F** (08) 8272 8491 **www.**smidgewines.com **Open** Not
Winemaker Matt Wenk **Est.** 2004 **Cases** 1000
Matt Wenk and Trish Callaghan have many things in common: their joint ownership of Smidge Wines, their marriage, and their real day jobs. Matt has a distinguished record as Flying Winemaker and, in Australia, working with Tim Knappstein and then Peter Leske at Nepenthe Wines. These days he is the winemaker for Two Hands Wines (and Sandow's End). Trish holds a senior position in one of the world's largest IT services companies, and in 2003 was a finalist in the Australian Young Business Woman of the Year. The elegantly labelled wines are Le Grenouille (The Frog) Adelaide Hills Merlot, from a small vineyard in Verdun, and The Tardy Langhorne Creek Zinfandel which (and I quote) 'is named The Tardy in honour of Matt's reputation for timekeeping (or lack thereof)'. Exports to the UK and the US.

ŶŶŶŶŶ **Adamo Barossa Valley Shiraz 2005** Aromatic notes of mint, spice and herbs, but the palate has more richness and density than expected, with ripe plum and blackberry essence; controlled extract. Screwcap. 15.1° alc. **Rating** 93 **To** 2020 $26
The Cellar-pod Adelaide Hills Viognier 2006 Attractive; while the varietal statement isn't particularly strong, has good line and length, the oak mere background scenery; 8 barrels made. Screwcap. 13.5° alc. **Rating** 92 **To** 2009 $26

ŶŶŶŶ **The Donald Barossa Valley Zinfandel 2005** Curious pine resin aromas which come through as part of the thundering herd of flavours and alcohol on the palate. Bravery needed. Screwcap. 15.7° alc. **Rating** 89 **To** 2015 $38
S Smitch Barossa Valley Shiraz 2005 Distinct confit/jam aromas, the over-the-top ripeness and alcohol making a major statement. In a style which will appeal to some, and not others. Cork. 15.5° alc. **Rating** 89 **To** 2020 $65
The Houdini 2005 Light- to medium-bodied; soft, sweet red fruits, reigned in by light tannins on the finish. Screwcap. 14.5° alc. **Rating** 87 **To** 2010 $16

Smithbrook   ★★★★★

Smithbrook Road, Pemberton, WA 6260 **Region** Pemberton
T (08) 9772 3557 **F** (08) 9772 3579 **www.**smithbrook.com.au **Open** Mon–Fri 9–4, w'ends by appt
Winemaker Michael Symons, Ashley Lewkowski **Est.** 1988 **Cases** 8000
Smithbrook is a major player in the Pemberton region, with over 60 ha of vines in production. Owned by Petaluma/Lion Nathan, but continues its role as a contract grower for other companies, as well as supplying Petaluma's needs and making relatively small amounts of wine under its own label. Perhaps the most significant change has been the removal of Pinot Noir from the current range of products, and the introduction of Merlot. The Far Flung second label offers great value. Exports to the UK, Canada and Japan.

ŶŶŶŶŶ **Pemberton Sauvignon Blanc 2007** Strong varietal sauvignon, with cut grass, nettle and bright acidity; good depth of fruit, and quite long and flavoursome on the finish. Screwcap. 13° alc. **Rating** 94 **To** 2009 $19
The Yilgarn Blanc 2007 A well-handled complex style; maintains freshness and focus amidst the complex toasty oak; very long, and quite mouthfilling, with very good balance on the finish. Screwcap. 13° alc. **Rating** 94 **To** 2009 $35

ŶŶŶŶ **Far Flung Corner Unwooded Chardonnay 2006** Gentle stone fruit, melon and a touch of grapefruit; good acidity provides life, length and zest. Screwcap. 14° alc. **Rating** 89 **To** 2009 $17

Far Flung Corner Cabernet Merlot 2006 Good hue; fresh, bright and breezy, with cassis-accented fruit; fine tannins. Screwcap. 13.5° alc. **Rating** 89 **To** 2011 $17
The Yilgarn Blanc 2006 The strong oak influence gives a wine with more exotic fruit character, and very noticeable toasty oak on the finish; lots of flavour, but less finesse. Sauvignon Blanc. Screwcap. 12.5° alc. **Rating** 88 **To** 2009 $28
Pemberton Merlot 2005 Good juicy merlot fruit; soft and approachable with a hint of cedar from the oak, and juicy plums on the palate. Screwcap. **Rating** 88 **To** 2010 $24

Smiths Vineyard   ★★★★★

27 Croom Lane, Beechworth, Vic 3747 **Region** Beechworth
T 0412 475 328 **F** (03) 5728 1603 **www**.smithsvineyard.com.au **Open** W'ends & public hols 10–5 or by appt
Winemaker Jeanette Henderson, Will Flamsteed **Est.** 1978 **Cases** 600
Pete and Di Smith established the first vineyard in Beechworth in 1978, with the encouragement of John Brown Jr of Brown Brothers. In 2003 the winery and vineyard was taken over by their daughter Sarah and husband Will Flamsteed. At 550 m, the 2.5-ha vineyard is predominantly chardonnay, with some cabernet sauvignon and merlot which make the estate wines. Will and Sarah made their first Beechworth Shiraz in 2006.

ΨΨΨΨΨ **Beechworth Chardonnay 2006** Very good colour; high quality wine from start to finish, with nectarine/white peach fruit and seamless oak; long, balanced finish. Screwcap. 13.8° alc. **Rating** 94 **To** 2015 $34
310 Beechworth Shiraz 2006 Crimson-purple; elegant, juicy black and red fruits, licorice and spice; silky and supple mouthfeel and good length. Screwcap. 14.4° alc. **Rating** 94 **To** 2021 $40

ΨΨΨΨΨ **Beechworth Cabernet Merlot 2005** Herbaceous style; spicy/earthy edges to the blackcurrant fruit; while only light- to medium-bodied, has plenty of intensity and length. Screwcap. 13.2° alc. **Rating** 90 **To** 2015 $30

Snobs Creek Wines   ★★★☆

486 Goulburn Valley Highway, via Alexandra, Vic 3714 **Region** Upper Goulburn
T (03) 5774 2017 **F** (03) 5774 2017 **www**.snobscreekvineyard.com.au **Open** W'ends 11–5, closed winter
Winemaker MasterWineMakers **Est.** 1996 **Cases** 3500
The vineyard is situated where Snobs Creek joins the Goulburn River, 5 km below the Lake Eildon wall. Originally planted in 1996, the vineyard has recently been increased to 16 ha. The varieties grown are pinot gris, pinot noir, shiraz, viognier, chardonnay, merlot and dolcetto; all manage to produce no more then 7.4 tonnes per hectare. Is described as a cool-climate vineyard in a landscaped environment.

ΨΨΨΨ **VSP Shiraz 2005** Light- to medium-bodied; many similarities to the varietal, but a touch more blackberry fruit at its core and on the finish. Screwcap. 14.5° alc. **Rating** 89 **To** 2012 $25
Dolcetto Syrah 2006 The Peter Lehmann blend; light- to medium-bodied; quite vibrant red fruits on the bouquet with additional notes of spice and blackberry on the palate. Screwcap. 14.5° alc. **Rating** 88 **To** 2011 $16
Lightly Wooded Chardonnay 2005 A delicate, light-bodied wine which has developed slowly; has some length, though not so much depth. Screwcap. 13.8° alc. **Rating** 87 **To** 2009 $18
Shiraz 2005 Light- to medium-bodied; very spicy, tangy, savoury wine moving quite rapidly to its peak. Screwcap. 14.5° alc. **Rating** 87 **To** 2009 $18
Shiraz Cabernet Merlot 2005 Despite its alcohol, light-bodied, with a mix of red berry, mint and spice aromas and flavours; difficult to see through the wine. Screwcap. 15° alc. **Rating** 87 **To** 2010 $20

Snowy Vineyard Estate ★★☆

125 Werralong Road, Dalgety, NSW 2628 **Region** Southern New South Wales Zone
T (02) 6456 5052 **F** 1800 021 986 **www**.snowywine.com **Open** 7 days 10–5
Winemaker Rob Howell **Est.** 1984 **Cases** 1500
This is the slightly renamed Snowy River Winery (briefly called Manfred's), the change
following its acquisition by David and Sue Lowe (no relation to David Lowe of Mudgee) in
2005. It continues to claim to be Australia's coldest climate vineyard (I'm not sure it is) and
to grow sieger rebe (correctly seigerrebe), rhein riesling (correctly riesling), mueller thurgau
(correctly muller thurgau) and sylvaner. The most fascinating wine is their Snow Bruska, 'a
medium-bodied blend of cabernet and rhein riesling with full fruit flavour'.

Somerset Hill Wines

540 McLeod Road, Denmark, WA 6333 **Region** Denmark
T (08) 9840 9388 **F** (08) 9840 9394 **www**.somersethillwines.com.au **Open** 7 days 11–5
summer, winter 11–4
Winemaker Graham Upson (red), Harewood Estate (James Kellie, white) **Est.** 1995
Cases 2000
Graham Upson commenced planting 11 ha of pinot noir, chardonnay, semillon, merlot and
sauvignon blanc in 1995, on one of the coolest and latest-ripening sites in WA. The limestone
cellar door sales area has sweeping views out over the ocean and to the Stirling Ranges,
with everything from Belgian chocolates to farm-grown mushrooms for sale (and, of course,
wine). Exports to Denmark, Russia and Poland.

ꔹꔹꔹꔹꔹ **Semillon 2007** A tightly wound bouquet of lemon and fresh cut grass; generously
textured, with great purity and focus on the very long finish; will reward patient
cellaring. Screwcap. 13° alc. **Rating** 94 **To** 2016 $21

Songlines Estates

PO Box 221, Cessnock, NSW 2325 **Region** Southeast Australia
T (02) 4934 3214 **F** (02) 4934 3214 **www**.songlinesestates.com **Open** Not
Winemaker David Fatches, John Duval **Est.** 2002 **Cases** 3500
This is another of the multinational, multi-talented boutique wine operations springing up
like mushrooms after autumn rain. The English end is represented by Martin Krajewski and
Esme Johnstone (big names in the UK) and by David Fatches and John Duval as McLaren
Vale winemakers. It becomes a little more complicated when one finds the vineyard address
is Gabriel's Paddocks in the Hunter Valley, and that Bylines Hunter Valley Chardonnay is one
of several wines produced. The majority come from old-vine vineyards in McLaren Vale and
from Coonawarra; however, samples were not submitted for tasting.

ꔹꔹꔹꔹ **Bylines Hunter Valley Chardonnay 2006** A full-bodied wine with ripe fruit
and generous French oak; lots of flavour in a somewhat old-fashioned style. Cork.
13° alc. **Rating** 89 **To** 2009 $55

 ## Sons & Brothers Vineyard ★★☆

PO Box 978, Orange, NSW 2800 **Region** Orange
T (02) 6366 5117 **www**.sonsandbrothers.com.au **Open** Not
Winemaker Chris Bourke **Est.** 1978 **Cases** 250
Chris and Kathryn Bourke do not pull their punches when they say, 'Our vineyard has had
a checkered history because in 1978 we were trying to establish ourselves in a non existent
wine region with no local knowledge and limited personal knowledge of grapegrowing and
winemaking. It took us about 15 years of hit and miss before we started producing regular
supplies of appropriate grape varieties at appropriate ripeness levels for sales to other NSW
wineries.' In 2001 their 2-ha vineyard produced their first commercial vintage of Cabernet
Shiraz (a 70%/30% blend). They mature the wine for five to six years before release, and use a
unique closure involving a stainless steel crown cap, an oxygen barrier foil and a small plastic
bidule, a variant of champagne closures used during tirage.

Sorby Adams Wines

Lot 18, Gawler Park Road, Angaston, SA 5353 **Region** Eden Valley
T (08) 8564 2741 **F** (08) 8564 2437 **www**.sorbyadamswines.com **Open** 7 days 10–5
Winemaker Simon Adams **Est.** 2004 **Cases** 5000
Simon Adams and wife Helen purchased a 3.2-ha vineyard in 1996, which had been planted by Pastor Franz Julius Lehmann (none other than Peter Lehmann's father) in 1932. Peter Lehmann always referred to it as 'Dad's Block'. They have added 0.25 ha of viognier which, as one might expect, is used in a shiraz viognier blend. Most recent plantings are of shiraz (2.5 ha), riesling (1.7 ha) and cabernet sauvignon (0.7 ha). Nonetheless, the top wines, The Family Shiraz and The Thing Shiraz, need no assistance from viognier. Only six barrels of The Thing are made each year, using the best grapes from Dad's Block. The name Sorby Adams has overtones of a chameleon: it comes from a female ancestor of long-serving Yalumba winemaker Simon Adams, whose full name is Simon David Sorby Adams.

ΨΨΨΨΨ **Individual Vineyard Eden Valley Cabernet Sauvignon 2005** Ripe cassis-accented fruit with complementary oak; fine ripe tannins; enjoyable style of cabernet, now or later. Screwcap. 14° alc. **Rating** 90 **To** 2015 $20

ΨΨΨΨ **The GT Eden Valley Gewurztraminer 2007** A closed bouquet, then some hints of lychee and spice on the palate; very difficult year for the variety, well-made. Screwcap. 13° alc. **Rating** 88 **To** 2011 $20

Soul Growers

34 Maria Street, Tanunda, SA 5352 (postal) **Region** Barossa Valley
T 0417 851 317 **Open** By appt
Winemaker James Lindner, Paul Lindner, David Cruickshank **Est.** 1998 **Cases** 600
James Lindner is a fifth-generation Barossan, working in every area of the wine industry since he left school. In 1998 he acquired a small property on the hills of Seppeltsfield, planting 1.6 ha of shiraz, 0.8 ha of grenache, 0.3 ha of mourvedre, and a little cabernet sauvignon and black muscat. The first three varieties are separately open-fermented and given two years barrel age before the wine is blended and bottled (without filtration or fining). Exports to Canada and Singapore.

ΨΨΨΨΨ **Barossa Valley Shiraz 2005** An immensely concentrated wine, exuding black fruits, licorice and spice from every pore, the oak and tannins in a back seat role, as is the alcohol (however improbable). Cork. 15.5° alc. **Rating** 94 **To** 2020 $50

ΨΨΨΨΨ **Barossa Valley Shiraz Grenache Mourvedre 2005** Medium-bodied; a ripe expression of varietal blend and of region; best sooner rather than later. Cork. 15.5° alc. **Rating** 90 **To** 2010 $29.50

ΨΨΨΨ **Barossa Valley Shiraz Cabernet 2005** Far less body and more spicy/savoury than the alcohol would suggest, though the colour is still fresh; not much structure. Cork. 15.5° alc. **Rating** 87 **To** 2012 $29.50

🍂 Souter's Vineyard

390 Happy Valley Road, Rosewhite, Vic 3737 **Region** Alpine Valleys
T (03) 5752 1077 **www**.happyvalley75.com.au/soutersvineyard/ **Open** Fri–Sun 10–4,
7 days in Jan
Winemaker Contract **Est.** 1983 **Cases** 300
Melbourne professional couple Kay and Allan Souter acquired the former Rosewhite Vineyard in late 2003. The vineyard, one of the oldest in the Alpine Valleys region, had been run down significantly owing to the age and ill health of the former owners, and the Souters have invested much time and effort in rehabilitating, retrellising and regrafting the vineyard to more suitable varieties. The first vintage was made in 2004, but alas there were no '07 wines thanks to frost and bushfire smoke taint.

ŢŢŢŢ **Alpine Valleys Shiraz 2004** Light- to medium-bodied; spicy, savoury overtones to dark fruit flavours; fine tannins; two years in oak. Cork. 13.5° alc. **Rating** 88 **To** 2013 $17.50
Alpine Valleys Cabernet Sauvignon 2004 Holding hue well; a strong mint/eucalypt overlay to the red fruit is a legitimate cool-climate style; does lack structure, however. Cork. 13.2° alc. **Rating** 87 **To** 2013 $20
White Gold 2006 An odd blend, with clear fruit flavours; good balance and length. Chardonnay (60%)/Gewurztraminer (40%). Diam. 11.4° alc. **Rating** 87 **To** 2010 $12.50

South Channel Wines   ★★★★

485 Bittern-Dromana Road, Red Hill, Vic 3937 (postal) **Region** Mornington Peninsula
T 0412 361 531 **F** (03) 9897 4310 **Open** Not
Winemaker Phil Kerney, Tony Lee (Contract) **Est.** 1997 **Cases** 1000
Melbourne orthopaedic surgeon David Booth planted a total of 4 ha of pinot noir, pinot gris and shiraz on a large property situated on warm, northern slopes overlooking Dromana and the busy South Channel leading to the port of Melbourne. 'At times,' says David Booth, 'the big ships seem to appear in the vineyard.' Other varieties are being trialled in a nursery section, and the range of wines may increase somewhere down the track.

ŢŢŢŢŢ **Mornington Peninsula Pinot Gris 2006** A clean wine with pear flesh, candied fruits, and quite generous mouthfeel; vibrant and clean on the finish; very good value. Screwcap. 13° alc. **Rating** 90 **To** 2009 $15
Mornington Peninsula Shiraz 2006 Very stemmy style, with cool spicy red fruits; very savoury and drying tannins, but the fruit is fine and complex, and once again good value for the money. Screwcap. 14.5° alc. **Rating** 90 **To** 2014 $15

ŢŢŢŢ **Mornington Peninsula Pinot Noir 2005** Bright colour; fresh and varietal red cherry bouquet, with a little spice and quite firm structure; very good value. Screwcap. 14° alc. **Rating** 89 **To** 2009 $15

Southpaw Vineyard   ★★★★

Level 1, 30 Flinders Street, Kent Town, SA 5067 **Region** McLaren Vale
T (08) 8132 1279 **F** (08) 8132 1288 **www.**southpawvineyard.com.au **Open** Not
Winemaker Kevin O'Brien **Est.** 2004 **Cases** 700
Henry and Lucy Rymill are both left-handed, so the choice of name was almost preordained. The same could not necessarily be said of their decision to buy a 6.5-ha shiraz vineyard in the Sellicks Foothills at the southern end of McLaren Vale. Henry comes from a distinguished line of vignerons in Coonawarra, and notwithstanding his alarm at 'a flooding wine lake that may overtake the rising sea … I nurtured a dangerous dream to one day have a vineyard of my own in McLaren Vale. Commonsense, accountants and half of me said don't do it. It's not fair on your family, it will take years to succeed, if at all, and you will become completely despondent. To make it all the more loopy we decided to go biodynamic.' Well, it's not time for suicide just yet, rather a deserved sense of satisfaction.

ŢŢŢŢŢ **McLaren Vale Shiraz 2005** Punchy, slightly earthy aromas and flavours, somewhere out of the McLaren Vale comfort zone, though there is a foundation of black cherry, blackberry, spice and bitter chocolate; has length. Screwcap. 14° alc. **Rating** 90 **To** 2013 $28

SpearGully Wines   ★★★★☆

455 Lusatia Park Road, Hoddles Creek, Vic 3139 (postal) **Region** Yarra Valley
T 0409 258 348 **F** (03) 5967 4496 **Open** Not
Winemaker Tony Jordan **Est.** 1999 **Cases** NA
SpearGully is the venture of Dr Anthony (Tony) and Michele Jordan, both prominent figures in the Australian wine industry, albeit in different fields. Tony Jordan has had a distinguished career, first as a lecturer and consultant, and thereafter as CEO of Domaine Chandon, broken

for several years as the senior technical director for the worldwide operations of Möet Hennessy, before returning to Domaine Chandon and the Yarra Valley. Wife Michele has spent many years in public relations, marketing and sales, based variously in the UK and Australia. They have established 2 ha of chardonnay and 1 ha of shiraz on the hillsides surrounding their home in the Upper Yarra Valley, and the wines have both domestic and international distribution, albeit in small quantities.

ਪੂੰਪੂੰਪੂੰਪੂੰਪੂੰ **Yarra Valley Chardonnay 2004** Still extremely youthful; seamless nectarine, melon, citrus and fine, French oak; excellent length and balance. Cork. 13° alc. **Rating** 94 **To** 2014 $30

ਪੂੰਪੂੰਪੂੰਪੂੰਪੂੰ **Shiraz 2003** An interesting medium-bodied multi-regional blend, with no single region dominating, although the vintage might be so accused. A complex wine in every respect; 18 months French oak; Yarra Valley/Heathcote/McLaren Vale/ Rutherglen. Cork. 13.5° alc. **Rating** 90 **To** 2013 $30

Spence   ★★★

760 Burnside Road, Murgheboluc, Vic 3221 **Region** Geelong
T (03) 5265 1181 **F** (03) 5265 1181 **Open** By appt
Winemaker Peter Spence **Est.** 1997 **Cases** 700
Peter and Anne Spence were sufficiently inspired by an extended European holiday, which included living on a family vineyard in Provence, to purchase a small property specifically for the purpose of establishing a vineyard and winery. It remains a part-time occupation; Peter is an engineering manager at the Ford product development palnt at Geelong, Anne a teacher, but presently full-time mother looking after two young children. They have planted 3.2 ha on a north-facing slope in a valley 7 km south of Bannockburn; the lion's share to three clones of shiraz (1.83 ha), the remainder to chardonnay, pinot noir and fast-diminishing cabernet sauvignon (which is being grafted over to viognier for use in the Shiraz). It seems to me Peter has had access to some friendly winemaking advice; if this is really cold turkey, great wines will be on their way.

ਪੂੰਪੂੰਪੂੰਪੂੰ **Oakbough Pinot Noir 2006** Light-bodied but fragrant and elegant, with precise line; lacks vinosity on the mid-palate. Screwcap. 13.3° alc. **Rating** 87 **To** 2009 $25
Oakbough Shiraz 2006 Bright colour; the viognier (6%) has far more impact than the cabernet (5%) in this lively light-bodied red, perhaps a little thin on the finish. Interesting. Screwcap. 13.6° alc. **Rating** 87 **To** 2011 $25

Spinifex   ★★★★★

PO Box 511, Nuriootpa, SA 5355 **Region** Barossa Valley
T (08) 8562 1914 **F** (08) 8562 1409 www.spinifexwines.com.au **Open** Not
Winemaker Peter Schell **Est.** 2001 **Cases** 3500
Peter Schell and Magali Gely are a husband and wife team from NZ who came to Australia in the early 1990s to study oenology and marketing respectively at Roseworthy College. Together they have spent four vintages making wine in France, mainly in the south where Magali's family were vignerons for generations near Montpellier. The focus at Spinifex is the red varieties which dominate in the south of France: mataro (more correctly mourvedre), grenache, shiraz and cinsaut. The wine is made in open fermenters, basket-pressed, partial wild (indigenous) fermentations, and relatively long post-ferment maceration. This is at once a very old approach, but nowadays à la mode. The wines are made at Spinifex's winery in Vine Vale, where Peter also makes wines for a number of clients to whom he consults. So far as I am concerned Spinifex out-Torbrecks Torbreck. Exports to the UK, the US, Canada, Belgium, Taiwan and Singapore.

ਪੂੰਪੂੰਪੂੰਪੂੰਪੂੰ **Shiraz Viognier 2006** Vibrant colour; perfect texture and structure, lip-smacking from the first sip; lifted, spiced plum fruit which gains thrust on the back-palate and finish. Diam. 14.5° alc. **Rating** 95 **To** 2021 $48

Indigene 2006 Vivid colour; floods the mouth with flavour the moment it enters, yet the flavours are not extravagant, and certainly not the least jammy; instead there is tobacco, spice and a touch of bitter chocolate to accompany the red and blackberry fruits. Shiraz/Mataro. Cork. 14.8° alc. **Rating** 95 **To** 2017 $44

Esprit 2006 Some development in colour; very lively, spicy and complex flavours which unite in a lingering savoury palate calling to the southern Rhône. Mataro/Grenache/Shiraz/Cinsaut. Diam. 14.5° alc. **Rating** 94 **To** 2013 $28

D.R.S. Vineyard 2006 Saturated purple; luscious, intense and rich; very good example of the variety, which will always transcend the winemaker's influence if it is well-grown. Durif. Cork. 15° alc. **Rating** 94 **To** 2015 $48

♟♟♟♟♀ **Lola 2007** An exotic blend of Semillon (50%)/Marsanne/Viognier/Ugni Blanc/Grenache Blanc/Vermentino with a myriad of aromas which fuse together on the dry but lip-smacking palate, with an unexpectedly juicy finish. Screwcap. 13° alc. **Rating** 92 **To** 2015 $19

Aimee Semillon 2007 Exotic style, relying on strong influence from the oak; good texture and a fresh ample finish. Semillon. Screwcap. 13.1° alc. **Rating** 90 **To** 2013 $23

Barossa Rose 2007 Salmon colour; a dry and complex rose with good flavour and weight; more than a passing nod to Provence. Screwcap. 13.5° alc. **Rating** 90 **To** 2010 $20

Papillon 2007 Bright and juicy, and pure red fruit aromas; a lively palate, with good flavour, texture and length. Grenache/Cinsaut/Mataro. Screwcap. 13.8° alc. **Rating** 90 **To** 2012 $25

🍇 SplitRock Vineyard Estate ★★★

6299 Putty Road, Howes Valley, NSW 2330 **Region** Hunter Valley Zone
T (02) 9667 5022 **F** (02) 9667 5023 **Open** By appt
Winemaker Hunter Wine Services (John Hordern) **Est.** 2006 **Cases** 3200
This is a semi-isolated vineyard on the historic Putty Road, well to the west of the main Hunter Valley vineyards. Peter Brueckner and vineyard manager John Feaks have 6 ha of semillon, chardonnay, verdelho, merlot and shiraz. The wines will be released either as single varietals (Semillon, Chardonnay and Verdelho) or as a Semillon blend and a Shiraz Merlot blend.

♟♟♟♟ **Estate Reserve Hunter Valley Semillon 2006** Classically tight and reserved, still hiding its future flavour in a secret place; the balance and length are good; simply needs time. Screwcap. 11° alc. **Rating** 89 **To** 2016 $10

Splitters Swamp Vineyards ★★★

Craigielee, Bolivia via Tenterfield, NSW 2372 **Region** New England
T (02) 6737 3640 **F** (02) 6737 3640 **Open** By appt
Winemaker Ravens Croft Wines, Symphony Hill Wines **Est.** 1997 **Cases** 550
Ken Hutchison and Mandy Sharpe have made a cautious entry, planting a 1-ha vineyard equally to shiraz, cabernet sauvignon and merlot. As knowledge of the region grows, and as their experience as vignerons increases, they intend to increase the size of the vineyard and plant additional varieties. In the meantime they are producing Shiraz, Cabernet Merlot and Merlot, which have won several bronze medals.

♟♟♟♟ **Cabernet Sauvignon 2006** Firm, blackcurrant flavours; likewise tannins; oak well handled. **Rating** 89 **To** 2012

Cabernet Merlot 2003 Retains good hue; light-bodied, but quite fresh blackcurrant and cassis; not much structure. **Rating** 88 **To** 2010 $18

Shiraz Cabernet Port 2005 Sweet, quite luscious; consumer-friendly. **Rating** 87 **To** 2009

Spring Ridge Wines ★★★

880 Darbys Falls Road, Cowra, NSW 2794 **Region** Cowra
T (02) 6341 3820 **F** (02) 6341 3820 **www**.springridgewines.com.au **Open** W'ends,
public hols or by appt
Winemaker Contract **Est.** 1997 **Cases** NA
Peter and Anne Jeffery have established 12.5 ha of shiraz, chardonnay, semillon, cabernet
sauvignon and merlot. They sell the greatest part of the grape production, having only a small
amount made under the Spring Ridge Wines label.

�♀♀♀♀   **Cowra Chardonnay 2006** Relatively early picking and 50% barrel
ferment/50% stainless steel ferment results in a more than usually elegant wine
from Cowra; light- to medium-bodied, well-balanced. Screwcap. 13.3° alc.
Rating 88 **To** 2010 $18
Cowra Shiraz 2006 Light but bright hue; light- to medium-bodied fresh plum
and cherry fruit; correctly, no attempt to force the pace. Screwcap. 14.6° alc.
Rating 87 **To** 2012 $18

Spring Vale Vineyards ★★★★☆

130 Spring Vale Road, Cranbrook, Tas 7190 **Region** East Coast Tasmania
T (03) 6257 8208 **F** (03) 6257 8598 **www**.springvalewines.com **Open** 7 days 10–4
Winemaker Kristen Cush, David Cush **Est.** 1986 **Cases** 10 000
Rodney Lyne progressively established 1.5 ha each of pinot noir and chardonnay and then
added 0.5 ha each of gewurztraminer and pinot gris; the latter produced its first crop in
1998. Spring Vale produces first-class wines when the frost stays away. In 2007 Spring Vale
purchased the Melrose Vineyard from Bishops Rock (not the Bishops Rock brand or stock),
with 3 ha of pinot noir, 1 ha each sauvignon blanc and riesling and 0.5 ha chardonnay, which
will double its production. Exports to the UK, the US, Canada and Malaysia.

♀♀♀♀♀   **Pinot Noir 2006** Black cherry and plum aromas and flavours; very fine tannins
and good acidity, oak a back seat passenger. **Rating** 94 **To** 2013 $40

♀♀♀♀�♀   **Chardonnay 2006** Nicely balanced and modulated; sweet stone fruit and fig;
subtle oak and good length. **Rating** 92 **To** 2012 $30
Pinot Gris 2007 Apple and pear aromas; unusual mouthfeel and weight, almost
viscous, but not sweet. Commendable. Screwcap. 12.8° alc. **Rating** 90 **To** 2009 $28

♀♀♀♀   **Chardonnay Junior 2007** Peach, nectarine and some citrus; has good mouthfeel
and length, with more richness than the alcohol might suggest. **Rating** 89
To 2012 $18
Pinot Junior 2007 Fresh, distinctly tangy; very much fruit-driven, with a brisk
finish; leathery/earthy notes ex pinot meunier. Drink now. Pinot Meunier (55%)/
Pinot Noir (45%). **Rating** 89 **To** 2010 $18
Gewurztraminer 2007 Pleasant wine, well-balanced and smooth, but almost no
varietal character. **Rating** 87 **To** 2010 $28

Squitchy Lane Vineyard ★★★

PO Box 208, Coldstream, Vic 3770 **Region** Yarra Valley
T (03) 5964 9114 **F** (03) 5964 9017 **www**.squitchylane.com.au **Open** Not
Winemaker Matt Aldridge (Contract) **Est.** 1982 **Cases** 1000
Owner Mike Fitzpatrick acquired his taste for fine wine while a Rhodes scholar at Oxford
University in the 1970s. Returning to Australia he guided Carlton Football Club to two
premierships as captain, then established Melbourne-based finance company Squitchy Lane
Holdings. The wines of Mount Mary inspired him to look for his own vineyard, and in '96
he found a 16-ha vineyard of sauvignon blanc, chardonnay, pinot noir, merlot, cabernet franc
and cabernet sauvignon planted in '82 just around the corner from Coldstream Hills and Yarra
Yering. Between then and 2003 the grapes were sold to well-known local wineries, but in
'04 he began to put in place a team to take the venture through to the next stage with wines
under the Squitchy Lane label, commencing with the '05 vintage, launched in '07.

♥♥♥♥ **Yarra Valley Sauvignon Blanc 2006** A firm wine with considerable depth, but muted varietal character – which may well suit some palates. Screwcap. 13° alc. **Rating** 87 **To** 2009 $22

Yarra Valley Pinot Noir 2006 Quite developed, and light-bodied; some tinned cherry fruit flavours with a savoury twist on the finish. Screwcap. 13° alc. **Rating** 87 **To** 2010 $30

Yarra Valley Cabernets 2005 Some sweet and sour notes to the fruit on a light- to medium-bodied palate; an old vineyard in need of a firm hand. Screwcap. 14° alc. **Rating** 87 **To** 2013 $27

St Aidan

754 Ferguson Road, Dardanup, WA 6236 **Region** Geographe
T (08) 9728 3007 **F** (08) 9728 3006 **www**.saintaidan.com **Open** W'ends & public hols 10–5 or by appt
Winemaker Mark Messenger (Contract) **Est.** 1996 **Cases** 1500
Phil and Mary Smith purchased their property at Dardanup in 1991, a 20-min drive from the Bunbury hospitals for which Phil Smith works. They first ventured into Red Globe table grapes, planting 1 ha in 1994–05, followed by 1 ha of mandarins and oranges. With this experience, and with Mary completing a TAFE viticulture course, they extended their horizons by planting 1 ha each of cabernet sauvignon and chardonnay in 1997. Half a hectare of muscat followed in 2001, and semillon and sauvignon blanc therafter.

♥♥♥♥♀ **Chardonnay 2005** A generous wine with quality oak, and very good concentration; unctuous on the finish, with good flavour and length. **Rating** 92 **To** 2011 $20

♥♥♥♥ **Geographe Cabernet Sauvignon 2004** Holding hue very well; light- to medium-bodied, with savoury leafy components, but the wine has good structure and length in a cool-grown spectrum. Cork. 13.5° alc. **Rating** 88 **To** 2013 $17

Geographe Cabernet Merlot 2005 Good hue; a bright wine, with a mix of leafy/minty and riper fruit flavours to the light-bodied palate. Screwcap. 13.5° alc. **Rating** 87 **To** 2012 $17

St Hallett

St Hallett Road, Tanunda, SA 5352 **Region** Barossa Valley
T (08) 8563 7000 **F** (08) 8563 7001 **www**.sthallett.com.au **Open** 7 days 10–5
Winemaker Stuart Blackwell, Toby Barlow **Est.** 1944 **Cases** 100 000
Nothing succeeds like success. St Hallett merged with Tatachilla to form Banksia Wines, which was then acquired by NZ's thirsty Lion Nathan. St Hallett understandably continues to ride the Shiraz fashion wave, with Old Block the ultra-premium leader of the band (using grapes from Lyndoch and the Eden Valley) supported by Blackwell (taking its grapes from Greenock, Ebenezer and Seppeltsfield). It has also had conspicuous success with its Eden Valley Rieslings, and its big-volume Poacher's range. Exports to all major markets.

♥♥♥♥♥ **Blackwell Barossa Shiraz 2006** Delivers immediate intensity from the first sip, blackberry fruit enhanced by nuances of licorice; has tremendous vitality and thrust to the long palate and finish. Screwcap. 14.5° alc. **Rating** 96 **To** 2026 $34.95

Blackwell Barossa Shiraz 2005 Perfectly ripened fruit; strong varietal character, but not at all jammy; blackberry, with notes of licorice and spice, finishing with fine-grained tannins. Cork. 14.5° alc. **Rating** 94 **To** 2020 $29

♥♥♥♥♀ **Old Block Barossa Shiraz 2004** Has sweet berry fruit on the fore-palate, then coasting along towards the finish; I wonder whether there were subliminal cork oxidation issues for what should have been a spectacular wine. 14.5° alc. **Rating** 92 **To** 2014 $70

Eden Valley Riesling 2007 As always, a quality wine, particularly given the limitations of the '07 vintage; classic regional citrus the main driver, backed up by firm acidity. Screwcap. 12.5° alc. **Rating** 91 **To** 2015 $21

Barossa Semillon 2005 Still moving towards maturity; crisp and firm, lemon, mineral, herb and grass intermingling; no phenolics. Screwcap. **Rating** 90 **To** 2015 $19

ΨΨΨΨ **Barossa Semillon 2006** Squeaky clean, with good texture and a bright lemony finish. Screwcap. **Rating** 89 **To** 2014 $19

Poacher's Blend Barossa Semillon Sauvignon Blanc 2007 Plenty of fresh-cut fruit flavours; good line, but does shorten fractionally on the finish; well-priced. Screwcap. 11.5° alc. **Rating** 88 **To** 2010 $15

Faith Barossa Shiraz 2006 Is quite aromatic, with spicy/leafy nuances on both bouquet and palate, framing the core of medium-bodied red fruits. Screwcap. 14.5° alc. **Rating** 88 **To** 2014 $21

Gamekeeper's Reserve Barossa Shiraz Grenache 2007 Full of bright raspberry fruit, framed by a little spice; juicy, lively and fresh. Screwcap. 14.5° alc. **Rating** 88 **To** 2012 $15

St Huberts

Cnr Maroondah Highway/St Huberts Road, Coldstream, Vic 3770 **Region** Yarra Valley **T** (03) 9739 1118 **F** (03) 9739 1096 **www**.sthuberts.com.au **Open** Mon–Fri 9–5, w'ends 10.30–5.30
Winemaker Greg Jarratt **Est.** 1966 **Cases** 10 000
A once famous winery (in the context of the Yarra Valley) which is now part of Foster's. The wines are now made at Coldstream Hills, and on an upwards trajectory. (I have no part in their making.)

ΨΨΨΨΨ **Yarra Valley Pinot Noir 2006** Deep colour; a very complex and powerful wine with ripe black cherry and plum fruit; arresting show style with multiple trophies and gold medals, but needs time. Screwcap. 13.5° alc. **Rating** 94 **To** 2016 $26.95

ΨΨΨΨΨ **Yarra Valley Cabernet Sauvignon 2006** Dense purple-red; chunky blackcurrant fruit on a medium- to full-bodied palate; good tannin and oak contribution; a wine yearning for a screwcap and a 30-year future. Cork. 14° alc. **Rating** 91 **To** 2016 $30.95

Yarra Valley Chardonnay 2006 Classic melon, nectarine and a hint of citrus, complexed by skilled use of French oak and partial mlf. Screwcap. 13.5° alc. **Rating** 90 **To** 2014 $23.95

ΨΨΨΨ **Yarra Valley Roussanne 2006** Good structure and texture; some pear, apple and talc flavours, though not particularly distinctive; will live and likely develop with bottle age. Screwcap. 13° alc. **Rating** 89 **To** 2012 $29.95

St Ignatius Vineyard

5434 Sunraysia Highway, Lamplough, Vic 3352 **Region** Pyrenees
T (03) 5465 3542 **F** (03) 5465 3542 **www**.stignatiusvineyard.com.au **Open** 7 days 10–5
Winemaker Enrique Diaz **Est.** 1992 **Cases** 1000
Silvia Diaz and husband Enrique began establishing their vineyard, winery and restaurant complex in 1992. They have planted 8 ha of shiraz, chardonnay, cabernet sauvignon, sauvignon blanc, merlot and sangiovese. The vineyard has received three primary production awards. Wines are released under the Hangmans Gully label. Exports to the UK.

St John's Road

PO Box 286, Rundle Mall, SA 5000 **Region** Barossa Valley
T (08) 8342 9070 **F** (08) 8342 9007 **www**.stjohnsroad.com **Open** Not
Winemaker Biscay Rd Vintners (Peter Schell), Rolf Binder (Christa Deans) **Est.** 2002
Cases 4500

Martin Rawlinson (with a background of politics and defence) and wife Vivienne (journalism and music) were running a small B&B-type establishment in France surrounded by vineyards. One thing led to another, and in 2002 they purchased a small vineyard in the Eden Valley, planted to 30-year-old riesling on lean, rocky soils. The following year they purchased a much larger property at Greenock, established by the Helbig family in the 1880s. In all, they had 24 ha of riesling, semillon, chardonnay, grenache, cabernet sauvignon and shiraz. Out of the blue Martin was diagnosed with motor neurone disease, dying in 2005. Says Vivienne, 'I am grateful that Martin had a chance to see and taste the realisation of his dream with the bottling of our 2003 Julia (named after their young daughter) and the other wines of the 2004 vintage'. Exports to the US, Canada and NZ.

ⵧⵧⵧⵧⵧ **Blood and Courage Greenock Shiraz 2006** A clean, supple and lively mix of red and black fruits, savoury nuances and very well-handled overall extract of tannins and oak. Well-priced. Screwcap. 14.5° alc. **Rating** 93 **To** 2015 $20
A Motley Bunch GSM 2006 Lively, fresh and fragrant; a spicy light- to medium-bodied array of red fruits in no way intimidated by alcohol; some clever sleight of winemaking hand. Screwcap. 15° alc. **Rating** 90 **To** 2011 $22

ⵧⵧⵧⵧ **Peace of Eden Riesling 2007** Bright straw-green; has classic Eden Valley lime and lemon aromas and flavours, but also shows the effects of the warm vintage; early developing. Screwcap. 12.5° alc. **Rating** 89 **To** 2011 $20

St Leonards Vineyard ★★★☆

St Leonards Road, Wahgunyah, Vic 3687 **Region** Rutherglen
T (02) 6033 1004 **F** (02) 6033 3636 www.stleonardswine.com.au **Open** Fri–Mon 10–5
Winemaker Dan Crane **Est.** 1860 **Cases** 20 000
An old favourite, relaunched in late 1997 with a range of premium wines cleverly marketed through a singularly attractive cellar door and bistro at the historic winery on the banks of the Murray. All Saints and St Leonards were wholly owned by Peter Brown, tragically killed in a road accident in late 2005. Ownership has passed to Peter Brown's children, Eliza, Angela and Nicholas, and it is the intention to keep the business in the family.

ⵧⵧⵧⵧ **Rutherglen Muscat NV** A reliably good value muscat that exhibits more youthful grapey muscat character than aged complexity. Cork. 18° alc. **Rating** 89 **To** 2015 $20

St Mary's ★★★

V & A Lane, Penola, SA 5277 **Region** Limestone Coast Zone
T (08) 8736 6070 **F** (08) 8736 6045 www.stmaryswines.com **Open** 7 days 10–4
Winemaker Barry Mulligan **Est.** 1986 **Cases** 4000
The Mulligan family has lived in the Penola/Coonawarra region since 1909. In 1937 a 250-ha property 15 km west of Penola, including an 80-ha ridge of terra rossa over limestone, was purchased for grazing. The ridge was cleared, the remainder of the property was untouched and is now a private wildlife sanctuary. In 1986 Barry and Glenys Mulligan planted shiraz and cabernet sauvignon on the ridge, followed by merlot in the early '90s. Exports to the UK, the US, Canada, Belgium, Hong Kong and China.

St Michael's Vineyard ★★★★☆

503 Pook Road, Toolleen, Vic 3521 **Region** Heathcote
T (03) 5433 2580 **F** (03) 5433 2612 **Open** By appt
Winemaker Mick Cann **Est.** 1994 **Cases** 300
Owner/winemaker Mick Cann has established just over 4 ha of vines on the famous deep red Cambrian clay loam on the east face of the Mt Camel Range. Planting began in 1994–95, with a further extension in 2000. Shiraz (2.5 ha), merlot (1.25 ha) and petit verdot (0.3 ha) are the main varieties, with a smattering of cabernet sauvignon and semillon. Part of the grape production is sold to David Anderson of Wild Duck Creek, the remainder made by Mick Cann, using open fermentation, hand-plunging of skins and a basket press, a low-technology

but highly effective way of making high-quality red wine. The period poster-style labels do the wines scant justice. No samples received, the rating is that of last year.

St Regis
35 Princes Highway, Waurn Ponds, Vic 3216 **Region** Geelong
T (03) 5241 8406 **F** (03) 5241 8946 **www**.stregis.com.au **Open** 7 days 11–5
Winemaker Peter Nicol **Est.** 1997 **Cases** 600
St Regis is a family-run boutique winery focusing on estate-grown Shiraz, Chardonnay and Pinot Noir. Each year the harvest is hand-picked by members of the family and friends, with Peter Nicol (assisted by wife Viv) the executive, onsite winemaker. While Peter has a technical background in horticulture, he is a self-taught winemaker, and has taught himself well, also making wines for others.

Staindl Wines ★★★★☆
63 Shoreham Road, Red Hill South, Vic 3937 (postal) **Region** Mornington Peninsula
T (03) 9813 1111 **Open** Not
Winemaker Phillip Jones (Contract) **Est.** 1982 **Cases** 500
As often happens, the establishment date for a wine producer can mean many things. In this instance it harks back to the planting of the vineyard by the Ayton family, and the establishment of what was thereafter called St Neots. Juliet and Paul Staindl acquired the property in 2002, and, with the guidance of Phillip Jones, have since extended the plantings of pinot noir. In all there are now 2 ha of pinot noir, 0.7 ha of chardonnay and 0.3 ha of riesling. The vineyard is run on a low chemical regime, headed towards biodynamic viticulture. Paul Staindl says, 'It's all good fun and lots of learning'. I would add it's also more than slightly demanding.

Mornington Peninsula Riesling 2006 Has much more intensity, line and length than most maritime-grown rieslings; tight citrus, pear and apple flavours, then a crisp, dry finish. Screwcap. 12.3° alc. **Rating** 94 **To** 2016 $25

Mornington Peninsula Chardonnay 2005 Obvious bottle development under the cork seal is understandable; a rich peaches and cream style, with nutty oak. 13.5° alc. **Rating** 90 **To** 2011 $32

Stanton & Killeen Wines
Jacks Road, Murray Valley Highway, Rutherglen, Vic 3685 **Region** Rutherglen
T (02) 6032 9457 **F** (02) 6032 8018 **www**.stantonandkilleenwines.com.au
Open Mon–Sat 9–5, Sun 10–5
Winemaker Michael Oxlee, Brendan Heath **Est.** 1875 **Cases** 20 000
The tragic and premature death of Chris Killeen was much mourned by his numerous admirers, myself included. However, son Simon is already studying wine science, and 18-year-old daughter Natasha is likely to enrol in a wine marketing course. In the meantime Michael Oxlee, Chris's assistant for 15 years, continues the winemaking, with assistance from Brendan Heath, who spent a similar time with Campbells. Exports to the UK, the US and other major markets.

Rare Rutherglen Muscat NV Deep brown, olive-rimmed; has fantastic flair and style; in the mouth, there is still a core of fresh muscat fruit encased in a complex web of nutty, raisin-accented rancio, spirit the hidden scalpel. **Rating** 96 **To** 2009 $100
Rutherglen Durif 2005 Deep colour; it is impossible not to be impressed with the power of this variety, especially when made by winemakers as skilled as the late Chris Killeen. The secret is to control the extract, and give the wines the freedom to fully express themselves. Diam. 15° alc. **Rating** 94 **To** 2020 $30
Rutherglen Vintage Port 2003 Rich and lusciously complex, thanks to 45% of four Portuguese varieties, the remainder shiraz and durif; flavours of dark chocolate, licorice and spice, the palate sweet, but drying off appropriately on the finish. Cork. **Rating** 94 **To** 2024

Grand Rutherglen Muscat NV Full olive-brown; clear-cut rancio aligns with clean spirit and spicy/grapey fruit; excellent balance and structure, the tannins subliminal, but giving another dimension to the flavour; very long, fine finish. **Rating** 94 **To** 2009 $75

ŶŶŶŶŶ **Tawny Port NV** Medium red-tawny; the bouquet is clean with nice butterscotch overtones and, like the palate, shows positive but not aggressive rancio. **Rating** 93 **To** 2009 $27

Classic Rutherglen Tokay NV Light to medium golden-brown; great clarity and freshness, with honey and tea leaf aromas; lively and vibrant with similar finesse and harmony to the Campbell wines. Finishes with excellent acidity and a clean, crisp aftertaste. **Rating** 92 **To** 2009 $27

Classic Rutherglen Muscat NV Has a great display of grapey varietal fruit, skillfully combining younger and older material. Fine tannins give the wine extra structure and intensity. **Rating** 92 **To** 2009 $27

ŶŶŶŶ **Rutherglen Muscat NV** Bright tawny, with a faint crimson blush; high-toned spirit on the bouquet lifts rather than obscures the fruit; intense, raisiny yet fresh. **Rating** 89 **To** 2009 $16.50

Steels Creek Estate   ★★★★

1 Sewell Road, Steels Creek, Vic 3775 **Region** Yarra Valley
T (03) 5965 2448 **F** (03) 5965 2448 www.steelsckestate.com.au **Open** W'ends & public hols 10–6, or by appt
Winemaker Simon Peirce **Est.** 1981 **Cases** 400
A 1.7-ha vineyard (chardonnay, shiraz, cabernet sauvignon, cabernet franc and colombard), family-operated since 1981, is located in the picturesque Steels Creek Valley with views towards the Kinglake National Park. Red wines are made onsite, white wines with the assistance of consultants. Visitors can view the winemaking operations from the cellar door.

ŶŶŶŶŶ **Yarra Valley Chardonnay 2006** Strong toasty oak aromas, with ripe pear and melon coming through behind; finer and more balanced on the palate, with a fresh, vibrant and almost racy finish. Screwcap. 13.5° alc. **Rating** 93 **To** 2012 $22

Stefani Estate

389 Heathcote-Rochester Road, Heathcote, Vic 3523 **Region** Heathcote
T (03) 9570 8750 **F** (03) 9579 1532 www.stefaniestatewines.com.au **Open** By appt
Winemaker Mario Marson **Est.** 2002 **Cases** 2860
Stefano Stefani came to Australia in 1985. Business success has allowed Stefano and wife Rina to follow in the footsteps of Stefano's grandfather, who had a vineyard and was an avid wine collector. The first property they acquired was at Long Gully Road in the Yarra Valley, with pinot grigio, cabernet sauvignon, chardonnay and pinot noir. The next was in Heathcote, where he acquired a property adjoining that of Mario Marson, built a winery and established 8.5 ha of vineyards, planted predominantly to shiraz, then cabernet sauvignon and merlot and a mixed block of cabernet franc, malbec and petit verdot. In 2003 a second Yarra Valley property was purchased where Dijon clones of chardonnay and pinot noir have been planted. Mario Marson (ex Mount Mary) oversees the operation of all the vineyards and is also the winemaker. He is also able to use the winery to make his own brand wines, completing the business link. Exports to China.

ŶŶŶŶŶ **The Gate Yarra Valley Cabernet Sauvignon Merlot 2006** Bright colour; touches of cassis and cedar, and plenty of black olive; good weight, and fine-grained tannins on the finish. Cork. **Rating** 94 **To** 2015 $40

ŶŶŶŶŶ **Heathcote Vineyard Shiraz 2005** Dense, dark and brooding; has plenty of depth, but needs time to soften and open up. Cork. 14.5° alc. **Rating** 90 **To** 2016 $40

Stefano Lubiana ★★★★★

60 Rowbottoms Road, Granton, Tas 7030 **Region** Southern Tasmania
T (03) 6263 7457 **F** (03) 6263 7430 **www.**slw.com.au **Open** Sun–Thurs 11–3
(closed some public hols)
Winemaker Steve Lubiana **Est.** 1990 **Cases** NFP
When Stefano (Steve) Lubiana moved from the Riverland to Tasmania, he set up a
substantial contract sparkling winemaking facility to help cover the costs of the move and
the establishment of his new business. Over the years, he has steadily decreased the amount
of contract winemaking, now focusing on his estate-grown wines from 18 ha of beautifully
located vineyards sloping down to the Derwent River. Exports to Italy, Sweden, Korea,
Indonesia and Japan.

TTTTT **Estate Pinot Noir 2005** A relatively quiet bouquet, but springs into life on the
spicy palate, both intense and very long; excellent acidity on the finish. Diam.
13.5° alc. **Rating** 95 **To** 2012 $52
Sasso Pinot Noir 2005 Colour development obvious; aromatic spicy foresty
bouquet; has outstanding length; with complex sous bois dark fruits and superfine
but persistent tannins. **Rating** 95 **To** 2013 $87.90

TTTT **Estate Chardonnay 2004** Quite developed colour; complex, but has a broken
line, with the flavours heading off in different directions. Screwcap. 13.5° alc.
Rating 88 **To** 2010 $49

Steinborner Family Vineyards ★★★★☆

91 Siegersdorf Road, Tanunda, SA 5352 **Region** Barossa Valley
T 0414 474 708 **F** (08) 8522 4898 **www.**sfvineyards.com.au **Open** By appt
Winemaker David Reynolds, Neil Doddridge, Sally Blackwell **Est.** 2003 **Cases** 2000
This is a partnership between David and Rebecca Reynolds, and Rebecca's parents, Michael
and Heather Steinborner. They say 'David, hailing from UK/Irish heritage and with a chance
meeting in Tokyo (with Rebecca), brings some fresh blood to the Steinborner clan. He
oversees (or does himself wherever possible) much of both the vineyard and wine production.'
The oldest vines include some 80-year-old shiraz, and all the other varieties of semillon,
viognier, durif and marsanne are planted on the typical sand over clay profile of Vine Vale, one
of the noted subregions of the Barossa Valley.

TTTTT **Caroliene Semillon Sauvignon Blanc 2007** The Adelaide Hills sauvignon
blanc component plays a significant role, though the semillon is very crisp, too; the
finish is delicious, with lime/lemon acidity a major surprise. Top value. Screwcap.
12.8° alc. **Rating** 94 **To** 2010 $17

TTTTY **Caroliene Barossa Valley Semillon 2007** Very much the new style of Barossa
semillon, lively, crisp and fresh, suggesting even lower alcohol than it has; good life
and length, will develop well. Screwcap. 12.8° alc. **Rating** 90 **To** 2015 $16
Deutsche Barossa Shiraz 2005 Retains bright crimson hue; harmonious
flavours and texture, supple and smooth, perhaps just a fraction ripe with
some confiture notes, but enjoyable nonetheless. Cork. 14.7° alc. **Rating** 90
To 2013 $27.50

TTTT **Ancestry Barossa Shiraz Viognier 2004** Pleasant medium-bodied palate,
with soft, approachable red fruits influenced by the 3% viognier. Cork. 14° alc.
Rating 88 **To** 2013 $27.50

Stella Bella Wines ★★★★★

PO Box 536, Margaret River, WA 6285 **Region** Margaret River
T (08) 9757 6377 **F** (08) 9757 6022 **www.**stellabella.com.au **Open** Not
Winemaker Janice McDonald **Est.** 1997 **Cases** 50 000

This enormously successful, privately owned winemaking business produces wines of true regional expression with fruit sourced from the central and southern parts of Margaret River. Owns or controls more than 80 ha of vineyards, recently acquired a 3000-tonne (potential) winemaking facility at Karridale and a cellar door in the pipeline, just minutes from the township at the original Isca vineyard. It's hard to imagine the wines getting better, but we shall see. Exports of Stella Bella, Suckfizzle and Skuttlebutt labels to the UK, the US, Canada, China, Hong Kong and Singapore.

ŶŶŶŶŶ **Suckfizzle Margaret River Sauvignon Blanc Semillon 2005** A very complex wine, maturing with unusual grace; barrel fermentation and maturation has not subdued the intense fruit; power with finesse; long finish. Screwcap. 13° alc. **Rating** 95 **To** 2011 $45

Cabernet Sauvignon Merlot 2005 An aromatic bouquet of red fruits, then a palate bursting with flavour, led by cassis/redcurrant, followed by perfectly balanced tannins and sure French oak. Screwcap. 14° alc. **Rating** 95 **To** 2019 $25

Suckfizzle Margaret River Cabernet Sauvignon 2005 Complex, medium-bodied, blackcurrant cassis fruit, fine ripe tannins and cedary oak all seamlessly joined on the fluid and long palate. Screwcap. 14° alc. **Rating** 95 **To** 2020 $50

Semillon Sauvignon Blanc 2007 A complex bouquet and palate, suggesting barrel ferment components which, however, don't impinge on the line and flow of the fruit through to the finish. Screwcap. 13° alc. **Rating** 94 **To** 2009 $19.99

Margaret River Chardonnay 2006 A brilliantly clean, precise and fresh chardonnay showing just how much can be achieved with early picking; the oak has been absorbed in Chablis style. Screwcap. 12.5° alc. **Rating** 94 **To** 2015 $28

ŶŶŶŶŶ **Sauvignon Blanc 2007** The wine's strength lies in the texture, structure and balance more than any effusive varietal expression; all-purpose food style. Screwcap. 13° alc. **Rating** 93 **To** 2010 $22

Margaret River Sangiovese Cabernet Sauvignon 2006 The sour cherry and unique tannins of the sangiovese dominate the cabernet sauvignon, no mean feat; for lovers of all things Italian. Screwcap. 13.5° alc. **Rating** 91 **To** 2014 $30

Skuttlebutt Sauvignon Blanc Semillon 2007 A spotlessly clean bouquet leads into a rich palate with an abundance of tropical fruit needing no prop of sweetness. Screwcap. 13° alc. **Rating** 91 **To** 2009 $16

Margaret River Shiraz 2006 White pepper, licorice and lively red fruit aromas; the spice follows through on the palate, with a fine, lingering finish. Screwcap. 13.5° alc. **Rating** 91 **To** 2014 $27

Margaret River Tempranillo 2006 Bright crimson; a mix of cherry, raspberry and lemon rind, with a nice savoury twist to the finish; overall balance and length are good. Screwcap. 14° alc. **Rating** 90 **To** 2012 $30

ŶŶŶŶ **Skuttlebutt Sauvignon Blanc Semillon 2006** A fresh, crisp mix of minerals, grass and kiwifruit; good balance and length. Easy access. Screwcap. 12.5° alc. **Rating** 89 **To** 2009 $16

Step Road Winery/Beresford Wines   ★★★★

Davidson Road, Langhorne Creek, SA 5255 (postal) **Region** Langhorne Creek
T (08) 8537 3342 **F** (08) 8537 3357 **www**.steprd.com **Open** Not
Winemaker Scott McIntosh, Justin Coates **Est.** 1998 **Cases** 200 000
Step Road has 100 ha of vineyard at Langhorne Creek, and 40 ha in the Adelaide Hills. In a sign of the times, it is an environmentally aware winery: all liquid waste is stored in plastic-lined dams, treated to remove chemicals and salinity and then recycled as irrigation for the vineyard. All solid waste from the grapes (skins, stalks and seeds) is mulched and returned to the vineyards, reducing irrigation requirements by 25%. Exports to the UK, the US, Canada, Germany, Malaysia and NZ.

ŶŶŶŶŶ **Step Road Langhorne Creek Shiraz 2005** Deep, dense colour; lives up to the promise of its colour, showing much in common with McLaren Vale; blackberry fruit, dark chocolate and licorice supported by soft but persistent tannins; controlled oak. Screwcap. 14.5° alc. **Rating** 94 **To** 2025 $20

♟♟♟♟ **Beresford McLaren Vale Cabernet Sauvignon 2005** Blackcurrant, mint and leaf aromas; the flavours stay in the blackcurrant spectrum, supported by controlled tannins. Screwcap. 14.5° alc. **Rating** 88 **To** 2012 $18
Beresford Highwood Shiraz 2005 Light- to medium-bodied; has some structure and flavour complexity, with savoury, spicy edges to light-framed black fruit flavours. Screwcap. 14.5° alc. **Rating** 87 **To** 2009 $14

Stephen John Wines ★★★★

Sollys Hill Road, Watervale, SA 5452 **Region** Clare Valley
T (08) 8843 0105 **F** (08) 8843 0105 www.stephenjohnwines.com **Open** 7 days 11–5
Winemaker Stephen John **Est.** 1994 **Cases** 10 000
The John family is one of the best known in the Barossa Valley, with branches running Australia's best cooperage (AP John & Sons) and providing the former chief winemaker of Lindemans (Philip John) and the former chief winemaker of Quelltaler (Stephen John). Stephen and Rita John have now formed their own family business in the Clare Valley, based on a 6-ha vineyard overlooking Watervale, and supplemented by grapes from a few local growers. The cellar door is a renovated 80-year-old stable full of rustic charm. Exports to the UK, Canada, France, Malaysia and Singapore.

♟♟♟♟♟ **Dry Grown Clare Valley Shiraz 2006** Dense, impenetrable purple-red, the bouquet and palate following logically, with prune, blackberry, plum and licorice flavours; soft tannins and oak. Cork. 14° alc. **Rating** 92 **To** 2014 $25

♟♟♟♟ **Watervale Riesling 2007** Ripe apple, citrus and mineral aromas; a well-balanced, relatively light-bodied, palate. Screwcap. 12° alc. **Rating** 89 **To** 2013 $25
Traugott Clare Valley Cuvee NV The percentages are not stated, but a quite attractive medium-bodied sparkling red, not too oaky, though it is a little sweet; some will love that aspect. Shiraz/Pinot Noir. **Rating** 87 **To** 2012 $25

Sticks ★★★★

179 Glenview Road, Yarra Glen, Vic 3775 **Region** Yarra Valley
T (03) 9730 1022 **F** (03) 9730 1131 www.sticks.com.au **Open** 7 days 10–5
Winemaker Rob Dolan, Travis Bush **Est.** 2000 **Cases** 60 000
In 2005 the former Yarra Ridge winery, with a 3000-tonne capacity, and 25 ha of vineyards planted mainly in 1983, was acquired by a partnership headed by Rob 'Sticks' Dolan. The estate production is significantly supplemented by contract-grown grapes sourced elsewhere in the Yarra Valley. He is making all the Sticks wines here, and also provides substantial contract-making facilities for wineries throughout the Yarra Valley. Exports to the UK, the US and other major markets.

♟♟♟♟♟ **Yarra Valley Sauvignon Blanc 2007** Clean, fresh and lively; clear-cut varietal character in a fresh citrus/gooseberry/passionfruit spectrum; not intense, but has length. Screwcap. 11.5° alc. **Rating** 92 **To** 2009 $16
Pinot Noir 2006 Bright red fruits with lots of toasty oak; plenty of weight and good silky texture on the finish. Screwcap. **Rating** 92 **To** 2013 $38

♟♟♟♟ **Chardonnay 2006** Pale lemon; nice varietal aromas; plenty of oak here, and will benefit with some bottle age; good flavour and length. Screwcap. **Rating** 89 **To** 2013 $28
Cabernet Sauvignon 2006 Very oaky, but with good fruit beneath; a little raw now and needs time, but the potential is certainly there. Screwcap. **Rating** 89 **To** 2016 $28

Stone Coast Wines ★★★☆

18 North Terrace, Adelaide, SA 5000 (postal) **Region** Wrattonbully
T (08) 8239 4949 **F** (08) 8239 4959 www.stonecoastwines.com **Open** Not
Winemaker Steve Maglieri, Scott Rawlinson, Simon Greenleaf **Est.** 1997 **Cases** NA

The development of the 33 ha of cabernet sauvignon and 11 ha of shiraz (with an addition of 0.5 ha of pinot gris planted in 2004) which constitutes the vineyard was exceptionally difficult. It is situated on a terra rossa ridge top, but had unusually thick limestone slabs running through it, which had caused others to bypass the property. A 95-tonne bulldozer was hired to deep-rip the limestone, but was unequal to the task, and ultimately explosives had to be used to create sufficient inroads to allow planting. Only 15% of the production from the vineyard is used by the formidably skilled winemaking team. Exports to the UK, the US, Canada and Germany.

♀♀♀♀♀ **The Struggle Limestone Coast Shiraz 2003** Has improved significantly since Oct '05, the red fruits asserting themselves; good tannins, and still has time. Screwcap. 14° alc. **Rating** 90 **To** 2013 $25

♀♀♀♀ **Wrattonbully Pinot Gris 2006** Flavour-neutral, but is well made, and does have both length and balance. Screwcap. 13.4° alc. **Rating** 87 **To** 2009 $25
Wrattonbully Pinot Gris 2007 Gentle pear and citrus, lengthened by pleasing lemony acidity. Screwcap. 13° alc. **Rating** 87 **To** 2009

Stonebrook Estate   ★★★☆

1191 Vasse-Yallingup Road, Quindalup, WA 6280 **Region** Margaret River
T (08) 9755 1104 **F** (08) 9755 1001 **www.**stonebrookestate.com **Open** By appt
Winemaker John Durham (Consultant) **Est.** 1997 **Cases** 1000
Perth lawyer Jonathan Meyer decided on a seachange in 1992, moving with his family to their beach house at Dunsborough. From the outset, the intention was to establish a vineyard, and a property was selected in 1996; planting of 7.4 ha of chardonnay, cabernet sauvignon and merlot began in '97. Most of the production is sold, part made under the Stonebrook Estate label, and a small amount under the second label, Station Gully.

♀♀♀♀♀ **Small Block Margaret River Chardonnay 2006** Pure grapefruit and toast aromas; the richly textured palate is persistent and finishes with a little buttered toast. Screwcap. 13.5° alc. **Rating** 90 **To** 2010 $25

Stonehaven

Riddoch Highway, Padthaway, SA 5271 **Region** Padthaway
T (08) 8765 6166 **F** (08) 8765 6177 **www.**stonehavenvineyards.com.au **Open** 7 days 10–4
Winemaker Susanne Bell **Est.** 1998 **Cases** NFP
It is, to say the least, strange that it should have taken 30 years for a substantial winery to be built at Padthaway. However, when Hardys (as it was then known) took the decision, it was no half measure: $20 million was invested in what was the largest greenfields winery built in Australia for more than 20 years. It is capable of processing 10 000 tonnes of fruit each vintage, and the barrel hall (exactly 1 acre in size) can hold 15 000 barrels (equivalent to 500 000 dozen bottles). In fact many of the wines are made in small batches, and the winery has had significant show success with wines which can offer spectacular value for money. Exports to all major markets.

♀♀♀♀♀ **Fatherwoods Cabernet Sauvignon 2006** Racks the intensity of the Best on Ground up several notches, but the flavour and overall style is in the same family. Screwcap. 14° alc. **Rating** 95 **To** 2026 $50
Hidden Sea Shiraz 2005 Very good colour; licorice, spice, cherry and plum coalesce on the palate; has line, texture and length; good oak. **Rating** 94 **To** 2015 $21
Best on Ground Coonawarra Cabernet Sauvignon 2006 Fragrant blackcurrant fruit on the bouquet and medium-bodied palate; firm but ripe tannins extend the finish considerably, oak also in on the act. Screwcap. 14° alc. **Rating** 94 **To** 2021 $30
Rat & Bull Cabernet Shiraz 2006 Very good colour; a powerful wine, with layers of black fruits, oak and tannins; good balance, long future. Gold medal, Limestone Coast Wine Show '07. **Rating** 94 **To** 2020 $25

ŸŸŸŸŸ **Stepping Stone Cabernet Sauvignon 2006** Vibrant colour; as usual, significantly over-delivers, making cabernet sauvignon a pleasure to drink young without compromising its varietal character. Screwcap. 13.5° alc. **Rating** 92 To 2016 $16
Hidden Sea Limestone Coast Chardonnay 2006 Scores for its depth and breadth of ripe fruit flavour; controlled oak and good length. **Rating** 90 To 2011 $21
Hidden Sea Shiraz 2006 Medium- to full-bodied; plenty of powerful black fruit, but not abrasive; as yet, a fraction one-dimensional, but will gain in bottle. **Rating** 90 To 2015 $21
Hidden Sea Limestone Coast Cabernet Sauvignon 2004 Retains good hue; fresh red fruit characters dominate a silky, supple medium-bodied palate; good length and finish. Cork. 13° alc. **Rating** 90 To 2014 $18.50

ŸŸŸŸ **Wrattonbully Shiraz 2006** A powerful, concentrated, brooding wine with blackberry fruits; still settling down and needs time. **Rating** 89 To 2014 $33.50
Hidden Sea Limestone Coast Cabernet Sauvignon 2005 Pleasant medium-bodied palate, with ripe black and red fruits; somewhat oaky, however. **Rating** 87 To 2014 $21

Stonehurst Cedar Creek ★★★★★

Wollombi Road, Cedar Creek, NSW 2325 **Region** Lower Hunter Valley
T (02) 4998 1576 **F** (02) 4998 0008 **www.**cedarcreekcottages.com.au **Open** 7 days 10–5
Winemaker Monarch Winemaking Services **Est.** 1995 **Cases** 400
Stonehurst (subtitled Cedar Creek) has been established by Daryl and Phillipa Heslop on a historic 220-ha property in the Wollombi Valley, underneath the Pokolbin Range. They have 6.5 ha of vineyards, planted to chambourcin, semillon, chardonnay and shiraz, all organically grown. A substantial part of the business, however, is the six self-contained cottages on the property. Skilled contract winemaking has produced great results. Exports to Tonga and Fiji.

ŸŸŸŸŸ **Reserve Hunter Valley Chardonnay 2006** Very well made; excellent handling of oak to frame melon and white peach fruit; supple mouthfeel; good line and length. Screwcap. 13.5° alc. **Rating** 94 To 2013 $25
Hunter Valley Shiraz 2005 Elegant medium-bodied palate, with both focus and effortless length; delicious mouthfeel, courtesy of appropriate alcohol and fine tannins; will age with grace. Screwcap. 13.5° alc. **Rating** 94 To 2025 $25

ŸŸŸŸŸ **Hunter Valley Chardonnay Semillon 2007** Impressively assembled and balanced, with both varieties making positive contributions along with a dash of French oak, good length. Screwcap. 12.5° alc. **Rating** 91 To 2014 $18

ŸŸŸŸ **Hunter Valley Semillon 2007** Clean and fresh, with strong lemongrass notes, good length and brisk acidity; good development potential. Screwcap. 10° alc. **Rating** 89 To 2015 $18
Hunter Valley Rose 2007 Fragrant red and black cherry fruit balanced by crisp acidity on the fresh finish. Screwcap. 13.5° alc. **Rating** 88 To 2009 $18

Stonewell Vineyards ★★★★☆

Stonewell Road, Tanunda, SA 5352 **Region** Barossa Valley
T (08) 8563 3624 **F** (08) 8563 3624 **www.**stonewell.com.au **Open** By appt
Winemaker Troy Kalleske **Est.** 1965 **Cases** 260
Owners John and Yvonne Pfeiffer, together with daughters Lisa and Tammy, are the fifth and sixth generations of this Barossa winegrowing family. John and Yvonne transformed what was an unviable mixed fruit and farming property into 50 ha of mainstream grape varieties; the vineyards are in the Stonewell area, noted for producing high-quality shiraz. The grapes were sold for many years, but in 2004 specially selected small parcels were contract-made under the Daughters of the Valley label – dedicated to John and Yvonne's four daughters who, after growing up in the Barossa Valley, have now returned to continue the family business. No samples received, the rating is that of last year.

Stoney Rise ★★★★★

Hendersons Lane, Gravelly Beach, Tas 7276 **Region** Northern Tasmania
T (03) 6394 3678 **F** (03) 6394 3684 **www**.stoneyrise.com **Open** Thurs–Mon 11–5
Winemaker Joe Holyman **Est.** 2000 **Cases** 1500

This is the venture of Joe and Lou Holyman. The Holyman family has been involved in vineyards in Tasmania for 20 years, but Joe's career in the wine industry, first as a sales rep, then as a wine buyer, and more recently working in wineries in NZ, Portugal, France, Mount Benson and Coonawarra, gave him an exceptionally broad-based understanding of wine. In 2004 Joe and Lou purchased the former Rotherhythe vineyard, which had been established in '86, and was in a somewhat rundown state by the time it was purchased. They set about restoring the vineyard to its former glory, with 3 ha of pinot noir and 1 ha of chardonnay. There are two ranges: the Stoney Rise wines focusing on fruit and early drinkability, the Holyman wines with more structure, more new oak and the best grapes, here the focus on length and potential longevity. The 2006 Pinots had spectacular success at the Tas Wine Show '07. Exports to the UK.

🍷🍷🍷🍷🍷 **Pinot Noir 2006** Fresh and vibrant, with a complex array of aromas and flavours from dark cherry to dark plum; a gentle sprinkle of spice to complete a beautiful palate. Trophy Tas Wine Show '08. Screwcap. 14° alc. **Rating** 96 **To** 2014

Holyman Pinot Noir 2006 Strong colour typical of the vintage; very complex, with some toasty barrel ferment characters, and an abundance of pinot fruit to continue developing over the next 5+ years. Gold, Tas Wine Show '08. Screwcap. 13.5° alc. **Rating** 94 **To** 2013 **$45**

🍷🍷🍷🍷 **Riesling 2007** Some colour development, and seems riper than the alcohol suggests; perhaps stressed fruit; finishes short. Screwcap. 12° alc. **Rating** 88 **To** 2010 **$25**

Stonier Wines ★★★★★

Cnr Thompson's Lane/Frankston-Flinders Road, Merricks, Vic 3916
Region Mornington Peninsula
T (03) 5989 8300 **F** (03) 5989 8709 **www**.stoniers.com.au **Open** 7 days 11–5
Winemaker Geraldine McFaul **Est.** 1978 **Cases** 25 000

One of the most senior wineries on the Mornington Peninsula, now part of the Petaluma group, which is in turn owned by Lion Nathan of NZ. Wine quality is assured, as is the elegant, restrained style of the Chardonnay and Pinot Noir. Exports to all major markets.

🍷🍷🍷🍷🍷 **KBS Vineyard Chardonnay 2005** Fine citrus, melon and nectarine fruit leads the band; surges in the mouth, with focused intensity running right through its length; bright acidity. Screwcap. 14.5° alc. **Rating** 96 **To** 2015 **$60**

Reserve Mornington Peninsula Chardonnay 2006 Complex, intense aromas and flavours; perfectly ripened white peach and nectarine fruit, the winemaking inputs seamless; long finish. Screwcap. 13.5° alc. **Rating** 95 **To** 2014 **$40**

Mornington Peninsula Chardonnay 2006 Fresh and lively, with melon and stone fruit in a crisp basket of natural acidity, supported by subtle oak. Screwcap. 13.5° alc. **Rating** 94 **To** 2010 **$24**

🍷🍷🍷🍷½ **Cuvee 2003** Pale green-straw; as ever, intense lime citrus flavours; very linear and long, but not as deep or complex as others at this price; could well develop with further time on cork. 12.5° alc. **Rating** 92 **To** 2011 **$45**

Mornington Peninsula Pinot Noir 2006 A delicate and understated pinot in typical Stonier style; clear varietal expression, but really needs more substance. Screwcap. 14° alc. **Rating** 90 **To** 2011 **$26**

Reserve Mornington Peninsula Pinot Noir 2006 Typically light colour; elegant, with strong briar, forest floor and savoury components, and small red fruits; in a particular style. Screwcap. 13.5° alc. **Rating** 90 **To** 2014 **$50**

ŢŢŢŢ   **Windmill Vineyard Pinot Noir 2005** A pale and relatively advanced colour; pleasant pinot flavours, but lacks intensity, and may have some brettanomyces issues. Screwcap. 14.5° alc. **Rating** 88 **To** 2009 $60

Stringy Brae of Sevenhill

Sawmill Road, Sevenhill, SA 5453 **Region** Clare Valley
T (08) 8843 4313 **F** (08) 8843 4319 **www**.stringybrae.com.au **Open** 7 days 11–5
Winemaker O'Leary Walker **Est.** 1991 **Cases** 3500
Donald and Sally Willson began planting their vineyard in 1991, having purchased the property in '83. In 2004 daughter Hannah Rantanen took over day-to-day management from Donald. A slip of the finger last year increased plantings from 10 ha to 70 ha – the former figure was correct, and Stringy Brae is still of modest proportions, with 2.8 ha riesling and 3.6 ha each of shiraz and cabernet sauvignon. No samples received, the rating is that of last year. Exports to the UK, the US, Canada and Singapore.

Stringybark
★★★☆

2060 Chittering Road, Chittering, WA 6084 **Region** Perth Hills
T (08) 9571 8069 **F** (08) 9561 6547 **www**.stringybarkwinery.com.au **Open** Wed–Sat 12–late, Sun 9–8
Winemaker Lilac Hill Estate (Steven Murfitt) **Est.** 1985 **Cases** 750
Bruce and Mary Cussen have a vineyard dating back to 1985, but the development of the cellar door and restaurant complex is far more recent. The vineyard consists of 2 ha of verdelho, chardonnay and cabernet sauvignon. Impressive contract winemaking makes its mark.

ŢŢŢŢ   **Chittering Chardonnay 2007** A brassy, almost grassy, bouquet, with good depth of flavour and a rich, ripe palate. Screwcap. 13.8° alc. **Rating** 89 **To** 2009 $21.90
Rose 2007 Cleverly made, relying largely upon the juxtaposition of a little residual sugar and crisp acidity; light red fruit somewhere in the background. **Rating** 87 **To** 2009 $22.50

Stuart Wines

105 Killara Road, Gruyere, Vic 3770 (postal) **Region** Yarra Valley
T (03) 5964 9312 **F** (03) 5964 9313 **www**.stuartwinesco.com.au **Open** Not
Winemaker Peter Wilson **Est.** 1999 **Cases** 70 000
The Indonesian Widjaja family have major palm oil plantations in Java, with downstream refining. Hendra Widjaja was sent to Australia to establish a vineyard and winery, and he initially chose the Yarra Valley for the first vineyard, thereafter establishing a larger one in Heathcote. The Yarra Valley vineyard has 12 varieties, the Heathcote seven – shiraz, nebbiolo, tempranillo, merlot, cabernet sauvignon, viognier and chardonnay; the two vineyards cover 128 ha. Since 2004 all the wines have been made at a new winery at Heathcote. While the major part of the production is exported, there are also direct sales in Australia. Wines are released under the Cahillton, White Box and Buddha's Wine labels; 50¢ per bottle of the proceeds of sales of all of the Buddha's Wine are donated to the Buddha's Global Childrens Fund, www. buddhaswine.com.au. No wines were submitted for review in this year's *Companion*, because of the cumulative effects of smoke taint, drought and frost decimating yield and quality. The tasting notes are those from the 2008 *Wine Companion*, as the wines reviewed there are still available. Exports to Germany, the Netherlands, Indonesia, China and NZ.

ŢŢŢŢŢ   **Cahillton Yarra Valley Chardonnay 2005** Melon, nectarine, white peach and barrel ferment oak aromas; the complex palate follows suit, with excellent depth and mouthfeel from the well-judged use of mlf; long and well-balanced. Cork. 15° alc. **Rating** 94 **To** 2014 $30
White Box Heathcote Shiraz 2005 Generous medium- to full-bodied with quite lush, but in no sense over-ripe or jammy, blackberry, spice and chocolate fruit. The tannins are fully ripe, the oak subtle; really pleasurable mouthfeel. Screwcap. 14.8° alc. **Rating** 94 **To** 2019 $18

ŸŸŸŸ♀ **Buddha's Wine Yarra Valley Tempranillo 2006** Has more structure and texture than average, although the tannins are light; the flavours, melding tangy citrus with sweeter cherry fruit, are also correct. Cork. 13.3° alc. **Rating** 90 **To** 2012 $18.50

ŸŸŸŸ **White Box Heathcote Merlot Cabernet 2005** Distinctly more minty and savoury than the Cabernet Merlot; since merlot ripens earlier than cabernet, not easy to understand why this should be so; overall texture and weight is quite good. Cork. 14.2° alc. **Rating** 89 **To** 2013 $18
Buddha's Wine Yarra Valley Shiraz Mataro Viognier 2005 Light-bodied; as one might expect, a fragrant and complex bouquet; spicy notes dominate both the bouquet and palate, mocha and chocolate joining in on the mid-palate and finish. Cork. 14.8° alc. **Rating** 88 **To** 2015 $17.50
Cahillton Yarra Valley Shiraz 2004 Shares many things with Buddha's Shiraz, and has developed rather quickly for a wine at this price-point; soft, light- to medium-bodied sweet fruit; fine, ripe tannins. Cork. 14.5° alc. **Rating** 88 **To** 2010 $30
Buddha's Wine Yarra Valley Tempranillo 2005 Similar to the '06, likewise with some texture to the spice, cherry and plum fruit; well-balanced. Cork. 13.5° alc. **Rating** 88 **To** 2008 $16.50

Studley Park Vineyard ★★★

5 Garden Terrace, Kew, Vic 3101 (postal) **Region** Port Phillip Zone
T (03) 9254 2777 **F** (03) 9853 4901 **www**.studleypark.com **Open** Not
Winemaker Llew Knight (Contract) **Est.** 1994 **Cases** 250
Geoff Pryor's Studley Park Vineyard is one of Melbourne's best-kept secrets. It is on a bend of the Yarra River barely 4 km from the Melbourne CBD, on a 0.5-ha block once planted to vines, but for a century used for market gardening, then replanted with cabernet sauvignon. A spectacular aerial photograph shows that immediately across the river, and looking directly to the CBD, is the epicentre of Melbourne's light industrial development, while on the northern and eastern boundaries are suburban residential blocks.

Stumpy Gully

1247 Stumpy Gully Road, Moorooduc, Vic 3933 **Region** Mornington Peninsula
T (03) 5978 8429 **F** (03) 5978 8419 **www**.stumpygully.com.au **Open** W'ends 11–5
Winemaker Wendy Zantvoort, Frank Zantvoort, Michael Zantvoort **Est.** 1988 **Cases** 7500
Frank and Wendy Zantvoort began planting their first vineyard in 1988, Wendy having enrolled in the viticulture course at CSU. Together with son Michael, the Zantvoorts look after all aspects of grapegrowing and winemaking. The original vineyard has 9 ha of vines, but in establishing the 20-ha Moorooduc vineyard the Zantvoorts have deliberately gone against prevailing thinking, planting it solely to red varieties, predominately cabernet sauvignon, merlot and shiraz. They believe they have one of the warmest sites on the Peninsula, and that ripening will in fact present no problems. In all they now have 10 varieties planted on 40 ha, producing 18 different wines (Peninsula Panorama is their second label). Exports to all major markets.

ŸŸŸŸŸ **Magic Black Reserve Pinot Noir 2005** Powerful and intense, with excellent balance between masses of dark plum/black cherry fruit and more savoury notes; good length. Deserves the Reserve tag, the price (and the name). Screwcap. 14.5° alc. **Rating** 94 **To** 2012 $48

ŸŸŸŸ♀ **Mornington Peninsula Chardonnay 2006** A cool-grown style, with hints of citrus and plenty of minerality; clean and fresh on the finish, with just a hint of almond at the end. Screwcap. 14.3° alc. **Rating** 90 **To** 2013 $20
Mornington Peninsula Pinot Grigio 2007 Aromas of citrus and almonds, with fresh, crisp and clean fruit and acidity on the savoury finish. Screwcap. 13.1° alc. **Rating** 90 **To** 2010 $22

ＹＹＹＹ   **Mornington Peninsula Pinot Noir 2006** Lots of briar, earth and forest notes throughout the red and black cherry fruit; needs just a little more strength to carry all of these complex inputs. Screwcap. 13.8° alc. **Rating** 89 **To** 2013 $25

Mornington Peninsula Sauvignon Blanc 2007 An unusual touch of anise on the bouquet; a firm gooseberry/grassy palate, and a clean finish. Screwcap. 13.2° alc. **Rating** 88 **To** 2009 $18

Mornington Peninsula Marsanne 2007 Hints of honeyed fruit on the bouquet, and some nice texture from oxidative fruit handling, as well as some nutty complexity. Screwcap. 14.8° alc. **Rating** 87 **To** 2012 $22

Sugarloaf Creek Estate

20 Zwars Road, Broadford, Vic 3658 **Region** Goulburn Valley
T (03) 5784 1291 **F** (03) 5784 1291 **www**.sugarloafcreek.com **Open** First Sun of month 10–5, or by appt
Winemaker Munari Wines **Est.** 1998 **Cases** 600
The 2-ha vineyard, planted exclusively to shiraz, was established by the Blyth and Hunter families in the 1990s, the first vintage in '01. While situated in the Goulburn Valley, it is in fact near the boundary of the Upper Goulburn, Goulburn Valley and Macedon Ranges regions, and the climate is significantly cooler than that of the major part of the Goulburn Valley.

ＹＹＹＹ   **Shiraz 2005** Enters the mouth without too much fuss, but the alcohol takes over the whole scene thereafter; for disciples of Robert Parker. Screwcap. 16.5° alc. **Rating** 87 **To** 2015 $18

Sugarloaf Ridge ★★★

336 Sugarloaf Road, Carlton River, Tas 7173 **Region** Southern Tasmania
T (03) 6265 7175 **F** (03) 6266 7275 **www**.sugarloafridge.com **Open** Fri–Mon 10–5 Oct–May
Winemaker Winemaking Tasmania (Julian Alcorso) **Est.** 1999 **Cases** 300
Dr Simon Stanley and wife Isobel are both microbiologists, but with thoroughly unlikely specialities: he in low-temperature microbiology, taking him to the Antarctic, and she in a worldwide environmental geosciences company. Sugarloaf Ridge is an extended family business, with daughter Kristen and husband Julian Colville partners. Since 1999, multiple clones of pinot noir, sauvignon blanc, pinot gris, viognier and lagrein have been planted, and 1580 native trees, 210 olive trees and 270 cherry trees have also helped transform the property.

ＹＹＹＹＹ   **Pinot Noir 2005** Complex aromas of dark berry, spice and forest, then a tangy, savoury palate with an acid twist on the finish. **Rating** 90 **To** 2011 $40

ＹＹＹＹ   **Pinot Noir 2006** Overtones of mint, and yet the fruit is quite soft until the finish, where it is picked up by some acidity. **Rating** 87 **To** 2011

Summerfield

5967 Stawell-Avoca Road, Moonambel, Vic 3478 **Region** Pyrenees
T (03) 5467 2264 **F** (03) 5467 2380 **www**.summerfieldwines.com **Open** 7 days 9–5.30
Winemaker Mark Summerfield **Est.** 1979 **Cases** 8000
A specialist red wine producer, the particular forte of which is Shiraz. The red wines are consistently excellent: luscious and full-bodied and fruit-driven, but with a slice of vanillin oak to top them off. Founder Ian Summerfield has now handed over the winemaking reins to son Mark, who, with consulting advice, produces consistently outstanding and awesomely concentrated Shiraz and Cabernet Sauvignon, both in varietal and Reserve forms. The red wines are built for the long haul, and richly repay cellaring. Exports to the US and the UK.

ＹＹＹＹＹ   **Reserve Shiraz 2006** Complex aromas, with fruit, oak, licorice and spice intermingling; excellent vinosity and generosity on the medium- to full-bodied palate; no dead fruit; good finish. Cork. 14.5° alc. **Rating** 94 **To** 2021 $50

Reserve Cabernet 2005 Rich, mouthcoating fruit ranging through regional mint, blackcurrant and a mix of dark chocolate and mocha/cedar oak; the tannins are particularly soft and fine. Cork. 14.9° alc. **Rating** 94 **To** 2017 $50

Reserve Cabernet 2006 While full-bodied, has more texture and refinement, and better oak than the varietal; considerable length and good line; if only Summerfield would reverse the closures. Cork. 14° alc. **Rating** 94 **To** 2020 $50

ȚȚȚȚȚ **Shiraz 2006** Herbal mint and spice overtones to predominantly blackberry and black cherry fruit; has more elegance than usual, with life and thrust to the palate; difference in style more than quality. Screwcap. 14.5° alc. **Rating** 93 **To** 2016 $30

Cabernet 2006 Typically, a lusciously rich and softly dense wine, with fruitcake and lashings of black fruit flavours easily handling the oak; ripe tannins. Screwcap. 14.5° alc. **Rating** 90 **To** 2016 $30

Tradition 2006 The medium-bodied blend of Merlot/Shiraz/Cabernet Sauvignon/Cabernet Franc works well, with gentle cassis and red berry fruits and a slightly savoury twist to the finish. Screwcap. 14° alc. **Rating** 90 **To** 2014 $30

ȚȚȚȚ **Merlot 2006** Medium- to full-bodied; regional red wine, varietal character the last cab off the rank; generous fruit and soft mouthfeel. Screwcap. 14.5° alc. **Rating** 88 **To** 2015 $30

Summit Estate

291 Granite Belt Drive, Thulimbah, Qld 4377 **Region** Granite Belt
T (07) 4683 2011 **F** (07) 4683 2600 **www.**summitestate.com.au **Open** 7 days 9–5
Winemaker Paola Cabezas Rhymer **Est.** 1997 **Cases** 2500
Summit Estate is the public face of the Stanthorpe Wine Co, owned by a syndicate of 10 professionals who work in Brisbane, and share a love of wine. They operate the Stanthorpe Wine Centre, which offers wine education as well as selling wines from other makers in the region (and, of course, from Summit Estate). The 17-ha vineyard is planted to chardonnay, marsanne, pinot noir, shiraz, merlot, tempranillo, petit verdot and cabernet sauvignon, and they have set up a small, specialised contract winemaking facility. Exports to the UK.

ȚȚȚȚ **Reserve Cabernet 2005** Strong, savoury earthy components, but well within varietal expectations; commendable Qld cabernet. Quality cork. 13.4° alc. **Rating** 89 **To** 2015 $24

Verdelho 2007 Light, fresh and crisp; well made, though not much depth to the flavour; redeemed by a clean, relatively lively finish. Screwcap. 13.8° alc. **Rating** 87 **To** 2009 $16

Sunnyhurst Winery

Lot 16 Doust Street, Bridgetown, WA 6255 **Region** Blackwood Valley
T (08) 9761 4525 **F** (08) 9761 4525 **www.**sunnyhurst.com.au **Open** 7 days 10–6
Winemaker Mark Staniford **Est.** 2000 **Cases** NA
Mark and Lainie Staniford purchased a 110-year-old stone house surrounded by extensive gardens on the outskirts of Bridgetown in 1999. It gave Mark Staniford the opportunity of realising a lifelong dream of making wine after he opened WA's first specialist wine shop in North Fremantle in 1965. He has established 0.25 ha each of semillon, sauvignon blanc, cabernet sauvignon and merlot, the original intention being to make the equivalents of white and red Bordeaux respectively. Both red and white wines are pressed in hand-operated basket presses, the whites barrel-fermented, the reds mainly open-fermented.

ȚȚȚȚ **Cabernet Merlot 2005** Medium-bodied, but quite intense blackcurrant and cassis fruit; has good length and finish; early picking a plus. Twin top. 13.9° alc. **Rating** 89 **To** 2012 $26

Cabernet Sauvignon 2005 Firm, fresh, in similar style to the other Sunnyhurst reds; juicy varietal fruit does the talking on the light- to medium-bodied palate. Twin top. 13.9° alc. **Rating** 88 **To** 2013 $26

Blackwood Valley Merlot 2005 Savoury and very earthy, but also very persistent; olive tones and lingering tannins. Twin top. 13.8° alc. **Rating** 87 To 2011 $22

Surveyor's Hill Winery

215 Brooklands Road, Wallaroo, NSW 2618 **Region** Canberra District
T (02) 6230 2046 www.survhill.com.au **Open** W'ends & public hols, or by appt
Winemaker Brindabella Hills Winery (Dr Roger Harris) **Est.** 1986 **Cases** 1000
The Surveyor's Hill vineyard is on the slopes of the eponymous hill, at 550 m to 680 m above sea level. It is an ancient volcano, producing granite-derived coarse-structured (and hence well-drained) sandy soils of low fertility. Former grape sales to Kamberra have ceased, and the wines are made by Dr Roger Harris.

Semillon Chardonnay 2005 In Surveyor's Hill style, slow-developing, but doesn't look as if it will ever gain real complexity or, more importantly, thrust; pleasant now. Screwcap. 12° alc. **Rating** 87 To 2009 $15
Touriga Nacional Cabernet Franc 2004 Light-bodied, with some of the cedar and tobacco characters of the Loire Valley cabernet franc, even though this is only one-third of the blend; an exercise for the brain, not the heart or stomach. Screwcap. 13.1° alc. **Rating** 87 To 2011 $18

Sutherland Estate ★★★★☆

2010 Melba Highway, Dixons Creek, Vic 3775 **Region** Yarra Valley
T 0402 052 287 **F** (03) 9762 1122 **Open** 7 days 10–5 summer, or Thurs–Sun & public hols
Winemaker Alex White (Contract) **Est.** 2000 **Cases** 2000
The Phelan family (father Ron, mother Sheila, daughter Catherine and partner Angus Ridley) established Sutherland Estate in 2000, when they acquired a mature 2-ha vineyard at Dixons Creek. Later that year they planted another 3.2 ha, including a small amount of tempranillo. Catherine and Angus are in the final year of the part-time viticulture and oenology course at CSU; in the meantime, Angus is gaining further experience as a winemaker at Coldstream Hills. The DHV range is estate-grown on Daniel's Hill Vineyard. No samples received, the rating is that of last year.

 # Sutherlands Creek Wines

PO Box 1665, Geelong, Vic 3220 **Region** Geelong
T (03) 5281 1811 **F** (03) 5281 1877 www.sutherlandscreek.com **Open** Not
Winemaker Fred Meeker **Est.** 2000 **Cases** 12 500
The five investor-owners of Sutherlands Creek bring a wide range of international business backgrounds to the venture, spanning the UK, Hong Kong, Asia and Australia. The total investment in the venture was $12 million; there are two separate vineyard properties, together planted to pinot noir (16 ha); viognier (5 ha); shiraz, zinfandel and sauvignon blanc (2 ha each); and 1 ha each of pinot gris and semillon. In addition there is a 2.4-ha planting of 42 varietals, rootstocks and clones at the Russells Bridge Vineyard, including varieties such as gamay, nebbiolo, mourvedre and roussanne. A winery has been built, which will be expanded in the years ahead if the need arises.

Rose 2006 Attractive, gently spicy strawberry fruit; good length and balance, finishing with citrussy acidity. Screwcap. 13° alc. **Rating** 89 To 2009 $16.95
Zinfandel 2005 Strong colour; rich black fruits and licorice supported by ripe tannins; curiously, seems to show warm region characteristics; perhaps just the variety. Cork. 14° alc. **Rating** 89 To 2010 $26.95
Pinot Noir 2005 Savoury, spicy, stemmy aromas and flavours; just enough fruit to carry it over the line. Cork. 14.5° alc. **Rating** 87 To 2009 $29.95

Sutton Grange Winery   ★★★★☆

Carnochans Road, Sutton Grange, Vic 3448 **Region** Bendigo
T (03) 5474 8277 **F** (03) 5474 8294 **www**.suttongrangewines.com **Open** Mon–Fri 9–4,
w'ends 11–5
Winemaker Gilles Lapalus **Est.** 1998 **Cases** 3000
The 400-ha Sutton Grange property is a thoroughbred stud acquired in 1996 by Peter
Sidwell, a Melbourne businessman with horse racing and breeding interests. A lunch visit to
the property by long-term friends Alec Epis and Stuart Anderson led to the decision to plant
14 ha of syrah, merlot, cabernet sauvignon, viognier and sangiovese, and to the recruitment
of French winemaker Gilles Lapalus, who just happens to be the partner of Stuart Anderson's
daughter. The winery, built from WA limestone, was completed in 2001. Exports to the UK,
Belgium, France and Malaysia.

♀♀♀♀♀ **Estate Syrah 2005** Deep-coloured and complex, with abundant red and black
fruits, considerable toasty oak and firm tannins; a big mouthful of wine. Cork.
Rating 94 **To** 2025 $50

♀♀♀♀♀ **Fairbank Syrah 2005** A slightly reduced bouquet, but good fruit concentration,
with red fruits and savoury spicy aromas and flavours; quite tannic, but really bright,
and a certain European edge to the finish. Screwcap. **Rating** 93 **To** 2020 $25
Fairbank Viognier 2006 A hint of sulphur on the bouquet, with spicy aromas
alongside a little apricot kernel fruit; quite generous, with good acidity to keep the
palate lively. Screwcap. 14° alc. **Rating** 90 **To** 2011 $28

♀♀♀♀ **Fairbank Rose 2007** Complex barrel-fermented style, with early-picked
Cabernet/Shiraz/Merlot; bone-dry, and with good texture; a cerebral rose.
Screwcap. 13° alc. **Rating** 89 **To** 2010 $20

Swings & Roundabouts   ★★★★

2807 Caves Road, Yallingup, WA 6232 **Region** Margaret River
T (08) 9756 6640 **F** (08) 9756 6736 **www**.swings.com.au **Open** 7 days 10–5
Winemaker Mark Lane **Est.** 2004 **Cases** 30 000
The Swings name comes from the expression used to encapsulate the eternal balancing
act between the various aspects of grape and wine production. Swings aims to balance the
serious side with a touch of fun. There are now four ranges overseen by winemaker Mark
Lane: Kiss Chasey, Life of Riley, Swings & Roundabouts and the top shelf Laneway.

♀♀♀♀♀ **Margaret River Semillon Sauvignon Blanc 2007** Fine and precise, with
varietal herbaceous notes and ample fruit that follows through to the even finish.
Screwcap. 12.5° alc. **Rating** 90 **To** 2010 $19

♀♀♀♀ **The Life of Riley Chenin Blanc 2007** An aromatic tangy, passionfruit-accented
bouquet, the palate following suit; cloys just a little on the finish. Screwcap. 13° alc.
Rating 88 **To** 2012 $17
Margaret River Cabernet Merlot 2005 Quite ripe with blueberries and
cassis; fairly tannic, but with good flavour depth and flavour. Screwcap. 14.5° alc.
Rating 88 **To** 2014 $19
Laneway Margaret River Sangiovese 2007 Bright and juicy cherry fruit;
high levels of acid and tannin, with good focus; very tannic, so needs food.
Screwcap. 14° alc. **Rating** 88 **To** 2012 $25
Margaret River Shiraz 2005 Fresh redcurrant, spice and quite lifted; medium-
bodied, with good flavour and persistence on the finish. Screwcap. 14.5° alc.
Rating 87 **To** 2012 $19
The Life of Riley Shiraz Viognier 2005 Vibrant, spicy light-bodied, cherry-
flavoured wine ready to roll right now. Screwcap. 14° alc. **Rating** 87 **To** 2010 $17

Swooping Magpie

860 Commonage Road, Yallingup, WA 6282 **Region** Margaret River
T 0417 921 003 **F** (08) 9756 6227 **www.**swoopingmagpie.com.au **Open** By appt
Winemaker Mark Standish (Contract) **Est.** 1998 **Cases** 2000
Neil and Leann Tuffield have established their 2-and-a-bit-ha vineyard in the hills behind
the coastal town of Yallingup. The name, they say, 'was inspired by a family of magpies who
consider the property part of their territory'. One ha each of semillon and cabernet franc is
supplemented by purchased sauvignon blanc, chenin blanc and merlot to produce the wines.
The Tuffields have obtained planning approval for a cellar door, due to open early 2009.
Exports to the US.

ΨΨΨΨΨ **Margaret River Semillon 2007** Generous flavour and structure, strongly, though
not excessively, influenced by barrel ferment and 9 months in French oak; good
length in Margaret River style. Screwcap. 13.6° alc. **Rating** 90 **To** 2014 $20

ΨΨΨΨ **Margaret River Cabernet Franc 2005** Very savoury cedar, tobacco, earth and
spice; extremely fine tannins are a distinct plus. Screwcap. 14.5° alc. **Rating** 88
To 2012 $20
Margaret River Cabernet Merlot 2004 Powerful but slightly reduced, and
has high tannin levels; time may come to its aid. Screwcap. 14° alc. **Rating** 87
To 2014 $17

Sylvan Springs

RSD 405 Blythmans Road, McLaren Flat, SA 5171 (postal) **Region** McLaren Vale
T (08) 8383 0500 **F** (08) 8383 0499 **Open** Not
Winemaker Brian Light (Consultant) **Est.** 1974 **Cases** 4500
The Pridmore family has been involved in grapegrowing and winemaking in McLaren
Vale for four generations, spanning over 100 years. The pioneer was Cyril Pridmore, who
established The Wattles Winery in 1896, and purchased Sylvan Park, one of the original
homesteads in the area, in 1901. The original family land in the township of McLaren Vale
was sold in '78, but not before third-generation Digby Pridmore had established vineyards (in
'74) near Blewitt Springs. When he retired in '90, his son David purchased the 45-ha vineyard
(planted to 11 different varieties) and, with sister Sally, began assisting with winemaking in
'96. Exports to the US and Canada.

ΨΨΨΨ **Hard Yards McLaren Vale Shiraz 2005** Very good concentration of fruit, with
a slight herbal edge; good overall flavour, but quite tannic, and lacks vibrancy on
the finish. Screwcap. 14.5° alc. **Rating** 89 **To** 2016 $14.90
Dirty Girl's McLaren Vale Semillon Sauvignon Blanc 2007 Fresh and
vibrant, with cut and dried grass on the palate; good flavour. Challenging brand
name. Screwcap. 13° alc. **Rating** 87 **To** 2010 $14
Filthy Boy's McLaren Vale Cabernet Sauvignon Merlot 2005 Bright and
varietal with a hint of cedar and juicy cassis fruits; early-drinking style. Even more
arresting. Screwcap. 13.5° alc. **Rating** 87 **To** 2012 $14

Symphonia Wines

1019 Snow Road, Oxley, Vic 3678 **Region** King Valley
T (03) 5727 3888 **F** (03) 5727 3853 **www.**sammiranda.com.au **Open** At Sam Miranda
Winemaker Sam Miranda **Est.** 1998 **Cases** 3000
Peter Read and his family were veterans of the King Valley, commencing the development
of their vineyard in 1981 to supply Brown Brothers. As a result of extensive trips to both
Western and Eastern Europe, Peter Read embarked on an ambitious project to trial a series
of grape varieties little known in this country. The process of evaluation and experimentation
produced a number of wines with great interest and no less merit. In 2005 Rachel Miranda
(wife of Sam Miranda), with parents Peter and Suzanne Evans, purchased the business, and
intends to keep its identity intact and separate from the Sam Miranda brand.

ΨΨΨΨϘ **King Valley Saperavi 2006** Typically dense colour and equally dense flavours of dark berries and licorice, yet manages a certain elegance thanks to immaculate balance of fruit, oak and tannins. Screwcap. 14.5° alc. **Rating** 93 **To** 2020 $24
Las Triadas Winemakers Reserve Tempranillo 2006 Fragrant red fruit aromas, but moving more to spicy black fruit flavours on the medium-bodied palate, then a tangy, faintly lemony, finish. Screwcap. 13.8° alc. **Rating** 90 **To** 2013 $24

ΨΨΨΨ **King Valley Albarino 2006** Symphonia continues its varietal trail blazing role, here combined with astute winemaking; notes of white peach and granny smith apples tied with good acidity. Screwcap. 12° alc. **Rating** 89 **To** 2011 $25
King Valley Tannat 2005 A more savoury and spicy wine than the Saperavi, medium- rather than full-bodied; a fragrant, lifted bouquet, and a brisk finish side-steps the tough tannins of the variety. Screwcap. 14° alc. **Rating** 89 **To** 2014 $24

Symphony Hill Wines   ★★★★☆

2017 Eukey Road, Ballandean, Qld 4382 **Region** Granite Belt
T (07) 4684 1388 **F** (07) 4684 1399 **www.**symphonyhill.com.au **Open** 7 days 10–4
Winemaker Mike Hayes **Est.** 1999 **Cases** 6000
Ewen and Elissa Macpherson purchased what was then an old table grape and orchard property in 1996. In partnership with Ewen's parents, Bob and Jill Macpherson, they developed 4 ha of vineyards, while Ewen completed his Bachelor of Applied Science in viticulture (2003). The vineyard has been established using state-of-the-art technology; vineyard manager and winemaker Mike Hayes has a degree in viticulture and is a third-generation viticulturist in the Granite Belt region. Between Hayes and Ewen Macpherson, a trial block of 50 varieties has been established, including such rarely encountered varieties as picpoul, tannat and mondeuse. The quality of the '06 reds is excellent. Exports to Singapore.

ΨΨΨΨΨ **Reserve Granite Belt Cabernet Sauvignon 2006** Deep colour; richer and deeper than the Winemakers' Blend; classic cabernet fruit with perfectly integrated cedary oak and the tannins essential for top cabernet sauvignon; long life ahead. Screwcap. 14.5° alc. **Rating** 94 **To** 2026 $45

ΨΨΨΨϘ **Reserve Granite Belt Shiraz 2006** Very well made; harmonious fruit, oak and tannins on the medium-bodied palate; good line and length. Screwcap. 14.5° alc. **Rating** 92 **To** 2016 $45
Reserve Sauvignon Blanc 2007 Has totally unexpected intensity and thrust to the mix of mineral, gooseberry, kiwifruit and herbs; clear-cut acidity and good length. Bolivia, NSW. Screwcap. 11.5° alc. **Rating** 91 **To** 2010 $25
Winemakers' Blend Granite Belt Cabernet Sauvignon 2006 Bright crimson-purple; a bright and zesty palate with vibrant blackcurrant and cassis fruit thrusting through vigorously to the finish. Screwcap. 14.9° alc. **Rating** 91 **To** 2016 $35
Reserve Granite Belt Petit Verdot 2006 Impressively made, in full-bodied mode as befits the variety, but without aggressive extract; dark berry fruits, tonnes of cedar and spice join the tannins on the finish. Screwcap. 14.9° alc. **Rating** 91 **To** 2020 $35
Reserve Granite Belt Merlot 2006 Lively and fresh, with light-bodied raspberry and cassis fruit carefully captured in an appropriately light- to medium-bodied palate and finish. Screwcap. 13.9° alc. **Rating** 90 **To** 2013 $35

ΨΨΨΨ **Reserve Granite Belt Pinot Noir 2006** Surprise packet; both in terms of structure and flavour verging on medium- to full-bodied dry red, but will benefit from extended cellaring. Screwcap. **Rating** 89 **To** 2014 $45
Danying Shiraz Cabernet Sauvignon 2005 A supple, medium-bodied palate with nicely integrated blackberry, redcurrant fruit and mocha oak; soft tannins. Screwcap. 13.5° alc. **Rating** 89 **To** 2015 $25
Chardonnay 2006 White and yellow peach flavours with some oak inputs; betrayed by a rather hard finish. Screwcap. 13° alc. **Rating** 87 **To** 2009 $20

Pinot Gris 2007 Considerable power, especially on the finish, giving the illusion of more alcohol; demands food to tame it. Screwcap. 13.5° alc. **Rating** 87 To 2009 $30

Reserve Verdelho 2007 Light- to medium-bodied; typical varietal fruit salad flavours; good balance, and no alcohol heat. Screwcap. 13.8° alc. **Rating** 87 To 2010 $25

Syrahmi ★★★★★

PO Box 438, Heathcote, Vic 3523 **Region** Heathcote
T 0407 057 471 **Open** Not
Winemaker Adam Foster **Est.** 2004 **Cases** 550
Adam Foster worked as a chef in Vic and London before moving to the front of house and becoming increasingly interested in wine. He then worked as a cellar hand with a who's who from Australia and France, including Torbreck, Chapoutier, Mitchelton, Domaine Ogier, Heathcote Winery, Jasper Hill and Domaine Pierre Gaillard. He became convinced that the Cambrian soils of Heathcote could produce the best possible shiraz, and since 2004 has purchased grapes from Heathcote Winery, using the full bag of open ferment techniques with 30% whole bunches, extended cold soak, wild yeast and mlf and hand-plunging, then 13 months in French oak. Bottled unfined and unfiltered.

♥♥♥♥♥ **Petite Priere Heathcote Shiraz 2006** Rich, velvety black fruits and licorice; no issues from a very difficult pregnancy and birth (neither volatile acidity nor aldehydes); soft, spicy/savoury tannins; good oak. Screwcap. 14° alc. **Rating** 94 To 2021 $45

T'Gallant ★★★★☆

1385 Mornington–Flinders Road, Main Ridge, Vic 3928 **Region** Mornington Peninsula
T (03) 5989 6565 **F** (03) 5989 6577 **www**.tgallant.com.au **Open** 7 days 10–5
Winemaker Kevin McCarthy **Est.** 1990 **Cases** 40 000
Husband-and-wife consultant winemakers Kevin McCarthy and Kathleen Quealy carved out such an important niche market for the T'Gallant label that in 2003, after protracted negotiations, it was acquired by Beringer Blass. The acquisition of a 15-ha property, and the planting of 10 ha of pinot gris gives the business a firm geographic base, as well as providing increased resources for its signature wine. La Baracca Trattoria is open 7 days for lunch and for specially booked evening events.

♥♥♥♥♥ **Tribute Mornington Peninsula Pinot Noir 2005** Deceptively light colour; has very good focus, intensity and even better length; spice, cherry and plum all intermingle. Screwcap. 13° alc. **Rating** 94 To 2012 $27.99

♥♥♥♥♀ **Juliet Pinot Noir 2007** Fragrant spicy foresty components along with cherry fruit, savoury elements coming again on the long finish. Screwcap. 12.5° alc. **Rating** 91 To 2013 $19.95

Chardonnay 2006 Crisp, lively and fresh, with good thrust to the nectarine and grapefruit flavours, the barrel ferment component adding to texture rather than flavour. Screwcap. 13.5° alc. **Rating** 90 To 2014 $30.95

Juliet Pinot Noir 2006 Has well-focused, clear-cut and quite intense varietal fruit on both bouquet and palate; is a tad simple, but is excellent value. Screwcap. 13.5° alc. **Rating** 90 To 2011 $18.95

♥♥♥♥ **Juliet Pinot Grigio 2007** A well-balanced, totally dry palate; light-bodied in true seafood style, running no interference; low alcohol also a plus. Screwcap. 11.5° alc. **Rating** 89 To 2009 $14

Tribute Pinot Gris 2007 Powerful wine, with abundant mouthfeel, ripe pear at the heart; the back label assertion of 10-year cellaring future is challenging. Screwcap. 14.5° alc. **Rating** 89 To 2010 $32.95

Juliet Moscato 2007 Extreme style; mix with 50% soda water, chill to near freezing, and have the equivalent of a low-strength beer to guzzle on the beach on a hot summer's day. Screwcap. 6° alc. **Rating** 87 To 2009 $18.95

Imogen Pinot Gris 2007 Varietal pear and clove flavours clear enough, but lacks thrust and clarity. Screwcap. 14.5° alc. **Rating** 87 **To** 2009 $21.95

Premium Moscato 2007 Very smart packaging; pink fizz in strawberry and lemon flavours just fun; serve very cold. Cork. 6° alc. **Rating** 87 **To** 2009 $20.95

Tahbilk

Goulburn Valley Highway, Tabilk, Vic 3608 **Region** Nagambie Lakes
T (03) 5794 2555 **F** (03) 5794 2360 **www.**tahbilk.com.au **Open** Mon–Sat 9–5, Sun 11–5
Winemaker Alister Purbrick, Neil Larson, Alan George **Est.** 1860 **Cases** 120 000
A winery steeped in tradition (with National Trust classification), which should be visited at least once by every wine-conscious Australian, and which makes wines – particularly red wines – utterly in keeping with that tradition. The essence of that heritage comes in the form of the tiny quantities of Shiraz made entirely from vines planted in 1860. In 2005 Tahbilk opened its substantial wetlands project, with a series of walks connected (if you wish) by short journeys on a small punt. Exports to the UK and the US.

🍷🍷🍷🍷🍷 **Eric Stevens Purbrick Shiraz 2002** Bright colour; clearly superior grapes have been well-handled in the winery, giving the wine a level of sweet red and black fruits well above the norm; ripe tannins and high quality oak. Arguably the best shiraz since 1962. Cork. **Rating** 96 **To** 2027 $69.95

Eric Stevens Purbrick Cabernet Sauvignon 2002 Pleasant earthy/cedary aromas; springs into life on the palate, supple and smooth, yet full of life, with perfect balance and length. This really is a breakthrough for Tahbilk. Cork. **Rating** 96 **To** 2027 $69.95

1927 Vines Marsanne 1999 Bright, pale straw-green; layers of flavour turn around honeysuckle fruit and lemony acidity; great length and fully deserves its show success. The bottom of the cork was ominously soggy. 12° alc. **Rating** 95 **To** 2011 $31.45

1860 Vines Shiraz 2002 A light but youthful colour with no sign of browning; has very good balance and length, albeit in the usual restrained style; oak and tannins provide a well-judged support role; 254 dozen from the only vineyard of this age without replaced (hence younger) vines. Cork. 13.5° alc. **Rating** 95 **To** 2022 $128

🍷🍷🍷🍷🍷 **Marsanne 2007** Clean and fragrant; more varietal fruit and flavour than most young marsannes from France or Australia; mineral, spice and honeysuckle cohabit on a long, crisp finish. A classic in the making. Screwcap. 12.5° alc. **Rating** 93 **To** 2017 $14.90

Nagambie Lakes Riesling 2007 Clean and vibrant, showing lemon zest and nice texture on the finish; good value. Screwcap. 12.5° alc. **Rating** 90 **To** 2015 $16.45

Viognier 2006 Has benefited from a year in bottle, gaining weight and complexity; apricot, toast and a touch of honey, then good acidity. Screwcap. 14.5° alc. **Rating** 90 **To** 2009 $18.95

Shiraz 2004 Bright, clear colour; fresh and lively cherry and plum fruit, soft tannins and gentle oak; a new Tahbilk face without loss of flavour. Screwcap. 15° alc. **Rating** 90 **To** 2019 $21.50

🍷🍷🍷🍷 **Viognier 2007** Well made; varietal flavour is achieved without loss of finesse, freshness and length; a delicate apricot and citrus mix with crisp acidity. Screwcap. 14° alc. **Rating** 89 **To** 2010 $18.95

Cabernet Sauvignon 2004 Firm, youthful medium-bodied palate with clear varietal fruit largely uninfluenced by new oak; overall, slightly lean-flanked. Screwcap. 14.5° alc. **Rating** 89 **To** 2013 $21.50

Tallarook

140 Ennis Road, Tallarook, Vic 3659 **Region** Upper Goulburn
T (03) 5793 8344 **F** (03) 5793 8399 **www**.tallarook.com **Open** By appt
Winemaker Terry Barnet **Est.** 1987 **Cases** 1200
Tallarook has been established on a property between Broadford and Seymour at an elevation
of 200–300 m. Since 1987, 11 ha of vines have been planted, mainly to chardonnay, shiraz
and pinot noir, but with significant amounts of marsanne, roussanne and viognier. The
second label Terra Felix was sold in 2005, and the quality of the Tallarook wines has risen
significantly. The 2007 vintage was destroyed by frost, an unfortunately common story.
Exports to the UK and Germany.

Chardonnay 2005 Quite savoury, with citrus fruits, toast and a persistent mineral
undercurrent; creamy and rich, with a long toasty/nutty finish; still very fresh for
age. Screwcap. 13.5° alc. **Rating** 92 **To** 2010 $25
Marsanne 2005 Honeysuckle fruits, blended with spicy and toasty oak; good
concentration and depth of fruit, and the palate opens up slowly, but with very
good length; very nutty on the finish. Screwcap. 14.5° alc. **Rating** 90 **To** 2012
$27.50
Roussanne 2006 Quite tight and very minerally; all secondary character as you
would expect with such a strong European influence; fine, fresh and with just a
little savoury grip on the finish. Screwcap. 13.5° alc. **Rating** 90 **To** 2009 $27.50

Marsanne 2006 Wild yeast, barrel ferment and 10 months in older French oak
has augmented the honeysuckle and mineral notes of the fruit; has length, and will
age well. Screwcap. 13° alc. **Rating** 89 **To** 2014 $27.50
Chardonnay 2006 Understated style, with more textural play from wild yeast,
barrel fermentation in older oak and lees stirring giving nutty/creamy characters,
but with subdued fruit. Screwcap. 13.5° alc. **Rating** 87 **To** 2011 $25

Tallis Wine

PO Box 10, Dookie, Vic 3646 **Region** Central Victoria Zone
T (03) 5823 5383 **F** (03) 5828 6532 **www**.talliswine.com.au **Open** Not
Winemaker Richard Tallis, Gary Baldwin (Consultant) **Est.** 2000 **Cases** 2000
Richard and Alice Tallis have 25 ha under wine, with 16 ha shiraz, 5 ha cabernet sauvignon,
2 ha viognier, 1 ha merlot and a small planting of sangiovese and nebbiolo. While most of
the grapes are sold, they have embarked on winemaking with the aid of Gary Baldwin, and
have had considerable success. The philosophy of their winemaking and viticulture is minimal
intervention to create a low-input and sustainable system; use of environmentally harmful
sprays is minimised.

Dookie Hills Sangiovese 2006 Has well above-average intensity and length
with strong sour cherry, tobacco and spice flavours running through the long
palate. Screwcap. 14.4° alc. **Rating** 90 **To** 2013 $18

Dookie Hills Merlot 2006 Medium-bodied, with ripe cassis fruit offset by quite
persistent tannins; still in two parts, and needs time. Screwcap. 14.6° alc. **Rating** 87
To 2013 $18

Taltarni

339 Taltarni Road, Moonambel, Vic 3478 **Region** Pyrenees
T (03) 5459 7900 **F** (03) 5467 2306 **www**.taltarni.com.au **Open** 7 days 10–5
Winemaker Loïc Le Calvez **Est.** 1972 **Cases** 80 000
After a hiatus of two years or so following the departure of long-serving winemaker and
chief executive Dominique Portet, Taltarni gathered momentum and inspiration with a new
winemaking team. Major changes in the approach to the vineyards; major upgrading of
winery equipment and investment in new oak barrels; a long-term contract for the purchase
of grapes from the Heathcote region; and the release of a flagship wine, Cephas, are the visible
signs of the repositioning of the business. Exports to all major markets.

♥♥♥♥♥ **Heathcote Shiraz 2005** Great colour; shows the depth of flavour without excessive alcohol possible in Heathcote; blackberry, licorice and dark chocolate, with ripe tannins and oak seamlessly integrated. Screwcap. 14.5° alc. **Rating** 95 To 2025 $42.25

Estate Pyrenees Shiraz 2005 Medium- to full-bodied; very good structure, texture and balance; harmonious black fruits woven through quality oak and fine but ripe and positive tannins. Cork. **Rating** 94 To 2014 $30.95

♥♥♥♥♥ **Three Monks Fume Blanc 2007** A complex regional blend (Vic/Tas) and partial barrel ferment plus 6 months in oak playing a role; quite ripe tropical fruit but good acidity; well made. Screwcap. 12.5° alc. **Rating** 91 To 2010 $21.95

Three Monks Cabernet Merlot 2006 A firm, savoury wine, with elements of briar and cassis on the quite long, tannic and even finish. Screwcap. **Rating** 90 To 2016 $21.95

Estate Pyrenees Cabernet Sauvignon 2005 Elegant medium-bodied wine, with a classic interplay between blackcurrant fruit and savoury/earthy characters from the tannins. Cork. **Rating** 90 To 2020 $30.95

Brut Tache 2006 Has more red fruit flavours (strawberry) than the Brut, 'stained' (French tache) by the addition of pinot noir dry red wine; good balance and length. Cork. 13° alc. **Rating** 90 To 2010 $23.95

♥♥♥♥ **Brut 2006** Not clear how long on lees; certainly has good stone fruit profile from Chardonnay/Pinot Noir; meritorious length and balance. Vic/Tas. Cork. 13° alc. **Rating** 89 To 2012 $23.95

T Series Sauvignon Blanc Semillon 2007 Dry style; very clean and well made, with good texture and lightness on the finish. Screwcap. 12.5° alc. **Rating** 87 To 2010 $14.95

T Series Chardonnay Pinot Noir NV Clean, crisp and with a nice creamy mouthfeel; a fresh aperitif style. Cork. 12.5° alc. **Rating** 87 To 2009 $14.95

Tamar Ridge   ★★★★★

Auburn Road, Kayena, Tas 7270 **Region** Northern Tasmania
T (03) 6394 1111 **F** (03) 6394 1126 **www.**tamarridge.com.au **Open** 7 days 10–5
Winemaker Andrew Pirie, Tom Ravech, Matt Lowe **Est.** 1994 **Cases** 75 000
Gunns Limited, of pulp mill fame, purchased Tamar Ridge in 2003. With the retention of Dr Richard Smart as viticultural advisor, the largest expansion of Tasmanian plantings is now underway, with 137 ha of vines in several vineyards in the vicinity of the winery. Richard Smart has constructed a micro-vinification winery, with $1.9 million (including a Federal grant of $900 000) as funding to employ a number of doctor of philosophy students. Their subjects are multifaceted, ranging from clonal trials to canopy trials. A further development at Coombend, on the east coast, is also underway. Dr Andrew Pirie became CEO and chief winemaker in 2005, adding further lustre to the brand. Exports to the UK, the US and other major markets.

♥♥♥♥♥ **Kayena Vineyard Pinot Noir 2005** Stacked full of pinot varietal fruit from start to finish, but is in no sense cumbersome or heavy; great length and structure. Screwcap. 14° alc. **Rating** 95 To 2012 $30

Botrytis Riesling 2006 As ever, hyper-concentrated and rich; luscious, sweet lime juice and pineapple fruit balanced by lingering acidity. Screwcap. **Rating** 94 To 2016 $25

♥♥♥♥♥ **Riesling 2006** Firm apple, mineral flavours; long palate, bone-dry finish. Needs time. Screwcap. 12.5° alc. **Rating** 91 To 2014 $22

Kayena Vineyard Sauvignon Blanc 2007 A clean and bright bouquet; ripe, but less than the alcohol suggests; a full, smooth, tropical palate. Screwcap. 13.5° alc. **Rating** 90 To 2009 $22

Alvarinho 2007 Fresh and lively; some nuances of pear and apricot; crisp acidity and good length. Screwcap. **Rating** 90 To 2011 $25

Kayena Vineyard Pinot Noir 2006 Fleshy plum, spice and black cherry fruit has savoury overtones to give complexity, ripe tannins adding to the structure and length. Screwcap. 14° alc. **Rating** 90 **To** 2013 $28

🍷🍷🍷🍷 **Devil's Corner Pinot Grigio 2007** More personality than many; ripe pear, apple and lychee with a drizzle of lemon; firm finish. Screwcap. 13° alc. **Rating** 89 **To** 2009 $17

Kayena Vineyard Pinot Gris 2007 High-flavoured pinot gris, with clearly delineated pear and musk flavours on a long, richly textured, slightly sweet palate. Screwcap. **Rating** 89 **To** 2010 $25

Devil's Corner Pinot Noir 2007 Direct, fresh and light, with red cherry and strawberry fruit; simple but appealing for immediate consumption. Screwcap. 13.5° alc. **Rating** 89 **To** 2010 $18

Devil's Corner Sauvignon Blanc 2007 A clean and tightly drawn wine, with good concentration and texture across the mid-palate, the finish long and fresh. Screwcap. 13° alc. **Rating** 88 **To** 2010 $17

Devil's Corner Chardonnay 2007 Pleasant unoaked style, with stone fruit flavours and good balance. Screwcap. 13° alc. **Rating** 87 **To** 2010 $18

Tambo Estate ★★★

96 Pages Road, Bumberrah, Vic 3902 **Region** Gippsland
T (03) 5156 4921 **F** (03) 5156 4291 **Open** W'ends by appt
Winemaker Alistair Butt **Est.** 1994 **Cases** 680
Bill and Pam Williams returned to Australia in the early 1990s after seven years overseas, and began the search for a property which met the specific requirements for high-quality table wines established by Dr John Gladstones in his masterwork *Viticulture and Environment*. They chose a property in the foothills of the Victorian Alps on the inland side of the Gippsland Lakes, with predominantly sheltered, north-facing slopes. They planted a little over 5 ha of chardonnay (the lion's share of the plantings with 3.44 ha), sauvignon blanc, pinot noir, cabernet sauvignon and a splash of merlot. Until 1999 the grapes were sold to other producers in the region, and part continues to be sold. They have been rewarded with high-quality Chardonnay and Pinot Noir.

🍷🍷🍷🍷 **Gippsland Lakes Cabernet Sauvignon 2005** A medium-bodied display of earth, mint, leaf and cassis overtones to the mainframe of blackcurrant fruit; firmish tannins. Screwcap. 14.6° alc. **Rating** 87 **To** 2012 $25

Tamburlaine ★★★★★

358 McDonalds Road, Pokolbin, NSW 2321 **Region** Lower Hunter Valley
T (02) 4998 7570 **F** (02) 4998 7763 www.mywinery.com **Open** 7 days 9.30–5
Winemaker Mark Davidson, Simon McMillan, Patrick Moore **Est.** 1966 **Cases** 80 000
A thriving business which, notwithstanding the fact that it has doubled its already substantial production in recent years, sells over 90% of its wine through the cellar door and by mailing list (with an active tasting club members' cellar program offering wines which are held and matured at Tamburlaine). The maturing of the estate-owned Orange vineyard has led to a dramatic rise in quality across the range. Both the Hunter Valley and Orange vineyards are now Australian Certified Organic. Exports to the UK, the US, Sweden, Denmark, Japan, China and Nepal.

🍷🍷🍷🍷🍷 **Members Reserve Hunter Semillon 2007** Super-intense and lively; tremendous thrust to the tightly focused palate, lemony acidity extending the long finish. Screwcap. 10.2° alc. **Rating** 96 **To** 2020 $26

Members Reserve Orange Riesling 2007 A very fragrant and flowery bouquet of citrus and apple blossom; the palate follows in emphatic style; early development, but of undoubted quality. Surprise. Screwcap. 12.7° alc. **Rating** 94 **To** 2013 $26

Members Reserve Orange Chardonnay 2007 Has more intensity, purity and length than the Hunter Valley, although barrel ferment inputs similar; grapefruit and stone fruit run through the long finish. Screwcap. 12.7° alc. **Rating** 94 **To** 2015 $26

♀♀♀♀♀ **Members Reserve Hunter Verdelho 2007** Exceptional thrust and vibrancy to the palate; full of citrus fruit salad ranging from citrus mandarin to grapefruit. A verdelho with attitude. Screwcap. 13.1° alc. **Rating** 93 **To** 2012 $26
Members Reserve Orange Merlot 2006 Well made from fairly intense fruit, balanced between cassis and black olive; medium-bodied, with good length. One of the better merlots going around. Screwcap. 14.8° alc. **Rating** 92 **To** 2016 $32
Members Reserve Hunter Syrah 2006 A powerful, medium- to full-bodied wine with blackberry fruit, savoury tannins and a jab of alcohol which the palate does absorb; from 40-year-old vines around the winery. Time ahead. Screwcap. 15° alc. **Rating** 91 **To** 2026 $40
Members Reserve Hunter Chardonnay 2007 Rich and complex, with obvious barrel ferment inputs to the peachy fruit on the mid-palate; a pleasantly grippy finish. Screwcap. 13.5° alc. **Rating** 90 **To** 2012 $26
Members Reserve Orange Syrah 2006 Elegant, medium-bodied, with bright red fruits on both bouquet and palate; has length and persistence; utterly belies its alcohol. Screwcap. 15.3° alc. **Rating** 90 **To** 2016 $32
Members Reserve Hunter Cabernet Merlot 2006 Far purer and more correct varietal expression as a young wine than usual; lively red fruits and fine acidity, the oak and tannins barely visible. Screwcap. 13.7° alc. **Rating** 90 **To** 2013 $32

♀♀♀♀ **Members Reserve Orange Sauvignon Blanc 2007** Moderately intense, with a mix of herbal notes and some tropical passionfruit flavours; slightly tough finish. Screwcap. 12.7° alc. **Rating** 88 **To** 2010 $26
Members Reserve Orange Cabernet Sauvignon 2006 Despite high alcohol, distinct herbal/briar/earth notes persist on the palate, the alcohol then heating the finish. Not at peace with itself. Screwcap. 15.7° alc. **Rating** 88 **To** 2016 $32

Taminick Cellars   ★★★☆

339 Booth Road, Taminick via Glenrowan, Vic 3675 **Region** Glenrowan
T (03) 5766 2282 **F** (03) 5766 2151 **www**.taminickcellars.com.au **Open** Mon–Sat 9–5, Sun 10–5
Winemaker Peter Booth, James Booth **Est.** 1904 **Cases** 4000
Peter Booth is a fourth-generation member of the Booth family, who have owned this winery since Esca Booth purchased the property in 1904. He makes massively flavoured and very long-lived red wines, most sold to long-term customers and through the cellar door.

♀♀♀♀♀ **Liqueur Muscat NV** Deep colour with defined muscat florals, and rich fruitcake aromas; quite deep and complex, with a well-handled touch of freshness to the finish. Cork. 18.4° alc. **Rating** 91 **To** 2020 $15

Tanjil Wines   ★★★★☆

1171 Moe Road, Willow Grove, Vic 3825 (postal) **Region** Gippsland
T (03) 9773 0378 **F** (03) 9773 0378 **www**.tanjilwines.com **Open** Not
Winemaker Robert Hewet, Olga Garot **Est.** 2001 **Cases** 1200
Robert Hewet and Olga Garot planted 3 ha of pinot noir and pinot grigio on a north-facing slope at an altitude of 200 m between the Latrobe and Tanjil valleys. The cool climate allows the vines to grow without irrigation, yields are kept low and the wines are made onsite using traditional methods and minimal intervention. The modest prices do not reflect the quality of the wines. No Pinot Noir was made in 2007 due to smoke taint, but the '05 and '06 Pinots are still currently available. Exports to the US.

🍷🍷🍷🍷🍷 **Gippsland Pinot Noir 2006** A very pure, elegant and well-balanced wine, needing just a fraction more complexity. Screwcap. 13.8° alc. **Rating** 91 **To** 2013 $15
Gippsland Pinot Noir 2005 Generous sweet plum and black cherry fruit; smooth and supple; combines complexity and finesse, although charry oak is a little obvious. Screwcap. 13.2° alc. **Rating** 91 **To** 2009 $15

Tapanappa ★★★★★

PO Box 174, Crafers, SA 5152 **Region** Various SA
T 0419 843 751 **F** (08) 8370 8374 **www**.tapanappawines.com.au **Open** Not
Winemaker Brian Croser **Est.** 2002 **Cases** 2500

The Tapanappa partners are Brian Croser (formerly of Petaluma), Jean-Michel Cazes of Chateau Lynch-Bages in Pauillac and Societe Jacques Bollinger, the parent company of Champagne Bollinger.The partnership has three vineyard sites in Australia, the 8-ha Whalebone Vineyard at Wrattonbully (planted to cabernet sauvignon, shiraz and merlot 30 years ago) and the 4.7 ha of Tiers Vineyard (chardonnay) at Piccadilly in the Adelaide Hills (the remainder of the Tiers Vineyard chardonnay continues to be sold to Petaluma) and the most recent, the 4 ha Foggy Hill Vineyard on the southern tip of the Fleurieu Peninsula (pinot noir). Exports to all major markets.

🍷🍷🍷🍷🍷 **Tiers Vineyard Chardonnay 2006** Bright lemon-green; lovely line and focused fruit with complex cashews and fine citrus fruits on the long, generous finish; great texture, and very supple. Cork. 13.5° alc. **Rating** 95 **To** 2018 $75
Whalebone Vineyard Cabernet Shiraz 2005 Finely constructed, with bright fruits supported by classy oak; full-bodied with ample levels of black fruits and superfine tannins, yielding a supple and surprisingly approachable young wine. May surprise with its longevity. Cork. 13.5° alc. **Rating** 94 **To** 2020 $75

Tapestry ★★★★☆

Olivers Road, McLaren Vale, SA 5171 **Region** McLaren Vale
T (08) 8323 9196 **F** (08) 8323 9746 **www**.tapestrywines.com.au **Open** 7 days 11–5
Winemaker Jon Ketley **Est.** 1971 **Cases** 15 000

After a relatively brief period of ownership by Brian Light, the former Merrivale Winery was acquired in 1997 by the Gerard family, previously owners of Chapel Hill. It has 40 ha of 30-year-old vineyards, 6.5 ha in McLaren Vale and 33.5 ha in Bakers Gully. Less than half the grapes are used for the Tapestry label.Very limited tastings for this edition. Exports to the UK, the US, Canada, Singapore, Hong Kong, India and NZ.

🍷🍷🍷🍷🍷 **McLaren Vale Chardonnay 2006** Ripe clean fruit on the bouquet, with oak in the background; well made and well balanced. **Rating** 90 **To** 2010 $18

Tar & Roses/Trust ★★★★☆

1 Foy Street, Euroa, Vic 3666 (postal) **Region** Central Victoria Zone
T 0427 310 214 **www**.trustwines.com.au **Open** Not
Winemaker Don Lewis, Narelle King **Est.** 2004 **Cases** 500

Tar & Roses is one of the more interesting new arrivals on the Australian winemaking scene, even though the partners, Don Lewis and Narelle King, have been making wine together for many years at Mitchelton and – for the past three years – Priorat, Spain. Don Lewis came from a grape growing family in Red Cliffs, near Mildura, and in his youth was press-ganged into working in the vineyard. When he left home he swore never to be involved in vineyards again, but in 1973 found himself accepting the position of assistant winemaker to Colin Preece at Mitchelton, where Don remained until his retirement 32 years later. Narelle, having qualified as a chartered accountant, set off to discover the world, and while travelling in South America met a young Australian winemaker who had just completed vintage in Argentina, and who lived in France. The lifestyle appealed greatly, so on her return to Australia she obtained her winemaking degree from CSU, thereafter being offered work by Mitchelton as a bookkeeper and cellarhand. Together they are making wines which are a mosaic of Australia, Italy and Spain in their inspiration.

ŶŶŶŶŶ **Tar & Roses Miro 2004** Bright purple hue; blueberries on the bouquet with spicy fruit and good texture on the palate; a little chunky, but a fun wine to be enjoyed for its youthful Spanish flair. From Priorat, Spain. Cork. 14.5° alc. Rating 92 To 2012 $49

Tar & Roses Heathcote Tempranillo 2006 Very bright red fruits with a touch of mint; good texture and very clean and vibrant; quite long too, with savoury drying tannins on the finish. Screwcap. 13.5° alc. Rating 91 To 2009

Tar & Roses Heathcote Shiraz 2006 Bright and juicy blueberry fruits, with a hint of briar, and some attractive lifted florals; good flavour and weight. Screwcap. 14.5° alc. Rating 90 To 2014

Trust Shiraz 2006 Elegant and lively, with complexity coming from multiple fruit sources more than from texture; skilled handling of extract gives light- to medium-bodied wine excellent length. Screwcap. 14.2° alc. Rating 90 To 2015

ŶŶŶŶ **Tar & Roses Heathcote Sangiovese 2006** A little minty, but with sour cherry fruit; not overly varietal, but the strict tannins may convince you otherwise. Screwcap. 15° alc. Rating 88 To 2009

Tarrawarra Estate ★★★★★

Healesville Road, Yarra Glen, Vic 3775 **Region** Yarra Valley
T (03) 5962 3311 **F** (03) 5962 3887 www.tarrawarra.com.au **Open** 7 days 11–5
Winemaker Clare Halloran, Bruce Walker **Est.** 1983 **Cases** 18 000
Clare Halloran has lightened the Tarrawarra style, investing it with more grace and finesse, but without losing complexity or longevity. The opening of the large art gallery (and its attendant café/restaurant) in early 2004 added another dimension to the tourism tapestry of the Yarra Valley. The gallery is open Wed–Sun, and as the *Michelin Guide* says, it is definitely worth a detour. Tin Cows is the second label, with most of the grapes for the Chardonnay and Pinot Noir estate-grown. The ratings for the Tin Cows range speak for themselves. Exports to the UK, the US, Canada, France, Denmark, Slovakia, Hong Kong, Malaysia and Singapore.

ŶŶŶŶŶ **Chardonnay 2004** An elegant wine, seamlessly weaving fruit, oak and lees influences through the melon fruit and creamy cashew flavours. (The word 'Reserve' is on the label from the '05 vintage.) Screwcap. 13.8° alc. Rating 94 To 2012 $50

Tassell Park Wines ★★★★

Treeton Road, Cowaramup, WA 6284 **Region** Margaret River
T (08) 9755 5440 **F** (08) 9755 5442 www.tassellparkwines.com **Open** 7 days 10.30–5
Winemaker Peter Stanlake (Consultant) **Est.** 2001 **Cases** 4000
One of the light brigade of newcomers to the Margaret River region. Ian and Tricia Tassell have 7 ha of sauvignon blanc, chenin blanc, semillon, cabernet sauvignon, merlot, shiraz and petit verdot. Their white wines have proved so successful that some of the red varieties are being grafted over to white varieties, with the emphasis on their trophy-winning Sauvignon Blanc Semillon.

ŶŶŶŶŶ **Margaret River Sauvignon Blanc Semillon 2007** Like the Sauvignon Blanc, earned a string of medals from wine shows,; has good intensity and line, with fresh minerally lemony flavours. Screwcap. 12.9° alc. Rating 90 To 2012 $20

Margaret River Cabernet Sauvignon 2005 Strongly varietal, with intense blackcurrant fruit and persistent tannins; does have length and balance, and will go the distance. Screwcap. 13.6° alc. Rating 90 To 2020 $25

ŶŶŶŶ **Private Bin Margaret River Shiraz 2005** A firm medium-bodied palate, with berry, mint, spice, pepper and leaf all running through the bouquet and sharply defined palate; brisk finish. Screwcap. 13.7° alc. Rating 89 To 2017 $32

Margaret River Sauvignon Blanc 2007 Won 7 bronze and silver medals in '07; a trade-off between a trace of sweaty reduction on the bouquet and delicate gooseberry and passionfruit flavours. Screwcap. 12.8° alc. **Rating** 88 **To** 2009 $22

Margaret River Shiraz 2007 Deep colour; a similarly powerful palate of ripe blackberry fruit; early in its life still to settle down, but seems the product of a warm vintage. Screwcap. **Rating** 88 **To** 2015 $23

Margaret River Cabernet Sauvignon Merlot 2005 Another string of bronzes attesting to a medium-bodied wine with just enough savoury fruits and length of palate to appeal with roast lamb. Screwcap. 13.9° alc. **Rating** 87 **To** 2012 $22

Tatachilla

151 Main Road, McLaren Vale, SA 5171 **Region** McLaren Vale
T (08) 8323 8656 **F** (08) 8323 9096 **www**.tatachillawines.com.au **Open** Mon–Fri 12–5, Sat & public hols 11–5
Winemaker Fanchon Ferrandi **Est.** 1903 **Cases** 50 000
Tatachilla was reborn in 1995 but has had an at-times tumultuous history going back to 1903. Between 1903 and '61 the winery was owned by Penfolds. It was closed in 1961 and reopened in '65 as the Southern Vales Co-operative. In the late 1980s it was purchased and renamed The Vales but did not flourish; in '93 it was purchased by local grower Vic Zerella and former Kaiser Stuhl chief executive Keith Smith. After extensive renovations, the winery was officially reopened in 1995 and won a number of tourist awards and accolades. It became part of Banksia Wines in 2001, in turn acquired by Lion Nathan in '02. Exports to all major markets.

ƳƳƳƳƳ **Foundation Shiraz 2004** Intensely focused and structured, with a thrusting array of black and red fruits driving through a very long palate and finish without missing a beat. Badly stained cork a worry. Cork. **Rating** 95 **To** 2020 $60

ƳƳƳƳƳ **McLaren Vale Shiraz 2006** Rich, robust, mouthfilling wine, with black fruits, bitter chocolate and earth all demanding to be heard; balanced tannins and oak complete the picture. Screwcap. 14.5° alc. **Rating** 90 **To** 2020 $22.95

McLaren Vale Cabernet Sauvignon 2006 Strongly regional, with a pleasing ripeness to the black fruits and a touch of chocolate making the wine easy to enjoy right from the word go. Screwcap. 14.5° alc. **Rating** 90 **To** 2016 $22.95

ƳƳƳƳ **Partners Cabernet Sauvignon Shiraz 2006** Generously structured and proportioned, with supple blackberry and blackcurrant fruit at a level way in excess of the price. Screwcap. 14.5° alc. **Rating** 89 **To** 2012 $15

Keystone McLaren Vale Chardonnay 2007 Has good focus, concentration and structure, all fruit-derived; nectarine and a touch of citrus supported by firm acidity. Screwcap. 13.5° alc. **Rating** 89 **To** 2011 $21

Keystone McLaren Vale Shiraz Viognier 2006 Hard to resist the charms of a carefree wine such as this, with a charge of fresh, spicy fruit and the typical viognier lift. Screwcap. 14° alc. **Rating** 89 **To** 2011 $17.95

Tatler Wines

477 Lovedale Road, Lovedale, NSW 2321 **Region** Lower Hunter Valley
T (02) 4930 9139 **F** (02) 4930 9145 **www**.tatlerwines.com **Open** 7 days 9.30–5.30
Winemaker Monarch Winemaking Services, Ross Pearson, Alasdair Sutherland, Jenny Bright (Contract) **Est.** 1998 **Cases** 5000
Tatler Wines is a family-owned company headed by Sydney hoteliers Theo and Spiro Isak (Isakidis). The name comes from the Tatler Hotel on George Street, Sydney, which was purchased by James (Dimitri) Isak from the late Archie Brown, whose son Tony is general manager of the wine business. Together with wife Deborah (whom he met at the Tatler Hotel many years ago) he now runs the vineyard, cellar door, café and accommodation. The 40-ha property has 13 ha of shiraz, semillon and chardonnay.

ΨΨΨΨΨ **Over the Ditch Hunter Valley Marlborough Semillon Sauvignon Blanc 2007** The blend works to perfection, the 40% Marlborough Sauvignon Blanc giving the wine great thrust to the passionfruit and gooseberry flavour components, 60% Semillon the backbone of the mineral and grass. Screwcap. 11.5° alc. **Rating** 94 **To** 2010 $24
The Nonpariel Hunter Valley Shiraz 2006 Elegant and supple, the medium-bodied palate with a delicious array of red and black fruits, gossamer tannins and controlled oak. Screwcap. 13.6° alc. **Rating** 94 **To** 2026 $42

ΨΨΨΨΨ **Nigel's Hunter Valley Semillon 2007** Spotlessly clean; vibrant, positively flavoured mineral grass/lemongrass; acidity spot-on; will develop very well over 5 years. Screwcap. 10.4° alc. **Rating** 92 **To** 2012 $20

ΨΨΨΨ **McLaren Vale Shiraz 2006** Medium-bodied; strongly regional impact of dark chocolate, with red and black fruit successfully carrying the alcohol; the oak and tannins are good. Screwcap. 15.2° alc. **Rating** 89 **To** 2016 $22

Tawonga Vineyard

2 Drummond Street, Tawonga, Vic 3697 **Region** Alpine Valleys
T (03) 5754 4945 **www.**tawongavineyard.com **Open** By appt .
Winemaker John Adams **Est.** 1993 **Cases** 500
Diz and John Adams' vineyard is at the head of the Kiewa Valley, looking out over the mountains of the area. It is on a northeast slope with a mixture of deep, red loam/clay and shallow red loam over ancient river stone soils, at an altitude of 365 m. Over the years, the Shiraz has won many wine show medals, not surprising given the extensive Flying Winemaker experience of John Adams. Commencing in France in 2000, he has recently extended his consultancy work to Abruzzo, Italy and La Mancha, Spain. This comes in handy when, as in 2007, the Tawonga vintage was destroyed by bushfire smoke taint.

 # Tayloroo Farm Wines

★★★

PO Box 711, Heathcote, Vic 3523 **Region** Central Victoria Zone
T (03) 5433 3240 **Open** Not
Winemaker Mount Burrumboot Estate (Cathy Branson) **Est.** 2005 **Cases** 50
Michelle and Nick Taylor purchased a 32-ha property from a very traditional Italian family, which was mostly used for grazing and cropping, but with a 2-ha oasis of ancient olive trees, fruit trees of every description and almond trees surrounding 0.8 ha of shiraz and interplanted riesling and chardonnay (with a few more interplants of table grapes and unknown varieties). The entire property is run organically, with no chemical sprays whatsoever. Frost destroyed the 2007 vintage, but a good vintage followed in '08.

ΨΨΨΨ **Lite White 2006** Very light-bodied, crisp and clean; no particular fruit expression; a summer's day at the beach; bonus points for what it doesn't have (alcohol, oak, phenolics) and for its left-field take. Screwcap. 9.5° alc. **Rating** 87 **To** 2009

Taylors

Taylors Road, Auburn, SA 5451 **Region** Clare Valley
T (08) 8849 1111 **F** (08) 8849 1199 **www.**taylorswines.com.au **Open** Mon–Fri 9–5,
Sat & public hols 10–5, Sun 10–4
Winemaker Adam Eggins, Helen McCarthy **Est.** 1969 **Cases** 580 000
The family-founded and owned Taylors continues to flourish and expand, its vineyards now total over 500 ha, by far the largest holding in Clare Valley. There have also been substantial changes both in terms of the winemaking team and in terms of the wine style and quality, particularly through the outstanding St Andrews range. With each passing vintage, Taylors is managing to do the same for the Clare Valley as Peter Lehmann is doing for the Barossa Valley. Off the pace with this year's submissions; rated on previous years, and (indirectly) on value. Exports (under the Wakefield brand due to trademark reasons) to all major markets.

ⵗⵗⵗⵗⵗ St Andrews Cabernet Sauvignon 2003 Age in barrel and bottle enhances the cedary nuances of the wine, and softens the persistent tannins; needed a little more strength in the underlying fruit. Screwcap. 14.5° alc. **Rating** 92 **To** 2015 $70
Clare Valley Shiraz 2006 Complex layers of black fruit flavours interwoven by ripe tannins on the medium- to full-bodied palate; American oak fits well in the overall profile. Good value. Screwcap. 14.5° alc. **Rating** 90 **To** 2012 $17
Adelaide Hills Clare Valley Gewurztraminer 2007 Perfumed and intense spice and rose petal nuances; good weight and density to clearly expressed varietal fruit. Screwcap. 14° alc. **Rating** 90 **To** 2010

ⵗⵗⵗⵗ Adelaide Hills Clare Valley Pinot Noir 2007 Well made; some Clare dry red characters, but the Adelaide Hills wins the day. Rich, with much to offer the casual pinot drinker, at a fair price. Screwcap. 14.5° alc. **Rating** 89 **To** 2009 $17
Clare Valley Riesling 2007 Subdued bouquet typical good texture and structure; ripe citrus fruit around a stoney/minerally core. Screwcap. 13° alc. **Rating** 89 **To** 2013 $18.95
Clare Valley Chardonnay 2005 Opens nicely with melon and peach fruit largely untrammelled by oak, but – as ever in the Clare Valley – falters on the finish. Screwcap. 14.5° alc. **Rating** 89 **To** 2011 $17.95
Jaraman Clare Valley Adelaide Hills Chardonnay 2005 A smooth, generously proportioned wine which by and large carries its alcohol well; ripe peach fruit and integrated oak. Screwcap. 15° alc. **Rating** 89 **To** 2010 $24.95
Promised Land Cabernet Merlot 2006 Has fresh and quite vibrant red fruit flavours so typical of the vintage; great early drinking. Screwcap. 14.5° alc. **Rating** 89 **To** 2010 $13
80 Acres Clare Valley Shiraz Viognier 2005 A powerful entry to the palate, with plum and black fruits doing the talking, and suppressing the viognier; a little tough, but should develop. Screwcap. 14.5° alc. **Rating** 88 **To** 2011 $15
Promised Land Shiraz Cabernet 2005 A thoroughly honest, traditional style, with plenty of ripe (not jammy) fruit, but trailing away somewhat on the finish. Screwcap. 14.5° alc. **Rating** 87 **To** 2009 $13

Te-aro Estate   ★★★★☆

Lot 501 Fromm Square Road, Williamstown, SA 5351 **Region** Barossa Valley
T (08) 8524 6116 **F** (08) 8524 7289 **www**.te-aroestate.com **Open** By appt
Winemaker Rod Chapman, Mark Jamieson **Est.** 1919 **Cases** 2000
Te-aro Estate has been in the Fromm family since 1895, when Carl Hermann Fromm purchased the land and married Elizabeth Minnie Kappler. In 1919, with the aid of a crowbar, they planted 2 ha of Madeira clone semillon and a shiraz block of 1.2 ha, both of which remain in production to this day. Te-aro is not a Maori name, nor are the Fromms related to the Marlborough (NZ) Fromm family. It is a Latin-derived phrase meaning 'to plough'. With a second family-developed property now also owned by Te-aro Estate, the Fromms' main occupation is grape production for others from the 56 ha of estate vines, some of which are dry-grown. Exports to the UK, the US, Singapore and Japan.

ⵗⵗⵗⵗⵗ Harold's Creek Barossa Valley Cabernet Sauvignon 2006 Good depth to the blackcurrant fruit; very clear varietal fruit definition and ripe tannins; the Barossa Valley can't always do this. Screwcap. **Rating** 94 **To** 2020 $22

ⵗⵗⵗⵗⵗ Barossa Valley Shiraz Cabernet 2006 Fragrant black fruit aromas, and a lively palate with juicy red and black fruits, supported by fine tannins. Screwcap. **Rating** 90 **To** 2016 $18
Two Charlies G.S.M. 2006 Good colour; has richness and structure deriving from the shiraz and mourvedre components, plus the juiciness of grenache. Nice wine. Screwcap. **Rating** 90 **To** 2016 $22

ⵗⵗⵗⵗ Harold's Creek Barossa Valley Shiraz 2006 Blackberry, dark plum and a touch of chocolate; a robust, medium- to full-bodied style, with solid tannins; needs time to knit together. Screwcap. **Rating** 89 **To** 2016 $22

Crocket's Block Barossa Valley Grenache 2006 It is curious how light-bodied wines come from dry grown Barossa grenache; hard to imagine how large yields can possibly come into play. Screwcap. **Rating** 87 **To** 2009 $25
Saddleback Barossa Valley Merlot 2006 Ripe, slightly stewy fruit; not varietal, but it is powerful. Screwcap. **Rating** 87 **To** 2011 $18

Temple Bruer   ★★★★

Milang Road, Strathalbyn, SA 5255 **Region** Langhorne Creek
T (08) 8537 0203 **F** (08) 8537 0131 **www**.templebruer.com.au **Open** Mon–Fri 9.30–4.30
Winemaker David Bruer, Vanessa Altmann **Est.** 1980 **Cases** 10 000
Always known for its eclectic range of wines, Temple Bruer (which also carries on a substantial business as a vine propagation nursery) has seen a sharp lift in wine quality. Clean, modern redesigned labels add to the appeal of a stimulatingly different range of red wines. Part of the production from the 19.2 ha of estate vineyards is sold to others, the remainder made under the Temple Bruer label. The vineyard is now certified organic and organic wines are an increasingly important part of the business. Exports to the US and Japan.

🍷🍷🍷🍷 **Preservative Free Organic Langhorne Creek Shiraz Malbec 2007** Vivid colour; attractive, soft, juicy berry fruits, malbec especially suited to the style; very good example. Screwcap. 14° alc. **Rating** 89 **To** 2009 $18

Tempus Two Wines   ★★★★☆

Broke Road, Pokolbin, NSW 2321 **Region** Lower Hunter Valley
T (02) 4993 3999 **F** (02) 4993 3988 **www**.tempustwo.com.au **Open** 7 days 9–5
Winemaker Liz Jackson **Est.** 1997 **Cases** 100 000
Tempus Two is the name for what was once Hermitage Road Wines. It is a mix of Latin (Tempus means time) and English; the change was forced on the winery by the EU Wine Agreement and the prohibition of the use of the word 'hermitage' on Australian wine labels. It has been a major success story, production growing from 6000 cases in 1997 to over 100 000 cases today. Its cellar door, restaurant complex (including the Oishii Japanese restaurant), and small convention facilities are situated in a striking building. The design polarises opinion; I like it. Exports to all major markets.

🍷🍷🍷🍷🍷 **Zenith Semillon 2003** Highly attractive perfumed bouquet; intense juicy flavour on the palate, still with a touch of CO_2; exceptional length. Ready. Screwcap. 11° alc. **Rating** 94 **To** 2011 $25

🍷🍷🍷🍷🍷 **Copper Wilde Chardonnay 2006** Rich, ripe and slightly brassy fruit, but squeaky clean and showing appealing texture; the finish is fine, rich and clean. Screwcap. 13.5° alc. **Rating** 90 **To** 2012 $19.95

🍷🍷🍷🍷 **Vine Vale Barossa Shiraz 2006** Medium- to full-bodied; has plenty of black fruit flavour and pleasing grip on the finish; just a touch four square. Diam. 14° alc. **Rating** 89 **To** 2016 $29.95
Copper Moscato 2007 This is surely the ultimate in absurd packaging, presented in one of the humungus heavyweight dark bottles (and attendant metal label), all for a wine no one can take seriously, worth $10 or so. Crown Seal. 7° alc. **Rating** 87 **To** 2009 $25
Pewter Botrytis Semillon 2005 As famous for the 250 ml phallic bottle in which it is presented as for the wine, which would be $60 in a normal 750 ml bottle, which would stop buyers in their tracks. Diam. 10.5° alc. **Rating** 87 **To** 2009 $20

Ten Minutes by Tractor   ★★★★★

1333 Mornington–Flinders Road, Main Ridge, Vic 3928 **Region** Mornington Peninsula
T (03) 5989 6455 **F** (03) 5989 6433 **www**.tenminutesbytractor.com.au **Open** 7 days 11–5
Winemaker Richard McIntyre, Martin Spedding **Est.** 1999 **Cases** 4800

The energy, drive and vision of Martin Spedding has transformed Ten Minutes by Tractor since he acquired the business in early 2004. He has entered into long-term leases of the three original vineyards, thus having complete management control over grape production courtesy of vineyard manager Alan Murray, who has been involved with those vineyards since 1999. A fourth vineyard has been added on the site of the new cellar door and restaurant; its first vintage was 2008, and it has been managed organically since day one. It is being used to trial various organic viticultural practises which will ultimately be employed across all of the plantings. Martin is completing a wine science degree at CSU, and has taken over active winemaking alongside Richard McIntyre (the latter as an all-important mentor). The restaurant has one of the best wine lists to be found at any winery. Exports to the UK, Hong Kong and Singapore.

♙♙♙♙♙ **10X Mornington Peninsula Sauvignon Blanc 2007** Whole bunch pressing, wild yeast and fermentation and 9 months in barrel have had a marked impact, taking the wine towards white Bordeaux, the depth of fruit carrying the winemaking inputs. Left of centre. Screwcap. 13.5° alc. **Rating** 94 **To** 2012 $28
Wallis Vineyard Mornington Peninsula Chardonnay 2006 Highly focused, but lighter than McCutcheon notwithstanding higher alcohol, with slightly more tangy fruit; 100% mlf here too, but with fewer question marks. Screwcap. 13.5° alc. **Rating** 94 **To** 2013 $50
McCutcheon Vineyard Mornington Peninsula Pinot Noir 2006 Light, bright hue; precisely sculpted and structured, with black and red cherry supported by fine, savoury tannins and oak. Screwcap. 13.8° alc. **Rating** 94 **To** 2013 $65

♙♙♙♙♙ **McCutcheon Vineyard Mornington Peninsula Chardonnay 2006** Powerful, layered and textured; minerally, almost savoury characters, the oak seamlessly welded with the fruit; altogether cerebral style; was 100% mlf too much? Screwcap. 13° alc. **Rating** 92 **To** 2012 $50
10X Mornington Peninsula Chardonnay 2006 Subdued grapefruit and nectarine aromas; very fine on the palate, with real focus and subtle oak influence. Screwcap. 13.5° alc. **Rating** 91 **To** 2014 $30
Mornington Peninsula Pinot Noir 2006 More developed than McCutcheon; light-bodied, savoury, spicy wine, its strength lying in its length; for the purist. Screwcap. 13.8° alc. **Rating** 91 **To** 2012 $55
10X Mornington Peninsula Pinot Gris 2007 A highly worked wine, wild yeast, barrel-fermented and matured in older French oak; strong textural play, not flavour enhancing. Screwcap. 14° alc. **Rating** 90 **To** 2011 $28
10X Mornington Peninsula Pinot Noir 2006 Ripe and varietal, with red cherry fruits, and plenty of spice; well-handled toasty oak persists on the fine and juicy finish. Screwcap. 14° alc. **Rating** 90 **To** 2011 $36

Terra Felix   ★★★★
PO Box 2029, Wattletree Road, Malvern East, Vic 3134 **Region** Upper Goulburn
T (03) 9807 9778 **F** (03) 9923 6167 **www.**terrafelix.com.au **Open** Not
Winemaker Terry Barnett **Est.** 2001 **Cases** 12 000
Terra Felix was for many years a brand of Tallarook Wines, jointly owned by the Riebl family and by Peter Simon, Stan Olszewski and John Nicholson. In 2005 it was decided to separate the businesses, with Luis Riebl now solely concerned with the production of the Tallarook wines. Peter Simon and Stan Olszewski had run the Stanley Wine Company in Clare over 20 years ago, leaving it in the early 1980s, but always harbouring a desire to be involved in the industry as owners. They have worked hard to establish export markets as well as on-premise distribution in Australia, with one-third of the production exported to the UK, the US, the Netherlands and China. Grapes continue to be sourced from Tallarook, and also supplemented by other local growers.

♙♙♙♙♙ **Shiraz Viognier 2007** Highly perfumed and lifted floral notes accompany the spicy black and red fruits; medium-bodied with good concentration, and vibrant acidity; very good value. Screwcap. 14.1° alc. **Rating** 92 **To** 2014 $16

E'Vette's Block Mourvedre 2007 Twenty per cent of juice was run-off before fermentation, adding to the fruit profile but without unbalancing the tannins; good plum and black fruit flavours. Screwcap. 14.1° alc. **Rating** 90 **To** 2012 $16.50

ŶŶŶŶ **Viognier 2007** While not especially varietal, the aromas and flavours come together well; apricot and quince, with a pleasingly fresh finish. Screwcap. 14.2° alc. **Rating** 89 **To** 2011 $16

Shiraz Viognier 2006 Light- to medium-bodied; a juicy berry style, as ever the fruit sweetness enhanced by the viognier; structurally a little simple. Screwcap. 13.9° alc. **Rating** 89 **To** 2011 $15

Mourvedre 2006 A deceptive bright, light red colour; likewise the entry to the mouth with small red fruit flavours before the tannins jump on you. A wine to keep you guessing. Screwcap. 14.4° alc. **Rating** 87 **To** 2010 $15

Chardonnay 2007 A cool example, with stone fruits and a strong core of minerality; a fresh, early-drinking style. Screwcap. 14° alc. **Rating** 87 **To** 2009 $16

La Vie En Rose 2007 Bright, fresh red cherry/strawberry/plum fruit; a direct, linear style; dry finish. Mourvedre. Screwcap. 13° alc. **Rating** 87 **To** 2009 $16

Terrace Vale

149 Deasys Road, Pokolbin, NSW 2321 **Region** Lower Hunter Valley
T (02) 4998 7517 **F** (02) 4998 7814 **www.**terracevale.com.au **Open** 7 days 10–4
Winemaker Alain Leprince **Est.** 1971 **Cases** 14 000
In 2001, the Batchelor family (headed by former AMP chief executive Paul Batchelor) acquired Terrace Vale. In late 2004 Terrace Vale (and its various second labels and brands) was merged with Cheviot Bridge/The Long Flat Wine Co, of which Paul Batchelor is now non-executive chairman. Marketing in Australia and overseas is undertaken by Cheviot Bridge.

ŶŶŶŶŶ **Old Vine Hunter Valley Semillon 2006** Abundant flavour and intensity; lemon/lemon cake flavours on the mid-palate, then a perfectly balanced twist of acidity on the finish; surprise packet. Screwcap. 10.8° alc. **Rating** 94 **To** 2016 $19.95

ŶŶŶŶŶ **Old Vine Shiraz 2005** Rich, ripe and rounded; soft, velvety black fruit and tannins. Screwcap. 12.4° alc. **Rating** 91 **To** 2015 $24.95

ŶŶŶŶ **Declared Vintage Hunter Valley Shiraz 2005** A savoury, earthy medium-bodied wine in uncompromisingly regional style; plenty of flavour, but finishes somewhat short. Screwcap. 13° alc. **Rating** 89 **To** 2015 $44.95

Tertini Wines

PO Box 445, Chester Hill, NSW 2162 **Region** Southern Highlands
T (02) 4878 5162 **F** (02) 4878 5197 **www.**tertiniwines.com.au **Open** Not
Winemaker High Range Vintners **Est.** 2000 **Cases** 3000
When Julian Tertini began the development of Tertini Wines in 2000, he followed in the footsteps of Joseph Vogt 145 years earlier. History does not relate the degree of success that Joseph Vogt had, but the site he chose then was, as it is now, a good one. Tertini has 1.8 ha each of riesling and pinot noir, 1 ha each of arneis, chardonnay and cabernet sauvignon, and 0.6 ha of merlot and 0.2 ha of lagrein. It is early days, but the indications are that the earlier ripening varieties – notably riesling – will be most suited. Exports to all major markets.

ŶŶŶŶ **Tertini & Knight Pinot Noir 2006** Light but bright hue; has more red fruits than the other Tertini pinots, and a silky note to the palate and finish. Screwcap. **Rating** 88 **To** 2012 $38

Eighteen 55 Berrima Valley Pinot Noir 2006 Like all the Tertini pinots, very light in colour and body, but does have length and surprising intensity. Screwcap. **Rating** 87 **To** 2010 $25

Teusner ★★★★★

29 Jane Place, Tanunda, SA 5352 (postal) **Region** Barossa Valley
T (08) 8563 0898 **F** (08) 8563 0898 **www.**teusner.com.au **Open** By appt tel 0409 351 166
Winemaker Kym Teusner **Est.** 2001 **Cases** 12 000
Teusner is a partnership between former Torbreck winemaker Kym Teusner and brother-in-law Michael Page, and is typical of the new wave of winemakers determined to protect very old, low-yielding, dry-grown Barossa vines. Kym Teusner was crowned *Gourmet Traveller* Young Winemaker of the Year in 2007. The winery approach is based on lees ageing, little racking, no fining or filtration, and no new American oak. The reasonably priced wines are made either from 100% shiraz or from Southern Rhône blends. Exports to the UK, the US, the Netherlands, Israel, Hong Kong, Singapore, Malaysia and Japan.

ŢŢŢŢŢ **Albert 2005** Fruit flavours in the black spectrum, with licorice and hints of dark chocolate; has hallmark silky mouthfeel, together with line and length; controlled alcohol a blessing. Cork. 14.5° alc. **Rating** 95 **To** 2020 $45
The Riebke Ebenezer Road Barossa Valley Shiraz 2006 Highly aromatic, with the type of lift often found with viognier; vibrant red fruits with splashes of blackberry and spice; good mouthfeel. Screwcap. 14.5° alc. **Rating** 94 **To** 2016 $19

ŢŢŢŢŢ **Avatar 2005** A complex wine, sweet fruit of the grenache gains strength from the shiraz and mataro; good balance. Grenache (55%)/Shiraz (25%)/Mataro (20%) Cork. 14.5° alc. **Rating** 92 **To** 2013 $26

ŢŢŢŢ **Salsa 2007** A spicy, aromatic entry to the light-bodied palate; a cunning twist of sweetness on the finish. Rose. Screwcap. 13.5° alc. **Rating** 87 **To** 2009 $20.50

The Blok Estate ★★★★

Riddoch Highway, Coonawarra, SA 5263 **Region** Coonawarra
T (08) 8737 2734 **F** (08) 8737 2994 **www.**blok.com.au **Open** 7 days 10–5
Winemaker Kopparossa Wines (Gavin Hogg) **Est.** 1999 **Cases** 2000
The Trotter family (Luke, Rebecca, Gary and Ann) purchased The Blok Estate in 2005, and have significantly increased production. The cellar door is in a renovated, old stone home surrounded by gardens.

ŢŢŢŢŢ **Coonawarra Riesling 2006** Fragrant and pure, with more lime and apple juice flavours; good length and balance, still delicate. Screwcap. 11° alc. **Rating** 90 **To** 2012 $18

ŢŢŢŢ **Coonawarra Riesling 2007** In Coonawarra mode, delicate apple and citrus blossom aromas and flavours; crisp, bone-dry palate still to build texture. Screwcap. 11.5° alc. **Rating** 89 **To** 2013 $16

The Cups Estate ★★★★★

269 Browns Road, Fingal, Vic 3939 **Region** Mornington Peninsula
T 1300 131 741 **F** (03) 9886 1254 **www.**thecupsestate.com **Open** 7 days 10–5
Winemaker Moorooduc Estate, Pfeiffer, Kilchurn Wines **Est.** 1999 **Cases** 2500
Joe Fisicaro has returned to his roots after a career as a financial executive, establishing The Cups Estate near Rye. The name comes from the rolling dune region of the Peninsula known as 'the cups country'; the soils are light, with relatively low fertility, but drainage is excellent. Wind and frost have been problems, and the composition of the 6.15-ha vineyard has been somewhat modified by a grafting program placing more emphasis on early ripening varieties. Exports to Japan.

ŢŢŢŢŢ **Raimondo Reserve Mornington Peninsula Pinot Noir 2006** Definitely the big brother (or sister, perhaps) of the varietal, with greater depth and intensity to flavours in the same family; positively luscious, and very long. Diam. **Rating** 95 **To** 2015 $35

Mornington Peninsula Pinot Noir 2006 Complex, multifaceted aromas, the dark plum and oriental spice notes repeated on the palate; good line and balance. Diam. **Rating** 94 **To** 2013 $25

Mornington Peninsula Shiraz 2006 Fragrant and spicy, with quite sweet (not jammy) fruit flavours, more in the red spectrum than black; fine-grained tannins to a medium-bodied, elegant cool-climate style. Diam. **Rating** 94 **To** 2016 $25

ŢŢŢŢŢ **Mornington Peninsula Chardonnay 2007** Pale straw-green; an aromatic and flowery, fruit-driven bouquet leads directly into the strongly minerally palate, oak in the background; needs a few years to build flesh. Diam. **Rating** 92 **To** 2015 $30

Mornington Peninsula Pinot Rose 2007 Red cherry and strawberry aromas and flavours; a crisp and dry finish provides both length and balance. Screwcap. **Rating** 91 **To** 2008 $18

Mornington Peninsula Merlot 2006 More advanced colour than the Shiraz; medium-bodied, with herb, black olive tapenade flavours on the mid-palate, tightening nicely on the finish. Good value. Diam. **Rating** 90 **To** 2012 $18

Mornington Peninsula Blanc de Noir 2006 Pale rose colour; fresh and lively red fruit flavours tinged with citrus; not complex, but nonetheless delicious time on cork may build the texture. Cork. **Rating** 90 **To** 2012 $30

The Deanery Vineyards ★★★☆

PO Box 1172, Balhannah, SA 5242 **Region** Adelaide Hills
T (08) 8390 1948 **F** (08) 8390 0321 **Open** Not
Winemaker Duncan Dean (Sangiovese), Phil Christiansen (Shiraz), Petaluma (Sauvignon Blanc) **Est.** 1995 **Cases** 500

The Dean family – Pat and Henry, and sons Duncan, Nick and Alan – purchased a 30-ha dairy farm at Balhannah in late 1994, and planted 6.5 ha of chardonnay, sauvignon blanc and semillon in the spring of '95, subsequently adding 0.67 ha of shiraz. Pinot noir and a tiny block of sangiovese were also planted at a property at Piccadilly. A further 8 ha are now being developed on a third property, adjacent to the original Balhannah holding. Alan Dean, a CSU-trained viticulturist and former Petaluma vineyard manager, is in charge of the vineyards, working alongside brother Duncan. The primary aim of the business is contract grapegrowing, the purchasers including some high-profile names.

ŢŢŢŢŢ **Quartz Block Adelaide Hills Sauvignon Blanc 2007** Has a very considerable depth of flavour in a tropical passionfruit spectrum; good outcome for the vintage. Screwcap. 13.2° alc. **Rating** 90 **To** 2009 $18

ŢŢŢŢ **Bull Paddock Adelaide Hills Shiraz 2004** In similar style to the '05; plenty of congenial flavour suggesting a warm site in the Adelaide Hills; badly stained cork a worry. 14.3° alc. **Rating** 88 **To** 2011 $16

Bull Paddock Adelaide Hills Shiraz 2005 Shows fully ripe fruit flavours in an atypical fashion for Adelaide Hills, trying to head back down the hill to McLaren Vale. Screwcap. 14.6° alc. **Rating** 87 **To** 2012 $18

The Grapes of Ross ★★★

PO Box 14, Lyndoch, SA 5351 **Region** Barossa Valley
T (08) 8524 4214 **F** (08) 8524 4214 **Open** Not
Winemaker Ross Virgara **Est.** 2006 **Cases** 2500

Ross Virgara spent much of his life in the broader food and wine industry, and finally took the plunge into commercial winemaking in 2006. The grapes come from a fourth-generation family property in the Lyndoch Valley, and the aim is to make fruit-driven styles of quality wine. His fondness for frontignac led to the first release of 2006 Moscato, followed by two Roses, a Merlot Cabernet and an Old Bush Vine Grenache.

ŢŢŢŢ **Black Rose Barossa Valley Shiraz 2006** Abounds with flavour of plum, blackberry and mocha/vanilla oak; easy access style courtesy of soft tannins and alcohol sweetening; now or later. Screwcap. 15.8° alc. **Rating** 89 **To** 2013 $28

Old Bush Vine Barossa Valley Grenache 2006 Fresh, light- to medium-bodied wine made from 40-year-old bush vines in the southern Barossa; simple structure, but the red fruit flavours do have length. Screwcap. 15.8° alc. **Rating** 88 **To** 2013 $18

The Growers ★★★★

392 Wildwood Road, Yallingup, WA 6282 **Region** Margaret River
T (08) 9755 2121 **F** (08) 9755 2286 **www**.thegrowers.com **Open** 7 days 10–5
Winemaker Philip May **Est.** 2002 **Cases** 15 000
The Growers (once AbbeyVale) has had a turbulent history since it was founded in 2002, with legal disputes between various partners making life complicated. In February 2006 all that was put behind it, and it is now a syndicate of 17 growers with vineyards spread across all six regions in South West Australia, and 400 ha planted to all the major varieties. Five shareholders have key vineyards in the Margaret River region, where it is based. The wines are released in four tiers: Peppermint Grove at the $12–$15 entry point; The Growers Reward (Margaret River) at $15–$25; The Growers Limited Release Reward (single vineyard, single varietal Margaret River) at $20–$30; and The Growers Palate, with six wines identically vinified across three different styles to showcase single region vineyard expression at $30. It's an interesting concept, already gaining significant exports into all parts of Asia.

ꝐꝐꝐꝐꝐ **The Growers Palate Western Australia Shiraz 2004** A fragrant bouquet and entry to the palate; there is synergy with sweeter fruit notes offset by fine but persistent tannins; parcels from the five regions. Screwcap. 14° alc. **Rating** 92 **To** 2015 $30
The Growers Palate Geographe Shiraz 2004 Spicy black cherry, blackberry and licorice in a medium-bodied frame; good length and balance; has a powerful presence. Screwcap. 14.5° alc. **Rating** 92 **To** 2015 $30
Frankland River Riesling 2004 Bright, pale green-straw, developing slowly but surely, with a mineral/chalk backbone to the citrus, apple and pear flavours. Screwcap. 13.5° alc. **Rating** 91 **To** 2013
The Growers Palate Great Southern Shiraz 2004 Quite intense, although only medium-bodied; notes of wild herb, spice and licorice; fine but persistent tannins add to the structure. Screwcap. 14° alc. **Rating** 91 **To** 2013 $30
The Growers Palate Pemberton Shiraz 2004 A dark cherry/blackberry mix, the tannins making a quite unexpected statement and certainly adding to the structure. Screwcap. 14° alc. **Rating** 90 **To** 2013 $30

ꝐꝐꝐꝐ **Reward Chardonnay 2006** Attractive wine; nicely ripened stone fruit, with the depth expected of Margaret River which compensates for the lack of oak. Sophisticated label. **Rating** 89 **To** 2010
The Growers Palate Margaret River Shiraz 2004 Some young vine characters evident in a light- to medium-bodied wine; delicate fruit is interwoven with savoury/earthy tannins. Screwcap. 13.5° alc. **Rating** 89 **To** 2011 $30
The Growers Palate Blackwood Valley Shiraz 2004 Fresh, elegant, light-bodied, light-coloured wine; cherry and raspberry red fruit flavours; minimal tannins and oak. Not forced. Screwcap. 13° alc. **Rating** 89 **To** 2011 $30

The Islander Estate Vineyards ★★★★★

PO Box 96, Parndana, SA 5220 **Region** Kangaroo Island
T (08) 8553 9008 **F** (08) 8553 9228 **www**.iev.com.au **Open** By appt
Winemaker Jacques Lurton **Est.** NA **Cases** 5000
Established by one of the most famous Flying Winemakers in the world, Bordeaux-born, trained and part-time resident Jacques Lurton, who has established 10 ha of close-planted vineyard. The principal varieties are sangiovese and cabernet franc; then lesser amounts of semillon, viognier, grenache, malbec and merlot. The wines are made and bottled at the onsite winery, in true estate style. The flagship wine (Yakka Jack) is an esoteric blend of sangiovese and cabernet franc. Exports to the US, France, Denmark, Sweden, Norway, China and Japan.

ŸŸŸŸŸ **Old Rowley Bush Vine Grenache 2005** Light but vivid and clear red purple; a highly aromatic wine, in a class and style of its own, reflecting the cool King Island climate and sophisticated winemaking; great mouthfeel, balance and length. Screwcap. 13.5° alc. **Rating** 95 **To** 2011 $43.90

Bark Hut Road Kangaroo Island Cabernet Shiraz Viognier 2005 Shows winemaker Jacques Lurton's Bordeaux upbringing, even with the shiraz and viognier components; great understanding of tannins which shape the structure and style, yet aren't the least aggressive. Screwcap. **Rating** 94 **To** 2020 $37.50

Majestic Plough Kangaroo Island Malbec 2005 Exceptional colour; very interesting wine; does have the opulence and confit notes of good malbec, but has the mid-palate and the structure all others miss. Screwcap. 14.5° alc. **Rating** 94 **To** 2025 $43.90

ŸŸŸŸŸ **Winelife Zone Kangaroo Island Shiraz 2005** Superb colour; delicious fresh medium-bodied wine, with all the aromas and tastes expected of cool-grown shiraz (red fruits, spice and pepper) and a silky, fine and long palate. Underpriced. Screwcap. 14.5° alc. **Rating** 90 **To** 2011 $16

Wally White Kangaroo Island Semillon Viognier 2006 Very well made, barrel ferment and maturation a means to an end; the wine has seamless line and balance, but poses the question which variety is meant to augment the other – or is it both? Perhaps time will tell. Screwcap. 14° alc. **Rating** 90 **To** 2015 $43.90

ŸŸŸŸ **Yakka Jack Cabernet Franc Sangiovese 2005** A savoury bouquet; red and black fruits on the palate, with a briary undercurrent; quite tannic, with an earthy, high-acid finish. Cork. 14° alc. **Rating** 89 **To** 2015 $72.90

Winelife Zone Kangaroo Island Sangiovese 2005 Strongly varietal, with sour cherry and even a twist of lemon zest; fruit carries through to the finish instead of obscuring tannins. Screwcap. 14° alc. **Rating** 87 **To** 2010 $16

The Lake House Denmark   ★★★★

106 Turner Road, Denmark, WA 6333 **Region** Denmark
T (08) 9848 2444 **F** (08) 9848 3444 **www.**lakehousedenmark.com.au **Open** 7 days 11–4
Winemaker Harewood Estate (Jamie Kellie) **Est.** 1995 **Cases** 3000
When Gary Capelli and partner Leanne Rogers purchased the vineyard (formerly known as Jindi Creek) in 2005, it had 5.2 ha planted 10 years earlier to no less than eight mainstream varieties, headed by chardonnay (2 ha) and pinot noir and merlot (0.8 ha each). They have since moved to incorporate biodynamic principles into the vineyard.

ŸŸŸŸŸ **Pinot Noir 2006** Shows a greater volume of ripe pinot fruit aroma and flavour than many from the Great Southern, but not quite enough texture. Screwcap. 13° alc. **Rating** 91 **To** 2012 $34.95

Semillon Sauvignon Blanc 2007 Generously endowed with flavours ranging through tropical/passionfruit and grass/green pea; has length. Screwcap. 13.5° alc. **Rating** 90 **To** 2009 $23.95

Merlot 2006 Has considerable thrust and life; red fruits and snow pea; fine, lingering tannins; very good for the vintage. Screwcap. 14° alc. **Rating** 90 **To** 2014 $26.95

ŸŸŸŸ **Classic White 2007** Peach and nectarine from Chardonnay appropriately dominate the palate; the other varieties, Sauvignon Blanc/Semillon/Riesling providing flavour.complexity and texture, nullifying the boredom of unoaked chardonnay. Screwcap. 14.5° alc. **Rating** 89 **To** 2009 $21.95

Unwooded Chardonnay 2007 Gentle white peach/nectarine/honeydew melon flavours, with a twist of grapefruit on the finish. Screwcap. 14.5° alc. **Rating** 88 **To** 2009 $20.95

Frankland Shiraz 2006 Bright hue; a fresh, light-bodied palate with cherry and plum fruit and minimal tannins. Screwcap. 14° alc. **Rating** 88 **To** 2012 $30

The Lane Vineyard
★★★★☆

Ravenswood Lane, Hahndorf, SA 5245 **Region** Adelaide Hills
T (08) 8388 1250 **F** (08) 8388 7233 **www**.thelane.com.au **Open** 7 days 10–4.30
Winemaker Charlotte Hardy, John Edwards **Est.** 1993 **Cases** 30 000
With their sales and marketing background, John and Helen Edwards opted for a major
lifestyle change when they began establishing the first of the present 28.1 ha of vineyards in
1993. Initially, part of the production was sold to Hardys, but now some of the wine is made
for release under The Lane label (until 2003, Ravenswood Lane). A joint venture with Hardys
has been terminated, which has resulted in the Starvedog Lane brand being owned by Hardys,
and a revamped Ravenswood Lane label (and a new, cheaper Off The Leash label) carrying the
flag for The Lane. John Edwards has applied to build a 500-tonne winery, and plans to open
a cellar door and café. Exports to all the UK, the US, Ireland and China.

ꝯꝯꝯꝯꝯ **Reunion Adelaide Hills Shiraz 2003** An appealing mix of spice, pepper, cedar
and finely structured black fruits; remarkably fresh for the vintage; good tannins
and oak. Screwcap. 13.5° alc. **Rating** 93 **To** 2015 $49
Ravenswood Lane Single Vineyard Adelaide Hills Sauvignon Blanc 2007
Initially innocuous, then the palate unfolds, with remarkable thrust and drive
to the herbaceous/mineral/gooseberry fruit. Screwcap. 14° alc. **Rating** 92
To 2010 $25
Ravenswood Lane Single Vineyard Adelaide Hills Shiraz Viognier 2005
A sultry, leathery, spicy, plummy bouquet, with similar flavours on the medium-
bodied palate, plus some juicy apricot notes from the viognier; fine tannins.
Screwcap. 14° alc. **Rating** 91 **To** 2015 $30
Gathering Adelaide Hills Sauvignon Blanc Semillon 2007 Good structure,
touches of chalk and slate giving the wine some authority and length to the citrus,
lemon and gooseberry flavours. Screwcap. 13.5° alc. **Rating** 90 **To** 2012 $30
Ravenswood Lane Single Vineyard Adelaide Hills Pinot Gris 2007 Pale
blush pink; very good varietal fruit in a classic pear/musk/spice spectrum plus a
touch of mineral on the finish. Screwcap. 13.5° alc. **Rating** 90 **To** 2011 $30

ꝯꝯꝯꝯ **Beginning Adelaide Hills Chardonnay 2007** A carefully constructed barrel-
fermented chardonnay, the fruit and oak woven together seamlessly; yet to open
up and develop richness. Screwcap. 13.5° alc. **Rating** 89 **To** 2013 $39
19th Meeting Adelaide Hills Cabernet Sauvignon 2003 Spicy cedary
savoury overtones to the fruit, which seems riper than the alcohol would suggest;
still can't escape the clutches of '03. Screwcap. 13° alc. **Rating** 89 **To** 2013 $49
Ravenswood Lane Adelaide Hills Chardonnay 2007 Well-balanced and
light-bodied melon and citrus fruit with integrated oak; simply a little light-on.
Screwcap. 13° alc. **Rating** 88 **To** 2012 $30
Ravenswood Lane Single Vineyard Adelaide Hills Pinot Gris 2006 Must
surely set an Australian record price (this at cellar door). A well-balanced wine, in
Evian style, and little more to say. Screwcap. 14° alc. **Rating** 87 **To** 2009 $39
Ravenswood Lane Single Vineyard Adelaide Hills Viognier 2006 Good
mouthfeel (no phenolics or oiliness) but marginal varietal character; only hints of
peach and apricot. Screwcap. 14° alc. **Rating** 87 **To** 2010 $30
Off the Leash Max Adelaide Hills Shiraz Viognier 2006 Most remarkable
for its back label story which I'm not sure I fully understand; savoury/spicy/earthy,
the softening influence of viognier not obvious. Screwcap. 13.5° alc. **Rating** 87
To 2012 $25

The Little Wine Company
★★★☆

825 Milbrodale Road, Broke, NSW 2330 (postal) **Region** Lower Hunter Valley
T (02) 6579 1111 **F** (02) 6579 1440 **www**.thelittlewinecompany.com.au **Open** Not
Winemaker Ian Little, Suzanne Little **Est.** 2000 **Cases** 13 000
Having sold their previous winery, Ian and Suzanne Little moved in stages to their new
winery at Broke. The Little Wine Company is part-owner of the 20-ha Lochleven Vineyard

in Pokolbin, and contracts three vineyards in the Broke-Fordwich area. It also has access to the Talga Vineyard in the Gundaroo Valley near Canberra.

ΨΨΨΨ   **Olivine Verdelho 2007** Well above-average intensity of fruit flavour; an array of tropical and citrus flavours; good length, and a clean, bright finish. Hunter Valley. Screwcap. 13.5° alc. **Rating** 91 **To** 2012 $19
Olivine Viognier 2007 Clear-cut varietal character; ripe apricot, musk and dried fruit notes; has length, and is not too heavy or phenolic. Screwcap. 13° alc. **Rating** 90 **To** 2010 $19

ΨΨΨΨ   **Olivine Gewurztraminer 2007** Bright colour, with no bronze; well-constructed, but struggles to show clear varietal character; just a waft of lychee and spice. Screwcap. 12.5° alc. **Rating** 88 **To** 2009 $19
Olivine Sangiovese 2005 Spicy, savoury sour cherry/red cherry/plum fruit; has surprising length and aftertaste. Region of origin not specified. Screwcap. 13.5° alc. **Rating** 88 **To** 2009 $19

The Minya Winery   ★★★

Minya Lane, Connewarre, Vic 3227 **Region** Geelong
T (03) 5264 1397 **F** (03) 5264 1097 **www.**theminya.com.au **Open** Public hols, or by appt
Winemaker Susan Dans **Est.** 1974 **Cases** NA
Geoff Dans first planted vines in 1974 on his family's dairy farm, followed by further plantings in '82 and '88 lifting the total to 4 ha. Grenache is a highly unusual variety for this neck of the woods. The concerts staged in summer sound appealing.

ΨΨΨΨ   **Cabernet Sauvignon Shiraz Merlot 2006** Deep purple hue; medium-bodied; has balanced, though not so much depth. Cork. 12.5° alc. **Rating** 87 **To** 2011 $25

 ## The Old Faithful Estate   ★★★★★

c/- PO Box 235 (Kangarilla Road), McLaren Vale, SA 5171 **Region** McLaren Vale
T 0419 383 907 **F** (08) 8323 9747 **Open** By appt
Winemaker Nick Haselgrove, Warren Randall **Est.** 2005 **Cases** 2500
This is a 50/50 joint venture between American John Larchet (with one half) and a quartet of Nick Haselgrove, Warren Randall, Warren Ward and Andrew Fletcher (with the other half). Larchet has long had a leading role as a specialist importer of Australian wines into the US, and guarantees the business whatever sales it needs there. The shiraz, grenache and mourvedre come from selected blocks within Tinlins wine resources, with which the quartet has a close association. It's a winning formula.

ΨΨΨΨΨ   **Top of the Hill McLaren Vale Shiraz 2006** Has more depth and structure, more regional in expression than the Cafe Block; a nice touch of blackberry; excellent length courtesy of fine tannins. Diam. 14.5° alc. **Rating** 95 **To** 2026 $75
Northern Exposure McLaren Vale Grenache 2006 Deep crimson; has the power, texture and tannin grip which only comes from McLaren Vale, the fruit in a black, rather than red, spectrum. From 60-year-old dry-grown vines on terra rossa. Diam. 14.5° alc. **Rating** 94 **To** 2021 $75
Sandhill McLaren Vale Grenache 2006 From 50-year-old vines on sandy soil, with more red fruit notes and more elegant, but still the unique regional power, focus and length; finer, but more intense, than Northern Exposure. Diam. 14.5° alc. **Rating** 94 **To** 2017 $75

ΨΨΨΨΨ   **Almond Grove McLaren Vale Mourvedre 2006** A massive wine, with all the grainy/rocky tannins which mourvedre is noted for and hence is usually used as a blend component. Long life ahead. Diam. 14° alc. **Rating** 93 **To** 2021 $75
Cafe Block McLaren Vale Shiraz 2005 A bright and fresh medium-bodied palate, which opens with quite sweet black fruits, then moves through to a spicy, tangy, savoury finish; 50-year-old vines. Cork. 14.5° alc. **Rating** 91 **To** 2020 $75

Top of the Hill McLaren Vale Shiraz 2005 Very similar style to Cafe Block, with slightly more developed colour; opens with sweet fruit then spicy cake and bitter chocolate finish. Cork. 14.5° alc. **Rating** 90 **To** 2020 $75
Cafe Block McLaren Vale Shiraz 2006 Fully ripe, juicy berry fruit in a predominantly red spectrum; fine tannins and oak. Diam. 15° alc. **Rating** 90 **To** 2020 $75
Northern Exposure McLaren Vale Grenache 2005 Unforced, fresh raspberry and red cherry fruits; supple, fine tannins and gentle extract; 60-year-old vines. Cork. 14.5° alc. **Rating** 90 **To** 2014 $75

♀♀♀♀ **Almond Grove McLaren Vale Mourvedre 2005** Retains good hue; dark berry fruits with the lingering tannins expected of the variety, but needs more mid-palate push. Cork. 14.5° alc. **Rating** 89 **To** 2014 $75

The Poplars Winery   ★★★

Riddoch Highway, Coonawarra, SA 5263 **Region** Coonawarra
T (08) 8736 3130 **F** (08) 8736 3163 **www.**thepoplarswinery.com **Open** 7 days 9–6
Winemaker Jonathon Luestner **Est.** 2006 **Cases** NA
A new name in Coonawarra, but in fact a long-term and highly successful cornerstone of the region. It is part of Coonawarra Developments Pty Ltd, which is in turn the owner of Chardonnay Lodge, the only large-scale (and ever-growing) accommodation complex in the heart of Coonawarra. Founded by the Yates family 22 years ago, it remains in that ownership, now offering 38 large suites and a deservedly popular restaurant. Most recently, and in a way most significantly, Coonawarra Developments has also purchased the former Jamiesons Run Winery from Foster's. The adjacent 4 ha of vineyard opposite the winery, and adjacent to Chardonnay Lodge, will underpin one of the most diverse tourism developments in SA on the 22-ha property.

♀♀♀♀ **Cabernet Merlot 2005** Excellent colour; plenty of presence and length in a ripe blackcurrant spectrum; fractionally dry tannins. 13.7° alc. **Rating** 89 **To** 2014 $24
Coonawarra Unoaked Chardonnay 2007 Has enough varietal expression and fruit weight to get over the line; stone fruit-driven; does shorten somewhat on the finish. Screwcap. 12° alc. **Rating** 87 **To** 2010 $17

The Ritual   NR

233 Haddrill Road, Baskerville, WA 6056 (postal) **Region** Peel
T 0417 095 820 **F** (08) 9296 0681 **Open** Not
Winemaker John Griffiths **Est.** 2005 **Cases** 3000
The Ritual is the product of a partnership between two Perth wine identities. John Griffiths is winemaker, and Bill Healy owns the 40-ha Orondo Farm Vineyard in Dwellingup, where John Griffiths obtains much of the grapes for his own (Faber) and other labels. The modest line-pricing and simplicity of the product range reflect no more than sober experience. Exports to the UK.

The Standish Wine Company

PO Box 498, Angaston, SA 5353 **Region** Barossa Valley
T (08) 8564 3634 **F** (08) 8564 3634 **www.**standishwineco.com **Open** Not
Winemaker Dan Standish **Est.** 1999 **Cases** 800
Dan Standish is an extremely experienced winemaker, adding work in the Napa and Sonoma valleys in California, La Rioja in Spain and the Rhône Valley in France to his domestic winemaking. In 1999 he was able to negotiate a small parcel of 96-year-old shiraz from his parents' vineyard in the Vine Vale subregion of the Barossa Valley. This produces 300 cases of The Standish, a wild yeast, open-fermented and basket-pressed shiraz matured in French oak for 30 months. The Standish, which uses his Rhône Valley experience led to the creation of The Relic, Shiraz (93%)/Viognier (7%) co-fermented, otherwise made with similar techniques.

ŶŶŶŶ♀ **The Relic Single Vineyard Shiraz Viognier 2004** A brooding monster of a wine! Incredibly concentrated, powerful and intense, with fruitcake spice enveloping a massive core of fruit; the palate is almost syrupy, and so rich that a great deal of time will be needed to see this wine come around; if in fact it ever does. Cork. 14.5° alc. **Rating** 93 **To** 2030
The Standish Single Vineyard Barossa Valley Shiraz 2003 Very youthful colour; massively proportioned, with lots of flavour and plenty of depth; very clean and quite fruit-sweet, with a mere hint of toastiness in the background; long and rich. Cork. 14.5° alc. **Rating** 92 **To** 2020

 The Story Wines ★★★★★

7 St Leonard Place, St Kilda, Vic 3182 (postal) **Region** Grampians
T 0411 697 912 **F** (03) 9534 8881 **www**.thestory.com.au **Open** Not
Winemaker Rory Lane **Est.** 2004 **Cases** 400
Over the years I have come across winemakers with degrees in atomic science, innumerable doctors with specialities spanning every human condition, town planners, sculptors and painters, the list going on and on, and Rory Lane adds yet another, a degree in ancient Greek literature. He says that after completing his degree, and 'desperately wanting to delay an entry into the real world, I stumbled across and enrolled in a postgraduate wine technology and marketing course at Monash University, where I soon became hooked on ... the wondrous connection between land, human and liquid.' Vintages in Australia and Oregon germinated the seed, and he ultimately zeroed in on the Grampians, where he purchases small parcels of high quality grapes for his one and only wine, Shiraz, making it in a small factory shell where he has assembled a basket press, a few open fermenters, a mono pump and some decent French oak.

ŶŶŶŶŶ **Westgate Vineyard Grampians Shiraz 2006** A spotlessly clean bouquet, then a palate with perpetual movement as the lively, spicy flavours wash back and forth, and a wonderful finish and aftertaste; more elegant, less power. Screwcap. 14° alc. **Rating** 96 **To** 2026 $36
Grampians Shiraz 2006 Lusciously dense and rich, a velvet cascade of black fruit flavours supported by a fine net of ripe tannins and well-handled oak; will age superbly. Screwcap. 14° alc. **Rating** 95 **To** 2026 $20

ŶŶŶŶ♀ **Grampians Shiraz 2005** Plenty of blackberry, plum and chocolate fruit on a medium-bodied palate, with fine, ripe tannins in support; good oak. Screwcap. 14.5° alc. **Rating** 91 **To** 2015 $19

The Tiers Wine Co ★★★

28 Chalk Hill Road, McLaren Vale, SA 5171 **Region** McLaren Vale
T (08) 8323 8946 **F** (08) 8323 9644 **www**.tierswines.com.au **Open** Mon–Fri &
public hols 10–5
Winemaker Claudio Curtis, Phillip Reschke **Est.** 1990 **Cases** 50 000
In 1956 the Curtis family emigrated from Italy to Australia, and purchased its first vineyard land from one Clarence William Torrens Rivers. They renamed it Clarence Hill. Further land was acquired in the 1980s and '90s, establishing the Landcross Estate and California Rise vineyards, which, together with Clarence Hill, now have over 100 ha in production. Claudio Curtis (who has a science degree from Adelaide University) manages wine production and sales. Wines are released under the Clarence Hill, Landcross Estate and Martins Road labels. Exports to the UK, the US, the Netherlands and China.

ŶŶŶŶ **Clarence Hill McLaren Vale Cabernet Sauvignon 2005** Powerful, firm, ripe wine; continuing concern over heavily staining sides of Diams; if all is well, cellaring worthwhile. **Rating** 88 **To** 2012 $25
Clarence Hill McLaren Vale Shiraz 2005 Medium-bodied; very earthy overall character with some dark chocolate and spices; persistent tannins; very stained Diam. 14.5° alc. **Rating** 87 **To** 2012 $25

 ## The Trades

13/30 Peel Road, O'Connor, WA 6161 (postal) **Region** Warehouse
T (08) 9331 2188 **F** (08) 9331 2199 **Open** Not
Winemaker Contract **Est.** 2006 **Cases** 1000

Thierry Ruault and Rachel Taylor have run a wholesale wine business in Perth since 1993, representing a group of top-end Australian and imported producers. By definition, the wines they offered to their clientele were well above $20 per bottle, and they decided to fill the gap with a contract-made Shiraz from the Adelaide Hills, and a Sauvignon Blanc from Margaret River, selling at $17.50. This is, without question, a virtual winery.

ŸŸŸŸ **Butcher's Adelaide Hills Shiraz 2004** Light- to medium-bodied but with good intensity to the spicy savoury aromas and flavours; also has length, even though little depth. Screwcap. 14° alc. **Rating** 89 **To** 2012 $17.50

The Wanderer

2850 Launching Place Road, Gembrook, Vic 3783 **Region** Yarra Valley
T (03) 5968 1622 **F** (03) 5968 1699 **Open** By appt
Winemaker Andrew Marks **Est.** 2005 **Cases** 500

Andrew Marks is the son of Ian and June Marks, owners of Gembrook Hill, and after graduating from Adelaide University with a degree in oenology he joined Southcorp, working for six years at Penfolds (Barossa Valley) and Seppelt (Great Western), as well as undertaking vintages in Coonawarra and France. He has since worked in the Hunter Valley, Great Southern, Sonoma County in the US and Costa Brava in Spain – hence the name of his business. He made the 2005 wines at Gembrook Hill, lending a hand with the Gembrook Hill vintage while doing so.

The Willows Vineyard

Light Pass Road, Light Pass, Barossa Valley, SA 5355 **Region** Barossa Valley
T (08) 8562 1080 **F** (08) 8562 3447 **www.**thewillowsvineyard.com.au **Open** Wed–Mon 10.30–4.30, Tues by appt
Winemaker Peter Scholz, Michael Scholz **Est.** 1989 **Cases** 6500

The Scholz family have been grapegrowers for generations and have 40 ha of vineyards, selling part and retaining the remainder of the crop. Current generation winemakers Peter and Michael Scholz make smooth, well-balanced and flavoursome wines under their own label, all marketed with bottle age. Exports to the UK, the US, Canada, NZ and Singapore.

ŸŸŸŸŸ **Bonesetter Barossa Shiraz 2005** Significantly deeper colour than the varietal; proclaims its class from the word go, the blackberry and plum fruit beautifully complemented by cedary French oak; long, perfectly balanced finish. Cork. 15° alc. **Rating** 94 **To** 2020 $56

ŸŸŸŸŸ **Barossa Valley Riesling 2007** Fragrant blossom and spice aromas flow through to a juicy palate and crisply dry finish. Rewarded for early picking. Value. Screwcap. 11° alc. **Rating** 90 **To** 2012 $14
Barossa Valley Shiraz 2005 A medium-bodied mix of gently sweet black and red fruits in traditional Barossa Valley style, supported by vanillin oak and ripe tannins. Screwcap. 15° alc. **Rating** 90 **To** 2020 $26

ŸŸŸŸ **Barossa Valley Cabernet Sauvignon 2005** Strongly earthy savoury overtones come through on both bouquet and palate, although there is a bed of red and blackcurrant fruit. Screwcap. 14.5° alc. **Rating** 89 **To** 2017 $26
Single Vineyard Barossa Valley Semillon 2005 Elements of toast and honey starting to emerge; slightly loose texture; better sooner than later. Screwcap. **Rating** 87 **To** 2010 $15

The Wine & Truffle Co   ★★★★

PO Box 1538, Osborne Park, WA 6916 **Region** Pemberton
T (08) 9777 2474 **F** (08) 9204 1013 www.wineandtruffle.com.au **Open** 7 days 10–4.30
Winemaker Mark Aitken **Est.** 1997 **Cases** 12 000
Owned by a group of investors from various parts of Australia who share the common vision
of producing fine wines and black truffles. The winemaking side is under the care of Mark
Aitken, who, having graduated as dux of his class in applied science at Curtin University in
2000, joined Chestnut Grove as assistant winemaker in 2002. He now is contract maker for
the Wine & Truffle Company, as well as working for Chestnut Grove. The truffle side of the
business is under the care of former CSIRO scientist Dr Nicholas Malajcsuk. He has overseen
the planting of 13 000 truffle-inoculated hazelnut and oak trees on the property, which has
now produced truffles, some of prodigious size. Exports to Denmark and Singapore.

 Reserve Pemberton Riesling 2005 Developing with assurance; gentle orange
blossom and lime zest flavours with a streak of mineral providing structure.
Screwcap. 13° alc. **Rating** 90 **To** 2015 $23
Reserve Chardonnay 2006 Bold with plenty of sweet fruit, and good flavour
on the finish. **Rating** 90 **To** 2010 $25
Icon Series Pemberton Cabernet Franc 2005 Dense purple; an unusually
full-bodied cabernet franc, seemingly much riper than the alcohol suggests; still
needs time to open up. Screwcap. 13.9° alc. **Rating** 90 **To** 2015 $35

Sauvignon Blanc 2007 Light, fresh and bright in a herbaceous mould; crisp
seafood style. Screwcap. 13.3° alc. **Rating** 89 **To** 2009 $17.50

Third Child   ★★★

134 Mt Rumney Road, Mt Rumney, Tas 7170 (postal) **Region** Southern Tasmania
T 0419 132 184 **F** (03) 6223 8042 **Open** Not
Winemaker John Skinner, Rob Drew **Est.** 2000 **Cases** 250
John and Marcia Skinner planted 2.5 ha of pinot noir and 0.5 ha of riesling in 2000. It is
very much a hands-on operation, the only concession being the enlistment of Rob Drew (on
an adjoining property) to help John Skinner with the winemaking. When the first vintage
(2004) was reaching the stage where it was to be bottled and labelled, the Skinners could not
come up with a name and asked their daughter Claire. 'Easy,' she said. 'You've got two kids
already; considering the care taken and time spent at the farm, it's your third child.'

 Benjamin Daniel Pinot Noir 2006 A multi-clone blend as opposed to the
single clone 2051 wine, supporting the French point that a mixture of clones
will always be better than a single clone; there is strong black cherry fruit and
green, stemmy notes needing to integrate; nonetheless an impressive achievement.
Screwcap. 13° alc. **Rating** 89 **To** 2012 $25

Thistle Hill   ★★★

74 McDonalds Road, Mudgee, NSW 2850 **Region** Mudgee
T (02) 6373 3546 **F** (02) 6373 3540 www.thistlehill.com.au **Open** Mon–Sat 9.30–4.30,
Sun & public hols 9.30–4
Winemaker Lesley Robertson, Robert Paul (Consultant) **Est.** 1976 **Cases** 3500
The Robertson family owns and operates Thistle Hill. The estate-grown wines are made
onsite with the help of Robert Paul, whatever additional assistance is needed is happily
provided by the remaining wine community of Mudgee. The vineyard, incidentally, is
registered by the National Association for Sustainable Agriculture Australia (NASAA), which
means no weedicides, insecticides or synthetic fertilisers – the full organic system. Hail and
drought severely reduced the 2007 vintage. Exports to the UK, Canada and Japan.

Thomas Vineyard Estate ★★★★

PO Box 490, McLaren Vale, SA 5171 **Region** McLaren Vale
T (08) 8557 8583 **F** (08) 8557 8583 **www**.thomasvineyard.com.au **Open** Not
Winemaker Trevor Tucker **Est.** 1998 **Cases** 1000
Merv and Dawne Thomas thought long and hard before purchasing the property on which
they have established their vineyard. It is 3 km from the coast of the Gulf of St Vincent on the
Fleurieu Peninsula, with a clay over limestone soil known locally as 'Bay of Biscay'. They had
a dream start to the business when the 2004 Shiraz won the trophy for Best Single Vineyard
Wine (red or white) at the McLaren Vale Wine Show '05, the Reserve Shiraz also winning
a gold medal.

 Estate Reserve McLaren Vale Shiraz 2006 Powerful and resolutely closed,
with a well of dark fruits which will likely open up with time. Diam. 14.6° alc.
Rating 90 **To** 2015 $40

Thomas Wines ★★★★★

c/- The Small Winemakers Centre, McDonalds Road, Pokolbin, NSW 2321 **Region**
Lower Hunter Valley
T (02) 6574 7371 **F** (02) 6574 7371 **www**.thomaswines.com.au **Open** 7 days 10–5
Winemaker Andrew Thomas **Est.** 1997 **Cases** 3000
Andrew Thomas came to the Hunter Valley from McLaren Vale, to join the winemaking team
at Tyrrell's. After 13 years with Tyrrell's, he left to undertake contract work and to continue
the development of his own winery label, a family affair run by himself and his wife, Jo. To
date the Semillon has come from the renowned vineyard of Ken Bray, but the plan is to add
other single vineyard wines, simply to underline the subtle differences between the various
subregions of the Hunter. With 12 months to run on his current lease of the Hungerford Hill
winery on the corner of Broke Road, Andrew Thomas is building a winery on a 10-ha block
on Hermitage Road. The winery will be completed for the 2009 vintage, with a cellar door
due to open within the next two years. Says Andrew 'Finally, we will have a spiritual home
and true destination for Thomas Wines'. Exports to Canada and Singapore.

 Kiss Limited Release Hunter Valley Shiraz 2006 Strong crimson; classic
Hunter at the start of a long life (the cork is high quality) with all the black fruits,
structure, texture and balance to guide it though the decades. 14.3° alc. **Rating** 95
To 2026 $50
Braemore Individual Vineyard Hunter Valley Semillon 2007 Herb, grass
and mineral aromas; a focused and intense palate, with abundant fruit weight
accented by citrussy acidity; long finish. Screwcap. 11° alc. **Rating** 94 **To** 2017 $25
Sweetwater Individual Vineyard Hunter Valley Shiraz 2006 Fragrant, lively
and wonderfully juicy with the most expressive shiraz imaginable, offering so
much now there seems no reason to give it the 10 years it will take to reach its
peak. Cork. 13.8° alc. **Rating** 94 **To** 2016 $32

The O.C. Individual Vineyard Hunter Valley Semillon 2007 Citrus peel
aromas; a generous palate, unusually full and round for a young semillon, but has
balance. Early-drinking style. Screwcap. 12° alc. **Rating** 92 **To** 2012 $20

Thompson Estate ★★★★★

Harmans Road South, Wilyabrup, WA 6284 **Region** Margaret River
T (08) 9386 1751 **F** (08) 9386 1708 **www**.thompsonestate.com **Open** Wed–Sun 10–5
Winemaker Various contract **Est.** 1998 **Cases** 4000
Cardiologist Peter Thompson planted the first vines at Thompson Estate in 1994, inspired
by his and his family's shareholdings in the Pierro and Fire Gully vineyards, and by visits to
many of the world's premium wine regions. A total of 15 ha has been established: cabernet
sauvignon, cabernet franc, merlot, chardonnay and pinot noir. The Thompsons have split the
winemaking between specialist winemakers: Cabernet Merlot by Mark Messenger of Juniper
Estate (previously of Cape Mentelle), Pinot Noir by Flying Fish Cove, and Pinot Chardonnay
by Harold Osborne of Fraser Woods. Exports to the UK, the US and other major markets.

ŸŸŸŸŸ **Margaret River Cabernet Sauvignon 2004** Brightly coloured; has real depth and complexity, as floral aromas drift over cassis and cedar; the tannins are ample, very fine and ripe, drawing out the palate to a very long, even and harmonious finish. Cork. 14° alc. **Rating** 95 **To** 2020 $38

Margaret River Semillon Sauvignon Blanc 2007 A seamless wine, with fleshy citrus fruit and a hint of dried straw; lovely texture, and really vibrant, fine and long on the finish. Screwcap. 13° alc. **Rating** 94 **To** 2012 $22

Andrea Reserve Margaret River Cabernet Merlot 2005 Deep crimson; a very poised example of this blend, with cassis fruit, black olives and a little hint of toasty oak; the palate is polished, and vibrant, with great focus and terrific line; very long on the finish. Screwcap. 14.5° alc. **Rating** 94 **To** 2020 $35

ŸŸŸŸŸ **Margaret River Cabernet Merlot 2004** A pleasing blend, more in the red fruit spectrum, with a little savoury twist to the finish, and the merlot providing plumpness on the mid-palate. Screwcap. 14° alc. **Rating** 90 **To** 2012 $28

ŸŸŸŸ **Margaret River Chardonnay 2006** Very creamy and mealy oak aromas; but the palate tightens up with a real citrus twist on the finish; just lacks a little concentration. Screwcap. 14.5° alc. **Rating** 89 **To** 2012 $38

Thorn-Clarke Wines   ★★★★★

Milton Park, Gawler Park Road, Angaston, SA 5353 **Region** Barossa Valley
T (08) 8564 3036 **F** (08) 8564 3255 **www**.thornclarkewines.com **Open** Mon–Fri 9–5
Winemaker Derek Fitzgerald **Est.** 1997 **Cases** 80 000
Established by David and Cheryl Clarke (née Thorn), and son Sam. Thorn-Clarke is one of the largest Barossa grapegrowers, with 270 ha across four vineyard sites. Shiraz (136 ha), cabernet sauvignon (49 ha) and merlot (20 ha) are the principal plantings, with lesser amounts of petit verdot, cabernet franc, nebbiolo, chardonnay, riesling and pinot gris. As with many such growers, most of the grape production is sold, but the best is retained for the Thorn-Clarke label. Thorn-Clarke has become a serial trophy and gold medal winner, with a wholly enviable track record. Exports to all major markets.

ŸŸŸŸŸ **William Randell Barossa Valley Shiraz 2005** Deep, dark and compelling, loaded with fruitcake, charry oak and dark fruits; full-bodied with plenty of ripe tannins, and an ample amount of sweet fruit on the finish. Cork. 15° alc. **Rating** 94 **To** 2020 $49

Shotfire Quartage 2006 Stacked full of ripe, though not overripe blackberry and plum fruit; soft tannins and perfectly managed oak. Yet another gold medal performance for Quartage, this time National Wine Show '07. Screwcap. 14.9° alc. **Rating** 94 **To** 2016 $20

ŸŸŸŸŸ **Sandpiper Barossa Shiraz 2006** Vibrant, precocious and juicy fruit; nice acid provides a fresh and lively finish, with good focus. As ever, great value. Screwcap. 14° alc. **Rating** 90 **To** 2012 $15

Sandpiper Barossa Cabernet Sauvignon 2006 Strong varietal aromas, with blackcurrant and cassis fruit; the palate is full-bodied, fleshy and quite firm on the finish. Likewise, value plus. Screwcap. 13.5° alc. **Rating** 90 **To** 2015 $15

Shotfire Ridge Barossa Valley Shiraz 2006 Good colour; full-bodied, with plenty of sweet fruit and sweet oak on the bouquet and palate; typically complex, with strong tannin and oak in support. Screwcap. 14° alc. **Rating** 90 **To** 2021 $23

ŸŸŸŸ **Sandpiper Brut Reserve Pinot Noir Chardonnay NV** Quite tight fruit, with citrus and hints of wild berries; simple but clean and attractive. Cork. 12.5° alc. **Rating** 88 **To** 2012 $15

Sandpiper Eden Valley Riesling 2007 A strong mineral overtone defines this wine; good weight and texture, but the line breaks at the end. Screwcap. 12.5° alc. **Rating** 87 **To** 2012 $14.95

Sorriso Barossa Rose 2007 A nicely focused red fruit bouquet, with good flavour and freshness on the palate, and a pleasingly dry finish. Screwcap. 12.5° alc. **Rating** 87 **To** 2010 $15

3 Drops ★★★★

PO Box 1828, Applecross, WA 6953 **Region** Mount Barker
T (08) 9315 4721 **F** (08) 9315 4724 **www**.3drops.com **Open** Not
Winemaker Robert Diletti (Contract), John Wade (Consultant) **Est.** 1998 **Cases** 4500
The 3 Drops are not the three owners (John Bradbury, Joanne Bradbury and Nicola Wallich),
but wine, olive oil and water, all of which come from the property, a substantial vineyard
at Mount Barker. The 16 ha are planted to riesling, sauvignon blanc, semillon, chardonnay,
cabernet sauvignon, merlot, shiraz and cabernet franc. The business expanded significantly in
2007 with the purchase of the 14.7-ha Patterson's Vineyard. Exports to the UK and Canada.

ΨΨΨΨΨ **Mount Barker Riesling 2007** The palate has lime, quince and fine, minerally
acidity; the generous mouthfeel complements the persistent finish. Screwcap.
13° alc. **Rating** 92 **To** 2015 $20

ΨΨΨΨ **Mount Barker Sauvignon Blanc 2007** Clear varietal aromas in a gooseberry
and asparagus spectrum; the palate is a trifle edgy on the finish. Screwcap. 13.5° alc.
Rating 89 **To** 2009
Mount Barker Chardonnay 2006 Light-bodied; oak is more evident on the
bouquet than the palate, where grapefruit and stone fruit flavours lead the band;
bright finish. Screwcap. 13.5° alc. **Rating** 89 **To** 2010 $23
Mount Barker Shiraz 2005 A savoury wine with a dark and quite meaty
personality; the black fruits are vibrant and fleshy on the medium-bodied palate.
Screwcap. 14.5° alc. **Rating** 89 **To** 2014 $23

Three Willows Vineyard ★★★

46 Montana Road, Red Hills, Tas 7304 **Region** Northern Tasmania
T 0438 507 069 **www**.threewillowsvineyard.com.au **Open** By appt
Winemaker Philip Parés **Est.** 2002 **Cases** 100
Philip Parés and Lyn Prove have planted a micro-vineyard, with 1.5 ha of pinot noir, pinot
gris, baco noir (a hybrid) and chardonnay. It is 50 km west of Launceston near Deloraine on
a gentle north-facing slope at an elevation of 220–250 m. The present tiny production will
peak at around 250 cases, sold to in-house guests at the B&B accommodation, and by mail
and phone order.

ΨΨΨΨ **Cool Climate White 2006** Has retained remarkable freshness and life, the
unholy trinity of Chardonnay (54%)/Muller Thurgow (sic) (25%)/Pinot Gris
(21%) forming an unexpected union. Diam. 12.8° alc. **Rating** 87 **To** 2010 $20

Three Wise Men ★★★★★

Woongarra Estate, 95 Hayseys Road, Narre Warren East, Vic 3804 **Region** Port Phillip Zone
T (03) 9796 8886 **F** (03) 9796 8580 **www**.threewisemen.com.au **Open** Thurs–Sun 9–5
by appt
Winemaker Graeme Leith **Est.** 1994 **Cases** 800
The Three Wise Men label was conceived to make a top-quality single-vineyard Pinot Noir
grown at Woongarra Estate, a well-drained, cool and moist site close to the Yarra Valley.
An agreement between the Jones's of Woongarra and Passing Clouds (see separate entries)
winemaker Graeme Leith means that the wine is made at Passing Clouds at Kingower,
near Bendigo. A variety of winemaking techniques are used, varying according to vintage
conditions. Each of the partners takes half of the resulting wine and sells it through their
respective cellar doors.

ΨΨΨΨΨ **Pinot Noir 2006** More elegant than the Passing Clouds label, though made there;
has excellent structure and length, with a mix of spicy red and black small berry
fruits and thrust to the long finish. Diam. **Rating** 94 **To** 2013

Three Wishes Vineyard ★★★★

604 Batman Highway, Hillwood, Tas 7252 **Region** Northern Tasmania
T (03) 6331 2009 **F** (03) 6331 0043 **www.**threewishesvineyard.com.au **Open** 7 days
11–5 Boxing Day to Easter or by appt
Winemaker Bass Fine Wines **Est.** 1998 **Cases** 600

Peter and Natalie Whish-Wilson began the establishment of their vineyard in 1998 while they were working in Hong Kong, delegating the management tasks to parents Rosemary and Tony Whish-Wilson until 2003. Peter and Natalie took a year's sabbatical to do the first vintage, with their children aged six and four also involved in tending the vines. The seachange became permanent, Peter completing his wine growing degree from CSU in 1996. The original 2.8 ha of pinot noir, chardonnay and riesling are being extended by the planting of a further ha of pinot noir.

ŶŶŶŶ   **Riesling 2007** Quite lifted florals on the bouquet; the palate has good flavour on entry, falling away a little on the finish. Screwcap. 12° alc. **Rating** 88 **To** 2013 $27
       Pinot Noir 2006 Bright red fruits on the bouquet, and quite silky tannins; the oak needs to settle down, as does the fierce acidity. Screwcap. 14° alc. **Rating** 88 **To** 2012 $35

Tibooburra Wines ★★★★

Stringybark Lane, Yellingbo, Vic 3139 (postal) **Region** Yarra Valley
T 0418 367 319 **F** (03) 5964 8577 **www.**tibooburra.com **Open** Not
Winemaker Paul Evans, Timo Mayer (Contract) **Est.** 1996 **Cases** 1500

The Kerr family has done much with Tibooburra since they began assembling their 1000-ha property in 1967. They have established a champion Angus herd, planted a 33-ha vineyard in '96 on elevated northern and northwest slopes, established a truffliere in 2001 to supply Japanese and northern hemisphere restaurants with black truffles, and launched the Tibooburra Wines label in '02. Four generations have been, or are, involved in the business. Most of the grapes are sold. Plantings (in descending order) are pinot noir, chardonnay, shiraz, sauvignon blanc, merlot and cabernet sauvignon, and the quality of the early releases is all one could possibly ask for.

ŶŶŶŶŶ   **Yarra Valley Shiraz 2006** Elegant and lively, the medium-bodied palate with a range of spicy black fruits, and fine, savoury tannin in immaculately balanced support. Diam. 13.5° alc. **Rating** 93 **To** 2016 $28
       Yarra Valley Sauvignon Blanc 2007 Quite intense aromas and flavours; herb, grass and fresh gooseberry; minerally acidity extends the length and finish of a wine with attitude. Screwcap. 12.5° alc. **Rating** 91 **To** 2010 $22
       Yarra Valley Chardonnay 2006 Relatively light-bodied and restrained, leaning towards Chablis; length and persistence are its long suits. Screwcap. 13° alc. **Rating** 90 **To** 2013 $22

ŶŶŶŶ   **Yarra Valley Pinot Noir 2006** Light-bodied; spicy stemmy overtones at the least ripe end of the spectrum; not up to expectations. Screwcap. 13° alc. **Rating** 88 **To** 2010 $28
       Yarra Valley Merlot 2006 The most robust of the Tibooburra range from '06, which is strange. Considerable extract and tannins make this a cellaring rather than drinking proposition for the short term. Diam. 13° alc. **Rating** 88 **To** 2015 $28

Tidswell Wines ★★★★☆

PO Box 94, Kensington Park, SA 5068 **Region** Limestone Coast Zone
T (08) 8363 5800 **F** (08) 8363 1980 **www.**tidswellwines.com.au **Open** Not
Winemaker Ben Tidswell, Wine Wise Consultancy **Est.** 1997 **Cases** 7000

The Tidswell family (now in the shape of Andrea and Ben Tidswell) has two large vineyards in the Limestone Coast Zone near Bool Lagoon; in total there are 140 ha, the lion's share planted to shiraz and cabernet sauvignon, with smaller plantings of merlot, chardonnay, semillon and sauvignon blanc. Fifty percent of the vineyards are organically certified, and more will be converted in due course. Wines are released under the Jennifer, Heathfield Ridge and Caves Road labels. Exports to the US, Canada, Denmark, Germany and Japan.

ŢŢŢŢŢ **Jennifer Cabernet Sauvignon 2004** An attractive, clear fruit-driven style; very pure cabernet flavour; fine, silky tannins and 24 months in French oak are unobtrusive. Named in memory of Ben Tidswell's late sister. Cork. 14.5° alc. **Rating** 94 **To** 2021 $29.50

ŢŢŢŢŢ **Heathfield Ridge Shiraz 2004** Attractive blackberry, cherry, licorice and spice fruit with balanced and integrated mocha oak; very good tannins and length. Cork. 14.5° alc. **Rating** 91 **To** 2014 $19.95

ŢŢŢŢ **Heathfield Ridge Cabernet Sauvignon 2003** Some confit/jammy notes to the fruit, but does have plenty of flavour. Cork. 14° alc. **Rating** 88 **To** 2014 $19.95
Caves Road Chardonnay 2006 Tangy grapefruit flavours in typical regional style; slightly grippy finish. Screwcap. 14° alc. **Rating** 87 **To** 2010 $15.50
Caves Road Shiraz 2005 A mix of leafy, spicy, minty bramble notes; does have length, and fine tannins. Screwcap. 14.5° alc. **Rating** 87 **To** 2011 $15.50

Tiger Ranch Wines   ★★★

116 Allisons Road, Lower Barrington, Tas 7306 (postal) **Region** Northern Tasmania
T (03) 6492 3339 **F** (03) 6492 3356 www.tigerranch.com.au **Open** Not
Winemaker Neil Colbeck **Est.** 2000 **Cases** NFP
Neil Colbeck developed a fascination with fine wine during his time as sommelier at Hayman Island between 1987 and '90. At that time the Island was at its zenith, with a cellar of over 38 000 bottles worth $750 000. All good things have to come to an end, and when he returned to Tasmania in '90, he planted his first vineyard. In 2000 Tiger Ranch was relocated to Lower Barrington and a new vineyard established. While this was coming into being, grapes were purchased from Lake Barrington Estate; it has to be said that Neil Colbeck's DIY winemaking has not been entirely successful, although it is early days. Tiger Ranch not only produces wine; it has an Arabian horse stud, breeds border collie working dogs and is home to Brian Colbeck's very beautiful watercolour and ink bird paintings, which Gould would not be ashamed of.

ŢŢŢŢ **Chardonnay 2007** A fine bouquet with some mineral elements, followed by citrus fruits on the palate; has good weight and length, and will develop. **Rating** 88 **To** 2013 $20

Tilbrook   ★★★★★

17/1 Adelaide Lobethal Road, Lobethal, SA 5241 **Region** Adelaide Hills
T (08) 8389 5318 **F** (08) 8389 5315 www.marketsatheart.com/tilbrookestate
Open Fri–Sun 11–5 & public hols, or by appt
Winemaker James Tilbrook **Est.** 2001 **Cases** 1500
James and Annabelle Tilbrook have 4.4 ha of multi-clone chardonnay and pinot noir, and 0.4 ha of sauvignon blanc at Lenswood. The winery and cellar door are in the old Onkaparinga Woollen Mills building in Lobethal; this not only provides an atmospheric home, but also helps meet the very strict environmental requirements of the Adelaide Hills in dealing with winery waste water. English-born James Tilbrook came to Australia in 1986, aged 22; a car accident led to his return to England. Working for Oddbins and passing the WSET diploma set his future course. He returned to Australia, met wife Annabelle, purchased the vineyard and began planting the vineyard in 1999. Plantings are continuing for the Tilbrook label, and for the moment the major part of the 1999 plantings of chardonnay and pinot noir is sold to Foster's. Core releases not submitted for this edition; rating from last year. Exports to the UK.

Tim Adams ★★★★☆

Warenda Road, Clare, SA 5453 **Region** Clare Valley
T (08) 8842 2429 **F** (08) 8842 3550 **www**.timadamswines.com.au **Open** Mon–Fri 10.30–5,
w'ends 11–5
Winemaker Tim Adams **Est.** 1986 **Cases** 50 000
After almost 20 years slowly and carefully building the business, based on 11 ha of the Clare
Valley classic varieties of riesling, semillon, grenache, shiraz and cabernet sauvignon, Tim and
wife Pan Goldsack decided to increase their production from 35 000 to 50 000 cases. Like
their move to a total reliance on screwcaps, there is nothing unexpected in that. However, the
makeup of the new plantings is anything but usual: they will give Tim Adams more than 10 ha
of tempranillo and pinot gris, and about 3.5 ha of viognier, in each case with a very clear idea
about the style of wine to be produced. Exports to all major markets.

ŸŸŸŸŸ **Clare Valley Pinot Gris 2007** A totally unexpected flavour profile; an intense
mix of citrus/mandarin flavours, then cleverly offset acidity and residual sugar.
Screwcap. 13.5° alc. **Rating** 92 **To** 2009 $22
The Aberfeldy 2005 Traditional medium- to full-bodied Clare Valley style, bold
and flavoursome, driven as much by two years in American oak as by its abundant
black fruits. Screwcap. 14.5° alc. **Rating** 92 **To** 2015 $55

Tim Gramp ★★★★☆

Mintaro/Leasingham Road, Watervale, SA 5452 **Region** Clare Valley
T (08) 8344 4079 **F** (08) 8342 1379 **www**.timgrampwines.com.au **Open** W'ends &
public hols 11–4
Winemaker Tim Gramp **Est.** 1990 **Cases** 6000
Tim Gramp has quietly built up a very successful business and by keeping overheads to a
minimum, provides good wines at modest prices. Over the years the estate vineyards have
expanded significantly to their present level of 16 ha (shiraz, riesling, cabernet sauvignon and
grenache). Exports to the UK, Taiwan, Malaysia and NZ.

ŸŸŸŸŸ **McLaren Vale Shiraz 2005** Great colour, with an array of dark fruits, well-
handled toasty oak and good fruit weight on the palate; firm tannins on the finish.
Screwcap. 15° alc. **Rating** 92 **To** 2020 $26.50
Watervale Riesling 2007 Solid, ripe fruit flavour and structure; some tropical
canned pineapple notes; early developing typical of the vintage. Screwcap.
12.5° alc. **Rating** 90 **To** 2012 $19.50

ŸŸŸŸ **Watervale Cabernet Sauvignon 2004** Light- to medium-bodied; cedary,
earthy bottle-developed characters starting to emerge alongside a splash of redcurrant; balanced tannins and oak. Screwcap. 14.5° alc. **Rating** 88 **To** 2012 $19.90

Tim McNeil Wines ★★★

PO Box 1088, Clare, SA 5453 **Region** Clare Valley
T (08) 8843 4348 **F** (08) 8843 4272 **www**.timmcneilwines.com.au **Open** Not
Winemaker Tim McNeil **Est.** 2004 **Cases** 300
When Tim and Cass McNeil established Tim McNeil Wines, Tim had long since given up his
teaching career, and graduated with a degree in oenology from Adelaide University in 1999.
During his university years he worked at Yalumba, before moving with Cass to the Clare Valley
in 2001, spending four years as a winemaker at Jim Barry Wines before moving to Kilikanoon
in '05, where he currently works as a winemaker alongside Kevin Mitchell. The McNeils have
a 16-ha property at Watervale which includes 3.2 ha of mature, dry-grown riesling, and intend
to plant shiraz, currently purchasing that variety from the Barossa Valley. A cellar door facility
is under construction, and will open by the end of 2008.

ŸŸŸŸ **Barossa Shiraz 2005** Well-made classic Barossa shiraz; dark-fruited, quite chewy
and with nice depth to the fruit; needs a little more precision on the finish.
Screwcap. 15° alc. **Rating** 89 **To** 2016 $24.95

Clare Valley Riesling 2007 A very dry style, with fresh lime juice on the palate, and with mouthwatering acidity on the finish. Screwcap. 12.5° alc. **Rating** 88 **To** 2014 $19.95

Tim Smith Wines

PO Box 446, Tanunda, SA 5352 **Region** Barossa Valley
T (08) 8563 0939 **F** (08) 8563 0939 **Open** Not
Winemaker Tim Smith **Est.** 2001 **Cases** 1000
Tim Smith aspires (and succeeds) to make wines in the mould of the great producers of Côte Rôtie and Chateauneuf du Pape, but using a New World approach. It is a business in its early stages, with only four wines, a Shiraz, Botrytis Semillon, Viognier and Grenache/Shiraz/Mourvedre. Exports to the UK and the US.

⧠⧠⧠⧠⧠ **Barossa Mataro Grenache Shiraz 2005** Deep, clear colour; few better than this from the Barossa; no jujube fruit whatsoever, all falling in the black fruit range; perfect tannin and oak balance. Screwcap. 14.5° alc. **Rating** 96 **To** 2020 $27

⧠⧠⧠⧠⧠ **Adelaide Hills Viognier 2007** Quiet but clean aroma; the palate refreshed by citrussy acidity surrounding the core of apricot and musk fruit; obvious development potential. Screwcap. 14° alc. **Rating** 90 **To** 2013 $27

Timmins Wines

7 Durham Street, Hunters Hill, NSW 2110 (postal) **Region** Hunter Valley/Orange
T (02) 9816 1422 **F** (02) 9816 1477 **Open** Not
Winemaker John Timmins **Est.** 2001 **Cases** 350
Unusually, this is a micro-wine operation without its own vineyard. Pharmacist John Timmins completed his Bachelor of Applied Science (Wine Science) degree in 2003, and is using his qualifications to make wines in small volumes from grapes grown in the Hunter Valley and Orange. Exports to Singapore.

⧠⧠⧠⧠ **Hunter Valley Shiraz 2005** Punches above its alcohol weight, with ripe plum and prune aromas and flavours, but then thins out on the finish. Screwcap. 13.5° alc. **Rating** 87 **To** 2011 $25

Tin Shed Wines

PO Box 504, Tanunda, SA 5352 **Region** Eden Valley
T (08) 8563 3669 **F** (08) 8563 3669 **www.**tinshedwines.com **Open** Not
Winemaker Andrew Wardlaw, Peter Clarke **Est.** 1998 **Cases** 3000
Proprietors Andrew Wardlaw and Peter Clarke weave all sorts of mystique in marketing the Tin Shed wines. They say, 'our wines are handmade so we can only produce small volumes; this means we can take more care at each step of the winemaking process ... most bizarre of all we use our nose, palette (sic) and commonsense as opposed to the safe and reliable formula preached by our universities and peers'. The Tin Shed newsletter continues with lots of gee-whizz, hayseed jollity, making one fear the worst, when the reality is that the wines (even the Wild Bunch Riesling, wild-fermented without chemicals) are very good. No samples received, the rating is that of last year. Exports to the UK, the US, NZ and Japan.

Tinderbox Vineyard

Tinderbox, Tas 7054 **Region** Southern Tasmania
T (03) 6229 2994 **Open** By appt
Winemaker Hood Wines (Andrew Hood) **Est.** 1994 **Cases** 240
Liz McGown may have retired from specialist nursing (five years ago), but is busier than ever, having taken on the running of the 400-ha Tinderbox fat lamb and fine merino wool property after a lease (which had run for 22 years) terminated. Liz describes Tinderbox as a vineyard between the sun and the sea, and looking out over the vineyard towards Bruny Island in the distance, it is not hard to see why. The attractive label was designed by Barry Tucker, who was so charmed by Liz's request that he waived his usual (substantial) fee.

▼▼▼▼▼ **Pinot Noir 2006** Strong colour; abundant plum, spice and sous bois fruit, fully ripe notwithstanding the low alcohol; good length and finish. Screwcap. 12.8° alc. **Rating** 94 **To** 2013

Tinkers Hill Vineyard
84 Sugarloaf Lane, Beechworth, Vic 3747 **Region** Beechworth
T (03) 5728 3327 **F** (03) 5728 1360 **www**.tinkershillwines.com.au **Open** Fri–Mon 11–5, or by appt
Winemaker Andrew Doyle **Est.** 2000 **Cases** 255
James and Rhonda Taylor have established 1.35 ha of shiraz, chardonnay and cabernet sauvignon. The cellar door is situated in the Chiltern Mt Pilot National Park, close to the Woolshed Falls, one of Beechworth's main natural attractions. Small quantities of Barbera are sourced from within the region, the Merlot coming from their daughter's Cirko V winery (see separate entry). Classy packaging is a feature.

Tinklers Vineyard ★★★★
Pokolbin Mountains Road, Pokolbin, NSW 2320 **Region** Lower Hunter Valley
T (02) 4998 7435 **F** (02) 4998 7469 **www**.tinklers.com.au **Open** 7 days 10–5
Winemaker Usher John Tinkler **Est.** 1997 **Cases** 1000
Three generations of the Tinkler family have been involved with the property since 1942. Originally a beef and dairy farm, vines have been both pulled out and replanted at various stages along the way, and part of the adjoining old Ben Ean Vineyard acquired, the net result being a little over 41 ha of vines. The major part of the production is sold as grapes to McWilliam's, but when Usher John Tinkler returned from CSU in 2001, he turned the tractor shed into a winery, and since then the wines have been made onsite.

▼▼▼▼▽ **School Block Hunter Valley Semillon 2006** Bright green-straw; high-flavoured, verging on tropical, and quite soft in the mouth, but not flabby; has developed quickly, but not alarmingly. Screwcap. 11.5° alc. **Rating** 91 **To** 2012 $18
U & I Reserve Shiraz 2004 A lively and elegant shiraz which clearly expresses the terroir of the Hunter Valley; a mix of spice, earth and leather alongside gentle blackberry fruit, and controlled oak. Screwcap. 13.8° alc. **Rating** 91 **To** 2019 $25

▼▼▼▼ **Poppys Vineyard Chardonnay 2006** Medium- to full-bodied; a good depth of peachy fruit and balanced oak; doesn't show the alcohol. Screwcap. 14° alc. **Rating** 89 **To** 2010 $20

Tintilla Wines
725 Hermitage Road, Pokolbin, NSW 2320 **Region** Lower Hunter Valley
T (02) 6574 7093 **F** (02) 9767 6894 **www**.tintilla.com.au **Open** 7 days 10.30–6
Winemaker James Lusby **Est.** 1993 **Cases** 4000
The Lusby family has established a 10-ha vineyard (merlot, shiraz, sangiovese, semillon and cabernet sauvignon) on a northeast-facing slope with red clay and limestone soil. They have also planted an olive grove producing four different types of olives, which are cured and sold from the estate.

▼▼▼▼▼ **Angus Hunter Semillon 2007** Typical subdued bouquet but comes alive on the intense and highly focused citrussy palate; great thrust and drive. Long future. Screwcap. 10.5° alc. **Rating** 94 **To** 2017 $22

▼▼▼▼▽ **Chardonnay 2007** Skilled winemaking on display; seamless fruit and oak; nectarine and citrus fruit, with great thrust to the finish and aftertaste. Screwcap. **Rating** 93 **To** 2014 $25
Reserve Hunter Valley Shiraz 2006 Bright colour; medium-bodied, firm and youthful, the tightly wound texture needing years to unfurl, but the essential balance is there. Screwcap. 13° alc. **Rating** 91 **To** 2020 $28

♀♀♀♀ **Rosato di Jupiter Hunter Valley Sangiovese 2007** A welcome bone-dry
rose, with a mix of spice, cherry and tar aromas and flavours befitting the variety;
clean, crisp finish. Screwcap. 13° alc. **Rating** 88 **To** 2010 $20
Catherine de 'M Hunter Valley Sangiovese Merlot 2005 Clever blending
of the varieties with similar light- to medium-bodied, savoury profiles; food style,
and even then, best with Italian. Screwcap. 13° alc. **Rating** 88 **To** 2012 $25.60

Tizzana Winery ★★★

518 Tizzana Road, Ebenezer, NSW 2756 **Region** South Coast Zone
T (02) 4579 1150 **F** (02) 4579 1216 **www.**tizzana.com.au **Open** W'ends & public
hols 12–6, or by appt
Winemaker Peter Auld **Est.** 1887 **Cases** 1000
Tizzana has been a weekend and holiday occupation for Peter Auld for many years now. It
operates in one of the great historic wineries, built (in 1887) by Australia's true renaissance
man, Dr Thomas Fiaschi. The wines may not be great, but the ambience is. Moreover, the
cabernet sauvignon and shiraz have been replanted on the same vineyard as that first planted
by Fiaschi in 1885. Peter Auld has also developed Tizzana as a wine education centre.

♀♀♀♀ **Ambrose Aleatico Rose 2007** A musky, off-dry style which is clearly varietal
in character, and a little rough around the edges; 1000 bottles. Screwcap. 11.5° alc.
Rating 87 **To** 2009 $20

Tobin Wines ★★★

34 Ricca Road, Ballandean, Qld 4382 **Region** Granite Belt
T (07) 4684 1235 **F** (07) 4684 1235 **www.**tobinwines.com.au **Open** 7 days 10–5
Winemaker Adrian Tobin, David Gianini **Est.** 1964 **Cases** 1000
In the early 1960s the Ricca family planted table grapes, planting shiraz and semillon in
1964–66, which are said to be the oldest vinifera vines in the Granite Belt region. The Tobin
family (headed by Adrian and Frances Tobin) purchased the vineyard in 2000 and have
substantially increased plantings. There are now nearly 10 ha planted to semillon, verdelho,
chardonnay, sauvignon blanc, shiraz, merlot, cabernet sauvignon and tempranillo, with some
remaining rows of table grapes. The emphasis has changed towards quality bottled wines,
with some success.

♀♀♀♀ **Liqueur Muscat NV** Bright and varietal, with good flavour and nice level of
sweetness for the fruit. Zork. 17.5° alc. **Rating** 89 **To** 2009 $25
Max Shiraz 2006 Good colour, with plenty of sweet fruit, plus spice and raw
oak on the bouquet and palate; needs a little time. Diam. 13.5° alc. **Rating** 88
To 2013 $24

Tokar Estate ★★★☆

6 Maddens Lane, Coldstream, Vic 3770 **Region** Yarra Valley
T (03) 5964 9585 **F** (03) 5964 9587 **www.**tokarestate.com.au **Open** 7 days 10–5
Winemaker Paul Evans **Est.** 1996 **Cases** 5000
Tokar Estate is one of many vineyards on Maddens Lane, Leon Tokar having established
12.4 ha of now mature pinot noir, shiraz, cabernet sauvignon and tempranillo. All the wines
are from the estate, badged Single Vineyard (which they are) and have performed well in
regional shows, with early success for the Tempranillo.

♀♀♀♀♀ **Cabernet Sauvignon 2005** Attractive earthy, cedary, dark chocolate nuances to
the base of blackcurrant fruit, the tannins in good balance. Nice wine. Screwcap.
14° alc. **Rating** 90 **To** 2015 $30

♀♀♀♀ **Yarra Valley Chardonnay 2006** Well-made wine, with typical Yarra profile of
stone fruit and length of flavour; that said, needs a little more zest. Screwcap.
13.5° alc. **Rating** 89 **To** 2012 $24

Pinot Noir 2006 Ripe plum and black cherry fruit, riper than the alcohol suggests, needs time to lose some of its puppy fat. Screwcap. 13.5° alc. **Rating** 89 To 2013 $24

Shiraz 2006 Medium- to full-bodied; generous blackberry and plum fruit in a fully ripened mode, but also with ripples of licorice and spice; perhaps a touch too ripe. Diam. 14.5° alc. **Rating** 89 To 2015 $28

The Aria Tempranillo Cabernet Sauvignon Shiraz 2005 A ludicrously shaped and doubtless very expensive bottle is the most striking thing about a blend which really doesn't have a great deal of logic, though the wine is pleasant enough. Diam. 14.5° alc. **Rating** 87 To 2010 $95

Tollana   ★★★★

GPO Box 753, Melbourne, Vic 3001 **Region** Barossa Valley
T 1300 651 650 **Open** Not
Winemaker Andrew Baldwin **Est.** 1888 **Cases** 10 000
Tollana survived a near-death experience during the turbulent days of the Rosemount management of Southcorp; where it will ultimately fit in the Foster's scheme of things remains to be seen, but in the meantime, Tollana is back in business producing Riesling, Viognier, Shiraz and Cabernet Sauvignon.

ΨΨΨΨΩ **Bin TR16 Adelaide Hills Eden Valley Shiraz 2006** Well constructed and balanced components, with spicy black cherry and blackberry fruit, fine-grained tannins and French oak. Screwcap. 14° alc. **Rating** 90 To 2016 $19.95

ΨΨΨΨ **Bin TR222 Adelaide Hills Cabernet Sauvignon 2005** A courageous decision to forsake Eden Valley for Adelaide Hills for this variety; nonetheless, an elegant wine, with pure, verging on puritanical, cabernet fruit; worth cellaring, perhaps. Screwcap. 14° alc. **Rating** 89 To 2017 $19.95

Tom's Waterhole Wines   ★★★

'Felton', Longs Corner Road, Canowindra, NSW 2804 **Region** Cowra
T (02) 6344 1819 **F** (02) 6344 2172 **www.tomswaterhole.com.au Open** 7 days 10–4
Winemaker Graham Kerr **Est.** 1997 **Cases** 1000
Graham Timms and Graham Kerr started the development of Tom's Waterhole Wines in 1997, progressively establishing 6 ha of shiraz, cabernet sauvignon, semillon and merlot, completing the planting program in 2001. They have decided to bypass the use of irrigation, so the yields will always be low.

ΨΨΨΨ **Semillon 2006** Organic grapes; some bottle development adding weight; fair balance and overall flavour. Screwcap. 10.5° alc. **Rating** 87 To 2010 $12

Tomboy Hill   ★★★★★

204 Sim Street, Ballarat, Vic 3350 (postal) **Region** Ballarat
T (03) 5331 3785 **Open** Not
Winemaker Scott Ireland (Contract) **Est.** 1984 **Cases** 1200
Former schoolteacher Ian Watson seems to be following the same path as Lindsay McCall of Paringa Estate (also a former schoolteacher) in extracting greater quality and style than any other winemaker in his region, in this case Ballarat. Since 1984 Watson has slowly and patiently built up a patchwork quilt of small plantings of chardonnay and pinot noir. In the better years, the single-vineyard wines of Chardonnay and/or Pinot Noir are released; Rebellion Chardonnay and Pinot Noir are multi-vineyard blends, but all 100% Ballarat. I have a particular fondness for the style not necessarily shared by others. Exports to the UK and Canada.

ΨΨΨΨΨ **The Tomboy Ballarat Goldfields Pinot Noir 2006** Here the cherry and plum varietal fruit drives the wine from start to finish, the savoury spicy notes simply adding to the excellent texture and length, the oak likewise. Screwcap. 13.5° alc. **Rating** 96 To 2015 $70

Garibaldi Farm Ballarat Goldfields Chardonnay 2006 Superfine and elegant; tightly focused nectarine grapefruit and melon has swallowed up the French oak; very long finish. Screwcap. 13.3° alc. **Rating** 95 **To** 2016 $36

Smythes Creek Ballarat Goldfields Pinot Noir 2006 Also has elements of spice, mint and stem on the bouquet, but on the equally intense and very long palate the red cherry, strawberry and raspberry fruits are in abundance. Screwcap. 13.3° alc. **Rating** 95 **To** 2015 $48

Rebellion Ballarat Goldfields Chardonnay 2006 Slightly less intense fruit than Garibaldi, but has similar focus and length; fruit-driven from start to finish, with perfect balance. Screwcap. 13.3° alc. **Rating** 94 **To** 2015 $30

� **Rebellion Ballarat Goldfields Pinot Noir 2006** Good hue; notes of spice, stem and oak on the bouquet; a particularly intense, spicy savoury palate, the varietal fruits at its heart. Screwcap. 13.3° alc. **Rating** 93 **To** 2014 $35

Tombstone Estate   **NR**

5R Basalt Road, Dubbo, NSW 2830 **Region** Western Plains Zone
T (02) 6882 6624 **F** (02) 6882 6624 **Open** Fri–Mon & school hols 10–5, or by appt
Winemaker Ian Robertson **Est.** 1997 **Cases** 300
The ominously named Tombstone Estate has been established by Rod and Patty Tilling, who have planted 2 ha of chardonnay, pinot noir, shiraz, cabernet sauvignon, sangiovese, barbera and muscat. The wine is made onsite, and the cellar door offers barbecue and picnic facilities.

Tomich Hill Wines

87 King William Road, Unley, SA 5061 (postal) **Region** Adelaide Hills
T (08) 8272 9388 **F** (08) 8373 7229 **www.**tomichhill.com.au **Open** Not
Winemaker John Tomich, Tim Knappstein (Contract) **Est.** 2002 **Cases** 2000
There is an element of irony in this family venture. Patriarch John Tomich was born on a vineyard near Mildura, where he learnt firsthand the skills and knowledge required for premium grapegrowing. He went on to become a well-known Adelaide ear, nose and throat specialist. He has taken the wheel full circle with postgraduate studies at the University of Adelaide, resulting in a diploma in winemaking in 2002, and now venturing on to the Master of Wine revision course from the Institute of Masters of Wine. His son Randal is a cutting from the old vine (metaphorically speaking), having invented new equipment and techniques for tending the family's 80-ha vineyard in the Adelaide Hills near Woodside; resulting in a 60% saving in time and fuel costs. Most of the grapes are sold, but the amount of wine made under the Tomich Hill brand is far from a hobby.

♀♀♀♀♀ **Adelaide Hills Pinot Noir 2006** Complex morello cherry and plum aromas; good intensity and length, with lovely silky mouthfeel. Screwcap. 13° alc.
Rating 94 **To** 2012 $26.50

♀♀♀♀♀ **Adelaide Hills Pinot Gris 2007** Attractive juicy style, with good movement in the mouth; delicious flavours, ranging from pear to near-tropical; '07 seemed to be kind to pinot gris. Screwcap. 13° alc. **Rating** 92 **To** 2009 $24.50

Adelaide Hills Gewurztraminer 2007 An elegant and lively palate; light rose petal lychee characters throughout, lemony acidity on the finish adding authority. Screwcap. 13° alc. **Rating** 91 **To** 2012 $24.50

♀♀♀♀ **Adelaide Hills Sauvignon Blanc 2007** A pleasant mix of tropical and stone fruit aromas and flavours; medium intensity and length. Screwcap. 12.8° alc.
Rating 89 **To** 2009 $22

Toms Cap Vineyard   ★★★

322 Lays Road, Carrajung Lower, Vic 3844 **Region** Gippsland
T (03) 5194 2215 **F** (03) 5194 2369 **www.**tomscap.com.au **Open** 7 days 10–5
Winemaker Owen Schmidt (Contract) **Est.** 1994 **Cases** 600

Graham Morris began the development of the vineyard in 1992 on a 40-ha property surrounded by the forests of the Strzelecki Ranges, the Ninety Mile Beach at Woodside, and the Tarra Bulga National Park, one of the four major areas of cool temperature rainforest in Vic. The vineyard has 2.4 ha of cabernet sauvignon, chardonnay, sauvignon blanc and riesling. In 2007 a 100-seat restaurant was opened offering a variety of local and overseas foods.

ϷϷϷϷ   **Riesling 2007** Very developed colour; abundant flavour, just a little rough around the edges. Screwcap. 13.1° alc. **Rating** 87 **To** 2011 $18

Toolangi Vineyards   ★★★★★

PO Box 5046, Glenferrie South, Vic 3122 **Region** Yarra Valley
T (03) 9822 9488 **F** (03) 9804 3365 **www**.toolangi.com **Open** Not
Winemaker Various contract **Est.** 1995 **Cases** 10 000
Garry and Julie Hounsell acquired their property in the Dixons Creek subregion of the Yarra Valley, adjoining the Toolangi State Forest, in 1995. Plantings have taken place progressively since then, with 13 ha now in the ground. The primary accent is on pinot noir and chardonnay, accounting for all but 2.8 ha, which is predominantly shiraz and a little viognier. As only half the vineyards are bearing, production is supplemented by chardonnay and pinot noir from the Coldstream subregion, cropped at 2 tonnes per acre. Winemaking is (or was) by Tom Carson of Yering Station, Rick Kinzbrunner of Giaconda and Matt Harrop of Shadowfax, as impressive a trio of winemakers as one could wish for. A 24-ha property was acquired in late 2005, and further chardonnay planted.

ϷϷϷϷϷ   **Estate Yarra Valley Chardonnay 2006** Crisp and tight, the aromas and flavours built around a minerally rather than oaky structure; terrific drive to the nectarine fruit, and a very long finish. Screwcap. 13.5° alc. **Rating** 96 **To** 2016 $40
Estate Yarra Valley Chardonnay 2005 Pale straw-green; immaculate balance of supple, smooth nectarine fruit and perfectly integrated oak. 14° alc. **Rating** 95 **To** 2013 $35
Reserve Yarra Valley Chardonnay 2006 More colour than the other Chardonnays, ultra-complex, with strong winemaking fingerprints giving a warm toasty/nutty/creamy texture. Screwcap. 14.2° alc. **Rating** 94 **To** 2013 $80
Estate Yarra Valley Pinot Noir 2005 An ultra-fragrant, almost flowery, bouquet; considerable intensity to the complex spicy dark berry aromas of the palate, and good length. Screwcap. 14° alc. **Rating** 94 **To** 2012 $35

ϷϷϷϷϿ   **Reserve Yarra Valley Shiraz 2005** An elegant, medium-bodied wine, winning by subtle persuasion rather than brute force; silky tannins and fine cherry/plum fruit; fully priced. Diam. 14° alc. **Rating** 93 **To** 2015 $70
Yarra Valley Chardonnay 2006 Clean, fresh and bright, the innate complexity of texture not immediately obvious in an elegant wine, with neat balance between fruit and oak. Screwcap. 13.5° alc. **Rating** 92 **To** 2012 $25

ϷϷϷϷ   **Yarra Valley Pinot Noir 2006** Light-bodied, bright and fresh, with interesting textural play from forest floor characters, but needs more sweet fruit; wanders away on the finish. Screwcap. 13° alc. **Rating** 89 **To** 2011 $25
Yarra Valley Shiraz 2005 Clear colour; a mix of spicy/earthy notes to the light- to medium-bodied fruit; has line and length. Screwcap. 14° alc. **Rating** 89 **To** 2009 $23
Yarra Valley Pinot Noir 2005 Light-bodied, with a strongly savoury/spicy cast, and not enough pinot fruit to carry it through. Screwcap. 13° alc. **Rating** 88 **To** 2009 $24

Toorak Winery   ★★★

Vineyard 279, Toorak Road, Leeton, NSW 2705 **Region** Riverina
T (02) 6953 2333 **F** (02) 6953 4454 **www**.toorakwines.com.au **Open** Mon–Fri 10–5
Winemaker Robert Bruno **Est.** 1965 **Cases** 200 000

A traditional, long-established Riverina producer with a strong Italian-based clientele around Australia. Production has been increasing significantly, utilising 150 ha of estate plantings and grapes purchased from other growers, both in the Riverina and elsewhere. Wines are released under the Willandra Estate, Toorak Estate and Amesbury Estate labels. While, in absolute terms, the quality is not great, the low-priced wines in fact over-deliver in many instances. Exports to Russia, China and Singapore.

♟♟♟♟   **Willandra Estate Leeton Selection Shiraz 2007** Sophisticated winemaking obvious in achieving maximum colour and flavour; does finish short, but at this price that is a carping criticism. Screwcap. 13.5° alc. **Rating** 87 **To** 2010 $12

Topper's Mountain Vineyard   ★★★

5 km Guyra Road, Tingha, NSW 2369 **Region** New England
T (02) 6723 3506 **F** (02) 6723 3222 **www**.toppers.com.au **Open** By appt
Winemaker Contract **Est.** 2000 **Cases** 500
This is yet another New England venture, owned by the Kirkby and Birch families, with Mark Kirkby having the primary management responsibilities. Planting began in the spring of 2000, with 1.1 ha, the remaining 8.9 ha following in the spring of '02. Varieties planted include chardonnay, gewurztraminer, sauvignon blanc, semillon, riesling, tempranillo and shiraz.

♟♟♟♟   **Nebbiolo 2006** Far better balanced than many other nebbiolos; fine tannins; cedar, rose and tar; faint touch of sweetness ex glycerol; commendable. **Rating** 89 **To** 2012
Thunderbolt's Riesling Traminer 2005 Not much intensity but has balance and a fresh finish. **Rating** 87 **To** 2009 $14

Torbreck Vintners   ★★★★★

Roennfeldt Road, Marananga, SA 5352 **Region** Barossa Valley
T (08) 8562 4155 **F** (08) 8562 4195 **www**.torbreck.com **Open** 7 days 10–6
Winemaker David Powell **Est.** 1994 **Cases** 50 000
Of all the Barossa Valley wineries to grab the headlines in the US, with demand pulling prices up to undreamt of levels, Torbreck stands supreme. David Powell has not let success go to his head, or subvert the individuality and sheer quality of his wines, all created around very old, dry-grown, bush-pruned vineyards. The top trio are led by The RunRig (Shiraz/Viognier); then The Factor (Shiraz) and The Descendant (Shiraz/Viognier); next The Struie (Shiraz) and The Steading (Grenache/Mataro Shiraz). Notwithstanding the depth and richness of the wines, they have a remarkable degree of finesse. Exports to all major markets.

♟♟♟♟♟   **The RunRig 2004** A fragrant and complex bouquet; shiraz, viognier and oak all coalesce in a rich, velvety, mouthfilling and sensuous wine; oak is somewhere in the background. I do wish the Woodcutters had a cork and RunRig the screwcap. Cork. 14.5° alc. **Rating** 96 **To** 2019 $225
The Descendant 2005 Immaculate structure, texture and balance; likewise black-fruited shiraz with a subliminal viognier twist, plus licorice and spice; tannins ripe and perfectly weighted. Cork. 14.5° alc. **Rating** 96 **To** 2025 $125
The Factor 2005 Superb colour; exceptional mouthfeel courtesy of fine, ripe tannins seamlessly woven through the velvet curtain of black fruits; the flavours echo repeatedly around the mouth. Cork. 14.5° alc. **Rating** 96 **To** 2030 $125
The Struie 2006 Faintly dull edges to the colour; but the palate proclaims the quality of the wine, flush with blackberry, spice and bitter chocolate, tannins and oak exactly positioned. Cork. 14° alc. **Rating** 94 **To** 2014 $48.50
The RunRig 2005 Has all the expected vibrancy and complexity of flavour in this wine; rounded and velvety fruit sweetness (not residual sugar) backed by ripe tannins and just the right amount of oak. Cork. 14.5° alc. **Rating** 94 **To** 2018 $225

♟♟♟♟♟   **The Gask 2006** Medium-bodied; a savoury spicy earthy edge to the bouquet and palate, the texture fine and supple; the tannins have been managed to perfection. Cork. 13.5° alc. **Rating** 92 **To** 2013 $75

The Steading 2005 Ultra-fragrant, ultra-juicy aromas; a cupboard of spices join in on the palate; subtle tannins; southern Rhône-style. Cork. 14.5° alc. **Rating** 91 To 2013 $40

Woodcutters Barossa Valley Semillon 2006 Clean and fresh; carries its alcohol well, although there is a slight hit on the finish; any oak used is not visible. Screwcap. 14° alc. **Rating** 90 **To** 2011 $17.50

Woodcutters Shiraz 2006 Clean, fresh, medium-bodied wine with neatly balanced black fruits, tannins and a touch of oak. Screwcap. 14.5° alc. **Rating** 90 To 2014 $18.50

Cuvee Juveniles 2007 Clean and fresh; a light- to medium-bodied, fruit-driven array of red and black fruits; fine-grained tannins; good length. Grenache/Mourvedre/Shiraz. Screwcap. 14.5° alc. **Rating** 90 **To** 2012 $25

Torzi Matthews Vintners

Cnr Eden Valley Road/Sugarloaf Hill Road, Mount McKenzie, SA 5353 **Region** Eden Valley **T** (08) 8565 3393 **F** (08) 8565 3393 **www**.torzimatthews.com.au **Open** By appt **Winemaker** Domenic Torzi **Est.** 1996 **Cases** 2100

Domenic Torzi and Tracey Matthews, former Adelaide Plains residents, searched for a number of years before finding a 6-ha block at Mt McKenzie in the Eden Valley. The block they chose is in a hollow and the soil is meagre, and they were in no way deterred by the knowledge that it would be frost-prone. The result is predictably low yields, concentrated further by drying the grapes on racks and reducing the weight by around 30% (the Appassimento method is used in Italy to produce Amarone-style wines). Two wines are made, both under the Frost Dodger label: Eden Valley Riesling and Eden Valley Shiraz, the Shiraz wild yeast-fermented and neither fined nor filtered. Exports to the UK, the US, Denmark and Singapore.

ΨΨΨΨΨ **Frost Dodger Eden Valley Riesling 2007** Bright fresh-cut green apple with a drizzle of lime juice; a long, lively palate; fresh finish. Screwcap. 12° alc. **Rating** 94 To 2020 $20

Frost Dodger Eden Valley Shiraz 2005 Powerful, clear-cut regional shiraz, with blackberry, licorice, spicy pepper and a touch of dark chocolate; fine tannins and perfect oak integration. Screwcap. 14.5° alc. **Rating** 94 **To** 2025 $30

ΨΨΨΨ **Schist Rock Shiraz 2006** Dark fruits with a mix of dark chocolate and mocha; good balance, with fine but gently savoury tannins; great value. Screwcap. 14° alc. **Rating** 92 **To** 2016 $16.95

Totino Wines

982 Port Road, Albert Park, SA 5014 (postal) **Region** Adelaide Hills **T** (08) 8268 8066 **F** (08) 8268 3597 **Open** Not **Winemaker** Scott Rawlinson **Est.** 1992 **Cases** NA

Don Totino migrated from Italy in 1968, and at the age of 18 became the youngest barber in Australia. He soon moved on, into general food and importing and distribution. Festival City, as the business is known, has been highly successful, recognised by a recent significant award from the Italian government. In 1998 he purchased a run-down vineyard at Paracombe in the Adelaide Hills, since extending the plantings to 29 ha of chardonnay, pinot grigio, sauvignon blanc, sangiovese, shiraz and cabernet sauvignon. Various members of his family, including daughter Linda, are involved in the business.

ΨΨΨΨΨ **Adelaide Hills Shiraz 2005** Excellent purple-crimson; quite luscious black cherry and plum and spice aromas and flavours; certainly not over-extracted. Screwcap. 14° alc. **Rating** 93 **To** 2020

ΨΨΨΨ **Paracombe Creek Adelaide Hills Sauvignon Blanc 2007** Crisp, crunchy, almost gritty, texture with lemon zest flavours; unusual (especially for the vintage) but refreshing. Screwcap. 13° alc. **Rating** 89 **To** 2010

Adelaide Hills Pinot Grigio 2007 Within the context of the variety, has good flavour in pear/apple/spice spectrum; cleansed by crisp citrussy acidity on the finish. Screwcap. 13° alc. **Rating** 89 **To** 2009

Adelaide Hills Chardonnay 2006 Very light but fresh nectarine and citrus fruit; subtle oak; fair length; may develop further. Screwcap. **Rating** 88 **To** 2013
Adelaide Hills Cabernet Sauvignon 2004 Light- to medium-bodied; strong herb and olive overtones to the blackcurrant and cassis fruit; its main strength is the length of the palate. Screwcap. 13.5° alc. **Rating** 87 **To** 2012
Adelaide Hills Sangiovese 2004 Light-bodied, with very savoury/sour cherry flavours; best sooner rather than later. Screwcap. 13.5° alc. **Rating** 87 **To** 2010

Tower Estate ★★★★★

Cnr Broke Road/Hall Road, Pokolbin, NSW 2320 **Region** Lower Hunter Valley
T (02) 4998 7989 **F** (02) 4998 7919 **www.**towerestatewines.com.au **Open** 7 days 10–5
Winemaker Scott Stephens, Jeff Byrne **Est.** 1999 **Cases** 10 000
Tower Estate was founded by the late Len Evans, with the 5-star Tower Lodge accommodation and convention centre part of the development. It is anticipated there will be little day-to-day change in either part of the business. Tower Estate will continue to draw upon varieties and regions which have a particular synergy, the aim being to make the best possible wines in the top sector of the wine market. Exports to the UK, Denmark, Russia, Singapore, Hong Kong, Japan and Canada.

ŸŸŸŸŸ Hunter Valley Semillon 2006 An exceptionally intense wine with a cascade of citrus, grass and minerally flavours; has great length and a sparkling finish. Cork. 10.5° alc. **Rating** 96 **To** 2013 $26
Museum Release Hunter Valley Semillon 1999 Vibrant yellow-green; totally delicious, still retaining freshness and delicacy; touches of toast and lemon run through a lingering finish. When first tasted in '00, was given only 90 points. This is what age can do, cork permitting. 10.5° alc. **Rating** 95 **To** 2012 $45
Museum Release Hunter Valley Semillon 2001 Great green-straw; a complex, toasty/honey overlay to citrus fruit on the palate; long, lingering finish. Cork. 12° alc. **Rating** 95 **To** 2013 $45
Adelaide Hills Sauvignon Blanc 2007 Pale straw-green; pronounced herb and dried grass aromas; considerable depth on the palate with some richer tropical fruits; good length. Screwcap. 13.5° alc. **Rating** 94 **To** 2009 $32
Tasmania Pinot Noir 2006 Vivid crimson-purple sets the scene for a pinot with an elevated bouquet and palate; high-profile plum fruit, and zesty acidity. Tamar Valley; new French clones. Cork. 13.5° alc. **Rating** 94 **To** 2014 $58

ŸŸŸŸŸ Hunter Valley Semillon 2007 A firm, still relatively closed palate; lanolin, herb, mineral and grass notes are all scrunched up in a tight ball of flavour; will open up in time. Screwcap. 11° alc. **Rating** 90 **To** 2017 $26
Adelaide Hills Chardonnay 2005 Light- to medium-bodied and elegant; gentle stone fruit and a twist of citrus supported by fairly obvious oak. Cork. 14° alc. **Rating** 90 **To** 2010 $32

ŸŸŸŸ Hunter Valley Chardonnay 2005 Soft, peachy/nutty flavours; good balance, but will continue rapid development. Cork. 14° alc. **Rating** 89 **To** 2010 $32
Hunter Valley Verdelho 2007 Strong tropical fruit salad flavours on a rich palate; a singularly powerful example of the variety. Screwcap. 14° alc. **Rating** 89 **To** 2010 $22
Hunter Valley Shiraz 2005 Youthful hue; light- to medium-bodied, especially for the year; also a youthful palate with a small vinous footprint; may blossom with age, but not easy to tell. Cork. 13.5° alc. **Rating** 89 **To** 2015 $42
Barossa Shiraz 2004 Unconvincing colour; the Barossa Valley with a Hunter Valley graft! Light- to medium-bodied, with savoury flavours; perhaps going through a change in life. Cork. 14° alc. **Rating** 88 **To** 2014 $42

Train Trak   ★★★★☆

957 Healesville–Yarra Glen Road, Yarra Glen, Vic 3775 **Region** Yarra Valley
T (03) 9730 1314 **F** (03) 9427 1510 **www**.traintrak.com.au **Open** Wed–Sun
Winemaker Contract **Est.** 1995 **Cases** 6000

The unusual name comes from the Yarra Glen to Healesville railway, which was built in 1889 and abandoned in 1980 – part of it passes by the Train Trak vineyard. The 15.95-ha vineyard is planted (in descending order) to pinot noir, cabernet sauvignon, chardonnay and shiraz. The restaurant makes exceptional pizzas in a wood-fired oven. Exports to Japan.

ỸỸỸỸỴ **Yarra Valley Chardonnay 2006** Well made, allowing the regional expression of chardonnay (built around length not depth) to express itself in the smooth nectarine and melon fruit, the oak minimal. Screwcap. 13.5° alc. **Rating** 90 **To** 2012 $25

ỸỸỸỸ **Yarra Valley Shiraz 2005** Spice, bracken, earth and licorice, plus some vanilla on a light- to medium-bodied palate; ready now. Screwcap. 15° alc. **Rating** 87 **To** 2010 $27

Yarra Valley Cabernet Sauvignon 2005 A blend of earthy/savoury characters with sweeter blackcurrant fruit, making for some sweet and sour characters. Screwcap. 14.5° alc. **Rating** 87 **To** 2012 $25

Tranquil Vale   ★★★

325 Pywells Road, Luskintyre, NSW 2321 **Region** Lower Hunter Valley
T (02) 4930 6100 **F** (02) 4930 6105 **www**.tranquilvalewines.com.au **Open** Thurs–Mon 10–5, or by appt
Winemaker Phil Griffiths **Est.** 1996 **Cases** 2500

Phil and Lucy Griffiths purchased the property sight unseen from a description in an old copy of the *Weekend Australian* found in the Australian High Commission Office in London. The vineyard they established is on the banks of the Hunter River, opposite Wyndham Estate, on relatively fertile, sandy clay loam. Competent winemaking has resulted in good wines, some of which have already had show success. Exports to the UK.

Trentham Estate   ★★★★★

Sturt Highway, Trentham Cliffs, NSW 2738 **Region** Murray Darling
T (03) 5024 8888 **F** (03) 5024 8800 **www**.trenthamestate.com.au **Open** 7 days 9.30–5
Winemaker Anthony Murphy, Shane Kerr **Est.** 1988 **Cases** 60 000

Remarkably consistent tasting notes across all wine styles from all vintages attest to the expertise of ex-Mildara winemaker Tony Murphy, making the Trentham wines from his family vineyards. All the wines offer great value for money. Only time will tell where the business will head in the future if the dire predictions for the Murray Darling prove accurate, but the broadening of the net gives a strong lead. Exports to the UK, Canada, Denmark, Germany, Belgium and NZ.

ỸỸỸỸỸ **Yarra Valley Chardonnay 2006** Highly polished and finely structured wine, showing the synergy between Tony Murphy's winemaking skills and Yarra Valley chardonnay; very pure and long. Bravo. Screwcap. 13° alc. **Rating** 94 **To** 2013 $25

Heathcote Shiraz 2005 Tony Murphy shows his masterly ability to unlock the terroir and character of the regions in the Trentham range; supple black fruits and singing tannins on the finish. Screwcap. 14.5° alc. **Rating** 94 **To** 2025 $25

ỸỸỸỸỴ **Mornington Peninsula Pinot Noir 2005** Retains excellent hue; powerful and complex, with strong dark plum and forest floor characters; very long palate, will improve further. Screwcap. 14° alc. **Rating** 93 **To** 2014 $25

Chardonnay 2006 A beautifully crafted wine, lifting it out of its regional limitation and above its price bracket; melon, peach, fig and a touch of French oak. Screwcap. 13.5° alc. **Rating** 91 **To** 2010 $14.50

Pinot Noir 2006 Very good colour; quite simply the best pinot noir on the market sub-$15; clear-cut cherry, strawberry varietal fruits and silky mouthfeel. Delicious drink now style. Screwcap. 13.5° alc. **Rating** 91 **To** 2010 $12.50

Petit Verdot 2006 Attractive red and black fruit flavours, the tannins particularly well-controlled; a civilised and harmonious version of a variety which can be aggressive. Screwcap. 13.5° alc. **Rating** 90 **To** 2012 $18

ÏÏÏÏ **Cellar Reserve Shiraz 2004** Good structure and weight, but for once Tony Murphy's hand faltered slightly with an overdose of American oak on both bouquet and palate. Screwcap. 14° alc. **Rating** 89 **To** 2013 $20

La Famiglia Nebbiolo 2005 Ah, that ever-elusive nebbiolo, best understood by thinking of it in pinot noir terms; light-coloured, spicy cherry fruits and gossamer tannins. Screwcap. 13.5° alc. **Rating** 88 **To** 2010 $14.50

La Famiglia Pinot Grigio 2007 As ever, Tony Murphy conjures up that little bit extra on the bouquet, although the palate does show the limitations on warm-grown pinot gris. Screwcap. 12.5° alc. **Rating** 88 **To** 2009 $14.50

Shiraz 2005 In typical Trentham style, fragrant and with fresh, light- to medium-bodied red fruit flavours; easy drinking, no forcing. Screwcap. 14.5° alc. **Rating** 88 **To** 2010 $15

Cabernet Sauvignon Merlot 2005 Tony Murphy gives that little bit extra to the lift of the wine; bright colour; fresh cassis and blackberry flavours; smooth and supple. Screwcap. 13.5° alc. **Rating** 88 **To** 2012 $14.50

Noble Taminga (375 ml) 2003 Botrytis is evident, as is richness and sweetness, but the wine definitely needed more acidity to lift it into higher points. Screwcap. 11° alc. **Rating** 88 **To** 2009 $12.50

Sauvignon Blanc 2007 While not particularly expressive in varietal terms, does have good texture and structure, fresh, crisp and minerally. Screwcap. 13° alc. **Rating** 87 **To** 2009 $12.50

Two Thirds Semillon Sauvignon Blanc 2007 Nicely balanced; almost inevitably lacks fruit depth and intensity, but has lively lemony flavour with ultra-low alcohol. Screwcap. 8.5° alc. **Rating** 87 **To** 2009 $12.50

Viognier 2006 Quite elegant and delicate, though varietal expression is slightly muted; does have length. Screwcap. 13.5° alc. **Rating** 87 **To** 2009 $18

La Famiglia Vermentino 2007 Tight, fresh, crisp lemon and herb aromas; a lively finish with good acidity, all helped by moderate alcohol. Screwcap. 11.5° alc. **Rating** 87 **To** 2009 $14.50

La Famiglia Moscato 2007 Intensely grapey and unashamedly sweet; 50% soda water, drink ice-cold on a hot summer day. Screwcap. 6° alc. **Rating** 87 **To** 2009 $12.50

Murphy's Lore Shiraz Cabernet 2006 Offers honest flavour; black and red fruits with a subliminal hint of sweetness; fair price. Screwcap. 13.5° alc. **Rating** 87 **To** 2009 $10

La Famiglia Nebbiolo 2004 No doubting the variety, nor, in a sense, its durability; savoury/spicy/earthy notes predominate, with little twists of sweet fruit. Screwcap. 12.5° alc. **Rating** 87 **To** 2011 $14.50

Trevelen Farm ★★★★

302 Weir Road, Cranbrook, WA 6321 **Region** Great Southern
T (08) 9826 1052 **F** (08) 9826 1209 **www.**trevelenfarmwines.com.au **Open** Fri–Mon 10–4.30, or by appt
Winemaker Harewood Estate (James Kellie) **Est.** 1993 **Cases** 2500
John and Katie Sprigg, together with their family, operate a 1300-ha wool, meat and grain-producing farm, run on environmental principles with sustainable agriculture at its heart. As a minor, but highly successful, diversification they established 5 ha of sauvignon blanc, riesling, chardonnay, cabernet sauvignon and merlot in 1993, adding 1.5 ha of shiraz in 2000. The quality of the wines is as consistent as the prices are modest, and visitors to the cellar door have the added attraction of both garden and forest walks, the latter among 130 ha of remnant bush home to many different orchids. Exports to Japan, Malaysia and Hong Kong.

ÏÏÏÏÏ **Riesling 2007** Strong mineral aromas, with nectarine and good flesh on the finish. Screwcap. 13° alc. **Rating** 90 **To** 2014 $18

Frankland Reserve Shiraz 2006 A lifted, spicy wine with good concentration and a fleshy mid-palate; quite long and smooth; good flavour. Screwcap. 14.5° alc. **Rating** 90 **To** 2015 $25

♟♟♟♟ **Katie's Kiss Soft Sweet Riesling 2007** As its name suggests, gently sweet, with good varietal definition and length. Screwcap. 10.9° alc. **Rating** 88 **To** 2014 $14

Trevor Jones/Kellermeister ★★★★★

Barossa Valley Highway, Lyndoch, SA 5351 **Region** Barossa Valley
T (08) 8524 4303 **F** (08) 8524 4880 **www.**kellermeister.com.au **Open** 7 days 9–6
Winemaker Trevor Jones, Matthew Reynolds **Est.** 1996 **Cases** 28 000
Trevor Jones is an industry veteran, with vast experience in handling fruit from the Barossa Valley, Eden Valley and the Adelaide Hills. His business operates on two levels: Kellermeister was founded in 1979 with the emphasis on low-cost traditional Barossa wine styles. In '96 he expanded the scope by introducing the ultra-premium Trevor Jones range, with a strong export focus. Exports to the US, France, Switzerland, Macau, Singapore, Malaysia and Japan.

♟♟♟♟♟ **Trevor Jones Reserve Wild Witch Barossa Valley Shiraz 2004** Excellent hue; a multi-dimensional wine in both flavour and texture wreathed in a gossamer web which holds everything in place. Black fruits, licorice, dark chocolate and mocha, the tannins ripe and perfectly balanced. The heaviest bottle in the world, but, oh for a screwcap. Cork. 14.8° alc. **Rating** 96 **To** 2024 $70
Trevor Jones Reserve Wild Witch Barossa Valley Shiraz 2001 Very good hue; aromatic blackberry and black cherry fruit; admirable intensity and length, with fine tannins and quality oak. Cork. 14° alc. **Rating** 95 **To** 2021 $50
Trevor Jones Reserve Wild Witch Barossa Valley Shiraz 2005 Deep, bright colour; very complex, with layered fruit, licorice, leather and chocolate; despite its weight and concentration, is supple and harmonious. Cork. 14.9° alc. **Rating** 94 **To** 2025 $62.50

♟♟♟♟♟ **Trevor Jones Dry Grown Barossa Shiraz 2005** Redolent of dark fruits and mocha, the wine has plenty of concentration, but lacks a little mid-palate vinosity. Screwcap. 14.6° alc. **Rating** 90 **To** 2018 $38.50

♟♟♟♟ **Trevor Jones Boots Barossa Grenache Merlot Cabernet 2006** Sweet-fruited grenache on the bouquet and palate, with a little savoury twist on the finish. Screwcap. 14.5° alc. **Rating** 87 **To** 2014 $16.50

Tuck's Ridge ★★★★★

37 Shoreham Road, Red Hill South, Vic 3937 **Region** Mornington Peninsula
T (03) 5989 8660 **F** (03) 5989 8579 **www.**tucksridge.com.au **Open** 7 days 11–5
Winemaker Peninsula Winemakers **Est.** 1985 **Cases** 4000
Tuck's Ridge has changed focus significantly since selling its large Red Hill vineyard. Estate plantings are now an eclectic mix of chardonnay (2 ha), pinot noir (1.2 ha) and albarino (0.7 ha), and contract grape purchases have been reduced. Quality, not quantity, is the key. Exports to the US, Hong Kong and Singapore.

♟♟♟♟♟ **Buckle Vineyard Chardonnay 2006** Has great purity, finesse, intensity and length, grapefruit and nectarine creating the movement, oak merely the vehicle; will be long-lived. Screwcap. 13.4° alc. **Rating** 96 **To** 2016 $60
Buckle Vineyard Pinot Noir 2006 Exceptional colour; a very powerful wine, with as much drive and velocity as any Central Otago pinot; satsuma plum and black cherry; very fine tannins run through the palate giving great structure; will be long-lived. Screwcap. 13.5° alc. **Rating** 96 **To** 2020 $60
Turramurra Vineyard Chardonnay 2006 Similar brilliant green-yellow to Buckle Vineyard Chardonnay; a very complex wine, profound and deep; wild yeast, barrel ferment, lees and some mlf (?) influence all sustained by melon, fig and nectarine fruit. Screwcap. 13.5° alc. **Rating** 94 **To** 2013 $60

Buckle Vineyard Pinot Noir 2005 Holding hue well; most attractive silk and velvet texture; delicious red fruit flavours, and a long finish. Screwcap. 13.5° alc. **Rating** 94 **To** 2012 $60

Mornington Peninsula Pinot Noir 2006 Very good colour; convincing texture and structure to the seductive mix of black and red berry fruits; an excellent back palate opening like the proverbial peacock's tail; long aftertaste. Screwcap. 13.6° alc. **Rating** 94 **To** 2015 $35

Hurley Vineyard Pinot Noir 2006 Dramatically lighter colour than Buckle Vineyard; fragrant and pure, with the tightness and acidity of many '04 red burgundies. A fascinating contrast in style, but doesn't quite get there. Perhaps time is the answer. Screwcap. 14° alc. **Rating** 92 **To** 2013 $60

Mornington Peninsula Chardonnay 2006 Clean and varietal, with good fruit weight; just a little one-dimensional, but clean and well made. **Rating** 88 **To** 2010 $29

Tulloch ★★★★★

'Glen Elgin', 638 De Beyers Road, Pokolbin, NSW 2321 **Region** Lower Hunter Valley **T** (02) 4998 7580 **F** (02) 4998 7226 **www**.tulloch.com.au **Open** 7 days 10–5
Winemaker Jay Tulloch, Monarch Winemaking Services, Jim Chato **Est.** 1895 **Cases** 40 000
The revival of the near-death Tulloch brand continues apace, production up from 30 000 cases. Angove's, the national distributor for the brand, has invested in the business, the first time the Angove family has taken a strategic holding in any business other than its own. Inglewood Vineyard (aka Two Rivers) also has a shareholding in the venture, and is the primary source of grapes for the brand. A lavish cellar door and function facility has opened, and Jay Tulloch is in overall control, with his own label, JYT Wines, also available at the cellar door. The return of the classic Dry Red and Private Bin Dry Red labels (only slightly rejigged) brings back memories of the great wines of the 1950s and '60s, and is a sign of the continuing resurgence of this brand. Exports to Belgium, Finland, Phillippines, Singapore and China.

EM Limited Release Chardonnay 2006 Bright green-yellow; elegant and restrained, but with excellent focus to the nectarine and white peach fruit; subtle oak; from the Two Rivers Vineyard. Screwcap. 13.5° alc. **Rating** 94 **To** 2011 $28

Pokolbin Dry Red Private Bin Shiraz 2006 A classy young Hunter shiraz with decades of development in front of it, still showing primary black fruits; good oak and tannin support for the long, intense palate. Screwcap. 13.5° alc. **Rating** 94 **To** 2026 $40

Limited Release Julia Semillon 2006 A classic young semillon taking the first few steps along an extended development pathway; lemon, grass and slate flavours; certain improvement. Screwcap. 10° alc. **Rating** 93 **To** 2016 $28

Cellar Door Release Hunter Valley Petit Verdot 2006 Usual deep colour; firm, concise blackcurrant and spice characters on both bouquet and palate; good structure; shades of the 1930 Wyndham Estate Cabernet Petit Verdot. Screwcap. 13° alc. **Rating** 90 **To** 2015 $22

Vineyard Selection Hunter Valley Verdelho 2007 Has better than average depth to the appealing fruit salad flavours and offsetting lemony acidity. Screwcap. 13° alc. **Rating** 90 **To** 2011 $20

Hector of Glen Elgin Shiraz 2004 Light- to medium-bodied; sweet plum and blackberry mixed with more earthy regional notes, and a touch of oak; still developing slowly. Screwcap. **Rating** 90 **To** 2014 $38

Pokolbin Dry Red Shiraz 2006 Attractive, lively and fresh black cherry and plum plus a touch of blackberry; good length and acidity; will develop regional character with age. Screwcap. 13.5° alc. **Rating** 90 **To** 2016 $25

Hunter Valley Semillon Sauvignon Blanc 2007 Hunter semillon with a twist of gooseberry and citrus; a bright, lively and fresh wine. Screwcap. 11.5° alc. **Rating** 89 **To** 2009 $16

Cabernet Sauvignon 2006 Light-bodied; fresh redcurrant fruit, slightly simple, but sensibly made and not forced to be what it is not. Screwcap. 13.5° alc. **Rating** 87 **To** 2011 $16

Turkey Flat ★★★★★

Bethany Road, Tanunda, SA 5352 **Region** Barossa Valley
T (08) 8563 2851 **F** (08) 8563 3610 **www**.turkeyflat.com.au **Open** 7 days 11–5
Winemaker Julie Campbell **Est.** 1990 **Cases** 25 000

The establishment date of Turkey Flat is given as 1990 but it might equally well have been 1870 (or thereabouts), when the Schulz family purchased the Turkey Flat vineyard, or 1847, when the vineyard was first planted to the very old shiraz which still grows there today alongside 8 ha of equally old grenache. Plantings have since expanded significantly, now (in total) comprising shiraz (24 ha), grenache (10.5 ha), cabernet sauvignon (4.7 ha), mataro (3.7 ha) marsanne (2.2 ha), viognier (1 ha), roussanne (0.6 ha) and dolcetto (0.5 ha). Exports to the UK, the US and other major markets.

🍷🍷🍷🍷🍷 **Barossa Valley Shiraz 2006** Dense deep purple-crimson; a sumptuously rich cascade of black fruits and some Christmas cake spices, yet miraculously retains elegance thanks to restraint in winemaking. Oh for a screwcap. Cork. 14.5° alc. **Rating** 96 **To** 2026 $45

Butchers Block Barossa Valley Marsanne Viognier 2005 Excellent texture and structure; a backbone of minerally acidity carries the alcohol with ease, and also the pear, apricot and green apple flavours. Has matured beautifully since tasted in Feb '06, still with years in front of it. Screwcap. 14.5° alc. **Rating** 94 **To** 2013 $22

Barossa Valley Rose 2007 Blush-pink; the complex base wine varieties pay dividends; while fresh and light, there are layers of strawberry, raspberry and cherry fruits; fruity rather than sweet. Screwcap. 13° alc. **Rating** 94 **To** 2009 $23

Butchers Block Barossa Valley Shiraz Grenache Mourvedre 2006 Fragrant and vibrant; while light- to medium-bodied, has pure raspberry and red cherry fruit running through the length of the palate without the cosmetic characters of many Barossa grenaches; 90-year-old vines. Screwcap. 14.5° alc. **Rating** 94 **To** 2014 $30

Barossa Valley Mourvedre 2006 Has far deeper colour than the Hewitson mourvedres; robust and powerful black fruits, with elements of the savoury/spicy/fairly sour tannins and flavour nuances. Will definitely repay 10+ years cellaring. Cork. 14.5° alc. **Rating** 94 **To** 2018 $35

Barossa Valley Sparkling Shiraz NV Rich, layered and concentrated black fruits; perfectly controlled dosage, and deserves as long as possible in bottle. Blend 3, disgorged Nov '06. Crown. 13° alc. **Rating** 94 **To** 2017 $40

🍷🍷🍷🍷½ **Barossa Valley Cabernet Sauvignon 2006** Deeply coloured; luscious blackcurrant and cassis; a strongly regional-accented structure and flavour; needs time to shed its puppy fat. Cork. 14.5° alc. **Rating** 93 **To** 2021 $40

Butchers Block Barossa Valley Marsanne Viognier 2007 Barrel ferment and maturation in French oak plus the blend give Rhône overtones, minerally notes giving the wine lightness. Screwcap. 13.5° alc. **Rating** 91 **To** 2013 $23

Barossa Valley Grenache 2006 Light, bright colour; fresh juicy berry fruit; serve slightly chilled on a summer's day for a great lunch red; enjoy for its freshness. Screwcap. 15° alc. **Rating** 91 **To** 2011 $27

🍷🍷🍷🍷 **Pedro Ximinez (375 ml) NV** Seemingly fairly youthful, albeit strong expressive, fruit meets spirit in an as-yet unresolved Indian arm wrestle. Cork. 17° alc. **Rating** 89 **To** 2009 $30

Turner's Crossing Vineyard ★★★★★

PO Box 103, Epsom, Vic 3551 **Region** Bendigo
T (03) 5448 8464 **F** (03) 5448 7150 **www**.turnerscrossing.com **Open** W'ends tel (03) 5944 4599
Winemaker Sergio Carlei **Est.** 2002 **Cases** 10 000

The name of this outstanding vineyard comes from local farmers crossing the Loddon River in the mid-to late 1800s on their way to the nearest town. The 40-ha vineyard was planted in 1999 by former corporate executive and lecturer in the business school at La Trobe University, Paul Jenkins. However, Jenkins' experience as a self-taught viticulturist dates back to 1985, when he established his first vineyard at Prospect Hill, planting all the vines himself. The grapes from both vineyards have gone to a who's who of winemakers in Central Victoria, but an increasing amount is being made under the Turner's Crossing label, not surprising given the exceptional quality of the wines. Phil Bennett and winemaker Sergio Carlei have joined Paul Jenkins as co-owners of the vineyard, with Sergio putting his money where his winemaking mouth is. Exports to the UK, the US, Canada, Singapore and Taiwan.

ŶŶŶŶŶ **Bendigo Shiraz Viognier 2006** Crimson-purple; a strikingly opulent wine, the 95% Shiraz/5% Viognier doing all the talking, with a rippling cascade of black fruits and almost powdery but persistent ripe tannins; maturation in older oak exactly the right call. Screwcap. 14.5° alc. **Rating** 95 **To** 2021 $26
The Cut Shiraz 2005 Powerful full-bodied wine, with an uncompromising thrust of black fruits, licorice and some spice; the tannins and oak are present, but largely incidental; demands time. Diam. **Rating** 94 **To** 2020 $75
Bendigo Cabernet Sauvignon 2005 Classy medium- to full-bodied cabernet, with a seamless marriage of blackcurrant fruit and earthy nuances, the texture excellent and the palate long. Diam. **Rating** 94 **To** 2018 $26

Twelve Acres

Nagambie-Rushworth Road, Bailieston, Vic 3608 **Region** Goulburn Valley
T (03) 5794 2020 **F** (03) 5794 2020 **Open** Thurs–Mon 10.30–5.30
Winemaker Peter Prygodicz, Jana Prygodicz **Est.** 1994 **Cases** 300
The property name comes from the fact that the original subdivision created a tiny 12-acre block in the midst of 1000-acre properties, giving rise to the local nickname of 'Bastard Block', less suited for a winery brand. When purchased in 1987, it was completely overgrown, and Peter and Jana Prygodicz have done all the work themselves, doing it the tough way without any mains power, relying on a generator and solar panels.

24 Karat Wines ★★★★

PO Box 165, Mosman Park, WA 6912 **Region** Margaret River
T (08) 9383 4242 **F** (08) 9383 4502 **www.24karat.com.au Open** Not
Winemaker Claudia Lloyd, Bruce Dukes (Contract) **Est.** 1998 **Cases** 1000
In 1979 Dr Graham Lloyd, a qualified metallurgist, established his now world-leading metallurgical services company Ammtec, with particular expertise in gold mining. By 1997 he was ready for a new challenge, and as he and his family had a long association with the Augusta area, the idea of a vineyard was natural. He found an 82-ha property in Twenty Four Road, Karridale, and acquired the property in 1997. He then did what many fail to do: in 1998 signed a 15-year contract with Brookland Valley for sale of the grapes, but including a right to retain 10% for his own label. It has 46 ha spread across the major varieties of the region, importantly including 8.7 ha of six clones (including the outstanding French Dijon clones) of chardonnay all planted in individual blocks. The vineyard is managed with biodynamic principles, and the driving force is to procure quality-based bonus grape payments from Brookland Valley. Graham and Penny Lloyd's younger daughter Claudia is a winemaker with both Australian and overseas experience, and the expectation is that she will have a long-term involvement with the business.

ŶŶŶŶŶ **Margaret River Sauvignon Blanc Semillon 2006** Lighter, but tighter and brighter than the '07, with flavours more in a grassy/lemony spectrum; clean finish. Screwcap. 12.5° alc. **Rating** 90 **To** 2009 $17

ŶŶŶŶ **Margaret River Sauvignon Blanc Semillon 2007** Sauvignon blanc is dominant, with soft, tropical stone fruit aromas and flavours, and the impression of sweetness on the back-palate. Screwcap. 13° alc. **Rating** 89 **To** 2009 $18

Margaret River Chardonnay 2006 A well-balanced, light- to medium-bodied wine with nectarine, white peach and well-integrated oak. Screwcap. 13° alc. **Rating** 89 **To** 2012 $29

Two Hands Wines ★★★★★

Neldner Road, Marananga, SA 5355 **Region** Various
T (08) 8562 4566 **F** (08) 8562 4744 **www**.twohandswines.com **Open** 7 days 10–5
Winemaker Matthew Wenk **Est.** 2000 **Cases** 20 000
The 'hands' in question are those of SA businessmen Michael Twelftree and Richard Mintz, Twelftree in particular having extensive experience in marketing Australian wine in the US (for other producers). On the principle that if big is good, bigger is better, and biggest is best, the style of the wines has been aimed fairly and squarely at the palate of Robert Parker Jr and the *Wine Spectator's* Harvey Steiman. Grapes are sourced from the Barossa Valley, McLaren Vale, Clare Valley, Langhorne Creek and Padthaway. The retention of cork closures, the emphasis on sweet fruit, and the soft tannin structure, all signify the precise marketing strategy of what is a very successful business. Exports to the UK, the US and other major markets.

ΨΨΨΨΨ **Max's Garden Heathcote Shiraz 2006** More aromatic and with red fruits joining the blackberry; a fine, gently savoury palate, with little or no sweetness to contend with. Cork. 14.5° alc. **Rating** 95 **To** 2020 $60
Ares Barossa Valley Shiraz 2005 Has the explosive impact of the late Maria Callas, jam-packed with juicy black fruits and the hot breath of alcohol; take it on her/its terms, or not at all. Cork. 15.4° alc. **Rating** 94 **To** 2029 $125
Gnarly Dudes Barossa Valley Shiraz 2006 Strong blackberry and prune fruit, with plenty of attitude; there are some appealing savoury spicy notes which add to the length of the wine. Screwcap. 15.1° alc. **Rating** 94 **To** 2016 $27
Bella's Garden Barossa Valley Shiraz 2006 More opulent and fleshy than Gnarly Dudes, leaving no corner of the mouth untouched; the fruit, oak and tannins carry the alcohol. Cork. 15.2° alc. **Rating** 94 **To** 2021 $60
Sophie's Garden Padthaway Shiraz 2006 The lightest of the premium range in terms of colour and body, but does have appealing spicy elements; is not unduly sweet, and has good length. Cork. 14.5° alc. **Rating** 94 **To** 2016 $60
Zippy's Block Barossa Valley Shiraz 2006 The extra $30 partially goes to the cost of the world's heaviest wine bottle, and partially to the atomic power of the alcohol. For they who have everything. Cork. 16.5° alc. **Rating** 94 **To** 2021 $90
Aphrodite Barossa Valley Cabernet Sauvignon 2005 Lusciously rich and thick, very ripe blackcurrant confit topped with creamy oak and a drizzle of chocolate/mocha; a carefully engineered style. High-quality cork. 15.8° alc. **Rating** 94 **To** 2015 $125

ΨΨΨΨΨ **Bad Impersonator Barossa Valley Shiraz 2006** A generous, bold, medium- to full-bodied wine with rich, ripe fruit tempered by French oak and integrated, ripe tannins. Screwcap. 14.5° alc. **Rating** 93 **To** 2021 $45
Samantha's Garden Clare Valley Shiraz 2006 Very concentrated, dense black fruits and dark chocolate; the alcohol warmth posing a question, but the wine just gets away with it. Cork. 15.7° alc. **Rating** 93 **To** 2021 $60
Harry & Edward's Garden Langhorne Creek Shiraz 2006 Radically different aroma and flavour profile, with spice, leaf and mint added to the red and black fruits on a relatively firm palate. Cork. 14.8° alc. **Rating** 93 **To** 2016 $60
Lily's Garden McLaren Vale Shiraz 2006 Has more texture and definition than the Angel's Share, the common feature being the sweet fruit (plus oak, of course). Cork. 14.8° alc. **Rating** 92 **To** 2016 $60
Angel's Share McLaren Vale Shiraz 2006 Filled to the brim with ripe, sweet fruit, sweet oak and soft tannins; a lot of skilled winemaking lies behind this wine. Screwcap. 14.8° alc. **Rating** 90 **To** 2020 $27

♈♈♈♈ The Bull and The Bear Barossa Valley Shiraz Cabernet 2006 Well named, for there is much stamping of the ground with this effusive, high-toned and largely unsettled wine, needing time for the combatants to resolve their differences. Screwcap. 15.4° alc. **Rating** 89 **To** 2016 $45

Brave Faces Barossa Valley Shiraz Grenache 2006 Shiraz provides the structure and the blackberry fruits, allowing the grenache to add its note of sweet red fruit; nicely composed. Screwcap. 15° alc. **Rating** 89 **To** 2014 $27

Two Rivers

2 Yarrawa Road, Denman, NSW 2328 (postal) **Region** Upper Hunter Valley **T** (02) 6547 2556 **F** (02) 6547 2546 **www**.tworiverswines.com.au **Open** 7 days 11–4 **Winemaker** First Creek Winemaking Services **Est.** 1988 **Cases** 15 000

A significant part of the viticultural scene in the Upper Hunter Valley, with over 160 ha of vineyards established, involving a total investment of around $7 million. Part of the fruit is sold under long-term contracts, and part is made for the expanding winemaking and marketing operations of Two Rivers, the chief brand of Inglewood Vineyards. The emphasis is on Chardonnay and Semillon, and the wines have been medal winners at the Hunter Valley Wine Show. It is also a partner in the Tulloch business, together with the Tulloch and Angove families, and supplies much of the grapes for the Tulloch label. A contemporary cellar door has recently opened, adding significantly to the appeal of the Upper Hunter Valley as a wine-tourist destination.

♈♈♈♈♈ Reserve Hunter Valley Chardonnay 2005 Medium-bodied; smooth, long melon, stone fruit and peach flavours; good use of quality oak. Top gold, Hunter Valley Wine Show '06. Screwcap. 13.5° alc. **Rating** 94 **To** 2013 $18

♈♈♈♈♈ Reserve Hunter Valley Semillon 2005 Bright green-straw; still delicate and relatively unevolved, but the balance and length are good; will reward cellaring. Screwcap. 11° alc. **Rating** 90 **To** 2015 $18

♈♈♈♈ Stone's Throw Hunter Valley Semillon 2006 Clean, fresh and lively; lemon citrus flavours run through the length of the palate and finish. Screwcap. 11° alc. **Rating** 89 **To** 2013 $14

Reserve Hunter Valley Shiraz 2005 Bright, limpid colour; a fresh, light- to medium-bodied palate with red and black cherry fruit, balanced oak and tannins; will gain regionality with bottle age. Screwcap. 14° alc. **Rating** 89 **To** 2015 $22

Twofold

142 Beulah Road, Norwood, SA 5067 (postal) **Region** Clare Valley/Heathcote **T** 0418 544 001 **Open** Not **Winemaker** Neil Pike, Sergio Carlei (Contract) **Est.** 2002 **Cases** 800

This is the venture of brothers Nick and Tim Stock, both of whom have had a varied background in the wine industry (primarily at the marketing end, whether as sommeliers or in wholesale) and both of whom have excellent palates. Their contacts have allowed them to source a single-vineyard riesling from Sevenhill in the Clare Valley, and a single-vineyard shiraz from Heathcote, both under ongoing arrangements. As one might expect, the quality of the wines is excellent.

♈♈♈♈♈ Clare Valley Riesling 2007 A highly fragrant bouquet, especially for the vintage, ranging through citrus and a gruner-veltliner-like touch of pepper/spice, the palate zesty, with good minerality and a clear, dry finish. Screwcap. **Rate** 95 **To** 2013, $24

Heathcote Shiraz 2005 An elegant, medium-bodied version of Heathcote shiraz; has savoury aspects to the plum and blackberry fruit, with cedary French oak sustaining the back-palate and finish. Screwcap. **Rate** 94 **To** 2015 $38

Tyrrell's   ★★★★★

Broke Road, Pokolbin, NSW 2321 **Region** Lower Hunter Valley
T (02) 4993 7000 **F** (02) 4998 7723 **www**.tyrrells.com.au **Open** 7 days 8.30–5
Winemaker Andrew Spinaze, Mark Richardson **Est.** 1858 **Cases** 500 000
One of the most successful family wineries, a humble operation for the first 110 years of its
life which grew out of all recognition over the past 40 years. In 2003 it cleared the decks by
selling its Long Flat range of wines for an 8-figure sum, allowing it to focus on its premium,
super-premium and ultra-premium wines: Vat 1 Semillon is one of the most dominant wines
in the Australian show system, and Vat 47 Chardonnay is one of the pace-setters for this
variety. It has an awesome portfolio of single-vineyard Semillons released when 5–6 years
old. Exports to all major markets.

ᵠᵠᵠᵠᵠ **Single Vineyard HVD Hunter Semillon 2001** Classic Semillon, both in
terms of its maker and region; starting to pick up honey and lemon, toast in the
background; a lovely cleansing finish; excellent length. Cork. 10.7° alc. **Rating** 96
To 2016 $45

Museum Release Vat 1 Hunter Semillon 2002 Pale straw-green; a very fresh
and tingling wine, with exceptional thrust to the juicy lemony palate and finish;
good cork can do a good job. **Rating** 96 **To** 2017 $50

Winemaker's Selection Vat 9 Hunter Shiraz 2006 Deeper colour, richer
and rounder in the mouth, with blackberry joining the red fruits of the 4 Acres;
doesn't require explanation, just a lovely wine; vines 36 to 127 years old. Cork.
13.5° alc. **Rating** 96 **To** 2026 $60

Single Vineyard Stevens Hunter Semillon 2003 Has startling intensity
and depth to the fruit; an ultra-powerful style; some vines planted 1863. Cork.
10.9° alc. **Rating** 95 **To** 2013 $30

Vat 1 Hunter Semillon 2000 When the cork permits, is brilliantly crisp, fresh
and lively, with an incredibly long finish; trophy Best White Wine National Wine
Show '06. 11.1° alc. **Rating** 95 **To** 2015 $52

Rufus Stone Heathcote Shiraz 2006 An elegant, medium-bodied palate, with
wonderful black cherry and spice fruit, perfectly matched by seamless tannins and
oak. Great finesse. Gold, National Wine Show '07. Screwcap. 14.8° alc. **Rating** 95
To 2021 $23.95

Double Barrel 24 McLaren Vale Shiraz 2006 Serious stuff indeed; plenty of
toasty oak, and the core of fruit is dark and brooding, but not at all heavy; chewy
and thick on the palate, with terrific length, and the many layers of the wine to
open on the palate over a long period of time. Diam. **Rating** 95 **To** 2020 $90

Single Vineyard Stevens Hunter Semillon 2004 A complex, slightly tangy
bouquet is reflected by the lively, crisp and lingering palate; very different style to
HVD, should live longer. Screwcap. **Rating** 94 **To** 2017 $30

Single Vineyard HVD Hunter Semillon 2004 Rich and full-flavoured, typical
of the HVD Vineyard, the generosity of the fruit balanced and tied up with a bow
of acidity. Screwcap. **Rating** 94 **To** 2014 $35

Single Vineyard HVD Hunter Semillon 2003 Lightly browned toast aromas
starting to develop; crammed to the gills with almost sweet lemon juice on the
palate; no need to wait. Cork. 11° alc. **Rating** 94 **To** 2013 $46.95

Single Vineyard Belford Chardonnay 2005 An altogether superior
chardonnay from the Hunter Valley; very fresh, with excellent acidity underpinning
the stone fruit flavours; integrated French oak. Screwcap. 13.5° alc. **Rating** 94
To 2012 $30

Vat 47 Hunter Chardonnay 2006 Pale bright straw-green; elegant wine,
with masterful integration and balance of melon/nectarine fruit and oak;
totally harmonious. Screwcap. **Rating** 94 **To** 2013 $50

Single Vineyard Stevens Shiraz 2004 Bright colour; deceptively light-
to medium-bodied, still with fresh red and black fruits, regional character yet to
make its appearance; sweet tannins. Screwcap. 13.5° alc. **Rating** 94 **To** 2029 $30

Winemaker's Selection 4 Acres Hunter Valley Shiraz 2006 Light, brilliantly clear colour; light-bodied and fresh; predominantly red fruits; has not been tricked up in any way; only understood in context of wines such as the 1872 Craiglee Hermitage at even lower alcohol; 127-year-old vines. Screwcap. 12.4° alc. **Rating** 94 **To** 2036 $45

Vat 8 Hunter Mudgee Shiraz Cabernet 2004 Has the elegance Tyrrell's achieved with all its '04 reds; supple and smooth blackberry and cassis fruit, with minimal oak interference. Cork. 13.5° alc. **Rating** 94 **To** 2019 $52

ΨΨΨΨΨ **Lost Block Semillon 2007** Has the extra degree of fruit flavour typical of '07, but without sacrificing finesse; fine, long, lemony fruit, then crisp acidity. Great bargain. Screwcap. 11° alc. **Rating** 93 **To** 2012 $13

Single Vineyard Stevens Shiraz 2005 Medium-bodied and strongly regional; just when you think the wine lacks enough fruit, the thrust and drive of the palate tells you otherwise. Screwcap. **Rating** 91 **To** 2015 $30

Old Winery Hunter Valley Semillon 2007 Full-flavoured, moving towards some stone fruit characters, but is not phenolic or flabby; gold Melbourne Wine Show '07. Undoubted bargain. Screwcap. 10.5° alc. **Rating** 90 **To** 2012 $12

Rufus Stone Heathcote Shiraz 2005 Medium-bodied, elegant wine; blackberry, spice and dark chocolate (figuratively) borrowed from McLaren Vale; superfine tannins supported by French oak. Screwcap. 14.7° alc. **Rating** 90 **To** 2018 $20

Double Barrel 24 McLaren Vale Shiraz 2005 Certainly shows a year in barrel (used?) and then another year in new oak; the winemakers thought the fruit justified the expense; I am not convinced. Cork. 14.5° alc. **Rating** 90 **To** 2015 $99

ΨΨΨΨ **Rufus Stone McLaren Vale Shiraz 2005** The high alcohol does show through in comparison to the Heathcote version and doesn't deliver extra flavour; expected chocolate and vanilla characters. Screwcap. 15.8° alc. **Rating** 89 **To** 2015 $20

Fordwich Hunter Valley Verdelho 2007 Has some appealing juicy fruit flavours with a twist of lemon; clean finish. Screwcap. 13.5° alc. **Rating** 88 **To** 2010 $20

Uleybury Wines ★★★☆

Uley Road, Uleybury, SA 5114 **Region** Adelaide Zone
T (08) 8280 7335 **F** (08) 8280 7925 **www.**uleybury.com **Open** 7 days 10–5
Winemaker Tony Pipicella **Est.** 1995 **Cases** 15 500
The Pipicella family – headed by Italian-born Tony – has established nearly 45 ha of vineyard near One Tree Hill in the Mt Lofty Ranges; 10 varieties have been planted, with more planned. Daughter Natalie Pipicella, who has completed the wine marketing course at the University of SA, was responsible for overseeing the design of labels, the promotion and advertising, and the creation of the website. Exports to the UK, Canada, Denmark, China, Singapore and Japan.

ΨΨΨΨ **Basket Press Cervo 2005** Typical Uleybury; massively dense and ripe; I can't cope with the alcohol, others can. Cork. 15.5° alc. **Rating** 88 **To** 2015 $25

Basket Press Sangiovese 2005 Good colour; savoury, very spicy red fruits and savoury, lemony tannins. Screwcap. 14° alc. **Rating** 87 **To** 2009 $15.50

Ulithorne

The Middleton Mill, 29 Mill Terrace, Middleton, SA 5213 **Region** McLaren Vale
T (08) 8554 2411 **F** (08) 8554 2433 **www.**ulithorne.com.au **Open** Fri–Sun 8 am–midnight or by appt
Winemaker Brian Light, Natasha Mooney (Contract) **Est.** 1971 **Cases** 800
The changes have continued apace for Ulithorne. Sam Harrison and partner Rose Kentish have sold the vineyard (but with the right to select and buy part of the production each vintage) and have purchased the Middleton Mill on the south coast of the Fleurieu Peninsula.

It is now their home, and Sam has resumed full-time painting while Rose is running a wine bar in the Middelton Mill with Ulithorne and other local wines, beers and platters of regional food on offer. Exports to the UK, the US and other major markets.

🍷🍷🍷🍷🍷 **Paternus McLaren Vale Cabernet Shiraz 2006** Dense colour; intense, but not extractive, simply reflecting the low-yielding vines; a mix of red and black fruits, touches of chocolate and oak. Screwcap. 14.5° alc. **Rating** 94 **To** 2021 $35

🍷🍷🍷🍷🍷 **Frux Frugis McLaren Vale Shiraz 2006** Some colour development; rich soft black fruits with some caramel elements; even palate feel and flow with some fruit sweetness ex alcohol. Screwcap. **Rating** 91 **To** 2016 $45

 # Umamu Estate

PO Box 1269, Margaret River, WA 6285 **Region** Margaret River
T (08) 9757 5058 **F** (08) 9757 5058 **www**.umamuestate.com **Open** Not
Winemaker Bruce Dukes (Contract) **Est.** 2005 **Cases** 7500
Chief executive Charmaine Saw explains 'my life has been a journey towards Umamu. An upbringing in both eastern and western cultures, graduating in natural science, training as a chef, combined with a passion for the arts, and experience as a management consultant have all contributed to my building the business creatively yet professionally.' The palindrome Umamu, says Saw, is inspired by balance and contentment. In practical terms this means an organic approach to viticulture and a deep respect for the terroir. When Charmaine Saw purchased the property in 2004 the substantial plantings dated back to '78, with cabernet sauvignon (7 ha), shiraz (4.1 ha), chardonnay (3.5 ha), merlot (2 ha), semillon and sauvignon blanc (1.5 ha each) and cabernet franc (0.7 ha), the maiden vintage under the Umamu label following in '05.

🍷🍷🍷🍷🍷 **Margaret River Chardonnay 2006** Highly fragrant nectarine and grapefruit aromas and flavours; strongly fruit-driven, but not simple; excellent length. Screwcap. 13.5° alc. **Rating** 94 **To** 2014 $48

🍷🍷🍷🍷 **Margaret River Cabernet Merlot 2005** The fresh, savoury, slightly minty aspects are heightened by early picking, but not at the cost of structure: overall, well-handled. Screwcap. 13° alc. **Rating** 89 **To** 2013 $25
Margaret River Semillon Sauvignon Blanc 2005 Some light oak infusion has softened the fruit line to make an attractive, early-drinking style. Screwcap. 13° alc. **Rating** 87 **To** 2009 $22
Margaret River Shiraz 2005 Light-bodied bright, lively and fresh red fruits, just reaching the threshold of ripeness; probably best enjoyed now as one step up from a rose. Screwcap. 13° alc. **Rating** 87 **To** 2009 $25

Unavale Vineyard

10 Badger Corner Road, Flinders Island, Tas 7255 **Region** Northern Tasmania
T (03) 6359 3632 **F** (03) 6359 3632 **Open** By appt
Winemaker Andrew Hickinbotham (Contract) **Est.** 1999 **Cases** 200
Roger and Bev Watson have pioneered viticulture on Flinders Island, planting 1 ha of pinot noir, and 0.5 ha each of chardonnay, sauvignon blanc, riesling and cabernet sauvignon. The windswept environment has slowed the development of the vines, and will always keep yields low, but production will rise over the next few years. Two quite lovely wines from 2006 will hopefully point the way for the future given the struggle the Watsons have to grow and protect the grapes. No samples received, the rating is that of last year.

Undercliff

Yango Creek Road, Wollombi, NSW 2325 **Region** Lower Hunter Valley
T (02) 4998 3322 **F** (02) 4998 3322 **www**.undercliff.com.au **Open** 7 days 10–5, or by appt
Winemaker David Carrick **Est.** 1990 **Cases** NA

Peter and Jane Hamshere are the new owners of Undercliff, but it continues to function as both winery cellar door and art gallery. The wines, produced from 2.5 ha of estate vineyards, have won a number of awards in recent years at the Hunter Valley Wine Show and the Hunter Valley Small Winemakers Show.

ŢŢŢŢ **Semillon 2002** Green-gold; still has a firm and crisp structure, the fruit slow to develop; not sure whence now. Cork. 11.2° alc. **Rating** 88 **To** 2012 $18

Upper Reach Vineyard ★★★☆

77 Memorial Avenue, Baskerville, WA 6056 **Region** Swan Valley
T (08) 9296 0078 **F** (08) 9296 0278 **www.**upperreach.com.au **Open** 7 days 11–5
Winemaker Derek Pearse **Est.** 1996 **Cases** 5000
This 10-ha property on the banks of the upper reaches of the Swan River was purchased by Laura Rowe and Derek Pearse in 1996. The original vineyard was 4 ha of 12-year-old chardonnay, which has been expanded by 1.5 ha of shiraz, 1 ha of cabernet sauvignon, 0.5 ha each of verdelho and merlot and 0.2 ha of graciano. All wines are estate-grown. The fish on the label, incidentally, is black bream, which can be found in the pools of the Swan River during the summer months. Exports to the UK.

ŢŢŢŢ **Reserve Swan Valley Chardonnay 2006** Maximises the potential of Swan Valley chardonnay, with astute barrel ferment oak handling; stone fruit and spice, the finish just a little green. Quality packaging. Screwcap. 13.5° alc. **Rating** 89 **To** 2012 $25
Reserve Swan Valley Chardonnay 2007 Rich and ripe, with dried figs and peaches on the bouquet; plenty of oak and nutty fruit on the palate; generous and full. Screwcap. 13.5° alc. **Rating** 89 **To** 2011 $25
Verdelho 2007 Pronounced fruit salad and banana varietal aromas; plenty of weight and flavour in a similar flavour spectrum; soft finish, easy access. Screwcap. 13° alc. **Rating** 88 **To** 2009 $17

Vale Wines ★★★★

2914 Frankston-Flinders Road, Balnarring, Vic 3926 **Region** Mornington Peninsula
T (03) 5983 1521 **F** (03) 5983 1942 **www.**valewines.com.au **Open** 7 days 11–5
Winemaker John Vale **Est.** 1991 **Cases** 400
After a lifetime in the retail liquor industry, John and Susan Vale took a busman's retirement by purchasing a grazing property at Balnarring in 1991. They planted a little under 0.5 ha of cabernet sauvignon (since grafted over to gewurztraminer), and John Vale undertook what he describes as 'formal winemaking training' before building a 20-tonne winery in 1997. In 2000 they extended the plantings with 1.4 ha of tempranillo, riesling and durif, seeking to move outside the square. In the meantime the wine range has been extended by the purchase of chardonnay and pinot grigio from local growers.

ŢŢŢŢŢ **Chardonnay 2005** A quite developed and toasty bouquet, with fresh fruit coming to the fore on the palate; has abundant flavour, and ready to drink now. ProCork. 12.7° alc. **Rating** 90 **To** 2010 $25
Pinot Grigio 2005 A rich style wine, with plenty of flavour and depth; expected development, but still quite fresh and crisp on the finish. ProCork. 12.6° alc. **Rating** 90 **To** 2010 $18

Valhalla Wines ★★★

163 All Saints Road, Wahgunyah, Vic 3687 **Region** Rutherglen
T (02) 6033 1438 **F** (02) 6033 1728 **www.**valhallawines.com.au **Open** Fri–Sun & public hols 10–5, or by appt
Winemaker Anton Therkildsen **Est.** 2001 **Cases** 2000
This is the highly focused venture of Anton Therkildsen and wife Antoinette Del Popolo. They acquired the property in 2001, and in '02 began the planting of shiraz (1.6 ha) and durif (0.9 ha). They intend to expand the vineyard with marsanne, viognier, grenache, mourvedre

and riesling, reflecting their primary interest in the wines of the Rhône Valley. For the time being, they are relying on contract grown grapes to develop these wine styles. The straw bale winery was built in 2007, underlining their desire for sustainable viticulture and biodiversity, with minimal use of sprays and annual planting of cover crops between the rows. A worm farm and the composting of grape skins and stalks completes the picture.

ΨΨΨΨ **Rutherglen Shiraz 2005** Very ripe prune and confit plum flavours with elements of dead fruit and some alcohol sweetening; certainly not short on flavour. Cork. 15° alc. **Rating** 87 To 2014 $25

Vardon Lane/Kanta

22–26 Vardon Lane, Adelaide, SA 5000 (postal) **Region** Adelaide Hills
T (08) 8232 5300 **F** (08) 8232 2055 **Open** Not
Winemaker Egon Muller, Stephen Pannell **Est.** 2005 **Cases** 1400
This is the ultimate virtual winery, a joint venture between famed Mosel-Saar-Ruwer winemaker (and proprietor) Egon Muller, Michael Andrewartha from Adelaide's East End Cellars, and Armenian-born vigneron and owner of La Corte from Italy's Puglia region, Vahe Keushguerian. A three-year search for the perfect riesling site ended almost where the journey began, at the Shaw & Smith Adelaide Hills vineyard. Muller arrived on the day of picking to oversee the whole production, carried out at Shaw & Smith with input from Steve Pannell and Shaw & Smith's winemaker, Daryl Catlin. The grapes were crushed and cold-soaked for up to 16 hours, the juice settled without enzyme and kept at 12°C until spontaneous fermentation began. Small wonder that the wine is so different from other Australian Rieslings, and even more different from the gloriously fine wines which Muller makes at home. Exports to the UK, the US and Germany.

ΨΨΨΨΨ **Kanta Egon Muller Adelaide Hills Riesling 2007** All about texture not flavour; late-picked but dry, with green apple and herb flavours, is outside normal Australian parameters. Wild yeast and extended lees contact. Screwcap. 13.4° alc. **Rating** 90 To 2012 $31

Vasse Felix

Cnr Caves Road/Harmans Road South, Cowaramup, WA 6284 **Region** Margaret River
T (08) 9756 5000 **F** (08) 9755 5425 **www**.vassefelix.com.au **Open** 7 days 10–5
Winemaker Virginia Willcock **Est.** 1967 **Cases** 150 000
Vasse Felix was the first winery to be built in the Margaret River. Owned and operated by the Holmes à Court family since 1987, the winery and vineyard have been carefully developed. Recent acquisitions of a neighbouring vineyard and property within the Willyabrup subregion will ensure the dynamic Virginia Willcock will have the ability to craft wines of the highest calibre for many years to come. Exports to all major markets.

ΨΨΨΨΨ **Heytesbury Margaret River Chardonnay 2006** A superbly balanced and composed wine; has all the depth and richness of Margaret River at its best, with succulent nectarine and melon fruit; balanced acidity and oak on the long palate and finish. Screwcap. 13° alc. **Rating** 96 To 2020 $45
Margaret River Classic Dry White 2007 Clean and bright; has intense grassy, citrus and mineral flavours, the palate driving through to a long finish; a wine with velocity. Screwcap. 12° alc. **Rating** 95 To 2012 $20
Margaret River Semillon 2007 Constructed around lemon, herb and grass, backed by firm acidity on a bone-dry finish; long palate. Screwcap. 12.5° alc. **Rating** 94 To 2015 $25
Margaret River Sauvignon Blanc Semillon 2007 Fresh cut grass aromas, with abundant citrus fruits on the palate, and a touch of nettle on the finish; good concentration. 12.5° alc. **Rating** 94 To 2012 $25
Margaret River Chardonnay 2006 Aromatic fruit with a hint of oak on the bouquet; abundant nectarine, melon and grapefruit flavour, with a seamless infusion of gentle oak; skilful use of partial barrel ferment and mlf. Screwcap. 13° alc. **Rating** 94 To 2015 $25

Vasse River Wines

c/- Post Office, Carbunup, WA 6280 **Region** Margaret River
T (08) 9755 1111 **F** (08) 9755 1011 **www**.vasseriver.com.au **Open** Not
Winemaker Sharna Kowalczuk, Jane Dunkley **Est.** 1993 **Cases** 7000
This is a major and rapidly growing business owned by the Credaro family; 90 ha of
chardonnay, semillon, verdelho, sauvignon blanc, cabernet sauvignon, merlot and shiraz have
been planted on the typical gravelly red loam soils of the region. The wines are released
under two labels: Vasse River for the premium, and Carbunup Estate (not to be confused
with Carbunup Crest) for the lower-priced varietals. Exports to the US and Canada.

ᵀᵀᵀᵀᵀ **Beach Head Margaret River Semillon Sauvignon Blanc 2007** Has the life,
crispness and drive missing from most eastern states '07s; the 75/25 blend works
perfectly, lengthening the palate and brightening the finish. Value plus. Screwcap.
13.2° alc. **Rating** 92 **To** 2010 $14.50
Margaret River Chardonnay 2006 Bright green-yellow; a superfine bouquet
and palate, with white peach and melon within a minerally wedding ring, oak
sotto voce. Excellent value. Screwcap. 13.2° alc. **Rating** 92 **To** 2015 $18.30
Margaret River Chardonnay 2007 More complex than Beach Head, with
a wider array of stone fruits and a judicious input of barrel ferment giving good
texture and length. Value. Screwcap. 13.6° alc. **Rating** 91 **To** 2012 $18.30

ᵀᵀᵀᵀ **Beach Head Margaret River Chardonnay 2007** Good chardonnay at
the price, thanks largely to the benison of the Margaret River; straightforward
nectarine fruit and good balance. Screwcap. 13.5° alc. **Rating** 87 **To** 2010 $14.50
Margaret River Cabernet Merlot 2005 An overall savoury, briary cast to
the wine; fine texture, but needed more berry fruit. Screwcap. **Rating** 87
To 2012 $18.50

Velo Wines

755 West Tamar Highway, Legana, Tas 7277 **Region** Northern Tasmania
T (03) 6330 3677 **F** (03) 6330 3098 **Open** 7 days 10–5
Winemaker Micheal Wilson, Winemaking Tasmania (Julian Alcorso) **Est.** 1966 **Cases** 1800
The story behind Velo Wines is fascinating, wheels within wheels. The 0.9 ha of cabernet
sauvignon and 0.5 ha of pinot noir of the Legana Vineyard were planted in 1966 by Graham
Wiltshire, legitimately described as one of the three great pioneers of the Tasmanian wine
industry. Fifteen years ago Micheal and Mary Wilson returned to Tasmania after living in
Italy and France for a decade. Micheal was an Olympic cyclist, following which he joined
the professional ranks, racing in all of the major European events. Imbued with a love of
wine and food, they spent 'seven long hard years in the restaurant game'. Somehow, Micheal
found time to become a qualified viticulturist, and was vineyard manager for Moorilla
Estate based at St Matthias. Wife Mary spent five years working in wine wholesaling for
leading distributors. In 2001 they purchased the Legana Vineyard planted so long ago, and
have painstakingly rehabilitated the 40-year-old vines. They have built a small winery where
Micheal makes the red wines, Julian Alcorso makes the white wines, sourced in part from
0.6 ha of estate riesling and from grapes grown on the East Coast.

ᵀᵀᵀᵀᵀ **Wooded Chardonnay 2006** A rich, generously fruited wine, with white and
yellow peach fruit; good barrel ferment notes, and a clean, fresh finish. Screwcap.
13.5° alc. **Rating** 90 **To** 2014 $25
Pinot Noir 2006 Medium-bodied; a focused style, with dark fruits and some
stemmy notes coming through on a savoury finish; overall complexity. Screwcap.
13.5° alc. **Rating** 90 **To** 2013 $25

ᵀᵀᵀᵀ **Pinot Gris 2007** Pink blush; very ripe fruit aromas and flavours and a flick of
residual sugar on the finish; crowd pleaser (for some of the crowd). **Rating** 89
To 2009 $25

Vercoe's Vineyard

PO Box 145, Cessnock, NSW 2325 **Region** Lower Hunter Valley
T 0410 541 663 **F** (02) 6574 7352 **www**.vercoesvineyard.com.au **Open** Not
Winemaker Monarch Winemaking Services **Est.** 2002 **Cases** 700
In the mid-1960s a young John Vercoe toyed with the idea of establishing a wine bar, but it took another 30 years for his interest in wine to translate itself into Vercoe's Vineyard. Together with wife Elizabeth, and adult children, the property on the evocatively-named Sweetwater Ridge was purchased in 1999. After three years of soil preparation, 1.8 ha of verdelho was planted in 2002, followed by merlot (1.3 ha) and semillon and chardonnay (0.8 ha each).

TTTTT **Hunter Valley Verdelho 2006** Good length and intensity; typical tropical fruit salad flavours, lifted from the ruck by good lemony acidity. Value, and will benefit from time in bottle. Screwcap. 13.5° alc. **Rating** 90 **To** 2012 $11

Veronique

PO Box 599, Angaston, SA 5353 **Region** Barossa Valley
T (08) 8565 3214 **Open** Not
Winemaker Domenic Torzi **Est.** 2004 **Cases** 1500
Peter Manning, general manager of Angas Park Fruits, and wife Vicki, moved to Mt McKenzie in the 1990s. His wine consumption soon focused on Barossa shiraz, and he quickly became a close drinking partner of all things shiraz with Domenic Torzi. By 2004 the Mannings decided it was high time to produce a Barossa shiraz of their own, and, with the help of Torzi, sourced grapes from three outstanding blocks. The vineyards also include mataro and grenache (thoroughly excusable in the context) and sauvignon blanc.

TTTTT **Regions Barossa Shiraz 2006** Concentrated black fruits with a strong spicy/savoury streak inclining the wine to the dry side rather than luscious; attractive alternative style. Lyndoch/Greenock/Eden Valley. Screwcap. 14.5° alc. **Rating** 90 **To** 2015 $19

Victory Point Wines ★★★★☆

121 Rosalie Street, Shenton Park, WA 6008 (postal) **Region** Margaret River
T (08) 9381 5765 **F** (08) 9388 2449 **www**.victorypointwines.com **Open** By appt
Winemaker Keith Mugford, Ian Bell (Contract) **Est.** 1997 **Cases** 2500
Judith and Gary Berson (the latter a partner in the Perth office of a national law firm) have set their aims high. With viticultural advice from Keith and Clare Mugford of Moss Wood, they have established their 12-ha vineyard without irrigation, emulating those of the Margaret River pioneers (including Moss Wood). The plantings comprise 4.47 ha chardonnay, the remainder the Bordeaux varieties, with cabernet sauvignon (6 ha), merlot (2 ha), cabernet franc (1.5 ha) and malbec and petit verdot (0.3 ha each).

TTTTT **Margaret River Chardonnay 2007** The combination of Burgundy clones 76, 95, 96 and 277 plus the Mendoza clone is a potent one; highly aromatic and pure chardonnay has absorbed the French oak, and the wine has a prodigiously long palate. Screwcap. 13.5° alc. **Rating** 96 **To** 2020 $40

TTTT **Margaret River Cabernet Sauvignon Cabernet Franc Malbec Petit Verdot 2005** The Bordeaux varietal background is clear enough, but the tannins are somewhat dry and abrasive; needed more fining, and it is not certain time will be enough. Screwcap. 13.3° alc. **Rating** 88 **To** 2015 $33

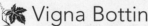 Vigna Bottin

14 Clifton Court, McLaren Vale, SA 5171 (postal) **Region** McLaren Vale
T (08) 8323 8126 **F** (08) 8323 0026 **Open** Not
Winemaker Paolo Bottin **Est.** 1998 **Cases** 400

The Bottin family migrated to Australia in 1954 from Treviso in northern Italy, where they were grapegrowers. The family began growing grapes in McLaren Vale in 1970, focusing on mainstream varieties for sale to wineries in the region. When son Paolo and wife Maria made a trip back to Italy in 1998, they were inspired to do more, and, says Paolo, 'My love for barbera and sangiovese was sealed during a vintage in Pavia. I came straight home to plant both varieties in our family plot. My father was finally happy!' They now trade under the catchy phrase 'Italian Vines, Australian Wines', and in the short time they have been producing their Italian varietals, have won a gold medal, two silvers and a bronze at the Australian Alternative Wine Show.

ΨΨΨΨΨ **McLaren Vale Sangiovese 2005** Plenty of depth and power; spicy, savoury cherry fruit, with abundant structure and length. Screwcap. 14.5° alc. **Rating** 90 To 2014 $22

McLaren Vale Barbera 2005 Very good hue; shows what can be achieved, with a savoury blackberry, dark cherry and anise melange of flavours; good length. Screwcap. 14.3° alc. **Rating** 90 **To** 2015 $22

ΨΨΨΨ **McLaren Vale Sangiovese 2004** Distinctly savoury with the cherry fruit starting to fade somewhat; nonetheless, a distinctive wine with good structure. Gold medal, Alternative Varieties Wine Show '06. Screwcap. 15.4° alc. **Rating** 88 To 2009 $22

McLaren Vale Barbera 2004 A lemony twist to the fruit, itself in a dark spectrum; touches of cedar and cigar box. Screwcap. 14.3° alc. **Rating** 87 To 2009 $22

Viking Wines   ★★★★☆

RSD 108 Seppeltsfield Road, Marananga, SA 5355 **Region** Barossa Valley
T (08) 8562 3842 **F** (08) 8562 4266 **www**.vikingwines.com **Open** 7 days 11–5
Winemaker Rolf Binder, Kym Teusner (Contract) **Est.** 1995 **Cases** 1500
With 50-year-old, dry-grown and near-organic vineyards yielding of 1–1.5 tonnes per acre, Viking Wines was 'discovered' by Robert Parker with inevitable consequences for the price of its top Shiraz. There are 5 ha of shiraz and 3 ha of cabernet sauvignon. The Odin's Honour wines (made by sister company Todd-Viking Wines) also come from old (20–100 years) dry-grown vines around Marananga and Greenock. Exports to the US, the UK, Singapore and France.

ΨΨΨΨΨ **Grand Barossa Valley Shiraz 2005** Deep colour; concentrated but refined and delicious blackberry fruit with notes of dark chocolate, spice and mocha; excellent length; from 50-year-old estate vines. Diam. 14° alc. **Rating** 94 **To** 2018

Villa Caterina Wines   ★★★

4 Wattletree Road, Drumcondra, Geelong, Vic 3215 (postal) **Region** Geelong
T (03) 5278 2847 **F** (03) 5278 4884 **Open** Not
Winemaker Ernesto Vellucci **Est.** 2001 **Cases** 300
Ernesto Vellucci was born in Italy where his parents brought him up in the traditional and cultural way of Italian winemaking. He is qualified as an industrial chemist, with years of working with laboratory equipment and techniques. He offers the only wine laboratory services in Geelong with microbiological testing facilities and gas chromatography, directed to the detection of brettanomyces/dekkera yeasts. His small production is made from purchased grapes.

 Vincognita   ★★★★☆

PO Box 778, McLaren Vale, SA 5171 **Region** Southern Fleurieu
T (08) 8370 5737 **F** (08) 8556 9113 **www**.vincognita.com.au **Open** Not
Winemaker Peter Belej, Carrie Belej (Consultant) **Est.** 1999 **Cases** 900

Vigneron-owner Peter Belej moved from Ukraine as a boy with his family, and grew up on the family vineyards at Gol Gol in NSW. After 40 years he decided to move to the Fleurieu Peninsula. Here he has planted 40 ha on the Nangkita Vineyard, with 14 ha of shiraz, 8 ha each of cabernet sauvignon, merlot and sauvignon blanc, 2 ha of viognier and one row of zinfandel. Daughter Carolyn (Carrie) Belej is a winemaker with Foster's, but directs the winemaking at Vincognita on a consultant basis. The sheer consistency of the quality of the wines is as impressive as the sub-$20 price tags, but in March 2008 the Nangkita Vineyard was listed for sale (www.wineryforsale.com.au).

ŶŶŶŶŶ **Nangkita Vineyard Madeleine's Fleurieu Viognier 2006** An unusually elegant expression of viognier; has apricot and stone fruit flavours without any hint of oily phenolics. Two trophies, McLaren Vale Wine Show '06. Screwcap. 13° alc. **Rating** 94 **To** 2010 $19

ŶŶŶŶŶ **Nangkita Vineyard Fleurieu Shiraz 2005** Has similar sweet fruit to the McLaren Vale Shiraz, but the overall style is quite different, finer, spicier and medium-bodied, with a particularly long finish. Screwcap. 14.5° alc. **Rating** 93 **To** 2020 $19

Nangkita Vineyard Fleurieu Shiraz 2006 Attractive medium-bodied palate with a distinctive silky texture to the black cherry and plum fruit; good oak and tannin management in a flavoursome but elegant wine. Value. Screwcap. 14° alc. **Rating** 93 **To** 2018 $19

McLaren Vale Shiraz 2006 From very old vines at Willunga; quite aromatic and luscious, with blackberry, raspberry, dark chocolate and mocha oak; balanced tannins dry the finish nicely. Screwcap. 14.5° alc. **Rating** 92 **To** 2020 $19

Nangkita Vineyards Fleurieu Cabernet Sauvignon 2005 Good hue; an elegant, medium-bodied wine, with delicious cassis and blackcurrant fruit; fine tannins, integrated oak. Screwcap. 14.5° alc. **Rating** 92 **To** 2020 $19

Nangkita Vineyard Madeleine's Fleurieu Viognier 2007 Picked when very ripe with shrivel in the grapes, yet shows no phenolic heaviness, just clear varietal fruit and good mouthfeel. Gold medal, Sydney Wine Show '08 a surprise, but exceptional value. Screwcap. 14° alc. **Rating** 90 **To** 2012 $19

McLaren Vale Shiraz 2005 Dense colour; very ripe fruit with confit flavours on the full-bodied palate; lashings of chocolate, mocha and vanilla. Screwcap. 14.5° alc. **Rating** 90 **To** 2020 $19

Bullseye Fleurieu McLaren Vale Shiraz 2004 Medium-bodied, but has quite intense black fruits, with notes of spice and dark chocolate; persistent but ripe tannins on a long finish. Screwcap. 14.5° alc. **Rating** 90 **To** 2014 $14.90

Vinden Estate ★★★

17 Gillards Road, Pokolbin, NSW 2320 **Region** Lower Hunter Valley
T (02) 4998 7410 **F** (02) 4998 7175 **www**.vindenestate.com.au **Open** 7 days 10–5
Winemaker Guy Vinden, John Baruzzi (Consultant) **Est.** 1998 **Cases** 4000
Sandra and Guy Vinden have a beautiful home and cellar door, with landscaped gardens, and 3.6 ha of merlot, shiraz and alicante bouschet, with the Brokenback mountain range in the distance. The winemaking is done onsite, using estate-grown red grapes; semillon and chardonnay are purchased from other growers. The reds are open-fermented, hand-plunged and basket-pressed.

ŶŶŶŶ **Estate Reserve Hunter Valley Verdelho 2007** Mainstream varietal fruit salad flavours with good intensity and length. Screwcap. 13.5° alc. **Rating** 88 **To** 2010 $23

Vinea Marson

PO Box 222, Heathcote, Vic 3523 **Region** Heathcote
T (03) 5433 2768 **F** (03) 5433 2768 **www**.vineamarson.com **Open** Not
Winemaker Mario Marson **Est.** 2000 **Cases** 1350

Owner-winemaker Mario Marson spent many years as the winemaker viticulturist with the late Dr John Middleton at the celebrated Mount Mary. He purchased the Vinea Marson property in 1999, on the eastern slopes of the Mt Camel Range, and in 2000 planted syrah and viognier, plus Italian varieties, sangiovese, nebbiolo and barbera. Since leaving Mount Mary, he has undertaken vintage work at Isole e Olena in Tuscany, worked as winemaker at Jasper Hill vineyard, and as consultant and winemaker for Stefani Estate. Exports to Sweden and the Maldives.

005 **Syrah 2006** Deep crimson; super-rich and concentrated, with ripples of flavours and layers of texture; blackberry, licorice, spice, pepper and plum are joined by exemplary oak and tannins. Cork. 14.5° alc. **Rating** 96 **To** 2021 $39
Rose 2006 Slightly more colour and flavour than the '07, both tasted at the same time; here small berry fruits and spices do the talking; no sign of tiredness; points deliberately generous. Diam. 13.5° alc. **Rating** 94 **To** 2009 $20
Sangiovese 2006 Light bright colour; typical of the best sangiovese a la Australia; sour cherry fruit with an enveloping web of fine tannins, the fruit coming again on the finish. Cork. 14° alc. **Rating** 94 **To** 2012 $33
Sangiovese 2005 The wine is slightly more savoury than the '06, but otherwise a twin; there is no question about the drinkability of the wines, but they do demand food; cherries come again on the finish. Cork. 13.5° alc. **Rating** 94 **To** 2011 $33

004 **Nebbiolo 2006** Almost painfully pure, grown and made without any concessions to other red wines; the flavour structure does have (if obscure) links to pinot, but the pleasure factor has no links; has great length and persistence. Cork. 13.5° alc. **Rating** 93 **To** 2016 $39
Syrah 2005 Retains crimson hue; super-elegant, medium-bodied wine, with focus, line, length and balance all in place. Cork. 14° alc. **Rating** 93 **To** 2015 $39
Rose 2007 Pale salmon; a thinking man's rose, with great texture and structure; light red fruits and rose petals, with perfect acidity. Diam. 13.5° alc. **Rating** 92 **To** 2010 $20

004 **Nebbiolo 2005** The more complex of the Nebbiolos, but by far the hardest to love. Others will have to enjoy this one. Cork. 14° alc. **Rating** 89 **To** 2012 $39

Vinecrest   ★★★★☆

Cnr Barossa Valley Way/Vine Vale Road, Tanunda, SA 5352 **Region** Barossa Valley
T (08) 8563 0111 **F** (08) 8563 0444 **www.**vinecrest.com.au **Open** 7 days 11–5
Winemaker Mos Kaesler **Est.** 1999 **Cases** 10 000
The Mader family has a long connection with the Barossa Valley. Ian Mader is a fifth-generation descendant of Gottfried and Maria Mader, who immigrated to the Barossa Valley in the 1840s, and his wife, Suzanne, is the daughter of a former long-serving vineyard manager for Penfolds. In 1969 Ian and Suzanne established their Sandy Ridge Vineyard, and more recently the Turrung Vineyard (together a total of 30 ha), a few mins from Tanunda. Having been grapegrowers for 30 years, in 1999 they established Vinecrest, using a small portion of the production from their vineyards. Vinecrest was purchased by the Indian drinks conglomerate Champagne Indage in March 2008. No samples received, the rating is that of last year. Exports to the US, Japan, Malaysia, Hong Kong and Singapore.

Vineyard 28   ★★★

270 Bagieau Road, Harvey, WA 6220 **Region** Geographe
T (08) 9733 5605 **F** (08) 9733 4500 **Open** 7 days 10–5
Winemaker Contract **Est.** 1998 **Cases** 1000
In 1997 Mark and Pippa Cumbers decided to leave Melbourne (where they had worked and become wine lovers) and return to Mark's home state of WA. They chose a 4-ha property on coastal tuart sands, and planted cabernet sauvignon (0.8 ha) and nebbiolo, sauvignon blanc and chenin blanc (0.4 ha each). Nebbiolo was planted as a point of difference, but has so far proved as difficult to come to terms with here as elsewhere. Plantings have since increased further with muscat a petit grains and arneis.

♟♟♟♟   **Geographe Nebbiolo 2006** An interesting wine; that no-compromise, direct line of nebbiolo, with similar line and texture to cool-grown pinot, and red cherry flavours. Screwcap. **Rating** 87 **To** 2014 $18

Vinifera Wines   ★★★

194 Henry Lawson Drive, Mudgee, NSW 2850 **Region** Mudgee
T (02) 6372 2461 **F** (02) 6372 6731 **www.**viniferawines.com.au **Open** 7 days 10–5.30
Winemaker Tony McKendry, Frank Newman **Est.** 1997 **Cases** 2000
Having lived in Mudgee for 15 years, Tony McKendry (a regional medical superintendent) and wife Debbie succumbed to the lure; they planted their small (1.5-ha) vineyard in 1995. In Debbie's words, 'Tony, in his spare two minutes per day, also decided to start Wine Science at CSU in 1992.' She continues, 'His trying to live 27 hours per day (plus our four kids!) fell to pieces when he was involved in a severe car smash in 1997. Two months in hospital stopped full-time medical work, and the winery dreams became inevitable.' Financial compensation finally came through and the small winery was built. The vineyard is now 11 ha, including 2 ha of tempranillo and 1 ha of graciano.

♟♟♟♟   **Mudgee Graciano 2007** Light-bodied, but neatly balanced parcel of spices and earths, tannins helping shape both the flavour and structure. Screwcap. 13° alc. **Rating** 89 **To** 2014 $27
Limited Release Semillon 2006 Has a firm structure, with the first hints of honey and toast starting to emerge, and more to come. Screwcap. 11° alc. **Rating** 88 **To** 2013 $22

Vinrock

23 George Street, Thebarton, SA 5031 (postal) **Region** McLaren Vale
T (08) 8408 8955 **F** (08) 8408 8966 **www.**vinrock.com **Open** Not
Winemaker Serafino (Scott Rawlinson) **Est.** 2004 **Cases** 5000
Owners Don Luca, Marco Iannetti and Anthony De Pizzol all have a background in the wine industry, none more than Don Luca, a former board member of Tatachilla. He also planted the 30-ha Luca Vineyard in 1999. The majority of the grapes are sold, but since 2004 limited quantities of wine have been made from the best blocks in the vineyard. Exports to Malaysia and Singapore.

♟♟♟♟♟   **McLaren Vale Shiraz 2006** Has supple mouthfilling juicy black fruits and a coating of dark chocolate; fine, ripe tannins; well made. Cork. 14.5° alc. **Rating** 90 **To** 2014 $24
McLaren Vale Grenache 2006 Less concentrated than most from McLaren Vale, but has delicious fruit on the faintly spicy medium-bodied palate; light tannins clean up the finish. Screwcap. 14.5° alc. **Rating** 90 **To** 2012 $21

♟♟♟♟   **McLaren Vale Cabernet Sauvignon 2006** Neatly assembled and balanced wine, with quite luscious redcurrant and blackcurrant fruit; the tannins are balanced, but the American oak jars. Cork. 14.5° alc. **Rating** 89 **To** 2014 $24

Vintara

Fraser Road, Rutherglen, Vic 3685 **Region** Rutherglen
T 0447 327 517 **F** (02) 6032 7098 **www.**vintara.com.au **Open** 7 days 10–5
Winemaker Michael Murtagh **Est.** 2005 **Cases** 1500
Michael Murtagh (and wife Lisa) are long-term industry professionals, Michael adding 150 years of family ownership in Rutherglen for good measure. His great-grandfather arrived from Ireland 150 years ago and named his property Tara, a mystical hill in Ireland which was the meeting place of kings. The view from the 47-ha vineyards owned by Michael and Lisa prompted the name Vintara, which is a veritable patchwork quilt of 15 varieties; only shiraz (13.6 ha) is over 5 ha, many 1 ha or less. Most of the grapes are sold, but Vintara makes Riesling, Viognier, Sangiovese, Tempranillo, Shiraz, Petit Verdot, Merlot and Durif.

🍷🍷🍷🍷 **Petit Verdot 2006** Fresh black fruits on the mid-palate, then powerful tannins, typical of the variety, on the finish. Screwcap. 13.8° alc. **Rating** 88 **To** 2021 $20
Merlot 2006 Deep colour; abundant sweet, dark fruit flavours and some sweetness on the finish; all pleasant, but no vestige of varietal character. Screwcap. 12.9° alc. **Rating** 87 **To** 2009 $19

Vintner's Nest Wines ★★★★☆

692 Rowella Road, Rowella, Tas 7270 **Region** Northern Tasmania
T (03) 6394 7179 **F** (03) 6394 7206 **Open** Sept–May 7 days 11–5
Winemaker Chris Beanlands, Kristen Cush **Est.** 1996 **Cases** 650
Chris and Judy Beanlands have established a typical Tasmanian micro-vineyard with 0.75 ha each of chardonnay and pinot noir, and 0.25 ha each of cabernet sauvignon and merlot. The chardonnay was planted in 1996, the pinot noir and cabernet in the next year and the merlot in 2000. No samples received, the rating is that of last year.

Virgara Wines ★★★

Lot 11 Heaslip Road, Angle Vale, SA 5117 **Region** Adelaide Plains
T (08) 8284 7688 **F** (08) 8284 7666 **www**.virgarawines.com.au **Open** Mon–Fri 9–5, w'ends & public hols 10–5
Winemaker Tony Carapetis **Est.** 2001 **Cases** 10 000
In 1962 the Virgara family, with father Michael, mother Maria and 10 children ranging from one to 18 years old, migrated to Australia from southern Italy. Through the hard work so typical of many such families, in due course they became market gardeners on land purchased at Angle Vale (1967) and in the early '90s acquired an existing vineyard in Angle Vale. This included 25 ha of shiraz, the plantings since expanded to over 68 ha of alicante, cabernet sauvignon, grenache, malbec, merlot, riesling, sangiovese, and sauvignon blanc. In 2001 the Virgara brothers purchased the former Barossa Valley Estates winery, but used it only for storage and maturation, as the first wine (made in '02 from 40-year-old shiraz) was made by the Glaetzer family. The death of Domenic Virgara in a road accident led to the employment of former Palandri winemaker (and, before that, Tahbilk winemaker) Tony Carapetis, and the full commissioning of the winery. Exports to Canada, China, Thailand and Vietnam.

🍷🍷🍷🍷 **Adelaide Plains Cabernet Sauvignon 2006** Very ripe black fruits in a somewhat rustic full-bodied mode, but no technical issues; great with a barbecued butterfly-cut leg of lamb. Screwcap. 14.5° alc. **Rating** 87 **To** 2012 $18

Virgin Block Vineyard ★★★

Caves Road, Yallingup, WA 6282 **Region** Margaret River
T (08) 9755 2394 **F** (08) 9755 2357 **www**.virginblock.com **Open** 7 days 10–5
Winemaker Bruce Dukes, Anne-Coralie Fleury (Contract) **Est.** 1995 **Cases** 3000
Virgin Block has been established on a 30-ha property, 3 km from the Indian Ocean, and is surrounded by large Jarrah and Marri forests.

🍷🍷🍷🍷 **Sauvignon Blanc Semillon 2007** Neatly balanced mix of herb and riper tropical fruit flavours; has particularly good length. Screwcap. 13° alc. **Rating** 89 **To** 2010 $18

Virgin Hills ★★★★☆

Salisbury Road, Lauriston via Kyneton, Vic 3444 **Region** Macedon Ranges
T 1800 777 444 **www**.virginhills.com.au **Open** Not
Winemaker James Campkin **Est.** 1968 **Cases** 1500
Changes of ownership of Virgin Hills have confused a number of people, myself included. It is now owned by Michael Hope, but is a standalone business totally separate from Hope Estate in the Hunter Valley. The brand continues, as does the distinctive white and gold label. The change is the splitting of the varieties, previously blended, into two wines. Exports to the UK, the US, Canada, Norway and Sweden.

ŸŸŸŸŸ **Cabernet Sauvignon 2005** Quite savoury, with a bright core of cassis and minerals; full-bodied, pure and very long finish. Cork. 14.5° alc. **Rating** 93 To 2016 $38
Shiraz Malbec 2005 Quite savoury and pure; dark-fruited, with a mineral core running through to the finish; fine and firm. A long future. Cork. 13.5° alc. **Rating** 92 To 2016 $38

🍇 Voice of the Vine   ★★★★

155 Coolart Road, Tuerong, Vic 3915 **Region** Mornington Peninsula
T (03) 5979 7771 **F** (03) 5979 8977 **www**.voiceofthevine.com.au **Open** First Sat of month 11–4
Winemaker Mac Forbes, Jeremy Magyar (Contract) **Est.** 2000 **Cases** 3300
Terry and Merylyn Winters have invested a substantial amount of money in their 33-ha property on the Coolart Hills, with views over Westernport Bay to French Island, Tortoise Head, Phillip Island, Gippsland and Mt Baw Baw. As well as over 14 ha of vines (predominantly five clones of pinot noir on a variety of spacings and trellises) they have established extensive botanical gardens incorporating three lakes, a bushland area and adjoining wetlands. The lagoons serve a practical purpose as well as an aesthetic one, providing irrigation water from over 30 megalitres of storage. Winemaking and viticulture have been developed by consultants with an interesting blend of youth and broad-based experience in Australia and Europe.

ŸŸŸŸŸ **Acappella Pinot Noir 2006** Strong colour; has considerable thrust to the spiced plum fruit and crisp acidity along with a touch of forest; will develop. Screwcap. 13.5° alc. **Rating** 93 To 2014 $55
Chardonnay 2005 An understated, light-bodied style, with no strident oak to worry about; gentle melon and nectarine fruit. Diam. 13° alc. **Rating** 90 To 2010 $33
Pinot Noir 2006 A somewhat reduced bouquet, but a powerful palate with plum, black cherry and spice running through to a long finish; aerate when serving. Screwcap. 13.5° alc. **Rating** 90 To 2012 $29.50

ŸŸŸŸ **Riesling 2005** A definite impact from barrel ferment on the bouquet and palate, perhaps augmented by bottle development; crisp minerally acidity again dominant. Cork. 12° alc. **Rating** 89 To 2013 $25.50
Riesling 2006 An interesting style, with some textural benefit from partial barrel ferment in aged barriques, although lingering minerally acidity is the main driver on the palate. Diam. 11° alc. **Rating** 89 To 2014 $25.50
Sauvignon Blanc 2005 Has held on and developed well; a complex mix of tropical fruit, lychee and gooseberry; good finish. Diam. 12.5° alc. **Rating** 89 To 2009 $26.50
Chardonnay 2006 Barrel ferment oak tends to sit on top of the fruit on both the bouquet and palate; lively, zesty, citrus-tinged fruit does help the long finish. Screwcap. 13° alc. **Rating** 89 To 2012 $33
Acappella Sauvignon Blanc 2006 Some bottle development evident; plenty of ripe fruit on the mid-palate, but then an abrupt finish. Diam. 12° alc. **Rating** 88 To 2009 $29.50
Acappella Pinot Noir 2005 A strongly stemmy/foresty/briary/earthy wine, which needed more ripeness to the mid-palate fruit. Cork. 13° alc. **Rating** 88 To 2011 $49.50

Voyager Estate   ★★★★★

Lot 1 Stevens Road, Margaret River, WA 6285 **Region** Margaret River
T (08) 9757 6354 **F** (08) 9757 6494 **www**.voyagerestate.com.au **Open** 7 days 10–5
Winemaker Cliff Royle **Est.** 1978 **Cases** 35 000
Voyager Estate has come a long way since it was acquired by Michael Wright (of the mining family) in 1991. It now has a high-quality 103-ha vineyard which means it can select the best parcels of fruit for its own label, and supply surplus (but high-quality) wine to others.

The Cape Dutch-style tasting room and vast rose garden are a major tourist attraction. For inexplicable reasons, the portfolio of wines did not arrive for this edition, but Voyager's track record means I have no hesitation in maintaining its top rating. Exports to the UK, the US and other major markets.

♥♥♥♥♥ Margaret River Sauvignon Blanc Semillon 2007 A fragrant, delicate bouquet ranging through tropical to passionfruit to citrus; a long and fine palate, fruit speaking all the way through to the finish. Screwcap. 12.8° alc. **Rating** 95 **To** 2011 $24

♥♥♥♥ Margaret River Chenin Blanc 2007 Lifted by a hint of residual sweetness, though this is in turn balanced by acidity; ripe custard apple and peach mix; clever winemaking. Screwcap. 13° alc. **Rating** 89 **To** 2009 $20

Wagga Wagga Winery   NR
RMB 427 Oura Road, Wagga Wagga, NSW 2650 **Region** Riverina
T (02) 6922 1221 **F** (02) 6922 1101 **www**.waggawaggawinery.com.au **Open** Wed–Sun 11–late
Winemaker Peter Fitzpatrick **Est.** 1987 **Cases** 2000
Planting of the 5.5-ha vineyard, 200 m from the Murrumbidgee River and just 15 mins from Wagga Wagga, began in 1987, with further plantings in the '90s and the current decade. Chardonnay, riesling, shiraz, cabernet sauvignon, cabernet franc and touriga have been established.

Walden Woods Farm   NR
469 Donald Road, Armidale, NSW 2350 (postal) **Region** New England
T (02) 6772 8966 **Open** Not
Winemaker Scott Wright (Contract), Doug Hume **Est.** 2001 **Cases** 65
Doug Hume and Nadine McCrea have established 0.3 ha of close-planted pinot gris, using certified organic growing and management techniques from the outset. The necessarily small production sells out quickly by word of mouth, phone and mail orders.

Wallaroo Wines   ★★★
PO Box 272, Hall, ACT 2618 **Region** Canberra District
T (02) 6230 2831 **F** (02) 6230 2830 **www**.wallaroowines.com.au **Open** Not
Winemaker Roger Harris (Contract) **Est.** 1996 **Cases** 800
Leading international reporters and journalists Carolyn Jack and Philip Williams purchased the property on which they have subsequently established Wallaroo Wines in 1996, after a five-year sojourn in Japan led to a desire for space. They retained leading viticultural consultant Di Davidson to evaluate the property and recommend varieties, and she quickly encouraged them to proceed. In 1997 they planted 2 ha of riesling, 4 ha of cabernet sauvignon and 6 ha of shiraz, leading to the first vintage in 2000. Much of the production has been done by remote control, as they lived in the UK from 2000–05, Philip as the European correspondent for the ABC covering the Iraq war, the Madrid bombing and the Beslan siege, all making the return to Wallaroo and its elegant house especially rewarding.

♥♥♥♥ Canberra District Riesling 2007 Quite an exotic style, with florals and spice playing a prominent role; the palate is quite rich, with generous mouthfeel and fruit on the finish. Screwcap. 12.5° alc. **Rating** 89 **To** 2009 $25

Wandin Valley Estate
Wilderness Road, Lovedale, NSW 2320 **Region** Lower Hunter Valley
T (02) 4930 7317 **F** (02) 4930 7814 **www**.wandinvalley.com.au **Open** 7 days 10–5
Winemaker Matthew Burton **Est.** 1973 **Cases** 5000

After 15 years in the wine and hospitality business, owners Phillipa and James Davern have decided to offer the property as a going concern, with vineyard, winery, accommodation, function centre, cricket ground and restaurant in the package, aiming to keep its skilled staff as part of the business, and ensure that all existing contracts are ongoing. Ironically, being offered for sale just as the overall quality has increased. Exports to Denmark and Japan.

🍷🍷🍷🍷🍷 **Bridie's Reserve Hunter Valley Shiraz 2005** An elegant wine, with very considerable length to the finely structured black cherry, plum and blackberry flavours of the palate; fine, savoury tannins; low alcohol commendable. Cork. 13° alc. **Rating** 94 **To** 2020 $35

🍷🍷🍷🍷🍷 **Reserve Hunter Valley Chardonnay 2006** A complex bouquet leads into a long, well-balanced and focused palate; stone fruit with touches of cashew and cream provide enticing mouthfeel and a supple finish. Screwcap. 13.5° alc. **Rating** 92 **To** 2011 $30
Shiraz 2005 A savoury, earthy, leathery regional style, showing more colour development than Bridie's Reserve; a good savoury finish with fine, ripe tannins. Screwcap. 14° alc. **Rating** 90 **To** 2015 $18

🍷🍷🍷🍷 **Hunter Valley Verdelho 2007** Classic fruit salad flavours, but with more length and intensity than usual in the first months of its life; drink while it retains its zesty youth. Screwcap. 14° alc. **Rating** 89 **To** 2009 $18
Pavilion Hunter Valley Rose 2007 Brilliant purple-puce; has an extra degree of complexity and flavour without the penalty of phenolics, and a balanced, relatively dry finish; 15% barrel-fermented in old American oak. Screwcap. 14° alc. **Rating** 89 **To** 2009 $20

Wangolina Station ★★★

Cnr Southern Ports Highway/Limestone Coast Road, Kingston SE, SA 5275
Region Mount Benson
T (08) 8768 6187 **F** (08) 8768 6149 **www**.wangolina.com.au **Open** 7 days 10–5
Winemaker Anita Goode **Est.** 2001 **Cases** 3000
Four generations of the Goode family have been graziers at Wangolina Station, but now Anita Goode has broken with tradition by becoming a vigneron. She has planted a total of 9 ha of vines, with a little over 3 ha of shiraz, 2.6 ha of sauvignon blanc and 1.6 ha of cabernet sauvignon.

Wanted Man ★★★★☆

c/- Jinks Creek Wines, Tonimbuk Road, Tonimbuk, Vic 3815 (postal) **Region** Heathcote
T (03) 5629 8502 **F** (03) 5629 8551 **www**.wantedman.com.au **Open** Not
Winemaker Andrew Clarke, Peter Bartholomew **Est.** 1996 **Cases** 2000
The Wanted Man vineyard was planted in 1996, and has been managed by Andrew Clarke since 2000, producing Jinks Creek's Heathcote Shiraz. That wine was sufficiently impressive to lead Andrew Clarke and partner Peter Bartholomew (a Melbourne restaurateur) to purchase the vineyard in 2006, and give it its own identity. It is a substantial vineyard, with 6 ha of shiraz, 1.5 ha each of merlot and marsanne, 1 ha of viognier and 0.3 ha of dolcetto. The quirky Ned Kelly label is the work of Mark Knight, cartoonist for the *Herald Sun*. Exports to the UK, the US and other major markets.

🍷🍷🍷🍷🍷 **Premium Shiraz 2006** Vibrant hue; a strong personality of red and dark fruits, and a core of earth and minerals; builds across the palate; is distinctly tannic and chewy, but at the same time harmonious with the fruit on offer. Diam. 14.5° alc. **Rating** 94 **To** 2020 $70

🍷🍷🍷🍷🍷 **Marsanne Viognier 2007** Clean, crisp and quite reserved; a fine example of a Rhône Valley blend; the palate takes time to build; surprisingly long, and manages to hold interest for the entire journey. Screwcap. 13.5° alc. **Rating** 92 **To** 2014 $35

ℙℙℙℙ   **Shiraz 2006** Deep purple-red; smooth blackberry and black cherry fruit, but a curious lack of texture and structure. Screwcap. 13.6° alc. **Rating** 89 **To** 2014 $30

Wantirna Estate

Bushy Park Lane, Wantirna South, Vic 3152 **Region** Yarra Valley
T (03) 9801 2367 **F** (03) 9887 0225 **www**.wantirnaestate.com.au **Open** Not
Winemaker Maryann Egan, Reg Egan **Est.** 1963 **Cases** 800
Situated well within the boundaries of the Melbourne metropolitan area, Wantirna Estate is an outpost of the Yarra Valley. It was one of the first established in the rebirth of the valley. Maryann Egan has decided it is time to come in from the cold, and have the wines rated (father Reg had declined), self-evidently a very sensible decision. Exports to Hong Kong, Singapore and Japan.

ℙℙℙℙℙ   **Lily Pinot Noir 2006** Fragrant and delicate spice and red cherry fruit; just when you think there is not enough there, the considerable length and aftertaste tell otherwise; easy to miss. Diam. 14° alc. **Rating** 94 **To** 2012 $55
Amelia Cabernet Sauvignon Merlot 2005 Fragrant berry aromas; a supple and smooth palate, with perfectly ripened cassis and blackcurrant fruit; fine tannins and quality oak. Diam. 14.2° alc. **Rating** 94 **To** 2017 $50

ℙℙℙℙℙ   **Isabella Chardonnay 2006** Bright green-straw; simply doesn't show its alcohol, rather a delicate restraint; firm, citrus/grapefruit/nutty palate, with subtle barrel ferment inputs. Diam. 14° alc. **Rating** 93 **To** 2014 $50

ℙℙℙℙ   **Hannah Cabernet Franc Merlot 2005** Light- to medium-bodied; aromatic leaf and cedar notes, then a spicy red fruit palate; Chinon style. Diam. 14.2° alc. **Rating** 89 **To** 2012 $115

Warburn Estate

700 Kidman Way, Griffith, NSW 2680 **Region** Riverina
T (02) 6963 8300 **F** (02) 6962 4628 **www**.warburnestate.com.au **Open** Mon–Fri 9–5, Sat 10–4
Winemaker Sam Trimboli, Moreno Chiappin, Carmelo D'Aquino **Est.** 1969
Cases 1.25 million
Warburn Estate, doubtless drawn in part by the success of Casella's yellowtail, has seen its production soar to 1.25 million cases. It draws on 1000 ha of vineyards, and produces an encyclopaedic range of wines exported to all major markets. The wines tasted are a tiny part of its large number of wines.

ℙℙℙℙℙ   **Stephendale Shiraz 2006** A direct outcome of the then-grape surplus, allowing a wine of this quality to come onto the market; medium-bodied, with good texture and mouthfeel to the blackberry, licorice and plum fruit; restrained American oak. Bargain. Barossa. Screwcap. 14° alc. **Rating** 91 **To** 2011 $11

ℙℙℙℙ   **Premium Reserve Cabernet Merlot 2006** Highly fragrant and perfumed, to the point of outright confection in a mint/chocolate/cola spectrum. However, abundant flavour tied off with a minerally finish. **Rating** 89 **To** 2012 $9
The Singing Tree Shiraz 2006 Good fruit from 80-year-old Hilltops vines submerged in all-encompassing vanillin oak. Cork. 15° alc. **Rating** 88 **To** 2016 $35
1164 Family Reserve Barossa Valley Merlot 2004 Good colour; a firm, slightly extractive style, relatively low pH leading to a hard-edged palate. Screwcap. 14.5° alc. **Rating** 87 **To** 2011 $24.95

Warrabilla

Murray Valley Highway, Rutherglen, Vic 3685 **Region** Rutherglen
T (02) 6035 7242 **F** (02) 6035 7298 **www**.warrabillawines.com.au **Open** 7 days 10–5
Winemaker Andrew Sutherland Smith **Est.** 1990 **Cases** 10 000

Andrew Sutherland Smith and wife Carol have built a formidable reputation for their wines, headed by the Reserve trio of Durif, Cabernet Sauvignon and Shiraz, quintessential examples of Rutherglen red wine at its best. Their 18.5-ha vineyard has been extended with the planting of some riesling and zinfandel. Andrew spent 15 years with All Saints, McWilliam's, Yellowglen, Fairfield and Chambers before setting up Warrabilla, and his accumulated experience shines through in the wines.

ΨΨΨΨΨ **Reserve Cabernet Sauvignon 2006** Elegant in body, though the decision to use 100% American oak (rather than a mix of French and American) is quixotic; has some tension and length between cassis fruit and (doubtless adjusted) acidity. Diam. 14.5° alc. **Rating** 94 **To** 2030 $22

Reserve Durif 2006 Dwarfed by the Parola's, but still a huge wine; here some structure expresses itself in a range of black fruits; again, not extractive in a conventional sense. 16° alc. **Rating** 94 **To** 2030 $22

Reserve Durif 2007 Saturated purple; has that unique structure of the Warrabillas, with fruit that is so dense it does not admit light and shade; however, the dark chocolate, licorice, maraschino cherry and prime fruit flavours are good. Heavily stained Diam. 16.4° alc. **Rating** 94 **To** 2013 $22

ΨΨΨΨΨ **Reserve Shiraz 2006** The still very high alcohol (but lower than Parola's) results in more expression; plum, prune, blackberry and a touch of licorice; has spent a perfunctory 10 months in French and American oak which has barely made an impression. Diam. 16° alc. **Rating** 93 **To** 2030 $22

Limited Release Parola's Cabernet Sauvignon 2006 An ever-interesting interaction between terroir and variety, which works far better than it should. Lots of cassis and blackcurrant, tannins soft and not over-extracted. Diam. 15° alc. **Rating** 93 **To** 2030 $30

Reserve Cabernet Sauvignon 2007 Crimson-purple; thick, chewy texture and structure although, as usual, the tannins are ripe and soft; juicy blackcurrant fruit has largely absorbed the French and American oak. Diam. 15.6° alc. **Rating** 92 **To** 2017 $22

Reserve Shiraz 2007 Unique wine; the saturated colour, the alcohol and the fruit all suggest it should be a forbidden drink for the next 10 years, but it doesn't work that way. What you do need is a roasted ox on a barbecue. Diam. 16.6° alc. **Rating** 91 **To** 2017 $22

Limited Release Parola's Shiraz 2006 Opaque purple-red; extremely concentrated and dense, just as the extreme alcohol would suggest. This really is pushing the envelope too far, however spectacular it may be; sweet licorice fruit, but the tannins are not aggressive. Diam. 17° alc. **Rating** 90 **To** 2030 $30

ΨΨΨΨ **Limited Release Parola's Durif 2006** It is impossible to judge or point this wine by conventional standards; almost viscous, and certainly velvety; the extraordinary alcohol actually robs the wine of structure at this stage. Perhaps 50 years in bottle will put matters right. Diam. 18° alc. **Rating** 89 **To** 2080 $30

Warramate   ★★★★★

27 Maddens Lane, Gruyere, Vic 3770 **Region** Yarra Valley
T (03) 5964 9219 **F** (03) 5964 9219 **www**.warramatewines.com.au **Open** 7 days 10–6
Winemaker David Church **Est.** 1970 **Cases** 1500
A long-established and perfectly situated winery reaping the full benefits of its 37-year-old vines; recent plantings have increased production. All the wines are well made, the Shiraz providing further proof (if such be needed) of the suitability of the variety to the region; has moved to another level since son David Church took the full mantle of winemaker.

ΨΨΨΨΨ **White Label Yarra Valley Shiraz 2006** Complex, with layers of flavour and especially fine, velvety texture; medium-bodied with lovely poise, focus and finesse to the finish. Screwcap. 13.5° alc. **Rating** 94 **To** 2016 $45

Yarra Valley Cabernet Merlot 2005 A pure example of cabernet; vibrant, deep and complex, with elements of cedar, and almost ethereal florals; lovely palate weight and texture, with silky, supple tannins driving through on the finish. Screwcap. 13.5° alc. **Rating** 94 **To** 2016 $35

ŶŶŶŶ♀ **Black Label Yarra Valley Shiraz 2006** Vibrant, fresh and juicy red berry fruits, with a dash of clove thrown in for good measure; vibrant and fleshy on the finish. Screwcap. 13.5° alc. **Rating** 90 **To** 2014 $20

ŶŶŶŶ **Black Label Yarra Valley Cabernet Sauvignon 2006** Essency cassis on the bouquet, with cabernet structure following on the palate; very juicy, and showing the young vine character as a fleshy, forward fruit component. Screwcap. 13.5° alc. **Rating** 89 **To** 2012 $20

Warraroong Estate ★★★☆

247 Wilderness Road, Lovedale, NSW 2321 **Region** Lower Hunter Valley
T (02) 4930 7594 **F** (02) 4930 7199 **www.**warraroongestate.com **Open** Thurs–Mon 10–5
Winemaker Andrew Thomas **Est.** 1978 **Cases** 3500
'Warraroong' is an Aboriginal word for 'hillside', reflecting the southwesterly aspect of the property, which looks back towards the Brokenback Range and Watagan Mountains. The label design is from a painting by Aboriginal artist Kia Kiro who, while coming from the NT, is now living and working in the Hunter Valley. The mature vineyard plantings were extended in 2004 with a little over 1 ha of verdelho. Exports to Japan.

ŶŶŶŶ♀ **Hunter Valley Semillon 2007** Has the glorious green colour scattered here and there throughout this vintage; a very complex wine with layers of fruit; has balance and length. **Rating** 93 **To** 2015 $22

ŶŶŶŶ **Hunter Valley Shiraz 2006** Medium-bodied, with red fruits and a hint of leather; good flavour and bright fruit on the soft finish. Screwcap. 13.8° alc. **Rating** 88 **To** 2014 $22
Hunter Valley Malbec 2005 Quite rich and ripe; good fruit weight and texture; a little simple, but fleshy on the finish. Screwcap. 12.5° alc. **Rating** 88 **To** 2012 $22

Warrenmang Vineyard & Resort ★★★★★

Mountain Creek Road, Moonambel, Vic 3478 **Region** Pyrenees
T (03) 5467 2233 **F** (03) 5467 2309 **www.**warrenmang.com.au **Open** 7 days 10–5
Winemaker Luigi Bazzani, Sean Schwager **Est.** 1974 **Cases** 14 000
Luigi and Athelie Bazzani continue to watch over Warrenmang as a newly, partially underground, barrel room with earthen walls has been completed, and production has increased over the past two years. National distribution was put in place in 2007, and Warrenmang now exports to over a dozen countries. However, after 30 years at the helm, the Bazzanis do have the combined winery and holiday complex on the market.

ŶŶŶŶŶ **Luigi Tribute 2005** Dense purple-red, the wine encased in a massive bottle; a core of delicious blackberry and blackcurrant fruit, then a display of fine, ripe tannins (plus oak) on the finish. Cork. 15° alc. **Rating** 95 **To** 2020 $96
Grand Pyrenees 2005 Dense colour; massively concentrated full-bodied wine in traditional Warrenmang style, with black fruits, dark chocolate and licorice; firm tannins; no dead or overripe fruit characters. Cabernet Franc/Cabernet Sauvignon/Merlot/Shiraz. Cork. 15° alc. **Rating** 94 **To** 2020 $35

ŶŶŶŶ **Bazzani Vinello Dolcetto Nebbiolo Barbera 2005** Light, fresh and lively red fruits, spice and virtually no tannins to worry about; casual drinking right now. Cork. 14° alc. **Rating** 87 **To** 2009 $20

Water Wheel

Bridgewater-on-Loddon, Bridgewater, Vic 3516 **Region** Bendigo
T (03) 5437 3060 **F** (03) 5437 3082 **www**.waterwheelwine.com **Open** Mon–Fri 9–5,
w'ends & public hols 12–4
Winemaker Peter Cumming, Bill Trevaskis **Est.** 1972 **Cases** 45 000
Peter Cumming, with more than two decades of winemaking under his belt, has quietly
built on the reputation of Water Wheel year by year. The winery is owned by the Cumming
family, which has farmed in the Bendigo region for 50+ years, with horticulture and
viticulture special areas of interest. The wines are of remarkably consistent quality and modest
price. Exports to the UK, the US and other major markets.

ＹＹＹＹＹ **Bendigo Shiraz 2006** A dense and rich wine with black fruits and a slight
minty overtone; fairly robust, the tannins needing to soften somewhat. Screwcap.
Rating 90 **To** 2018 $18

Watershed Wines

Cnr Bussell Highway/Darch Road, Margaret River, WA 6285 **Region** Margaret River
T (08) 9758 8633 **F** (08) 9757 3999 **www**.watershedwines.com.au **Open** 7 days 10–5
Winemaker Severine Logan **Est.** 2002 **Cases** 76 000
Watershed Wines has been established by a syndicate of investors, and no expense has
been spared in establishing the vineyard and building a striking cellar door, and a 200-seat
café and restaurant. Situated towards the southern end of the Margaret River region, its
neighbours include Voyager Estate and Leeuwin Estate. Exports to the UK, the US and
other major markets.

ＹＹＹＹＹ **Shiraz 2005** Impeccably made, with clever use of barrel ferment oak inputs to
lively, spicy black fruits; good structure and depth. **Rating** 93 **To** 2015 $24.95
Awakening Margaret River Sauvignon Blanc 2007 Complex, with a strong
mineral current to the quite fleshy and generous fruit; well-handled oak treatment
has added an extra dimension. Screwcap. 13° alc. **Rating** 92 **To** 2012 $32.95

ＹＹＹＹ **Shades Margaret River Unoaked Chardonnay 2007** Ideal unwooded style,
the fruit with a flowery/estery lift, the palate precise and quite long. Screwcap.
Rating 89 **To** 2009 $16.95

Waterton Vineyards

PO Box 125, Beaconsfield, Tas 7270 **Region** Northern Tasmania
T (03) 6394 7214 **F** (03) 6394 7614 **www**.watertonhall.com.au **Open** Not
Winemaker Winemaking Tasmania (Julian Alcorso) **Est.** 2006 **Cases** 140
Jennifer Baird and Peter Cameron purchased this remarkable property in 2002. Waterton
Hall was built in the 1850s, and modified extensively by well-known neo-gothic architect
Alexander North in 1910. The property was owned by the Catholic church from 1949–96,
variously used as a school, a boys home and retreat. Following its sale the new owners planted
1 ha of riesling at the end of the 1990s, and Jennifer and Peter extended the vineyard with
1 ha of shiraz, electing to sell the riesling until '06, when part was made under the Waterton
label. The plans are to use the existing buildings to provide a restaurant, accommodation and
function facilities.

ＹＹＹＹＹ **Riesling 2006** Another '06 riesling to have changed out of all recognition;
fragrant apple blossom aromas, then a lively palate with a delicious twist of lemony
acidity on the finish; fresh aftertaste; gold Tas Wine Show '08. Screwcap. 11.7° alc.
Rating 95 **To** 2014 $26.50
Dessert Riesling 2007 A long and brilliantly defined wine, with quince and
lime intermingling, with exceptional acidity and focus on the long finish. Gold,
Tas Wine Show '08. **Rating** 95 **To** 2016 $24.50

ＹＹＹＹ **Riesling 2007** Riper, more weighty than '06; ripe tropical passionfruit with a
big blurred finish. **Rating** 89 **To** 2010 $24.50

Watson Wine Group

PO Box 6243, Halifax Street, Adelaide, SA 5000 **Region** Coonawarra
T (08) 8338 3200 **F** (08) 8338 3244 **www**.rexwatsonwines.com **Open** Not
Winemaker Roger Harbord **Est.** 1997 **Cases** 80 000
Rex Watson commenced business in the Australian wine industry in 1991 and began
growing wine grapes in Coonawarra in '97. In 1999 he commenced planting the most
significant modern vineyard development in Coonawarra. In less than five years this was built
into a venture that now controls and manages almost 400 ha over three vineyards, all close
to the historic township of Coonawarra and well within the Coonawarra GI. Exports to the
US, Canada, Sweden, Singapore, Malaysia, India, Sri Lanka, Taiwan, China and NZ.

ꙮꙮꙮꙮ **Rex Watson Coonawarra Petit Verdot Shiraz 2007** Crimson-purple thanks
to the petit verdot; light- to medium-bodied, with fresh juicy plum, black cherry
and blackberry flavours; fine tannins and just a whisk of oak; drink asap; bargain.
Screwcap. 14.5° alc. **Rating** 89 **To** 2010 $13.95
Rex Watson Three Sons Coonawarra Sauvignon Blanc 2007
Considerable CO_2 early in its life; however, does have an attractive mix of
citrus and gently tropical fruit, with a touch of sweetness. Screwcap. 12.5° alc.
Rating 88 **To** 2009 $17.95
Rex Watson Wish Coonawarra Blanc de Blancs NV A zesty chardonnay
fizz, with lots of fresh lemons, and plenty of vibrant acidity; quite creamy and even
on the finish. Cork. 11.5° alc. **Rating** 88 **To** 2009 $22.95
Rex Watson Coonawarra Sauvignon Blanc 2007 Ripe tropical fruit, with
a nice touch of lemon juice. Screwcap. 12.5° alc. **Rating** 87 **To** 2009 $13.95

Wattle Ridge Vineyard

Loc 11950 Boyup-Greenbushes Road, Greenbushes, WA 6254 **Region** Blackwood Valley
T (08) 9764 3594 **F** (08) 9764 3594 **www**.wattleridgewines.com.au **Open** Thurs–Mon 10–4
Winemaker Contract **Est.** 1997 **Cases** 1500
James and Vicky Henderson have established 6.25 ha of vines at their Nelson Vineyard,
planted to riesling, verdelho, merlot and cabernet sauvignon. The wines are sold by mail
order and through the cellar door, which also offers light meals, crafts and local produce.
Exports to Canada and Japan.

Wattlebrook Vineyard

Fordwich Road, Broke, NSW 2330 **Region** Lower Hunter Valley
T (02) 9929 5668 **F** (02) 9929 5668 **www**.wattlebrook.com **Open** Not
Winemaker Andrew Margan (Contract) **Est.** 1994 **Cases** 1500
Wattlebrook Vineyard was founded by NSW Supreme Court Justice Peter McClellan and
family in 1994, with a substantial vineyard lying between the Wollemi National Park and
Wollombi Brook. The family planted another major vineyard, in 1998, on Henry Lawson
Drive at Mudgee, to shiraz, merlot and cabernet sauvignon. The Wollombi Vineyard is
planted to chardonnay, semillon, verdelho, cabernet sauvignon and shiraz. The wines have
been consistent medal winners at various local wine shows.

ꙮꙮꙮꙮꙮ **Bird's Keep Hunter Valley Shiraz 2006** Red and dark fruits, with a little
Hunter earthiness; medium-bodied and with good fruit concentration. Screwcap.
13.6° alc. **Rating** 90 **To** 2015 $22

 # Waurn Ponds Estate

Nicol Drive North, Waurn Ponds, Vic 3217 **Region** Geelong
T (03) 5227 2143 **F** (03) 5227 2111 **www**.waurnpondsestate.com.au **Open** Mon–Fri 10–4
Winemaker Duncan MacGillivray **Est.** 2001 **Cases** 4500

A somewhat unusual venture, owned by Deakin University, but managed by winemaker Duncan MacGillivray. Two ha each of chardonnay, pinot noir, cabernet sauvignon and shiraz, and 1 ha each of viognier, riesling, sauvignon blanc, merlot and petit verdot were planted in 2002. Grapes from the early vintages were sold to other Geelong wineries, notably Scotchmans Hill, but from 2005, encouraged by the quality of the grapes, increasing quantities have been retained for wines under the Waurn Ponds Estate label.

ŸŸŸŸŸ **Chardonnay 2006** Fragrant nectarine and grapefruit; an elegant and supple palate, with strong varietal presence, and good length. 13° alc. **Rating** 92 **To** 2015 $17.50
Riesling 2007 Bright, crisp and minerally; good length and balance, with a pleasingly dry finish. Cork. 13° alc. **Rating** 90 **To** 2011 $16
Sauvignon Blanc 2007 Aromatic and clean, a lively palate freshened by a touch of CO_2; citrus/passionfruit/grassy flavours; good length. Cork. 13° alc. **Rating** 90 **To** 2009 $17.50
Reserve Shiraz 2006 Abundant rich, sweet black fruits, with touches of licorice and prune; velvety mouthfeel, sweetness from the alcohol. Bottle variation from cork. 15° alc. **Rating** 90 **To** 2016 $30

ŸŸŸŸ **Geelong Shiraz 2005** Highly aromatic, with plenty of spice and red fruits; a little simple, but a good drink. Cork. 14° alc. **Rating** 87 **To** 2014 $17.50

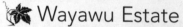

Wayawu Estate ★★★★

1070 Bellarine Highway, Wallington, Vic 3221 **Region** Geelong
T (03) 5250 4457 **www**.wayawawinerybb.com.au **Open** Tues–Sun 10–5
Winemaker John Henry, Stephanie Henry **Est.** 2004 **Cases** NFP
In 2004 John and Stephanie Henry planted 0.5 ha of shiraz, with four different clones. Both vineyard and winery are onsite, and the results so far have been impressive. The name comes from northeast Arnhem Land, and means 'where the land touches the Milky Way'. The Henrys have been given permission by Arnhem Land artist, Nami Maymuru-White, to reproduce one of her paintings of the Milky Way on their label.

ŸŸŸŸŸ **Harry's Shiraz 2006** Medium-bodied; a smooth and supple mix of blackberry, licorice and cedary oak, supported by ripe tannins; needed a touch more density. **Rating** 92 **To** 2014

Wedgetail Estate ★★★★★

40 Hildebrand Road, Cottles Bridge, Vic 3099 **Region** Yarra Valley
T (03) 9714 8661 **F** (03) 9714 8676 **www**.wedgetailestate.com.au **Open** W'ends & public hols 12–5, or by appt. Closed from 25 Dec – reopens Australia Day w'end
Winemaker Guy Lamothe **Est.** 1994 **Cases** 1500
Canadian-born photographer Guy Lamothe and partner Dena Ashbolt started making wine in the basement of their Carlton home in the 1980s. The idea of their own vineyard started to take hold, and the search for a property began. Then, in their words, 'one Sunday, when we were "just out for a drive", we drove past our current home. The slopes are amazing, true goat terrain, and it is on these steep slopes that in 1994 we planted our first block of pinot noir.' While the vines were growing – they now have 5.5 ha in total – Lamothe enrolled in the winegrowing course at CSU, having already gained practical experience working in the Yarra Valley (Tarrawarra), the Mornington Peninsula and Meursault (Burgundy). The net result is truly excellent wine. Exports to the UK, Canada and Singapore.

ŸŸŸŸŸ **Single Vineyard Yarra Valley Chardonnay 2006** Elegant, finely boned and typically long in the mouth, a defining feature of the Yarra Valley; oak has not been allowed to usurp fruit flavour. Screwcap. 13° alc. **Rating** 94 **To** 2013 $34
Reserve Pinot Noir 2006 The flavours move towards plum from the cherry of the varietal; lots of structure and depth; cellar this and drink the other. Reversing the closures would have been smart. Diam. 13° alc. **Rating** 94 **To** 2015 $65

🍷🍷🍷🍷🍷 Single Vineyard Yarra Valley Pinot Noir 2006 Bright and clear; has distinct but appealing spicy characters throughout the light-bodied yet long palate; elegant and unforced, for early drinking. Screwcap. 13.5° alc. **Rating** 92 **To** 2011 $42

🍷🍷🍷🍷 Single Vineyard Yarra Valley Shiraz 2006 Fragrant, spicy light-bodied cool-grown shiraz; might well surprise with its longevity, but there is no need for patience. Screwcap. 14° alc. **Rating** 89 **To** 2014 $35
The North Face 2006 Potent wine; some dusty earthy (reductive?) overtones to the mainframe of black and redcurrant fruit. Cabernet Sauvignon/Merlot. Screwcap. 13.5° alc. **Rating** 88 **To** 2012 $30

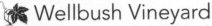 # Wellbush Vineyard ★★★☆
659 Huntly-Fosterville Road, Huntly, Vic 3551 **Region** Bendigo
T (03) 5448 8515 **Open** W'ends by appt
Winemaker Mandurang Valley Wines (Wes Vine), Greg Dedman (Contract), David Wallace **Est.** 2006 **Cases** 410
David and Lynn Wallace purchased the 10-ha property in 2006, which brought with it a long history. In the early years of the last century it was a Chinese market garden, the hand-built ponds remaining today. In 1975 the first chardonnay, shiraz, cabernet sauvignon and merlot vines were planted, with further plantings of shiraz in '98, and an addition to the cabernet sauvignon the following year brought the vineyard to its present level of 2.4 ha. The Wallaces (David having studied for his Bachelor of Applied Science (wine science) at CSU) have been progressively rehabilitating and retrellising the vineyard, building a 50-megalitre dam to provide reliable water in the seemingly endless drought years. They say 'our aims and aspirations are to produce the best quality grapes we possibly can and eventually produce our own handcrafted wines, give up our day jobs and grow old ungracefully in our beautiful vineyard.' A small onsite winery will be part of that plan.

🍷🍷🍷🍷🍷 Handpicked Bendigo Shiraz 2006 Medium-bodied; lively spicy/savoury edges to blackberry and licorice fruit, with a sprightly finish. From 1975 plantings. Screwcap. 14° alc. **Rating** 90 **To** 2016 $22

🍷🍷🍷🍷 Handpicked Bendigo Cabernet Sauvignon 2006 A powerful wine, with blackcurrant fruit and fractionally green/hard tannins. More work in barrel fining needed. Screwcap. 14° alc. **Rating** 88 **To** 2014 $22

Wellington Vale Wines ★★★
'Wellington Vale', Deepwater, NSW 2371 (postal) **Region** New England
T (02) 6734 5226 **F** (02) 6734 5226 **Open** Not
Winemaker Preston Peak (Rod McPherson), Mike Hayes (Symphony Hill Wines)
Est. 1997 **Cases** 200
David and Dierdri Robertson-Cuninghame trace their ancestry (via David) back to the Duke of Wellington, with Cuninghame Senior being the ADC to the Duke, and his son, Arthur Wellesley-Robertson, the godson. Arthur Wellesley migrated to Australia and took up the land upon which Wellington Vale is situated in 1839. Planting began in 1997 with 0.7 ha of semillon, 1 ha of pinot noir and 0.3 ha of riesling. The first vintage was in 2000, and the subsequent vintages have won bronze medals at the competitive Australian Small Winemakers Show.

Welshmans Reef Vineyard ★★★☆
Maldon-Newstead Road, Welshmans Reef, Vic 3462 **Region** Bendigo
T (03) 5476 2733 **F** (03) 5476 2537 **www**.welshmansreef.com **Open** W'ends & public hols 10–5 or by appt
Winemaker Ronald Snep **Est.** 1986 **Cases** 2000
The Snep family (Ronald, Jackson and Alexandra) began developing Welshmans Reef Vineyard in 1986, planting cabernet sauvignon, shiraz and semillon. Chardonnay and merlot were added in the early 1990s, with sauvignon blanc and tempranillo later. The 6-ha vineyard

is certified organic. For some years the grapes were sold to other wineries, but in the early 1990s the Sneps decided to share winemaking facilities established in the Old Newstead Co-operative Butter Factory with several other small vineyards. When the Butter Factory facility closed down, the Sneps built a winery and mudbrick tasting room onsite, 6 km north of Newstead.

ŸŸŸŸŸ **Shiraz 2005** Robust and full-bodied, with a collage of licorice, spice, blackberry and plum; controlled tannins, and copes well with the alcohol. Screwcap. 14.8° alc. **Rating** 92 **To** 2020 $20

Wendouree ★★★★★
Wendouree Road, Clare, SA 5453 **Region** Clare Valley
T (08) 8842 2896 **Open** By appt
Winemaker Tony Brady **Est.** 1895 **Cases** 2000
The iron fist in a velvet glove best describes these extraordinary wines. They are fashioned with passion and precision from the very old vineyard with its unique terroir by Tony and Lita Brady, who rightly see themselves as custodians of a priceless treasure. The 100-year-old stone winery is virtually unchanged from the day it was built; this is in every sense a treasure beyond price.

ŸŸŸŸŸ **Cabernet Malbec 2005** Deepest colour of the three Wendourees, with cassis and blackcurrant aromas bursting out of the glass; has the greatest depth, richness and dimension to the blackcurrant and anise fruit, the tannins and oak also having their say. Cork. **Rating** 96 **To** 2030
Shiraz 2005 Bright, clear crimson; medium-bodied, supple and smooth, remarkably so for Wendouree; has great length and elegance, revealing ever more of its future with each sip. Cork. **Rating** 95 **To** 2025
Shiraz Mataro 2005 Slightly lighter colour than the Shiraz, but similar brilliant hue; the mataro/mourvedre tannins are evident, but not trenchantly so; nonetheless, needs 5–10 years to fully unfurl its sails. Cork. **Rating** 94 **To** 2023

Were Estate ★★★☆
Cnr Wildberry Road/Johnson Road, Wilyabrup, WA 6280 **Region** Margaret River
T (08) 9755 6273 **F** (08) 9755 6195 **www**.wereestate.com.au **Open** 7 days 10.30–5
Winemaker Ian Bell, Amanda Kramer **Est.** 1998 **Cases** 5000
Owners Diane and Gordon Davies say, 'We are different. We're original, we're bold, we're innovative.' This is all reflected in the design of the unusual back labels, incorporating pictures of the innumerable pairs of braces which real estate agent Gordon Davies wears on his Perth job; in the early move to screwcaps for both white and red wines; and, for that matter, in the underground trickle irrigation system (plus a move towards to organic methods) in their Margaret River vineyard which can be controlled from Perth. Exports to the US, Philippines and Singapore.

 Semillon Sauvignon Blanc 2007 Has the intensity missing from many '07 regional blends; partial barrel ferment of the semillon component adds authority to the grass, herb and citrus flavours; dry finish. Screwcap. 13.9° alc. **Rating** 90 **To** 2012 $18

West Cape Howe Wines ★★★★★
678 South Coast Highway, Denmark, WA 6333 **Region** Denmark
T (08) 9848 2959 **F** (08) 9848 2903 **www**.westcapehowewines.com.au **Open** 7 days 10–5
Winemaker Gavin Berry, Dave Cleary, Imogen Casey **Est.** 1997 **Cases** 55 000
After a highly successful seven years, West Cape Howe founders Brenden and Kylie Smith moved on, selling the business to a partnership including Gavin Berry (until 2004, senior winemaker at Plantagenet) and viticulturist Rob Quenby. As well as existing fruit sources, West Cape Howe now has the 80-ha Lansdale Vineyard, planted in 1989, as its primary fruit source. The focus now will be less on contract winemaking, and more on building the very strong West Cape Howe brand. Exports to the UK, the US and other major markets.

ΨΨΨΨΨ **Great Southern Riesling 2007** Combines delicacy and power; fine, taut, lemon, lime and mineral flavours; a long, lingering, zesty finish. Great potential. Screwcap. 12° alc. **Rating** 95 **To** 2020 $19

Styx Gully Chardonnay 2006 Complex aromas of cool-climate chardonnay and barrel ferment inputs; an intense palate with focus and line, fruit to the fore, but with above-average complexity. Screwcap. 13° alc. **Rating** 95 **To** 2011 $24

Great Southern Sauvignon Blanc 2007 Fragrant and lively gooseberry and passionfruit flavours; crisp acidity and excellent length. Screwcap. 12.5° alc. **Rating** 94 **To** 2011 $19

Shiraz 2005 Delicious plum, blackberry and spice fruit in perfect balance with tannins and oak; medium-bodied and elegant, a tiny percentage of viognier part of the secret. Sensational value. Screwcap. 13.5° alc. **Rating** 94 **To** 2015 $16

ΨΨΨΨΨ **Cabernet Merlot 2005** Clear purple-red; abundant cassis and blackcurrant fruit, with touches of spice and subtle oak; fine, ripe tannins; very good mouthfeel. Screwcap. 13.5° alc. **Rating** 93 **To** 2015 $16

Rose 2007 Totally delicious; a fresh cascade of strawberry and small berry red fruits with a twist of citrussy acidity; a wine to be gulped. Merlot/Pinot Noir. Screwcap. 13.5° alc. **Rating** 92 **To** 2009 $16

Semillon Sauvignon Blanc 2007 Enters quietly but progressively builds up flavour around the structural core of semillon, moving through to gooseberry and citrus flavours. Screwcap. 12.5° alc. **Rating** 92 **To** 2010 $16

Book Ends Great Southern Cabernet Sauvignon 2006 Highly perfumed redcurrant and cassis fruits and a little cedar; good depth and weight of cabernet on the finish, especially for the vintage. Screwcap. 13.5° alc. **Rating** 92 **To** 2015 $24

Viognier 2006 Vibrant white peach and apricot aromas and flavours, with attractive acidity on the finish; a superior example. Screwcap. 12.5° alc. **Rating** 91 **To** 2010 $19

Great Southern Tempranillo 2007 Lively juicy red fruits, with an almost heady perfume; a fun wine with lovely texture, and a savoury tannic finish that gets you back for more. Screwcap. 13° alc. **Rating** 91 **To** 2012 $19

Unwooded Chardonnay 2007 An excellent example of cool-climate unoaked chardonnay; grapefruit and mandarin flavours, generous and satisfying, but neatly trimmed by acidity. Screwcap. 13° alc. **Rating** 90 **To** 2011 $16

Two Steps Great Southern Shiraz Viognier 2006 Lifted and highly perfumed, displaying savoury characters; medium-bodied, with real brightness on the finish. Screwcap. 13.5° alc. **Rating** 90 **To** 2012 $24

Cabernet Merlot 2006 Focused varietal cabernet fruit and some cedar; fine and quite aromatic on the palate, with correct expression on the finish. Screwcap. 13.5° alc. **Rating** 90 **To** 2013 $16

Westend Estate Wines ★★★★

1283 Brayne Road, Griffith, NSW 2680 **Region** Riverina
T (02) 6969 0800 **F** (02) 6962 1673 **www.**westendestate.com **Open** Mon–Fri 8.30–5, w'ends 10–4
Winemaker William Calabria, Bryan Currie, Sally Whittaker **Est.** 1945 **Cases** 250 000
Along with a number of Riverina producers, Westend Estate is making a concerted move to lift both the quality and the packaging of its wines. Its leading 3 Bridges range, which has an impressive array of gold medals to its credit since being first released in 1997, is anchored in part on 20 ha of estate vineyards. Bill Calabria has been involved in the Australian wine industry for more than 40 years, and is understandably proud of the achievements both of Westend and the Riverina wine industry as a whole. Exports to all major markets.

ΨΨΨΨΨ **3 Bridges Winemakers Selection Durif 2005** Has an abundance of luscious, stewed plum fruit without going over the top; smooth and supple; two gold medals no surprise. Cork. 15° alc. **Rating** 91 **To** 2012 $19.95

3 Bridges Limited Release Reserve Shiraz 2005 Still retains remarkable freshness and vibrancy to the long, quite juicy palate; a nice touch of oak into the bargain. Cork. 14.5° alc. **Rating** 90 **To** 2015 $24.95

3 Bridges Reserve Botrytis 2006 Unctuously rich crème caramel, glacé apricot and peach, with soft acidity to provide balance. Cork. **Rating** 90 **To** 2012 $29.95

3 Bridges Golden Mist Botrytis 2005 Glowing gold; luscious and rich cumquat mandarin and peach fruit, with good balancing acidity. Gold medal, Melbourne Wine Show '07; drink asap. Screwcap. 11° alc. **Rating** 90 **To** 2009 $19.95

ŶŶŶŶ **Richland Pinot Grigio 2007** Has more fragrance and freshness than many, making its haul of silver and bronze medals understandable; enjoy while it keeps that freshness; very good value. Screwcap. 11.5° alc. **Rating** 89 **To** 2009 $10.95

3 Bridges Winemakers Selection Shiraz 2005 A soft, but ripe, palate, with sweet fruit and soft tannins; a vinous representation of the proverbial dumb blonde. **Rating** 89 **To** 2011 $19.95

3 Bridges Winemakers Selection Durif 2006 Dark crimson; chock-full of flavour, winning gold and silver at Melbourne and Rutherglen shows respectively no surprise; to be fair, does have length, and carries its alcohol well. Diam. 15° alc. **Rating** 89 **To** 2012 $19.95

Outback Semillon Sauvignon Blanc 2007 Herbaceous overtones are well within varietal expectations; a lively, zippy mid-palate, then a firm, dry finish. **Rating** 88 **To** 2010 $7.95

3 Bridges Cabernet Sauvignon 2006 Clear-cut cabernet fruit expression with blackberry cassis and a touch of olive backed by quite firm tannins. Cork. **Rating** 88 **To** 2014 $19.95

3 Bridges Limited Release Reserve Durif 2006 Dense purple-red; a massive wine, with high extract and alcohol; either a barbecue ox, or faith and patience, needed. Cork. 15° alc. **Rating** 88 **To** 2016 $29.95

Richland Sauvignon Blanc 2007 Clean, fresh and lively aromas; well made, tending neutral on the palate, but does have length. Screwcap. 12° alc. **Rating** 87 **To** 2009 $10.95

Richland Viognier 2007 Surprisingly attractive fruit salad aromas and flavours, with a crisp finish. Nice wine at the price, but little varietal expression evident. Screwcap. 14.5° alc. **Rating** 87 **To** 2009 $10.95

3 Bridges Limited Release Reserve Shiraz 2006 Medium-bodied; an impressive Riverina shiraz, with plenty of varietal fruit, the Achilles Heel a distinctly hot finish. Cork. 15° alc. **Rating** 87 **To** 2012 $29.95

Richland Merlot 2007 Clever making and early bottling keeps the freshness of small red berry fruits; absolutely simple but good value. Screwcap. 14° alc. **Rating** 87 **To** 2009 $10.95

Western Range Wines   ★★★★★

1995 Chittering Road, Lower Chittering, WA 6084 **Region** Perth Hills
T (08) 9571 8800 **F** (08) 9571 8844 **www**.westernrangewines.com.au **Open** Wed–Sun 10–5
Winemaker Ryan Sudano **Est.** 2001 **Cases** 40 000
Between the mid-1990s and 2001, several prominent West Australians, including Marilyn Corderory, Malcolm McCusker, and Terry and Kevin Prindiville, established approximately 125 ha of vines (under separate ownerships) in the Perth Hills, with a kaleidoscopic range of varietals. The next step was to join forces to build a substantial winery. This is a separate venture, but takes the grapes from the individual vineyards and markets the wine under the Western Range brand. The wines are made and sold at four levels: Lot 88, Goyamin Pool, Julimar and Julimar Organic. The label designs are clear and attractive. Exports to Canada, France, Switzerland, Poland, Russia, China and Japan.

ŶŶŶŶŶ **Julimar Limited Release Chardonnay 2006** Particularly fine and delicate given its Chittering origin; very well made, keeping the focus on stone fruit and citrus flavours. Screwcap. 14.5° alc. **Rating** 94 **To** 2011 $25

Julimar Perth Hills Shiraz Viognier 2005 Smooth and supple, with enhanced red fruits, cherries and plums; has low oak impact, and good length. Chittering Valley. Cork. 14° alc. **Rating** 94 **To** 2013 $22

ΨΨΨΨΥ **Julimar Viognier 2006** An interesting wine, introducing aromas and flavours outside the normal spectrum; a mix of pawpaw and citrus, long finish. Screwcap. 14° alc. **Rating** 92 **To** 2010 $22

Julimar Perth Hills Shiraz Viognier 2006 A fragrant bouquet so typical of the blend; the medium-bodied palate has juicy red fruits, well-handled tannins and oak input. Long finish. Screwcap. 14.5° alc. **Rating** 92 **To** 2015 $22

ΨΨΨΨ **Julimar Premium Selection Liquid Gold Liqueur Muscat 2002** Pale gold; exceedingly luscious, verging on viscous, sweet grapey flavours; great on vanilla ice cream or with a dash of soda with ice blocks. Cork. 18° alc. **Rating** 88 **To** 2009 $34

Goyamin Pool Old Vine Grenache 2006 Clear-cut grenache varietal character from start to finish; juicy berry aromas and flavours, with tannins all but absent. For early consumption. Screwcap. 14.5° alc. **Rating** 88 **To** 2009 $17.50

Goyamin Pool Cabernet Malbec 2006 Bright, fresh juicy fruits, the malbec component obvious, the tannins largely invisible. Screwcap. 14° alc. **Rating** 88 **To** 2009 $17.50

Westgate Vineyard   ★★★★★

180 Westgate Road, Armstrong, Vic 3377 **Region** Grampians
T (03) 5356 2394 **F** (03) 5356 2594 www.westgatevineyard.com.au **Open** At Garden Gully
Winemaker Bruce Dalkin **Est.** 1997 **Cases** 500
Westgate has been in the Dalkin family ownership since the 1860s, the present owners Bruce and Robyn being the sixth-generation owners of the property, which today focuses on grape production, a small winery and 4-star accommodation. There are 14 ha of vineyards, progressively established since 1969, including a key holding of 12 ha of shiraz; most of the grapes are sold to Mount Langi Ghiran and others, but a small amount of high-quality wine is made under the Westgate Vineyard label. No red wines available due to drought and bushfires, previous rating stands. Exports to Singapore.

ΨΨΨΨΥ **Riesling 2007** Attractive lime, mineral and spice aromas; crisp, fresh flavours with lemony acidity to close. Screwcap. 12.8° alc. **Rating** 90 **To** 2013 $22

Westlake Vineyards   ★★★★★

PO Box 638, Nuriootpa, SA 5355 **Region** Barossa Valley
T (08) 8565 6249 **F** (08) 8565 6208 www.westlakevineyards.com.au **Open** Not
Winemaker Troy Kalleske (Contract), Darren Westlake **Est.** 1999 **Cases** 300
Darren and Suzanne Westlake tend 19 ha of shiraz, 6.5 ha of cabernet sauvignon, 2 ha of viognier and 1.5 ha of petit verdot planted on two properties in the Koonunga area of the Barossa Valley. The soil is red-brown earth over tight, heavy red clay with scatterings of ironstone and quartz, and the vines yield between 2.5 and 7.5 tonnes per ha, dropping to a miserable 1 tonne per ha in 2007. They, and they alone (other than with some help in the pruning season), work in the vineyards, and have a long list of high-profile winemakers queued up to buy the grapes, leaving only a small amount for production under the Westlake label. And while 1999 is shown as the establishment date, Suzanne's great-great-grandparents migrated from Prussia in 1838, and she is Shawn Kalleske's cousin.

ΨΨΨΨΨ **Eleazar Barossa Valley Shiraz 2005** Much darker than Albert's Block, with more tar, leather and savoury notes; loaded with fruit, and there is a brooding quality that needs time to be fully realised; a heroic wine that carries itself with poise. Cork. 15.7° alc. **Rating** 95 **To** 2025 $55

Albert's Block Barossa Valley Shiraz 2005 Big, soft and supple, with lots of mocha, blackberries and bright red berry fruit; very concentrated, yet very fine, with supple mouthfeel. Cork. 15° alc. **Rating** 94 **To** 2018 $30

Wharncliffe

Summerleas Road, Kingston, Tas 7050 **Region** Southern Tasmania
T 0438 297 147 **F** (03) 6229 2298 **Open** W'ends by appt
Winemaker Hood Wines (Andrew Hood) **Est.** 1990 **Cases** 125
With total plantings of 0.75 ha, Wharncliffe could not exist without the type of contract-winemaking service offered by Andrew Hood, which would be a pity, because the vineyard is beautifully situated on the doorstep of Mt Wellington, the Huon Valley and the Channel regions of southern Tasmania.

♀♀♀♀♀ **Unwooded Chardonnay 2005** Elegant and fresh, with citrus, stone fruit and melon flavours; perfect balance and finish; good unwooded style. **Rating** 90 To 2010 $18

♀♀♀♀ **Pinot Noir 2005** Slightly dull, uninspiring colour; light-bodied, early-picked and early-drinking style; at least it is well-balanced, and not forced. **Rating** 88 To 2009 $20

Whinstone Estate

295 Dunns Creek Road, Red Hill, Vic 3937 **Region** Mornington Peninsula
T (03) 5989 7487 **F** (03) 5989 7641 **www**.whinstone.com.au **Open** W'ends & public hols 11–4, Jan 7 days
Winemaker Ewan Campbell, Maitena Zantvoort (Contract) **Est.** 1994 **Cases** 500
Ken and Leon Wood began the development of their vineyard in 1994, planting 1 ha of chardonnay, 0.8 ha of pinot gris, 0.6 ha of pinot noir, 0.4 ha of sauvignon blanc and a few rows of melon (a grape of Muscadet, France). Initially the grapes were sold to other makers in the region, with a small amount made under the Whinstone label for friends and family. Demand has grown and, with it, production.

♀♀♀♀ **Mornington Peninsula Pinot Noir 2007** Cherry and hints of rhubarb; soft, fleshy and ripe with a little stem evident on the finish. Screwcap. 14° alc. **Rating** 88 To 2009 $25
Barrel Fermented Mornington Peninsula Chardonnay 2007 Nectarine and lemon fruit aromas; clean and focused with vibrant acidity on the finish. Screwcap. 13.5° alc. **Rating** 87 To 2012 $23

Whiskey Gully Wines

Beverley Road, Severnlea, Qld 4352 **Region** Granite Belt
T (07) 4683 5100 **F** (07) 4683 5155 **www**.whiskeygullywines.com.au **Open** 7 days 9–5
Winemaker Rod MacPherson (Contract) **Est.** 1997 **Cases** NA
Close inspection of the winery letterhead discloses that The Media Mill Pty Ltd trades as Whiskey Gully Wines. It is no surprise, then, to find proprietor John Arlidge saying, 'Wine and politics are a heady mix; I have already registered the 2000 Republic Red as a voter in 26 marginal electorates and we are considering nominating it for Liberal Party pre-selection in Bennelong'. Wit to one side, John Arlidge has big plans for Whiskey Gully Wines: to establish 40 ha of vineyards, extending the varietal range with petit verdot, malbec, merlot, semillon and sauvignon blanc. So far, these plans are moving very slowly, but the quality of the wine is not, soaring upwards.

♀♀♀♀♀ **Rep Red 2005** Very good colour; generous mouthfilling wine, very well made; balanced fruit and oak; tannins supple; flowing mouthfeel. Cabernet Sauvignon/Shiraz. **Rating** 94 To 2014 $24

♀♀♀♀♀ **Black Rod Shiraz 2005** Attractive cool-grown shiraz; red and black fruits, licorice, spice; fine tannins; slightly sweet **Rating** 93 To 2013 $26
Upper House Cabernet Sauvignon 2005 Powerful wine; dense fruit and oak; dark chocolate, blackcurrant; lacks light and shade. **Rating** 90 To 2012 $26
Nectar Colombard 2006 Glowing yellow-green; rich, bordering viscous; very sweet, but retains varietal acidity. **Rating** 90 To 2010 $25

ΨΨΨΨ **Reserve Chardonnay 2005** Nectarine, yellow peach; needs more acidity; resinous oak **Rating** 87 **To** 2009 $25
Nectar 2006 Well made; the wine has far more interest and flavour than many, not just reliance on sweetness but on sweet citrus and spice flavours. Colombard. Screwcap. 11° alc. **Rating** 87 **To** 2010 $25

Whispering Brook

Hill Street, Broke, NSW 2330 **Region** Lower Hunter Valley
T (02) 9818 4126 **F** (02) 9818 4156 **www.**whispering-brook.com **Open** By appt
Winemaker Nick Patterson, Susan Frazier **Est.** 2000 **Cases** 1000
Susan Frazier and Adam Bell say the choice of Whispering Brook was the result of a 5-year search to find the ideal viticultural site (while studying for wine science degrees at CSU). Some may wonder whether the Broke subregion of the Hunter Valley needed such persistent effort to locate, but the property does in fact have a combination of terra rossa loam soils on which the reds are planted, and sandy flats for the white grapes. The partners have also established an olive grove and accommodation for six–14 guests in the large house set in the vineyard. Exports to the UK, Japan and Southeast Asia.

ΨΨΨΨ **Hunter Valley Rose 2007** Brilliant colour; a vibrant and fresh cascade of red fruits, and a lingering, dry finish. Screwcap. 12.2° alc. **Rating** 89 **To** 2009 $19
Hunter Valley Shiraz 2005 Medium-bodied; leathery earthy regional notes starting to appear on the long palate and finish; ready sooner rather than later. Diam. 14° alc. **Rating** 88 **To** 2011 $24

Whispering Hills ★★★★

580 Warburton Highway, Seville, Vic 3139 **Region** Yarra Valley
T (03) 5964 2822 **F** (03) 5964 2064 **www.**whisperinghills.com.au **Open** 7 days 10–6
Winemaker Murray Lyons **Est.** 1985 **Cases** 1500
Whispering Hills is owned and operated by the Lyons family (Murray, Marie and Audrey). Murray (with a degree in viticulture and oenology from CSU) concentrates on the vineyard and winemaking, Marie (with a background in sales and marketing) and Audrey take care of the cellar door and distribution of the wines. The 3.5-ha vineyard was established in 1985 (riesling, chardonnay and cabernet sauvignon), with further plantings in '96, and some grafting in '03. Exports to Japan.

ΨΨΨΨΨ **Shiraz 2006** A sweet-fruited wine with luscious dark fruits/fruitcake on the palate; rich, ripe and warm on the finish, with just a little heat evident. Screwcap. 14° alc. **Rating** 90 **To** 2014 $25

ΨΨΨΨ **Yarra Valley Riesling 2007** Showing nutty oxidative aromas, with interesting texture; good acidity, and a more savoury personality than many Australian Rieslings. Screwcap. 12.5° alc. **Rating** 88 **To** 2015 $18

Whistler Wines

Seppeltsfield Road, Marananga, SA 5355 **Region** Barossa Valley
T (08) 8562 4942 **F** (08) 8562 4943 **www.**whistlerwines.com **Open** 7 days 10.30–5
Winemaker Troy Kalleske, Christa Deans, Ben Glaetzer **Est.** 1999 **Cases** 7700
Whistler Wines had a dream start at the Barossa Valley Wine Show 2000, when its '00 Semillon won trophies for Best Dry White and for Most Outstanding Barossa White Table Wine. Add to that sales to the distinguished US importer Weygandt-Metzler, and it is no surprise to find the sold out sign going up on the extremely attractive (modern) galvanised iron cellar door building. The operation is based on 5 ha of shiraz, 2 ha each of semillon and merlot and 1 ha of cabernet sauvignon, with an additional 4 ha of grenache, mourvedre and riesling planted in '01. The hope is to gradually increase production to match existing demand. Exports to the US, Canada, Denmark, Taiwan and Thailand.

ŶŶŶŶŶ **Barossa Shiraz 2005** Rich, ripe blackberry and satsuma plum fill the palate and carry the alcohol remarkably well; long finish. Screwcap. 15° alc. **Rating** 93 To 2015 $27

The Reserve Estate Grown Barossa Shiraz 2005 At the ripe/full end of the spectrum, but avoids excessive confit/jam notes; does need time for the flush of primary fruit to subside, but has the structure to reach its peak. Cork. 15° alc. **Rating** 91 To 2020 $48

Barossa Cabernet Sauvignon 2005 Has the tangy, savoury characters which seem to mark the vintage, adding to the length and complexity of the core of varietal fruit. Screwcap. 14.5° alc. **Rating** 91 To 2020 $22

Whistling Eagle Vineyard ★★★★

2769 Heathcote-Rochester Road, Colbinabbin, Vic 3559 **Region** Heathcote
T (03) 5432 9319 **F** (03) 5432 9326 **www**.whistlingeagle.com **Open** By appt
Winemaker Ian Rathjen **Est.** 1995 **Cases** 1000
This is a remarkable story; owners Ian and Lynn Rathjen are fourth-generation farmers living and working on the now famous Cambrian red soil of Heathcote. Henning Rathjen was lured from his birthplace in Schleswig Holstein by the gold rush, but soon decided farming provided a more secure future. In 1858 he made his way to the Colbinabbin Range, and exclaimed 'We have struck paradise'. Amongst other things, he planted a vineyard in the 1860s, expanding it in the wake of demand for the wine. He died in 1912, and the vineyards disappeared before being replanted in '95, with 20 ha of immaculately tended vines. The core wine (first made in 1999) is Shiraz, with intermittent releases of Sangiovese, Viognier, Cabernet Sauvignon and Semillon.

ŶŶŶŶŶ **Viognier 2006** Abundant varietal fruit on both bouquet and palate; peach, apricot and honeysuckle intertwined with a clear-cut finish, courtesy of lemony acidity. Classy label design. Screwcap. 13.5° alc. **Rating** 92 To 2013 $30

Eagles Blood Heathcote Shiraz 2005 Savoury, spicy notes are slightly at odds with the high alcohol; a base of ripe, black cherry and blackberry fruit plus vanilla oak ties the palate together. Cork. 15.2° alc. **Rating** 91 To 2015 $45

White Dog Farm ★★★

2035 Chittering Road, Lower Chittering, WA 6084 **Region** Perth Hills
T (08) 9571 8880 **www**.whitedogfarm.com.au **Open** W'ends & public hols 12–4
Winemaker Bella Ridge Wines (Alon Arbel) **Est.** 2007 **Cases** 225
When Joanne and Peter Gunn purchased the 17-ha property now known as White Dog Farm, it had first been used for forestry timber, and, once the trees were gone, planted to cereal crops. Within a year of purchasing the property (named in honour of their former dog) they had begun planting 2 ha of cabernet sauvignon and 0.25 ha of merlot plus a total of 400 olive trees with five different varieties used to produce the estate olive oil.

ŶŶŶŶ **Chittering Valley Methode Champenoise 2005** Commendable restraint in both fruit extract of the cabernet sauvignon base and in the low level of dosage sweetness. Cork. 12° alc. **Rating** 87 To 2009 $26.50

White Rock Vineyard ★★★★

1171 Railton Road, Kimberley, Tas 7304 (postal) **Region** Northern Tasmania
T (03) 6497 2156 **F** (03) 6497 2156 **Open** At Lake Barrington Estate
Winemaker Winemaking Tasmania (Julian Alcorso), Phil Dolan **Est.** 1992 **Cases** 150
Phil and Robin Dolan have established White Rock Vineyard in the northwest region of Tasmania, which, while having 13 wineries and vineyards, is one of the least known parts of the island. Kimberley is 25 km south of Devonport in the sheltered valley of the Mersey River. The Dolans have planted 2.4 ha of pinot noir, chardonnay, riesling and pinot gris, the lion's share going to the first two varieties. It has been a low-profile operation not only because of its location, but because most of the grapes are sold, with only Riesling and Chardonnay being made and sold through local restaurants and the cellar door at Lake Barrington Estate.

ỸỸỸỸỸ **Riesling 2006** Has developed very well over the past 12 months, miraculously retaining its generosity, but also seemingly gaining focus and length; delicious wine. **Rating** 92 **To** 2014

Whitechapel Wines

Gerry Semmler Road, Lyndoch, SA 5351 **Region** Barossa Valley
T 0438 822 409 **F** (08) 8342 4028 **www.**whitechapelwines.com.au **Open** By appt
Winemaker Trevor Jones **Est.** 1997 **Cases** 950
The Colovic family, headed by Adelaide insolvency lawyer David Colovic, purchased the small, run-down Whitechapel property at Lyndoch in 1997 as a retirement occupation for Tom Colovic. The idea was to renovate the building, but instead most of the time was spent establishing the immaculately tended 4.5 ha shiraz vineyard. The grapes were initially sold to another Barossa winemaker, but since 2001 small batches of the grapes have been made for the Whitechapel label. The name Tom's Lot for the wine was almost inevitable.

ỸỸỸỸ **Tom's Lot Shiraz 2005** A slight savoury character frames the dark fruits of the palate; medium-bodied with prominent acidity on the finish. Cork. 14° alc. **Rating** 89 **To** 2014 $24

 # Whitfield Estate

198 McIntyre Road, Scotsdale, Denmark, WA 6333 **Region** Great Southern
T (08) 9840 9016 **F** (08) 9840 9016 **www.**whitfieldestate.com.au **Open** 7 days 10–5
Winemaker West Cape Howe (Gavin Berry, Dave Cleary) **Est.** 1994 **Cases** 1000
Graham and Kelly Howard acquired the Whitfield Estate vineyard (planted in 1994) in 2005. They have 2.4 ha of chardonnay and 2 ha of shiraz, with some of the grapes sold to other producers. They in turn acquire semillon, merlot and cabernet sauvignon from other vineyards, thus making Unwooded Chardonnay, Catriona's Chardonnay, Semillon Sauvignon Blanc, Cabernet Merlot, Cabernet Sauvignon, Rose and (most recently) Shiraz.

ỸỸỸỸ **Semillon Sauvignon Blanc 2006** Tangy, zesty bitter lemon rind flavours; does have length and intensity. The back label recommends drinking with 'anti pesto'. Screwcap. 12° alc. **Rating** 87 **To** 2009 $16
Unwooded Chardonnay 2006 No question cool-grown chardonnay is best suited to the unwooded style; has grapefruit/stone fruit flavours, and a clean finish. Screwcap. 12.9° alc. **Rating** 87 **To** 2009 $12
Catriona's Chardonnay 2006 Strong, toasty barrel ferment aromas and flavours surround nectarine and citrus fruit; complex wine. Screwcap. 13.5° alc. **Rating** 87 **To** 2013 $25
Cabernet Sauvignon 2005 Minty, leafy, berry fruits with some sweet and sour characters; does have fair length, however. Screwcap. 14.4° alc. **Rating** 87 **To** 2012 $20

Whitsend Estate ★★★☆

52 Boundary Road, Coldstream, Vic 3770 **Region** Yarra Valley
T (03) 9739 1917 **F** (03) 9739 0217 **www.**whitsend.com.au **Open** By appt
Winemaker Oakridge (David Bicknell, Adrian Rodda) **Est.** 1998 **Cases** 500
In 1998 the Baldwin family established a 13-ha vineyard on northwest-facing slopes above the Coldstream aerodrome. Ross utilised his engineering background to meticulously plan and develop the project, whilst nurturing an ambition to grow the finest fruit possible. Most of the fruit is sold to a nearby winery, with a small select amount being retained for the Whitsend label. Exports to Canada, Japan and Indonesia.

ỸỸỸỸ **Yarra Valley Shiraz Viognier 2006** A lifted bouquet, with bright red fruits the focus; a little spice on the palate, and good straightforward flavour. Screwcap. 13.9° alc. **Rating** 89 **To** 2014 $30

⚜ Whyworry Wines   ★★★★☆

376 Kingstown Road, Uralla, NSW 2358 **Region** New England
T (02) 6778 4147 **F** (02) 6778 4147 **www**.whyworrywines.com.au **Open** W'ends 10–4
Winemaker Gary McLean, Sean Cassidy **Est.** 2000 **Cases** 3000
Whyworry was originally a sheep station set up after the Second World War to produce
superfine merino wool for export to the Italian market. Owners Darryl and Robyn Carter
have now ventured into grapegrowing, having planted 14 ha of chardonnay, verdelho,
sauvignon blanc, riesling, gewurztraminer, pinot noir, merlot, shiraz, pinot gris, pinotage (the
odd man out), and viognier. The vines are 1150 m above sea level on a property 3.5 km west
of Uralla, in turn, just south of Armidale.

🍷🍷🍷🍷🍷 **Sauvignon Blanc 2006** Clean, fresh, lively gooseberry/grass; crisp minerally
acidity; good length and finish. **Rating** 91 **To** 2009 $18

🍷🍷🍷🍷 **Verdelho 2007** Strongly citrus-accented bouquet and palate; not mainstream
varietal; has length. **Rating** 87 **To** 2009 $18
Shiraz Rose 2006 Spicy red cherry; some sweetness; a little over-extracted.
Rating 87 **To** 2009 $16
White Port 2007 Lightly fortified; points for lateral thinking; quite good balance.
Rating 87 **To** 2009 $20

Wicks Estate Wines   ★★★★★

555 The Parade, Magill, SA 5072 (postal) **Region** Adelaide Hills
T (08) 8331 0211 **F** (08) 8431 3300 **www**.wicksestate.com.au **Open** Not
Winemaker Tim Knappstein, Leigh Ratzmer **Est.** 2000 **Cases** 6000
Tim and Simon Wicks had a long-term involvement with orchard and nursery operations
at Highbury in the Adelaide Hills prior to purchasing the 54-ha property at Woodside in
1999. They promptly planted fractionally less than 40 ha of chardonnay, riesling, sauvignon
blanc, shiraz, merlot and cabernet sauvignon, following this with the construction of a
state-of-the-art winery in early 2004. The vast experience of Tim Knappstein, supported by
Adelaide University graduate in oenology, Leigh Ratzmer, has predictably produced wines
of impressive quality. Exports to the US, China, Singapore and Hong Kong.

🍷🍷🍷🍷🍷 **Eminence Adelaide Hills Shiraz Cabernet 2005** Super-elegant, fine and
long; cassis, redcurrant and blackcurrant coalesce; fine tannins and good oak for
a light- to medium-bodied wine; 75% Shiraz. Screwcap. 14.5° alc. **Rating** 95
To 2020 $60
Adelaide Hills Shiraz 2005 Classic cool-climate shiraz, with aromatic, almost
flowery, aromas and flavours of blackberry, licorice, spice and cracked pepper; fine
tannins and good length. Screwcap. 14.5° alc. **Rating** 94 **To** 2015 $19

🍷🍷🍷🍷🍷 **Adelaide Hills Riesling 2007** Ripe apple and citrus characters on both bouquet
and palate; finishes with a subliminal touch of sweetness making it an easily
accessible style. Screwcap. 12.5° alc. **Rating** 90 **To** 2012 $16

🍷🍷🍷🍷 **Adelaide Hills Sauvignon Blanc 2007** A clean bouquet, then a light, firm
and crisp palate with mineral and grass flavours; a partial victim of a challenging
vintage. Screwcap. 13° alc. **Rating** 89 **To** 2009 $18
Adelaide Hills Unwooded Chardonnay 2007 Light- to medium-bodied;
fresh nectarine and citrus fruit; has length, and is a good example of the unwooded
style. Screwcap. 13° alc. **Rating** 88 **To** 2009 $16
Adelaide Hills Cabernet Sauvignon 2005 Bright colour; light- to medium-
bodied, cool-grown cabernet flavours of sweet cassis fruit without green notes,
but also without much structure. Screwcap. 14.5° alc. **Rating** 88 **To** 2010 $19

wightwick   ★★★★☆

323 Slatey Creek Road North, Invermay, Vic 3352 **Region** Ballarat
T (03) 5332 4443 **F** (03) 5333 4556 **www**.wightwick.com.au **Open** By appt
Winemaker Simon Wightwick **Est.** 1996 **Cases** 250

wightwick might best be described as an angels on a pinhead exercise. Keith and Ann Wightwick planted the tiny estate vineyard to 0.12 ha of chardonnay and 0.29 ha of pinot noir in 1996. In 2003 they purchased a 20-year-old vineyard at Cottlesbridge (1.5 ha chardonnay and 0.5 ha cabernet sauvignon); most of the grapes from this vineyard are sold to other producers, a small of amount of cabernet sauvignon being retained for the wightwick label. Son Simon Wightwick works as a viticulturist and winemaker in the Yarra Valley, and looks after the vineyards on weekends (using organic principles) and the micro-winemaking during the Yarra Valley vintage. The Pinot Noir is hand-plunged, basket-pressed, with racking via gravity, and minimal fining.

Wignalls Wines

448 Chester Pass Road (Highway 1), Albany, WA 6330 **Region** Albany
T (08) 9841 2848 **F** (08) 9842 9003 **www.**wignallswines.com.au **Open** 7 days 11–4
Winemaker Rob Wignall, Michael Perkins **Est.** 1982 **Cases** 9000
A noted producer of Pinot Noir which extended the map for the variety in Australia, since 2004 a welcome return to top form. The white wines are elegant, and show the cool climate to good advantage. A winery was constructed in 1998 and uses the production from the 16 ha of estate plantings. Exports to Denmark, Indonesia, Japan, Taiwan and Singapore.

ΨΨΨΨΨ **Albany Chardonnay 2007** Grapefruit and well-handled toasty oak aromas; good flesh on the palate, with some stone fruits coming through on the finish. Screwcap. 14.5° alc. **Rating** 94 **To** 2014 $28

ΨΨΨΨΨ **Albany Pinot Noir 2007** Deep colour and bright; very ripe fruit, bordering overripe, but good flavour; some alcohol evident on the finish. Screwcap. 15° alc. **Rating** 90 **To** 2011 $30

ΨΨΨΨ **Albany Sauvignon Blanc 2007** Plenty of varietal fruit expression on both bouquet and palate; a little congestion on the finish. Screwcap. 13.5° alc. **Rating** 88 **To** 2009 $17.50

Wild Cattle Creek Winery

473 Warburton Highway, Wandin North, Vic 3139 **Region** Yarra Valley
T 0412 621 102 **F** (03) 5967 1182 **www.**wildcattlecreek.com **Open** Wed–Sun 11.30–5, or by appt
Winemaker Jeff Wright **Est.** 1996 **Cases** 1000
This is the (much-altered) reincarnation of Langbrook Estate Vineyard, continuing under the ownership of Graeme and Ingrid Smith together with daughter Tonia and husband Luke. It has 12 ha of pinot noir, chardonnay, sauvignon blanc, pinot gris, cabernet sauvignon and merlot, and the Sauvignon Blanc, in particular, has had significant show success. A Shiraz (made from contract-grown grapes) has been added to the range.

Wild Dog

South Road, Warragul, Vic 3820 **Region** Gippsland
T (03) 5623 1117 **F** (03) 5623 6402 **www.**wilddogwinery.com **Open** 7 days 10–5
Winemaker Mal Stewart **Est.** 1982 **Cases** 3600
An aptly named winery which produces somewhat rustic wines from the 12 ha of estate vineyards; even the Farringtons (the founders) say that the 'Shiraz comes with a bite', but they also point out that there is minimal handling, fining and filtration. Following the acquisition of Wild Dog by Gary and Judy Surman, Mal Stewart was appointed winemaker with a far-ranging brief to build on the legacy of the previous owners. As the tasting notes indicate, there is much to be confident about. Exports to China.

ΨΨΨΨΨ **Gippsland Chardonnay 2006** Fresh and lively thanks in part to early picking, with flavours of grapefruit and nectarine; subtle oak, good length. Has developed well over the past 12 months. Screwcap. **Rating** 90 **To** 2013

Gippsland Sparkling Shiraz 2006 Notwithstanding its youth, has plenty going for it, the shiraz base neither oaky nor too sweet; however, needs a minimum of 5 years to start showing its best. Cork. 14° alc. **Rating** 90 To 2013 $25

ΨΨΨΨ Gippsland Riesling 2007 Starts with a crisp and bright mix of herb, mineral and lime on a light-bodied palate; overall a little lean. Screwcap. 12° alc. **Rating** 89 To 2013 $20

Gippsland Wild Ice Liqueur Riesling 2007 Very clever winemaking, intense and bright lemon zest fruit; very clean spirit. Screwcap. **Rating** 89 To 2009 $19

Gippsland Shiraz 2006 Spicy cool-grown style, with notes of herb amid black fruits and licorice and olive; overall a little lean. Screwcap. **Rating** 87 To 2014 $20

Wild Duck Creek Estate ★★★★★

Spring Flat Road, Heathcote, Vic 3523 **Region** Heathcote
T (03) 5433 3133 **F** (03) 5433 3133 **Open** By appt
Winemaker David Anderson **Est.** 1980 **Cases** 4000
The first release of Wild Duck Creek Estate from the 1991 vintage marked the end of 12 years of effort by David and Diana Anderson. They began planting the 4.5-ha vineyard in 1980, made their first tiny quantities of wine in '86, the first commercial quantities of wine in '91, and built their winery and cellar door facility in '93. Exports to the US (where Duck Muck has become a cult wine), the UK and other major markets.

ΨΨΨΨΨ Springflat Heathcote Shiraz Pressings 2005 Despite lower alcohol, impressive richness and depth; velvety blackberry, plum and some licorice; one cannot help but ask why it was not back-blended with the standard Springflat. The tannins are soft, not rough, and in perfect balance. Diam. 14.5° alc. **Rating** 95 To 2020 $125

Reserve Heathcote Shiraz 2005 Dense purple-red; luscious, plush, rounded and rich flavours, the alcohol contributing sweetness more than heat; the tannins are soft, oak somewhere in the mix. Diam. 16° alc. **Rating** 95 To 2020 $125

The Blend 2005 An impressive blend of varieties, five vineyards and two regions (Yarra Valley merlot); a delicious and supple cascade of red and black flavours; long finish. Cabernet/Merlot. Diam. 14.5° alc. **Rating** 95 To 2020 $39.95

Reserve Heathcote Cabernet Sauvignon 2005 Fragrant cassis and blackcurrant fruit, with hints of spice and cedar; plush, mouthfilling fruit remarkable at this alcohol level; excellent tannins and oak. Diam. 14° alc. **Rating** 95 To 2020 $130

Springflat Heathcote Shiraz 2005 A faint hint of reduction on the bouquet, but nonetheless with complex spice, leaf and berry aromas; the palate throws off the uncertainty of the bouquet with a velvety array of black fruits, licorice and spice; oak and tannins balanced. Screwcap. 15.5° alc. **Rating** 94 To 2020 $49.95

ΨΨΨΨΨ Yellow Hammer Hill Heathcote Shiraz Malbec 2005 A clean aromatic bouquet; opens in the mouth with ripe, but not jammy, fruit in a black spectrum, firm tannins on the finish a mild surprise. Needs time. Screwcap. 14.5° alc. **Rating** 93 To 2020 $39.95

Alan's Vat 1 Heathcote Cabernets 2005 Floral and scented aromas; although medium-bodied, has potent flavours ranging through blackcurrant to mulberry to mint plus savoury notes; just a trifle edgy. Diam. 14° alc. **Rating** 92 To 2017 $54.95

Homestead Merlot 2004 No doubting the variety; stemmy/foresty/olivaceous characters are spun through the base of blackcurrant fruit; fine tannins. Diam. 13.5° alc. **Rating** 91 To 2014 $29.95

Wild Geese Wines ★★★

PO Box 1157, Balhanna, SA 5242 **Region** Adelaide Hills
T (08) 8388 4464 **F** (08) 8388 4464 **Open** Not
Winemaker Patrick O'Sullivan **Est.** 2000 **Cases** 400

Patrick, a graduate of CSU, and Amanda O'Sullivan (and two business partners) have established a trial planting of four clones of merlot, and have found the difference between each of the clones to be substantial. The Wild Geese name, incidentally, comes from the Irish emigres who fled religious and political persecution in the 18th century to settle elsewhere.

Wild Orchid Wines

PO Box 165, Boyup Brook, WA 6244 **Region** Blackwood Valley
T (08) 9767 3058 **F** (08) 9767 3058 **www.**wildorchidwines.com.au **Open** Not
Winemaker Brad Skraha, Sharna Kowalczuk (Contract) **Est.** 1997 **Cases** 1000
Orest and Robyn Skraha, along with son Brad and his wife Kirsten, have established a little under 16 ha of chardonnay, semillon, shiraz, merlot and cabernet sauvignon. Most of the grapes are sold, with small premium parcels contract-made for the Wild Orchid brand. Brad completed his Bachelor of Science in viticulture and oenology at Curtin University, then gained experience at Howard Park (Margaret River) and Chappellet winery in the Napa Valley. Exports to Singapore.

Wildwood

St John's Lane, Wildwood, Bulla, Vic 3428 **Region** Sunbury
T (03) 9307 1118 **F** (03) 9331 1590 **www.**wildwoodvineyards.com.au **Open** 7 days 10–5
Winemaker Dr Wayne Stott **Est.** 1983 **Cases** 800
Wildwood is just 4 km past Melbourne airport, at an altitude of 130 m in the Oaklands Valley, which provides unexpected views back to Port Phillip Bay and the Melbourne skyline. Plastic surgeon Dr Wayne Stott has taken what is very much a part-time activity rather more seriously than most by completing the wine science degree at CSU.

🍷🍷🍷🍷🍷 **Chardonnay 2007** A nutty, slightly savoury wine, quite elegant on entry; the wine builds flavour and leaves a savoury, nutty, yet fresh finish. Screwcap. 12.5° alc. **Rating** 90 **To** 2012 $25

Wili-Wilia Winery **NR**

80 Scrubby Camp Road, Emu Flat, Vic 3455 **Region** Macedon Ranges
T (03) 5433 5367 **www.**wwwinery.com.au **Open** W'ends & public hols 10–5
Winemaker Cobaw Ridge (Alan Cooper) **Est.** 1996 **Cases** 500
Rod Schmidt and Jacquie Bliss have established their 3.5-ha vineyard (gewurztraminer, chardonnay, pinot noir, shiraz and cabernet sauvignon) at the extreme northern end of the Macedon Ranges region, abutting the southern perimeter of the Heathcote region. For better or worse, they have to use the Macedon Ranges GI, but the wines achieve a greater degree of ripeness than those from the coolest parts of the Macedon Ranges. The wines have been well made, first by Mark Nicol (now gone to Oregon) and, since 2007, at Cobaw Ridge.

Wilkie Estate

Lot 1, Heaslip Road, Penfield, SA 5121 **Region** Adelaide Plains
T (08) 8284 7655 **F** (08) 8284 7618 **www.**wilkieestatewines.com.au **Open** 7 days 10–5
Winemaker Trevor Spurr **Est.** 1990 **Cases** NA
Trevor and Bill Spurr have 17.5 ha of organic-certified vineyards planted to verdelho, cabernet sauvignon, merlot and ruby cabernet. They make the wine onsite, and have established exports to the UK and Belgium.

🍷🍷🍷🍷🍷 **Organic Adelaide Cabernet Merlot 2004** Deep colour, its richness and varietal authenticity from an area not predisposed to these varietals; a great advert for organic grapes, ripe tannins a further plus. Screwcap. 14.5° alc. **Rating** 90 **To** 2014 $14.50

Will Taylor Wines

1B Victoria Avenue, Unley Park, SA 5061 **Region** Southeast Australia
T (08) 8271 6122 **F** (08) 8271 6122 **Open** By appt
Winemaker Various contract **Est.** 1997 **Cases** 1500
Will Taylor is a partner in the leading Adelaide law firm Finlaysons, and specialises in wine
law. He and Suzanne Taylor have established a classic negociant wine business, having wines
contract-made to their specifications. Moreover, they choose what they consider the best
regions for each variety; thus Clare Valley Riesling, Adelaide Hills Sauvignon Blanc, Hunter
Valley Semillon and Yarra Valley Pinot Noir. Exports to the UK, Canada, Hong Kong, China
and Singapore.

♥♥♥♥♥ **Hunter Valley Semillon 2001** Glowing yellow-green; lovely citrus and lemon
cake flavours; long, well-balanced finish; 5 years since its first release (a re-release)
makes all the difference. Cork. 10.6° alc. **Rating** 94 **To** 2011 $26

♥♥♥♥♡ **Coonawarra Cabernet Sauvignon 2005** Mainstream Coonawarra cabernet,
with plenty of drive and length; opens with dusty earthy overtones before the fruit
clicks in, supported by French oak. Cork. 15° alc. **Rating** 91 **To** 2020 $36

Willespie

NR

555 Harmans Mill Road, Wilyabrup via Cowaramup, WA 6284 **Region** Margaret River
T (08) 9755 6248 **F** (08) 9755 6210 **www**.willespie.com.au **Open** 7 days 10.30–5
Winemaker Kevin Squance **Est.** 1976 **Cases** 8500
Willespie has produced many attractive white wines over the years, typically in brisk,
herbaceous Margaret River style; all are fruit- rather than oak-driven. The wines have had
such success that the Squance family (which founded and owns Willespie) has substantially
increased winery capacity, drawing upon an additional 24 ha of estate vineyards now in
bearing. Exports to the UK, Japan and Singapore.

William Downie

121 Yarragon South Road, Yarragon, Vic 3823 (postal) **Region** Yarra Valley
T (03) 5634 2216 **F** (03) 5634 2216 **www**.williamdownie.com.au **Open** Not
Winemaker William Downie **Est.** 2003 **Cases** 500
William Downie spends six months each year making wine in Burgundy, the other six based
in the Yarra Valley with De Bortoli. He uses purchased grapes from older vines to make the
wines, avoiding the use of pumps, filtration and fining. The striking label, designed by artist
Reg Mombassa, has helped obtain listings at The Prince Wine Store and elsewhere. In the
2006 *Gourmet Traveller* Wine Winemaker of the Year Awards, Bill Downie was awarded the
Kemeny's Medal for the Best Young Winemaker 2006. His boss at De Bortoli, Stephen
Webber, goes a little further when he says, 'Downie is the best winemaker in Australia'.

♥♥♥♥♡ **Yarra Valley Pinot Noir 2006** Faintly hazy colour; an understated style, with
sotto voce complexity to its mix of dark fruits and savoury/foresty flavours; good
length and acidity. Diam. 13° alc. **Rating** 92 **To** 2013 $45

Willow Bridge Estate

Gardin Court Drive, Dardanup, WA 6236 **Region** Geographe
T (08) 9728 0055 **F** (08) 9728 0066 **www**.willowbridge.com.au **Open** 7 days 11–5
Winemaker David Crawford **Est.** 1997 **Cases** 40 000
The Dewar family has followed a fast track in developing Willow Bridge Estate since
acquiring the spectacular 180-ha hillside property in the Ferguson Valley in 1996: 70 ha of
chardonnay, semillon, sauvignon blanc, shiraz and cabernet sauvignon were planted, with
tempranillo added in 2000. The winery is capable of handling the 1200–1500 tonnes from
the estate plantings. Not too many wineries in Australia better the price/value ratio of the
mid-range wines of Willow Bridge. Exports to the UK, the US and other major markets.

ΨΨΨΨΨ **Reserve Sauvignon Blanc 2007** A clean bouquet leads into a palate with exceptional zest and thrust for a warm vintage; tingling citrus and kiwifruit flavours run through the long palate. Screwcap. 12° alc. **Rating** 94 **To** 2010 $20
Rose 2007 Fragrant cherry fruit on the bouquet and palate, which is fine and dry, with excellent length. Screwcap. 12.9° alc. **Rating** 94 **To** 2009 $15.50
Family Reserve Shiraz Viognier 2005 Vibrant colour; elegantly sumptuous, the viognier doing its job to perfection; masses of primary red fruit flavours, and a fine finish. Screwcap. 14.5° alc. **Rating** 94 **To** 2020 $28
Black Dog Shiraz 2005 Very refined, cerebral style, with a finesse and purity utterly at odds with its alcohol; a splendid array of black fruits, spice and pepper which have consumed the French oak. Cork. 15° alc. **Rating** 94 **To** 2025 $60

ΨΨΨΨῪ **Reserve Semillon 2007** Skilled winemaking; barrel ferment in new and 1-year-old French oak plus 4 months on lees hasn't taken away the sparkle and finesse of the fruit; good length. Screwcap. 12.5° alc. **Rating** 93 **To** 2014 $20
Sauvignon Blanc Semillon 2007 Sauvignon blanc pulls the wine into a tropical spectrum of passionfruit and pineapple, semillon providing the mineral backbone. Screwcap. 13° alc. **Rating** 90 **To** 2010 $15.50

ΨΨΨΨ **Cabernet Merlot 2006** Bright, clear colour; fresh, zippy redcurrant and blackcurrant fruit on a light- to medium-bodied palate drives the wine, rather than tannins or oak. Screwcap. 13.5° alc. **Rating** 89 **To** 2014 $15.50
Unwooded Chardonnay 2007 Fresh, crisp and clean; good structure and balance, although the flavours are on the light side. Screwcap. 13.5° alc. **Rating** 88 **To** 2009 $15.50
Family Reserve Shiraz Viognier 2006 Despite the viognier, doesn't have the usual silky structure of Willow Bridge reds, the tannins a little out of line on the finish; may settle down. Screwcap. 14° alc. **Rating** 88 **To** 2015 $28
Reserve Tempranillo 2006 It doesn't seem to matter where tempranillo is grown in Australia, a similar mix of red fruits and a dash of lemon juice is the result, this a lunch style for a sunny day. Screwcap. 13.5° alc. **Rating** 88 **To** 2010 $20

Willow Creek Vineyard ★★★★★

166 Balnarring Road, Merricks North, Vic 3926 **Region** Mornington Peninsula
T (03) 5989 7448 **F** (03) 5989 7584 **www.**willow-creek.com.au **Open** 7 days 10–5
Winemaker Phil Kerney **Est.** 1989 **Cases** 7000
A significant presence in the Mornington Peninsula area, with 12 ha of vines planted to cabernet sauvignon, chardonnay, pinot noir and sauvignon blanc. The grape intake is supplemented by purchasing small, quality parcels from local growers. Salix restaurant is out of the ordinary, winning a Chef's Hat from *The Age Good Food Guide*, and with a wine list which includes wines from all 31 of Burgundy's Grand Cru vineyards. The wines from Willow Creek aren't bad, either. Exports to the US and Norway.

ΨΨΨΨΨ **Tulum Mornington Peninsula Chardonnay 2006** A modern, elegant style; whole bunch pressing, wild yeast and only partial mlf result in a wine of great finesse, freshness and length, finishing with citrussy acidity. Screwcap. 13.5° alc. **Rating** 95 **To** 2013 $39.95
Cistercia Mornington Peninsula Chardonnay 2006 A distinctly creamy bouquet, supported by citrus and hints of hazelnut; good flavour, depth and creamy mouthfeel on the finish. Cork. 13.5° alc. **Rating** 94 **To** 2012 $50
Eremetes Mornington Peninsula Syrah 2006 A lifted, fragrant style; a little oaky now, but will see integration with time; ample fine-grained tannins on the finish. Cork. 14° alc. **Rating** 94 **To** 2014 $65
Tulum Mornington Peninsula Cabernet Sauvignon 2005 Ripe and varietal, with a leafy edge; very fine palate, with lots of bright red and dark fruits; fine and silky on the finish; should age gracefully. Screwcap. 14° alc. **Rating** 94 **To** 2015 $35

ΨΨΨΨΨ **WCV Mornington Peninsula Shiraz 2006** Lifted spice and red fruits; cool, fragrant and textural, with lovely focus; this wine should really appeal to those who like a European angle to their wines. Screwcap. 14° alc. **Rating** 93 **To** 2012 $25
Tulum Mornington Peninsula Pinot Noir 2006 An elegant wine, with cherry red fruits, hints of spice and plenty of fine-grained tannins; quite long and expansive. Screwcap. 14° alc. **Rating** 93 **To** 2011 $35
Benedictus Mornington Peninsula Pinot Noir 2006 Dominated by oak at this point, with cola aromas suppressing the elegant red fruits of the wine; better on the palate, but a little less oak may have been the order of the day, time will tell. Cork. 14° alc. **Rating** 92 **To** 2012 $50
WCV Mornington Peninsula Pinot Noir 2006 Clean, straightforward and varietal; cherries and spice, with fine acid and velvety texture. Screwcap. 14° alc. **Rating** 90 **To** 2010 $25

ΨΨΨΨ **WCV Mornington Peninsula Chardonnay 2007** Highly pungent bouquet and distinctly herbaceous; the wine is clean and reflects a little regional sweet and sour characteristic. Screwcap. 13.5° alc. **Rating** 89 **To** 2011 $22
WCV Strathbogie Foothills Shiraz Cabernet 2006 Spicy and full of red fruits; clean and fleshy, with a little kick of cabernet on the finish. Screwcap. 14° alc. **Rating** 89 **To** 2012 $25
WCV Mornington Peninsula Pinot Saignee 2007 A savoury rose with strong varietal pinot aromas; hints of earth and stem; quite dry on the finish. Screwcap. 13.5° alc. **Rating** 88 **To** 2009 $22

Willunga 100 Wines ★★★★☆

Kangarilla Road, McLaren Vale, SA 5171 **Region** McLaren Vale
T (08) 8323 8649 **F** (08) 8323 7622 **www**.libertywine.co.uk **Open** By appt
Winemaker Nick Haselgrove, Warren Randall **Est.** 2005 **Cases** 12 000
This is a joint venture between Blackbilly and Liberty Wines UK, the latter a well-known importer of quality wines from Australia. It is a grape-to-retail venture, the foundation being grapes supplied by 400 ha of McLaren Vale vineyards, with a particular emphasis on viognier, shiraz, grenache and cabernet sauvignon. Almost all the wine is exported to the UK and Europe, with limited amounts sold in Australia by mail order; has hit the scene running with outstanding value for money.

ΨΨΨΨΨ **McLaren Vale Cabernet Shiraz 2006** Brilliant colour; medium- to full-bodied; has abundant black fruits in a positive palate with good drive and complexity; ripe tannins and good oak handling. Screwcap. 14° alc. **Rating** 94 **To** 2016 $18

ΨΨΨΨΨ **McLaren Vale Grenache 2006** Voluminous juicy fruit aromas and flavours are unequivocally varietal, though needs a little more structure/conviction. Screwcap. 14.5° alc. **Rating** 90 **To** 2009 $18

Willy Bay ★★★★

PO Box 193, Inglewood, WA 6932 **Region** Geographe
T (08) 9271 9890 **F** (08) 9271 7771 **www**.willybay.com.au **Open** Not
Winemaker Peter Stanlake **Est.** 2003 **Cases** 1500
Willy Bay Wines is jointly owned and run by the Siciliano and Edwards families, who have established 6.5 ha of shiraz, 2.8 ha of cabernet sauvignon and 1.7 ha of chardonnay. While some of the wine names are borrowed from cricket (I suppose I am meant to know why, but don't) there is nothing ambiguous about wine quality, with even higher scores in prospect.

ΨΨΨΨΨ **French Cut Semillon Sauvignon Blanc 2006** Has good weight and concentration; the ripe fruit has the strength to carry barrel ferment inputs through to a long finish. Screwcap. **Rating** 90 **To** 2011 $22

ΨΨΨΨ **Fine Leg Chardonnay 2006** Ripe brassy fruit, with toffee aromas from the lavish oak treatment. Screwcap. 14° alc. **Rating** 87 **To** 2012 $24

Wilson Vineyard   ★★★★★

Polish Hill River, Sevenhill via Clare, SA 5453 **Region** Clare Valley
T (08) 8843 4310 **www**.wilsonvineyard.com.au **Open** W'ends 10–4
Winemaker Dr John Wilson, Daniel Wilson **Est.** 1974 **Cases** 4000
After working at the shoulder of his father John for many years, Daniel Wilson took
responsibility for the winemaking in 2003. The Wilson Vineyard of today is a far cry from that
of 10 years ago, taking its place in the upper echelon of the Clare Valley.

ҮҮҮҮҮ **Polish Hill River Museum Riesling 2003** Great colour; gloriously intense lime
juice and toast aromas and flavours surround a spine of tingling acidity. Perfection.
Has blossomed since Sept '03. Screwcap. **Rating** 96 **To** 2013 $36

ҮҮҮҮҮ **Clare Valley Merlot Malbec 2005** An interesting, lively blend, with good
velocity in the mouth; blackcurrant, redcurrant, raspberry, mocha, cedar and spice
all make their mark. 66/34. Screwcap. 14.5° alc. **Rating** 93 **To** 2013 $24.50
Polish Hill River Riesling 2007 Shows some of the restrained minerally, spicy
characters of the Grosset Polish Hill; well-balanced, good length, but needs time.
Screwcap. 14° alc. **Rating** 90 **To** 2015 $22

ҮҮҮҮ **Hand Plunge Clare Valley Shiraz 2005** A massive wine; potent prune aromas
flow through into the imposing palate, deriving much of its impact from alcohol.
Screwcap. 16° alc. **Rating** 88 **To** 2015 $35
DJW Clare Valley Riesling 2007 Developed colour; full flavour, but not in the
same class as prior vintages; a short-term proposition. Screwcap. 14° alc. **Rating** 87
To 2009 $19.50

Wily Trout   ★★★★

Marakei-Nanima Road, via Hall, NSW 2618 **Region** Canberra District
T (02) 6230 2487 **F** (02) 6230 2211 **www**.wilytrout.com.au **Open** 7 days 10–5
Winemaker Dr Roger Harris, Andrew McEwen (Contract) **Est.** 1998 **Cases** 3000
The 19.5-ha Wily Trout vineyard shares its home with the Poachers Pantry, a renowned
gourmet smokehouse. The quality of the wines is very good, and a testament to the skills of
the contract winemakers. The northeast-facing slopes, at an elevation of 720 m, provide some
air drainage and hence protection against spring frosts.

ҮҮҮҮҮ **Canberra District Shiraz 2005** Has plenty of pepper and red fruits; high levels
of acid and fine tannins produce a refreshing wine that is sure to age gracefully.
Screwcap. 14.3° alc. **Rating** 93 **To** 2015 $34

Wimbaliri Wines   ★★★★

3180 Barton Highway, Murrumbateman, NSW 2582 **Region** Canberra District
T (02) 6227 5921 **F** (02) 6227 5921 **Open** 7 days 11–5
Winemaker John Andersen **Est.** 1988 **Cases** 600
John and Margaret Andersen moved to the Canberra District in 1987 and began establishing
their vineyard at Murrumbateman in '88; the property borders highly regarded Canberra
producers Doonkuna and Clonakilla. The vineyard is close-planted with a total of 2.2 ha
planted to chardonnay, pinot noir, shiraz, cabernet sauvignon and merlot (plus a few vines
of cabernet franc).

ҮҮҮҮҮ **Gravel Block Shiraz 2005** Deep but bright colour; powerful, focused black
fruits, spice and licorice; a slight tang to the finish, with very good tannins and oak
management on a long finish. Value. Diam. **Rating** 93 **To** 2020 $22

Winbirra Vineyard

173 Point Leo Road, Red Hill South, Vic 3937 **Region** Mornington Peninsula
T (03) 5989 2109 **F** (03) 5989 2109 **www**.winbirra.com.au **Open** 1st w'end month &
public hols 11–5, or by appt
Winemaker Tuerong Winery **Est.** 1990 **Cases** 1300
Winbirra is a small, family-owned and run vineyard which has been producing grapes since
1990, between then and '97 selling the grapes to local winemakers. Since 1997 the wine has
been made and sold under the Winbirra label. There is 1.5 ha of pinot noir (with three clones)
at Red Hill and 1.5 ha each of viognier and pinot gris on a second site at Merricks.

ΨΨΨΨ   **Mornington Peninsula Viognier 2007** A gentle introduction through the
bouquet, but gathers pace on the palate, with an array of apricot and other stone
fruit flavours; good length and balance. Screwcap. 14° alc. **Rating** 89 **To** 2011
$26.50
Mornington Peninsula Pinot Noir 2006 Good colour; interesting wine; opens
with quite sweet plummy mid-palate, then a distinctly briary earthy finish. A
somewhat wild ride. Diam. 14° alc. **Rating** 89 **To** 2012 $35

Winburndale

116 Saint Anthony's Creek Road, Bathurst, NSW 2795 **Region** Central Ranges Zone
T (02) 6337 3134 **F** (02) 6337 3106 **www**.winburndalewines.com.au **Open** By appt
Winemaker Mark Renzaglia, David Lowe (Consultant) **Est.** 1998 **Cases** 2500
Michael Burleigh and family acquired the 200-ha Winburndale property in 1998: 160 ha is
forest, to be kept as a nature reserve; three separate vineyards have been planted under the
direction of viticulturist Mark Renzaglia. The winery paddock has 2.5 ha of shiraz facing
due west at an altitude of 800–820 m; the south paddock, with north and northwest aspects,
varying from 790–810 m, has chardonnay (1.2 ha), shiraz (1 ha) and cabernet sauvignon
(3.5 ha). The home paddock is the most level, with a slight north aspect, and with 1.2 ha
each of merlot and cabernet franc. The name derives from Lachlan Macquarie's exploration
of the Blue Mountains in 1815. No samples received, the rating is that of last year. Exports
to the US and Denmark.

Windance Wines

2764 Caves Road, Yallingup, WA 6282 **Region** Margaret River
T (08) 9755 2293 **F** (08) 9755 2293 **www**.windance.com.au **Open** 7 days 10–5
Winemaker Damon Eastaugh, Liz Reed **Est.** 1998 **Cases** 4000
Drew and Rosemary Brent-White own this family business, situated 5 km south of Yallingup.
A little over 7 ha of cabernet sauvignon, shiraz, sauvignon blanc, semillon and merlot have
been established, incorporating sustainable land management and organic farming practices
where possible. The wines are exclusively estate-grown, pricing fairly reflecting quality.

ΨΨΨΨΨ   **Margaret River Shiraz 2006** Sophisticated winemaking; strong suggestion
of barrel fermentation; fleshy blackberry and plum fruit; particularly long finish.
Screwcap. 14° alc. **Rating** 93 **To** 2011 $36
Margaret River Shiraz 2007 Vibrant purple hue; a young and juicy, raspberry-
laden wine; medium-bodied and with nice weight and texture; slightly savoury
on the finish. Screwcap. 14.2° alc. **Rating** 93 **To** 2015 $25
Margaret River Merlot 2007 Bright-fruited bouquet, with spicy plums and a
hint of briar; fine, juicy and fragrant on the clear-cut palate. Screwcap. 14.5° alc.
Rating 90 **To** 2009 $25

ΨΨΨΨ   **Margaret River Chardonnay 2007** Ultra-pale colour; grapefruit, melon and
apple flavours; crisp finish. Unwooded. Screwcap. 13.2° alc. **Rating** 87 **To** 2009 $18

Windowrie Estate

Windowrie Road, Canowindra, NSW 2804 **Region** Cowra
T (02) 6344 3234 **F** (02) 6344 3227 www.windowrie.com **Open** At the Mill,
Vaux Street, Cowra
Winemaker Folkert Jansen **Est.** 1988 **Cases** 20 000
Windowrie Estate was established in 1988 on a substantial grazing property at Canowindra,
30 km north of Cowra and in the same viticultural region. A portion of the grapes from the
116-ha vineyard are sold to other makers, but increasing quantities are being made for the
Windowrie Estate and The Mill labels; the Chardonnays have enjoyed show success. The
cellar door is in a flour mill built in 1861 from local granite. It ceased operations in 1905 and
lay unoccupied for 91 years until restored by the O'Dea family. Exports to the UK, Ireland,
Canada, Denmark, Holland, Japan and China.

♥♥♥♥♥ **The Mill Limited Release Central Ranges Sangiovese 2006** Good colour;
major surprise; distinctive cherry, as much as sour cherry, fruit with the tannins
no higher than is necessary to give structure. Delicious example at a bargain price.
Cork. 14.5° alc. **Rating** 90 **To** 2012 $17.95

♥♥♥♥ **The Mill Chardonnay 2006** Attractive peach and melon fruit, with a touch of
citrussy acidity to lengthen the palate; subliminal oak. Screwcap. 14° alc. **Rating** 89
To 2010 $14.95
The Mill Central Ranges Shiraz 2006 Sourced from 'various vineyards in the
Central Ranges', and skilfully done to provide a wine with plenty of rich and
succulent black fruits. Twin top. 14.5° alc. **Rating** 89 **To** 2012 $14.95
Deep River Central Ranges Chardonnay 2007 Strong green-yellow;
mouthfilling peachy fruit, the finish showing signs of relatively high alcohol;
seemingly unoaked. Screwcap. 14° alc. **Rating** 87 **To** 2009

Windows Margaret River

4 Quininup Road, Yallingup, WA 6282 (postal) **Region** Margaret River
T (08) 9755 2719 **F** (08) 9755 2719 www.windowsmargaretriver.com **Open** Not
Winemaker Christopher Davies, Barbara Davies **Est.** 1996 **Cases** 5000
Len and Barbara Davies progressively established 1.5 ha of cabernet sauvignon, 1 ha each of
chenin blanc and shiraz, and 0.5 ha each of semillon and merlot, selling the grapes. In 2006 the
decision was taken to move to winemaking. Since Barbara Davies is a qualified winemaker and
works with her son Chris (as assistant winemaker and vineyard manager) the decision wasn't
hard to make. It has been rewarded with considerable show success for its consistently good,
enticingly priced, wines. Exports to Taiwan, Malaysia, Singapore, China and Hong Kong.

♥♥♥♥♥ **Sauvignon Blanc 2007** A mix of tropical and gooseberry fruit, with above-
average depth of flavour, but a slightly soft, bland finish. Trophy Cowra Wine Show
'07. Screwcap. 13.5° alc. **Rating** 92 **To** 2009 $18.95
Semillon Sauvignon Blanc 2006 Light-bodied; semillon provides the
framework and length, sauvignon blanc some tropical notes, then a citrussy finish.
Screwcap. 12° alc. **Rating** 90 **To** 2010 $18.95
Shiraz 2005 Has a strong, cool savoury streak; good flavour and line; a quite firm
and long finish. Screwcap. 14.3° alc. **Rating** 90 **To** 2014 $22

♥♥♥♥ **Sauvignon Blanc Semillon 2007** A mix of citrus and gooseberry aromas and
flavours; firm finish, some mineral. Screwcap. 13° alc. **Rating** 88 **To** 2012 $18.95

WindshakeR Ridge

PO Box 106, Karrinyup, WA 6921 **Region** Swan District
T (08) 6241 4100 **F** (08) 9240 6220 www.windshaker.com.au **Open** Not
Winemaker Ryan Sudano **Est.** 2003 **Cases** 4000

The Moltoni family has owned a 2000-ha farming property for three generations. Robert Moltoni is the driving force, establishing WindshakeR Ridge in 2003. The 25 ha vineyard (carnelian, semillon, shiraz and verdelho) is 9 km north of Gingin, and looks out over the hills to the sea. Moltoni is an accomplished poet, and I cannot help but quote one of his poems: 'Easterlies whistle through the gums/Crashing over silent ridges/Bathing vines in Namatjira Crimson/WindshakeR, WindshakeR, WindshakeR/The ghost winds whisper down/Off the red plains to the sea.' Exports to the US and China.

ŸŸŸŸ **Carnelian 2005** Bright hue; plenty of red and black fruits, the tannins needing to soften and integrate. Carnelian is a cross between cabernet sauvignon, carignan and grenache bred in the US. Screwcap. 14° alc. **Rating** 87 **To** 2012 $13.50
Carnelian 2006 Light- to medium-bodied; sweet cherry and plum on entry to the palate, then persistent tannins; needs to come together, but should do so. Screwcap. 14° alc. **Rating** 87 **To** 2011 $19.50

wine by brad ★★★★

PO Box 475, Margaret River, WA 6285 **Region** Margaret River
T 0409 572 957 **F** (08) 9757 1897 **www**.winebybrad.com.au **Open** Not
Winemaker Brad Wehr, Clive Otto **Est.** 2003 **Cases** 2500
Brad Wehr says that wine by brad 'is the result of a couple of influential winemakers and shadowy ruffians deciding that there was something to be gained by putting together some pretty neat parcels of wine from the region, creating their own label, and releasing it with minimal fuss'. In 2007 a premium range was introduced under the Mantra label, with separately sourced grapes.

ŸŸŸŸŸ **Margaret River Cabernet Merlot 2005** Medium-bodied; supple, round and smooth cassis, mulberry and blackberry fruit; good tannin and oak management. Screwcap. 13.5° alc. **Rating** 92 **To** 2020 $25
Margaret River Semillon Sauvignon Blanc 2007 A relatively subdued bouquet, but with plenty of intensity, drive and movement on the palate, with zesty lemony acidity. Screwcap. 13° alc. **Rating** 90 **To** 2011 $25

ŸŸŸŸ **Mantra Revelation Margaret River Sauvignon Blanc 2007** Faintly blurred tropical aromas are reflected on the palate, with light passionfruit and grassy fruit; has redeeming length. Screwcap. 13° alc. **Rating** 87 **To** 2009 $19.95
Mantra Affirmation Margaret River Semillon Sauvignon Blanc 2007 All the activity is in the mouth, with vibrant citrussy/minerally acidity giving a sherbet mouthfeel. Screwcap. 13° alc. **Rating** 87 **To** 2010 $19.95

Wines of Willochra ★★☆

PO Box 1108, North Haven, SA 5018 **Region** Southern Flinders Ranges
T 0409 043 229 **F** (08) 8341 9529 **Open** Not
Winemaker Jeanneret (Ben Jeanneret) **Est.** 2004 **Cases** 675
Darren Meyers (with the help of wife Deborah and children Mitchell and Amanda) has established this 4-ha shiraz vineyard just south of Wilmington in the Southern Flinders Ranges which they say is 'considered as the most northern commercial vineyard in the driest state in the driest continent on earth'.

Winetrust Estates ★★★★

PO Box 541, Balgowlah, NSW 2093 **Region** Southeast Australia
T (02) 9949 9250 **F** (02) 9907 8179 **www**.winetrustestates.com **Open** Not
Winemaker Andrew Peace, Rob Moody **Est.** 1999 **Cases** 35 000
Mark Arnold is the man behind Winetrust Estates, drawing on a lifetime of experience in wine marketing. It is a virtual winery operation, drawing grapes from three states and five regions using contract winemakers according to the origin of the grapes (either contract-grown or produced under a joint venture). The top-of-the-range Picarus red wines come

from the Limestone Coast; the other ranges are Ocean Grove and Firebox, covering all the major varietal wines plus a few newcomers. Exports to the US, Canada, China, Japan, Singapore, Hong Kong and Thailand.

ΨΨΨΨΨ **Picarus Wrattonbully Shiraz 2006** Medium- to full-bodied; rich, plush blackberry and spice fruit accompanied by ripe tannins; good length. Screwcap. 13.5° alc. **Rating** 92 **To** 2016 $20
Picarus Padthaway Chardonnay 2006 Light- to medium-bodied, understated wine with gentle stone fruit flavours woven through French oak with some creamy/nutty characters. Screwcap. 13.5° alc. **Rating** 90 **To** 2012 $18.50

ΨΨΨΨ **Picarus Clare Valley Riesling 2006** Quite full-flavoured, with ripe citrus fruit, but does shorten on the finish. Screwcap. 12.5° alc. **Rating** 87 **To** 2011 $17.50
Picarus Wrattonbully Cabernet Sauvignon 2006 A powerful, but somewhat rustic, underworked palate with black fruits; has a rough sort of balance, and should improve with time in bottle. Screwcap. 13.5° alc. **Rating** 87 **To** 2016 $20

Winstead

75 Winstead Road, Bagdad, Tas 7030 **Region** Southern Tasmania
T (03) 6268 6417 **F** (03) 6268 6417 **Open** By appt
Winemaker Neil Snare **Est.** 1989 **Cases** 350
The good news about Winstead is the outstanding quality of its extremely generous and rich Pinot Noirs, rivalling those of Freycinet for the abundance of their fruit flavour without any sacrifice of varietal character. The bad news is that production is so limited, with only 0.8 ha of pinot noir and 0.4 ha riesling being tended by fly-fishing devotee Neil Snare and wife Julieanne.

ΨΨΨΨΨ **Pinot Noir 2005** Good hue and depth; excellent texture, balance and mouthfeel; convincing mesh of ripe plum fruit and gently spicy tannins, fine finish. **Rating** 94 **To** 2011
Reserve Pinot Noir 2005 Distinctly firm and more youthful style, still to open up as it will in due course to emulate the varietal; has length, all it needs is time. **Rating** 94 **To** 2012 $45

ΨΨΨΨΨ **Riesling 2005** Bright green-straw; developing slowly but surely, with a mix of lime, mandarin and apple; good length and balance. Screwcap. 12° alc. **Rating** 90 **To** 2012 $20

ΨΨΨΨ **Riesling 2006** Still showing some CO_2, but has a strong, minerally personality; has a great track record of improving with age. **Rating** 89 **To** 2011
Pinot Noir 2006 Essency pinot fruit, hints of confiture on the bouquet; nice texture, good length. **Rating** 89 **To** 2011

Winter Creek Wine

PO Box 170, Williamstown, SA 5351 **Region** Barossa Valley
T (08) 8524 6382 **F** (08) 8524 6382 **www.**wintercreekwine.com.au **Open** By appt
Winemaker David Cross **Est.** 2000 **Cases** 1500
David and Pam Cross acquired their small vineyard at Williamstown in the cooler foothills of the southern Barossa Valley in 2000, in time for their first vintage that year. There are 2 ha of shiraz, and 1 ha of 70-year-old grenache. More recently they have added a Sauvignon Blanc and a Chardonnay to the Winter Creek range, the grapes purchased from the Adelaide Hills. The wines are exported to the US and Denmark, appreciated in the US for their elegance rather than their alcohol.

ΨΨΨΨΨ **The Old Barossa Blend Grenache Shiraz 2005** Very savoury, earthy, grenache-dominant (75%) wine, which does, however, have very good thrust and length to the medium-bodied palate. Ready now. Screwcap. 14° alc. **Rating** 90 **To** 2012 $25

Vintage Fortified Shiraz 2006 A take-no-prisoners style, but the naked power has good foundations, with neutral spirit and a dry Portuguese-style finish. Could really surprise with 10 years in bottle. Screwcap. 20° alc. **Rating** 90 **To** 2018 $20

♀♀♀♀ **Adelaide Hills Sauvignon Blanc 2007** A solid mix of herb, grass and riper fruit; has flavour but is slightly short. Screwcap. 12.5° alc. **Rating** 87 **To** 2009 $18

Wirra Wirra   ★★★★★

McMurtrie Road, McLaren Vale, SA 5171 **Region** McLaren Vale
T (08) 8323 8414 **F** (08) 8323 8596 **www**.wirrawirra.com **Open** Mon–Sat 10–5, Sun & public hols 11–5
Winemaker Samantha Connew, Alexia Roberts **Est.** 1969 **Cases** 150 000
Long respected for the consistency of its white wines, Wirra Wirra has now established an equally formidable reputation for its reds. Right across the board, the wines are of exemplary character, quality and style, The Angelus Cabernet Sauvignon and RSW Shiraz battling with each other for supremacy. Long may the battle continue under the direction of new managing director Andrew Kay following the retirement of highly respected Tim James, particularly in the wake of the death of the universally loved co-founder/owner Greg Trott in early 2005. In Dec '07 Wirra Wirra purchased the 20-ha Rayner Vineyard (with blocks dating back to the 1950s) which had hitherto supplied Brokenwood with the grapes for its eponymous icon shiraz. Exports to all major markets.

♀♀♀♀♀ **RSW McLaren Vale Shiraz 2005** An exceptionally intense and long palate; red and black fruits with strong overtones of regional chocolate supported by fine tannins; 20 months in oak. French (65%)/American (35%). Screwcap. 14.5° alc. **Rating** 96 **To** 2025 $60
RSW McLaren Vale Shiraz 2006 It is hard to visualise a wine with more regional character than this, dark chocolate a translucent veil for the blackberry fruit; has outstanding texture and structure on the back palate and finish. Screwcap. 14.5° alc. **Rating** 95 **To** 2021 $60
The Angelus McLaren Vale Cabernet Sauvignon 2006 Very good colour; an elegant and complex mix of blackcurrant fruit, cassis, cedar and dark chocolate, the tannins ripe and perfectly balanced. Screwcap. 14.5° alc. **Rating** 95 **To** 2026 $60
The Lost Watch Adelaide Hills Riesling 2007 A fresh and vivacious bouquet leads into fine passionfruit and citrus flavours on the palate; elegant but intense. Screwcap. 12.5° alc. **Rating** 94 **To** 2015 $16.50
Hiding Champion Sauvignon Blanc 2007 Opens quietly, progressively building intensity through to the back-palate, finish and aftertaste; grass, citrus and a touch of passionfruit. Screwcap. 13.5° alc. **Rating** 94 **To** 2009 $19.99
The Angelus McLaren Vale Cabernet Sauvignon 2005 A complex mix of ripe and juicy blackcurrant, cedar, black olives and toasty oak; plenty of flavour, and good length. Screwcap. 14.5° alc. **Rating** 94 **To** 2020 $55

♀♀♀♀♀ **Woodhenge McLaren Vale Shiraz 2006** Deeply coloured with dark chocolatey fruits; full-bodied and deep, with a savoury, dry and firm finish. Screwcap. 14.5° alc. **Rating** 93 **To** 2020 $35
Catapult McLaren Vale Shiraz Viognier 2006 Great colour; highly aromatic with florals and dark roasted meats on offer; dense and chewy, with a fine, even finish. Screwcap. 14.5° alc. **Rating** 92 **To** 2015 $20
Scrubby Rise Shiraz Cabernet Sauvignon Petit Verdot 2006 A lively, medium-bodied palate with a generous mix of blackberry, blackcurrant and cherry, the tannins and oak spot-on. Screwcap. 14.5° alc. **Rating** 91 **To** 2012 $15
The 12th Man Adelaide Hills Chardonnay 2006 Tightly structured, nectarine, grapefruit and apple flavours; minimal oak and a long finish; still to fully flower. Screwcap. 13° alc. **Rating** 91 **To** 2012 $24.50
The 12th Man Adelaide Hills Chardonnay 2007 More like an opening batter in the Matthew Hayden mould, powerful and full-flavoured; lots of nectarine fruit and not short of willow oak. Screwcap. 13.5° alc. **Rating** 90 **To** 2011 $24.50

Scrubby Rise Sauvignon Blanc Semillon Viognier 2007 Has more intensity and drive than most of such blends; very attractive citrus tang and zest on the finish; a faint echo of barrel ferment. Screwcap. 13° alc. **Rating** 90 **To** 2009 $15
Mrs Wigley Rose 2007 A user-friendly style from start to finish; bright strawberry fruit and a touch of sweetness on the back palate. Screwcap. 12.5° alc. **Rating** 90 **To** 2009 $16.50
Church Block McLaren Vale Cabernet Sauvignon Shiraz Merlot 2005 An honest wine, strongly regional and stoutly constructed, with black fruits, a touch of bitter chocolate, and well-balanced tannins. Screwcap. 14.5° alc. **Rating** 90 **To** 2018 $20

ŸŸŸŸ **Scrubby Rise Shiraz Cabernet Sauvignon Petit Verdot 2007** As usual, over-delivers expectations with its multifaceted aromas and flavours, the tannins tamed by clever winemaking to allow the blackberry/mulberry/raspberry fruits free reign. Screwcap. 14.5° alc. **Rating** 89 **To** 2014 $16.50
Church Block McLaren Vale Cabernet Sauvignon Shiraz Merlot 2006 Notwithstanding the blend (50/30/20) it is the region which comes through most clearly, transcending all varieties; medium-bodied, with dark chocolate and some oak influence to the black fruits. Screwcap. 14.5° alc. **Rating** 89 **To** 2014 $20
Mrs Wigley Moscato 2007 Exactly as the cellar door ordered; fizzy, giggly and grapey sweet. Technically not wine – alcohol is too low. Crown Seal. 5.5° alc. **Rating** 87 **To** 2009 $17.95

Wirruna Estate ★★★

419a Lake Road, Bethanga, Vic 3691 **Region** North East Victoria Zone
T (02) 6040 4808 **F** (02) 6040 6046 **www**.wirrunawines.com **Open** By appt
Winemaker John Woodhouse **Est.** 1997 **Cases** 1650
John and Sandra Woodhouse have established 1.5 ha of each of shiraz, durif and marsanne on the banks of Lake Hume. The varieties were chosen because of their compatibility with the hot, dry summers, while the Wirruna name is an Aboriginal word for the sunset depicted on the labels. Son-in-law Manfred Walch works as assistant winemaker during vintage, and John, Sandra and Manfred work on the property in a part-time capacity for most of the year. Picking, done over three weekends, is a family and friends affair.

ŸŸŸŸ **JW Family Reserve Shiraz 2004** Very ripe prune, licorice and plum flavours suggest higher alcohol; dips on the back-palate but kicks again on the finish and aftertaste. Screwcap. 14° alc. **Rating** 87 **To** 2012 $16
JW Family Reserve Durif 2004 Dense colour; dense black fruits and dark chocolate, with the edge of presumably late-corrected acidity present in most of the Wirruna reds. Screwcap. 14° alc. **Rating** 87 **To** 2012 $20

Wise Wine ★★★★★

Lot 4 Eagle Bay Road, Dunsborough, WA 6281 **Region** Margaret River
T (08) 9756 8627 **F** (08) 9756 8770 **www**.wisewine.com.au **Open** 7 days 10–5
Winemaker Amanda Kramer, Andrew Bromley **Est.** 1986 **Cases** 18 000
Wise Vineyards, headed by Perth entrepreneur Ron Wise, is going from strength to strength, with 18 ha at the Meelup Vineyard in Margaret River, 10 ha at the Donnybrook Vineyard in Geographe, and leases on the Bramley and Bunkers Bay vineyards, with a total of almost 40 ha. Wine quality is consistently very good, often outstanding. Exports to the US, Vietnam, Singapore and Taiwan.

ŸŸŸŸŸ **Pemberton Sauvignon Blanc 2007** A delicious array of passionfruit, grapefruit and gooseberry aromas and flavours; long palate, finishing with citrussy acidity. Screwcap. 13.5° alc. **Rating** 95 **To** 2009 $29
Semillon Sauvignon Blanc 2007 Fragrant citrus and passionfruit aromas; perfect clarity and great intensity to the long palate and lingering aftertaste. Screwcap. 13.5° alc. **Rating** 95 **To** 2009 $17

Single Vineyard Chardonnay 2006 Has the pure and elegant Wise style, initially deceptively light, but intensity unfurling with each sip of stone fruit and grapefruit flavours plus a touch of creamy lees. Screwcap. 14° alc. **Rating** 95 **To** 2012 $45

ŸŸŸŸŸ **Eagle Bay Shiraz 2005** Fragrant, fresh and lively red cherry, plum and raspberry aromas and flavours; light- to medium-bodied, but has length and poise, the oak nicely restrained. Screwcap. 14° alc. **Rating** 92 **To** 2015 $30

ŸŸŸŸ **The Bramley Cabernet Sauvignon 2004** Unusually for Wise, fails to live up to expectations; by no means a poor wine, but its antecedents (Bramley plantings 1965 and '66) plus 20-year-old Eagle Bay fruit suggest more. Screwcap. 14° alc. **Rating** 89 **To** 2013 $45
Single Vineyard Donnybrook Verdelho 2007 Classy winemaking provides a perfectly balanced wine; the varietal fruit, however, is far from emphatic. Screwcap. 13.5° alc. **Rating** 88 **To** 2009 $29

Witchcliffe Estate ★★★★☆

Wickham Road, Witchcliffe, WA 6285 **Region** Margaret River
T (08) 9757 6279 **F** (08) 9757 6279 **www**.witchcliffe-estate.com.au **Open** 7 days (summer), Wed–Sun (winter) 11–5
Winemaker Peter Stanlake **Est.** 2003 **Cases** 2000
While the establishment date of Witchcliffe Estate is shown as 2003, the 8-ha vineyard of semillon, sauvignon blanc, chardonnay and shiraz was planted in the early '90s. Tony and Maureen Cosby acquired the 69-ha property in 2000, at which time it was best known as the Margaret River Marron Farm. The Cosbys still farm marron on a small scale, selling both at the farm gate, and through the cellar door. It has been a very impressive start.

ŸŸŸŸŸ **Margaret River Semillon Sauvignon Blanc 2007** Good fruit, with intense tropical flavours framed by a little fresh cut grass; well-balanced finish. Screwcap. 12.7° alc. **Rating** 94 **To** 2011 $16.50

🍃 Witches Falls Winery ★★★★

79 Main Western Road, North Tamborine, Qld 4272 **Region** Granite Belt
T (07) 5545 2609 **F** (07) 5545 0189 **www**.witchesfalls.com.au **Open** 7 days 10–4
Winemaker Jon Heslop, Richard Abraham **Est.** 2004 **Cases** 6500
This is the venture of Jon and Kim Heslop, and former Brisbane lawyer-turned-winemaker Richard Abraham. Abraham's conversion is more recent than that of Jon Heslop, who has 12 years' experience in the wine industry, the first three as a sales representative for Orlando Wyndham, before realising he wanted to make his own wine, rather than sell someone else's. His career began as a cellarhand with Richmond Grove, before moving to the Hunter Valley as a winemaker at Tamburlaine, and says 'I was influenced by Rod Kemp of Lake's Folly, PJ Charteris of Brokenwood and Andrew Thomas of Thomas Wines' which is not a bad trio. In 2004 he moved back to Qld with his wife to establish Witches Falls Winery, and was joined in '05 by Richard Abraham, who is currently undertaking a degree in applied science (oenology) at CSU, a degree which Jon Heslop already has under his belt. The only estate plantings are of durif; the other wines are made from contract-grown grapes.

ŸŸŸŸŸ **Falls Prophecy Cabernet Sauvignon 2005** Strong colour; classy medium-bodied wine, with classic varietal fruit and seamlessly integrated and balanced tannins, and cedary oak; lingering finish. Screwcap. 14.2° alc. **Rating** 94 **To** 2015 $45

ŸŸŸŸ **Wild Fermented Granite Belt Chardonnay 2007** Full barrel fermentation has diminished varietal fruit expression, although it has added to the nutty, creamy texture; swings and roundabouts. Screwcap. 13.1° alc. **Rating** 87 **To** 2010 $25

Witchmount Estate

557 Leakes Road, Rockbank, Vic 3335 **Region** Sunbury
T (03) 9747 1055 **F** (03) 9747 1066 **www**.witchmount.com.au **Open** Wed–Sun 10–5
Winemaker Steve Goodwin **Est.** 1991 **Cases** 6800
Gaye and Matt Ramunno operate Witchmount Estate in conjunction with its Italian
restaurant and function rooms. A little under 19 ha of vines have been established since 1991,
with an eclectic array of eight varieties ranging from mainstream to barbera and tempranillo.
The quality of the wines has been consistently excellent, the prices very modest. Exports to
Canada and Singapore.

ŸŸŸŸŸ **Cabernet Sauvignon 2004** Dark fruits and earthy/savoury nuances; full-bodied
and quite tannic, but ample fruit to support the structure, and the finish is long.
Screwcap. 14.5° alc. **Rating** 92 **To** 2015 $26

ŸŸŸŸ **Cabernet Merlot 2005** Dense colour; a very powerful and tight wine, still quite
austere, with earthy notes to the well of black fruits, the softening influence of
merlot nowhere to be seen yet. Screwcap. 14.5° alc. **Rating** 89 **To** 2015 $26
Barbera 2005 An earthy bouquet, the palate with medium-bodied
concentration; spicy/earthy and quite dry on the finish, with a brambly personality.
Screwcap. 14° alc. **Rating** 89 **To** 2012 $26
Olivia's Paddock Chardonnay 2006 Quite cool chardonnay fruit on the
bouquet, with more savoury nutty characters dominating the long finish. Screwcap.
14° alc. **Rating** 88 **To** 2012 $26

WJ Walker Wines

Burns Road, Lake Grace, WA 6353 **Region** Central Western Australia Zone
T (08) 9865 1969 **Open** 7 days 10–4
Winemaker Porongurup Winery **Est.** 1998 **Cases** 700
Lake Grace is 300 km due east of Bunbury, one of those isolated viticultural outposts which
are appearing in many parts of Australia these days. There are 1.5 ha of shiraz and 0.5 ha of
chardonnay.

ŸŸŸŸŸ **Lake Grace Shiraz 2005** A spotless, fruit-driven bouquet leading into a medium-
bodied palate, with black cherry, plum and spice; has life and movement; fine tannins
and gentle oak. Great value. Screwcap. 13.5° alc. **Rating** 92 **To** 2015 $15

ŸŸŸŸ **Lake Grace Shiraz 2006** Rich plummy fruit; soft tannins and lots of American
oak. **Rating** 87 **To** 2013 $18

Wolf Blass

Bilyara Vineyards, 97 Sturt Highway, Nuriootpa, SA 5355 **Region** Barossa Valley
T (08) 8568 7300 **F** (08) 8568 7380 **www**.wolfblass.com.au **Open** Mon–Fri 9.15–5,
w'ends & public hols 10–5
Winemaker Chris Hatcher (Chief), Caroline Dunn (Red), Mat O'Leary (White)
Est. 1966 **Cases** 4 million
Although merged with Mildara and now under the giant umbrella of Foster's, the brands
(as expected) have been left largely intact. The white wines are particularly impressive, none
more so than the Gold Label Riesling. After a short pause, the red wines have improved out
of all recognition thanks to the sure touch (and top palate) of Caroline Dunn. All of this has
occurred under the leadership of Chris Hatcher, who has harnessed the talents of the team
and encouraged the changes in style. Exports to all major markets.

ŸŸŸŸŸ **Gold Label Adelaide Hills Shiraz Viognier 2005** Has evolved out of all
recognition over the past 12 months. Highly perfumed and wonderfully rich
and deep, an absolutely brilliant finish and aftertaste. Screwcap. 15° alc. **Rating** 96
To 2020 $24.95

White Label Specially Aged Release Eden Valley Riesling 2002 Very restrained given its age, genesis in the cool vintage; doesn't have quite the same striking allure of Lehmann Reserve or Heggies Contour from the same vintage; very good wine, nonetheless. Screwcap. **Rating** 94 **To** 2014 $39.95

White Label Chardonnay 2004 Shares many attributes with the '03 White Label; complex, with strong barrel ferment characters, and a great volume of nectarine fruit on the mid-palate. Gold, National Wine Show '07. **Rating** 94 **To** 2011 $39.95

White Label Chardonnay 2003 Very complex wine with some funky Burgundian barrel ferment characters; has abundant fruit on the mid-palate, and great length. Altogether stylish. **Rating** 94 **To** 2011 $39.95

Platinum Label Barossa Shiraz 2005 A deep and densely flavoured wine, with abundant black fruits and dark chocolate overtones; excellent control of tannin and oak, with some barrel ferment hints. **Rating** 94 **To** 2025 $157.95

Black Label Cabernet Sauvignon Shiraz Malbec 2005 Saturated colour; in typical modern Black Label style, oozing dark black fruits, ripe tannins and an abundance of new oak all tied together. Screwcap. 15.3° alc. **Rating** 94 **To** 2025 $129.95

ΨΨΨΨΨ **Gold Label Sauvignon Blanc 2007** A relatively subdued bouquet, but picks up pace on the palate, with an attractive mix of sweet tropical and citrus fruit; harmonious finish. Screwcap. 12° alc. **Rating** 93 **To** 2009 $21.99

Gold Label Adelaide Hills Cabernet Sauvignon Merlot Cabernet Franc 2005 A very fragrant bouquet, almost floral; a similarly fresh array of red and black fruits with nuances of spice and licorice on the palate; oak a touch assertive, but will settle down. Screwcap. 14.5° alc. **Rating** 92 **To** 2017 $24.95

White Label Chardonnay 2002 Vivid green-gold; obviously made for delayed release, because still tight and minerally; will it ever fully flower? Perhaps. Screwcap. **Rating** 91 **To** 2015 $39.95

Grey Label McLaren Vale Shiraz 2006 An opulent wine in every respect; fruit, oak, alcohol and berry and dark chocolate fruit; while medium- to full-bodied, it is soft; for early or later consumption. Screwcap. 15° alc. **Rating** 91 **To** 2016 $40.95

Gold Label Adelaide Hills Chardonnay 2006 Supple and smooth, showing some early stages of development; white peach and nectarine, gentle oak. Screwcap. 13° alc. **Rating** 90 **To** 2013 $24.95

Gold Label Coonawarra Cabernet Sauvignon 2005 Made despite Wolf's refusenik view of Coonawarra; a classic Coonawarra cabernet style, with cassis, mulberry and blackcurrant; good oak handling, and has length. PS, he did sign the label. Screwcap. 14.5° alc. **Rating** 90 **To** 2015 $24.95

ΨΨΨΨ **Yellow Label Riesling 2006** Achieves good depth of flavour without coarseness; a gently ripe basket of citrus and some tropical fruits; ready now. Screwcap. 12.5° alc. **Rating** 89 **To** 2010 $16.95

Gold Label Barossa Shiraz 2006 Quite how well this wine escapes the scar of the high alcohol is beyond me; however, has supple fruit and strong oak in true Blass style. Screwcap. 15.5° alc. **Rating** 89 **To** 2014 $24.95

Grey Label Langhorne Creek Cabernet Sauvignon 2006 Good depth and hue to the colour; very powerful, full-bodied with unexpected firm and persistent tannins; may or may not achieve balance with prolonged cellaring. Screwcap. 14.5° alc. **Rating** 89 **To** 2020 $40.95

Red Label Semillon Sauvignon Blanc 2007 Clean, positive and quite juicy aromatic flavours in a citrus spectrum; subliminal touch of sugar adds to the length. Screwcap. 12.5° alc. **Rating** 88 **To** 2009 $13.95

Red Label Cabernet Merlot 2006 Good structure and texture for the price; red berry fruits, fine tannins and balanced oak. Screwcap. 13.5° alc. **Rating** 88 **To** 2012 $13.95

Yellow Label Sauvignon Blanc 2007 Well made and balanced; gentle varietal fruit in a tropical spectrum; modest finish. Screwcap. 12° alc. **Rating** 87 To 2009 $16.99

Red Label Traminer Riesling 2007 Similar purpose-designed wine to Rosemount Traminer Riesling headed to Chinese restaurants or takeaway. Screwcap. 11° alc. **Rating** 87 To 2009 $13.95

Red Label Shiraz Cabernet Sauvignon 2006 Simple but fresh black and red berry fruits is all the market demands, tannins and oak all but absent. Screwcap. 13.5° alc. **Rating** 87 To 2009 $13.95

Yellow Label Cabernet Sauvignon 2006 Relatively light-bodied, but has good cabernet fruit and deceptive length; balanced tannins likewise. Screwcap. 13.5° alc. **Rating** 87 To 2012 $16.95

Wolseley Wines ★★★

1790 Hendy Main Road, Paraparap, Vic 3240 **Region** Geelong
T 0412 990 638 **www**.wolseleywines.com **Open** W'ends & public hols 11–6
Winemaker Will Wolseley **Est.** 1992 **Cases** 2500
Will Wolseley grew up in Somerset, England, and from an early age made blackberry wine at home. He came to Australia in 1986 and enrolled in wine science at CSU, gathering vintage experience at various wineries over the next five years. A two-year search for an ideal vineyard site resulted in the acquisition of property on the gently sloping hills of Paraparap, inland from Bells Beach, Torquay. He established 6.5 ha of pinot noir, cabernet sauvignon, chardonnay, shiraz, cabernet franc and semillon. Hail storms, frost and drought delayed the first commercial vintage until 1998, but the solar-powered winery is now in full production.

 # Wombat Lodge NR

c/- 21 Princes Street, Cottesloe, WA 6011 (postal) **Region** Margaret River
T 0418 948 125 **F** (08) 9284 4455 **Open** Not
Winemaker Sandstone Wines (Jan McIntosh) **Est.** 1997 **Cases** 500
It pays to have a keenly developed sense of humour if you are a small winemaker committed to producing the very best possible wine regardless of cost and market constraints. The short version (and I quote) is 'Warick (sic) Gerrard, owner/consumer; Jan McIntosh, winemaker and life partner; Danny Edwards, viticulture and adopted son; 60 ha of central Wilyabrup land, two houses and 60 cows; 4 ha of spoilt vines and 500 cases of red wine. There is a much longer version, underlining Danny Edwards' freedom to organically grow the vines with limited irrigation limiting yield and maximising quality, and Jan MacIntosh's freedom to buy as much French oak as she wishes.' The outcome is four clones of cabernet sauvignon, merlot, cabernet franc, malbec and petit verdot in the 500-case make up, selling for the ludicrously low price of $120 per case plus postage.

Wonga Estate ★★★★☆

204 Jumping Creek Road, Wonga Park, Vic 3115 **Region** Yarra Valley
T (03) 9722 2122 **F** (03) 9722 1715 **www**.wongaestate.com.au **Open** Mon–Sat 9–5, Sun 10–5 by appt
Winemaker Greg Roberts, Sergio Carlei (Consultant) **Est.** 1997 **Cases** 900
Greg and Jady Roberts developed their 1.8-ha vineyard in 1997 with a minor expansion in 2002. The wines are made at the onsite micro-winery by Greg Roberts with assistance from Sergio Carlei. Since 2002 the range has been expanded with shiraz grown in the Colbinabbin area of Heathcote, open-fermented and basket-pressed. Limited production has not stopped the listing of the wines at an impressive range of Melbourne, Yarra Valley and Brisbane restaurants.

 Heathcote Shiraz 2005 Deep crimson-purple; classic Heathcote in the big style, abounding with black fruits in a soft, rounded palate; can be enjoyed now or in 20 years. Cork. 15° alc. **Rating** 94 To 2025 $55

ŢŢŢŢ̣̣ **Yarra Valley Chardonnay 2006** Has more richness and weight than the alcohol would suggest, with ripe stone fruit carrying the barrel ferment oak inputs well; does shorten slightly. Cork. 13° alc. **Rating** 90 **To** 2011 $25

Wood Park   ★★★★

263 Kneebones Gap Road, Markwood, Vic 3678 **Region** King Valley
T (03) 5727 3367 **F** (03) 5727 3682 www.woodparkwines.com.au **Open** At Milawa Cheese Factory 7 days 10–5
Winemaker John Stokes **Est.** 1989 **Cases** 12 000
John Stokes planted the first vines at Wood Park in 1989 as part of a diversification program for his property at Bobinawarrah, in the hills of the Lower King Valley, east of Milawa. The vineyard is managed with minimal chemical use, winemaking a mix of modern and traditional techniques. In an unusual twist, Stokes acquires his chardonnay from cousin John Leviny, one of the King Valley pioneers, who has his vineyard at Meadow Creek. The quality of the wines made in 2004 and subsequent vintages is very impressive. Exports to China and NZ.

ŢŢŢŢ̣̣ **Cabernet Sauvignon Shiraz 2006** Pleasant spicy fruit, with good flavour and depth; overall clean and vibrant. Screwcap. 14.5° alc. **Rating** 90 **To** 2014 $22

Woodeneye Estate   ★★★

Lot 13 Dewry Avenue, Irymple, Vic 3498 **Region** Murray Darling
T 0419 518 846 **F** (03) 5024 6126 www.woodeneye.com.au **Open** Thurs–Sun 11–5 or by appt
Winemaker Steve Glasson **Est.** 1990 **Cases** 1000
Steve and Debi Glasson purchased their 12-ha vineyard at Irymple in 1990. It was largely planted to sultana, and in 1992 they took the decision to remove all but 0.6 ha of 65-year-old grenache. They replanted the vineyard to chardonnay, cabernet sauvignon, shiraz and merlot, leading to the first vintage in 2003. In the meantime Steve Glasson had completed a winemaking course through La Trobe University at Bundoora, and made the wine in an insulated shed on the property. A new winery and cellar door on the property next door, which the Glassons also own, was completed in time for the 2007 vintage.

ŢŢŢŢ **Chardonnay 2006** A totally remarkable unwooded chardonnay from a region which shouldn't be able to do this; elegant, fine and quite racy. Drink today. Screwcap. 12.7° alc. **Rating** 89 **To** 2009 $12
Shiraz 2005 Another wine to over-deliver for its background; light-bodied, but showing what can be achieved with small winery hand plunging of open vats and use (not abuse) of oak. Screwcap. 13.5° alc. **Rating** 87 **To** 2010 $15

Woodlands   ★★★★★

3948 Caves Road, Wilyabrup, WA 6284 **Region** Margaret River
T (08) 9755 6226 **F** (08) 9755 6236 www.woodlandswines.com **Open** 7 days 10.30–5
Winemaker Stuart Watson, David Watson **Est.** 1973 **Cases** 5500
The quality of the grapes, with a priceless core of 6.8 ha of cabernet sauvignon, planted more than 30 years ago, more recently joined by merlot, malbec, cabernet franc, pinot noir and chardonnay, has never been in doubt. The two estate vineyards (the second on Puzey Road, called Woodlands Brook Vineyard) total 14.67 ha, all except 1 ha being the Bordeaux varieties. Whatever the shortcomings of the 1990s, these days Woodlands is producing some spectacular wines in small quantities. The larger volume Cabernet Sauvignon is also of very high quality, and Woodlands is now a major player in the top echelon of Margaret River producers. Exports to the UK and other major markets.

ŢŢŢŢŢ **Colin Margaret River Shiraz 2005** A classic example of cabernet with leafy notes sitting gracefully on top of cassis and a little black olive complexity; rich yet fine on the palate, with plenty of fine-grained tannins; oak dominates now, but will offer real pleasure with time. Screwcap. 13.5° alc. **Rating** 96 **To** 2020 $100

Reserve de la Cave Margaret River Cabernet Franc 2006 Highly aromatic floral bouquet, underscored by red fruits; medium-bodied and fleshy, with very good focus and energy on the finish; very precise. Screwcap. 13° alc. **Rating** 95 To 2016 $65

Chloe Reserve Margaret River Chardonnay 2006 A complex wine with lovely concentration, especially for the vintage; grapefruit and nectarine are framed by toasty high quality oak; very fresh and very fine with good acidity on the toasty finish. Screwcap. 13.5° alc. **Rating** 94 To 2014 $55

Reserve de la Cave Margaret River Merlot 2006 Complex and compelling fruit with lovely concentration, lifted florals, complex cedar and fine and quite full on the palate; very oaky, but works well with the fruit on offer. Screwcap. 13° alc. **Rating** 94 To 2015 $65

ÏÏÏÏÏ **Emily Special Reserve 2006** A fine cedar bouquet, with redcurrant and black olive notes; medium-bodied, with gravelly tannin and a long savoury finish. Screwcap. 13° alc. **Rating** 93 To 2016 $35

Margaret River Chardonnay 2007 Bright and crisp grapefruit aromas, with just a light touch of oak evident; fresh, vibrant and tightly wound with good concentration; should age gracefully. Screwcap. 13.5° alc. **Rating** 92 To 2012 $20

Reserve de la Cave Margaret River Malbec 2006 Quite essency bouquet; dark fruits, layered with florals and just a little spice; fine and firm on the long and even finish. Screwcap. 12.5° alc. **Rating** 92 To 2015 $65

Margaret River Cabernet Sauvignon Merlot 2006 Bright and clear red-purple; a very fragrant bouquet with red fruits and a touch of leaf; an elegant, light- to medium-bodied unforced palate; best drunk while young. Screwcap. 13° alc. **Rating** 91 To 2010 $20

Margaret 2006 Subdued bouquet; red fruits and a little spice; a fine and focused finish. Cabernet Sauvignon/Merlot/Malbec. Screwcap. 13° alc. **Rating** 91 To 2015 $39.50

Reserve de la Cave Margaret River Pinot Noir 2006 Red fruits and lots of stem and toasty oak; very soft, and quite savoury with good acid, and good varietal expression on the finish. Screwcap. 12° alc. **Rating** 90 To 2011 $65

Woodside Valley Estate ★★★★★

PO Box 332, Greenwood, WA 6924 **Region** Margaret River
T (08) 9345 4065 **F** (08) 9345 4541 **www**.woodsidevalleyestate.com.au **Open** Not
Winemaker Kevin McKay **Est.** 1998 **Cases** 1500
Woodside Valley has been developed by a small syndicate of investors headed by Peter Woods. In 1998 they acquired 67 ha of land at Yallingup, and have now established 19 ha of chardonnay, sauvignon blanc, cabernet sauvignon, shiraz, malbec and merlot. The experienced Albert Haak is consultant viticulturist, and together with Peter Woods, took the unusual step of planting south-facing in preference to north-facing slopes. In doing so they indirectly followed in the footsteps of the French explorer Thomas Nicholas Baudin, who mounted a major scientific expedition to Australia on his ship *The Geographe*, and defied established views and tradition of the time in (correctly) asserting that the best passage for sailing ships travelling between Cape Leeuwin and Bass Strait was from west to east. Exports to the UK, the US, Singapore and Japan.

ÏÏÏÏÏ **Baudin Cabernet Sauvignon 2005** As with most in this range, very correct and precise; medium-bodied, the blackcurrant fruit seamlessly welded with fine, savoury tannins and quality oak; long finish. Diam. 14° alc. **Rating** 95 To 2025 $56

Le Bas Chardonnay 2006 An elegant, tight and long palate, with grapefruit and white peach all intermingling, the oak perfectly balanced and integrated. Diam. 14° alc. **Rating** 94 To 2015 $42

Bonnefoy Shiraz 2005 A stylish, lively, medium-bodied wine with remarkably intense and spicy black cherry and blackberry fruit; quality oak and tannins round off the picture. Diam. 14° alc. **Rating** 94 To 2020 $50

🍷🍷🍷🍷 **Rissy Merlot 2005** Light but bright colour; a lively wine, but seems to have been picked just a little too early; while the flavours are correct, not enough mid-palate vinosity. Diam. 13° alc. **Rating** 89 **To** 2013 $49

Woodstock ★★★★☆

Douglas Gully Road, McLaren Flat, SA 5171 **Region** McLaren Vale
T (08) 8383 0156 **F** (08) 8383 0437 **www**.woodstockwine.com.au **Open** Mon–Fri 9–5, w'ends, hols 12–5
Winemaker Scott Collett, Ben Glaetzer **Est.** 1974 **Cases** 30 000
One of the stalwarts of McLaren Vale, producing archetypal and invariably reliable full-bodied red wines, spectacular botrytis sweet whites and high-quality (14-year-old) Tawny Port. Also offers a totally charming reception-cum-restaurant, which does a roaring trade with wedding receptions. Has supplemented its 22 ha of McLaren Vale vineyards with 10 ha at its Wirrega Vineyard, in the Limestone Coast Zone. Exports to the UK and other major markets.

🍷🍷🍷🍷🍷 **The Stocks Single Vineyard McLaren Vale Shiraz 2005** Good colour; ripe, plush and flush with black cherry, blackberry and dark chocolate fruit; both tannins and oak are balanced and integrated. Screwcap. 14.5° alc. **Rating** 94 **To** 2025 $50

🍷🍷🍷🍷🍷 **McLaren Vale Cabernet Sauvignon 2005** Shows both regional and varietal character; blackcurrant, a dusting of chocolate, and well-pitched tannins; good balance and length. Screwcap. 14.5° alc. **Rating** 91 **To** 2015 $22

🍷🍷🍷🍷 **McLaren Vale Shiraz 2005** Same alcohol as The Stocks, but nowhere near as intense (not surprising, of course); does have savoury/earthy/chocolatey regional edges. Screwcap. 14.5° alc. **Rating** 89 **To** 2015 $22

Woody Nook ★★★★

506 Metricup Road, Wilyabrup, WA 6280 **Region** Margaret River
T (08) 9755 7547 **F** (08) 9755 7007 **www**.woodynook.com.au **Open** 7 days 10–4.30
Winemaker Neil Gallagher **Est.** 1982 **Cases** 5000
This improbably named and not terribly fashionable winery has produced some truly excellent wines over the years, featuring in such diverse competitions as Winewise, the Sheraton Wine Awards and the WA Wine Show. Cabernet Sauvignon has always been its strong point, but it has a habit of also bobbing up with excellent white wines in various guises. Since 2000 owned by Peter and Jane Bailey; Neil Gallagher continues as viticulturist, winemaker and minority shareholder. Exports to the UK, the US, Canada, Singapore, Hong Kong and Bermuda.

🍷🍷🍷🍷🍷 **Gallagher's Choice Margaret River Cabernet Sauvignon 2004** Still has very fresh cabernet cedar and cassis fruit; tightly structured, with plenty of tannin and persistent black fruit on the finish. Cork. 14.5° alc. **Rating** 93 **To** 2016 $50.95
Margaret River Shiraz 2004 Cool and clean, with plenty of spice and red berry fruits; quite tannic, but plenty of fruit to carry it through on the generous finish. Cork. 14.5° alc. **Rating** 91 **To** 2015 $40.95

🍷🍷🍷🍷 **Margaret River Shiraz 2005** Clean shiraz fruit, dominated by high levels of toasty oak; has flavour and persistence; but lacks finesse. **Rating** 87 **To** 2013 $28.95

Woolybud ★★★★

Playford Highway, Parndana, SA 5220 **Region** Kangaroo Island
T (08) 8559 6110 **F** (08) 8559 6031 **Open** Not
Winemaker Dudley Partners **Est.** 1998 **Cases** 1300
The Denis family moved to their sheep-farming property, Agincourt, west of Parndana, in 1986. Like many others, the downturn in the wool industry caused them to look to diversify their farming activities, and this led to the planting of cabernet sauvignon, shiraz and sauvignon blanc, and to the subsequent release of their Woolybud wines. The wines are available by mail order.

Kangaroo Island Cabernet Sauvignon 2005 Densely coloured; the depth and richness of the palate lives up to the colour, with blackcurrant, blackberry and bitter chocolate; good tannins. Value. Screwcap. 14° alc. **Rating** 92 **To** 2020 $19.50
Kangaroo Island Sauvignon Blanc 2007 A clean bouquet; good varietal expression on the palate with gooseberry/tropical/passionfruit flavours; has balance, length and a good finish. Screwcap. 12.9° alc. **Rating** 90 **To** 2010 $19

Woongarra Estate ★★★★☆

95 Hayseys Road, Narre Warren East, Vic 3804 **Region** Port Phillip Zone
T (03) 9796 8886 **F** (03) 9796 8580 **www.**woongarrawinery.com.au **Open** Thurs–Sun 9–5 by appt
Winemaker Bruce Jones, Sergio Carlei **Est.** 1992 **Cases** 3000
Dr Bruce Jones, and wife Mary, purchased their 16-ha property many years ago; it falls within the Yarra Ranges Shire Council's jurisdiction but not within the Yarra Valley wine region. In 1992 they planted 1 ha of sauvignon blanc, small patches of shiraz and a few rows of semillon. Over 1 ha of sauvignon blanc and pinot noir followed in 1996 (mostly MV6, and some French clone 114 and 115) with yet more 114 and 115 pinot noir in 2000, lifting total plantings to 3.2 ha of pinot noir, 1.4 ha of sauvignon blanc and a splash of the other two varieties. Success has also come with Three Wise Men Pinot Noir (a joint venture between Woongarra and Passing Clouds – see separate entry). No samples received, the rating is that of last year.

Word of Mouth Wines ★★★★

Campbell's Corner, 790 Pinnacle Road, Orange, NSW 2800 **Region** Orange
T (02) 6362 3509 **F** (02) 6365 3517 **www.**wordofmouthwines.com.au **Open** Fri–Sun & public hols 11–5
Winemaker David Lowe, Jane Wilson (Contract) **Est.** 1991 **Cases** 3000
Word of Mouth Wines acquired the former Donnington Vineyard in 2003, with its 16 ha of mature vineyards. The planting mix has been changed to place emphasis on white varieties; there are now 4 ha of pinot gris, 3 ha of chardonnay, 2 ha each of pinot noir and merlot, 1.7 ha each of sauvignon blanc and riesling and 1 ha of viognier. More recently, Pinnacle Wines (with just over 1 ha of viognier, 1.6 ha of pinot noir, plus a little riesling) was acquired by Word of Mouth Wines.

 Orange Sauvignon Blanc 2007 Clean fresh flowery aromas, then a very lively passionfruit and snow pea-accented palate, the acidity giving thrust through to the finish. Screwcap. 12.8° alc. **Rating** 91 **To** 2010 $22
NF Orange Chardonnay 2007 Light, early picked, but intense citrus and stone fruit aromas and flavours deliberately kept away from oak, with Chablis as the model. Has length, will improve. Screwcap. 12.5° alc. **Rating** 90 **To** 2012 $22

 Orange Merlot 2005 A light-bodied mix of small red berry fruits and earthy/briary/foresty notes; for merlot lovers. Screwcap. 13.6° alc. **Rating** 87 **To** 2010 $24

Wordsworth Wines ★★★★☆

Cnr South Western Highway/Thompson Road, Harvey, WA 6220 **Region** Geographe
T (08) 9733 4576 **F** (08) 9733 4269 **www.**wordsworthwines.com.au **Open** 7 days 10–5
Winemaker Lamont's (Digby Leddin, Rachael Robinson), Western Range Wines (Ryan Sudano) **Est.** 1997 **Cases** 5000
David Wordsworth has established a substantial business in a relatively short space of time: 27 ha of vines have been planted, with cabernet sauvignon (10 ha), shiraz (5 ha) and verdelho (4 ha) predominant, and lesser amounts of zinfandel, petit verdot, chardonnay and chenin blanc. The winery features massive jarrah beams, wrought iron and antique furniture, and the tasting room seats 80 people. The wines have had show success. Exports to the US.

ϷϷϷϷϙ **Geographe Shiraz 2006** An achievement for a difficult vintage, with considerable texture, weight and length to the black fruits, and a long, textured finish. Cork. 14.5° alc. **Rating** 91 **To** 2015 $25

Wovenfield

PO Box 1021, Subiaco, WA 6904 **Region** Geographe
T (08) 9481 3250 **F** (08) 9481 3076 **www**.wovenfield.com **Open** W'ends 10–5
Winemaker Rienne Buck, Damien Hutton **Est.** 1997 **Cases** 600
Martin Buck, together with daughter Rienne, purchased an old dairy farm in 1996, and with advice from an experienced local viticulturist, Phil Gumbrell, came up with a three-stage planting program. Five hectares of shiraz and semillon were planted in 1997; 7.5 ha of merlot and cabernet sauvignon in '98; and in 2002 a further 3.5-ha, northwest-facing paddock was partially planted with viognier on a trial basis, the planting extended in '05 after a successful outcome. Nor have they rested there; in 2004 1.85 ha of merlot and cabernet sauvignon were grafted over to sauvignon blanc, and a small amount of tempranillo planted. They have also formed a highly successful winemaking team, the wines made at the small winery established on the property. Exports to Singapore.

ϷϷϷϷϷ **Reserve Shiraz Viognier 2006** Deeper, denser colour than the varietal; a very considerable volume of plush black fruits; licorice and spice all lifted by the touch of viognier. Screwcap. 14.5° alc. **Rating** 94 **To** 2021 $25

ϷϷϷϷϙ **Lone Barrel Viognier 2006** Good focus, mouthfeel and length, a mix of pear and citrus, the oak subliminal; price parity with the varietal curious. Screwcap. 13.9° alc. **Rating** 91 **To** 2011 $20
Viognier 2006 Has more overt fruit than the Single Barrel, but is still supple and generous, and avoids phenolics; gold Geographe Wine Show '07. Screwcap. 14.1° alc. **Rating** 90 **To** 2010 $20

ϷϷϷϷ **Shiraz Viognier 2006** Fragrant and vibrant, the influence of the viognier very marked, giving a near-citrus tang to the fruit profile; has length. Screwcap. 14.5° alc. **Rating** 89 **To** 2014 $25
Sauvignon Blanc 2007 Very light, but the mix of passionfruit and citrus is appealing; drink asap. Screwcap. 12.5° alc. **Rating** 87 **To** 2009 $15
Verdelho 2007 A generous wine, with abundant ripe fruit; overall sweetness great appeal to cellar door visitors. Screwcap. 13.6° alc. **Rating** 87 **To** 2010 $15
Viognier 2007 Lots of tropical apricot fruit, full in the mouth, and with some non-specific impression of sweetness, plus some phenolics on the finish. Not an easy variety. **Rating** 87 **To** 2010 $20

Wright Family Wines

'Misty Glen', 293 Deasey Road, Pokolbin, NSW 2320 **Region** Lower Hunter Valley
T (02) 4998 7781 **F** (02) 4998 7768 **www**.mistyglencottage.com.au **Open** 7 days 10–4
Winemaker Contract **Est.** 1985 **Cases** 1200
Jim and Carol Wright purchased their property in 1985, with a small existing vineyard in need of tender loving care. This was duly given, and the semillon, chardonnay and cabernet sauvignon revived. In 2000, 1.5 ha of shiraz was planted; 1.5 ha of chambourcin was added in '02, lifting total plantings to 7.5 ha. Carol has been involved in the wine industry since the early 1970s, and is now helped by husband Jim (who retired from the coal mines in '02), and by children and grandchildren. Wines are released under the Misty Glen Cottage label.

ϷϷϷϷ **Misty Glen Cottage Chardonnay 2007** Developed yellow-green; very rich yellow peach and melon fruit; ready now and won't hold. Screwcap. 13.7° alc. **Rating** 87 **To** 2010 $26.50
Misty Glen Cottage Hunter Valley Chambourcin 2006 Strictly for immediate consumption, with light-bodied juicy red fruits and no structure; serve slightly chilled on a hot day. Screwcap. 13° alc. **Rating** 87 **To** 2009 $26.50

Wright Robertson of Glencoe   NR

'Waratah Ridge', New England Highway, Glencoe, NSW 2365 **Region** New England
T (02) 6733 3255 **F** (02) 6733 3220 **www**.wrightwine.com **Open** Mon–Fri 9–5, Sat 10–4
Winemaker Scott Wright **Est.** 1999 **Cases** NA
Scott and Julie Wright began establishing their 4-ha vineyard (pinot noir, pinot gris, riesling, shiraz and cabernet sauvignon) in 1999, and now operate a winery making both their own wines and wines for three other producers. They also purchase grapes from other growers; an estate-grown Organic Syrah is the flagship wine.

Wroxton Wines

Flaxman's Valley Road, Angaston, SA 5353 **Region** Eden Valley
T (08) 8565 3227 **F** (08) 8565 3312 **www**.wroxton.com.au **Open** By appt
Winemaker Bethany Wines **Est.** 1995 **Cases** 60
Ian and Jo Zander are third-generation grapegrowers on the 200-ha Wroxton Grange property, which was established in 1845 in the high country of the Eden Valley. The Zander family purchased the property in 1920, and planted their first vines that year; since '73 an extensive planting program has seen the progressive establishment of riesling (15.4 ha), shiraz (10.5 ha), chardonnay (6.9 ha), semillon (2.5 ha) and traminer (2 ha). The majority of the grapes are sold, the best parcels from the mature vineyards retained to produce single vineyard wines.

ŸŸŸŸŸ **Single Vineyard Eden Valley Riesling 2003** Bright, light green-yellow; lime and apple blossom aromas; a finely wrought palate with lime, apple and mineral flavours; has developed superbly, with a minimum of another 5 years peak drinking. Screwcap. 12.5° alc. **Rating** 95 **To** 2015 $20

ŸŸŸŸ **Single Vineyard Eden Valley Shiraz 2002** Shows expected development; earthy bramble and spicy notes, but also some sweet fruit and mocha oak; ready now but will hold for a few years. Quality cork. **Rating** 89 **To** 2011 $25

Wyndham Estate   ★★★★

700 Dalwood Road, Dalwood, NSW 2335 **Region** Lower Hunter Valley
T (02) 4938 3444 **F** (02) 4938 3555 **www**.wyndhamestate.com **Open** 7 days 10–4.30 except public hols
Winemaker Sam Kurtz **Est.** 1828 **Cases** 1 million
This historic property is now merely a shop front for the Wyndham Estate label. The Bin wines often surprise with their quality, representing excellent value; the Show Reserve wines, likewise, can be very good. The wines come from various parts of South East Australia, sometimes specified, sometimes not.

ŸŸŸŸŸ **George Wyndham Shiraz Grenache 2005** Unexpectedly, the strongest and richest of the George Wyndham trio, with buckets of red fruits and just enough tannins to provide structure. Screwcap. **Rating** 90 **To** 2017 $19.95

ŸŸŸŸ **Bin 555 Shiraz 2005** Medium-bodied; has attractive black fruits, with spice and some touches of charry oak; shortens fractionally on the finish. Screwcap. 14.5° alc. **Rating** 89 **To** 2009 $14.99
George Wyndham Shiraz Cabernet 2005 A pleasing mix of cassis, blackcurrant and black cherry to a medium-bodied, fruit-driven wine with good length. Screwcap. 14° alc. **Rating** 89 **To** 2015 $19.95
George Wyndham Shiraz 2004 A blend of SA and Hunter material; some earthy notes from the latter, licorice and dark chocolate from SA; plenty of flavour to a well-balanced wine. Cork. 15° alc. **Rating** 88 **To** 2014 $19.95
Bin 777 Semillon Sauvignon Blanc 2007 Unusual herb and lemongrass aromas and flavours, almost earthy; bone-dry, and does have some appeal as a food wine. Screwcap. 13.5° alc. **Rating** 87 **To** 2009 $14.99

Wynns Coonawarra Estate ★★★★★

Memorial Drive, Coonawarra, SA 5263 **Region** Coonawarra
T (08) 8736 2225 **F** (08) 8736 2208 **www**.wynns.com.au **Open** 7 days 10–5
Winemaker Sue Hodder **Est.** 1897 **Cases** NFP
Large-scale production has not prevented Wynns from producing excellent wines covering
the full price spectrum, from the bargain basement Riesling and Shiraz through to the
deluxe John Riddoch Cabernet Sauvignon and Michael Shiraz. Even with steady price
increases, Wynns offers extraordinary value for money. The large investments since 2000
in rejuvenating and replanting key blocks under the direction of Allen Jenkins, and skilled
winemaking by Sue Hodder, has resulted in wines of far greater finesse and elegance than
most of their predecessors. Exports to the UK and other major markets.

ＰＰＰＰＰ **John Riddoch Cabernet Sauvignon 2005** Wonderfully precise and clear
varietal fruit in a ripe, but not overripe, mould; cassis and redcurrant flavours; fine
tannins and quality oak. **Rating** 96 **To** 2021 $75.95
Messenger Vineyard Cabernet Sauvignon 2005 A powerful wine, with
considerable depth and structure; blackcurrant fruit with good tannin and oak
management. Trophy Limestone Coast Wine Show '07. **Rating** 95 **To** 2020 $38.95
Riesling 2006 Fine, fresh and crisp; intense lime zest, apple and mineral; great
length, and a great future. Top gold, National Wine Show '07. Screwcap. 12.5° alc.
Rating 94 **To** 2016 $14
Johnson's Block Single Vineyard Shiraz Cabernet 2004 An intense wine;
a hint of reduction which does not impinge on the overall quality; still very
youthful, with years of development, having already improved out of sight since
Mar '06. Screwcap. 13.5° alc. **Rating** 94 **To** 2024 $34.95

ＰＰＰＰＰ **Cabernet Shiraz Merlot 2006** Brilliant crimson; lively, vibrant and fresh
array of red and black fruits; fine tannins and controlled oak on the long, balanced
finish; now or whenever the fancy takes you. Screwcap. 14° alc. **Rating** 93
To 2021 $20.95
Cabernet Sauvignon 2005 A delicious wine; generous, supple blackcurrant
fruit bolstered by fine, ripe tannins and judicious oak; long finish. Cork. 14.5° alc.
Rating 92 **To** 2020 $35.99
Shiraz 2006 Light- to medium-bodied, but all the components of fruit, oak and
tannins are well-balanced; gentle black fruits and soft tannins, will improve with
age. Tasted when 18 months old. Cork. 14° alc. **Rating** 91 **To** 2014 $18.95
Chardonnay 2006 Typical Wynns style, gentle and basically understated; melon,
fig and some creamy/cashew notes. Screwcap. 13° alc. **Rating** 90 **To** 2012 $15.95
Chardonnay 2007 In normal sotto voce style for Wynns, fruit and oak seamlessly
welded; white peach and a dusting of oak; good length and balance. Screwcap.
13° alc. **Rating** 90 **To** 2012 $17.95

Xabregas ★★★★

Cnr Spencer Road/Hay River Road, Narrikup, WA 6326 **Region** Mount Barker
T (08) 9321 2366 **F** (08) 9327 9393 **www**.xabregas.com.au **Open** By appt tel 0409 532 255
Winemaker The Vintage Wineworx (Dr Diane Miller, Greg Jones) **Est.** 1996 **Cases** 16 000
In 1996 stockbrokers Terry Hogan and Eve Broadley, the major participants in the Spencer
Wine Joint Venture, commenced a viticulture business which has now grown into three
vineyards totalling 120 ha on sites 10 km south of Mount Barker. The varieties planted are
riesling, chardonnay, sauvignon blanc, cabernet sauvignon, cabernet franc, merlot and shiraz. As
well as being contract growers to Houghton, Howard Park and Forest Hill, they act as contract
managers to surrounding vineyards, and are investors in the vintage Wineworx contract
winemaking facility. The wines are modestly priced. Exports to the UK, NZ and China.

ＰＰＰＰＰ **Show Reserve Chardonnay 2006** Punches well above its alcohol, with quite
intense melon and stone fruit on the mid-palate, followed by lingering, citrussy
acidity, oak in the background. Screwcap. 12.9° alc. **Rating** 90 **To** 2012 $23.20

Show Reserve Shiraz 2005 A powerful wine; strong structure supports the blackberry, plum, licorice and spice fruit; appropriate oak. Screwcap. 15.5° alc. **Rating** 90 **To** 2020 $23.95

ȲȲȲȲ **Riesling 2007** A clean, but relatively unexpressive bouquet; a light, crisp palate only unfurling on the finish and aftertaste, with some citrus fruit. Screwcap. 12.2° alc. **Rating** 88 **To** 2012 $14.95
Show Reserve Sauvignon Blanc 2007 A faintly reduced bouquet; a light palate with citrus and gooseberry fruit, and a crisp finish. Screwcap. 11.8° alc. **Rating** 87 **To** 2009 $22.95
Cabernet Merlot 2004 Developed colour; quite intense, but very savoury/ earthy overtones to the fruit, and distinctly savoury tannins; somehow, has enough fruit to convince. Screwcap. 14° alc. **Rating** 87 **To** 2011 $15.95
Show Reserve Cabernet Sauvignon 2005 Plenty of varietal aroma and flavour, but persistent, dry tannins need to soften before the fruit dies; no guarantee they will. Cork. 14.6° alc. **Rating** 87 **To** 2015 $22.95

Xanadu Wines

Boodjidup Road, Margaret River, WA 6285 **Region** Margaret River
T (08) 9757 2581 **F** (08) 9757 3389 **www.**xanaduwines.com **Open** 7 days 10–5
Winemaker Glenn Goodall **Est.** 1977 **Cases** 65 000
Xanadu fell prey to over-ambitious expansion and to the increasingly tight trading conditions in 2005 as wine surpluses hit hard. The assets were acquired by the Rathbone Group, completing the Yering Station/Mount Langi Ghiran/Parker Coonawarra Estate/Xanadu group. The prime assets were (and are) the 130 ha of vineyards and a winery to match. The increasing production is matched by exports to 18 markets, led by the UK and the US.

ȲȲȲȲȳ **Dragon Margaret River Unoaked Chardonnay 2007** A cool bouquet of lemon zest and a little mineral note; nice weight, and fresh and vibrant on the finish. Screwcap. 13.5° alc. **Rating** 90 **To** 2012 $16

ȲȲȲȲ **Dragon Margaret River Shiraz 2006** Highly fragrant spicy shiraz bouquet, with red fruit framed by a drying minerally palate. Screwcap. 13.5° alc. **Rating** 88 **To** 2012 $16

Yabby Lake Vineyard

1 Garden Street, South Yarra, Vic 3141 (postal) **Region** Mornington Peninsula
T (03) 9251 5375 **F** (03) 9639 1540 **www.**yabbylake.com **Open** Not
Winemaker Tom Carson, Tod Dexter, Larry McKenna (Consultant) **Est.** 1998 **Cases** 3350
This high-profile wine business is owned by Robert and Mem Kirby (of Village Roadshow) who have been landowners in the Mornington Peninsula for decades. In 1998 they established Yabby Lake Vineyard, under the direction of vineyard manager Keith Harris; the vineyard is on a north-facing slope, capturing maximum sunshine while also receiving sea breezes. The main focus is the 21 ha of pinot noir, 10 ha of chardonnay and 5 ha of pinot gris; the 2 ha each of shiraz and merlot take a back seat. Tod Dexter (former long-term winemaker at Stonier) and Larry McKenna (ex Martinborough Vineyards and now the Escarpment in NZ) both have great experience. The arrival of the hugely talented Tom Carson as Group Winemaker can only add lustre to the winery and its wines.

ȲȲȲȲȲ **Roc Mornington Peninsula Shiraz 2004** Very good colour; made only in small quantities from a small estate block in the best vintages; an utterly delicious wine, the fruit totally seductive, singing in the mouth; cool-climate shiraz doesn't come better than this. Diam. 14.5° alc. **Rating** 97 **To** 2019 $90
Mornington Peninsula Pinot Noir 2006 Good hue; very pure pinot in a light- to medium-bodied frame of spiced red and black fruits coming through strongly on its long palate and aftertaste. Screwcap. 14° alc. **Rating** 95 **To** 2013 $50

Mornington Peninsula Chardonnay 2006 Superfine, minimalist, style, the focus on texture, structure and length rather than primary fruit; overall, subdued now, but will build with time in bottle. Screwcap. 13.5° alc. **Rating** 94 To 2016 $40

Red Claw Mornington Peninsula Pinot Noir 2006 Good colour and hue; an attractive mix of plum, cherry and spice; good mouthfeel, balance and length; quality oak. Screwcap. 14° alc. **Rating** 94 To 2012 $29

♟♟♟♟♀ **Red Claw Mornington Peninsula Pinot Noir 2007** Well-shaped and balanced, with silky, plummy fruit and restrained oak; good now, but plenty of development potential. Screwcap. **Rating** 92 To 2013 $29

Red Claw Mornington Peninsula Chardonnay 2006 A long, fresh and tightly focused palate, with grapefruit and nectarine flavours to the fore; good line and length. Screwcap. 13° alc. **Rating** 90 To 2012 $25

Red Claw Mornington Peninsula Chardonnay 2007 A powerful wine, with supple but intense melon and stone fruit augmented by barrel ferment and good acidity. Screwcap. **Rating** 90 To 2013 $25

Red Claw Mornington Peninsula Pinot Gris 2006 A quiet bouquet, but an intense and lively palate, ranging through lychee, pear and citrus flavours; dry finish. Screwcap. 14.5° alc. **Rating** 90 To 2010 $25

♟♟♟♟ **Mornington Peninsula Pinot Gris 2007** Well made, and has more texture than many; likewise has grainy pear and varietal fruit; but it's a very ambitious price. Screwcap. 14.6° alc. **Rating** 89 To 2010 $40

Red Claw Mornington Peninsula Pinot Gris 2007 Solid wine, plenty of flavour and substance, but pedestrian mouthfeel/structure. Screwcap. **Rating** 87 To 2009 $25

Yacca Paddock Vineyards   ★★★☆

PO Box 824, Kent Town, SA 5071 **Region** Adelaide Hills
T (08) 8362 3397 **F** (08) 8363 3797 **www**.yaccapaddock.com **Open** Not
Winemaker Mr Riggs Wine Company **Est.** 2000 **Cases** 500
Filmmakers Kerry Heysen-Hicks and husband Scott Hicks have left little to chance in establishing Yacca Paddock Vineyards. The vineyards (22 ha) were established under the direction of leading viticulturist Geoff Hardy, and the wines are made by equally illustrious winemaker Ben Riggs. The vineyard is at an altitude of 350 m, and all of the vines are netted. In descending order of size the rainbow selection of varieties is chardonnay, pinot noir, tempranillo, merlot, cabernet sauvignon, riesling, sauvignon blanc, shiraz, arneis, dolcetto, tannat and durif. No samples received.

Yaldara Wines   ★★★★☆

Hermann Thumm Drive, Lyndoch, SA 5351 **Region** Barossa Valley
T (08) 8524 0200 **F** (08) 8524 0240 **www**.yaldara.com.au **Open** 7 days 10–5
Winemaker James Evers, Peter Ruchs **Est.** 1947 **Cases** 500 000
At the very end of 1999 Yaldara became part of the publicly listed Simeon Wines, the intention being that it (Yaldara) should become the quality flagship of the group. Despite much expenditure and the short-lived stay of at least one well-known winemaker, the plan failed to deliver the expected benefits. In 2002 McGuigan Wines made a reverse takeover for Simeon, and the various McGuigan brands will (presumably) fill the role intended for Yaldara.

♟♟♟♟♟ **The Farms Barossa Valley Shiraz 2004** Very good winemaking; blackberry, plum, licorice and dark chocolate coalesce with quality American oak, the tannins perfectly balanced and integrated. Cork. 15° alc. **Rating** 94 To 2019 $70

Yalumba ★★★★★

Eden Valley Road, Angaston, SA 5353 **Region** Barossa Valley
T (08) 8561 3200 **F** (08) 8561 3393 **www**.yalumba.com **Open** Mon–Fri 8.30–5, Sat 10–5, Sun 12–5
Winemaker Louisa Rose (chief), Brian Walsh, Alan Hoey, Peter Gambetta **Est.** 1849
Cases 950 000
Family-owned and run by Robert Hill Smith, Yalumba has been very successful in building its export base, but has long had a commitment to quality and has shown great vision in its selection of vineyard sites, new varieties and brands. It has always been a serious player at the top end of full-bodied (and full-blooded) Australian reds, and was the pioneer in the use of screwcaps (for Pewsey Vale Riesling). While its 940 ha of estate vineyards are largely planted to mainstream varieties, it has taken marketing ownership of Viognier. However, these days its own brands revolve around the Y Series, having divorced Oxford Landing, and established a number of stand-alone brands across the length and breadth of SA, and the Victorian Redbank brand.

ҮҮҮҮҮ **FDW[7c] Adelaide Hills Chardonnay 2006** A beautiful light- to medium-bodied chardonnay, pointing the direction for Australia in the future with this variety; perfectly delineated varietal fruit from the superb Burgundy clones 76 and 95; oak appropriately subtle. Screwcap. 13° alc. **Rating** 96 **To** 2014 $23.95
The Virgilius Eden Valley Viognier 2005 A very interesting wine; despite its well-deserved icon status, is relatively low in alcohol, and has much more finesse than most prior vintages; it is also ageing slowly and with grace. Best yet. Screwcap. 13.5° alc. **Rating** 96 **To** 2012 $44.95
The Virgilius Eden Valley Viognier 2006 Immediately proclaims its class and power on the first whiff of the bouquet; an emphatic varietal statement on the palate, with pear, apricot and musk tied by citrussy acidity, barrel ferment adding texture and structure. Screwcap. 14.5° alc. **Rating** 96 **To** 2013 $44.95
The Reserve 2001 Exceptional colour for a 7-year-old; medium- to full-bodied, opening with a supple array of black fruits in the mouth, then firming up with ripe tannins on the finish. Screwcap. 14.5° alc. **Rating** 95 **To** 2021 $109.95
Eden Valley Semillon Sauvignon Blanc 2007 More aromatic than many from the vintage; attractive citrus characters run throughout, then a breezy, zesty finish. Screwcap. 12° alc. **Rating** 94 **To** 2012 $17.95
Wild Ferment Eden Valley Chardonnay 2006 A hint of French funk on the bouquet adds to the appeal; melon, stone fruit and acidity flow seamlessly across the palate; excellent line and balance. Screwcap. 13.5° alc. **Rating** 94 **To** 2014 $17.95
Hand Picked Barossa Tempranillo Grenache Viognier 2006 Intense red fruit aromas with a touch of viognier apricot; considerable volume of flavour on the palate, veering towards darker fruits; very good structure and balance. All three components co-fermented. Screwcap. 13.5° alc. **Rating** 94 **To** 2011 $28.95

ҮҮҮҮҮ **Hand Picked Shiraz Viognier 2005** Good colour; medium-bodied, with attractive lifted fruit aromas and flavours, fine tannins and good length. Super-weight bottle and rather ratty cork. 14.5° alc. **Rating** 93 **To** 2012 $28.95
Barossa Valley Shiraz Viognier 2005 A fragrant bouquet, then an array of cherry, plum, licorice and spice on the flowing, fruit-driven, medium-bodied palate. Cork. 14.5° alc. **Rating** 92 **To** 2010 $17.50
Y Series Viognier 2006 Shows the long experience of Yalumba with this variety; fresh, if light, honeysuckle and apricot aromas and fore-palate, then a twist of citrussy acidity on the finish. Screwcap. 13.5° alc. **Rating** 90 **To** 2009 $11.95
Eden Valley Viognier 2006 Typical flavour and style profile of Yalumba viognier; abundant apricot, nectarine and white peach fruit, with an emphatic finish. Screwcap. 14.5° alc. **Rating** 90 **To** 2009 $21.95
Galway Vintage Traditional Shiraz 2005 Medium-bodied; a thoroughly enjoyable wine with more than sufficient fruit flavour and structure; fine tannins and good length; best for some time. Screwcap. 14° alc. **Rating** 90 **To** 2012 $13.95

Y Series Shiraz Viognier 2006 Fresh, lively, zesty red fruit aromas and flavours, with minimal tannins; ideal summer red, could be served slightly chilled. Screwcap. 14° alc. **Rating** 90 To 2009 $11.95

🍷🍷🍷🍷 **Oxford Landing Sauvignon Blanc 2007** Runs true to form; Yalumba achieves clear-cut citrus and grass varietal character in a theoretically difficult environment; has immaculate balance, even if it is not particularly intense. Fresh finish. Unbeatable value. Screwcap. 11.5° alc. **Rating** 89 To 2009 $7.95

Barossa Shiraz 2005 An attractive, medium-bodied wine with plum and black cherry fruit; plenty of texture, the oak just a little assertive; vines 30–50 years old. Cork. 14.5° alc. **Rating** 89 To 2013 $17.95

Y Series Riesling 2007 Attractive citrus and tropical fruit aromas; a soft, full-flavoured palate with some canned pineapple notes. Very good value. Screwcap. 12.5° alc. **Rating** 88 To 2009 $11.95

Bush Vine Barossa Grenache 2006 Very typical Yalumba style, though does have some attractive grainy tannins to moderate the cosmetic regional fruit profile. Cork. 14.5° alc. **Rating** 88 To 2010 $17.95

Y Series Merlot 2006 Dark plum and hints of cedar on the bouquet; quite obvious tannins, and the fruit is a little subdued; not the sweet fruit many expect from merlot. Screwcap. 13.5° alc. **Rating** 88 To 2012 $11.95

Oxford Landing Chardonnay 2007 Voluminous peachy fruit; all about cheerful sunshine-in-a-bottle, out of fashion with critics, but not consumers; great value. Screwcap. 13.5° alc. **Rating** 87 To 2009 $7.95

Y Series Sauvignon Blanc 2007 Floral aromas with some passionfruit; plenty of flavour and life on the palate in a tropical spectrum; quite an achievement for the vintage. Cork. 10.5° alc. **Rating** 87 To 2009 $11.95

Y Series Shiraz 2006 A well put together, light- to medium-bodied wine, offering value at this price point; some spicy, savoury notes add interest. Screwcap. 14° alc. **Rating** 87 To 2011 $11.95

Oxford Landing Merlot 2006 A vibrant array of raspberry and cherry flavours; little to do with merlot, but a lovely, carefree any-time-of-day drink. Screwcap. 13.5° alc. **Rating** 87 To 2009 $7.95

Ringbolt Margaret River Cabernet Sauvignon 2005 Regional character is subdued either by young vines or generous yields; cassis, a touch of mint and persistent tannins. Cork. 14° alc. **Rating** 87 To 2011 $22.95

Y Series Cabernet Sauvignon 2006 Has pleasing cassis-accented cabernet fruit in a generally low profile style, the oak and tannins marked more by their absence than presence. Screwcap. 14° alc. **Rating** 87 To 2009 $11.95

Yalumba The Menzies (Coonawarra)   ★★★★★

Riddoch Highway, Coonawarra, SA 5263 **Region** Coonawarra
T (08) 8737 3603 **F** (08) 8737 3604 **www**.yalumba.com **Open** 7 days 10–4.30
Winemaker Peter Gambetta **Est.** 2002 **Cases** 5000
Like many SA companies, Yalumba had been buying grapes from Coonawarra and elsewhere in the Limestone Coast Zone long before it became a landowner there. In 1993 it purchased the 20-ha vineyard which had provided the grapes previously purchased, and a year later added a nearby 16-ha block. Together, these vineyards now have 22 ha of cabernet sauvignon and 4 ha each of merlot and shiraz. The next step was the establishment of 82 ha of vineyard in the Wrattonbully region, led by 34 ha of cabernet sauvignon, the remainder equally split between shiraz and merlot. The third step was to build The Menzies Wine Room on the first property acquired – named Menzies Vineyard – and to offer the full range of Limestone Coast wines through this striking rammed-earth tasting and function centre. Exports to all major markets.

🍷🍷🍷🍷🍷 **The Menzies Coonawarra Cabernet Sauvignon 2004** A high-toned bouquet of cassis and herbs, the palate with finely sculpted blackcurrant and cassis fruit, tannin and oak support spot-on. Cork. 14° alc. **Rating** 94 To 2015 $42.95

The Menzies Coonawarra Cabernet Sauvignon 2005 Perfectly presented cassis and blackcurrant fruit; tannins and oak in the back seat; supple mouthfeel. **Rating** 94 **To** 2018 $46.95

☆☆☆☆☆ **Mawson's Wrattonbully Sauvignon Blanc 2007** Voluminous tropical strawberry fruit in strong varietal mode; good intensity and length. Screwcap. 12° alc. **Rating** 93 **To** 2009 $14.95

Wrattonbully Vineyards Tempranillo 2006 A delicious, fresh and supple panoply of red fruits and spices with gentle tannins; a seductive wine in every respect. Screwcap. 14° alc. **Rating** 92 **To** 2010 $18.55

Smith & Hooper Wrattonbully Cabernet Merlot 2005 Clean, fresh, subtle fruit in a blackcurrant/redcurrant spectrum; medium-bodied, with superfine tannins and good oak handling. Cork. 14.5° alc. **Rating** 92 **To** 2011 $16.95

Mawson's Hill Wrattonbully Cabernet Sauvignon 2005 A well-composed and balanced wine, driven by a fresh mix of red and black fruits, tannins and oak a simple backdrop. Over-delivers on price. Screwcap. 14.5° alc. **Rating** 91 **To** 2011 $14.95

The Retreat Cabernet Shiraz 2005 Firm cabernet fruit profile, the shiraz (14%) largely irrelevant; blackcurrant fruit with slightly austere tannins; classic tightness. **Rating** 91 **To** 2015 $24.95

Smith & Hooper Wrattonbully Merlot 2005 Fragrant and spicy; flavours are predominantly in the cassis/redcurrant/raspberry spectrum; ultra-fine tannins are ripe, and there is just a whisper of varietal black olive adding to the positive finish. Cork. 14.5° alc. **Rating** 90 **To** 2011 $16.95

☆☆☆☆ **Mawson's Bridge Block 7A Wrattonbully Sauvignon Blanc 2007** Full of somewhat broad, sweet tropical fruit; drink asap. Screwcap. 12° alc. **Rating** 87 **To** 2009 $14.95

Yangarra Estate ★★★★

Kangarilla Road, McLaren Vale, SA 5171 **Region** McLaren Vale
T (08) 8383 7459 **F** (08) 8383 7518 **www**.yangarra.com **Open** By appt
Winemaker Peter Fraser **Est.** 2000 **Cases** 17 000
This is the Australian operation of Kendall-Jackson, one of the leading premium wine producers in California. In 2000 Kendall-Jackson acquired the 172-ha Eringa Park vineyard from Normans Wines (97 ha are under vine, the oldest dating back to 1923). The renamed Yangarra Estate is the estate base for the operation, which has, so it would seem, remained much smaller than originally envisaged by Jess Jackson. Exports to the UK, the US, Canada, Ireland and Korea.

☆☆☆☆☆ **Single Vineyard McLaren Vale Shiraz 2006** Bright and vibrant with strong chocolate flavours to complement the concentrated black fruits; rich and chewy on the finish, and quite complex. Screwcap. 15° alc. **Rating** 93 **To** 2018 $28

Cadenzia McLaren Vale Grenache Shiraz Mourvedre 2005 Rich and spicy, with good fruit concentration; sweet fruits and a little spice; good acid and fine-grained tannins; bright focused red fruit on the finish. Screwcap. 15° alc. **Rating** 91 **To** 2015 $28

High Sands McLaren Vale Grenache 2005 A super-rich, ripe and concentrated array of prune, plum, dark chocolate and leather with considerable structure reflecting the high alcohol. Cork. 15.5° alc. **Rating** 90 **To** 2017 $60

Cadenzia McLaren Vale Grenache Shiraz Mourvedre 2006 Deep colour, with complex savoury aromas to complement the vibrant red cherry fruits; quite silky, and a touch of spice on the finish. Screwcap. 15° alc. **Rating** 90 **To** 2014 $28

☆☆☆☆ **Single Vineyard McLaren Vale Roussanne 2007** Dried straw and a hint of honeysuckle; a fraction short, but nice flavour; potential for this variety in McLaren Vale. Screwcap. 13° alc. **Rating** 87 **To** 2009 $21

Single Vineyard McLaren Vale Shiraz 2005 Warm-fruited with ample levels of dark fruits; good flavour, but lacks focus on the finish. Cork. 15° alc. **Rating** 87 To 2014 $28

Yarra Burn

60 Settlement Road, Yarra Junction, Vic 3797 **Region** Yarra Valley
T (03) 5967 1428 **F** (03) 5967 1146 **www.**yarraburn.com.au **Open** 7 days 10–5
Winemaker Mark O'Callaghan **Est.** 1975 **Cases** NFP
The headquarters of Constellation's very substantial Yarra Valley operations centring on the large production from its Hoddles Creek vineyards. The new brand direction has taken shape; all the white and sparkling wines are sourced from the Yarra Valley; the Shiraz Viognier is a blend of Yarra and Pyrenees grapes. Exports to the UK and the US.

ŸŸŸŸŸ **Cellar Release Pyrenees Shiraz 2003** A mix of supple red and black fruits, and firm but ripe tannins; from a single vineyard, with no sign of drought stress; very well made, the oak perfectly judged. Cork. 13.5° alc. **Rating** 94 To 2018 $30

ŸŸŸŸŸ **Sauvignon Blanc Semillon 2007** Clean, lively and fresh from start to finish; clear-cut fruit flavours in a citrus/lemon/passionfruit spectrum; crisp, lingering finish. Screwcap. 12.5° alc. **Rating** 92 To 2011 $24
Pinot Noir Chardonnay Rose 2004 Similar intensity and structure to the standard, but slightly more red fruits and slightly less lemon citrus. Cork. 13° alc. **Rating** 92 To 2013 $27.50
Bastard Hill Hoddles Creek Pinot Noir 2006 Profoundly atypical for Bastard Hill; light in colour, body and texture; positively delicate, with fresh red fruits and a touch of spice. Screwcap. 13.5° alc. **Rating** 91 To 2012 $59
Cellar Release Pyrenees Shiraz 2006 A full-bodied palate, crammed with black fruits, licorice and a healthy slab of tannins to provide structure and longevity; patience needed for the wine to show its best. Cork. 14° alc. **Rating** 91 To 2020 $32
Pinot Noir Chardonnay Pinot Meunier 2006 Fragrant stone fruit aromas, a posy of the Yarra Valley; fresh, clean palate, not complex, but has good length and balance. Worth cellaring. Cork. 12.5° alc. **Rating** 91 To 2012 $27.50
Viognier 2007 An even and supple palate picks up all the good parts of the variety, stone fruit and a hint that honey/honeysuckle may be around the corner. Screwcap. 13.5° alc. **Rating** 90 To 2012 $25.50
Shiraz Viognier 2006 Has plenty of structure and depth to the lush black and red fruits with the usual viognier lift. Pyrenees/Yarra Valley/Heathcote. Screwcap. 13.5° alc. **Rating** 90 To 2012 $24
Pinot Noir Chardonnay Pinot Meunier 2005 A smooth, supple sparkling, with a mix of stone fruit and spicy strawberries; good length. Yarra Valley/Tasmania/Tumbarumba. Cork. 13° alc. **Rating** 90 To 2009 $21.99

ŸŸŸŸ **Third Light Chardonnay 2006** A well-crafted light- to medium-bodied palate, with fresh varietal fruit to the fore, though not especially complex. Screwcap. 13° alc. **Rating** 89 To 2011 $16.99
Pinot Gris 2007 Clear varietal character; pear, spice and citrus on a long, focused palate, but without complexity, of course. Screwcap. 13.5° alc. **Rating** 89 To 2011 $25.50
Cabernet Sauvignon 2005 Oak seems to play a prominent role in this wine, encircling the gently ripe blackcurrant fruit. Cork. 14° alc. **Rating** 89 To 2017 $28.50
Third Light Pinot Noir Chardonnay NV Fresh, lively and zesty; not complex, but has good balance in a light-bodied mode. Cork. 12.5° alc. **Rating** 87 To 2009 $18.50

Yarra Park Vineyard

4 Benson Drive, Yering, Vic 3770 **Region** Yarra Valley
T (03) 9739 1960 **F** (03) 9841 7522 **www**.yarrapark.com.au **Open** By appt
Winemaker Mac Forbes (Contract) **Est.** 1996 **Cases** 750
Stephen and Rosalind Atkinson established 1 ha each of chardonnay and cabernet sauvignon, and 0.5 ha of sauvignon blanc, between 1996 and '97. The vineyard is run on organic principles, with heavy mulching and what is technically termed Integrated Pest Management. Yields are deliberately kept low. Until 2006 the wines were made by Phil Kerney at Willow Creek on the Mornington Peninsula, but since '07 have been made by Mac Forbes. The vineyard is situated in what the Atkinsons call 'the golden mile', 1 km to the north of Mount Mary. One particular claim to fame was the sale of a barrel of 2003 Cabernet Sauvignon (the first) for $11 000.

ΨΨΨΨΨ **Sauvignon Blanc 2005** Still very pale; remarkably fresh and delicate, with fine-spun mouthfeel and gentle tropical fruit; perfect balance; wild yeast, 15% barrel ferment. Screwcap. 13° alc. **Rating** 94 **To** 2009 $27.50

ΨΨΨΨΨ **Chardonnay 2006** A well-crafted wine, with a seamless integration of fruit and oak; has good thrust and length in a medium–bodied frame. Screwcap. 13° alc. **Rating** 93 **To** 2012 $30
Cabernet Sauvignon 2005 Quite developed; attractive spicy, cedary, blackberry and mulberry fruit; soft tannins. Cork. 14° alc. **Rating** 90 **To** 2015 $35

Yarra Ridge

GPO Box 753, Melbourne, Vic 3001 **Region** Yarra Valley
T 1300 651 650 **Open** Not
Winemaker Joanna Marsh **Est.** 1983 **Cases** 37 000
Now part of the Foster's group, Yarra Ridge wines continue to be made in the Yarra Valley, and aged at Seppelt (Great Western) under the guidance of Joanna Marsh. The white wines will be crushed and pressed in the Yarra Valley, and fermented at Seppelt; the reds will be pressed and fermented at Sticks, and sent to Great Western for mlf and finishing.

ΨΨΨΨ **Chardonnay 2007** Light-bodied, but does have some of the focus and length expected from the Yarra, with nectarine and citrus fruit on the finish. Screwcap. 13° alc. **Rating** 89 **To** 2009 $21.95
Sauvignon Blanc 2007 Modest intensity and length, likewise varietal character; well-balanced. Screwcap. 11.5° alc. **Rating** 87 **To** 2009 $21.95
Pinot Noir 2006 Strong colour; plenty of flavour in a four square mode, the extract somewhat over the top; age may possibly help. Screwcap. 14° alc. **Rating** 87 **To** 2012 $22.95

Yarra Yarra

239 Hunts Lane, Steels Creek, Vic 3775 **Region** Yarra Valley
T (03) 5965 2380 **F** (03) 5965 2086 **www**.yarrayarravineyard.com.au **Open** By appt
Winemaker Ian Maclean **Est.** 1979 **Cases** NFP
Despite its small production, the wines of Yarra Yarra found their way onto a veritable who's who of Melbourne's best restaurants, encouraging Ian Maclean to increase the estate plantings from 2 ha to over 7 ha in 1996 and '97. Demand for the beautifully crafted wines continued to exceed supply, so the Macleans have planted yet more vines and increased winery capacity. Exports to the UK and Singapore.

Yarra Yering

Briarty Road, Coldstream, Vic 3770 **Region** Yarra Valley
T (03) 5964 9267 **F** (03) 5964 9239 **Open** Sat 10–5, Sun 2–5 while stocks last
Winemaker Dr Bailey Carrodus, Mark Haisma **Est.** 1969 **Cases** 10 000

Bailey Carrodus makes extremely powerful, occasionally idiosyncratic, wines from his 40-year-old, low-yielding unirrigated vineyards. Both red and white wines have an exceptional depth of flavour and richness, although my preference for what I believe to be his great red wines is well known. As he has expanded the size of his vineyards, so has the range of wines become ever more eclectic, none more so than the only Vintage Port being produced in the Yarra Valley. Exports to the UK, the US and other major markets.

🍷🍷🍷🍷🍷 **Dry Red No. 2 2005** Deeply coloured; has more focus and intensity than the Underhill, with more spice and more complexity to the fruit; the texture, likewise, is excellent. Cork. 15° alc. **Rating** 95 **To** 2020

Dry Red No. 1 2005 Altogether stylish, the whole character and impact radically different to the shiraz side of the portfolio; bright and lively cassis and blackcurrant; not the least bit green, and has very good length. Cork. 13° alc. **Rating** 95 **To** 2020

Pinot Noir 2005 Deeply coloured; rich, plush and mouthcoating, with deep, sweet, plum fruit which takes you to the edge of dry red, but doesn't go over; very good fruit, oak and tannin balance; heroic pinot. Cork. 14° alc. **Rating** 94 **To** 2015

Portsorts 2004 Inky purple-black; tremendously complex, concentrated and powerful; more suitable for a 50th anniversary/birthday than a 21st; layer upon layer of black fruits, and not too sweet. Cork. 22° alc. **Rating** 94 **To** 2050 **$65**

🍷🍷🍷🍷½ **Underhill Shiraz 2005** Medium-bodied, supple and smooth; while the fruit is ripe, with confit plum and redcurrant flavours, it carries the alcohol well; soft tannins and quality oak also help. Cork. 15° alc. **Rating** 93 **To** 2015

Yarrabank ★★★★★

38 Melba Highway, Yarra Glen, Vic 3775 **Region** Yarra Valley
T (03) 9730 0100 **F** (03) 9739 0135 **www**.yering.com **Open** 7 days 10–5
Winemaker Michel Parisot, Darren Rathbone **Est.** 1993 **Cases** 5000

The 1997 vintage saw the opening of the majestic winery, established as part of a joint venture between the French Champagne house Devaux and Yering Station. Until 1997 the Yarrabank Cuvee Brut was made under Claude Thibaut's direction at Domaine Chandon, but thereafter the entire operation has been conducted at Yarrabank. There are now 4 ha of dedicated 'estate' vineyards at Yering Station; the balance of the intake comes from other growers in the Yarra Valley and southern Vic. Wine quality has been quite outstanding, the wines having a delicacy unmatched by any other Australian sparkling wines. Exports to all major markets.

🍷🍷🍷🍷🍷 **Late Disgorged 1999** Incredibly bright green-straw; as fresh and lively on its feet as the colour suggests, with aromas and flavours of spice, citrus, apple and brioche; brilliant finish. Zero dosage. Cork. 12.5° alc. **Rating** 96 **To** 2009 **$45**

Cuvee 2003 Very good mousse; despite 4 years on lees, wonderfully fresh, crisp, lively and delicate; rose petals, stone fruit and strawberry float somewhere in the background. Pinot Noir/Chardonnay; no mlf; multi-region. Cork. 12.5° alc. **Rating** 95 **To** 2009 **$38**

YarraLoch ★★★★★

58 Stead Street, South Melbourne, Vic 3205 **Region** Yarra Valley
T (03) 9696 1604 **F** (03) 9696 8387 **www**.yarraloch.com.au **Open** By appt
Winemaker Sergio Carlei **Est.** 1998 **Cases** 4500

This is the ambitious project of successful investment banker Stephen Wood. He has taken the best possible advice, and has not hesitated to provide appropriate financial resources to a venture which has no exact parallel in the Yarra Valley or anywhere else in Australia. Twelve ha of vineyards may not seem so unusual, but in fact he has assembled three entirely different sites, 70 km apart, each matched to the needs of the variety/varieties planted on that site. The 4.4 ha of pinot noir are on the Steep Hill Vineyard, with a northeast orientation, and a shaley rock and ironstone soil. The 4 ha of cabernet sauvignon have been planted on a vineyard at Kangaroo Ground, with a dry, steep northwest-facing site and abundant sun exposure in the warmest part of the day, ensuring full ripeness of the cabernet. Just over

3.5 ha of merlot, shiraz, chardonnay and viognier are planted at the Upper Plenty vineyard, 50 km from Kangaroo Ground. This has an average temperature 2° cooler and a ripening period 2–3 weeks later than the warmest parts of the Yarra Valley. Add the winemaking skills of Sergio Carlei, and some sophisticated (and beautiful) packaging, and you have a 5-star recipe for success.

ΥΥΥΥΥ **The Collection Heathcote Shiraz 2005** Seductively smooth and supple, with layers of red cherry, plum and blackberry fruit; harmonious oak and tannins. Cork. 14° alc. **Rating** 95 **To** 2025 $40

Yarra Valley Chardonnay 2006 Fine and focused pear flesh aromas, with hints of toast and cashews; the palate has great thrust, with lively acidity on the finish; fine, yet generously textured. Screwcap. 13° alc. **Rating** 94 **To** 2014 $35

Stephanie's Dream SV 2005 Lively and lifted aromas and flavours, with a mix of red and black fruits, spice and fine tannins, all with the usual viognier enhancement. Shiraz/Viognier (3%). Diam. 14° alc. **Rating** 94 **To** 2015 $40

Stephanie's Dream Yarra Valley Merlot 2005 Strong Bordeaux overtones to a classically severe exposition of merlot; herb and olive characters alongside cassis fruit; firm, savoury tannins. Diam. 14° alc. **Rating** 94 **To** 2013 $50

Yarra Valley Cabernets 2005 A quite intense and long palate in a Bordeaux mould, with notes of cedar, earth and briar; reflects the particular type of approach to maceration and tannins; excellent length. Cork. 14° alc. **Rating** 94 **To** 2017 $25

ΥΥΥΥΡ **Arneis 2006** Apple blossom aromas; a lively palate, with more fruit intensity than usual for the variety, ranging through citrus to pear; long finish. Screwcap. 13° alc. **Rating** 92 **To** 2009 $25

Shiraz Viognier 2005 A big, robust wine without the usual silky mouthfeel of most shiraz viogniers; dark fruits, spice, licorice and quite firm tannins. Patience should reward. Diam. 14° alc. **Rating** 91 **To** 2015 $35

Viognier 2007 Varietal apricot and cinnamon spice aromas and flavour; quite rich on the palate, but has assertive acidity to clean it up on the finish. Screwcap. 13.8° alc. **Rating** 90 **To** 2009 $25

Arneis 2007 Pale colour; restrained pear flesh aromas, with hints of dried straw; fine on entry but fleshes out across the palate, and has lovely vibrancy on the finish. Screwcap. 12.5° alc. **Rating** 90 **To** 2009 $25

Yarra Valley Pinot Noir 2005 Holding hue well; spotlessly clean plum and black cherry fruit surrounded by a strong savoury net. Screwcap. 13.5° alc. **Rating** 90 **To** 2012 $30

Morpheus Merlot 2005 A very impressive bottle encases this wine, and the concentration is definitely there; very ripe red fruits, with a little tomato leaf green edge; the palate is fresher, with depth, weight and structure; does the bottle justify the price? Diam. 14° alc. **Rating** 90 **To** 2014 $100

ΥΥΥΥ **Rose 2007** Salmon-pink; very savoury, almost spicy personality; bone-dry and with good persistence; a lean style. Screwcap. 12° alc. **Rating** 88 **To** 2009 $20

Yarrambat Estate ★★★☆

45 Laurie Street, Yarrambat, Vic 3091 (postal) **Region** Yarra Valley
T (03) 9717 3710 **F** (03) 9717 3712 **www**.yarrambatestate.com.au **Open** Not
Winemaker John Ellis (Contract) **Est.** 1995 **Cases** 1800
Ivan McQuilkin has a little over 2.6 ha of chardonnay, pinot noir, cabernet sauvignon and merlot on his vineyard in the northwestern corner of the Yarra Valley, not far from the Plenty River. It is very much an alternative occupation for McQuilkin, whose principal activity is as an international taxation consultant to expatriate employees. While the decision to make wine was at least in part triggered by falling grape prices, hindsight proves it to have been a good one, because some of the wines have impressed. In 2006 the vineyard-grown grapes were supplemented with shiraz from Heathcote. There are no cellar door sales; the conditions of the licence are that wine sales can only take place by mail or phone order.

ΥΥΥΥ♀   **Pinot Noir 2004** Developed, but holding on well; supple and smooth spicy red and black fruits, has a bright finish and good length. Screwcap. 13.5° alc. **Rating** 90 To 2012 $15

ΥΥΥΥ   **Chardonnay 2005** Supple and smooth stone fruit and melon, minimal oak influence, but has good structure and very good length. Screwcap. 13.5° alc. **Rating** 89 To 2013 $12.50

Merlot Cabernet 2004 Bright clear red–purple; light-bodied, extremely fresh and lively, like all the Yarrambat Estate wines, looking younger than it is; has length, not texture or structure. Screwcap. 13° alc. **Rating** 87 To 2012 $17.50

Yarrh Wines   ★★★

Greenwood Road, Murrumbateman, NSW 2582 **Region** Canberra District
T (02) 6227 1474 **F** (02) 6227 1584 **www**.yarrhwines.com.au **Open** Sep–June w'ends & public hols 11–5
Winemaker Fiona Wholohan **Est.** 1997 **Cases** 3000
It is probably best to quickly say that Yarrh is Aboriginal for running water, and is neither onomatopoeic nor letters taken from the partners names, the partners being Fiona Wholohan, Neil McGregor and Peta and Christopher Mackenzie Davey. The vineyard was planted in three stages between 1997 and 2000, and there are now 6 ha of cabernet sauvignon, shiraz, sauvignon blanc, riesling, pinot noir and sangiovese (in descending order of importance), and all of the wines are estate-grown, and competently made by Fiona Wholohan. Exports to Norway and China.

ΥΥΥΥ   **Canberra District Riesling 2006** Mineral, herb and spice aromas; bright, fresh mineral-accented palate; developing very slowly, fruit still to emerge. Screwcap. 11.8° alc. **Rating** 89 To 2014 $16

Canberra District Rose 2007 A dry, savoury, tangy, lemony blend of Sangiovese (42%)/Cabernet Sauvignon (41%)/Merlot (17%), the first two driving a food-style rose with attitude. Screwcap. 12° alc. **Rating** 88 To 2009 $16

Canberra District Pinot Noir 2006 Has enough varietal character to satisfy, although the line of the palate is somewhat indistinct, the oak a little assertive. Screwcap. 14° alc. **Rating** 87 To 2011 $20

🍇 Yelland & Papps   ★★★★★

PO Box 256, Greenock, SA 5360 **Region** Barossa Valley
T (08) 8562 8434 **F** (08) 8562 8434 **www**.yellandandpapps.com **Open** Not
Winemaker Michael Papps **Est.** 2005 **Cases** 450
This is the venture of Michael and Susan Papps (née Yelland) set up after their marriage in 2005. Susan decided she did not want to give up her surname entirely, and thus has been able to keep her family name in the business. Michael has the technical background, having lived in the Barossa Valley for more than 20 years, working at local wineries, bottling facilities and wine technology businesses. Susan, who grew up on the Yorke Peninsula, headed to New York for a year, working and studying at the Windows of the World Wine School. The quantity of wine made is limited by the scarcity of the high quality grapes which they have managed to secure from the Greenock area for their wines.

ΥΥΥΥΥ   **Greenock Barossa Valley Shiraz 2005** A very interesting wine; seems to have more cool-climate characteristics (black fruits, pepper and spice) until the finish and aftertaste pull it back to its birthplace; masses of personality. Screwcap. 14.5° alc. **Rating** 95 To 2025 $30

Greenock Barossa Valley Shiraz 2006 A fragrant and lively medium-bodied wine, the black fruit flavours juicy and fresh; a silky mouthfeel and finish. Screwcap. 14.5° alc. **Rating** 94 To 2020 $30

Barossa Valley Cabernet Sauvignon 2006 Bright purple; quite luscious but perfectly ripened cassis and blackcurrant fruit; fine, ripe tannins, perfectly judged French oak maturation. Delicious. Screwcap. 14.5° alc. **Rating** 94 To 2020 $30

ŶŶŶŶŶ **Old Vine Barossa Valley Grenache 2006** As ever, has the sweet confit fruit of
Barossa Valley grenache, but has been sensitively made, the extract controlled, and
French (not American) oak used. Screwcap. 14.5° alc. **Rating** 92 **To** 2016 $30
Barossa Valley Grenache Rose 2007 Tangy, juicy, almost citrussy red fruits on
a bright, clean and long palate; has real attitude and personality. Screwcap. 12.5° alc.
Rating 90 **To** 2009 $17

Yellowglen ★★★★

77 Southbank Boulevard, Southbank, Vic 3006 **Region** Ballarat
T 1300 651 650 **F** (03) 9633 2002 **www.**yellowglen.com.au **Open** Not
Winemaker Charles Hargrave **Est.** 1975 **Cases** NFP
It may come as a surprise to some (it certainly did to me) that Yellowglen is the clear leader
in the value share of the sparkling wine category in Australia, with 22%, and growing at over
15% per annum, way in front of Jacob's Creek in no. 2 position at 8.2%, and with zero growth.
It is this dominant position (and a spread of RRP prices from $12.99 for Yellow up to $26.99
for Vintage Perle) which underpins its separate listing. Exports to the UK and the US.

ŶŶŶŶŶ **Limited Release Perle Rose NV** Deliciously delicate and fresh, the red
grape components obvious; a long, satisfying finish. Pinot Noir/Pinot Meunier/
Chardonnay. Cork. 12° alc. **Rating** 91 **To** 2010 $28.95
Perle 2005 Lively and fresh small fruits, both white and red; impact of lees
contact not marked, but the wine does have good length and merits further time
on cork for the adventurous. Cork. 12° alc. **Rating** 90 **To** 2012 $28.95

Yengari Wines

117 High Street, Taradale, Vic 3447 **Region** Beechworth
T (03) 5423 2828 **F** (03) 5423 2828 **www.**yengari.com.au **Open** Fri–Sun 10–6
Winemaker Tony Lacy **Est.** 1998 **Cases** 500
Tony Lacy currently sources fruit from small family-owned vineyards in Beechworth,
Coonawarra, Heathcote, Macedon Ranges, Yarra Valley and Tamar Valley, making Reserve
and single-vineyard wines for the Yengari label and varietal blends for the Garden Street
and Green Ant labels. Tony Lacy owns a vineyard in Beechworth, currently in development
stage, and leases an organic vineyard in Kyneton, where his Yengari Wine & Produce Store is
located in the historic Taradale General Store. Exports to Japan and Germany.

ŶŶŶŶ **Dookie Shiraz 2005** Floral, lifted red fruits on the bouquet and palate; a little
spicy, cool and fine on the finish. Cork. **Rating** 88 **To** 2014
Uleybury Shiraz 2004 Quite savoury, with clearly defined blackberry fruit and
a little lift of floral aromas; quite chewy on the palate. Cork. 14.2° alc. **Rating** 88
To 2016

 # Yeowarra Hill ★★★★

152 Drapers Road, Colac, Vic 3250 **Region** Geelong
T (03) 5232 1507 **F** (03) 5231 1037 **Open** By appt
Winemaker Ian Deacon, Lee Evans (Contract) **Est.** 1998 **Cases** 400
Bronwyn and Keith Thomas planted 1.6 ha (two-thirds pinot noir, one-third chardonnay)
over 1998 and '99. They say the early vintages were consumed by family and friends, and as
the vines have gained maturity and moved to full-cropping, part of the production has been
sold to other wineries in the region. The business is part of a function venue, which has
expansive views of Colac, with the vineyard in the foreground.

ŶŶŶŶŶ **Chardonnay 2006** Highly focused cool-grown style, with fruit to the fore;
excellent length and fruit sweetness well within style. **Rating** 91 **To** 2014 $18
Limited Release Chardonnay 2007 Has good length and intensity to the
finely drawn melon and citrus fruit, oak playing a minor support role; well made.
Screwcap. 12.5° alc. **Rating** 90 **To** 2014

Yering Farm   ★★★★

St Huberts Road, Yering, Vic 3770 **Region** Yarra Valley
T (03) 9739 0461 **F** (03) 9739 0467 **www.**yeringfarmwines.com **Open** 7 days 10–5
Winemaker Alan Johns **Est.** 1988 **Cases** 5000
Former East Doncaster orchardist Alan Johns acquired the 40-ha Yeringa Vineyard property in 1980; the property had originally been planted by the Deschamps family in the mid-19th century and known as Yeringa Cellars. The plantings now extend to 12 ha, and the wines are made onsite, enjoying consistent show success.

ΨΨΨΨΨ **Chardonnay 2005** An attractive, complex bouquet with a touch of French funk; a rich, textured wine, with well above-average depth, but (as with the Reserve) a little short. Screwcap. **Rating** 92 **To** 2013 $28
John's Estate Reserve Chardonnay 2006 While barrel ferment oak is present, is primarily driven by ripe stone fruit and melon; rich in the mouth, but a touch short. Screwcap. **Rating** 90 **To** 2014 $45

ΨΨΨΨ **Farmyard Unoaked Chardonnay 2006** Fresh, crisp, basically minerally style; some grapefruit flavour; bright finish. Screwcap. **Rating** 88 **To** 2009 $20

Yering Range Vineyard   NR

14 McIntyre Lane, Coldstream, Vic 3770 **Region** Yarra Valley
T (03) 9739 1172 **F** (03) 9739 1172 **Open** By appt
Winemaker Domaine Chandon **Est.** 1989 **Cases** 300
Yering Range has 2 ha of cabernet sauvignon under vine; part is sold and part is made under the Yering Range label.

Yering Station   ★★★★★

38 Melba Highway, Yarra Glen, Vic 3775 **Region** Yarra Valley
T (03) 9730 0100 **F** (03) 9739 0135 **www.**yering.com **Open** 7 days 10–5
Winemaker Willy Lunn, Darren Rathbone **Est.** 1988 **Cases** 60 000
The historic Yering Station (or at least the portion of the property on which the cellar door sales and vineyard are established) was purchased by the Rathbone family in 1996 and is now the site of a joint venture with French Champagne house Devaux. A spectacular and very large winery has been erected which handles the Yarrabank sparkling wines and the Yering Station and Yarra Edge table wines. It has immediately become one of the focal points of the Yarra Valley, particularly as the historic Chateau Yering, where luxury accommodation and fine dining are available, is next door. Yering Station's own restaurant is open every day for lunch, providing the best cuisine in the Valley. In July 2008, winemaker Tom Carson moved to take up the position of Group Winemaker/General Manager of Heathcote Estate and Yabby Lake Vineyard, with overall responsibility for winemaking at those two properties. His replacement is William (Willy) Lunn, a graduate of Adelaide University with more than 24 years' cool-climate winemaking experience around the world, including Petaluma, Shaw & Smith and Argyle Winery (Oregon). Exports to all major markets.

ΨΨΨΨΨ **Reserve Yarra Valley Chardonnay 2005** Restrained elegance and length; grapefruit, nectarine and melon with a near-invisible web of oak; extreme length. Screwcap. 13.5° alc. **Rating** 96 **To** 2015 $64
Yarra Valley Chardonnay 2006 A complex wine, bringing together strong stone fruit, melon and citrus cool-climate characters augmented by barrel ferment oak and lees inputs. Bargain. Screwcap. 13° alc. **Rating** 95 **To** 2011 $23
Yarra Valley Pinot Noir 2006 Classic pinot noir bouquet, flavour and structure, the oak much less obvious than prior releases, fruit more to the front without sacrificing finesse. Outstanding value. Screwcap. 13.5° alc. **Rating** 95 **To** 2013 $24
Reserve Yarra Valley Pinot Noir 2006 A lovely young pinot; aromatic and spicy, with fine tannins and tremendous length. **Rating** 95 **To** 2014 $75

Yarra Valley Shiraz Viognier 2006 Great colour, and a perfumed bouquet to a vibrant and fresh wine, the viognier lift working to perfection with the medium-bodied fruit; long finish. Screwcap. 14.5° alc. **Rating** 95 **To** 2016 $24

MVR Marsanne Viognier Roussanne 2006 A totally convincing blend of the three principal Rhône white varieties; distinct honeysuckle aromas, then a vibrant, citrussy finish to the palate. Screwcap. 14° alc. **Rating** 94 **To** 2016 $24

ŶŶŶŶ♀ **ED Pinot Noir Rose 2007** A classic inheritance from the best roses of Provence; low alcohol also sharpens the focus of a savoury, spicy, bone-dry palate. Screwcap. 11.5° alc. **Rating** 92 **To** 2009 $19

Yarra Valley Cabernet Sauvignon 2005 Medium-bodied, showing some early development for a complex but seamlessly fused marriage of blackcurrant fruit and cedary French oak. Screwcap. 14.5° alc. **Rating** 92 **To** 2011 $24

Mr Frog Chardonnay 2006 A thoroughly cheerful and sprightly second label, the wine still very youthful and pale in colour; light melon fruit with just a hint of cashew; well priced. Screwcap. 13° alc. **Rating** 90 **To** 2010 $15

ŶŶŶŶ **Mr Frog Cabernet Shiraz Merlot 2005** A mix of juicy and more savoury fruits in easy brasserie style. Screwcap. 15° alc. **Rating** 87 **To** 2009 $15

Yeringberg ★★★★★

Maroondah Highway, Coldstream, Vic 3770 **Region** Yarra Valley
T (03) 9739 1453 **F** (03) 9739 0048 **www.**yeringberg.com **Open** By appt
Winemaker Guill de Pury, Sandra de Pury **Est.** 1863 **Cases** 1200
Makes wines for the new millennium from the low-yielding vines re-established in the heart of what was one of the most famous (and infinitely larger) vineyards of the 19th century. In the riper years, the red wines have a velvety generosity of flavour which is rarely encountered, yet never lose varietal character, while the long-lived Marsanne Roussanne takes students of history back to Yeringberg's fame in the 19th century. Exports to the UK, the US, Switzerland, Singapore, Indonesia and Hong Kong.

ŶŶŶŶŶ **Yarra Valley Marsanne Roussanne 2006** Spotlessly clean; the wine is a born-in-the-purple stayer, fabulously tight and focused; in 10 years will still look like a 5-year-old and live for further decades if the Diam lives up to its hopes. 13.5° alc. **Rating** 96 **To** 2025 $40

Yarra Valley Chardonnay 2006 A rich and complex wine from the bouquet to the palate and finish; opulent oak and ripe cashew, fig and peach fruit. For those who want a big bang for their buck. Cork. 13.5° alc. **Rating** 94 **To** 2012 $40

Yarra Valley Pinot Noir 2005 Light but bright colour; an intense and focused palate with wild strawberry/forest notes; silky texture, then a long and persistent finish. Cork. 13.5° alc. **Rating** 94 **To** 2012 $60

ŶŶŶŶ♀ **Yeringberg 2005** Medium-bodied; a wide spectrum of aromas and flavours from red berry to spice to mint and leaf; fine, persistent tannins; European feel. Cabernet Sauvignon/Cabernet Franc/Merlot/Malbec. Cork. 14.5° alc. **Rating** 90 **To** 2020 $60

Yilgarnia

1847 Redmond West Road, Redmond, WA 6327 **Region** Denmark
T (08) 9845 3031 **F** (08) 9845 3031 **www.**yilgarnia.com.au **Open** 7 days 11–late (from late '08)
Winemaker Harewood Estate (James Kellie) **Est.** 1997 **Cases** 3000
Melbourne-educated Peter Buxton travelled across the Nullarbor and settled on a bush block of 405 acres on the Hay River, 6 km north of Wilson Inlet. That was over 40 years ago, and for the first 10 years Buxton worked for the WA Department of Agriculture in Albany. While there, he surveyed several of the early vineyards in WA, and recognised the potential of his family's property. Today there are 10 ha of vines in bearing, with another 6 ha planted in 2002 and '03. All the vineyard plantings (eight varieties in all) are on north-facing blocks, the geological history of which stretches back two billion years. A cellar door is planned for late 2008.

ŸŸŸŸŸ **Reserve Denmark Shiraz 2003** Light but fresh colour; a seductive array
of spices attest to the cool-grown origins, the fruits in a red cherry/raspberry
spectrum, backed by fine tannins. Screwcap. 13° alc. **Rating** 93 **To** 2023 $24.95

ŸŸŸŸ **Denmark Sparkling Shiraz NV** A four-vintage blend, with spicy leathery
earthy characters; one of those very rare Sparkling Shirazs which could have
done with a higher dose of sweetness, rather than less. Cork. 14.5° alc. **Rating** 89
To 2012 $33.95
Denmark Sauvignon Blanc 2007 A positive bouquet with a mix of herb,
citrus and gooseberry, the palate quite rich but slightly phenolic. Screwcap. 14° alc.
Rating 87 **To** 2009 $15.95
Remembrance Methode Champenoise 2005 A blend of Chardonnay/
Cabernet Sauvignon strictly for those looking for something different, and a
devilish wine for the options game; the redcurrant fruit of the cabernet is
obvious once you know. Cork. 13.5° alc. **Rating** 87 **To** 2010 $33.95

🍇 Yuroke Vineyards   ★★★☆

830 Craigieburn Road, Yuroke, Vic 3063 **Region** Sunbury
T (03) 9333 3308 **F** (03) 9333 3308 **Open** By appt
Winemaker Diggers Rest (Mark Matthews) **Est.** 1997 **Cases** 1000
Robyn and Peter Simmie planted 5.6 ha of shiraz and 2.4 ha of pinot noir (and a few rows
of cabernet, and few vines of chardonnay) in 1997 and '99. Initially, the grapes were sold
to Southcorp, but are now partly vinified for the Yuroke Vineyards label. It seems that I was
indirectly responsible for the plantings of pinot (in preference to cabernet sauvignon), good
advice at the time, but who knows what in the future. Not surprisingly, Shiraz is the wine
which has received most accolades.

ŸŸŸŸŸ **Shiraz 2005** Deep colour; good focus, structure and mouthfeel to the medium-
bodied palate; offers spicy plum and blackberry fruit, fine tannins and well-
integrated oak. Screwcap. 14.5° alc. **Rating** 90 **To** 2014 $24

🍇 Z4 Wines   ★★★

PO Box 58, Campbell, ACT 2612 **Region** Canberra District/Tumbarumba
T (02) 6248 6445 **F** (02) 6249 8482 **www**.z4.com.au **Open** Not
Winemaker Greg Gallagher, Steve Thompson (Contract) **Est.** 2007 **Cases** 600
Z4 Wines is the venture of the very energetic Bill Mason and wife Maria. The name derives
from the Mason's four children, each having a Christian name starting with 'Z'. Bill Mason
has been distributing wine in Canberra since 2004, with a small but distinguished list of
wineries, which he represents with considerable marketing flair.

ŸŸŸŸ **Zoe Tumbarumba Riesling 2006** Floral wild herb/flowers on the bouquet;
soft, slightly off-dry palate balanced by good acidity; easy style. Screwcap. 11.5° alc.
Rating 89 **To** 2011 $13.95
Zarah Canberra District Sauvignon Blanc Riesling 2007 A somewhat
esoteric blend, justified in the end by the tangy, citrussy finish which lifts the wine
from mediocrity. Screwcap. 12° alc. **Rating** 87 **To** 2009 $13.95

Zappa-Dumaresq Valley Vineyard   **NR**

Bruxner Highway, Tenterfield, NSW 2372 **Region** New England
T (02) 6737 5281 **F** (02) 6737 5293 **www**.dumaresqvalleyvineyard.com.au **Open** 7 days 9–5
Winemaker Contract **Est.** 1997 **Cases** 2500
Three generations of the Zappa family have been involved in the establishment of what is
now a very large mixed farming property on 1600 ha, all beginning when the first generation
arrived from Italy in the late 1940s to work as cane-cutters in Qld. Today, Martin and
Amelia, with three of their sons and their wives, have a property sustaining 120 cattle, 5000

superfine wool Merino sheep, 140 ha of fresh produce, 250 ha of cereal crops and a 25-ha vineyard. The vineyard was progressively established between 1997 and 2000, with plantings of chardonnay, semillon, sauvignon blanc, shiraz, merlot, cabernet sauvignon, barbera and tempranillo. Exports to Japan.

Zarephath Wines

424 Moorialup Road, East Porongurup, WA 6324 **Region** Porongurup
T (08) 9853 1152 **F** (08) 9853 1151 **www**.zarephathwines.com **Open** Mon–Sat 10–5, Sun 12–4
Winemaker Robert Diletti **Est.** 1994 **Cases** 3000
The 9-ha Zarephath vineyard is owned and operated by Brothers and Sisters of The Christ Circle, a Benedictine community. They say the most outstanding feature of the location is the feeling of peace and tranquility which permeates the site, something I can well believe on the basis of numerous visits to the Porongurups. Exports to the UK, the US and NZ.

♟♟♟♟♟ **Chardonnay 2006** A very attractive fruit-driven style; nectarine and a touch of grapefruit; a fluid, seamless palate. **Rating** 94 **To** 2014 $25

♟♟♟♟ **Pinot Noir 2006** In typical light-bodied style of the region; cherry and plum fruit, the texture quite silky, but bordering dilute. **Rating** 87 **To** 2009 $25

Zema Estate

Riddoch Highway, Coonawarra, SA 5263 **Region** Coonawarra
T (08) 8736 3219 **F** (08) 8736 3280 **www**.zema.com.au **Open** 7 days 9–5
Winemaker Greg Clayfield **Est.** 1982 **Cases** 25 000
Zema is one of the last outposts of hand-pruning in Coonawarra, with members of the Zema family tending a 61-ha vineyard progressively planted since 1982 in the heart of Coonawarra's terra rossa soil. Winemaking practices are straightforward; if ever there was an example of great wines being made in the vineyard, this is it. The extremely popular and equally talented former Lindemans winemaker Greg Clayfield has joined the team, replacing long-term winemaker Tom Simons. Exports to the UK, the US and other major markets.

♟♟♟♟♟ **Family Selection Coonawarra Cabernet Sauvignon 2004** Has clearly managed the challenges of the vintage (the large crop); excellent texture and mouthfeel, with clear-cut blackcurrant and cassis fruit; tannins and oak precisely positioned on the finish. Cork. 14.5° alc. **Rating** 95 **To** 2020 $45
Family Selection Coonawarra Shiraz 2004 An elegant, classy wine; a fine mix of blackcurrant and cherries; silky mouthfeel and length; fine tannin and oak handling; a return to top form. Cork. 15.5° alc. **Rating** 94 **To** 2019 $45
Family Selection Coonawarra Cabernet Sauvignon 2005 Has very good concentration of pure cassis fruits, and a little regional mint; full-bodied and focused on the long and fine-grained tannin finish. ProCork. 15.5° alc. **Rating** 94 **To** 2020 $44.95

♟♟♟♟♀ **Merlot 2005** A pretty wine, with authentic varietal character and structure; has balance and length, but not quite enough intensity for top points. Screwcap. 14.5° alc. **Rating** 92 **To** 2014 $25

♟♟♟♟ **Shiraz 2005** Good colour and concentration; quite savoury/spicy dark fruits and vibrant acidity on the somewhat tannic finish. Cork. 15° alc. **Rating** 89 **To** 2018 $25.65
Coonawarra Cabernet Sauvignon 2005 Lifted, aromatic red fruits, and plenty of acid on the palate; very fresh, but lacks varietal intensity. Cork. 14.5° alc. **Rating** 88 **To** 2016 $25.65
Cluny 2005 A fraction stewy, though has complexity and some depth. Screwcap. 15° alc. **Rating** 88 **To** 2015 $20

Zig Zag Road

201 Zig Zag Road, Drummond, Vic 3461 **Region** Macedon Ranges
T (03) 5423 9390 **F** (03) 5423 9390 **www**.zigzagwines.com.au **Open** Fri–Mon 10–6
Winemaker Eric Bellchambers, Llew Knight **Est.** 1972 **Cases** 350
The dry-grown vines produce relatively low yields, and until 1996 the grapes were sold to
Hanging Rock Winery. In '96 the decision was taken to manage the property on a full-time
basis, and to make the wine onsite, using 0.25 ha each of riesling, merlot and pinot noir, and
1 ha each of shiraz and cabernet sauvignon. In 2002 Eric and Anne Bellchambers became
the third owners of this vineyard, planted by Roger Aldridge in '72. The Bellchambers have
extended the plantings of riesling and merlot, which will produce their first grapes by '09,
supplementing the older plantings of shiraz, cabernet sauvignon and pinot noir.

ŸŸŸŸ **Riesling 2006** More variety fruit than the '07, but still a very shy, slow-
developing style; offers light apple and citrus; dry finish. Screwcap. 12.2° alc.
Rating 88 **To** 2012 $22
Macedon Ranges Cabernet Sauvignon 2004 Against all logic, green citrussy
elements do not destroy the wine, but rather underline the cassis components;
however, I am sure not all will agree. Diam. 12.7° alc. **Rating** 87 **To** 2011 $22
Macedon Ranges Cabernet Merlot 2004 Vibrant, bright colour reflecting
low pH; a curate's egg, with clean light-bodied blackcurrant fruit, but a tart, green
finish; points for effort. Diam. 12.7° alc. **Rating** 87 **To** 2010 $22

Zilzie Wines

Lot 66 Kulkyne Way, Karadoc via Red Cliffs, Vic 3496 **Region** Murray Darling
T (03) 5025 8100 **F** (03) 5025 8116 **www**.zilziewines.com **Open** Not
Winemaker Mark Zeppel **Est.** 1999 **Cases** 100 000
The Forbes family has been farming Zilzie Estate since the early 1990s; it is currently run by
Ian and Ros Forbes, and sons Steven and Andrew. A diverse range of farming activities now
include grapegrowing, with 700 ha of vineyards. Having established a position as a dominant
supplier of grapes to Southcorp, Zilzie formed a wine company in 1999 and built a winery in
2000. It has a capacity of 16 000 tonnes, but is designed so that modules can be added to take
it to 35 000 tonnes. The business includes contract processing, winemaking and storage. The
recent expansion may face problems given the state of the Murray Darling Basin. Exports
to all the major markets.

ŸŸŸŸŸ **Shiraz 2006** A glorious bouquet, very complex and lively; a fine, intense and silky
mid-palate flows through to a very long finish. Gold, National Wine Show '07.
Cork. 14° alc. **Rating** 95 **To** 2016 $15

ŸŸŸŸŸ **Selection 23 Sauvignon Blanc 2007** A very considerable achievement for
Riverland fruit; abundant tropical flavours with balancing citrussy acidity; great
value. Screwcap. 11.5° alc. **Rating** 90 **To** 2009 $10

ŸŸŸŸ **Estate Chardonnay 2006** Has more restraint and finesse than most Riverland
chardonnays, though there is plenty of peachy fruit, the oak in restraint. Screwcap.
13.5° alc. **Rating** 88 **To** 2010 $15
Rose 2007 Very fresh and crisp, with a strong lemony/citrussy streak through the
red fruits; a bold, dry finish. Screwcap. 13.5° alc. **Rating** 88 **To** 2009 $15

Zitta Wines

26 Dover Street, Malvern, SA 5061 (postal) **Region** Barossa Valley
T 0419 819 414 **F** (08) 8272 3735 **www**.zitta.com.au **Open** Not
Winemaker Angelo De Fazio **Est.** 2004 **Cases** 1000
Owner Angelo De Fazio says that all he knows about viticulture and winemaking came from
his father (and generations before him). It is partly this influence that has shaped the label
and brand name: Zitta is Italian for 'quiet' and the seeming reflection of the letters of the
name Zitta is in fact nothing of the kind; turn the bottle upside down, and you will see it is

the word Quiet. The Zitta vineyard is on a property dating back to 1864, with a few vines remaining from that time, and a block planted with cuttings taken from those vines. In all there are 21.4 ha of shiraz of varying age, 1.75 ha of grenache, a dash of mataro, and a hectare of chardonnay. The property has two branches of the Greenock Creek running through it, and the soils reflect the ancient geological history of the site, in part with a subsoil of river pebbles reflecting the course of a long-gone river. Tradition there may be, but there is also some highly sophisticated writing and marketing in the background material and the website.

ŸŸŸŸŸ **Greenock Barossa Valley Shiraz 2005** Deep crimson; bright and focused, with fruit purity at its core; fine and long, with lively red fruits and fine-grained tannins on the finish. Cork. 14.5° alc. **Rating** 94 **To** 2018 $36.50

Zonte's Footstep

PO Box 53, Langhorne Creek, SA 5255 **Region** Langhorne Creek
T (08) 8537 3334 **F** (08) 8537 3231 **www**.zontesfootstep.com.au **Open** 7 days 10–5
Winemaker Ben Riggs **Est.** 1997 **Cases** 50 000
The 215-ha vineyard of Zonte's Footstep dates back to 1997 when a group of old school mates banded together to purchase the land and established the vineyard under the direction of viticulturist Geoff Hardy and long-term vigneron John Pargeter. Obviously enough, a large percentage of the grapes are sold to others, a small part skilfully made by Ben Riggs. While it is not clear who Zonte was, the footprint on the label is that of the Diprotodon or giant wombat, which inhabited the southeastern corner of SA for more than 20 million years until becoming extinct 10 000–20 000 years ago. The wine quality is as good as the prices are modest. Exports to the UK, the US, Canada, Ireland, France, Denmark and NZ.

ŸŸŸŸŸ **Langhorne Creek Pinot Grigio 2007** Pear and cinnamon aromas, the palate well balanced and quite long with good acidity; astonishingly, the judges awarded it South Australian Wine of the Year at the Hyatt/Advertiser Competition '07. Screwcap. 12.5° alc. **Rating** 90 **To** 2009 $18
Langhorne Creek Cabernet Malbec 2006 The juicy-fruity malbec works well with the open personality of Langhorne Creek cabernet, making this a thoroughly user-friendly, why wait, style. Screwcap. 14.5° alc. **Rating** 90 **To** 2012 $15
Langhorne Creek Sangiovese Barbera 2007 A trendy label blend, but there is substance to the wine, with more fruit strength and structure than usual; the sangiovese tannins are perfect. Screwcap. 14.5° alc. **Rating** 90 **To** 2013 $18

ŸŸŸŸ **Langhorne Creek Shiraz Viognier 2007** Perfumed, typical fruit flavours of the blend; throws the emphasis onto that fruit and away from structure into a cheerful early-drinking style. Screwcap. 14.5° alc. **Rating** 89 **To** 2012 $18
Dry Rose 2007 A fresh, vibrant and juicy personality; quite dry on the finish, and plenty of flavour; enjoy on the patio watching the sunset. Cabernet Sauvignon/ Petit Verdot. Screwcap. 13.5° alc. **Rating** 88 **To** 2010 $15
Langhorne Creek Verdelho 2007 Good varietal aroma and flavour; a mix of fruit salad and citrus; doesn't aspire to complexity. Screwcap. 13.5° alc. **Rating** 87 **To** 2010 $15

Index

♀	**Cellar door sales**
⑪	**Food:** lunch platters to à la carte restaurants
⊨	**Accommodation:** B&B cottages to luxury vineyard apartments
♩	**Music events:** monthly jazz in the vineyard to spectacular yearly concerts

Beechworth (Vic)

Yarra Valley/Strathbogie Ranges (Vic)